Praise for Robert B. Strassler's

THE LANDMARK HERODOTUS

"*The Landmark Herodotus* may well be the greatest English-language edition ever published. Lush with maps and illustrations, amplified with useful marginal comments, and fortified with easy-to-read but unobtrusive foot-notes, it's a book that scholars will value, students can use, and general readers will cherish."
—*The Boston Phoenix*

"A worthy occasion for celebrating Herodotus' contemporary importance.... The headings, index and footnotes let you know precisely where you are... providing a set of landmarks far more detailed than anything Herodotus could have found during his tours.... And the probing introduction by Rosalind Thomas increases readers' knowledge and curiosity."
—*The New York Times*

"A lucid new rendition [with] countless maps, photographs, annotations and appendices."
—*Newsday*

"The neophyte reader will certainly get a great deal ... from *The Landmark Herodotus*: an up-to-date translation, a superb analytic index, several background essays by experts that are the last word on current scholarship, intelligent illustrations geared to the text, running lessons in Mediterranean geography, occasional useful notes, and a handy glossary."
—Peter Green, *The New York Review of Books*

"Strassler helps readers unlock the mysteries of the Greek author's accont of the Persian Wars, offering detailed maps, margin notes, twenty-one appendices written by top scholars and more."
—*Rocky Mountain News*

"Unites under one cover, a new, lucid translation ... along with copious marginal notations and indexes, maps and over twenty highly useful appendices."
—*The News and Observer* (Raleigh)

ROBERT B. STRASSLER is an independent scholar whose articles have appeared in the *Journal of Hellenic Studies*. He holds an honorary Doctorate of Humanities and Letters from Bard College and is chairman of the Aston Magna Foundation for Music and the Humanities. He lives in Brookline, Massachusetts.

ANDREA L. PURVIS, translator, holds a Ph.D. in Classical Studies from Duke University and has taught in Duke University's Department of Classical Studies. She is the author of *Singular Dedications: Founders and Innovators of Private Cults in Classical Greece* and co-author of *Four Island Utopias*. She lives in Durham, North Carolina.

THE LANDMARK

HERODOTUS

THE HISTORIES

A New Translation by Andrea L. Purvis
with Maps, Annotations, Appendices, and Encyclopedic Index

Edited by Robert B. Strassler

With an Introduction by Rosalind Thomas

ANCHOR BOOKS
A Division of Random House, Inc. • New York

TO

GEORGE L. CAWKWELL

FIRST ANCHOR BOOKS EDITION, JUNE 2009

Copyright © 2007 by Robert B. Strassler

All rights reserved. Published in the United States by Anchor Books, a division of Random House, Inc., New York, and in Canada by Random House of Canada Limited, Toronto.

Anchor Books and colophon are registered trademarks of Random House, Inc.

Library of Congress Cataloging-in-Publication Data

Herodotus.
[History. English]
The landmark Herodotus : the histories / edited by Robert B. Strassler ;
translated by Andrea L. Purvis.
    p. cm.
Includes bibliographical references and index.
ISBN 978–0–375–42109–9
1. History, Ancient. 2. Greece—History—To 146 B.C. I. Strassler, Robert B., 1937–
II. Purvis, Andrea L. III. Title.
D58.H4713 2007
930—dc22   2007024149

Anchor ISBN: 978-1-4000-3114-6

Designed by Kim Llewellyn
Maps by Topaz Maps, Inc.
Index by Margot Levy
Photo research by Ingrid MacGillis
Author photograph © Clemens Kalischer

www.anchorbooks.com

Printed in the United States of America
10 9 8 7 6 5 4 3 2 1

CONTENTS

INTRODUCTION

Rosalind Thomas

1. Opening Remarks

§1.1. Herodotus' *Histories* trace the conflict between the Greeks and the Persians which culminated in the Persian Wars in the great battles of Thermopylae, Salamis, Plataea, and Mycale (480–479),[a] a generation or so before he was writing. He described his theme as comprising both the achievements of Greeks and barbarians, and also the reasons why they came into conflict (Book 1, Proem). This suggests that he sought the causes of the conflict in factors that took one back deep into the past and into the characteristics of each society. He implies that he saw the deep-seated causes in cultural antagonism of Greek and non-Greek, but he went out of his way to describe the achievements and customs of many non-Greek peoples with astonishing sensitivity and lack of prejudice. The *Histories* are the first work in the Western tradition that are recognizably a work of history to our eyes, for they cover the recent human past (as opposed to a concentration on myths and legends), they search for causes, and they are critical of different accounts. Herodotus' own description of them as an inquiry, a "*historiē*," has given us our word "history," and he has been acknowledged as the "father of history." He also has a claim to be the first to write a major work on geography and ethnography. His interests were omnivorous, from natural history to anthropology, from early legend to the events of the recent past: he was interested in the nature of the Greek defense against the Persians, or the nature of Greek liberty, as well as in stranger and more exotic tales about gold-digging ants or other wondrous animals in the East. The *Histories* are the first long work in prose (rather than verse) which might rival the Homeric epics in scale of conception and length. Shorter works in prose had appeared before, but the *Histories* must in their time have been revolutionary.

§1.2. Who, then, was Herodotus? As with most ancient Greek authors, we have little reliable information, and the later ancient biographers may have invented biographical "facts" by drawing from the content of the *Histories* themselves, as was common in ancient biographies of writers. He was born in Halicarnassus[a] in Asia Minor,[b] now modern Bodrum in western Turkey. He spent much of his life in exile,

Intro.1.1a All dates in this edition of Herodotus and in its supporting materials are B.C.E. (Before the Common Era), unless otherwise specified.

Intro.1.2a Halicarnassus: Map Intro.1.
Intro.1.2b Asia Minor (Asia): Map Intro.1, locator.

spending some time in Samos,[c] some in Athens,[d] and apparently ending up in Thurii,[e] the Athenian Panhellenic colony founded in south Italy (Aristotle in the fourth century knew him as Herodotus of Thurii). The *Histories* themselves provide the evidence for his extensive travels in the Greek world, Asia Minor, Phoenicia, Egypt and North Africa,[f] and perhaps the Black Sea[g] (see below). Unlike in many modern travelogues, the main focus of interest is not on the traveling itself but on the information it yields, so again the personal elements are not extensive. His life spanned much of the fifth century: here there is no reason to doubt the ancient tradition that he was born at roughly the time of the Persian Wars (480–479), and he probably lived into the 420s, since the *Histories* make references to events in Greece early in the Peloponnesian War of 431–404. It is usually thought that he was active as researcher and writer from the 450s to the 420s. The *Histories* clearly constituted a life's work.

2. The Historical Background

§2.1. The beginning of this period saw the triumph of the Greek mainland states over the might of the Persian Empire, first in the initial invasion of 490 and the battle of Marathon,[a] then in the second invasion of 480/79, with the battles of Thermopylae, Salamis, Plataea, and finally Mycale[b] in Asia Minor. This unexpected victory resonated in Greek consciousness through the fifth century and indeed beyond, and it is important to recall this when reading Herodotus, who was researching a generation or two after the Greek victory. It helped crystallize Greeks' attitudes to their own way of life and values, intensified their supreme distrust of monarchy and tyranny, and shaped their attitude to the Persians. In more practical terms, Athens' naval success in the Persian Wars and its enterprise immediately after led to the creation of the Athenian Empire, which started as an anti-Persian league and lasted for almost three-quarters of a century (479–404). As the Spartans[c] were increasingly reluctant to continue anti-Persian activity into the Hellespont and Asia Minor, the Athenians were free to create their maritime league composed of many smaller Greek states situated around the Aegean and up into the Hellespont.[d] Athenian power grew steadily and Athens even tried a disastrous expedition to help Egypt rebel against the Persian King. As her radical democracy developed from the 460s, conflict arose between her and the other powerful Greek states, particularly Corinth[e] and Sparta and the members of Sparta's Peloponnesian League. By the late 430s tensions had reached their height. War broke out in 431 between Athens and her allies and Sparta and hers. Athens was now a "tyrant city," the Corinthians claimed (*Thucydides* 1.122.3; generally, 1.68–71, 1.120–124), and Greece must now be freed from Athens. Greece had been freed from the Persians[f] only to be enslaved by Athens. The great historian of this later war, Thucydides, was successor and rival to Herodotus. As he makes his Athenian speakers remark in the opening book of his history, they are weary of pointing out that the Athenian Empire is justified

Intro.1.2c Samos: Map Intro.1.
Intro.1.2d Athens: Map Intro.1.
Intro.1.2e Thurii: Map Intro.1, locator.
Intro.1.2f Phoenicia, Egypt, and North Africa (Libya): Map Intro.2.
Intro.1.2g Euxine (Black) Sea: Map Intro.1, locator.
Intro.2.1a Marathon: Map Intro.1.

Intro.2.1b Battle sites of 480: Thermopylae and Salamis, of 479, Plataea and Mycale: Map Intro.1.
Intro.2.1c Sparta: Map Intro.1.
Intro.2.1d Aegean Sea: Map Intro.1. Hellespont: Map Intro.1, locator.
Intro.2.1e Corinth: Map Intro.1.
Intro.2.1f Persia: Map Intro.2.

on the grounds that the Athenians did most to defeat the Persians (e.g., *Thucydides* 1.73.2–75.2: "although we are rather tired of continually bringing up this subject [the Persian War]," 1.73.2). In other words, the Persian Wars were still very much a living part of Greek politics in the 430s and 420s and the period during which Herodotus was researching. They played an important role in the rhetoric and diplomacy of the time. Athens could and did claim that she had done more than any other Greek city to help Greece keep her freedom; Sparta and Corinth now asserted that Athens herself was enslaving Greece. Freedom is central to Herodotus' *Histories*, and it played a crucial part in inter-state political argument and antagonism in the later fifth century.

§2.2. Herodotus' *Histories* need to be seen in part against this background, even though in formal terms they describe events only down to the end of the Persian Wars in 479. For he takes as his explicit theme the conflict between the Greeks and the barbarians, as he puts it in the introduction, and after tracing this conflict back to the earliest times, he gradually works up to the full narrative of the Greek-Persian conflict in the Ionian[a] Revolt of 499–494 (Books 5–6), and to the two Persian invasions of mainland Greece of 490 and 480 (Books 6–9). Herodotus' *Histories* stop on the brink of the creation of the Athenian Empire: they end their main narrative at the point where the Greeks in Asia Minor, helped by the Greek fleet under the Spartan Leotychidas, have won a decisive victory against the Persian forces at Mycale in Asia Minor—on the very same day on which the Greek army in central Greece under Pausanias had won the victory at Plataea, which forced the Persians to withdraw entirely from Greece. The Asia Minor Greeks were taken into the anti-Persian alliance of the Greek allies (9.106), and the victorious Greek forces sailed up to the Hellespont to continue aggressive operations against Persia and free more Greek cities. The Spartans and Peloponnesians went home, fatally leaving the Athenians in charge (9.114; though they were to send another commander out later), and Herodotus' narrative ends with the Athenian actions in the Hellespont, which many scholars have seen as an ominous portent of the future (9.120).

§2.3. If we imagine Herodotus trying to collect accounts, to take oral testimony, and to gather personal or collective memories about the Persian Wars, then we can assume that he would have been talking to people who had actually been involved, who perhaps had fought in the war or whose relations had done so; and since the effects of the Persian Wars were still immediate and strong, and charges of Medism[a] still potent, it is hard to imagine that his research was either simple or straightforward. His claims to set the record straight and to record both the brave and the cowardly still had resonances for later generations. Plutarch still resented his remarks about certain Greek cities, particularly Corinth and Thebes,[b] several centuries later, in the late first century C.E., in his fascinatingly and curiously petty essay "On the Malice of Herodotus," where he also tried in his own way, rather ineffectually, to set the record straight. Excuses for why the Argives[c] did not help against the Persians

Intro.2.2a Ionia: Map Intro.1.
Intro.2.3a Those Greeks who accepted Persian rule and fought with the Persians were accused of "Medism" by those Greeks who fought against the Persians. That they were said to have "medized" is an extension of the Greek habit of using the words "Mede" and "Persian" interchangeably, although the Medes were a people quite distinct from the Persians.
Intro.2.3b Thebes (Boeotia): Map Intro.1.
Intro.2.3c Argos: Map Intro.1.

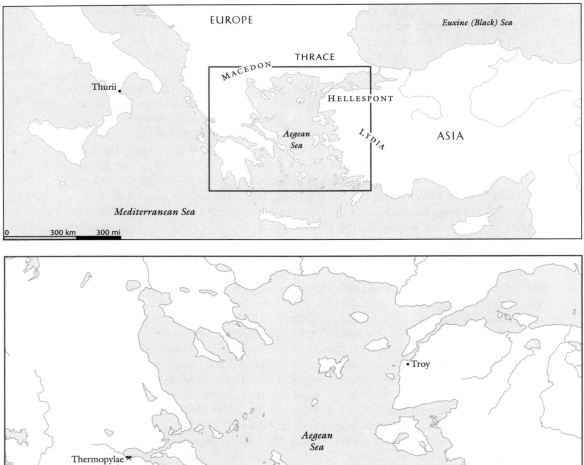

MAP INTRO.1*

*See the Editor's Preface and the Key to Maps for an explanation of map layout, symbols, and typography.

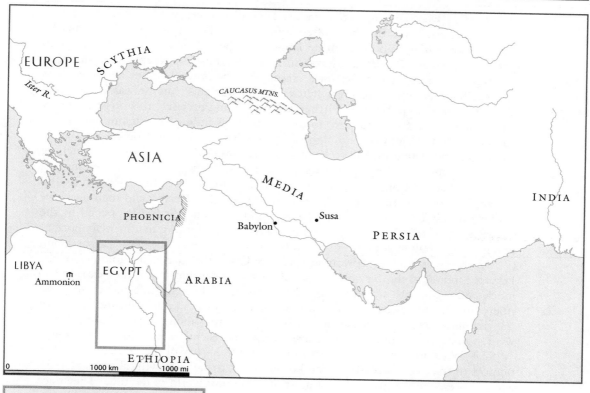

MAP INTRO.2

(7.148–152) were still important in the later fifth century and beyond. In fact, Herodotus knows well that he is often controversial. For instance, he notes that he is saying something unpopular in declaring that the Athenians in fact did most to defeat the Persians (7.139): modern historians would usually accept this opinion, so why was it so unpopular at the time? Presumably the prevailing view in Greece was that the Spartans were the great heroes of the war and thus he was challenging that. Even more important, the Athenians were using precisely this boast to justify their empire. The fact that Herodotus admitted his judgment was unpopular was not so much a straightforward sign of "pro-Athenian feelings" on his part as an acknowledgment that he had to have good reasons—which he does and which he gives at length—for going against the popular view. He may also have been hinting indirectly at some morals or warnings to be drawn from Greek history down to 479 and applied to the period after the wars. At any rate the *Histories* end their narrative oddly: the last but one paragraph reads, "and that was all that happened in the course of the year" (9.121).[d] It is as if he was discreetly hinting that many important things were certainly going to occur in the following years. The very last paragraph (9.122) takes us back to a warning given by Cyrus the Great, the founder of the Persian Empire, in the very early years of Persian expansion that if they expand too much and move into rich, luxurious lands, they will become soft and cease to be rulers. In this unexpected flashback, one could simply read a moralizing tale about the rise and decline of Persian might, but Herodotus' audience could also, if they were so minded, see in it a warning about the more recently arisen Athenian Empire.

§2.4. What are the *Histories*? Far more than the history of the Persian Wars, they purport to trace the Greek-barbarian hostility back to earliest mythical times (1.1–5), and they describe the geography of most of the known world of the time. They trace relations between peoples and cities in such a way as to describe much earlier history, and they describe the customs of many of the peoples of the inhabited world. The expansion of the Persian Empire into new areas serves as a peg for several large sections—often misleadingly called "digressions"—about the geography and peoples of those areas. The geographical and ethnographical details are often closely linked to the success or failure of those peoples in resisting the Persians (note particularly Book 4 on the Scythians). The section on Egypt runs to one very substantial book in its own right (note, though, that the book divisions were a later creation), and the Scythians[a] receive the second longest section. Ethiopians, Libyans, and Thracians[b] are described in detail. It might be tempting to see this in terms of modern disciplines and in some sort of hierarchy: is he an anthropologist, a historian, or a geographer? Is the geography subservient to the history, or, as the great early-twentieth-century German scholar Jacoby argued, did he start out as a geographer and only become a historian later in life? But there are huge problems with these ideas, the most pressing one being that they impose modern conceptions of modern disciplines on a writer writing at the "beginning," before history has even been defined or separated from anything else as a discipline. Herodotus helped create the concept of the discipline of "history," in part

Intro.2.3d Translation throughout the Introduction differs from that in this volume.
Intro.2.4a Scythia: Map Intro.2.

Intro.2.4b Ethiopia, Libya: Map Intro.2. Thrace: Map Intro.1, locator.

by stressing and criticizing his sources and accepted traditions, but it was his successor Thucydides who really solidified and in fact narrowed the idea of history as a critical study of past events (and only past events, as opposed to ethnography, mythology, or geography). This definition of "history" as the study of past political and military events is something of an anachronism for Herodotus, who, after all, included so much more in his "inquiry": we would be applying a later conception to an earlier achievement which was conceived in earlier and therefore different terms (see below). It also ignores the complex structure of his work and its overall unity, for in the *Histories* geography and customs have a large explanatory role in the course of events, and the interweaving of geography, ethnography, and the narrative of events is very finely done, not as one might expect if one or the other area was somehow tacked on later. Besides, "wonders" and achievements are "worthy of relation/telling" (*axiologotatoi*), in Herodotus' phrase, in their own right. Egypt was worthy of a longer description because it had more marvels than any other place (2.35.1). Wonders were simply part of his subject matter.

§2.5. Herodotus' own conception of his work is that it is a "*historiē*," a Greek word for "inquiry" which through Herodotus' own use has become our word for history. Not only did it not yet mean "history," but in the second half of the fifth century, *historiē* inquiry seems to have had particular connotations, as I hope I have shown in my book.[a] It was a term of "science" in the sense that it was accompanied by the desire to discover the truth about the world, with a degree of critical rigor, concern for proof, and respect for evidence (though hardly to the degree expected of modern science). We encounter the term "inquiry into nature" for natural science, or "inquiry into medicine" for the attempt to understand medicine and its relation to human nature. *Historiē* was an all-encompassing term that was by no means limited to research into the past; indeed Herodotus may have been the first to use it for research that included past human actions. Its appearance in his opening sentence was surely meant to signal to his audience that here was no rehash of the old myths, no mere uncritical retelling of stories, but a modern work of critical inquiry.

The opening paragraph of the proem sets out clearly that his subject was wide-ranging (I give a very literal translation):

> This is the publication [or display *apodexis*] of the inquiry of Herodotus of Halicarnassus, which he presents in the hope that the achievements of men should not be obliterated by time, nor that the great and wonderful deeds [*erga*] of both Greeks and barbarians should be without their due fame, and also for what reason they fought each other. (Book 1, Proem)

§2.6. The proem itself, then, states that his subject is the events and achievements of mankind, and that included both Greeks and barbarians. The final clause is similarly wide-open: for what reason or cause. How did he conceive of causation? The causes of the conflict could be sought in mythical origins, in the buildup of antagonism in earlier history, in geographical layout and proximity, in way of life, customs, and over-

---

Intro.2.5a   Rosalind Thomas, *Herodotus in Context: Ethnography, Science and the Art of Persuasion* (Cambridge, 2000).

all attitudes, for instance the conflicting values of Greeks and non-Greeks which are certainly visible in the *Histories*. The political and social strengths of different peoples change, too, in the course of the *Histories*, so that Greeks were not always free, and non-Greeks were worthy of investigation in their own right. His proem therefore describes the idea of his work in terms which could virtually encompass everything which actually appears in the *Histories*. Of course, writers are at liberty to do more or less than they promise at the start, but it is striking how wide-open Herodotus' themes are from the start. It is interesting to compare the way Thucydides opened his *History* with a far more focused summary, surely with an eye on his predecessor Herodotus:

> Thucydides the Athenian wrote [*xunnegrapse*] the history of the war between the Peloponnesians and the Athenians, beginning at the moment it broke out and believing that it would be a great war and more worthy of relation than any that had preceded it. (*Thucydides* 1.1.1: Crawley)

§2.7. Instantly it is obvious that this is to be a more concentrated, sharply focused account of a war—one war—and not the wider "inquiry," nor a baggy, all-encompassing account of everything that deserves to have its fame preserved. And he claims that his war was greater than earlier ones, which includes both the Trojan War, sung by Homer, and the Persian War. Rivalry with Homer and Herodotus is emphatically signaled. Turning back from Thucydides to Herodotus, we are struck by the wide-arching aims of the Herodotean proem: this was indeed going to encompass far more than the narrative of the Persian Wars alone.

§2.8. Here it may be useful to say something about the structure of the *Histories*, which is related to their all-encompassing and inclusive subject matter. As we saw above, the large sections on the geography and customs of various peoples tend to be pegged onto the larger narrative framework of conquest: when the Persians or before them, on a lesser scale, the Lydians[a] try to conquer a people, these people are described. Thus the history of the Medes, who conquered the Persians (1.102) but were later subjected by them, is included in the description of their relations with the Persians (1.95–104, the Medes rise up against Assyria; see also 1.123–130, Cyrus and the Persians rise up against the Medes).

§2.9. Right at the start of the *Histories* the grand theme of the conflict between Greeks and non-Greeks is launched, and the structure reflects this. We start immediately after the proem with a curious set of opening myths, contrary stories by learned Persians, Greeks, and Phoenicians, about mythical abductions of various women by Persians, Phoenicians, or Greeks (1.1–5): the tit-for-tat of wrongs and retaliations is thus traced right back to mythical times. But however we interpret this opening—probably a parody of a certain type of argument about causes of wars—Herodotus pulls the inquiry back onto safer ground almost immediately, into a period more susceptible to historical inquiry, by saying that he is not going to declare whether any of these mythical abductions happened in this way, but he is

Intro.2.8a   Lydia: Map Intro.1, locator.

going to proceed with the man he knows was the first to commit unjust acts against the Greeks (1.5.3). This marks a clear division between what he knows and the unstable and unreliable tales of a more distant past. He then proceeds to tell of Croesus of Lydia, who attacked the Greeks of Asia Minor in the mid-sixth century (1.6). This is the period safely within the range of historical knowledge. From now on in Book 1, the narrative thread follows Croesus' rise and fall as king of Lydia, the rise of the Median[a] kingdom and then that of the Persian Empire, the Persian conquest of Lydia and other territories, and the gradual escalation of hostility between Persia and the Greek world.

§2.10. It is, however, the numerous "flashbacks," frequently called "digressions," within this narrative that the modern reader often finds hard to follow. Attached to this main narrative are many inserted sections which explain circumstances, describe the relevant geography, trace how such a situation has arisen, or describe the state of a city which now becomes involved in the main narrative. A simple example occurs in the narrative of Croesus' expansionist plans. Croesus king of Lydia first inquires about possible allies, as part of his plan to go to war (1.56). This inquiry forms a peg for a description of the major Greek ethnic groups, the Dorians and Ionians (1.56–58). Then as "Croesus learned that the Athenians, inhabitants of the foremost city of the Ionians, were ruled at this time by the tyrant Peisistratos son of Hippocrates" (1.59.1), we are given an account of the mid-sixth-century factional strife in Athens and Peisistratos' three periods of power. We thus have an explanation within another explanation, a description hanging from another description, all of which are in fact important to our understanding of the train of events.[a] In a form of "ring composition," Herodotus returns neatly at the end of this to his main narrative and clearly signals the end of the section on Athens with the sentence "Such, Croesus learned, was the condition of the Athenians" (1.65.1). The ring is complete, and the ancient reader would be alerted to this by the very method of ring composition. The modern terms "digression" or "excursus" imply that these passages are less important, possibly off the point, getting off the main theme, but this is to impose modern conceptions of linear structure and relevance and an anachronistically negative slant. The nearest Herodotus gets to describing his principle is in Book 4 (30.1): "My account goes searching from the start for extra material [literally "additions"]." The word "additions" carries a more positive charge than "digression" and is the excuse for moving from the effects of the cold on cattle in Scythia to a different but equally odd fact about the impossibility of breeding mules in Elis. The searching for extra information is part and parcel of the wide-open nature of his inquiry.

3. The Intellectual and Moral World of Herodotus

§3.1. In all this it is hard to see Herodotus as anything but revolutionary: as the great scholar and historian Momigliano put it vividly, "There was no Herodotus

Intro.2.9a   Media: Map Intro.2.
Intro.2.10a And this information is also vital to our understanding of later events which Herodotus describes subsequently, when the Athenians drive out the last Peisistratid tyrant (5.65) and form a new rudimentary, democratic government (5.66), from which they draw the strength and will (5.78) to resist the Persians.

before Herodotus."[a] We can pick out earlier writers who pursued one or another element of the many areas of inquiry that appear in Herodotus' *Histories*. Of these Hekataios was the greatest, writing c. 500. He wrote a geographical work enumerating the peoples and places on a circumnavigation of the Mediterranean (*Periodos Gēs*) and tried to collect, systematize, and rationalize the many contradictory legends of the Greeks in a work called *Genealogies*. Other prose writers may have written short works on Lydian history and Persian history, but none of these have survived in anything but a few fragments, and in any case, the great mass of Herodotus' *Histories* draws on oral traditions and witnesses rather than written works. With the exception of Homer, the "predecessors" of Herodotus seem only to make Herodotus' achievement all the more monumental, and we can perhaps understand the *Histories* more if we view Herodotus not so much in comparison with the few shadowy writers somewhat before his time, but against the background of developments in his own contemporary world.

§3.2. The supreme model for a narrative on this scale was provided by Homer, the *Iliad* as a narrative of war, the *Odyssey* of travels. There are clear Homeric features in Herodotus from the very opening, where he declares that his aim is partly to ensure that fame (*kleos*) is preserved from the ravages of time. The larger structure owes something to Homer, and similarities bring out the Homeric resonances and parallels for Greek readers, who would have been very familiar with the epics. At the start of Xerxes' great invasion of Greece, there is a long catalog of his forces (7.61–99), which is clearly reminiscent of the great catalog of ships of the Greek forces at Troy[a] in the *Iliad* (*Iliad* 2.484–779). Dreams play a large part in the Xerxes narrative as he is persuaded to go ahead with his disastrous expedition against Greece by a series of dreams sent by the gods to ensure that, despite all arguments raised against the expedition, he nevertheless continues with his plans to invade Greece (Book 7, beginning). Similarly, early in the *Iliad*, Agamemnon is sent a deceptive dream which leads him to believe that the capture of Troy could be imminent (*Iliad* 2.1–40)—though here, as the circumstances and effects are so different, we may wonder if the deceptive dream is simply a feature of the Greek conception of how dreams and the divine may function in human life and, as such, common to both Homer and Herodotus. Herodotus uses phrases and expressions that are reminiscent of Homeric ones, and the practice of giving speeches to the actors in his *Histories* continues what is originally a Homeric practice.[b]

§3.3. Yet there are sharp differences between them, too, and Herodotus on several occasions distances himself from the Homeric account in such a way as to emphasize his superior methods and judgment. Writers began to write in prose (as opposed to verse) in the sixth century for serious attempts to elucidate the grand workings of the cosmos and to *distance* themselves from the dominant poetic tradition. Most early philosophy was in prose, and the early rationalization and ordering

Intro.3.1a   A. Momigliano, "The Place of Herodotus in the History of Historiography," Chapter 8 of his *Studies in Historiography* (London, 1966), 129.

Intro.3.2a   Troy: Map Intro.1.

Intro.3.2b   D. Boedeker, "Epic Heritage and Mythical Patterns in Herodotus," Chapter 5 in *Brill's*

Companion to Herodotus, and S. Hornblower, "Introduction," in Hornblower, ed., *Greek Historiography* (oxford, 1994), 65–7 on Homeric speech and rhythms. Note also S. Saîd, "Herodotus and Tragedy," Chapter 6 in *Brill's Companion to Herodotus*, for an excellent analysis of the tragic in Herodotus.

of the myths by writers such as Hekataios were written in a rather dry prose. By Herodotus' time, then, prose was the medium for serious investigation into the world, although Homer's authority was still enormous. We can often see Herodotus distancing his account and his whole approach from the Homeric vision. One example we saw above, where Herodotus proclaimed (effectively) that it was only the recent past that could properly be known as a subject of real knowledge (1.5.3). In Herodotus' idea that wisdom comes from travel, which he implies in his description of his own research and makes still clearer in the account of the travels of Solon the lawgiver (1.29–33), we might see echoes of the Homeric Odysseus, "who saw many cities and came to know their minds" (*Odyssey* 1.3). But Herodotus often demolishes traditions and criticizes myths. He takes apart the veracity of basic elements of Homer's *Iliad* in a remarkable section of Book 2, where he argues that Helen never reached Troy but remained in Egypt for the war, and he believes Homer rejected this version as inappropriate for epic (2.113–120). Herodotus often recorded traditions as they stood, as is often pointed out, but he also corrected them, and stressed that he had the truth. He seems deliberately to mark his distance from the great epics in his very opening sentence (Proem): "the publication of his inquiry" (*apodexis histories*) is an expression which belongs to the intellectual currents of the second half of the fifth century, and it is placed just before he expresses the desire to preserve the fame of great achievements, which is an entirely Homeric idea. Then the next five paragraphs (1.1–5) juxtapose legends of various women being seized in rationalized versions of the old legends, with accounts about the past which he characterizes as what "I know." The epic poet appealed to the Muse to give him his story: "Sing, goddess, of the wrath of Peleus' son Achilles" (*Iliad* 1.1), the oral poet calling upon the Muse for inspiration and the very material of his epic. Herodotus' opening, on the other hand, signals to his audience that his sources are actually his own inquiries, his own travels, his own experience (or *autopsy*). The hint at external sources of information is couched in terms of a new, entirely human-based search for knowledge.

§3.4. Herodotus' awareness of his sources, the way he actually mentions his methods and distinguishes between what he has seen and what he has only heard, enable him to delineate his work as a new kind of "inquiry." For instance, he emphasizes that the Egyptians keep records of the past and therefore are "the most learned" of any people he knows (2.77), and he claims the Egyptian priests as sources of information throughout Book 2. Or, more implausibly, he declares that he himself saw a great marvel at the site of the battle of Pelusium, where he was shown the Egyptian and Persian skulls which still lay there in separate piles, and he claims an identical experience at the battlefield of Papremis (3.12; see further below, §4, Herodotus' Reliability). This idea of novelty might at first seem paradoxical when he is recording past traditions and past *histories* (e.g., the past history of

Sparta, 1.65–68), and when many of his stories have the archaic ring of the folktale (the story of Polykrates' ring [3.40–42], the story of Solon's visit to Croesus [1.29–33], the rise and fall of Croesus in Book 1). But in many ways Herodotus' *Histories* show his immersion not only in the traditions of his times but also in the most exciting intellectual developments of the latter part of the fifth century. His inquiry was a significant part of the shared milieu in that period that included early medical investigations and speculation, philosophical experiments, sophistic arguments, and creative speculation of all kinds. His methods of inquiry and his own awareness of them reveal that he is very much a product of this intellectual climate. Today we expect historians to be aware of their methods and sources, but this practice only began in the latter part of the fifth century. It is visible in the texts of the early medical writers which were collected under the name of Hippocrates, and in the works of contemporary philosophers, and in general in this period, different methods of getting at the truth, with or without the help of visual evidence, were being investigated. Thucydides picked up Herodotus' methods and improved upon them, stating his methods in a more compressed and authoritative manner but with some of the same vocabulary (*Thucydides* 1.20–22). Had Herodotus not led the way, Thucydides' task would have been far harder.

§3.5. There are also links between different writers of the period in the treatment of certain topics. When Herodotus described in Book 4 the customs *(nomoi)* of the Scythians, an ethnic group which lived in what is now the Ukraine, he balanced this with an account of the geography of the area, which was remarkable for its many rivers. We know from the late-fifth-century essay "Airs, Waters, Places," attributed to the doctor Hippocrates, that Scythia was a focus of attention to those intent on linking climate and geography to the physical character of the human inhabitants: this link in turn determined their susceptibility to certain illnesses, particularly the Scythian "female disease." The Scythians turn up elsewhere in the Hippocratic corpus and seem to have been something of a cause célèbre as people whose physical constitution was extremely damp; the Libyans were the opposite, very hot and dry, and in Greek eyes, therefore, much healthier. Herodotus' work bears a fascinating and complex relationship to these ideas. He knows about these investigations and can employ the idea of environmental determinism himself (e.g., 1.142.1–2, 2.77, 9.122), but he does not borrow slavishly. On the contrary, he seems to criticize them implicitly, as when he stresses that the Scythians' nomadism was the really effective part of their strategy in resisting the Persians (4.46.2), or when he emphasizes that custom/law *(nomos)* is the governing principle in the character of a people (3.38). Here he tells of an experiment of the Persian King Darius, who asked a group of Greeks what it would take to persuade them to eat the bodies of their dead parents: they exclaimed that nothing could induce them to do such a thing. Darius then asked a group of Indians,[a] who were cannibals, what they would take to burn their parents' dead bodies (as the Greeks did), and they were equally horrified by the very idea. Thus, from this demonstration, Herodotus concludes that the famous

Intro.3.5a   Delos: Map Intro.1.

poet Pindar was right: "custom [*nomos*] is king of all" (3.38). Here custom is implicitly contrasted with nature and the environment. One of the primary interests of the various writers we call sophists was in the relation or opposition between nature and custom, *physis* and *nomos*. Medical writers linked geography and climate to health and constitution in a type of environmental determinism. So when Herodotus stresses the importance of *nomos* here, as he does also for an explanation of Spartan superior courage in a conversation between King Xerxes and the former Spartan king Demaratos (7.101–104), he is engaging in the same debate, and coming down on the side of *nomos* as the determining factor.

§3.6. Elsewhere he criticizes current theories with arguments and vocabulary which would have been thoroughly familiar to other contemporary intellectuals (whether we call them natural philosophers, sophists, or medical writers matters less here, since they overlap considerably in this period). For instance, he criticizes the Ionian writers who believed Egypt comprised only the Egyptian Delta: "If we think correctly about these things, then the Ionians do not think sensibly about Egypt; but if the opinion of the Ionians is correct, then I undertake to show that neither the Greeks nor the Ionians know how to count, who say that there are three parts to the earth, Europe, and Asia and Libya" (2.16: a deliberately inelegant but literal translation). His greatest tour de force in this vein is his long section about the different theories on the cause of the Nile River[a] flood, knocked down one after the other in Herodotus' most argumentative and polemical style (2.19–27). When Herodotus says in the first person, about the Macedonian[b] kings, "Now that these are Greeks . . . as they themselves say, I can affirm of my own knowledge, and indeed, I will demonstrate this later on, that they are Greeks" (5.22), when he talks of having proof and evidence, he is using the flamboyant, polemical, and demonstrative style that was fashionable in the latter part of the fifth century, particularly in the display lecture for a live audience and the investigation into natural philosophy and medicine.

§3.7. Knowing about fashionable theories, however, does not necessarily mean that someone accepts them. To say that Herodotus shared some of the ideas and language of the medical writers and sophists is not to affirm that he necessarily accepted all their views, still less the more radical ideas associated with certain sophists. He says in his own person that he believes *nomos* (custom, law) to be crucial to human society (3.38), which distances him from the most subversive sophists, who championed "nature" as more important in human morality, but he seems happy to declare one or the other custom that he describes to be an excellent one. He singles out the Babylonian marriage market practice to be "the wisest custom" of the Babylonians[a] (1.196). Sadly, it had fallen into disuse, he says, but they used to hold an auction in which the money offered by rich men to acquire the most beautiful women as wives was then redistributed as dowries to give to the less beautiful as a kind of compensation, so that everyone, rich and poor, beautiful and less beautiful, could thus find a mate. This is not the remark of someone who simply

Intro.3.6a Nile River: Map Intro.2, inset.
Intro.3.6b Macedon: Map Intro.1, locator.

Intro.3.7a Babylon: Map Intro.2.

accepts all human customs as equally good or worthy. He expresses disagreement with those who thought animal behavior could be used as a justification for human behavior: speaking of the Egyptian and Greek taboo against coupling in temples, he says that some said this was justifiable because animals did it, but "I do not agree with those who now defend their practice in this way" (2.64). It was a fashionable sophistic trick to defend the apparently indefensible on the grounds of animal behavior: such arguments and their often ridiculous implications are parodied by Aristophanes in *The Clouds* (1421–1431). Herodotus seems to know of such arguments, but he is firmly traditional: animal behavior is one thing, the world of humans another. He was part of the "Greek Enlightenment"[b] in many ways, but remained distant from the most radical or revolutionary theories of the sophists.

§3.8. Above all, he believed that there was a truth that could be discovered, or at least he was keen to affirm that he was finding out the truth: the *Histories* are full of statements of fact and corrections by Herodotus both to false anecdotes and to accepted tradition. Moreover, while he shared the late-fifth-century emphasis on human activities in determining the course of events, he believed, like most Greeks, that oracles would come true, and that the divine might affect the human world. This perhaps deserves some emphasis. Greek states and Greek citizens consulted the oracles, above all the oracle at Delphi,[a] about their future course of action, and if we believe the traditions, questions might be direct or roundabout, and the answers might range from an enigmatic riddle to the most straightforward directives about what deities to honor in order to achieve the desired result. Apollo at Delphi is portrayed repeatedly as foretelling the future (e.g., oracles for Argos and Miletus, 6.19, 6.77, 6.86), and it is striking that in Herodotus' *Histories* the oracle may be misunderstood or misinterpreted by the human actors, but the oracle, mouthpiece of the god, does not itself lie (the priestess may be bribed to give a false oracle, as in 5.63 and 5.66, but that is another matter). It is the fault of men if they willfully or arrogantly interpret an oracle in such a way as to defeat their original hopes. Croesus, for example, interpreted the oracle "You shall destroy a great empire" to mean that he himself would be successful against the Persians, whereas it actually meant the opposite, as the god Apollo pointed out to him afterward: the destroyed empire would be his own (1.53, 1.91). While the gods do not feature as actors in the historical narrative of the *Histories*, as they do in Homer, Herodotus does affirm that "It is plain from many pieces of evidence that the hand of god is active in human affairs." He makes this claim in his narrative of the last stages of the Persian Wars, and the final battle against the Persians at Mycale in Asia Minor. He states that "it is plain" if it is true that the rumor of the Greek victory at Plataea against the Persians managed to reach the Greek army fighting the Persians on the same day all the way across the Aegean at Mycale (9.100). There is a hint of caution here (note the careful expression), but we are left with the strong impression that the divine plan was indeed to encourage the Greeks fighting at Mycale, so that they would win the victory in Asia

Intro.3.7b "Greek Enlightenment" (here and later, in §5.9) is the term sometimes used to refer in shorthand to the upsurge in intellectual creativity and innovation in the second half of the fifth century associated with Periclean Athens, the emergence of the sophists, Thucydides, Euripides, and Socrates, the period envisaged as background to Socrates' discussions in most of Plato's dialogues. See, e.g., F. Solmsen, *Intellectual Experiments of the Greek Enlightenment* (Princeton, 1975).

Intro.3.8a Delphi: Map Intro.1.

as well as the crucial final battle on the Greek mainland. The hand of "the god" (unnamed) is also seen in the terrible storm off Euboea which did so much to reduce the superiority of the Persian fleet so that it should equal the Greek one (8.13).

§3.9. Herodotus' moral world is thus one which looks backward rather than forward and which often seems reminiscent of an older Greece. It is worth dwelling on this further. Modern readers are struck almost immediately in the *Histories* with the sense that men (and women) are punished by the gods, brought down, for excessively arrogant behavior or for the sins of their forefathers. The story of Croesus king of Lydia offers all of this, and its place as the main opening narrative suggests that Herodotus meant it to be emblematic in some way for the rest of the *Histories*. Croesus, the fabulously wealthy Lydian king, was anxious to show off his wealth and good fortune to Solon the Athenian, one of the many wise men who visited Croesus (1.29–34). Solon, however, was unimpressed, offering instead two examples of men of greater happiness: Tellus, who died bravely and received a public burial, and Cleobis and Biton, who died in their sleep after their strenuous efforts on behalf of their mother and the deity. From these examples he also draws the uncomfortable and paradoxical moral "Never call yourself happy until you are dead": man's life is buffeted constantly, and the gods are jealous; good fortune can change very suddenly (1.32). The gods seemed to punish Croesus for thinking himself the happiest of men, for Croesus continued in his high opinion of himself, misinterpreted in his arrogance the enigmatic oracle mentioned above which said "You shall destroy a great empire," attacked the Persians, and lost everything. Not only had he brought this misfortune on himself by his own arrogance, but it turns out that he was also suffering for the misdeeds of Gyges, an ancestor five generations back (1.90–91). When he accused the god Apollo of misleading him with the oracle, Apollo replied that he had managed to delay Croesus' fate for three years, but not even the gods could escape the fates.

§3.10. This awareness of the transience of human fortune and the jealous nature of the gods fits smoothly with the moral view of man's place in the world that we see in earlier poetry and much of Athenian tragedy. It is very Greek, very traditional, and to some extent Herodotus may have absorbed and continued it from the traditions which he recorded and reused; by definition these would tend to encapsulate traditional lines of morality, and the idea that the gods would punish arrogance. Yet the placing of this story of Solon and Croesus, as I have said, suggests that Herodotus meant the moral to have emphasis for his *Histories* as well, and it may be significant that the warning figure is a highly respected Athenian. At the start of the *Histories*, just before he turns to Croesus, he says he will "describe equally the small and the great cities of men. For the cities which were formerly great have most of them become small; and such as are powerful in my time were formerly weak. I shall therefore tell equally of both, knowing that human happiness [*eudaimonia*] never continues long in one place" (1.5). The instability of human fortune, then, was to be a central theme. It is this, followed by the Croesus tale, that persuades some scholars that Herodotus meant the warning to have force in his own day, and for the most powerful and most prosperous city of his time, the city of Athens. The virtue of Herodotus' narrative style and presentation is that he does not need to spell out a message: the implied moral lies there implicit in the text for anyone to see if they so wish, clothed in the garb of traditional and therefore unprovocative wisdom, and his exact intentions remain ambiguous.

§3.11. We should also consider here as an abiding force the motif of revenge and the dynamic of "tit for tat," more elaborately called "reciprocity," which readers will see in the often bewildering chains of explanations offered for actions and motives. This, too, seems to be an archaic or traditional motif and was probably embedded in the oral traditions of many cities as the explanation for an action or situation, with all the simplification that oral tradition brought to bear on complex historical forces. In a particularly complex example, the Spartans in the late sixth century help some Samian exiles to defeat the Samian tyrant because, we are told, the Samians had once helped them, the Spartans, in a struggle against the Messenians;[a] but the Spartans themselves see their action as revenge because the Samians had once stolen a bowl which Sparta had sent to Croesus (3.47). The Corinthians are also willing to help, because they had been insulted by the Samians generations before in a manner which Herodotus then explains (3.48–49). This rather crude form of explanation seems also to be a powerful traditional motif in explaining the behavior of individuals, though it is by no means the only form of causation in the *Histories*. The expansion of the Persian Empire can equally be defended in terms of the need to maintain the dynamism of the ruling power (7.8–9). The opening of Book 7 offers a spectrum of different forms of causation and explanation for the Persian invasion alongside the traditional motifs of reciprocity and revenge.

4. Herodotus' Reliability

§4.1. How far can we believe Herodotus' account? Are the *Histories* reliable, or some sections more reliable than others? Is the love of a good story sometimes more attractive for Herodotus than the quest for the truth? Herodotus' reliability has often been questioned, and some even wonder whether he was committed to giving historically accurate information at all. Could a serious historian really believe some of the implausible tales he recorded?—for instance, that an important stage in the Ionian Revolt against Persian power was launched by "the slave with the tattooed head"? For Histiaios, stuck in Susa,[a] sent a slave with a secret message tattooed onto his head and the hair grown over, to tell Aristagoras in Ionia that he should now revolt (5.35). Or that King Amasis of Egypt abandoned his alliance with Polykrates tyrant of Samos (late sixth century) because Polykrates was too fortunate and was therefore bound to meet a reversal? And then there is his curiosity about "marvels," exotic animals or

Intro.3.11a   Delos: Map Intro.1.
Intro.4.1a   Susa: Map Intro.2.

humans at the edges of the known world, of which his giant "gold-digging ants" of India are among the most notorious (3.102–105: this did not prevent Alexander the Great from looking for them, however, when he was in the vicinity [b]). And what about the Egyptian and Persian skulls neatly separated on the battlefield of Pelusium mentioned above (3.12), which enabled Herodotus to discover an interesting fact about skull thickness? The sometimes bewildering combination of serious political analysis and wondrous marvels has led to the nickname "father of history, father of lies." A more extreme accusation has been made that he deliberately and quite consciously gave false information or even made it up. A few modern scholars suspect that he goes much further than relaying doubtful information, and that he consciously invented material, stories, and even the very statements he gives about how he got his information (for example, the Egyptian priests cited as his sources in Book 2).[c] One or two have even doubted that he went to Egypt at all, despite his frequent remarks about what he saw there and though he repeatedly pressed upon the reader his own experiences, what he saw himself, as a reason for believing him. If we accept this skeptical view, our image of Herodotus the traveler and researcher would be left in total disarray. Yet, on the other hand, his integrity is also defended, sometimes vehemently. Occasionally he may be pulling the wool over his audience's eyes, we might admit, but then there are counterarguments, too. Perhaps (some scholars suggest) he has simply got things wrong, been misled by his informants, or been taken in by exotic travelers' tales; or perhaps he simply could not resist including some curious but questionable stories (the giant ant tale is said to be a Persian account).

§4.2. The disagreements and indeed the very controversy seem to hinge mainly on two questions: first, what do we think Herodotus meant to convey to his fifth-century audience, who may not have understood his statements in the way a modern reader might? And second, what was he in a position to hear, see, find out, and investigate in that period? For the first question, he clearly does indicate that he has carried out investigations himself, that he has traveled widely and questioned people, and it would seem most unlikely that he would have invented these practices completely when he was inventing the method of carrying out such research: the satire or parody of a genre is likely to be a comparatively late development within that genre, not an initial stage. For instance, early in Book 2, Herodotus gives a fascinating story about an experimental rearing of young babies organized by the Egyptian pharaoh Psammetichos in order to find out the first (natural) language, and the story he prefers is the one given him by the priests of Hephaistos at Memphis,[a] though the Greeks have their own versions of the story, and he comments further on the learned Egyptian priests with whom he conversed (2.2–3). This sounds like an elaborate, perhaps slightly labored, effort to stress new and thorough, if somewhat eccentric, methods of inquiry. One strand of the debate has criticized the way Herodotus loosely gives a version of events or motives as "what is said" by the Athenians, or the Corinthians, or the Egyptian priests, and if taken absolutely literally, these references are sometimes

Intro.4.1b   W. K. Pritchett, *The Liar School of Herodotus* (Amsterdam, 1993), 90ff., gives various attempted explanations (e.g., marmots' barrow debris dug from gold-bearing sands), all assuming there is some kernel of truth in the tale.

Intro.4.1c   Most particularly argued by D. Fehling, "Herodotus and His Sources," in *Citation, Invention and Narrative Art* (Leeds, 1989; translated and revised from German original of 1971).

Intro.4.2a   Memphis: Map Intro.2, inset.

puzzling or invite skepticism. However, not all the remarks about certain traditions need necessarily imply that he has gone to the most knowledgeable and direct source (which in itself would be unlikely for all cases). I would particularly emphasize phrases such as "the Athenians say," "but the Persians say," "the Corinthians say," which recur throughout the *Histories*. Taken literally, these expressions might imply that Herodotus talked to "the Athenians," or more likely, members of the Athenian elite, and that these were therefore his direct source, Herodotus giving us a tradition with mention of his source in an almost modern fashion. So some scholars interpret them. But it is almost invariably a piece of Athenian history that "the Athenians say," or a Samian version that "Samians say," all quite neat and logical. Should we take these literally? A more plausible interpretation[b] is that Herodotus usually means no more than "This is the Athenian tradition" or "This is the general Athenian version of events," "This version belongs to the Athenians," thus that he is signaling the social memory, the collective memory, and his audience would know this quite well. We shall return to this when we look at oral tradition below.

§4.3. Turning to the second question, we should not judge his account purely against modern standards of accuracy. It is occasionally suggested that because he is simply wrong in modern scientific terms, he cannot have seen what he says he has seen. His account of the Labyrinth in Egypt (2.148), a great "wonder," is hard to match up with the later description of Strabo and the foundations that are all that is left of this immense building—though a reconstruction is possible, and one might expect from its very name that casual observers like Herodotus might indeed find the grand plan hard to grasp.[a] The measurements of the Euxine (Black) Sea are not strictly accurate, though he says he was on the north coast (4.81), and it is strange that he has remarkably little to say about the great temples of Thebes and Luxor[b] in Egypt, which he says he visited (2.3, 2.54 or 2.55.1, 2.143, strongly implied). A more complex example, which tantalizes the modern reader into wondering what he really saw in Egypt, is the striking section where he claims that the Egyptians do everything the other way around to the rest of mankind: "The Egyptians themselves in their manners and customs seem to have reversed the ordinary practices of mankind. For instance, women attend market and are employed in trade, while men stay at home and do the weaving. Men in Egypt carry loads on their heads, women on their shoulders, women urinate standing up, men sitting down" and so on, and he continues in this vein for some time, moving gradually to a detailed account of the most remarkable of Egyptian practices like mummification (2.35–36, 2.37ff.). There are many theories about what Herodotus might have meant here which serve to defend or undermine his veracity. Despite all this, however—both antithesis and exoticism—he still believes that the Greeks learned a great deal from the Egyptians, including much Greek religious practice (he presents this as his own discovery), so they are hardly "opposite" in every respect. An even more notorious example is that of the flying snakes from Arabia,[c] whose skeletons he claims to have seen himself lying

---

Intro.4.2b See N. Luraghi, "Local Knowledge in Herodotus' *Histories*," Chapter 7, in N. Luraghi, ed., *The Historian's Craft in the Age of Herodotus* (Oxford, 2001), an excellent critique of Fehling, "Herodotus and His Sources."

Intro.4.3a See Alan Lloyd's commentary, *Herodotus, Book II*, Vol. III, on 2.148 for details of reconstruction.

Intro.4.3b Luxor (Thebes): Map Intro.2, inset.

in great piles at Bouto,[d] where they were killed by ibises as they entered Egypt (2.75–76). They have puzzled most commentators. What could he possibly have seen, if anything? (Guesses abound.) Yet he says he went to Bouto expressly to inquire about these snakes. Was he too credulous when being shown around by his Egyptian guides, or does some chain of stories and misunderstandings lie behind this that can only elude us now? He claims that his information about Egyptian history and much else comes from discussion with the Egyptian priests, but the accuracy of his accounts compared to modern knowledge of Egypt is quite patchy. His account of the process of mummification is astonishingly accurate, but could he really have talked to priests? Or to lower temple attendants he assumed were priests? Or did he simply talk to Greek intermediaries in Greek?[e]

§4.4. We need some common sense here, and we should not lose sight of an appreciation of what Herodotus was trying to achieve that was new. Scientific history was not yet invented, indeed "history" itself was not yet a discipline, traveling was difficult, geographical knowledge still mingled with what we would call mythical space, permanent notekeeping was probably difficult. Anyone with extensive travel experience knows how topography, places, and details can get inextricably confused, even (or especially) with the help of the camera. A superficial acquaintance with local culture can, in a travel account or guidebook, take on the veneer of a more profound understanding of what is essentially an alien culture. Modern travel writers frequently take shortcuts, despite the ease of modern travel. Moreover, the observer is likely to see things through the filter of his or her own culture: certain features will be picked out, others left unobserved, yet others misinterpreted. Just on these grounds alone, it seems hardly surprising if Herodotus sometimes has curious views of a place or people when compared to the full archaeological evidence now available. It is quite possible that the "Egyptian priests" to whom he talked lacked an entirely accurate picture of their country's history, and that the accounts attributed to them in the *Histories* might also represent an amalgam of Greek ideas of what the priests said and the priests' traditions seen inevitably through a Hellenizing lens. Then again, certain of the priests' traditions (as recounted by Herodotus) may in fact reflect developments in Egyptian temple culture of the fifth century.[a] Perhaps Herodotus did not describe the fabulous temple of Karnak[b] because he did not go there, or was not allowed in, or for some reason was only briefly in Thebes, or not at all (as above, he says he went there at 2.3; see also 2.143). Could he have lifted his famously odd description of the hippo, with its mane and tail "like a horse" (2.71), from his predecessor Hekataios, hoping that Hekataios had seen more of one than he had? Was this one of his shortcuts, and one that he did not realize would be detected because Hekataios had also taken a shortcut? Or were they both simply concocting the description from the very name *hippopotamos* ("river horse")? It is hard indeed to believe he went to Babylon, simply because his description is bizarre and exaggerated; and indeed he never quite says he did, only that he will not

Intro.4.3d Bouto: Map Intro.2, inset.
Intro.4.3e See Appendix C, The Account of Egypt, §7, a discussion of Herodotus' Egyptian sources, for his section on Egyptian history.
Intro.4.4a See, for instance, I. Moyer, "Herodotus and an Egyptian Mirage," *Journal of Hellenic Studies* 122 (2002), 70ff., for fifth-century Egyptian culture and Herodotus.
Intro.4.4b Karnak (Thebes): Map Intro.2, inset.

describe the yields of millet and sesame because no one would believe it unless they had been there themselves (1.193.4). And when he says, "The greatest wonder for me, after the city itself, I will now describe" (1.194.1), he is using an oddly oblique way of implying his own personal knowledge. So yes, Herodotus probably took a few shortcuts. But to go further and disbelieve all his claims to have seen what he says he saw, to deny all his assertions that he was trying to discover true accounts of the present or past, would certainly be extreme. Moreover, it would be surprising for someone to invent examples of conventions within a genre that did not yet exist, as I mentioned above: the parody of a genre is likely to be a relatively late development within that genre. The most interesting point is that he tried to describe foreign cultures, foreign monuments, and foreign mentalities at all, and that he did so with an open-mindedness which is astonishing.

§4.5. He was also contending with the frayed edges of the world as it was known to Greeks, the ends of Greek knowledge, where perhaps someone heard from someone else about the tribes or geography beyond the next horizon. What is striking, and would have been revolutionary in his day, was that he bothered to point out for his audience tales that he thought stretched credulity, and where his own knowledge gave out. In Book 2, he says he went down the Nile as far as Elephantine,[a] at the First Cataract: "I went to Elephantine and saw for myself; after that I rely on hearsay (*akouē*)" (2.29.1). It seems a little unlikely that he had really traveled as far as Elephantine, for he had just mentioned an absurd account of the sources of the Nile north of Elephantine with two conical mountains called Crophi and Mophi and fathomless springs which flow one toward Egypt, the other to Ethiopia (2.28), and he says he thinks the scribe who told him this was "playing" (*paizein*, 2.28). Yet far later accounts may corroborate the names as truly Egyptian: was Herodotus amalgamating folktales and topography? Or one tale with another?[b] Or his own experience with curious and not entirely compatible accounts from Egyptians? What is significant is that his curiosity did not stop even there, and he proceeded to add hearsay accounts of what lay beyond even Elephantine.

§4.6. We should also reckon with the extreme difficulty of fully appreciating an alien culture, as modern anthropologists are well aware. Outsiders' perceptions may be influenced, perhaps fatally, by their own preconceptions and theories, and the prejudices or assumptions of their own culture. Nor do local informants always give the most informed or most "official" account of local practices. Herodotus went to Egypt and Scythia with an array of Greek conceptions and expectations and to some extent he must have seen these cultures through Greek eyes: when he says that the Egyptians are quite the opposite in their customs to the rest of mankind, mankind seems primarily to be Greeks (2.35). The fascinating question that arises for the reader of Herodotus is how far he has combined common Greek perceptions, more educated Greek theories, and the awkward intrusion of the visual evidence, what he saw himself, that might correspond to neither of these. He made sense of the world in part in terms of the Greek division between Greeks and barbarians, but he transcended that dichotomy to such an extent that he could show noble barbarians and

Intro.4.5a   Elephantine (modern Aswan): Map 2.2, Egypt inset.
Intro.4.5b   See Appendix C for a discussion of the quality of Herodotus' account of Egypt. For more detailed information on that subject, see Lloyd's commentary, *Herodotus, Book II*.

praise barbarian customs. He could describe completely unfamiliar practices like the Scythian royal burials (4.71–73) or Egyptian mummification (2.86–90) in ways that correspond well to modern archaeological discoveries, and attribute much of Greek religious practice to Egyptian influence (e.g., 2.49–53). There were also models that were popular in Greek natural philosophy for understanding the world: the early Greek scientific division between the hot and the cold, the wet and the dry, seems to be there in his accounts of Scythia and Libya (note the large number of horned animals in Libya: Greek science held that horns grew best in hot and dry conditions). But which came first, the theoretical framework or the observation? Sometimes the theory. Some of his comments about the natural world seem bizarre now, but were taken seriously enough to deserve rebuttal by Aristotle (e.g., in *Generation of Animals* [755b6], he objects to Herodotus' "silly account" at 2.93 of how fish reproduce). We may also bear in mind that Greek natural science had its own interest in the apparently extraordinary, the obviously marvelous, as elements which demanded new explanation and further investigation.

§4.7. Wonders merited an account, however, in their own right, too: remarkable tales often appear in Herodotus precisely because they are marvelous. Some stories set in India and Arabia sound more like tall travelers' tales or, in the case of the spice harvesting of Arabia (3.107–112), exotic marketing tales. In any case Herodotus embraces the marvelous as a subject for his inquiry. On Egypt, he explains that he will describe it at great length because of the large number of remarkable things in the country, "and because of the fact that more monuments which are beyond description are to be found there than anywhere else. It is because of these that I will dwell on it at greater length" (2.35.1).

§4.8. Herodotus seems to have conceived of his task as covering the entire known world, mapping the vast expanses of the *oikoumenē*, the inhabited world, and mapping it in terms of what could be known and what could not, in terms of human activity and human inhabitants. He pointed out how far knowledge could reach, what was the furthest extent and the limit of human information. For instance, on the sources of the Nile he made a comparison with the Danube:[a] "Now as this river flows through regions that are inhabited, its course is perfectly well known; but of the sources of the Nile no one can give any account since Libya, the country through which it passes, is desert and without inhabitants. As far as it was possible to get information, I have given a description of the river" (2.34). On the edges of the *oikoumenē*, in particular, travelers' tales merged with myth: Hyperboreans—people living in the far north and mentioned by the poets—whose very existence Herodotus doubted (4.32–36), Libyans and the various inhabitants of the African desert which he charts going west (4.168–197), along with Lotus-eaters (4.177–178), dog-headed creatures, men without heads and therefore with eyes in their breasts (4.191) and people without names.

§4.9. His remarks about truth, falsehood, and probability are interesting here, for he notes quite emphatically for the reader what he considers unverifiable, and this serves to reinforce the information he gives elsewhere as correct. Thus "Ocean," the great river surrounding the known land mentioned by the poets, "takes the

Intro.4.8a   Danube (ancient Ister) River: Map Intro.1, locator.

matter into the realm of the invisible, which therefore admits of no refutation" (2.23, literal translation): thus one element of mythical and poetic geography is calmly set aside as beyond the possibility of proof! Other pieces of information about the edge of the world are hedged around with a careful marking of a train of informants, as with the travelers into the African interior who came across a crocodile-infested river flowing west to east, which must, Herodotus believes, be the Nile (2.32–33): he says that he got this account from the Cyrenaeans, who got it from Etearchos king of Ammon when he was at the oracle of Ammon[a] who told them what he had heard from the Libyan Nasamonians, whose wilder young men had explored the desert. In one of two possible proofs that Libya was surrounded by sea except for the Suez isthmus, he mentions the Phoenicians who sailed around Africa from east to west at the Egyptian pharaoh's behest, and insisted that the sun appeared on their right, i.e., to the north (4.42–43). Because of this statement, Herodotus declares that he does not believe them, but he relates it all the same, and for us the statement indicates their veracity and Herodotus' denial illustrates a limit of his geometrical knowledge. He may not be able to resist a good story at times, but he will often express disbelief or say that he is not sure (2.123.1, "the less plausible version should, since it was given, be declared"; more disingenuously perhaps on the politically delicate subject of Argive Medism,[b] 7.152.3, his method was to "repeat what was said"). There is a link here with his knowledge of current intellectual arguments mentioned above. He can express incredulity in modern, sophisticated language but have the best of both worlds in telling the story anyway. He mentions, for instance, the tale told by the "bald-headed men" who live beyond the Scythians: they say that the mountains beyond them, that is, in the far north, are inhabited by goat-footed men and beyond that, by men who sleep for six months of the year. Of the latter story, Herodotus says he thinks it "utterly incredible" (4.24–25). He can mention a story which amuses and fascinates while showing off his superior discernment in disbelieving it.

§4.10. It is remarkable that Herodotus does not simply follow the same vein of prejudice and simplification about various barbarian peoples that we see in other Greek writers of the time. He was influenced, like anyone, by the mentality of his age and culture, but he went far beyond that influence and often seems deliberately to puncture some prejudice about foreign peoples. As he says about Greek misunderstandings of the Egyptians, "the Greeks tell many silly stories without investigation and among them is the silly fable about Herakles" (in Egypt), which he proceeds to criticize on logical and rational grounds, since "the Greeks are utterly ignorant of the character and customs of the Egyptians" (2.45).

§4.11. But Egypt had fascinated Greeks for generations. Mentioned in Homer, it had become home to Greek traders and mercenaries who lived in Naucratis[a] and Memphis, controlled settlements in the Delta, from as far back as the late seventh century. Egypt was a source of exotic luxuries, ancient wisdom, and influential styles of monumental art. These were barbarians whom Greeks could admire. Of the other Near Eastern empires, Herodotus had a skimpy knowledge, but the Persians were another matter. They had attacked or conquered Greeks and were regarded with far

Intro.4.9a   Ammonion: Map Intro.2.
Intro.4.9b   Medism: see n. Intro.2.3a.
Intro.4.11a Naucratis: Map Intro.2, inset.

more hostility by them. It is all the more remarkable, then, how balanced and fair Herodotus is in his presentation of the Persians. He introduces the Persians as a people with some noble characteristics, for instance their abhorrence of lying (1.138), and some commendable customs, such as their rule that the king should not inflict the death penalty for a single fault (1.137). He carefully explains how, unlike the Greeks, they do not believe that the gods have human form (1.131). Cyrus the Great, who founded the Persian Empire, is depicted as an admirable ruler (though he yielded to excessive pride in the end), and to a lesser extent so is King Darius, who initiated the Persian invasion of 490. Cyrus' son Cambyses, however, is portrayed as totally without respect for normal conventions, let alone other peoples' beliefs, and Xerxes, the aggressor of the second Persian invasion, is also portrayed as the typical tyrant, prone to sudden and inexplicable bursts of brutality. It is undeniable that acts of autocratic atrocity are generally attributed to the Persian King. Yet Xerxes, seeing his great army about to invade Greece, is suddenly struck by the shortness of human life and, in an almost Solonian moment, realizes they will all be dead in a hundred years and bursts into tears (7.45–47). It is Cyrus who gives the wise advice about the perils of expansion and of acquiring riches which forms the very last paragraph of the *Histories* (9.122), the final words about the dangers of becoming soft and luxury-loving.

§4.12. Of course it is relatively easy to admit that your prime enemy (i.e., the Persians) had admirable traits as long as those traits were safely in the distant past and you can portray them as decadent and in decline in the present, the period in which you have defeated them. Yet it is striking that Herodotus portrays the Persians in Book 1 as courageous and fierce, and initially they are fighting for their freedom from the Medes (1.210.2, 1.126.5), though the Persian Empire in later Greek thought was regarded as antithetical to freedom. Herodotus insists that the Persian general Mardonios, on behalf of the Persian King, gave the Ionians democracy shortly after the disastrous Ionian Revolt (6.43.3). This was a claim which would have surprised an Athenian audience: Athenians behaved as if they had a monopoly on democracy. He once remarks slyly that the mainland Greeks were terrified of going east of the island of Delos,[a] for they thought that all the islands and the Asian coast were overrun with Persian soldiers (8.132.2). Here Herodotus was probably making a dig at the ignorance and fear of mainland Greeks; for Herodotus, who grew up in Halicarnassus, and his contemporaries who also lived on the western edge of the Persian Empire, were probably much more familiar with Persians than were the mainland Greeks, and much less naïve.

§4.13. It may also be the case that the in-between position of a place like Halicarnassus, partly Greek, partly Carian,[a] on the edge of both Athenian and Persian empires, enabled Herodotus to be reasonably evenhanded in his treatment of the Persian Empire. The recent publication of some remarkable Persian documents, the "Fortification Tablets,"[b] now confirm that Herodotus has a great deal of accurate information about the workings of the Persian Empire, including the Royal Road, its subject peoples, and many named Persian dignitaries and officials. His presentation of the Persians was far more sophisticated and rounded than the clichés that abound in

Intro.4.12a   Delos: Map Intro.1.
Intro.4.13a   Caria: Map Intro.1.
Intro.4.13b   Fortification Tablets: see Appendix M,

Herodotus on Persia and the Persian Empire, §3, n. M.3d.

political writings of other Greeks, particularly in the fourth century (Isocrates, Plato, Aristotle).[c] Five hundred years later, the first-century C.E. writer Plutarch was so disgusted by Herodotus' stance that he called him *philobarbaros*, "barbarian lover," in his strange essay "On the Malice of Herodotus." Indeed, Herodotus' curiosity about the customs and mores of non-Greek peoples from the Scythians to the Egyptians, not merely the main Persian antagonists, is a quite remarkable and original feature which was to exert a strong influence on Greek historians for centuries.

§4.14. To sum up, then, in many cases Herodotus' account was probably as reliable as his informants and sources—and probably in part replicated the oddities, distortions, and prejudices of his world and its traditions. In his accounts of distant and foreign lands, we need to recall that his subject matter does indeed include the marvelous. He may well have taken shortcuts occasionally, and included irresistible stories even though he did not quite believe them. His accounts, like any others, will have been influenced by his curiosity, prejudices, and particular interests. But we should not judge him rigidly or exclusively by modern standards. His preoccupation with true accounts and correct versions reveals that he was not merely peddling fictions. Some of the novelty of his achievement was precisely in the sustained and serious curiosity about non-Greek lands and peoples, and much of this, ridiculous though it may seem now, continued to be discussed by Greek writers like Aristotle interested in the *oikoumenē*, the inhabited world.

5. Oral Tradition and Historical Narrative

§5.1. Inquiring into existing foreign cultures and peoples is one thing, inquiring into the past is quite another: with the former there may be gulfs of comprehension, problems of perception and understanding, but if you were trying to investigate the past in the ancient Greek world, you were at the mercy of memory and tradition. The actual witnesses had died; there were few written sources to supplement the oral traditions. For events within living memory like the Persian Wars, there were plenty of informants, eyewitnesses and sons of participants, but the stories people were willing to give (as opposed to what they remembered privately) might be colored by the desire for personal fame or good reputation and political constraints. As we have seen, the conduct of the various Greek cities in the Persian Wars still continued to be political dynamite. Herodotus tried to find out the truth, and as he made clear, he wished to mark out the brave and courageous, and those who betrayed Greek liberty. Hence, for example, he carefully distinguishes which cities and which individuals fought most courageously at Salamis (8.93–95) and at the final mainland battle at Plataea (9.71–75). Their fame must be recorded for posterity.

§5.2. While the most thorough narrative covers the events leading up to the Persian Wars and the wars themselves, the *Histories* are also an important source for much early Greek history. In this one work he provides our main and earliest evidence for the Peisistratid tyranny of sixth-century Athens and the struggles which ended it (1.59ff.,

Intro.4.13c   The Athenian Isocrates, for instance, in his *Panegyricus* (c. 380), declared at some length that the Persians were servile in behavior, pampered by luxury, and degenerate (see Chapters 145, 150–155), while at the same time complaining, somewhat illogically, that the Persian King now controlled Greek destinies.

5.55–78). He even provides us with the main narrative account of Kleisthenes' reforms of 507, which gave Athens her moderate democracy (5.69–73): they can be supplemented with later documentary evidence, but the short paragraph at 5.69 is central. He provides the earliest and irreplaceable accounts of the great tyrannies of Greece, Kypselos and the Kypselids at Corinth, Polykrates of Samos, Orthagoras of Sicyon.[a] His treatment of early Spartan history is fundamental (if flawed, like all accounts of early Spartan history), and he records important traditions about some of the cities which played a part in the colonizing movement beginning in the eighth century, in which Greek communities were founded all around the Mediterranean. But these accounts are often more akin to anecdotal stories, or they have the rounded perfection of folktales without the historical credibility or political bite that we might wish.

§5.3. The fabulous story of how the infant Kypselos, the later tyrant of Corinth, was saved from murder by the ruling clan (5.92) has elements which can be found in folktales about "founding figures" across the world. Kypselos as a baby is hidden from certain murder in a chest (a *kypselos*) and spirited away to return later as ruler, a tale reminiscent of the tale of Moses in the bullrushes; the infancy of Cyrus the Great, who was to be exposed on a hillside when he was a baby; and the tale of Oedipus. In Herodotus' account of Cyrus' early years (1.108–123), he also refers to the "well-known tale" of the Persians that the baby Cyrus was suckled by a bitch, which he claims was a story put about by the real parents, who created the story to show his miraculous preservation. The version Herodotus prefers has a rationalized element in which a woman with the odd name Kyno ("bitch") wishes to save the baby Cyrus. We are clearly dealing with storytelling motifs which have grown up around certain figures, perhaps borrowed across cultures, and the amount of hard historical fact is probably minimal. It is just possible that Kypselos' name, which means "chest," points to a "kernel of truth," but we seem to be dealing with folktales and oral traditions which have survived generations. In addition to this, Herodotus has probably remolded the story yet again to suit his narrative, for it appears in a speech on the evils of tyranny (5.92).

§5.4. The impression of Herodotus' "naïveté," much of the famous Herodotean charm, the delight of the good story, the moralizing tales, are largely bound up with the presence of such folktales, which often form an important part of his narrative. These were the traditions of the Greeks, though, and it is simplistic to see them merely as signs of Herodotus' naïve credulity. The Greeks knew of their past from oral traditions, and in part from the poetic traditions (which themselves preserved or created some oral traditions). But events that occurred more than three generations ago would be only very loosely remembered and increasingly altered by the various oral traditions, unless they were embedded in the more lasting form of poetry; or they would be forgotten altogether. The Greeks had no formalized way of memorizing oral traditions of the recent past (epic dealt with the distant heroic past), so their traditions were particularly at the mercy of the vagaries of memory and the simplifying process of telling a good story. Above all, there had to be reasons of some kind not only to remember a tale but to pass it on down the generations. Those very reasons for transmitting the tales

Intro.5.2a Sicyon: Map Intro.1.

themselves play a part in the selection of the tales and the angles given to these tales which are passed on. Glorious achievements, for instance, are more keenly remembered than inglorious. A community will retain elements in the collective memory which may be different from those remembered by a family. There is a tendency for oral traditions to conform increasingly to communal fears and ideals, the ideals of the group; after all, one does not retell tales that an audience does not wish to hear.

§5.5. This explains why so many of the tales about the more distant past are noticeably more stylized than Herodotus' accounts of the recent past, the Ionian Revolt and the Persian Wars. Many tyrant tales were presumably transmitted in order to glorify the city's liberation from tyranny. Herodotus could omit these or retell them, while Thucydides chose instead to offer a concise and rationalized view of early Greek history down to the Persian Wars based on abstract theories about the growth of power (*Thucydides* 1.1ff.). We may presume that Herodotus relayed many of the traditions mostly as he heard them, though he may have altered them further to point out a moral or to fit what he thought plausible within his narrative. It is because he lacked Thucydides' distaste for such traditions that we are in the fortunate position of having a wealth of Greek oral traditions about the archaic age.

§5.6. As he wrote of events closer to his own period, Herodotus' narrative became more detailed. His account of the fall of the Athenian tyranny of the late sixth century and the eventual establishment of democracy is complex and sophisticated. It was not drawn (as used to be thought) from a single family source, and he was not taken in by the popular tradition of Athens, which glorified the tyrannicides even though they did not really end the tyranny. His account of the Ionian Revolt (499–495) is even more thorough. That, too, had important resonances in his day, for he claimed that the Persian King only thought of attacking Greece because Athens sent ships to help the Ionians free themselves. Only twenty ships, but "these ships were the beginning of evils for the Greeks," as he adds ominously and decisively (5.97; echoing Homer *Iliad* 5.62–65, 11.604). The account of the Ionian Revolt suffers from a curious emphasis on the petty and personal motifs of individuals who held responsible positions under the Persians, the tyrants Histiaios and Aristagoras, and it may well be that the tradition or, rather, various traditions were affected by the disastrous fact of failure. Since the revolt failed, memories were perhaps fragmented into recriminations, criticism of the Persian-backed tyrants, self-criticism for lack of discipline and organization. But even here we can be under no illusions about the importance of the revolt. Herodotus devoted considerable space to it, and while the reasons for its origins and failure do not entirely cohere, there can be no doubt that this was a politically charged narrative. The fate of the Ionian cities under the Athenian Empire was one that many cities regretted, others embraced, and it may have seemed important to Herodotus, who was from Asia Minor himself, to affirm that the Greeks of Asia Minor did in fact revolt: they had tried to gain freedom, they had not merely fought on the Persian side, but their geographical situation on the edge of the Persian Empire made it extremely difficult, if not impossible, to defeat the Persians, as discussions of the future of the Ionians attest (1.170, 9.106; see also 5.36).

§5.7. As he drew nearer his own time, Herodotus could use living witnesses, but he names very few. It is interesting that each of the witnesses he does name gives striking and surprising information. One was Thersandros, who told Herodotus about a banquet for Persian commanders he had attended in Thebes a few days before the battle of Plataea (9.16). His Persian neighbor at the banquet told him, weeping, that he thought the battle to come would leave few Persians alive. Herodotus also mentions an Archias, a Spartan whom he met in Sparta itself (3.54–55), who told him about the activities of his grandfather, also called Archias, whose bravery in the Spartan siege of Samos had been honored by the Samians with a public burial. A third named informant is Tymnes, an agent of a Scythian king, who tells him about the sage Anacharsis and his family (4.76).

§5.8. We can guess at other specific informants: Zopyrus, for instance, the grandson of the Zopyrus who helped Darius capture Babylon by a bizarre stratagem (3.160.2), for we have reason to believe that the younger Zopyrus visited Athens, and Herodotus could easily have met him there. Zopyrus could have given him access to inside information about the conspiracy by which Darius seized the Persian throne (3.71ff.). Many other informants remain unnamed, but Herodotus also stresses information that he received from Egyptian priests and other *logioi*,[a] such as the priests of Thebes and Dodona. There is little reason to doubt that Herodotus did talk to such people, the elite of their communities, though his "Egyptian priests" might have been quite lowly or the product of some misunderstanding of categories (for instance, he may have talked to people he took to be priests who were in fact more lowly). But we need also to take into account the vaguer, more nebulous general traditions and beliefs which can perhaps be called "social memory" or "collective memory," the general traditions that a community might have about its past, and which might be embedded in monuments or poetry. These surely existed, though it would probably still be elite members of such communities who relayed such traditions to Herodotus. Phrases such as "the Athenians say" may mean nothing more than that, as we saw above. Often these general traditions are cited so as to contrast them with the views of another group. For instance, the defamatory account of what the Corinthian contingent did at Salamis is presented as what the Athenians say, but the Corinthians deny that it has any truth at all (8.94). In fact, it is interesting that Herodotus felt that he needed to distinguish different traditions, different views of various groups, at all, and to mark this in the text. Thucydides, after all, mentioned virtually no informants, nor divergent views, perhaps in reaction to Herodotus. We cannot leave the *Histories* without a strong sense of separate polis traditions and diverging views. The author often leaves his audience to decide.

§5.9. It has been aptly said of Herodotus that "he did not invent his sources; he discovered the *problem* of sources."[a] This is where Herodotus' sense of his inquiry as belonging to the contemporary world intersects with his practice of distinguishing traditions and (occasionally) naming informants. His preoccupation with sources and evidence, with criticizing traditions, and his presentation of his inquiries in terms which sometimes mirror contemporary philosophical or scientific discussions

Intro.5.8a *Logioi* means those possessed of *logoi*, that is, "learned men."

Intro.5.9a R. L. Fowler, "Herodotus and His Contem- poraries," *Journal of Hellenic Studies* 116 (1996), 62–87: p. 86.

all indicate that his basic approaches to his inquiry—despite the marvels, oral traditions, and tall tales—belong to the intellectual currents of the latter part of the fifth century. The period of the "Greek Enlightenment"[b] saw an exploration of methods of arriving at the truth; the thinkers of the time developed new habits of argument, they explored the production of evidence and new ideas about what constituted proof and evidence. This is strikingly clear in early oratory and in the early medical writers, who were less concerned with abstract philosophical argument than with the business of diagnosing and curing patients. When he explicitly states and shares his methods, when he reveals a source or a group tradition or argues for his own view, and when he reveals or constructs his personality as an inquirer—all so absent from Thucydides—Herodotus seems to be identifying himself as belonging to the same late-fifth-century intellectual milieu. In the middle of Book 2, Herodotus says, "thus far I have relied on my own sight (*opsis*), and inquiry (*historiē*) and judgment (*gnōmē*), but from now on I rely on the accounts (*logoi*) given to me by the Egyptians, though with a little of my own autopsy (*opsis*)" (2.99.1), and with this he switches to the account of Egypt's past history. He is shifting from the type of knowledge that can be acquired by autopsy or "sight," experience and research, mostly Egyptian geography and social and religious practices, to the more problematic use of tradition or hearsay (*akouē*) for accounts of the past. In his very self-consciousness about this shift, and even more in the fact that he marks it explicitly, Herodotus was using the methods and style also familiar in the late-fifth-century medical world. We should presume that this was the now fashionable way of talking about the process of inquiry. But it was the radical achievement of Herodotus—so far as our evidence indicates—to apply those methods and that style to a sustained inquiry into the peoples of the inhabited world and to the narrative of the past itself.

§5.10. Herodotus' lasting achievement in the *Histories* was eventually to change the meaning of *historiē* "inquiry" for later generations to that of "history." This inquiry encompassed the longest and most sustained investigation yet attempted into the past, and especially the recent past, which was susceptible to rational inquiry, rather than the mythical periods which were the conventional material of poetry and which earlier mythographers had tried to rationalize. Since Herodotus' inquiry was also very much concerned with separating "true" accounts from false, with sifting arguments and traditions, and investigating causes (however conceived), above all the causes of the Greek-barbarian conflict, it can emphatically be seen as a work of history, and Herodotus thus as the first historian. But it is much more besides. While the geography and ethnography illuminate the historical processes and events, they are also there in their own right. For his own audience in the Greek world, his subject encompassed the whole of human activity in the known world of his day.

Rosalind Thomas
Balliol College
Oxford University

Intro.5.9b   Greek Enlightenment: see n. Intro.3.7a.

EDITOR'S PREFACE

Robert B. Strassler

Although I had a high opinion of Herodotus when I began work on this edition in 1997, I felt at that time that Thucydides was the greater historian of the two. That is no longer my view. In fact, I come away from completing this edition with a profound admiration for the *Histories* that transcends comparison with other works. Many elements of the narrative that at first appeared to me as weaknesses now appear to me to be remarkable achievements. What I initially saw as arbitrary digressions now stand revealed as cleverly inserted background material that often proves vital to a reader's understanding of later, sometimes much later, episodes. His omnivorous curiosity, which struck me as misplaced in a volume of history, now appears a fascinating and valuable asset to historical comprehension. And the vast scope of his tale in time and territory, which seemed so bewildering at first, proves in the end to be a fitting background for the epic scale of his climax. In short, I now recognize and admire the skill with which he crafted such a brilliant account of Persia's worldwide expansion and unexpected defeat at the hands of the mainland Greeks. I hope that many of those who read this volume (or any text of Herodotus, for that matter) will come to understand why I feel this way about Herodotus and will come to share my opinion.

Herodotus has been called the "father of history," and whether or not we would credit him with originating the field, we in the English-speaking world must admit that his work is the progenitor of much that we now call history. We are the cultural heirs, one might say the direct intellectual descendants, of Herodotus and other ancient Greek writers. For better or worse, our concepts and vocabularies for many disciplines—history, medicine, philosophy, mathematics, architecture, sculpture, theater, poetry, to name a few—have come down to us from these ancient Greeks, many of whom not only pioneered these fields but also produced brilliant works in them whose excellence is still recognized by us today, 2,400 years later. Herodotus is one of those, and the *Histories* is his masterpiece.

Our direct line of descent from his intellectual world, however, does not mean that everything he wrote can be easily understood by us. Although he says in his Proem that he had posterity in mind when he wrote, he could hardly have foreseen the immense changes that have occurred in human life over the last two and half millennia. Nor can he be faulted for this; who among us would have the temerity to predict what human life will look like two and a half millennia from now? Herodotus simply assumed that his readers would always be familiar with many elements of ancient Greek life about which he wrote and in which he lived. Thus he provided little explanation, elaboration, or background on what, to his ancient readers, would have been common and familiar aspects of life, but which today have become long-dead and forgotten customs and practices. The geography he describes has in some instances changed substantially over the centuries, and many of the cities and sites which figure in his narratives have disappeared or now exist under different names (which renders most modern maps useless and in some cases deceptive). Military tactics, religious rites, and political rules of ancient Greece are complete mysteries to current readers, who know nothing of rowed warships, animal sacrifices and other pagan religious rituals, or the rules and procedures of ancient Greek political institutions.

Unfortunately, current editions of Herodotus, although they may present skillful translations from the Greek, make little attempt to provide needed background information. They contain only a small number of often inadequate maps, sparse indexes, incomplete (and sometimes incorrect) chronologies, and few if any helpful appendices. There are exceptions to this blanket criticism, but no edition I know of makes a concerted or systematic effort to inform the reader of the general context, or about what some obscure but important elements of the text might mean, or even where and when the events described took place.

Modern readers who lack special schooling or assistance of some sort understand progressively less about what is happening as they proceed into the book and soon find the going arduous and confusing. After all, how much can readers expect to comprehend of a historical narrative if they are not informed of the date or location of many events, cannot envision the temporal or geographic relationship between events, or are unaware of the meaning and significance of important aspects of those events? This ignorance creates a barrier which obscures the readers' perception, diminishes their interest, and separates them from an essential quality of the narrative: its historicity. At its worst, the text becomes something like a literary exercise, a dreary recitation of disconnected incidents at unknown places concerning artificial characters whose names cannot be pronounced. At best, it reads like a modern fantasy novel, but all too often, it is a bad novel, a boring novel.

This transformation, or degradation, is particularly lamentable in the case of Herodotus, whose work, although it includes explicitly identified speculative and fabulous episodes, is truly a historical account of momentous and dramatic events that really took place. The Persians did mount attacks on mainland Greece, and they were repulsed. Arrow and spear heads have been collected from the battlefields of Thermopylae and Marathon and are now displayed in museums.[a] Many of the participants in this epic struggle—Greeks and Persians alike—were brave and intelligent men who acted and risked all without knowing what the future would hold;

EP.a   See Figure 6.117b.

and because Herodotus is a talented writer, his text can convey the dread that men feel when facing an unknown, ominous future. If he set out, as he says, to preserve for us the momentous deeds of real men in the real past, he has succeeded brilliantly. But if a reader today is unable to recognize that excellence, cannot perceive its power, and is not moved by the historical reality that lies at the heart of the text, then the reader has missed the essence of Herodotus, and of history.

This Landmark edition is an attempt to reduce the barriers between the general reader and Herodotus' text. It employs many of the same elements that were used eleven years ago in *The Landmark Thucydides*. Both editions, for example, contain a large number of maps, side notes, and footnotes, but since the two ancient texts differ significantly in scope and method, the number and nature of these and other features are not identical. In the section that follows I give a brief description and explanation of how the maps, notes, and the other features listed in this volume's contents page are to be read and used.

This volume contains 127 **maps** designed to support every episode of the narrative. Each one is located within or adjacent to the text it supports. Every known city, town, shrine, river, mountain, or other geographic feature that appears in the text is referenced in the text by a footnote to a nearby map. Those maps which display many labels employ a simple coordinate system to help readers search for a particular site. In the interest of clarity, each map displays the names of only those features that appear in the surrounding text. If the location of a place is unknown, the footnote says so. If we moderns are not sure of a site's location, our uncertainty is mentioned in the footnote and indicated on the map with a question mark. A few maps have been designed to support some of the appendices, and they are also placed into or adjacent to the relevant appendix text.

Although a number of maps are single images, most are double or triple, arranged in overlapping format from small scale (wide scope) to large scale (detailed scope). Thus the reader often finds a series of maps which are to be read from the top down, as their scale increases.

The first and topmost map is usually called a **locator map**, covering the widest and most easily recognized area. It is framed by a thin black border. Within the locator map a dark and slightly thicker rectangular outline identifies the location and boundaries of the **main map**. Occasionally, when the main map is of sufficient scope so as to be easily recognizable itself, the locator map is dispensed with and the main map becomes the topmost map. Many of the main maps contain one or two thick, light gray rectangular outlines indicating, in their turn, the location and edges of larger-scale **inset maps**. These maps (always with light gray borders) show areas of particular narrative interest in greater detail. All maps display simple distance scales in miles and kilometers.

Locating the correct map from the rectangular outlines is facilitated by map shape, common major sites labeled, prominent physical features (islands or coastlines), and border frame characteristics.

Following cartographic convention, water and other natural features such as islands and peninsulas are labeled with italics to distinguish them from cultural features, labeled with roman type. Centers of population are indicated using small dots and uppercase lettering designed to approximate their relative sizes and degrees of importance in the early fifth century. A **Key to Maps**[b] is located just before Herodotus' text begins with a complete legend of typography and symbols used, and an illustration of the map border frame system.

In the sample map to the right (Map 9.107, which means it is located in Book 9 by Chapter 107), the locator map stretches some 3,000 miles, from Italy to Baktria. The main map extends some 400 miles, centered on the Aegean Sea, and the inset map covers sixty miles of the Hellespont and Chersonese region.

Footnotes that cite labels found on the locator map show the word "locator." Those footnotes citing labels on main maps will show no other designation except for coordinates, if the main map has them. Any footnotes referring to an inset map will use the word "inset." If there are two inset maps, the footnote will identify which one is meant by an additional word such as "Egypt inset" or "Aegean inset." Sample footnotes referring to Map 9.107 illustrate those rules below.

> 9.108.2a Susa: Map 9.107, locator.
> 9.107.2b Halicarnassus: Map 9.107.
> 9.114.1c Abydos: Map 9.107, inset.

To assist the reader who wishes to rapidly locate a particular place, an index of all sites that appear on the maps in this book can be found in the final pages of this volume, along with a series of **Reference Maps**. Readers can quickly locate all important sites shown on the Reference Maps by their listing in the **Reference Map Directory**, which indicates the reference map number on which it can be found and the site's coordinates on that map. Sites mentioned only once in the text are included in the directory but they are often not shown on the Reference Maps for reasons of clarity and lack of space. Instead, the reader will be referred to a map within the text.

The authority for all the maps in this volume is the *Barrington Atlas of the Greek and Roman World*, edited by Richard J. Talbert and published by Princeton University Press in 2000. Readers who would seek larger, more accurate, and more detailed maps of any regions depicted in this edition of Herodotus should seek them in that atlas. In order to help those readers who do turn to the *Barrington Atlas*, all labels that appear on the maps of this volume are spelled exactly as they are in the atlas, so that no one seeking to find Cyme or Chalcidice in one volume will be confronted by Kyme or Khalkidike in the index of the other. Since the *Barrington Atlas* covers both the Greek and Roman periods, it employs an orthographic system in which place-names are transliterated into either Greek or Latin, and this apparently inconsistent set of transliterations is carried over into the maps of this volume. Some people may be bothered by this seemingly arbitrary bilingual labeling (although I

EP.b See Key to Maps located on page lxiv.

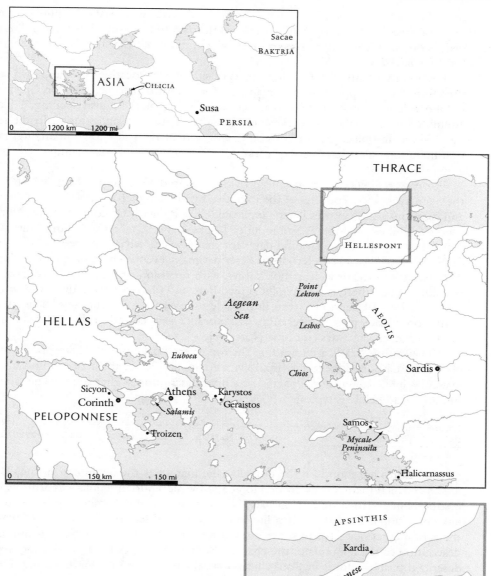

MAP 9.107

don't believe it will disturb the general reader). Anyone who wishes to pursue questions of map label orthography in this edition should consult Professor Talbert's discussion of ancient names presented on page xxv of the Introduction to the *Barrington Atlas.*

For all other names, that is, for names of sites whose locations are unknown and therefore do not appear on any maps, or for names of people, and for Greek or foreign nouns for which there is no commonly accepted English spelling, I have attempted to use only Greek transliterations, not Latin or English ones. In the few cases where an object, person, or country is particularly well known in an alternate transliteration—Pericles, Persia, trireme, and so forth—I have employed that common spelling.[c]

For easy reference, this volume provides a **Dated Outline of Text**, which lists the main events and episodes of the narrative by book and chapter, and applies dates and locations to the entries where applicable (and known). Of course, almost all the events described in Book 7, and in all of Books 8 and 9, take place during just two years, 480 and 479, so providing dates for them is fairly trivial. In the first six books of his *Histories,* however, Herodotus describes many events whose date and/or location is not known, or at least not known with precision or a reasonable degree of certainty. When there is a generally agreed date and place, they are displayed in the dated outline of Herodotus' text, in the side notes, and in the running heads found at the top of each page. Uncertainty or ignorance is indicated in the side notes and footnotes in various ways (see Side Notes below).

The **running heads** are found on the top of each page of text. They provide at a glance the dates and locations (if known and applicable) of the action found in the first complete chapter on the page, and a brief description of that action. The sample running head below is typical.

| BOOK FIVE 512? | PERINTHUS | *Megabazos conquers Perinthus* |

Side notes are found on the outside page margin at the beginning of the chapters into which the text was divided long ago by Alexandrian scholars. Normally, the first two lines of the side note display the book and chapter number and the date (if known or applicable). The third line shows in capital letters the location of where the action takes place (or in some cases, a topical title). Finally, there is a summary description of the contents of the chapter. Because the dates for a number of events described by Herodotus in Books 1 to 6 are unknown, or in dispute among scholars, and because he writes about customs and practices for which no date (and sometimes no location) is applicable, the data in the side notes must vary according to the circumstances. The sample side notes below, all drawn from Book 4, show the variations that may appear in the side notes.

EP.c   There are a few exceptions. The *Barrington Atlas* uses Latin "Mare" and "Lacus" for Sea and Lake, and in those cases I have used the English equivalents. Another exception occurs in the few instances where the *Barrington Atlas* uses a Greek name for a place or country that is very well known by its English equivalent. For example, where it uses "Persis," this edition uses the common "Persia."

There are also four or five unimportant sites located in one or two maps that are not found in the *Barrington Atlas,* and they are identified as such in the footnote which references them.

4.1
513
SCYTHIA
Darius marches against the Scythians.

This is the side note to Book 4, Chapter 1. It is a typical side note showing the date, 513 (B.C.E.; all dates in this volume are B.C.E. unless otherwise noted), and place, Scythia. Although Darius is not in Scythia when he decides to march, the important place to which the action refers is clearly Scythia.

4.2
SCYTHIA
How the blinded Scythian slaves
take milk from mares and separate it.

This chapter describes an element of Scythian culture (whether true or not is not in question here) to which no particular date could be applicable, so this side note has no date.

4.36
Herodotus mocks maps showing
the earth as round and Asia
equal to Europe in extent.

This chapter includes comments by Herodotus on some prevailing Ionian geographic concepts. It does not seem appropriate, helpful, or indeed possible to provide either a date or a location for the substance of this chapter, so this side note contains neither a date nor a location.

4.102
513?
EGYPT
The Scythians send messengers
to their neighbors.

This chapter relates an event which probably took place in the year 513, but about which scholars are not certain. The doubtful nature of the date is indicated by the question mark after the numbers.

4.160
?
LEUCON
King Arkesilaos quarrels with his
brothers and is killed after being
defeated by them in battle.

This chapter clearly describes a real event that took place in time so it should have a date, but the date is not known. The appropriateness of a date and our ignorance of it are signified by the lone question mark where a date should be. A plausible range might be given, and is given in a few instances, but I decided that in general, ranges of dates would not be a helpful elaboration. In this case it is obvious that the event must have occurred sometime after the Persian siege and capture of the city of Barke, which is thought to have occurred in 510.

4.155
BATTOS
The Cyrenaean
story of Battos.

This chapter describes the story of Battos, the man who was sent by the Delphic oracle to colonize Libya, who succeeded after many trials, and who even became king of the city of Cyrene. Since this saga took place over many years and in many location, I thought it best to head the chapter with a topical rather than a geographical sidenote.

The text of each chapter contains section numbers in **square brackets** [2] to mark the divisions into which scholars have traditionally divided the text for ease of search, analysis, and discussion.

Footnotes not only refer place-names in the text to nearby maps, as mentioned above, but they may serve to connect certain points in the text to other relevant sections, or to the work of other ancient writers and poets. They also cite particular paragraphs in the Introduction or in one or more of the appendices where the reader will find discussion of the topics or events footnoted. On occasion, they provide background information that does not appear in any of the appendices. They may also point out and briefly describe some of the major scholarly controversies over interpretation, translation, or corruption of the text.[d] A few explanatory footnotes are quite long and detailed, but they contain important information which could not be further condensed. Footnotes and map data are repeated throughout the work to assist those who will read only selections from it, or whose reading of the text is discontinuous.

Wherever possible and appropriate, I have converted Herodotus' original **units of distance** (stades, plethra, fathoms, cubits, etc.) into miles and feet, and provided footnotes citing the original ancient units listed in the Greek text. Unless the text indicates otherwise, I have made all conversion calculations assuming that Herodotus' intended "stade" was the Attic stade of 583 modern feet and his "cubit" to be the more or less standard cubit of one and a half feet. The reader should know, however, that we are not sure of the precise value for many of the ancient units he cites, that there were different "standard" stade and cubit units in use in the ancient Mediterranean world, and that Herodotus may well have intended one of these "others" when he generically names one. And finally, we cannot know how carefully and precisely he arrived at some of these measurements—many were clearly estimates, some were probably calculated guesses. Thus no decimal places can be ascribed to the numbers arrived at by my calculations, as no such precision is possible. I would advise any readers with

EP.d In the Introduction and Appendices, the authors
      may have used other or their own translations.

further questions concerning these matters to consult Thomas Martin's excellent Appendix J in this volume, "Ancient Greek Units of Currency, Weight, and Distance."

Herodotus' rare mention of **units of dry and wet measure** (artabe, choinix, medimnos) are stated in English transliteration and provided with modern American equivalents in footnotes. Currency is always stated in English transliteration of whatever units appear in the Greek text.

This edition of the *Histories* begins with an excellent and informative **Introduction** by Rosalind Thomas, in which she describes what is known of Herodotus himself, and where and how he and his work fit in the context of the intellectual world in which he lived and wrote.

It also contains some twenty-one of **Appendices** on various topics by a number of scholars. It is hoped that these will provide a sufficient minimum of explanatory and/or background information to help a general reader better understand and relate to the text. As was mentioned above, relevant paragraphs in the introduction and the individual appendices are cited by footnote throughout the text, so that the readers will know where to look for explanation or further information. A glance at the table of contents will show how many topics were deemed necessary for discussion in order to provide that minimum for the *Histories*. It is interesting to note that for Thucydides' work, which focuses almost exclusively on military and political history of the Greek world, what was thought to be sufficient background information for his reader was provided by just eleven appendices. Herodotus, who covers many aspects of life for several major cultures in a geographic area stretching from India to Spain and from Scythia to Ethiopia, required twenty-one, and we arguably could have used many more. Limitations of space, however, and our wish to write a book of, not about, Herodotus made it necessary to choose this select group from a vast range of possible topics.

To assist the reader who wishes to locate passages or subjects within the text, this edition offers the most thorough and complete **Index** that can be found to any English translation. There is, in addition, a **Glossary** of terms and a short **Bibliography** specifically designed for that general reader who might wish to read more about Herodotus or his world.

Finally, the book contains a number of **illustrations**. These are not intended to be just attractive ornaments; they have been chosen specifically to enhance the reader's sense of historicity of the text. For example, Figure 9.81b shows a vase painting by an Athenian artist of the late fifth century which depicts a very good likeness of a camel. Although camels are mentioned in several contexts in the *Histories*, I think it quite likely that the camels which served as models for this painter's very accurate depiction of what must to Greeks have been rare and exotic beasts were probably one of the camels (or a descendant) which Herodotus says accompanied Xerxes' army of invasion and which were captured by the Greeks and distributed with the rest of the spoils (9.81.2). Thus this vase painting may present a direct link to Xerxes' defeated army and adds an interesting element of verisimilitude to Herodotus' text.

The translation used in this edition is a new one by Andrea L. Purvis, who describes her work in her own **Translator's Preface** to this volume. I believe her translation is ideally suited for those who we hope will be the main readers of this edition. I did play a part in creating it, although, since I am not a scholar of ancient Greek and indeed can barely parse a simple sentence in that language, my role was a limited and subsidiary one. The only goal I could pursue in editing the translation with Andrea was to ensure that the resulting text would be clear, simple, and easily comprehensible for a modern reader. My narrow objective occasionally created difficulties for Andrea and led to some disagreements between us—she arguing for tighter fidelity to the Greek text and I for clarity in the English. I don't believe, however, that we were ever really far apart, and with time and iteration, we were always able to find a mutually agreeable compromise. As we came to know each other's methods and goals, our work pace increased and our problems diminished. I enjoyed our collaboration and learned a great deal from Andrea about ancient Greek and Herodotus. I am grateful to her for her many comments and suggestions, and it is fair to say that she contributed a good deal more to this edition than just the translation.

Years before Andrea Purvis began her translation for this book, I was able to download a text of Herodotus translated by A. D. Godley for the Loeb Classical Library[c] (Harvard University Press, 1920–1925), from the Perseus Project. I am grateful to both of these institutions, for this electronic text proved essential to the preliminary design of this volume's maps. Through that connection, a number of Godley's footnotes were incorporated into this volume and the editor sincerely regrets that inadvertently, these notes were not given proper attribution in the initial printings. That lapse has been rectified in this and all future editions.

In the acknowledgments I made for the Landmark edition of *Thucydides* eleven years ago, I tried to express my gratitude to all those who in the past had in any way contributed to my ability to create that edition. My debt to those who helped me long ago certainly remains, but I shall not now use that broad brush again. Here I will limit my thanks and acknowledgments to just those, and they are not few in number, who made specific contributions to this Landmark edition of Herodotus' *Histories*.

First among them I would rank George L. Cawkwell. His friendly review, comments, criticism, and suggestions helped me in more ways than I can list. Most of all, I am grateful for his constant encouragement, without which I am not sure I could ever have finished the job. George and his wife, Pat, always made me feel welcome at their home, and I greatly appreciated their hospitality whenever I came to Oxford. Because he did not wish to unduly influence my own thoughts on Herodotus, George did not disclose to me that he was writing a book on the Persian-Greek Wars until his work was published in 2005, by which time I had essentially completed my work on Herodotus' text. Then, at my urging, he generously agreed to write an appendix for this volume on the Ionian Revolt.

Paul Cartledge also encouraged me to undertake this project when I first mentioned it to him some ten years ago, and he has supported me in it ever since. A friend as well as a valued colleague, Paul contributed an excellent appendix to this volume on Sparta and much thoughtful advice and counsel.

EP.e   Loeb Classical Library® is a registered trademark
of the President and Fellows of Harvard College.

Indeed, it was at Paul's suggestion that I contacted Rosalind Thomas, who agreed to write the introduction to this volume. I feel fortunate that we obtained her services, as I believe she has written a brilliant, concise, and lucid essay on Herodotus, his work, and his times. Her text is perfect for the intended readership of this book, although I believe everyone will find it valuable. Her scholarship and good nature made her a pleasure to work with, and I feel greatly in her debt.

I would also like to thank the other scholars who contributed appendices to this volume. They are too many to name here, but they were all very helpful, and they labored under the constraints posed by this volume's space limitations. Thus, from complex topics about which they were experts, they had to draw concise narratives that, with a minimum of distortion, would provide both general background information and explanations of specific points raised by Herodotus' text. This required a great deal of skill on their part, and I believe they succeeded admirably.

Two of those scholars, Alan B. Lloyd and Everett L. Wheeler, deserve special mention for the extraordinary quality of the appendices they wrote. Lloyd's is a marvelous critical essay on Herodotus' account of Egypt. Wheeler's three appendices (and the contents of several long footnotes), clarify much about what is known and not known about Scythia, Scythians, and the whole Black Sea region. He summarizes for us the results of recent archaeological and anthropological research in that area, some of which confirm the accounts of Herodotus, and much of which does not.

For the excellent index to this volume we owe thanks to the talented efforts of Margot Levy. She brought patience, good humor, experience, and a great deal of indexing science to the task. She and I immediately agreed on what should be in an index and whom it should serve. I enjoyed editing the index with her, and I look forward to working with her on future Landmark editions.

An old friend, Ingrid MacGillis, helped me select illustrations for this book and conducted the correspondence and negotiations which secured the rights to print them. Anyone who has ever tried to do that will know what a frustrating and difficult process that can be, but Ingrid's language skills, patience, and tenacity proved equal to the task. She also helped by proofreading and editing. I am very happy to have had her assistance and support.

The excellent maps of this volume were drawn by professional cartographers Jonathan Wyss and Kelly Sandefer, who form the working team of Topaz Maps, Inc. We got along together very well. I would draw up a sketch map containing the sites that had to be displayed to illustrate a given episode of the text, and from that blueprint they would design and draw the clean and easily grasped maps (often an overlapping series of maps in different scales) that we now have. These maps provide readers with essential visual data for maintaining geographic orientation. They are vital to the purpose of this edition, and insofar as the edition will achieve its objective, much is owed to their attractive designs and skillful execution. I must also thank them for their unfailing courteous patience with which they responded to my hundreds of requests for changes, many of them quite picayune, and most of them to correct my own errors.

The maps are indeed wonderful, but no one made a more crucial contribution to the elegant and accommodating appearance of this volume than Kim Llewellyn, master page-designer and editor. I live in awe of her creative talents and her vast publishing experience. She truly knows how to make a text look pleasing and easy on the eye. To design and lay out each page of this volume, with its ubiquitous side notes, footnotes, maps, and multi-sized illustrations, requires the skills of a genius. I am fully convinced that there is no problem that might arise in these books that Kim cannot solve. It was a delight to work with her again, and I am profoundly grateful to her.

My thanks must also be expressed to the crew at Pantheon Books who supported this effort. Edward Kastenmeier, my chief editorial contact at Pantheon, has proved to be a helpful and reliable supporter. Many problems that could have become serious were somehow resolved in their early stages due to his skill and tact. Pantheon organized the excellent copyediting and proofreading of the text by Chris Jerome and Candy Gianetti—no small task—under Altie Karper and Lydia Buechler, and they did that job with skill and thoroughness. Andy Hughes, Avery Fluck, and Jonathan Sainsbury of the Art Department took special care in the reproduction of this volume.

Perhaps I could also mention that when the publisher of *The Landmark Thucydides* decided not to take on the projected *Landmark Herodotus*, my agent, Glen Hartley, immediately put me in touch with Pantheon, with whom a successful relationship was quickly established. Without Glen, I might still be looking for a publisher.

My thanks also go to John Marincola, who provided many helpful tips and suggestions, and to my assistant Sandra Kleiner, who keeps my voluminous drafts, correspondence, and notes in order when I, if left to myself, would completely lose control over them. I want to acknowledge the help I received from both Retina Vaughn and Skyler Balbus in developing a chronology from *The Cambridge Ancient History*. Professor Nino Luraghi was kind enough to give me expert advice on some of the art shown in this volume, for which I remain greatly in his debt. Last but not least among those who should be thanked is another old friend, Isabel Raphael, who made vital last-minute efforts to help me straighten out the Greek transliteration of the text's personal names. She not only brought the problem to my attention but worked with us to resolve it. I am most happy to acknowledge her important contribution.

Finally, I want to thank my family for once again enduring the eccentricity and churlishness which comes over me whenever I am stretched to the limit as I am by projects of this nature. I specifically owe a great deal to my son-in-law, David Herbstman, who was always willing to drop whatever he was doing and come to my rescue when a computer crash seemed to lose files or a recalcitrant printer threatened to ruin everything. Of course my thanks also go to my brother and business partner, David Strassler, to my son, Matthew, my daughter, Karen, and most of all to my wife, Toni, whose support and forbearance were essential. They create for me a milieu of relative peace and continuity without which I could not possibly work on such long-term projects as these Landmark editions.

R.B.S.

August 22, 2007

TRANSLATOR'S PREFACE

Andrea L. Purvis

My goal in creating this translation has been to transform the Greek of Herodotus into the most accurate and accessible rendition possible for readers of modern English. I have tried to remain faithful to the text in sense, tone, and style while striving for clarity. Where the text seemed ambiguous or vague, the final decision on its interpretation was often preceded by extensive research (see the list of commentaries and bibliography), and then discussions with Diskin Clay and Robert Strassler, who worked tirelessly with me in the process of revision. The reader will at times find alternative interpretations or clarification of terms in the notes. In the case of the Delphic oracles quoted by Herodotus, the intended obscurity has been preserved. The tone and style of Herodotus is alternately high and low, objective and subjective, analytic and whimsical, complicated and straightforward. My hope is that the reader will find him as engaging and enjoyable to read as he has been to translate.

I have translated the *Oxford Classical Text* edited by C. Hude (third edition, 1927), with the following exceptions:

1.58	many peoples	Reading *pollon* (mss.) instead of Pelasgon ("Pelasgians")
1.64.3	as tyrant of the Athenians	Reading Athenaion (mss.) instead of Atheneon ("Athens")
2.11.3	and that the other gulf,	Deleting "the Arabian gulf, as I am going to describe," extending with Schweighaeuser
2.27	from very warm places	Reading *choron*, with some mss., instead of *choreon* ("from very warm countries")
2.116.2	composed	Reading *poiese*, with mss., instead of *parepoiese* ("made a mistake")
2.145.4	about 1,000 years	Deleting *hexakosia* ("six hundred") with Wilamovitz, and bracketed in Hude, to agree with Herodotus' chronology at 2.44.4
2.175.5	contrition	Reading *enthumiston*, with mss., instead of *enthumeton* (meaning uncertain)
4.17ff	Alazones	Instead of Alizones, found in some mss.

4.154.1	Axos	Instead of Oaxos, found in some mss.
5.92.β.1	the Bacchiads	Reading *hoi* (the), with Madvig, for mss. *houtoi* ("these")
6.40.1	prior to this	Inserting *pro*, with Stein
7.36.2	triremes	Adopting the anonymous conjecture *triereon* instead of the mss. *trichou* ("in three places")
7.61.1	and breastplates	Inserting *kai thorakes*, with Biel
7.90	felt caps	Reading *kitarias*, Pauw, instead of *kithonas* ("tunics"), given in the mss.
7.123.2	Aisa	Reading Stein's conjecture for mss. Lisai
7.151	as they wished	Inserting *emmenein ethelousi*, included in some mss.
8.77.1	words	Reading *rhemata* (Stein) for mss. *pregmata* ("deeds")
9.15.2	but because of the absolute necessity to build a fortification	Deleting *boulomenos* ("wanting to"), with most mss.
9.85.2	priests	Retaining the readings of most mss., *ireas, irees*, instead of *irenes* ("young men")

DATED OUTLINE OF TEXT

Book 1

Proem, 1.1		Herodotus identifies himself, describes his subject, and states his purpose in writing the *Histories*.	450–420?
1.2–5	ASIA-GREECE	Abductions of various Greek and Asian women.	
1.6–29	**LYDIA**	***HISTORIES* BEGIN: CROESUS OF LYDIA**	**716–547/46**
1.7–12	LYDIA	Gyges kills Kandaules and becomes king of Lydia.	716?
1.13–14	LYDIA	Gyges is confirmed by Delphic oracle; his reign.	716–678
1.15	LYDIA	Ardys' reign; captures Priene, invades Miletus, Cimmerians.	678–629
1.16–17	LYDIA	Sadyattes' reign; drives out Cimmerians, takes Smyrna.	629–617
1.18–22	LYDIA-MILETUS	Alyattes' reign; makes peace with Miletus.	617–560
1.23	CORINTH	Periandros (r. 627–587) informs Thrasyboulos of the oracle.	
1.24	TARAS-CORINTH	The tale of Arion.	
1.25	LYDIA-DELPHI	Alyattes' gifts to Delphi.	617–560?
1.26–92	**LYDIA**	**CROESUS' REIGN: CONQUERS GREEKS IN ASIA; DEFEATED BY CYRUS**	**560–547/46**
1.29–33	LYDIA	Croesus and Solon.	
1.34–45	LYDIA	The story of Adrastus; death of Atys, Croesus' son.	
1.46–56	LYDIA	Croesus decides to attack Persia, tests oracles, rewards some.	550–?
1.57–58		Herodotus speculates on language of the Pelasgians.	
1.59–64	ATHENS	Peisistratos' rise to tyrannical power at Athens. (r. c. 561–556, 555?–?, 546–528)	
1.65	SPARTA	Lykourgos reforms and establishes the Spartan government.	
1.66–68	SPARTA	Spartan conflict with Tegea.	
1.69–70	SPARTA	Spartans agree to assist Croesus.	548–547
1.71–1.73	CAPPADOCIA	Lydians cross the Halys River into Persian-controlled territory.	547?
1.74–75	CAPPADOCIA	Thales predicts eclipse (585); diverts Halys River (547?).	

Book 3

Book 4

5.72	ATHENS	Kleomenes tries to impose Isagoras but is again driven out.	507
5.73	ATHENS-SARDIS	Athenian envoys offer earth and water to Persia for alliance.	507
5.74–76	ATTICA	Kleomenes tries again, but King Demaratos deserts him.	506
5.77–81	THEBES-ATTICA	Democratically strong Athens defeats Thebes and Chalcis.	506–505?
5.82–89	AEGINA-ATHENS	Quarrel with Epidauros leads Aegina to enmity with Athens.	498?
5.90–93	ATTICA	Kleomenes tries again with Hippias. His allies desert him.	504
5.94–96	SIGEION	Hippias takes refuge at Sigeion, intrigues with Persians.	504?
5.97	ATHENS	Athenians vote to help Aristagoras and Ionians, send twenty ships.	500/499
5.98	PAIONIA	Aristagoras persuades Paionians to leave Phrygia for home.	?
5.99–102	SARDIS	Ionians sack and burn Sardis but are defeated at Ephesus.	498
5.103	HELLESPONT	Hellespontine and Carian cities are made to join the Ionians.	498?
5.104–116	CYPRUS-IONIA	Cyprus revolts against Persia but is defeated on land and sea.	497–496
5.117–123	ASIA	Persians reconquer the Hellespont, Caria, Aeolis, and Ionia.	497–495
5.124–126	THRACE	Aristagoras flees to Thrace and is killed there by Thracians.	497–496?

Book 6

6.1–5	LESBOS-CHIOS	Histiaios arrives on the scene, is accused by Artaphernes.	496–494?
6.6–8	LADE	Persians concentrate at Miletus. Ionians decide to fight at sea.	494
6.9	MILETUS	Former tyrants promise Ionians good terms if they surrender.	494
6.10–12	LADE	Dionysios of Phocaea drills the Ionian fleet. They don't like it.	494
6.13–15	LADE	Samian ships flee as the battle opens, other Ionians also flee.	494
6.16	EPHESUS	Ephesians massacre Chian ship crews, thinking them pirates.	494
6.17	PHOENICIA-SICILY	Dionysios of Phocaea becomes a pirate against non-Greeks.	494
6.18–20	MILETUS	Persians take Miletus, enslave its people, resettle them.	494–?
6.21	ATHENS	Phrynichos fined by Athenians for play about fall of Miletus.	493/92
6.22–25	SAMOS-ZANCLE	Samians at Zancle; Persians restore son of Syloson.	494?
6.26–30	CHIOS-MYSIA	Histiaios is captured by the Persians and executed.	494?
6.31–33	ASIA-CYCLADES	Persians conquer nearby islands and the remaining cities.	493
6.34–38	CHERSONESE	How Miltiades son of Kypselos became tyrant c. 555.	died 519?
6.39	CHERSONESE	Hippias sends Miltiades son of Kimon to be ruler there.	516
6.40	CHERSONESE	Miltiades flees from Scythians (510), but returns to rule again (496–493).	
6.41	CHERSONESE	Miltiades flees from Persian (Phoenician) fleet.	493

Book 8

Key to Maps

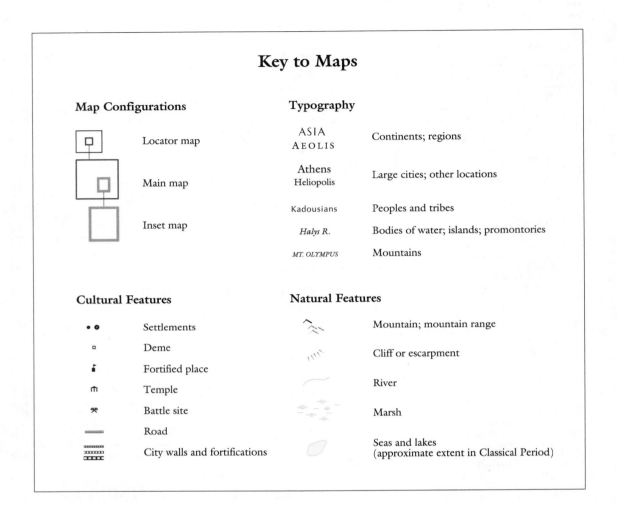

Map Configurations

Locator map

Main map

Inset map

Typography

ASIA
AEOLIS — Continents; regions

Athens
Heliopolis — Large cities; other locations

Kadousians — Peoples and tribes

Halys R. — Bodies of water; islands; promontories

MT. OLYMPUS — Mountains

Cultural Features

• ● — Settlements

▫ — Deme

ᴑ — Fortified place

ᛘ — Temple

⚔ — Battle site

═ — Road

▦ — City walls and fortifications

Natural Features

Mountain; mountain range

Cliff or escarpment

River

Marsh

Seas and lakes
(approximate extent in Classical Period)

Distance Conversions

Wherever possible and appropriate, I have converted Herodotus' original units of distance (stades, plethra, cubits, etc.) into miles and feet, and noted in a footnote the original units that are cited in the text. In calculating modern units, unless the text specifies other units, I have assumed the use of the Attic stade of 583 feet and the more or less standard cubit of one and a half feet. The reader should realize, however, that different "standard" stade and cubit units were in use in the ancient Mediterranean world, and Herodotus might have had one of them in mind when he gave his measurements, so that we can never know the actual lengths with any precision. See Appendix J, Units of Currency, Weight, and Distance.

Dates

All dates in this volume and in its supporting materials are B.C.E. (Before the Common Era), unless otherwise specified.

BOOK ONE

Theme: to record events & their causes *(handwritten, margin)*

Herodotus of Halicarnassus[a] here presents his research[b] so that human events do not fade with time. May the great and wonderful deeds—some brought forth by the Hellenes, others by the barbarians—not go unsung; as well as the causes that led them to make war on each other.[c]

Persian[a] authorities of the past claim that the Phoenicians[b] were responsible for the dispute. This is because, after they had come to and settled the land which they still inhabit from what is now called the Erythraean Sea,[c] they at once undertook long sea voyages and brought back cargo from Egypt,[d] Assyria,[e] and elsewhere, but more to the point, they came to Argos.[f]

[2] At this time in the land we now call Hellas,[a] Argos surpassed other places in all things, and when the Phoenicians reached Argos they set out their cargo for sale. [3] On the fifth or sixth day after their arrival, when they had sold almost everything, many women came down to the sea, in particular, the king's daughter. Her name, according to what the Hellenes also say, was Io daughter of Inachos. [4] The women were standing by the stern of the ship intent upon their purchases when the Phoenicians, inciting each other, rushed upon them. The greater part made their escape, but some were seized and carried off. Io herself was among the captives. The Phoenicians put the women on board their vessel and set sail for Egypt.

WOMEN ABDUCTING *(handwritten, margin)*

Proem
Herodotus states his general purpose in this brief preface.

1.1
Herodotus describes the origins of the conflict between Hellenes and barbarians as a series of abductions of women. The Argive woman Io was first.

Proem.a Halicarnassus: Map 1.3, the city in Asia Minor in which Herodotus grew up; Aristotle knew a version of this work in which Herodotus identified himself as from Thurii (Map 1.24), where he lived in his later years.

Proem.b These opening words crudely translated run: "What follows is a performance [literally 'display'] of the enquiries of Herodotus from Halicarnassus." (Gould). This almost certainly implies that Herodotus performed (read aloud) his text, in whole or in part, to an audience gathered to hear him.

Proem.c See Appendix Q, Herodotus and the Poets, §1–2.

1.1.1a Persia: Map 1.3.

1.1.1b Phoenicia: Map 1.3.

1.1.1c Erythraean Sea: Map 1.3. Herodotus recognizes only one sea south of Africa, Persia, and India and calls it, including the gulfs that extend north from it—the modern Red Sea and the Persian Gulf—the Erythraean Sea. However, on three occasions, he does call it the "Southern Sea" (2.11.3, 2.158, 3.17.1), and once he calls the modern Red Sea the "Arabian Gulf." See Appendix D, Herodotean Geography, §1–3.

1.1.1d Egypt: Map 1.3.

1.1.1e Assyria: Map 1.3.

1.1.1f Argos: Map 1.3.

1.1.2a Hellas: Map 1.3.

This is how Io came to Egypt according to the Persians (though the Hellenes disagree), and this was the very beginning of grievances.

They say that following these events, certain Hellenes whose names they cannot specify came to the port of Tyre,[a] in Phoenicia, and abducted the king's daughter Europa. These Hellenes would be Cretans.[b] And now the score was even.

[2] But after this, the Hellenes were responsible for a second crime. For they sailed in a warship to Aia in the territory of Colchis and on to the River Phasis.[a] And when they had finished the business that brought them there,[b] they abducted the king's daughter Medea. [3] So the Colchian king sent a messenger to Hellas to demand satisfaction for the abduction and the return of his daughter. The reply was that, since they had received no satisfaction for the abduction of Io of Argos, neither would they pay anything to them.

PARIS

They say that in the generation following these events Alexandros son of Priam[a] heard the stories and wanted to abduct a wife from Hellas for himself, quite confident that he would pay no penalty since the other side had not paid either. [2] And so he abducted Helen. The Hellenes decided that the first thing to do was to send messengers demanding the return of Helen and satisfaction for the abduction. When they made these proposals they were charged with the abduction of Medea, and besides, they said, how could they expect satisfaction from others when they themselves had neither paid nor surrendered her upon request?

Up to this point, there had been abductions only from each other, but after this the Hellenes were largely responsible for offenses. For they began to make war on Asia[a] before their enemies made war on Europe.[b] [2] Now the Persians think that the abduction of women is certainly an act only unjust men would perform, and yet once they have been abducted, it is senseless to make a fuss over seeking vengeance. It is the way of sensible people to have no concern for abducted women; it is quite obvious that the women would not have been abducted if they had not been compliant. [3] The Persians claim that while they themselves, Asiatics, thought nothing of the women being abducted, the Hellenes of Sparta, for the sake of a woman, mustered a huge expedition, went to Asia, and destroyed the power of Priam. [4] From that time on they have considered the Hellenes to be their enemies. For the Persians assume Asia and the barbarian tribes living there as their own, and anything Hellenic is separate and divergent from themselves.

The Persians claim that this is how it happened, and they find in the sack of Troy[a] the origin of their hostility toward the Hellenes. [2] But the Phoenicians disagree with the Persians about Io. They say that it was not by

---

1.2.1a Tyre: Map 1.3.
1.2.1b Crete (Creta): Map 1.3.
1.2.2a Aia in Colchis: site unknown. Colchis: Map
　　　1.3. Phasis River: Map 1.3.
1.2.2b The legendary capture of the Golden Fleece.

1.3.1a Alexandros son of Priam; also known as Paris.
1.4.1a Asia: Map 1.3.
1.4.1b Europe: Map 1.3.
1.5.1a Troy (Ilion/Ilium): Map 1.3.

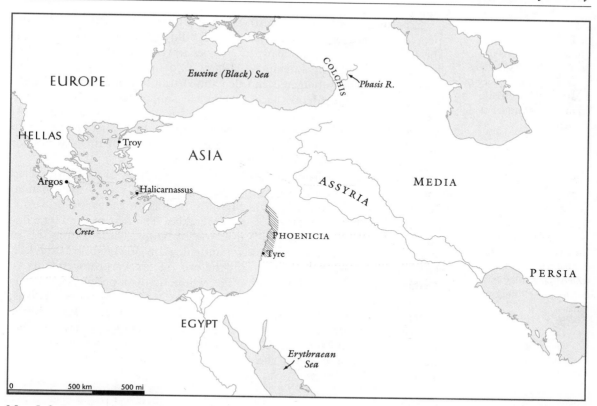

Map 1.3

abduction that they brought her to Egypt, but rather that she had inter-course with the captain of the ship in Argos, and when she realized she was pregnant, she was ashamed to face her parents and she voluntarily sailed away with the Phoenicians so that she would not be found out.

[3] These are the stories told by the Persians and Phoenicians. I myself have no intention of affirming that these events occurred thus or otherwise. But I do know who was the first man to begin unjust acts against the Hellenes. I shall describe him and then proceed with the rest of my story recounting cities both lesser and greater, [4] since many of those that were great long ago have become inferior, and some that are great in my own time were inferior before. And so, resting on my knowledge that human prosperity never remains constant, I shall make mention of both without discrimination.

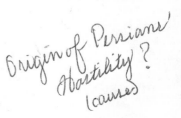

[handwritten margin notes: "Origin of Persians' Hostility? (cause)" and "HUMAN PROSPERITY"]

1.6
LYDIA
Herodotus begins the history of Croesus by recounting the history of Lydia, the first Asiatic country to conquer the Hellenes.

1.7
c. 716
LYDIA
The story of Croesus begins with the tale of how Gyges, the first Lydian ruler of his line, killed Kandaules and made himself king of Sardis.

GYGES & KANDAULES

Croesus was of Lydian[a] ancestry, the son of Alyattes, and the ruler of the peoples this side of the River Halys[b] (which flows from the south between the Syrians[c] and Paphlagonians,[d] then goes toward the north and empties into the sea called the Euxine[e]). [2] Now Croesus was the first barbarian known to us who subjugated and demanded tribute from some Hellenes,[a] although he made friends with others. He subjugated the Ionians, the Aeolians, and the Asian Dorians,[b] and made friends with the Spartans.[c] [3] Before the reign of Croesus, all Hellenes had been free. There had been an invasion by Cimmerians[a] into Ionia prior to Croesus, but this was not for the subjugation of cities, but rather a raid for plunder.

The rule passed from the Heraklids[a] to the family of Croesus, called the Mermnads, in the following way. [2] There was a man named Kandaules, known to Hellenes as Myrsilos; he was the monarch[a] of Sardis[b] and the descendant of Alkaios son of Herakles. The first of the Heraklids to become king of Sardis was Agron son of Ninos, who was the son of Belos, who was the son of Alkaios. Kandaules son of Myrsos was the last. [3] The kings who ruled this land before Agron were descendants of Lydus son of Atys, from whom the whole Lydian people derives its name; earlier they had been called Meionian. [4] From these Lydians, the Heraklids were entrusted with the rule, obtaining it through the sanction of an oracle.[a] The Heraklids were descendants of a slave-woman of Iardanos[b] and Herakles. They governed for twenty-two generations, 505 years, handing down the rule from father to son until it reached Kandaules son of Myrsos.

1.6.1a Lydia: Map 1.9. Here, as Herodotus begins his discussion of Croesus, he passes from myth to history. See Appendix Q, §7.

1.6.1b Halys River: Map 1.9. "This side of the river" clearly means west of the river, perhaps indicating a bit of unconscious Hellenocentrism. Another instance of this Hellocentricity occurs at. 1.28.1.

1.6.1c Syria (Cappadocia): Map 1.9. Not the Semitic Syrians, but Northern Cappadocians, who were known to the Hellenes as Syrians. Herodotus does not distinguish Anatolian from Semitic peoples. The distinction of two types of "Syrians," however, is clear in the ancient geographer Strabo (e.g., 1.12.3), who calls these Cappadocian/Pontic Syrians "White Syrians" and notes Syrians of darker complexions of the Taurus. "Syrian" in Greek (like "Arab" later) is a very elastic ethnic term.

1.6.1d Paphlagonia: Map 1.9.

1.6.1e Euxine (Black) Sea: Map 1.9.

1.6.2a Scholars have wondered how to reconcile this statement with others made by Herodotus in 1.14–16, where he says that Gyges (reigned 716–678) took Colophon, that Ardys (678–629) took Priene, and that Sadyattes (629–617) took Smyrna—Greek cities all, and "taken" well before the time of Croesus (560–547/46).

1.6.2b Ionians, Aeolians, Dorians, in Asia: Map 1.9. See Appendix K, Dialect and Ethnic Groups in Herodotus, §4–7.

1.6.2c Sparta: Map 1.9.

1.6.3a Cimmerians, possible original territory: Map 1.9. The Cimmerians remain a historical and archaeological enigma; they cannot be identified from any material remains. Neither on the Dniester (Tyras) River, where Herodotus sites a Cimmerian burial mound (4.11.4), nor in the Crimea as a whole is there any sign of occupation before the arrival of the Scythians. They are mentioned obscurely in Homer (*Odyssey* 11.14), and the writer Hekataios (fl. 500) already knew the Strait of Kerch as the Cimmerian Bosporus (Map 1.9). They invaded Asia Minor in the eighth century, plundered many cities, and came into conflict with Assyrians and Phrygians before being defeated by the Lydians at the end of the seventh century. (Wheeler) See also nn. 1.15.1d, 4.12.3b.

Hekataios was the author of geographical and historical accounts of Asia Minor and the East who wrote in the late sixth century, and was a source both used and criticized by Herodotus. He also plays a role in Herodotus' account of Ionian history. See 5.36, 5.125–126, and 6.137. See also Introduction, §3.1.

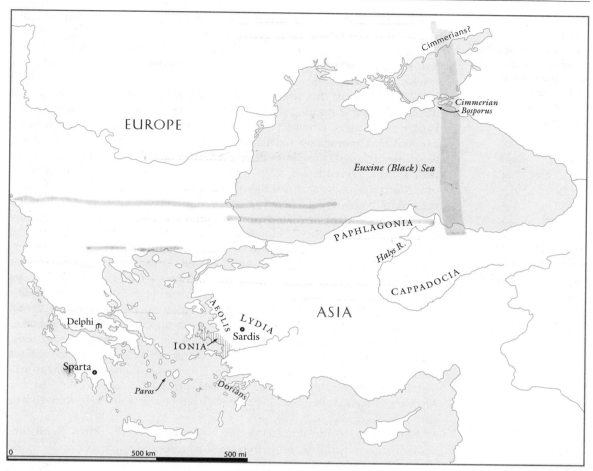

MAP 1.9

1.7.1a Heraklids, descendants of the hero Herak-
        les. This clan of Heraklid kings of Lydia are
        otherwise unknown. See Appendix L, Aris-
        tocratic Families in Herodotus, §3, 7, for
        more on the royal lines of Sparta, who also
        traced their origin to Herakles and were
        called Heraklids.
1.7.2a Herodotus uses the Greek word for
        "tyrant" to characterize Kandaules' office,
        but the meaning of that word may not

accurately describe his position. See Appendix T, Tyranny in Herodotus, §1.
1.7.2b Sardis: Map 1.9.
1.7.4a For an introduction to oracles, see
        Appendix P, Oracles, Religion, and Politics
        in Herodotus, §1, 8.
1.7.4b The Greek is ambiguous here. Some
        scholars have called her the daughter of
        Iardanos.

1.8

LYDIA

Kandaules wishes to show his wife naked to Gyges, his favorite bodyguard.

Now this Kandaules fell in love with his own wife and, being in love, thought he had the most beautiful of all women. Therefore, he used to tell his favorite among his bodyguards, Gyges son of Daskylos, not only about serious matters but [especially] about the beauty of his wife, and with extravagant praise.

[2] It was fated that things would turn out badly for Kandaules, and so this had not gone on long when he said to Gyges, "Since I don't think you believe me, Gyges, when I tell you about my wife's beauty (and it just so happens that people believe their ears less than their eyes), I am asking you to do something to make sure you see her naked." [3] Gyges responded with a sharp cry and said, "My Lord, what are you saying? Insanity! You order me to see your mistress naked? When a woman's dress is removed, so is her dignity. [4] People long ago recognized what principles are noble and good, and we should learn from them. Among them is this one: 'Look only at what belongs to you.' I do believe that she is the most beautiful of all women, and I beg you not to ask for what is against all decency."

(margin note: NOBLE & GOOD PRINCIPLES)

1.9

LYDIA

Gyges resists but is persuaded that the queen will not be aware of the insult.

Gyges said such things to thwart the king's desire, dreading the thought of how badly things could turn out for him because of this. Then Kandaules replied, "Don't worry, Gyges, and don't be afraid of me or my wife; I didn't tell you this to test you, and no harm will come to you from her. I have a plan and will make sure she has no idea you're watching her. [2] I will position you in the bedroom behind the open door. After I come in, my wife, too, will be there to go to bed. Next to the doorway is a chair. She will set each of her garments on it one by one as she takes them off, and you may watch unobserved. [3] But when she walks from the chair to the bed and her back is turned, be careful she doesn't see you and then you can go out through the door."

1.10

LYDIA

The queen does perceive Gyges and is shamed.

Since Gyges could not escape, he was won over. And when Kandaules thought it was bedtime, he led Gyges to the room, where before long the queen entered.

[2] While she came in and set down her garments, Gyges watched. And when she went toward the bed with her back turned, he slipped out from behind the door and went out. But the woman spied him as he left and, realizing that this was her husband's doing, she neither cried out, even though she felt shamed, nor let on that she knew, since she intended to get even with Kandaules. [3] For among the Lydians, as well as nearly all other barbarians, it is a great disgrace for even a male to be seen naked.

Thus she revealed nothing and remained silent for the time being.

1.11

LYDIA

The queen insists that Gyges must kill Kandaules and make himself king, or be killed himself.

But as soon as day dawned, she prepared her most faithful servants for what she intended and had Gyges summoned. He came at her request, assuming she knew nothing of what went on, just as he had always come to the queen whenever she had summoned him before. [2] When he arrived, she said, "Now, Gyges, there are two roads before you, and I shall let you choose which you want to take. Either kill Kandaules and have me and the

Gyges' Choice

kingdom of the Lydians,[a] or you yourself must die at once so that in the future you will never see things you should not see in your complete obedience to Kandaules. [3] At any rate, either he should die, since he planned the deed, or you should, since you saw me naked, which violated all decency."

At first Gyges was dumbstruck by what he heard; then he begged her not to force him to make such a choice. [4] Nevertheless, he could not persuade her, and when he saw that he really was confronted with the necessity to kill his master or to be killed by others, he decided that he would survive. He asked her, "Since you are compelling me to slay my master, please tell me how we're going to assault him." [5] "The attack will be made from the very place he revealed me naked," she replied, "and the assault will be made upon him in his sleep."[a]

Together they worked out the plan, and when night fell—for Gyges was not getting out of this; there was no escape—either he or Kandaules had to die—Gyges followed the woman to the bedroom. She gave him a dagger and hid him behind the same door. [2] Then, when Kandaules was sleeping, Gyges crept up, slew him, and obtained the woman and the kingdom. It is this Gyges that the poet Archilochus of Paros,[a] who lived at the same time, mentions in his verses.

Gyges was supported in obtaining the kingdom by an oracle[a] from Delphi.[b] For the Lydians thought that what had happened to Kandaules was dreadful and were up in arms. However, the partisans of Gyges and the rest of the Lydians came to an agreement: if the oracle declared him king, he would be king; if not, he would return the rule to the Heraklids. [2] The oracle did in fact declare for him, and thus Gyges became king. But the Pythia[a] added this: retribution would come from the Heraklids to the fourth descendant of Gyges.[b] The Lydians and their kings disregarded this part of the oracle until it actually came to pass.

Thus the Mermnads obtained the kingship by taking it from the Heraklids. When Gyges became king, he sent quite a few dedications off to Delphi, and of all the silver dedications in Delphi, most are his. Besides silver, he dedicated an unbelievable amount of gold. Most

1.12
LYDIA
The queen prepares the plot, and Gyges kills Kandaules.

1.13
680
LYDIA-DELPHI
Gyges' rule is confirmed by the Delphic oracle.

1.14
680
LYDIA-DELPHI
Gyges sends many gifts to Delphi. He captures Colophon. He reigns thirty-eight years.*

1.11.2a Lydia: Map 1.9.
1.11.5a For a brief review of the roles of women in Herodotus, see Appendix U, On Women and Marriage in Herodotus.
1.12.2a Paros: Map 1.9, also Map 1.59. Archilochus (c. 650) was second only to Homer in the ranking of poets by many ancient Greeks. One of his poems that has come down to us reads:

> I care not at all for the wealth of
>   Gyges rich in gold,
> Ambition has no grip on me at all,
>   nor do I envy
> The exploits of gods; no lust have
>   I for great kingly power;
> Such things lie far beyond my sight.

(Aristotle *Rhetoric* 3.17, 1418b28; Plutarch *de Tranquilitate Animi* 10 [*Moralia* 470b–c]; Fragment 19, West, quoting words spoken by a character called Charon the carpenter.) See Appendix Q, §4.
1.13.1a This prediction is recalled in 1.91.1. For some general background on oracles, and the Delphic oracle in particular, see Appendix P, §1, 5, 8.
1.13.1b Delphi: Map 1.9.
1.13.2a Pythia, the priestess at Delphi who pronounced the oracles while in a trance. See Appendix P, §9, 12.
1.13.2b Herodotus tells how this "retribution" came about to Gyges' descendant Croesus, in 1.86ff.
1.14* *The Cambridge Ancient History* says thirty-five years, from 680? to 645?

worthy of mention among them are the bowls; six golden bowls are his offerings; [2] they weigh thirty talents[a] and stand in the treasury of the Corinthians,[b] although the truth is that it is not the treasury of all the Corinthians, but of Kypselos son of Eetion.[c] Of all barbarians known to us, it was Gyges who first dedicated offerings to Delphi, after Midas son of Gordias, the king of Phrygia.[d] [3] Midas in fact dedicated a royal throne worth seeing, on which he sat when he gave judgments. This throne sits in the same place as Gyges' bowls. The gold and silver dedicated by Gyges is called "Gygian" by the Delphians, named after its dedicator.

[4] After Gyges had gained control of the government, he led his army in an invasion of Miletus[a] and Smyrna,[b] and he took Colophon.[c] But since no other great deed was done by him during his kingship of thirty-eight years, we shall bypass it, having mentioned so much already.[d]

But I will mention Ardys son of Gyges, who became king after him. It was this man who took Priene[a] and invaded Miletus. While he was ruling in Sardis,[b] the Cimmerians,[c] expelled from their homeland by Scythian[d] nomads, came into Asia[e] and took all of Sardis with the exception of the acropolis.[f]

1.15
645
LYDIA
Gyges' son Ardys takes Priene. Cimmerians invade Lydia. Ardys reigns forty-nine years.*

1.14.2a The "Attic" talent had a weight of approximately 57 pounds avoirdupois, the "Aeginetan" of about 82. We cannot be sure which one Herodotus refers to here. See Appendix J, Ancient Greek Units of Currency, Weight, and Distance, §11–13, 20.

1.14.2b Corinth: Map 1.18. At Delphi and other shrines, offerings of silver and gold objects and other valuable material accumulated to such a degree that these institutions became unique and tempting repositories of ready capital in ancient Greece.

1.14.2c Kypselos son of Eetion: tyrant of Corinth (657–627). For more on tyrants in ancient Greek politics, see Appendix T.

1.14.2d Phrygia: Map 1.18.

1.14.4a Miletus: Map 1.18, inset. An Ionian Greek city.

1.14.4b Smyrna: Map 1.18, inset. Once an Aeolian Greek city but then an Ionian Greek city. See 1.194.1.

1.14.4c Colophon: Map 1.18, inset. An Ionian city.

1.14.4d See Figure 1.14 of an Assyrian tablet recording an embassy from King Gyges of Lydia.

1.15* *The Cambridge Ancient History* says thirty years, from 645? to 615?

1.15.1a Priene: Map 1.18, inset. An Ionian Greek city.

1.15.1b Sardis: Map 1.18, inset.

1.15.1c Cimmerians, possible original territory: Map 1.18. See 1.6.3, 1.103, 1.105–106, 4.11–12. The Cimmerians' invasion caused much havoc in Asia Minor. They are mentioned in Assyrian and Babylonian documents in which they first appear c.

714 on the borders of the Kingdom of Urartu, which was Assyria's imperial rival in the eighth and seventh centuries. The Assyrians record that after their victory over the Cimmerians (679), a Cimmerian unit was incorporated into the Assyrian army. Literary sources assign the Cimmerians a role in the fall of the Phrygian kingdom c. 675, and Cimmerian attacks on Lydia began in 669 or 664–663. Gyges requested Assyrian support against the Cimmerians (660) and defeated them three years later. But in 644, the Cimmerians took Sardis and Gyges was killed. About four years later, Cimmerian power began to collapse with a failed attack on Assyrian possessions in Asia Minor and the death of their king Lygdamis. After the Lydian Alyattes defeated the Cimmerians c. 600 (1.16), the Cimmerians vanish from the sources. (Wheeler)

1.15.1d Scythians, home territory at that time: Map 1.18.

1.15.1e Asia: Map 1.18. Throughout this book, when Herodotus uses the word "Asia," he, like other Hellenes of his day, means the landmass that we call Asia Minor, occupied by modern Turkey.

1.15.1f The "acropolis" of a city ("acropolis" means upper or high city) was usually, as at Athens, a hill adjacent to or within the city which served as a fortification and on which often were located its most ancient and holy sites. See Figure 5.101 for a view of the acropolis (citadel) of Sardis as seen from the ruins of the temple of Artemis in the agora.

FIGURE 1.14. AN INSCRIBED
TABLET OF KING ASHURBANIPAL
OF ASSYRIA IN CUNEIFORM,
REPORTING AN EMBASSY FROM
KING GYGES OF LYDIA.

1.16
c. 629–c. 617
LYDIA
Ardys is succeeded by Sadyattes, who is succeeded by Alyattes.

1.17
c. 629–c. 617
LYDIA-MILETUS
Sadyattes continues the campaign against Miletus.

1.18
610
LYDIA-MILETUS
Alyattes succeeds Sadyattes and continues the war against Miletus. Alyattes reigns from 617 to 560.*

1.19
598?
LYDIA-MILETUS
The Lydians burn a Milesian temple. Alyattes falls ill and is told by the Delphic oracle to repair the temple.

When Ardys had been king for forty-nine years, Sadyattes son of Ardys succeeded him and ruled as king for twelve years,[a] followed by Alyattes son of Sadyattes. [2] This king made war on Cyaxares, the descendant of Deiokes, and on his army of Medes.[a] He drove the Cimmerians out of Asia, took Smyrna[b] (a colony founded from Colophon[c]), and invaded Klazomenai.[d] From the latter he did not come away as he wished but suffered a great defeat.

However, the deeds he performed while in power were most noteworthy, as follows. He made war on the Milesians, inheriting this war from his father. He attacked Miletus and laid siege to it in the following way. Whenever the crops on its land had ripened, he would thrust his army upon it, marching to the music of flutes, lyres, and the pipes of high and low tones. [2] When he came into Milesian territory, he neither tore down or burned the houses nor broke down the doors but instead allowed them to remain in place. After destroying the trees and crops on the land, he would turn back and depart. [3] He did this because the Milesians held control over the sea, so that a blockade by his army would accomplish nothing. The Lydian refrained from tearing down their houses so that the Milesians could set forth from them to sow and work the fields, and through their work he would have something to plunder.

In this way he waged war for eleven years, during which he inflicted two serious defeats on the Milesians, one at Limeneio[a] in their own territory, and another on the plain of the River Maeander.[b] [2] Now Sadyattes son of Ardys, who began the war, ruled for six of those eleven years during which he sent his army to invade Milesian territory. But during the next five years, Alyattes son of Sadyattes, who, as I said earlier, inherited the war from his father, applied himself to it strenuously. [3] None of the Ionians assisted the Milesians in the war, except for the Chians,[a] who did so in return for a similar favor, as the Milesians had previously helped the Chians in waging war against the Erythraeans.[b]

In the twelfth year, when the crops were being burned by the army, an unfortunate incident occurred. As soon as the crop caught on fire, it was driven by the wind against the temple of Athena of Assesos[a] and, once ignited, the temple was consumed by fire. [2] Although at first no one paid much attention to this event, later, when the army came back to Sardis, Alyattes became sick. When the sickness persisted for quite a long time, he

1.16.1a From 639 to 617. According to *The Cambridge Ancient History*, Sadyattes reigned for six years, from 615? to 610?
1.16.2a For more on the Mede Deiokes, see 1.96–101. Media: Map 1.3.
1.16.2b Smyrna: Map 1.18, inset.
1.16.2c Colophon: Map 1.18, inset.
1.16.2d Klazomenai: Map 1.18, inset.
1.18* *The Cambridge Ancient History* says sixty years, from 610 to 550.
1.18.1a Limeneio: location unknown. The word

is related to the word for "harbor," and thus probably designates the coastal area.
1.18.1b Maeander River: Map 1.18, inset.
1.18.3a Chios: Map 1.18, inset. An island occupied by Ionian Hellenes.
1.18.3b Erythrai (Ionia): Map 1.18, inset.
1.19.1a Assesos: site of a shrine near Miletus (Map 1.18, inset). Athena of Assesos is the Panhellenic goddess Athena, with an epithet derived from the locality, Assesos.

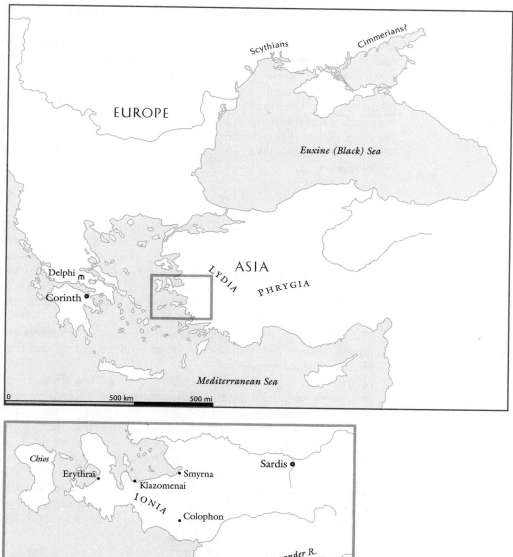

MAP 1.18

decided—whether on his own or upon the advice of someone else—to send sacred delegates to consult the oracle at Delphi[a] to ask the god about his sickness. [3] When they arrived at Delphi, the Pythia[a] denied them an oracular response until they had rebuilt the temple of Athena that they had burned down at Assesos in Milesian territory.

1.20

LYDIA-MILETUS

The Milesian version of the story.

I know this because I heard it from the Delphians, but the Milesians add further details. They say that Periandros son of Kypselos[a] found out about the oracle's reply to Alyattes and sent a messenger to disclose it to his closest guest-friend[b] Thrasyboulos,[c] the tyrant of Miletus[d] at the time, so that Thrasyboulos could make appropriate plans for the situation at hand armed by this knowledge.

So say the Milesians.

1.21

LYDIA-MILETUS

Alyattes rebuilds the temple and is deceived by a Milesian stratagem.

When Alyattes received the message, he at once sent a herald to Miletus, wanting to call a truce with Thrasyboulos and the Milesians for as long as it would take to rebuild the temple. The messenger arrived at Miletus, but meanwhile Thrasyboulos, completely informed about the whole story in advance, and surmising what Alyattes would do, had devised the following plan. [2] He had all the food in the city, including his own private supply, brought together into the public square; then he told the Milesians to watch for his signal, at which time they should all drink and carouse together.

1.22

LYDIA-MILETUS

The peace and friendship between Lydia and Miletus.

Thrasyboulos gave these orders so that the herald from Sardis would see it and tell Alyattes about the huge pile of food heaped up and the people having a good time there.

[2] And that is just what happened. The herald saw these things going on and, after communicating the Lydian message to Thrasyboulos, returned to Sardis. And as far as I can tell, this is the only reason for the turnabout to peace that followed. [3] Alyattes, you see, had hoped there would be a severe food shortage in Miletus and that the populace would be worn to the breaking point by their suffering. But when the herald returned, he heard from him just the reverse of what he had expected. After this, there was a reconciliation in which they became friends and military allies to each other; Alyattes built for Athena two temples in Assesos instead of one, and recovered from his sickness. That is how things turned out for Alyattes in his war against the Milesians and Thrasyboulos.

1.23

CORINTH

Periandros is tyrant of Corinth (c. 627–587). The tale of Arion.

Periandros, the man who informed Thrasyboulos of the oracle, was the son of Kypselos and tyrant of Corinth.[a] The Corinthians tell a story, and the people of Lesbos[b] agree with them, about the most amazing thing that

---

1.19.2a Delphi: Map 1.18. See Appendix P, §5, 8, 9.
1.19.3a Pythia, the priestess at Delphi who pronounced the oracles while in a trance. See Appendix P, §9, 12.
1.20.1a On Periandros (ruled from c. 627 to 587), see 1.23ff., 3.48. For a brief description of Greek tyranny, see Appendix T.
1.20.1b Guest-friendship (*xenia*): a bond of ritualized friendship, usually between aristocrats or prominent men of different cities. It

was passed down through generations and required hereditary privileges and obligations such as reciprocal hospitality and assistance. See Appendix T, §3.
1.20.1c On Thrasyboulos, see 5.92.ε–ζ. (The Greek letters indicate chapter subdivisions, ε (epsilon) and ζ (zeta).
1.20.1d Miletus: Map 1.18, inset.
1.23.1a Corinth: Map 1.24.
1.23.1b Lesbos: Map 1.24.

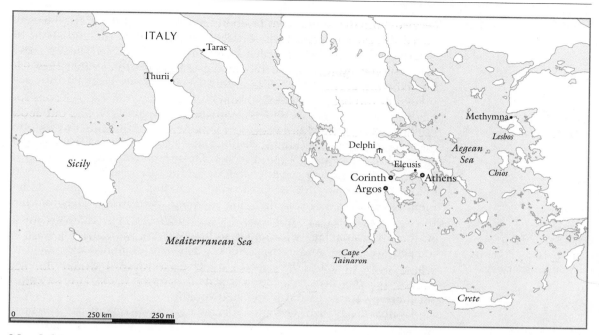

Map 1.24

happened during his lifetime: Arion of Methymna[c] was carried upon a dolphin and set on shore at Tainaron.[d] Arion was a lyre player second to none at that time, as well as the first person known to us to have created and named the dithyramb,[e] and to have produced it in Corinth.

They say that this Arion spent much of his time at the court of Periandros, but longed to sail to Italy[a] and Sicily.[b] He finally did so, and after he had earned a large amount of money there, he decided to return to Corinth. [2] So he sailed out from Taras,[a] and since he trusted no people more than Corinthians, he hired a boat of Corinthians. When these men were out at sea, they plotted to throw Arion overboard in order to get his money. Once Arion perceived this, he begged them to take his money but spare his life. [3] But he could not persuade them. The sailors ordered him to kill himself if he would have a grave on land or to get it over with immediately and to jump into the sea. [4] Arion, made desperate by their decision, asked one request of them. Would they permit him to sing for them from the stern in

ARION & THE DOLPHIN

1.24
TARAS-CORINTH
The tale of Arion and the dolphin.

1.23.1c   Methymna on Lesbos: Map 1.24; see also Map 1.149, AX.
1.23.1d   Cape Taineron: Map 1.24.
1.23.1e   The dithyramb is a song in honor of Dionysos, first mentioned by Archilochus (c. 680–640): "I know how to lead off the dithyramb when my mind is thunderstruck with wine." (Fragment 120 West) Herodotus

may mean that Arion was the first to adapt it to a circular choral performance.
1.24.1a   Italy: Map 1.24.
1.24.1b   Sicily: Map 1.24.
1.24.2a   Taras: Map 1.24.

15

full costume?[a] [5] He promised that as soon as his song was ended, he would kill himself. Delighted at the prospect of hearing the best of all singers, the sailors retreated from the stern to the middle of the ship. Arion put on his costume, picked up his lyre, stood on the deck, and performed the high-toned hymn.[a] When he finished the song, he leapt into the sea, still in full costume. [6] And the men sailed back to Corinth.[a]

But according to what they say, a dolphin took up Arion on its back and brought him to shore at Tainaron. There he stepped off the dolphin and made his way to Corinth in his costume, and when he arrived, he explained all that had happened. [7] In disbelief, Periandros did not allow Arion to leave, but kept him in custody while watching attentively for the crew of sailors. When they arrived in Corinth, he had them summoned and inquired whether they could tell him anything about Arion. They told him that Arion had been safe in Italy and prospering in Taras when they had left. As they were speaking, Arion appeared before them, just as he was when he jumped overboard. And in their shock, when cross-examined they could no longer deny what had happened. [8] The people of both Corinth and Lesbos[a] tell this story, and there is a dedication by Arion at Tainaron, a small bronze statue of a man upon a dolphin.[b]

1.25

LYDIA-DELPHI

Alyattes' gifts to Delphi.

Alyattes the Lydian died after concluding his war against the Milesians; he had reigned for fifty-seven years. [2] This man was the second of his family to make a dedication to Delphi;[a] when he was relieved of his sickness, he dedicated a large silver bowl and a welded iron stand, worth seeing among all the dedications at Delphi. It is the work of Glaukos of Chios,[b] the only man to discover the art of welding iron.

1.26

560

LYDIA

Croesus succeeds Alyattes as king of Lydia. Croesus reigns fourteen years, 560–547/46.

When Alyattes died, Croesus son of Alyattes[a] received the kingship at the age of thirty-five. It was he who attacked the Ephesians,[b] the first of the Hellenes to be attacked. [2] At the very time the Ephesians were besieged by him, they dedicated their city to Artemis[a] by tying a rope from the temple to the city wall; between the old sector of the city where the siege was in progress and where the temple is located, a distance of 4,081 feet.[b] These were the very first people Croesus attacked.[c] Afterward he attacked the Ionians[d] and the Aeolians[e] sepa-

1.24.4a Greek vase paintings that show a singer's costume could include a wreath for the head, a long embroidered robe, long sashes, and high-heeled boots.
1.24.5a The Orthian song, often sung in honor of Apollo.
1.24.6a Corinth: Map 1.24.
1.24.8a Lesbos: Map 1.24.
1.24.8b The statue is also mentioned by the travel writer Pausanias, who saw it six centuries later.
1.25.2a Delphi: Map 1.24.
1.25.2b Chios: Map 1.24.
1.26.1a Croesus is thought to have reigned from 560 to 546.
1.26.1b Ephesus, Ionia: Map 1.28, BX.
1.26.2a Artemis: chaste Greek goddess of the hunt.

1.26.2b Herodotus describes the distance between the temple and the city walls as "7 stades." See Distance Conversions, p. lxiv, and Appendix J, §6, 19.
1.26.2c According to Aelian, *Historical Miscellany* 3.26, Croesus reacted to the Ephesians' dedication of their city by granting them freedom, on the condition that their tyrant, Pindar, go into exile. The Ephesians thus obtained special status among the Hellenes in Asia Minor.
1.26.2d Ionia, Ionian region in Asia (Minor): Map 1.28, BX. See Appendix K, §4–10.
1.26.2e Aeolis, Aeolian region in Asia (Minor): Map 1.28, BX. See Appendix K, §4–10.

[handwritten: pretend he's executing justice]

rately, charging each with various offenses. For some he could think up greater offenses and would charge them accordingly; against others he would make petty accusations.

When the Hellenes in Asia had been subjugated and forced to pay tribute, he next set his mind on building ships and attacking the islanders in the Aegean Sea.[a] [2] But just as he had everything ready to begin building ships, some people say that Bias of Priene[a] came to Sardis,[b] although others say it was Pittakos of Mytilene.[c] Croesus asked him if there was any news concerning Hellas,[d] and it was this reply that put a stop to the shipbuilding. [3] "Sire, the islanders are buying up ten thousand horses and intend to attack you at Sardis." Croesus thought he was speaking the truth and said, "Oh, if only the gods did in fact make the islanders turn their minds to attacking the sons of Lydians with horses." [4] "Sire," he replied, "you seem to me quite eager to catch the islanders riding horses on the mainland, and this is a reasonable ambition. But as soon as the islanders learned you were going to build ships to use against them, what do you think they prayed for? Nothing other than to catch the Lydians on the sea and take revenge on you for the Hellenes on the mainland that you have enslaved." [5] Croesus was delighted by this reasoning; he thought the man spoke with shrewd sense, and was thus persuaded by him to cease building ships. Instead he made a friendly alliance with the Ionians who lived on the islands.

As time went on, nearly all the peoples dwelling on this side of the River Halys[a] were also subjugated. With the exception of the Cilicians[b] and Lycians,[c] Croesus subjugated and held under his sway all the rest: the Lydians, Phrygians, Mysians, Mariandynians, Chalybians, Paphlagonians, Thracians (both Thynian and Bithynian), Carians, Ionians, Dorians, Aeolians, and Pamphylians.[d]

When all these had been subjugated and Croesus was adding them to his Lydian empire, there arrived at Sardis, now at the very height of wealth, all the wise men of Hellas who were alive at the time, each coming with his own motives. Of particular note was Solon the

1.27
LYDIA
Croesus is dissuaded from fighting the Ionians at sea by the wisdom of Bias of Priene.

1.28
560–547
ASIA
Further conquests of Croesus.

1.29
SARDIS
Solon, having left Athens, arrives at Sardis.

1.27.1a Aegean Sea: Map 1.24.
1.27.2a Bias of Priene: one of the seven proverbial wise men of ancient Hellas. Priene: Map 1.28, BX.
1.27.2b Sardis: Map 1.28, BX.
1.27.2c Pittakos of Mytilene: one of the seven proverbial wise men of ancient Hellas. Mytilene: Map 1.28, AX.
1.27.2d Hellas: the region of Greek-speaking people in the ninth century, before their expansion to other parts of the Mediterranean shores, very much the same territory as that of modern Greece: Map 1.3.
1.28.1a Halys River: Map 1.28, AY. "This side of the river" clearly means west of the river, perhaps indicating a bit of unconscious Hellenocentrism. See also 1.6.1.

1.28.1b Cilicia: Map 1.28, BY. Definitely not west of the Halys River.
1.28.1c Lycia: Map 1.28, BX.
1.28.1d The places and peoples listed by Herodotus here are located on Map 1.28 as follows:

Lydia: BX.
Phrygia: BX.
Mysia: AX.
Mariandynia: AX.
Chalybes: AY.
Paphlagonia: AY.
Thynia, Thynian Thracians: AX.
Bithynia, Bithynian Thracians: AX.
Caria: BX.
Ionia: BX.
Dorians, region settled by, in Asia: BX.
Pamphylia: BX.

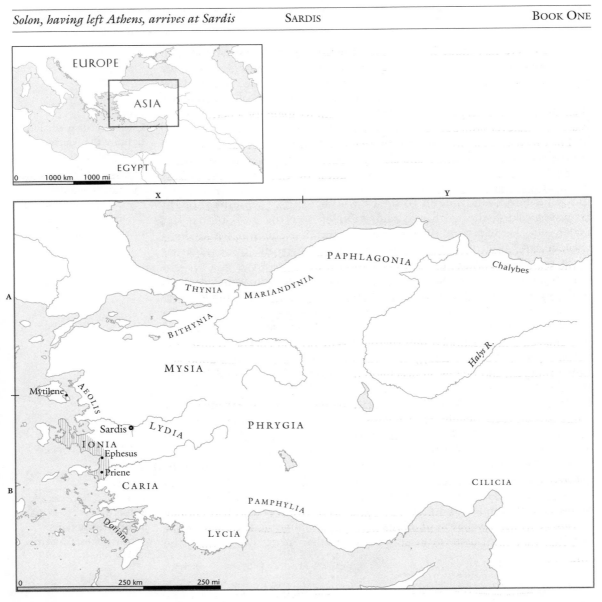

MAP 1.28

Athenian.[a] He had made laws for the Athenians at their request and then went abroad for ten years. He did have the excuse of wanting to do some sightseeing, but he really did it so that he could not be forced to repeal any of the laws he had made. [2] The Athenians could not do such a thing on their own because they had taken a solemn oath to abide for a period of ten years by whatever laws Solon would make.

For this reason, as well as for sightseeing, Solon went abroad and visited the court of Amasis in Egypt[a] and also the court of Croesus at Sardis.[b] When he arrived there, he was entertained as a guest by Croesus in the palace. Then, on the third or fourth day, Croesus gave orders to his servants to give Solon a tour through the treasuries and to point out all his great riches. [2] When Solon had viewed and inspected everything long enough, Croesus said to him, "My Athenian guest, word of your wisdom and travels has reached us even here. We hear you have wandered through much of the world in the search for knowledge, so I really can't resist asking you now whether you have yet seen anyone who surpasses all others in happiness and prosperity?" [3] He asked this in the hope that he would be declared the happiest and most prosperous of all, but Solon had no intention of flattering him. He spoke the plain truth. "Sire, that would be Tellus the Athenian." Croesus was amazed and questioned him sharply. "Why do you choose Tellus?" [4] Solon replied, "For one thing, he lived in a famous city and had good and noble children, and he saw all his children and grandchildren surviving him. Besides, he was well off, at least by our standards of living, and he ended his life in the greatest glory, [5] for he came to the aid of the Athenians in a battle against their neighbors in Eleusis[a] and forced them to flee before he died most nobly on the battlefield. The Athenians buried him at public expense in the very place he fell and gave him great honors."

As Solon spoke at length about Tellus' happiness and prosperity, he spurred Croesus to ask further who might be the next most happy man. Croesus was altogether certain he would win at least second place. But Solon said, "Cleobis and Biton. [2] These were Argives[a] who had enough resources to live on and in addition were physically fit, as is shown by the fact that they both won prizes at athletic contests, as well as by this story told about them.

1.30
SARDIS
Croesus asks Solon who is the most fortunate of men. Solon responds that Tellus the Athenian is most fortunate.

1.31
SARDIS
Provoked, Croesus asks Solon who is the next most fortunate, and Solon replies, Cleobis and Biton.

(handwritten margin note: ATHENIAN IDEAL or HAPPY LIFE)

1.29.1a Solon: another of the seven proverbial wise men of ancient Hellas. He was archon of Athens in 594–3. Some of his writings have survived to this day. This meeting between him and Croesus is certainly fictional, for Solon must have been dead many years before Croesus became king of Lydia in 560. For a review of his reforms at Athens, see Appendix A, The Athenian Government in Herodotus, §2–6. Athens: Map 1.24.

1.30.1a Egypt: Map 1.28, locator. Amasis, pharaoh 570–526. Herodotus has much more to say about Amasis in Books 2 and 3.
1.30.1b Sardis: Map 1.28, BX.
1.30.5a Eleusis: Map 1.24. Just who these neighbors were is moot. Some scholars think they were the Eleusinians, others believe they were Megarans; both at different times could be called "neighbors" to Athens.
1.31.2a Argos: Map 1.24.

"The Argives were having a festival for Hera,[b] and their mother had to be taken to the shrine in a wagon, but the oxen were not back from the fields in time to pull it. With time running out, the young men put themselves under the yoke and themselves hauled the wagon, with their mother riding in it, for five miles,[c] until they brought her all the way to the sanctuary. [3] Everyone who had gathered there for the festival watched them perform this feat; and then the god granted the young men the best possible departure from this life, showing clearly that it is better for a human being to be dead than to be alive.

"The Argive men crowded around them and showered praises on their strength, while the Argive women commended their mother for being blessed with such good sons. [4] Their mother was simply elated by her sons' feat and by all the praise. She stood before the statue of the goddess and said a prayer for Cleobis and Biton: that since they had shown her such great honor, let the goddess grant to them the best thing a human being could have. [5] After the prayer, they all sacrificed and had their feast. Then the young men fell asleep in that very sanctuary and never awoke again; this was the end of their lives. The Argives made statues of them and dedicated them at Delphi[a] to commemorate that they had proven themselves to be the best of men."

When Solon thus allotted his second place for happiness to these, Croesus now became annoyed. "My Athenian guest," he said, "are you disparaging my own happiness as though it were nothing? Do you think me worth less than even a common man?" Solon replied, "Croesus, you asked me about human concerns, and I know that the gods are jealous of human prosperity and disruptive of our peace. [2] Over a long period of time, a man will see and experience many things he would rather not. If we set the limit of a human life at seventy years, [3] these seventy cycles of seasons provide 25,200 days, without the intercalary months.[a] But if you want to make every other year a month longer so that the seasons occur at the proper time, add thirty-five intercalary months to the seventy years, and from these months you get 1,050 days. [4] All these days in the seventy years add up to 26,250, and any one of these days brings with it something completely unlike any other. And so, Croesus, human life is pure chance. [5] You seem to be very wealthy, and you rule over many people, but I cannot yet tell you the answer you asked for until I learn how you have ended your life. You see, the man who is very wealthy is no more happy and prosperous than the man who has only enough to live from day to day, unless good fortune stays with him and he retains his fair and noble possessions right up until he departs this life happily. For many wealthy people are unhappy, while many others who have more modest resources

[margin notes: better be dead than alive · GOOD DEATH · DEATH=BEST · HUMAN LIFE = CHANCE]*

1.32
SARDIS
Vexed, Croesus asks why Solon despises him. Solon points out that no one can be judged fortunate until he is dead.

1.31.2b   Hera, goddess consort of Zeus. See Figure 1.31, showing the remaining foundations of the temple of Hera in Argive territory.
1.31.2c   Herodotus writes "45 stades" here. See Appendix J, §6, 19.
1.31.5a   Delphi: Map 1.24.

1.32.3a   The "intercalary" month is a month periodically inserted to make the series of solar and calendar years eventually correspond. But Herodotus' reckoning here would make the average length of a year 375 days. (Godley)

FIGURE 1.31. FOUNDATION REMAINS OF THE TEMPLE OF HERA IN THE ARGOLID.

are fortunate. [6] The man who has great wealth but is unhappy outdoes the fortunate man in only two ways, while the fortunate man outdoes him in many ways. The former is more capable of gratifying his passions and of sustaining himself in adversity, but the fortunate man, although he does not have the same ability to sustain himself in adversity or passion, avoids these anyway by virtue of his good fortune. Moreover, he has no injury, no sickness, no painful experiences; what he does have is good children and good looks. [7] Now if, in addition to all these things, he ends his life well, too, then this is the man you are looking for; he alone deserves to be called happy and prosperous. But before he dies, refrain from calling him this—one should rather call him lucky.

FORTUNATE MAN = HAPPY MAN

(handwritten margin notes: "HAPPY MAN", "(son killed)", "FOR PRIDE", "CROESUS = PUNISHED CONCL. RE: HAPPY MAN")

[8] "Of course, it is impossible for one human being to receive all these blessings together, just as no one country can produce everything it needs by itself. What one has, the other lacks, and the one that has the most is the best. So, too, no one man can be self-sufficient either; he surely lacks something. [9] But the man who goes through life having the most blessings and then ends his life favorably, he is the man, sire, who rightly wins this title from me. We must look to the end of every matter to see how it will turn out. God shows many people a hint of happiness and prosperity, only to destroy them utterly later."

1.33
SARDIS
Croesus is displeased.

Solon did not please Croesus at all by telling him this, and Croesus dismissed him, thinking him worthless and extremely ignorant for overlooking the good things right before his eyes and telling him instead to look to the end of every matter.

1.34
SARDIS
Croesus tries to protect his son Atys from a death he foresaw in a dream.

But after Solon left, the god took a dreadful vengeance upon Croesus, apparently because Croesus had thought himself the happiest and most prosperous of men. Not long afterward, he had a terrible dream that accurately showed him the troubles about to descend upon his son. [2] Now Croesus had two sons, one disabled by muteness, the other, named Atys, who greatly surpassed his peers in everything. It was Atys that Croesus dreamed he would lose after he had been wounded by an iron spear.[a]

[3] When Croesus awoke he pondered the dream and became more and more apprehensive about it; he quickly found a wife for Atys, and although the young man had served as a general in the Lydian army before this, Croesus no longer permitted him to have anything to do with war. Further, he moved all the javelins, lances, and everything else men use in warfare from the men's hall into the bedrooms so that they could not hang above his son and perhaps fall upon him.

1.35
SARDIS
Adrastos arrives as a suppliant to the court of Croesus.

Just when his son was becoming occupied with his marriage, there arrived in Sardis a man caught up in bad luck, with blood guilt on his hands. He was a Phrygian of royal birth and came to Croesus' household in accordance with the local custom; he needed to obtain ritual purification because of his crime. And so Croesus performed this service for him. [2] The Lydian method of purification is similar to that of the Hellenes.[a] After Croesus had performed the customary rites, he asked who he was and where he was from in these words: [3] "Now, you, who are you? And from where in Phrygia have you come here as my suppliant? What man or woman did you murder?" And the man answered, "I am the son of Gordias son of Midas; my name is Adrastos.[a] I killed my brother unintentionally, and am here because I was banished by my father and am now deprived of everything." [4] Croesus replied with these words: "It so happens that you

1.34.2a Significant dreams were thought to be communications from the gods warning of threats and dangers, advising on cures for illness, imposing policies, or answering pressing questions, but in 7.16.β.2, Herodotus has Artabanos give a surprisingly rational explanation for them when

he advises Xerxes and says that "most of the visions visiting our dreams tend to be what one is thinking about during the day."
1.35.2a The ritual included pouring a young pig's blood over the murderer's hands.
1.35.3a The name means "unable to escape."

are descended from friends of mine; therefore you have found friends here and will lack for nothing in my home. You will do best to bear this misfortune as lightly as possible."

And so Adrastos lived for some time at the court of Croesus. Meanwhile, a huge monster of a boar appeared on Mount Olympus in Mysia,[a] from which it would set out to ravage the Mysians' fields. The Mysians often went out to attack it but could do it no harm and they suffered injuries from it instead. [2] At last, messengers from the Mysians went to Croesus and told him, "Sire, a very huge monster of a boar has appeared in our land and is destroying our fields. Although we are eager to catch it, we do not have the power to do so. And so now we ask you to please send us your son with a group of your best young men and your hunting dogs so that we can remove it from our land."

[3] As they were making this request, Croesus recalled the dream, and this was his reply. "About my son—do not bring up that subject again, because I would not send him with you. He has just been married, and this sort of thing is not his concern right now. I will, however, send with you a group of the best Lydians as well as my whole pack of hunting dogs, and I will order them to help you remove the beast from your land with their utmost determination."

With this reply the Mysians were satisfied. But Croesus' son had overheard the Mysians' request, and the young man came in after Croesus had refused to send him and confronted the king with these words: [2] "Before this, Father, I always enjoyed the best, the most noble status when I went to war or to the hunt, and I was held in high esteem. But now you exclude me from both, although I do not believe you have detected in me any cowardice or lack of bravery. How am I supposed to show my face when I visit the public square? [3] What kind of man will the citizens think I am? And my bride? What kind of man will she think she is living with? So either let me go on the hunt or give me a convincing reason why it is better that I follow your wishes in this matter."

Croesus replied, "My son, I am not doing this because I have detected cowardice or any other displeasing quality in you, but rather because I was visited by a dream, a vision in sleep, and it told me that you would live only a short time and would be killed by an iron spear. [2] And so, in light of the vision, I was eager for this marriage of yours and refused to send you on this expedition. I am trying to be careful in the hope that I can somehow rescue you from that fate while I live. You are my only true son, since I don't count the other one, the disabled one,[a] as my own."

1.36.1a Mount Olympus in Mysia: Map 1.46.
1.38.2a We are told more about this mute son of
        Croesus in 1.85.

1.36
LYDIA-MYSIA
The Mysians request help from Croesus against a monster boar.

1.37
SARDIS
Croesus' son Atys asks to be allowed to lead the expedition against the boar.

1.38
SARDIS
Croesus reveals his vision and fears.

CROESUS TRIES TO AVOID FATE

1.39
SARDIS
Atys points out that he will be fighting a boar, not men, and need not fear iron.

The young man responded, "Father, since you had such a dream, I forgive you for watching over me; but let me tell you that you missed something in the dream. [2] You said that in your dream I appeared to die by an iron spear. Well, what kind of hands does a boar have? Or what kind of spear could it use that you are so afraid? If the dream told you that I would die by its teeth or by some other means natural to this animal, then you ought to act as you are doing, but it told of a spear. So, since I will not be in a battle against men, please do let me go."

1.40
SARDIS
Croesus allows Atys to hunt.

"You win, my son," Croesus replied, "you have shown good judgment about the dream. And since you have won, I shall change my mind and will let you go on the hunt."

1.41
SARDIS
Croesus charges Adrastos to watch over Atys.

Then Croesus summoned Adrastos the Phrygian and told him, "Adrastos, I don't reproach you for your unpleasant bad luck. I have purified you and have taken you into my household and paid all your expenses. [2] Now you owe me favors for those I have done for you. I ask you to protect my son as he sets out on the hunt, in case any wicked thieves appear on the road to harm him. Moreover, as you are a strong man descended from illustrious ancestors, you should strive to do deeds that will win glory for yourself."

1.42
SARDIS
Adrastos promises to protect Atys.

Adrastos said in reply, "Sire, if the situation were different, I would not go on such an assignment, since anyone who has experienced the calamity that I have does not properly associate with those who are fortunate. I would not willingly go and really should restrain myself for many reasons. [2] But as matters stand, and I do owe you many favors, your wish is my command. You have ordered me to protect your son; therefore you can expect him to return home safe under my protection."

1.43
MYSIA
Atys is accidentally killed by Adrastos' spear.

After this he went off, taking with him a group of the best young men and the dogs. When they reached Mount Olympus,[a] they searched for the boar, and when they found the beast, they surrounded it and cast their spears at it. [2] But at that point, the supplicant stranger, Adrastos, the very man whom Croesus had purified of blood guilt, missed his mark while aiming his javelin at the boar and hit the son of Croesus. [3] Thus wounded by the iron spear, Atys fulfilled the prophecy of the dream. A messenger was sent to inform the king, who, upon his arrival at Sardis, soon told Croesus all about the hunt and the fate of his son.

1.44
SARDIS
Croesus is distraught.

Croesus was distraught at the news of the death of Atys and protested indignantly that the very man he had purified from murder had now slain his own son. [2] Furious at this stroke of bad fortune, he made fierce calls upon Zeus the Purifier, beseeching him to witness what he had suffered at the hand of his guest. Later he called on Zeus Protector of the Hearth and Zeus Protector of Friendship,[a] invoking the god in both roles at once.[b] He

1.43.1a Mount Olympus in Mysia: Map 1.46.
1.44.2a Guest-friendship (*xenia*): a bond of ritualized friendship, usually between aristocrats or prominent men of different cities. It was passed down through generations and required hereditary privileges and obligations such as reciprocal hospitality

and assistance. See Appendix T, §3.
1.44.2b Literally, "naming him as one and the same god," suggesting the importance of the various epithets defining one divinity in his or her various functions and demands for worship.

called upon Zeus Protector of Suppliants at the Hearth because he had not realized that the man he had welcomed and fed as a guest in his own home was to be his own son's murderer, and he called upon Zeus Protector of Friendship because he had sent Adrastos off as his son's guardian only to discover that he was his greatest enemy.

After this the Lydians came back carrying the corpse and behind them followed the murderer. Standing before the body of the young man, and offering himself up to Croesus, he stretched out his hands and begged Croesus to slay him over the dead youth, saying that to his earlier misfortune was now added the ruin of the man who had purified him, so that he could no longer bear to live. [2] As Croesus listened he began to pity Adrastos, although suffering such agony of his own, and he said to him, "My friend, I have already received full payment from you in that you have sentenced yourself to death. You are not the cause of my affliction; you did the deed, but you had no intention of doing it. In all likelihood this was done by one of the gods, who long ago, in fact, revealed to me what would happen in the future."

[3] Then Croesus gave his son an appropriate funeral. And when it was over and all was silent around the tomb, Adrastos, son of Gordias son of Midas, to his own brother a murderer, to his purifier a murderer, admitting to himself that he knew of no man suffering greater torment, slew himself upon the tomb.

For two years, Croesus sat and did nothing but grieve bitterly for the loss of his son. But his grief ended when he learned that the Persian Cyrus son of Cambyses had destroyed the empire of the Mede Astyages son of Cyaxares[a] and that the power of the Persians was steadily growing. He wondered if he would be able to check the Persian power before it became too strong. [2] With this in mind, he resolved to test the oracles of the Hellenes and the oracle in Libya and immediately sent sacred delegates to the following Hellenic oracles: to Delphi,[a] to Abai[b] in Phocis, to Dodona,[c] to the oracle of Amphiareion,[d] and Trophonios,[e] and to the Branchidai in the territory of Miletus.[f] [3] He also sent men to question the oracle of Ammon in Libya.[a] He dispatched these men to the different oracles in order to test them, so that if he found any that could know the truth, he could send a second time to ask if he should wage war against the Persians.[b]

Croesus gave his sacred delegates the following instructions for testing the oracles: that they were to count the days from their departure from Sardis until the hundredth day, on which they would then consult the

1.45
SARDIS
Adrastos kills himself on the tomb of Atys.

1.46
550–?
LYDIA
Croesus considers challenging the power of Persia. He decides to consult and to test a series of oracular shrines.

1.47
550–?
LYDIA
Croesus devises a means to test the oracles.

1.46.1a Cyrus' victory over Astyages took place in 550. Herodotus tells the "full" story of Astyages and Cyrus in 1.107–130.
1.46.2a Delphi: Map 1.46.
1.46.2b Abai: Map 1.46.
1.46.2c Dodona: Map 1.46. Dodona, an oracle of Zeus, was the oldest known oracle in Hellas.
1.46.2d Amphiareion, shrine to Amphiareios: Map 1.46. It is located in Oropos (Map 1.59, inset), a much disputed territory between Attica and Boeotia: Map 1.46. See also 8.134.
1.46.2e A shrine to Trophonios was located at Lebadeia: Map 1.46.
1.46.2f Didyma (Branchidai): Map 1.46. Branchidai refers to both the site of the sanctuary and temple of Apollo at Didyma, a little more than 20 miles from Miletus, and to the family from which the priests who administered the sanctuary were drawn. The family's ancestor Branchus was said to have founded the cult.
1.46.3a Ammonion, "the shrine to Ammon" in Libya: Map 1.46, locator.
1.46.3b See Appendix P, §7–9, 15.

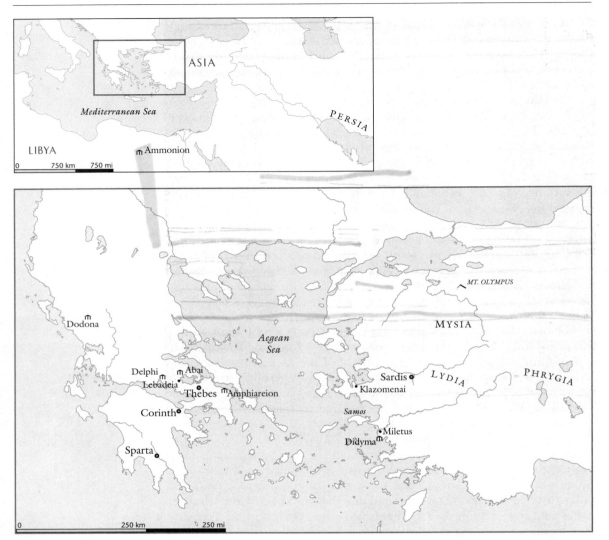

Map 1.46

oracles, asking what the Lydian king, Croesus son of Alyattes, happened to be doing just then. Then they were to record in writing whatever each of the oracles answered and bring that record back to him. [2] Except for the oracle of Delphi, the replies of the oracles are not reported, but at Delphi, as soon as the Lydians entered the inner shrine and posed their assigned question, the Pythia[a] spoke forth in verse:

1.47.2a   For a discussion of the Pythia at Delphi and the various other priests and priest- esses through whom Apollo spoke to the   human questioners, see Appendix P, §9. See also Figure 1.47, a vase painting of King Aigeus consulting an oracle.

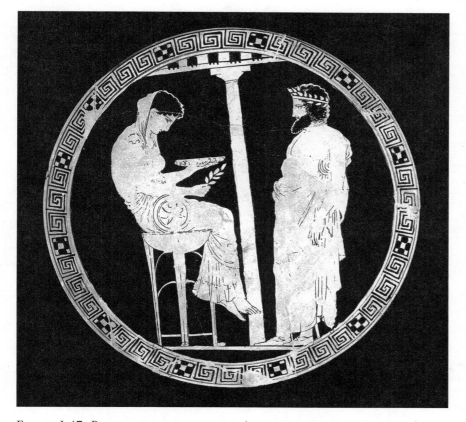

FIGURE 1.47. PAINTING FROM THE TONDO (ROUND INNER BOTTOM SURFACE) OF A CUP, SHOWING KING AIGEUS, A MYTHICAL KING OF ATHENS, CONSULTING THE ORACLE OF DELPHI. THE PROPHETESS SITS ON A TRIPOD, AND AN INSCRIPTION ON THE CUP IDENTIFIES HER AS THE GODDESS THEMIS, WHO WAS IN CHARGE OF THE ORACLE BEFORE APOLLO TOOK IT OVER. ATTIC RED-FIGURE KYLIX BY THE KODROS PAINTER, C. 440–30.

I know the number of grains of sand and the measures of the sea,
I understand the mute and hear the speechless.
Into the depth of my senses has come the smell of hard-shelled tortoise
Boiling in bronze with the meat of lamb,
Laid upon bronze below, covered with bronze on top.

Figure 1.51. Large bronze volute krater (vessel), made by Greek craftsmen and found in the grave of a Celtic princess in northeastern France. It holds 262 gallons and stands five feet four inches tall.

1.48
550–?
LYDIA-DELPHI
The Delphic oracle wins Croesus' approval.

The Lydians had these verses of the Pythia recorded, and left for Sardis. And when all the sacred delegates whom Croesus had sent out were present and ready with their oracular responses, he unfolded each one and studied what was written. None of them received his approval until he heard[a] the one from Delphi, whereupon he said a prayer of joy and declared that the only true oracle was at Delphi, since it alone had discovered what he was doing. [2] For after he had sent his sacred delegates off to the various oracles, he watched for the day he had appointed with a plan in mind that he thought would be impossible to discover and disclose: all by himself, he had chopped up a tortoise and a lamb, then boiled them together in a bronze cauldron covered by a bronze lid.

1.49
550–?
AMPHIAREION
Croesus also accepts the oracle of Amphiareion.

And this is just what the oracle from Delphi said in its response to Croesus. I cannot say what reply the oracle of Amphiareion gave to the Lydians after they went through the customary rites at the sanctuary since this is not reported, other than that he believed that he had found there a true oracle as well.[a]

1.50
550–?
LYDIA-DELPHI
Croesus tries to curry favor with the Delphic oracle by sacrifices and rich gifts.

After this he tried to please the god at Delphi with generous offerings. He sacrificed 3,000 of every kind of appropriate animal. He piled up gold- and silver-plated couches, golden libation cups, and purple garments, and then burned them on a huge pyre, hoping thereby to gain a bit more of the god's favor. He ordered all the Lydians to sacrifice according to their

1.48.1a   Herodotus uses the term "heard" probably because he envisions Croesus reading aloud, as was the norm for Hellenes at this time.

1.49.1a   Amphiareion, a healing shrine and oracle; see Appendix P, §4.

means. [2] After the sacrifice, Croesus melted down a great amount of gold and beat it into ingots, 117 in all, each measuring eighteen inches long, nine inches wide, and three inches high.[a] Of these, four were made of refined gold, weighing two and a half talents[b] each, and the rest were made of white gold, weighing two talents each. [3] He also had a statue of a lion made of refined gold, weighing ten talents. When the temple at Delphi burned down,[a] this lion fell from the ingots on which it had been sitting, and was set up in the treasury of the Corinthians; it now weighs six and a half talents, since three and a half talents melted off in the fire.[b]

When Croesus had finished preparing these offerings, he sent them to Delphi together with two bowls of enormous size: one of gold, which was set on the right of the temple entrance, and the other of silver, which was set on the left. [2] These also were moved when the temple burned down. The golden bowl is now displayed in the treasury of the Klazomenaians[a] and weighs eight and a half talents and twelve minas;[b] the silver one is in the corner of the temple's front hall and holds 600 amphoras.[c] I know this because they are now used by the Delphians for mixing wine at the Theophania festival.[d] [3] The Delphians say they are the work of Theodoros of Samos,[a] and I believe them, since they do not look to me like any ordinary pieces. In addition, Croesus sent four large silver storage jars, which are in the treasury of the Corinthians;[b] and he dedicated two vessels for sprinkling holy water, of gold and silver. Of these, the golden jar has an inscription that claims it is a dedication of the Spartans,[c] but that is incorrect, for [4] this, too, came from Croesus; but a Delphian inscribed it thus in order to ingratiate the Spartans. I know his name but will not mention it. There is, however, a statue of a boy with water flowing through his hands which is really from the Spartans, but neither of the sprinklers are theirs. [5] Together with these offerings, Croesus sent many other less remarkable items: these included some round cast objects of silver, a golden statue of a woman four and a half feet[a] tall, which the Delphians say is an image of Croesus' baker, and his own wife's necklaces and belts.

1.51
550–?
LYDIA-DELPHI
Croesus sends rich gifts to Delphi.

1.50.2a The Greek text measures the ingots in "palms," each palm being a little under 3 inches. See Appendix J, §4, 5, 19.
1.50.2b The Attic talent was a unit of weight (approximately 57 pounds) and money (6,000 drachmas). See Appendix J, §11–13, 20.
1.50.3a The temple at Delphi burned down in the year 584.
1.50.3b 6.5 Attic talents would amount to 370 modern pounds. See Appendix J, §11.
1.51.2a Klazomenai: Map 1.46.
1.51.2b The Attic talent; see n. 1.50.2b. There were 60 minas in each talent, so a mina weighed about 15 ounces. See Appendix J, §11.
1.51.2c One amphora could equal slightly more than 10 gallons (Appendix J, §18, 22), so

Herodotus would have us believe that this vessel held more than 6,000 gallons. See Figure 1.51 of a very large bronze vessel.
1.51.2d The Theophania festival was celebrated at Delphi in the spring to mark the return of the sun god. (How and Wells) See Appendix I, Classical Greek Religious Festivals, §5–12.
1.51.3a Theodoros of Samos: a famous goldsmith, maker of Polykrates' ring (3.41.1) and probably of the golden plane tree (7.27.1). Samos: Map 1.46.
1.51.3b Corinth: Map 1.46.
1.51.3c Sparta: Map 1.46.
1.51.5a Herodotus writes that the statue was "3 cubits" high. The cubit probably referred to here was approximately 1.5 feet long. See Appendix J, §4, 5, 19.

1.52
550–?
AMPHIAREION
Croesus' gifts to
the Amphiareion.

1.53
550–?
DELPHI
The Delphic oracle
advises Croesus that an
expedition against Persia
will destroy a great
empire!

1.54
550–?
SARDIS
Croesus is pleased by
the oracle's response.

1.55
550–?
DELPHI
Croesus asks the Delphic
oracle about war with
Persia again.

Those were his offerings to Delphi, but he also sent some things to the shrine of Amphiareios when he learned of this hero's valor and suffering.[a] He dedicated a shield made entirely of gold, as well as a spear of solid gold, shaft and spearhead alike. Both of these could still be seen in my day at Thebes,[b] displayed there in the temple of Ismenian Apollo.[c]

Croesus gave the following instructions to the Lydians who were to bring these gifts to the sanctuaries: they were to ask the oracles if he should wage war against the Persians and if there were any military forces he should add to his own as his friends and supporters. [2] When the Lydians arrived at their assigned locations, they dedicated the offerings, went to the oracles, and said, "Croesus king of the Lydians and other peoples, in the belief that yours is the only true oracle in the whole world, gives you gifts worthy of your prophetic insight, and asks whether he should wage war against the Persians and whether he should seek to add any military force to his own as an ally." [3] Both oracles concurred in their reply; they predicted that if Croesus were to wage war against the Persians, he would destroy a great empire, and they advised him to find the most powerful Hellenes and to make them his friends and supporters.

When the oracular responses were brought back to Croesus, he was overjoyed with the prophecies, confidently expecting that they foretold that he was going to destroy the empire of Cyrus, Then, having sent yet another mission to Delphi, and after having ascertained the size of the population of Delphi, Croesus gave each man of that city a present of two gold staters.[a] [2] In return, the Delphians granted to Croesus and the Lydians the privileges of priority in oracular consultation and exemption from fees, along with front-row places at their festivals. They also granted in perpetuity that any of the Lydians could become a Delphian citizen.[a]

After presenting the Delphians with these gifts, Croesus consulted the oracle for yet a third time. Evidently, once he felt sure that he had received truth from the oracle, he wished to use it to the full. This time he asked whether his reign would be long-lasting. [2] The Pythia[a] answered him as follows:

> . . . But[b] whenever a mule becomes king of the Medes,
> Then, tender-footed Lydian, flee by the pebbled River Hermus
> And do not delay, nor feel shame at being a coward.

1.52.1a Herodotus here refers to the legend of the hero Amphiareios. According to the *Thebaid* (Fragment 9, Davies, according to the *Oxford Classical Dictionary*), Amphiareios was one of the Seven Against Thebes, and when he fled from the battle, he was swallowed up by a cleft in the earth made by a thunderbolt from Zeus. The shrine was also dedicated to healing. As at Epidauros (but on a much smaller scale), suppliants would relax and sleep at the sanctuary, and the god would visit them in their sleep and either cure them or tell them what they must do to be cured. See Figure 1.52.

1.52.1b Thebes, Boeotia: Map 1.46.

1.52.1c An oracular shrine in Thebes. Herodotus mentions some of Croesus' additional gifts to various shrines in 1.90.

1.54.1a The stater was a unit of currency. See Appendix J, §14.

1.54.2a Croesus rewards Delphi, and he and all Lydians are rewarded by the citizens of Delphi: see Appendix P, §12.

1.55.2a Pythia, the priestess at Delphi who pronounced the oracles while in a trance. See Appendix P, §9, 12.

1.55.2b Quoted oracles sometimes begin with the word "but," perhaps indicating that the beginning of the oracle has been lost or omitted.

FIGURE 1.52. AMPHIAREION: VIEWS OF THE
REMAINS OF THE SMALL THEATER (ABOVE),
AND THE PORTICO COLONNADE (RIGHT), AT
THE SHRINE DEDICATED TO AMPHIAREIOS.
THE THEATER WAS THERE BECAUSE IT WAS
THOUGHT TO BE EFFECTIVE FOR HEALING.

1.56
550–?
SARDIS-HELLAS
Following the oracle's advice, Croesus seeks allies among the Hellenes.

These verses, when delivered to Croesus, delighted him more than ever before. He was confident that a man would always rule the Medes—never a mule—and therefore assumed that he and his descendants would rule forever.[a] After this, he began to investigate which Hellenes were most powerful in order to add them to his own forces as friends and supporters. [2] By making inquiries, he discovered that the most distinguished among them were the Spartans[a] of Dorian ancestry and the Athenians[b] of Ionian ancestry.[c] These were the eminent powers in antiquity as well. The Athenians, a Pelasgian[d] people, had occupied Attica[e] and never moved from it. The Hellenes who became Spartans, however, wandered extensively. [3] When Deukalion was king, these Hellenes inhabited the land of Phthia,[a] but under Doros son of Hellen, they dwelled in the land beneath Ossa and Olympus,[b] which is called Histiaiotis.[c] From there they were expelled by the Kadmeians and settled in Pindus,[d] where they were called Macedonians. From there they migrated into Dryopis,[e] and from Dryopis they finally came to the Peloponnese,[f] where they came to be called Dorians.

1.57
HELLAS
Herodotus' conjectures on the language of the Pelasgians.

I am unable to state with certainty what language the Pelasgians spoke, but we could consider the speech of the Pelasgians who still exist in settlements above Tyrrhenia in the city of Kreston,[a] formerly neighbors to the Dorians who at that time lived in the land now called Thessaliotis;[b] [2] also the Pelasgians who once lived with the Athenians and then settled Plakia and Skylake in the Hellespont;[a] and along with those who lived with all the other commmunities and were once Pelasgian but changed their names. If one can judge by this evidence, the Pelasgians spoke a barbarian[b] language. [3] And so, if the Pelasgian language was spoken in all these places, the people of Attica being originally Pelasgian, must have learned a new language when they became Hellenes.[a] As a matter of fact, the people of Krestonia and Plakia no longer speak the same language as their neighbors, but they both speak the same language, which shows that they continue to use the dialect they brought with them when they migrated to these lands.

1.56.1a A typical error in interpretation. See Appendix P, §8–9.
1.56.2a Sparta: Map 1.59, BX.
1.56.2b Athens: Map 1.59, BX and inset.
1.56.2c Doric and Ionian blood: see Appendix K, §7–9.
1.56.2d The Pelasgians are mentioned by Homer as specific ethnic groups in Thrace (*Iliad* 2.840, 17.301), Argos (*Iliad* 2.684), and Crete (*Odyssey* 19.177); Herodotus and later authors, however, use the term to describe the pre-Hellenic populations in general throughout the Aegean and Mediterranean. Herodotus mentions Pelasgians again at 2.50.1, 2.51.1–2, and 8.44.
1.56.2e Attica: Map 1.59, inset.
1.56.3a Phthia: Map 1.59, AX.
1.56.3b Mount Ossa and Mount Olympus: Map 1.59, AX.
1.56.3c Histiaiotis: precise location unknown.
1.56.3d Pindus Mountains: Map 1.59, AX.

1.56.3e Dryopis: Map 1.59, AX.
1.56.3f Peloponnese: Map 1.59, BX.
1.57.1a These Tyrrhenians could hardly be Etruscans, as some have surmised. There is a district called Krestonia in Thrace, north of Chalcidice and west of the Strymon River (Map 1.59, AX), but no Tyrrhenian tribe or town of Kreston is known in that district.
1.57.1b Thessaliotis, one of four districts in Thessaly, thought to be in the southern half of the country. Thessaly: Map 1.59, AX.
1.57.2a Plakia and Skylake: Map 1.59, AY. These towns are located east of Cyzicus (Map 1.59, AY) on the Propontis (Map 1.59, AY), which Herodotus here calls the Hellespont.
1.57.2b By "a barbarian language," Herodotus (and all Hellenes) meant only that the language was not Greek.
1.57.3a The new language that the people of Attica would have had to adopt to become Hellenes was of course Greek.

As for the Hellenes, it seems obvious to me that ever since they came into existence they have always used the same language. They were weak at first, when they were separated from the Pelasgians, but they grew from a small group into a multitude, especially when many peoples, including other barbarians in great numbers, had joined them. Moreover, I do not think the Pelasgians, who remained barbarians, ever grew appreciably in number or power.

Well, then, of these two peoples, Croesus learned that those in Attica were currently being oppressed and divided in political strife by Peisistratos son of Hippocrates, who was ruling Athens as a tyrant at the time.[a] Long before this, the tyrant's father Hippocrates had received a great portent when he attended the Olympic games,[b] in no official political capacity, but merely as a spectator. When he had sacrificed the victims,[c] the cauldrons, which had been set in place and filled with the meat and water, boiled and overflowed, although the fire had not yet been lit. [2] Chilon the Lacedaemonian happened to be at hand and saw the portent. He advised Hippocrates to avoid bringing into his household a childbearing wife, but if he already had one, to send her away and, further, if he happened to have a son, to disown him. [3] They say that Hippocrates refused to heed Chilon's advice, and that afterward Peisistratos was born to him.

Later, at Athens, two factions formed, one of the coastal district under the leadership of Megakles son of Alkmeon,[a] and another of the plains district under Lykourgos son of Aristoleides. Peisistratos then formed a third faction, intending to make himself the city's tyrant. When he had collected his partisans and made himself nominal leader of the hill district, he devised the following plan. [4] First, he wounded himself and his mules and drove his chariot into the center of town, claiming to be in flight from enemies who had attempted to kill him as he drove into the countryside. He then asked the Athenian people to grant him protection, reminding them of his many past achievements on their behalf, particularly his service as general in the war against Megara,[a] when he had captured Nisaia.[b] [5] The Athenian people, completely duped by Peisistratos, selected some of their city's men to serve as a bodyguard for him. These carried wooden clubs instead of spears as they followed him about, and they supported him when he revolted and took control of the acropolis.[a] From then on, Peisistratos ruled the Athenians, but he neither disrupted the existing political offices nor changed the laws. He managed the city in accordance with its existing legal and political institutions, and he provided it with moderate and good government.[b]

[handwritten margin notes: "PEISISTRATOS" and "type of ruler"]

1.58
HELLAS
Others may have adopted different languages, but not the Hellenes.

1.59
c. 561
ATHENS
The origins of Athens and the story of Peisistratos' rise to power at Athens. His first tyranny.

1.59.1a   About the year 560.
1.59.1b   Olympia: Map 1.59, BX. These games probably took place in 608 or 604. For the significance of the Olympic festival's athletic contests to ancient Greeks, see Appendix I, §12.
1.59.1c   The practice of sacrificing animals to the gods at sanctuary altars was a way to invoke the god's help or at least goodwill. It also provided meat for a feast.

1.59.3a   Megakles son of Alkmeon was a scion of the Alkmeonid family or clan; see Appendix L, §4, 11–13, 15.
1.59.4a   Megara: Map 1.59, inset.
1.59.4b   Nisaia: Map 1.59, inset. Nisaia was the port of Megara.
1.59.5a   Acropolis: see n. 1.15.1f and Glossary.
1.59.5b   On Peisistratos as tyrant of Athens, see Appendix A, §6, and Appendix T, §2, 5.

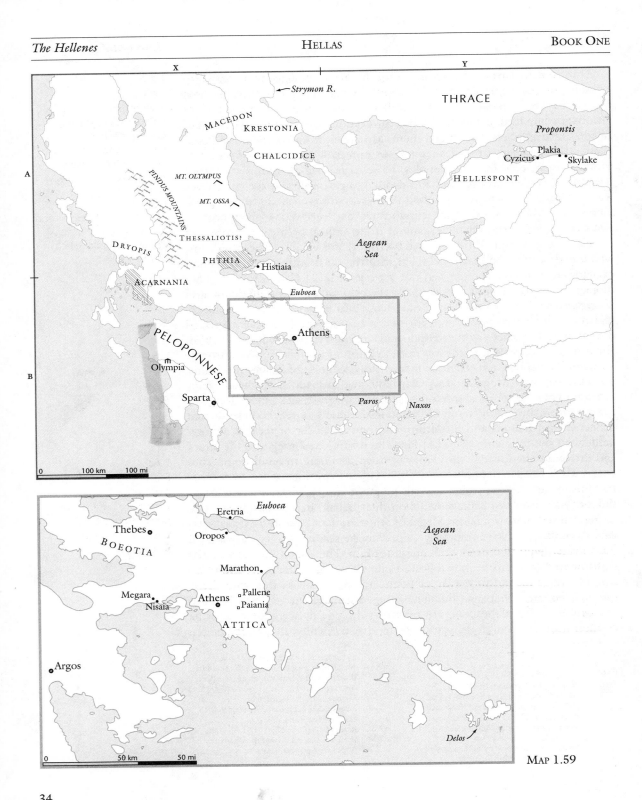

MAP 1.59

After a little while the partisans of Megakles united with those of Lykourgos, and together they drove out Peisistratos. Thus the first time Peisistratos took control of Athens and held the tyranny, his rule did not become deeply rooted and he lost it. However, the men who drove him out divided into quarrelsome factions once again, and [2] Megakles, who was particularly harassed by this factional strife, sent a message to Peisistratos offering to restore him to the tyranny if in return he would marry his daughter. [3] Peisistratos agreed to the terms and accepted the offer; they then, in order to help him return to power, contrived the silliest scheme I've ever heard of—particularly silly in this case, for long ago the Hellenes distinguished themselves from barbarians by their superior cleverness and freedom from naïve stupidity; moreover, they carried out this scheme against the Athenians, who were at the time reputed to surpass all other Hellenes in intellect!

[4] There was a woman named Phya in the deme of Paiania[a] who was almost six feet tall and strikingly beautiful. They dressed her up in a full set of armor, placed her in a chariot, showed her how to project a distinguished appearance, and then drove her into the city. They sent heralds on ahead of them to tell the people to remain in the city and to proclaim: [5] "Athenians, hail Peisistratos and welcome him joyfully, since Athena herself is bringing him home to her own acropolis, honoring him above all men." They repeated these words as they made their way onward, and before long the rumor that Athena was bringing Peisistratos home had reached the demes. In the city, people actually worshiped this woman in the belief that she was really the goddess,[a] and they welcomed Peisistratos back.

After recovering his tyranny in this way, Peisistratos married the daughter of Megakles in accordance with their agreement. But since he already had full-grown sons, and the Alkmeonids were said to be under a curse,[a] he did not want his new wife to bear his children, and so had intercourse with her in an indecent way. [2] His wife kept quiet about this at first, but later (I do not know whether she was questioned about it or not), she did tell her mother, who then told her husband. Megakles, responding to what he considered a grave insult by Peisistratos, flew into a terrible rage, and in his fury he ended his hostility with his political enemies and united with them. When Peisistratos learned what was being organized against him, he fled the country with all his supporters and went to Eretria,[a] where he took counsel with his sons. [3] Hippias' advice, that they should try to regain the

1.60
556
ATHENS
Driven out of power, Peisistratos returns for his second tyranny with the help of a fake Athena.

1.61
555?
ATHENS
Peisistratos returns to power for his third tyranny at Athens but is forced to leave once more.

[handwritten marginal notes: "What does this say abt belief in gods?" and "ATHENA SCHEME"]

1.60.4a Paiania: Map 1.59, inset. At the time of Peisistratos (mid-sixth century), "demes" signified the rural villages where the common people lived. Elsewhere in Hellas it retained that meaning, but in Athens, after the reforms of Kleisthenes in the year 508/7 (see 5.69), demes came to mean specific, politically and geographically defined districts. Every citizen of Athens was identified by name and by the deme in which he was born.

1.60.5a An event as extraordinary (and incredible) as this one does not appear again in Athenian political history. For a brief discussion of the incident and a possible rational explanation, see Appendix A, §6.

1.61.1a Curse of the Alkmeonids: see 5.70 and Appendix L, §11, 15.

1.61.2a Eretria, a city on the nearby island of Euboea: Map 1.59, inset.

tyranny, was adopted; and they then began to collect funds from cities that were in debt to them for any reason. Many cities provided large sums, but the Thebans[a] surpassed all the others in the amount of money they gave.

[4] To make a long story short, with the passage of time, they prepared everything for their return. From the Peloponnese[a] came Argive[b] mercenaries; and from Naxos,[c] a most enthusiastic volunteer named Lygdamis, who brought with him both money and men.

Setting out from Eretria, they returned in the eleventh year of their exile. The first place in Attica[a] they seized was Marathon.[b] There they camped and mustered their forces, as supporters from both the city and the demes[c] flocked to join them. These were men who found tyranny more welcome than freedom.

[2] Other Athenians of the city ignored Peisistratos, both while he had collected money and later, when he took Marathon; but when they heard that he and his army of returning exiles had left Marathon and were advancing on the city, they marched out against him in full force. [3] The two armies met at the sanctuary of Pallenian Athena and there took up their battle positions.[a]

[4] Just then, by divine guidance, a seer named Amphilytos the Acarnanian[a] was standing near Peisistratos and, coming closer, recited an oracle to him in verse:

> The net has been cast forth, and the snare is spread open;
> The tuna will swarm through the moonlit night.

Clearly the man who gave this oracle was divinely inspired, and Peisistratos grasped its meaning. He said he welcomed this prophecy, and went to lead his army on. The Athenians from the city had just finished their midday meal and were at their leisure, some playing dice, others sleeping. Peisistratos' men attacked and routed them. [2] While they were in flight, Peisistratos devised a clever plan to scatter the Athenians and prevent them from rallying again. He sent his sons on horseback toward the enemy, and when they caught up with those fleeing, they announced Peisistratos' instructions: that they should have no fear and that each of them should return to his own home.

The Athenians obeyed, and thus Peisistratos took Athens[a] for the third time and established the tyranny firmly now by employing numerous mercenaries and drawing increased revenues from both Attica itself and from the region of the River Strymon.[b] The children of some Athenians who had not fled at once but remained behind he took as hostages and placed them on Naxos. [2] For Peisistratos had also conquered this island

1.61.3a Thebes, Boeotia: Map 1.59, inset.
1.61.4a Peloponnese: Map 1.59, BX.
1.61.4b Argos: Map 1.59, inset.
1.61.4c Naxos (Aegean island): Map 1.59, BY.
1.62.1a Attica: Map 1.59, inset.
1.62.1b Marathon: Map 1.59, inset.
1.62.1c Demes: see n. 1.60.4a.

1.62.3a Pallene, Attica: Map 1.59, inset. The presumed location of the sanctuary of Pallenian Athena.
1.62.4a Acarnania: Map 1.59, BX.
1.64.1a Athens: Map 1.59, BX, and inset.
1.64.1b Strymon River in Thrace: Map 1.59, AX.

and had entrusted it to Lygdamis. In addition to all this, he purified the island of Delos[a] in accordance with some prophecies, digging up all the graves that lay within sight of the sanctuary and burying the remains in another more distant area of Delos. [3] And so Peisistratos ruled as tyrant of the Athenians, although some Athenians had fallen in battle against him, and others fled into exile from their own country with the Alkmeonids.

And so Croesus learned that the Athenians were being oppressed in this way at the time. But the Spartans,[a] he heard, had just emerged from great difficulties and were now waging war victoriously against the Tegeans.[b] Under their kings Leon and Hegesikles,[c] the Lacedaemonians[d] kept failing in their attempts against Tegea, although they had been victorious in all their other wars. [2] In a still earlier period, the Spartans experienced the worst government of nearly all the Hellenes, in both their domestic and their foreign affairs, as they lived in an enforced isolation from others. Their conversion from bad to good government occurred in the following way. Lykourgos, one of Sparta's most worthy men, went one day to the oracle at Delphi,[a] and as he entered the inner shrine there, the Pythia[b] spontaneously proclaimed: [3]

> You have come, Lykourgos, to my rich temple,
> You are dear to Zeus and to all on Olympus;
> Do I speak to a god or a man? I know not,
> Yet, I rather think to a god, Lykourgos.

[4] Some say that in addition to this, the Pythia dictated to him the laws that established the present Spartan way of life. The Lacedaemonians say, however, that Lykourgos, who became regent of his nephew King Leobates while the latter was a child, brought these new institutions from Crete[a] and implemented them in place of the old [5] as soon as he became regent. Having changed all the institutions, he was careful to see that the new rules and precepts would not be violated. Later, he established Sparta's military institutions: the platoons of citizens bound together by oath, the companies of thirty, and the system of communal messes.[a] And in addition, he set up the Board of Ephors and the Council of Elders.[b]

With these changes, they attained good government, and after Lykourgos died, they built a shrine in his honor and worshiped him with great reverence. And as their land was fertile and their population large, they soon thrived and became a flourishing people. Indeed, they were no longer

1.65
SPARTA
Sanctified by the Delphic oracle, Lykourgos reforms and stabilizes the Spartan government.

1.66
?
SPARTA-TEGEA
The Spartans are defeated at Tegea and bound with their own fetters.

1.64.2a Delos (Aegean island): Map 1.67.
1.65.1a Sparta: Map 1.67.
1.65.1b Tegea: Map 1.67.
1.65.1c Leon reigned at Sparta from 590 to 560, Hegesikles from 575 to 550.
1.65.1d Lacedaemonians: Herodotus uses the names Spartans and Lacedaemonians interchangeably. "Spartans," however, often refers specifically to citizens of the state of Sparta, whereas any inhabitant of the territory of Lacedaemon is a Lacedaemonian. See Appendix B, The Spartan State in War

and Peace, §5, 7, and n. B.7a.
1.65.2a Delphi: Map 1.67.
1.65.2b Pythia, the priestess at Delphi who pronounced the oracles while in a trance. See Appendix P, §9, 12.
1.65.4a Crete (Creta): Map 1.67.
1.65.5a The Spartan terms for these military institutions were Enomotiae, Triacades, and Syssitia. See Appendix N, Hoplite Warfare in Herodotus, §4.
1.65.5b The Spartan terms for these magistrates were ephors and gerousi. See Appendix B, §12–13.

content with peace, and because they assumed that they could prove themselves superior to the Arcadians,[a] they consulted the oracle at Delphi about all the land in Arcadia. [2] The Pythia replied:

> For Arcadia you ask me, you ask for much; I refuse to give it.
> Eaters of acorns, and many of them, dwell in Arcadia,
> And they will stop you. But not all will I grudge you;
> Tegea I will give you, a dance floor to tread,
> A beautiful plain to measure out with a line.

[3] When these verses were reported to the Lacedaemonians, their reaction was to forgo the rest of Arcadia and march on Tegea. Overlooking the ambiguity of the oracle, they brought shackles along with them, confident that they would enslave the Tegeans. [4] In the battle that took place, however, the Spartans were defeated, and all of them who were taken alive were made to work the plain of Tegea, measuring it out with a line and wearing the very shackles they had brought along with them. Those shackles are still, even in my day, hanging safe in Tegea, around the temple of Athena Alea.[a]

In all these earlier struggles against the Tegeans the Spartans were always defeated. But in Croesus' time, during the kingships of Anaxandridas and Ariston,[a] the Spartans kept winning all their wars. [2] You see, their defeat at the hands of the Tegeans led them to send sacred delegates to Delphi to inquire as to which god they should propitiate in order to defeat the Tegeans in war. And the Pythia's response instructed them to bring the bones of Orestes, the son of Agamemnon, back to Sparta. [3] But since they were unable to discover where Orestes' tomb was located, they sent another embassy to the god at Delphi to ask where Orestes was buried. When this embassy had made its inquiry, the Pythia replied: [4]

> There is a place called Tegea; it lies in Arcadia's plain,
> Where two winds blast by powerful force
> And stroke meets counterstroke, woe lies upon woe,
> The son of Agamemnon in this fertile earth lies.
> Tegea's guardian you will be when you have brought him home.

[5] When the Spartans heard this, they kept searching everywhere but came no closer to finding the hero's grave, until Lichas, one of the Spartans they call Agathoergi[a]—distinguished servicemen—found it. The "distinguished servicemen" are the five veterans of the Knights[b] who are discharged

1.67
SPARTA-DELPHI
The Spartans, defeated repeatedly by the Tegeans, apply to Delphi to find out how they might prevail. The oracle's reply is characteristically cryptic and puzzling.

Handwritten margin note: (SPARTA) AMBIGUITY OF ORACLE

1.66.1a Arcadia: Map 1.67.
1.66.4a Athena may have been the patron goddess of Athens, but she was worshiped by Greeks in all parts of the Hellenic world. The shackles mentioned by Herodotus were perhaps the same shackles that were seen hanging in Tegea's Temple of Athena Alea some 600 years later by Pausanias, a travel writer of the second century A.D. (*Description of Greece*, viii, 47.2).

1.67.1a Anaxandridas (II) is thought to have ruled from 560 to 520, Ariston from 550 to 515.
1.67.5a Agathoergi: This is the only passage in Greek literature where Agathoergi are mentioned.
1.67.5b Knights: thought to have been a royal bodyguard, who despite their name definitely fought as infantry and, at least in Herodotus' day and later, no longer rode horses.

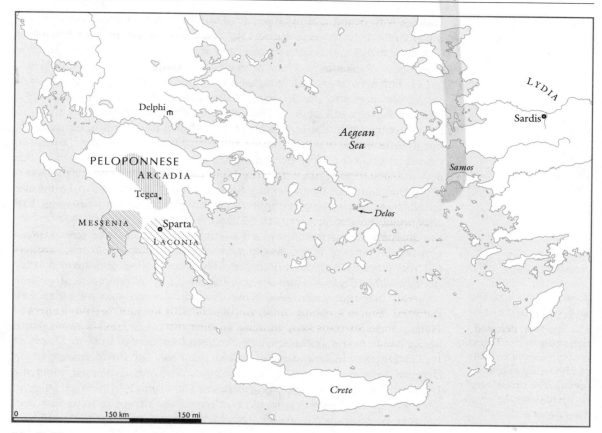

MAP 1.67

every year by reason of being the eldest, and who are sent out continually by the state on various assignments during that year.

When Lichas served on one of these assignments in Tegea, he made his discovery by both good luck and good sense. At that time, the Spartans were at peace with the Tegeans, and Lichas could visit a forge to observe iron being worked there. He watched the process in amazement. [2] The smith, noticing his reaction, paused from his work and said, "My Spartan guest, if you think iron-working is so amazing, I'm sure you would be extremely amazed if you had seen what I have seen. [3] I wanted to dig a well in the courtyard here, and as I was digging, I chanced upon a coffin more than ten feet long. I could not believe that people were once so much bigger than they are now, but when I opened the coffin I saw there a corpse the same size. After measuring it, I covered it up with earth again."

Thus the smith told what he had seen and Lichas, putting two and two together, concluded that all that he had heard conformed to the oracular

1.68
SPARTA-TEGEA
The Spartan Lichas finds the tomb of Orestes at Tegea, solves the oracle's riddle, and brings the bones back to Sparta.

response—here must be the grave of Orestes. [4] He realized that the smith's two bellows were the oracle's two winds, the anvil and hammer were the stroke and counterstroke, and the working of iron was the woe lying upon woe, since iron had been invented to the detriment of mankind. [5] Having arrived at these conclusions, he returned to Sparta[a] and related the whole matter to the Spartans. They then concerted a plan whereby a fabricated charge was asserted against Lichas, for which he was banished. So he returned to Tegea[b] and, reporting his bad luck to the smith, tried to rent out the courtyard, which, however, the smith would not permit. [6] But in time, Lichas succeeded in persuading the smith and made the courtyard his new residence. Then he dug up the bones and carried them back to Sparta. From that time on, whenever the Spartans and Tegeans met in battle, the Lacedaemonians were victorious. And by that time, the Spartans had conquered the greater part of the Peloponnese.[a]

1.69
548–547
LYDIA-SPARTA
Croesus requests an alliance with Sparta, and the Spartans agree to it.

These are the very things that Croesus learned, and so he sent messengers bearing gifts to Sparta in order to request a military alliance, instructing them on what they should say. When the messengers arrived, they declared, [2] "Croesus king of the Lydians and other peoples sent us here with this message: 'Lacedaemonians, the god's oracle told me to acquire the Hellene as friend and supporter. You, I have learned, are the leaders of Hellas, and so I invite you to comply with the oracle; and I am eager to become your friend and military ally without treachery or guile.'
[3] This was the message of Croesus, and the Lacedaemonians, having already heard of the oracle's response to Croesus, were pleased when the Lydians arrived and happily took oaths of friendship and military alliance. They in fact had become indebted to Croesus for a favor at an earlier date. [4] For the Lacedaemonians had once sent a mission to Sardis in order to purchase gold for a statue they wanted to have made. This statue, of Apollo, now stands in Laconian territory at Thornax.[a] And although they had intended to buy the gold, Croesus gave it to them instead, as a gift.

1.70
548–47
SPARTA-SAMOS
The Spartans make a huge bronze bowl and send it to Croesus, but it is diverted to Samos.

For this reason, and also because he had chosen them as friends in preference to all other Hellenes, the Spartans welcomed the alliance with Croesus; and not only were they ready to respond to his call, they even decided to repay him with a gift; so they made a bronze mixing bowl holding 300 amphoras,[a] covered with figures on the outside around the rim. [2] This bowl, however, never reached Sardis,[a] but there are two different accounts as to why it never arrived there. The Spartans say that the bowl was on its way to Sardis, but that when it reached a point just off the coast of the island of Samos,[b] the Samians, who knew about the bowl, attacked in their

1.68.5a   Sparta: Map 1.67.
1.68.5b   Tegea: Map 1.67.
1.68.6a   Peloponnese: Map 1.67. This statement by Herodotus is not true. Sparta had an alliance with many states of the Peloponnese that gave her hegemony there, perhaps, but she never conquered more than neighboring Messenia (Map 1.67).

1.69.4a   Thornax: precise location unknown. For Laconia, which was Spartan territory, see Map 1.67.
1.70.1a   The vessel held more than 3,120 gallons (1 amphora = about 10.4 gallons). See Appendix J, §18, 22.
1.70.2a   Sardis: Map 1.67.
1.70.2b   Samos: Map 1.67.

warships and stole it.[c] [3] The Samians, however, say that the Spartans who were bringing the bowl to Croesus did not get to Sardis on time, and when they found out that Sardis and Croesus had been captured,[a] they sold the bowl on Samos, where private citizens bought it and dedicated it in the sanctuary of Hera. And it may well be that when they returned to Sparta, the men who sold the bowl claimed that it had been stolen by the Samians. That is the story, then, concerning the bowl.

Meanwhile Croesus, who had misunderstood the oracle, was preparing an expedition to Cappadocia,[a] assuming that he would depose Cyrus and defeat the Persians. [2] While he was preparing for war against Persia, a Lydian named Sandanis, who was considered a sage even before this, achieved greater fame among the Lydians for the advice he now gave to Croesus. "Sire," he said, "you are preparing for war against the sort of men who wear leather trousers and leather for all their other garments as well. They eat not as much as they want, but as much as they have, since their land is rugged. [3] Moreover, they have no wine but drink water instead. They have no figs for dessert, nor anything else good to eat. Now if you should conquer them, what will you take from these people who have nothing at all? And then again, if they were to conquer you, think of how much you will lose: as soon as they taste our good life, they will never give it up and you will never get rid of them. [4] I for my part give thanks to the gods for not putting it into the minds of the Persians to make war on the Lydians." These words did not persuade Croesus, although it was true indeed that at that time the Persians really did lack luxuries and good things.

The Cappadocians are called Syrians by the Hellenes, and these Syrians, before the Persians became their rulers under Cyrus, were subject to the Medes.[a] [2] The empire of the Medes at that time was divided from that of the Lydians by the River Halys,[a] which rises from a mountain in Armenia,[b] flows through Cilicia,[c] and passes between the Matienians[d] on its right bank and the Phrygians[e] on its left. It then turns toward the north, to form the boundary separating the Syrian Cappadocians on its right from the Paphlagonians[f] on its left. [3] Thus the River Halys divides nearly all of Asia[a] between those regions

1.71
547?
LYDIA-CAPPADOCIA
Croesus invades Cappadocia, despite the advice of Sandanis to forgo it because the Cappadocians are poor.

1.72
HALYS RIVER
The Halys River is the boundary between the Median and Lydian empires.

1.70.2c   Piracy seems to have been a Samian specialty. The family of Aiakes, the father of Polykrates, made a very profitable living off it and so gained the tyranny of the city. At 3.47 Herodotus alludes to two celebrated captures by the Samians during the rule of Polykrates, whose younger brother, Syloson (3.39), had a suggestive name, Sulan (Greek), meaning "to plunder." The large number of archers in Polykrates' military forces is also suggestive, 1,000 for 100 pentekonters (3.39) being much greater than normal; perhaps they were used in piratical attacks. Piracy was widespread in early Hellas, as in *Thucydides* 1.4 and 1.5.

1.70.3a   Croesus and his capital were both captured by the Persians in 546 (1.81–85).

1.71.1a   Cappadocia: Map 1.75, AY.

1.72.1a   Media: Map 1.75, locator.

1.72.2a   Halys River: Map 1.75, AY. Herodotus' description of where this river flows has some correct elements. It does originate in mountains near Armenia, and does flow west and turn north, but it is very difficult to see how it can be said to flow both through Cilicia (which lies far to the south) and between Phrygia and Matiane, which are not at all contiguous.

1.72.2b   Armenia: Map 1.75, locator.

1.72.2c   Cilicia: Map 1.75, BY.

1.72.2d   Matienians (Matiane): Map 1.75, locator.

1.72.2e   Phrygia: Map 1.75, BY.

1.72.2f   Paphlagonia: Map 1.75, AY.

1.72.3a   Asia: Map 1.75, locator. When Herodotus and other ancient Hellenes spoke of Asia, they meant the land we call Asia Minor, now occupied by the state of Turkey.

in the south, facing the sea toward Cyprus,ᵇ and those northern regions facing the Euxine Sea.ᶜ It is here that the neck of the whole continent lies; it can be crossed by a man traveling without heavy baggage in five days.ᵈ

1.73
CAPPADOCIA
Reasons for Croesus' expedition against Cappadocia.

There were several reasons why Croesus wanted to wage war against Cappadocia. Of course he coveted more land and wanted to increase his own domain, and he was entirely confident that the oracle had predicted victory for him; but he also wished to punish Cyrus on behalf of Astyages, his brother-in-law. [2] Astyages son of Cyaxares had been king of the Medes until he was conquered by Cyrus son of Cambyses.

This is how Astyages came to be Croesus' brother-in-law. [3] A band of Scythian nomadsᵃ once emigrated into Median territory because of a feud. At this time, the ruler of the Medes was Cyaxares son of Phraortes son of Deiokes. He treated the Scythians well at first, since they had come to him as suppliants; indeed, his esteem for them grew so high that he entrusted some boys to them so that they would learn the Scythian language and the art of archery. [4] As time passed, the Scythians would often go hunting and bring some game back with them, but one time they happened to get nothing and returned empty-handed. Cyaxares, who had, as he now showed, the most violent of tempers, treated them very roughly this time, and even abused them physically. [5] After suffering this treatment from Cyaxares, the enraged Scythians, who felt they did not deserve such abuse, plotted to take one of their pupils, chop him to pieces, and prepare his flesh just as they would normally have prepared the game they caught in the hunt. They planned to bring the dish to Cyaxares and serve it up to him with the pretense that it was game from a hunt. Then, as soon as they had served it, they intended to flee with all speed to Sardis, to the court of Alyattes son of Sadyattes. [6] And this is just what happened. Cyaxares and the guests dining with him ate the meat, and the Scythians fled and became suppliants of Alyattes.

1.74
585
CAPPADOCIA?
A battle (and a war) between Lydians and Medes is halted by an eclipse of the sun.

Then, because Alyattes refused to surrender the Scythians to Cyaxares when he demanded their return, the Lydians and the Medes waged war against each other for five years. During this time, both the Medes and the Lydians won victories over each other, and they even engaged in a night battle of sorts.

[2] This happened in the sixth year of the war, as they continued to struggle with about equal success, when a battle broke out during which the day suddenly turned into night. The Ionians received a prediction of this eclipse from Thales of Miletus, who had determined that this was the year in which an eclipse would occur.ᵃ [3] The Lydians and the Medes,

---

1.72.3b Cyprus: Map 1.75, BY.
1.72.3c Euxine (Black) Sea: Map 1.75, AY.
1.72.3d Herodotus greatly underestimates this distance, which is close to 300 miles.
1.73.3a Scythia: Map 1.75, locator.
1.74.2a The date of this eclipse was May 28, 585. Miletus: Map 1.75, BX. Thales of Miletus (c. 600–546) was said by Herodotus to be of Phoenician descent (1.170.3). He was one of the legendary seven wise men of Hellas. In addition to his knowledge of

astronomy, he was a skilled engineer (1.75) and a political advisor (1.170). He was said to have founded systematic geometry from Egyptian techniques of land measurement. Four more of the seven wise men appear in Herodotus' text: Periandros of Corinth (1.20.1, 1.23.1, 3.48.2–53), Pittakos of Mytilene (1.27.2), Solon of Athens (1.29–33, 3.48.2–53.7), and Bias of Priene (1.27.2, 1.170.1).

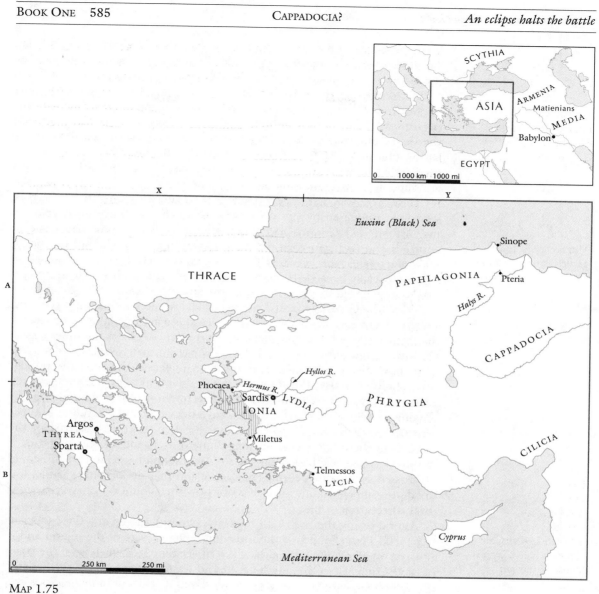

MAP 1.75

MOTIVE FOR CROESUS' DESIRE FOR WAR (handwritten margin note)

however, were astonished when they saw the onset of night during the day. They stopped fighting, and both sides became eager to have peace. The mediators in the ensuing reconciliation were Syennesis the Cilician[a] and Labynetos the Babylonian.[b] [4] These men vigorously pressured both sides to swear oaths and exchange marriage ties—namely, they decided that Alyattes would give his daughter Aryenis to Astyages son of Cyaxares—for they knew that treaties do not tend to remain in effect without the force of strong obligations. [5] These peoples make oaths just as the Hellenes do, except that in addition, they make small incisions on the surface of their arms and lick each other's blood.

1.75
547?
HALYS RIVER
The Hellenes believe that Thales assisted Croesus to cross the Halys River.

This, then, was that same Astyages,[a] the maternal grandfather of Cyrus, who was conquered by Cyrus for reasons which I shall explain later on in my history.[b] [2] Croesus had taken offense at what Cyrus had done to Astyages and had sent for oracles to advise him as to whether he should make war against the Persians. The ambiguous oracle[a] he received gave him hope, especially because he assumed that it referred to his own advantage, and so now he led his army into the domain of the Persians.

[3] When Croesus reached the River Halys,[a] he had his army cross the bridges that were already there; that, at least, is what I maintain, but according to the common account given by the Hellenes, Thales the Milesian was the one who got the army across. [4] They claim that Croesus was at a loss as to how his army would cross the river (since at the time the present bridges did not exist). Thales was there in the camp, they say, and he made the river then flowing to the left of the army flow also to its right [5] by digging a deep canal, starting from above the camp and extending it into a crescent that curved behind the camp; he then diverted this part of the canal from the original channel and shunted it around the camp and back into the existing riverbed. Thus the river was soon divided in two and could be crossed on either side. [6] They also claim that the original channel was dried up completely, but I disagree; for how then could they have crossed it on their return journey?

1.76
546?
PTERIA-CAPPADOCIA
An indecisive battle between Cyrus' Persians and Croesus' Lydians.

After crossing the river with his army, Croesus arrived at a Cappadocian[a] city called Pteria.[b] Pteria is the most impregnable part of the region and is situated on a line directly south of the city of Sinope,[c] which is on the coast of the Euxine Sea.[d] Camping here, he laid waste to the fields of the Syrians, [2] took the city of the Pterians and enslaved its citizens, and also took the surrounding towns, driving their Syrian inhabitants from their homes, although they had done nothing to offend him. Cyrus prepared to oppose Croesus by gathering together his own army and increasing its numbers by

1.74.3a Cilicia: Map 1.75, BY.
1.74.3b Babylon: Map 1.75, locator. This Baby-
          lonian king, whom Herodotus calls
          Labynetos, was in fact Nebuchadnezzar,
          who ruled Babylon from 604 to 562.
1.75.1a For more on Astyages, see 1.107–128.
1.75.1b Herodotus describes Cyrus' victory over
          Astyages in 1.123–129.

1.75.2a See the oracles described in 1.53.3 and
          1.55.2.
1.75.3a Halys River: Map 1.75, AY.
1.76.1a Cappadocia: Map 1.75, AY.
1.76.1b Pteria: Map 1.75, AY.
1.76.1c Sinope: Map 1.75, AY.
1.76.1d Euxine (Black) Sea: Map 1.75, AY.

enlisting all who dwelled along his march. [3] Before his army began to march, he had sent heralds to the Ionians[a] in an attempt to induce them to rebel against Croesus. Although the Ionians did not rebel, Cyrus arrived and prepared to fight with what troops he had; and so pitching his camp opposite that of Croesus in the territory of Pteria, they tried each other by force of arms. [4] The battle that took place there was fierce, with many falling on both sides. It finally ended when night fell, with neither side gaining the victory.

Croesus attributed his lack of success to the size of his army that had fought that day (for it was much smaller than the army of Cyrus), and so when Cyrus made no move to attack the next day, Croesus led his army back to Sardis[b] with the intention of summoning the Egyptians to carry out the terms of their oath. [2] (He had made this oath and a military alliance with Amasis king of Egypt even before he sought the Spartan[a] alliance.) He also planned to send for the Babylonians, with whom he had also concluded a military alliance when Labynetos was absolute ruler[b] of Babylon. [3] And he would send instructions to the Spartans to join him at an appointed time. He planned to spend the winter in Sardis and then, when spring arrived and these allied troops had joined with his own, he would again wage war against the Persians. [4] And so with this in mind, when he arrived at Sardis he sent heralds to his allies, ordering them to assemble at Sardis in four months. As for the mercenary army that had just fought the Persians, he dismissed and disbanded the entire force, never expecting that Cyrus, who had been no more successful than himself in the battle, would march against Sardis.

As Croesus was attending to all this, the area before the city gate suddenly swarmed with snakes, and at their appearance, the horses ceased grazing in the pastures and converged instead on this place and began to eat the snakes. When Croesus saw this, he considered it a portent, as in fact it was. [2] At once he sent sacred delegates to the Board of Telmessian Seers[a] who, when they arrived, learned from the Telmessians the portent's significance, but they did not succeed in delivering the message to Croesus. For before they sailed back to Sardis, Croesus was captured. [3] In any case, the Telmessians' interpretation was that a foreign army should be expected to arrive in Croesus' country and to conquer the native inhabitants, since the snake is an offspring of the earth and the horse is a warlike immigrant from a foreign land. Croesus had already been captured when the Telmessians gave this answer; but as yet they knew nothing of what was going on at Sardis or of what was happening to Croesus.

1.77
547/46
SARDIS
Croesus retreats to Sardis, summoning his Egyptian, Spartan, and other allies to join him in the spring.

1.78
547/46
LYDIA
A swarm of snakes in Lydia, and an explanation of it that arrives too late.

1.76.3a   Ionia: Map 1.75, BX.
1.77.1a   Sardis: Map 1.75, BX.
1.77.1b   Egypt: Map 1.75, locator.
1.77.2a   Sparta: Map 1.75, BX.
1.77.2b   Herodotus uses the Greek word *tyrannos*. The king Herodotus calls Labynetos here is probably Nabonidas, the last king of Babylon, who ruled from 556 to 538,

until Babylon was taken by Cyrus. See 1.188 and 1.191.
1.78.2a   Priests of Apollo at Telmessos in Lycia: Map 1.75, BY.

1.79
547/46
SARDIS
Cyrus' army follows
Croesus' forces to Sardis.

Even while Croesus was leading his army away after the battle in Pteria,[a] Cyrus recognized that Croesus intended to disband his army at the end of the march. After some deliberation, he realized that it would be advantageous for him to march against Sardis as quickly as he could, before the Lydian forces could assemble a second time. [2] Having made this decision, he led his army into Lydia[a] and marched so swiftly that he himself was the herald of his own arrival.

Croesus thus suddenly found himself in great difficulty, as events had turned out quite to the contrary of what he had expected. Nevertheless, he led the Lydian army out to battle, [3] for at that time, of all the peoples of Asia,[a] none had more bravery and strength in battle than the Lydians.[b] They fought on horseback, wielding long spears, and were excellent riders.

1.80
546
SARDIS
Cyrus' camels defeat the
Lydian cavalry and force
the Lydians to take
refuge behind the walls
of Sardis.

The two armies met on the vast plain in front of the city of Sardis. This plain is bare of vegetation, although several rivers, including the Hyllos,[a] flow through it. They join together into the largest river, called the Hermus,[b] which springs forth from the mountain sacred to the mother goddess Dindymene[c] and empties into the sea at Phocaea.[d] [2] When Cyrus saw the Lydians lining up for battle, he grew apprehensive at the number of their cavalry and, acting on the advice of a Mede named Harpagos, he brought together all the camels that had accompanied his army carrying food and equipment. He removed their baggage and mounted men on them dressed as horsemen and, after equipping them in this way, he ordered them to advance in front of the rest of his army toward the cavalry of Croesus. Then he commanded the infantry to follow after the camels, and he placed his entire cavalry behind the infantry. [3] When they had all reached their appointed positions, Cyrus exhorted them to kill every man who crossed their path, sparing none of the Lydians except for Croesus himself; him they should not kill, even if he tried to fight back while being captured. [4] Those were his orders. The reason he arranged for the camels to face the cavalry was that he knew that horses fear camels and can endure neither the sight nor the scent of them, so that the Lydian cavalry, upon which Croesus most relied, would thereby be rendered useless to him.

[5] And when they met in battle, as soon as the horses smelled and saw the camels, they wheeled around and fled, and Croesus' hopes were shattered. [6] The Lydians, however, did not react to this like cowards. When they perceived what was happening, they leapt off their horses and engaged the Persians on foot. Finally, after many had fallen on both sides, the Lydians were put to flight; although they reached safety behind the walls of Sardis, they were trapped there when the Persians laid siege to the city.

1.79.1a   Pteria: Map 1.75, AY.
1.79.2a   Lydia: Map 1.75, BX.
1.79.3a   Asia: Map 1.75, locator.
1.79.3b   The Hellenes believed that after the Lydians lost their freedom they became cowardly, effeminate, and devoted to pleasure and luxury. See 1.155–156.
1.80.1a   Hyllos River: Map 1.75, AY.

1.80.1b   Hermus River: Map 1.75, BX.
1.80.1c   Identified with the Phrygian and Lydian goddess Cybele. (Godley) Phrygia: Map 1.75, BY.
1.80.1d   Phocaea: Map 1.75, BX.

As the Persians settled down to their siege, Croesus, expecting that it would last a long time, sent out from the wall another group of messengers to his allies. While some had been sent earlier to order the allies to gather in Sardis in four months, he sent these to ask for help immediately, on the grounds that he was being besieged.

These requests were sent to all of his allies, but in particular, to Sparta.[a] But the Spartans, at that moment, were occupied with a conflict which had broken out with the Argives,[b] concerning a place called Thyrea.[c] [2] Thyrea had been the property of the Argolid, but the Spartans had seized it for themselves. At this time the land as far as Malis[a] in the west belonged to the Argives, both the mainland and the islands, including Cythera[b] and the rest. [3] The Argives came to defend their land as it was being seized, but before any battle took place there, they met with the Spartans and made an agreement that 300 men from each side would fight it out, and the side that prevailed would hold the land. All the other soldiers of each army were to return to their homes so that they would not be present at the contest and would not be able to come to the aid of their own men if they saw them losing. [4] After agreeing to these terms, they departed, and the picked men remaining from each side joined battle.

As the fighting went on, the two sides were so equally matched that, finally, as night fell, only three of the original 600 men were left, Alkenor and Chromius from the Argives and Othryades from the Spartans. [5] The two Argives ran back to Argos in the belief that they had won, but the Spartan, Othryades, stripped the Argive corpses and carried their armor to his own camp, where he kept to his assigned post. On the next day, both sides arrived to learn the outcome. [6] For a time, both claimed to have won; the Argives said that more of their men had survived, and the Spartans pointed out that these men had fled, while their own man had remained and stripped the corpses of the Argive dead.[a] [7] Finally, the dispute between them developed into a brawl and before long a full-fledged battle was under way. Although many fell on both sides in this fighting, the Spartans were ultimately victorious. From that time on, the Argives have always cut their hair short. Before this, their fixed custom had been to wear their hair long, but now they made a regulation and even pronounced a curse: that no Argive man could grow his hair long, and no Argive woman could wear gold, until Argos had won back Thyrea. [8] The Spartans established a contrary regulation: they had not previously worn their hair long, but from that time on they did so.[a] And they say that the one man left of the 300, Othryades, was

1.81
546
SARDIS
Croesus asks his allies for immediate help.

1.82
546
SPARTA-ARGOS
"The Battle of the Champions." Some 300 Spartans and 300 Argives battle over Thyrea.

1.82.1a   Sparta: Map 1.75, BX.
1.82.1b   Argos: Map 1.75, BX.
1.82.1c   Thyrea: Map 1.75, BX. Herodotus calls it Thyreatis.
1.82.2a   Malis, in the Peloponnese: site unknown. Apparently not connected with the peninsula which ends in Cape Malea: Map 1.92, BX.
1.82.2b   Cythera: Map 1.92.

1.82.6a   In hoplite warfare, the victor held the field and stripped the dead of their armor, while the defeated asked for, and were granted, a truce in which to recover the corpses of their dead. See Appendix N, §11.
1.82.8a   The Spartans wore their hair long to display their confidence, prowess, and military superiority.

ashamed to return to Sparta because his comrades had died; he killed himself there in Thyrea.

The Spartans were still occupied with this matter when the herald from Sardis arrived to ask them to assist Croesus, who was being besieged. Despite their conflict with the Argives, when they heard the news from the herald, they decided to go to his aid. Their preparations were complete, and their ships ready to sail, when another message arrived that the wall of the Lydians had been taken and Croesus was being held captive. So considering it a great disaster, they stopped the expedition.

This is how the Persians captured Croesus and Sardis.[a] When the fourteenth day of the siege arrived, Cyrus sent around his horsemen and proclaimed to his army that he would give a reward to the first man to scale the wall. [2] After this, the army tried to scale the walls but failed. Then, when all the rest had given up, a Mardian[a] named Hyroeades attempted to climb up at the part of the acropolis[b] where no guard had been posted, since it was so steep and apparently impenetrable there that no one had ever feared that the acropolis could be taken from there. [3] It was only at this part of the wall that Meles, an earlier king of Sardis, did not pass when he was carrying the lion borne to him by his concubine; he was following the judgment of the Telmessians,[a] who had determined that Sardis would be impregnable if a lion was carried around its wall. Meles carried the lion around the rest of the wall, but ignored this part because it was so steep it was thought to be impenetrable. It is on the side of the city that faces Mount Tmolus.[b] [4] It so happened that the day before, Hyroeades the Mardian had seen one of the Lydians climb down at this part of the acropolis and recover a helmet that had tumbled from above. Hyroeades watched him carefully and committed to memory what he saw. Then, the next day, he ascended the height at the same place with other Persians following behind. In this way, when many had made the climb, the acropolis of Sardis was taken and the whole city fell and was sacked.

What happened to Croesus himself was this. As I mentioned earlier,[a] he had a son who, although healthy in all other respects, was unable to speak. In the past, during peace and prosperity, Croesus had done everything for this boy and, among other things, sent a mission to Delphi[b] asking the oracle about him. [2] This is what the Pythia[a] said:

> Lydian of race, king of many, Croesus, you fool,
> Desire not to hear at home that prayed-for sound,
> Of your son's voice. Much better for you to be far from that:
> The day on which you hear it first will rob you of prosperity.

1.83
546?
SPARTA
The Spartans plan to assist Croesus but learn of his fall before help can be sent.

1.84
547/46
SARDIS
How the Persians captured Sardis.

1.85
SARDIS
The story of Croesus' mute son.

1.84.1a Sardis: Map 1.92.
1.84.2a The Mardi were a Persian tribe.
1.84.2b Acropolis of Sardis, a steep, fortified hill above the town; see n. 1.15.1f and Glossary.
1.84.3a Telmessians: priests of Apollo at Telmessos in Lycia: Map 1.75, BY.

1.84.3b Mount Tmolus: Map 1.92.
1.85.1a See 1.34.2.
1.85.1b Delphi: Map 1.92.
1.85.2a Pythia, the priestess at Delphi who pronounced the oracles while in a trance. See Appendix P, §9, 12.

[3] And indeed it turned out that when the wall was being taken, one of the Persians. who did not recognize Croesus, approached the king and was going to kill him; Croesus saw him coming but did nothing; in his misery he did not care that he would die by a stroke of violence. [4] But when his mute son saw the Persian approaching, he shouted out in fear and horror, "You there! Do not kill Croesus!" These were the first words he ever spoke, and after this, he could speak for the rest of his life.

When the Persians took Sardis and captured Croesus, he had ruled fourteen years and had been under siege fourteen days. And as the oracle predicted, he put an end to a great empire—his own. The Persians seized him and led him to Cyrus, [2] and to a huge pyre that the King had had them build, and they mounted Croesus bound in shackles on top of it, and with him, fourteen Lydian boys. Cyrus did this either to consecrate them as a sacrifice of victory offerings to some god, or to fulfill a vow, or perhaps, having found out that Croesus was god-fearing, he wanted to see if some divinity would save him from being burned alive. [3] As Croesus stood there on the pyre, despite the horror of his predicament, he thought of Solon and how divinely inspired he had been when he stated his maxim that no living human can be called truly happy and prosperous. Until then he had remained quiet, but when this occurred to him, he sighed deeply and groaned and repeated aloud "Solon," three times. [4] Cyrus heard this and ordered his interpreters to ask Croesus who was this man he had called by name. Croesus kept silent at first, but when they pressed him to answer, he said, "A man to whom I would pay a fortune if only he could talk to all tyrants."[a] Since his words were obscure to them, they questioned him again, asking what he meant, [5] and they continued to pester him until he told them what had happened when Solon the Athenian had visited him; indeed he related the whole story from beginning to end, even repeating Solon's very words, of how after the Athenian had seen all of the king's prosperity, he had still made light of it and refused to call Croesus a fortunate man. And now everything had turned out just as Solon had said, and indeed it was clear that his words applied no more to Croesus himself than to the whole human race, and especially to all those who consider themselves happy and prosperous. While Croesus related all this, the pyre had been lit and its edges were now burning. [6] Cyrus, after learning through the interpreters what Croesus had said, reflected that he, too, was human, and changed his mind about committing a living man to the fire, a fellow human being who had been blessed with happiness no less than he. Moreover, he began to fear retribution, and to contemplate the fact that nothing is really secure and certain for human beings. So he gave orders that the fire should be extinguished at once and that Croesus and the Lydian

1.86
SARDIS·
Croesus on the pyre recalls the words of Solon.

[handwritten margin notes: CROESUS ENDED HIS EMPIRE; CROESUS IS NEARLY BURNED; Cyrus has conversion]

1.86.4a Herodotus here uses the term *tyrannoi*, which meant to Hellenes persons who obtained power without traditional means or legitimate consent. To Easterners the term meant absolute rulers like the Persian King.

youths with him on the pyre be brought down. The Persians immediately tried to carry out his orders, but they were unable to get the fire under control.

1.87
SARDIS
Croesus prays to Apollo and is saved by a sudden rainstorm. He becomes an advisor to Cyrus.

Then, say the Lydians, as Croesus watched all the men attempting but failing to put out the mounting flames, he realized that Cyrus had changed his mind, and now called out to Apollo, beseeching him that if any of his gifts had ever pleased the god, to come now to his rescue and save him from the danger at hand. [2] And as he called on the god and began to weep, clouds suddenly converged out of the clear, calm sky, and a storm burst out, and rain poured down in floods, extinguishing the fire. Cyrus understood from this that Croesus must be a good man and dear to the gods. He had him brought down from the pyre and asked him, [3] "Croesus, who on earth persuaded you to wage war against me rather than to become my friend?" Croesus replied, "Sire, what I did was a blessing for you, but a curse for me. The one to blame is the god of the Hellenes; it is he who encouraged me to go to war. [4] Otherwise, no one could be so foolish as to prefer war to peace; in peace sons bury fathers; in war fathers bury sons. Surely this all happened by divine will."[a]

1.88
SARDIS
Croesus advises Cyrus that Sardis, which is now his city, is being plundered.

That is what he told Cyrus, and Cyrus ordered him to be freed and sat him at his side, treating him with great respect and both Cyrus and all those nearby stared at Croesus in wonder while he sat silently in contemplation. [2] But then, when he turned and saw the Persians ransacking the Lydians' city, he said, "Sire, should I keep quiet or tell you what I am thinking right now?" Cyrus told him to have no fear and to say whatever he wanted, so Croesus asked, "What is it that that mob of your soldiers is so busily doing?" Cyrus replied, "They are sacking your city and plundering your wealth." "No, sire, it is not my city," Croesus answered, "it is not my city, nor my wealth any longer that they are sacking, since after this nothing here belongs to me. It is, rather, your property they are plundering and looting."

1.89
SARDIS
Croesus advises Cyrus as to how to recover the plunder and preserve his army from corruption.

These words of Croesus' impressed Cyrus so much that he asked all those who were present to leave them alone. Then he asked Croesus what he thought Cyrus should do, in his own best interest, about the plundering. And Croesus answered, "Since the gods have given me to you as your slave, I think it only right that I speak out when I see where your advantage may lie. [2] Because the Persians are both poor and by nature rapacious, if you allow them to completely sack the city and seize all of its great wealth, this is what is likely to happen: whoever accumulates the most wealth will be most likely to rebel against you. So now, if you would act on my advice, [3] post some of your spearmen as sentries at each and every gate; have them take the plunder from the men carrying it off, and let them say that they must give a tenth part of it to Zeus. This way they will not hate you for taking things away from them by force, but will have to admit that you are acting justly, and they will willingly surrender what they have gathered."

1.87.4a The death of Croesus became a theme of legend. In addition to the version here recounted by Herodotus, Croesus was also thought to have been thrown or to have thrown himself on a funeral pyre, but to have been saved by Apollo and taken by the god to the land of the Hyperboreans. See Figure 1.91.

50

Cyrus was delighted with this advice; he lavishly praised Croesus for it and ordered his bodyguards to carry out this plan. Then he turned to Croesus and said, "Because you are of royal blood and are willing to help me in word and deed, now ask me for a gift, whatever you want, and you will have it at once." [2] Croesus replied, "My Lord, you could give me the greatest pleasure by allowing me to send these shackles to the god of the Hellenes, the one I honored above all other gods, and so that I might ask him if he typically deceives those who have treated him well." When Cyrus asked what complaint he had against the god that led him to make this request, [3] Croesus related the whole story—his queries, the oracular responses, and especially the dedications, and the oracle's encouragement for him to make war on the Persians. So he told the story, and at its conclusion he asked a second time for permission to reproach the god, and Cyrus laughed and said, "Of course I grant you this, Croesus, and indeed I shall grant any request you make to me in the future."

[4] So ~~Croesus~~ was able to send some Lydians to Delphi with orders to place the shackles at the temple's threshold and to ask the god if he was not at all ashamed that his oracle had encouraged Croesus to make war on the Persians with the goal of ending Cyrus' power, from which venture, however, the only victory offerings Croesus could dedicate were these shackles. And he instructed them, as they said these words, to point to the shackles and then to ask if the Hellenic gods were habitually ungrateful.

When the Lydians arrived and carried out their orders, the Pythia is said to have replied, "Fated destiny is impossible to avoid even for a god. Croesus had to atone for the wrong of his ancestor four generations ago. This ancestor was a bodyguard for his king, of the family line of the Heraklids. He was induced by a trick involving a woman to kill his master and usurp for himself a position that did not belong to him.[a] [2] Although Apollo[a] strove to delay the fall of Sardis until after Croesus was dead, he was unable to deflect the Fates. [3] Indeed, as a favor to Croesus, Apollo did gain as much as the Fates would concede: he deferred the fall of Sardis for three years. So let it be known to Croesus that his downfall and capture occurred three years later than his appointed destiny. And in addition, it was Apollo who rescued Croesus from burning on the pyre.[a]

[4] "And as to the oracles given to Croesus, his accusation is wrong. The one in which Apollo predicted that if he made war on the Persians he would destroy a great empire[a] was not considered wisely by Croesus, for if he had done so he would have realized that he should have sent again to ask whether it meant his own empire or that of Cyrus. So, since he misunderstood that oracle and failed to question the god further, let him admit that

1.90
SARDIS-DELPHI
Croesus receives permission to reproach the Delphic oracle for its misleading advice.

1.91
DELPHI
The Delphic oracle defends itself against Croesus' reproaches.

(handwritten marginalia: "FATE, RETRIBUTION, DESTINY")

1.91.1a   Apollo here refers to the killing of Kandaules by Gyges, a story told by Herodotus in 1.7–12. See Figure 1.91, a depiction of Croesus on the pyre.

1.91.2a   Herodotus uses the name Loxias here, a common epithet of Apollo, especially at Delphi. Its meaning and etymology are disputed and ultimately uncertain; the most common conjectures connect it with the quality of either ambiguity or light.

1.91.3a   See 1.87.2 for the divine rescue of Croesus.

1.91.4a   See 1.53 for the context in which this oracle was delivered.

FIGURE 1.91. A DEPICTION OF
CROESUS ON THE PYRE FROM
AN EARLY-FIFTH-CENTURY
ATTIC VASE PAINTING FOUND
IN ITALY.

here he himself is at fault. [5] Moreover, Croesus also misconstrued the
oracle from Apollo about the mule.[a] For the mule cited in the oracle is
Cyrus himself, who was born from parents of different peoples and different social stations. [6] His mother was noble, a Mede and the daughter of
Astyages king of the Medes, but his father was a Persian, subject to the rule
of the Medes and inferior to them, who, despite his rank, was able to marry
and live with the queen." This was the Pythia's answer to the Lydians,
which they brought back to Sardis and reported to Croesus. When he heard
it, he had to confess that it was he himself, and not the god, who was in the
wrong.[a]

That is the story of the empire of Croesus and the first conquest of
Ionia.[a] But, in addition to the numerous offerings by Croesus that I have
already mentioned, he dedicated many other gifts in Hellas[b] that are worthy
of note: there is a tripod of gold in Boeotian Thebes,[c] which he dedicated to
Ismenean Apollo; golden cows and many columns at Ephesus;[d] and a large

1.92
HELLAS
A list of Croesus'
offerings in Hellas.

1.91.5a   See 1.55.2 for the text of this oracle.
1.91.6a   See Appendix P, §15.
1.92.1a   Ionia: Map 1.92.
1.92.1b   By Hellas here (also at 2.182.1 and
         8.157.3), Herodotus means to include
         the Greek cities of Asia (Asia Minor):

Map 1.92, locator.
1.92.1c   Thebes, Boeotia: Map 1.92. See a depic-
         tion of a tripod in Figure 1.92.
1.92.1d   Ephesus: Map 1.92.

FIGURE 1.92. PHINTIAS'
GREEK PAINTING (C. 525?)
ON AN AMPHORA, HERAKLES
AND APOLLO STRUGGLING
FOR THE DELPHIC TRIPOD.

golden shield in the temple of Athena Pronaia at Delphi.[c] These still exist in my time, but some of his other gifts have been lost. [2] The offerings made by Croesus at Branchidai in Milesian[a] territory, I hear, are equal in weight and similar to the ones at Delphi. Those at Delphi and at Amphiareion[b] he dedicated as his own and as victory offerings from his ancestral wealth, but the rest of the gifts come from the property of a man he hated, a political opponent who, before Croesus became king, strongly supported Pantaleon as heir to the Lydian empire. [3] Pantaleon was the son of Alyattes, the brother of Croesus but by a different mother. For Croesus' mother was a wife of Alyattes from Caria,[a] while Pantaleon's mother was from Ionia. [4] When Croesus took control of the empire given to him by his father, he killed the man who had opposed him, by dragging him over a carding comb. He had earlier vowed to donate the man's property to the gods, and now he dedicated it as described here to the sanctuaries I have mentioned above, and that is all that I will say on the subject of Croesus' offerings.

1.92.1e Delphi: Map 1.92. The temple of Athena
    Pronaea refers to a sanctuary of Athena
    on the road to Delphi before one reaches
    the sanctuary of Apollo. The epithet
    Pronaea means "of the temple before" or
    "of the temple in front."

1.92.2a Miletus: Map 1.92. Branchidai (Didyma)
    was the shrine at Didyma (Map 1.92),
    south of Miletus. See n. 1.46.2f.
1.92.2b Amphiareion: Map 1.92.
1.92.3a Caria: Map 1.92.

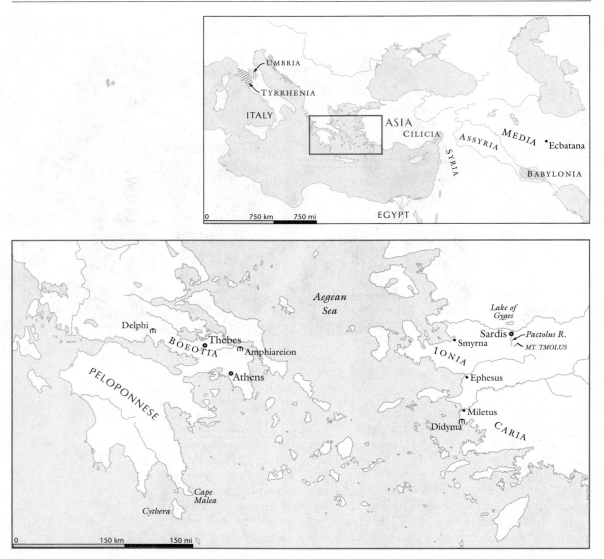

MAP 1.92

FIGURE 1.93. THE LARGE TOMB OF THE LYDIAN KING ALYATTES, LOCATED ABOUT SEVEN MILES NORTH OF THE RUINS OF THE LYDIAN CAPITAL OF SARDIS.

The Lydian land does not have as many extraordinary features to record as other places, except for the gold dust that is washed down from Mount Tmolus.[a] [2] And it has, in the tomb of Alyattes, father of Croesus, the greatest structure ever built, apart from those of the Egyptians and Babylonians.[a] The tomb's foundation is made of huge stones, on which has been piled a mound of earth.[b] It was built by the joint efforts of tradesmen, craftsmen, and prostitutes. [3] There are five stone monuments on top of the tomb that are still extant in my time, and their inscriptions record what each group contributed to the construction. A comparison of the records shows that the greatest contribution to the work was made by the prostitutes. [4] It is a fact that in Lydia, all daughters of the common people work as prostitutes; they accumulate their dowries while they work in this profession until they get married, when they give themselves away in marriage.[a] [5] The circumference of the tomb is almost 3,700 feet, and it is 1,300 feet wide.[a] A large lake is located near the tomb, which the Lydians say is always full of water, called the Lake of Gyges.[b] Such are the wonders of Lydia.

Except for the practice of prostituting their young girls, the Lydians have nearly the same customs as the Hellenes. They were the first of all people we know of to use coinage struck from gold and silver, and the first to become retailers of goods they did not themselves produce. [2] The

1.93
LYDIA
Herodotus describes the tomb of Alyattes.

1.94
LYDIA
Herodotus describes Lydian customs and achievements and how they founded Etruria.

1.93.1a   Mount Tmolus: Map 1.92. Some gold is still washed down by the Pactolus River (Map 1.92).
1.93.2a   Egypt and Babylonia: Map 1.92, locator.
1.93.2b   This burial mound is still quite intact and visible to the north of Sardis. See Figure 1.93.
1.93.4a   In the Hellenic world, fathers gave away their daughters with a dowry to husbands chosen by the family; here, women

collected their own dowries and so had freedom in choosing their husbands.
1.93.5a   Herodotus' dimensions are "6 stades" and "2 plethra" in circumference, "13 plethra" in width. The Attic stade is 583 feet long and the Attic plethron 100 feet long. See Appendix J, §6, 19.
1.93.5b   Lake of Gyges: Map 1.92. This lake is mentioned in Homer (*Iliad* II 864–886) and lies north of the tombs.

Lydians themselves say that they invented the games that are now popular among themselves as well as the Hellenes. They also say that they made these inventions during the same period in which they colonized Tyrrhenia,[a] and they give this account of how that happened.

[3] When Atys son of Manes was king, there occurred a severe famine throughout all of Lydia. For some time the Lydians tenaciously endured, but then, when they saw no end to it, they sought remedies, and different people came up with various solutions. That was when certain individuals among them invented dice, knucklebones,[a] ball games, and other sorts of games—with the exception of draughts,[b] which the Lydians do not claim to have invented. [4] With these inventions they adopted the following strategy against the famine. On one day they played games so that they did not crave food; on the next, they stopped playing and ate, and they lived this way for eighteen years.

[5] But when their troubles did not cease but became even more acute, the king decided to divide the whole Lydian population in half and draw lots to determine which half would remain and which would emigrate from the country. He appointed himself king of those whose lot it was to remain and named his son Tyrrhenos to be king of those who would have to depart. [6] Those whose lot it was to leave the country went down to the coast at Smyrna,[a] procured ships, and put on board all of their moveable goods and sailed away in search of new land in which to gain their livelihood. They sailed past the lands of many peoples until they finally reached the land of the Ombrikoi,[b] where they halted, built cities, and still dwell to this day. [7] Moreover, they changed their name from Lydians to Tyrrhenians, to commemorate the king's son who had led their expedition. The Lydians who did not emigrate, however, remained in Lydia and were enslaved by the Persians.

From here, our story demands that we inquire further about Cyrus and the Persians: who was this man who destroyed the empire of Croesus, and how did the Persians become leaders of Asia?[a] I shall write this account using as my sources certain Persians who do not intend to magnify the deeds of Cyrus but rather to tell what really happened, although I know of three other ways in which the story of Cyrus is told.

[2] The Assyrians[a] ruled inland Asia for 520 years, and the Medes[b] were the first to revolt from them. It would seem that they proved themselves to be truly courageous men by fighting the Assyrians for the cause of freedom, and they succeeded in casting off slavery and were liberated. Afterward, [the] other ethnic groups[c] freed themselves as the Medes had done.

1.95
?
MEDIA-PERSIA
The origins of Cyrus, the
Persians, and the Medes.

[handwritten margin note: QUESTION RE: CYRUS & PERSIA]

1.94.2a Tyrrhenia, possible location, if one assumes that Herodotus identifies the Tyrrhenians with the Etruscans in Italy. Tyrrhenia (Etruria): Map 1.92, locator. See n. 1.94.6b.
1.94.3a Dice have six sides, knucklebones four sides.
1.94.3b A board game comparable to backgammon.
1.94.6a Smyrna: Map 1.92.
1.94.6b Ombrikoi, possibly in Umbria: Map 1.92, locator. Herodotus refers to both the

region of modern Umbria and a wider area around it. In 4.49.2, he extends the "Ombrikoi" as far north as the Alps.
1.95.1a Asia: Map 1.92, locator.
1.95.2a Assyria: Map 1.92, locator.
1.95.2b Media: Map 1.92, locator.
1.95.2c Other ethnic groups: Cilicians, Babylonians, Syrians: Map 1.92, locator.

After those on the mainland had gained their freedom and attained self-government, they returned once again to the rule of tyrants. This happened to the Medes because of a shrewd man named Deiokes son of Phraortes. [2] He had conceived a passionate ambition to rule, and this is the story of how he went about fulfilling it.[a]

The Medes at that time dwelled in villages, and Deiokes, who had already attained a certain eminence in his own village, now earned even greater renown by his enthusiastic support of righteousness and his opposition to injustice, although he knew that injustice is a constant foe of what is right, and he did this at a time when anarchy prevailed in Media. His upright conduct was perceived by his fellow villagers, who chose him to be their judge. And Deiokes, always seeking to acquire power, performed his duties with such integrity and fairness that he received high praise from his fellow citizens. [3] When the Medes in the other villages heard of his unique reputation for honesty as a judge, they refused to submit to unjust verdicts, as they had in the past, but instead went to Deiokes, confident that they would receive a fair trial and judgment. Before long, they would not entrust themselves and their causes to anyone else.

More and more people came to him as they heard how truth prevailed in the trials that he conducted, and Deiokes, perceiving that the people had now become dependent on him for everything, was no longer willing to sit all day long, judging and giving decisions for others, as he had done before, while his own affairs were neglected and he himself received nothing at all from his labors. [2] And so, as robbery and anarchy became rife again throughout the villages, and even worse than before, the Medes met together to deliberate and make speeches about the current situation, and I presume that the friends of Deiokes spoke a great deal, arguing that [3] "since we cannot continue to live in this country under the present conditions, let us appoint a king to rule over us. That way our country will be well governed and we can return to our work without the threat of losing our homes due to anarchy." With speeches such as this they convinced one another to accept being governed by a king.

Without delay, they began to propose individuals whom they might appoint as king, but Deiokes was both proposed and highly praised by so many Medes that they finally consented to appoint him to be their king.

[2] Deiokes first ordered the Medes to build him a residence worthy of a king and to fortify it with bodyguards. They carried out these orders, constructing for him a monumental and secure palace in the very location he requested and entrusting to him a corps of bodyguards specially selected from all the Medes. [3] And now that Deiokes had secured his power, he commanded them to build a single great city for a capital, which they would maintain and take greater care of than their villages; and the

1.96
MEDIA
How Deiokes became an accepted judge by the Medes, as part of a plan to become king.

1.97
MEDIA
By refusing to give judgment, Deiokes induces the Medes to desire a king.

1.98
c. 700–647
MEDIA
Deiokes is chosen to be king. He orders the Medes to construct a fortress for him at Ecbatana. Deiokes reigns fifty-three years.*

1.96.2a   The account of Deiokes' rise to power illus-
          trates Herodotus' opinion on the disadvan-
          tages of autocratic rule. See Appendix T, §4.

1.98*   *The Cambridge Ancient History* says fifty-
        two years, from 727 to 675?

Medes obeyed him. He surrounded this city, now called Ecbatana,[a] with a series of massive concentric walls. [4] These ramparts were laid out so that each circle was elevated above the one in front by the height of the parapets. Although this arrangement was aided in part by the hill on which the site is located, it resulted more from human design and construction.[a] [5] There are, altogether, seven circular walls, and within the innermost one are located the palace and treasury. The outermost wall is about the length of the wall that surrounds Athens.[a] The parapets of the first circle are white; the second is colored black; the third, crimson; the fourth, dark blue; and the fifth, orange. [6] All these circles are painted thus in different colors, but of the innermost two, one parapet is plated with silver, the other with gold.

Deiokes had these fortifications built to surround his own dwelling only; he ordered the rest of the people to build their houses and to live outside the walls. When all of the construction was completed, Deiokes established the following ceremonial etiquette; he was the first one to do this. No one was allowed to enter into the presence of the king inside his palace. They must use messengers instead. And when the king came out, no one was to look directly at him, and anyone who laughed or spit in his presence[a] would incur disgrace. [2] His motive in creating all this formality was to create a distance between himself and his peers, because they had grown up with him and were not his inferiors in family lineage, competence, or valor. He expected that if they did not see him personally, they would in time come to accept him as different and distinguished from themselves, and thereby would not be moved by resentment to plot against him.

When he had established these points of royal etiquette, he took other steps to secure his position as tyrant, and he became a particularly severe guardian of justice. He conducted cases now by having petitioners write down their suits and send them inside to him, where he would render his judgments and send them out. [2] Deiokes also instituted other regulations. He had spies and informers scattered throughout his entire realm, and if he heard of anyone engaging in disorderly conduct, he would summon the offender and render judgment according to the severity of the crime.

And that is how Deiokes became the ruler of the Medes, whom he united into one people although they are composed of six tribes: the Busai, Paretakenoi, Stroukhates, Arizantoi, Budioi, and Magoi.

Deiokes died after ruling for fifty-three years,[a] and Phraortes his son inherited his rule over the Median kingdom. But Phraortes was not content to rule only the Medes,[b] and he made war on the Persians.[c] These were the first people he attacked and the first whom he made subject to the Medes.

1.99
MEDIA
Deiokes isolates himself from the people and his peers to forestall plots.

1.100
MEDIA
Deiokes is a harsh judge and rules with spies everywhere.

1.101
MEDIA
The six Median tribes.

1.102
647–625
MEDIA-ASIA
Phraortes succeeds Deiokes and reigns for twenty-two years.* He conquers the Persians and other Asians but is defeated and killed by the Assyrians.

1.98.3a　Ecbatana: Map 1.92, locator.
1.98.4a　Herodotus may be describing here a ziggurat, a common ancient Mesopotamian religious building.
1.98.5a　According to *Thucydides* 2.13, Athens' circuit wall was 60 stades, or about 6.6 miles, long. See Appendix J, §6, 19.
1.99.1a　With the amended text of Herwerden, rather than the manuscripts, which say "in anyone's presence."
1.102*　　*The Cambridge Ancient History* says twenty-one years, from 674 to 653.
1.102.1a　Deiokes died in 656. (Godley)
1.102.1b　Media: Map 1.103, BY.
1.102.1c　Persia: Map 1.103, BY.

[2] When he had both these mighty peoples under his rule, he began the further conquest of Asia,[a] attacking one tribe or group after another, until he made war even against the Assyrians,[b] who held sway over Nineveh.[c] The Assyrians had earlier ruled all of Asia, but their allies had rebelled, and they now stood alone. Nonetheless, they were still formidable, and when Phraortes led his army into battle against them, he and most of his troops were killed. Phraortes had ruled for twenty-two years.

When Phraortes died, the throne passed to Cyaxares son of Phraortes son of Deiokes.[a] He is said to have been much more devoted to war than his father and grandfather. He was in fact the first to divide his Asian subjects into regiments, and reorganize each group into separate contingents: the infantry armed with spears, the archers, and the cavalry. Before this all the soldiers had been jumbled together in a chaotic mass. [2] And it was he who was fighting the Lydians[a] at the time when day turned to night,[b] and who acquired for himself all of Asia east of the River Halys.[c] He mustered all the men under his rule and made war on Nineveh, hoping to destroy this city in revenge for his father's death. [3] He did defeat the Assyrians in battle, but while he was besieging Nineveh, a large army of Scythians attacked, led by the Scythian king Madyes son of Protothyes.[a] The Scythians had invaded Asia when they were chasing the Cimmerians[b] out of Europe,[c] and it was during their pursuit of the fleeing Cimmerians that they reached the land of the Medes.

It is a thirty-day journey for a traveler without heavy baggage from Lake Maeotis[a] to the River Phasis[b] and Colchis,[c] and from Colchis it is not much farther to cross into Media. To reach Media, one passes a single tribe in between, the Saspeires.[d] [2] The Scythians, however, did not enter Asia by this route but turned off to a much longer road inland, keeping the Cauca-

1.103
624–585
MEDIA-LYDIA-ASSYRIA
Cyaxares succeeds Phraortes. He fights the Lydians at the battle of the eclipse, and besieges Nineveh, although he is driven off by the Scythians. Cyaxares reigns forty years, from 624 to 585.

1.104
SCYTHIA-ASIA
How the Scythians entered Media and ruled Asia for twenty-eight (?) years.

1.102.2a Asia: Map 1.103, AX.
1.102.2b Assyria: Map 1.103, BY.
1.102.2c Nineveh: Map 1.103, BY.
1.103.1a The dates for Deiokes and Phraortes are murky indeed. Not even *The Cambridge Ancient History* (Vol. IV, 2nd Edition, pp. 18–21) can satisfactorily resolve the difficulty of Phraortes' reign, which seems to end in 653 (1.102 sidenote), and the beginning of the reign of Cyaxares, which is reasonably well documented from Babylonian sources as taking place in 625.
1.103.2a Lydia: Map 1.103, BX.
1.103.2b The eclipse of the sun mentioned in 1.74.2–3.
1.103.2c Halys River: Map 1.103, AX.
1.103.3a Assyrian records initially mention the Scythians in the early 670s, when the Assyrians allied with a Scythian king (Herodotus' Protothyes), who married a daughter of the Assyrian king Esarhaddon. Herodotus has Madyes, who succeeded his father Protothyes, thwart the Mede Cyaxares' siege of Nineveh. This would be congruent with a continued Assyrian-Scythian alliance, but the Median assault

on Nineveh and a Scythian victory over the Medes have no echo in Near Eastern sources. As Cyaxares ruled from 624 to 585, this siege would have to date after 624 but not later than 612, when Nineveh fell to the combined forces of the Medes and the Neo-Babylonians. It is generally agreed that in 612 the Scythians were allies of the Medes. A hint of a Median-Scythian alliance can be found in 1.73–74 on Scythians in Cyaxares' service. Perhaps Herodotus, whose sketchy knowledge of Median history has often invited criticism, has, in his efforts to make sense of his poor and poorly understood sources, invented an earlier siege of Nineveh. (Wheeler)
1.103.3b Cimmerians, mentioned in 1.6.3, n. 1.6.3a, 1.15.1, and n. 1.15.1c.
1.103.3c Europe: Map 1.103, AX.
1.104.1a Lake Maeotis (modern Sea of Azov): Map 1.103, AX. It is not a lake, but a northern gulf of the Euxine (Black) Sea.
1.104.1b Phasis River: Map 1.103, AY.
1.104.1c Colchis: Map 1.103, AY.
1.104.1d Saspeires, possible location: Map 1.103, AY.

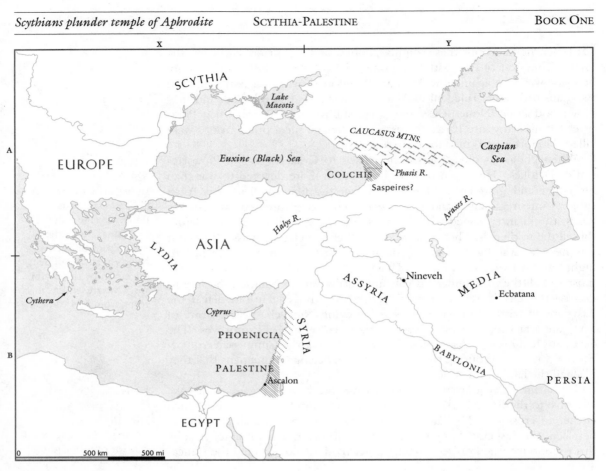

MAP 1.103

sus Mountains[a] on their right. And so now the Medes joined battle with the
Scythians and lost the fight as well as their power, while the Scythians
undertook the occupation of all Asia.

1.105

SCYTHIA-PALESTINE

Those Scythians who plun-
dered Aphrodite's oldest
temple in Ascalon, Pales-
tine, and their descendants,
have ever since suffered
from the female disease.

From here they advanced toward Egypt,[a] but when they reached Palestinian Syria,[b] Psammetichos king of Egypt met them and turned them back
with gifts and pleas not to advance farther.[c] [2] The Scythians then
retreated, and most of them passed by the Syrian city of Ascalon[a] without
doing any damage, but a few lingered behind and plundered the sanctuary

1.104.2a The Scythians apparently marched east-
          ward along the northern slope of the
          Caucasus Mountains (Map 1.103, AY),
          turning south between the east end of the
          range and the Caspian Sea (Map 1.103,
          AY). This was a frequently used invasion
          route into the Near East from north of
          the Caucasus in later times. (Wheeler)

1.105.1a Egypt: Map 1.103, BX.
1.105.1b Palestine, Syria: Map 1.103, BX.
1.105.1c There is no evidence for a Scythian raid
          into Palestine, or any interaction between
          the Scythians and King Psammetichos I
          (664–609) in Assyrian or Egyptian
          sources. (Wheeler)
1.105.2a Ascalon: Map 1.103, BX.

of Aphrodite Ourania.[b] [3] I have found out through inquiry that this is the oldest of all the temples of this goddess. In fact, her sanctuary on Cyprus[a] originated here, as the Cyprians themselves affirm, and the one on Cythera[b] was founded by the Phoenicians[c] coming from this Syrian region. [4] The goddess inflicted the female disease upon the Scythian plunderers of the sanctuary in Ascalon, and not only upon them, but upon their descendants for all time. And so the Scythians agree that because of this they have the disease, and visitors to the Scythian land can see among them those suffering from it, whom the Scythians call Enarees.[a]

The Scythians ruled Asia for twenty-eight years,[a] and life was disrupted everywhere because of their arrogance and brutality. In addition to the tribute that they exacted and imposed on everyone, they would ride through the land plundering and seizing whatever else they wanted.[b] [2] Then Cyaxares and the Medes held a feast for the greater part of them, got them drunk, and killed them. That is how the Medes won back their power and regained control over the same places they had ruled before. And they also captured Nineveh[a] (how they took it, I shall show elsewhere[b]), and made the Assyrians[c] subject to them, with the exception of the Babylonian[d] district. [3] After this, Cyaxares died, having ruled forty years, if we count the years of Scythian rule.

1.106
612
MEDIA
Cyaxares defeats the Scythians, captures Nineveh, and reestablishes Median rule.

FIGURE 1.106.
SCYTHIAN TRIPLE-EDGED JAVELIN HEAD FOUND AT PERSEPOLIS.

1.105.2b   Aphrodite Ourania (Heavenly Aphrodite): called Derketo at Ascalon, she was a mermaid and mother goddess.

1.105.3a   Cyprus: Map 1.103, BX.

1.105.3b   Cythera: Map 1.103, BX.

1.105.3c   Phoenicia: Map 1.103, BX.

1.105.4a   Enarees: "lacking manhood" (impotence, according to Hippocrates, but other interpretations have been suggested as well). Also see 4.67, where Herodotus calls some (literally) menwomen.

1.106.1a   Herodotus' version of a massive and sudden invasion from a base in the eastern Crimea is surely a myth. Scythians did reside in the northern parts of the Near East in the seventh century, but in the Caucasus region, where Scythian interaction with the natives produced the distinctive socketed triple-edged Scythian arrowheads (see Figure 1.106), which have a Transcaucasian origin, as do the Scythian daggers also mentioned in 4.70.1, 7.54.2, 7.67.1, 8.120.1, 9.107.2 and their iron battle-axes. In the eastern Crimea, however, there is no evidence for Scythians in the seventh century; and even in the sixth and fifth centuries, the traces of Scythian presence there are scattered and episodic. (Wheeler)

1.106.1b   Herodotus' supposed twenty-eight years of Scythian rule of the Near East does occur in a chaotic period when the Assyrian Empire fell, the Kingdom of Urartu disappeared, and Median and Neo-Babylonian (Chaldaean) Empires originated. The sources reflect this chaos: Assyrian records cease to provide historical information after 640, and the Babylonian chronicle of Nabopalassar begins with 616. Confirmation of Herodotus' view of a period of Scythian dominance in the Near East is therefore difficult. The fact itself is suspect, as Herodotus conveniently puts these events into the wider context of his theme of East-West conflict (4.1.1, 7.20.2): Darius I's Scythian campaign (513) avenged the Scythian invasion. Perhaps the best that can be said is that the Scythians clearly played a role as allies of various powers in the conflicts of the seventh century, but a Scythian defeat of the Medes and domination of Asia cannot be substantiated from other sources. (Wheeler)

1.106.2a   Nineveh: Map 1.103, BY. The collapse of the Assyrian states after the capture and sack of Assyria's capital was an earthshaking event in ancient western Asian history.

1.106.2b   The narrative of the capture of Nineveh by the Medes, which took place in 612, is not found in the text of Herodotus that has come down to us.

1.106.2c   Assyria: Map 1.103, BY.

1.106.2d   Babylonia: Map 1.103, BY.

1.107
584
MEDIA
Astyages succeeds
Cyaxares as king of Media
and rules from 584 to
550. He tries to escape
his fate by killing Cyrus,
the son of his daughter
Mandane.

1.108
MEDIA
Astyages charges
Harpagos with the task
of killing the newborn
grandson.

1.109
MEDIA
Harpagos decides not to
carry out Astyages'
instructions himself.

Astyages son of Cyaxares inherited the kingship. He had a daughter by the name of Mandane, and he dreamed that she urinated so copiously that she filled up his city and flooded all Asia besides. He told the Magis' dream interpreters about his dream, and when he learned from them the implication of its details, he became frightened. [2] Later, when Mandane had matured and reached the age for marriage, his fear of the dream led him to give her not to a Mede of his own rank, but to a Persian named Cambyses. This man, he discovered, was from a good family, had a peaceful disposition, and Astyages considered him much lower in status than even a middle-class Mede.[a]

In the first year of Mandane's marriage to Cambyses, Astyages had another dream-vision: he saw a vine growing from his daughter's genitals and covering all of Asia. [2] After this dream, too, he consulted the dream interpreters, and then he sent for his daughter to come back from Persia. She was with child, and after her arrival, he kept a close watch on her because he intended to kill the child she would bear. For the Magis' dream interpreters had revealed to him that the significance of the dream was that his daughter's child would replace Astyages as king. [3] To prevent this, when Cyrus was born he summoned Harpagos, a relative who looked after his affairs and whom he trusted more than any other Mede, and said, [4] "Harpagos, whatever matter I entrust to your care, be sure not to treat it lightly; nor should you choose to serve others and toss me aside, only to risk tripping yourself up later on. Take the son Mandane has borne, carry him home, and kill him; bury him however you like." [5] Harpagos replied, "Sire, you have never found anything in me to displease you, and I shall take care not to fail you in the future either; rather, if this is what you desire, it is my duty to serve you and to faithfully carry out your wishes."

That was the reply of Harpagos, after which the child was handed over to him, dressed up for his death. Harpagos wept on his way home, and when he entered his house, he told his wife all that Astyages had said. [2] And she asked him, "What do you intend to do now?" And he replied, "I will not comply with Astyages' plan. No, not even if he were to lose his mind and become more insane than he is now would I follow his orders and commit such a murder. [3] There are many reasons I will not murder this boy. First of all, he is related to me, and besides, Astyages is old and without a male heir. And then again, if the child and the sovereignty[a] were to pass to Astyages' daughter, whose son he seeks to have me kill, what is left for me but the gravest danger? Yet for the sake of my present security, the boy must die. The murderer, however, should come from the household of Astyages, not from mine."

Harpagos won't murder Cyrus

1.107.2a See 1.91.5, where Apollo explains to
Croesus how he failed to perceive that
the oracle's "mule" was Cyrus, the son
of Mandane and Cambyses, offspring of

two different races and unequal
social ranks.
1.109.3a Herodotus uses the word "tyranny"
here, in the sense of absolute rule.

After saying this, he at once sent a messenger to one of Astyages' herds-man, who, as he knew, grazed his herds in pastures and hills most suitable for his purpose, since they were full of wild beasts. His name was Mitra-dates, and he lived with his wife, a fellow slave whose name in Greek would have been Kyno, or bitch, but it was Spako in the Median language, for the Medes call a *kyno* a *spako.* [2] The foothills of the mountains where this herdsman pastured his cows are located north of Ecbatana[a] toward the Euxine Sea.[b] The Median[c] territory here, next to the Saspeires,[d] is covered by a thick canopy of trees; it is quite high and mountainous, while the rest of Media is completely flat.

[3] The herdsman who was summoned came with alacrity, and when he arrived, Harpagos said these words to him: "Astyages orders you to take this child and abandon it in the most desolate spot on the mountains so that it will die as quickly as possible. And he has ordered me to tell you that if you do not kill the child, but keep it alive somehow, you will suffer a very painful and violent death. And I have been appointed to inspect the child's corpse after its exposure."

Upon hearing this, the herdsman picked up the child and returned with it to his hut by the same road by which he had come. As it happened, his wife had been expecting to give birth any day, and it seems, as if by divine fate, that she did give birth after the herdsman had gone to the city. Each had been worrying about the other, he deeply concerned about his wife's labor and delivery, she anxious because it was unusual for Harpagos to send for her husband. [2] Upon his return, when she saw him standing there before her, after nearly giving up hope of ever seeing him again, she spoke first, asking him why Harpagos had sent for him so urgently. And Mitra-dates answered, "My dear wife, when I went to the city, I saw sights I wish I had never seen, and learned of things I wish had never happened to those we serve. I was astonished when I went inside to find that the entire house of Harpagos was filled with wailing. [3] As soon as I entered I saw lying before me a child gasping and crying, dressed up in gold and embroidered clothes. When Harpagos saw me, he ordered me to take the child at once and be gone, and to carry it to the part of the mountains most frequented by wild beasts, and to abandon it there. He said Astyages had imposed this task on me, and he threatened me fiercely with terrible consequences if I should fail to do it. [4] So I took the child and carried it away, thinking at first that it belonged to one of the household servants, and never suspecting where it really came from, although I was amazed by the gold and robes in which it was dressed and by the conspicuous wailing I heard in the house of Harpagos. [5] But I soon learned the whole story on the way back, from a servant who had handed over the infant and was escorting me out of the

1.110.2a   Ecbatana: Map 1.103, BY.
1.110.2b   Euxine (Black) Sea: Map 1.103, AX.
1.110.2c   Media: Map 1.103, BY.
1.110.2d   Saspeires, possible location: Map 1.103, AY.

1.110
MEDIA
Harpagos entrusts the task of killing the child to the cowherd Mitradates.

1.111
MEDIA
Mitradates takes the child and tells the whole story to his wife, who has herself just given birth.

city. It turns out that the child is the son of Astyages' daughter Mandane and Cambyses son of Cyrus, and it is Astyages who has commanded that he be killed. And as a matter of fact, here he is."

Whereupon the herdsman unwrapped the child and showed it to his wife; and when she saw the child, and how beautiful it was, she burst into tears and took hold of her husband's knees, imploring him not to expose the baby, but he told her that he had no alternative, since agents of Harpagos would come as inspectors, and he would be killed in a most dreadful way if they discovered that he had not killed it. [2] When she saw that she could not convince her husband, she said, "Well, then, since I am unable to persuade you not to expose it, and since it is absolutely necessary that a dead child be witnessed, let me propose another course we could take, for I, too, have given birth, but to a stillborn child. Take the dead child and expose it outside, [3] but let us raise the son of Astyages' daughter as our own. Our clever scheme will benefit us greatly: you will not be caught defying those you serve, our dead child will get a royal burial, and the surviving child will not lose his life."

The herdsman thought that his wife had given excellent advice for their present situation, and he carried it out at once. He handed over to his wife the child he had brought home to put to death, and then, taking the body of his own child and dressing it in all the adornments of the other infant, and placing it in the urn in which he had carried the other child, [2] he took it to the most desolate place on the mountains and left it there. Then, on the third day of the child's exposure, the herdsman went to the city, leaving behind one of his assistants to keep watch over the body. When he came to the house of Harpagos, he said he was ready to show the body of the child; [3] and Harpagos sent men from among his most trustworthy bodyguards, and it was they who, on his behalf, saw and buried the child of the herdsman. And so while the one infant lay buried, the other was raised by the herdsman's wife; he was later called Cyrus, although I'm sure she gave him some other name.

When the boy was ten years old, an event occurred which revealed his true identity. What happened was something like this. He was playing in the road with other boys his age in a village where the herds were tended, and in their game they chose him (the so-called son of the herdsman) to be their king. [2] He then appointed some of them to be builders, others to be bodyguards, a certain one of them to act as Eye of the King,[a] and another to have the honor of delivering messages; thus he assigned a position to each of them. [3] One of the boys who joined in this game was the son of Artembares, a man held in high esteem among the Medes. This boy refused to perform the task assigned by Cyrus, so Cyrus ordered the

1.112
MEDIA
Mitradates and his wife decide to raise the royal child and to expose the body of their own recently stillborn child.

1.113
MEDIA
Mitradates carries out his wife's plan.

1.114
MEDIA
The young Cyrus displays traits of kingship.

[handwritten margin note: YOUNG KING CYRUS = RECOGNIZED]

1.114.2a The King's Eye was "a real court official whose function was to report to the king directly on all matters concerning the kingdom. The Hellenes thought that the 'eyes and ears' of the king were a sort of spy system." (McNeal) See Appendix M, Herodotus on Persia and the Persian Empire, §8.

other boys to seize him, and when they obeyed, Cyrus punished the boy severely with a whip. [4] The boy was enraged at having to endure treatment so offensive to his sense of honor, and as soon as he was released, he returned to the city and complained to his father of the abuse he had received at the hands of Cyrus, though he did not call him that (since that was not yet his name), but rather "the son of Astyages' herdsman." [5] Infuriated by this affront, Artembares went straight to Astyages, bringing along his son, and described to the king the shocking treatment his boy had endured, pointing to his son's shoulders and saying, "Sire, this is how we have been outrageously insulted by the son of your slave, the herdsman."

When Astyages saw the bruises and heard this story, he wanted to punish the boy for the sake of Artembares' honor, and so he summoned the herdsman and his son. When they came into his presence, Astyages fixed his eyes on Cyrus and said, [2] "How could you, the son of this herdsman, dare to inflict such injury on the son of this man, who is foremost at my court?" And the boy answered, "My lord, I did this to him for just cause. For when the boys of the village, including this boy, were playing a game, they made me their king because I seemed to them the most suitable for this role. [3] All the other boys carried out my commands, but this one boy disobeyed and ignored them, for which he received punishment. So if I deserve some painful discipline for this, here I am."

As the boy spoke, Astyages became aware of a growing sense of recognition, noticing that his facial features resembled his own, that he spoke more like a free man than a slave, and that the time since the baby's exposure seemed to correspond to the boy's present age. [2] Amazed at this recognition, he was for a while speechless. But with difficulty, he at last regained his composure and, wanting to send Artembares away so that he could test the herdsman alone with questions, he dismissed Artembares, saying, "Artembares, I will take action so that you and your son will have no reason to complain." [3] And while the servants led Cyrus to an inner chamber at his order, Astyages asked the herdsman, who was now left behind alone, where and from whom, exactly, he had received the boy. [4] Mitradates answered that the boy belonged to himself and the woman who gave birth to him and with whom he still lived. Astyages remarked that Mitradates had not been very clever in adopting a course that would bring him to terrible torture, and as he spoke he signaled to his bodyguards to seize the man. [5] And as the herdsman was being led away to be tortured, he broke down and told the whole story from start to finish, telling the truth throughout, and concluding with entreaties and pleas for mercy and forgiveness.

1.115
MEDIA
Summoned to Astyages, Cyrus defends his "royal" acts.

1.116
MEDIA
Suspecting the true identity of the boy Cyrus, Astyages interrogates Mitradates and discovers the truth.

Astyages was now less interested in the fact that the herdsman had revealed the truth than in blaming Harpagos for an outrageous offense. So he ordered his bodyguards to summon him. [2] And when Harpagos appeared, Astyages asked him, "Harpagos, how did you put to death my daughter's son, the child I gave over to you?" Harpagos saw that the herdsman was there and so he decided not to lie, for fear of getting caught in cross-examination. He replied, [3] "Sire, when I received the child into my own hands, I considered how I could act in accordance with your wishes, give you no reason to find fault with me, and yet avoid being a murderer in the eyes of your daughter and yourself. [4] So this is what I did. I summoned this herdsman and gave the child to him, saying truthfully that it was you who ordered it to be killed. That is, after all, how you stated your instructions. Further, when I gave over the child, I instructed him to abandon it on a desolate mountain and to stay there and keep watch until the child died, threatening him with all sorts of punishments should he neglect to carry out these instructions. [5] Then, when he had carried out the orders and the child died, I sent my most trustworthy eunuchs, and it was they who saw the corpse for me and buried the child. That was the end of this matter, sire, and that was how the boy was put to death."

Harpagos had indeed disclosed the truth. And Astyages, at first concealing within himself his anger about what had happened, told Harpagos the herdsman's story just as he had heard it; and when the whole story had been repeated, he concluded by saying that the boy was still alive and that things had turned out well. "You see," he said, "what had been done to the boy made me suffer greatly, and further, being in conflict with my daughter was not something I could deal with lightly. And so, since our fortune has changed for the better, first send your own boy here to be with the newcomer, and then come and have dinner with me, since I intend to sacrifice an offering in thanks for the boy, to whichever gods this honor is due."

1.119
MEDIA
Astyages has the son of
Harpagos killed, cooked,
and served to Harpagos
at a banquet. After
learning the nature of his
meal, Harpagos retires
calmly, to plot revenge.

When Harpagos heard this, he prostrated himself before the king and made much of the fact that his offense had turned out to be opportune and that he was invited to dinner to celebrate these fortunate events. Then he went home, [2] and as soon as he arrived there he sent his only son, who was about thirteen years old, to go to Astyages and do whatever he ordered. Then he joyfully told his wife what had happened.

[3] Astyages, when the son of Harpagos came to him, slew him, and cut him limb from limb. Next he roasted some parts of the flesh and boiled other parts, then prepared them so that they were ready to serve. [4] When dinnertime came and Harpagos and the rest of the guests were present, tables full of lamb's meat were set before Astyages and the others, but to Harpagos was served the body of his son, except for the head, hands, and feet; these had been set aside and covered up in a basket. [4] When Harpa-

gos decided he had eaten enough, Astyages asked him if he had enjoyed the feast. Harpagos replied that he had certainly enjoyed it very much, and then those whose task it was set before him the head, hands, and feet of his son, still covered. Standing nearby, they ordered Harpagos to take off the cover and help himself to whatever he wanted. [6] Harpagos obediently took off the cover and saw the remains of his son, but instead of reacting with shock at the sight, he contained himself. When Astyages asked him whether he knew what meat he had eaten, [7] he replied that he knew, and that it was pleasing—as was everything that the king did. After replying thus, he picked up his son's remains and went home. There, I assume, he buried all the remains that he had been able to gather together.

That was the punishment Astyages inflicted on Harpagos. But he thought long and hard about Cyrus, and in trying to decide what to do about him, he summoned the same Magi whose interpretation of the dream had been sought before. When they arrived, Astyages asked them how they interpreted his vision now, and they said that their interpretation had not changed, that the boy would have been king if he had survived and had not died first. [2] Astyages then told them, "The boy has survived and is alive today, but while he was dwelling in the country, the boys of the village made him king in their game, and he performed and carried out all the functions that real kings do; he appointed bodyguards, porters, message-bearers, and all the rest. And what do you now think would be the significance of all this?" [3] And the Magi said, "If the boy still lives and has become king in some unforeseen way, you have nothing to fear from him, since he will not rule a second time. For even some of our prophecies come to very little significance, and some of them connected with dreams turn out to be completely trivial in the end." [4] "I myself," Astyages replied, "strongly agree with this explanation. When the boy was given the title of king, the dream was fulfilled, and I have no reason to fear him any longer. Nevertheless, do consider this matter carefully and give me advice as to how both my house and you can obtain the greatest degree of safety in regard to it." [5] To this the Magi responded, "Sire, it means a great deal to us that you continue to rule securely and successfully, because if your rule were to pass to this Persian boy, it will come into the hands of others, and the Persians will make us their slaves and despise us, since we are foreigners to them. But while you reign securely as our king and fellow citizen, we have our share of your rule and receive from you great honors. [6] Thus, we must by all means preserve you and your rule. And so in this present instance, if we perceived anything that might cause alarm, we would certainly notify and warn you of it. But as it is, the dream has been realized without consequence to you; we are encouraged by this and urge you to feel that way, too. But we do think that you should send this boy out of your sight and back to his parents in Persia."[a]

1.120

MEDIA

The Magi now decide that Astyages has nothing to fear from Cyrus.

1.120.6a Persia: Map 1.103, BY.

1.121
MEDIA
Astyages apologizes
to Cyrus.

As Astyages was very pleased to hear this, he called for Cyrus and said to him, "My boy, as a matter of fact, I must admit that I have wronged you because of a dream that was not fulfilled; thus by your own destiny you are alive today. So go back now to Persia with my blessing. I will send an escort along with you, and when you arrive there, you will find your father and mother to be very different from Mitradates the herdsman and his wife."

1.122
PERSIA
Astyages sends Cyrus
back to his true parents
in Persia.

Having said this, Astyages sent Cyrus off to the house of Cambyses. When the boy arrived there, his parents received him and took him in. And then, when they learned who he was, they welcomed him joyously, because they had lived all these years believing that he had died shortly after his birth. When they asked him how he had survived, [2] he told them the whole story, adding that he had not known his identity and had been very much mistaken about it, until he had learned the truth of his ordeal during his journey to his parents' home. Indeed, before that he had always thought of himself as the son of Astyages' herdsman, but on his way here he had learned the true story from his escort. [3] He also told them how he had been raised by the herdsman's wife Kyno, praising her so continually throughout all he said that her importance to the story of his life was obvious. His parents exploited this woman's name[a] in order to spread the rumor that when Cyrus had been exposed in the wild, a bitch had suckled and raised him, so that their son's survival would seem more divinely miraculous to the Persians. Certainly, from this beginning, that rumor has spread far and wide.

1.123
559
MEDIA-PERSIA
Harpagos cultivates Cyrus
while Astyages alienates
the Medes with harsh
treatment. Cyrus
becomes King of the
Persians in 559.

Cyrus grew into manhood and was the most stalwart of his peers—as well as the most popular. Meanwhile, Harpagos worked to establish ties with him by sending him gifts, although his real desire was for revenge on Astyages. He saw that his status as a mere private citizen, one who held no official position, meant that he would not be able to take vengeance on Astyages directly, and so, as he saw Cyrus grow into manhood, he formed an alliance with him, identifying Cyrus' ordeals with his own. [2] Even before this, he had achieved something toward his goal, for Astyages had begun to treat the Medes harshly, and Harpagos mingled with the most prominent Medes one by one and persuaded them to work to end the reign of Astyages and make Cyrus their leader instead. [3] Having thus prepared the ground, Harpagos now wanted to reveal his plan to Cyrus, who was still living in Persia; but since the roads were under guard there, he had to devise the following scheme to make it known to him.

[4] He procured a hare, slit open its belly just as it was, without skinning it, and inserted a scroll on which he had written his message. Then he sewed up the hare's belly and gave it with hunting nets to his most trusted servant, sending him off to the Persians in the guise of a hunter with

1.122.3a *Kyno* in Greek means "bitch" or "female
           dog."

instructions to give the hare to Cyrus. In addition, he was to give Cyrus oral instructions to split open the hare with his own hand and to be sure no one else was present when he did this.

These instructions were carried out, and Cyrus, finding the scroll inside, picked it up and read it. It said, "Son of Cambyses, the gods are watching over you; otherwise you could never have come into such good fortune. Now is the time to take revenge on Astyages, who chose to be your murderer. [2] For it was his will that you were to be killed, but by the will of the gods and myself, you are alive. I suppose that you have known for a long time of what I did for you and of how I suffered at the hands of Astyages because I did not kill you but instead gave you to the herdsman. Now, if you will take my advice you will come to rule the entire land over which Astyages now rules. If you will persuade the Persians to revolt and march against the Medes, [3] it will not matter whether I or another of the eminent Medes is appointed by Astyages to serve as general against you. You shall have anything you want, for these Medes will be the first to revolt against him and come over to your side, and they will strive to bring him down. And so, since all is in readiness for you here, make your move now and with all dispatch."

1.124
MEDIA-PERSIA
Harpagos secretly encourages Cyrus to lead a revolt against Astyages.

When Cyrus learned all this, he considered what might be the shrewdest way to persuade the Persians to revolt; his deliberations led him to conclude that the following course of action would be most effective, and he duly carried it out. He first wrote down on a scroll everything that he wanted to say to them. [2] Then, after convening an assembly of the Persians, he read from the scroll announcing that Astyages had appointed him general of the Persians. "And now, Persians," he said, "I command each and every one of you to reassemble here with a scythe."

1.125
PERSIA
Cyrus marshals the Persians and considers how to induce them to follow him in revolt.

[3] This was the proclamation of Cyrus. There are many tribes among the Persians, but it was only some of them that Cyrus assembled and persuaded by this speech to revolt against the Medes. These were the leading tribes, on which all the other Persians were dependent, namely, the Pasargadae, Maraphians, and Maspioi.[a] Of these, the Pasargadae are the most noble and include the family of Achaimenids, the Kings of Persia, who are descendants of Perseus.[b] [4] The other Persian tribes are those who are farmers, the Panthialaioi, Derousiaioi, and Germanioi; and those who are nomads, the Daoi, Mardians, Dropikans, and Sagartians.

When all had arrived there with their scythes, Cyrus ordered them to clear and prepare for cultivation a certain tract of wild land covered with thorn bushes, which measured about two to two and a quarter miles on each side;[a] they were to complete the work in one day. [2] After the Persians had carried out this task, he ordered them to return there on the

1.126
PERSIA
Cyrus offers the Persians a rich life if they will follow him in revolt against the Medes.

1.125.3a Of these, only the location of the Pasargadai is known, or at least indicated by the location of the city of Pasargadae: Map 1.142, locator.
1.125.3b The Hellenes believed that the Persians were descended from the hero Perseus; see 7.61.
1.126.1a Herodotus writes "18 to 20 stades" on a side. See Appendix J, §6, 19.

next day, bathed and refreshed. In the interval, Cyrus gathered together all of his father's flocks of goats and sheep and his herds of cattle. He sacrificed them and prepared to receive the army of Persians as his guests, setting out wine and food in addition for the most pleasant feast possible. [3] The next day when the Persians arrived, he provided a feast for them as they reclined in a meadow. After the meal, Cyrus asked them whether they preferred what they had the day before or what they had today. [4] They said that there was a big difference between the two: yesterday had been terrible—everything bad—while today everything had been pleasant and good. Picking up on their language, Cyrus began to disclose to them his project, saying, [5] "Men of Persia, here is where you stand: if you will obey me, you will have good days like today, but with the good multiplied many times over, and you will not have to work like slaves. If you do not obey me, however, you will have to perform countless labors fit for slaves, like those of yesterday. [6] So I appeal to you now: obey me and be free. In fact, I believe that it was by divine providence that I was born and that this opportunity was meant to fall into my hands. And I believe that you Persian men are in no way inferior to the Medes in war, nor in anything else. That is how things stand, so let us revolt against Astyages, and let us do it immediately."

Now, the Persians enthusiastically accepted Cyrus' offer to be their leader and approved his proposal that they should liberate themselves, since they had for a long time felt that to be ruled by the Medes was intolerable. When Astyages found out what Cyrus was doing, he sent a messenger and summoned him to the palace. [2] Cyrus commanded the messenger to report back to Astyages that he would be in the king's presence sooner than the king would wish. When Astyages heard this, he armed all the Medes, and because he was unbalanced by the god, he appointed Harpagos as his general, forgetting the outrage he had inflicted upon him previously. [3] And when the Medes went out to war and engaged in battle with the Persians, only some of them really fought, namely those who had no part in the plot of Harpagos and Cyrus. Of the others, some deserted to the Persians, but most deliberately played the coward and fled.

And so the army of the Medes fell apart in an inglorious rout. When Astyages learned of its disgraceful collapse, he immediately issued a threat to Cyrus: "Even though Cyrus has won a victory, he will not exult for long." [2] Having said just this, he first impaled the dream interpreters of the Magi who had advised him to send Cyrus away, and then he armed the Medes left in the city of Ecbatana,[a] including both the young and the old men, and led them out to do battle against the Persians. But Astyages also suffered a severe defeat: he lost the Medes he had led into battle and he himself was captured alive.

1.127
550?
MEDIA
Astyages appoints Harpagos general of the Median armies sent to fight the Persians. Many desert, others run away.

1.128
550
MEDIA
Astyages kills the Magi, and is captured in a final battle.

1.128.2a Ecbatana: Map 1.142, locator.

Harpagos came to see Astyages as a prisoner of war and stood there gloating over him and mocking him. Among his insulting taunts he reminded him in particular of that dinner at which Astyages had feasted him on his own son's flesh, asking him how he liked being a slave instead of a king. [2] Astyages looked him straight in the eye and asked if what Cyrus had done had been in reality the work of Harpagos. And Harpagos told him about the letter he had written to Cyrus and that he was in that sense the true author of the revolt. [3] Astyages then tried to show Harpagos that he was in fact the most foolish and unjust of all men; because if the revolt was really his doing, he was a fool never to have realized that he could have been king himself rather than to bestow the power on someone else; and most unjust, because he had enslaved all the Medes for revenge over a mere dinner, whereas, if [4] he really wished to give the kingship to someone else, it would have been more just to award this noble office to a Mede rather than a Persian. But now the Medes would become slaves instead of masters, through no offense of their own, and the Persians, the former slaves of the Medes, would become their masters.

1.129
MEDIA
Astyages criticizes Harpagos for helping the Persians to defeat the Medes out of personal anger.

Thus the reign of Astyages was brought to an end; he had ruled thirty-five years, and because of his cruelty, the Medes had to bend to the Persians. They had ruled Asia[a] east of the River Halys[b] for 128 years, if we exclude the Scythian occupation.[c] [2] Some years later, however, they regretted their submission to the Persians and revolted against the Persian King Darius,[a] but they were defeated in battle and again subjugated. After their successful revolt against Astyages, it was the Persians who then ruled this part of Asia. [3] Cyrus did not treat Astyages badly at all after this, but kept him by his side until Astyages died.

1.130
550–530
MEDIA-ASIA
Cyrus becomes the first Persian King of Asia. He reigns as Great King for twenty years, from 550 to 530.

This, then, is how Cyrus was born and raised, how he became King and later subjugated Croesus the Lydian, who had begun unjust acts against him. And as I said earlier, once Croesus had been subjugated, Cyrus ruled all of Asia.

How Cyrus became King

I have acquired knowledge about the customs of the Persians, and here is what I have learned. They do not erect statues, temples, and altars; they deem anyone who does these things a fool, and they feel this way, I presume, because unlike the Hellenes, they do not believe that the gods have human qualities. [2] It is their custom to climb the highest of their mountains and there to perform sacrifices to Zeus;[a] indeed they call the whole circle of the heavens Zeus. They also sacrifice to the sun, moon, earth, fire, water, and winds. [3] These latter have been the object of their sacrifices from the very beginning, but at some time later they also began to

1.131
PERSIA
Herodotus describes the religious beliefs of the Persians.

Customs of Persians

1.130.1a Asia: Map 1.142, locator.
1.130.1b Halys River: Map 1.142, locator.
1.130.1c The 128 years from 687 to 559. As to the supposed Scythian reign mentioned by Herodotus, see n. 1.106.1b.
1.130.2a Their revolt against Darius occurred in 520; the event is recorded in a cuneiform inscription. (Godley)
1.131.2a Herodotus is referring to Ahura Mazda (later called Ormazd), the supreme god of the Persians, worshiped on mountaintops, as was the Hellenes' Zeus.

sacrifice to Heavenly Aphrodite,[a] having learned to do this from the Assyrians[b] and Arabians.[c] The Assyrians call Aphrodite Mylitta,[d] the Arabians call her Alitta,[e] and the Persians call her Mitra.

1.132
PERSIA
The Persian method of sacrifice.

When the Persians sacrifice according to their traditions to these gods, they neither set up altars nor light fires, nor do they pour libations or play flutes, wear garlands, or use barley meal.[a] If someone wants to sacrifice to one of the gods, he leads an animal to a place that is free of pollution and calls upon the god, wearing a tiara made preferably of myrtle branches. [2] It is not permitted for an individual sacrificing privately to pray for himself alone; he must pray for the welfare of the King and the entire population of Persians, among whom he himself is, of course, included. He then divides the sacrificial victim into portions, boils the meat, and places it on a prepared bed of the softest grasses possible, preferably clover. [3] Once he has it all set out, a Magus[a] stands beside it and chants a history of the gods, which is how they refer to their invocation.[b] Indeed, it is not their custom to perform sacrifices without having a Magus present. Finally, after waiting a short time, the sacrificer takes away the meat and uses it as he sees fit.

1.133
PERSIA
Various customs of the Persians.

Of all the days of the year, one's own birthday is held in the most honor. On this day they claim the right to serve a larger feast than on any other day. The more fortunate among them serve the meat of oxen, horses, camels, and donkeys roasted whole in ovens, while the poor serve the meat of small animals such as sheep and goats. [2] They eat few main dishes but consume many desserts, and the latter are not served as one course, but at intervals throughout the meal. The Persians in fact say that the Hellenes are still hungry when they finish eating, since nothing worthwhile is served after the main dinner, and, they add, if something extra were to be served, the Hellenes would not stop eating so soon.

[3] Persians are quite devoted to drinking wine but are not permitted to vomit or urinate in anyone else's presence, and they are very careful about such things.

They are accustomed to deliberating on the most serious business while they are drunk, [4] and whatever decision they reach in these sessions, it is proposed to them again the next day by the host in whose house they had deliberated the night before. Then, if the decision still pleases them when they are sober, they act on it; if not, they give it up. Conversely, whatever provisional decisions they consider while sober, they reconsider when they are drunk.

1.131.3a Heavenly Aphrodite (Aphrodite Ourania); also mentioned in 1.105.2–3 and 3.8.1.
1.131.3b Assyria: Map 1.142, locator.
1.131.3c Arabia: Map 1.142, locator.
1.131.3d Mylitta: see also 1.199.
1.131.3e Alitta; but at 3.8.3, she is called Alilat.
1.132.1a All of these are elements of Greek rituals. On the use of barley meal in Greek sacrifice, see 1.160.5.
1.132.3a A "Magus" (plural Magi) is what the

Greeks called a Median priest. See Appendix M, §3. The Magoi are a tribe of the Medes; see 1.101.
1.132.3b Herodotus says the Persians called this chant a "theogony," which apparently meant that it was some type of genealogy of the gods, but most authorities agree that it was not exactly like a Greek theogony.

When Persians happen to meet each other on the street, one can tell whether or not they are equals simply by watching them. For instead of declaring a greeting to each other, they kiss each other on their mouths; and then, if one is inferior to the other, they kiss each other on their cheeks; but if one of them is of much lower status, he falls to the ground and prostrates himself before the other.[a] [2] They reserve the highest esteem for those who live closest to them, and secondly, those next to these, and so on; the farther they go from home, the less they esteem the inhabitants proportionally. And they hold in the slightest regard those who live farthest from them, in the belief that they themselves are by far the best of the human race in every way, and the rest partake of excellence in the same proportion to distance stated above; and so those who live the farthest away from them are felt to be the most inferior. [3] The Medes actually governed by a similar principle, collectively ruling over all peoples but exerting the most direct rule upon those situated closest to them, who in turn ruled their neighbors farther out. The Persians grant esteem by the same logic, for that nation also has a line of government and subordinate administration that descends progressively from self-rule to lower levels of delegation of authority in the same way.[a]

Of all men, the Persians especially tend to adopt foreign customs. For example, they wear the fashions of the Medes in the belief that the Medes' clothing is more beautiful than their own, and they wear Egyptian breastplates when they go to war. They inquire into the enjoyments of pleasure seekers in every nation and in particular have learned pederasty from the Hellenes. Each of them marries many legitimate wives but also acquires still more concubines.

A man's worth is demonstrated first of all by his valor in battle, but next to that, by fathering many sons, and the King sends gifts throughout the whole year to the man who in that year can show off the most sons. They believe that there is strength in numbers. [2] From the age of five to the age of twenty, they teach their sons just three things: to ride horses, to shoot the bow, and to speak the truth. Before the age of five, the sons spend all their time with the women and never come into their fathers' sight so that if the boy should die while still in the care of his nurse, his father will not be afflicted with grief.

Now I think this custom is worthy of praise, and there is another custom I commend as well: the King himself does not have anyone killed for a single offense, nor do any of the Persians inflict irremediable harm on any

1.134
PERSIA
Persian attitudes toward rank, neighbors.

1.135
PERSIA
Persians welcome foreign customs.

1.136
PERSIA
Persians educate their boys to ride well, shoot straight, and speak the truth.

1.137
PERSIA
Herodotus praises certain Persian laws.

1.134.1a This passage is crucial for understanding the Persian practice of self-abasement (*proskynesis*), so misunderstood by the Hellenes. For them, one abased oneself only in the presence of a god (normally a statue of a god). This sentence makes clear that in the Oriental world it was a matter simply of social distinction, not of religion (see also the recognition of Darius as King, 3.8.62, and Harpagos paying his respect, 1.119.1). When Persians did *proskynesis* before King Alexandros the Great, Hellenes in his entourage were outraged. Greeks liked righteously to refuse to submit (7.136.1) and made merry over such a sign of abjectness (8.48.4). But to address the King, submission was inevitable—many Hellenes, including Themistokles, fell into line, or rather to the ground. See Appendix M, §3 and n. M.3c.

1.134.3a Median governmental method: see Appendix M, §7.

of their household slaves for a single offense. But if, when they add up the wrongdoings and find that they outnumber and outweigh the good services rendered, then they act on their anger. [2] They say that no one ever kills his own father or mother, but that as often as such cases have occurred up to now, investigation invariably resulted in the finding that the child was either not the parent's natural offspring or else was the offspring of an adulterous union. The Persians think it most improbable that a true parent could ever be killed by his own son.

1.138
PERSIA
The Persians hate falsehoods and leprosy but revere rivers.

They are not permitted to even talk about anything which they are not permitted to do. They believe that the most disgraceful act a man may commit is to lie; after this, the next most shameful step is to incur debt. They cite many reasons for this belief, but it is true most of all, they say, because a man in debt inevitably tells lies.

Any citizen who has leprosy or the white sickness[a] may neither enter the city nor associate with other Persians; they claim that anyone who contracts these diseases has committed an offense against the sun. [2] Indeed, many Persians will drive out of the country any foreigners who may be stricken by these diseases, and they will do the same even to white pigeons, which they accuse of the same charge.

They never urinate or spit into rivers, nor will they wash their hands in them or allow others to do so; they treat rivers with the utmost veneration.[a]

1.139
PERSIA
All Persian names end in the same letter.

Another peculiarity of Persia which the Persians themselves fail to notice, but which we notice, is that their personal names, which correspond to personal qualities and magnificence, all end with the same letter, called *san* by the Dorians, *sigma* by the Ionians. And anyone who inquires into this will discover that not just some but all Persian names end in this letter.[a]

1.140
PERSIA
Various tales about Persian burial customs.

Up to this point I have given information for which I have certain knowledge. The subject of death, however, is not discussed openly and plainly, but is dealt with as though it should be concealed. For example, a Persian's corpse is not buried until it has been mauled by birds or dogs. [2] I know with certainty that this is the practice of the Magi, since they do this where all can see it. But the rest of the Persians cover the body with wax before burying it in the earth. The Magi differ a great deal from the rest of the human race, and particularly from those priests in Egypt [3] who think it impure to kill any living thing except for the purpose of sacrifice. The Magi, however, will kill everything with their own hands except dogs and human beings, and even compete with each other for the privilege of killing ants as well as snakes and all creatures that creep and fly. Since they have observed this custom from the very beginning, let it be. I shall now return to my earlier narrative.

1.138.1a　The "white sickness" is a type of leprosy which causes an efflorescence of the skin and turns the hair white.

1.138.2a　For an example of the worship of rivers, see 7.113.2.

1.139.1a　Greek versions of Persian names apparently did end in this letter, but the Persian spellings did not.

As soon as the Lydians[a] had been conquered by the Persians, the Ionians and Aeolians[b] sent messengers to Cyrus at Sardis[c] to convey their wish to be subject to him on the same terms on which they had formerly been subject to Croesus. Cyrus heard their proposal and responded by telling them a story. There was a flute player, he said, who saw some fish in the sea and played his flute to them, thinking they would come out onto the land. [2] But when his expectation proved to be mistaken, he took a fishing net, caught a great number of fish in it, and pulled them out of the sea. Then, watching the fish writhe and quiver on the ground, he said to them, "Stop dancing for me now, since you refused to come out and dance before, even when I played my flute for you." [3] Cyrus told this story to the Ionians and Aeolians because they had refused to obey the messengers he had sent to them asking them to rebel,[a] so since he had completed the Lydian affair without their help, [4] he was quite angry that they should now be ready and willing to obey him. When news of Cyrus' wrath was reported back to the Ionians, they all built walls and fortified their cities and assembled together at the Panionion[a]— all, that is, except the Milesians,[b] for Cyrus had sworn to an agreement with the Milesians alone, on the same terms that they had had with Croesus. But the rest of the Ionians decided by common consent to send messengers to Sparta[c] asking for help in their struggle against Cyrus.

Of all the people we know, these Ionians, who are members of the Panionion, have happened to build their cities in a region whose climate and skies are the most fair. [2] The regions north and south, as well as those east and west, do not have weather as fine as that of Ionia; some are oppressed by cold and dampness, others by heat and drought.

[3] The Ionians do not traditionally speak their dialect in the same way—they use in fact four different variants of their dialect in the following locations: Miletus is the southernmost of the Ionian cities, and next in order toward the north come Myous[a] and Priene;[b] these three cities lie in Caria,[c] and their inhabitants speak the same variant of the Ionian dialect. The next Ionian cities to the north—Ephesus,[d] Colophon,[e] Lebedos,[f] Teos,[g] Klazomenai,[h] and Phocaea[i]—are all located in Lydia: their citizens all speak in the same way, but their variant [4] is not the same as that of the first group of cities. Of the three remaining Ionian cities, two are on the islands of Samos[a] and Chios,[b] and Erythrai,[c] the other one, is

1.141
546
PERSIA-IONIA
After Cyrus refuses the offer of the Ionians and Aeolians to submit (on terms), they fortify their cities and appeal to Sparta for help.

1.142
IONIA
Herodotus describes the cities and dialects of Ionia.

1.141.1a	Lydia: Map 1.142, AY.	1.142.3a	Myous: Map 1.142, AY.
1.141.1b	Ionia and Aeolis: Map 1.142, AX, AY; see also Appendix K, §7–9.	1.142.3b	Priene: Map 1.142, AY.
		1.142.3c	Caria: Map 1.142, BY.
1.141.1c	Sardis: Map 1.142, AY.	1.142.3d	Ephesus: Map 1.142, AY.
1.141.3a	These messengers are referred to by Herodotus in 1.76.3, although there he writes that they were sent to the Ionians, and does not mention the Aeolians.	1.142.3e	Colophon: Map 1.142, AY.
		1.142.3f	Lebedos: Map 1.142, AX.
		1.142.3g	Teos: Map 1.142, AX.
		1.142.3h	Klazomenai: Map 1.142, AX.
1.141.4a	Panionion: Map 1.142, AY. A sanctuary for all Ionians, as Herodotus explains in 1.143.3.	1.142.3i	Phocaea: Map 1.142, AX.
		1.142.4a	Samos: Map 1.142, AX.
		1.142.4b	Chios: Map 1.142, AX.
1.141.4b	Miletus: Map 1.142, AY.	1.142.4c	Erythrai: Map 1.142, AX.
1.141.4c	Sparta: Map 1.146, locator.		

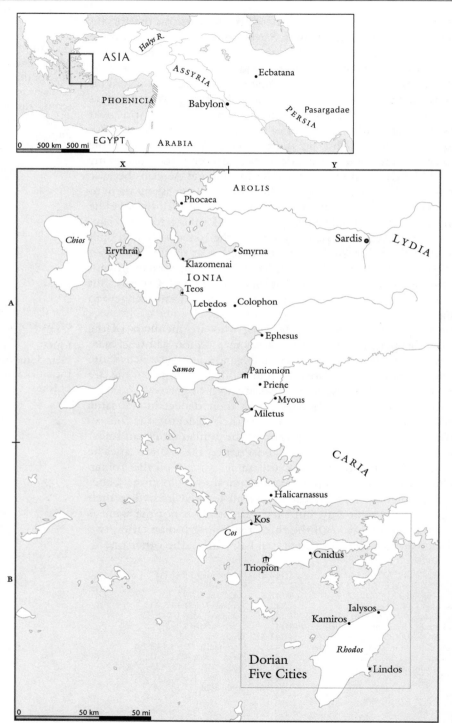

MAP 1.142

on the mainland. The Chians and Erythraians use a third distinct variant of the Ionian dialect, while the Samians speak a form of it that is unique to themselves. These then are the four variants of the Ionian dialect.[d]

And so of all the Ionians, the Milesians[a] alone were sheltered from distress by reason of their sworn alliance with Cyrus, and the islanders also were out of danger, because the Persians were themselves not seafarers and they had not yet conquered the Phoenicians.[b] [2] The Milesians had split off from the rest of the Ionians simply because the latter were the weakest and least important of the entire Hellenic people—who themselves lacked strength at this time. Indeed, Athens[a] was then the only significant Ionian city.

[3] Now these other Ionians[a]—including the Athenians—shunned the name and did not wish to be called Ionians, and even now many of them seem to me to be ashamed of the name. But these twelve cities gloried in it and even built a sanctuary just for themselves, calling it the Panionion,[b] and they decided in joint council that none of the other Ionians should share it with them (although none wanted to except the people of Smyrna[c]).[d]

In the same way the five cities of the Dorians (formerly known as the six cities of the Dorians) refuse to admit any neighboring Dorians to their Triopian sanctuary.[a] Moreover, they bar all those who break any of the rules of the sanctuary from participating in the rites and activities there. [2] In the games held in honor of Triopian Apollo they used to award tripods to the victors, but the victors were forbidden to take their prizes out of the sanctuary; they were required to dedicate them directly to the god there. [3] And so, when a man by the name of Agasikles of Halicarnassus[a] ignored the rule and, taking the tripod he had won to his home, hung it up on pegs there to display it, the other five cities, Lindos,[b] Ialysos,[c] Kamiros,[d] Kos,[e] and Cnidus,[f] prohibited Halicarnassus (which had been the sixth Dorian city) from any further participation in the games. That was the penalty they imposed on the Dorians of Halicarnassus.

It seems that the Ionians organized themselves into just twelve cities in Asia and have refused to admit any more because they had earlier been divided into twelve groups when they lived in the Peloponnese[a] before the Achaeans[b] drove them out. The first of these cities, going from east to west,

---

1.143
546
IONIA
The Milesians had a treaty with Persia. Those Ionians living on the islands had no fear of Persian naval power.

1.144
DORIAN ASIA
The five (or six) cities of the Dorians in Asia.

1.145
IONIA
The twelve Ionian cities derived their number from the twelve Ionian divisions of Achaea, where the Ionians lived before being driven out.

1.142.4d For more information on these dialects and variants, see Appendix K, §2–6.
1.143.1a Miletus: Map 1.142, AY.
1.143.1b Phoenicia: Map 1.142, locator. On Cambyses' campaign against Egypt in 525, he acquired control of Phoenicia and the Phoenician fleet, the strongest navy in the Mediterranean.
1.143.2a Athens: Map 1.46, BY.
1.143.3a Ionia in Asia: Map 1.142, AX.
1.143.3b Panionion: Map 1.142, AY.
1.143.3c Smyrna: Map 1.142, AY.
1.143.3d Herodotus, a Dorian from Halicarnassus, seems to have had a poor opinion of Ionians. He gave them no credit for having the courage to revolt, and he speaks constantly of the revolt as hopeless and as causing great ill for the Hellenes (see also

5.28, 5.30.1, 6.3, 6.19.2). They were, he thought, too soft to train properly before the crucial sea battle of Lade (6.12.2). He also found the reason for Kleisthenes' reform of the Athenian constitution to be contempt for the Ionians (5.69.1).
1.144.1a This Tropion sanctuary, which belonged to all of the five Dorian cities, was located on the end of the Cnidian peninsula: Map 1.142, BY.
1.144.3a Halicarnassus: Map 1.142, BY.
1.144.3b Lindos, Rhodos: Map 1.142, BY.
1.144.3c Ialysos, Rhodos: Map 1.142, BY.
1.144.3d Kamiros, Rhodos: Map 1.142, BY.
1.144.3e Kos: Map 1.142, BY.
1.144.3f Cnidus: Map 1.142, BY.
1.145.1a Peloponnese: Map 1.146, BX.
1.145.1b Achaea, Peloponnese: Map 1.146, AX.

borders on Sicyon[c] and is called Pellene;[d] next come Aigeira[e] and Aigai[f] where the River Krathis[g] flows and never dries up, and from which the river in Italy got its name. Next to these are Boura[h] and Helike,[i] where the Ionians took refuge when they were defeated by the Achaeans in battle; and then Aigion,[j] Rhypes,[k] Patrae,[l] Pharai,[m] and Olenos,[n] through which the large Peiros River[o] flows; and finally Dyme,[p] and, turning now inland to the southeast, Tritaia,[q] the only inland city.

1.146
IONIA
After intermixing
with other groups,
Ionians "today" are
heterogeneous.

The twelve divisions of the current Achaeans correspond to the twelve divisions of the Ionians, and so because of their earlier pattern of settlement, the Ionians organized themselves into twelve cities. It follows, then, that it is very foolish to claim that these Asian Ionians are in any way more Ionian or more noble in birth than any of the others. After all, a large number of them derive from the Abantes of Euboea,[a] who are not Ionians at all. Many other peoples are mixed in among them, including the Minyans of Orchomenus,[b] Kadmeians,[c] Dryopians,[d] Phocaeans,[e] Molossians,[f] Pelasgians from Arcadia,[g] and Dorians from Epidauros,[h] to name just a few!

[2] Those who set out from the Prytaneion of Athens[a] may have believed themselves to be the most nobly born of the Ionians, but they did not bring their own women with them to settle in their colony; what they did when they got there was to seize Carian[b] women after murdering their menfolk. [3] Because of these murders, the women compelled one another to take an oath to abide by a rule that they established, and which they handed down to their daughters: that they would never dine with their husbands nor even speak their new husbands' names out loud, because these men had murdered their fathers, their former husbands, and even their sons, and, having done this, took the women and lived with them.[a] This is what happened in Miletus.[b]

1.145.1c Sicyon: Map 1.146, BY.
1.145.1d Pellene: Map 1.146, BX.
1.145.1e Aigeira: Map 1.146, AX.
1.145.1f Aigai: Map 1.146, AX.
1.145.1g Krathis River, Achaea (modern Akrata River): Map 1.146, BX. In Italy, there is a Crathis River, whose mouth is at Sybaris: Map 5.44. See 5.45.
1.145.1h Boura: Map 1.146, AX.
1.145.1i Helike: Map 1.146, AX.
1.145.1j Aigion: Map 1.146, AX.
1.145.1k Rhypes: Map 1.146, AX.
1.145.1l Patrae: Map 1.146, AX.
1.145.1m Pharai: Map 1.146, AX.
1.145.1n Olenos: Map 1.146, AX.
1.145.1o Peiros River: Map 1.146, BX. Today Olenos is not located on the bank of the Peiros River.
1.145.1p Dyme: Map 1.146, AX.
1.145.1q Tritaia: Map 1.146, BX. Tritaia is certainly the most inland of those cities, but Pellene, Boura, Rhypes, and Pharai are also several miles from the coast.
1.146.1a Euboea: Map 1.146, AY.
1.146.1b Orchomenus, Boeotia: Map 1.146, AY.
1.146.1c Kadmeians (Phoenicians): There is

archaeological evidence that Phoenicians were among the earliest settlers at Thebes (Boeotia). Phoenicia: Map 1.142, locator.
1.146.1d Dryopians (Euboea): Map 1.146, AY.
1.146.1e Phocis: Map 1.146, AX.
1.146.1f Molossia: Map 1.146, locator.
1.146.1g Arcadia: Map 1.146, BX.
1.146.1h Epidauros: Map 1.146, BY.
1.146.2a The Prytaneion of Athens was a building in the center of the city containing the sacred hearth and serving both political and religious functions. Colonists took fire from the sacred hearth of their mother city to their new settlement. Athens: Map 1.146, BY.
1.146.2b Caria: Map 1.146, locator.
1.146.3a In traditional Greek marriage, a bride was given away to a husband by her father or male relative, who approved and arranged the marriage. The Carian women were certainly outraged by the loss of their loved ones, but perhaps they were also offended by the fact that their marriages were not strictly legal. For a discussion of women in Herodotus, see Appendix U.
1.146.3b Miletus: Map 1.149, BY.

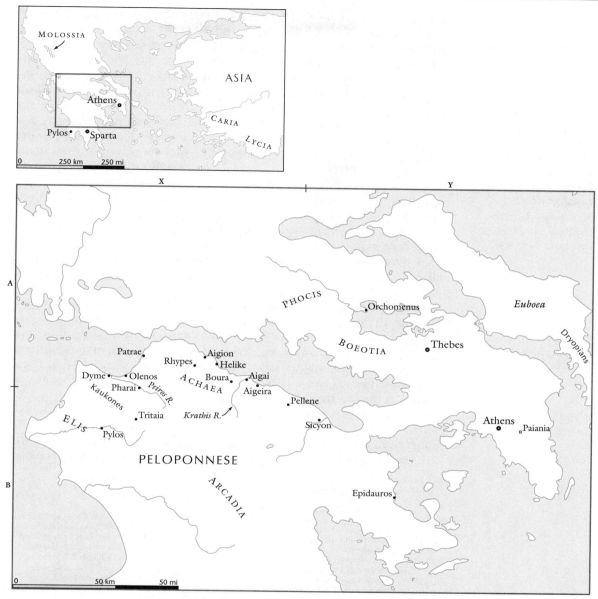

MAP 1.146

1.147
IONIA
Ionians apparently chose kings from old native lines.

Furthermore, some of the Ionians appointed Lycians[a] who were descendants of Glaukos son of Hippolochos as their kings; others appointed Kaukones from Pylos,[b] descendants of Kodros son of Melanthos; and still others appointed kings from both families at the same time. [2] But since the Ionians of Asia want to be called Ionians more than the others of that name, let them be known as the purebred Ionians, though actually all those who came from Athens and who celebrate the festival of the Apaturia[a] are Ionians. All of them do celebrate this festival except for the Ephesians[b] and the Colophonians,[c] who alone among the Ionians do not celebrate this festival and who offer as an explanation that they are prevented from doing so by some murder or other.

1.148
IONIA
Herodotus describes the Panionion and its ceremonial purpose.

The Panionion[a] is a sacred place in Mycale[b] facing toward the north, which the Ionians collectively decided to consecrate to Helikonian Poseidon.[c] Mycale forms a promontory jutting out from the mainland, extending toward the west just off the island of Samos.[d] Here the Ionians come from their various cities and gather together to celebrate the festival they named the Panionia. [2] All the festival names of the Ionians and those of all Hellenes, too, end in the letter "a," as all Persian names end in the letter "s."

1.149
AEOLIS
Description of the Aeolian cities of the Asian mainland.

These, then, are the Ionian cities. The Aeolian cities are Cyme[a] (the one also called Phrikonis), Larissa,[b] Neonteichos,[c] Temnos,[d] Killa,[e] Notion,[f] Aigiroessa,[g] Pitane,[h] Aegae,[i] Myrina,[j] and Gryneion.[k] These are the eleven old cities of the Aeolians; there used to be twelve of them on the mainland, but one, Smyrna,[l] was detached from them by the Ionians. [2] These Aeolians happened to settle on land that is more fertile but not as fair in climate as the Ionians' land.

1.150
AEOLIS-SMYRNA
How the Aeolians lost Smyrna.

This is how the Aeolians lost Smyrna. The people of Smyrna took in and sheltered some Ionian men who had been defeated in factional strife and exiled from Colophon, their home city. Once they were admitted into the city, the Colophonian exiles watched and waited until one day the people of

1.147.1a Lycia: Map 1.146, locator.
1.147.1b Pylos: Map 1.146, BX. Not Pylos in Messenia (Map 1.146, locator) but Pylos in Elis, near the Kaukones.
1.147.2a Apaturia: a three-day festival celebrated at most Ionian cities in late October and early November. During the rites, sacrifices to Zeus and Athena took place; youths were formally admitted as new members of their tribes; children were introduced to and registered in the community at specific stages of childhood, and citizenship was granted to them. See Appendix I for the role of ancient Greek festivals in forming and nurturing a sense of identity and citizenship.
1.147.2b Ephesus: Map 1.149, BY.
1.147.2c Colophon: Map 1.149, BY.
1.148.1a Panionion: Map 1.149, BY.

1.148.1b Mycale (Peninsula): Map 1.149, BY.
1.148.1c Dedicated to Poseidon of Helike (Achaea): Map 1.146, AX.
1.148.1d Samos: Map 1.149, BX.
1.149.1a Cyme: Map 1.149, AX. Perhaps Cyme is called Phrikonis from a nearby mountain in Aeolis of that name. Mount Phrikonis: Map 1.149, BX.
1.149.1b Larissa: Map 1.149, AX.
1.149.1c Neonteichos: Map 1.149, AX.
1.149.1d Temnos: Map 1.149, AY.
1.149.1e Killa: site unknown.
1.149.1f Notion: Map 1.149, BY.
1.149.1g Aigiroessa: site unknown.
1.149.1h Pitane: Map 1.149, AX.
1.149.1i Aegae: Map 1.149, AY.
1.149.1j Myrina: Map 1.149, AX.
1.149.1k Gryneion: Map 1.149, AY.
1.149.1l Smyrna: Map 1.149, BY.

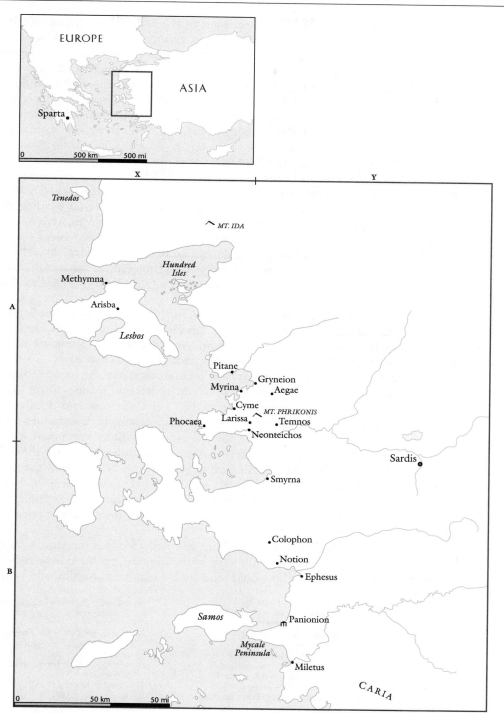

MAP 1.149

Smyrna went outside the city walls to hold a festival in honor of Dionysos. Then the Colophonians shut and locked the gates and took possession of the city. [2] When all the Aeolians rushed there to help the Smyrnaians recover their city, the two sides reached an understanding whereby the Ionians agreed to return to the Smyrnaians all of their moveable goods in the city, and the Aeolians agreed to abandon the site of Smyrna itself. The Smyrnaians carried out their part of the bargain, and the eleven Aeolian cities distributed the former Aeolians of Smyrna among themselves and made them citizens.

1.151
AEOLIS
Aeolian settlements
on the islands.

These, then, are the Aeolian cities of the mainland, from which I exclude those settlements in the region of Mount Ida,[a] which are separate. [2] The Aeolians inhabiting the islands have five cities on the island of Lesbos,[a] the people of the sixth one—Arisba[b]—having been enslaved by their Aeolian kinsmen from the city of Methymna.[c] The Aeolians also have one city on Tenedos[d] and another one on what is called the Hundred Isles.[e]

[3] These Aeolian islanders on Lesbos and Tenedos, like the Ionian islanders mentioned above, were not endangered by the initial advance of the Persians, but the rest of the cities resolved together to follow the Ionians wherever they should lead.

1.152
546?
SPARTA
The Spartans refuse
military help, but they
send a herald to warn
Cyrus not to molest the
Greek cities.

When the messengers of the Ionians and Aeolians arrived in Sparta[a] (and this all actually happened very quickly), they chose a Phocaean named Pythermos to speak for all of them. And he donned a purple cloak in order to arouse the curiosity of the Spartans and attract as many as possible to come and hear him. Then, taking an orator's stance, he made a long speech asking the Spartans to come to their defense against Cyrus. [2] The Lacedaemonians,[a] however, refused to heed this plea and decided against helping the Ionians against Cyrus, so the messengers departed. However, in spite of having turned the Ionians away, the Lacedaemonians dispatched some men in a penteconter[b]—I presume in order to spy on the affairs of Cyrus and the Ionians. And when they arrived at Phocaea,[c] they sent the most distinguished man with them, named Lakrines, to Sardis[d] to declare to Cyrus in the name of the Lacedaemonians that he must not inflict reckless damage on any city in Hellenic territory, since the Lacedaemonians would not tolerate it.

1.153
SARDIS
Cyrus asks who the Spartans
are and how numerous they
are. Cyrus leaves Sardis to
attack Babylon.

They say that when the herald had delivered this message, Cyrus questioned the Hellenes who were with him, asking them who were these Lacedaemonians who would send such a command to him, and how many

---

1.151.1a Mount Ida: Map 1.149, AX.
1.151.2a Lesbos: Map 1.149, AX.
1.151.2b Arisba: Map 1.149, AX.
1.151.2c Methymna: Map 1.149, AX.
1.151.2d Tenedos: Map 1.149, AX.
1.151.2e Hundred Isles (Hekatonnesoi): Map 1.149, AX. A group of small islands between Lesbos and the mainland.
1.152.1a Sparta: Map 1.149, locator.
1.152.2a Lacedaemonians: Herodotus uses the

names Spartans and Lacedaemonians interchangeably. See Appendix B, §5, 7, and n. B.7a.
1.152.2b Pentecontor, a ship like a trireme but of a simpler design, with one line of rowers instead of three, and a total of fifty oars. See Appendix S, Trireme Warfare in Herodotus.
1.152.2c Phocaea: Map 1.149, AX.
1.152.2d Sardis: Map 1.149, BY.

of them were there?[a] When he heard their response, he said to the Spartan herald, "I have never yet feared any men who have a place in the center of the city set aside for meeting together, swearing false oaths, and cheating one another, and if I live long enough, Lacedaemonians will have troubles of their own about which to converse, rather than those of the Ionians." [2] Cyrus thus insulted the Hellenes because of their custom of setting up agoras[a] in their cities for the purpose of buying and selling, which is unknown among the Persians, who do not use markets and, indeed, have no such place as an agora in any of their cities.

[3] After this, Cyrus entrusted control over Sardis to a Persian named Tabalos and assigned the management of the gold which had belonged to the Lydians and to Croesus to a Lydian named Paktyes. He himself marched to Ecbatana,[a] taking Croesus with him, considering the Ionians of no importance for the present. [4] For Cyrus was now planning to make expeditions himself against Babylon,[a] the Baktrians,[b] the Sacae,[c] and the Egyptians,[d] while assigning someone else to lead an army against the Ionians.

But after Cyrus had marched out of Sardis, Paktyes led the Lydians[a] in a revolt against Tabalos and Cyrus; and then, using all the gold he had from Sardis, he went down to the coast, where he hired mercenaries and persuaded the people living there to join his army. From there he marched on Sardis and besieged Tabalos, who found himself now confined to the acropolis of the city.

When word of the revolt reached Cyrus on his journey, he turned to Croesus and asked, "How will these events turn out for me, Croesus? It seems as though the Lydians will never cease to cause trouble for themselves and for others. Perhaps it might be best for me to reduce them to complete slavery, for now I feel like someone who has killed the father but spared the children.[a] [2] I took you, who were more than a father to the Lydians, into captivity, but I handed Sardis back to the Lydians themselves. So after that should I be surprised that they would rebel against me?" Thus Cyrus expressed his thoughts, and Croesus, in fear that he would expel the Lydians from Sardis, answered, [3] "Sire, what you said makes sense, but do not be so overcome by your anger that you may destroy an ancient city

1.154
c. 545
LYDIA
Lydia revolts against Persian rule.

1.155
SARDIS
Croesus saves Sardis from Cyrus' wrath by proposing to turn the Sardians into shopkeepers.

1.153.1a   It is interesting to note that Cyrus did not know who the Spartans were or how numerous they were. In short, he had probably never heard of them before. This is one of several indications that Persian knowledge of the peoples and geography west of Asia was quite limited.
1.153.2a   The agora was the civic center of a Greek polis, where all political, commercial, and much social activity took place. See Glossary.
1.153.3a   Ecbatana: Map 1.157, locator.
1.153.4a   Babylon: Map 1.157, locator.
1.153.4b   Baktrians (Baktria): Map 1.157, locator.
1.153.4c   There are two distinct ethnic groups

called Sakai or Sacae. The "Sacae" are Scythians, living to the east of Scythia; the other group, which, following the *Barrington Atlas*, I have called the "Sakai," were definitely not Scythians. They lived on the coast of the Indian Ocean near the mouth of the Indus River. It is not clear which of these groups Herodotus is identifying here. For both groups, see Map 1.157, locator.
1.153.4d   Egypt: Map 1.157, locator.
1.154.1a   Lydia: Map 1.157.
1.155.1a   Herodotus has Cyrus allude to a well-known Greek proverb: "Foolish is he who kills the father but leaves the children behind."

whose people were guiltless before and are guiltless even now, despite the present situation. For what happened before was my doing, and I bear the guilt for it on my own head. But right now, it is Paktyes who does you wrong; he is the man you left in charge of Sardis. You should make him pay the penalty [4] and pardon the rest of the Lydians. You could prevent them from being rebellious or a threat to you in the future by ordering the following steps: prohibit them from possessing weapons of war, order them to wear tunics under their cloaks and soft boots, instruct them to play the lyre and the harp, and tell them to educate their sons to be shopkeepers. If you do this, sire, you will soon see that they will become women instead of men and thus will then pose no danger or threat to you of any future rebellion."

1.156

LYDIA

Cyrus decides to follow Croesus' advice about the Lydians.

Croesus gave this advice to Cyrus because he realized that these conditions would be better for the Lydians than those which they would face if they were enslaved and sold. He knew that if he did not put forth a compelling case, he would not be able to persuade Cyrus to change his mind, and he was worried that even if the Lydians did manage to emerge unharmed from their present danger, they might someday rebel from the Persians again and then they would certainly be destroyed. [2] Cyrus, however, was so pleased with this plan that his anger abated and he said he would follow Croesus' advice. He then summoned a Mede named Mazares and told him to order the Lydians to carry out the steps which Croesus had advised and in addition to enslave all those who had joined the war against the Persians in Sardis with the Lydians, and above all to take Paktyes alive and bring him back to Cyrus.

1.157

SARDIS-CYME

Sardis is taken by the Persians. Paktyes, leader of the revolt, escapes to Cyme. The Persians demand his surrender.

Cyrus was still on his journey to Ecbatana[a] when he gave these orders, and now he continued his march into the heartland of Persia.[b] As for Paktyes, when he learned there was a Persian army nearby and closing in on him, he was stricken with fear and left at once, fleeing to Cyme.[c] [2] Mazares the Mede, who marched on Sardis with a part of Cyrus' army, discovered upon his arrival that Paktyes and his followers had fled. So his first act was to compel the Lydians to follow Cyrus' instructions, and when they carried out these orders, the Lydians changed their entire way of living. [3] Mazares next sent messengers to Cyme to demand that Paktyes be handed over to him. The Cymaeans resolved to refer this question to the god at Branchidai[a] and to ask for advice. For a long-established oracle existed there which all the Ionians and Aeolians[b] traditionally consulted. Its location is in Milesian territory overlooking the harbor called Panormos.[c]

1.158

CYME

The Cymaeans consult the oracle at Branchidai.

And so the men of Cyme sent sacred delegates to consult the oracle at Branchidai and asked what course of action concerning Paktyes would be pleasing to the gods. The oracle's response to this question was that they

1.157.1a Ecbatana: Map 1.157, locator.
1.157.1b Persia: Map 1.157, locator.
1.157.1c Cyme: Map 1.157.
1.157.3a Branchidai (Didyma): Map 1.157. See n. 1.46.2f.

1.157.3b Ionians and Aeolians: see Appendix K, §7–9.
1.157.3c Panormos: Map 1.157.

Map 1.157

should hand over Paktyes to the Persians. When the Cymaeans heard the report of the oracle, a majority of them were inclined to hand him over; [2] but a distinguished citizen named Aristodikos son of Herakleides prevented the Cymaeans from doing this, because he distrusted the oracular response, suspecting that the sacred delegates were not telling the truth. Finally another group of sacred delegates, which included Aristodikos, were sent to the oracle to inquire about Paktyes.

1.159
BRANCHIDAI
Aristodikos, chosen to question the oracle at Branchidai, elicits the same response from the god and a threat that obedience will lead to destruction for impiety.

(margin handwritten note: IMP. of protecting guest)

When they arrived at Branchidai, they consulted the oracle, choosing Aristodikos to present the question: "Lord[a] Apollo, Paktyes the Lydian has come to us as a suppliant, trying to escape a violent death at the hands of the Persians. And now the Persians demand that we surrender him to them. [2] Even though we fear the power of the Persians, we have not dared to hand over the suppliant to his enemies until you have specifically revealed the correct course of action to us." To this inquiry, the god made the same response as before, ordering them to hand over Paktyes to the Persians.

[3] Aristodikos had expected this response and was prepared to react to it. He walked around the entire circuit of the temple, chasing away all the sparrows and the rest of the birds nesting there. It is said that as he did this, a voice came out of the inner chamber and reached the ears of Aristodikos, saying, "You, most ungodly man, how dare you rob my temple of its suppliants?" Aristodikos without hesitation replied, [4] "So, Lord Apollo, do you strive to protect your own suppliants while ordering the Cymaeans to give up theirs?" The god answered, "Indeed I do, so that you will all be destroyed the sooner for your impiety and thus never again consult oracles about the surrender of suppliants."[a]

1.160
MYTILENE-CHIOS
The Cymaeans send Paktyes to Mytilene and then to Chios. The Chians deliver him to the Persians.

When the Cymaeans received the report of this exchange, they decided that they wanted neither to be destroyed for handing over Paktyes, nor to be besieged for keeping him, so they sent him off to Mytilene.[a] [2] Mazares then sent a message to the Mytilenians ordering them to hand over Paktyes; and they made ready to do so, for a specified price. I do not know the exact amount, since it was never paid, [3] for when the Cymaeans found out what the Mytilenians intended to do, they sent a boat to Lesbos[a] and conveyed Paktyes to Chios.[b] But there he was torn from the sanctuary of Athena Poliochos[c] and handed over to the Persians by the Chians—also for a price. [4] They gave him up in exchange for the possession of Atarneus,[a] a district in the territory of Mysia[b] on the mainland opposite Lesbos. Once the Persians had taken Paktyes into their custody, they kept him under guard and looked forward to presenting him to Cyrus. [5] As for the Chians, a long time passed before any of them would use barley meal from Atarneus in any of their sacrifices to the gods, or use its grain in any cakes they baked for the gods. In fact, all the produce from this place was barred from all sacred rituals.

1.161
545?
IONIA
Priene is enslaved, Magnesia pillaged.

Now having captured Paktyes, Mazares proceeded to make war on those who had joined in the siege of Tabalos at Sardis.[a] He first captured Priene[b] and enslaved its inhabitants, then he invaded the entire plain of the River Maeander[c] and gave it over to his army to plunder, just as he also gave over the territory of Magnesia.[d] After having accomplished these things, he died suddenly of an illness.

1.159.1a Herodotus uses the word *anax*, which means either "lord" or "master" but is used for heroes and gods, especially for Apollo.
1.159.4a Inscrutable oracles: see Appendix P, §8–9.
1.160.1a Mytilene: Map 1.157.
1.160.3a Lesbos: Map 1.157.
1.160.3b Chios: Map 1.157.
1.160.3c Athena the Guardian of the City, another aspect of this multifaceted goddess.
1.160.4a Atarneus: Map 1.57.
1.160.4b Mysia: Map 1.157.
1.161.1a Sardis: Map 1.157.
1.161.1b Priene: Map 1.157.
1.161.1c Maeander River: Map 1.157. See Figure 1.161.
1.161.1d Magnesia (on the Maeander): Map 1.157.

FIGURE 1.161. VIEW OF TEMPLE REMAINS FROM PRIENE, OVERLOOKING THE MAEANDER RIVER PLAIN, WHICH IN ANCIENT TIMES WAS COMPLETELY UNDER WATER.

After Mazares died, command of the army passed to his successor, Harpagos. A Mede by origin, this Harpagos was the same man who had been served that offensive meal by Astyages, the king of the Medes,[a] and who had subsequently helped Cyrus to obtain the kingship.[b] [2] Now that Cyrus had appointed him general, Harpagos went to Ionia,[a] where he captured the cities there by investing them with earthworks. For whenever he had forced the people of a city to shut themselves up within their walls, he would then pile mounds of earth[b] up against the walls as he laid siege to the city.

His initial attack was against the Ionian city of Phocaea.[a] Now the Phocaeans were the first of the Hellenes to make long sea voyages; they are the ones who opened up the Adriatic,[b] Tyrrhenia,[c] Iberia,[d] and Tartessos[e] to the Hellenes. [2] They did not sail in round-sided ships,[a] but in penteconters. When they went to Tartessos, they made friends with the king of the Tartessians, whose name was Arganthonios. He ruled as

1.162
545?
IONIA
The Persians under
Harpagos capture
Ionian cities by means
of earthworks.

1.163
PHOCAEA
Description of early
Phocaean sea voyages.

1.162.1a   See 1.117–119 for a description of the
            "offensive meal" served to Harpagos.
1.162.1b   See 1.123–129 for how Harpagos helped
            Cyrus overthrow the rule of the Medes.
1.162.2a   Ionia: Map 1.166, inset.
1.162.2b   This is an example of Persia's adoption of
            Mesopotamian technology and science, in
            this case siege equipment and procedures,
            to use against the Greeks, whose cities
            had heretofore been impregnable against
            each other and against the weapons and
            tactics of hoplite warfare. See Appendix
            O, The Persian Army in Herodotus, §9.
            See also Figure 1.162a, showing the
            current remains of the siege mound that

was constructed by the Assyrians against
Lachish, Judea, which they captured in
704; and Figure 1.162b, showing a detail
of the representation of that siege from a
frieze in Sennacherib's palace.

1.163.1a   Phocaea: Map 1.166, inset.
1.163.1b   Adriatic Sea: Map 1.166.
1.163.1c   Tyrrhenia (Etruria): Map 1.166.
1.163.1d   Iberia: Map 1.166, locator.
1.163.1e   Tartessos: Map 1.166, locator.
1.163.2a   By "round-sided" ships, Herodotus
            means merchant ships, which were
            broad-beamed and propelled mostly by
            sails. See Appendix S, §3–5, 21.

FIGURE 1.162A. THE MOUND BUILT BY ASSYRIANS AT LACHISCH, JUDEA, AS PART OF THE SIEGE WORKS BY WHICH THEY CAPTURED THE FORTRESS IN 704. THE PERSIANS ADOPTED ADVANCED SIEGE TECHNOLOGY AND METHODS FROM THE ASSYRIANS THEY CONQUERED AND USED THEM TO GOOD EFFECT AGAINST THE GREEK CITIES OF ASIA.

tyrant[b] of Tartessos for 80 years, and lived for all of 120 years. [3] The Phocaeans became such good friends with this man that he urged them to leave Ionia behind and settle wherever they wished in his country; then, when he could not persuade them to do that, and learning that the growing power of the Mede[a] was beginning to threaten them, he gave them a very generous amount of money to build a wall around their city.[b] [4] In fact, the circumference of the wall they built measures a great number of stades[a] and it is constructed entirely of huge stones fitted securely together.

That is how the Phocaeans built their wall. And now Harpagos led his army there, but as he prepared to besiege the Phocaeans, he sent them a proposal to

1.164

c. 545

PHOCAEA

The Phocaeans build a city wall but decide, when besieged by Harpagos, to leave their city and settle elsewhere.

1.163.2b For a description of a Greek tyrant, see Appendix T, §1.

1.163.3a "Mede" here might refer to the Persian King Cyrus or the Persians collectively, because Herodotus and many of his Greek contemporaries sometimes used the term "Mede" or "Median" for Persian. In this case, where we are not sure when the relationship between the

Phocaeans and Tartessos developed, the use of the term "Mede" may indeed apply to the Medes before their conquest by Cyrus the Persian.

1.163.3b Perhaps this anecdote serves to illustrate the Greek reliance upon city walls at that time, and their ignorance of effective Persian siege craft.

1.163.4a See Appendix J, §6, 19.

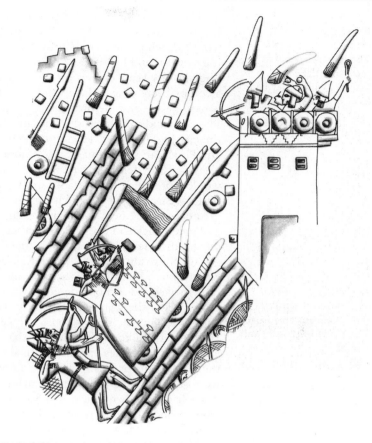

Figure 1.162b. Drawing of a detail from an Assyrian frieze in the palace of Sennacherib portraying the capture of Lachisch in 704. It shows a sophisticated mobile battering ram that ascends on plank pathways set into the siege mound built by the attackers. By this means the ram (one of many shown) closes with and batters down the walls. The defenders are shown throwing torches down to burn the rams, but the attackers pour water over the top and front of the vehicles to prevent ignition. Archers and slingers support the attack.

the effect that he would be quite satisfied if they would demolish just one of their wall towers and consecrate[a] one building. [2] The Phocaeans, distressed at the thought of slavery, replied by saying they wanted one day to deliberate, promising that they would then give him an answer. But they demanded that while they were deliberating, he would lead his army some distance away from the wall. Harpagos replied that although he knew quite well what they intended to do, he would nevertheless allow them to deliberate.

[3] And so while Harpagos marched his army away from the wall, the Phocaeans hauled their penteconters down to the sea and loaded them with all of their women, children, and moveable goods; and they took their statues and other offerings from their sanctuaries, all except those of bronze or stone and the inscriptions, which they left. Once the ships were loaded, they boarded them and sailed to Chios.[a] The Persians thus gained possession of Phocaea, but it was an empty city—there were no Phocaeans in it.

1.164.1a Herodotus uses a word here referring to the dedication of property to the gods, but which "probably means in this instance that the Phocaeans were supposed to declare solemnly that one house to be the king's property, a material and symbolic sign of submission." (McNeal)

1.164.3a Chios: Map 1.166, inset.

1.165
c. 545
CORSICA
The Phocaeans sail to their city Alalie on Corsica, which they had built twenty years earlier.

The Phocaeans first tried to buy the Oinoussai Islands[a] from the Chians, but the Chians refused to sell them. They were afraid that the Phocaeans would develop the islands into a center of commerce that would exclude their own island from trade. So the Phocaeans set sail for Corsica (Kyrnos),[b] since twenty years earlier, on the advice of a prophecy, they had established a colony there called Alalie,[c] and anyway, [2] by this time, Aganthonios had passed away.[a] But before starting out for Alalie, they first sailed back to Phocaea[b] and murdered the Persian garrison who had been left in charge of the city by Harpagos. Having done this deed, they resolutely laid curses on any Phocaean who remained behind and did not accompany them on their journey. [3] Then they sank into the sea a mass of iron[a] and swore that they would not return until it appeared again. But as they set out for Kyrnos, a pitiful yearning for their city and the customs of their land seized the greater part of them, so many of the Phocaeans broke their recent oaths and sailed back to Phocaea. The others, however, honored their pledge and, setting their sails, began their voyage from Oinoussai.

1.166
539
CORSICA
"Kadmeian" victory of the Phocaeans at sea over a combined Etruscan and Carthaginian naval force.

After arriving on Corsica, they lived for five years with those who had come earlier, sharing their settlement and building sanctuaries. During that time they raided and plundered all the neighboring settlements until they had so provoked the Tyrrhenians[a] and Carthaginians[b] that each of these powers agreed to furnish sixty ships to wage war against the Phocaeans. [2] In response, the Phocaeans manned sixty ships of their own and went out to engage their enemies on what is called the Sardinian Sea.[a] The Phocaeans won the battle, but for them it was a Kadmeian victory,[b] since forty of their ships were destroyed and the twenty remaining were rendered useless because their beaks had been bent back.[c] [3] So they sailed back to Alalie, picked up their women and children, took on board as many of their other possessions as their ships could carry and, leaving Corsica behind, sailed to Rhegion.[a]

1.167
CAERE
The Etruscan city Caere kills its Phocaean prisoners.

The Carthaginians and Tyrrhenians divided by lot all the men taken prisoner from the ships they had destroyed, who were more numerous than those who had escaped. They brought them to shore at Caere[a] and there stoned them to death. After this event all living things in Caere that

1.165.1a Oinoussai Islands: Map 1.166, inset.
1.165.1b Corsica: Map 1.166. Herodotus calls this island "Kyrnos."
1.165.1c Alalie: Map 1.166.
1.165.2a See 1.163.3 for the offer made by Aganthonios, tyrant of Tartessos, for the Phocaeans to settle in his country, which they had refused.
1.165.2b Phocaea: Map 1.166, inset.
1.165.3a This method of making a most solemn oath occurs elsewhere in ancient Greek history, and it is possible, although by no means certain, that ritual required the iron to be red-hot.
1.166.1a Tyrrhenia (Etruria): Map 1.166.
1.166.1b Carthage: Map 1.166. Herodotus calls the Carthaginians "Karchedonioi."
1.166.2a Sardinian Sea: Map 1.166.

1.166.2b A "Kadmeian" victory was one in which the victor suffered crushing losses, like a later "Pyrrhic victory." Such a victory proverbially derives from the two sons of Oedipus, Eteocles and Polynices, who slaughter each other in the war of the Seven Against Thebes. (How and Wells)
1.166.2c Beaks bent back refers to the bronze rams at the prows of the ships that were disabled. See Appendix S, §12.
1.166.3a Rhegion: Map 1.166.
1.167.1a Caere: Map 1.166. Herodotus calls this city "Agylla." The Romans called it "Caere," which was close to the Etruscan name for this Etruscan city. The text here is uncertain. It is possible that some of it has been lost.

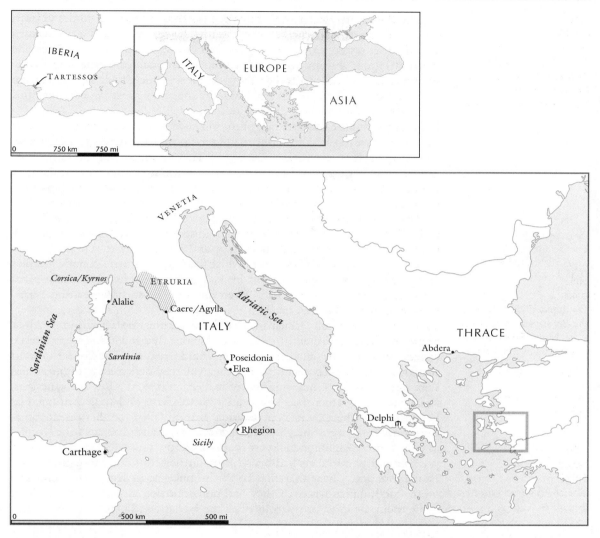

MAP 1.166

passed nearby the place where the remains of the Phocaeans who had been stoned to death lay, whether they were flocks, oxen, or human beings, would suffer strokes and become twisted and crippled. [2] The Caereans sent to Delphi[a] wishing to set right their offense and did what the Pythia ordered, as they still do today: they sacrifice to the Phocaeans who were stoned to death as to heroes and hold athletic and equestrian competitions in their honor.[b]

[3] That was the ultimate fate of those Phocaeans, but the others who fled to Rhegion[a] set out later from there and took possession of a city in Oinotrian territory which is now called Elea.[b] [4] They founded this city after they learned from a Poseidonian[a] man that the Pythia had not meant for them to found a city on the island of Corsica, but rather to institute the worship of the hero of that name.[b] That is what happened to the Phocaeans of Ionia.

The people of Teos[a] reacted to Harpagos in a similar way. When, by his earthworks, he had taken their wall, he discovered that they were already gone, for they had boarded their ships and sailed away to Thrace.[b] There they founded the city of Abdera,[c] which had actually been founded earlier by Timesios of Klazomenai,[d] but he had not been able to hold the place against the Thracians, who had driven him out. Now, however, the Teians in Abdera honor him as a hero.[e]

These were the only Ionians who refused to tolerate slavery and left their homeland. Like them, all of the Ionians who stayed behind (except for the Milesians) faced the challenge of resisting Harpagos. These men fought courageously for their country. But they suffered defeat and conquest and then stayed in their cities, submitting to Persian rule. [2] But the Milesians, as I mentioned earlier, had sworn an oath to Cyrus and thus continued to live in peace. That, then, is how Ionia[a] was enslaved for the second time. And once Harpagos had conquered the mainland Ionians, the Ionian islanders[b] grew frightened and also submitted to Cyrus.

Although the Ionians had been hit hard, they continued to gather at the Panionion, and I hear that Bias of Priene once proposed to the Ionians a most practical plan which, if they had only followed his advice, would have made them the most prosperous of all the Hellenes. [2] He counseled them to set sail together on a voyage to Sardinia[a] and, once there, to found a city that would belong to all Ionians. Thus they would set themselves free from slavery and become prosperous through their possession of the largest of all islands and in their rule over others. But he predicted that there would be no freedom for them in the future if they remained in Ionia. [3] This was

1.168
TEOS-ABDERA
The Teians also leave Ionia and found Abdera in Thrace.

1.169
545
IONIA
All the Ionians are conquered except the Milesians, who have a treaty with the Persians.

1.170
IONIA
Bias of Priene advises the Ionians to leave en masse and found a single city on Sardinia for all Ionians.

1.167.2a Delphi: Map 1.166.
1.167.2b Communal atonement through sacrifice.
1.167.3a Rhegion: Map 1.166.
1.167.3b Elea: Map 1.166. Herodotus' text here calls the place "Hyele," not Elea.
1.167.4a Poseidonia, Italy: Map 1.166. Poseidonia was called "Paestum" by the Romans.
1.167.4b Kyrnos was the son of Herakles. The island Herodotus calls "Kyrnos" is modern Corsica.

1.168.1a Teos: Map 1.166, inset.
1.168.1b Thrace: Map 1.166.
1.168.1c Abdera: Map 1.166.
1.168.1d Klazomenai: Map 1.166, inset.
1.168.1e It was customary for ancient Greek cities to worship their founders as cult heroes.
1.169.2a Ionia: Map 1.166, inset.
1.169.2b See 1.142.3–4 for a list of the Ionian cities on the mainland and on the nearby islands.
1.170.2a Sardinia (Sardo in the Greek): Map 1.166.

the plan that Bias of Priene proposed to the Ionians after their defeat. But even prior to their defeat, another good plan had been proposed by Thales of Miletus, a Phoenician by descent. He recommended that the Ionians establish a single central council house in Teos (for Teos is at the midpoint of Ionia), and that the other cities be treated as though they were demes.[a]

Well, then, such were the plans they proposed.

When Harpagos had finished subjugating Ionia,[a] he marched against the Carians,[b] the Caunians,[c] and the Lycians,[d] bringing Ionian and Aeolian[e] troops along with him. [2] The Carians came to the mainland from the Cyclades islands.[a] Long ago they had occupied the islands as subjects of Minos[b] and were called the Leleges. As far back as I have been able to trace them by hearsay, they paid no tribute to Minos but did provide the manpower for his ships whenever he needed them. [3] Inasmuch as Minos conquered a great deal of territory and was successful in war, the Carians became by far the most famous of all peoples at that time. [4] The Hellenes, in fact, adopted three of their inventions for their own use. The Carians taught them how to tie plumes to helmets, to decorate shields with devices, and to attach handles to shields. Indeed, they were the first to use shield handles; until then anyone who bore a shield manipulated it not by handles, but rather by a leather strap worn around the neck and left shoulder.[a] [5] Many years later, the Dorians[a] and Ionians expelled the Carians from the islands, and so they came to the mainland. At least that is what the Cretans say happened, but the Carians themselves say they are indigenous to the mainland and have always had the name they do now. [6] As proof, they point to the ancient sanctuary of Carian Zeus in Mylasa,[a] which the Mysians[b] and Lydians[c] share with them as kinsmen of the Carians, since Mysos and Lydos were brothers of Car.[d] These, in fact, are the only ones who share the sanctuary; no one belonging to any other group is admitted to it, not even those who speak the same language as the Carians.

The Caunians, although they seem to me to be indigenous to their region, claim that they originally came from Crete. Their language resembles the Carians', or perhaps that of the Carians resembles theirs; this I cannot judge for certain. Their customs, however, are very different from those of the Carians and everyone else. For all of them—men, women, and children—believe that the most excellent and beautiful way to pass the time is to gather

1.171
545
CARIA
Harpagos continues the conquest of Asia Minor. Herodotus describes the origins of the Carians.

1.172
CAUNUS
Herodotus describes the origins and some customs of the Caunians.

1.170.3a   Herodotus means that the cities would stand in the same relation to the central council as, for instance, the Athenian demes stand in relation to the council in Athens, meaning the cities would no longer be autonomous. See Appendix A, §7.
1.171.1a   Ionia: Map 1.173.
1.171.1b   Caria: Map 1.173 and inset.
1.171.1c   Caunus: Map 1.173, inset.
1.171.1d   Lycia: Map 1.173 and inset.
1.171.1e   Aeolis: Map 1.173.
1.171.2a   Cyclades (islands): Map 1.173.
1.171.2b   Minos to the Hellenes was a mythical ruler of a legendary seafaring culture and empire based on the island of Crete

(Creta): Map 1.173.
1.171.4a   This is the management of the Homeric "man-covering" shield, as described in the *Iliad*. The shield is not carried on the arm, but hangs by a belt which passes over the left shoulder and under the right armpit; it can be shifted so as to protect the breast or back.
1.171.5a   Dorians: see Appendix K, §7–9.
1.171.6a   Mylasa: Map 1.173, inset.
1.171.6b   Mysia: Map 1.173.
1.171.6c   Lydia: Map 1.173.
1.171.6d   This is an excellent example of the Greek habit of explaining the present through the names of ancestors.

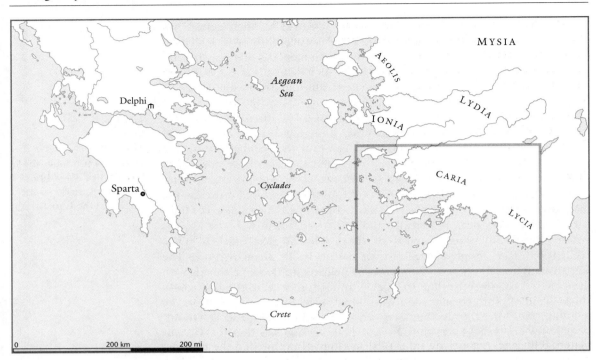

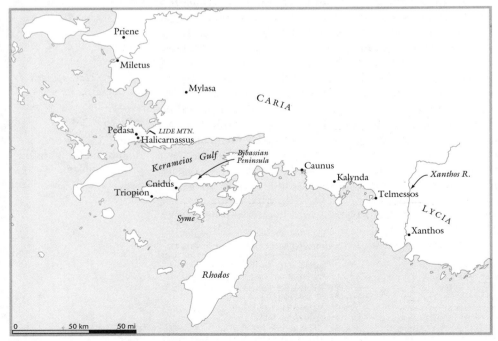

MAP 1.173

together with friends of the same age and to drink. [2] Moreover, sometime after the worship of foreign gods had spread throughout their land, they decided to reject all of them and honor only their own ancestral gods. So all the Caunians in the prime of life armed themselves and, striking at the air with their spears, chased the foreign gods all the way to the border of the Kalyndans.[a] In this way, they claim, they threw out the foreign gods.

The Lycians did come from Crete in ancient times. Actually, barbarians occupied all of Crete long ago. [2] But Sarpedon and Minos, the sons of Europa, quarreled over the kingship of Crete, and when Minos prevailed in this strife, he drove out Sarpedon and his supporters. Expelled from Crete, they came to Milyas in Asia. For the land the Lycians now inhabit was once called Milyas, and the Milyans were at that time called Solymoi. [3] Sarpedon ruled them for a time. And they were called by the name they brought with them from Crete, the same name that their neighbors still call the Lycians today: the Termilai. In the course of time, they acquired the name Lycians from Lykos son of Pandion. He, too, was driven out of his homeland, Athens, by his brother Aigeus and came to the Termilai and to Sarpedon. [4] The customs of the Lycians are partly Cretan and partly Carian. But they have one unique custom of their own which is not observed among any other people. They name themselves after their mothers and not their fathers. [5] If one person asks another who he is, he will recite his maternal lineage, recounting his mother and grandmother and the mothers before her. And if a native free woman has children by a slave, their children are considered legitimate; but if a native free man has a foreign wife or concubine, their children have no civic status or civic rights.

Now the Carians did not distinguish themselves in opposing Harpagos; indeed they submitted to him without performing any glorious deeds, and the same can be said, too, of all the Hellenes who lived in that region of Asia: none displayed valor. [2] Among the Hellenes dwelling in this area were the Cnidians,[a] colonists from Lacedaemon,[b] whose settlement faces the sea and is called Triopion.[c] Their territory begins at the Bybassian Peninsula,[d] which, except for a narrow land bridge to the mainland, is completely surrounded by water. [3] The Kerameios Gulf[a] borders the peninsula on the north, the sea off Syme[b] and Rhodos[c] on the south. The narrow isthmus connecting the Cnidian territory to the mainland is about 3,000 feet[d] wide.

While Harpagos was subjugating Ionia, the Cnidians tried to dig through this strip of land, with the intent of making their own land an island, since all the territory to the west of where they were digging belonged to them. [4] But the extent to which the huge crew of Cnidians who worked here on the

1.173
LYCIA
The origins of the Lycians and their unusual matriarchal family lines.

1.174
CNIDUS
The Cnidians, advised by Delphi, cease work on the ditch that would turn their peninsula into an island.

1.172.2a Kalynda: Map 1.173, inset.
1.174.2a Cnidus: Map 1.173, inset.
1.174.2b Lacedaemon (Sparta): Map 1.173.
    Herodotus uses the names Spartans
    and Lacedaemonians interchangeably.
    "Spartans," however, often refers specifi-
    cally to citizens of the state of Sparta,
    whereas any inhabitant of the territory
    of Lacedaemon is a Lacedaemonian. See

Appendix B, §5, 7, and n. B.7a.
1.174.2c Triopion: Map 1.173, inset.
1.174.2d Bybassian Peninsula (on which Cnidus is
    located): Map 1.173, inset.
1.174.3a Kerameios Gulf: Map 1.173, inset.
1.174.3b Syme: Map 1.173, inset.
1.174.3c Rhodos: Map 1.173, inset.
1.174.3d Herodotus writes "5 stades" here. See
    Appendix J, §6, 19.

canal suffered injuries seemed almost supernatural. They were injured all over their bodies, but especially in their eyes, because of the smashing of rock. So they sent sacred delegates to Delphi[a] to ask why this was happening. [5] The Cnidians claim that the Pythia gave them this response in trimeter verses:

> Do not wall off the isthmus; do not dig through the isthmus;
> Had Zeus wished it to be an island, he would have made it thus himself.

[6] When the Cnidians received this response from the Pythia, they stopped digging and gave themselves up without resistance to Harpagos, who at that moment was advancing toward them with his army.

Above Halicarnassus[a] and inland from it live the Pedasians.[b] Whenever they or their neighbors have been threatened by some calamity or other, their priestess of Athena would grow a long beard, and this omen had occurred three times in the past.[c] These were the only men in this region of Caria who resisted Harpagos for a time, and they also gave him more trouble than all the others by fortifying a mountain called Lide.[d] But in time the Pedasians, too, were conquered.

When Harpagos led his army onto the plain of Xanthos,[a] the Lycians attacked him suddenly and fought, a few against many, and with great valor. They were defeated, however, and forced to retire inside their walls. Once trapped in their city, they gathered together their women, children, possessions, and servants on the acropolis[b] and set fire to it, burning up everything. [2] Then, having sworn powerful oaths, the men of Xanthos went forth again to do battle against Harpagos. They all died fighting. [3] And so, the present-day Lycians who claim to be Xanthians are mostly immigrants, with the exception of eighty families, whose ancestors at the time of the battle happened to be abroad and thus survived. That is how Harpagos took Xanthos. He took Caunus[a] in a similar way, since the Caunian response to Harpagos was much like that of the Lycians.

Thus Harpagos laid waste to the regions in southern Asia;[a] meanwhile, Cyrus himself set upon the northern regions, subjugating all the peoples; and none of them were spared. The greater part of them we shall pass by without comment, but I shall tell of those who gave him the most trouble, and who are also the most noteworthy.

After Cyrus had subjected all of the mainland of Asia to his rule, he attacked the Assyrians.[a] There are, no doubt, many great cities of Assyria, but the strongest and most notable was Babylon,[b] where the royal palace was established after the overthrow of Nineveh.[c] Let me describe what the city is

---

1.175

?

CARIA

Among the Carians, only the Pedasians held out for a while against Harpagos.

1.176

?

LYCIA

The Lycians resist Harpagos to the end, burning down their city and killing their families and themselves.

1.177

?

ASIA

Harpagos and Cyrus continue conquests.

1.178

539

BABYLON

Cyrus attacks Babylon. Herodotus describes that city.

1.174.4a Delphi: Map 1.173.
1.175.1a Halicarnassus: Map 1.173, inset.
1.175.1b Pedasa: Map 1.173, inset.
1.175.1c Herodotus tells the same story in 8.104, but there he tells us it has occurred only twice before.
1.175.1d Mount Lide: Map 1.173, inset.
1.176.1a Xanthos River: Map 1.173, inset.
1.176.1b Acropolis: see n. 1.15.1f and Glossary.

1.176.3a Caunus: Map 1.173, inset.
1.177.1a Asia: Map 1.183. When Herodotus and other ancient Hellenes spoke of Asia, they meant the land we call Asia Minor, now occupied by the modern state of Turkey.
1.178.1a Assyria: Map 1.183.
1.178.1b Babylon: Map 1.183.
1.178.1c Nineveh: Map 1.183.

like. [2] Situated on a vast plain, it is shaped like a square measuring thirteen and a half miles on each side, with a perimeter of about 55 miles;[a] that is how large the urban area of Babylon is. And it is designed like no other city known to us. [3] First, a deep, wide moat full of water surrounds it and forms its outer boundary. Next there is a wall 76 feet in width, 304 feet in height. The royal cubit is three fingers longer than the common cubit.[a]

I must also reveal what use they made of the earth dug from the moat, and how they constructed the wall. While they were digging the moat, they took the clay thus excavated from it and made it into bricks, and when they had molded a sufficient number, they baked the bricks in kilns. [2] Then, using hot bitumen[a] as mortar, they built up the banks of the moat and stuffed reed mats in between at intervals of every thirty layers. Next, they built the wall using the same method. [3] Along the top edge of the wall, they built one-story chambers facing each other, leaving a space about the size of a passageway for a four-horse chariot between each. Around the wall they installed 100 gates all of bronze, including the pillars and the lintels. [4] There is another city that lies eight days away from Babylon called Is.[a] Here there is a small river of the same name which flows into the River Euphrates.[b] It is this River Is that gives forth with its water the many lumps of bitumen from which they obtained what they needed for the wall in Babylon.

That is how the wall around Babylon was built. The city has two districts, for the River Euphrates divides it in half through the middle. This river is large, deep, and swift. [2] The wall on either bank extends down to the river at an angle and from this point turns to form a drywall brick rampart along each bank of the river. [3] The town itself is full of houses three and four stories high. Its streets are laid out in straight lines; they all run either at right angles or parallel to the river. [4] At the end of each street leading to the river, there is a little gate set into the rampart; all the streets in this direction have these gates, which are made of bronze and which open on the other side onto the river itself.

While the outer wall is the city's main defense, there is another wall within it extending around the city which is not much weaker but is narrower than the outer one. [2] In the center of one of the city's two districts, they have built the royal palace, fortified and surrounded by a huge impregnable wall. In the other district they built the sanctuary of Zeus

1.179
BABYLON
Description of Babylon continues.

1.180
BABYLON
Description of Babylon continues.

1.181
BABYLON
Description of Babylon continues.

1.178.2a Herodotus writes that the wall was a "square 120 stades on a side." See Appendix J, §6, 19. In Attic stades, that would be a square city of Babylon measuring more than 13.2 miles on a side. These colossal dimensions and the fact that archaeological excavations suggest that the city may not have been built in the shape of a square have led some scholars to question whether Herodotus ever visited Babylon at all. See Introduction, §4.4.

1.178.3a Herodotus writes these dimensions as "50 royal cubits" wide and "200 royal cubits" high. The royal cubit measures 20.5 inches, so Herodotus is describing a wall approximately 76 feet wide and 304 feet high. Of course that is simply not plausible. See Appendix J, §4, 5, 19. Whether Herodotus ever actually went to Babylon is a problem which scholars continue to debate; many seem to feel that he did actually go there.

1.179.2a Bitumen: naturally occurring tar, asphalt, or heavy oil residues found by surface oil seeps in ancient times.

1.179.4a Is (Hit): Map 1.183.

1.179.4b Euphrates River: Map 1.183.

Belos,[a] which has a bronze gate and is shaped like a square, measuring 1,170 feet on each side.[b] It survives up to my time. [3] In the center of the sanctuary there is a solid tower, 583 feet[a] in length and in width, and upon this tower stands another tower, and another upon that and so on, rising to a height of eight towers. [4] On the outside they built a ramp leading upward around the towers in a circle.[a] Somewhere in the middle of the ascent is a shelter with benches where people climbing up may sit and rest. [5] On top of the highest tower stands a large temple, and within it is a huge bed generously covered with fine blankets, and next to it, a golden table. But no statue is erected there, and no one passes the night there except for one woman, the one whom the god has chosen out of all the native-born women of the land. So say the Chaldaeans, the priests of the god.

And these same priests claim—though it sounds incredible to me—that the god himself visits the temple and sleeps on the bed, just as the Egyptians claim that the same thing happens in Egyptian Thebes. [2] For there, too, the woman lies in the temple of Theban Zeus, and both women are said to engage in intercourse with no human men at all. The same claim is made about the oracular priestess of the god in Lycian Patara,[a] whenever he is there, that is, since the oracle is not always in use. But whenever the god is there, he lies with her at night inside his temple.

The same sanctuary in Babylon contains another temple below the one just described. Here there is a huge statue of Zeus, seated and made of gold. And next to him is set a table, also of gold, as are his footstool and throne. The Chaldaeans say that 800 talents[a] of gold were used to make all of this. [2] Outside the temple stands a golden altar. There is also another altar, a large one upon which full-grown animals are sacrificed. For it is not permitted to sacrifice anything on the golden altar but suckling animals. And upon the larger altar the Chaldaeans also burn 1,000 talents of frankincense every year when they celebrate the festival for this god. At the time of Cyrus, there was still a solid-gold statue eighteen feet[a] high in this precinct. [3] I myself did not see it but am reporting what is said by the Chaldaeans. Darius son of Hystaspes had designs on this statue but did not dare remove it; Xerxes son of Darius, however, did take it and killed the priest who was trying to forbid him to disturb the sacred image. In addition to the decoration of the sanctuary that I have already described, there are also many privately dedicated offerings here.

There were many rulers of Babylon who have further adorned the city with walls and sanctuaries. Some of these I will mention in my history of Assyria,[a] but of particular interest were two women rulers. The first of these

1.182
BABYLON
Description of Babylon continues.

1.183
BABYLON
Description of Babylon continues.

1.184
BABYLON
Two famous female rulers of Babylon.

1.181.2a Zeus Belos: Bel or Baal, the greatest god of the Assyrian pantheon.
1.181.2b Herodotus writes "2 stades" in length. See Appendix J, §6, 19.
1.181.3a Herodotus writes "1 stade" in height and width. See Appendix J, §6, 19.
1.181.4a Herodotus here is quite accurately describing a ziggurat, a not uncommon Mesopotamian temple.
1.182.2a Herodotus refers to Apollo, who was said to alternate giving oracles at Patara (Map

1.183), on the coast east of Xanthos in the winter, and on Delos in the summer.
1.183.1a The talent was a unit of weight that varied from place to place in the ancient world. See Appendix J, §11–13, 20.
1.183.2a Herodotus writes that it is "12 cubits" high. See Appendix J, §4, 5, 19.
1.184.1a A promise which Herodotus never fulfilled. There is no evidence that Herodotus ever wrote an "Assyrian history," as no ancient author ever indicates knowledge of it.

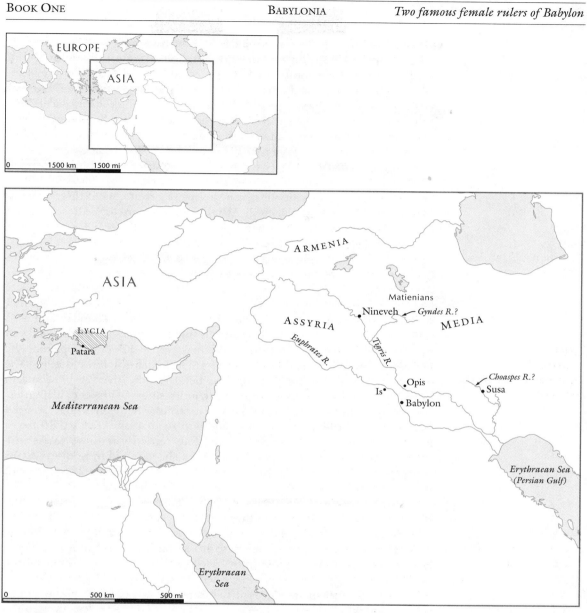

MAP 1.183

ruled five generations earlier than the other, and she was called Semiramis. It was she who created the spectacular dikes one sees throughout the plain. Before the dikes were constructed, the river regularly flooded the entire plain.

1.185

BABYLONIA

Constuction projects of the Babylonian queen Nitokris.

The queen who ruled after her was called Nitokris, and she was more intelligent than the earlier queen. She not only left behind memorials which I shall describe, but also perceived that the power of the Medes[a] was aggressive and menacing and that they had already taken a number of cities, Nineveh[b] in particular. And so she took as many defensive, precautionary measures as she could. [2] First, she diverted the River Euphrates,[a] which had been flowing straight through the center of the city. She did this by having channels dug farther upstream so that the river curved three times as it approached a certain village in Assyria called Arderikka.[b] After that, and even now, whoever travels to Babylon[c] from the north arrives at this village three times in three days while sailing down the River Euphrates.

[3] After completing this task, she also built up dikes on each bank of the river which are themselves worth seeing for their size and height. [4] And far upstream from Babylon, she ordered a basin to be dug out for a lake not far from from the river and consistently excavated to the depth at which water appeared. She made its circumference about 46 miles[a] and used the earth that was dug from the basin to build up dikes along the banks of the river. [5] When the excavation of the basin had been completed, she had stones brought in and lined up to form a circular rim around it. [6] She undertook both of these projects, the bends in the river and the marsh excavation, so that the river would flow more slowly with its course interrupted by many curves, and thus navigation into Babylon would proceed along a meandering course; and in addition to that, travelers would face a long detour around the lake itself. [7] She carried out these works in a region of the country through which ran the shortest and most direct access routes from Media, in order to prevent the Medes from having contact with her people and thereby gaining intelligence about her affairs.

1.186

BABYLON

Nitokris constructs brick river embankments and a bridge over the Euphrates at Babylon.

In this way she protected her city by digging soil from its depths, and at the same time she achieved another feat. Since the time of earlier kings, the two districts of the city had always been separated by the river flowing between them, and if anyone wanted to cross from one to the other, he had to cross by boat, which I suppose must have been annoying. But Nitokris made provision for this problem, too. For when the basin for the lake was dug, she left behind another memorial from this same project. [2] She quarried huge stones,[a] and when the excavation of the basin was complete, she diverted the entire flow of the river into it. As the basin filled, the old riverbed dried up, and during this dry period she built up the banks of the river in the city and

1.185.1a   Media: Map 1.183.
1.185.1b   Nineveh: Map 1.183.
1.185.2a   Euphrates River: Map 1.183.
1.185.2b   Arderikka: location unknown.
1.185.2c   Babylon: Map 1.183.
1.185.4a   Herodotus writes that this circumference is "420 stades." See Appendix J, §6, 19.

1.186.2a   Probably from the north, shipped down the Euphrates, and not from the basin, since large stones were scarce or nonexistent in Babylonia (How and Wells; Sayce).

constructed steps out of kiln-baked bricks that led from the little gates down to the river, in the same manner in which she had built the wall. Then, using the huge stones that she had quarried, and fastening them together with iron and lead, she built a bridge roughly in the center of the city. [3] During the day she had wooden platforms laid over the bridge, so that the Babylonians could cross over to either side. But at night they used to remove the platforms to prevent anyone from going back and forth and stealing from each other. [4] And so when the area that had been dug was filled up by the river and became a lake, and the bridge had been completed to perfection, she diverted the River Euphrates back to its old bed from the lake. Thus the excavated area became a marsh, which seemed to suit its intended purpose, and a bridge had been provided for the city's inhabitants.

This same queen also devised a clever ruse. She had a tomb for herself built in midair above the portal over the most frequented gate of the city and had this inscription engraved on the tomb: [2] "If any king of Babylon who comes after me needs money, let him open this tomb and take as much money as he wants. Let him not, however, open it unless he is truly in need. If he opens it for any other reason it will not go well with him."[a] [3] This tomb remained undisturbed until the kingship passed to Darius, who thought it was just terrible not to use this gate and not to take the money that was lying there with its inscription inviting someone to take it. [4] He refused to use the gate because if he drove through it, a corpse would be over his head.[a] [5] When he opened the tomb, however, he found no money inside, just the corpse and an inscription which read: "You would not open up the graves of the dead if you were not so insatiable and shamefully greedy." This, then, is the sort of queen she is said to have been.

Cyrus went to war against the son of Nitokris, who had the same name as his father, Labynetos,[a] and had inherited the kingdom of the Assyrians. When the great King goes out to war, he goes well equipped with food and herds from home, and especially with water drawn from the River Choaspes,[b] which flows past Susa.[c] The King drinks from this river only and none other. [2] Each time he marches out he is accompanied by numerous four-wheeled chariots, driven by mules, which carry silver jars holding water from the River Choaspes that has been boiled.

1.187
BABYLON
The tomb of Nitokris.

1.188
539
BABYLON
Cyrus attacks Nitokris' son Labynetos of Babylon.

1.187.2a This text says literally that to open the tomb without true need "is not the better course," which is familiar from Greek religious contexts, both in alternatives presented to an oracle to learn "the better course" of action, and in curses connected with tombs and disturbing the dead, where it implies a threat of divine retribution. Herodotus has the Persian King Darius use the same phrase at 3.71.2 and 3.82.5.

1.187.4a A practice which would have violated Persian (Zoroastrian) religion. Darius had no qualms about coming in contact with the corpse inside the tomb. That contradiction can be explained: Herodotus was told about Darius' refusal to use the gate and thus his annoyance with the tomb, but made up the other details of the story to help make sense of it to a Greek. (John Dillary, "Darius and the Tomb of Nitokris," *Classical Philology* 87 [1992] 30–38.)

1.188.1a Other reliable sources call this king Nabonidas, not Labynetos, but apparently this change in spelling reflects an occasional tendency in ancient Greek to change the letter/sound "N" to "L."

1.188.1b Choaspes River, possible location: Map 1.183.

1.188.1c Susa: Map 1.183.

1.189
539
BABYLONIA
Cyrus tames the Gyndes
River with canals.

When Cyrus was advancing to Babylon,[a] he came to the River Gyndes,[b] which, having its source in the land of the Matienians,[c] flows through the land of the Dardaneans[d] and empties into the River Tigris.[e] The Tigris flows past the city of Opis[f] and empties into the Erythraean Sea.[g] Now to cross the River Gyndes requires boats, and when one of Cyrus' sacred white horses audaciously stepped into the river and tried to cross it, the river's current swept him underwater and carried him off. [2] Cyrus was extremely angry at the river for its insolence and threatened that he would weaken it so much that in the future, women would be able to cross it easily without even getting their knees wet. [3] Having made this threat, he postponed his expedition against Babylon and divided his army into two units, one for each side of the river. Then, surveying with a rope, he marked out the ground for 180 channels on each side of the Gyndes and leading from it in every direction. [4] Because his labor force was large, this work was finally accomplished, but not until they had spent the whole summer there working on it.

1.190
539
BABYLON
Cyrus defeats the
Babylonians and
besieges the city.

Thus Cyrus punished the River Gyndes by dividing it into 360 channels. At the first signs of spring, he advanced toward Babylon. The Babylonians marched out and awaited him, and when Cyrus drew near the city, they joined battle with him. They were defeated, however, and forced to retire within the city walls. [2] Because the Babylonians had noted earlier how Cyrus was not at all peaceful, and had watched him attack and conquer so many other nations, they had prepared in advance for a siege by stockpiling enough food to last them many years. For this reason they were not at all concerned by the siege, and after much time had gone by and Cyrus had made no further progress, he found himself at an impasse.

1.191
539
BABYLON
Cyrus lowers the level of
the Euphrates and takes
the city by surprise.

Then, whether someone suggested it to him because he was at an impasse or whether he realized what had to be done himself, this is what he did. [2] Posting the main part of his army at the location where the river flows into the city, and another part of his army at the opposite end, where the river exits the city, he gave orders to the army that whenever they saw that the river had become fordable, they should enter the city via the riverbed. When he had thus assigned them to their posts, he marched away with that part of his army that was useless for battle. [3] When he arrived at the lake basin, he duplicated what the queen of the Babylonians had done to the river and lake basin. For he diverted the river through a channel into the lake basin, which had become a marsh, and thus made the river fordable as its waters subsided.

[4] When the Persians who were posted by the city saw the River Euphrates drop to about the level of midthigh for a man, they entered

1.189.1a Babylon: Map 1.183.
1.189.1b Gyndes River, possible location: Map 1.183.
1.189.1c Matienians (Matiane): Map 1.183.
1.189.1d Dardanean country referred to here is unknown.
1.189.1e Tigris River: Map 1.183.
1.189.1f Opis: Map 1.183.
1.189.1g Erythraean Sea here refers to what is now called the Persian Gulf: Map 1.183.

Herodotus recognizes only one sea south of Africa, Persia, and India and calls it, including the gulfs that extend north from it—the modern Red Sea and the Persian Gulf—the Erythraean Sea. However, on three occasions, he does call it the "Southern Sea" (2.11.3, 2.158, 3.17.1), and once he calls the modern Red Sea the "Arabian Gulf." See Appendix D, Herodotean Geography, §1–3.

~~Babylon according to Cyrus' plan.~~ [5] Now if the Babylonians had been able to surmise what Cyrus was doing, they could have allowed the Persians to enter the city by the riverbed and then destroyed them utterly. For they could have locked all the little gates leading to the river and, by climbing onto the ramparts extending along the riverbanks, would have caught the Persians there as if they had been so many fish in a barrel. [6] But as it was, the Persian maneuver took them by surprise. Because the city is so immense, its inhabitants say that when the Babylonians at the edges of the city were taken, those Babylonians who lived in the center were unaware of their capture because they happened to be celebrating a festival at that moment, and so they sang and danced and enjoyed themselves until they found out all too well what had happened. This is how Babylon fell to the Persians the first time.

I shall explain many sources of Babylonian power, but of particular interest is the following: the Great King of the Persians and his army receive a share of their support, besides the regular tribute, from each of the lands that he rules. Of the twelve months of the year, Babylonian territory provides his support for four months, all the rest of Asia for eight. [2] Thus the territory of Babylon[a] equals one third of all Asia in terms of power and resources.

That the government of the Babylonian province, which the Persians call a satrapy, is by far the most powerful of all the Persian satrapies can be shown from the fact that Tritantaichmes son of Artabazos, who ruled this province for the King, received daily revenues of a full artabe of silver. [3] (An artabe is a Persian unit of measure holding three choinikes more than the Attic medimnos.)[a] And besides the warhorses he maintained, he had his own private herd of 800 stallions and 16,000 mares, one stallion for breeding with every 20 mares. [4] And he kept such a great number of Indian hunting dogs that four large villages on the plain were assigned to provide food for the dogs and were exempt from other taxes. Such were the perquisites of the governor of Babylon.

The land of Assyria[a] receives just enough rainfall to nurture the roots of the country's crops. Then, as the plants come into leaf and the fruit ripens, they are watered with river water—not as in Egypt, where the river itself rises onto the fields, but the farmers bring river to crops, by hand-worked shadoofs.[b] [2] For the entire Babylonian territory, just as in Egypt, is crisscrossed by channels. The largest of these channels is navigable by ships and flows toward the winter sun.[a] From the Euphrates[b] it flows into the Tigris River,[c] on whose banks is situated the city of Nineveh.[d] Of all lands known to us, this one is by far the best in producing the crops of Demeter.[e] [3] It does

1.192
BABYLON
Herodotus describes the wealth of Babylon.

1.193
MESOPOTAMIA
Herodotus describes the irrigation agriculture of Mesopotamia and its astounding fecundity.

1.192.2a Babylon: Map 1.199. Herodotus says "Assyrian" here, using that term interchangeably with "Babylonian."
1.192.3a The artabe = 50 quarts.
The medimnos = 48 quarts.
The choinix = 1 quart.
These figures are approximate in U.S. dry measure quarts. See Appendix J, §17, 21.
1.193.1a Assyria: Map 1.199. See n. 1.192.2a.
1.193.1b Shadoof: a bucket attached to a lever which

revolves around a post; used sometimes in series, to lift water in order to irrigate fields. See Figure 1.193 of shadoofs in use.
1.193.2a The direction is southeast, from which rises the winter sun.
1.193.2b Euphrates River: Map 1.199.
1.193.2c Tigris River: Map 1.199.
1.193.2d Nineveh: Map 1.199.
1.193.2e Crops of Demeter are grain.

FIGURE 1.193. THE PHOTOGRAPH SHOWS A SINGLE SHADOOF IN USE. THE DRAWING SHOWS SHADOOFS ARRANGED IN TIERS TO RAISE WATER TO GREATER HEIGHTS.

not at all support the growth of trees such as the fig, grape, or olive, but it bears such good crops of Demeter that it gives a 200-fold return, and when it yields its best, it produces a 300-fold return.[a] The stalks of wheat and barley here easily measure four fingers in width. [4] I know how large the returns from growing millet and sesame are but will not mention them: I am well aware that even the account of the crops already described meets with great incredulity. from those who have not visited the territory of Babylon themselves. The Babylonians use no olive oil but make oil from sesame instead. They have palm trees growing throughout the entire plain; the majority of these bear fruit from which food, wine, and honey are made.

1.193.3a Such returns would have seemed incredibly, fabulously high to Hellenes, whose return on planting cereal grains was much lower.

[5] They tend their date palm trees by the same method used for figs: they tie the nonedible fruit of the trees, called males by the Hellenes, to the date-bearing palms so that the gallfly[a] will enter the date and ripen it, preventing it from falling off the tree while still unripe. For the male trees carry gallflies in their fruit, just as do wild figs.

I shall now describe the greatest of all marvels here, after the city of Babylon itself. The boats which float down the river to Babylon are completely circular in form and made of leather. [2] The Armenians[a] who live upstream from Assyria construct the ribs of the boat out of cut willow branches and stretch around them watertight skins to complete the hull. They form neither a stern nor a prow for the boat, but shape it into a circle like a shield. Then they stuff the entire boat with reeds, fill it with cargo, and release it to drift with the current down the river. Their most common cargo is made up of jars full of Phoenician date-palm wine. [3] The boats are guided by men standing and wielding two long oars, one drawing his oar in as the other pushes his out. These boats are constructed in all sizes, from small to very large. The largest of them can hold freight weighing up to 5,000 talents.[a] Each boat carries a live donkey; the larger boats hold several donkeys. [4] With these they sail to Babylon, and when they arrive, they sell their cargo and auction off the ribs and reeds from the boats; but they load the skins onto the donkeys and lead them back to Armenia, [5] for it is impossible for them to sail the boats back up the river due to its swift current. This is why the boats are made not of wood but of skins. So they ride the donkeys back to Armenia, and when they arrive, they make other boats in the same way.

Such are their boats. For clothing, they wear a long linen tunic reaching down to their feet, and over this another tunic of wool, around which they drape a short white cloak. Their shoes are peculiar to this country but resemble Boeotian[a] sandals. They grow their hair long, bind their heads with turbans, and perfume their entire bodies. [2] Each man wears a signet ring and carries a handcrafted staff topped with an apple, rose, lily, eagle, or some other design. In fact, it would be very unusual to find a man with a staff that did not have an emblem. This, then, is how they dress.

I shall describe their customs, beginning with the one I consider the wisest, which I hear is also still followed among the Enetoi of Illyria.[a] It used to be observed once each year in every village. All the girls of marriageable age were assembled together in one place, and a crowd of men would form a circle around them [2] while an auctioneer had the women stand up one by one and sold them, beginning with the most beautiful. When this young woman was sold for a large amount of gold, he would then put up for sale the second most beautiful. The women were sold for

1.194
MESOPOTAMIA
Herodotus describes the skin boats used to carry cargo down the rivers of Mesopotamia and then disassembled and carried back upriver on mules.

1.195
MESOPOTAMIA
Mesopotamian clothing.

Babylonian Customs
1.196
BABYLONIA
Babylonian customs: the auctioning of wives.

1.193.5a   Gallfly: the *Cynips psenes*.
1.194.1a   Armenia: Map 1.199.
1.194.3a   The talent was a unit of weight that varied from place to place in the ancient world. See Appendix J, §11–13, 20.

1.195.1a   Boeotia: Map 1.204, inset.
1.196.1a   Enetoi of Illyria: the Venetians on the Adriatic Sea, Map 1.166. See 5.9.2.

the purpose of marriage.[a] All the wealthier Babylonian men of marriage-able age would try to outbid each other for the prettiest girls. The more humble among them did not seek beauty in the women they bid for, because the homelier ones came with a monetary reward as an incentive for someone to marry them. [3] And when the auctioneer finished selling the most beautiful of the young women, he had the most unattractive stand up, or a crippled girl, if there was any among them, and these would be offered for sale with the announcement that they would go to whoever would accept the smallest amount of gold and marry them, and the auction would continue in this way until the last woman was finally matched up with the man who agreed to accept the least for her. The gold for these arrangements came from the sale of the beautiful girls, and thus the attractive provided the dowries to help marry off the unattractive and crippled. No one was permitted to marry his daughter to any man because he preferred him, nor could any groom take away the young woman he had bought until he had appointed a guarantor, who would ensure that he would marry her. [4] Only then could he take her home with him. If the couple could not get along, it was customary to pay back the gold. Anyone who wished to participate in the auction was permitted to purchase a young woman, even if he came from another village. [5] This was their finest custom; however, it is no longer observed. Quite recently they began to observe another one, to prevent anyone from treating their women unjustly or taking them to the other city.[a] For after the Babylonians had been conquered by the Persians, they were ruined and became impover-ished, so that now every commoner who cannot make a living prostitutes his daughters.

Here is another custom of theirs, which is the second wisest. They do not use physicians; instead they carry their sick people out into the public square and allow people to approach the sick person and advise him about his illness. Some may themselves have suffered from the same illness that the sick person has, or have seen someone else who did. They go to the sick person and give advice, encouraging him to do whatever they themselves or others they may know have done to be cured of a similar illness. And it is not permitted for anyone to leave the side of a sick person before having inquired what illness he suffers from.

They use honey to preserve the bodies of the dead, and their funeral songs resemble those of Egypt.[a]

After a Babylonian has intercourse with his wife, he sits before burning incense and his wife does the same, opposite him. At sunrise they both

1.197
BABYLONIA
Babylonian public
medicine.

1.198
BABYLONIA
Babylonian burial and
purification customs.

1.196.2a Herodotus uses a word here that connotes a union of houses, a joining together, which would seem synony-mous with marriage.

1.196.5a It is not clear exactly what Herodotus means here by "the other city." Perhaps he means that the Babylonians did not want their women to become slaves to the Persians and be carried off from Babylon to the Persian capital (Ecbatana under Cyrus, Susa under Darius).

1.198.1a Egypt: Map 1.199.

bathe, and they refrain from touching any vessel or jar that contains food until they have bathed. The Arabians[b] follow the same rules in these matters.

Surely the most disgusting of all Babylonian customs is the following. Once in her life, every woman of the country must sit down in the sanctuary of Aphrodite and have intercourse with a stranger. Many of the wealthier women, haughty in their pride, think they are too good to mingle with the rest and ride to the sanctuary in covered chariots with large groups of servants following them, and they simply stand there waiting. [2] But the majority sit in the sacred precinct of Aphrodite wearing wreaths made of cord on their heads. Women are continually entering and leaving this place. Paths run through the crowd of women in every direction, on which the men walk as they make their selections. [3] Whenever a woman comes here and sits down, she may not return home until one of the strangers has tossed silver into her lap and has had intercourse with her outside the sanctuary. When he tosses the silver, he must say, "I call on you in the name of the goddess Mylitta." (The Assyrians call Aphrodite Mylitta.) [4] The silver can be of any amount, for no law regulates this matter; but the women cannot refuse, and the silver then becomes sacred property. Indeed, a woman must follow the first man who tosses silver at her and may not reject him. Then, after they have had intercourse and she has thus discharged her duty to the goddess, she returns home. But after this event, no matter how much you give her, she will refuse you. [5] Those women who are tall and beautiful leave quickly, but unattractive women may wait for a long time, unable to fulfill the prescribed obligation. In fact, some have had to remain for up to three or four years. A custom similar to this is observed in some regions of Cyprus.[a]

These, then, are the customs established and observed by the Babylonians. There are also three tribes among them who eat nothing but fish. First they catch them and dry them in the sun; then they prepare them by placing them in a mortar, grinding them down with a pestle, and then squeezing the ground fish through a linen cloth. After this, one can either knead the fish meal into a cake and eat it or bake it into a type of bread.

After Cyrus had conquered the Babylonians, he next set his heart on the conquest of the Massagetai.[a] This nation is reported to be populous and warlike and to inhabit a land situated toward the rising of the sun in the east, across and beyond the River Araxes,[b] which corresponds with that of the Issedonians.[c] Some say they are a Scythian[d] tribe.

1.199
BABYLONIA
Babylonian ritual prostitution.

1.200
BABYLONIA
Babylonian tribes that eat only dried fish.

1.201
MASSAGETAI
Cyrus decides to conquer the Massagetai.

1.198.1b Arabia: Map 1.199.
1.199.5a Cyprus: Map 1.199.
1.201.1a Massagetai, approximate location of territory: Map 1.199.
1.201.1b Herodotus cannot mean the Araxes River (Map 1.199) in this instance. It flows into the Caspian Sea. He must have confused the Araxes with either the Oxus

or the Jaxartes, which both flow into the Aral Sea (Map 1.199).
1.201.1c Issedones, possibly mythical group of nomads, located in ancient writings somewhere in what is now Kazakhstan. They are also mentioned in 4.26.
1.201.1d Scythia: Map 1.204. Herodotus treats them at length in 4.1–20.

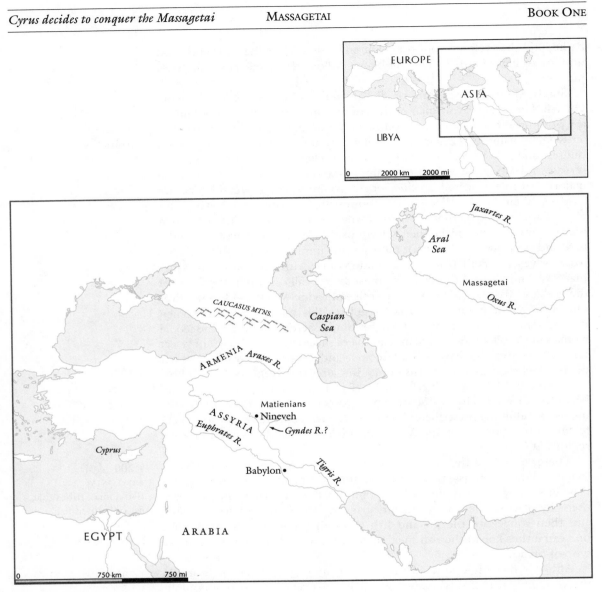

MAP 1.199

The River Araxes[a] is variously claimed to be larger or smaller than the Ister.[b] They say that there are many islands in it similar in size to the island of Lesbos[c] and that the inhabitants of these islands dig up and eat all sorts of roots in the summer and have discovered a tree whose fruit they store away when ripe for winter consumption. [2] They have also discovered other trees bearing fruit which they use when they gather together in groups. They sit in a circle around a fire and throw this fruit into it, inhaling the fumes as the fruit burns; they then become intoxicated by the vapors just as Hellenes become intoxicated with wine. They add more of the fruit to the fire and become even more intoxicated until they reach a point where they stand up and begin to sing and dance. This, then, is said to be their way of life.

[3] The River Araxes flows out from the land of the Matienians,[a] as does the Gyndes,[b] which Cyrus divided into 360 channels.[c] It flows out through forty mouths, of which all but one end up in swamps and shallows. They say that in these swamps live people who eat raw fish and are accustomed to wearing sealskins as clothing. [4] One of the mouths of the Araxes runs through open country and into the Caspian Sea.[a] The Caspian Sea is a self-contained body of water; it has no point of contact with that other sea, the one which is navigated by the Hellenes[b] and which, together with the sea located outside the Pillars of Herakles[c] called the Atlantic[d] and the one to the south called the Erythraean,[e] in fact constitute one single united sea.

The Caspian, however, has no connection to this other sea. It takes fifteen days to cross its length in a sailing ship with oars, and eight days to traverse it at its widest point. The Caucasus mountain range,[a] the greatest in area and highest of all mountains, extends along the western edge of this sea. And many peoples of all kinds live on it, the majority subsisting entirely on the wild produce of the forests. [2] It is said that here the leaves of the trees have a special quality when they are crushed, mixed with water, and then used to paint images on clothing. These images do not wash out but wear with the cloth itself, as though woven into it from the beginning. It is also said that these people engage in intercourse out in the open, just like animals.

While the Caucasus Mountains enclose the Caspian to the west, toward the east and the rising sun a boundless plain stretches out as far as the eye can see. The Massagetai possess the largest share of this great plain, and it was against this people that Cyrus had now conceived a desire for war. [2] There were significant reasons that motivated him and which led him to face this

1.202
ARAXES RIVER
Description of the Araxes River, the Caspian Sea.

1.203
CASPIAN SEA
Description of the Caspian Sea and the Caucasus Mountains.

1.204
CASPIAN PLAIN
The Massagetai inhabit the plains to the east of the Caspian Sea.

1.202.1a The Araxes River of the chapter must be the one that empties into the Caspian Sea (Map 1.99), as Herodotus says in 1.202.4.
1.202.1b Ister (modern Danube) River: Map 1.199.
1.202.1c Lesbos: Map 1.204, inset. A ridiculous idea. Lesbos is one of the larger Greek islands.
1.202.3a Matienians (Matiane), approximate location of territory: Map 1.199.
1.202.3b Gyndes River, possible location: Map 1.199.
1.202.3c For the 360 channels by which Cyrus crossed the Gyndes, see 1.189.3–1.190.1.

1.202.4a Caspian Sea: Map 1.204. Herodotus here refutes a common geographical conception of his time that the Caspian and Euxine (Black) Seas were both open to the Atlantic Ocean.
1.202.4b Mediterranean Sea: Map 1.204.
1.202.4c Pillars of Herakles (modern Straits of Gibraltar): Map 1.204.
1.202.4d Atlantic Ocean: Map 1.204.
1.202.4e Erythraean (Red, Southern) Sea: Map 1.204. See n. 1.1.1c.
1.203.1a Caucasus Mountains: Map 1.204.

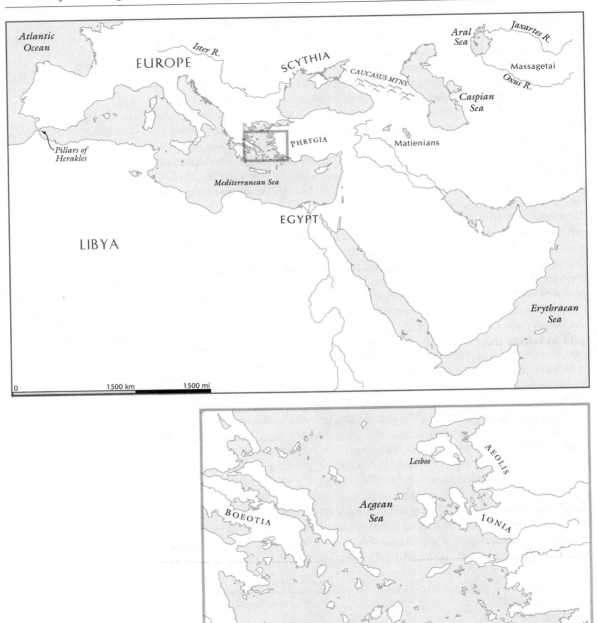

MAP 1.204

prospect with confidence: the first of these was his birth, which seemed more than human, and the second the good fortune that had always attended him throughout his campaigns, for wherever he had waged war, he had encountered only nations who had proved incapable of resisting his conquest.

The Massagetai at this time were ruled by a woman named Tomyris,[a] whose husband had died and who was now their queen. Cyrus sent a message to her pretending courtship and claiming that he wanted her to be his wife. Tomyris astutely grasped his real intention—that he was courting not her but the kingship over the Massagetai. She refused his proposal. [2] After this, having failed to win by deceit, Cyrus led his army to the River Araxes[a] and began overt hostilities against the Massagetai by constructing a bridge of boats so that his army could cross it. He also built towers on the boats that were to serve as the soldiers' transport.[b]

While he was building the bridge, Tomyris sent a herald to him with this message: "King of the Medes,[a] cease your labors; you cannot know whether this project will prove to be advantageous to you. So stop; be satisfied with reigning over your own people and endure the sight of me ruling over the subjects that I have now. However, I assume that you will not follow my advice, as you would find anything preferable to living in peace. Well, if your heart is so strongly set on a trial of strength with the Massagetai, come on then and we shall oblige you; but you need not labor more to build a bridge. Give us three days to retreat from the river, and then you may proceed to invade my territory. Or, if you would prefer to admit us into your territory, you do the same."

When he had heard this message, Cyrus summoned the leading men of the Persians to meet with him and set before them the whole issue, requesting advice on which course he should take. Their vote was unanimous: they recommended that he admit Tomyris and her army into Persian territory.

Now Croesus was present at this meeting, and he disagreed with this decision, offering his own opinion to counter the prevailing one. "Sire, you know, as I told you earlier, that since Zeus gave me to you, I would always strive, to the best of my ability, to avert any harm to you and your house that I could envision. My suffering, though joyless for me, has taught me many lessons. [2] If you think yourself an immortal and that you command an immortal army, no opinion of mine will mean anything to you. But if you realize that you are human and command an army of human beings, consider first that there is a cycle in human affairs, and as it goes around it does not permit the same person to enjoy good fortune forever. [3] Therefore, I have an opinion opposite to that of these men concerning this matter. For if you permit the enemy to enter your territory and are defeated, you will risk losing

1.205
530
QUEEN TOMYRIS
The Massagetai are ruled by Queen Tomyris, who spurns Cyrus' overtures.

1.206
530
QUEEN TOMYRIS
Tomyris offers to cross the Araxes River and do battle in Persian territory or to permit Cyrus to cross unopposed. Cyrus considers her offer.

1.207
530
ARAXES RIVER
Croesus advises Cyrus to cross the river and seek battle in enemy territory. He also devises a stratagem to defeat the enemy with opulence and wine.

Cycle in human affairs

1.205.1a The queen as a worthy opponent: see Appendix U, §2.
1.205.2a The Araxes River referred to here, which separates Cyrus' kingdom from the Massagetai, must be either the Oxus or the Jaxartes (Map 1.199), both of which flow into the Aral Sea: Map 1.204.
1.205.2b Herodotus may mean here that towers

were built on some of the boats that were to transport the soldiers and that these would then be moored at the enemy's side to protect the bridge against attack.
1.206.1a This is another instance where, like many of his Greek contemporaries, Herodotus uses the term "Medes" for Persians.

your whole empire. For if the Massagetai should win, it is quite obvious that they will not retreat but will march on your other provinces. [4] And even if you defeat them there, you will not gain as much from the victory as you could have gained had you crossed the river [and] defeated the Massagetai on their own territory, and pursued them as they fled. Just as they might have done great harm to you had they defeated you here, your victory there will permit you to advance directly into the empire of Tomyris. [5] And apart from all that, it would be an intolerable disgrace for Cyrus son of Cambyses to concede the initiative to a woman and to retreat before her. For these reasons, I think you should cross the river, advance as far as they make way for you, and then endeavor to gain the advantage over them by means of the following scheme. [6] I hear that the Massagetai have had no experience of all the amenities and the finer things in life which the Persians enjoy. So I propose that you should deal with these men in the following way: slaughter many cattle—and be generous about it. Have the cattle prepared to serve as a feast in our camp, along with generous provisions of undiluted wine and food of every sort. [7] When everything is prepared, leave behind the worst part of your army and retreat at once with the rest to the river. For in my judgment, the Massagetai, when they see the many good things to eat and drink there, will turn their attention to these delights and thereby create an opportunity for us to perform great deeds of valor."

Cyrus, faced with these two conflicting opinions, chose to follow the counsel of Croesus. So he sent a message to Tomyris telling her to withdraw so that he could cross into her territory, and she retreated as promised. Then Cyrus placed his son, Cambyses, whom he intended to be heir to his kingdom, into the hands of Croesus, ordering his son to honor Croesus and treat him well in the event that his crossing over into Massagetai territory did not succeed. After giving these instructions, he sent them both back to Persia and then crossed the river with his army.

After crossing the river, and with the onset of night, Cyrus slept in the territory of the Massagetai, and in his sleep he had a dream in which he seemed to see Darius, the eldest son of Hystaspes son of Arsames, who was an Achaimenid,[a] bearing wings on his shoulders, one of them casting a shadow over Asia, the other over Europe. [2] The eldest son of Hystaspes son of Arsames, who was an Achaimenid, was named Darius. He was now about twenty years old at the most, and had been left behind in Persia because he was too young to go to war at the time. [3] When Cyrus awoke, he thought about this vision; and once he decided it was of great significance, he summoned Hystaspes and, taking him aside by himself, said, "Hystaspes, your son has been caught plotting against me and my empire. I shall explain how I know this for certain. [4] The gods care for me and reveal all the future to me. Well, last night in my sleep I saw your eldest son bearing wings on his shoulders, one of them casting a shadow over Asia, the

1.208
530
ARAXES RIVER
Cyrus decides to follow Croesus' advice.

1.209
530
Cyrus dreams that Darius has become ruler of Asia and Europe.

1.209.1a The Achaimenids were descendants of Achaimenes, who gave his name to the Persian royal family, whose members were eligible to become kings.

other over Europe. [5] There is no escape from the inevitable interpretation of this dream—your son is certainly plotting against me. You must go back to Persia at once and see to it that your son is prepared for examination by me after I have conquered here and returned home."

Cyrus really believed that Darius was plotting against him when he said this, but in fact a divinity was trying to reveal to him in advance that he was about to die right there and that Darius would ultimately succeed to his throne.

[2] At any rate, Hystaspes replied to him, "Sire, may no man born a Persian ever plot against you, but if someone has done so, may he die as soon as possible. It was you who made the Persians free men instead of slaves, and rulers of all instead of subjects ruled by others. [3] So if a dream has revealed that my son is intriguing against you, I shall surrender him so that you may do with him whatever you wish." After having made this reply, Hystaspes crossed back over the Araxes and returned to Persia to keep an eye on his son Darius for Cyrus.

Cyrus advanced beyond the Araxes for one day and then, following the advice of Croesus, [2] he set up the banquet there. After that, he and his most competent Persian troops marched some distance back toward the Araxes, leaving behind the most unfit part of his army. These men left behind were then attacked by one third of the Massagetaian army, and although they defended themselves, they were massacred. After the Massagetai had finished killing their enemies, they saw the feast that had been set before them, and turning eagerly to it, they fell to eating and drinking until they fell asleep, fully sated. [3] At this point, the Persians made their assault and slew many of them. But they captured even more of them alive, including Spargapises, the son of Queen Tomyris, who was a general of the Massagetai.

When Tomyris learned what had happened to her army and her son, she sent a herald to Cyrus with this message: [2] "Bloodthirsty Cyrus, do not gloat over what has happened here. You Persians indulge yourselves with the fruit of the vine to the point of madness, so that as the wine descends into your bodies, ugly words flow up and out of you. By such means you have tricked me and have taken my son prisoner, but not by supremacy in battle. [3] Well, then, I urge you to follow this advice: return my son to me and, despite the damage you have cunningly wreaked upon a third part of the army of the Massagetai, you may leave this land unharmed. If you do not do this, I swear by the Sun, the Lord of the Massagetai, that I will satisfy your thirst for blood, insatiable as you are."

When this message was reported to Cyrus, he ignored it. But when the effects of the wine wore off from Spargapises son of Queen Tomyris and he discovered the terrible nature of his predicament, he begged Cyrus to set him free from his bonds. Cyrus granted this favor to him, and as soon as he was free and had regained the use of his hands, he killed himself.

Thus did he meet his end.

1.210
Cyrus misinterprets the dream.

1.211
530
MASSAGETAI
Croesus' stratagem succeeds. The Persians destroy one third of the Massagetai force and capture Tomyris' son, Spargapises.

1.212
530
MASSAGETAI
Tomyris asks Cyrus to return her son and leave the country.

1.213
530
MASSAGETAI
Spargapises kills himself.

1.214
530
MASSAGETAI
The Persian army is
destroyed and Cyrus
killed in a great battle
with the Massagetai.

1.215
MASSAGETAI
Dress, armor, and
customs of the
Massagetai.

1.216
MASSAGETAI
Customs of the
Massagetai.

Tomyris, when she saw that Cyrus had ignored her advice, gathered her entire army and attacked him. What happened then was, in my judgment, the most violent of all battles ever fought by barbarians; this is what I heard about how it was waged. [2] It is said that the battle began with each side shooting arrows at each other while still far apart. Then, when their supply of arrows was exhausted, they fell upon each other at close quarters with spears and daggers. For a long time they fought fiercely and neither side was willing to flee. But at last the Massagetai prevailed. [3] A large part of the Persian army perished in this battle, and in particular, Cyrus himself met his end. He had reigned for twenty-nine years.

[4] Tomyris then filled a wineskin with human blood and searched for the corpse of Cyrus among the Persians' dead. When she found him, she thrust his head into the wineskin, and as she thus abused the corpse, she declared to it: "I am alive and have conquered you in battle, but you have ruined me by taking my son through guile. Well, then, just as I threatened, I will slake your thirst for blood." Of the many stories told about the death of Cyrus, this account seems to me to be the most credible version.

The Massagetai resemble the Scythians in the clothing they wear and in their general way of life. They arm themselves as both cavalry and infantry and fight as archers and spearmen, but their customary weapon is the battle-axe.[a] They use gold and bronze for all their war gear—bronze for their spearheads, arrowheads, and battle-axes; gold for the decorations on their belts and chest bands. [2] Likewise, they attach breastplates of bronze around the chests of their horses but use gold for the bridles, bits, and the bosses on the cheek straps. They use no iron or silver at all, since these metals are not found in their land, although gold and silver are abundant there.

These are the type of customs they follow: Each man marries one woman, but all men share these women in common. Some Hellenes claim that it is the Scythians who do this, but it is really the Massagetai, not the Scythians, who have this custom. If one of the Massagetai should desire a particular woman, he hangs his quiver on the front of her wagon, has intercourse with her, and he has nothing to fear. [2] A man's life ends on the day they assign to him, for whenever someone grows very old, all his relatives assemble and sacrifice him together with some sheep. Then, after stewing the meat, they feast on it, [3] believing this to be the most blessed way to end one's life. If someone dies from an illness, they do not eat his flesh but bury him in the ground, deeming it a misfortune that he did not attain the perquisites of being sacrificed and eaten. They do not sow crops but subsist on animals and fish, which thrive abundantly in the River Araxes, [4] and they drink milk. The sun is the only god they worship; they sacrifice horses to him, thinking it fitting that the swiftest of gods should be offered the swiftest of all mortal beings.

1.215.1a Herodotus uses the Scythian word *sagaris*, here translated as "battle-axe." It also appears in 5.4.3 and 7.64.2.

BOOK TWO

W hen Cyrus died, the kingship was inherited by Cambyses. He was the son of Cyrus by Cassandane daughter of Pharnaspes. Cassandane had died before Cyrus, and he had grieved for her with great sorrow and ordered all of his subjects to grieve for her, too. [2] As the son of this woman and Cyrus, Cambyses considered the Ionians[a] and Aeolians[b] as his slaves whom he had inherited from his father, and when he made his expedition to Egypt,[c] he took with him these Hellenes who were under his rule, along with the rest of his subjects.

Now, before Psammetichos became king, the Egyptians used to believe that they were the earliest humans. But upon assuming the kingship, Psammetichos became eager to ascertain which people were really the first; and ever since his reign, the Egyptians consider that the Phrygians[b] lived before they did, but that they themselves existed prior to all the rest of humanity. [2] Unable to find a means of discovering who were the first humans by making inquiries, Psammetichos devised an experiment. He selected two newborn children from ordinary people and gave them to a shepherd to take into his flocks and raise according to the following instructions: no one was to utter a word in their presence; the shepherd should place them in a secluded hut by themselves and at appropriate intervals bring in the goats, give the children their fill of milk, and then tend to the rest of their needs. [3] The reason he gave these instructions was because he wished to listen to the children after they had outgrown their inarticulate crying and to find out what word they would speak first. And everything turned out as he planned, for the shepherd had followed his orders for two years when one day, as he opened the door and entered, both children rushed at him with outstretched hands, crying out "*bekos.*" [4] At first the shepherd kept quiet about having heard this, but when the word *bekos* was repeated again and again as he came and went in his care for the children, he told his master. At his command the shepherd brought the children into his presence, and

2.1
530
Cambyses succeeds Cyrus and prepares to attack Egypt.

2.2
EGYPT
Psammetichos (r. 664–610) of Egypt determines by experiment that Phrygians were the earliest people on earth.

2.1.2a   Ionia: Map 1.204, inset.
2.1.2b   Aeolis: Map 1.204, inset.
2.1.2c   Egypt: Map 1.204. See Appendix C, The
        Account of Egypt: Herodotus Right and
        Wrong, §1.
2.2.1b   Phrygia: Map 1.204.

Psammetichos himself heard the word. When he inquired which people might use the word *bekos*, he discovered that the word *bekos* means "bread" in the Phrygian language. [5] Thus the Egyptians accepted this evidence and concluded that the Phrygians are older than themselves. I heard this account from the priests of Hephaistos at Memphis.ᵃ Hellenes tell many different silly stories—for example, there is one that Psammetichos cut out the tongues of some women and made the children live with them.

2.3
EGYPT
Herodotus lists some of his Egyptian sources.

Such are the stories told about how the children were raised. But I heard other things in Memphis, too, when I conversed with the priests of Hephaistos. And I also went to Thebesᵃ and Heliopolis,ᵇ since I wanted to see if they agreed with what was said in Memphis. For of all the Egyptians, the Heliopolitans are said to be the most learned in tradition. [2] I have no desire to relate what I heard about matters concerning the gods, other than their names alone, since I believe that all people understand these things equally. But when my discussion forces me to mention these things, I shall do so.

2.4
EGYPT
The Egyptian calendar is superior to the Greek. Herodotus is told that the first ruler of all Egypt is Min, who is thought to have reigned c. 3000.

As to all matters concerning the human world, they were in agreement. They said that the Egyptians were the first of all peoples to discover the year, by dividing up the seasons into twelve parts to total one year, and that they discovered how to do this from the stars. The Egyptians seem to me to be much wiser than the Hellenes in the way they regulate the timing of the seasons. While the Hellenes attempt to preserve the timing of the seasons by inserting an intercalary month every other year, the Egyptians divide the year into twelve months of thirty days each and add just five days each year beyond that number, and thus their seasons do return at the same periods in the cycle from year to year.

[2] They said that the Egyptians were also the first to establish the tradition of identifying namesᵃ for the twelve gods, and that the Hellenes adopted this practice from them. They were also the first to assign altars, statues, and temples to the gods and to carve their figures in relief on stone. The priests in fact demonstrated with proofs that these claims were valid, but they could only assert that the first man to be king of Egypt was Min.ᵇ [3] During his reign, they said, all Egypt was swamp except for the district of Thebes, and none of it protruded above water beyond what is now the lake of Moeris,ᵃ which lies at a seven-day voyage upriver from the sea.

2.5
EGYPT
Egypt consists of mud deposited by the Nile River.

It seemed to me that they accurately described the nature of their land. For even if one has not heard about it in advance, it is obvious to anyone with common sense when he sees it for himself: the Egypt to which the Hellenes sail is land that was deposited by the river—it is the gift of the river to the Egyptians, as is also the area south of the lake as far as a three-day voyage upriver. Although they said nothing further about this, there is

2.2.5a   Memphis: Map 2.6, Egypt inset.
2.3.1a   Thebes, Egypt: Map 2.6, Egypt inset.
2.3.1b   Heliopolis: Map 2.6, Egypt inset. The name means City of the Sun; in Egyptian, the House/Abode of Ra/Re.
2.4.2a   Herodotus uses a word which literally means "epithet" here. He probably

means that the Egyptians were the first to use specific and particular names for each divinity in contrast to *theoi*/gods—a collective designation.
2.4.2b   Min is Menes. See 2.99.
2.4.3a   Lake Moeris: Map 2.6, Egypt inset.

something more to add; [2] the nature of Egypt is such that if you are in a boat one whole day's sail distant from the land and you let down a sounding line, you will bring up mud even to the depth of eleven fathoms.[a] This shows just how far the alluvial deposit of the land extends.

The length of the Egyptian seacoast, as we Hellenes define the territory of Egypt, is 60 schoinoi,[a] from the Gulf of Plinthine[b] to Lake Serbonis,[c] along which extends Mount Casius.[d] It is from this place that the 397 miles are measured. [2] Whoever possesses very little property here measures his land in fathoms; those who have somewhat more, in stades; those who have much, in parasangs; and those who have an extremely sizeable portion, in schoinoi. [3] A parasang is equal to thirty stades; each schoinos, an Egyptian unit of measure, is equal to sixty stades.[a] Thus the coast of Egypt is 397 miles in length.[b]

From the coast, Egypt extends inland as far as Heliopolis in a broad expanse, entirely flat, wet, and muddy. The road from the sea to Heliopolis is about as long as the road leading from the Altar of the Twelve Gods at Athens[a] to the temple of Olympian Zeus in Pisa.[b] [2] If one measured the length of both these roads, one would discover that they are not exactly equal in length, but that the difference between them is negligible, no more than one and a half miles by which the road from Athens to Pisa is shorter than the 165 miles[a] which is the full length of the road from the sea to Heliopolis.

From Heliopolis, Egypt becomes narrow as one travels farther inland. For on one side, toward Arabia,[a] there extends a mountain range from north to south, and toward the south it winds all the way to the sea called Erythraean.[b] In these mountains are the stone quarries from which the stones for the pyramids near Memphis were cut. The mountain range ends

2.6
EGYPT
Length of the Egyptian seacoast.

2.7
EGYPT
A description of the dimensions of Egypt.

2.8
NILE VALLEY
Mountains border both sides of the narrow Nile valley above Heliopolis.

2.5.2a   The fathom = 6 feet. See Distance Conversions, p. lxiv, and Appendix J, Ancient Greek Units of Currency, Weight, and Distance, §4, 5, 19. Herodotus' measurement is wrong; a depth of 11 fathoms is encountered much nearer the coast of Egypt than a full day's sail.

2.6.1a   Herodotus' "60 schoinoi" comes to approximately 397 miles. Schoinoi (*skhoinoi*): literally, "ropes," were an Egyptian unit of measurement whose length can vary. See Appendix J, §5–7, 19. Herodotus occasionally shows off his knowledge of foreign terms and units of measure.

2.6.1b   Plinthine Gulf: Map 2.6, Egypt inset.

2.6.1c   Lake Serbonis: Map 2.6, Egypt inset. Herodotus calls it the Serbonian Marsh in 3.5.2.

2.6.1d   Mount Casius: Map 2.6, Egypt inset.

2.6.3a   The fathom = 6 feet.
The Attic stade = 583 feet.
The parasang (30 stades or .5 schoinos) = 17,490 feet = 3.3 miles.
The schoinos (60 stades) = 34,980 feet = 6.6 miles.
But Herodotus may have had different units in mind when he made his estimate. See Appendix J, §4–7, 19.

2.6.3b   If one schoinos = 60 stades, then the "60 schoinoi" of the coast of Egypt would equal 3,600 stades, or about 397 miles. This is a significant overestimate. Just under 300 miles would be more accurate.

2.7.1a   Athens: Map 2.6, Aegean inset.

2.7.1b   Pisa (Olympia): Map 2.6, Aegean inset.

2.7.2a   Herodotus actually writes that the difference between the two distances (Athens to Pisa and the Egyptian coast to Heliopolis) is negligible, that between Ayhens and Pisa (Olympia) being barely one percent less than the 1,500 stades which he says separate the Egyptian coast from Heliopolis. The distances are not really equivalent at all. The 1,500 stades between the Egyptian coast and Heliopolis would come to some 165 miles, whereas the the length of the road from Athens to Pisa (Olympia) is closer to 110 miles. Of course, the coast of Egypt has extended a good deal farther north into the sea today than it was in Herodotus' day. See Appendix C, §3.

2.8.1a   Arabia: Map 2.6. The Arabian mountains extend along the western bank of the Nile.

2.8.1b   Erythraean Sea, in this case the sea to the east of the Nile, i.e., the modern Red Sea: Map 2.6 and Egypt inset.

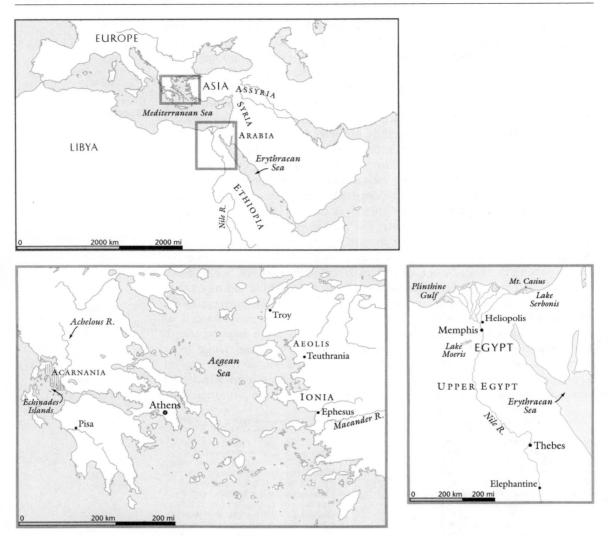

MAP 2.6

here at the quarries and slopes down toward the Erythraean Sea. This is the broadest part of the range, so I am told, requiring a two-month journey[c] from east to west, and at its eastern extremity the land produces frankincense. [2] Such is this mountain range, but there is another one on the Libyan side of Egypt where the pyramids are located, which is composed of stone. It is coated with sand and it extends parallel to the Arabian mountain to the south. [3] From Heliopolis[a] to the south, the land area of Egypt is not large but becomes a narrow strip which is so long that it requires a four-

2.8.1c There is no place where it can be a two-   2.8.3a Heliopolis: Map 2.6, Egypt inset.
month journey from the Nile west across
this mountain range to the Red Sea.

120

day journey upstream by boat in order to traverse it; it seemed to me that the distance between these mountains, from the Arabian to the one called "Libyan,"[a] was no more than twenty-two miles[b] at its narrowest part. After that, Egypt widens out again.[c]

A nine-day boat voyage upstream is required to go south from Heliopolis to Thebes;[a] the distance between them is 517 miles.[b] [2] If we now sum up the various distances I have mentioned above, we find that the length of the Egyptian coast is 397 miles, and the distance inland from the coast to Thebes is 675 miles. Then there is an additional distance of 200 miles[a] between Thebes and the city called Elephantine.[b]

I believe the priests were right when they said that much of the land of Egypt is an alluvial deposit. For the flat plain between the mountains mentioned earlier, which extends above the city of Memphis,[a] appeared to me to have once been a gulf of the sea, just as were the regions (to compare the small with the great) around Ilium,[b] Teuthrania,[c] Ephesus,[d] and the plain of the River Maeander.[e] [2] For although these rivers also produced alluvial deposits which form the land around them, none of them can be compared in size to even one of the five mouths of the Nile.[a] [3] There are other rivers, too, which, though they do not compare to the Nile in size, have produced significant effects. Among their names I can mention above all the Achelous,[a] which flows through Acarnania[b] and empties into the sea. It has already linked half of the Echinades Islands[c] to the mainland.

Not far from Egypt, in Arabia,[a] there is a gulf that runs up from what is called the Erythraean Sea;[b] I shall describe its dimensions. [2] Its length is such that a ship powered by oars would require forty days to go from its innermost corner to the open sea, and at its widest point, the gulf can be crossed in just half a day. It is a sea whose level rises and falls every day. [3] I believe that perhaps present-day Egypt was once a gulf just like this, which would have extended from the sea in the north toward Ethiopia[a] in the south, and that the other gulf extending from the Southern Sea north toward

2.9
EGYPT
The dimensions of Egypt.

2.10
EGYPT
The Nile is similar to, but much greater than, other rivers.

2.11
EGYPT
Herodotus speculates that an original "Egyptian Gulf" was silted up by the Nile River over the ages.

2.8.3a Libya: Map 2.6. The "Libyan" side of the Nile is the western side.
2.8.3b Herodotus writes that the narrowest part is "200 stades" (22 miles); the actual distance is more like 12 miles. See Appendix J, §6, 19.
2.8.3c Egypt can hardly be said to widen out significantly anywhere south of the Delta.
2.9.1a Thebes (Egypt): Map 2.6, Egypt inset.
2.9.1b Herodotus writes this distance as "4,680 stades," equal to "81 schoinoi," which is slightly different from his earlier statement (2.6.3) that 1 schoinos equals 60 stades. His 4,680 stades would equal 517 miles, an overestimate, as the actual distance is closer to 450 miles. See Appendix J, §5–7, 19.
2.9.2a Herodotus' measurements in stades: Egyptian coast length, 3,600 stades; Egyptian coast to Thebes, 6,120 stades; Thebes to Elephantine, 1,800 stades. See Appendix J, §6, 19.
2.9.2b Elephantine (modern Aswan): Map 2.6, Egypt inset.

2.10.1a Memphis: Map 2.6, Egypt inset. Herodotus mentions this flat, wet, and muddy area in 2.7.1.
2.10.1b Ilium (Troy/Ilion): Map 2.6, Aegean inset.
2.10.1c Teuthrania: Map 2.6, Aegean inset.
2.10.1d Ephesus: Map 2.6, Aegean inset.
2.10.1e Maeander River: Map 2.6, Aegean inset.
2.10.2a Nile River: Map 2.6, Egypt inset. The Nile has seven mouths, but Herodotus has omitted here the two allegedly artificial ones, the Bolbinic and the Bucolic. See 2.17.
2.10.3a Achelous River: Map 2.6, Aegean inset.
2.10.3b Acarnania: Map 2.6, Aegean inset.
2.10.3c Echinades Islands: Map 2.6, Aegean inset.
2.11.1a Arabia: Map 2.6.
2.11.1b The "gulf" in Arabia here is the modern Red Sea, labeled "Erythraean Sea" on Map 2.6. Generally what Herodotus calls the Erythraean Sea or "the Southern Sea" is the entire modern Indian Ocean.
2.11.3a Ethiopia: Map 2.19, locator.

Syria[a] nearly ran together with it at their extremities, but they were separated from each other by a small strip of land passing between them. [4] Now then, if the Nile's flow were diverted into this Arabian gulf, what would prevent it from filling up the gulf with silt in 20,000 years? For my part, I suppose it might fill it up with silt in only 10,000 years. Well, then, given all the years that passed before I was born, why could not a gulf much larger than this have been silted up by a river as great and powerful as the Nile?[a]

And so I believe what I have been told about the land of Egypt, and I found myself convinced when I saw how the Delta of Egypt juts out from the adjacent lands, the seashells that appear on the mountains, and the salt coating its surfaces so that even the pyramids are damaged by its erosion, and that the only mountain in Egypt containing sand is the one above Memphis. [2] Furthermore, Egyptian soil is unlike that of Arabia, of Libya, and of Syria (for the Syrians inhabit the coast of Arabia). It is black and friable, since it is composed of mud and alluvial deposit washed down from Ethiopia by the river, [3] whereas, as we know, the soil of Libya is redder and more sandy while that of Syria consists more of clay and rock.

Another significant proof about this land was told to me by the priests: when Moeris was king, the Nile would flood the region below[a] Memphis[b] whenever it reached the level of at least twelve feet. When I heard this from the priests, Moeris had been dead for not quite 900 years. But now, if the river does not rise at least twenty-three or twenty-four feet,[c] it does not overflow onto the land. [2] And I think that if this land keeps rising in elevation proportionally to its increase in area, and if the Nile does not wash over it, the Egyptians who inhabit the regions below Lake Moeris,[a] and especially the region called the Delta,[b] would then for the rest of time suffer the same exposure to famine that they claim may someday threaten to strike the Hellenes. [3] For when they heard that all the land of the Hellenes is watered by rain and not by rivers, they said that someday the Hellenes would be disappointed in their hopes for rain and would suffer a miserable starvation. What they meant was that if the god decides not to send rain, but instead a long drought, the Hellenes would all die of hunger, since they have no means of obtaining water other than from Zeus alone.[a]

The Egyptians were also correct in saying this about the Hellenes. But let me describe to you now the situation of the Egyptians. If the land below Memphis, which is increasing in area, as I mentioned earlier, should also increase proportionally in height as time passes, how could the Egyptians

---

2.12
EGYPT
Egyptian soil is clearly alluvial.

2.13
EGYPT
Egypt's soil is annually irrigated by the Nile, whereas in Greece, crops are watered by more random rainfall.

2.14
EGYPT
Egyptian agriculture requires little effort.

2.11.3a   Syria: Map 2.6.
2.11.4a   These are impressive speculations from Ionian concepts of geology. See Appendix C, §3.
2.13.1a   "Below" in this context means to the north, the direction in which the Nile River flows (downstream). Conversely, the Egyptians considered "above" to be to the south, or upstream, the exact opposite of our standard cartographic convention.
2.13.1b   Memphis: Map 2.19.

2.13.1c   Herodotus writes that the earlier flood level was "8 cubits" and the current one was "15 or 16 cubits." There were several different-sized cubits in use in the ancient world, but the levels above are based on a cubit of 1.5 feet. See Appendix J, §4, 5, 19.
2.13.2a   Lake Moeris: Map 2.19.
2.13.2b   Nile Delta: Map 2.19.
2.13.3a   Zeus was considered the god responsible for bringing rain to the Greeks, who often said "Zeus rains" rather than "it rains."

dwelling here do anything but go hungry if their land does not receive rain and their river will not be able to water the fields either. [2] For as it is now, at least, they obtain crops from the earth with less labor than all other peoples and the rest of the Egyptians, too, since they do not have to break the soil into furrrows with the plow, nor use the hoe, nor do any other work that the rest of mankind must do in order to produce grain. Rather, whenever the river rises spontaneously, it waters the fields, and once it has watered them, it subsides again; then each man sows his field and puts pigs onto it to tread the seed into the earth. From this point they have only to harvest the grain and thresh it, again by means of pigs, and thus they obtain their food.

Now, if we were to consider the opinions of the Ionians about Egypt, we would have to deal with their claim that Egypt is the Delta alone, by which they mean the area extending for 276 miles[a] along the coast from the watchtower of Perseus[b] to the Pelusian saltworks;[c] and then that from the coast inland as far as the city of Kerkasoros,[d] where the Nile splits and flows to Pelusium and to Canobus.[e] They claim that the rest of what I would call Egypt[f] is Libya[g] on the one side and Arabia[h] on the other. In considering this account, we should point out that this land did not exist for the Egyptians at an earlier time. [2] For we have already established that the Delta, as the Egyptians themselves say, and I agree, is alluvial and has, so to speak, just recently appeared above the sea. Well, then, if they had no land in the beginning, why did they bother to think that they might have been the first humans? Moreover, it would not have been necessary for them to conduct the experiment on the children to discover what language they would speak first.[a] [3] I do not think that the Egyptians came into being at the same time as the land the Ionians call the Delta, but rather that they have always existed, beginning from the time when the human race was born, and although many stayed behind as the land extended farther, many others gradually moved downstream on it. And therefore long ago, Thebes[a] was called Egypt and had a perimeter of 676 miles.[b]

Now, if my understanding of these matters is correct, then the Ionians' conception of Egypt is absurd, and even if their view of Egypt were correct, their simple arithmetic would be all wrong! For when they claim that the

2.15
EGYPT
The Ionians are mistaken. Egypt originated in Thebes and spread into the recently formed alluvial delta.

2.16
IONIA
The Ionians divide the world into three parts, but the Egyptian Delta lies between Asia and Africa.

2.15.1a Herodotus writes "40 schoinoi." The schoinos = about 6.6 miles. See nn. 2.6.1a and 2.6.3a and Appendix J, §5–7, 19.
2.15.1b Watchtower of Perseus, location unknown; thought to have been somewhere to the east of the Bolbitinic Mouth of the Nile (Map 2.19), but erroneously placed by Herodotus farther west near the Canobic Mouth (Kanobikon Stoma; Map 2.19).
2.15.1c Pelusian saltworks; presumably near Pelusium: Map 2.19.
2.15.1d Kerkasoros: Map 2.19.
2.15.1e Canobus (Canopus): Map 2.19. Herodotus is thought to be criticizing the position of Hekataios, the author of geographical and

historical accounts of Asia Minor and the East. Hekataios wrote in the late sixth century and was a source both used and criticized by Herodotus. He also plays a role in Herodotus' account of Ionian history. See 5.36, 5.125–126, and 6.137. See also Introduction, §3.1.
2.15.1f Egypt: Map 2.19, locator; in this case what Herodotus considers to be Egypt.
2.15.1g Libya: Map 2.19 and locator.
2.15.1h Arabia: Map 2.19, locator.
2.15.2a This experiment is described in 2.2.2–4.
2.15.3a Thebes, Egypt: Map 2.19, locator.
2.15.3b Herodotus writes "6,120 stades." See Appendix J, §6, 19.

whole earth is made up of three parts—Europe,[a] Asia,[b] and Libya—[2] they in fact should add the Delta of Egypt as a fourth part. Indeed, by their own definition, the Nile is what divides Asia and Libya; but the fact is that the Nile splits and flows around the Delta from its apex, so that the Delta itself lies between Asia and Libya.[a]

2.17
EGYPT
Herodotus lists the channels of the Nile Delta.

Let me dismiss the view of the Ionians now and instead describe to you my own opinions on these matters. I believe it best to characterize Egypt as all the territory inhabited by Egyptians, just as Cilicia[a] is populated by the Cilicians and Assyria[b] by the Assyrians; and as we have seen, there are no boundaries between Asia and Libya other than the boundaries of the land which is inhabited by the Egyptians. [2] If we follow the belief commonly held by the Hellenes, we will accept that all Egypt, beginning at the First Cataract[a] of the Nile River and the nearby city of Elephantine,[b] is divided by the Nile into two halves along its length; [3] and since the Nile flows from the Elephantine to the sea, the land on one side of the river should be called Libya and that on the other side Asia. But although the Nile flows as a single stream from Elephantine to Kerkasoros,[a] from that city it splits into three branches. [4] One branch turns east toward the dawn and enters the sea at what is called the Pelusian[a] Mouth; another extends west toward the sunset and ends in what is called the Canobic[b] Mouth. And the Nile has a third branch that continues in a straight line north. Thus, as the river arrives at the apex of the Delta, it splits the Delta in half on its course to the sea. This branch carries quite a substantial volume of water and is quite famous: it terminates at what is called the Sebennytic[c] Mouth. [5] There are also two other mouths, which split off from the Sebennytic branch and lead to the sea, whose names are the Saitic[a] and the Mendesian.[b] [6] The Bolbitinic[a] and the Bucolic[b] Mouths are not natural in origin; their channels were excavated.[c]

2.18
EGYPT
The god Ammon confirmed that all who lived in the Nile valley are Egyptians and must observe their ways.

My own conception of the extent of Egypt is confirmed by an oracle from Ammon, which I learned about after I had formed my own judgment about this land.[a] [2] The inhabitants of the cities of Mareia[a] and Apis,[b] on

2.16.1a Europe: Map 2.19, locator.
2.16.1b Asia: Map 2.19, locator.
2.16.2a Herodotus addresses a problem of definition posed by Greek (Ionian) geographical thinking: if the Nile is the boundary between Asia and Libya (Africa), then what is the Egyptian Delta? See Appendix C, §3, and Appendix D, Herodotean Geography, §1, 3.
2.17.1a Cilicia: Map 2.19, locator.
2.17.1b Assyria: Map 2.19, locator.
2.17.2a The First Cataract (Herodotus writes *katadoupoi*, literally "the thunderers"): A cataract is an area of fast currents and rapids through which boats cannot safely pass. The First Cataract of the Nile—the northernmost one, i.e., the first one encountered as one goes upstream (south) on the Nile River.
2.17.2b Elephantine (modern Aswan), the Egyptian city located at the First Cataract: Map 2.19, locator.
2.17.3a Kerkasoros: Map 2.19.

2.17.4a Pelusian Mouth of the Nile River: Map 2.19.
2.17.4b Canobic Mouth (Kanobikon Stoma) of the Nile River: Map 2.19.
2.17.4c Sebennytic Mouth of the Nile River: Map 2.19.
2.17.5a Saitic Mouth of the Nile River, possible location, if Herodotus means what is known as the "Tanitic" Mouth: Map 2.19.
2.17.5b Mendesian Mouth of the Nile River: Map 2.19.
2.17.6a Bolbitinic Mouth of the Nile River: Map 2.19.
2.17.6b Bucolic Mouth of the Nile River: Map 2.19.
2.17.6c The statement that the Bolbitinic and Bucolic Mouths of the Nile are not natural is almost certainly false.
2.18.1a Herodotus uses an oracle to settle an issue of geography. See Appendix P, Oracles Religion, and Politics in Herodotus, §7–9.
2.18.2a Mareia: Map 2.19.
2.18.2b Apis: Map 2.19.

the border of Libya,[c] used to think they were Libyans, not Egyptians, and were aggrieved by the Egyptian sacred rites that required them to abstain from eating the meat of cows. So they sent to the oracle of Ammon, claiming they had nothing in common with the Egyptians, that they lived outside the Delta and did not resemble them in any respect; therefore, they said, they wanted to be permitted to consume all foods. [3] But the god did not allow them to do this; he defined Egypt as the entire area watered by the Nile as it rises over the land, and Egyptians as those who live downstream of the city of Elephantine and who drink the water of this river. That was the oracle's reply.

The Nile overflows onto the land whenever it is in full flood, not only on the Delta but also in some places of the regions called Libya and Arabia, even as far as a two-day journey on either side of the river, sometimes more, sometimes less. I was unable to obtain any information about the nature of the river from either the priests or anyone else. [2] I especially wanted to learn from them why the Nile begins to flood the land at the summer solstice and continues in flood for 100 days before receding and subsiding back into its riverbed, where for the rest of the year it remains shallow for the whole winter until the summer solstice arrives again.[a] [3] None of the Egyptians whom I asked could give me any information as to what power the Nile possesses which gives it a nature contrary to that of other rivers and why the Nile River alone of all other rivers has no cool breezes that blow from it.

Certain Hellenes, however, wanting to win fame for their cleverness, have expressed three different explanations concerning this river, two of which I do not consider worth mentioning, except to report their main arguments. [2] One of them claims that the Etesian winds[a] are the cause of the river's flood, as they prevent the Nile from flowing out into the sea. But often the Etesian winds do not blow, and the Nile floods at the same time anyway. [3] Further, if the Etesians were the cause, all the other rivers that also flow in a direction opposite to these winds should behave the same way as the Nile does, and actually to a greater degree, as they are smaller and have weaker currents. But there are many rivers in Syria as well as in Libya which do not at all behave as does the Nile.[a]

The second explanation is even less knowledgeable than the one just mentioned and, if I may say so, more astonishing. Its claim is that the Nile causes this phenomenon because it flows from Ocean, and that Ocean flows around the entire world.[a]

2.19
EGYPT
NILE FLOOD
No one answers Herodotus' inquiries as to why the Nile, unlike other rivers, floods in summer.

2.20
EGYPT
NILE FLOOD
The Greek opinion that the Etesian winds cause the flood is ridiculous.

2.21
EGYPT
NILE FLOOD
The second hypothesis: the Nile flows from Ocean.

2.18.2c Libya (Africa): Map 2.19 and locator.
2.19.2a Most rivers flood in the spring, swollen from melting snow, and are at a low level during the summer solstice (September 21), but the Nile, fed by winter monsoon rains far to the south in Ethiopia, unknown to Egyptians and Greeks alike, doesn't flood in Egypt until many months later, at the summer solstice. See Appendix C, §3.

2.20.2a Etesian winds: *Etesian* means "occurring annually." The winds blow from the north and west every summer.
2.20.3a As a matter of fact, there are almost no rivers other than the Nile that flow from south to north into the Mediterranean.
2.21.1a Homer (*Iliad*, Book 18, lines 607–608) describes Ocean as covering the entire outer rim of the shield of Achilles.

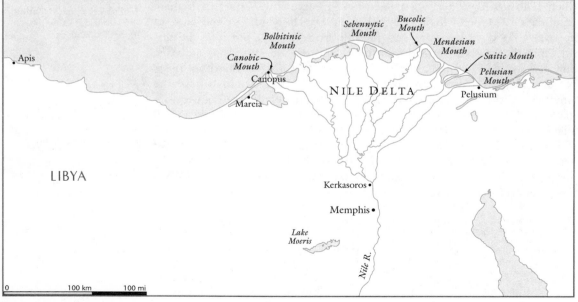

Map 2.19

The third theory, though ostensibly much more plausible, is in fact the most erroneous. Indeed, this theory makes no sense at all when it claims that the Nile's flood comes from melting snow which flows from the interior of Libya through the middle of Ethiopia[a] and then issues forth into Egypt.[b] [2] Well, now, how could its flood come from melting snow if its water flows from the warmest regions to those which are for the most part cooler? A man could at least try to think logically about such things: it is certainly improbable that the Nile's flood comes from snow, and the first and most important evidence for this is provided by the fact that the winds blowing from this region are warm. [3] Second, the land has no rain or ice; but after a snowfall there would have to be rain within five days,[a] and therefore, if these regions received snow, they would also receive rain. Third, the people are black because of the burning heat of the sun. [4] And kites and swallows do not migrate but stay there year round, while in Scythia,[a] when winter arrives, the cranes fly away and migrate to these southern regions for their winter habitat; so if any snow fell at all in this land through which the Nile flows, none of the above phenomena could occur, as logical necessity requires.

And the man who spoke of Ocean,[a] transporting his story into the realm of the unknown, cannot possibly be refuted. For I, at least, have no certain knowledge that such a river Ocean exists; I think, rather, that Homer or one of the poets before him invented the name and introduced it into his poetry.

If one were to say, however, that after finding fault with the opinions already proposed about the unknown, one should declare his own ideas, I shall reveal to you why I think the Nile floods in summer.[a] I believe that during the winter the sun is driven off its usual course by storms and travels to the region of the sky above Libya. [2] Now—to state this opinion very briefly—wherever the sun god approaches closely and hovers is likely to become dehydrated and to have its native rivers and streams shrink and dry up.

Indeed—to present my idea now in greater detail—the sun causes the following effects when he passes over Libya: as the upper air becomes dry over the land which is exposed to the sun and lacks cool breezes, the sun produces a result similar to that which he normally does during our summer, when he is directly overhead. [2] That is to say, he draws water toward himself which he later releases back into the region of the sky far above Libya. There the winds seize this moisture and scatter it into mist and rain, which

2.22
EGYPT
NILE FLOOD
A very plausible Greek opinion, that the Nile flood derives from melting snow, is obviously wrong.

2.23
Herodotus doubts the existence of Ocean.

2.24
EGYPT
NILE FLOOD
Herodotus gives his own idea about why the Nile floods in summer.

2.25
EGYPT
NILE FLOOD
Herodotus believes the winter sun in the Libyan south dries up the Nile, which thus runs fullest when the summer sun is in the north.

2.22.1a Ethiopia: Map 2.19, locator.
2.22.1b Egypt: Map 2.19, locator. Of the theories mentioned by Herodotus, this is the closest to being correct, but neither he nor his contemporaries had any evidence to know that.
2.22.3a There is no known authority for this assertion. (Godley)

2.22.4a Scythia: Map 2.19, locator.
2.23.1a Herodotus here is probably referring to Hekataios; see n. 2.15.1a.
2.24.1a Although Herodotus says he will tell here why he thinks the Nile floods in summer, he seems to focus hereafter on why the Nile differs from other rivers in not flooding in winter.

explains why the south and southwest winds, which blow from this region, are naturally the rainiest of all winds.[a] [3] It seems to me, however, that the sun does not release all the water of the Nile that he takes up in a single year, but that some is left around him as a residue.[a] As winter abates, the sun returns to midheaven and thereafter draws water from all the other rivers equally. [4] So until the onset of summer, the other rivers flow in full force as heavy rain pours into their waters and scours the land where it falls into ravines and gullies. But in summer the rains stop; these rivers dry up and become weak as their water is drawn up by the sun. [5] The Nile, on the other hand, which, unlike the other rivers, receives none of its water from winter rain and which in fact loses water to the sun in that season, is thus the only river that regularly flows at a much lower level in winter than in summer. For in summer, its waters are drawn up by the sun just like all other bodies of water, but it alone suffers evaporation in winter. Thus I believe it is the sun which causes these effects.[a]

And, in my personal opinion, the sun is likewise responsible for the dryness of the air in Egypt,[a] as it scorches this place on its course. Thus in Libya,[b] there is perpetual summer. [2] But if the positions of the seasons were interchanged, and if the region of the sky where the north wind and winter are now should move to the position of where the south wind and the south are, the sun would be driven from midheaven by winter, and the new north wind would go to the regions of the sky above Europe,[a] just as it now (as the south wind) goes above Libya. And I suppose that, as it passed through Europe, it would have the same impact on the Ister[b] as it now does on the Nile.[c]

As to why cool breezes do not blow from the Nile, I am of the opinion that it is unlikely for them to blow at all from very warm places; cool breezes normally arise from quite cold places.

Well, then, let these things be as they are now and have been ever since the beginning. I consulted Egyptians, Lydians, and Hellenes about the sources of the Nile, but no one I talked to professed to know anything about it, except for a scribe of the sacred treasury of Athena[a] in the Egyptian city of Sais.[b] [2] For my part, I thought this man was joking when he presented himself to me as one who knew exactly where the sources were. He said that there are two mountains called Krophi and Mophi, whose peaks rise to points, which are situated between the city of

2.26
EGYPT
NILE FLOOD
The sun keeps Libya in constant summer heat; if the positions of Europe and Libya were reversed, the sun would then affect the Ister as it now does the Nile.

2.27
EGYPT
Cool breezes arise from cool places.

2.28
EGYPT
NILE SOURCES
Herodotus inquires about the sources of the Nile.

2.25.2a   The south and southwest winds are wet in Greece but not in Egypt.
2.25.3a   Perhaps this reflects the contemporary theory that the sun and the stars were fed by water.
2.25.5a   This translation has added to the original text a few phrases, such as names of seasons, to help clarify the author's meaning. One should note the scientific rigor of this discussion of the Nile's sources. Although Herodotus' own theory is certainly wrong, it is

true that from the Northern Hemisphere, the sun does appear to move south in winter and to return in summer.
2.26.1a   Egypt: Map 2.19, locator.
2.26.1b   Libya (Africa): Map 2.19 and locator.
2.26.2a   Europe: Map 2.19, locator.
2.26.2b   Ister (Danube) River: Map 2.19, locator.
2.26.2c   Nile River: Map 2.19 and locator.
2.28.1a   Athena is the Egyptian Nt, called Neith in Greek.
2.28.1b   Sais: Map 2.31, inset.

Syene[a] in the Thebaid[b] and Elephantine.[c] [3] The sources of the Nile are bottomless and originate between these mountains. Half of this water flows to Egypt toward the north, the other half to Ethiopia and the south. [4] He said that Psammetichos king of Egypt decided to conduct an experiment to test whether the sources are really bottomless. He had a rope many thousands of fathoms long woven and let it down there, but it did not reach the bottom. [5] The scribe actually showed, insofar as I understood him (and if what he said was true at all), that the water dashing against the mountains there produced powerful eddies and back currents which would prevent a sounding line from reaching the bottom when it was let down.

But I could learn nothing from anyone else. However, I did learn as much as I could by traveling to the city of Elephantine and seeing it for myself, but I investigated the region beyond that point through hearsay alone.[a] [2] From Elephantine, as one travels inland, the ground rises steeply, and so here one must bind one's boat securely on either side, as though it were an ox, in order to advance. If the rope should break, the boat is instantly gone, carried away by the force of the current. [3] The voyage[a] to this place takes four days, and here the Nile winds and curves like the Maeander.[b] There are eighty miles[c] one must sail through by this method. But then you reach a level plain, where the Nile flows around an island called Tachompso.[d] [4] Half of this island is inhabited by Ethiopians from Elephantine, the other half by Egyptians. Adjacent to the island is a huge lake, whose surrounding land is used for pasture by Ethiopian nomads. If you sail through here, you will come to the channel of the Nile that flows into this lake. [5] Then, disembarking beside the river, you make a forty-day journey by foot. For there are many reefs just below the surface as well as sharp rocks jutting out of the Nile through which one cannot sail. [6] But after traveling through this land for forty days, you can embark on a boat again and then sail for twelve days until you arrive at a large city by the name of Meroe.[a] [7] It is said that this city is the metropolis[a] of the Ethiopians. Here the only gods the people worship are Zeus and Dionysos,[b] and they give great honor to them. They have established an oracle of Zeus, and they make war whenever the god tells them to do so via his divine utterances, and they march wherever he orders them to go.

2.29
EGYPT-ETHIOPIA
Herodotus travels up the Nile to Elephantine and describes the journey beyond to Meroe in Ethiopia.

2.28.2a The location of this Syene near Thebes is unknown. There is a Syene (Map 2.31, inset) just across the Nile from the island called Elephantine, at the First Cataract.
2.28.2b Thebaid: the district around the city of Thebes, Egypt: Map 2.31, inset.
2.28.2c Elephantine (modern Aswan): Map 2.31, inset.
2.29.1a Some scholars have questioned whether Herodotus could actually have gone as far south as Aswan, site of the First Cataract on the Nile, particularly since he fails to mention the huge, extraordinary temples at Thebes, but others argue that he did mention the temples at Thebes at 2.143;

they give various explanations for the omission, or find it unimportant. See Appendix C, §8, and Introduction, §4.3, 4.4.
2.29.3a The voyage from Elephantine to Tachompso (See n. 2.29.3d.).
2.29.3b Maeander River: Map 2.31, AY.
2.29.3c Herodotus writes "12 schoinoi." See n. 2.6.3a and Appendix J, §5–7, 19.
2.29.3d Tachompso: Map 2.31, BY.
2.29.6a Meroe, Ethiopia, approximately 750 miles south of Syene: Map 2.31, BY.
2.29.7a Metropolis, the "mother city" from which colonies were founded.
2.29.7b Zeus and Dionysos, the Greek equivalents of Ammon and Osiris.

2.30
ETHIOPIA
The tale of the Egyptians who deserted Egypt for Ethiopia and civilized the Ethiopians.

If you spend the same amount of time traveling from this city as you spent coming from Elephantine to the metropolis of the Ethiopians, you will reach the Deserters. Their name is Asmach, which, translated into the Greek, means "those who stand to the left of the king." [2] The story goes that these Deserters were 240,000 Egyptians of the warrior class who revolted and came over to the Ethiopians.[a] They had originally been assigned by King Psammetichos to garrison various cities: one garrison was placed in the city of Elephantine[b] to guard against the Ethiopians, another in Pelousian Daphnai[c] against the Arabians[d] and Syrians,[e] and another in Mareia,[f] against the Libyans.[g] [3] These same garrisons were later taken over by the Persians and were still in these positions in my time, for the Persians have garrisons in both Elephantine and Daphnai. Well, no one released these Egyptians from their garrison duty for three years, so they deliberated with each other, worked out a plan together, revolted from Psammetichos, and went off to Ethiopia. [4] When Psammetichos found out about this, he pursued them, and when he caught up with them, he begged them at length not to abandon their ancestral gods, and then he implored them not to leave their women and children. It is reported, however, that one of them exposed himself and, pointing to his genitals, said that wherever these were, they would not lack for wives and children. [5] These men, then, went to Ethiopia and presented themselves to the king of the Ethiopians. And here is how he rewarded them. Some of the Ethiopians had become hostile, and he ordered the Deserters to drive these people out and live on their land. Thus they made their home among the Ethiopians, and the latter became more civilized by learning the manners and customs of the Egyptians from them.

2.31
NILE SOURCES
The sources of the Nile lie beyond the limits of our knowledge.

Beyond its course in Egypt, the Nile is known to extend as far as a four-month journey by boat and by foot, for that is how many months are spent if one adds up the segments I have described as one travels from Elephantine to these Deserters. At that point the river flows in from the west and the setting sun.[a] But about the region beyond this, no one can say anything with certainty, for that land is uninhabited due to the scorching heat of the sun.

2.32
LIBYA
Herodotus recounts the tale of the Nasamonian youths who traveled across the Libyan desert to a land of black pygmies.

I did hear something, however, from some inhabitants of Cyrene[a] who claimed that they had gone to the oracle of Ammon and had conversed with Etearchos king of the Ammonians,[b] and that, after discussing various topics with him, they came to the subject of the Nile and the fact that no one knew its source. Etearchos said that at one time some Nasamonians had come to him; [2] these people are Libyans who inhabit Syrtis[a] and the territory a short distance to the east of Syrtis. [3] These Nasamonians were asked if they had

2.30.2a Ethiopia: Map 2.31, BY.
2.30.2b Elephantine (modern Aswan): Map 2.31, inset.
2.30.2c Daphnai near Pelusium: Map 2.31, inset.
2.30.2d Arabia: Map 2.31, BY.
2.30.2e Syria: Map 2.31, AY.
2.30.2f Mareia: Map 2.31, inset.
2.30.2g Libya (Africa): Map 2.31, BX.
2.31.1a The Nile does not turn west, but doing

so would render its course symmetrical to that of Europe's great river, the Ister (Danube). See Appendix D, §4.
2.32.1a Cyrene: Map 2.31, AY.
2.32.1b Ammonians from the Shrine of Ammon: Map 2.31, BY. The oracle at Ammon is located in the modern oasis of Siwa.
2.32.2a Gulf of Syrtis: Map 2.31, AY.

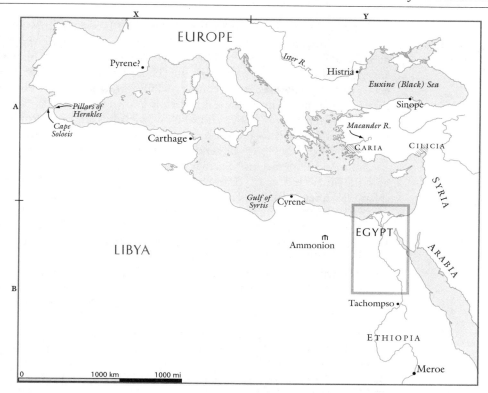

MAP 2.31

any information about the uninhabited regions of Libya, and they replied that they had living among them some sons of their chieftains who were bold and daring and who, when they had grown to manhood, invented some wild and adventurous schemes. In particular, they chose by lot five of their number to go to the uninhabited desert regions of Libya in order to find out whatever they could about them that was not already known before.

[4] The territory of Libya and of its many tribes stretches from Egypt at the sea in the north to the promontory of Soloeis,[a] which is the border of Libya, and extends along the whole coast except for the areas inhabited by Hellenes and Phoenicians.[b] Farther inland, in the regions away from the sea and the inhabited coast, Libya is full of wild animals. And even farther inland lies a sandy desert, extremely dry and barren of all life.

[5] Well, these youths were sent off by their peers well equipped with water and food, and they came first to the inhabited regions, and, passing beyond these, arrived at a land full of wild animals; then, making their way through the desert, they proceeded toward the west and, [6] after crossing an extensive tract of sandy desert for many days, they at last saw trees growing on a plain. As they approached to pick the fruit hanging from the trees, they were attacked and taken captive by little men, that is, people shorter in stature than men. Neither the Nasamonians nor their captors could understand each other's language. [7] They were led through vast swamps, and once they had passed through these, they arrived at a city in which all the people were the same height as their captors and had black skin. Alongside the city was a large river, flowing from the west toward the sunrise, in which crocodiles were visible.

As for this story told by the Ammonian Etearchos, let that be as much as I will reveal of it, except, as the Cyrenaians said, that he claimed that the Nasamonians returned home and that the people they had reached were all sorcerers. [2] Etearchos believed that the river flowing alongside their city must be the Nile,[a] and good sense requires this inference, too. For the Nile flows from Libya and cuts Libya in half. And, if I can make judgments about the unknown from what is known, I can conclude that it is equal to the Ister[b] in the distance it flows from its source. [3] For the River Ister begins in the country of the Celts and the city of Pyrene[a] and flows through the middle of Europe,[b] bisecting it. The Celts are outside the Pillars of Herakles,[c] bordering the Kynesians, who dwell at the edge, farther toward the

2.32.4a   Cape Soloeis: Map 2.31, AX.

2.32.4b   The Hellenes referred to here lived in the area of Cyrene (Map 2.31, AY), and the Phoenicians lived in the region dominated by Carthage (Map 2.31, AX).

2.33.2a   Nile River: Map 2.31, inset. Any such river could not be the Nile. Perhaps it might be the Niger, which also has crocodiles and flows for much of its course from west to east, These characteristics might have led Herodotus to conclude that it was the Nile.

2.33.2b   Ister (Danube) River: Map 2.31, AY.

What Herodotus appears to mean is that as the Nile, according to him, flows first from west to east and then turns northward, so these rivers, one crossing Africa, the other Europe, correspond to each other in a manner conforming to Greek concepts of geographic symmetry. See Appendix D, §1–4.

2.33.3a   Pyrene (Pyrenaeum), possible location: Map 2.31, AX.

2.33.3b   Europe: Map 2.31, AX.

2.33.3c   Pillars of Herakles (modern Straits of Gibraltar): Map 2.31, AX.

2.33

NILE-ISTER COMPARISON Herodotus thinks the river seen by the Nasamonians was probably the Nile and speculates on its symmetry with the Ister River in Europe.

setting sun than all other inhabitants of Europe. [4] The Ister flows through the whole of Europe and ends at the Euxine Sea,[a] where colonists who came from Miletus[b] inhabit Istria.[c]

While the Ister is well known because it flows through inhabited territory, no one can say anything about the sources of the Nile. For the part of Libya through which it flows is uninhabited desert. All that can possibly be learned about its course from inquiry has been stated here. It issues forth into Egypt, and Egypt lies approximately opposite to the mountains of Cilicia.[a] [2] From there to Sinope[a] on the Euxine Sea, it is a five-day journey for a man traveling without heavy baggage. And Sinope lies opposite to the mouth of the Ister. Thus I conclude that the Nile's course through all of Libya is equal in length to that of the Ister. Enough said, then, concerning the Nile.[b]

I am going to extend my account of Egypt at some length here and give additional details about it, because this country has more marvels and monuments that defy description than any other.[a] [2] Together with the contrary nature of Egypt's climate and its unique river, the manners and customs established by the Egyptians are at least in most respects completely opposite to those of other peoples. For example, the women of Egypt go to the marketplace and sell goods there while their men stay at home and do the weaving, which they also do differently from other peoples, who push the woof up from below while the Egyptians push it down. [3] Here the men carry loads on their heads and the women bear them on their shoulders. Women urinate standing up, men sitting down. They ease themselves inside the house, but eat out in the streets, and justify this with the explanation that one ought to take care of base necessities in private, but those that are not base, in public. [4] No woman serves as a priestess of any deities, male or female—only men serve as the priests. No constraint forces unwilling sons to support their parents, but women are forced to provide for them, even if they do not want to do so.[a]

Elsewhere, priests of the gods wear their hair long, but in Egypt they shave their heads. And although the rest of the human race expresses mourning, especially those closest to the deceased, by cutting their hair at once, Egyptians allow their shaved hair to grow both on the head and the chin just after a death. [2] Other peoples isolate their animals from contact with their daily civilized life, but the Egyptians live together with their animals. The principal food of everyone else consists of wheat and barley, but

2.34
NILE-ISTER COMPARISON
Herodotus compares the Nile to the Ister River.

2.35
EGYPT
Herodotus begins to describe the customs of the Egyptians.

2.36
EGYPT
More customs of the Egyptians.

2.33.4a Euxine (Black) Sea: Map 2.31, AY.
2.33.4b Miletus: Map 2.48, Hellas inset.
2.33.4c Istria (Histria): Map 2.31, AY.
2.34.1a Cilicia: Map 2.31, AY.
2.34.2a Sinope: Map 2.31, AY.
2.34.2b This passage provides an interesting and revealing glimpse into Herodotus' view of the geography of his world and into some of the "logical" inferences he could draw from it. See Appendix D, §1–4.
2.35.1a This statement reveals a great deal about marvels, a subject which greatly interests

Herodotus and his public. See Appendix C, §5, 8.
2.35.4a Although Herodotus' description of Egyptian customs and manners is mostly correct, he is sometimes wrong and often mistaken in drawing such a rigid and complete dichotomy (highly valued in ancient Greek thought) between those of the Greeks and those of the Egyptians, which are not so clean and neat in practice. See Appendix C, §4.

an Egyptian would consider this an absolutely disgraceful diet; their bread is made from hulled, single-seeded wheat, which some call emmer.[a] [3] And they knead dough with their feet, but lift up mud and even dung with their hands. The Egyptians practice circumcision, while all other peoples (except for those who have learned it from the Egyptians) let their genitals remain as they are at birth. Each man owns two garments, each woman owns one. [4] While others attach the rings of their sails and the lines on the outside, the Egyptians attach them on the inside. The Hellenes write letters and calculate numbers by moving their hand from left to right, but the Egyptians write their letters and numbers from right to left; what's more, the Egyptians claim that their method is the "right" one, the Greek way a "left-handed" one. They write with two different scripts, one called "sacred," the other called "public."[a]

Of all peoples, they are the most exceedingly pious, with customs such as these: they drink from bronze cups that they wash every day, not just this one or that one, but all of them. [2] They are especially strict about always wearing freshly laundered linen garments. They circumcise their men for the sake of cleanliness, esteeming purity above beauty. Their priests shave their entire bodies every other day to prevent lice or any other vermin from hiding on their bodies as they worship the gods.

[3] Their priests wear only linen garments and sandals made of papyrus;[a] they are not permitted to acquire any other kinds of garments or sandals. They bathe with cold water twice daily and twice nightly, and they must perform an incredible number of religious observances. [4] They do, however, receive a considerable number of benefits. For example, they don't have to pay anything of their own for their living expenses. Their food, which is considered sacred, is cooked for them, and each one of them receives a generous allowance of beef and goose meat every day; they are also provided with wine made from grapes. Fish, however, they are not even permitted to taste. [5] Beans are not sown much at all by the Egyptians, and they generally will not eat those that do grow there, whether raw or cooked. But the priests, who believe this pulse[a] to be unclean, cannot even endure the sight of them. Many priests serve each of the gods, although there is a chief priest for each deity, whose son succeeds him in that office when he dies.

They believe that bulls belong to Epaphos,[a] and therefore they examine them with great care. If they see even a single black hair, they consider the animal unclean. [2] A priest appointed for this purpose searches the body of the bull, both as it stands and as it lies on its back, and also pulls out its tongue to see if it is clear of certain prescribed marks (which I shall explain in another

2.37
EGYPT
Religious customs
of the Egyptians.

2.38
EGYPT
Egyptian method for
certifying the purity of
sacrificial bulls.

2.36.2a Herodotus is wrong here. The Egyptians used barley on a large scale.

2.36.4a There are three scripts, really: hieroglyphic, hieratic (derived from hieroglyphic), and demotic, a simplified form of hieratic (Godley), of which Herodotus

appears to be ignorant.

2.37.3a For more about the papyrus plant, see 2.92.5.

2.37.5a Pulse: a porridge made with beans and/or lentils.

2.38.1a Epaphos is the Greek name for the god Apis.

account).[a] Then he inspects the hairs of the tail to see if they have grown in naturally, [3] and if, after this thorough examination, the bull is deemed clean, the priest marks it by twisting papyrus around its horns, plastering on sealing clay, and then stamping it with his signet ring. After this, the bull is led away. The penalty for sacrificing a bull that has not been thus marked is death.[a]

They sacrifice the designated animal in the following way: after leading it to the sacrificial altar, they light the fire and pour wine upon both the altar and the victim. Then, as they invoke the god, they slash the animal's throat and, after having thus slaughtered it, cut off its head. [2] The body of the victim is then skinned, but they invoke many curses on its head before they take it away. Those who have a market where Hellenes live and work as merchants take the head there and sell it to them. But those who have no Hellenes living nearby throw the head into the river. [3] They invoke those many curses on the bull's head so that any evil that is about to happen either to those performing the sacrifice or to all of Egypt will be diverted onto the head of the bull. [4] Because of this belief, no Egyptian will taste the head of any animal. All Egyptians practice the same custom concerning the heads of sacrificial cattle and pour libations of wine in every one of their rituals.

2.39
EGYPT
Religious animal sacrifice in Egypt.

Their traditional methods of removing and burning the entrails, however, differ according to the sacrificial victim. They celebrate the goddess they believe to be the greatest[a] with a festival in her honor, which is also their most important festival, and which I will now describe.

[2] When they skin a bull, they pronounce a prayer over all the intestines they have removed, but leave the rest of them and its fat in the body. Then they cut off the legs, the tip of its loins, the shoulders, and the neck. [3] When they have finished this task, they fill the remaining cavity of the bull's body with bread they consider pure, and with honey, raisins, figs, frankincense, myrrh, and other fragrant substances. When it is filled completely, they burn up the entire carcass, all the while pouring oil over it copiously. [4] They fast before they sacrifice, and while the victim is burning, they beat their breasts in mourning; but when they have finished beating their breasts, the entrails that remain are served as a meal.

2.40
EGYPT
One method of preparing the sacrificed animal.

Egyptians sacrifice only ritually pure bulls and male calves. They are not permitted to sacrifice female animals, as these are considered sacred to Isis. [2] Their statue of Isis has a woman's body with horns like a cow's, just as the Hellenes portray Io; and all Egyptians venerate cows more than any other animals by far. [3] Because Hellenes do eat cows, no Egyptian man or woman will kiss a Greek man on the mouth, nor will they use a Greek man's knife, his cooking skewers, or his cooking pot. And they will not taste the meat of a bull, even one deemed ritually pure, if it has been butchered with a Greek knife.

2.41
EGYPT
Cows are sacred and may not be killed. Rules for disposal of dead cows and bulls.

2.38.2a   This other account either is the text of 3.28 or is not available to us—perhaps an unfulfilled promise.

2.38.3a   The great sanctity of Apis emphasizes the magnitude of the blasphemy of King

Cambyses when he kills the bull later in the main narrative (3.28–30).

2.40.1a   Their greatest goddess is probably Isis (2.61) or Artemis/Bastet (2.59).

[4] When their cattle die, they dispose of them as follows: the cows they toss into the river, but the bulls are buried in the ground by inhabitants of the outskirts of the city, with one or both horns protruding as a marker. When the body has rotted and the appointed time has arrived, a barge[a] comes to each city from an island called Prosopitis.[b] [5] This island lies in the Delta and measures sixty miles[a] in circumference. There are in fact many cities on this island of Prosopitis, but the one from which the barges come to take up the bones of the bulls is called Atarbechis.[b] And here they have dedicated a sanctuary sacred to Aphrodite.[c] [6] From this city, many people travel to other Egyptian cities in order to dig up the bones, which they then bring back and bury, all of them in one place. When other animals die naturally—and the Egyptians do not kill these other animals either—they bury them just as they do the bulls, for that is their traditional belief and custom about these matters.

2.42
EGYPT
Regional sacrificial practices
and taboos in Egypt.

All those who have established a sanctuary of Theban Zeus, or who are of the Theban nome,[a] sacrifice goats but not sheep. [2] For Egyptians do not all worship the same gods in the same way. Only the gods Isis and Osiris (the latter of whom they say is Dionysos) are worshiped in the same manner by all Egyptians. For example, those who have a sanctuary of Mendes[a] or are of the Mendesian district sacrifice sheep but not goats. [3] Now the Egyptians and all who follow their practice abstain from sacrificing sheep and claim that their custom originated in this manner: Herakles[a] had an overwhelming desire to see Zeus, who did not want to be seen by him. Finally, since Herakles kept insisting, Zeus devised the following scheme. [4] He skinned a ram, cut off its head, wrapped himself in the fleece, and placed the head in front of his own face, and showed himself thus to Herakles. That is why the Egyptians fashion the statue of Zeus with the head of a ram. The Ammonians,[a] who are colonists from both Egypt[b] and Ethiopia[c] and who speak a combination of both languages, apparently received this tradition from the Egyptians. [5] And since the Egyptians call Zeus by the name of Ammon, it seems to me that the Ammonians also received their name from the appellation of this god. So that is why the Thebans[a] do not sacrifice rams but consider them their sacred animals. [6] On one day of the year, at a festival of Zeus, they

2.41.4a   Herodotus uses a non-Greek word, *baris* (for barge), twice in this chapter. He uses it again in 2.60.1, 2.60.2, 2.96.5, and 2.179.1. Herodotus occasionally inserts non-Greek terms throughout his *Histories*.
2.41.4b   Prosopitis (Prosopites) was an island probably formed between the Canobic (Kanobikon) and Sebennytic channels of the Nile, in the south of the Delta. Its precise location is unknown. For the mouths of the Nile's Canobic and Sebennytic channels, see Map 2.48, Nile Delta inset.
2.41.5a   Herodotus writes "9 schoinoi." See Appendix J, §5–7, 19.
2.41.5b   Atarbechis: Map 2.48, Nile Delta inset.
2.41.5c   Aphrodite in this case is the Egyptian goddess Hathor.

2.42.1a   Herodotus here and later in this chapter uses the word *nome* for district, or county, or unit of local government. The Theban nome (Thebes): Map 2.48, locator.
2.42.2a   Herodotus identifies the Egyptian god Mendes with the Greek god Pan; they both share goatlike qualities. See 2.46.
2.42.3a   The Greeks identified Herakles with the Egyptian god Shu (called Chonsu-Neferhotep at Thebes). (Godley)
2.42.4a   Ammonians: from the shrine of Ammon in the Egyptian desert. See Map 2.48, locator.
2.42.4b   Egypt: Map 2.48, locator.
2.42.4c   Ethiopia: Map 2.48, locator.
2.42.5a   Thebans of the Theban nome (Nomos Thebaios). See n. 2.42.1a.

cut up a single ram and skin it, just as Zeus is supposed to have done in the story. Then they dress the statue of Zeus in its hide and bring another statue, one of Herakles, to stand next to it. When this has been done, they first beat their breasts and circle the sanctuary in mourning for the ram, and then they bury it in a sacred tomb.

Now to turn again to Herakles, I have heard it said that he was one of the twelve Egyptian gods, but about the other Herakles, the one known to the Hellenes, I was unable to learn anything anywhere in Egypt. [2] Moreover, the fact is that the Egyptians did not take the "name of Herakles" from the Hellenes, but that the Hellenes (that is, those Hellenes who established the name of Herakles as the son of Amphitryon[a]) took it from the Egyptians; this can be demonstrated by many proofs, especially by the fact that both parents of Herakles, Amphitryon and Alkmene, were of Egyptian descent.[b] In addition, the Egyptians claim that they do not know the names "Poseidon" or "the Dioskouroi";[c] so they do not recognize or accept them among their other gods. [3] If they had taken the name of a divinity from the Hellenes, they would surely retain a vivid memory of it, rather than having no memory of it at all. And if in fact the Egyptians and the Hellenes were both making sea voyages at that time, as I think most likely to have been the case, the Egyptians would certainly have become acquainted with the names of these gods (Poseidon and the Dioskouroi) better than that of Herakles. [4] The Egyptians do, however, recognize a certain Herakles, a god of great antiquity; as they themselves say, it was 17,000 years prior to the reign of Amasis[a] when their number of gods expanded from eight to twelve to include Herakles among them.

Since I wished to know something definite about all this from any source I could find, I sailed to Tyre in Phoenicia[a] when I learned that there was a sanctuary sacred to Herakles there. [2] And I saw that it was decorated lavishly with many offerings; in particular, I saw two pillars in it, one of refined gold, the other of emerald so magnificent that it glowed in the dark. When I asked the priests of the god how long it had been since the sanctuary had been established, [3] I discovered that they did not agree with the Hellenes, for they said that the sanctuary was founded at the same time that Tyre was settled, and that Tyre had been inhabited for 2,300 years. I also saw in Tyre another sanctuary of Herakles, this one bearing the epithet "Thasian." [4] And so I went to Thasos[a] and found there a sanctuary of Herakles founded by Phoenicians who had set sail in search of Europa[b] and had colonized Thasos, which happened in fact five generations of men earlier than the birth of Herakles son of Amphitryon, in Hellas. [5] And so this research shows clearly that Herakles is an ancient divinity. The Hellenes I consider the most orthodox are those who have founded and maintained two distinct sanctuaries of Herakles, sacrificing to one as an

2.43
EGYPT
Concerning the Egyptian antiquity of Herakles. Evidence and proofs.

2.44
PHOENICIA
Herodotus travels to Phoenicia inquiring about Herakles. More evidence and proofs.

2.43.2a   The Greek poets Homer and Hesiod.
2.43.2b   They were of Egyptian descent through their grandfather Perseus, a descendant of Aigyptos; see 2.91 and 6.53.
2.43.2c   Poseidon and the Dioskouroi were gods of the sea and helpers to sailors.
2.43.4a   Amasis reigned in Egypt from 570 to 526.
2.44.1a   Tyre, Phoenicia: Map 2.48, locator.
2.44.4a   Thasos: Map 2.48, Hellas inset.
2.44.4b   Europa: see 1.2.1.

immortal with the epithet "Olympian," and to the other as a hero, with offerings appropriate to the dead.[a]

2.45
Greek myths about Herakles show them to be ignorant of the Egyptians.

The Hellenes tell many different naïve stories, and their myth of Herakles is especially foolish. They say he came to Egypt and was crowned by the Egyptians, who then let him direct a procession as a sacrificial victim to Zeus; he kept silent for a while, but when they led him up to the altar, he turned on them and with his great strength he murdered them all. [2] The Hellenes who tell this story, it seems to me, are entirely ignorant of the nature and customs of the Egyptians: these people are forbidden by sacred law to sacrifice their domestic animals, apart from sheep, bulls, male calves that are ritually clean, and geese, so how could they conceivably sacrifice human beings? [3] And furthermore, how could it be humanly possible for Herakles, a single man and human, as they say, to murder many thousands of men at one time? Having said so much about this, I pray that both the gods and the heroes may look upon us favorably.

2.46
EGYPT
Mendesian worship of Pan and treatment of goats.

Well, the Egyptians that I mentioned earlier,[a] the ones who do not sacrifice goats, and especially male goats, refrain from doing so for this reason. The Mendesians count Pan as one of the eight gods who, they say, existed before there were twelve gods. [2] Indeed, painters and sculptors depict and carve the image of Pan just as the Hellenes do, with the head of a goat and the legs of a male goat, although they do not believe that he really looks like this, but rather that he resembles the other gods. Why they depict him in this way, however, I should prefer not to mention. [3] The Mendesians venerate all goats, but the male goats more than the female goats, and the herdsmen of male goats receive greater honors. Of all these goats, one is considered the most important, and when he dies, the entire Mendesian district goes into solemn mourning. [4] Both this goat and Pan are called Mendes by the Egyptians. During my lifetime there occurred in this nome[a] a bizarre phenomenon: a goat had intercourse with a woman out in public. This incident became notorious.

2.47
EGYPT
Egyptian customs relating to pigs.

The Egyptians consider the pig an unclean animal. In the first place, if anyone is passing by a pig and so much as touches it, he goes immediately to the river and submerges himself in it entirely, clothes and all; furthermore, of all the Egyptians, it is only the swineherds, even though they are native-born, who do not enter any sanctuary in Egypt. And no one will give his daughter in marriage to one of them, nor marry one of their daughters; so the swineherds must intermarry among themselves. [2] Egyptians do not sacrifice pigs to any of their gods except Selene and Dionysos,[a] to both of whom they offer sacrifice together during the full moon. After the sacrificial ceremony they feast on the meat. As to the reason for their aversion to pigs

---

2.44.5a　Homer describes a dual Herakles (*Odyssey* 11.601ff.). His "shade" is seen in the world of the dead, but "he himself" is an immortal among the gods of heaven.
2.46.1a　Mentioned in 2.42.2.
2.46.4a　Nome Mendesios: Map 2.48, Nile Delta inset.

2.47.2a　Selene and Dionysos are the Egyptian Isis and Osiris. Because Herodotus feels that the Egyptians came to know and name the gods first, then transmitted their knowledge to the Greeks, he finds identity between the gods of the Egyptian and Greek pantheons. See Appendix C, §2, 4.

at other festivals, there is an account given by Egyptians which, though I know it, would not be very proper for me to divulge here.

[3] This is how they sacrifice pigs to Selene. Whenever someone performs this ritual, he gathers together the tip of the tail, the spleen, and the membrane enclosing the entrails, wraps them all up inside the fat surrounding the animal's belly, then burns it completely in the fire, as in a funeral offering. The rest of the meat they consume on the same night of the full moon during which they sacrificed the victim; on any other day they would refuse to even taste it. Their poor people, because they cannot afford to sacrifice real pigs, bake cakes molded in the shape of pigs and sacrifice these instead.

On the eve of the festival of Dionysos, each Egyptian slaughters a young pig in front of the entrance to his home and then gives it back to the swineherd who sold it to him to take away. [2] The Egyptians celebrate the festival of Dionysos in nearly the same way as the Hellenes do, except they do not have choral dances. And instead of phalluses they have their own invention—marionettes as tall as one and a half feet,[a] which the women carry around through the villages; these marionettes have genitals that move up and down and are not much smaller than their entire bodies. A flute player leads the way, and the women follow, singing praises of Dionysos. [3] There is a sacred story which explains why the genitals are so large and why they are the only part of the marionettes that move.

> 2.48
> EGYPT
> The Egyptian festival of Dionysos.

Now it seems to me that Melampous son of Amythaon was not ignorant of this sacrificial ritual. I think, rather, that he was actually quite familiar with it, for it was Melampous who disclosed the name of Dionysos to the Hellenes, and who taught them how to sacrifice to him and perform his phallic procession. Strictly speaking, he did not reveal everything to them, but the sages who were his descendants completed the revelation. And so it is Melampous who taught the Hellenes the phallic procession for Dionysos which they practice today. [2] What is more, I would argue that Melampous, being a clever man, acquired the art of prophecy by himself and then, utilizing information from Egypt, introduced many different rites to the Hellenes, among them those for Dionysos, although along the way he made a few changes. I would certainly not claim that it is by chance that the rite performed for the god in Egypt resembles so closely that carried out in Hellas. If that were true, then this rite would be more similar to other Greek rites in character and would not be considered a recent introduction. [3] Nor would I assert that the Egyptians took this or any other custom or ritual from the Hellenes. But I rather suspect that Melampous learned about Dionysos chiefly from Kadmos of Tyre[a] and those who accompanied him on the journey from Phoenicia[b] to the land now called Boeotia.[c]

> 2.49
> EGYPT-HELLAS
> How the Dionysian rite was transmitted to the Greeks.

2.48.2a Herodotus writes "1 cubit." There were several standard measures for the cubit, but the one probably referred to here = approximately 1.5 feet. See Appendix J, §4, 5, 19.

2.49.3a Tyre: Map 2.48, locator. In Greek myths and in Euripides' play *The Bacchae*, Kadmos was the grandfather of Dionysos.

2.49.3b Phoenicia: Map 2.48, locator.

2.49.3c Boeotia: Map 2.48, Hellas inset.

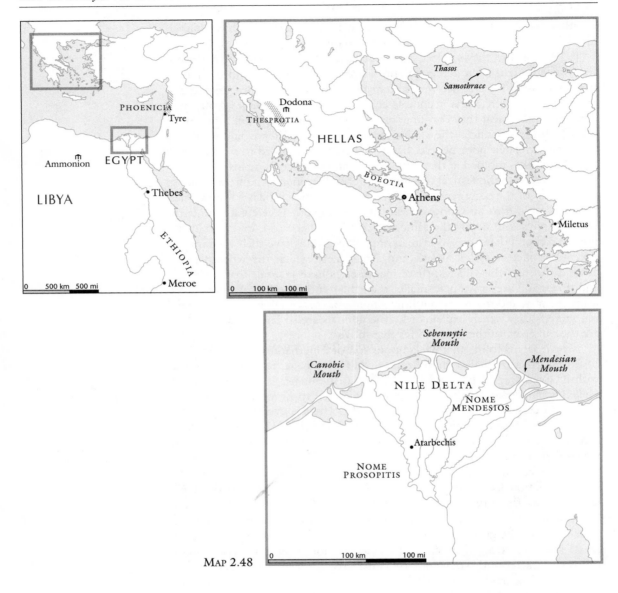

MAP 2.48

By making inquiries, I discovered that the names of the gods came to Hellas from barbarians,[a] and I myself concluded that they derive specifically from Egypt, for [2] the names of the gods have been known in Egypt since the earliest times, except for Poseidon and the Dioskouroi (as I mentioned earlier),[a] as well as Hera, Histia, Themis, the Graces, and the Nereids. Here I am reporting what the Egyptians themselves say, and this leads me to believe that the gods whose names they deny knowing were named by the Pelasgians[b]—all except for Poseidon, since this god was introduced to the Hellenes by the Libyans, who alone, among all peoples, have always honored him and have possessed the name of Poseidon from the beginning. And as to the Dioskouroi, the Egyptians do not believe in heroes at all.

These customs, in addition to others which I shall describe, have been adopted by the Hellenes from the Egyptians. But they learned to make their statues of Hermes with an erect phallus from the Pelasgians, not the Egyptians. The Athenians[a] were the first of all Hellenes to embrace this practice, and the others adopted it later from them. [2] And since already at that time the Athenians were considered as Hellenes and the Pelasgians had settled in their land, the Pelasagians, too, were believed to be Hellenes.[a] Whoever has been initiated into the secret rites of the Kabeiroi[b] performed by the Samothracians[c] (who adopted them from the Pelasgians) will know what I mean. [3] For the same Pelasgians who settled in Athenian territory had earlier inhabited Samothrace, and it was from them that the Samothracians adopted those mysteries. [4] And so the Athenians were the first of the Hellenes to make statues of Hermes with an erect phallus, and they learned this from the Pelasgians. There exists a sacred story about Hermes that was told by the Pelasgians; its details are revealed in the mysteries at Samothrace.

But I heard at Dodona[a] that long ago the Pelasgians, when they made sacrifices, used to pray to the gods, but they could not address prayers to any one of them by name or epithet because they had not yet learned or heard of these. They called them gods because they believed that it was the gods who had ordered and allotted all things.[b] [2] But after the passage of quite a long time, they did learn the names of the gods from Egypt, all except for Dionysos, whose name they learned much later on. Then they consulted the oracle at Dodona about these names. This oracle, which is

2.50
EGYPT-HELLAS
Most knowledge of the gods came to Greece from Egypt and Libya.

2.51
EGYPT-HELLAS
The Pelasgian origin of the phallic images of Hermes.

2.52
EGYPT-HELLAS
The Pelasgians learned the names of the gods from Egypt.

2.50.1a   Herodotus, like other Greeks of his time, uses the term "barbarian" in a non-pejorative sense to mean non-Greek. The term usually refers to language but can apply to such factors as ethnicity, customs, and religion as well. There are instances in which it is used pejoratively, but that is generally not the case.
2.50.2a   Reported at 2.43.2.
2.50.2b   The Pelasgians were thought by the Greeks to have been the original inhabitants of what became Greece (or Hellas) after the Greeks (or Hellenes) arrived.
2.51.1a   Athens: Map 2.48, Hellas inset.
2.51.2a   For more on the Pelasgians, see n. 1.56.2d and 1.57ff.

2.51.2b   The Kabeiroi varied in number in different areas of Greece and were probably worshiped from a very early time. In Samothrace they were thought to be Hermes and Hephaistos, but Herodotus calls them "sons of Hephaistos" at 3.37. They were believed to be associated with fertility and also protection of sea travelers.
2.51.2c   Samothrace: Map 2.48, Hellas inset.
2.52.1a   Dodona: Map 2.48, Hellas inset.
2.52.1b   This sentence, if read literally, contains the following pun, which is difficult to render in English: They called them gods [*theoi*] because the gods [*theoi*] set [*thentes*] all things in order and continued to maintain the allotment of all things.

thought to be the most ancient of all Greek oracles, was in fact the only one that existed at the time. [3] When the Pelasgians asked this oracle whether they should agree to these names that came from barbarians, the oracle answered agreeably that they should indeed use them.[a] And so from then on they used the specific names of the gods when they prayed to them at sacrifice. Later on, the Pelasgians passed these names on to the Hellenes.

2.53
850?
HELLAS
Also Hesiod and Homer taught the Greeks about the gods 400 years ago.

But the origin of each of the gods, or whether they always existed, and what they look like: all of this was unknown until just recently—only yesterday, so to speak. [2] For I believe that Hesiod and Homer were contemporaries who lived no more than 400 years before my time.[a] These were the poets who composed for the Hellenes the theogony,[b] assigned to the gods their epithets, defined their particular honors and skills, and described what they look like. [3] Those poets who are said to have lived earlier than these men actually lived later; at least that is what I think. Of the claims stated here, I heard the former one[a] directly from the priestesses at Dodona; the latter one, concerning Hesiod and Homer, is my own opinion.

2.54
EGYPT-HELLAS
The Egyptian explanation for the oracles in Dodona and Libya.

The Egyptians[a] tell this story about the oracles in Hellas[b] and Libya.[c] The priests of Theban Zeus say that the Phoenicians[d] abducted two priestesses from Thebes[e] and that they learned how one of them was sold into Libya, the other into Hellas, and that the two women became the first founders of oracles among these peoples. [2] When I asked them how they knew this had really happened, they replied that they had carried out an extensive search for these women and, though they were unable to find them, they did later learn what they had just told me about them.

2.55
DODONA
The priestesses of Dodona's explanation for the oracles there and in Libya.

That at least is what I heard from the priests in Thebes, but the priestesses of Dodona told me that two black doves flew from Egyptian Thebes and that one went to Libya, the other to Dodona. [2] Perching on the oak tree at Dodona, the one dove proclaimed with a human voice that an oracle of Zeus should be established on that spot. The people of Dodona assumed that this was a divine command and accordingly did as they were told. [3] They say that the dove that went to Libya ordered the Libyans to establish an oracle of Ammon there. This, too, is an oracle of Zeus. That is the account I received from the priestesses of Dodona, of whom the eldest is named Promeneia, the second eldest Timarete, and the youngest Nikandra. And the other Dodonaians around the sanctuary agreed with them.

2.56
DODONA
Herodotus' own explanation for the oracles at Dodona and Libya.

But I have my own opinion about these claims. If the Phoenicians really did abduct the priestesses and sell one into Libya and the other into Hellas, I think that Thesprotia[a] was probably the region of what is now called Hellas (but formerly Pelasgia) into which the woman was sold. [2] Then it is reasonable to expect that, as a slave there, she founded the sanctuary of Zeus under the grow-

2.52.3a	The repetition of "agree" in this sentence reflects another pun in the Greek, with the same verb used in different forms: *anelontai/aneile*. Oracles can verify names. See Appendix P, §9.	2.53.2b	Theogony: the genealogy of the gods.
		2.53.3a	The claim Herodotus just made in 2.52.
		2.54.1a	Egypt: Map 2.48, locator.
		2.54.1b	Hellas (Greece): Map 2.48, Hellas inset.
2.53.2a	Modern scholars believe that Homer and Hesiod lived about 200 years before Herodotus' time.	2.54.1c	Libya: Map 2.48, locator.
		2.54.1d	Phoenicia: Map 2.48, locator.
		2.54.1e	Thebes, Egypt: Map 2.48, locator.
		2.56.1a	Thesprotia: Map 2.48, Hellas inset.

FIGURE 2.55. VIEW DOWN THE VALLEY FROM THE THEATER AT THE DODONA SHRINE TO ZEUS.

ing oak tree of Dodona. She had, after all, been a handmaid to the sanctuary of Zeus in Thebes, and in this way she maintained a memorial to that god when she came from there to Hellas. [3] At this sanctuary, then, she introduced the oracle as soon as she understood the Greek language, and she also said that her sister had been sold in Libya by the same Phoenicians who had sold her.

I assume that the woman was called a dove by the Dodonaians because she was a barbarian[a] and sounded to them like a bird when she spoke. [2] Thus they interpreted her speech so long as she spoke in a barbarian language, but after a while they say that the dove spoke with the voice of a human. I believe what really happened was that the woman now spoke to them intelligibly in Greek. How could a dove possibly speak with the voice of a human? And furthermore, the Dodonaians, by claiming that the dove was black, show that she was an Egyptian. [3] Finally, the method of divination in Egyptian Thebes resembles the one used in Dodona;[a] and the Dodonaian art of divination from sacrificial victims also came from Egypt.

2.57
DODONA
Herodotus' further explanation of the Dodonaian myth concerning its foundation.

2.57.1a   The term "barbarian" was used by Greeks as a non-pejorative term which simply meant non-Greek. See n. 2.50.1a.

2.57.3a   Dodona: Map 2.48, Hellas inset. See Fig-

ure 2.55, the theater and the view down the valley from it at Dodona, the site of a major Greek oracle and sanctuary to Zeus.

In any case, the Egyptians were the first of all peoples to hold public religious festivals, pageants, and processions escorting divine images, and the Hellenes learned about these rituals from them. My proof for this assertion is that Egyptian ceremonies have obviously been held for a very long time, but those of the Hellenes have been instituted only recently.[a]

The Egyptians come together to celebrate major festivals not just once but many times a year. The most popular festival takes place at the city of Boubastis[a] in honor of Artemis. Their second most popular festival honors Isis at the city of Bousiris,[b] an Egyptian city situated in the center of the Delta [2] where the most important sanctuary of Isis is located. Isis in the Greek language is Demeter. [3] Their third most popular festival is at the city of Sais[a] in honor of Athena; their fourth, at Heliopolis[b] in honor of Helios; their fifth, at the city of Bouto[c] in honor of Leto; and their sixth, at the city of Papremis[d] in honor of Ares.

Here is what they do on their way to Boubastis. Men sail with women, large crowds of them together in each barge.[a] Throughout the entire journey, some of the women play castanets, some of the men play flutes, and the rest of them, both men and women, sing and clap their hands. [2] Whenever they approach some city along the way to Boubastis, they skirt the shore with their barge, and while some of the women continue as before, others shout at the women of the city, mocking and ridiculing them, and some dance, and still others stand up and lift their robes, exposing themselves. They do this at every city along the river, [3] and when they arrive at Boubastis, they celebrate their holiday by performing huge sacrifices. They consume more grape wine at this festival than at any other time of the year, and according to what the native inhabitants say, there may be as many as 700,000 men and women (but no children) gathered together here.

That is how this festival is celebrated. I have already described how the one at the city of Bousiris in honor of Isis is observed,[a] and the fact that they beat their breasts in mourning after the sacrifice. All the men and women there, countless thousands of people, do this together. But it would be blasphemous for me to identify who it is for whom they mourn.[b] [2] Those Carians[a] who live in Egypt go so much further than the Egyptians in their mourning that they cut their faces with knives, and thereby reveal themselves to be foreigners, not Egyptians.

2.58.1a As in his discussion of the names of the gods, Herodotus assumes that since the Egyptian festivals were celebrated earlier, the Greeks must have learned about them from the Egyptians. See Appendix C, §2.

2.59.1a Boubastis: Map 2.67, inset. The "city of Bastet," where the cat-headed goddess Bastet (Pasht), identified by Herodotus with Artemis, was worshiped. (Godley)

2.59.1b Bousiris: Map 2.67, inset.

2.59.3a Sais: Map 2.67, inset.

2.59.3b Heliopolis: Map 2.67, inset.

2.59.3c Bouto is mentioned many times in Herodotus' text. There are two Egyptian cities of that name. This citation refers to the Bouto which lies in the northwestern sector of the Nile Delta and was the site of the oracle of Leto. Both Boutos are shown on Map 2.67, inset.

2.59.3d Papremis: Map 2.67, inset.

2.60.1a Herodotus uses the foreign word *baris* here for "barge," as he does in 2.41.4, 2.60.2, 2.96.5, and 2.179.1.

2.61.1a At 2.40.

2.61.1b Apparently they mourn for Osiris. Compare 2.86.2 and 2.132.2.

2.61.2a Caria: Map 2.67.

When they congregate in the city of Sais for the festival sacrifices, there is a certain night on which they all light many lamps in the open air, in a circle around the houses. The lamps they use are saucers filled with salt and oil that have a wick floating on top; they burn all night long, and that is why the festival is called the Feast of the Burning Lamps. [2] Even the Egyptians who do not attend this festival in person observe the night of the sacrifice by lighting lamps, too, and so they burn them not only in Sais but throughout all Egypt as well. There is a sacred story which explains why this night is honored and associated with light.

When they go to Heliopolis and Bouto, they perform only sacrifices. In Papremis, they have sacrifices and sacrificial victims as elsewhere, but in addition, they perform the following ritual: as soon as the sun goes down, a few of the priests attend to the sacred image, while many other priests stand at the entrance to the sanctuary holding wooden clubs; opposite them stands a crowd of more than 1,000 men who are fulfilling their vows, and who are also holding clubs. [2] On the day previous to this, the sacred image is carried in a small gilded wooden shrine to another sacred building. And now the few priests left with the image pull a four-wheeled wagon containing both the shrine and the image inside it to the sanctuary. But those priests standing before the gates do not allow them to enter, and those who are bound by their vows assist the god by striking the others who resist them. [3] The battle intensifies as they wield their wooden clubs; heads are bashed, and I think that many must die from their wounds, although the Egyptians deny that anyone actually dies.

[4] According to the native Egyptians, the reason for the customs of this festival is that the mother of the god Ares used to live in this sanctuary; and when Ares, who grew up apart from his mother, reached adulthood, he wanted to mingle with[a] her. But his mother's servants, having never seen him before, warded him off and did not permit him to approach her. So he returned with a group of people from another city and, after beating up the servants, went in to be with his mother. That is why, they say, it is customary to have a fight at this festival in honor of Ares.[b]

The Egyptians were the first to observe religious prohibitions against having intercourse with women in sanctuaries and against even entering sanctuaries, if one has not washed after having had intercourse with women. Almost all other peoples, in fact, except for the Egyptians and the Hellenes, do have intercourse in sanctuaries and do enter them unwashed after just having had intercourse with women, believing as they do that people are just like animals. [2] Because they see all types of animals and birds mounting each other in the temples and precincts of the gods, they assume that the animals would not do this unless the god approved of it. Now I find this explanation to be quite disagreeable.

2.63.4a   The literal translation "mingle with" can ambiguously indicate either social interaction (as at 1.123.2, of Harpagos and the Medes) or sexual intercourse.

2.63.4b   It is uncertain which Egyptian deity Herodotus identifies with Ares, the Greek god of war. (Godley)

2.65
EGYPT
Egyptian veneration for
and care of animals.

But it must be admitted that the Egyptians are excessively scrupulous in these and in many other religious matters.

[2] Although Egypt shares a border with Libya,[a] it does not have many wild animals, and all the animals that do live there are considered sacred.[b] Some live with people in their households; others do not. But if I should tell why they are sacrosanct, I would cross into the topic of divine matters, which I am especially trying to avoid.[c] Up till now, I only mentioned this subject when I was forced to do so, and even then I merely touched its surface.

[3] The customs of the Egyptians regarding animals are as follows.[a] Separate caretakers are appointed for the raising and feeding of each type of animal. These caretakers are Egyptians, both men and women, and children inherit these offices from their parents. [4] The people in the cities take vows and pray to the god to whom the animal belongs. Then they shave off all, half, or a third of their children's hair from their heads. This hair is then weighed in a balance scale, and its weight in silver is given to the caretaker of the animals. She then procures fish equal in value to the sum of silver, slices them up, and gives it to the animals to eat. [5] That is the sort of care and feeding the animals receive. Whenever someone kills an animal, if he did it intentionally, the penalty is death; if the deed was unintentional, the priests assign whatever penalty they wish. But whoever kills an ibis or a hawk, no matter whether it was intentional or not, is sentenced to death.

2.66
EGYPT
Egyptian household cats.

Many animals live with these people, but many more would do so if it were not for the fate of the cats. When the female cats have given birth, they no longer associate with the males, who, however, still seek intercourse with them, but without success. [2] So in response, the males outsmart the females by stealing away and then killing their offspring, although they do not eat them after killing them. The females, bereft of their babies, feel a desire for more and so go back to the males, for they are fond of offspring.

[3] And whenever a fire breaks out, some divine seizure comes over the cats. The Egyptians stand at intervals and try to keep the cats safe, but if they fail to extinguish the fire, the cats slip between or leap over them and rush into the flames. [4] When this happens, the Egyptians are overcome by intense grief. All those who live in a household where a cat has died a natural death shave their eyebrows. For the death of a dog, however, they shave their entire body and head.[a]

2.67
EGYPT
Embalming and ritual burial
of cats and other animals.

When cats die, they are taken to sacred buildings and, after being embalmed, are buried in the city of Boubastis.[a] Everyone buries dogs, how-

2.65.2a Libya: Map 2.67. Not the modern state Libya, but what we call the continent of Africa.
2.65.2b Almost all of the animals Herodotus describes in these chapters were then unknown to Greeks.
2.65.2c Compare this statement with what Herodotus says in 2.3.2.
2.65.3a Here Herodotus begins his description of Egyptian zoology. See Appendix C, §5.
2.66.4a These anecdotes are quite untrue, but

there were no domestic cats in Greece in Herodotus' day, so his ignorance or gullibility here, and that of his Greek audience, can perhaps be forgiven. His interest, however, stems from his fascination with marvels and paradoxes. See Introduction, §2.4, 3.4, 4.1, 4.6, 4.7, 4.14, 5.9.
2.67.1a Boubastis: Map 2.67, inset. Cats are buried in other places in Egypt as well. See Figure 2.67, an elegantly wrapped and embalmed Egyptian cat.

FIGURE 2.67. EMBALMED EGYPTIAN CAT. DOMESTIC CATS WERE AN EXOTIC SPECIES UNKNOWN TO THE GREEKS.

ever, in sacred tombs located in their own cities. They bury ichneumons[b] just as they do dogs. They take the bodies of shrew-mice and hawks to the city of Bouto,[c] and ibises to Hermopolis.[d] [2] Egyptian bears, which are rare, and wolves, which are not much larger than foxes, are buried on the spot where they are found lying.

    The nature of the crocodile is such that it eats nothing during the four winter months. It has four feet and lives both on dry land and in the water. Although it lays and hatches its eggs on land and generally spends the greater part of the day on dry ground, it stays in the river all night, since the water is warmer than the open air and the dew. [2] Of all mortal creatures we know, this one grows from the smallest to the largest size, for its egg is not much larger than that of a goose, and the size of its newly hatched offspring is proportional to the egg, yet it grows to a length of twenty-five feet[a] or more. [3] It has the eyes of a pig, enormous teeth, and tusks proportional to its body. And it alone of all animals has no tongue. Nor does it move its lower jaw, but it is the only animal that brings its upper jaw down to meet its lower jaw. [4] It has strong claws and an impenetrable hide on its back. In water it is blind, but in the open air extremely sharp-sighted. Whenever it spends time in the water, the inside of its mouth fills up completely with leeches. And although other birds and animals avoid it, the plover lives at peace with it, since the crocodile receives benefits from it. [5] When the crocodile emerges from the water onto land and opens its jaws (and as a rule, it faces the west as it does this), the plover enters its mouth and devours the leeches, while the crocodile, seeming to enjoy this service, does no harm at all to the plover.

2.68
EGYPT
Herodotus describes
the Nile crocodile.

2.67.1b   The ichneumon is a mongoose.
2.67.1c   Bouto: Map 2.67, inset. See n. 2.59.3c.
2.67.1d   Hermopolis: Map 2.67, inset.
2.68.2a   Herodotus writes "17 cubits." The com-

mon cubit, to which he may be referring here = about 1.5 feet (see Appendix J, §4, 5, 19). The largest Nile crocodiles are about 20 feet long.

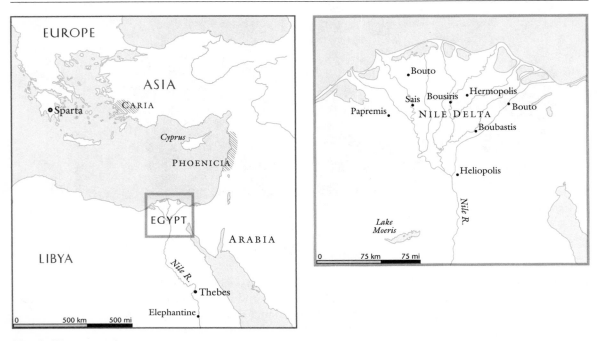

MAP 2.67

2.69
EGYPT
Variations in Egyptian
treatment of crocodiles.

Crocodiles are sacred to some Egyptians but not to all; there are some who actually treat them as enemies. Those who live around Thebes[a] and Lake Moeris[b] believe fervently in their sacred status. [2] At both places, they choose one crocodile to raise and feed, taming it completely, inserting pendants of glasslike jewels and gold in its ears and adorning its front feet with bangles. They feed it specially reserved food and sacrificial offerings, and give it the best treatment possible for as long as it lives. And when these animals die, they embalm them and bury them in sacred tombs. [3] The people living around the city of Elephantine,[a] however, do not believe crocodiles are sacred, and they even eat them. The Egyptians call these animals not crocodiles but *khampsai*.[b] "Crocodiles" is the name that was given to them by the Ionians,[c] who likened them in form to the lizards they call "crocodiles" that are found on the dry stone walls of Ionia.

2.69.1a Thebes, Egypt: Map 2.67.
2.69.1b Lake Moeris: Map 2.67, inset.
2.69.3a Elephantine (modern Aswan): Map 2.67.
2.69.3b *Khampsai*: the Greek *kroko-deilos* (*krokodeilos*) is Ionic for a lizard; the more common Greek term is *sau-ra* (*saura*) or *sau-ros* (*sauros*). (Godley)

2.69.3c The Ionians were among the first Greek settlers in Egypt; see 2.154.

There are many methods of catching crocodiles, but I shall write of only one, which seems to me most worthy of telling. The hunter hangs the back of a pig on his hook as bait and casts out into the middle of the river. Then, standing at the edge of the river, he holds a live piglet and strikes it. [2] The crocodile, hearing the piglet's cry, rushes toward the sound and comes upon the pig's back on the hook. He gulps it down, and they pull the crocodile in. When they have dragged it all the way to shore, the hunter first of all attempts to smear mud over its eyes, and if he succeeds in doing this, the rest becomes quite easy, but if not, he faces an arduous and difficult struggle.

2.70
EGYPT
Crocodile hunting.

The hippopotamus[a] is thought to be sacred by the people of the nome of Paprece,[b] but not by other Egyptians. This is what it looks like: it has four feet with cloven hooves like an ox, a blunt snout, a mane like a horse, conspicuous tusks, and a horse's tail. It neighs. It is the size of the largest ox, and its hide is so thick that once it is dried, spear shafts are crafted from it.

2.71
EGYPT
Hippopotami.

There are also otters in the river, and these, too, are believed to be sacred. The only fish they consider sacred is the one called "scaly" and the eel. These creatures are holy to the god of the Nile. In addition, among Egyptian birds, the "fox-goose"[a] is believed to be sacred.

2.72
EGYPT
Otters and other sacred animals.

But there is another sacred bird called the phoenix.[a] I myself have not seen it, except in paintings, for it rarely visits Egypt; indeed, the people of Heliopolis[b] say that it comes only once every 500 years. [2] They claim that a phoenix visits them when its father has died. The paintings, if they are accurate, depict a bird in shape and size very much like an eagle, with both golden and red feathers. [3] They also say, though it seems incredible to me, that when the phoenix sets out from Arabia toward the sanctuary of Helios, it carries the corpse of its own father plastered up in myrrh and buries it there in the sanctuary. [4] Thus it transports its father, but in order to do that, it first shapes some myrrh into an egg as heavy as it can carry. It then attempts to fly with it and keeps adjusting the size of the egg until its weight is just right. Then the phoenix hollows out the egg and places the body of its father inside it. It fills in the gap thus created with additional myrrh, so that when its father is laid within, the egg weighs the same as before. When the egg is completely plastered shut, the phoenix carries it to Egypt to the sanctuary of Helios. At least that is what they claim about this bird.

2.73
EGYPT
The phoenix.

Around Thebes there are sacred snakes which are not harmful to humans but small in size, with two horns growing from the top of their head.[a] When they die, they are buried in the sanctuary of Zeus, since the Egyptians state that these snakes are sacred to Zeus.

2.74
THEBES
Sacred snakes.

2.71.1a   The Greek *hippopotamos* literally means "horse of the river." It is obvious from his description of the animal that Herodotus never saw one.
2.71.1b   Papremis: Map 2.67, inset.
2.72.1a   The fox-goose is probably the *Chenalopex aegyptiaca*, or "smn-goose" as it appears

frequently on monuments. (Lloyd)
2.73.1a   The phoenix is not a real bird but a mythological creature.
2.73.1b   Heliopolis: Map 2.67, inset.
2.74.1a   Herodotus must refer here to the horned viper, which is not known to have been sacred.

2.75
ARABIA
The ibis and the
winged serpent.

There is a place in Arabia somewhat near the city of Bouto,[a] and I went to this site in order to learn about the winged serpents.[b] When I arrived there, I saw the bones and spines of serpents in such huge quantities as to beggar description. The spines lay in heaps, and there were quite a few of these heaps, too. Some of them were large, some smaller, and others smaller still. [2] The place where these bones lay is at a narrow mountain pass leading onto a vast plain which borders the plain of Egypt. [3] The story goes that, when spring arrives, winged serpents fly from Arabia toward Egypt, but at this mountain pass they encounter ibis birds, which not only do not let them pass but which kill them. [4] Because of this service, the Arabians say, the ibis is highly honored by the Egyptians, and the Egyptians agree that this is why they hold these birds in such high esteem.

2.76
ARABIA
A description of the ibis
ends Herodotus' account
of sacred animals.

The ibises who fight these serpents are entirely jet black, with the legs of a crane and a very hooked beak; they are the size of our krex.[a] But there are really two kinds of ibis. The other kind tends to flock nearer to humans. [2] It has no feathers on its head and throat (which are black in color), but has white feathers everywhere else, except for the tips of its wings and tail, which are all jet black. Its legs and beak resemble those of the other kind of ibis. [3] The snake has a form like that of the water snake, and bears wing-like membranes that lack feathers, quite similar to the wings of a bat. I think I've said enough now about sacred animals.

2.77
EGYPT
Egyptian skills in history
and preservation of the past.
Their habits regarding
health and foods.

The Egyptians who live in the agricultural region[a] foster the preservation of historical memory more than all other peoples and are by far the most learned about tradition of all those I have questioned.

[2] This is how they live. Every month for three days in a row, they purge themselves, seeking health by means of vomiting and enemas; they believe that all human illnesses are caused by the ingestion of food. [3] For this and other reasons as well, the Egyptians are the healthiest of all peoples after the Libyans, and I think another reason for this is their climate, which lacks seasonal variations. For illnesses fall upon people mostly when they experience changes of all kinds, but especially changes of weather.[a]

[4] These Egyptians eat bread made from spelt, and they call these loaves *kyllestis*.[a] The wine they drink is made from barley, since there are no vineyards there.[b] They consume some fish raw, either dried in the sun or

2.75.1a   Bouto (of the Eastern Delta near the Arabian, desert): Map 2.67, inset. This is the only citation in which Herodotus refers to this city. All other citations of Bouto refer to the city of Leto in the northwest Delta.
2.75.1b   Winged serpents or snakes: see also 3.107.
2.76.1a   Krex: a bird which scholars have not definitively identified. Likely candidates are the corncrake and the black-winged stilt.
2.77.1a   Apparently much of the outer Delta was too marshy for cultivation at that time. Herodotus contrasts the customs of these Egyptians with those of Egyptians who lived in the marshes, i.e., closer to the seacoast, in

2.92. This "agricultural region" therefore probably includes at least the southern half of the Delta and all of cultivable Egypt south of the Delta.
2.77.3a   This reflects Greek preconceptions, as described in the Hippocratic Corpus, a body of ancient Greek medical texts.
2.77.4a   Spelt is a coarse form of wheat. Herodotus uses a foreign word here, *kyllestis*, perhaps to show off his knowledge of other languages.
2.77.4b   There were vineyards in the north and west of the Delta region, which Herodotus is apparently not including in this "agricultural region."

cured with salt, [5] and they also use salt to cure small birds, ducks, and quails. All the rest of the birds and fish they have in Egypt, except for those designated as sacred, they eat baked or boiled.

At drinking parties of wealthy Egyptians, they always follow the end of their dinner by having a man carry around a corpse made of wood inside a coffin. The wooden corpse is crafted so as to be most realistic, both in the way it is painted and in the way it is carved, and it measures altogether one to three feet[a] in length. As the man displays it before each of the guests, he says, "Look at this as you drink and enjoy yourself, for you will be like this when you are dead."

2.78
EGYPT
Egyptian symposia.

They remain faithful to their ancestral customs and add nothing new to them. Among their noteworthy traditions is one song in particular about "Linos," who is celebrated in song in Phoenicia,[a] Cyprus,[b] and elsewhere, but who bears a different name in each nation. [2] He corresponds to the one whom the Hellenes invoke in their song as Linos.[a] Among the many things about Egypt that amaze me, I find one of the most astonishing to be where they obtained the name of their "Linos Song;" for it is clear that they have always sung this song. Among the Egyptians, Linos is called Maneros. [3] The Egyptians say he was the only son of the first Egyptian king, and that when he died an untimely death, he was honored by the Egyptians with this dirge, which, they claim, was their first and at that time their only song.

2.79
EGYPT
The origin of the Egyptian version of the Linos Song.

Another Egyptian custom resembles one practiced by the Spartans[a] alone among the Hellenes. Young people make way and stand aside for their elders when they happen to meet them, and even get up from their seats when elders approach. [2] Unlike any of the Hellenes, however, the Egyptians do not exchange verbal greetings on the street; instead they bow down and lower their hand to their knee.

2.80
EGYPT
Courtesies of young to old, and uncommon greetings.

They wear linen tunics they call *kalasiris*, which are fringed with tassels around their legs. Over these garments they drape white woolen cloaks. When they enter sanctuaries or when they are buried, however, they never wear wool, for to do so would offend their religious sensibility. [2] In this they agree with the ritual practices called Orphic and Bacchic, which are in reality Egyptian and Pythagorean, for the participants in these rites also find it religiously offensive to be buried in woolen garments, and there is a sacred story concerning this.[a]

2.81
EGYPT
Egyptian clothing.

The Egyptians have discovered which month and day is sacred to each of the gods, and they can tell by the day on which each man is born what will happen to him during his life, how he will die, and what sort of person he will be. Those Hellenes who are skillful poets have exploited these discoveries.

2.82
EGYPT
Egyptian knowledge of sacred days and portents.

2.78.1a   Herodotus writes "1 to 2 cubits." There
          were several cubits in use in the ancient
          world, all of them equaling between 1.5
          and 2 feet. See Appendix J, §4, 5, 19.
2.79.1a   Phoenicia: Map 2.67.
2.79.1b   Cyprus: Map 2.67.
2.79.2a   "The Linos Song" was a hymn for a slain
          youth (said to typify the departure of

early summer). The Semitic refrain *ai
lenu*, "alas for us," becomes the Greek *ai
linos*, from which comes the name Linos.
(Godley)
2.80.1a   Sparta: Map 2.67.
2.81.2a   About this ancient story Herodotus tells
          us nothing more, and nothing more is
          known of it.

[2] In addition, the Egyptians have noted more portents than any other people in the world. For when they observe a portent, they carefully write down the outcome, and if something similar to that portent occurs later, they believe it will be followed by the same outcome.

2.83
EGYPT
Divination.

They treat prophecy as an art that belongs not to human beings, but only to certain gods. Indeed, there are oracles in Egypt of Herakles, Apollo, Athena, Artemis, Ares, and Zeus; but of all their oracles, they honor that of Leto in the city of Bouto[a] the most. Their modes of divination are not uniform, however, but differ from place to place.

2.84
EGYPT
Egyptian medicine.

The art of medicine is divided so that each physician treats just one illness and no more. Doctors are everywhere, as there are specific physicians for the eyes, the head, the teeth, the abdomen, and still others for illnesses that are invisible.

2.85
EGYPT
Burial customs.

Now I will describe the way they mourn and bury their dead. When someone highly esteemed in their household dies, the women of that household plaster their heads and faces all over with mud. Then, leaving the corpse at home, they wander throughout the city beating their chests, binding up their garments and exposing their breasts;[a] and they are accompanied by all their female relatives. [2] The men also beat their chests and bind up their garments. When they have finished performing this ritual, they carry the body away to be embalmed.

2.86
EGYPT
The most costly methods of the Egyptian embalmers.

There are men in Egypt whose profession it is to embalm corpses. [2] Whenever a body is brought to them, they display painted wooden replicas of corpses to those who brought it, and they describe the most elaborate method of embalming, using an image whose name I will not reveal in this context, since I would consider that a religious offense. Then they demonstrate a second method which is inferior to the first but cheaper, and also a third, the cheapest of all. Having explained all this to their clients, the embalmers ask them to select the method by which they wish to have the body prepared. [3] After they have agreed on the price,[a] the clients then depart, leaving the embalmers alone in their quarters to perform their craft. The most elaborate method is performed in the following way. First, they draw out part of the brain through the nostrils with a curved iron implement; then they extract the rest by pouring in drugs. [4] After this, they make a slit with a sharp Ethiopian stone along the flank, from which they extract the entire contents of the abdomen. Then, when they have cleaned and washed out the abdominal cavity with Phoenician date-palm wine, they clean it once more with crushed spices. [5] Next, they fill the abdomen with pure ground myrrh, cassia, and other fragrant substances, except for frankincense, and then they stitch it up again. When all this has been done,

2.83.1a　Bouto (in the northwest delta): Map 2.67, inset.
2.85.1a　Apparently they used belts to keep their garments from falling down when the women exposed their breasts.
2.86.3a　Herodotus' use of the word "price" here

implies a money exchange, but the Egyptian economy had always functioned on the basis of barter, and much of it continued to do so after money was introduced by the Assyrians, or even later under the Persians.

they embalm the body by covering it completely with natron[a] for seventy days—it is not permitted to embalm for longer than this— [6] and when the seventy days are up, they bathe the body and wrap all of it up in bandages cut from fine linen and smeared with gum, which the Egyptians generally use in place of glue. [7] Then the corpse is handed over to the relatives, who enclose it in a hollow wooden coffin crafted to resemble a human which they have had made for this purpose, and once the coffin is closed, they stow it away in a burial chamber, standing it upright against a wall.

That is the most expensive method they employ for embalming corpses, but for those who wish to avoid the highest costs and to accept a cheaper method, they embalm them in the following way: [2] when they have filled syringes with oil of cedar, they introduce the oil into the bowels through the anus, so that they neither make cuts in the body nor remove the belly; after the oil has been injected, they stop up the orifice to prevent it from flowing back out, and then they embalm the body for the set number of days. On the last day, they let out the oil, [3] which is so potent that it flushes out along with it the now completely dissolved abdominal contents and the internal organs. The natron has by then dissolved the flesh, so that now all that is left of the corpse is skin and bones. After this, they return the body with no further ado.

For the third and least expensive method of embalming, which is performed for the poor, they rinse out the bowels with oil of radish, embalm the body in natron for seventy days, and then return it to be carried away.

But when wives of prominent men or very beautiful or noteworthy women die, they do not deliver their bodies to be embalmed at once. They give them over only on the second or third day after their death [2] so that the embalmers do not have intercourse with the dead woman's body, for they say that one was once caught in the act of having intercourse with a woman's fresh corpse, and that this crime was disclosed by his co-worker.

If anyone, Egyptian or foreigner, is snatched away by a crocodile or has clearly drowned due to the force of the river itself, it is absolutely necessary that the inhabitants of whatever city to which the body floats have it embalmed, laid out, and buried in a sacred tomb in the best manner possible. No one, not even friends or relatives, are permitted to touch the corpse except for the priests of the Nile themselves; their hands alone come in contact with the body during its burial, on the grounds that its status is above and beyond that of a human.

The Egyptians avoid practicing the customs of the Hellenes, and, to tell the whole truth, they shun those of everyone else in the world as well. All Egyptians preserve their own customs this way except for those in the great city of Chemmis,[a] in the Theban nome, close by Neapolis.[b] [2] Here

---

2.87
EGYPT
Less expensive embalming methods.

2.88
EGYPT
The cheapest method of embalming.

2.89
EGYPT
Protection of female corpses.

2.90
EGYPT
Special treatment for crocodile or drowning victims.

2.91
EGYPT
The cult of Perseus in Egypt.

2.86.5a   "Natron is 'natural soda,' a compound of sodium carbonate and sodium bicarbonate mixed with varying proportions of sodium sulphate and sodium chloride [common salt]." (Lloyd)

2.91.1a   Chemmis: Map 2.97.

2.91.1b   Neapolis: site unknown, but if it was in the Theban nome (see n. 2.42.1a), it would obviously be in the vicinity of Thebes, which would make it very far indeed from Chemmis. Thebes: Map 2.97.

there is a square sanctuary of Perseus[a] son of Danae, surrounded by palm trees. The entrance gates of the sanctuary are made of massive stones, in front of which stand two huge stone statues. Within this enclosure is a temple, and inside it is a statue of Perseus. [3] The people of Chemmis say that Perseus often appears to them throughout their land, frequently within his temple. And they say that one of the sandals that he has worn also turns up there, three feet[a] long, and that whenever it appears, all Egypt flourishes. [4] Regardless of what they say, they certainly honor Perseus in a traditional Greek way: they hold athletic contests, which include the whole range of competitive events, and they offer as prizes cattle, cloaks, and hides. [5] When I inquired as to why Perseus tends to appear only to them, and why they, apart from all other Egyptians, celebrated with athletic games, they replied that Perseus originated from their own city, since Danaos and Lynkeus, both of Chemmis, sailed off to Hellas, and from them is traced the bloodline from which Perseus is descended. [6] They say that Perseus came to Egypt for the same reason that the Hellenes believe: to take the head of the Gorgon[a] out of Libya. They further claim that he came into their presence and acknowledged them all as his kinsmen; that he had come to Egypt well acquainted with the name of the city Chemmis, since he had heard all about it from his mother, and that it was to carry out his order that they established the athletic games in his honor.

2.92
EGYPT
Local Nile plant foods for the inhabitants of the Nile Delta.

All these customs are observed by those Egyptians who dwell upstream (or inland) of the marshes. The inhabitants of marsh country in fact follow some of the same customs as the rest of the Egyptians; for example, each of them lives with one wife, just as the Hellenes do.

They have, however, discovered their own ways to economize on the cost of food. [2] Whenever the river floods and transforms the plains into a sea, many lilies grow in the water which the Egyptians call the lotus. After they pick these, they dry them in the sun and crush their centers, which are quite similar to the centers of poppies. Then they make loaves of it which they bake in the fire. [3] The root of the lotus is also edible, and somewhat sweet, round, and about the size of an apple. [4] There are other lilies, too, similar to roses. These also grow in the river, and the fruit sprouts up from them in a separate flower which grows adjacent to and out of the root. The fruit is very similar in shape to the comb of wasps. Within the fruit are kernels that grow as large as olive pits, and these they enjoy both fresh and dried as snacks. [5] Furthermore, they pull up the yearly growth of the papyrus plant from the marshes and cut off the upper part to use for various purposes, but they either eat or sell

2.91.2a   Perseus, hero of Ionian Greek myth.
          See 6.53–54, 7.61.3, 7.150.
2.91.3a   Herodotus writes that this sandal was
          "2 cubits" long, the same length as the
          "footprint of Herakles" in 4.82. The
          common cubit = about 1.5 feet. See

2.91.6a   Appendix J, §4, 5, 19.
          One of Perseus' most famous feats was
          to slay the monstrous Gorgon Medusa
          by cutting off her head without looking
          directly at her but only at her reflected
          image in a shiny shield.

the lower part that is left, which grows up to a length of eighteen inches.[a] Those who prefer to make the best use of the papyrus, however, bake it in a red-hot oven and eat it cooked that way. There are other people in the marshes who live only on fish that they catch; they remove the guts, dry the fish in the sun, and eat them.

The fish that swim together in schools are not born in the river branches of the Delta. When they have grown to maturity in the lakes, the urge to breed incites them to go out to sea in schools. The males lead the way, shedding their seed as they go, while the females follow, swallowing the seed, and thereby conceiving. [2] After the females have been impregnated, they all swim back again, each school to its former home. But the males no longer swim in front as before; now the leadership passes to the females, who lead in the schools and behave as the males did, shedding their eggs (which are like millet seeds), a few at a time, while the males follow, devouring many of these "seeds," which are actually fish. [3] Indeed, it is only those that are not swallowed which survive and grow into mature fish. Now, it is a fact that the fish which are caught while they swim out to sea appear bruised on the left sides of their heads, and those caught on their return are bruised on the right. [4] This happens to them because they cling close to the land on the left as they swim down to sea and keep to the same bank on their way back, adhering to the shore so closely that they bump against it as they swim, apparently so that they will not lose their way in the current.[a] [5] When the Nile begins to rise and water starts to seep through the banks of the river, the recesses and lowlands flood first. Suddenly, they are full of water, and immediately after that they teem with small fish. [6] I think I understand how these fish come to be there. When the Nile's level was falling in the previous year, fish laid eggs in the mud before departing with the last of the water. Then, when the next flood occurred and water washed over the eggs, they hatched immediately, and thus the fish were born. That, at least, is my explanation concerning the fish.

The Egyptians who live around the marshes use oil extracted from the fruit of the castor oil plant, which the Egyptians call *kiki*. They sow seeds of this castor oil plant along the banks of the river and lakes. There is a type of castor oil plant that grows wild in Hellas, without cultivation, [2] but in Egypt the seeds that are sown bear an abundance of fruit, although they give off a foul stench. When these plants are harvested, some people cut them up and press out the oil; others roast them and then extract and collect the oil by boiling them. The oil is thick and serves as well as olive oil when used in lamps, but it does give off a strong odor.

2.93
EGYPT
Herodotus describes the reproduction of school fish and tells of the sudden appearance of fish in newly flooded areas in the Nile valley.

2.94
EGYPT
Egyptian cultivation and use of the castor berry.

2.92.5a   Herodotus writes "1 cubit." For a brief discussion of the excursus into Egyptian botany here and at 2.94, see Appendix C, §6.

2.93.4a   According to Lloyd, this description is based on the habits of the Nile bream,

but it is very misleading. See Appendix C, §5.

2.95
EGYPT
Egyptian methods of
mosquito protection.

The vast numbers of mosquitoes in Egypt have led people here to contrive certain defenses against them. People dwelling inland of the marshes use towers in which they climb up to sleep, since the mosquitoes are unable to fly so high because of the winds. [2] Others who live in the vicinity of the marshes use their fishnets instead of towers. Each of them owns a net with which he catches fish during the day, which at night he arranges around his bed so that he can sleep underneath it. [3] If one goes to bed wrapped up in a cloak or a linen blanket, the mosquitoes bite right through them, but they do not even begin to try to bite through a net.[a]

2.96
EGYPT
The construction of Nile
acacia boats and their use
with rafts and stone anchors.

The boats they use to carry freight are made of acacia wood,[a] which exudes drops of gum; this tree is most similar in form to the Cyrenaean lotus. They cut planks of wood three and a half feet[b] long from this tree and set them together like bricks. They build their ships by inserting long, closely set dowels to fasten the wooden planks together, and when they have thus constructed a boat, they place cross-planks over it. They do not put in any ribs at all but actually caulk the joints inside with papyrus. [3] Only one steering oar is made, which is inserted through the keel. Their masts are made of acacia wood, their sails of papyrus. With these boats they cannot sail upstream in the river unless a fresh, strong wind prevails; otherwise, they must be towed along from the shore. But here is how they sail downstream. [4] They construct a door-shaped raft of tamarisk, stitch it together with matted reeds, and tie it by a rope to the front of the boat, so that the boatman can let it float on ahead. In addition, they take a stone that weighs about two talents[a] and has a hole bored through it and tie that to the back of the boat. [5] The raft moves swiftly forward with the rushing current and thus pulls the *baris* (for this is what the Egyptians call these boats), while the stone is dragged behind and, being deep under the water, helps to keep the boat steady. They have a large number of these boats, some of which can carry many thousands of talents in weight.

2.97
EGYPT
During the Nile flood,
the towns are on hills like
Aegean islands.

Whenever the Nile overflows onto the land, all of Egypt becomes a sea, except for the cities which alone project above water, quite like the islands in the Aegean Sea.[a] When this happens, the Egyptians who now must travel by ferry are no longer constrained to sail through the river channels, but can go directly over the middle of the plain. [2] A voyage upstream from Naucratis[a] to Memphis[b] passes right beside the pyramids[c] themselves, whereas normally one would go via the apex of the Delta by the city of

---

2.95.3a These fine fishnets were probably folded several times to keep out at least most of the mosquitoes. The nets were quite large and were also used to catch birds.

2.96.1a Either *Acacia nilotica* or *Mimosa nilotica*.

2.96.1b Herodotus writes "2 cubits." The common cubit = about 1.5 feet. See Appendix J, §4, 5, 19.

2.96.4a Talent, a unit of weight, equal to about 57 pounds, according to the system in use at Athens. See Appendix J, §11–13, 20.

2.97.1a Aegean Sea: Map 2.97.

2.97.2a Naucratis: Map 2.97, inset.

2.97.2b Memphis: Map 2.97, inset.

2.97.2c Pyramids (general location): Map 2.97, inset. See Figure 2.97, a photograph of the flooding Nile in the vicinity of the pyramids.

FIGURE 2.97. A NINETEENTH-CENTURY PHOTOGRAPH OF AN EGYPTIAN VILLAGE DURING THE ANNUAL NILE FLOOD. SINCE THE EARLY TWENTIETH CENTURY THE DAMMING OF THE NILE HAS PREVENTED FLOODS.

Kerkasoros.[d] And if at this season you sail from the sea by Canobus[e] to Naucratis, you can go directly over the plain and pass by the cities of Anthylla[f] and Archandropolis,[g] as the latter is called.

Of these two cities, the one named Anthylla is notable as the one selected to provide shoes for the wife of the reigning ruler of Egypt.[a] This has been the case ever since Egypt became subject to Persia.[b] [2] It seems to me that the other city, Archandropolis, may have acquired its name from the son-in-law of Danaos—Archandros son of Phthios the son of Achaios—for it is called the city of Archandros. Perhaps it was named after some other Archandros, but at any rate, its name is not Egyptian.

2.98
EGYPT
The cities of Anthylla and Archandros.

2.97.2d   Kerkasoros: Map 2.97, inset.
2.97.2e   Canobus (Canopus): Map 2.97, inset.
2.97.2f   Anthylla: Map 2.97, inset.
2.97.2g   Archandropolis: Map 2.97, inset. Herodotus actually calls this city "the city of Archandros" here and in 2.98.
2.98.1a   In Herodotus' day the reigning ruler was probably the Persian satrap of Egypt.

2.98.1b   King Cambyses of Persia conquered Egypt in 525. See 3.1–13.

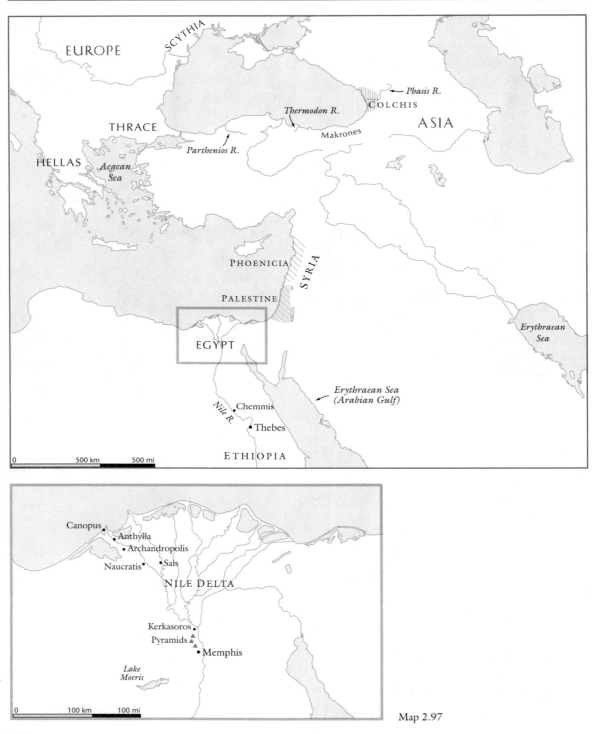

Map 2.97

Up to this point, what I have said about Egypt has been the result of my own observation, judgment, and research,[a] but from here on, I am going to report the words of the Egyptians just as I heard them, although again I shall on occasion add something of my own observation.[b]

[2] The priests told me that the first king of Egypt was named Min[a] and that it was he who sheltered the area which became Memphis[b] with dikes. Before this, the whole river flowed alongside the sandy mountain toward Libya (to the west), but Min dammed up the river at the bend some eleven miles[c] south of Memphis, which thereby dried up the old riverbed and diverted the river to a new channel that flowed between the mountains. [3] Even today, this bend of the Nile is still very carefully maintained by the Persians, who reinforce the banks every year so that its stream remains confined behind them. For if the river were to break out of the dykes at this point, its flow would threaten to flood all of Memphis. [4] And so this Min, the first man to become king, waited until the area he had closed off was dried up and then founded the city called Memphis there in the narrow region of Egypt.[a] [5] He then excavated a lake outside the city which extended from the river to the north and west to form a boundary just as the Nile itself does to the east. Finally, when that was done, he built the sanctuary of Hephaistos[a] at Memphis, which is huge and quite remarkable.

After this king, the priests related from a papyrus roll the names of 330 other kings of Egypt. In all these generations,[a] every one was an Egyptian man except for eighteen who were Ethiopians, and one who was a local woman. [2] The name of the woman who became queen was the very same as the Babylonian queen, Nitokris.[a] They said that she avenged her brother, whom the Egyptians had killed during his reign as king. Although they gave the crown to her after his murder, she sought revenge and destroyed many Egyptians by the following treacherous scheme. [3] She built a very large underground chamber, announced its opening ceremonies, and invited those Egyptians whom she knew to be the most guilty in the murder of her brother

2.99
EGYPT
Herodotus now ends his eyewitness account and describes what he learned from others. The story of how the king Min (r. c. 3000?) founded Memphis.

2.100
EGYPT
There have been 330 kings of Egypt. The story of queen Nitokris' revenge.

2.99.1a As in Herodotus' Proem (precedes Book 1), "This work sets forth the research . . . ," the word he uses for "research" here can mean oral inquiry, but in this case, and often elsewhere in Herodotus, it implies not only asking questions, but also confirming or refuting hypotheses by investigation. (Lloyd, vol. 1, p. 82). See Introduction, §2.5–6.

2.99.1b For comment on Herodotus' attempt here and later to describe the history of Egypt, see Appendix C, §7.

2.99.2a See 2.4.2–3 for Min and the swampy condition of Egypt in his time.

2.99.2b Memphis: Map 2.97, inset. Herodotus' account of the origins of Memphis is quite wrong. Archaeological research (Lloyd) has revealed that the first city of Memphis was built a good deal to the north of the city that existed in Herodotus' day.

2.99.2c Herodotus writes "100 stades." See Appendix J, §6, 19.

2.99.4a Herodotus is alluding to his argument at 2.15, where he describes the territory of Egypt as originating in the region south of the Delta, and the formation of the Delta as a recent phenomenon. This city was therefore founded before there was a delta.

2.99.5a Hephaistos is the Egyptian god Ptah.

2.100.1a Herodotus follows the common tendency of Greek historians to assume that each rule lasts for one generation, i.e., 30 to 40 years. In fact, he defines this principle more specifically in 2.142.2, where he states that there are three generations of men in one century.

2.100.2a The Babylonian Nitokris was mentioned at 1.185–87.

to attend them—all the while cleverly hiding her true intentions. Then, while the many guests there were enjoying the feast, she suddenly let the river burst in from a huge secret conduit. [4] That is about all they said of her, except that after she had accomplished this feat, she threw herself into a chamber full of ashes so that she herself would not become the object of vengeance.

2.101
EGYPT
King Moeris (Amenemhet III of the XII Dynasty) ruled from 1844 to 1797.

Concerning the other kings, they said that none of them had shown any brilliance or had accomplished any achievements worthy of note except for the last one, who was called Moeris. [2] He produced a memorial to himself by his construction of the monumental entrance facing the north at the sanctuary of Hephaistos. He also excavated a lake,[a] whose circumference I shall reveal later, and built pyramids within it whose size I shall mention when I describe the lake. Such were his many achievements, while none of the others accomplished a thing.

2.102
EGYPT
The expeditions of Sesostris by sea and land.

And so, passing over these rulers, I shall commemorate King Sesostris, who came after them. [2] The priests said that he first of all set sail in long ships from the Arabian Gulf[a] and conquered the inhabitants along the Erythraean Sea,[b] and that he continued to sail out until he arrived at a sea no longer navigable due to its shallows. [3] Then, according to the priests' report, he returned to Egypt and assembled a large army with which he marched through Asia,[a] conquering every nation that he encountered. [4] Now, for those he encountered who struggled bravely and fiercely for their freedom, he set up pillars in their lands with inscriptions declaring his name, his native land, and how he had subdued them with his might. [5] And for those whose cities he took easily and without a fight, he inscribed the same words on the pillars as he did for the courageous peoples, but added an image of female genitals, wishing to publicize their impotence.[a]

2.103
EGYPT-SCYTHIA-THRACE
Sesostris' victory over the Scythians and Thracians.

That is what he did as he marched through the continent, until he crossed over from Asia and into Europe,[a] where he conquered the Scythians[b] and the Thracians.[c] It seems to me that his army went no farther than the territories of these nations, for while he apparently erected pillars in their countries, he does not seem to have done so farther than this. [2] From these places he turned back, and when he came to the River Phasis[a] where—although here I cannot speak with certainty—either King Sesostris himself left a part of his army behind to settle this land, or some of his soldiers who had grown weary of the journey decided to stay and reside in the vicinity of the River Phasis.

2.101.1a   Of course, the Egyptians are quite wrong about this. Lake Moeris was not man-made. Herodotus describes this lake in 2.149.
2.102.2a   Arabian Gulf (modern Red Sea): Map 2.97.
2.102.2b   Erythraean Sea; in this case the body of water now called the Indian Ocean, from which the Arabian Gulf, the modern Red Sea, extends north: Map 2.97. See n. 1.1.1d.
2.102.3a   Asia here is presumably not limited to Asia Minor, which is what Herodotus

normally means by that name, but the entire landmass north and east of Egypt: Map 2.97.
2.102.5a   None of this material about Sesostris is true, except as Egyptian nationalist propaganda to counter and outshine the conquests of the Persians. See Appendix C, §7.
2.103.1a   Europe: Map 2.97.
2.103.1b   Scythia: Map 2.97.
2.103.1c   Thrace: Map 2.97.
2.103.2a   Phasis River: Map 2.97.

And it is indeed obvious that the Colchians[a] are really Egyptians.[b] I say this because I noticed this resemblance myself and then I heard about it from others, too. As I considered the matter, I questioned both peoples and it turned out that they did remember each other, although the Colchians remembered the Egyptians more than the Egyptians the Colchians. [2] The Egyptians stated that they believed the Colchians were from the army of Sesostris. I myself had also guessed that; first, because they are black-skinned and wooly-haired (although this in itself proves nothing, since others are like this, too), but even more because, of all peoples, only the Colchians, the Egyptians, and the Ethiopians[a] have practiced circumcision from the very earliest times. [3] The Phoenicians[a] and the Syrians of Palestine[b] agree that they have learned this practice from the Egyptians. And the Syrians who live around the River Thermodon[c] and the River Parthenios,[d] with their neighbors the Makrones,[e] claim they learned it only recently from the Colchians. These are the only peoples that practice circumcision, and it is clear that they do it the same way as the Egyptians. [4] But of the Egyptians and Ethiopians, I cannot say which of the two learned it from the other, since it is evidently a very ancient practice. However, there is, I think, convincing proof that people who have had close contact with Egypt learned circumcision from the Egyptians: those Phoenicians who have had close contact with the Hellenes no longer imitate Egyptians as regards their genitals, but instead leave the genitals of the next generation of sons uncircumcised.

But now let me cite further evidence that the people of Colchis and the Egyptians resemble each other. Of all peoples, only these two produce linen by the same, distinctive method. Moreover, their whole way of life and their languages are quite similar. Linen from Colchis is called "Sardonian" by the Hellenes, while they refer to the linen that comes from Egypt as "Egyptian."[a]

As to the pillars that Sesostris king of Egypt is said to have erected throughout his lands, the majority are evidently no longer in existence, but I myself saw some of them in Palestinian Syria[a] that had the previously mentioned inscription and depiction of the genitals of a woman. [2] And in the neighborhood of Ionia[a] there are two figures carved into rock faces by this man along the main routes one would travel when going from Ephesus[b] to Phocaea,[c] and from Sardis[d] to Smyrna.[e] [3] On each rock face is carved the image of a man about seven feet tall,[a] holding a spear in his

2.104
EGYPT-COLCHIS
Herodotus' evidence that the Colchians are Egyptians descended from Sesostris' army.

2.105
EGYPT-COLCHIS
Further evidence of resemblance.

2.106
PALESTINE-IONIA
Herodotus saw pillars of Sesostris in Palestine and Ionia.

2.104.1a Colchis: Map 2.97.
2.104.1b Egypt: Map 2.97. This identification of Egyptians with Colchians is, of course, entirely wrong.
2.104.2a Ethiopia: Map 2.97.
2.104.3a Phoenicia: Map 2.97.
2.104.3b Palestine: Map 2.97.
2.104.3c Thermodon River: Map 2.97.
2.104.3d Parthenios River: Map 2.97.
2.104.3e Makrones, territory of: Map 2.97.
2.105.1a This similarity of language is untrue, but the reference exemplifies Herodotus'

interest in language.
2.106.1a Palestinian Syria: Map 2.97.
2.106.2a Ionia: Map 2.112, AX.
2.106.2b Ephesus: Map 2.112, AX. These carved reliefs still exist, but they do not have some of the features Herodotus ascribes to them.
2.106.2c Phocaea: Map 2.112, AX.
2.106.2d Sardis: Map 2.112, AX.
2.106.2e Smyrna: Map 2.112, AX.
2.106.3a Herodotus gives the size of the figure as "4 cubits" and a "span." See Appendix J, §4, 5, 19.

right hand and a bow in his left, and the rest of his costume corresponds to these weapons, for it has both Egyptian and Ethiopian features.[b] [4] There is an inscription carved from one shoulder to the other across the figure's chest in sacred Egyptian characters[a] which reads, "I acquired possession of this land by the strength of my shoulders." Who this man is and where he is from, however, are not made clear on either image, [5] which has led certain people to conjecture that it is an image of Memnon,[a] but they are quite wrong, as records elsewhere clearly indicate that these are the work of Sesostris.

2.107
EGYPT
Sesostris and his wife thwart the plot of his brother.

The priests said that, as Sesostris was returning to Egypt, bringing many people with him from the nations he had conquered, he stopped at Daphnai[a] in Pelusium,[b] where his brother, to whom he had entrusted the rule of Egypt, invited him and his children for a visit. While he was there, his brother stacked wood on all sides of his house and set it on fire. [2] As soon as Sesostris realized what was happening, he consulted his wife, whom in fact he had brought along with him. She advised him to stretch two of their six children across the pyre to form a bridge over the flames that the rest of them could use to save themselves. That is what Sesostris did, so that, although two of his children were thus burned up completely, the rest escaped to safety with their father.

2.108
EGYPT
Sesostris uses captives taken on his campaigns to construct temples and canals.

After he returned to Egypt, Sesostris took vengeance on his brother and compelled the multitude of people he had brought back from the conquered countries to perform harsh labor. [2] It was they who hauled the enormous stones that were conveyed to the sanctuary of Hephaistos during the reign of this king. In addition, these were the people who dug the numerous canals which now exist in Egypt and who thereby unwittingly eliminated all horses and chariots from Egypt. [3] Although the country had previously been quite suitable for horses and for cross-country travel by chariots, now the many extensive canals which Sesostris built cut and divided the country everywhere so that neither horse nor chariot could be used. [4] The king carved up his land with canals in order to provide good water to all Egyptians whose cities were not situated along the river; those who lived at inland sites had previously suffered water shortages whenever the river receded, which had forced them to drink rather brackish water from wells.[a]

2.109
EGYPT
Sesostris divides the land and taxes it accordingly. From his work, the Greeks learn land measurement.

They said that Sesostris was also the king who made distributions of land to all Egyptians, giving to each a square plot of equal size and creating public revenue by ordering everyone to pay an annual tax. [2] Whenever the river destroyed a part of someone's plot, that man would declare his loss to the king, and the king would then send examiners to measure how much land had been lost, so that the man could be required to pay a tax propor-

2.106.3b   The spear is associated with Egypt, the bow with Ethiopia. Two such figures have been discovered in the pass of Karabel, near the old road from Ephesus to Smyrna. They are not at all Egyptian in appearance, however. (Godley)
2.106.4a   Herodotus would seem to be referring here to Egyptian hieroglyphs.
2.106.5a   Memnon: not the historical pharaoh in this case but the Homeric Memnon from Ethiopia.
2.107.1a   Daphnai: Map 2.112, BY.
2.107.1b   Pelusium: Map 2.112, BY.
2.108.4a   The canal system of Egypt is in fact much older than Herodotus' account.

tional to what was left. [3] And it seems to me that geometry was invented here and then passed on from Egypt to Hellas,[a] although it was from the Babylonians that the Hellenes learned of the hemispherical sundial with its pointer and the twelve divisions of the day.[b]

Sesostris was the only Egyptian king to rule Ethiopia.[a] As a memorial to his reign, he erected in front of the sanctuary of Hephaistos two stone statues forty-five feet tall, representing himself and his wife, and also statues of his four surviving children, each of them thirty feet tall.[a] [2] A long time after this the priest of Hephaistos refused to permit Darius the Persian to put up a statue in front of these, declaring that the Persian's deeds did not equal those achieved by Sesostris the Egyptian, for Sesostris had not only conquered as many nations as he had, but had gone even farther and had subdued Scythia, which Darius had not been able to subjugate. [3] Therefore, it was not right that someone whose deeds did not surpass those of Sesostris should erect offerings in front of his. Darius, they say, agreed with this.[a]

They say that when Sesostris died, his son Pheros[a] inherited the kingdom. He performed no military feats, but was blinded in the following incident: during his reign the river flooded over the land to a greater extent than ever before; it rose to a height of twenty-seven feet,[b] and when it overflowed the fields, the wind drove it to surge in waves like a sea. [2] They say that this king, in reckless arrogance, took a spear and cast it into the eddies in the middle of the river, and that immediately afterward, his eyes were afflicted with disease and he became blind. His blindness continued for ten years until, in the eleventh year, there came an oracular response from the city of Bouto[a] stating that the duration of his punishment was over now and that he would regain his sight by washing his eyes with the urine of a woman who had been with her husband alone, having had no experience of any other men. [3] And so he first tried this with the urine of his own wife, but this failed to restore his sight. He then tried all other women, one after the other, and when he finally regained his sight, he brought together into one city—which is now called Red Soil—all the women he had tried except for the one whose urine had restored his sight. When they were gathered together there, he set them all on fire along with the city itself. [4] But he took as his own wife the woman with whose urine he had washed his eyes and

---

2.109.3a Herodotus is wrong here. Geometry in the strict sense is a Greek invention. What the Egyptians had from early times was surveying techniques for laying out and apportioning land.

2.109.3b A point to make here is that the Persian Empire as a world state was a main conduit through which Greeks, particularly Ionian Greeks, discovered elements of Egyptian, Mesopotamian, and other foreign science, religion, and culture.

2.110.1a This statement is not correct: there are other Egyptian pharaohs who ruled Ethiopia.

2.110.1b Herodotus writes that these statues are, respectively, "30 cubits" and "20 cubits" tall. The common cubit = about 1.5 feet. See Appendix J, §4, 5, 19.

2.110.3a This invented incident reveals the propagandist dimension of the Sesostris legend.

2.111.1a The word means Pharaoh, but is used here as a proper name.

2.111.1b Herodotus writes "18 cubits."

2.111.2a Bouto: Map 2.112, BY. The oracle came from the sanctuary of Leto. See 2.83, 2.155.

regained his sight. And having thus escaped the affliction of blindness, he dedicated offerings at all the prominent sanctuaries, but his most noteworthy offerings were the two spectacular monolithic stone spits, each of them 150 feet long and twelve feet wide,[a] which he dedicated to the sanctuary of Helios.

From Pheros, the priests said, rule over the kingdom passed to a man of Memphis, whose name in Greek is Proteus.[a] His precinct still exists in Memphis to this day; it is quite beautiful and lavishly decorated, and lies to the south[b] of the sanctuary of Hephaistos. [2] Phoenicians from Tyre[a] live around it, and the whole area is called the Camp[b] of the Tyrians. Within the precinct of Proteus is a sanctuary named after Foreign Aphrodite, which I suppose is really a sanctuary of Helen daughter of Tyndareus,[c] since I have heard the report that Helen stayed with Proteus, and furthermore, because the sanctuary is named Foreign Aphrodite and none of the other sanctuaries of Aphrodite have the epithet "Foreign."

When I inquired about the stories in regard to Helen, the priests told me that Alexandros,[a] having abducted Helen from Sparta,[b] sailed away toward his own land, but when he reached the Aegean Sea,[c] violent winds drove him off course from there into the sea toward Egypt.[d] Since these winds did not let up, he soon found himself off the coast of Egypt at the Canobic Mouth of the Nile[e] and the nearby saltworks. [2] On the shore there was—and in fact there still is—a sanctuary of Herakles to which anyone's servant may flee for asylum, have himself branded with sacred marks, and devote himself to the service of the god. If he does this, no one is permitted to lay hands on him. This custom has been in effect since the beginning, and it is still the rule in my time. [3] Well, when the attendants of Alexandros learned of this law, they immediately abandoned him, went to the sanctuary, and sat as suppliants before the god. There they maliciously denounced Alexandros, relating the whole story of what had happened to Helen and the injustice he had committed against Menelaos. They made these accusations to the priests and to the guard assigned to this mouth of the Nile, whose name was Thonis.

2.111.4a Herodotus writes that these objects, which must have been obelisks, were "100 cubits" long and "8 cubits" wide. If so, 8 cubits (12 feet) would have been "the width of each of the four sides at the base." (Woods, Waddell) See Appendix J, §4, 5, 19.

2.112.1a A king of Egypt named Proteus is a fiction based on the ancient Greek poet Homer.

2.112.1b Herodotus says literally "south wind" for "south," following the ancient Greek practice of expressing directions in terms of personifications of divinities and mythical figures. North and south were often identified by winds, which were considered divine; the north wind (Boreas) will later be mentioned

as a god. See Appendix D, §3.

2.112.2a Tyre: Map 2.112, AY.

2.112.2b Herodotus uses a word here that is generally used for military camps.

2.112.2c This Helen daughter of Tyndareus is also the famous "Helen of Troy."

2.113.1a This Alexandros is more commonly known today as Paris, although in early Greek literature he was called Alexandros more frequently. It is he who abducted Helen from her husband King Menelaos, which served as the ostensible cause of the Trojan War. See 1.3.

2.113.1b Sparta: Map 2.112, AX.

2.113.1c Aegean Sea: Map 2.112, AX.

2.113.1d Egypt: Map 2.112, BY.

2.113.1e Canobic Mouth (Kanobikon Stoma) of the Nile River: Map 2.112, BX.

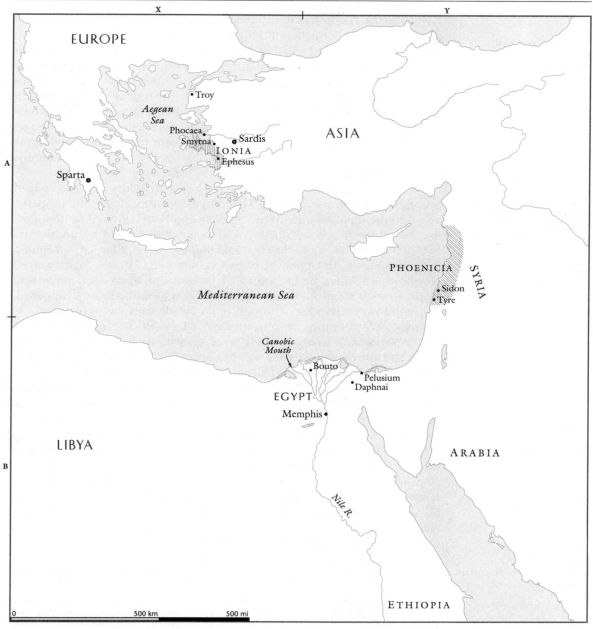

Map 2.112

2.114
EGYPT
Proteus demands that
Alexandros be arrested and
brought to him.

As soon as Thonis had heard their story, he sent a message to Proteus at Memphis.[a] [2] "A foreigner of the Trojan[a] race has arrived after committing an ungodly outrage in Hellas; he has seduced the wife of the very man who had taken him in as his guest,[b] and then went off with her, taking with him a fortune in property belonging to his host. He was driven away from his own land by the wind and has thus arrived here. So, shall we allow him to sail away with impunity, or shall we take for ourselves what he has stolen and brought here with him?" [3] In reply, Proteus sent back this message: "This man, and I don't care who he is, has committed a most impious act against his own host; seize him and bring him before me so I can examine him and find out what he might have to say for himself."

2.115
EGYPT
Outraged by Alexandros'
impious behavior, Proteus
orders him to depart and to
leave Helen and all the
stolen property in Egypt for
her husband to retrieve.

As soon as he heard this, Thonis arrested Alexandros, secured control over his ships, and took him to Memphis along with Helen, the property, and even the suppliants. [2] When all these had been delivered to him, Proteus asked Alexandros who he was and from where he had begun his voyage. Alexandros related his lineage, told him the name of his native country, and moreover described how he had set sail from it.[a] [3] Next, Proteus asked him how and where he had obtained Helen. And when Alexandros here began to stray from the truth and failed to say what had really happened, the suppliants refuted him, recounting the whole story of his injustice. [4] At the end of the story, Proteus spoke: "If I myself did not consider it of crucial importance to avoid killing strangers who have been caught by the winds and driven against their will to my land, I would already have punished you on behalf of that Hellene, for you are clearly the most wicked of men—one who accepted hospitality and then committed the most impious outrage. You dallied with your host's wife, but that was not enough for you. No—after having given wings to her passion, you stole her away and sailed off. [5] And even that did not satisfy you, for you also brought here a great deal of your host's property, which you had plundered. [6] As it is, however, since I do believe it crucial that we refrain from killing strangers, you shall live; but I shall not surrender this woman and property for you to take with you when you depart. I shall keep them safe for the Hellene until he wants to come and get them back himself. You must sail away with your company to some other land within three days' time. And if you do not obey my command, you will be treated as enemies."

2.116
Herodotus quotes Homer in
evaluating the Egyptian story
of Helen.

According to the priests, that is the way Helen came to Proteus. And it seems to me that Homer had also heard this version of the story. But since

2.114.1a Memphis: Map 2.112, BY.
2.114.2a Herodotus does not use the term
           "Trojan" here or elsewhere, but rather
           "Teukrian," which refers to a people who
           lived in the Troad—the region in which
           the city of Troy (Map 2.112, AX) is situ-
           ated. Scholars believe the "Teukrians" are
           probably the Tekkri of the Egyptian mon-
           uments, who came to the aid of the Hit-
           tites, along with other allies, from the
           western part of Asia Minor.

2.114.2b To steal a wife or any property from one's
           host was, in Greek eyes, both a criminal
           and an impious act. For more information
           on the relational obligations between
           guest and host, especially in the custom-
           ary institutions of "guest-friendship," see
           the Glossary and Appendix T, Tyranny in
           Herodotus, §3.
2.115.2a Alexandros (Paris) sailed originally from
           his home city, Troy (Ilion/Ilium): Map
           2.112, AX.

it was not as appropriate for epic composition as the other one which he adopted, he rejected it, but he did reveal here and there that he nevertheless knew this version, too.[a] [2] And it is clear that he accordingly composed (and nowhere contradicted) a version of the wanderings of Alexandros in the *Iliad* which told of how he was driven off course as he was bringing Helen home with him, and that in his various travels he came to Sidon in Phoenicia.[a] [3] Homer mentions this in the "Heroism of Diomedes" within these verses:

> Robes there were, of rich color and pattern, crafted by women,
> Sidonian women, Alexandros their escort (he looked like a god),
> on that very same journey over the vast, broad sea
> when he brought back Helen of noble birth.[a]

[4] Homer also mentions this version in the *Odyssey*, in these verses:

> Such drugs did the daughter of Zeus possess, drugs clever
> And good, given to her by the bed-mate of Thon
> Polydamna of Egypt, where the grain-giving fields bear forth
> many drugs; and once mixed, some bring much good,
> but others, much pain.[a]

[5] And in other verses, Menelaos says to Telemachus:

> The gods kept me in Egypt, though I yearned to come here,
> All because I neglected to offer them oxen, hundreds of oxen.[a]

[6] In these verses Homer shows that he knew of Alexandros' wandering to Egypt. For Syria[a] and Egypt share a border, and the Phoenicians, to whom Sidon belongs, live in Syria.

These verses make it clear that the *Cypria*[a] cannot be a poem by Homer, but must have been composed by someone else, as does also a particular passage of the *Cypria*, in which Alexandros and Helen arrive at Ilium (Troy) on the third day of their voyage from Sparta, having sailed under fair breezes on a calm sea, while in the *Iliad* Homer says that he was driven off course with her. But for now, let us bid farewell to this discussion of the verses of Homer and the *Cypria*.

2.117
The *Cypria* poem
cannot be by Homer.

2.116.1a Here, and in the next chapters through 2.120, Herodotus displays his knowledge of epic Greek poetry, analyzing the sources, evaluating their plausibility, rejecting some while stating and supporting his own conclusions. See Appendix Q, Herodotus and the Poets, §5–6.
2.116.2a Sidon, Phoenicia: Map 2.112, AY.
2.116.3a *Iliad* 6.289–292.
2.116.4a *Odyssey* 4.227–230.
2.116.5a *Odyssey* 4.351–352.
2.116.6a Syria: Map 2.112, AY.
2.117.1a The *Cypria* was one of the epic poems of the Trojan War cycle dealing with Alexandros' abduction of Helen and their flight, with Aphrodite's help, from Sparta. It was attributed by some in ancient times to Homer, but later to another poet, Stasinus.

2.118
A reconciliation of the Egyptian and Homeric stories.

When I asked the priests whether the Hellenes' account of what happened at Troy was fictitious, they claimed that they knew the truth of this affair because Menelaos himself was the source of their information. [2] They said a large army of Hellenes did in fact go to Troy in support of Menelaos after the abduction of Helen. After the Hellenes disembarked and set up their camp, they sent messengers to Troy, with Menelaos himself among them. [3] When they entered the city, they demanded the return of Helen as well as the property which Alexandros had stolen before he left. They asked for justice in return for the injustices that had been done them. But the Trojans told the same story then as they did afterward, both sworn to oath and not, that neither Helen nor the property they demanded were located in Troy. All these were really in Egypt, they said, and so it would be unjust for them to pay a penalty for what Proteus the Egyptian king had in his possession. [4] And so the Hellenes, thinking they were being mocked, besieged Troy until they captured it. But when they had taken the city and were unable to find Helen there, the Hellenes remembered the story they had been told before and, now believing it, sent Menelaos off to Proteus.

2.119
EGYPT
The Egyptian story of Menelaos' impious acts in Egypt.

So Menelaos had come to Egypt, had sailed upstream to Memphis,[a] and related the whole truth about the affair to the Egyptians. He was treated with great hospitality, and he regained Helen unharmed and recovered all his property. [2] Once he had obtained all this, however, he subsequently behaved so dreadfully that he proved to the Egyptians that he was a most unjust man. For when he was ready to sail away and was prevented from doing so by adverse weather which persisted for a long time, he committed the ungodly act [3] of seizing two children from local people and killing them as sacrificial victims. Afterward, when the Egyptians found out what he had done, he fled straight to Libya[a] in his ships, hated and pursued. But where he went from there the Egyptians did not know. They said that they knew some of these details from their own inquiries and others from what had happened to them directly, which of course they knew with certainty.

2.120
Herodotus gives his own judgment on the moral of the tale of the Trojan War.

That is what the Egyptian priests said, and I agree with their argument, considering that if Helen had been in Troy, the Trojans would certainly have returned her to the Hellenes, whether Alexandros concurred or not. [2] For neither Priam nor his kin could have been so demented that they would have willingly endangered their own persons, their children, and their city just so that Alexandros could have Helen. [3] Surely the Trojans would have realized this even in the first years of the war and would have given her up. After all, many Trojans were being killed whenever they joined combat with the Greeks, and the sons of Priam himself were dying in every battle, two or three at a time, and sometimes even more. And I believe—if the verses themselves can be used as evidence—that even if Priam himself had been living with Helen, he would certainly have returned her to the Achaeans in order to bring their troubles to an end. [4] In fact, since the kingship was not even going to devolve upon Alexandros, he could not

2.119.1a Memphis: Map 2.112, BY.   2.119.3a Libya: Map 2.112, BX.

have hoped to control matters in Priam's old age. It was Hector, both older and more of a man than Alexandros, who was to inherit the crown when Priam died, and he would never have entrusted affairs of state to a brother who committed injustices, and especially not if doing so were to bring great evils upon himself and on all the Trojans. [5] And so it is clear that they did not have Helen and therefore could not give her back; and that when they said this to the Hellenes, they were telling the truth; but the Hellenes did not believe them. This all took place—and here I am declaring my own opinion—because a divine force arranged matters so that the Trojans, by their total ruin and destruction, would clearly demonstrate to all humans the fundamental truth that when great injustices are committed, retribution from the gods is also great. That, at least, is what I think.[a]

After Proteus died, I was told, Rhampsinitos[a] received the kingship. He left as his memorial the monumental gateway facing west at the sanctuary of Hephaistos, and in front of it he set up two statues thirty-eight feet[b] tall. The Egyptians call the one standing on the north side "Summer"[c] and the one on the south side "Winter." They honor the one called "Summer" with great respect and homage but treat the one called "Winter" in just the opposite way.

This king amassed great wealth in silver, which none of his royal descendants could surpass or even come close to. In order to store his money in a safe place, he had a stone chamber constructed, with one of its walls extending to the outside of his living quarters. Now the man who built it devised a secret plan and accordingly constructed it so that one of the stones in the wall could easily be removed by two men, or even one. [2] After the chamber was completed, the king stored his treasure in it.

Years went by, and when the builder was approaching the end of his life, he summoned his two sons and described how he had provided for them by building the king's treasury according to his own skillful design so that they would be well taken care of. He explicitly described to them the removable stone, giving them measurements of its position, and he said that if they remembered it, they would become the real controllers of the king's treasury.

[3] When he died, his sons did not delay in setting to work. At night they went to the palace and easily discovered and removed the stone set in the building and took away much of the treasure they found there.

The next time the king happened to open the chamber, he was surprised to find the coffers much reduced in treasure, but he could not accuse any person of having broken in, since the seals were secure and the chamber

2.121
EGYPT
The reign of Rhampsinitos.[*]

2.121.α[*]
RHAMPSINITOS
The story of the clever theft of Rhampsinitos' treasure.

2.121.β
RHAMPSINITOS
The story of the theft of Rhampsinitos' treasure continues.

2.120.5a This chapter shows Herodotus' ability to take a critical stance toward traditional material. It is also a clear statement of his religious posture.

2.121[*] Rhampsinitos is thought to be a composite of the Ramses pharaohs of the XIX and XX dynasties, c. 1320–1069.

2.121.1b Herodotus writes "25 cubits." A common cubit = about 1.5 feet. See Appendix J, §4, 5, 19.

2.121.1c They called the north one "Summer" presumably because northerly winds (the Etesians) blow in summer." (Lloyd)

2.121.α[*] This chapter in the *Histories* has subdivisions indicated by Greek letters in alphabetic sequence. That sequence (with the letters' Latin equivalents) is as follows: α (a), β (b), γ (g), δ (d), ε (e), ζ (z).

had been locked.[a] When he opened it two or three times again and the treasure seemed to dwindle each time—for the thieves did not give up their plundering—he gave orders that traps were to be made and set around the coffers containing the treasure.

[2] So the thieves came just as before; one of them entered, and when he got close to a coffer, he was at once caught in a trap. As soon as he realized how bad his situation was, he called out to his brother, describing to him what had happened, and asked him to enter quickly and to cut off his head so as to prevent him from being recognized and identified, which would ruin his brother along with himself. His brother thought this to be sensible advice and so he complied, and after securing the stone back in position, he returned home, carrying his brother's head.

2.121.γ
RHAMPSINITOS
The story of the theft of Rhampsinitos' treasure continues.

The next morning the king entered the chamber and was astounded to see the headless body of the thief in the trap, but still no damage done to the chamber, nor any sign of how someone might have gone in or out. Completely baffled by what he saw, the king now decided to carry out yet another scheme. He had the corpse of the thief hung from the wall and appointed guards to watch over it, instructing them to arrest and bring to him anyone they saw mourning and lamenting. [2] When the thief's corpse was hung, his mother was terribly disturbed. She spoke to her surviving son, ordering him to come up with a plan to take down his brother's body and bring it home, no matter what the risks. She even threatened that if he did not do so, she would go to the king herself and inform him that it was her son who had stolen the king's treasure.

2.121.δ
RHAMPSINITOS
The story of the theft of Rhampsinitos' treasure continues.

The son tried to persuade her not to take such a dangerous course, but she continued to badger and abuse him until finally he devised the following stratagem. He loaded full wineskins on some donkeys and drove them to where the men were guarding the hanging corpse. Here he lightly tugged on two or three of the knotted necks of the wineskins just enough to loosen them; [2] and when the wine started flowing out, he beat his head and yelled loudly that he had no idea which donkey to attend to first. When the guards saw so much wine gushing out, they all ran into the road with jars and filled them with the flowing wine, believing it to be their windfall. [3] Meanwhile the thief shouted insults at everyone and everything, pretending to be furious, but as the guards tried to console him he began to act as though he were calming down and relenting. Finally, he drove the donkeys off the road and readjusted their packs. [4] The guards began to chat with him at length, and someone began to imitate his anger and to mock it, which brought him around to laugh with them, so that now, in good humor, he gave them another of the wineskins. At this point they reclined just as they were, intending to drink all of it right there, and they invited him to stay and drink with them. He

2.121.β.1a "Egyptians' doors were normally locked   stamped with the name of the owner."
            by means of bolts or keys and could,   (Lloyd)
            where necessary, be sealed by mud seals

agreed, of course, and lingered there with them. [5] And as they became more warm and friendly in their drinking, he gave them yet one more of the wineskins. This heavy drinking made the guards quite drunk, so that before long they were overcome by drowsiness and fell asleep on the very spot where they were drinking. [6] The thief waited until the middle of the night and then took down his brother's body and, by way of insult, shaved the right cheek of each guard.[a] Then he set the corpse on the backs of the donkeys and drove them home, having thus carried out his mother's command.

When it was reported to the king that the thief's corpse had been stolen away, he became enraged, and hoping to find some means, however extreme, by which this thief would be found, he is supposed to have devised the following scheme, although I find it difficult to believe. [2] He put his own daughter into a brothel and ordered her to receive all men alike, but before coupling with any of them, she was to require them to tell her the most clever and the most impious deeds they had ever committed, and whoever told her of deeds resembling those of the thief was to be arrested and prevented from leaving. [3] And so she began to carry out her father's orders, but the thief learned the reason for what she was doing and decided that he would try to outdo the king in shrewdness, so here is what he did: [4] he cut off the arm of a fresh corpse at the shoulder, concealed it under his cloak, and went to see the king's daughter. When he entered her chamber, she asked him the same question she had asked all the others, and he told her that the most evil deed that he had ever committed was to cut off the head of his brother,[a] who had been caught in a trap within the king's treasury; and that his most clever deed was to deceive the guards and make them drunk so that he could take down the corpse of his brother from where it was hanging. [5] When she heard this, she tried to seize him, but in the darkness the thief stretched out the arm of the corpse in front of his own, and she grasped hold of it, believing that she had hold of the thief's hand. The thief immediately let go of the unattached arm she clutched and, fleeing swiftly through the door, was gone.

When this exploit was reported to the king, he was so astounded at the cleverness and daring of this man that he sent an announcement throughout all of his cities that he would grant this man a free pardon and great rewards if he would come to the king and reveal himself. [2] The thief, taking the king at his word, appeared before him, and Rhampsinitos was so

2.121.ε
RHAMPSINITOS
The story of the theft of Rhampsinitos' treasure continues.

2.121.ζ
RHAMPSINITOS
The story of the theft of Rhampsinitos' treasure continues.

2.121.δ.6a This seems to contradict Herodotus' earlier claim that Egyptians were clean-shaven (2.36.1), but Egyptian police were not shaven, or these may have been foreign mercenaries.

2.121.ε.4a To mutilate a corpse, which he had done to acquire the arm, and particularly to harm the corpse of a relative, even though he had been asked to do it, went against all religious sentiments (both Greek and Egyptian) about the power and sanctity of human remains, which had to be respected and treated according to very specific rules. An example of this in ancient Greece is the truce that was always granted after a battle by the victors to the vanquished so that the latter could recover and properly bury the corpses of their fallen warriors.

amazed and impressed by him that he united him with his daughter, regarding him as the most intelligent of men. And as he esteemed Egyptians above all other races, he esteemed this man more than any other Egyptian.

2.122
RHAMPSINITOS
The festival of Demeter.

They say that after these events King Rhampsinitos descended into what the Hellenes think of as Hades while he was still alive, and that once there he played dice with Demeter,[a] winning some games and losing others before returning to the world above with a gift from her—a golden handkerchief. [2] They told me that when Rhampsinitos came back from his journey to the underworld, the Egyptians celebrated a festival to commemorate his return. I know for a fact that this festival is still observed in my time, but I cannot say whether that is the true reason they celebrate this festival. [3] On the day of the festival, the priests weave a new robe. They blindfold one of their number, and as he holds the robe, he is led by the other priests up to the road that leads to the sanctuary of Demeter, where he is released. They say that this blindfolded priest is then led by two wolves to the sanctuary of Demeter, more than two miles[a] from the city, and that the wolves then lead him back from the sanctuary to the same place.

2.123
EGYPT
Recording what others have told him, Herodotus describes an Egyptian theory of reincarnation.

Well, then, let these accounts told by the Egyptians be put to use by anyone who finds such things credible. My entire account is governed by the rule that I write down precisely what I am told by everyone, just as I heard it.[a]

The Egyptians say that Demeter and Dionysos[b] reign over those in the underworld.

[2] The Egyptians are in fact the first to have claimed that the human soul is immortal and that each time the body perishes, it enters at birth another living being; and whenever it has gone through the lives of all types of creatures living on land or sea, or flying in the air, it again enters at birth the body of a human. This cycle is said to take 3,000 years. [3] There are certain Hellenes—some who lived earlier, some later—who have adopted this theory as though it were their very own; I know their names but shall not write them down.[a]

2.124
2596–2573
CHEOPS–IV DYNASTY
Cheops' reign is harsh due to the construction of the Great Pyramid.

The priests said that as long as Rhampsinitos was king, Egypt was well governed in every respect and flourished remarkably. But after him Cheops became king, and under his rule the Egyptians suffered all kinds of misfortunes.[a] First of all, he closed down all the sanctuaries and prevented the Egyptians from performing sacrifices; then he commanded all Egyptians to do forced labor for him. [2] Some were assigned to haul stones to the Nile[a] all the way from the quarries in the mountains of Arabia.[b] Once these stones had

2.122.1a Herodotus here equates Demeter with the Egyptian Isis.
2.122.3a Herodotus writes "20 stades" from the city. See Appendix J, §6, 19.
2.123.1a A general statement by Herodotus of his method and policy.
2.123.1b Herodotus here equates Demeter and Dionysos with the Egyptian Isis and Osiris.
2.123.3a The Pythagoreans believed in the transmigration of souls.

2.124.1a Herodotus has confused the periods of the various pharaohs. The pyramid builders of the IV Dynasty—Cheops, Chephren, and Mykerinos—lived almost 1,500 years before the Ramses of the XIX and XX dynasties. See Appendix C, §7.
2.124.2a Nile River: Map 2.112, BY.
2.124.2b Mountains of Arabia: the range of hills on the Nile River's east bank (Arabian side).

FIGURE 2.124A. A VIEW OF THE GREAT PYRAMID OF CHEOPS (KHUFU?), ILLUSTRATING ITS GREAT HEIGHT AND STEEPNESS, WHICH INSPIRED HERODOTUS WITH AWE (AS IT DOES MANY OF US TODAY). NOTE THE CAMEL WITH RIDER (LOWER LEFT) WHICH PROVIDES SCALE.

FIGURE 2.124B. THE EDITOR AND HIS WIFE IN FRONT OF THE SOUTHERN PYRAMID OF SNEFRU (THE BENT PYRAMID AT DAHSHUR) IN SUMMER 1963. IT SHOWS THE ORIGINAL SMOOTH LIMESTONE SKIN THAT ONCE COVERED OTHER EGYPTIAN PYRAMIDS AND CERTAINLY DID SO WHEN HERODOTUS SAW THEM. IT ALSO ILLUSTRATES THE HUGE SIZE OF THE BLOCKS USED IN ITS CONSTRUCTION.

been conveyed across the river in boats, others were commanded to unload them and haul them to the so-called Libyan ridge.[c] [3] They worked in gangs of 100,000 men on each project, rotating in three-month shifts. For ten years the people labored and wore themselves out with just the construction of the causeway on which they hauled the stones, and I suppose this causeway was almost as great a project as the pyramids themselves, [4] since it is 3,900 feet long, 60 feet wide, 50 feet tall at its highest point,[a] and made from hewn stone sculpted with figures. So ten years were spent building all this, as well as the underground chambers in the ridge on which the pyramids stand. Cheops had these built as his burial vaults, and he directed a channel of the Nile to flow around them so as to form an island. [5] The pyramid itself took twenty years to complete; it measures 800 feet on each of its four sides, and 800 feet in height, constructed of hewn stones fitted together with the utmost precision. None of the stones measures less than thirty feet.[a]

This pyramid was built like a flight of stairs, which some call battlements, others platforms. [2] When they had completed the foundation level, they lifted the rest of the stones by means of a device made of short pieces of wood, raising them from the ground up to the first tier of stairs. [3] When a stone had been lifted to the first tier, it was mounted onto another lifting mechanism standing on that tier, and from there it was hoisted to the second tier and to yet another machine. [4] Either they employed as many devices as there were tiers, or perhaps they used one single machine that was easy to move from one tier to the next after they had removed the stone. I give both explanations here exactly as they were presented to me.[a]

[5] After the structure was complete, they finished off[a] the top tiers first and worked downward so that the lowest tiers at ground level were finished last. [6] On the pyramid are written the quantities of radishes, onions, and garlic consumed by the workers, and to the best of my recollection, the interpreter said, as he read the inscriptions, that the total cost

2.124.2c Libyan mountains: the range of hills on the west (Libyan side) of the Nile.

2.124.4a Herodotus writes that this ramp is "5 stades" long, "10 fathoms" wide, and "8 fathoms" tall at its highest point. He appears to have confused the then existing causeway with the ramp that was built for the purpose of constructing the pyramid, which was removed after construction was completed. See Appendix J, §4–6, 19.

2.124.5a Herodotus writes that the pyramids are "8 plethra" square and "8 plethra" in height. A plethron = 100 feet, so Herodotus' measurements of the base dimensions are not that far off: the Great Pyramid of Cheops at ground level is a square 756 feet on each side. Its height, however, is just 481 feet. The corners of

the structure are lined up with the cardinal directions with remarkable precision. The individual stones are indeed immense; some weigh up to 60 tons, none less than 2 tons. See Figures 2.124a and b. See Appendix J, §5–6, 19.

2.125.4a The description of this construction technique is probably false. There is no evidence of such devices. Herodotus may be influenced by Greek practices here.

2.125.5a That is, the stones which were used to fill up the angles of the steps and make the side of the pyramid a smooth inclined plane were fitted and finished from the top down. The pyramids built by Cheops, Chephren, and Mykerinos are now known as the Great Pyramids of Giza, near modern Cairo. (Godley)

of these items was 1,600 talents of silver.[a] [7] If this was really the case, how much more are they likely to have spent on the iron with which they worked,[a] and on the bread and clothing for the workers? And inasmuch as they built all this in the period of time stated earlier, I assume that the rest of the work—the cutting and transport of the stones, as well as the underground excavation and construction—must have required a substantial period of time.

The priests said that Cheops sank to such depths of wickedness that when he ran short of money, he placed his own daughter in a brothel and ordered her to charge a certain sum of silver, although they neglected to tell me the exact amount she was to demand. She did as her father ordered, but, intending to leave behind a memorial of her own, she asked each man who came to her for the gift of one stone. [2] And from these stones, they said, was built the pyramid that stands in the middle of the three that are situated in front of the great pyramid. Each of its sides measures 150 feet.[a]

The Egyptians said that Cheops reigned for fifty years,[a] and that, when he died, the kingdom passed to his brother Chephren, who continued to manage affairs in much the same way as Cheops had done, both in building a pyramid and in other respects, except that the size of his pyramid did not quite equal that of his brother's. I myself actually measured them. [2] Chephren's pyramid has neither an underground chamber nor a channel flowing from the Nile to surround it as does the earlier one, which also has a conduit built inside it through which flows a channel around the island on which they say Cheops himself lies buried. [3] Chephren built the course of his pyramid of colored Ethiopian stone[a] to measure forty feet less than the other pyramid, and he placed it nearby. Both of them stand on the same ridge, which is approximately 100 feet high.[b]

They said that Chephren reigned for fifty-six years.

They calculate that the Egyptians suffered extreme hardships for all of 106 years and that for this length of time, all the sanctuaries were shut down and remained closed. The Egyptians hate the very memory of these

2.126
2596–2573
CHEOPS–IV DYNASTY
Needing money, Cheops prostituted his daughter.

2.127
2573–2517
CHEPHREN–IV DYNASTY
The harsh reign of Chephren and a description of his pyramid.

2.128
EGYPT
Egyptians hate the memory of these kings.

2.125.6a   The talent was a unit of weight and money. Sixteen hundred talents was an astronomical sum to ancient Greeks. See Appendix J, §11–13, 20. No similar inscription has been found at the Great Pyramid of Cheops, or at any other pyramid in Egypt, and since Egypt's economy at that time did not use money but worked on a system of barter of commodities and services, one cannot help but wonder whether the translator who told Herodotus that the inscriptions commemorated in silver the cost of radishes, onions, and garlic consumed by the project was either totally incompetent or perhaps was pulling the leg of the "father of history." See also the tale told in 2.126.

2.125.7a   Herodotus is mistaken here. No iron

was used in the construction of the pyramids.

2.126.2a   Herodotus writes "1.5 plethra" on each side.

2.127.1a   Actually, Cheops' reign was not for fifty years, but for only twenty-three years—from 2596 to 2573; and he was succeeded by his brother Dedefre. Only after Dedefre's reign ended did Cheops' son Chephren become pharaoh.

2.127.3a   Ethiopia: Map 2.140, BY. By "Ethiopian stone" here, Herodotus undoubtedly means a reddish or sometimes darker granite that is quarried from Aswan, some 400 miles upstream from the Great Pyramids.

2.127.3b   Herodotus writes this height as 100 feet—Greek feet! See Appendix J, §6, 19.

2.129
2517–2511
MYKERINOS–IV DYNASTY
The benign reign of
Mykerinos. The death of
his daughter and her
entombment in a hollow
wooden cow.

2.130
2517–2511
MYKERINOS–IV DYNASTY
More about the cow tomb
and the gigantic wooden
statues of nude women.

2.131
2517–2511
MYKERINOS–IV DYNASTY
A contrary tale of Mykerinos
and his daughter. An obvious
falsehood.

2.132
2517–2511
MYKERINOS–IV DYNASTY
The gilded cow, described
by Herodotus as he saw it.

two kings so intensely that they will not even speak their names. Instead, they call another man the pyramid builder—one Philitis, who pastured cattle in these regions at the time.

After Chephren's death, they say that Mykerinos son of Cheops became king.[a] He disapproved of his father's policies, so he opened up the sanctuaries and allowed the people, now worn to the breaking point by their suffering, to go back to their occupations and to make sacrifices. Moreover, of all the kings of Egypt, his judicial decisions were the most equitable. [2] The Egyptians praise him more than any other king they have ever had, not only because he was in many ways a good judge, but especially because he was magnanimous to those who would find fault with his verdicts. If this occurred, the king would donate compensation from his own funds so as to satisfy the one who had complained. [3] Now, despite the fact that Mykerinos practiced clemency toward the citizens, he did not thereby escape trouble. He suffered his first misfortune when his daughter died. She was the only child of his house, and he reacted with extremely painful grief at this event. He desired to bury his daughter in a manner more extravagant than most, so he had a hollow wooden cow built and gilded, and then he buried his deceased daughter inside it.

This cow, however, was not buried in the ground; in fact it was still visible in my time, in the city of Sais,[a] lying in an ornately decorated chamber of the palace. All day and every day they burn incense of every kind beside it, and all night and every night a lamp burns next to it. [2] Close by this cow, but in a different room, stand statues of the concubines of Mykerinos, or so said the priests in the city of Sais. These are gigantic statues made of wood, about twenty in number, and they are carved so as to resemble naked women. But as to who these women really might be, I cannot say—I only report what they have told me.

Some people tell the following story about the cow and these gigantic statues: they say that Mykerinos fell in love with his own daughter and had intercourse with her against her will; [2] and that afterward she hanged herself in grief, and he buried her in the cow. But her mother cut off the hands of the girl's serving maids who had surrendered her to her father, and so now the statues of these women have suffered the very same punishment inflicted upon the women when they were alive. [3] I think they were talking total nonsense when they said this, particularly in their explanation of the statues' hands, for I myself saw that the images' hands had simply fallen off with time and were still plainly visible to me at the feet of the statues.[a]

The cow is covered almost completely in a crimson robe, but its neck and head are exposed and gilded with a thick layer of gold. Between the horns is set a lifelike image of the circle of the sun, also of gold. [2] The cow is not standing up but is shown falling to its knees. It is as big as a large cow in real

---

2.129.1a See Figure 2.129, a statue of Mykerinos
            (Menkaure) and his wife.
2.130.1a Sais: Map 2.140, BY.

2.131.3a Here is another example of Herodotus'
            use of critical faculties.

FIGURE 2.129. STATUE OF
MYKERINOS (MENKAURE)
AND HIS WIFE.

life. Each year, during the festival when they beat their breasts in mourning for the god whom I never name in this context,[a] they carry the cow out of the chamber [3] into the broad light of day, for they say that as the girl was dying, she requested from her father that she look upon the sun once a year.

After the ordeal of his daughter's death, the king suffered a second misfortune. An oracle came to him from the city of Bouto[a] predicting that he would live only six more years and would die in the seventh.[b] [2] In much distress, the king sent to the oracle a reply that reproached the god with a complaint: his father and uncle had shut down the sanctuaries, had paid no respect to the gods, and had destroyed humans, yet they had lived a long time, while he himself, who respected the gods, was destined to meet his end so quickly. [3] The oracle replied with a second message, saying that this was in fact why his life was being cut short, as he was not doing what he should, for the Egyptians were bound by fate to suffer hardships for 150 years.[a] The two kings preceding him had understood this, but he had not.

2.133
2517–2511
MYKERINOS–IV DYNASTY
Mykerinos attempts to prove wrong the oracle's prediction of his death.

2.132.2a Osiris, see also 2.61.
2.133.1a Bouto: Map 2.140, BY.
2.133.1b Seven years, a significant number in Egypt.

2.133.3a These arguments of Mykerinos and the oracle reflect very Greek thinking.

[4] Upon hearing this, Mykerinos, surmising that he had already been condemned, arranged for numerous lamps to be made and lit whenever night fell. Then he drank and enjoyed himself without stopping day or night, and he wandered into the marshes and groves to find the most suitable settings for youthful pleasures. [5] This behavior was all part of a plan to prove the oracle wrong; for by turning his nights into days, he extended the six allotted years to twelve.

This king, too, left behind a pyramid, but one much smaller than that of his father, for it was 280 feet[a] on each of its four sides. Half of it was made of Ethiopian stone.[b] Some of the Hellenes mistakenly claim that this pyramid is really that of a woman, the courtesan Rhodopis, [2] but they obviously make this claim without even knowing who Rhodopis was, for if they knew anything about her, they would never have attributed to her the construction of such a large pyramid, which must have cost countless thousands of talents. Moreover, Rhodopis was at her prime during the reign of Amasis[a] rather than during the period in question. [3] She lived, in fact, very many years after these kings had built their pyramids and left them behind as memorials. She was a Thracian[a] by race and served as the slave of Iadmon the Samian[b] son of Hephaistopolis. Aesop the storyteller was her fellow slave,[c] and he, too, belonged to Iadmon, which is quite obvious from [4] the fact that when the Delphians repeatedly announced by command of the oracle that whoever wanted compensation to be paid for the life of Aesop[a] should come forward and take it, no one appeared but Iadmon, although a different one, the grandson of the first Iadmon. From this I conclude that Aesop must have been the slave of Iadmon.

Rhodopis was brought to Egypt[a] by Xanthes of Samos. There she was freed by a man from Mytilene[b] so that she could work at her occupation. He was Charaxos son of Skamandronymos, the brother of Sappho the lyric songstress.[c] [2] Thus Rhodopis stayed in Egypt, and since she was well endowed with the blessings of Aphrodite, she acquired a large fortune— large for a Rhodopis that is, but certainly not the kind of fortune that would support the construction of a pyramid. [3] Anyone who wishes may still view one tenth of her fortune and therefore judge that her wealth was indeed not so large. For when Rhodopis wished to leave behind in Hellas a memorial to herself, she had objects made and dedicated in commemoration of herself at

2.134.1a   Herodotus writes that the sides of this pyramid are 20 (Greek) feet short of "3 plethra." A plethron = about 100 feet. The true measurement is 365.5 feet. (Lloyd)
2.134.1b   Ethiopia: Map 2.140, BY. For "Ethiopian stone," see n. 2.127.3a.
2.134.2a   Amasis reigned in Egypt from 570 to 526.
2.134.3a   Thrace: Map 2.140, AX.
2.134.3b   Samos: Map 2.140, AX.
2.134.3c   Aesop, the author of instructive fables.
2.134.4a   An early story (almost certainly not historical) related that the Delphians, insulted by Aesop, got revenge by planting a sacred drinking bowl in his baggage and then accusing him of theft of sacred objects. They had him executed (the usual punishment for sacrilegious theft) but then found that their land bore no crops. To rectify the situation, they were instructed to make com- pensation for his death, and they announced this offer at the Greek religious festivals.
2.135.1a   Egypt: Map 2.140, BY.
2.135.1b   Mytilene: Map 2.140, AX.
2.135.1c   Sappho, the most famous poetess of ancient Greece, lived in Lesbos c. 612–550.

Delphi[a]—objects which no one else had ever thought to dedicate to a sanctuary. [4] She commissioned smiths to craft many spits of iron large enough to impale oxen, as many as amounted to the value of a tenth of her estate, and then she sent them to Delphi. There they are still piled up behind the altar dedicated by the Chians,[a] which faces the temple itself.

[5] In Naucratis,[a] courtesans somehow tend to be especially endowed by Aphrodite. For in addition to the fame of Rhodopis, which is known to all the Hellenes, there is also another woman from that place named Archidike, who is also celebrated in song throughout Hellas, although she is less notorious than the other. In any case, after Charaxos freed Rhodopis he returned home to Mytilene, and Sappho denounced him harshly with much mockery in a song. So ends my account of Rhodopis.

The priests said that after Mykerinos, Asychis became king of Egypt. He built the monumental entrance facing the rising sun, by far the largest and most beautiful of all, at the sanctuary of Hephaistos. For while all the entrance gates do have reliefs carved on them and countless other spectacular architectural features, this one has many more than the others. [2] In the reign of this king, a law was established for the Egyptians to deal with the decline in commercial activity and the means of exchange. According to this law, an Egyptian could get a loan by declaring his father's corpse as security. Appended to this law was the stipulation that the creditor could assume possession of the whole grave site of the debtor as well, and added to this, a penalty was imposed also upon anyone who pledged this kind of security but who was unwilling to pay back his debt, that when he died, he would have no grave in the burial place of his ancestors nor any other grave; and his descendants could not be buried either.[a]

[3] This king wanted to surpass the kings of Egypt who ruled before him, so he left behind a pyramid as his memorial,[a] but had it constructed out of bricks, with an inscription engraved in stone upon it which reads: [4] "Do not think less of me than other pyramids, which are made of stone. I, in fact, surpass them as much as Zeus surpasses the other gods. For my construction was accomplished by plunging a pole down into a lake and gathering the clay that clung to the pole, from which the bricks were then molded." That is what this king achieved.

After him, a blind man became king; he was from the city of Anysis[a] and his name was Anysis, too. In his reign, the Ethiopians[b] and their king, Sabakos,[c] attacked Egypt with a huge force. [2] The blind king fled to the

2.136
945–924
ASYCHIS–XXII DYNASTY
The works of King Asychis (called Seshonq by the Egyptians).

2.137
ANYSIS–XXIII DYNASTY
The blind king Anysis is followed by the Ethiopian Sabakos, who ruled Egypt for fourteen years (716–702), not, as Herodotus says, for fifty years.

2.135.3a   Delphi: Map 2.140, AX.
2.135.4a   Chios: Map 2.140, AX.
2.135.5a   Naucratis: Map 2.140, BY.
2.136.2a   Herodotus is thinking in terms of the Greek money-based economy. He is unaware that there was no money in pharaonic Egypt, just barter.
2.136.3a   Asychis, also known as Sheshonq I, did not build a pyramid.
2.137.1a   Anysis, possible location: Map 2.165, AY. Anysis may represent the pharaohs

of the XXIII dynasty, who ruled from 818 to 715.
2.137.1b   Ethiopia: Map 2.140, BY.
2.137.1c   Three Ethiopian kings form the XXV dynasty, which ruled Egypt for fifty-two years, from 716 to 664. These kings are: Sabakos, 716–702, Shabataku, 702–690, and Taharqa (the Tirhaka of the Old Testament), 690–664.

marshes, leaving the field to the Ethiopian, who then reigned as king of Egypt for fifty years. He accomplished the following: [3] whenever an Egyptian committed some transgression, the king, who was averse to having anyone killed, instead judged each case according to the severity of the injustice done and then imposed on the offender the task of piling up a quantity of soil on the land of the city from which he came. In this way, the cities rose even higher in elevation than before. [4] For the cities rose above the original level of the land first because of the soil deposited from the work of those who excavated the channels of the Nile during the reign of King Sesostris, and secondly, during the reign of this Ethiopian king, who created quite a large increase in their elevation. [5] There are other cities in Egypt that have increased in elevation, but I think the city in the district of Boubastis[a] received the greatest accumulation of soil. It is here that the very remarkable sanctuary of Boubastis is located, and although there are larger and more opulent sanctuaries, none is more pleasurable to behold than this one. Boubastis in Greek means Artemis.

I could best describe the sanctuary as an island, except for its entrance. Two channels of the Nile extend around it as far as the entrance of the sanctuary on either side of it, without meeting each other. Each channel is 100 feet wide and shaded by trees. [2] The entrance gates are sixty feet tall and adorned with quite noteworthy figures nine feet[a] tall. The sanctuary is situated in the center of the city, and one can walk around it and look down into it from all sides because the city has risen in elevation with the accumulation of soil over time, but the sanctuary has remained undisturbed since it was first built, and therefore it is possible to look down into it.[b] [3] Surrounding it is a dry wall carved with reliefs, and within that wall is a grove of very tall trees growing around a large temple which contains the cult statue. The sanctuary is square and measures 583 feet on each side.[a] [4] Extending from the entrance is a stone road about 1,750 feet long and 400 feet wide,[a] leading through the marketplace to the east. Trees so tall that they seem to touch the sky grow on either side of the road, which continues until it reaches the sanctuary of Hermes. That is what the sanctuary of Boubastis looks like.

The priests said that the Ethiopian king finally fled and disappeared from Egypt because he had a vision in his sleep in which he thought he saw a man standing over him, advising him to assemble the priests of Egypt and to cut them all in half. [2] He said that through this dream, the gods seemed to be hinting that he might be about to commit a sacrilege, for which he would then suffer some disaster from either gods or

2.137.5a	Boubastis: Map 2.140, BY.
2.138.2a	Herodotus writes that they measured "6 cubits." The common cubit = about 1.5 feet. See Appendix J, §4, 5, 19.
2.138.2b	For the same reason, one looks down into or at many ancient temples in cities today. See Figure 2.138, which illustrates the phenomenon of rising Egyptian land levels due to flooding.
2.138.3a	Herodotus writes "1 square stade." The Attic stade = about 583 feet. See Appendix J, §6, 19.
2.138.4a	Herodotus writes "3 stades" long and "4 plethra" wide. The plethron = about 100 feet. See Appendix J, §5–6, 19.

FIGURE 2.138. THE TEMPLE WHOSE ROOF HERODOTUS SAYS HE LOOKED DOWN UPON FROM GROUND LEVEL IS NO LONGER STANDING. IT IS KNOWN, HOWEVER, THAT IT WAS ABOUT 2,000 YEARS OLD AT THE TIME HE MADE THAT STATEMENT. AS HE POINTS OUT, THE ANNUAL NILE FLOOD (AND THE EFFECT OF MUD-BRICK URBAN RENEWAL) CAUSED THE SURFACE OF THE LAND TO RISE SUBSTANTIALLY OVER THE YEARS, LEAVING THE TEMPLE, AS IT WERE, IN A PIT. THIS PHOTOGRAPH IS OF A PTOLEMAIC TEMPLE AT ESNA, EGYPT, WHICH TODAY IS ALSO A LITTLE MORE THAN 2,000 YEARS OLD. SINCE ONE CAN LOOK DOWN UPON ITS ROOF FROM CURRENT GROUND LEVEL, IT DISPLAYS A PARALLEL EXAMPLE OF THE PROCESS HERODOTUS SO GRAPHICALLY DESCRIBED.

men.[a] He would avoid this calamity, however, by leaving the country now, since the time for him to rule over Egypt had passed, [3] for when he was still in Ethiopia, the oracle that the Ethiopians consult[a] had told him that he had to reign in Egypt for fifty years. So now, since that much time had gone by and the vision in the dream had disturbed him, Sabakos willingly departed from Egypt.

2.140
BLIND KING
The blind king Anysis returns, having hid in the marshes.

When the Ethiopian had gone, the blind king came back from the marshes and again began to rule. For fifty years he had lived in the swamps on an island that he had created by heaping up ash and soil. He had commanded certain Egyptians to bring food to him without the knowledge of the Ethiopian, and when they came, he would order them to bring some ashes with their next offering of food. [2] No one before Amyrtaios[a] was able to find this island; for more than 700 years, the kings who lived before Amyrtaios could not find it. This island's name is Elbo,[b] and it measures more than 5,800 feet[c] in every direction.

2.141
702–690
SETHOS
Sethos (Shabataka) the priest becomes king. He repels the Assyrians with the help of mice sent by the god.

After this king, a priest of Hephaistos reigned whose name was Sethos.[a] He despised and slighted the Egyptian warrior class, thinking he would have no need of them. He offended their honor in many ways, and even took away the twelve choice plots of arable land that each of them had received from earlier kings. [2] After this, Sennacharib king of the Arabians[a] and Assyrians[b] led a large army against Egypt, and naturally the warrior class refused to assist Sethos. [3] Caught in a dreadful quandary, the priest entered the inner shrine, bewailing to the cult statue the great dangers that confronted him. He wept until at last sleep descended upon him, and in a dream he seemed to see the god standing over him and reassuring him that he would not suffer anything dreadful when he challenged the Arabian army, since he, the god himself, would send assistance to the king. [4] Trusting in this dream, the king took with him the Egyptians who were willing to follow him and made his camp at Pelusium,[a] since it was at this point that the enemy would enter Egypt. Not one man from the warrior class followed him; those who accompanied him were shopkeepers, craftsmen, and merchants of the marketplace. [5] But after the enemy had

---

2.139.2a Significant dreams were thought to be communications from the gods warning of threats and dangers, advising on cures of illness, imposing policies, or answering pressing questions. But Herodotus has Artabanos give a surprisingly rational explanation for them when he advises Xerxes, where he says that "most of the visions visiting our dreams tend to be what one is thinking about during the day." (7.16.β.2).
2.139.3a This oracle is described in 2.29 as at Meroe: Map 2.31, BY.
2.140.2a Amyrtaios was an anti-Persian rebel. See 3.1.3 and *Thucydides* 1.110.2.
2.140.2b Elbo Island: location unknown.
2.140.2c Herodotus writes "10 stades." The Attic

stade = about 583 feet. See Appendix J, §6, 19.
2.141.1a There is no record of a pharaoh named Sethos at this time. The pharaoh who lived contemporaneously with Sennacharib was named Shabataka, who reigned from 702 to 690.
2.141.2a Arabia: Map 2.140, BY.
2.141.2b Assyria: Map 2.140, AY. Sennacharib became king of Assyria in 704. He invaded Palestine more than once, but it is not clear that he actually did invade Egypt. If he did, he was repulsed by the Ethiopian king Shabataka, and Herodotus' informants may have wanted to tell him that an Egyptian accomplished this, not a foreigner.
2.141.4a Pelusium: Map 2.140, BY.

X

Y

THRACE

HELLAS

ASIA

ASSYRIA

Delphi

Lesbos

Mytilene

Chios

Ephesus

Samos

A

Mediterranean Sea

PALESTINE

Bouto

Pelusium

Naucratis

Sais

Boubastis

EGYPT

Lake Moeris

ARABIA

LIBYA

B

Nile R.

Thebes

Elephantine

ETHIOPIA

0   500 km   500 mi

Map 2.140

arrived and night had fallen, an army of field mice[a] swarmed through their camp and chewed up their quivers, bowstrings, and even the handles of their shields, so that on the next day, the enemy found themselves deprived of their weapons and defenseless; many fell as they tried to flee. [6] Today the stone image of this king stands in the sanctuary of Hephaistos holding a mouse in his hand and declaring in an inscription: "Whoever looks at me, let him venerate the gods."

2.142
EGYPT
From what he has seen and heard, Herodotus estimates the age of Egypt from its king list to be 11,340 years.

The Egyptians and the priests told me this much of their history, but they also showed me that from the first king to the last one mentioned—the priest of Hephaistos—there had passed 341 generations of men, and that in each generation there had been one priest and one king. [2] Now 300 generations of men is equivalent to 10,000 years, since there are 3 generations of men in 100 years, and the 41 remaining generations in addition to the 300 add up to 11,340 years. [3] And they said that in all of those 11,340[a] years, as well as in the years of the kings who reigned later, no god had ever appeared there in human form. [4] They did say that on four occasions during this period, the sun had changed its normal course: twice it rose from the place where it normally sets, and twice it set where it normally rises. But Egypt was not affected in any way on those occasions; indeed, nothing strange occurred on land or in the river, nor in regard to illnesses or deaths.

2.143
HEKATAIOS
Hekataios is mocked for his claim of (recent) descent from the gods, whereas Egyptians trace a lineage of 345 generations without gods.

Earlier, Hekataios the author[a] had traced his own genealogy, connecting his lineage to a god in the sixteenth generation before him, and had then gone to Thebes in Egypt, where the priests of Zeus gave him the same tour they gave to me[b] (although I had not traced my own genealogy). [2] They led me into a large inner hall and displayed the giant wooden statues there, counting them out to the very number I just stated, for it is their practice that each high priest erects a statue of himself in this hall during his lifetime. [3] As they enumerated and pointed out the statues, the priests explained how each one was the son of the priest who had preceded him; and they went through all of them, beginning with the image of the most recently deceased, until they had presented each and every one. [4] Moreover, they not only counted up the statues, but they responded with their own extensive genealogy to Hekataios' claim that his lineage could be traced back to a god in the sixteenth generation before him. They refused to believe that a human was ever born from a god, and they gave their own genealogy as

2.141.5a This is Herodotus' version of the Jewish story of the pestilence which destroyed the Assyrian army before Jerusalem. Mice are a Greek symbol of pestilence; it is Apollo Smintheus (the mouse god) who sends and then ends the plague in Homer, *Iliad* I. (Godley)
2.142.3a Herodotus stresses here the Egyptian records spanning what for Greeks were stupendous spans of time. See Appendix C, §2, 7.
2.143.1a Hekataios, the author of geographical and historical accounts of Asia Minor and the East who wrote in the late sixth cen-

tury, was a source both used and criticized by Herodotus. He also plays a role in Herodotus' account of Ionian history. See 5.36, 5.125–126, and 6.137; also Introduction, §3.1.
2.143.1b A direct assertion by Herodotus that he actually went to Thebes, although—despite his interest in marvels and extraordinary sights—he fails to explicitly identify the temple of Karnak with its spectacular dimensions, or some of the other great temples of Luxor. See n. 2.29.1a and Appendix C, §8.

support for this assertion, recounting how each of the giant statues represented a *piromis*[a] born from a *piromis*, until they had pointed out 345[b] statues; but none of these, they said, was connected to either a god or to a hero. In Greek, the term *piromis* means a "good and noble man."

And in this way they demonstrated that all of the images there represented human beings like themselves, completely distinct from the gods. [2] They said, however, that prior to these men, gods had dwelled in Egypt among human beings and had ruled there; indeed there had always been one of them who governed with supreme power. The last of these to reign over Egypt was Horus son of Osiris, whom the Hellenes name Apollo. It was he who had subdued Typhon[a] and became the last of these divine kings of Egypt. His father Osiris is called Dionysos by the Hellenes.

The Hellenes believe that Herakles, Dionysos, and Pan are the youngest of the gods.[a] But the Egyptians hold that Pan[b] is the most ancient of these three and belongs to the first group of gods, called "The Eight Gods." Herakles belongs to the second group, called "The Twelve Gods," and Dionysos belongs to the third, who were born from "The Twelve." [2] I have already shown how many millennia the Egyptians say intervened between Herakles and King Amasis.[a] They count back still more years from Amasis to Pan, but fewer years before they come to Dionysos; in all, they calculate that 15,000 years separate the latter from King Amasis. [3] The Egyptians claim they are absolutely certain of the truth of these calculations, since they have always counted and always recorded the years.

[4] The Hellenes believe, however, that from the time of that Dionysos who is said to be the son of Semele daughter of Kadmos, to my own day, only about 1,000 years have passed; and that the interval from Herakles son of Alkmene to the present is about 900 years; and that Pan son of Penelope (for the Hellenes say Pan was born of her and the god Hermes) occurred more recently still, after the time of the Trojan War, which took place about 800 years ago.[a]

As far as I am concerned, one may espouse either of these versions, whichever one he finds more credible. In any case, my own opinion has

2.144
GOD-KINGS
All of the long line of Egyptian priests were men, not gods, but long ago gods did live and rule in Egypt.

2.145
CHRONOLOGY
Herodotus discusses the chronology of Greek and Egyptian gods.

2.146
Herodotus' opinion about when the Greeks learned of Pan and Dionysos.

2.143.4a *Piromis*: another instance in which Herodotus uses a foreign word in his narrative.
2.143.4b Apparently, Hekataios' count of the statues comes to four more (345) than the number recorded by Herodotus (341). Perhaps Hekataios was shown those statues representing kings who came after the 11,340 years, the period in which Herodotus seems to be interested at this time. It is also possible that someone miscounted such a large number of images, or even that both authors relied here on two diverse versions of someone else's (possibly fictional) account. Clearly, Herodotus is ridiculing the genealogical pretensions of Greeks like Hekataios.

2.144.2a Typhon: Seth in Egyptian, the god of destruction. In Greek mythology, Typhon is a monster subdued by Zeus.
2.145.1a Compare 2.43ff. to 2.145–146. In both sections, Herodotus is contrasting and challenging Greeks' beliefs and chronology of the gods with those of the Egyptians.
2.145.1b The Greek god Pan is the Egyptian deity Mendes; see also 2.46.
2.145.2a Some 17,000 years (2.43.4). Amasis reigned in Egypt from 570 to 526.
2.145.4a Herodotus thus dates the Trojan War to c. mid-thirteenth century. Note how much more recently these events of Greek mythology are supposed to have taken place in comparison to the millennia calculated by the Egyptians.

already been revealed.[a] If these gods had become manifest and had grown old in Hellas just as Herakles son of Amphitryon did, one could claim that they were really just men, but were named after earlier gods. [2] As it is, however, the Hellenes say that as soon as Dionysos was born, Zeus sewed him up in his thigh and carried him to Nysa, above Egypt in Ethiopia;[a] but they cannot say where Pan went after his birth. So it is quite clear to me, at least, that the Hellenes learned the names of these gods later than those of the rest, and that they attribute to each of them a birthdate corresponding to the time when they first learned of him.

2.147
EGYPT
TWELVE KINGS
Herodotus adds new sources. The reign of Twelve Kings in Egypt.

Well, that is what the Egyptians said. Now let me relate what others told me, with the agreement of the Egyptians, about what happened in Egypt; and I will again add something of my own observations.

[2] After being liberated from Ethiopian rule and following the reign of the priest of Hephaistos, the Egyptians, who could not live without a king, divided all Egypt into twelve districts and appointed twelve kings to rule them. [3] Many of these kings formed alliances through intermarriage and obeyed certain laws during their reigns. They agreed not to depose one another, nor to pursue power that might set one of them above another, and they promised to always remain the best of friends and allies. [4] They made these rules and upheld them with rigorous care because of what an oracle had declared to them when they had first been appointed to their kingships:[a] that the one who would pour a libation out of a bronze libation cup in the sanctuary of Hephaistos would become king over all Egypt. And indeed it was their custom to meet together at all the sanctuaries.

2.148
LABYRINTH
Herodotus describes what he has seen and heard of the great labyrinth.

They also decided that a memorial should be left to commemorate them all collectively, and so they had a labyrinth[a] constructed a short distance south of Lake Moeris near the city that is named after crocodiles.[b] Of all the wonders I have seen, this labyrinth truly beggars description. [2] If someone were to put all the walls and splendid architecture of Hellas together, all these would still clearly fall short of this labyrinth in labor and expense,

2.146.1a   Herodotus is referring to his account in 2.43ff. There he seems to say that the name of Herakles refers to two beings, one a god, the other a hero, and that the Greeks took the name of the Egyptian god and gave it to their hero. Here he says the names Dionysos and Pan each refer to one being, a god to whom the Greeks have mistakenly assigned a mortal mother. This is also made clear elsewhere, when he says Osiris is Dionysos and Mendes is Pan. See Appendix C.

2.146.2a   Nysa, Ethiopia: site unknown. Ethiopia: Map 2.140, BY. Note again, as also more fully explained in n. 2.13.1a, that in the Egyptian context, "above" is upstream or south, toward Ethiopia. There were numerous sites called Nysa,

in Greece, Libya, Arabia, and later even India, which were claimed to be the home of Dionysos as a child and the birthplace of viticulture. See 3.97, where Nysa is called a mountain.

2.147.4a   Herodotus uses the word for "tyrannies" here, which we have translated as "kingships."

2.148.1a   This "labyrinth" exists. It was a rectangular group of buildings, supposed to have been near the pyramid of Hawara. It has been thoroughly excavated, but it is largely ruined and in very bad condition. It is thought to have been built by Amenemhet III (1842–1797) of the XII Dynasty.

2.148.1b   Krokodilopolis, literally the "City of the Crocodiles": Map 2.155, Egypt inset.

although the temples in Ephesus[a] and Samos[b] are certainly remarkable. [3] The pyramids, as I have mentioned, also defy description, and each of them could match many great buildings of the Hellenes, but the labyrinth surpasses even the pyramids.

[4] It has twelve roofed courtyards with gates; six of the gates are situated in a row facing north, the other six exactly opposite them facing south. These structures are entirely surrounded by an exterior enclosing wall. Inside there are two sets of 1,500 chambers, one underground, the other directly over it and aboveground—3,000 chambers altogether. [5] I myself saw the aboveground chambers and walked all the way through them, so I can rely on my direct observation when I report on these. About the underground chambers, however, I must depend on what I learned from others, for the Egyptians in charge were quite unwilling to show them to me, claiming they contained the tombs of the kings who had originally built this labyrinth, and also tombs of sacred crocodiles. [6] Thus what I relate about the underground chambers comes from hearsay. But I saw the upper chambers myself, and they are superhuman feats of construction. I was struck with awe and wonder by the intricate passageways that lead through vestibules and the paths that zigzag through the courtyards; I passed from courtyards to chambers and from chambers to corridors of columns, and then from the corridors of columns into other vestibules leading to other chambers and out again to other courtyards. [7] The roof sheltering the entire complex is made of stone, as are the walls, which are covered with reliefs. Each courtyard is surrounded by columns of white stone fitted together with the utmost precision, and at the end of the labyrinth, near its corner, stands a pyramid 240 feet[a] tall and engraved with enormous figures. The passage leading into the pyramid is constructed underground.

While the labyrinth is truly a wonder, the body of water called Lake Moeris,[a] on whose shores this labyrinth was built, is even more amazing. Its circumference measures 397 miles,[b] equaling the length of the coast of Egypt itself, but in this case extending from north to south. Its depth is 50 fathoms[c] at its deepest point. [2] This is clearly a man-made lake[a] which has been excavated, for roughly at its center stand two pyramids, each of them rising 50 fathoms above the surface of the water and extending just as far underwater. On top of each sits a giant stone statue on a throne. [3] Thus the pyramids measure a total of 100 fathoms[a] in height, and 100 fathoms equals just a stade or six plethra; the length of a fathom is equal to six feet, or four cubits; four palms equal one foot, and six palms equal one cubit. [4]

2.149
LAKE MOERIS
Description of the
wonders of Lake Moeris.

2.148.2a Ephesus: Map 2.155, Aegean inset. The site of a later huge temple to Artemis.
2.148.2b Samos: Map 2.155, Aegean inset. The site of a huge temple to Hera.
2.148.7a Herodotus writes "40 fathoms." A fathom = about 6 feet. See Appendix J, §4–5, 19.
2.149.1a Lake Moeris: Map 2.155, Egypt inset.

2.149.1b Herodotus writes the distance as "3,600 stades" or "60 schoinoi." The actual circumference of the lake is about 170 miles.
2.149.1c Fifty fathoms = about 300 feet.
2.149.2a Herodotus is wrong about the origins of the lake. It is clearly a natural lake.
2.149.3a One hundred fathoms = about 600 feet.

The water in the lake does not originate from here—for this region is terribly dry—but rather from the Nile, and is drawn here through canals, flowing into the lake for six months and back out to the Nile for the other six months of the year. [5] During the months when the water is flowing out, the lake contributes to the royal treasury one talent of silver a day, which is the value of its daily catch of fish. But when the water is flowing into the lake, it contributes only twenty minas[a] a day.

2.150
LAKE MOERIS
How the earth excavated in the digging of Lake Moeris disappeared.

The local inhabitants said that this lake also flows underground as far as Syrtis[a] in Libya. The western part of the lake turns inland along the mountain range south of Memphis.[b] [2] When I noticed that there was no soil heaped up from the excavation of the lake, I became concerned about this, so I asked the local inhabitants near the lake what had happened to the soil that had been excavated. They showed me where it had been taken and easily convinced me, for I had heard of a similar case which had occurred at Nineveh of the Assyrians.[a] [3] The great wealth of Sardanapalos[a] king of Nineveh was kept in a subterranean treasury, and some thieves who plotted to steal it measured the distance from their homes to the royal palace and dug a tunnel through to it. They threw the soil excavated from this tunnel into the Tigris River,[b] which flows past Nineveh; they did this every night until they had accomplished their goal. [4] This is the same procedure, they told me, that is followed by the Egyptians in the case of their lake, except that they carried it out by day rather than at night. As the Egyptians dug, they conveyed the soil to the Nile, where it was received and dispersed by its waters. That is how they say this lake was excavated.

2.151
664–610
PSAMMETICHOS
Psammetichos innocently fulfills the oracle and is driven into the marshes.

Now the Twelve Kings ruled and maintained their compact with equity and justice until, in the course of time, they met to sacrifice together at the sanctuary of Hephaistos. On the last day of that festival, as they were about to pour libations, the high priest brought out the golden libation cups customarily used for this purpose, but he miscounted them and brought only eleven instead of twelve. [2] There stood Psammetichos, the last of the kings, without a libation cup, so he took off his helmet, which was bronze, held it out to be filled, and poured his libation. Now all the other kings happened to be wearing helmets, too, [3] and Psammetichos had held out his helmet with no intent of treachery, but the kings grasped the connection between what he had done and what the oracle had declared to them—that the one who poured a libation from a bronze cup would become the sole king of Egypt. Once they had recalled this oracle, they investigated the matter, and after having discovered that the act of Psammetichos had been entirely unpremeditated, they decided it would not be just for them to kill him. So they resolved instead to strip him of most of his power and banish

2.149.5a Twenty minas = one-third of a talent.
　　　　　See Appendix J, §11–13, 20.
2.150.1a Gulf of Syrtis: Map 2.155.
2.150.1b Memphis: Map 2.155, Egypt inset.
2.150.2a Nineveh, Assyria: Map 2.155.
2.150.3a Sardanapalos; often identified as Asshur-

banipal, who ruled the Assyrian empire
from 668 to 627, but some scholars
think he may represent a composite of
Assyrian kings.
2.150.3b Tigris River: Map 2.155.

him to the marshes, and ordered that he was not to leave the marshes or to have any dealings with the rest of Egypt.

This Psammetichos had also left Egypt once before, when he fled from the Ethiopian[a] Sabakos, who had killed his father Nekos. On that occasion, Psammetichos went to Syria,[b] and when the Ethiopian had departed because of his dream, the Egyptians from the province of Sais[c] brought him back from exile. [2] After that, he began to reign,[a] but then the eleven kings turned against him on account of the helmet, and he was banished a second time, this time to the marshes. [3] Thinking that he had been grievously abused, he set his mind on taking revenge on these men who had banished him. He sent a delegation to the city of Bouto[a] to consult the oracle of Leto, the most truthful and accurate source of prophecy in Egypt. The response was that vengeance would come through bronze men appearing from the sea. [4] Now Psammetichos was profoundly skeptical of this prediction that bronze men would arrive from the sea and become his allies. But only a short while later, some Ionians[a] and Carians[b] who had sailed out for plunder were driven off course to Egypt and forced to land there. When they disembarked, they put on bronze body armor, so that an Egyptian who had never seen men armed in bronze delivered a message to Psammetichos in the marshes that bronze men had come from the sea and were plundering the land. [5] Recognizing that the oracle had been fulfilled, Psammetichos made friends with the Ionians and Carians and, promising them great rewards, persuaded them to join him. Thus he won them over as his allies, and with their help as well as that of Egyptian volunteers, he deposed the other kings.[a]

Once Psammetichos had become ruler of all Egypt, he built a monumental gateway for Hephaistos in Memphis which faces south, and opposite this a courtyard for Apis, in which the god is fed and tended whenever he manifests himself in Egypt.[a] The courtyard is entirely surrounded by a colonnade covered with reliefs, and what supports the roof is not columns, but giant statues eighteen feet[b] tall. Apis in Greek is Epaphos.

To the Ionians and Carians who had helped him Psammetichos gave plots of land on which they could settle; the plots were separated by the Nile, and he named these properties "The Camps." In addition, he gave them all the other rewards he had ever promised to them. [2] Moreover, he entrusted Egyptian children to them to be taught the Greek language, and it is from these Egyptians who thus learned the language that the present-day interpreters in Egypt are descended. [3] The Ionians and Carians inhabited these

2.152
664–610
PSAMMETICHOS–XXVI DYNASTY
With the help of Ionians and Carians, Psammetichos becomes sole king of Egypt.

2.153
664–610
PSAMMETICHOS–XXVI DYNASTY
Psammetichos becomes king of Egypt.

2.154
EGYPT
The subsequent history of the Ionians and Carians in Egypt, and their importance to Greek knowledge of Egyptian history.

2.152.1a Ethiopia: Map 2.155.
2.152.1b Syria: Map 2.155.
2.152.1c Sais: Map 2.155, Egypt inset.
2.152.2a Psammetichos (I) began to rule as one of the Twelve Kings, but then reigned as the first of the XXVI Dynasty. In all, he governed in Egypt from 664 to 610. He began as a vassal of Assyria, and it is possible that Gyges king of Lydia may have helped him to win independence from Assyria by sending him Carian and Greek

mercenaries. (Lloyd)
2.152.3a Bouto: (northwest Delta): Map 2.155, Egypt inset.
2.152.4a Ionia: Map 2.155, Aegean inset.
2.152.4b Caria: Map 2.155, Aegean inset.
2.152.5a Psammetichos controlled all of Egypt by 656. (Lloyd)
2.153.1a Apis would appear as a bull calf. See 2.38.
2.153.1b Herodotus writes "12 cubits." A common cubit = about 1.5 feet. See Appendix J, §4–5, 19.

properties for a long time. They were located near the sea just north of the city of Boubastis,[a] on the mouth of the Nile called the Pelusian;[b] but later King Amasis[c] moved both of them from there and settled them in Memphis to become his personal guards against the Egyptians. [4] It is due to the settlement of these men in Egypt and our contact with them that we Hellenes have precise knowledge about all the events that took place there, beginning with the reign of Psammetichos down to the present. These were the first speakers of a foreign language to settle in Egypt. [5] The ramps for their ships and the ruins of their dwellings were still visible even in my time. That is how Psammetichos gained control of Egypt.

I have already mentioned the Egyptian oracle on many occasions, and since it is worthy of note, I shall now describe it. This oracle is at the sanctuary of Leto in Egypt. It is built in a great city that one passes when sailing inland and upstream from the sea via the Sebennytic branch of the Nile.[a] [2] As I said earlier, Bouto[a] is the name of the city where the oracle is located, and in that city there is also a sanctuary of Apollo and Artemis. The temple precinct of Leto at the oracle is quite large in itself, with monumental gates rising to a height of sixty feet.[b] [3] But let me turn to what I think is the greatest wonder of everything to be seen there: the temple of Leto within this precinct is constructed from a single block of stone, and each wall is of equal dimensions, sixty feet in height and length. This structure is covered with a roof made of another huge block of stone, with a cornice[a] measuring six feet.

Of everything I was shown in the sanctuary, this temple was the most amazing of all; but another marvel there, among those second in importance to the temple, would be the island called Chemmis.[a] [2] This is located near the sanctuary of Bouto in a deep and broad lake. The Egyptians say that this island floats, although I myself did not see it float or move and frankly, whenever I hear that an island actually floats, I wonder if it can be true. [3] In any case, on this island there is a large temple of Apollo with three altars, and there are groves of palms and many other trees, some fruit-bearing and others not. [4] The Egyptians explain that the island was not floating when Leto, who is one the eight firstborn gods, lived here at the city of Bouto where the oracle is now. Then, they say, Isis gave the young Apollo to Leto

2.154.3a Boubastis: Map 2.155, Egypt inset.
2.154.3b Mouth of the Pelusian branch of the Nile River: Map 2.155, Egypt inset. This location lay on the invasion route into Egypt from the north and east, which the Egyptians must always have closely guarded.
2.154.3c King Amasis ruled from 570 to 526.
2.155.1a Sebennytic branch of the Nile River: Map 2.155, Egypt inset.
2.155.2a Bouto (northwest Delta): Map 2.155, Egypt inset. See 2.83. This city might have been on the coast in Herodotus' day, but a modern atlas shows Bouto to be inland and not at all at or near the Sebennytic branch of the Nile. Indeed, it is shown as closer to the Bolbitinic branch. These branches have certainly changed

their course over 2,500 years, but it is also possible that Herodotus was misinformed or failed to correctly understand an interpreter, or that he might have confused one city with another, or perhaps even that he invented the location.
2.155.2b Herodotus says these gates were "10 fathoms" high. See Appendix J, §4, 5, 19.
2.155.3a "Cornice" in this instance probably means overall height or thickness, but it could mean that the roof's edges project out six feet beyond the walls. Herodotus says the cornice measured "4 cubits." See Appendix J, §2-5, 19.
2.156.1a Chemmis Island in the city of Bouto: Map 2.155, Egypt inset. This is not the nearby city of Chemmis.

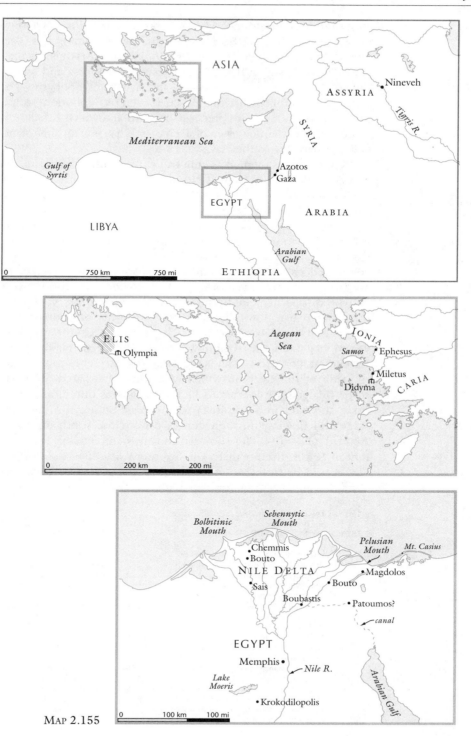

MAP 2.155

as her ward for her to look after and protect, and since Typhon was searching everywhere to find this son of Osiris, she hid him on this island, which is said to be floating now. [5] They say Apollo and Artemis are the children of Dionysos and Isis, and that Leto became their nurse and savior. Apollo in Egyptian is Horus, Demeter is Isis, and Artemis is Boubastis.[a] [6] It is from this account and no other that Aeschylos son of Euphorion[a] stole a version of the story that none of his predecessors used and which I shall now reveal: he made Artemis the daughter of Demeter. That is why this island became a floating island, or so they say.

Psammetichos reigned as king of Egypt for fifty-four years, during which he besieged Azotos,[a] a great city of Syria,[b] for twenty-nine years, until he finally captured it, but Azotos held out against a siege longer than any other city that we know of.

Nechos,[a] the son of Psammetichos, became the next king of Egypt. He was the first to undertake the digging of a canal leading from the Nile to the Erythraean Sea;[b] Darius the Persian was the second, and it was he who completed its excavation. This canal is so long that it takes four days to sail from one end to the other, and it is wide enough for two triremes to be rowed together side by side.[c] [2] Water from the Nile[a] is brought into the canal, which flows slightly south of the city of Boubastis[b] and past the Arabian city of Patoumos[c] before it enters the Erythraean Sea. The excavation began in the region where the Egyptian plain borders Arabia.[d] Extending along this plain is the ridge that stretches to the south opposite the side of the river on which Memphis[e] is situated. That is where the stone quarries are located.[f] [3] The canal was dug along the foot of this ridge and runs in a line from west to east before turning away from the ridge and flowing through gorges toward the south until it reaches the Arabian Gulf. [4] The shortest and most direct line from the Mediterranean Sea in the north to the Southern Sea, also called the Erythraean Sea, would be from Mount Casius,[a] on the boundary between Egypt and Syria,[b] straight to the Arabian Gulf, and would be precisely 115 miles[c]

2.157
664–610
PSAMMETICHOS–XXVI DYNASTY
Psammetichos' reign lasts fifty-four years.

2.158
610–595
EGYPT
NECHOS II–XXVI DYNASTY
Nechos II becomes king. He begins the construction of the canal from the Nile to the Red Sea.

2.156.5a   The goddess' name was actually Bastet, not Boubastis.
2.156.6a   Aeschylos son of Euphorion: famous Athenian tragic dramatist (c. 525?–456). Seven of his tragedies survive in their entirety, but not the one mentioned here.
2.157.1a   Azotos (Ashdod?), Syria: Map 2.155.
2.157.1b   Syria: Map 2.155.
2.158.1a   This Nechos is better known as Nechos II.
2.158.1b   The canal ran from near Boubastis (Map 2.155, Egypt inset) apparently to the Arabian Gulf (modern Red Sea). Inscriptions recording Darius' construction of it have been found nearby. (Godley) This is another instance in which Herodotus uses the name Erythraean Sea for either the modern Red Sea or the Persian Gulf. In this case, he means the Red Sea, which he also calls the Arabian Gulf (Map 2.155).

It is, after all, a narrow body of water lying between Arabia and Egypt which extends north from what he conceived to be the great Erythraean or Southern Sea: see n. 1.1.1d.
2.158.1c   Some authorities say the canal was about 100 miles long and 100 feet wide. Its precise route is unknown.
2.158.2a   Nile River: Map 2.155, Egypt inset.
2.158.2b   Boubastis: Map 2.155, Egypt inset.
2.158.2c   Patoumos (the biblical Pithom), possible-location: Map 2.155, Egypt inset.
2.158.2d   Arabia: Map 2.155.
2.158.2e   Memphis: Map 2.155, Egypt inset.
2.158.2f   On the stone quarries, see 2.8.
2.158.4a   Mount Casius: Map 2.155, Egypt inset.
2.158.4b   Egypt and Syria: Map 2.155.
2.158.4c   Herodotus writes "1,000 stades." The true distance today is closer to 70 miles. See Appendix J, §6, 19.

long. [5] That would be the most direct path, but the canal is much longer because of its many twists and turns. During the excavations which occurred in the reign of Nechos, 120,000 Egyptians lost their lives. But in the middle of the excavation, Nechos stopped the work when an oracle confronted him with the bad news that he was laboring for the future benefit of barbarians. The Egyptians call all who do not speak their language "barbarians."[a]

Having discontinued work on the canal, Nechos turned his attention to military projects. He had triremes built both for the Mediterranean Sea and for the Erythraean Sea in the Arabian Gulf, where slipways can still be seen today, [2] and put these to use as he needed them. He also engaged the Syrians[a] in a land battle and won a victory at Magdolos.[b] After this, he captured Gaza,[c] a great city in Syria, [3] and he dedicated the clothes he happened to be wearing while he achieved these victories to Apollo at Branchidai in Milesia.[a] After ruling for sixteen years altogether, he met his end and passed on the government to his son Psammis.

While Psammis reigned as king of Egypt, envoys came from Elis[a] who boasted that the Eleans had instituted the most equitable and noble games in the world at Olympia,[b] and that they believed that not even the Egyptians, the wisest of men, had invented anything to rival these games. [2] Upon their arrival in Egypt, the Eleans had announced the purpose of their visit, at which point the king summoned an assembly of those Egyptians said to be the wisest in the land. Once they had gathered together, these men questioned the Eleans, who told them everything relevant to the performance of their games. Then, once they had explained it all, they stated that they had come to find out whether the Egyptians could invent anything more equitable than these games. [3] After deliberating together, the Egyptians asked the Eleans if their own citizens were allowed to compete in these games. The Eleans replied that all Hellenes who wanted to do so, including their own citizens, were permitted to compete. [4] The Egyptians then said that they had fallen short of complete fairness when they had established these games, for it was impossible that they would not favor their fellow citizens in a competition and consequently be unfair to outsiders. If, however, they had really come to Egypt intending to establish truly impartial games, then they would advise the Eleans to forbid any of their own citizens from competing, and hold the games exclusively for visiting contestants. That is what the Egyptians suggested to the Eleans.

2.159
610–595
NECHOS II–XXVI DYNASTY
Nechos halts work on the canal to wage war successfully against the Syrians.

2.160
595–589
ELIS-EGYPT
Under King Psammis, Egyptians counsel the Eleans on how to achieve fairness in the Olympic games.

2.158.5a "Barbarians" is the term used by Greeks for non-Greeks, and Herodotus here extends this kind of usage to the Egyptians. He cannot mean literally that they used the term "barbarians" since that is a Greek word. He means that, like the Greeks, the Egyptians divided the world into themselves and all others.
2.159.2a Syria: Map 2.155.
2.159.2b Magdolos: Map 2.155, Egypt inset.
2.159.2c Gaza: Map 2.155. Herodotus calls the

place Cadytis. Lloyd points out that the "Cadytis" mentioned at 3.5 must be the site of Gaza, and that the Greek word "agrees perfectly with the Egyptian and Akkadian names for Gaza."
2.159.3a Branchidai (Didyma), the shrine at Didyma south of Miletus: Map 2.155, Aegean inset. See 1.46.2.
2.160.1a Elis: Map 2.155, Aegean inset.
2.160.1b Olympia: Map 2.155, Aegean inset.

Psammis reigned in Egypt for only six years, as he died soon after launching a military expedition into Ethiopia. He was succeeded by his son, Apries, who, [2] compared with the preceding kings, proved to be the most fortunate of all, with the exception only of his forefather Psammetichos. Apries governed for twenty-five years,[a] during which he led an army against Sidon[b] and fought a naval battle against the Tyrians.[c] [3] But it was fated that things would turn out badly for him,[a] which is clear from an incident which I shall describe briefly now but will relate at greater length when I tell of Libya.[b]

[4] Apries sent a large army against Cyrene,[a] and suffered a severe defeat. The Egyptians who were there blamed him for this calamity and revolted against him, believing that he had intentionally sent them to a disaster which he had clearly foreseen in order that, once they were destroyed, he would thereafter be able to govern the remaining Egyptians with greater confidence and safety. And so they returned home fiercely hostile to him and, after having recruited the friends and family of the men who had died, they revolted openly against the king.

When Apries learned of this revolt, he sent Amasis to put an end to it by negotiating with the rebels. After Amasis arrived, he sought to restrain the Egyptians, but while he was speaking to that effect, one of the Egyptians standing behind him placed a helmet on his head and stated that he had placed it there to crown him king. [2] Now perhaps Amasis was not exactly opposed to this gesture, as his subsequent actions reveal. After the rebels had appointed him king of the Egyptians, he began to make preparations to march against Apries, [3] and when Apries learned what the rebels and Amasis were up to, he sent a man who was preeminent among his Egyptian supporters, by the name of Patarbemis, with instructions to bring Amasis back to him alive. But when Patarbemis arrived and summoned Amasis to meet with him, Amasis, who happened to be sitting on his horse at that moment, lifted himself from the saddle, broke wind, and told Patarbemis to take that message back to Apries. [4] They say that Patarbemis nevertheless demanded that Amasis return to the king, since the king had summoned him. Amasis replied that he had been preparing to do just that for a long time now and that Apries would soon have nothing to complain about, since he was going to be there with the king forthwith

2.161.2a   Apries is thought to be the Hophra of
the Old Testament. Herodotus is mistaken about his twenty-five-year rule: he reigned from 589 to 570. Scholars have found elements of both agreement and conflict between Herodotus' account here and other ancient sources and are not certain about the details of his expedition to Phoenicia or its outcome. Herodotus is also wrong about the end of Apries. Lloyd recently deciphered a monument which says he was deposed in 570 but survived until 568, when he drowned in a military operation on the

Nile during an attempt by the Babylonian Nebuchadrezzar II to restore him.
2.161.2b   Sidon: Map 2.165, locator.
2.161.2c   Tyre: Map 2.165, locator.
2.161.3a   Very little is known about the successes and good fortune of Apries' rule before his fated demise, but it is a fairly common theme in Herodotus and other ancient Greek writers for rulers to enjoy an excess of prosperity which engenders hubris before succumbing to disaster.
2.161.3b   See 4.159.
2.161.4a   Cyrene: Map 2.165, locator.

and would be bringing others, too. [5] Patarbemis understood from this reply and from the preparations that he could observe what Amasis intended to do, so he left in haste, wishing to reveal these developments to the king as quickly as possible. Now when Apries saw that Patarbemis had returned without Amasis, he gave him no chance at all to speak, but in a fit of temper ordered that his ears and nose be immediately cut off; [6] and when the rest of the Egyptians who were still supporting Apries saw their most distinguished peer subjected to such a dishonorable insult, they immediatedly revolted, too, and, joining the other side, presented themselves to Amasis.

Faced with this wider rebellion, Apries, who still had a huge and remarkable palace in the city of Sais,[a] now armed his 30,000 Carian and Ionian[b] mercenaries and marched with them against the Egyptians. [2] So the foreign troops of Apries were going to do battle against Egyptians, and the Egyptian soldiers of Amasis were going to fight against foreigners. Both sides advanced to the city of Momemphis[a] intending to try each other's strength in combat.

In Egypt there are seven classes of people. These are the priests, the men called warriors, the cowherds, the swineherds, the shopkeepers, the interpreters, and the helmsmen; each one is named for its particular skill. [2] The warriors called Calasiries and Hermotybies are drawn from separate nomes,[a] as all Egypt is divided into nomes.

The Hermotybies come from the following nomes: the Bousirites,[a] Saites,[b] Chemmites,[c] Papremites,[d] the island called Prosopitis,[e] and half of Natho.[f] Their population, at its maximum, could number up to 160,000. Of all these men, not one has learned any manual occupation; instead, they are free to devote all their attention to military service.

The nomes of the Calasiries are the Thebaios,[a] Boubastites,[b] Aphthites,[c] Tanites,[d] Mendesios,[e] Sebennytes,[f] Athribites,[g] Pharbaithites,[h] Thmouites,[i] Onouphites,[j] Anytios,[k] and Myekphorites,[l] situated on an island which lies opposite the city of Boubastis.[m] [2] Their population at its maximum could number as many as 250,000. These men are also forbidden to practice any

2.163
570?
MOMEMPHIS
The forces of Apries and Amasis meet at Momemphis.

2.164
EGYPT
Herorotus describes the class system of Egypt.

2.165
EGYPTIAN NOMES
About the nomes and numbers of the Hermotybian warriors.

2.166
EGYPTIAN NOMES
About the nomes and numbers of the Calasirian warriors.

2.163.1a Sais: Map 2.165, AX.
2.163.1b Ionia and Caria: Map 2.165, locator.
2.163.2a Momemphis: Map 2.165, BX. Momemphis lay on a canal from the Canobic channel (Kanobikon) of the Nile to the Mareotic Lake. (How and Wells, i, 248) Lake Mareotis: Map 2.165, AX.
2.164.2a Egyptian nomes are administrative provinces or districts of long standing in Egypt.
2.165.1a Nome Bousirites: Map 2.165, AY.
2.165.1b Nome Saites: Map 2.165, AX.
2.165.1c Nome Chemmites?: Map 2.165, AX.
2.165.1d Nome Papremites: Map 2.165, BX.
2.165.1e Nome Prosopitis: Map 2.165, BX.
2.165.1f Natho: Map 2.165, BY.
2.166.1a Nome Thebaios: see Thebes, Map 2.175, locator.
2.166.1b Nome Boubastites: Map 2.165, BY.

2.166.1c Aphthites' location is uncertain but there is reason to believe it is the XIV nome of Lower Egypt. (Lloyd)
2.166.1d Nome Tanites: Map 2.165, AY.
2.166.1e Nome Mendesios: Map 2.165, AY.
2.166.1f Nome Sebennytes: Map 2.165, AY.
2.166.1g Nome Athribites: Map 2.165, BY.
2.166.1h Nome Pharbaithites: Map 2.165, AY.
2.166.1i Nome Thmouites, presumably around the city of Thmouis: Map 2.165, AY.
2.166.1j Nome Onouphites: Map 2.165, AX.
2.166.1k Nome Anytios: presumably located around the city of Anytis, which is probably an alternate form of Anysis (Map 2.165, AY), mentioned in 2.137.1.
2.166.1l Myekphorites, possible location: Map 2.165, BY.
2.166.1m Boubastis: Map 2.165, BY.

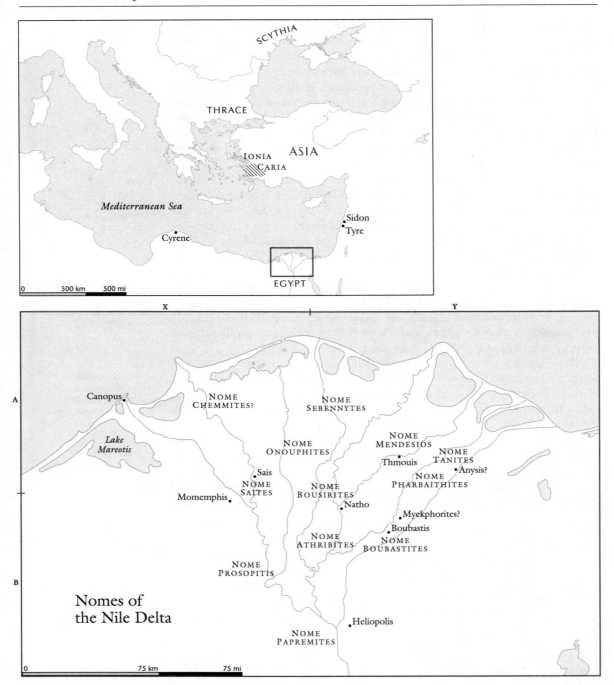

MAP 2.165

Nomes of
the Nile Delta

craft, but engage only in military pursuits, and their sons inherit this status directly from their fathers.

I have observed that in addition to the Hellenes, the Thracians,[a] Scythians,[b] Persians,[c] Lydians,[d] and nearly all barbarians also believe that those of their citizens who learn crafts, together with their offspring, are less honorable than the others; and that they consider those who have nothing to do with handicrafts to be noble, especially those who are free to focus solely on warfare, [2] but at any rate, all the Hellenes have learned this attitude, especially the Spartans,[a] and of all the Hellenes, it is the Corinthians[b] who despise manual skills the least.

Except for the priests, who had their own special rights,[a] only the warriors in Egypt had privileges reserved for themselves alone. Each soldier received choice plots of tax-exempt land, equal to twelve arouras (the aroura is equal to 100 square Egyptian cubits, and the Egyptian cubit happens to be the same length as the Samian cubit).[b] [2] These plots of land were reserved for every one of them, and they took turns reaping the fruits of the land, so that the plots were tended by different men each year. Units of the Calasiries and the Hermotybies, 1,000 of each, served as bodyguards for the king each year. Besides the produce from the plots of land, each man serving as a bodyguard was also given a daily allowance of about five pounds of baked bread, two pounds of beef, and four cups of wine. These privileges and rations were granted to each successive group of bodyguards.

When Apries and his mercenaries arrived at the city of Momemphis, they met Amasis with his army of Egyptians and fought a great battle. The foreigners fought well, and it was only because of their inferiority in numbers that they were defeated. [2] Now it is said that Apries believed that no god had the power to put an end to his reign; and thus he thought to himself that his position was firmly established and secure. But in fact his forces were defeated in battle, and he himself was taken prisoner and conducted to the city of Sais,[a] to the dwelling that had once been his, but which was now the palace of Amasis. [3] For a time, he was given room and board in the palace and Amasis treated him well, until finally the Egyptians complained that Amasis' good treatment of Apries was unjust both to Amasis and to them, as Apries was both his and their worst enemy. Rather than treat him well, they argued, he should surrender Apries to them, and when Amasis did turn Apries over to them, the Egyptians strangled him and buried him in his ancestral grave.[a] [4] This grave is located in the sanctuary of Athena,[a] adjacent to the hall on the left as one enters. The people of Sais buried all the kings from their province within this sanctuary. [5] And as a matter of fact, the tomb of Amasis is there also, although farther away from the hall

2.167
ARTISANS
Herodotus remarks on the nearly universal low status of artisans and high status of warriors.

2.168
WARRIOR CLASS
Each warrior was supported by an allotment of twelve acres.

2.169
570?
MOMEMPHIS-SAIS
Apries is defeated and captured at Momemphis and is killed later. Herodotus describes the tomb of Amasis.

2.167.1a Thrace: Map 2.165, locator.
2.167.1b Scythia: Map 2.165, locator.
2.167.1c Persia: Map 2.175, locator.
2.167.1d Lydia: Map 2.175, AY.
2.167.2a Sparta: Map 2.175, BX.
2.167.2b Corinth: Map 2.175, AX.
2.168.1a On privileges of the priests, see 2.37.4.
2.168.1b This aroura = 2,735.29 square meters

(Lloyd), which = 28,529 square feet = .65 acre. See Appendix J, §2, 4.
2.169.2a Sais: Map 2.165, AX.
2.169.3a This narrative is inaccurate in a number of aspects. The demise of Apries is a case in point. See n. 2.161.2a.
2.169.4a Herodotus equates Athena to the Egyptian goddess Neith.

than the tombs of Apries and his ancestors. It lies in the courtyard of the sanctuary amid a large stone colonnade adorned with pillars crafted to resemble palm trees and other costly decorations. Inside this colonnade stands a double door, enclosing the tomb within.

Also in the sanctuary of Athena at Sais is the tomb of one whose name I consider it religiously offensive to mention in this context. This tomb is situated behind the temple of Athena and extends along the full length of one of the temple walls. [2] In this precinct stand huge stone obelisks, and nearby there is a lake edged all around with a rim of stone and skillfully constructed; I believe it is equal in size to the one in Delos[a] called "the Wheel."

It is on this lake that they have nocturnal performances reenacting the sufferings of the god, which the Egyptians call the mysteries. Now, although I know all the details of these rites, may my reverence ensure that they remain unspoken.[a] [2] I feel the same way about the rite of Demeter which the Hellenes call the Thesmophoria,[a] so may my reverence ensure that they also remain unspoken, except for that which one can say without offense to religion.[b] [3] The daughters of Danaos were the ones who brought this ritual from Egypt and taught it to Pelasgian women.[a] Later the ritual died out when the original population was displaced from the Peloponnese[b] by the Dorians; and only the Arcadians[c] who remained preserve it still.

And so after Apries had been deposed, Amasis[a] became king. He was from the Saitic nome,[b] and Siouph[c] is the name of his native city. [2] The Egyptians at first despised Amasis and paid him no respect, since he had formerly been a common man and was not from a prominent family. But then Amasis won them over by his cleverness and sensible tact. [3] Among his countless valuable possessions was a golden foot basin, in which Amasis himself and all his dinner guests always washed their feet. Well, Amasis broke this basin into pieces and had them reworked into a statue of a divinity, which he erected at the busiest location in the city. And the Egyptians frequently visited the statue and worshiped it with reverence. [4] When Amasis learned how the Egyptian citizens were reacting to the statue, he summoned them and revealed that the statue had come from the foot basin into which they had previously vomited, urinated, and placed their dirty feet, but now they were worshiping it with reverence. [5] Then without further ado, he told them that he himself had turned out just like the foot-basin: he had been a common man before, but now he was their king. And

---

2.170.2a　Delos: Map 2.175, BX.
2.171.1a　"May my reverence ensure that they remain unspoken" is a metrical phrase which might have been part of a hymn or ritual prayer. It is also used again in this chapter (2.171.2) regarding the mysteries of Demeter.
2.171.2a　Thesmophoria: a women's ritual in honor of Demeter, conducted outside the city walls with no men present, which on at least two occasions mentioned by Herodotus (6.16.2, 6.138) led to unforeseen and unpleasant results. See

Appendix U, On Women and Marriage in Herodotus, §7.
2.171.2b　See Appendix P, §7.
2.171.3a　Pelasgians were considered by the Greeks to have been the first inhabitants of "Hellas." See n. 1.56.2d.
2.171.3b　Peloponnese: Map 2.175, BX.
2.171.3c　Arcadia: Map 2.175, AX.
2.172.1a　Amasis, XXVI Dynasty, ruled from 570 to 526.
2.172.1b　Nome Saites: Map 2.175, inset.
2.172.1c　Siouph: location unknown.

that is how he won over the Egyptians so that they considered it just to become his slaves.

Amasis established the following daily routine for himself. He worked diligently on serious matters of government from dawn until the peak market hour,[a] but after that he would drink and banter with his drinking companions. [2] His close friends and family were disturbed by this behavior and admonished him: "Sire, you are not conducting yourself properly by pursuing worthless pastimes. You ought to be seated solemnly upon your stately throne, transacting affairs of state throughout the day; that way, the Egyptians would know that they were being governed by a competent man, and your reputation would improve. But as it is, you are not acting at all like a king." [3] Amasis retorted: "When archers need to use their bows, they string them tightly, but when they have finished using them, they relax them. For if a bow remained tightly strung all the time, it would snap and be of no use when someone needed it. [4] The same principle applies to the daily routine of a human being: if someone wants to work seriously all the time and not let himself ease off for his share of play, he will go insane without even knowing it, or at the least suffer a stroke. And it is because I recognize this maxim that I allot a share of my time to each aspect of life." That is how Amasis answered them.

It is said that even before he was in office, Amasis loved to drink and crack jokes and was not at all a serious man; and further, whenever he ran out of supplies for drinking and enjoying himself, he would steal some more. When those he robbed claimed he had taken their goods and he denied it, they would bring him to whatever oracle happened to be nearby; and although he was caught many times by the oracles, there were many other times when he got away with it. [2] After he became king, he ignored those oracles that had released him from the charge of thievery and made no provision for their upkeep. Nor would he go to sacrifice to their gods, since he considered them to be worthless, as they presided over false oracles. But he took special care of all the oracles that had denounced him as a thief, believing their gods to be genuine, as they had provided oracles that did not lie.[a]

Amasis built a marvelous monumental gateway at the sanctuary of Athena in Sais.[a] It was constructed of such huge stones, and so many of them, that he surpassed all other builders by far. Further, he dedicated gigantic statues and a male sphinx of enormous length, and transported other stones of immense proportions in order to make repairs in the sanctuary. [2] He had some of these stones brought from the quarries near Memphis[a] and others, the immense ones, from the city of Elephantine,[b] which is a twenty-days' sail from Sais. [3] But of all his works, the one that I find the most amazing is that he transported from the city of Elephantine a chamber

2.173
570–526
AMASIS–XXVI DYNASTY
Amasis conducts business in a relaxed manner and justifies it as wise.

2.174
AMASIS–XXVI DYNASTY
More anecdotes about Amasis.

2.175
SAIS
AMASIS–XXVI DYNASTY
Herodotus describes the works of Amasis at Sais, particularly a major shrine made of one block of stone.

2.173.1a   Peak market hour would be about 9:00–10:00 a.m.
2.174.2a   They were not all trustworthy. See Appendix P, §14.
2.175.1a   Sais: Map 2.175, inset. Here Herodotus apparently refers to a temple of the god-

dess Nit and equates her with Demeter; In 2.122, he equates the goddess Isis with Demeter.
2.175.2a   Memphis: Map 2.175, inset.
2.175.2b   Elephantine (modern Aswan): Map 2.175, locator.

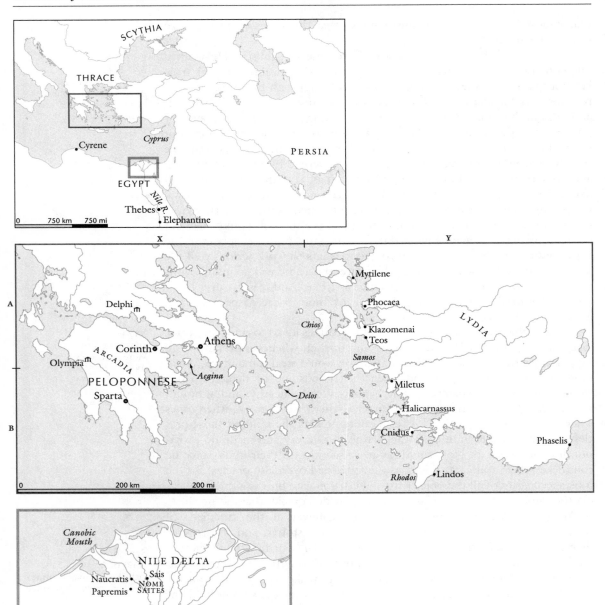

MAP 2.175

made from a single stone, whose transport downstream required three years by 2,000 men, all of them helmsmen under his orders. On the outside, this monolithic chamber measures thirty-two feet in length, twenty-one feet in width, and twelve feet in height. [4] Those are the external measurements of this monolithic chamber. On the inside, it measures almost twenty-nine feet in length, eighteen feet in width, and eight feet in height.[a] This chamber is situated beside the entrance to the sanctuary. [5] They say that the reason it was not dragged inside the sanctuary was that as they were hauling it in, the master builder sighed heavily at how much time had already been spent and at how tired he was of the project, which filled Amasis with such contrition[a] that he did not allow him to drag it any farther. Then again, there are some who say that one of the men lifting the chamber with a lever was killed under it, and that this was why it was not hauled inside the sanctuary.

Amasis also dedicated spectacular works of enormous dimensions at all the other noteworthy sanctuaries. In particular, he dedicated at Memphis a gigantic recumbent statue seventy-five feet long, which lies in front of the sanctuary of Hephaistos, along with two other gigantic statues of Ethiopian stone[a] standing upon the same base on either side of it, each of them twenty feet tall.[b] [2] In Sais there is another statue of stone just as big and in the same position as the one in Memphis. Amasis is also the man who was responsible for constructing and completing the sanctuary of Isis in Memphis; this sanctuary is huge and very much worth seeing.

It is said that during the reign of Amasis, Egypt prospered from both the river's floods over the land and the land's yield of produce to its people, and the number of its inhabited cities increased to 20,000 in all. [2] He is the king who established the law requiring each Egyptian every year to declare how he made his living to the governor of his nome. If someone failed to do this, or if he revealed that his livelihood was not a just and honest one, his punishment was death. Solon the Athenian[a] took this law and established it for the Athenians; it is an admirable law, and may it always remain in force.

Amasis became fond of Hellenes in general, and he displayed a special warmth for those who came to Egypt by giving them the city of Naucratis[a] in which to live. For those Hellenes who came by sea to visit but not to settle there, he granted land on which they could erect altars and build precincts for their gods. [2] Now the greatest, most famous, and most popular of these precincts is called "the Hellenion,"[a] which was

2.176
AMASIS–XXVI DYNASTY
Other monuments of Amasis in Egypt

2.177
AMASIS–XXVI DYNASTY
Egyptian prosperity under Amasis.

2.178
c. 615
NAUCRATIS
Herodotus describes Greek settlements at Naucratis in Egypt under Amasis (570–526). Greeks were first established at Naucratis by c. 615.

2.175.4a Herodotus writes that the external dimensions were "21, 14, and 8 cubits." The internal dimensions were "18 cubits and 1 pygon, and 12 and 5 cubits." A pygon is a short cubit, .8 of a cubit. See Appendix J, §4, 5, 19.
2.175.5a The translation is based on the Greek *enthumiston* (manuscripts), rather than *enthumeton*. (Bakker; Hude)
2.176.1a "Ethiopian stone" is red granite quarried from Aswan.

2.176.1b Both measurements in feet here refer to "Greek" feet. See Appendix J, §4, 6, 19.
2.177.2a Solon: archon at Athens 594–3, famous for his political and economic reforms as well as for his poetry. See Appendix A, The Athenian Government in Herodotus, §2–6. Athens: Map 2.175, AX. See 1.29ff. and n. 1.29.1b.
2.178.1a Naucratis: Map 2.175, inset.
2.178.2a Hellenion, in the city of Naucratis.

founded jointly by the Ionian cities of Chios,[b] Teos,[c] Phocaea,[d] and Klazomenai,[e] the Dorian cities of Rhodes,[f] Cnidus,[g] Halicarnassus,[h] and Phaselis,[i] and one Aeolian city, Mytilene.[j] [3] This precinct belongs to these cities, which also provide the magistrates who superintend the trading post. All other cities that claim these privileges in fact have no share in them at all. In addition, a precinct of Zeus was founded separately by some Aeginetans,[a] as was a precinct of Hera by some Samians[b] and a precinct of Apollo by some Milesians.[c]

2.179
NAUCRATIS
Naucratis was the sole Egyptian trading port of entry.

A long time ago, Naucratis was the one and only trading post in Egypt, and if anyone arrived at another mouth of the Nile,[a] he had to swear he had come there unwittingly or by accident, and take an oath that he would direct his ship to the Canobic Mouth;[b] if the winds prevented him from sailing there, he then had to transport his cargo by barge[c] all around the Delta until he reached Naucratis, which shows just how highly that city was regarded.

2.180
DELPHI
Amasis and Greeks from Egypt contribute large sums to the temple at Delphi.

When the Amphiktyones[a] contracted to build the present temple at Delphi from start to finish for 300 talents[a] (after the earlier one had burned down by accident),[b] the responsibility of paying a fourth of the expenses was imposed on the Delphians. [2] So the Delphians made their way from city to city seeking donations, and through their travels they received quite a large gift from Egypt, for Amasis gave them 1,000 talents of alum, and the Hellenes living in Egypt gave them 20 minas.[a]

2.181
AMASIS–XXVI DYNASTY
The tale of Amasis and the Greek woman Ladike from Cyrene.

Amasis also forged an alliance and a pact of friendship with the Cyrenaeans and thought that marrying a woman from Cyrene[a] would be good, either because he had his heart set on a Greek wife, or perhaps for the sake of his friendship with the Cyrenaeans. [2] And so he married a woman named Ladike, identified by some as the daughter of Battos son of Arkesilaos,[a] and by others as the daughter of Kritoboulos, a distinguished citizen

2.178.2b   Chios: Map 2.175, AY.
2.178.2c   Teos: Map 2.175, AY.
2.178.2d   Phocaea: Map 2.175, AY.
2.178.2e   Klazomenai: Map 2.175, AY.
2.178.2f   Rhodes: Map 2.175, BY.
2.178.2g   Cnidus: Map 2.175, BY.
2.178.2h   Halicarnassus: Map 2.175, BY.
2.178.2i   Phaselis: Map 2.175, BY.
2.178.2j   Mytilene: Map 2.175, AY.
2.178.3a   Aegina: Map 2.175, AX.
2.178.3b   Samos: Map 2.175, AY.
2.178.3c   Miletus: Map 2.175, BY.
2.179.1a   Nile River: Map 2.175, locator.
2.179.1b   Canobic Mouth of the Nile River: Map 2.175, inset.
2.179.1c   Herodotus uses a foreign word, *baris*, for "barge" here and in 2.41.4, 2.60.1, 2.60.2, and 2.96.5, perhaps to demonstrate his cosmopolitanism to his Greek audience, perhaps to intimidate them with his knowledge of other languages, since Greeks were notorious for their inability or unwillingness to learn foreign languages.

2.180.1a   Amphiktyones: a Greek league made up representatives of tribal groups (*ethne*; an alternative to *poleis*/city-states) organized to maintain, protect, and defend the sanctuary.
2.180.1a   The talent was a unit of weight and money that varied from place to place in the ancien world. See Appendix J, §11–13, 20.
2.180.1b   The temple burned down in 548/47; see also 1.50.3 and 5.62.
2.180.2a   Alum: aluminum potassium sulfate, used for medicinal purposes and for treating leather. One thousand talents of it would amount to more than 25 tons; and 20 minas, probably of silver, were one-third of a talent, or 2,000 drachmas. See Appendix J, §11–13, 20.
2.181.1a   Cyrene: Map 2.175, locator.
2.181.2a   As the daughter of Battos son of Arkesilaos, she was undoubtedly a princess. For the Battiad line of rulers of Cyrene, see Appendix L, Aristocratic Families in Herodotus, §9.

of Cyrene. But when Amasis went to bed with her, he was unable to have intercourse, and thus subsequently resorted to his other wives. [3] When this happened again and again, Amasis summoned Ladike and told her, "You have cast a spell on me, woman, and for that you will suffer the most terrible death any woman has ever suffered." [4] Ladike denied this accusation and tried to appease him but did not succeed. Then she made a silent vow to Aphrodite that if Amasis engaged in intercourse with her that very night—for that was the only remedy for her predicament—she would send a statue dedicated to the goddess to Cyrene. She made her vow, and at once Amasis succeeded in having intercourse with her, as he did also from that time on whenever he went to her, and he developed a deep affection for her thereafter. [5] Ladike then fulfilled her vow to the goddess; she had a statue made and sent to Cyrene, where it was still standing in good condition in my time, set up outside the town of Cyrene. And when Cambyses took over Egypt and found out from Ladike who she was, he sent her to Cyrene unharmed.

Amasis also dedicated offerings to other sanctuaries in the Greek world:[a] he offered a gilded statue of Athena and a painted image of himself in Cyrene; to Athena in Lindos[b] he sent two stone statues and a spectacular breastplate of linen; to Hera on Samos[c] he sent a pair of wooden images of himself, which were set up in the huge temple there and were still standing in my time behind the doors. [2] His gifts to Samos acknowledged his bond of guest-friendship[a] with Polykrates son of Aiakes, while those he sent to Lindos had nothing to do with guest-friendship but were given because the sanctuary of Athena in Lindos is said to have been founded by the daughters of Danaos when they came to shore there after running away from the sons of Aigyptos. Those, then, were the offerings that Amasis dedicated. He was also the first man to capture Cyprus[b] and subject it to payment of tribute.

2.182
570–526
AMASIS–XXVI DYNASTY
Amasis' offerings in Greece are described. He conquers Cyprus.

2.182.1a   Herodotus here means Greece in the wider sense of the term, as at 1.92.1.
2.182.1b   Lindos: Map 2.175, BY.
2.182.1c   Samos: Map 2.175, AY.
2.182.2a   Guest-friendship (*xenia*): a bond of ritualized friendship, usually between aristocrats or prominent men of different cities. It was passed down through generations and required hereditary privileges and obligations such as reciprocal hospitality and assistance. See Appendix T, §3.
2.182.2b   Cyprus: Map 2.175, locator.

BOOK THREE

‖t was against this Amasis that Camby-
ses son of Cyrus was preparing to wage war, with an army of his other
subjects, including Ionian and Aeolian Hellenes. He was marching against
Egypt[a] because of what happened after he had earlier sent a herald to ask
Amasis for his daughter. He had made this request on the advice of an
Egyptian doctor who resented Amasis for having chosen him out of all the
physicians in Egypt to be delivered to Persia and thus tearing him away
from his wife and children. And this had occurred because Cyrus had sent a
request to Amasis for the best physician in Egypt who specialized in the
treatment of the eyes. [2] It was because of this grievance that the Egyptian
advised Cambyses to ask Amasis for his daughter; he hoped thereby that
Amasis would either suffer anguish if he gave her to him or become the
enemy of Cambyses if he did not.

Amasis, disturbed and apprehensive about the power of the Persians,
could not refuse Cambyses, but neither could he bring himself to give up
his daughter, since he knew well that Cambyses intended to take her not as
a wife, but as a concubine. [3] After carefully considering all these matters,
he decided on the following course of action. The daughter of Apries, the
former king, was very tall and attractive, and the only surviving daughter of
that family; her name was Nitetis. Amasis dressed her up in fine clothing
and gold and then sent her off to Persia on the pretense that she was his
own daughter. [4] After a while, when Cambyses kept greeting the girl by
her patronymic (as the daughter of Amasis), she said to him, "Sire, you
have no idea how you have been duped by Amasis; he decked me out in
finery and sent me off to you on the pretense that he was giving up his own
daughter, when in reality I am the daughter of Apries, his former master,
whom he murdered when the Egyptians revolted." [5] And so, according
to the Persians, it was this little speech that caused Cambyses son of Cyrus
to become extremely enraged with Egypt.

3.1
525?
PERSIA
The Persians say that the
deceit of Amasis infuriated
Cambyses, who then
attacked Egypt.

3.1.1a   Egypt: Map 3.5.

**3.2
525?
PERSIA
The Egyptian version
of the story is false.**

The Egyptians, however, claim that Cambyses was one of their own kinsmen, born of this daughter of Apries. Cyrus, not Cambyses, they say, sent the request to Amasis for his daughter. [2] But they are incorrect, for they are well aware of the rule (and if anyone at all knows Persian customs, it is the Egyptians) that it is not permitted for an illegitimate son to become king while a legitimate son is still living; and furthermore, Cambyses was not the son of an Egyptian woman, but the son of Kassandane daughter of Pharnaspes, who was an Achaimenid.[a] The Egyptians are simply distorting the facts in an attempt to link themselves to the house of Cyrus.

**3.3
525?
PERSIA
Yet another Persian tale
explains Cambyses' anger
against Egypt.**

So much for that story. Another account is also told, though in my opinion it is unbelievable. This version claims that when some Persian woman came to visit the wives of Cyrus and saw Kassandane with her tall and attractive children standing beside her, she was filled with admiration and praised them extravagantly. Kassandane, the wife of Cyrus, then said to her, [2] "Although I am the mother of these children, Cyrus treats me disgracefully, while he honors his new wife, whom he acquired from Egypt." When Kassandane expressed her annoyance at Nitetis in this way, Cambyses, her eldest son, said, [3] "Well, then, mother, when I become a man, I shall turn Egypt upside down from top to bottom." He was only about ten years old when he said this, and his statement amazed the women who heard him. And they say that when Cambyses reached adulthood and became King, he remembered this incident and so made war on Egypt.[a]

**3.4
525?
PERSIA
Phanes from Halicarnassus
advises Cambyses.**

Another event also occurred that was relevant to the launching of this campaign. There was a man of Halicarnassus[a] named Phanes serving as one of Amasis' mercenaries. He was both a man of good judgment and a brave warrior in battle. [2] For some reason Phanes had been offended by Amasis and had fled from Egypt by ship, eager to go and have a talk with Cambyses. Amasis, who realized that Phanes was not only one of his more important mercenaries, but also a man in possession of precise information concerning Egypt, made a serious effort to track him down and capture him. He sent his most reliable eunuch in a swift trireme[a] in pursuit of him, and this eunuch did catch up with Phanes in Lycia[b] but did not succeed in bringing him back to Egypt, since Phanes cleverly evaded him. [3] He first made his guards drunk and then left for Persia,[a] reaching Cambyses just as he was getting ready to begin his campaign against Egypt, but still uncertain about the march across the desert. Phanes gave him a full account of the state of affairs with Amasis and revealed a method by which he could march to Egypt, advising him first to send a petition to the king of the Arabians[b] asking him to provide a safe passage for his army through the country.[c]

3.2.2a Cyrus was an Achaimenid, now the ruling
       house of Persia.
3.3.3a The real reason why Cambyses attacked
       Egypt, we must guess (for there is no
       evidence other than Herodotus' pretty
       story), is that Persia had embarked on a
       policy of imperial expansion, and Egypt,
       which was both ancient and rich and now
       on Persia's border, was next in line.
3.4.1a Halicarnassus, the city in which Herodotus

was born: Map 3.5.
3.4.2a Trireme: the most common ancient warship
       in the sixth and fifth centuries. See Appendix
       S, Trireme Warfare in Herodotus, §3–8.
3.4.2b Lycia: Map 3.5.
3.4.3a Persia: Map 2.175, locator.
3.4.3b Arabia: Map 3.5.
3.4.3c This demonstrates Persian military logistical
       skills. See Appendix O, The Persian Army in
       Herodotus, §11.

This desert is apparently the only land route leading into Egypt. From Phoenicia[a] to the boundary of the city of Gaza,[b] the land belongs to the Syrians called Palestinians.[c] [2] And from the city of Gaza, which, I believe, is not much smaller than Sardis,[a] and continuing past the coastal trading posts as far as the city of Ienysos[b] extends the territory of Arabia; then from Ienysos to Lake Serbonis,[c] along which Mount Casius[d] stretches down to the sea, the territory is again Syrian. [3] Lake Serbonis, where, as the story goes, Typhon lies hidden,[a] is where one enters Egyptian territory. The region lying between the city of Ienysos and Mount Casius with Lake Serbonis is sufficiently wide to require up to a hard three-days' journey through extremely arid country.

Now I would like to explain something that very few people who sail to Egypt understand. Although clay jars full of wine are imported into Egypt from all parts of Hellas[a] and Phoenicia throughout each year, there is virtually not even one empty wine jar to be seen there. [2] Where, one might well ask, have all these wine jars gone? The answer is that each demarch[a] must collect every jar from his city and bring them all to Memphis,[b] where the people of Memphis then fill them with water and transport them to the desert region of Syria just mentioned. Thus a jar makes its way to Egypt, is emptied there, and is then carried to Syria, to be deposited where all the rest of them have been stored.

Now after the Persians conquered Egypt, they established this system of stored water along the desert road mentioned earlier. [2] But before this time there was no water available at all, and so Cambyses, after acquiring information from Phanes, the Halicarnassian visitor, sent messengers to the Arabian king, asking him for a safe-conduct for his army, which he obtained by exchanging pledges with him.

The Arabians, who regard pledges made to their fellow men with special reverence, enter into a pledge in this way. Between the two men who wish to make the pledge stands another man, who cuts the palm of each along the thumb with a sharp stone. Then, taking a small strip of cloth from the cloak of each man, he daubs seven stones that have been set up between them with their blood, and as he does so, he invokes Dionysos and Ourania.[a] [2] Upon completion of this ceremony, the man offering the pledge commends the visitor or fellow citizen who is receiving his pledge to his own friends and family, who then consider themselves as rightful guarantors

---

3.5.1a Phoenicia: Map 3.5.
3.5.1b Gaza: Map 3.5. Herodotus calls Gaza Cadytis.
3.5.1c Palestine: Map 3.5.
3.5.2a Sardis: Map 3.5.
3.5.2b Ienysos' precise location is unknown, although known to be somewhere on the route between Palestine and Egypt.
3.5.2c Lake Serbonis: Map 3.5. Called Serbonian Lake in 2.6.1.
3.5.2d Mount Casius: Map 3.5.
3.5.3a Hot winds and volcanic action were attributed by Greek mythology to Typhon, cast

down from heaven by Zeus and "buried" in hot or volcanic regions. Typhon came to be identified with the Egyptian god Set, and the legend grew that he was buried in the Serbonian marsh. (Godley)
3.6.1a Hellas: Map 3.5.
3.6.2a Demarch: a Greek term for an Egyptian village administrator subordinate to the nomarch.
3.6.2b Memphis: Map 3.5.
3.8.1a Aphrodite Ourania is Heavenly Aphrodite. See also 1.105.2–3, 1.131.1.

MAP 3.5

3.9
ARABIA
Credible and incredible
stories of how the Arabians
provided water to
Cambyses' army.

of the pledge, too. [3] The Arabians believe that Dionysos and Ourania are the only gods who exist, and they claim that they cut their hair to look just like the haircut of Dionysos. They shear the hair around the head in a ring and shave under the temples. Dionysos they call Orotalt; Ourania, Alilat.

And so, when the Arabian king had made a pledge to the messengers who had come from Cambyses, he devised the following plan. He ordered camel skins to be filled with water and loaded onto all his camels which he drove to the desert region where they waited for the army of Cambyses. [2] That is the more trustworthy account of his scheme, but there is another, less credible version which should also be mentioned since it is in fact related by some people. According to this version, there is a great river in Arabia by the name of Corys,[a] which flows into what is called the Erythraean Sea.[b] From this river, it is said, the king of the Arabians took pipelines he had stitched together from untanned cowhides and other skins and extended them into the desert. He used the pipelines to carry water to the desert, where he had huge cisterns dug to collect and store it. The distance from the river to this desert is a journey of twelve days. He is said to have transported water through three of these pipelines to three different sites.

Psammenitos son of Amasis positioned his army at the mouth of the Nile that is called Pelusian[a] and there he awaited Cambyses. [2] For Cambyses did not manage to find Amasis alive when he marched to Egypt, as Amasis had already died after having reigned forty-four years, in all of which time nothing very unusual had happened. When he died he was embalmed and buried in the tomb complex which he himself had built at the sanctuary.[a] [3] But while Psammenitos son of Amasis reigned, the greatest portent of all occurred in Egypt: Thebes[a] received rain, which had never happened, neither before this nor afterward up to my time, according to the Thebans. It simply does not rain in Upper Egypt at all, but at that time a light sprinkle of rain did fall on Thebes.

The Persians marched across the desert and took up their position near the Egyptians in preparation for meeting them in battle. At that point, the Greek and Carian[a] mercenaries of the Egyptian king, who resented Phanes' leading a foreign army into Egypt, schemed to punish him in the following way. [2] They took the sons of Phanes, whom he had left behind in Egypt, into the camp, and after placing a wine bowl between the two armies, they led each of the sons up to it in full view of their father and cut their throats over the bowl, one by one. [3] When they had thus slaughtered each of the boys in turn, they added wine and water to the blood, and then each of the mercenaries drank from the bowl. Thus fortified, they went forth into battle in which the fighting became quite fierce, so that a large number of men fell on both sides, but finally the Egyptians were routed.

I saw something that amazed me here[a] and was told about it by the local inhabitants. The bones of those who died in this battle lie scattered in distinct areas reflecting the respective positions where the men of the two armies fell during the battle; thus the bones of the Persians lie on one side, just as they fell there originally, and those of the Egyptians on the other side. The skulls of the Persians are so soft that if you should decide to tap one with merely a pebble, you would pierce right through it. But Egyptian skulls are so very hard that you would have difficulty breaking through one by striking it with a rock. [2] They said the reason for this, which I, at any

3.10
526
THEBES
Amasis dies and is succeeded by Psammenitos. It rains in Thebes.

3.11
525
EGYPT
Slaughter of the sons of Phanes. The Egyptians are routed in battle.

3.12
EGYPT
An explanation for why Egyptian skulls are hard and Persians skulls brittle.

3.9.2a   Corys River: no great river exists in this part of Arabia.
3.9.2b   Erythraean Sea in this case is the modern Red Sea: Map 3.16.
3.10.1a Pelusian mouth of the Nile River: Map 3.16, inset. The easternmost mouth.
3.10.2a This tomb complex is mentioned in 2.169.5.

3.10.3a Thebes (Thebai), Egypt: Map 3.16, inset. In modern times there is sometimes a little rain at Thebes (modern Luxor). (Godley)
3.11.1a Caria: Map 3.5.
3.12.1a This reflects on Herodotus' personal travels.

rate, found convincing, is that Egyptians begin having their heads shaved from early childhood, and that the bone then thickens with exposure to the sun. [3] For the same reason, they do not go bald. There are fewer bald men in Egypt than there are anywhere else, which is a fact that anyone can observe for himself. [4] Exposure to sunshine, then, is the reason they have hard skulls, and the Persians conversely have soft skulls because they shade themselves from early childhood, wearing *tiaras*,[a] felt caps. So much, then, for this observation; I did, however, see a parallel to this phenomenon among the bodies of the men who fought and died at Papremis,[b] where Achaimenes son of Darius was defeated by Inaros of Libya.

When the Egyptians were routed in battle,[a] they fled in panicky disorder and did not stop until they had shut themselves up in Memphis. Cambyses sent a Mytilenian[b] ship up the river carrying a Persian herald to invite the Egyptians to enter into an agreement. [2] But when the Egyptians saw the boat approaching Memphis, they all rushed together out of the wall and destroyed the ship, tearing the men of its crew limb from limb and taking what was left back inside the wall with them. [3] After this, the Egyptians endured a siege for a time but finally surrendered. Their neighbors the Libyans[a] were quite alarmed at what had happened to Egypt and surrendered without a fight, agreeing to the payment of tribute and sending gifts to Cambyses. The citizens of Cyrene[b] and Barke[c] shared the same fears as the Libyans and yielded similarly. [4] But while Cambyses welcomed the gifts from the Libyans, he was displeased with those from the Cyrenaeans because, I suppose, they were so meager; the Cyrenaeans had sent only 500 minas[a] of silver. He picked up the money with his own hands and distributed them throughout his army.

Nine days after Cambyses had taken control over Memphis, he seated Psammenitos king of Egypt (who had reigned six months) and other Egyptians in front of the entrance to the town as an insult, and he tested the spirit of Psammenitos in this way. [2] He had the daughter of the former king dressed like a slave and sent out carrying a jug to get water, along with other girls (selected daughters of the most eminent men), and all dressed the same way as the daughter of Psammenitos. [3] As the girls walked past their fathers they cried out and wept, and all the other fathers, seeing their children so degraded, answered their cries and wept with their own, but Psammenitos, after seeing and recognizing his daughter, only bent down in silence to the ground.

3.12.4a *Tiara* was a Persian word for headgear with which Hellenes were apparently quite familiar, although to them it might describe anything from caps to turbans, depending on how it was wrapped.
3.12.4b Papremis: Map 3.16, inset.
3.13.1a Herodotus refers here to the battle that took place near the Pelusian mouth of the Nile between the forces of Psammenitos and Cambyses, mentioned at 3.11.3.
3.13.1b Mytilene, Lesbos: Maps 3.5, 3.16.
3.13.3a Libya: Map 3.16.
3.13.3b Cyrene: Map 3.16.

3.13.3c Barke, a colony of Cyrene: Map 3.16.
3.13.4a Five hundred minas in silver = 50,000 drachmas. A trireme with a crew of 200 men, each earning half a drachma a day, required 3,000 drachmas (½ talent) for each month of operations at sea. So 500 minas was only enough to keep one trireme operating for about eight months. Since there were no mina coins, Cambyses must have distributed the money as drachmas. See Appendix J, Ancient Greek Units of Currency, Weight, and Distance, §11–13, 20.

[4] After the girls had gone by with their water, Cambyses sent out the son of Psammenitos with 2,000 other Egyptians the same age, bound with ropes around their necks and bits in their mouths. [5] They were being led in this manner in order to pay the penalty for the Egyptians' destruction of the Mytilenians and their ship at Memphis. For the decision of the royal judges[a] was that for each member of the ship's crew, ten eminent Egyptians should be put to death in return.[b] [6] Psammenitos saw them passing by and realized that his son was being led to his death, but while the other Egyptians seated around him were crying and openly expressing their anguish, he behaved just as he had in the case of his daughter.

[7] When the young men had gone by, too, it happened that an elderly man passed them, one of Psammenitos' former drinking companions, who had lost his property and was now a pauper, possessing nothing except whatever alms he could beg from the army. As Psammenitos son of Amasis and the other Egyptians were sitting in front of the entrance to the town, this man walked past them, and when Psammenitos saw him, he burst into a flood of tears, called out to his friend by name, and beat himself on the head. [8] Cambyses had stationed guards nearby who reported to him everything that Psammenitos did as each group went by, and now Cambyses was surprised at Psammenitos' last reaction; so he sent a messenger to him to say, [9] "Your master Cambyses asks you, Psammenitos, why you neither cried out nor wept when you saw your daughter being degraded and your son marching off to his death, but you have granted this honor instead to a beggar who, as I hear from others, is no relation to you." That was the question of Cambyses to which Psammenitos responded: [10] "Son of Cyrus, my family's misfortunes were too horrible for me to weep over, but the grief of my friend was worthy of my tears. He has fallen from great prosperity into the life of a beggar, just as he arrives at the threshold of old age." It is said that when this answer was reported to him by the messenger, Cambyses thought that it was an excellent reply. [11] The Egyptians also say that Croesus wept when he heard it—for he happened to be accompanying Cambyses in Egypt—and that also the Persians who were present wept. Cambyses was overcome with pity and at once ordered that his men remove the son of Psammenitos from those about to die and save him, and then have Psammenitos rise and be conducted to the King.

The men who went for his son discovered that he was no longer alive, since he had been the first to be slain. They did, however, allow Psammenitos to stand up and then led him to Cambyses. [2] From that time on he suffered no violence from Cambyses, and if only he had known how to restrain himself from making trouble, he would have received Egypt back again, to serve as its administrator for the Persians, for it is the Persian custom to honor the sons of kings and to return the administration of

3.15
525–?
EGYPT
Psammenitos loses his opportunity to rule again by raising a revolt. He dies.

3.14.5a See 3.31.3 where royal judges are
          discussed.
3.14.5a This shows that the ship was a trireme,

which would have had a crew of 200 men.
See Appendix S, §3–8.

affairs to sons, even sons of fathers who have revolted. [3] One may conclude that this is so from many examples, including that of Thannyras son of Inaros, who recovered the government that had been his father's earlier, or that of Pausiris son of Amyrtaios, who also received the former government of his father, even though no one ever created more trouble for the Persians than did Inaros and Amyrtaios.ª [4] But be that as it may, Psammenitos did scheme to make trouble, and he paid the price for it. For he was caught inciting the Egyptians to revolt, and when this was made known to Cambyses, Psammenitos drank the bloodª of a bull and died instantly. And so that is how he ended his life.

3.16
525?
SAIS
Cambyses abuses the dead
body of Amasis, violating
customs of both Egyptians
and Persians.

From Memphis,ª Cambyses came to the city of Sais,ᵇ and there he accomplished exactly what he had hoped to do. As soon as he entered the home of Amasis, he ordered that the corpse of Amasis be removed from its tomb. When this had been done, he ordered that the corpse be whipped, plucked of its hair, stabbed, and subjected to every other kind of outrage as well. [2] His men eventually became very weary as they continued to perform these commands, because the corpse, having been embalmed, withstood this treatment and would not fall apart. So Cambyses next ordered them to burn it, which was an outrage against religion, for the Persians believe that fire is a god. [3] Actually, the burning of corpses contravenes the customs and laws of both of these peoples. The Persians, in accordance with the belief just mentioned, say that it is wrong to offer up a human corpse to a god; while the Egyptians believe that fire is a living and breathing animal, one which devours everything it receives until it is full of food, then perishes together with what it has eaten, [4] and it is entirely contrary to Egyptian custom and law to give over corpses to wild animals. That is precisely why they embalm them, in order to prevent them from being consumed by worms. Thus Cambyses had commanded his men to do something contrary to the customs of both Persians and Egyptians.ª

[5] However, the Egyptians say that Amasis' body was not the one which suffered this abuse, but rather that it was an Egyptian of about the same stature whose corpse the Persians mutilated, thinking that it was Amasis. [6] For, they say, Amasis had heard an oracular prophecy about what would happen after he died, and so to prevent what was impending, he ordered that a man who had died, the one the Persians did eventually whip, be buried just inside his tomb at the door, and commanded his son to bury his own body in the deepest recess of the tomb. [7] Now it seems to me that these orders of Amasis to place the other man's corpse in the

3.15.3a   The revolt of the Egyptians Inaros and
          Amyrtaios against the Persian governor
          lasted from 460 to 455. (Godley)
3.15.4a   The blood was supposed to coagulate and
          choke the drinker. (How and Wells; Asheri;
          Godley)
3.16.1a   Memphis: Map 3.16, inset.
3.16.1b   Sais: Map 3.16, inset.
3.16.4a   Herodotus' account of Cambyses'

mistreatment of the Egyptians is not
supported by other evidence. As a rule,
Persians were very careful to respect the
local religion and customs of the cultures
which they had conquered. Some scholars
(Asheri) have suggested that Herodotus'
disparaging stories about Cambyses may
reflect Egyptian hostility to the Persian
King who had conquered them.

Map 3.16

tomb never really happened at all, but that the Egyptians make this claim to save appearances.

After this, Cambyses planned three campaigns—one against the Carthaginians,[a] another against the Ammonians,[b] and the third against the long-lived Ethiopians[c] living in Libya at the Southern Sea.[d] [2] After careful deliberation, he resolved to divide his forces, sending his navy against the Carthaginians and dividing his land troops, sending some of them against the Ammonians. To the Ethiopians he would first send spies, allegedly for the sole purpose of bearing gifts for their king, but whose true mission was to observe everything they could and to determine whether the so-called Table of the Sun really did exist in the land of these Ethiopians.

The Table of the Sun is said to be something like this. There is a meadow which lies at the approach to the town filled with boiled meat from every kind of four-footed animal. During the night, the current magistrates of the town procure the meat and set it in this meadow, and during the day anyone who wishes may come there to feast on it. The local inhabitants, however, claim that it is the earth itself which gives forth the meat on each occasion it appears. Such is the description that is given of the Table of the Sun.[a]

Once Cambyses decided to send the spies, he immediately sent for the Fish-eaters[a] from Elephantine,[b] who knew the Ethiopian language. [2] When his men had set out to go after the Fish-eaters, he ordered his navy to sail against Carthage. But the Phoenicians[a] refused to do so, for they said they were bound by solemn oaths and would commit no impiety by fighting the sons of their own people. Without the cooperation of the Phoenicians the rest of the navy was inadequate for this campaign. [3] So the Carthaginians escaped being enslaved by the Persians, for Cambyses did not think it right to apply undue pressure on the Phoenicians, both because they had surrendered to the Persians voluntarily and because the Persian naval power depended entirely on them. The Cyprians[a] had also surrendered to the Persians voluntarily and were taking part in this campaign against Egypt as well.

After the Fish-eaters had come from Elephantine and met with Cambyses, he sent them to the Ethiopians with instructions about what they should say, and he gave them gifts to take there: a purple cloak, a necklace of twisted gold, bracelets, an alabaster pot of perfume, and a jar of Phoenician date-palm wine. The Ethiopians to whom Cambyses sent these gifts are reputed to be the tallest and most beautiful of all peoples. [2] It is also said that their

3.17.1a Carthage: Map 3.16. Carthaginians: in Greek, Karkhedonians.
3.17.1b Ammonians, from the shrine of Ammon in the Egyptian desert, the Ammonion: Map 3.16.
3.17.1c Ethiopia: Map 3.16, inset. "Long-lived Ethiopians" (the Macrobians in Greek): see 3.23. They are a largely mythical people; see also 3.114.
3.17.1d Southern (Erythraean) Sea: Map 3.16. This is one of three instances in which

Herodotus calls the Erythraean Sea by this name. See also 2.11.3 and 2.158.4.
3.18.1a This story may be an indication of offerings made to the dead or of a region of great fertility. In Homer's *Odyssey*, the gods are fabled to feast with the Ethiopians. (Godley)
3.19.1a The Fish-eaters: in Greek, Ikhthyophagoi.
3.19.1b Elephantine (modern Aswan): Map 3.16, inset.
3.19.2a Phoenicia: Map 3.16.
3.19.3a Cyprus: Map 3.16.

laws and customs are different and completely unlike those of anyone else, particularly in respect to their kingship, for they select the tallest of their men who possesses strength to match his size to reign as their king.

When the Fish-eaters arrived in Ethiopia, they presented the gifts to the king with these words: "Cambyses King of the Persians wishes to become your friend and ally[a] and has sent us here with orders to talk with you and present to you these gifts, which are the things he himself enjoys most." [2] The Ethiopian, realizing that they had come as spies, replied, "You are not telling the truth: the King of Persia did not send you here bearing gifts because he puts great value on becoming my ally. You have really come to spy on my kingdom, and he must be an unjust man. If he were just, he would not have set his heart on a country other than his own, nor would he be trying to force people who have not harmed him at all into slavery. But in any case, give him this bow and repeat to him these words: [3] 'The king of the Ethiopians offers this advice to the king of the Persians. Whenever Persians can draw a bow as large as this one as effortlessly as I can, then do make war on the long-lived Ethiopians with your superior numbers. But until then, thank the gods for not directing the minds of the sons of Ethiopians toward the acquisition of land other than their own.'"

After saying this, he released the bow and gave it to the men who had come to him. Then, picking up the purple cloak, he asked what it was and how it had been made. The Fish-eaters told him the truth, explaining the purple dye and the dyeing process, and he responded by saying that these people were deceitful and so were their cloaks. [2] Next, he asked about the gold, the twisted necklace, and the bracelets. As the Fish-eaters described these items as jewelry, the king burst out laughing. He had thought they were shackles, and he told them that among his people, shackles were stronger than these. [3] Third, he asked about the perfume. When they had reported to him how it was manufactured and used for anointment, he gave the same comment he had given about the cloak. But when he came to the wine and learned how it was made, he found great delight in the drink and asked what the king ate and what was the longest life span of a Persian man. [4] They said he ate bread, related how wheat was grown, and set eighty years as the longest life span for a man. To this the Ethiopian replied that it was no wonder they survived only a few years if they subsisted on manure,[a] and they would not even be able to live that long if they did not restore themselves with the drink; and as he made this remark to the Fish-eaters, he pointed to the wine, for at least in this one respect he admitted that his own people were inferior to the Persians.

3.21
ETHIOPIA
The Ethiopian king receives the Persian spies with defiance.

3.22
ETHIOPIA
The Ethiopian king disdains the Persian cloak and jewelry but admires the wine.

3.21.1a   Here and in 3.21.2, the word "ally" translates *xeinos*, which means guest-friend. Guest-friendship (*xenia*) was a bond of ritualized friendship, usually between aristocrats or prominent men of different cities. It was passed down through generations and required hereditary privileges and obligations such as reciprocal hospitality and assistance. See Appendix T, §3.

3.22.4a   The grain produced by the manured soil. (Godley)

3.23
ETHIOPIA
The envoys are taken to
see wonders of Ethiopia.

The Fish-eaters in turn then asked the king about the life span and diet in his country, and he told them that most of his people lived to the age of 120 years, and some even surpassed this age. Their food, he said, was boiled meat, and their drink was milk. [2] When the spies expressed amazement at this life span, he led them to a spring in which they bathed and became smoother and sleeker, just as though it consisted of olive oil and it smelled as though it consisted of violets. [3] The spies said that the liquid of this spring was so light that there was nothing that could float on top of it, neither wood nor anything lighter than wood; indeed, everything sank down to its depths. This liquid, if it truly is anything like it is described, would be the chief reason that the people who use it are so long-lived. [4] Leaving the spring, he led them to the men's prison, where the prisoners were all bound in shackles made of gold, for to these Ethiopians, the rarest and most highly valued metal of all is copper. After observing the prison, the spies also viewed the so-called Table of the Sun.

3.24
ETHIOPIA
Ethiopians bury their dead
in pillars of alabaster.

Last of all, they saw the Ethiopian coffins, which are said to be made of crystal in the following way. [2] When they have dried the corpse, whether according to the Egyptian method or otherwise, they plaster the whole body with gypsum, then decorate it with paint to resemble the appearance of the person as closely as possible. Next they enclose it in a hollow column of crystal, which they excavate in great quantities and which is easy to work. [3] The painted corpse is visible from where it is placed in the middle of the column, and while it has every appearance of being the natural body itself, it gives off no unpleasant odor or any other unseemly effect. [4] The closest relatives of the deceased keep the column in their home for one year, offering it a portion of everything as first fruits and sacrificing to it. After one year, the columns are carried out and set up around the city.

3.25
524?
EGYPT
Cambyses marches
precipitously against the
Ethiopians, but the
expedition runs out of
food and he withdraws it.

When the spies had seen everything, they departed and, returning to Cambyses, gave him their report. As soon as he heard it, he became enraged and commenced his expedition against the Ethiopians[a] without ordering any provision for food, nor giving any rational consideration to the fact that he was about to lead his army to the edges of the earth. [2] Instead, since he was clearly out of his mind after the report of the Fish-eaters, he immediately led out his entire land force except for the Hellenes there, whom he ordered to remain behind. [3] When he reached Thebes[a] in the course of this march, he separated out about 50,000 men of his army and instructed them to reduce the Ammonians[b] to total slavery and to set fire to the oracle of Zeus. Then he continued on his way toward the Ethiopians, leading the rest of his army. [4] But before they had gone through a fifth of the journey, they ran out of all their food, and after their provisions were gone, they consumed the pack animals, until they ran out of these, too. [5] Now if Cambyses, when he had learned of this, had

3.25.1a   Ethiopia: Map 3.16, inset.
3.25.3a   Thebes, Egypt: Map 3.16, inset.
3.25.3b   Ammonians, from the shrine of Ammon

in the Egyptian desert, the Ammonion:
Map 3.16.

changed his mind and turned his army back, he would have been a wise man, despite all his errors at the beginning. But, in fact, he took no notice of it at all and continued marching forward. [6] For a while, his soldiers took what they could get from the land and survived by eating grasses, but when they reached the desert sand, some of the men committed a horrible deed. They chose by lot one man out of every ten and devoured them. [7] When Cambyses learned of this, he was terrified at the thought of them devouring one another, and so he finally gave up the expedition against the Ethiopians and turned back. By the time he had returned to Thebes he had lost much of his army. From Thebes he went down to Memphis[a] and allowed the Hellenes to sail away.

So that was the outcome of the expedition against the Ethiopians. As for those dispatched from Thebes to wage war against the Ammonians, they traveled with guides, and it is known that they reached the city of Oasis.[a] This city belongs to Samians said to be of the Aeschrionian tribe,[b] and it lies a seven-days' journey through the desert sand from Thebes. In Greek, Oasis is called the Islands of the Blessed.[c] [2] It is said that the troops reached this place, but no one except for the Ammonians and those who heard the report of the Ammonians is able to report anything more about them. Apparently they never reached the Ammonians, nor did they ever return to Egypt. [3] The Ammonians themselves say that when the troops left Oasis, they marched across the sand until they stopped somewhere between Oasis and the Ammonians, and while they were having breakfast there, a strong wind of extraordinary force blew upon them from the south, pouring over them the sand it was carrying and burying them in dunes in such a way, it is said, that they completely disappeared. That, at least, is what the Ammonians claim to have happened to this army.

After Cambyses had arrived back at Memphis, an epiphany of Apis,[a] who is called Epaphos by the Hellenes, occurred among the Egyptians. As soon as this epiphany occurred, the Egyptians put on their finest clothes and began to celebrate a festival. [2] When Cambyses observed the Egyptians celebrating, he strongly suspected that they were rejoicing at his miserable military failure, and he summoned the governors of Memphis to his presence. When they arrived, he asked them why the Egyptians had not celebrated any comparable festivities when he had been in Memphis before but were reveling now, when he had returned after losing the greater part of his army. [3] They told him that the god, whose epiphany customarily

3.26
THEBES
The Persian army against the Ammonians is lost in the desert.

3.27
CAMBYSES' MADNESS
Apis comes to Egypt and the Egyptians celebrate, which offends Cambyses.

3.25.7a Memphis: Map 3.16, inset.
3.26.1a Oasis: Map 3.16, inset.
3.26.1b The modern name of this place is El Khargeh. Aeschrion is a known proper name on the island of Samos, but the tribe is not heard of elsewhere.
3.26.1c The Islands of the Blessed: Greek mythological isles sometimes said to be located in the Atlantic ("beyond the Pillars of Herakles"), but in general, remote islands were considered to be a kind of paradise

where those whom the gods favored spent their afterlife. They were analogous to an oasis in that they had fertile soil and fair weather, and were remote and surrounded by an area devoid of fertility and life.
3.27.1a Epiphany of Apis: the god Apis appeared among the Egyptians. Epaphos, son of Zeus and Io, is the Greek deity that Herodotus equated with Apis or Hapi, the bull god of Memphis. See 2.38.1.

occurred rarely and at long intervals, had just now appeared to them and that all the Egyptians joyously participated in a festival whenever he appeared. Upon hearing this, Cambyses asserted that they were lying and that his custom was to punish liars with death.

So he killed them all and then summoned the priests into his presence. When the priests replied to him in just the same way, he said that if some benign god had arrived among the Egyptians, he was not going to miss seeing him; and so he ordered the priests to conduct Apis to him, and they went to get him. [2] Apis (Epaphos) is a calf born of a cow which can then no longer conceive any more calves. The Egyptians say that a beam of light from heaven possesses the cow, and as a result, she gives birth to Apis, [3] who can be recognized by certain markings: its body is black, but it bears a white square on its forehead and an image shaped like an eagle on its back. It has double hairs on its tail and a beetle-shaped mark beneath its tongue.

The priests led Apis to Cambyses, and he, being somewhat insane, drew his dagger and struck it in the thigh, although he had aimed for its belly. Then he burst out laughing and said to the priests: [2] "You are pathetic people! Is this what your gods are like, flesh and blood that can feel the prick of iron? Well, then, this god is worthy of you Egyptians. But do not think you will get away with making me a laughingstock." Having said this, he instructed his men who were responsible for inflicting punishments to give the priests a good whipping, and then to kill any Egyptians they could find celebrating. [3] The festivities of the Egyptians were indeed broken off; the priests were punished; and Apis, suffering from the gash on his thigh, grew weaker and weaker lying in the sanctuary until he died of his wound. The priests buried him secretly, so that Cambyses would not know of it.[a]

The Egyptians say that right after this incident, Cambyses went completely insane because of his crime, though he had not been entirely in his right mind before, either. And the first of his evil deeds was committed against his brother Smerdis,[a] born of the same father and mother as himself. Cambyses had sent him back to Persia[b] out of jealousy, since Smerdis was the only Persian who had managed to draw the bow which the Fish-eaters brought back from the Ethiopian king. He was able to draw it back as far as two fingers' breadth,[c] while none of the other Persians could draw it at all. [2] After Smerdis had left for Persia, an apparition appeared to Cambyses as he slept, in which, they say, he thought he saw a messenger who had come from Persia announcing that Smerdis was sitting on the royal throne and touching heaven with his head. [3] Cambyses reacted to this dream by becoming frightened for himself. He worried that it meant that his brother would kill him and take over the government, so he sent Prexaspes to Persia

3.29.3a   There is no independent evidence that supports Herodotus' assertion that Cambyses was insane. See n. 3.16.4a.
3.30.1a   Smerdis, also known as Bardiya (another case of Greek name variations;

Aeschylus calls him Mardos).
3.30.1b   Persia: Map 3.45, locator.
3.30.1c   Two fingers' breadth, almost one inch.

in order to kill his brother. Prexaspes was the man he trusted the most of all the Persians, and he indeed did go to Susa[a] and kill Smerdis; some say he did this by taking him out hunting, others that he conducted him to the Erythraean Sea[b] and there drowned him.

That is what they say was the first of Cambyses' evil deeds. The second occurred when he slew his sister. She had accompanied him to Egypt and was not only his sister by both his parents but also the woman with whom he lived. I will tell you how he came to marry her. [2] Before this time, it was not at all the custom of Persians to live with their sisters.[a] But Cambyses had fallen in love with one of his sisters and wanted to marry her. Since what he wanted was unconventional, he summoned the officials called the royal judges[b] and asked if there was any law that would sanction a man's marrying his own sister. [3] The royal judges are men selected from all Persians to serve in this capacity until they die or are found guilty of some injustice. They judge lawsuits and are the interpreters of ancestral ordinances and institutions, and every question is referred to them for judgment. [4] So they responded to Cambyses' question with an answer that was both just and safe: they said they had discovered no law that would sanction marriage between a man and his sister, but they had found another law stating that the king of the Persians was permitted to do whatever he wanted. [5] Thus they did not break the law because of their fear of Cambyses, but in order that they would not destroy themselves by protecting the law, they discovered another one that supported the king in his desire to marry his sister. [6] At that particular time then, Cambyses married the sister he had fallen in love with, but a little while later, he married his other sister, too. Of these two sisters, it was this more recent wife who accompanied him to Egypt and who was killed by him.

There are two versions of how she died, just as in the case of Smerdis.

The Hellenes say that Cambyses had pitted a lion cub against a puppy, and that this wife of his viewed the fight with him. When it appeared that the puppy had begun to lose the fight, another puppy, its brother, broke its chain and went to its brother's side and the two of them together then prevailed over the lion cub. [2] Cambyses enjoyed watching this fight, but his wife sat beside him in tears. Noticing this, Cambyses asked why she was crying, and she replied that it made her weep to see the puppy defending its brother, as she recalled Smerdis and realized he would not be able to defend Cambyses in the future. [3] The Hellenes say that Cambyses slew her because of this remark.

But the Egyptians say that as this woman was sitting next to him at the dinner table, she took a head of lettuce and stripped it of its outer leaves,

3.31
CAMBYSES' MADNESS
Cambyses, who married two of his sisters, kills the younger one.

3.32
CAMBYSES' MADNESS
Two tales of the death of the sister of Cambyses.

3.30.3a Susa: Map 3.45, locator.
3.30.3b Erythraean Sea: in this case probably the Persian Gulf (Map 3.45, locator), which is the closest part of the "Southern Sea" (Indian Ocean) to Susa.

3.31.2a Sister brides: see Appendix M, Herodotus on Persia and the Persian Empire, §9.
3.31.2b A standing body of seven. See the Book of Esther, 1:14. (Godley) The royal judges mentioned also at 3.14.5.

and then asked her husband whether the lettuce was better stripped of its leaves or thick and full. When he answered "thick and full," she said, [4] "But you have stripped the house of Cyrus bare, just like this lettuce." Cambyses flew into a rage at this remark and leapt upon her. She was pregnant at the time; she miscarried and then died.

3.33
CAMBYSES' MADNESS
Cambyses suffers from the "sacred" disease from birth.

Thus Cambyses directed his madness against his closest relatives, whether because of his crime against Apis or for some other reason, as there are so many afflictions that tend to get the better of humans. As a matter of fact, Cambyses is said to have had a certain serious illness from birth, which some call the sacred disease.[a] In any case, it would not be at all improbable that someone who had a serious illness of the body would also suffer from an unhealthy mind.

3.34
CAMBYSES' MADNESS
Judgments of Cambyses by Prexaspes, Croesus, and some Persians.

And now he directed his madness against other Persians, too. For it is said that he had the following conversation with Prexaspes, whom he honored most among the Persians, who carried messages for him, and whose son served as a cup bearer to the King, an office of considerable honor. Cambyses is reported to have said to Prexaspes, [2] "Prexaspes, what kind of man do the Persians think I am? What do they say about me?" He replied, "My lord, they give you high praise in all things, except they say that you are excessively fond of wine." [3] What Prexaspes said about the opinions of the Persians enraged Cambyses, and he responded: "So if the Persians now say that I am out of my mind in my addiction to wine, and that I am not sane, well, then, their earlier claims about me could not have been true either." [4] For prior to this, Cambyses had asked both his Persian counselors and Croesus what kind of man they thought he was in comparison to his father Cyrus, and the Persians had answered that he was a better man than his father, since he had everything that his father had before him, and in addition had acquired control of Egypt and the sea.[a] [5] But Croesus, who was beside the King, was not satisfied with their verdict and said to Cambyses, "In my opinion, son of Cyrus, you do not seem to be like your father, for he, you know, had sired a son such as you to leave behind." Cambyses was delighted at hearing this and praised Croesus for his judgment.

3.35
CAMBYSES' MADNESS
Cambyses kills Prexaspes' son in another mad, cruel act.

So now Cambyses recalled this conversation and said angrily to Prexaspes, "Well, then, you will find out whether the Persians are telling the truth or whether they are really out of their minds themselves. [2] There stands your son on the porch; if I manage to hit him in the middle of his heart, that will show that the Persians talk nonsense; and if I should miss the mark, you may declare that the Persians are telling the truth and that it is I who am not sane." [3] Having said this, he drew his bow and shot an arrow at the boy, who fell to the ground. Cambyses ordered that the boy's body

3.33.1a The sacred disease is epilepsy, called "sacred" because of the similarity between epileptic and prophetic seizures.
3.34.4a When Cambyses moved against Egypt, he

acquired control over Phoenicia, which gave the Persians the most powerful navy in the Mediterranean.

be slit open and his wound examined. When the arrow was found within the heart, Cambyses burst into laughter and with great glee said to the boy's father, [4] "So, Prexaspes, it is clear that I am not mad, and that it is the Persians who are out of their minds. Now tell me, have you ever seen anyone in the world who hit his mark so successfully?" Prexaspes, observing that the man was indeed insane and fearing for himself, said, "My lord, I do believe that not even God himself could shoot so well." [5] That was what Cambyses did then, but at another time he took twelve Persians, peers of the first rank, and for no good reason at all had them buried alive up to their heads.[a]

When Cambyses did this, Croesus the Lydian decided it was the right moment to admonish him with these words: "Sire, do not yield to your youthful temper in everything, but rather stop and restrain yourself. Surely prudence is a good and noble trait, and forethought is also wise. But you have killed your own citizens for no good reason at all, and you have also killed children. [2] If you continue to commit such crimes, you will have to be careful that the Persians do not revolt against you. Your father Cyrus often ordered and instructed me to admonish you and to suggest to you whatever advice I found noble and good." Now Croesus tried to show that he meant well by this counsel, but Cambyses turned on him, saying: [3] "How can you have the audacity to counsel me, when you managed your own inherited land so successfully! And you advised my father so well by recommending that he cross the River Araxes and attack the Massagetai,[a] although they had offered to cross into our territory. You ruined yourself by being a poor leader of your country, and you also brought ruin to Cyrus, who trusted you. But you will certainly not go unpunished any longer! I have been waiting a long time now for an excuse to get my hands on you!" [4] With these words, he took his bow to shoot Croesus down, but Croesus jumped up and ran outside. And then, since he was not there for Cambyses to shoot with his arrow, the King told his servants to capture and kill him. [5] The servants were familiar with Cambyses' character, however, so they hid Croesus away, thinking that if Cambyses changed his mind and sought for Croesus, they would bring him forth and then receive gifts as their reward for saving his life; and if the King did not repent or ask for Croesus, they would then put him to death. [6] Cambyses did actually miss Croesus not much later, and when his servants noticed this, they announced to him that Croesus was still alive. Cambyses said he was happy that Croesus was alive, both for the sake of Croesus and for himself, but the men who had preserved Croesus had disobeyed their King and could not be allowed to get away with it: they deserved to die. And so he killed them.

3.36
CAMBYSES' MADNESS
When Croesus tries to advise Cambyses, the King reacts with fury and orders the Persians to kill him, but they, knowing Cambyses to be mad, forbear killing Croesus.

3.35.5a "Up to their heads" could also be translated "on their heads," but the former is
a common method of punishment in the
East. (How and Wells)

3.36.3a For Croesus' advice to Cyrus to cross the
Araxes River, where he was defeated and
killed, see 1.201–214. Territory of the
Massagetai: Map 1.204.

3.37

CAMBYSES' MADNESS
Cambyses commits mad
acts against all, and
sacrilegious acts against
the dead and the gods.

3.38

CAMBYSES' MADNESS
Herodotus believes Cambyses
to be mad. He tells the
anecdote of conflicting
Greek and Indian customs
concerning the treatment
of the bodies of the dead.

3.39
525
SAMOS
The Spartans wage war
against Polykrates of Samos.
How he became tyrant and
grew powerful and defeated
the Lesbians who had come
to the aid of the Milesians.

Such were the many acts of madness that Cambyses committed against the Persians and his allies. Indeed, while he was staying in Memphis,[a] he even opened up ancient graves and inspected the corpses. [2] And he also went to the sanctuary of Hephaistos and subjected its cult statue to mockery and derision. This statue of Hephaistos resembles the *pataikoi* which the Phoenicians fasten onto the prows of their triremes. For anyone who has not seen them, I would describe them as representations of pygmies. [3] Cambyses also went into the sanctuary of the Kabeiroi,[a] where no one other than the priest is allowed to enter according to the laws of gods and men. Here he subjected the statues to a long session of mockery and then burned them. These statues resemble that of Hephaistos, and they are said to represent his sons.

I am convinced by all the evidence that Cambyses was seriously deranged. Otherwise he would not have endeavored to mock what is sacred and customary. For if someone were to assign to every person in the world the task of selecting the best of all customs, each one, after thorough consideration, would choose those of his own people, so strongly do humans believe that their own customs are the best ones. [2] Therefore only a madman would treat such things as a laughing matter. There are many weighty proofs which confirm that all people have these strong attachments to their own customs, but let me describe this particularly interesting one: [3] During his reign, Darius summoned the Hellenes at his court and asked them how much money they would accept for eating the bodies of their dead fathers. They answered that they would not do that for any amount of money. [4] Later, Darius summoned some Indians called Kallatiai, who do eat their dead parents. In the presence of the Hellenes, with an interpreter to inform them of what was said, he asked the Indians how much money they would accept to burn the bodies of their dead fathers. They responded with an outcry, ordering him to shut his mouth lest he offend the gods. Well, then, that is how people think, and so it seems to me that Pindar was right when he said in his poetry that custom is king of all.[a]

While Cambyses was waging war against the Egyptians, the Lacedaemonians[a] were conducting a campaign, too, against Samos[b] and Polykrates son of Aiakes, who, by leading an insurrection, had taken control of Samos.[c] [2] At first he divided the city into three parts so that he could share it with his brothers, Pantagnotos and Syloson. But then he killed Pantagnotos and

---

3.37.1a Memphis: Map 3.16, inset.
3.37.3a Kabeiroi: see n. 2.51.2b.
3.38.4a Pindar (518–438) was a lyric poet active
       in the first half of the fifth century until
       c. 446. He was especially known for the
       victory odes he composed for victorious
       athletes throughout the Greek world.
3.39.1a Lacedaemon is Sparta: Map 3.45, BX.
       Herodotus uses the names Spartans and
       Lacedaemonians interchangeably. "Spar-
       tans," however, often refers specifically to

citizens of the state of Sparta, whereas any
inhabitant of the territory of Lacedaemon
is a Lacedaemonian. See Appendix B, The
Spartan State in War and Peace, §5, 7,
and n. B.7a.
3.39.1b Samos: Map 3.45, AY. This war probably
       took place in 532.
3.39.1c Polykrates is thought to have taken over
       the government of Samos c. 532. See
       Appendix T, Tyranny in Herodotus.

drove out Syloson, the younger one, and in this way took possession of all Samos for himself. He had also forged an alliance of friendship with Amasis king of Egypt through exchanges of gifts. [3] In no time at all, the power of Polykrates grew markedly, and his fame resounded throughout Ionia[a] and the rest of Hellas. For wherever he led his army, everything turned out well. He had a navy of 100 penteconters[b] and 1,000 archers, [4] and he raided and plundered everyone without exception.[a] In fact, he once said that he could better ingratiate a friend by returning what he had taken than by never taking it in the first place. He captured a great number of the islands and many towns on the mainland as well, and among his conquests were the people of Lesbos,[b] whom he vanquished with his fleet when they had gone out in full force to help the Milesians.[c] Following their defeat, he bound them in chains and had them dig the entire trench encircling the city wall of Samos.[d]

　　Now Amasis did not fail to notice Polykrates' exceptionally good fortune, and it worried him; so when his luck continued to improve still further, Amasis wrote him a letter and sent it to Samos. The letter said, "From Amasis to Polykrates: [2] It is a pleasure to hear that a friend and ally is doing well, but I am not pleased by your exceptional good fortune, since I know that god is jealous. Actually, what I sincerely want for both myself and for those I care about is good fortune in one matter but failure in another, and thus a life of continually alternating fortune rather than of success in everything. [3] For I have never yet heard of anyone enjoying good fortune in all things who did not ultimately die in total disaster.[a] And so now listen to me and deal with your perpetual good fortune as I advise. [4] You must think about what you have and select your most valuable possession, whatever would most break your heart were you to lose it; and then throw that object away so that it will never reach a human being again. If, after this, your good fortune persists and does not alternate with suffering, apply the remedy I have suggested once again."

　　When Polykrates read this letter, he realized that Amasis had given him very good advice, so he searched for the one heirloom in his possession whose loss would most afflict his heart and selected a signet ring that he wore, an emerald set in gold which had been crafted by Theodoros of Samos son of Telekles.[a] [2] And so when he decided that this ring was the object he should throw away, he manned a penteconter, got on board, and ordered the men to put out to sea. When they had reached a distance far from Samos, he took off his ring and, as all the men sailing with him looked on, tossed it into the sea. That done, he sailed home and mourned his loss.

3.40
525?
EGYPT
The extraordinary good fortune of Polykrates and its effect upon his relationship with Amasis of Egypt, who advises him to beware of too much success.

3.41
SAMOS
Following Amasis' advice, Polykrates throws his signet ring into the sea.

3.39.3a　Ionia: Map 3.45, AY.
3.39.3b　Penteconter: an early warship with one line of twenty-five rowers on each side of the ship.
3.39.4a　It is thought that Polykrates' reknown, wealth, and power depended upon piracy.
3.39.4b　Lesbos: Map 3.45, AY.
3.39.4c　Miletus: Map 3.45, BY.

3.39.4d　Samos, city of: Map 3.45, BY.
3.40.3a　Another example of Herodotus' view on fortune. See 1.32 for Solon's discussion of the same point with Croesus.
3.41.1a　This is the same craftsman of Samos, Theodoros son of Telekles, who built the great bowl described in 1.52.3.

3.42
SAMOS
Polykrates' ring returns
to him inside a fish.

But then, four or five days later, a fisherman caught a huge and beautiful fish; and thinking that it was only right to present it to Polykrates as a gift, he took it to the doors of Polykrates' home and announced that he wished to be admitted into the presence of Polykrates. When this request was granted, he offered the fish to Polykrates with these words: [2] "Sire, when I caught this fish, I did not think it right to take it to market, although I do make my living by my own labor. Instead, I decided it was worthy of you and your rule. So I bring this fish and give it to you now as a present." Polykrates was delighted to hear this little speech and replied, "You are very kind; I thank you twice over, both for your words and for your gift, and I invite you to dine with us." [3] The fisherman went home very flattered by the esteem shown him by Polykrates. But when the servants cut open the huge fish, they discovered the ring of Polykrates within its belly. [4] As soon as they saw it, they took it out and gleefully brought it to him and, as they gave it to him, explained how they had found it. Polykrates realized that this was an act of god, so he wrote down everything he had done and what had happened to him, then sent the whole story in a letter to Egypt.

3.43
EGYPT
Amasis realizes that
Polykrates is doomed.

When Amasis read this letter, he realized that it was impossible for one person to rescue another from what he was destined to experience: he knew that Polykrates was not going to continue to enjoy good fortune in everything and come to a happy end, since even what he had attempted to throw away had been restored to him. [2] So Amasis sent a herald to Samos to announce that he was breaking off their alliance of friendship. He did this so that when severe and dreadful misfortune should finally strike Polykrates, Amasis' spirit would not be tortured with anguish, as it would be for a friend and ally.[a]

3.44
525?
SAMOS
Polykrates sends potential
rebels to assist Cambyses,
asking him not to send
them back.

Well, then, it was against this most fortunate man, Polykrates, that the Spartans were now waging war, in response to a request for help from the Samian exiles who later founded Kydonia in Crete.[a] These Samian exiles had needed military assistance because Polykrates had earlier sent off a herald (without the knowledge of the Samians) to Cambyses son of Cyrus, just when he was mustering forces for his expedition against Egypt; the message conveyed by the herald was that Cambyses should send to Samos for troops from Polykrates. [2] When Cambyses received this appeal, he readily complied, dispatching a request that Polykrates provide him with a naval force to support his campaign against Egypt. Polykrates then picked out those of his citizens whom he suspected as the most likely to revolt against him, and sent them out on forty triremes with instructions to Cambyses that they should not be permitted to return.

3.43.2a Herodotus is mistaken here. It is thought
that it was Polykrates who broke off this
Samian-Egyptian friendship when he
decided to ally with Cambyses, as
described in 3.44, probably because

Cambyses, by conquering Phoenicia, had
become much stronger than Egypt and
now could wield sea power that could
directly threaten Samos.
3.44.1a Kydonia, Crete (Creta): Map 3.45, BX.

Now some say that the Samians sent by Polykrates did not reach Egypt, but instead, when their ships came to Karpathos,[a] that they deliberated among themselves and decided they should sail no farther. Others say that they did arrive in Egypt and were put under guard there but managed to escape. [2] Then, it is said, they sailed back to Samos, where Polykrates engaged them with his fleet in a naval battle. The returning men won this battle and disembarked onto the island, but here they were defeated in a battle on land, and so they sailed away to Sparta. [3] There are others who say that they were victorious over Polykrates when they returned from Egypt, but I cannot believe this is correct, for they would not have found it necessary to request help from the Spartans if they had defeated or been capable of defeating Polykrates on their own. Furthermore, it contradicts all logic to believe that someone who had large numbers of mercenaries and local archers to assist him could be defeated by the few Samians who returned from Egypt.[a] [4] Polykrates then took the children and wives of his subjects and crowded them together into a shipshed[a] he had been keeping ready, so that, if they should turn into traitors and go over to the men who had returned, he could set them on fire, together with the shipsheds.

The Samians who had been driven into exile by Polykrates arrived in Sparta and stood before the ruling authorities. They made a speech whose length matched the extent of their needs. The Spartans responded that they had forgotten what was said at the beginning and did not understand what was said after that. [2] After this reception the Samians stood up to speak again, but this time they brought a sack with them and said nothing except that the sack needed barley meal. The Spartans now answered that the "sack" was superfluous to their speech, but they did resolve to help them.[a]

The Spartans then made their preparations and set out on a campaign against Samos.[a] According to the Samians, they did this to repay a favor, since the Samians had previously come to their aid with their ships against the Messenians.[b] But the Spartans say that they embarked on the campaign not so much to defend those Samians who had asked for help, but because they wanted to exact vengeance for the seizure of the bowl[c] that they had been taking to Croesus, and of the breastplate which Amasis king of Egypt

3.45
525?
SAMOS
The Samians return, but after they are defeated by the forces of Polykrates, they sail to Sparta.

3.46
SPARTA
The Samians at Sparta learn to speak laconically.

3.47
525
SAMOS
Sparta sends an army to Samos, but less, they say, to help the Samians than to avenge the robbery of a bowl.

3.45.1a Karpathos: Map 3.45, BY.
3.45.3a Scholars have pondered this remark about the "few" Samians. The crews of forty fully manned triremes would have numbered 8,000 men, which is no small number. More likely these boats were penteconters, of which Herodotus has told us Polykrates had 100 (at 3.39.3). If that were the case, the Samians who manned such a fleet would have numbered 2,000.
3.45.4a Shipsheds were large buildings in which boats could be built or dragged up out of

the water to remain dry during the winter months or to undergo repairs and maintenance. See Appendix S, §8.
3.46.2a The Spartans meant that the Samians could have simply pointed to the sack and deleted that word from their speech. This episode is a parody of the famous Spartan "laconic" manner of speaking, in which brevity and bluntness were sought and applauded.
3.47.1a Samos: Map 3.45, AY.
3.47.1b Messenia: Map 3.45, BX.
3.47.1c For the story of this bowl, see 1.70.

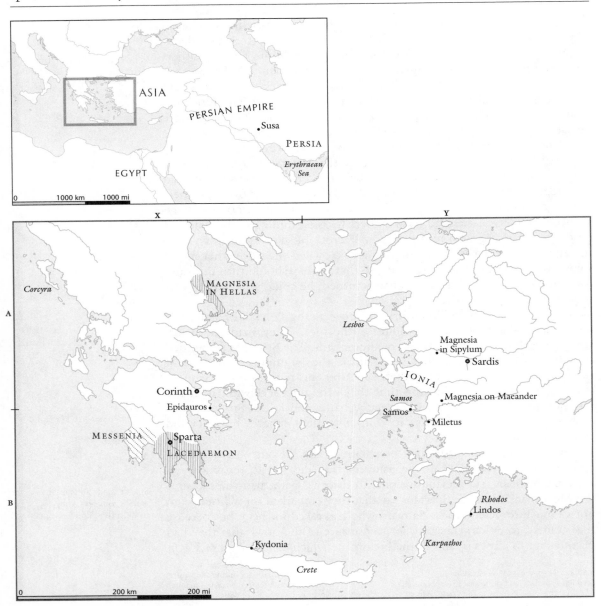

MAP 3.45

had sent to them as a gift.[d] [2] The Samians had stolen the breastplate the year before they had seized the bowl; the breastplate was made of linen closely woven with a multitude of figures and embroidered with gold and cotton fibers.[a] Every single thread of this breastplate inspires amazement, for it has a delicate weave of 360 filaments, all of them conspicuous. Amasis also dedicated another breastplate like this one to Athena in Lindos.[b]

The Corinthians[a] also were eager to participate in the expedition against Samos.[b] They, too, had been outraged by the Samians in the generation prior to this expedition, about the same time as the theft of the bowl. [2] For Periandros son of Kypselos[a] had sent 300 sons of the leading men of Corcyra[b] to Alyattes in Sardis[c] in order to be castrated, but when the Corinthians transporting the boys put in at Samos, and the Samians learned the reason for their journey to Sardis, they first taught the boys how to become suppliants through contact with the sacred ground of the sanctuary of Artemis. [3] Then they kept watch to ensure that no one would try to drag the suppliants away from the sanctuary. And when the Corinthians tried to prevent the boys from obtaining food, the Samians created a festival— which they still celebrate in the same way today—in which, during the entire time that the boys were suppliants, the Samians set up choruses of young men and women at nightfall, and made it the rule that these choruses would bring along snacks of sesame and honey, so that the Corcyrian boys could then snatch them and thus have something to eat.[a] [4] They kept this up until the Corinthians in charge of guarding the boys went away and left the boys there. Then the Samians delivered the boys back to Corcyra.

Now the Corinthians would not have participated in the expedition against Samos for this reason if relations between the Corinthians and Corcyrians had been friendly when Periandros died.[a] But in fact they had been feuding with each other, although they were one and the same people, ever since they had colonized the island of Corcyra.[b] [2] So that is why the Corinthians felt a long-standing resentment against the Samians. Now the reason Periandros had picked out these sons of the most eminent Corcyrians and sent them to Sardis to be castrated was in order to get revenge on the Corcyrians for an earlier arrogant act that they had committed against him, which indeed had started all the trouble.

3.48
525
Corinth
Why the Corinthians joined the Spartan expedition against Samos.

3.49
Corinth
Corinth's bad relationship with Corcyra.

3.47.1d Some scholars believe that Sparta's real reason for attacking Samos was to prevent it from "medizing" (allying with Persia) and thus to impede further Persian encroachment into Greek territories.

3.47.2a Amasis' dedication of this breastplate is also described in 2.182.1. Herodotus calls cotton literally "wool from wood or trees."

3.47.2b Lindos, Rhodes: Map 3.45, BY.

3.48.1a Corinth: Map 3.45, AX.

3.48.1b Corinth was probably a member of the Peloponnesian League at this time but apparently was not obliged to join this expedition. Perhaps one reason it did join was that its trade may have suffered from Samian piracy. For more on the Pelopon-

nesian League, see Appendix B, §20.

3.48.2a Periandros son of Kypselos (625–585): one of the seven wise men of Hellas (see n. 1.74.2a). There is a chronological problem with this story, as is often the case with Herodotus' accounts about the sixth century, as the events mentioned ("the insult") happened c. 550. (How and Wells)

3.48.2b Corcyra: Map 3.45, AX.

3.48.2c Sardis: Map 3.45, AY.

3.48.3a An example of the use of inviolate religious festivals to gain political ends; see Appendix I, Classical Greek Religious Festivals, §12.

3.49.1a Periandros died in 585.

3.49.1b Corinth is supposed to have colonized the island of Corcyra in 734.

After Periandros had killed his wife Melissa,[a] he suffered another unfortunate event. He had two sons by Melissa, one of them seventeen years old, the other eighteen. [2] Their maternal grandfather Prokles, the tyrant of Epidauros,[a] sent for them to visit him and treated them with affection, as was proper and reasonable, given that they were the sons of his daughter. When he was sending them back home, he said, [3] "Do you know, boys, who killed your mother?" Now the elder boy gave no thought to this remark, but the younger boy, whose name was Lykophron, was so distressed upon hearing it that when he came back to Corinth he refused to speak to his father, and neither responded to his conversation nor answered him when he asked a question, because he felt this man was his mother's murderer. At last Periandros drove him out of the house in anger and frustration.

After driving Lykophron out, he questioned his elder son about what their grandfather had said to them. The boy related how Prokles had affectionately welcomed them, but at first he did not remember what he had said before sending them away, since he had not grasped its meaning. Periandros said that it was impossible that Prokles had not suggested something to them and persisted with his questions, until at last his son remembered and told him about that question, too. [2] Periandros grasped its meaning and, unwilling to show weakness, sent a messenger to where the son he had driven out was then living, forbidding the people to make him welcome in their houses any longer. [3] Thus the boy was driven out of one house after another, only to be driven out again since Periandros kept issuing threats to those who had received him, ordering them to shut him out. And so, when he was expelled by one friend, he would go to the house of another, and even though they were afraid to do so, they would admit him, since he was the son of Periandros.

Finally, Periandros issued a proclamation that whoever took his son in or talked to him would have to pay a specified amount as a sacred fine to Apollo. [2] After this proclamation, no one would talk to Lykophron or admit him into their home, and not even he himself thought it was right to try to do what was forbidden, but carried on as best he could, lurking around the stoas.[a] [3] Finally, on the fourth day, when Periandros saw him reduced to a state of squalor and hunger, he felt sorry for him and, putting aside his anger, went up to Lykophron and said, "Son, which of these ways of life is the better choice: the squalor you have as a result of the way you are acting, or holding the tyranny and all the fine things I have now and which are yours to inherit, if only you conform to the wishes of your father? [4] Although you are my son and the prince of the prosperous city of Corinth, you have chosen the life of a vagabond, opposing and raging against me, the one person of all whom you should least treat this way. If some unfortunate event has happened in our family, for which you blame me, know that it affects me most directly, since I myself carried it out. [5] So now that I hope you have learned how much better it is to be envied than pitied, as well as what it is like to seethe in fury against your parents and those better than you, come back home!" [6] In this way, Periandros tried to prevail upon his son, but the boy gave no reply except to say that his father now owed a fine to the god for having conversed with him. At that point Periandros realized that his son's problem was insurmountable and impossible to solve. So he sent him out of his sight on a ship bound for Corcyra,[a] since he ruled that island, too. [7] After sending him off, Periandros waged war against his father-in-law Prokles, on the grounds that he was the one most responsible for his present predicament, and in the campaign Periandros captured Epidauros and took Prokles himself prisoner.

Time went by and when Periandros realized that he had passed his prime and admitted to himself that he was no longer capable of supervising and managing the government, he sent a summons to Corcyra, bidding Lykophron to return and assume the tyranny. For he saw no potential in his older son, who appeared rather sluggish and dull. [2] But Lykophron did not think it worthwhile to even interview the messenger. And so Periandros, still trying to maintain a connection with his younger son, sent his sister, the daughter of Periandros, who he thought could make the most effective attempt to persuade him. [3] When she arrived, she said, "Young man, do you really want the tyranny to fall to others and your father's house to be plundered, rather than to return and have it all for yourself? Come home and stop punishing yourself. [4] Obstinate pride is a handicap: do not try to heal one wound by creating another. Many people have preferred the appearance of justice to justice itself; and many others, while seeking the interests of their mother, have thrown away their patrimony. The power of a tyranny can easily slip from one's grasp: there are many who lust after it. Your father is now an old man and past his prime, so do not give away your own precious possessions to others." [5] These seductive words were exactly what her father had instructed her to say to Lykrophron, but he replied that he absolutely would not come to Corinth as long as he knew his father still lived there. [6] When Periandros heard the report of this visit, he sent a third messenger to bid Lykophron to come to Corinth and succeed him in the tyranny, saying that he himself was willing to go to Corcyra. [7] Lykophron agreed to these terms, and while Periandros arranged to go to Corcyra, he prepared to go to Corinth. But when the Corcyrians learned about each of these arrangements, they killed the young man to prevent Periandros from coming to their land. And so in retaliation for this deed, Periandros sought to get revenge against the Corcyrians.

3.53
CORINTH-CORCYRA
The Corcyrians kill Lykophron, which is the reason Periandros seeks vengeance against them.

3.52.6a   Corcyra: Map 3.45, AX.

3.54
525
SAMOS
The Spartans lay siege
to Samos.

The Lacedaemonians[a] went to Samos[b] with a huge force and besieged Samos by assaulting the wall at the tower which faces the sea and lies at the entrance to the city. But Polykrates himself then counterattacked with a large force of his own and drove them away. [2] Then a great number of Samians, along with their mercenaries, charged down from the upper tower on the mountain ridge and engaged the attacking Lacedaemonians, but after a short time they were forced to retreat, and the Lacedaemonians followed, chasing and killing them.

3.55
525
SAMOS
The Spartan Archias,
whose grandson Herodotus
has met, is killed and given
a public funeral by the
Samians.

Now if the rest of the Lacedaemonians who were there that day had been the equals of Archias and Lykopes, Samos would have been taken, for only Archias and Lykopes pursued the Samians as they fled within their wall; but then these two were trapped within the city of the Samians and, unable to escape, died there. [2] I myself met another Archias, the grandson of this Archias and the son of Samios in Pitane[a] (for that was his district), who honored his Samian guest-friends[b] more than all the others. He said his father had been given the name Samios because he was the son of that Archias who had died gallantly in Samos. And so now this later Archias honored the Samians because they had buried his grandfather at public expense.

3.56
525
SAMOS
The Spartans give up the
siege and leave Samos.

After the Lacedaemonians had besieged Samos for forty days without making any progress, they returned to the Peloponnese.[a] [2] There is an asinine account that has been spread about that Polykrates gave them a large sum of gilded lead Samian coins[a] that he had struck, which they accepted and for that reason departed. This was the first time that the Lacedaemonians had ever led an army into Asia.[b]

3.57
524?
SIPHNOS
Needing money, the anti-
Polykrates Samians retire
to rich Siphnos. Herodotus
describes the sources of
Syphnian wealth and the
Delphic oracle to Siphnos.

Just as the Lacedaemonians were about to abandon them, the Samians, who had started this war against Polykrates, sailed away to Siphnos[a] [2] because they needed money; and at that time, due to gold and silver mines on their island, the Siphnians had reached the peak of their prosperity and had become the wealthiest of all the islanders. Indeed, the mines were so productive that the tithe deposited in the Siphnian treasury at Delphi[a] was the equal to that of the wealthiest of treasuries. Each year, the Siphnians divided the profits from the mines among themselves.[b] [3] While they were building their treasury, they consulted the oracle about whether their present prosperity would last a long time. The Pythia replied:

3.54.1a Lacedaemon (Sparta): Map 3.45, BX.
3.54.1b Samos: Map 3.45, AY.
3.55.2a Pitane, a village of Sparta also mentioned at
         9.53. Sparta: Map 3.59. This remark
         certainly indicates that Herodotus traveled
         to Sparta. See Appendix B, §15.
3.55.2b Guest-friendship (*xenia*): a bond of ritual-
         ized friendship, usually between aristocrats
         or prominent men of different cities. It was
         passed down through generations and
         required hereditary privileges and obliga-
         tions such as reciprocal hospitality and
         assistance. See Appendix T, §3.
3.56.1a Peloponnese: Map 3.59.
3.56.2a Lead-gilt coins: see Appendix J, §8.
3.56.2b Asia: Map 3.59, locator. Samos was consid-
         ered Asian. The Achaean Lacedaemonians

had participated in the Trojan War, after
which the Dorians were thought to have
invaded the Peloponnese.
3.57.1a Siphnos: Map 3.59.
3.57.2a Delphi: Map 3.59. Many cities and individ-
         uals dedicated precious and valuable works
         and bullion to Panhellenic sanctuaries such as
         Delphi, and small buildings called treasuries
         were built by individual cities to house the
         dedications of their own citizens. See Appen-
         dix I, §7–9. See also Figure 7.139, of the
         restored Athenian treasury at Delphi.
3.57.2b Compare this division of the profits among
         the citizens to what the Athenians vote to
         do in 7.144 with windfall profits from silver
         mines at Laurium.

FIGURE 3.57. DETAIL FROM THE NORTH FRIEZE OF THE TREASURY OF SIPHNOS AT DELPHI, DEPICTING THE BATTLE OF THE GODS AGAINST GIANTS. IT ALSO DEPICTS THE OVERLAPPING SHIELD-WALL OF A HOPLITE FRONT LINE.

> When city hall is white
> And the agora white-browed, then should the wary man
> Beware: of wooden ambush, and a herald in red.

At that time both the agora and the city hall of the Siphnians were adorned with Parian marble.[a]

The Siphnians were unable to interpret this oracle, neither immediately after it was given nor later, when the Samians came. For as soon as the Samian ships put in at Siphnos, they sent ambassadors in one of their ships to the city. [2] Now in the old days all ships were painted red, and so this was precisely what the Pythia had predicted to the Siphnians when she bade them beware of wooden ambush and a herald in red. [3] When the ambassadors arrived at the city of Siphnos, they requested a loan of ten talents[a] from the Siphnians, but the Siphnians denied their request. The Samians then proceeded to ravage the island. [4] When the Siphnians found out about this, they armed themselves without delay and ran out to defend their

3.58
524?
SIPHNOS
The Samians defeat the Siphnians and take 100 talents from them.

3.57.3a   Paros: Map 3.59. Parian marble is pure
          white in color.
3.58.3a   A talent was a unit of weight. A talent of

gold or silver was a very large value used
in financial calculations. See Appendix J,
§11–13, 20.

land. In the battle that followed, the Siphnians were defeated, and after it was over, many of them found themselves cut off from their town by the Samians, who were then able to exact 100 talents from the Siphnians.

3.59
524
KYDONIA, CRETE
The Samians settle in Kydonia on Crete, but are captured and enslaved by the Aeginetans and Cretans (519).

With this money, the Samians bought from the people of Hermione[a] the island of Hydrea,[b] which lies off the coast of the Peloponnese,[c] and entrusted it to the care of the people of Troizen.[d] The Samians themselves settled in Kydonia on Crete,[e] although they had originally intended to sail to Zacynthus[f] and to expel the Zacynthians from their island. [2] These Samians then remained on Crete and prospered for five years. They are the ones who built the sanctuaries that now exist in Kydonia, including the temple of Diktyne.[a] [3] But in the sixth year, the Aeginetans[a] with the Cretans conquered them in a naval battle and enslaved them. They cut off the boarhead images from the prows of the Samian ships and dedicated them to the sanctuary of Athena in Aegina. [4] This was done by the Aeginetans in revenge for the severe damage that the Samians had inflicted upon them when they attacked Aegina earlier, during the reign of King Amphilkrates, although the Samians had also suffered much in that campaign. In any case, that was their reason for this attack.

3.60
SAMOS
Herodotus describes the three great engineering feats of the Samians.

I have given a rather lengthy account of the Samians because they achieved the three greatest engineering works of all the Hellenes. First, they dug a tunnel through a 900-foot-high mountain; [2] it is 4,080 feet long and 8 feet high and wide. Another channel, 30 feet deep and 3 feet wide, was dug along the entire length of the tunnel, into which water is sent through pipes directly into the city of Samos from a huge spring. [3] The builder in charge of designing and excavating this tunnel was a Megarian,[a] Eupalinos son of Naustrophos.[b] That is one of the three works; the second is a mole around the harbor in the sea, 120 feet[c] deep, with a length of over 1,200 feet.[d] [4] The third achievement is the largest of all the temples[a] we have ever seen; its first architect was a local man, Rhoikos son of Philes. So that is why I went on at some length about the Samians.

3.61
528?
SUSA
The rebellion against Cambyses by Patizeithes and his brother, the latter of whom impersonates Smerdis.

After Cambyses son of Cyrus lost his mind, and while he dawdled near Egypt, two brothers who were Magi revolted against him. Cambyses had

3.59.1a Hermione: Map 3.59.
3.59.1b Hydrea: Map 3.59.
3.59.1c Peloponnese: Map 3.59.
3.59.1d Troizen: Map 3.59.
3.59.1e Kydonia, Crete (Creta): Map 3.59.
3.59.1f Zacynthus: Map 3.59.
3.59.2a Diktyne: a Cretan goddess, protectress of hunters and seafarers; sometimes identified with Artemis.
3.59.3a Aegina: Map 3.59. This took place probably in 519.
3.60.3a Megara: Map 3.59.
3.60.3b This tunnel, which is indeed a marvel of ancient engineering, still exists, and its entrances can still be seen (see Figures 3.60a and b). It has been investigated by archaeologists and engineers in modern times and was found to have been excavated from both sides of the mountain

and designed so precisely that the two tunnels were only slightly misaligned when they met in the center. It was probably built in the early 520s.
3.60.3c Herodotus writes that the mole is "20 fathoms" deep (1 fathom = 6 feet), and "2 stades" long. See Distance Conversions, p. xliv, and Appendix J, §4–6, 19.
3.60.3d Herodotus writes that the mountain is "1.5 stades" high and the tunnel is "7 stades" long. Along the whole of its length another channel has been cut that is "20 cubits" deep and 3 feet wide. All other dimensions of the work are given in Greek feet. See Appendix J, §4–6, 19.
3.60.4a The temple of Hera at Samos, whose ruins still illustrate its immense size. Samos: Map 3.59.

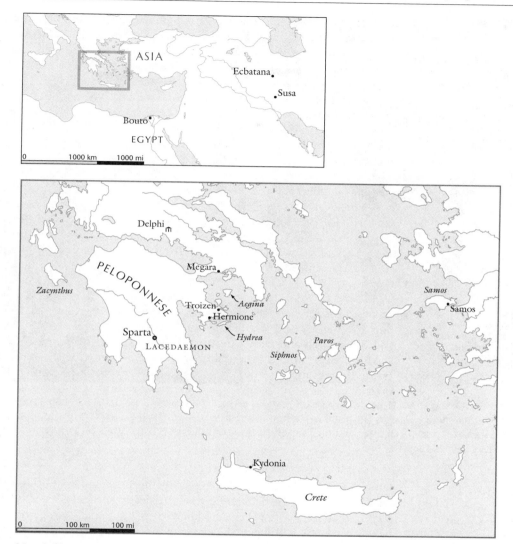

Map 3.59

FIGURE 3.60A. ONE OF THE ENTRANCES TO EUPALINOS' TUNNEL ON SAMOS (LEFT), BUILT IN THE SIXTH CENTURY TO CARRY WATER FROM A SPRING ON THE OTHER SIDE OF THE MOUNTAIN INSIDE THE CITY WALLS. THE MEETING POINT OF THE TWO TUNNELS (RIGHT), WHICH EUPALINOS HAD DUG FROM OPPOSITE SIDES OF MOUNT KASTRO. THEY ARE OFFSET BY ONLY A FEW FEET.

left one of these Magi in Persia to manage his household, and this is the one who revolted. When he learned that the death of Smerdis was being kept secret, that only a few Persians knew of it, and that the majority firmly believed he was still living, [2] he was induced by these circumstances to make an attempt on the throne. This was his scheme. His brother, the man who, as I mentioned, joined him in the revolt, bore a striking resemblance to Smerdis son of Cyrus, the brother of Cambyses, whom Cambyses had killed. Not only did he look like Smerdis, but his name was Smerdis! [3] Patizeithes, the Magus who had been left in charge of the household, assured his brother that he would take care of everything and led him to the throne and sat him upon it. This done, he sent out heralds to different places, including Egypt, to proclaim to the army that from now on the troops must obey Smerdis son of Cyrus, not Cambyses.

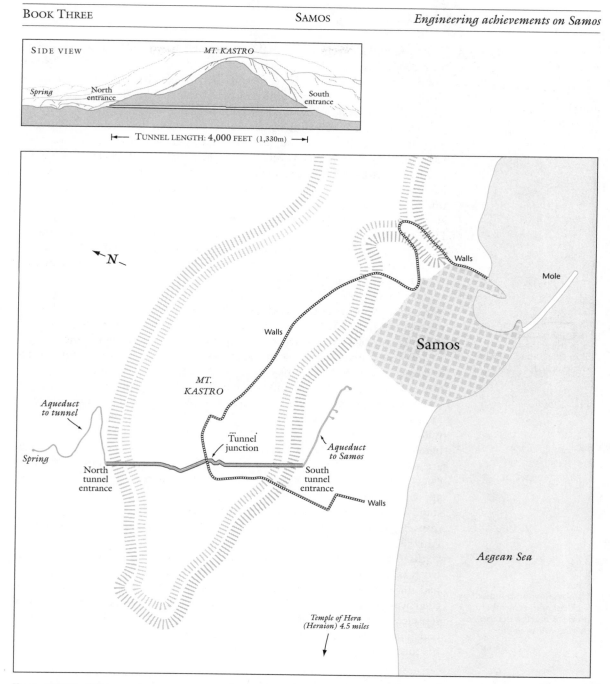

FIGURE 3.60B. THE PATH OF THE TUNNEL EUPALINOS CUT THROUGH MOUNT KASTRO TO BRING WATER INSIDE THE CITY WALLS OF SAMOS.

So the heralds went off to make the proclamation, and the one who had been sent to Egypt, finding Cambyses and his army at Ecbatana[a] in Syria, stood among them and recited the proclamation as he had been instructed by the Magus. [2] When Cambyses heard the herald, he believed he was telling the truth and concluded that Prexaspes, the man he had sent to kill Smerdis, had betrayed him by failing to carry out his orders. Glaring at Prexaspes, he said, "So is this how you have performed the task I assigned to you?" [3] Prexaspes answered, "My lord, it cannot be true that your brother Smerdis has revolted against you, or that you could have any reason for a serious or trivial quarrel with him, for I did just as you ordered, and I buried him with my own hands. [4] If the dead have risen, you had better also watch out that Astyages the Mede[a] does not revolt against you as well. However, if the world goes on as it did before, then that man will certainly never be a source of mischief again. Now, I think we should pursue, apprehend, and question this herald about who sent him here to proclaim that we should obey this King Smerdis."

Cambyses was pleased to hear this argument. At once, the herald was pursued and apprehended, and when he was brought before them, Prexaspes said to him, "You, who say that you have come as a messenger from Smerdis son of Cyrus, now tell the truth and no harm will come to you. Did Smerdis give you these instructions in person, or was it one of his servants?" [2] The herald answered, "Well, actually, I have not seen Smerdis son of Cyrus since King Cambyses marched off to Egypt. It was the Magus whom Cambyses appointed to be guardian of his household who instructed me to make this announcement, but he did claim that Smerdis son of Cyrus was the one who ordered that I declare it to you." [3] Everything the herald had said was true. Cambyses now turned to Prexaspes and said, "You are acquitted of blame, Prexaspes, since you are a good and noble man who obeyed your King. But which of the Persians has revolted against me and appropriated the name of Smerdis?" [4] Prexaspes replied, "I think I understand what has happened, sire. It is the Magi who have revolted: the man responsible is the one whom you expected to manage your household, Patizeithes, and his brother Smerdis."

As Cambyses heard the name Smerdis, he was suddenly struck by the truth of his dream as it was revealed in this account; for in the dream he had thought he saw someone reporting to him that Smerdis was sitting on the royal throne and touching heaven with his head. [2] Now realizing how senseless had been his brother's death, he wept for Smerdis. And when he had finished weeping, he leapt upon his horse in a fit of exasperation at all his misfortune, intending to lead his army immediately against the Magi in

3.62.1a   Ecbatana in Syria: location unknown.
3.62.4a   Astyages: the last king of the Medes who   ruled over Persians, whose story
Herodotus tells in Book 1.

Susa.[a] [3] But as he jumped up, the tip of his sword's scabbard fell off, and the bare blade stabbed his thigh, in the very same spot he had earlier struck Apis the god of the Egyptians.[a] Convinced that he had been mortally wounded, Cambyses asked what the name of this city was; and when they told him it was Ecbatana, [4] he recalled an earlier oracle that he had received from the city of Bouto[a] which had predicted that he would end his life in Ecbatana. Of course he had always believed that he would die as an old man in Median Ecbatana, where the seat of his government was located,[b] but as it turned out, the oracle had clearly meant Syrian Ecbatana after all. [5] And indeed, when his inquiry led him to discover the city's name, he was so overwhelmed by the misfortune that the Magus had inflicted on him and by his wound that he regained his sanity. After piecing together the significance of the oracle, he said, "It is here that Cambyses son of Cyrus is fated to meet his end."

That was what he said then; but about twenty days later, he sent for the most notable Persians there with him and told them, "Persians, I have reached the point where I must reveal to you the darkest secret of all my affairs. [2] When I was in Egypt, an apparition appeared to me in my sleep—oh, how I wish I had never seen it! I dreamt that I saw a messenger from home who told me that Smerdis was sitting on the royal throne and touching heaven with his head. [3] Frightened that my brother would rob me of my rule, I acted more hastily than wisely. It turns out that in the nature of things human, it is not possible to prevent what is destined. But fool that I was, I sent Prexaspes to Susa to kill Smerdis, and when the evil deed was done, I lived without fear, never thinking that with Smerdis dead, some other person would rise against me. [4] Therefore, because of my mistaken belief about all that was going to happen, I have killed my own brother for no good reason, and still I have been deprived of my kingship. For it was Smerdis the Magus who the divine force in my dream predicted would revolt against me. [5] And so I have committed a crime. Smerdis son of Cyrus, the one man who would be most obliged to defend me against the Magi's disgraceful treatment, has met his end in an unholy manner at the hands of his closest relative. He is no longer among the living, and the two Magi, the one I left as manager of my household and his brother Smerdis, now control your kingdom. [6] Smerdis is now dead, but for you and your future, Persians, my most pressing obligation as my life ends is to inform you about my wishes. And as I place these demands upon you—all of you, and especially the Achaimenids[a] who are present—I call upon the gods of the royal house. Do not allow sovereignty to pass to the Medes again. If they have acquired it by guile, you must take it away by guile; if they have

3.65
522
SYRIA
Cambyses describes his murder of his brother Smerdis to the Persians and charges them with taking the crown back from the Mede usurper Smerdis.

Magi = median priest

3.64.2a Susa: Map 3.59, locator.
3.64.3a For Herodotus' description of Cambyses' blow to Apis, see 3.29.1.
3.64.4a Bouto: Map 3.59, locator.
3.64.4b Ecbatana in Media: Map 3.59, locator. Ecbatana, the capital of Media, was the

Persian capital in the summer; Susa was the winter capital. See Appendix P, Oracles, Religion, and Politics in Herodotus, §8.
3.65.6a Cyrus was an Achaimenid, now the ruling house of Persia.

taken it by some act of brute force, you must recover it by brute force, and must do so with all your might. [7] If you do this, may the earth bring forth fruit, and may your wives and your flocks bear offspring, and may you live in freedom for eternity. But if you fail to recover our rule or do not even try to recover it, then I curse you to suffer a fate entirely opposite to this, and further, wish for every Persian an end of life like my own." Having said this, Cambyses now wept again over everything that had happened to him.

When the Persians saw their king weeping, they all tore the clothing they were wearing and began to wail uncontrollably. [2] Later, when his bone became gangrenous and the flesh of his thigh decayed, Cambyses son of Cyrus died after reigning a total of seven years and five months. He had sired no children at all, male or female. [3] The Persians who were there were profoundly skeptical that the Magi were in control of the government; they assumed that Cambyses said what he did about the death of Smerdis to discredit his brother and turn all Persia against him.

Their confidence that Smerdis son of Cyrus was really the man enthroned as King was that Prexaspes now strongly denied that he had ever killed Smerdis, since it was not safe, now that Cambyses was gone, for him to say that he had killed the son of Cyrus with his own hand. [2] And so, with Cambyses dead, the Magus who was appropriating the name of Smerdis son of Cyrus reigned confidently for seven months, a term which, if added to Cambyses' reign, completed a full eight years. [3] During these months, he performed many generous deeds to benefit his subjects, proclaiming to all the nations he ruled that they would be exempt from military service and taxes for three years, so that naturally everyone in Asia, except for the Persians, greatly mourned his loss when he died.

So that is what he proclaimed as he began to rule. But his identity was revealed seven months later, and it happened something like this. There was a man named Otanes son of Pharnaspes who was the equal of the most eminent Persians in both lineage and wealth. [2] This Otanes was the first to suspect that the Magus was not Smerdis son of Cyrus, and who he really was. He arrived at this conclusion from the fact that the King never wandered away from the citadel, nor summoned any of the notable Persians into his presence. [3] These suspicions led Otanes to send a message to his own daughter Phaidymie. She had been taken by Cambyses as a wife and was now being kept by the Magus, who was living with her as well as the rest of Cambyses' wives. In the message Otanes asked his daughter whom she was sleeping with: was it Smerdis son of Cyrus or someone else? [4] She responded that she did not know; she had never seen Smerdis son of Cyrus, nor could she identify the man who was sleeping with her, either. Otanes then sent a second message to her: "If you yourself cannot recognize Smerdis son of Cyrus, ask Atossa who is this man who is living with her as well as with you. I would expect that she can certainly recognize her own brother." [5] To this message his daughter replied, "I am unable to converse with Atossa, or any other woman who had their places by her side, since, whoever this man is, as soon as he took over the kingship, he dispersed the women and lodged each of us in separate quarters."

Upon hearing this, Otanes now saw the situation more clearly, so he sent a third message to Phaidymie saying: [2] "My daughter, you are of noble birth and must assume whatever risks your father asks of you. For if this man is not Smerdis son of Cyrus, but is really the impostor whom I suspect, he must not escape punishment for sleeping with you and holding sovereignty over the Persians: he must pay dearly for it. [3] So here is what you must do. When you go to bed with him and can be certain that he is fast asleep, then feel his ears. If he has ears, you may consider yourself the companion of Smerdis son of Cyrus, but if the man has no ears, then you are in bed with Smerdis the Magus." [4] Phaidymie sent back a reply saying that she would indeed be taking a great risk if she carried out his plan, for if he had no ears and she was caught in the act of feeling for them, she knew that he would absolutely obliterate her. Nonetheless, she promised her father that she would attempt it, [5] and she fulfilled her promise. Now, Smerdis the Magus had no ears because Cyrus son of Cambyses, while he ruled, had punished him for some grave offense by cutting off his ears. [6] So Phaidymie, as she was the daughter of Otanes, duly fulfilled her promise the next time it was her turn to approach the Magus (for in Persia, the women visit their men in rotation). When she had gone to bed with him and he had fallen into a deep sleep, she felt for his ears and with no difficulty whatsoever, indeed quite effortlessly, she discovered that he had no ears at all. At daybreak, she sent a message to her father, revealing what she had learned.

Otanes then invited Aspathines and Gobryas to join him; these were the leading Persians and the men he thought he could best trust for his purpose. He reported the whole story to them and, since they had already developed suspicions of their own, they accepted Otanes' story. [2] They then resolved that each one of them would bring the man he trusted most into their group. Otanes introduced Intaphrenes; Gobryas, Megabyzos; and Aspathines, Hydarnes. [3] Thus they already numbered six when Darius son of Hystaspes, whose father was a satrap of the Persians, arrived in Susa from Persia. Upon his arrival, the six Persians decided to include Darius in their conspiracy, too.

3.69
521?
SUSA
Otanes' daughter discovers and reports that the Smerdis with whom she sleeps has no ears, and thus identifies him as the Magus.

3.70
521?
SUSA
A cabal of seven Persians is formed.

3.71
521
SUSA
Darius demands that the conspirators act immediately.

3.72
521
SUSA
Darius explains how they will pass the guards and get to Smerdis.

These seven men met, pledged their good faith to each other, and discussed what they should do. When the moment came for Darius to state his opinion, he said, [2] "I used to believe that I alone knew that it was the Magus who now reigned and that Smerdis son of Cyrus was dead. My ambition to contrive the death of the Magus myself is the very reason that I came here. But since I have discovered that I am not the only one, that all of you are aware of this, too, I suggest that we act immediately without delay, for that would be the better course." [3] Otanes responded to this statement, "Son of Hystaspes, you come from a noble father, and you will probably show yourself to be no less of a man than he is, but do not rush into this attack recklessly; rather think carefully about how to go about it. I think we should attack only after we have increased our numbers." [4] To this Darius replied, "You men must realize that the plan suggested by Otanes will lead to your utter destruction, for someone, motivated by hopes of private gain, will surely report us to the Magus. [5] You really should have done the deed by yourselves, but since you resolved to tell me your suspicions and to ask my advice, I say that we do the deed today, and if we do not act this very day, you can be sure that I shall be the first to denounce you to the Magus!"

Observing Darius' agitation, Otanes said to him, "Since you are compelling us to act hastily and are not allowing further delay, tell us yourself how you think we might attempt to enter the palace and attack them. Surely, whether or not you have seen them for yourself, you know that guards are posted everywhere, so how shall we make our attack?" [2] Darius replied, "Otanes, many plans cannot be revealed in speech, but only in action, just as there are plans that can be described, but nothing glorious comes from them. You all know that the palace guards stationed there are not difficult to pass. [3] First of all, every one of us here, because of our rank and standing, could easily get past them—partly because they respect us, partly because they fear us. Secondly, I myself have the most appropriate pretext by which we may pass them: the claim that I have just arrived from Persia and wish to disclose certain intelligence from my father to the King. [4] For where a lie must be told, let it be told.[a] We strive for the same goal whether we lie or tell the truth. Some people lie hoping to gain by convincing their listeners to believe them; others tell the truth hoping that greater trust will thereby be placed in them. Our goal is the same, though the methods we practice to reach it may differ. [5] If there were nothing to gain, a truthful man would be just as likely to lie as a liar would be to tell the truth. Now then, we will see to it that any guard watching the gates who is willing to let us pass will be rewarded in the future; but whoever tries to resist us

3.72.4a Darius defends the use of a tactical lie here probably because of the traditional Persian insistence on telling the truth and abhorrence of lying. See 1.136.2 and 1.138.1.

let him be marked as our enemy, and then let us push our way through and keep to the task at hand."

After this speech, Gobryas said, "Friends, when will we ever have a better opportunity to recover our rule or, failing to win it back, to die in the attempt? For although we are Persians, we are ruled now by a Mede, a Magus no less, and one who has no ears! [2] Those of you who were with Cambyses when he was ill and dying surely recall the curses he called down upon us if we did not try to win back our rule, even though at the time we did not believe what he said but thought he was trying to discredit his brother. [3] But now, I cast my vote to follow Darius' counsel that we not depart from this meeting for any purpose other than to proceed directly against the Magus." That is what Gobryas said, and they all agreed with him.

3.73
521?
SUSA
Gobryas agrees, and they all consent to follow Darius' plan immediately.

While these men were deciding their course, other events were coincidentally taking place. The Magi decided to make Prexaspes their friend, since he had suffered undeserved abuse at the hands of Cambyses, who had shot and killed his son with his arrow; they also courted him because he alone knew that Smerdis son of Cyrus was really dead, for he had killed him with his own hand; and furthermore, Prexaspes was regarded by the Persians with the greatest esteem. [2] So for all these reasons they summoned him and worked on persuading him to be their friend through the exchange of pledges and oaths, asking him to swear that he would never expose the deception they had foisted on the Persians, and for this pledge they promised to give him everything, and countless times over, in return. [3] Finally, no sooner had the Magi succeeded in obtaining his promise to do as they wished in this than they proposed a second request; they asked if he would, after they themselves had summoned all the Persians together below the wall of the palace, climb up on the tower and proclaim to the Persians that they were being ruled by none other than Smerdis son of Cyrus. [4] They asked him to do this because he was—believe it or not—the man the Persians trusted most, and because he had so often stated publicly that Smerdis son of Cyrus still lived, denying that he had murdered him.

3.74
521?
SUSA
The Magi bribe Prexaspes to join them and help their cause.

Prexaspes said that he was ready and willing to carry out this request also, so the Magi summoned the Persians, had Prexaspes climb up to the tower, and told him to speak. But what they had asked him to say, he intentionally forgot. Instead, he narrated the ancestral lineage of Cyrus, from Achaimenes to Cyrus, and he concluded by enumerating all the good and noble deeds that Cyrus had accomplished for the Persians. [2] After this detailed account, he then disclosed the truth, stating that he had concealed it before (since it had been unsafe for him to tell what had really happened

3.75
521?
SUSA
Prexaspes agrees to help the Magi but instead publicly exposes them and kills himself.

then), but that necessity compelled him to reveal it now. And he then told them how he had been forced by Cambyses to kill Smerdis son of Cyrus, and revealed that the Magi were now reigning. [3] Finally, he threatened the Persians with many curses if they failed to recover their rule and to punish the Magi. After that, he hurled himself headfirst down from the tower. Thus Prexaspes ended his life as he had lived it: an admirable man.

The seven Persians, having concluded their meeting, set out at once to attack the Magi. With a prayer to the gods, they went on their way, knowing nothing of what Prexaspes had done. [2] But when they reached the mid-point of their journey, they heard the news and they stopped, stood to the side of the road, and once again deliberated. Otanes and his men strongly urged delay; no attack should be attempted, they argued, while affairs were in such upheaval. Darius and his supporters opposed delay, wishing to proceed at once to carry out the plan that they had decided upon before. [3] In the middle of their heated argument, seven pairs of hawks pursuing and pecking violently at a pair of eagles appeared above them. When they saw this, they all approved of Darius' plan and, emboldened by this omen of the birds, continued on toward the palace.

At the gates, events turned out much as Darius had predicted, for the guards showed great respect to these high-ranking Persians and suspected nothing of what they were going to do. So they passed by the guards without even being questioned, escorted by some sort of divine guidance. [2] But when they came to the courtyard, they encountered the eunuchs who served as royal messengers, who inquired about their purpose in coming here, uttered dire threats of what they would do to the guards for having allowed them to pass this far, and tried to keep the seven conspirators from advancing any farther. [3] But the conspirators, with a brisk shout to signal their assault, instantly drew their daggers and stabbed the eunuchs right then and there as they tried to hold them back. Then they dashed into the men's quarters.

At the time, both of the Magi[a] happened to be inside, discussing what Prexaspes had done. When they noticed the noise of the eunuchs shouting and all the commotion, both of them leapt to their feet, realizing what was going on, and immediately prepared to defend themselves. [2] One of them seized his bow before anyone could stop him; the other took up his spear; and the fight with the conspirators began. Since the struggle took place at close quarters—they were practically on top of each other—the bow was of no use at all to the Magus who had picked it up. The other one, however, did manage to make use of his spear, and struck Aspathines in the thigh and Intaphrenes in the eye. Intaphrenes in fact later lost his eye from this wound but did not die from it. [3] While one Magus was busy inflicting

3.78.1a   "Both" here presumably refers to
          Patizeithes and his brother Smerdis.

these injuries, the other, since his bow was useless to him, fled to a bedroom within the men's quarters, hoping to lock the door behind him. [4] But two of the seven conspirators, Darius and Gobryas, followed him closely and attacked him there. Gobryas wrestled him down, and as they were locked together in a tangled heap, Darius stood over them, hesitating because of his concern that in the darkness he might strike Gobryas by accident. [5] Gobryas noticed him standing there doing nothing and asked why he did not join in the fight. "I'm worried I might strike you," Darius replied. "Go ahead," said Gobryas, "thrust a sword through both of us!" And so Darius obeyed, thrusting his dagger through, and he managed to hit the Magus alone.

After the conspirators had killed both Magi, they cut off their heads and, leaving their own wounded men there, since they were too weak to go with them but could help guard the acropolis, the other five ran outside carrying the heads of the Magi. There, with great shouts they called out to the other Persians, describing all that had happened and showing them the heads. As they spread the news, they also killed every Magus they found in their path. [2] When the Persians learned from them about the Magi's criminal fraud and what had just occurred, they decided it was right for them to join in the killing, too, so, drawing their daggers, they slew every Magus they found, and if nightfall had not ended the slaughter, there would not have been a single Magus left alive. [3] The Persians commemorate this day as their most important public holiday and celebrate it with a great festival they call the Murder of the Magi. And during this entire day all Magi must keep within their houses—none are permitted to appear outside.

Five days later, when the commotion had subsided, the men who had revolted against the Magi consulted with one another about the whole state of affairs. Now there are some Hellenes who do not believe the following speeches took place at all, but they certainly did.

[2] Otanes encouraged them to place the government in the hands of all the Persians, saying, "I think it best that we no longer be ruled by one of ourselves as a monarch, since that kind of government is neither pleasant nor good. You have seen how Cambyses became outrageously arrogant, and you have all experienced the insolence of the Magus directly. [3] How could monarchy be a harmonious and coherent system when it permits the ruler to do whatever he wishes, to be accountable to no one? Even the best of men, if placed in this position of power, would lose his normal mental balance, for arrogance will grow within him as he enjoys all the good things at hand, as will envy, too, which is always a fundamental component of human nature. [4] All evil lies in these two traits, and he manifests both of them. Glutted as he is with arrogance, he carries out many reckless deeds

3.79
521
SUSA
Many Magi are slain. The Persians still celebrate this day with a great festival.

3.80
SUSA
The Persians discuss what form of government to adopt. Otanes speaks for a democracy.

All persuasive

and will then commit more outrageous acts out of envy! Since he possesses all good things, the tyrant ought to be entirely free from envy, but instead, he behaves just the opposite toward the citizens, for he envies the best men if they survive and live around him, while he derives pleasure from the worst people in town. But he himself is the best of men when it comes to accepting slander. [5] And indeed, his character is most inconsistent in nature, for if you admire him to a moderate degree, he is vexed that he is not being treated with sufficient deference, but if you treat him subserviently, then he becomes annoyed by your obsequiousness. And the worst of all his traits is that he overturns ancestral customs; he uses brute force on women, and he kills men without trial.[a] [6] The rule of the majority, however, not only has the most beautiful and powerful name of all, equality,[a] but in practice, the majority does not act at all like a monarch. Indeed, the majority chooses its magistrates by lot,[b] it holds all of these officials accountable to an audit, and it refers all resolutions to the authority of the public. I therefore propose that we abandon monarchy and raise the majority to a ruling position, for in the many is the whole."[c]   *rule of few*

3.81
521?
SUSA
The Persians discuss what form of government to adopt. Megabyzos speaks for an oligarchy.

Drawn by lots.

Next, Megabyzos urged them to turn to oligarchy, saying, "I am in favor of what Otanes says in his attempt to put an end to tyranny, but when he tells us to transfer power to the majority, he has strayed far from good judgment. For nothing can be both more unintelligent or insolent than the worthless, ineffectual mob. [2] If men want to escape the arrogance of a tyrant, it is absolutely intolerable that they should then fall victim to the arrogance of the undisciplined common people.[a] For whatever the tyrant may do, he at least knows what he is doing, whereas the people have no idea of what they are doing. How could someone who has not been educated, who has never seen anything good or decent, be knowledgeable about anything? He pushes and shoves and stumbles into affairs without thought, like a raging torrent. [3] So let those who are hostile to the Persians be governed by the people, while we pick out the

3.80.5a These remarks may represent Herodotus' true attitude toward tyranny. See Appendix T, §4.
3.80.6a Herodotus uses the complex Greek word *isonomia* here, and not the word *democratia*. Originally, *isonomia* meant equal apportionment (from *iso*, "equal," plus the verb *nemo*, "to distribute"), but at this time, the word mainly conveyed the sense of equality. Over time, it came to mean equality before the law, which implies that no one is above the law—that all have equal access to the law and its protection, even though they are not necessarily equal economically or politically. Finally, it is the law, not the whim of the monarch, that rules all.
3.80.6b The Athenian democracy chose its magistrates by lot, but that was not a general trait of all democratic governments.
3.80.6c This phrase was used or adapted by later authors, and could also be translated:

"The plurality is really the totality" or "in numbers lies everything." In other words, the majority of the people constitutes the whole state. Otanes' general argument, which employs both historical example and theoretical reasoning, reflects developments in political theory, rhetoric, and philosophy.
3.81.2a "Common people" and "people" (below) are translations of the Greek word *demos*, used here for the first time in the debate. The basic sense of the word is "district," which extends then to people of a district, especially common people of the country districts surrounding the urban center; and then, in a political context, the sovereign people. Otanes, who argued in favor of democracy, did not employ the words *demos* or *democratia*, but rather *plethos* (the majority) and *koinon* (authority of the public, common consent).

best men to make up an intimate company and endow it with power and authority. We ourselves will of course belong to this company, and the best men are most likely to make the best decisions." That, then, was the opinion of Megabyzos.

mob rule

The third to express his opinion was Darius, who said, "What Megabyzos claimed about the majority seems right to me, but what he said about oligarchy seems wrong. For if we compare the best examples in theory of these three types of government—the best democracy, the best oligarchy, and the best monarchy—I declare that monarchy surpasses the other two by far. [2] For obviously nothing can be better than the one man who is the best. And since he has the best judgment, he would be a blameless administrator of the majority, and thus, too, he would best be able to maintain silence about his plans to oppose enemies. [3] In an oligarchy, on the other hand, many men strive to achieve excellence, and thus private rivalries tend to become public hostilities. For each man wants to be the head of affairs and desires that his own opinions prevail; so that they ultimately become extremely hostile toward one another, which leads to the emergence of factions, which in turn produces bloodshed, and which then results in the establishment of a monarchy. This progression, then, also demonstrates just how much monarchy excels the others. [4] Then again, when the people rule, incompetence will always and inevitably be the result. While this incompetence is present, these inept men do not themselves engage in public hostilities, but instead form strong friendships among one another as they incompetently manage the commonwealth together. This situation goes on until one of them steps forth as leader of the people and stops the others from continuing such actions, after which this man is much admired by the people. And because of this admiration he is effectively declared to be a monarch, which again proves that monarchy is the best of the three. [5] But I can summarize my argument by one statement: Where did our freedom come from, who gave it to us? Did it come from the people, from an oligarchy, or from a monarchy? Well, then, in my opinion, since we were freed by one man, we should preserve that form of government. Moreover, we should not let go of our ancestral traditions, which are fine just as they are, for that would not be the better course."

3.82
SUSA
The Persians discuss what form of government to adopt. Darius speaks for a monarchy.

Crazy

Always rule by 1 man.

These were the three opinions presented at the meeting, and after the other four of the seven men decided in favor of the last one, Otanes, despite his eagerness to establish isonomy,ᵃ recognized that he had lost the argument, and he now addressed them all: [2] "My comrades, it is clear that one of us must become King, and whether he who will be entrusted with the administration of the kingdom is chosen by lot, by the majority of the Persians, or by some other method, I shall not compete with you, for I wish neither to rule nor to be ruled. So I now withdraw from this contest on the following condition: that neither I nor my descendants will be subject to

3.83
521
SUSA
Four of the seven vote for monarchy. Otanes asks to withdraw from the election that will determine which of them shall become King.

3.83.1a   Isonomy: see n. 3.80.6a.

you." [3] When he had stated this requirement, the other six agreed to it, and so he took no part in the competition among them but stood aside with an attitude of neutrality. And even now, Otanes' family is the only free one among the Persians; it submits to rule only as much as it wants to, although it does not transgress Persian laws.

The remaining six then deliberated about how they could most fairly establish one of themselves in the position of King. First they all agreed that if the kingship did go to one of them, Otanes and his descendants would be granted yearly allotments of Median clothing and every other gift thought to be most honorable in Persia. They decided to grant him these gifts because he had been the first to plan the conspiracy and bring them all together. [2] And in addition to these perquisites for Otanes, they resolved to establish other privileges that they would share in common: they agreed that any one of the seven would be allowed to go into the palace without an official to announce him, unless the King happened to be sleeping with a woman at the time, and that the King would not be permitted to marry a woman from any families other than their own. [3] Concerning the selection of the King, they decided that at sunrise, they would all mount their horses and ride just outside the city, and the man whose horse made the first sound would have the kingship.

Now Darius had a clever groom, whose name was Oibares, and when the meeting had dispersed, Darius went to him and said, "Oibares, this is what we have decided to do about the kingship: we are all going to mount our horses just as the sun rises, and the man whose horse makes the first sound will obtain the royal power. So now, if you have any skill at all with horses, devise a plan to assure that we and no one else obtain this prize." [2] Oibares replied, "My lord, if that is what will determine whether or not you become King, have no fear. You may be confident that no one but you will be King, since I know just the remedy required for this situation." "Well, then," said Darius, "if you do know of such a trick, do not save it for another day. Now is the time to use it, for our contest will take place with the next dawn." [3] After Oibares had heard this, he waited till nightfall and took the mare Darius loved most to the area just outside the city and tied her there securely. Then he led Darius' stallion to her and walked him around the mare repeatedly, brushing him up against her as he did so, until he finally allowed the stallion to mount her.

As dawn began to break, the six men, as they had agreed, mounted their horses and rode out to the area just outside the city. Just as they approached the place where the mare had been tied the night before, Darius' stallion ran up to the spot and whinnied. [2] At the very same time, lightning appeared and thunder sounded out of the clear sky like a signal of agreement, which added a perfect conclusion to the decision for Darius.[a] The

Margin notes

3.84
SUSA
The seven agree on how to honor Otanes in the future, and how to determine which of the six remaining shall become King.

3.85
SUSA
Darius' groom devises a scheme to win the kingship for him.

3.86
SUSA
The stratagem works, and Darius wins the contest.

3.86.2a　Thunder as a divine signal: see Appendix
　　　　　P, §2.

FIGURE 3.88. A CARVED
RELIEF OF KING DARIUS
ON HIS THRONE, FROM HIS
PALACE AT PERSEPOLIS.

other men immediately dismounted from their horses and prostrated themselves before Darius.

That is how some people tell the story of Oibares' scheme, but there is a
different version, told by others, who are also Persians. They say that
Oibares rubbed the genitals of this mare with his hand and then kept his
hand covered in his trousers. At sunrise, when the horses were about to be
released, he took out his hand and held it to the nostrils of Darius' stallion,
which, upon smelling it, immediately snorted and whinnied.

And so Darius son of Hystaspes was appointed King. All the people of
Asia whom Cyrus and later Cambyses had conquered were subject to him,
except for the Arabians. They had never submitted to Persian slavery but
had become allies instead, since they had allowed Cambyses to pass into

3.87
SUSA
An alternate version
of the stratagem.

3.88
521
PERSIAN KINGDOM
Darius becomes the King.

249

Egypt.[b] For the Persians could not have invaded Egypt without the consent of the Arabians.

[2] Darius married eminent Persian women, among whom the first were Atossa and Artystone, both daughters of Cyrus. Atossa had earlier been the wife of her brother Cambyses and then had been left to the Magus, while Artystone was a virgin. [3] In addition, Darius married the daughter of Smerdis son of Cyrus, whose name was Parmys, and also the daughter of Otanes who had revealed the identity of the Magus.

The power of Darius pervaded everything and everywhere in his realm. The first thing he did was to set up a stone and have a relief carved on it in which was depicted a man on horseback with an inscription which said, "Darius son of Hystaspes acquired possession of the kingship of the Persians by the merit of his horse [and here he placed the name of the horse] and of his groom Oibares."

Next he established twenty satrapies, which is what they call provinces in Persia, and after he had designated the provinces and the governors in charge of them, he assigned to each nation the tribute it would pay to him, organizing nations together with the peoples on their borders, and combining more distant peoples into various single satrapies with one another. [2] He divided up the provinces and the annual revenues of tribute as follows: those peoples who used silver were asked to pay with the Babylonian talent, and those using gold, with the Euboean talent. The Babylonian talent is equal to 78 minas.[a] [3] There had been no fixed assessment of tribute in the reign of Cyrus, nor again in the reign of Cambyses; instead, these kings were paid in gifts. Because Darius imposed tribute and enforced other policies similar to this, the Persians say that Darius was a retailer, Cambyses a master of slaves, and Cyrus a father: Darius tended to conduct all his affairs like a shopkeeper, Cambyses was harsh and scornful, but Cyrus was gentle and saw to it that all good things would be theirs.

From the first provincial district:[a] the Ionians, the Magnesians of Asia, the Aeolians, Carians, Lycians, Milyans, and Pamphylians, all of whom were assessed as a single unit for payment of tribute, came 400 talents of silver. From the second provincial district—the Mysians, Lydians, Lasonians, Kabalians, and Hytennai—came 500 talents. [2] From the third provincial district—the people of the southern coast of the Hellespont, the Phrygians, Thracians in Asia, Paphlagonians, Mariandynians, and Syrians—came tribute of 360 talents. [3] From the fourth provincial district, the Cilicians, came 360 white horses, one for each day, and 500 talents of silver, of which 140 were used to support the cavalry guarding Cilician territory and 360 were sent to Darius.

3.88.1b The Arabian cooperation with Cambyses was described in 3.5–9. Egypt, Arabia: Map 3.91.
3.89.2a For more on the silver Babylonian talent

and the gold Euboean talent, see Appendix J, §11.
3.90.1a Provinces 1–4: Map 3.90.

MAP 3.90. PERSIAN PROVINCES 1–4 IN THE ORDER LISTED BY HERODOTUS.

First Province
Ionians
Magnesians of Asia
Aeolians
Carians
Lycians
Milyans
Pamphylians

Second Province
Mysians
Lydians
Lasonians, location unknown

Kabalians
Hytennai, possibly a mountain tribe
    of Pisidia

Third Province
Hellespontine Phrygians
Asian Thracians
Paphlagonians
Mariandynians
Cappadocian Syrians

Fourth Province
Cilicians

FIGURE 3.91. RELIEF OF A PERSIAN GUARD. ONE OF THE ACHAEMENID KING'S ELITE GUARD, CALLED THE TEN THOUSAND IMMORTALS. THE FRAGMENT WAS PART OF A LONG FRIEZE DEPICTING A SINGLE FILE OF THE IMMORTALS LOCATED IN THE PALACE OF XERXES AT PERSEPOLIS AND WAS CARVED DURING HIS REIGN (484–464). MOST LIKELY IT WAS ONCE BRIGHTLY PAINTED WITH HUES OF YELLOW, BLUE, AND PURPLE.

3.91
PERSIAN KINGDOM
The inhabitants of provinces
5–8 and their respective
tributes are listed.

The fifth provincial district[a] began at the city of Posideion (which had been founded by Amphilochos son of Amphiareios[b] on the border between the Cilicians and the Syrians) and extended to Egypt, but it excluded Arabia,[c] since that country was exempt from payment of tribute. From this district came 350 talents. All of Phoenicia, Syria (the one called Palestinian), and Cyprus lie within this province. [2] From the sixth provincial district, which is Egypt, the Libyans bordering Egypt, Cyrene, and Barke (since the latter two are assigned to the province of Egypt), came 700 talents plus silver from the sale of fish obtained from Lake Moeris;[a] [3] and also 120,000 measures of grain, which was supplied to the Persian garrison and their mercenaries stationed at the White Fort of Memphis.[a]

3.91.1a   Provinces 5 and 6: Map 3.91.
3.91.1b   Herodotus refers here to the legendary
          hero Amphiareios. According to Statius'
          epic poem the *Thebaid*, Amphiareios was
          one of the Seven Against Thebes, who fled
          from the battle and was swallowed up by a

cleft in the earth made by a thunderbolt
from Zeus. (Fragment 9, Davies, according to the *Oxford Classical Dictionary*)
3.91.1c   Arabia: Map 3.91.
3.91.2a   Lake Moeris: Map 3.91.
3.91.3a   Memphis: Map 3.91.

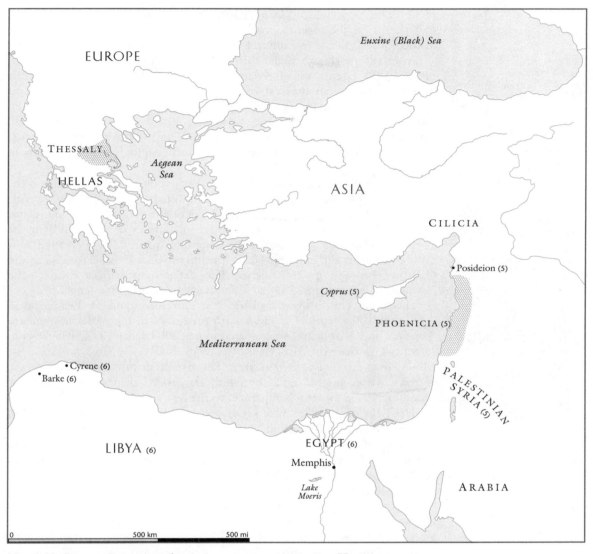

MAP 3.91. PERSIAN PROVINCES 5 AND 6 IN THE ORDER LISTED BY HERODOTUS.

Fifth Province
Posideion
Phoenicia
Palestinian Syria
Cyprus

Sixth Province
Egypt
Libya
Cyrene
Barke

3.92

PERSIAN KINGDOM
The inhabitants of provinces
9–12 and their respective
tributes are listed.

3.93

PERSIAN KINGDOM
The inhabitants of provinces
13–16 and their respective
tributes are listed.

3.94

PERSIAN KINGDOM
The inhabitants of provinces
17–20 and their respective
tributes are listed.

3.95

PERSIAN KINGDOM
Herodotus calculates
the value of Darius'
annual tribute.

3.96

SUSA
How the King
handles bullion.

[4] The Sattagydians, Gandarians, Dadikai, and Aparytai contributed 170 talents, as the seventh provincial district.[a] From the eighth provincial district: Susa, and the remaining territory of the Kissians, came 300 talents.

From the ninth provincial district, Babylonia and the rest of Assyria, came 1,000 talents of silver and 500 eunuch boys. From the tenth province—Ecbatana, the rest of Median territory, the Parikanians,[a] and the Orthokorybantians—came 450 talents. [2] The eleventh provincial district, which comprised the Caspians, Pausikai, Pantimathnoi, and Dareitai together, contributed 200 talents. The twelfth provincial district, which extends from the Baktrians as far as the Aigloi, paid 360 talents in tribute.

From the thirteenth provincial district: the people of the Paktyike and the Armenians with their neighbors as far as the Euxine Sea, came 400 talents. [2] From the fourteenth provincial district—the Sagartians,[a] Sarangians, Thamanaians, Outians, Mykians, and the inhabitants of the islands in the Erythraean Sea (settled there by the King and called "The Deported"[b])— came 600 talents altogether. [3] The fifteenth provincial district, the Sacae and Caspians, brought in 250 talents. The sixteenth provincial district—the Parthians, Chorasmians, Sogdians, and Areians—paid 300 talents.

The seventeenth provincial district, the Parikanians and the Ethiopians of Asia, paid 400 talents. The eighteenth provincial district—the Matienians, Saspeires, and Alarodians—was ordered to pay 200 talents. [2] The nineteenth provincial district—the Moschians, Tibarenoi, Makrones, Mossynoikians, and Mares—was assessed at 300 talents. The twentieth provincial district—the Indians, whose population is by far the largest of all peoples we know— accordingly paid more in comparison to the rest: 360 talents of gold dust.

The Babylonian silver, when measured against the Euboean standard of weight, comes to 9,880 talents. Since gold is calculated to be thirteen times the value of silver, the gold dust is found to be worth 4,680 Euboean talents. [2] When all these are added together as Euboean talents, the sum total of yearly tribute paid to Darius comes to 14,560 talents (I have not counted fractional amounts).[a]

This was the tribute sent to Darius from Asia[a] and a few areas of Libya.[b] As time went on, however, additional tribute came from the islands[c] and Europe[d] as far as Thessaly.[e] [2] The King uses the following method of storing his tribute income. After it has been melted down, it is poured into clay jars, and whenever a vessel is filled up, its clay is removed. Then, whenever he needs money, he strikes off and coins as much as he needs at the time.

3.91.4a Provinces 7–20: Map 3.94.
3.92.1a The location of the Parikainians of the
          tenth province is unknown. Another
          "Parikanians" is listed as in the Seven-
          teenth province (3.94.1) and their possi-
          ble location is shown on Map 3.94.
3.93.2a Sagartians: nomad Persian tribe
          mentioned in 1.125.
3.93.2b Herodotus is using the term for the
          peoples or individuals who were trans-

planted from the western into the eastern
part of the Persian Empire. (Godley)
3.95.2a For more on these conversion formulae,
          see Appendix J, §11–13, 20.
3.96.1a Asia (in this case, not just Asia Minor):
          Map 3.91.
3.96.1b Libya (Africa): Map 3.91.
3.96.1c Islands of the Aegean Sea: Map 3.91.
3.96.1d Europe: Map 3.91.
3.96.1e Thessaly: Map 3.91.

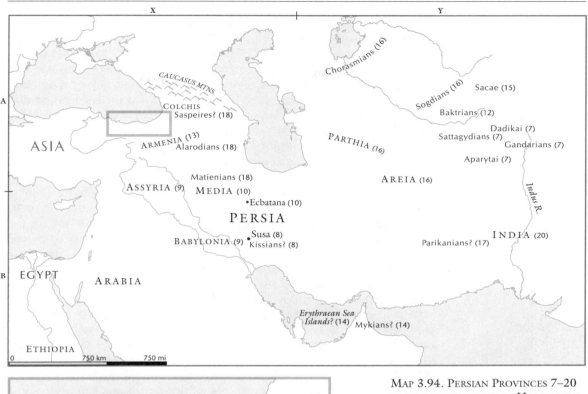

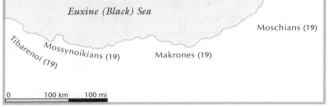

MAP 3.94. PERSIAN PROVINCES 7–20
IN THE ORDER LISTED BY HERODOTUS.

Seventh Province
Sattagydians, AY
Gandarians (Gandaris), AY
Dadikai, AY
Aparytai, AY

Eighth Province
Susa, BX
Kissians, possible location, BX

Ninth Province
Babylonia, BX
Assyria, AX

Tenth Province
Ecbatana, BX
Media, AX
Parikanians, location unknown
Orthokorybantians, location
 unknown

Eleventh Province
Caspians, location unknown
Pausikai, location unknown
Pantimathnoi, location unknown
Dareitai, location unknown

Twelfth Province
Baktrians (Baktrianoi), AY
Aigloi, location unknown

Thirteenth Province
Paktyike near Armenia, location unknown
Armenia, AX

Fourteenth Province
Sagartians, location unknown
Sarangians, location unknown
Thamanaians, location unknown
Outians, location unknown
Mykians, possible location, BY
Erythraean Sea Islands, possible location, BY

Fifteenth Province
Sacae, Eastern Scythians, AY
Sogdiana, AY
Caspians, location unknown

Sixteenth Province
Parthians (Parthia), AY
Chorasmians, AY
Sogdians, AY
Areians (Areia), AY

Seventeenth Province
Parikanians, possible location, BY
Ethiopians of Asia, location unknown

Eighteenth Province
Matienians (Matiane), AX
Saspeires, possible location, AX
Alarodians, AX

Nineteenth Province
Moschians (Moschoi), inset
Tibarenoi, inset
Makrones, inset
Mossynoikians, inset
Mares, location unknown

Twentieth Province
Indians (India), BY

255

3.97
PERSIAN KINGDOM
Herodotus lists those peoples who pay no tribute and who instead regularly bring gifts to the King.

That is the list of provinces and assessment of tribute to each one. One country not included in that list is Persia,[a] because the Persians are exempt from any payment of tribute. [2] There were also others for whom tribute was not assessed, but these instead brought gifts.[a] Among them were the Ethiopians[b] living near Egypt,[c] who had been conquered by Cambyses during his march to the long-lived Ethiopians; and also the residents around holy Nysa,[d] who celebrate festivals to Dionysos. This people and those living near them use the same seed as the Kallantian Indians,[e] but the people living around Nysa live in underground dwellings. [3] Every other year, both these peoples contributed two quarts[a] of unrefined gold, 200 logs of ebony, five Ethiopian boys, and twenty large elephant tusks, and they still do so in my time. [4] The Colchians[a] also agreed to give a gift, as did their neighbors extending all the way to the Caucasus Mountain[c] (for the territory subject to Persia begins at this mountain; the regions beyond the Caucasus toward the north wind still pay no attention at all to the Persians). These peoples sent 100 boys and 100 girls every four years, as they still do today. [5] Finally, the Arabians[a] gave 1,000 talents of frankincense each year, and all these gifts came to the King in addition to the tribute.

3.98
INDIA
How the Indians obtain their gold. There are many Indian peoples with different languages and customs.

The gold dust mentioned earlier which was sent to the king is derived from gold obtained in great quantities by the Indians in a way that I shall soon describe.[a] [2] The area of India lying nearest the rising sun is a tract of sand. Of all the peoples we know and can speak of with certainty, the Indians in Asia dwell farthest to the east and closest to the sunrise. For east of the Indians lies an uninhabitable desert of nothing but sand. [3] There are many nations in India, and they do not all speak the same language. Some of them are nomads; others are not. Some live in the marshland of the river[a] and eat raw fish. They catch fish from reed boats, each one of which is built from a single section of reed. [4] The clothing of these Indians is made from rushes which they cut and gather from the river. They weave the rushes together like a mat, and wear them like a sort of breastplate.

3.99
INDIA
Indian cannibals.

To the east of these Indians lives another group of Indians called Padaioi, who are nomads and who eat raw meat. They are said to observe a custom that when any resident of their village—whether man or woman—becomes ill, that person is killed. If a man becomes sick, his closest male associates kill him, claiming that as his illness consumes him, his flesh is being spoiled. When he denies that he is sick, they will disagree; they will kill him and then feast on his body. [2] In the same way, when a woman becomes ill, she, too, is put to death, but by the women closest to her. If anyone manages to reach

3.97.1a   Persia: Map 3.94, BX.
3.97.2a   Giving a gift acknowledged a sort of feudal superiority, which thereby constituted a claim to protection. The payment of tribute would have put them in the position of subjects; offering a gift enabled them to preserve that of allies. (Blakesley)
3.97.2b   Ethiopia: Map 3.94, BX.
3.97.2c   Egypt: Map 3.94, BX.
3.97.2d   Nysa in Ethiopia, location unknown. See n. 2.146.2a.
3.97.2e   Kallantian Indians: location unknown.
3.97.3a   Herodotus states the volume here as "2 choinikes." See Appendix J, §17, 21.
3.97.4a   Colchis: Map 3.94, AX.
3.97.4c   Caucasus Mountains: Map 3.94. AX.
3.97.5a   Arabia: Map 3.94, BX.
3.98.1a   India: Map 3.94, BY. Herodotus describes how the Indians collect this gold in 3.102–105.
3.98.3a   Indus River: Map 3.94, AY.

old age, they sacrifice him and feast on his body; but not many people live this long, since everyone who falls sick before old age is killed.

Other Indians follow quite different customs. There are some who kill no living creature at all; nor do they sow seeds. It is not their usual practice to acquire and keep houses. They eat grasses and also a plant that grows from the earth without cultivation, whose husk contains a seed within it about the same size as a millet seed. They gather and boil this, husk and all, then consume it. Among these Indians, whoever falls ill goes to a deserted place and lies down there. No one cares whether he is ill or has died.

It is the practice of all these Indians I have described up till now to have intercourse out in the open just like animals; and they all have the same color of skin, which is similar to that of the Ethiopians. [2] The seed they ejaculate into their wives is not white like that of the rest of men, but black like their skin and like the semen of the Ethiopians. These Indians live toward the south, and farther away from the Persians than the others, so that they never became subject to King Darius.

There are other Indians who live around the borders of the city of Kaspatyros and the territory of Paktyike,[a] beyond the other Indians and toward the north. Their manner of life closely resembles that of the Baktrians.[b] These are the most warlike of the Indians, and they are also the ones who go out to gather the gold, traveling to a region that is uninhabitable due to the sand. [2] Now in this desert of sand live huge ants, smaller than dogs but larger than foxes. Some of these ants were captured and brought to the Persian court. The ants in India make their dwellings underground by mounding up the sand, just as ants do in Hellas, and they also look very much the same. But here the mounded sand contains gold,[a] [3] so the Indians set out to collect this sand. Each of them yokes three camels together, placing a female in the middle and a male on either side as one does with trace horses. The Indian rides the female; he has taken great pains to find a female that has given birth as recently as possible, and he drags her away from her young[a] and then yokes her. Their female camels are as swift as horses and much stronger when it comes to carrying heavy burdens.

I shall not describe the general appearance of the camel, since Hellenes already know what this animal looks like.[a] But I shall tell about something that they do not know: that the camel has four thighs and knees on its hind legs, and its genitals protrude through its hind legs and toward the tail.

3.102.1a Kaspatyros and Paktyike, possible locations: Map 3.110.
3.102.1b Baktria: Map 3.110.
3.102.2a For a plausible and ingenius explanation for this apparently fabulous tale of huge ants in India whose nest mounds contain gold, see M. Peissel, *The Ant's Gold* (Harvill Press, London, 1984). Also see M. Peissel, *Geographic Journal* Vol. 150, 1984, p. 145ff., which recounts a tale from a resident of the Indus River valley about marmots (animals like prairie dogs in the United States) whose burrows contained high concentrations of gold dust.

3.102.3a The reason for taking the female away from her recently born young is made clear in 3.105.2.
3.103.1a Herodotus' assumption that Hellenes were familiar with this exotic animal is noteworthy. Possibly, the camels which had accompanied Xerxes' army and which, he says, were captured and distributed as spoils had already become familiar sights around Greece because they were put on view along with other Persian exotica. See Figure 9.81b for a fifth-century Attic representation of a camel.

3.104
INDIA
The sun's heat is stronger earlier in the day in India than elsewhere.

So that is the way the Indians yoke their camels in preparation for their journey. Then they calculate when they should ride out so that their plundering will take place during the hottest time of the day, since the ants then disappear underground because of the intense heat. [2] In this region, the sun is unbearably hot in the morning, not at midday as it normally is elsewhere. It ascends in the sky until the time when the marketplace empties[a] and during that time it blazes far hotter than at midday in Hellas, and it becomes so hot, they say, that the Indians then douse themselves with water. [3] At midday the heat is about the same for Indians as it is for people elsewhere. In the afternoon, as the sun begins to go down in India, it becomes like the morning sun elsewhere, and after this, it grows cooler as it descends until it becomes very cold indeed at sunset.

3.105
INDIA
The Indians gather the gold-bearing sand from the ants and escape on camels.

The Indians ride to the site of the gold, carrying sacks with them, which they fill with sand swiftly so that they can begin their ride back again as quickly as possible. They do this, the Persians say, because the ants smell the men immediately, and once their presence is detected, they will pursue them. They also say that these ants can move faster than anything, so that if the Indians did not get a head start on their return journey while the ants were still rallying for the chase, none of them would ever arrive home safely. [2] The male camels are said to run more slowly than the females, and so when they start to drag on the female, they are turned loose, though not both of them at once. Meanwhile, the female recalls the young she left behind and so does not at all slacken her pace out of weakness. That, according to the Persians, is how the Indians acquire most of their gold; the other gold they obtain is mined from their own territory, but in smaller amounts.

3.106
INDIA
The margins of the inhabited world have the finest resources. India is the most distant land to the east.

Somehow the edges of the inhabited world have been endowed with the best and finest resources, just as Hellas[a] has been endowed with much the finest of temperate climates. [2] As I have just explained, India[a] is situated on the eastern edge of the inhabited world, and here living creatures, whether four-footed animals or winged birds, are far larger than those in other places, except for the horses, which are called Nesaian[b] horses and are smaller than those of Media.[c] In addition, gold is present in immense quantities—some of it mined, some washed down by the river, and some plundered from ants, as I have related. [3] Moreover, there are trees in India which grow wild and produce crops of wool which surpass sheep's wool in beauty.[a] Indians actually wear clothing made from wool harvested from these trees.

3.107
ARABIA
Arabia, the southernmost country, grows unique products.

And again, at the southern edge of the inhabited world lies Arabia,[a] which is the only place on earth where frankincense grows; the other rare crops found there are myrrh, cassia, cinnamon, and *ledanon*.[b] All these, except myrrh, are very difficult for the Arabians to gather. [2] They collect frankincense by burn-

3.104.2a	About midmorning, 10:00–11:00 a.m.
3.106.1a	Hellas: Map 3.110.
3.106.2a	India: Map 3.110.
3.106.2b	In 7.40.2, Herodotus writes that there is a large plain in Media called the Nesaian Plain; it is presumably the place from which these horses came,

but its location is not known.
3.106.2c Media: Map 3.110.
3.106.3a Herodotus calls cotton literally, "wool from wood or trees."
3.107.1a Arabia: Map 3.110.
3.107.1b *Ledanon* (Arabian *ladanon*): rock-rose resin.

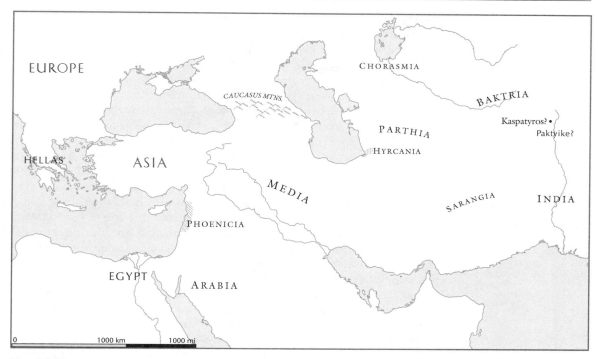

MAP 3.110

ing styrax,[a] which the Phoenicians[b] export to Hellas. It is only by burning this substance that they can gather the frankincense, since great numbers of winged serpents which are small and have variegated markings—the very same serpents that go out to invade Egypt[c]—carefully guard each tree. Only the smoke from burning styrax will drive them away from these trees.

The Arabians say that the entire world would be filled with these snakes if it were not for a certain phenomenon that happens to them, and which, I believe, also happens to vipers. [2] And this phenomenon indeed makes sense: for divine providence in its wisdom created all creatures that are cowardly and that serve as food for others to reproduce in great numbers so as to assure that some would be left despite the constant consumption of them, while it has made sure that those animals which are brutal and aggressive predators reproduce very few offspring. [3] The hare, for example, is hunted by every kind of beast, bird, and man, and so reproduces prolifically. Of all animals, she is the only one that conceives while she is

3.108
Herodotus notes that weak animals are prolific and that the strong ones bear few offspring.

3.107.2a Styrax: also known as storax, an aromatic resin from trees of the genus *Liquidambar*.
3.107.2b Phoenicia: Map 3.110.
3.107.2c Winged serpents of Egypt (Map 3.110): see 2.75.

already pregnant; her womb can contain at the same time young that are furry, bare of fur, just recently formed, and still being conceived. [4] That is the sort of pregnancy the hare has, but the lioness, since she is the strongest and boldest of animals, gives birth to only one offspring in her entire life, for when she gives birth she expels her womb along with her young. This happens because when the lion cub starts to move inside its mother, it lacerates the womb with claws that are sharper than those of any other beast, and as it grows, its scratches penetrate deeper and deeper, so that near the time of birth there is nothing at all of the womb left intact.

3.109
ARABIA
Unusual practices of vipers and winged serpents that limit their procreation.

Likewise, if vipers and the Arabian winged serpents were to live out their natural life spans, humans could not survive at all. What happens is that when they pair up and mount each other, and the male is in the very act of ejaculation, the female grasps hold of him by his neck and clings there, not letting him go until she has eaten clean through it. [2] Thus the male dies, but the female pays a penalty for treating him this way; for the young in her womb exact vengeance for the male by eating through their mother, and thus leave the womb in birth only after completely devouring the womb. [3] Conversely, other kinds of serpents that are not harmful to humans give birth by laying eggs and hatching huge broods of offspring. Now while vipers exist throughout the entire world, winged serpents only seem to be numerous because they are all crowded together in Arabia and nowhere else.

3.110
ARABIA
Arabian method of gathering cassia to make frankincense.

So much for the snakes and how the Arabians obtain their frankincense. They also acquire cassia, and they do it in the following way: before they go out for it, they bind leather hides and skins all over their entire bodies and faces, leaving only their eyes exposed. They cover themselves like this because cassia grows in a shallow lake within and around which dwell winged beasts that look very much like bats. These beasts cry out with a dreadful screeching and are quite hostile and aggressive, so the men must ward off these creatures from their eyes while they gather the cassia.

3.111
ARABIA
The peculiar way the Arabians gather cinnamon.

The way they collect cinnamon is even more fantastic. They cannot say where it comes from and what land produces it originally, except that some of them try to argue from probability that it sprouts in the lands where Dionysos grew up. [2] At any rate, it is said that huge birds carry the stalks, which we have learned from the Phoenicians to call cinnamon, to nests of clay that they have built hanging from steep mountains completely inaccessible to men. [3] But the Arabians have surmounted this problem rather cleverly. They cut up the limbs of dead cattle, donkeys, and other beasts of burden into pieces as large as they can carry, scatter them in the area under the nests, and then move out of the way. The birds swoop down for the limbs of the beasts and take them back to their nests, but the nests cannot bear the weight and so crash to the ground, where the men then collect the cinnamon that comes down along with them. That is how they obtain the cinnamon which eventually reaches other lands.

There is an even more astounding method of gathering ledanon, called *ladanon*[a] by the Arabians. For although it has the most pleasant fragrance itself, it comes from the most foul-smelling source. It is found in the beards of male goats clinging there like glue after the goats have been foraging in the bushes that produce it. This substance is used in many perfumes, but the Arabians most often use it to burn as incense.

So much for the incense and spices of Arabia, except to say that the fragrance emanating from this country is divinely sweet. Also worth marveling at are the two kinds of sheep in Arabia, both of which are found nowhere else. One type has long tails, no less than four and a half feet[a] in length, so that if the sheep were left alone to drag them, they would suffer trauma from the traction of their tails scraping the ground.[b] But all the shepherds know how to employ their carpentry skills to assist the sheep. They build small carts and securely attach the tail of each animal to a cart. The other type of sheep has a broad tail, reaching even one and a half feet[c] in width.

In the region where the sun sets at the end of day lies Ethiopian territory, at the southwest edge of the inhabited world.[a] This land produces much gold, enormous elephants, all kinds of wild trees, ebony, and men who are most tall, handsome, and long-lived.

Those, then, are the peripheral regions of Asia and Libya. I cannot speak with certainty, however, about the marginal regions which lie toward the west, in Europe.[a] But I surely do not believe that there is a river that the barbarians call Eridanos which flows into the sea toward the north wind and, as they say, is the source of our amber. Nor am I certain of the existence of the Cassiterides Islands,[b] from which we get our tin. [2] For one thing, the very name "Eridanos" proves the story wrong, since it is a Greek, not a barbarian, word, made up by some poet. Moreover, despite all my efforts to research the matter, I have been unable to find anyone who could say that he actually saw for himself that a sea exists on the far side of Europe. In any case, the far edges of the world are the source of the tin and amber that come to us.[a]

It is clear that gold exists in by far the greatest quantities to the north of Europe, but I cannot say with certainty how it comes to be there. It is reported that there are one-eyed men called Arimaspians who snatch it away from griffins,[a] [2] but I cannot believe in the existence of one-eyed men who are born that way, and who would still have in all other respects a nature just like that of other humans. In any case, these peripheral regions

3.112	ARABIA Where the Arabians find *ladanon*.
3.113	ARABIA Arabian sheep with strange tails.
3.114	ETHIOPIA Ethiopian products.
3.115	EUROPE Herodotus admits ignorance of western Europe: of the sources there of amber and tin.
3.116	EUROPE Herodotus' theory about outlying lands.

3.112.1a   *Ladanon*: the Arabian word for rock-rose resin.
3.113.1a   Herodotus writes "3 cubits." There were several standard measures for the cubit, but he is probably referring here to one that equaled approximately 1.5 feet. See Appendix J, §4, 5, 19.
3.113.1b   In Greek, there is a pun on the words for "trauma" and "traction."
3.113.1c   Herodotus writes "1 cubit."
3.114.1a   This "Ethiopia" may be a different one from the Ethiopia south of Egypt, although

it, too, is at an edge of the earth. See Appendix D, Herodotean Geography, §4.
3.115.1a   Europe: Map 3.110.
3.115.1b   The Cassiterides Islands are thought to be the British Isles, one of the few sources of tin for the ancient Mediterranean world, which required tin to mix with copper to make bronze.
3.115.2a   See Appendix D, §4.
3.116.1a   A griffin is a fantastic beast with the body of a lion and the beak and wings of an eagle. See Figure 4.152.

which surround and enclose the rest of the earth on all sides quite reasonably contain the very things we value as most beautiful and rare.

In Asia there is a plain enclosed by mountains on all sides, and these mountains have five ravines in them. This plain once belonged to the Chorasmians[a] and lay on the borders of the territory of the Chorasmians, Hyrcanians,[b] Parthians[c], Sarangians,[d] and Thamanaians.[e] But since the Persians took control, it belongs to the King. [2] Out of this surrounding mountain range flows a large river whose name is Aces. At one time, it used to provide water to the regions just mentioned, as it was divided into five channels, each leading to one of the regions through a ravine. But when these people became subject to the Persians, [3] the King blocked the mountain ravines and set up sluice gates at each one. Now the water has no outlet but is enclosed within, and the plain inside the mountain has become a sea, as the river flows in but has no way out. [4] The people who were once accustomed to using this water no longer have it and so suffer great adversity. For while the god does send them rain during the winter, just as everywhere else in the world,[a] they are in constant need of water in the summer as they sow their millet and sesame. [5] And so, whenever they are left with no water, they go with their wives to the Persians and stand at the door of the King, shouting and howling. Then the King instructs those who need water most to open the gates leading to their territory. And when their land is sated with water, these gates are closed again, and others who need it most are instructed to open their gates. I know from what I have heard that the King makes a huge sum of money when he opens a gate, and this is in addition to his tribute. That is how things are there.

Of the seven men who had revolted against the Magus,[a] one of them, Intaphrenes, met his death soon after the revolt, when he committed the following outrageous act. He had entered the palace wishing to consult with the King, and it was the rule that those who had revolted against the Magus had free access to the King without being formally announced unless the King happened to be having intercourse with a woman at that time. [2] And so Intaphrenes, as one of the seven, felt it was all right for him to go in to the King without anyone announcing his entry. But the gatekeeper and the royal messenger did not allow him to pass, telling him that the King at that moment was with a woman. Intaphrenes thought they were lying, however, so drawing his dagger,[a] he cut off their ears and noses and attached them to his horse's bridle, which he tied around their necks before releasing them.

In this state they showed themselves to the King and told him the cause of their suffering. Darius, fearing that the other six had shared in this act by common consent, sent for each one and questioned them individually about

3.117.1a   Chorasmia: Map 3.110.
3.117.1b   Hyrcania: Map 3.110.
3.117.1c   Parthia: Map 3.110.
3.117.1d   Sarangia: location unknown.
3.117.1e   Thamanaians: location of territory unknown.
3.117.4a   Perhaps Herodotus wrote this before visiting Egypt, where, as he describes the

climate, the god does not send rain at all, just a Nile flood in the late summer.
3.118.1a   Herodotus describes the revolt of these seven in 3.70.
3.118.2a   Herodotus uses the Persian word *akinakes*, a dagger or short sword.

their attitudes toward the deed of Intaphrenes and asked them whether they condoned what had been done. [2] When he had ascertained that Intaphrenes had not acted with their approval, he had Intaphrenes arrested along with his children and all his male relatives, as he strongly suspected that Intaphrenes had taken his relatives into a plot to revolt against him. After Darius had imprisoned and condemned them all to death, but while they yet awaited execution, [3] the wife of Intaphrenes began to hang around the doors of the King, weeping and wailing. Her persistence finally persuaded Darius to take pity on her, and he sent a messenger to tell her, "Woman, Darius the King grants that you may save one of your relatives who are imprisoned, whichever one you decide to select out of all of them." [4] She thought about it for a moment and then answered, "If the King is really granting me one life among all of those imprisoned, I choose my brother." [5] Darius was surprised at her reply and he sent this message back to her: "Woman, the King asks: what was your reasoning in passing over your own husband and children to pick out your brother to be the one who survives, since he is certainly more of a stranger to you than your children, and less dear to you than your husband?" [6] And she replied to the King's question: "Sire, I may have another husband and, god willing, other children, if I should lose the ones I have now. But since my mother and father are no longer alive, I could never have another brother. That was the reasoning behind my answer to you." [7] Darius thought this woman had answered very well, and was so delighted by her that he released not only the man she had pleaded for, but also her eldest son. He killed all the others, and that is how one of the seven soon met his death.

While Cambyses was still alive but ill, the following incident occurred. Oroites, a Persian whom Cyrus had appointed as governor of Sardis,[a] was now overcome by an impulse to commit an impious and unholy act. For though Polykrates of Samos had never offended him by word or deed, and in fact had never met him face to face, Oroites was seized by a desire to capture and destroy him. Most people say he did this because [2] one day while Oroites and another Persian named Mitrobates, who governed the provincial district of Daskyleion,[a] were sitting at the doors of the King, the two men began to quarrel over their respective merits. Mitrobates then reproached Oroites, saying: [3] "Do you actually consider yourself a man? You who failed to add the island of Samos[a] to the King's realm, although it lies adjacent to your province and is so very easy to subdue that one of its natives, who now rules it as a tyrant, revolted and took it over with only fifteen hoplites?" [4] Now, some people say that Oroites became so painfully distressed at this harsh criticism that he began to desire revenge, not so much against the man who had made the remark, but against Polykrates, who now became the man whom Oroites sought to destroy in any way possible, since he was the cause of this censure against him.

3.120
517/16?
SARDIS
Oroites, governor of Sardis, is goaded into destroying Polykrates of Samos.

3.120.1a   Sardis: Map 3.134.
3.120.2a   Daskyleion: Map 3.134.

3.120.3a   Samos: Map 3.134.

Others, though they are fewer in number, say that Oroites sent a herald to Samos to make some request or other (exactly what he wanted is not mentioned), and that when the herald arrived, Polykrates happened to be reclining on his banquet couch in the men's dining hall; Anakreon of Teos[a] was there, too. [2] Somehow, whether intentionally or by accident, Polykrates scorned the interests of Oroites, for when the herald came up and spoke to Polykrates, he happened to be facing the other way and he neither turned around nor gave the herald any answer.

Both these stories are told to explain the death of Polykrates, and you may believe whichever one you prefer. In any case, Oroites based himself at Magnesia,[a] which is situated above the River Maeander,[b] and when he learned that Polykrates planned to rule the sea, he sent a Lydian, Myrsos son of Gyges, to Samos with a message; and indeed, [2] Polykrates is the first Hellene we know of who ever attempted to control the sea, except, of course, for Minos of Knossos[a] and anyone who might have ruled the sea before Minos. But in what is told about the human race,[b] Polykrates was the first in this respect; and he had high hopes to rule Ionia[c] and the islands.[d] [3] Well, when Oroites learned that this is what Polykrates intended to accomplish, he sent a message to him saying, "From Oroites to Polykrates: I hear that you are making big plans, but that you lack funds to support your ambitions. If you do as I suggest, you will not only set yourself on the right track, but you will also save me. For I have reports that make it quite clear to me that King Cambyses is planning to kill me. [4] So now I ask you to transport me and my money away fom here; you may keep some of the money for yourself and allow me to keep the rest of it. With this money, you will be able to become ruler of all Hellas,[a] and if you do not believe what I have said about the money, send the man you trust most here, and I shall prove it."

This message delighted Polykrates, and he was quite willing to follow Oroites' advice. His passion for the money was especially intense, for the first thing he did was to send a citizen named Maiandrios son of Maiandrios, who was his secretary, to investigate the matter. This was the same man who, not very long afterward, dedicated the furnishings from Polykrates' dining hall, which are quite spectacular, to the sanctuary of Hera.[a]

[2] When Oroites found out that an inspector was coming, he filled eight chests with stones, except for a small space at the very top brim, on top of which he piled gold, and then tied the chests shut and kept them ready. Maiandrios came, viewed the chests, and then reported back to Polykrates.

3.121.1a Anakreon of Teos: lyric poet (570–485), famous for his songs of love and wine, and active also at the court of the Peisistratids after the death of Polykrates.
3.122.1a Magnesia (on the Maeander): Map 3.134.
3.122.1b Maeander River: Map 3.134.
3.122.2a Knossos, Crete (Creta): Map 3.134. Minos was the legendary king of Crete.
3.122.2b By "the human race," Herodotus means the historical period rather than mythical times.
3.122.2c Ionia: Map 3.134.
3.122.2d The islands: the Cyclades and other islands of the Aegean Sea: Map 3.134.
3.122.4a Hellas: Map 3.134.
3.123.1a The very large temple to Hera on Samos was famous throughout the Greek world.

Polykrates then prepared to visit Magnesia himself, although oracles as well as his friends and family tried repeatedly to dissuade him from doing so. His daughter even had a vision in her sleep in which she saw her father suspended in the air and being bathed by Zeus and anointed by Helios.[a] [2] After this dream she tried every way she could think of to prevent Polykrates from going to Oroites; and in particular, while he was boarding his pente-conter,[a] she uttered ominous words to him. In reply, he threatened that if he did return home safely, she would remain an unmarried virgin for a long time, but her response to this was to pray that his threat would be fulfilled, for she preferred to be a virgin for a very long time than to lose her father.

Polykrates disregarded all advice, however, and sailed to Oroites, bring-ing along with him many companions, including Democedes son of Kalliphon, who originally came from Croton;[a] he was a physician whose skill surpassed all other physicians practicing this art in his time. [2] After Polykrates arrived in Magnesia, he was brutally killed, which neither he nor his ambitions deserved. For with the exception of the tyrants of Syracuse, not one of the other Greek tyrants can compare with Polykrates in terms of magnificence. [3] But Oroites killed him in a way too disgusting to relate and hung his body from a stake. Of Polykrates' followers, he let all who were Samian citizens go, bidding them to be thankful to him for their free-dom; but the foreigners and those who had been born slaves were kept there and became slaves of Oroites. [4] As Polykrates hung suspended, he completely fulfilled his daughter's vision, for he was bathed by Zeus when it rained, and anointed by Helios (the Sun) as he released the moisture from his body. Thus all the prosperity and fortune of Polykrates came to an end, just as Amasis king of Egypt had prophesied.[a]

Not long afterward, retribution for Polykrates of Samos came to Oroites. After the death of Cambyses, and during the reign of the Magi, Oroites remained in Sardis and offered no help at all to the Persians as the Medes were usurping their rule. [2] Instead, he took advantage of the disorder then prevailing to kill Mitrobates, the governor of Daskyleion[a]—the man who had reproached him on the subject of Polykrates—and also Mitrobates' son Kran-aspes, both of whom were men of high distinction among the Persians. For example, when a courier came to Oroites from Darius, and Oroites found the message displeasing, he ordered his men to ambush the courier on his return, and he had them kill him and remove all traces of both his body and his horse.

But after Darius had secured his rule, he conceived the desire to punish Oroites for all his offenses, especially for the sake of Mitrobates and his son.

3.124
517/16?
SAMOS
Polykrates decides to sail to Oroites, against the advice of his friends, diviners, and daughter.

3.125
517/16?
MAGNESIA
Polykrates sails to Magnesia, where the Persian Oroites kills him.

3.126
?
SARDIS?
Oroites offers no help to the Persians against the Magi, and even kills a messenger from Darius.

3.127
516?
SUSA
Darius asks for a Persian volunteer to kill or capture Oroites.

3.124.1a   Significant dreams were thought to be communications from the gods warning of threats and dangers, advising on cures for illness, imposing policies, or answering pressing questions, but in 7.16.β.2 Herod-otus has Artabanos give a surprisingly rational explanation for them when he advises Xerxes and says that "most of the visions visiting our dreams tend to be what   one is thinking about during the day."

3.124.2a   Penteconters: ships powered by 50 oars; one line of 25 rowers on each side of the vessel. See Appendix S, Trireme Warfare, §4, 12.

3.125.1a   Croton: Map 3.134, locator.

3.125.4a   Amasis made this prediction in 3.43, after the episode of the return of the ring.

3.126.2a   Daskyleion: Map 3.134.

But he did not think it a good idea to directly confront him by sending an army against him, since Darius himself had only recently begun to rule and the state of affairs was still quite unsettled. Further, he learned that Oroites possessed great military and political strength, 1,000 Persians and a province that included Phrygia, Lydia, and Ionia.[a] [2] Instead, Darius summoned the most notable Persians and said to them, "Persians, which one of you could promise to accomplish what I want by cunning rather than violence or turmoil? An act of shrewdness, not force, is needed here. [3] Which of you could either bring Oroites to me alive, or simply kill him? He has never helped Persia, but to the contrary has done us great harm. For one thing, he annihilated two of our number, Mitrobates and his son; and he further displayed intolerable arrogance by killing those whom I sent to summon him to present himself to me. So before he can commit any worse crimes against Persia, we must see to it that death overtakes him."

3.128
516?
SARDIS
Bagaios draws the lot and uses letters from Darius to persuade Oroites' Persian guards to kill him, which they do.

That was Darius' request, and thirty of the men there took up his challenge, each one of them ready and willing to carry out his order. When they began to contend with one another to obtain the honor, Darius intervened and told them to draw lots. This they did, and the one man who won the job was Bagaios son of Artontes. [2] Having acquired his position by lot, he set to work in this way: he took many scrolls and, after writing various things on them, sealed them with the stamp of Darius and went off to Sardis, taking the scrolls along with him. [3] When he had arrived and gained an audience with Oroites, he opened the scrolls one by one and gave each to the royal secretary to read aloud (for all Persian governors have royal secretaries). He did this as a trial of the bodyguards, to test how they might respond to a revolt against Oroites. [4] When he observed how they regarded the scrolls with great respect and awe, and what was written on them with even more reverence, he handed over another, which contained these words: "Persians, King Darius forbids you to serve as bodyguards of Oroites." Upon hearing this, they relaxed their guard of Oroites and let down their spears. [5] When Bagaios saw that they had been won over by this scroll, he grew more confident and gave over to the secretary the very last of the scrolls, on which was written, "King Darius instructs the Persians in Sardis to kill Oroites." Hearing this, the bodyguards at once drew their daggers[a] and killed him. And that is how retribution for Polykrates of Samos came to Oroites.

3.129
SUSA
Democedes of Croton is brought in chains to cure the injured ankle of Darius.

The property of Oroites was confiscated and taken to Susa.[a] Not long afterward, King Darius was out hunting and sprained his foot as he dismounted from his horse. [2] Apparently, the sprain was quite severe, for the bone was dislocated from its socket. It was his custom to always keep the Egyptian[a] physicians, who were thought to be the best in the art of medicine, close at hand, so he consulted them first. But they employed violent

---

3.127.1a Phrygia (Hellespontine), Lydia, and Ionia seem to correspond to the first three Persian provinces (listed at 3.90) but were probably not yet divided this way at the time. See Map 3.90.

3.128.5a Herodotus uses the Persian word *akinakes*, a dagger or short sword.
3.129.1a Susa: Map 3.134, locator.
3.129.2a Egypt: Map 3.134, locator.

remedies to treat it, and by twisting his foot they caused even more damage. [3] For seven days and seven nights Darius was kept awake by the constant pain. On the eighth day, as his condition continued to deteriorate, someone who had been in Sardis[a] earlier and had heard of the skill of Democedes of Croton told Darius about him, so the King ordered that Democedes be brought to him as quickly as possible. He was found among the slaves of Oroites in a state of utter neglect, and he was brought out into the open still dragging his chains and dressed in rags, and presented to the King.

As he stood there, Darius asked him if he knew the art of medicine, but Democedes tried to deny that he did, fearing that if he revealed himself as a physician, he could forget about ever seeing Hellas again. [2] But it was obvious to Darius that Democedes knew not only the art of medicine, but the art of concealment as well, so he ordered the men who had brought him there to fetch whips and instruments of torture. At that point Democedes began to reveal more about himself. He said that his knowledge was not exactly proficient, but that he had obtained a trifling amount of skill through his association with a physician. [3] Finally he yielded to Darius' wishes and employed Greek remedies, following vigorous treatments with gentle ones,[a] and he made sure that Darius got some sleep, so that in a short time, although Darius had earlier given up hope that he could ever have a normal foot again, he restored him to health. [4] In return, Darius gave him a present of two pairs of golden chains, which prompted Democedes to ask Darius if what he really meant by this was to dispense a double punishment to him for bringing him back to health. Delighted by this little joke, Darius sent him off to his wives, escorted by the eunuchs; and when the eunuchs informed the women that this was the man who gave life back to the King, [5] each woman dipped a bowl into a chest of gold and presented it to Democedes. Indeed, they gave him such an extravagant amount that one of the servants, whose name was Skiton, collected an enormous sum of gold just by picking up the staters[a] that fell from the bowls as he followed behind.

Democedes, who was originally from Croton, came to the court of Polykrates in the following way: his father in Croton continually irritated him by his fierce temper, and when Democedes could tolerate him no longer, he left home and went to Aegina.[a] Here he settled down, and in his first year he surpassed the other physicians there, even though he lacked all of the equipment and instruments used in the art of medicine. [2] In the second year, the Aeginetans hired him at state expense and paid him one talent.[a] The third year, the Athenians hired him for 100 minas, and in the fourth year, Polykrates hired him for two talents.[b] That is how he came to Samos,[c] and it is largely because of him that physicians from Croton became highly esteemed. [3] Indeed, during this time, physicians of Croton were said to be the best

3.130
SUSA
Democedes cures the King and receives riches in return.

3.131
How Democedes came to the court.

3.129.3a Sardis: Map 3.134.
3.130.3a It is unclear whether the "vigorous treatments" are those of the Egyptians or his own.
3.130.5a These staters are gold coins. See Appendix J, §14.
3.131.1a Aegina: Map 3.134.
3.131.2a The Aeginetan talent = about 82 Attic *minas* (60 of which composed the Attic talent). (Godley) See Appendix J, §11–13, 20.
3.131.2b Polykrates' offer of two talents was worth 120 minas.
3.131.2c Samos: Map 3.134.

throughout Hellas,[a] while the Cyreneaeans[b] were second best, just as the Argives[c] were reputed to be the best musicians in this period.

3.132
SUSA
Democedes becomes an influential man at the court but is not allowed to return to Greece.

So after healing Darius completely, Democedes had the largest house in Susa and became a regular dinner guest of the King. And he lacked for nothing except permission to return to Hellas. [2] When the Egyptian physicians who had previously tried to treat the King were about to be impaled because they had proved to be inferior to a Hellene, Democedes appealed to the King on their behalf and saved them. He also rescued a prophet of Elis[a] who had followed Polykrates to Sardis and was being neglected among the captive slaves. So Democedes really did have very great influence with the King.

3.133
SUSA
Atossa calls on Democedes to cure her.

Soon after this, Atossa, the daughter of Cyrus and one of the wives of Darius, developed a growth on her breast, which then burst and spread. While it was smaller, she had concealed it out of shame and told no one about it, but now that it had grown much worse, she sent for Democedes and showed it to him. [2] He told her he would cure her, provided that she swear to return the favor by doing whatever he asked, which, he assured her, would be nothing that could compromise her modesty.

3.134
SUSA
Honoring her pledge to Democedes, Atossa goads Darius into attacking Greece, taking Democedes as a counselor. Darius decides to first send spies to Greece.

So he restored Atossa to health and instructed her about what it was that he wanted her to do. Atossa then went to bed with Darius, and as she was lying with him, she presented this proposal to him: "Sire, although you possess such great power, you are doing nothing to acquire either new nations or additional power for Persia. [2] It is reasonable to expect that a man who is young and the master of great wealth will display his power openly so that the Persians will know they are being ruled by a real man. There are actually two reasons why you should do this: not only so that the Persians realize their leader is a man, but also to keep them so occupied in war that they have no leisure to conspire against you. [3] For now is the time, while you are young, that you can achieve something since, as the body grows, so does the mind, but as it ages, the mind ages with it, too, and thus loses its edge." [4] Of course, in telling Darius all this, she was following Democedes' instructions. Darius responded, "My wife, I intend to do exactly what you have said, for I have already formed a plan to build a bridge from this continent to the other one[a] and to conduct a military campaign against the Scythians.[b] This will in fact be carried out within a short time." [5] Atossa then said, "Let the Scythians wait a while; they will still be there whenever you want to attack them. In my opinion, you should lead an army first against Hellas. For I have heard accounts of that land and have set my heart on obtaining Laconian[a] women to wait on me as servants, and I would also like to have Argive, Athenian, and Corinthian[b] women, too. Moreover,

3.131.3a Hellas: Map 3.134.
3.131.3b Cyrene: Map 3.134, locator.
3.131.3c Argos: Map 3.134.
3.132.2a Elis: Map 3.134.
3.134.4a The other continent is Europe: Map 3.134, locator.
3.134.4b Scythia: Map 3.134, locator.
3.134.5a Laconia: Map 3.134. Laconian women

here mean Spartan women. Herodotus uses the names Spartans and Laconians interchangeably. "Spartans," however, often refers specifically to citizens of the state of Sparta, whereas any inhabitant of the territory of Laconia is a Laconian. See Appendix B, §5, 7, and n. B.7a.

3.134.5b Corinth: Map 3.134.

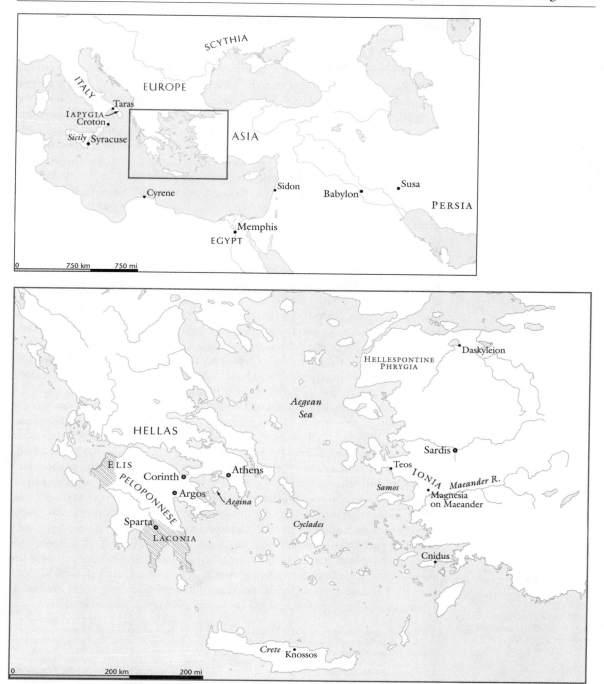

MAP 3.134

you have a man who is perfectly suited to act as your guide and to inform you of every detail about Hellas—the same man who healed your foot." [6] "My wife," Darius now replied, "since you prefer that we first make an attempt on Hellas, I think the better course would be to begin by sending some Persians there to spy out the place for me, along with the man you mentioned, so that they can see and learn everything about the Hellenes for us, and after I have become fully informed, I shall go against them myself." That is what he told her, and it was no sooner said than done.[a]

3.135
SUSA
Darius organizes the reconnaissance and sends Democedes with others to the coast.

As soon as day dawned, he summoned fifteen eminent Persians and ordered them to accompany Democedes on a journey along the coast of Hellas, and he instructed them specifically to make sure by all means that Democedes did not escape and to bring him back. [2] Next, he summoned Democedes himself and requested that he act as guide to the Persians, show them all of Hellas, and then return to Susa.[a] And he ordered Democedes to take along with him all of his moveable property, which he could give to his father and brothers, explaining that he would replace them with other items, many times over. In addition to the gifts, he told him, he would also contribute a merchant ship and fill it with all sorts of valuable goods to sail along with him. [3] I believe that Darius made this promise without guile, but Democedes feared that the King was trying to test him and so was reluctant to accept everything that was being offered. He said he would leave his own property behind where it was, so that he could have it when he returned, but he would accept the merchant ship that Darius had promised for his brothers. After Darius had given him the same instructions that he had given to the Persians, he sent them off to the sea.

3.136
TARAS
Democedes escapes the Persian escort and returns to Croton.

They went down to the coast of Phoenicia, to the city of Sidon,[a] where they immediately manned two triremes and filled a large Phoenician merchant ship[b] with all sorts of good things. When their preparations were complete, they sailed for Hellas, where they put in along the coast, made observations, and recorded them. When they had observed the greater part of Hellas and its most notable sites, they sailed to Italy and went ashore at Taras.[c] [2] There, out of kindness for Democedes, Aristophilides, the king of the Tarantines, removed the steering oars from the Median[a] ships and placed the Persians in confinement with the excuse that they were spies. While they endured this treatment, Democedes went off to Croton.[b] And it was not until after he had arrived in his home town that Aristophilides released the Persians and gave back the steering oars that he had taken from their ships.

3.137
CROTON
The Persians attempt but fail to recapture Democedes and leave without him.

The Persians then sailed in pursuit of Democedes and soon arrived at Croton, where they found him in the marketplace and seized him. [2]

3.134.6a   Despite this conversation and the reconnaissance expedition which followed it, Darius attacked Scythia first, in 513 (4.1ff.), many years before his first assault on Greece in 492 (6.43–45).
3.135.2a   Susa: Map 3.134, locator.
3.136.1a   Sidon: Map 3.134, locator.
3.136.1b   Herodotus actually calls this a round boat,

because merchant ships were often characterized as "round" to distinguish them from warships, which were called "long boats."
3.136.1c   Taras: Map 3.134, locator.
3.136.2a   Median ships: this is another example of the Greek practice of using the names Persian and Mede interchangeably.
3.136.2b   Croton: Map 3.134, locator.

Some of the Crotonians feared the power of Persia and were ready to let the Persians take him, but others struggled to hold him there and in turn began to strike the Persians with sticks. When this happened, the Persians made this speech: "Men of Croton, consider what you are doing: you are trying to help a man who is running away from the King. [3] How do you think King Darius will like being the object of such an outrageous offense? If you repulse us, there can be no good outcome for you. What city will we attack first? And what city will we enslave first?" [4] Their speech, however, did not persuade the Crotonians, so the Persians had to let Democedes go free and also to leave behind the merchant ship they had brought along. And so, without him, they sailed back toward Asia,[a] since they did not seek to learn more about Hellas lacking their guide. [5] As they were sailing out, however, Democedes told them to tell Darius that he had made arrangements to marry the daughter of Milon, for the name of Milon the wrestler meant a great deal to the King, and the reason is, I suppose, that Democedes had spent a large sum of money and was eager for this marriage to show Darius that he was highly esteemed in his own land, too.

After setting out from Croton, the Persians were shipwrecked on the coast of Iapygia[a] and enslaved there, but a Tarantine exile named Gillos rescued them and brought them back to King Darius. Darius was prepared to give Gillos anything he wanted as a reward for this deed. [2] Gillos related the story of his misfortune and asked to be returned from exile to Taras. But he did not wish to cause trouble for Hellas by having a huge expedition sail to Italy[a] on his account, so he said that the Cnidians[b] alone would suffice to take him back, thinking that the Cnidians, who were friends and allies of the Tarantines, could best accomplish his return. [3] Darius kept his promise and carried out his part of the plan by sending a messenger to Cnidus with orders for the Cnidians to take Gillos back to Taras. The Cnidians obeyed Darius but could not make the Tarantines comply and had no power to use force against them. [4] So that is what happened, and these were the first Persians to come from Asia to Hellas, serving as spies for the reasons I have related.

3.138
IAPYGIA
Shipwrecked and enslaved in Iapygia, the Persians are rescued by Gillos, a Tarantine exile.

After this, King Darius seized Samos.[a] This was the first of the cities he conquered, Greek or barbarian, and this was the reason why he captured it. At the time that Cambyses son of Cyrus was leading his army in Egypt,[b] many Hellenes came to Egypt—some probably for trade, others to fight in the war, and others merely to see the sights of this country for themselves. Among the latter was Syloson son of Aiakes, who was the brother of Polykrates and who was now in exile from Samos. [2] Syloson met with a stroke of good fortune in Egypt. One day he put on a red cloak and went to the marketplace in Memphis,[a] where Darius happened to see him. At that time, Darius served as a bodyguard of Cambyses and was not yet a person

3.139
515
EGYPT
Darius conquers Samos. The story of Darius and the red cloak of Syloson.

3.137.4a Asia: Map 3.134, locator.
3.138.1a Iapygia: Map 3.134, locator.
3.138.2a Italy: Map 3.134, locator.
3.138.2b Cnidus: Map 3.134.

3.139.1a Samos: Map 3.134.
3.139.1b Egypt: Map 3.134, locator.
3.139.2a Memphis: Map 3.134, locator.

of any great importance, but he was greatly moved by a desire to have the cloak, so he approached Syloson and offered to buy it. [3] Syloson, who could see how passionately Darius desired the cloak, and inspired by some divine fortune, replied: "I shall not sell this cloak at any price, but if you absolutely must have it, I shall give it to you." Darius gladly accepted his decision and accepted the garment, while Syloson recognized that his own naïve generosity had cost him his cloak.

3.140
SUSA
Syloson asks Darius to deliver Samos to him to rule.

As time passed, Cambyses died; the Seven revolted against the Magi, and of the Seven, Darius obtained the kingship.[a] When Syloson learned that the kingship had now come to the very man who had asked for his cloak and had received it from him as a gift, he journeyed to Susa[b] and sat down before the doors of the King, declaring himself to be a benefactor of Darius. [2] Upon hearing this, the gatekeeper reported it to the King, who said in surprise, "Well, who is this Greek benefactor to whom I am supposedly indebted? I have just recently begun to rule and hardly any Hellenes have ever journeyed all the way to our court, and I know of nothing that could be considered an obligation to any of them. Nevertheless, do admit him, so that I may see what he means by this statement." [3] The gatekeeper brought Syloson in, and as he stood before the King, the interpreters asked him who he was and what he had done to justify his claim to be a benefactor of the King. Syloson then told the whole story of the red cloak and how he was the man who had given it to the king. [4] To this, Darius responded, "Most noble of men, you are the one man who gave me something when I had no power, and even though it was but a trifle, it was a favor equal to someone giving me a gift of great value now. In return, I offer you countless sums of gold and silver, so that you will never regret your kindness to Darius son of Hystaspes." [5] Syloson replied, "Sire, give me neither gold nor silver, but instead restore my country Samos to me, for ever since my brother Polykrates died at the hands of Oroites, it has been the possession of our slave. So this is what I request from you, and that you accomplish it without murder or enslavement."

3.141
515
SAMOS
Darius sends an army.

Upon hearing this request, Darius sent off an army commanded by Otanes, one of the Seven, with instructions to carry out precisely whatever Syloson requested. So Otanes went down to the sea and embarked his troops.

3.142
516?
SAMOS
Maiandrios, delegate of Polykrates, tries to return the rule of Samos to its citizens but is criticized as lowborn.

The man who at that time controlled Samos was Maiandrios son of Maiandrios, who had earlier been delegated by Polykrates to rule it in trust for him in his absence. And although Maiandrios wanted to show himself to be the most just of men, his wish was not fulfilled. [2] The first thing he did after the death of Polykrates was announced was to dedicate an altar to Zeus the Liberator, and he marked off the boundaries of its precinct, which

3.140.1a　Herodotus tells the story of the revolt of the Seven and how Darius obtained the kingship in 3.70–88.
3.140.1b　Susa: Map 3.134, locator.

3.140.5a　This "slave" was Maiandros son of Maiandros, secretary to Polykrates who was deceived by Oroites two years earlier. See 3.123.

still exists at the entrance to the city today. Having completed this project, he next called an assembly of everyone in town and said to them, [3] "As you already know, I have been entrusted with the scepter and all the power of Polykrates, and by virtue of that delegation I am granted the authority to rule over you now. However, to the best of my ability, I shall not do anything to anyone that I would censure my neighbor for doing. I was not pleased to see Polykrates lording it over his equals, nor would I like anyone else to behave in that manner. So now that Polykrates has fulfilled his destiny, I am placing the government in the hands of the public, and I proclaim that equality under the law[a] is now yours. [4] All I ask for myself is the privilege to take six talents[a] from the estate of Polykrates and to assume the priesthood of Zeus the Liberator, since it is I who dedicated his sanctuary and bestowed on you your liberty." [5] After this proclamation to the Samians, one of them stood up and said, "Of course you are not at all worthy to rule over us; you were baseborn to begin with, and now you are a scoundrel to boot! Instead of what you propose, you must render an account of the money you have already had under your control."

The man who said this, whose name was Telesarchos, was highly esteemed among the townspeople, and his statement led Maiandrios to realize that if he relinquished power, someone else would soon make himself tyrant. So he decided not to give up power but instead withdrew to the acropolis, from which he then sent for the citizens one by one, on the pretext of rendering to them an account of the money, but really in order to have them arrested and imprisoned. [2] After they had been incarcerated, Maiandrios fell ill, and his brother Lycaretos, who expected that Maiandrios would die, killed all the prisoners in order to secure his power in Samos with less resistance. And so it seems the Samians did not want to be free.

Therefore, when the Persians who were bringing back Syloson arrived in Samos, no one raised a hand against them. Indeed, partisans of Maiandrios and Maiandrios himself said they were ready to leave the island under a truce. Otanes agreed to such a truce, and as he began to formalize it with libations, the Persians of highest rank there had chairs set up and sat upon them facing the acropolis.

Now Maiandrios the tyrant had a somewhat crazy brother whose name was Charilaos; he had committed some transgression or other, for which reason he was then being confined in a dungeon. And now, as he was creeping through his dungeon, he overheard what was going on, and when he saw the Persians sitting there peacefully, he shouted out that he would like to have a talk with Maiandrios. [2] Maiandrios heard this and ordered that he be released and brought to him. As soon as Charilaos was taken to him,

3.143
516?
SAMOS
Maiandrios changes his mind and imprisons his enemies.

3.144
515?
SAMOS
The Persians arrive, and Maiandrios offers to leave Samos.

3.145
515?
SAMOS
Charilaos reviles his brother Maiandrios and offers to resist the Persians.

3.142.3a Herodotus uses the Greek word *isonomia* here, "equality under the law." See 3.80.6 and n. 3.80.6a for more on the meanings of this word.
3.142.4a Six talents would have been a large fortune

for a private individual. It was worth 36,000 drachmas when something close to one drachma was a day's wages for a skilled laborer. See Appendix J, §10–16, 20.

he attempted to persuade Maiandrios to attack the Persians, reviling him with insults such as: "You, the most despicable of all men, how can you be so unjust to me, your own brother, and think it right to imprison me in a dungeon when I have done nothing to deserve it, but you merely look on as the Persians are casting you out and rendering you homeless. You don't have the nerve to punish them, when they would be so easy to subdue. [3] Well, if you are afraid of them, give me your mercenaries and I shall exact vengeance on them for having come here. As for you, I am ready and willing to send you away from this island."

3.146
515?
SAMOS
Maiandrios escapes while Charilaos attacks the Persians. They suffer heavy initial losses but rally and besiege Charilaos in the acropolis.

That was Charilaos' proposal, and Maiandrios accepted it. I suppose he did this not because he had reached such a state of idiocy that he could believe his own forces might prevail over those of the King, but rather out of spite against Syloson because he was unwilling to allow Syloson to recover the city intact and without any effort on his part. [2] By provoking the Persians, he hoped to damage Samos as much as possible before relinquishing it, knowing full well that if the Persians suffered harm there, they would feel bitter toward the Samians. He did this knowing also that he could safely escape from the island whenever he chose to leave, since he had earlier built a hidden tunnel that led from the acropolis to the sea.[a] [3] So Maiandrios sailed away from Samos, and Charilaos armed all the mercenaries, opened up the gates, and let them loose on the Persians, who, believing that they had secured an agreement of total compliance, expected nothing like this to happen. But the mercenaries fell upon the most notable Persians who were sitting there and proceeded to kill them. [4] As they were doing this, the rest of the Persian army ran to their aid, and the mercenaries were then pushed back and confined on the acropolis.

3.147
515?
SAMOS
The angry Persians disobey Darius and kill all the Samians they take.

When the general Otanes saw that the Persians had suffered severe losses, he forgot all about the instructions Darius had given him as he sent him off, namely, not to kill any Samian nor to enslave anyone, but to give back the island without inflicting any harm. Instead, he gave his troops the order to kill every man and child alike in Samos. [2] So while some of the troops besieged the acropolis, the others killed everyone in their path, regardless of whether they found them in a sanctuary or not.

3.148
515?
SPARTA
Maiandrios sails to Sparta and uses his wealth to try to bribe King Kleomenes, who, frightened that he would bribe someone, has the ephors expel him from Sparta.

Maiandrios, after escaping from Samos, sailed to Lacedaemon.[a] He had taken what he could when he left, and when he got there, he set out his silver and gold cups and had his servants polish them while he went out to engage in conversation with Kleomenes[b] son of Anaxandridas, who was king of Sparta, and to bring him to his house. When Kleomenes looked at the cups, he was struck with wonder and amazement. Maiandrios would then tell him to take for himself as many of them as he wanted. [2] After Maiandrios had said this two or three times, Kleomenes proved himself to

3.146.2a   For the "real" tunnel at Samos, see 3.60.
3.148.1a   Lacedaemon (Sparta): Map 3.134.
3.148.1b   For a brief discussion on the career and

the policies of Kleomenes, see Appendix B, §21–24.

be the most just of men, in that he refused to take what Maiandrios was trying to give away to him. But he realized that Maiandrios would find a way to take revenge on him by offering the gifts to others in the community; so he went to the ephors and said that it would be better for Sparta if the Samian visitor were made to leave the Peloponnese[a] so that he could not persuade him or any other Spartan to become corrupt.

The ephors complied and proclaimed the banishment of Maiandrios. As for Samos, the Persians swept it clean as with a net[a] and then handed it over to Syloson both ruined and devoid of inhabitants. Later, however, Otanes the general helped to resettle the island because of a dream he had and a disease which attacked his genitals.

After the navy sailed off to Samos,[a] the Babylonians[b] revolted. They had prepared for this rebellion well in advance, for during the entire period of disorder when the Magus ruled and the Seven revolted, they were making preparations for a siege, and somehow no one noticed them doing it. [2] When they did revolt openly, each man set aside his mother and one woman he selected from his household to prepare his food. These women were saved; all the other women were brought together and strangled in order to prevent them from consuming the supply of food.

When Darius learned about the revolt, he collected his entire army and launched a campaign against the Babylonians. When he arrived there, he laid siege to the city, but the Babylonians were not at all worried. They climbed up to the parapets and danced there, shouting. [2] One of them, indeed, was heard to proclaim, "Why do you sit there, Persians, instead of going away? For you will not conquer us until mules give birth." Of course, he never expected that a mule would give birth.

A year and seven months passed, and Darius became quite distressed when he found that his entire army could not manage to take Babylon, although he had tried every clever scheme and maneuver he could think of. But even after attempting many stratagems, including the one that Cyrus had used successfully against Babylon,[a] he still could not capture the city. The Babylonians maintained the highest state of alert, and he simply could not overpower them.

Then, in the twentieth month, Zopyros, the son of the Megabyzos who was one of the seven slayers of the Magus, was confronted by a strange portent: one of his supply mules gave birth. When this was reported to

3.149
515?
SAMOS
A deserted Samos is given to Syloson.

3.150
522–521
BABYLON
The Babylonians revolt against Darius.

3.151
522–521
BABYLON
Darius besieges Babylon.

3.152
522–521
BABYLON
The Babylonians hold out nineteen months.

3.153
522–521
BABYLON
A mule of Zopyros gives birth.

3.148.2a Peloponnese: Map 3.134. This anecdote is thought to reflect a visit that took place in 517 by Maiandrios to Sparta to request Spartan assistance against the Persians before their attack, not afterward; his request was refused by Kleomenes and the ephors.

3.149.1a The phrase translated as "swept it clean as with a net . . . ruined and devoid of inhabitants" is explained at 6.31. The Persians would supposedly form a line holding hands and march over the land, catching

everyone as with a fishing dragnet.
3.150.1a Samos: Map 3.134.
3.150.1b Babylon: Map 3.134, locator. According to the course of Herodotus' narrative, the revolt would seem to have taken place some considerable time after Darius' accession (531). But the Behistun inscription apparently makes it one of the earliest events of his reign. See Appendix M, §2 and n. M.2a.
3.152.1a For Cyrus' successful stratagem, see 1.191.

Zopyros, he went in disbelief to see the foal for himself. He forbade those who had also seen it to tell anyone else about it. Then, carefully considering the import of this event, [2] he recalled that at the beginning of the siege, a Babylonian had declared that when mules gave birth, the wall would be taken. In light of that statement, Zopyros began to think that Babylon could now be taken, because clearly it was a god who had motivated both that man in saying what he did and who had caused his own mule to give birth.

3.154
522–521
BABYLON
Zopyros mutilates himself to fool the Babylonians.

Convinced that Babylon was fated to be conquered now, Zopyros went to Darius and asked him whether he considered the capture of Babylon to be a matter of crucial importance. Learning that this goal was indeed highly important, he began to think of some way that he might be the one to capture it and to perform this feat by himself alone, for among the Persians such noble deeds are highly honored as a means to elevation in rank to greatness. [2] Yet he could think of no way by which he would be able to subdue the city except by mutilating himself and going over to the Babylonians as a deserter. Thereupon, treating it as a trivial matter, he proceeded to mutilate himself irreversibly; he cut off his own nose and ears as well as tufts of his hair, whipped himself, and then went to Darius.

3.155
522–521
BABYLON
Zopyros describes his stratagem to Darius.

When Darius saw his most eminent man so mutilated, he was horrified. He leapt up from his chair with a cry and asked who in the world had so mutilated him and what might he have done to provoke it. [2] Zopyros answered, "The man you ask about does not exist; only you have power great enough to do this to me. However, no one other than I myself has actually committed this deed, because I thought it intolerable to watch Assyrians mocking Persians." [3] Darius replied, "You are a most outrageous fool, to label the most shameful deed with the fairest name and claim that you have done this irreparable damage to yourself because of our enemies under siege! You must be an idiot! How can you expect that the enemy will submit to us any sooner because you are now mutilated? How could you have harmed yourself like this unless you have completely taken leave of your senses?" [4] Zopyros replied, "If I had consulted with you about what I intended to do, you would have denied me permission to do it. As it is, I have done it to myself and shall bear the burden of it. Now, unless you fall short on your part, we are going to take Babylon. I shall go as I am to the wall posing as a deserter and claim that I have suffered this abuse at your hands. I think my condition will convince them that what I say is true, and that they will then give me command of an army.

[5] "Your role will be to wait until I have entered the city; then, on the tenth day after that, you should select from your army the least effective

troops, whose loss will mean little, and post 1,000 of them at the portal called the Gates of Semiramis. Next, on the seventh day after that, station 2,000 more of these selected troops for me at the portal called the Gates of the Ninevites. Then wait twenty more days and leave 4,000 troops standing at the portal called the Gates of the Chaldaeans. Do not allow these last nor any of the earlier troops to have any means of defense except for hand knives, but let them at least carry those. [6] After the twentieth day, immediately order the rest of the army to surround the wall, placing the Persians at the portals called the Gates of Belos and the Gates of Kissia. I ask you to do all this because I think that once I have performed impressive achievements for the Babylonians, they will entrust everything else to me, including the command of the gates; and then I and the Persians will see to what must be done next."

Upon concluding his instructions, he went toward the gates, turning from side to side in a shifty manner just as a true deserter would do. When the guards posted on the towers saw him, they descended from the wall and, opening the gates slightly, asked who he was and what he wanted in coming there. He declared that he was Zopyros and that he was deserting to their side. [2] When the gatekeepers heard this, they led him to the public assembly of the Babylonians, where he stood before them and stated his complaints against the Persians. He claimed that Darius was responsible for the injuries (which had actually been self-inflicted) as a punishment for his having counseled Darius to send his army away, since it was obvious that they were unable to take Babylon. [3] "But now," he told them, "I have come here, Babylonians, to do the greatest good to you, and the worst evil to Darius and his army. For I certainly will not permit him to mutilate me in this manner and not pay a price for it. After all, I know all the details of his plans intimately." That is what Zopyros said to them.

Seeing this highly esteemed Persian with his nose and ears cut off and covered with blood from having been whipped, the Babylonians believed that he was telling the truth, that he really had come to be their ally, and so they were ready and willing to grant him any position he wanted. When he asked for the command of an army [2] and this had been granted to him, he carried out the arrangements he had made with Darius exactly as they had planned. On the tenth day he led out the army of Babylonians and encircled the first group of 1,000 men that he had instructed Darius to post there, and he slaughtered them. [3] The Babylonians, learning that he had performed deeds equal to his words, were overjoyed and grew ever more ready and willing to do whatever he told them to do. So, allowing the prearranged number of days to pass, he again selected some Babylonians, led them out, and slaughtered Darius' unit of 2,000 soldiers. [4] Upon seeing this deed, all that any of the Babylonians could talk about was

3.156
522–521
BABYLON
Zopyros deserts to the Babylonians, who accept his story that Darius had mutilated him.

3.157
522–521
BABYLON
As planned, Zopyros leads the Babylonians to victories that fully win their trust, and so he gains command of the guard of the walls.

to praise Zopyros. And after waiting for the specified number of days to go by, he again led out the army to the designated gate and encircled and slaughtered the 4,000 troops that had been stationed there. Following this accomplishment, Zopyros became so completely idolized by the Babylonians that he was duly appointed commander in chief and guard of the wall.

Finally, as they had arranged, Darius made his attack around the wall, and it was then that the deceit of Zopyros was fully revealed. For as the Babylonians climbed up the wall and were warding off the attack by Darius' army, Zopyros opened the portals called the Gates of Belos and Kissia and let the Persians come inside. [2] Some of the Babylonians noticed what had been done and fled to the sanctuary of Zeus Belos.[a] Others failed to notice and remained at their posts until they, too, realized that they had been betrayed.

Thus Babylon was taken a second time.[a] When Cyrus took Babylon earlier, he left the city walls and gates intact, but Darius stripped away its wall and tore down all the gates. He then impaled 3,000 of the highest-ranking Babylonians, but he returned their city to the rest of the citizens and allowed them to live there. [2] Moreover, Darius had the foresight to ensure that they would have wives, so that they would have descendants who would continue their race after them, for the Babylonians had strangled their own wives, as was mentioned at the beginning, with a view to conserving the supply of grain. So now Darius ordered the neighboring peoples to assign women to Babylon, appointing a specific number to be sent from each, with the result that a total of 50,000 women went to the city. The present-day Babylonians are descended from these women.

In Darius' judgment, no Persian ever surpassed Zopyros in noble service rendered, neither before nor after this, except for Cyrus alone, since no Persian ever thought himself worthy to be compared with Cyrus. And it is said that Darius would often express his opinion that he would prefer to have Zopyros unmaimed by his unsightly wounds than to have twenty Babylons in addition to the one he had. [2] He bestowed high honors on Zopyros. In fact, he gave him the sort of gifts Persians value most throughout each year, as well as Babylon to administer tribute-free for his entire life, and many other gifts in addition. The son of Zopyros was the Megabyzos who led the campaign in Egypt against the Athenians and their allies.[a] This Megabyzos had a son Zopyros, who deserted Persia and went over to the Athenians.[b]

3.158
522–521
BABYLON
During an assault, Zopyros opens gates for the Persians to enter.

3.159
522–521
BABYLON
Darius retakes Babylon.

3.160
BABYLON
Darius honors Zopyros for the rest of his life. The careers of Zopyros' son and grandson.

3.158.2a   Zeus Belos: Bel or Baal, the greatest god of the Assyrian pantheon. See 1.181.1a.
3.159.1a   The first Persian conquest of Babylon was carried out by Cyrus in the year 539 (see 1.191).
3.160.2a   Megabyzos defeated the Athenians and their allies in Egypt in 454. See *Thucydides* 1.109.
3.160.2b   Some scholars have speculated that this Zopyros was Herodotus' source here, but there were many other possible sources.

BOOK FOUR

F ollowing the capture of Babylon,[a] Darius led an army against Scythia.[b] For Asia[c] was flourishing; it had both numerous fighting men and ample revenues, and Darius had developed a desire to punish the Scythians for having earlier invaded Media[d] and having conquered those who had tried to oppose them; for in doing this, the Scythians had been the unjust aggressors. [2] As I mentioned earlier, the Scythians had invaded in pursuit of the Cimmerians, and they remained and ruled inland Asia for twenty-eight years,[a] interrupting the rule of the Medes, who had held the power there before they arrived. [3] Thus for twenty-eight years the Scythians were absent from their own land, and when they returned after so much time had passed, they found trouble there that was no less serious than their confrontation with the Medes: they found a large army there prepared to oppose them. For during their long absence, their wives had resorted to consorting with the slaves.

The Scythian custom is to blind all their slaves to conform with the process by which they obtain the milk that they drink.[a] To get their milk, they take a flutelike tube made of bone and, inserting it into the mare, they blow through it, while others milk the mare at the same time. They say that they do this because the ducts of the mare become full when air is blown into them, and then the udders descend. [2] They pour the mare's milk

4.1
513
SCYTHIA
Darius marches against the Scythians to avenge a previous attack by the Scythians on Asia.

4.2
SCYTHIA
How the blinded Scythian slaves take milk from mares and separate it.

4.1.1a Babylon: Map 4.7. Darius captured Babylon in 521.
4.1.1b Scythia: Map 4.7, Crimea inset. Most scholars believe Darius' campaign against Scythia took place in 513.
4.1.1c Asia: Map 4.7.
4.1.1d Media: Map 4.7.
4.1.2a Herodotus' supposed twenty-eight years of Scythian rule of the Near East does occur in a chaotic period, when the Assyrian Empire fell, the Kingdom of Urartu disappeared, and Median and Neo-Babylonian (Chaldaean) Empires originated. The sources reflect this chaos: Assyrian records cease to provide historical information after 640, and the Babylonian chronicle of Nabopalassar begins with 616. Confirmation of

Herodotus' view of a period of Scythian dominance in the Near East is therefore difficult. The fact itself is suspect, as Herodotus (4.1.1, 7.20.2) conveniently puts these events into the wider context of his theme of East-West conflict: Darius I's Scythian campaign (513) avenged the Scythian invasion. Perhaps the best that can be said is that the Scythians clearly played a role as allies of various powers in the conflicts of the seventh century, but a Scythian defeat of the Medes and domination of Asia cannot be substantiated from other sources. (Wheeler)
4.2.1a The Scythian practice of blinding slaves cannot be confirmed from any other sources.

into deep wooden pails, and then place the blind slaves at intervals around the pails and make them stir the milk. Then they skim off what rises to the top, which they value more than what sinks to the bottom. That is the reason they blind everyone they capture, since they are a nomadic and not an agricultural people.[a]

So the slaves and the Scythian women raised a new generation to adulthood, and when their offspring realized the circumstances of their birth, they tried to oppose the return of the Scythians from Media. [2] First of all, they attempted to block access to their land by digging a broad trench[a] all the way from the Tauric Mountains[b] to Lake Maeotis[c] at its widest extent. Then they took up their blocking positions against the Scythians and engaged them in battle when they tried to invade. [3] There were many battles, but the returning Scythians were unable to gain anything by fighting until one of them said, "What are we doing, Scythians? While we fight our own slaves, we are being killed and reduced in numbers, and by killing them, we will have fewer left to rule over in the future. [4] Therefore let us stop using spears and arrows and take up instead our horsewhips and advance upon them with those. For as long as they saw us holding weapons, they considered themselves our equals as sired by men who were our equals. But when they see us wielding whips instead of weapons, they will realize that they are our slaves; and once they become aware of that, they will not stand their ground."

Upon hearing this suggestion, the Scythians carried it out, and their opponents, astounded by what they saw approaching, abandoned all thought of battle and fled. That is how the Scythians once ruled Asia, were driven out by the Medes, and then came back to their own land. But now Darius wanted to punish them and began mustering an army to march against them.

According to the Scythians, theirs is the youngest of all nations, and it came into existence in the following way. The first man born in this land, when it was still uninhabited, was named Targitaos. They say that the parents of this Targitaos were Zeus and the daughter of the River Borysthenes, though that does not sound credible to me. Nevertheless, that is their claim. [2] From such stock, then, came Targitaos, and to him were born three sons: Lipoxais, Arpoxais, and the youngest of them, Colaxais. [3] While they reigned, certain objects made of gold fell from the sky: they were a plow, a yoke, a battle-axe,[a] and a cup. When these objects came to rest on Scythian ground, they were seen first by the eldest son, who, wanting to take them up, approached where they lay. But as he came near them,

4.3
SCYTHIA
Conflict between the returning Scythians and their former slaves.

4.4
SCYTHIA
The Scythians return home. Darius resolves to punish them.

4.5
SCYTHIA
The myth of Scythian national origin.

4.2.2a Herodotus' claim that the Scythians are not agricultural is contradicted in 4.17 and elsewhere. Some Scythians were settled or almost so and quite agricultural. See Appendix G, The Continuity of Steppe Culture, §5.
4.3.2a This trench, which Herodotus describes as running north–south, cannot be identified from any archaeological evidence. There are

remains of walls and ditches in the region, but they are of later date and do not fit Herodotus' description here.
4.3.2b Tauric Mountains: Map 4.7, Crimea inset.
4.3.2c Lake Maeotis (modern Sea of Azov): Map 4.7, Crimea inset.
4.5.3a Battle-axe: Herodotus uses a Scythian word here, *sagaris*, as he did at 1.215.1.

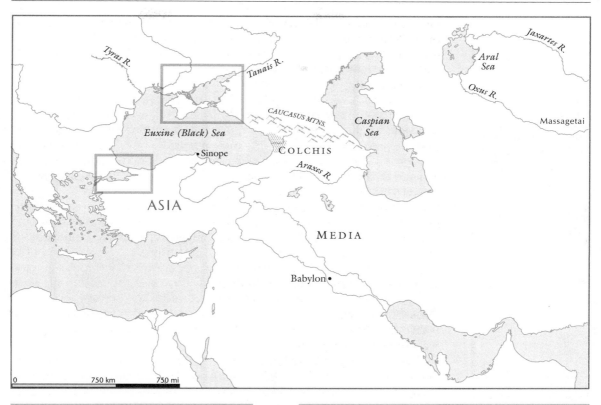

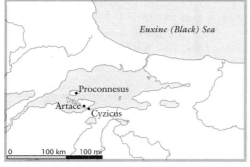

MAP 4.7

283

the gold caught on fire, [4] so he left them there; and when the second son approached, the same thing happened. Thus the burning gold drove both of them away; but when the third and youngest son approached, the fire stopped burning and went out, so he carried the gold home, and the elder brothers reacted to this event by agreeing to surrender the entire kingdom to the youngest.

4.6
SCYTHIA
The origin of the tribes of Scythia.

From Lipoxais were descended the Scythians known as the tribe of the Auchatai; from the middle brother, Arpoxais, the tribes of the Katiaroi and Traspies; and from the youngest, the royal tribe, called the Paralatai. [2] The name of all these tribes collectively is Skolotoi, derived from the king's name, but the Hellenes have named them Scythians. So that is how the Scythians explain the origin of their race.

4.7
SCYTHIA
Other myths and strange facts the Scythians tell about themselves.

They say that the entire interval between the birth of their race and the reign of their first king, Targitaos, and Darius' crossing over to their land was no more than 1,000 years. The kings guard the sacred gold objects with great care; each year they approach this treasure reverently and offer large, rich sacrifices to it. [2] According to the Scythians, if the person tending the sacred gold at this festival should fall asleep at this time in the open air, he will not live out the year. And in return for the performance of this duty, the man appointed to do it is granted as much land as he can ride his horse around in a single day. Since Scythia is vast, Colaxais established three separate kingdoms within it for his sons and made the kingdom sheltering the gold treasure the largest. [3] The region above this land, toward the north, is inaccessible to anyone trying to get very far into it, nor is it open to view, because both the land and the air are full of feathers, which obscure one's vision.[a]

4.8
How Herakles came to Scythia before it was inhabited by the Scythians.

That is how the Scythians describe themselves and the land north of them. But the Hellenes who inhabit the Pontic region on the coast of the Euxine Sea[a] say that Herakles came to this land before it was inhabited by the Scythians as it is now, when he was driving the cattle of Geryon.[b] [2] According to the Hellenes, Geryon lived far from the Pontus on the island Erytheia, near Gadeira[a] outside the Pillars of Herakles[b] in Ocean. The story is that Ocean flows around the entire earth,[c] beginning at the rising sun, but no evidence is produced to prove this theory. [3] When Herakles came from there to the land now called Scythia, the cold winter and frost overtook him, and he drew his lion's skin around him and fell asleep. Meanwhile, by divine fortune, his horses disappeared from where they had been grazing while yoked to his chariot.

4.7.3a By "feathers" here Herodotus means snow, as he explains in 4.31.
4.8.1a "Pontic region" means the region of the Pontus, the Euxine (Black) Sea: Map 4.7 and Cyzicus inset.
4.8.1b The cattle of Geryon: the tenth and last Labor of Herakles was to carry off these red cattle after slaying Geryon, their monster-owner,

and both the shepherd Eurytion and Orthus, the two-headed dog, who guarded them.
4.8.2a Gadeira (modern Cádiz): Map 4.18, locator.
4.8.2b Pillars of Herakles (modern Straits of Gibraltar): Map 4.18, locator.
4.8.2c Homer (*Iliad* 18.607–608) describes Ocean as covering the entire outer rim of the shield of Achilles.

When Herakles awoke, he searched everywhere in the land and kept going until he reached the place called Hylaia.[a] There he found a cave, and within it, a creature that was half girl, half viper.[b] From her hips up, she was a woman; from her legs down, a serpent. [2] At first Herakles just marveled at the sight of her, but then he asked her if she had seen his horses wandering anywhere. She declared that his horses were actually in her possession, but she would not return them until he had intercourse with her. So on these terms, Herakles had intercourse with her. [3] But she delayed returning the horses to him, as she wished to spend as much time as possible with Herakles, while all he wanted was to take his horses and leave. At last she gave them back, saying, "When your horses came here, I kept them safe for you, and you in return have rewarded me with the three sons I have had by you. [4] But tell me what you think I should do when they grow up: shall I settle them here (for I rule over this land), or shall I send them away to you?" That was her question; and they say that he replied, [5] "When you see that the boys have reached manhood, you will not go wrong if you follow these instructions. Have the one you see drawing this bow and girding himself with this belt (as I shall show you) become an inhabitant of this land. But those who fall short of this requirement should be sent away from this land. If you do these things, you will not only carry out my orders, but you will make yourself happy as well."

So to demonstrate what he meant, Herakles drew one of his bows (until then he carried two) and showed her how he put on the belt, which had a golden libation cup hanging from its clasp. Then, after giving her the bow and the belt, he left. And when the boys reached manhood, she gave them their names: the firstborn she called Agathyrsos; the one who followed, Gelonos; and the youngest, Scythes. Then, remembering the advice of Herakles, she did as she had been instructed. [2] And indeed two of the boys, Agathyrsos and Gelonos, could not manage the trial set before them, so they were expelled by their mother and disappeared from the land. But Scythes, the youngest, performed the task and remained there. [3] The descendants of Scythes son of Herakles have succeeded ever since to the kingship of the Scythians, and because of the original libation bowl, the Scythians still to this day wear cups hanging from their belts. As for the mother of Scythes, this is the only role she is reported to have had in the origin of this race. And so that is the version of the story given by the Hellenes of the Pontic region.

But there is yet another account, to which I myself am most partial. According to this theory, the Scythians were nomads who originally lived in Asia until, pressured in war by the Massagetai, they left Asia and crossed the

4.9
The Greek myth of Herakles and the snake goddess in what is now Scythia.

4.10
The Greek myth of Herakles and the snake goddess in what is now Scythia concludes.

4.11
Herodotus' preferred tale of how the Scythians took possession of their country.

4.9.1a   Hylaia (the name means "woodlands"):
         Map 4.18, AX.
4.9.1b   See Figure 4.9 for a representation of the

Scythian snake goddess or snake-footed goddess.

285

FIGURE 4.9. THE SCYTHIAN SNAKE GODDESS
AS DEPICTED ON A HORSE'S GOLD FOREHEAD
ORNAMENT FROM THE CIMALKA KURGAN
(TOMB) IN BULGARIA.

Araxes River[a] into Cimmerian territory. Indeed, the land now inhabited by Scythians is said to have belonged to the Cimmerians a long time ago. [2] While the Scythians were approaching to attack with their large army, the Cimmerians discussed what to do and finally split into two groups of different and vehemently held opinions. The common people proposed to leave the land; they felt no need to endanger themselves by fighting against so many invaders. The royal Cimmerians, whose proposal was the more noble of the two, thought they should fight to the end in defense of their land. [3] Each side refused to be persuaded by the other. The people decided to leave without a fight and give over their country to the invaders, while the royal Cimmerians, as they contrasted all the good things they had experienced there with all the bad things they could expect to happen to them if they fled, resolved not to run away with the people, but to die and lie buried in their own land. [4] Since this was their decision, the royal Cimmerians divided themselves into two equal groups and fought with each

4.11.1a　Herodotus uses the name Araxes for both the Armenian river, which flows into the Caspian Sea, and probably also the Jaxartes (modern Syr-Darya), which flows into the Aral Sea. Since later ancient writers frequently confused the Tanais (modern Don) River with the Jaxartes, it is possible that Herodotus refers here to the Tanais River. See nn. 1.201.1b, 1.202.1a, and 1.205.2a. For all these locations, see Map 4.7.

other until they all lay dead. Then they were buried by the Cimmerian people beside the Tyras River,[a] where their tombs are still visible. After the burial, the people departed from the land, so that when the Scythians invaded, the country they took was completely deserted.

But even today in Scythia, one can still see the Cimmerian walls, the river crossings called Cimmerian ferries, a region called Cimmeria, and the strait that is called the Cimmerian Bosporus.[a] [2] It is obvious that the Cimmerians, in their flight into Asia[a] to escape the Scythians, established a settlement on the peninsula on which the Greek city of Sinope[b] is now situated, while the Scythians in pursuit of them clearly went way off course and invaded Media.[c] [3] The Cimmerians continually stayed near the coast in their flight, while the Scythians in pursuit kept the Caucasus[a] on their right, which turned their course into the interior of Asia, so that they invaded Media.[b] So this is yet another story, and one that is told by both Hellenes and barbarians alike.

Then there is Aristeas son of Kaystrobios of Proconnesus,[a] who composed verses in which he claims to have been inspired by Phoibos Apollo and to have visited the land of the Issedones.[b] Above the Issedones, he says, live the Arimaspians, one-eyed men; above them dwell the gold-guarding griffins;[c] and above the griffins, the Hyperboreans,[d] whose land extends all the way to the sea. [2] With the exception of the Hyperboreans, all these peoples, beginning with the Arimaspians, attacked their neighbors in successive waves, so that the Issedones were pushed out by the Arimaspians, the Scythians by the Issedones, and the Cimmerians living along the sea to the south[a] were forced by the Scythians to leave their country, too. So not even Aristeas' story agrees with what the Scythians say about their land.

I have already mentioned where the author of this account came from; and now I shall tell you what I heard about him in Proconnesus and Cyzicus.[a] Aristeas, they say, was in lineage the equal or superior of any citizen in his town. One day he entered a fuller's shop in Proconnesus and died there, so the fuller locked up his workshop and went to announce to Aristeas' relatives that he had died. [2] The news of his death quickly spread throughout

4.12
Names in Scythian territory that reflect the past presence of the Cimmerians.

4.13
Herodotus cites Aristeas' poems which describe his visit to the land of the Issedones and beyond. At the end of a series of invasions, the Scythians pushed the Cimmerians to the south.

4.14
Herodotus relates a story about Aristeas the poet.

4.11.4a Tyras (modern Dniester) River: Map 4.7.
4.12.1a The Cimmerian name survives in Crimea in the Cimmerian Bosporus, the narrow entrance or straits to Lake Maeotis (modern Sea of Azov) from the Euxine (Black) Sea; and the Cimmerian ferry, which is probably the narrowest part of the straits. For all these locations, see Map 4.7, Crimea inset.
4.12.2a Asia (Minor): Map 4.7.
4.12.2b Sinope: Map 4.7.
4.12.2c Media: Map 4.7.
4.12.3a Caucasus Mountains: Map 4.7.
4.12.3b Herodotus' account of the route by which the Cimmerians entered Colchis and Asia is absurd in at least two respects: it is hardly likely that they would flee eastward from their settlements on the Tyras (modern Dniester) River to escape invaders from the east, and it would have

been geographically impossible for them to come down the eastern shore of the Euxine (Black) Sea, as the northwest Caucasus Mountains end abruptly and steeply at the water's edge. (Wheeler) For all these locations, see Map 4.7. For more on the Cimmerians, see nn. 1.6.3a and 1.15.1c.
4.13.1a Proconnesus: Map 4.7, Cyzicus inset.
4.13.1b Issedones: location of territory unknown. See 4.26.
4.13.1c The Arimaspians and griffins were mentioned in 3.116. A griffin is a mythical beast with the body of a lion and the beak and wings of an eagle.
4.13.1d On the Hyperboreans, see 4.32–36.
4.13.2a The "sea to the south" is in this case the Euxine (Black) Sea: Map 4.7 and Cyzicus inset.
4.14.1a Cyzicus: Map 4.7, Cyzicus inset.

the city, but a man of Cyzicus objected. He had just come from the city of Artace,[a] and he claimed to have just met and talked with Aristeas, who was on his way to Cyzicus. So he vehemently denied that Aristeas was dead. Meanwhile, the relatives of Aristeas went for his body at the fuller's shop, bringing along what they needed to take up the corpse for burial. [3] But when the place was opened, Aristeas was nowhere to be seen, dead or alive. Seven years later, he appeared in Proconnesus, composed the verses that Hellenes now call the *Arimaspea*, and, after he had finished them, disappeared a second time.

That is the story told in these cities, but I know also what happened to the Metapontines in Italy[a] some 240 years after the second disappearance of Aristeas. I calculated this interval myself by adding up the years between his appearance in Proconnesus and his appearance in Metapontum. [2] The Metapontines say that Aristeas himself appeared in their land and that he ordered them to erect an altar to Apollo and to set up beside it a statue identified with the name of Aristeas of Proconnesus. For, he said, of all the Italiotes it was to them alone and to their land that Apollo had come; and that he himself had followed the god, not as Aristeas, as he now appeared, but then in the form of a crow. [3] After saying this, he disappeared. The Metapontines relate that they then sent an inquiry to Delphi[a] asking the god what this apparition of a man really meant. The Pythia ordered them to obey the apparition and said that if they did, things would turn out the better for them. [4] So when they received this response, they did as they had been told. And still today, in their agora, the statue with the name of Aristeas stands beside the cult image of Apollo, surrounded by bay laurel trees. That is what I have to say about Aristeas, and let it be enough.

No one knows exactly what exists beyond this land which I have begun to describe. For I have been unable to find anyone who says he has actually seen it with his own eyes. Not even Aristeas, of whom I have just spoken, said he went any farther than the Issedones—even in his poetry. He said that his account of the region to the far north came from hearsay and that it was the Issedones who told him these things. [2] Nevertheless, I shall relate all the certain information we have been able to gather concerning these most distant regions.

Starting from the trading post of the Borysthenites,[a] which lies at the midpoint of the coast of Scythia, the first inhabitants are the Kallipidai,[b] who are Greek Scythians. Beyond them live another people called the Alazones.[c] Both these and the Kallipidai practice the same customs as Scythians do in all respects except that they sow and eat grain, as well as

4.15
The story of Aristeas with Apollo on his visit to Metapontum.

4.16
SCYTHIA
Herodotus lacks eyewitness reports of lands north of Scythia, but he will tell what he has heard.

4.17
SCYTHIA
People who live to the northwest of the Borysthenites. Herodotus begins his description of Scythian lands, which continues through 4.36.

4.14.2a　Artace: Map 4.7, Cyzicus inset. A Milesian colony, Artace was the port of Cyzicus, to the west of the city.
4.15.1a　Metapontum, Italy: Map 4.18, locator. See Figure 4.15 of the remains of a temple at Metapontum.
4.15.3a　Delphi: Map 4.33.
4.17.1a　Port of the Borysthenites, also called Village

of the Borysthenites, another Milesian colony, which the Hellenes called Olbia ("Fortunate"): Map 4.18, AX. It was the most important Greek center north of the Euxine (Black) Sea: Map 4.18, BX. (Godley)
4.17.1b　Kallipidai, location of territory: Map 4.18, AX.
4.17.1c　Alazones: Map 4.18, AX.

FIGURE 4.15. PARTIAL ROWS OF DORIC COLUMNS ARE ALL THAT REMAINS OF THE TEMPLE AT METAPONTUM, ITALY.

onions, garlic, lentils, and millet. [2] Above the Alazones live the Scythian plowmen,[a] who grow grain not for their own consumption, but for sale. Above these live the Neurians,[b] but the region beyond them toward the north is uninhabited by humans, as far as we know. Those, then, are the peoples along the Hypanis River,[c] to the west of the Borysthenes River.[d]

On the opposite side of the Borysthenes River, beginning from the coast, lies first of all Hylaia.[a] Next, farther inland, dwell the Scythian farmers,[b] called Borysthenites by the Hellenes who live near the Hypanis River, but called Olbiapolitai by themselves. [2] These Scythian farmers inhabit the region extending a three-days' journey to the east, up to the river named Panticapes,[a] and an eleven-days' sail up the Borysthenes toward the north. The region above them is uninhabited for a great distance, [3] but beyond dwell the Maneaters,[a] who are in no way Scythian, but a completely distinct people. Beyond them the land now becomes truly deserted and no human nation lives there, as far as we know.

East of the Scythian farmers, across the Panticapes River, dwell Scythian nomads,[a] who neither sow seed nor plow. This entire region is bare of trees except for Hylaia. The nomads inhabit the territory extending a fourteen-days' journey to the east, up to the Gerros River.[b]

4.18
SCYTHIA
Those who live to the northeast of the Borysthenites.

4.19
SCYTHIA
Nomadic Scythian country.

4.17.2a Scythian plowmen, possible location of territory: Map 4.18, AX.
4.17.2b Neurians, possible location of territory: Map 4.18, AX.
4.17.2c Hypanis (modern Bug) River: Map 4.18, AX.
4.17.2d Borysthenes (modern Dnieper) River: Map 4.18, AX.
4.18.1a Hylaia (the name means "woodlands"): Map 4.18, AX. The *Barrington Atlas* shows it on the same side (west) of the Borysthenes River, but on the opposite side of the Hypanis River.
4.18.1b Scythian farmers: Map 4.18, AX. Olbiapolitai are citizens of Olbia.

4.18.2a Panticapes River, possible location: Map 4.18, AX.
4.18.3a Maneaters (Androphagoi), possible location of territory: Map 4.18, AX. Archaeologists have uncovered evidence of cannibalism in the area Herodotus says the Androphagoi inhabited. See 4.100; Appendix E, Herodotus and the Black Sea Region, §10; and Appendix F, Rivers and Peoples of Scythia, §4.
4.19.1a Scythian nomads, possible location of territory: Map 4.18, AX.
4.19.1b Gerros River, possible location: Map 4.18, AX. Scholars do not agree on the identification of this river or the region.

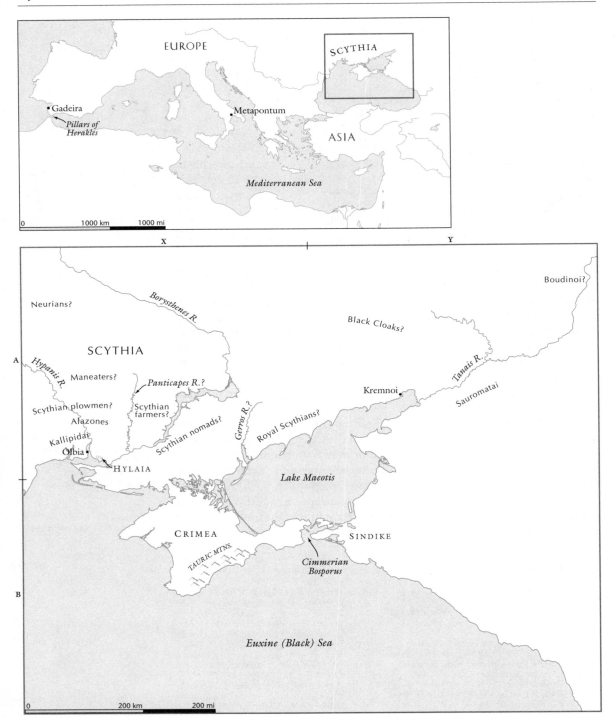

EUROPE

SCYTHIA

• Gadeira

Pillars of Herakles

• Metapontum

ASIA

Mediterranean Sea

0   1000 km   1000 mi

X   Y

Boudinoi?

Borysthenes R.

Neurians?

Black Cloaks?

SCYTHIA

A

Hypanis R.

Maneaters?

Panticapes R.?

Tanais R.

Kremnoi •

Sauromatai

Scythian plowmen?

Scythian farmers?

Alazones

Gerros R.?

Scythian nomads?

Royal Scythians?

Kallipidai

Olbia •

HYLAIA

Lake Maeotis

CRIMEA

SINDIKE

TAURIC MTNS.

Cimmerian Bosporus

B

Euxine (Black) Sea

0   200 km   200 mi

MAP 4.18

Across the Gerros are the districts called Royal, inhabited by the most noble and also the most numerous Scythians, who consider the rest of the Scythians their slaves. They live as far south as the Tauric land,[a] and as far east as the trench[b] dug by the sons of the blind slaves, and up to the trading post called Kremnoi[c] on Lake Maeotis.[d] And a portion of their territory extends to the Tanais River.[e] [2] Above the Royal Scythians,[a] toward the north, live the Black Cloaks,[b] another non-Scythian people. Beyond them are lakes and land uninhabited by humans, as far as we know.

Across the Tanais River, the land is no longer Scythian. The first land one comes to belongs to the Sauromatai,[a] who inhabit the territory beginning from the [northern tip] of Lake Maeotis and extending a fifteen-days' journey toward the north. All this land is bare of trees, wild or cultivated. Above this and occupying a second district are the Boudinoi,[b] who inhabit land that is completely and thickly covered with all kinds of shrubs.

Above the Boudinoi to the north, one first encounters a land that is completely deserted as far as a seven-days' journey, but the region after this desolate stretch, toward the east, is inhabited by the Thyssagetai,[a] a people both numerous and distinct. They live by hunting. [2] Adjoining them in the same region dwell people called the Iyrkai,[a] who live by hunting in the following way. The hunter climbs a tree—and dense trees cover this entire region—to lie in wait, while the horse each man has trained lies stretched out on its belly below in readiness, as does his dog. When the hunter sees an animal from the tree, he shoots his arrow at it, mounts his horse, and chases it, with the dog next to him in pursuit. [3] Beyond and to the east of these people dwell other Scythians, who came to this land after they had revolted from the Royal Scythians.

All the Scythian territory described thus far is flat and has deep soil, but from this point on it becomes stony and rugged. [2] If one travels a long distance through this rugged territory, one reaches a people who dwell in the foothills of high mountains. These people are said to be bald from birth, male and female alike; they have snub noses and large chins, speak a language of their own, wear clothing like the Scythians', and live off the produce they obtain from trees. [3] The name of the tree from which they obtain their sustenance is *pontikon*. It is about the size of a fig tree and bears

4.20
SCYTHIA
Peoples of eastern Scythia.

4.21
SAUROMATAI
Farther east is no longer Scythia.

4.22
SCYTHIA
Herodotus describes the hunting methods of the Iyrkai.

4.23
SCYTHIA
A legendary people called the Argippaioi, who have been visited by both Hellenes and Scythians.

4.20.1a Tauric land (modern Crimea): Map 4.18, BX. Herodotus implies the Royal Scythians' political control over a vast area. This is fiction.
4.20.1b For this trench, see 4.3.2.
4.20.1c Kremnoi (the word means "cliffs"): Map 4.18, AY. See also 4.110.
4.20.1d Lake Maeotis (modern Sea of Azov): Map 4.18, BX.
4.20.1e Tanais (modern Don) River: Map 4.18, AY.
4.20.2a Royal Scythians, possible location of territory: Map 4.18, AX.
4.20.2b Black Cloaks, possible location of territory: Map 4.18, AY. Called Melanchlainoi in Greek, they are mentioned in

Hekataios, who wrote a geographical description of the world c. 500 from which Herodotus borrows extensively, although he does not say so. Herodotus does mention Hekataios in 2.143, 5.36, 5.125, 5.126 and 6.137. See Introduction, §3.1.
4.21.1a Sauromatai, approximate location of territory: Map 4.18, AY.
4.21.1b Boudinoi, possible location of territory: Map 4.18, AY.
4.22.1a Thyssagetai: location of territory unknown. The Thyssagetai are mentioned in a late-fourth-century inscription from Olbia.
4.22.2a Iyrkai: location of territory unknown.

a fruit the size of a bean, which encloses a pit. When the fruit becomes ripe, they strain it through cloth and derive from it a thick black substance that flows out, called *askhy*. This they either lick up or drink mixed with their milk, and the thickest part, the lees, they compress into cakes and eat. [4] They have few flocks, because the land here is not very good pasturage. Each man lives beneath a tree and during the winter covers the tree with waterproof white felt, which he removes for the summer. [5] No human ever tries to harm these people, for they are said to be sacred and they possess no weapons at all. Furthermore, they are the ones who decide disputes for the neighboring peoples, and any exile can take refuge with them and no one will harm him. This people's name is Argippaioi.

4.24
Travel to these distant lands requires seven interpreters.

Now we have very thorough information about much of the land up to and including these bald men, for some of the Scythians, from whom it is not difficult to get information, have actually reached them, as have also some of the Hellenes from the trading post on the Borysthenes and from the other Pontic trading posts. Any Scythians who come this far must deal through seven interpreters and seven languages.

4.25
Beyond the Argippaioi nothing is really known. There are tales of men with goats' feet—but Herodotus does not believe them.

So there is reliable information concerning the land as far as these people, but what lies beyond the land of the bald men, no one can say for certain. For steep and high mountains which no one can climb cut off access to the land beyond the bald men. Though it sounds incredible to me, the bald men say that goat-footed men live on the mountains, and that if one goes beyond them, one will find other people who sleep for six months at a time. This latter claim I do not accept at all. [2] But it is known for certain that to the east of the bald men is a region inhabited by Issedones.[a] Of what lies beyond the bald men and the Issedones, toward the north, nothing is known, except for what they themselves tell us.

4.26
SCYTHIA
Customs of the Issedones.

The Issedones are said to observe the following custom: whenever a man's father dies, all his relatives bring their flocks and sacrifice them. Next they chop up the animals and the body of the father, mix all the meat together, and then set it all out for a feast. [2] After having plucked the hair from the father's head, they clean it, gild it, and thereafter treat it as a precious image, to which they offer lavish sacrifices annually. Indeed, sons perform this rite for their fathers, just as the Hellenes have their annual ritual commemorating the birthday of the dead. In other respects, these people are said to be civilized and righteous, and their women share power equally with their men.

4.27
SCYTHIA
Scythian tales of one-eyed men and griffins.

While the Issedones themselves are well known, we must rely on what they tell us for our knowledge of what lies beyond them—the one-eyed men and the gold-guarding griffins.[a] It is from the Issedones that the Scythians have received their account. The rest of us, because we have heard it from the Scythians, customarily call those people Arimaspians, which is a Scythian word. For the Scythians use the word *arima* for "one" and *spou* for "eye."

4.25.2a Issedones: location of territory
         unknown.

4.27.1a One-eyed men and gold-guarding
         griffins: see 4.13.1.

This entire land I am describing experiences such harsh winters that for eight months the frost is intolerable, and you could not create mud by pouring water on the ground unless you light a fire. The sea freezes over, as does the whole Cimmerian Bosporus;[a] and the Scythians who live within the trench conduct expeditions over the ice, driving their wagons across to the land of the Sindi.[b] [2] Winter continues like this for eight months, and the remaining four months of the year are cold here, too. But the winter differs from winters in all other regions in that during this season here there is no appreciable rainfall, while in summer it never stops raining. [3] And at the time when thunder occurs elsewhere,[a] it does not happen here, but instead is frequent in summer. If thunder does occur during the winter, the Scythians regard it with amazement and consider it a portent, as they do also in the event of earthquakes, no matter whether they occur in summer or winter. [4] While horses can tolerate the Scythian winter, mules and donkeys cannot bear it at all here, although elsewhere horses standing on ice suffer frostbite on their legs, whereas mules and donkeys are able to tolerate it.

I think that this is why the oxen here do not grow horns, and there is a verse in Homer's *Odyssey* that supports my opinion:

And Libya, where lambs grow horns straightway from birth.[a]

This statement is correct in that horns do grow quickly in hot climates, while in extremely cold climates cattle either do not grow horns at all or else just barely grow them.[b]

Those, then, are the effects of the cold in Scythia. But I find it amazing (since from the beginning of my account I have sought out additional information) that no mules can be born in the land of Elis,[a] although the climate there is not cold and there is no other obvious reason for this. The Eleans themselves say that it is because of a curse that no mules are born in their land. [2] So whenever mating season approaches, they drive out their mares to neighboring territory, where the mares then go to the male donkeys and, after becoming pregnant, are driven back again.

Now here is my own opinion concerning the feathers that the Scythians say fill up the air and obstruct both visibility and travel through their country. In the upper regions of this land, snow falls continually, although, as is reasonable to expect, less in the summer than in the winter. [2] Whoever has observed heavy snow falling knows what I mean when I say that the snow resembles feathers, and so I think the Scythians and surrounding

4.28
SCYTHIA
The Scythian winter.

4.29
SCYTHIA
Northern hornless cattle explained.

4.30
ELIS
The mysterious inability of mules to reproduce in Elis.

4.31
SCYTHIA
The tale of falling feathers explained as thick northern snow.

4.28.1a Cimmerian Bosporus (modern Strait of Kerch): Map 4.18, BY. The idea of an entire sea freezing over so that wagons could be driven over it must have seemed implausibly extreme to many Hellenes of the Mediterranean coast.
4.28.1b Sindi (Sindike), location of territory: Map 4.18, BY.
4.28.3a Elsewhere refers to Hellas, or the Aegean region, where it rains in winter and not in summer.
4.29.1a *Odyssey* 4.85.
4.29.1b Remains of hornless cattle have been found in what was Scythia, but Herodotus' explanation for why they are hornless is certainly false.
4.30.1a Elis: Map 4.33.

peoples describe the snow as feathers because they note the similarity between the two. It is because the winters there are so severe that the far northern regions of this land are uninhabitable. That, then, is the fullest account that can be given about these matters.

But about the Hyperboreans, neither the Scythians nor any other inhabitants of this region have anything to say, except perhaps for the Issedones; but I suppose they say nothing about them either, since if they did, the Scythians would repeat it, just as they do the Issedones' account of the one-eyed men. The Hyperboreans are mentioned by Hesiod[a] and also by Homer in the *Epigonoi*[b]—if Homer actually did compose those verses.

But the Delians[a] have by far the most to say about them. They tell how the Hyperboreans send sacred offerings bound in stalks of wheat to Scythia, and these offerings are received in succession by each neighboring country until they are brought as far west as the Adriatic Sea.[b] [2] From there they are sent southward, and the first of the Hellenes to receive them are the people of Dodona,[a] who send them on to the Malian Gulf.[b] Then they cross over to Euboea,[c] where one city sends them on to the next until they reach Karystos.[d] The Karystians take them to Tenos,[e] passing by Andros,[f] and the Tenians bring them to Delos. [3] That is how, it is said, the sacred objects come to Delos. But initially the Hyperboreans sent two girls to carry the offerings. Their names, according to the Delians, were Hyperoche and Laodike. The Hyperboreans also sent along with them an escort of five of their men for their safety; these men are now called Perpherees and are granted high honors on Delos. [4] But the girls and men sent by the Hyperboreans did not return home again, and the Hyperboreans, perturbed and afraid that if they continued to send others they would never get them back again either, wrapped their offerings in stalks of wheat, took them to the borders of their land, and laid a strict obligation upon their neighbors to send them on to the next people. [5] They say that in this way, the offerings are sent forth and finally arrive at Delos. I myself know of a practice similar to this, performed by Thracian[a] and Paionian[b] women: whenever they sacrifice to Royal Artemis,[c] they never fail to include an offering of a wheat stalk.

I know that the Thracian and Paionian women do this, but at Delos, the girls and boys cut their hair in honor of the Hyperborean virgins who died there. Before marriage, the girls cut off a lock of their hair, wind it around a spindle, and place it upon the tomb. [2] The tomb is located within the

4.32
SCYTHIA
There is very little known about the Hyperboreans.

4.33
DELOS
The Delian tale about the gifts sent to them from the Hyperboreans.

4.34
DELOS
Herodotus knows the Delian rites in honor of the Hyperboreans.

4.32.1a   Hesiod, Greek poet of seventh-century Boeotia: Map 4.33.
4.32.1b   The *Epigonoi*: one of the poems belonging to the Trojan War cycle. The Epigonoi were the sons of those who fought in a war that is supposed to have taken place just before the Trojan War, known as the Seven Against Thebes.
4.33.1a   Delos: Map 4.33. This Delian story about the Hyperboreans is additional evidence of the known fact that trade routes from the earliest times linked northern and southeastern Europe. Amber in particular

was carried from the Baltic to the Aegean. (Godley)
4.33.1b   Adriatic Sea: Map 4.33, locator.
4.33.2a   Dodona: Map 4.33.
4.33.2b   Malian Gulf: Map 4.33.
4.33.2c   Euboea: Map 4.33.
4.33.2d   Karystos: Map 4.33.
4.33.2e   Tenos: Map 4.33.
4.33.2f   Andros: Map 4.33.
4.33.5a   Thrace: Map 4.33.
4.33.5b   Paionia: Map 4.33.
4.33.5c   Royal Artemis is Artemis Basileia, probably the same as Thracian Bendis.

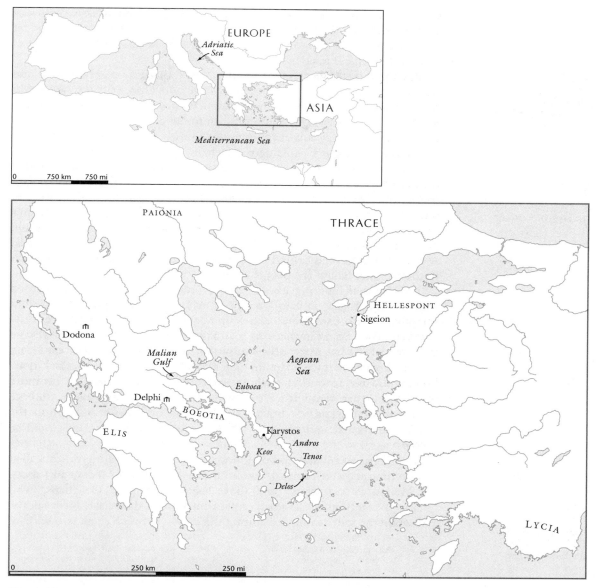

MAP 4.33

sanctuary of Artemis,[a] to the left of the entrance, and has an olive tree growing over it. All the boys, too, wind some of their hair around a plant shoot and set it on the tomb. Those are the honors that the inhabitants of Delos give to these maidens.

But the same Delians say that even before the time of Hyperoche and Laodike, other Hyperborean maidens, Arge and Opis, had traveled down through the same peoples and arrived at Delos. [2] They had come to pay Eileithuia what they had vowed in return for an easy delivery in childbirth.[a] Arge and Opis, they say, arrived together with the gods themselves and were granted various honors by the Delians. [3] The women collect donations for them and sing their names in the hymn that Olen of Lycia[a] composed for them. And the Delians have taught the islanders and Ionians to sing the hymn naming Opis and Arge and to collect donations for them, too. Olen, after arriving from Lycia, composed the other ancient hymns sung on Delos as well. [4] In addition, they place the ashes from the thigh offerings that have been burned on the altar upon the grave of Opis and Arge, which is located behind the sanctuary of Artemis, facing east and next to the banquet hall of the people of Keos.[a]

Let that conclude my account of the Hyperboreans, for I shall not tell the story of Abaris, said to have been a Hyperborean who went around the whole world carrying an arrow and eating nothing. But if there really are Hyperboreans, then there are also Hypernotians.[a] [2] And it makes me laugh when I see so many people nowadays drawing maps of the earth and not one of them giving an intelligent representation of it. They draw Ocean flowing around the whole earth, portray the earth to be more perfectly circular than if it were drawn with a compass, and make Asia[a] the same size as Europe.[b] I, however, will show by a brief description the actual size of each, and what they should look like and how they should be drawn.[c]

The Persians[a] inhabit the region extending to the Southern Sea, called the Erythraean.[b] Above them, toward the north, live the Medes,[c] and above the Medes, the Saspeires,[d] and above the Saspeires, the Colchians,[e] who inhabit the land up to the northern sea[f] into which the Phasis River[g] flows. Those are the four nations inhabiting the region between these two seas.

4.35
DELOS
The Delian myth of Arge and Opis, the early Hyperborean maidens.

4.36
Herodotus mocks maps showing the earth as round and Asia equal to Europe in extent.

4.37
Four nations which span from one sea to the other.

4.34.2a This sanctuary of Artemis has been located by archaeologists.
4.35.2a Eileithuia is the goddess of childbirth.
4.35.3a Lycia: Map 4.33. Olen was a semimythical poet from Lycia. By another tradition, he was thought to be a Hyperborean. His hymns to Apollo were in hexameter, which might date him, if he is real at all, to the eighth century.
4.35.4a Keos: Map 4.33.
4.36.1a Hyperborean was thought to mean "beyond the north wind," so Hypernotian would designate people living beyond the south wind.
4.36.2a Asia (Asia Minor): Map 4.39, locator.

4.36.2b Europe: Map 4.33, locator.
4.36.2c See Appendix D, Herodotean Geography, §1–3.
4.37.1a Persia (homeland): Map 4.39, locator.
4.37.1b Erythraean Sea (not the modern Red Sea in this instance but the modern Persian Gulf and the Indian Ocean): Map 4.39, locator.
4.37.1c Media: Map 4.39, BY.
4.37.1d Saspeires, possible location: Map 4.39, AY.
4.37.1e Colchis: Map 4.39, AY.
4.37.1f Northern sea: here, Herodotus means the Pontus, the Euxine (Black) Sea: Map 4.39, AX. See also n. 4.42.2f.
4.37.1g Phasis River: Map 4.39, AY.

From here, two peninsulas which I shall now describe extend to the sea. [2] One peninsula begins in the north from the Phasis River and stretches along the Pontus[a] and the Hellespont[b] until it reaches the sea at Sigeion[c] in the Troad. The southern coast of this same peninsula extends along the coast from the Myriandic Gulf,[d] which lies near Phoenicia,[e] to the Triopion Cape.[f] Thirty nations inhabit this peninsula.

4.38
Herodotus describes
Asia as a peninsula.

That is the extent of the first peninsula. The second one begins from Persian territory and extends to the Erythraean Sea. It includes Persia, followed by Assyria[a] and then Arabia.[b] It ends at the Arabian Gulf[c] (though it does not actually end here except by convention[d]), to which Darius had extended the canal he had dug from the Nile.[e] [2] Now from Persia to Phoenicia there is a large area of flat land. But from Phoenicia this peninsula stretches down beside the Mediterranean Sea[a] and Syria,[b] then reaches Egypt,[c] where it ends. Within this peninsula there are only three nations.

4.39
Persia, Assyria, and
Arabia are described
as a second peninsula.

That is the extent of Asian territory from Persia to the west. To the east beyond the Persians, Medes, Saspeires, and Colchians, Asia's southern border is the Erythraean Sea and its northern border is the Caspian Sea[a] and the Araxes River, which flows in the direction of the sunrise.[b] [2] Asia is inhabited as far as India,[a] but the territory east of India is uninhabited, and no one can say what sort of land exists there.

4.40
What lies to the
east of the Persians.

This, then, is the extent of Asia. Libya[a] occupies another peninsula, for Libya is the land one comes to going west right after Egypt. This peninsula is narrow at Egypt, for the distance between the Mediterranean Sea to the Erythraean Sea here measures only 110 miles.[a] But after this narrow tract of land, the peninsula called Libya becomes very broad.

4.41
Another peninsula includes
Egypt and Libya.

And so I am astonished by the way some people have delineated the boundaries of Libya, Asia, and Europe;[a] since these lands actually differ quite a bit in size. In length, Europe stretches out along both the other landmasses, while in width, any attempt to compare it to the others seems futile to me.[a] [2] For it is clear that Libya is surrounded by water except for

4.42
Libya, Asia, and Europe
are not equal, as some have
mapped them. An account
of the circumnavigation of
Africa by Phoenicians.

4.38.2a Pontus, the Euxine (Black) Sea: Map 4.39, AX. Herodotus is describing Asia Minor (modern Turkey).
4.38.2b Hellespont: Map 4.39, BX.
4.38.2c Sigeion: Map 4.33.
4.38.2d Myriandic Gulf: Map 4.39, BY.
4.38.2e Phoenicia: Map 4.39, BY.
4.38.2f Cape Triopion: Map 4.39, BX.
4.39.1a Assyria: Map 4.39, BY.
4.39.1b Arabia: Map 4.39, locator.
4.39.1c Arabian Gulf (modern Red Sea): Map 4.39, locator.
4.39.1d Herodotus seems to object to the conventional division because the landmasses are connected and therefore the continent does not really end.
4.39.1e On this canal, see 2.158.
4.39.2a Mediterranean Sea: Map 4.39, BX. Here and at 4.41 Herodotus calls the Mediterranean simply "this sea," referring to the sea closest to himself and his audience.

4.39.2b Syria: Map 4.39, BY.
4.39.2c Egypt: Map 4.39, locator.
4.40.1a Caspian Sea: Map 4.39, AY.
4.40.1b Araxes River: Map 4.39, AY. Here Herodotus is very clear in identifying the Armenian Araxes, which flows east into the Caspian Sea. See also n. 4.11.1a.
4.40.2a India: Map 4.39, locator.
4.41.1a Libya (modern Africa): Map 4.39, locator.
4.41.1b Herodous writes "100,000 fathoms." This would equal 1,029 stades or 113 miles, a gross overestimate. The true distance today is closer to 70 miles. See 1.158.4 and Distance Conversions, p. lxiv, and Appendix J, Ancient Greek Units of Currency, Weight, and Distance, §4, 5, 19.
4.42.1a Herodotus means that since the northern boundaries of Europe are unknown, one cannot compare its size in width to the other landmass.

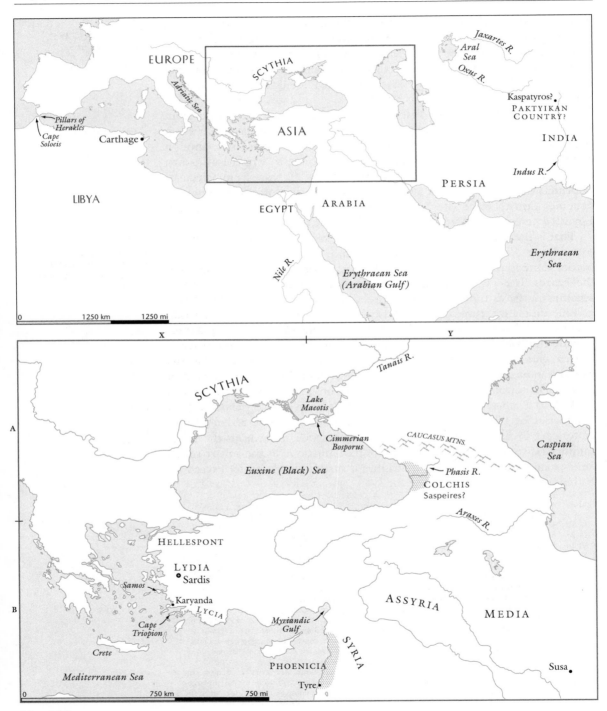

MAP 4.39

where it borders Asia. The first one we know of to have discovered this fact was Nechos king of Egypt.[a] After he had stopped excavation work on the canal, which extended from the Nile[b] to the Arabian Gulf, he sent some Phoenicians off on boats with orders to sail around Libya and back through the Pillars of Herakles[c] into the Mediterranean Sea[d] and to return by that route to Egypt. [3] And so the Phoenicians set out from the Erythraean Sea[a] and sailed the Southern Sea. Whenever autumn came, they would put in to shore at whatever region of Libya they happened to have reached in order to sow seeds. There they would wait for the harvest, [4] and after reaping their crops, they would sail on again. This they did for two years, and in the third, they came around through the Pillars of Herakles and returned to Egypt. They mentioned something else which I do not find credible, though someone else may: that when they were sailing around Libya, the sun was on their right side as they went.[a]

That is how knowledge of this land was first obtained. The next people to speak on this subject are the Carthaginians.[a]

But there is also the story of an Achaimenid Persian named Sataspes son of Teaspes. He was sent by his mother to sail around Libya but failed to accomplish the feat, returning because he feared the length of the voyage and the desolate nature of the land. [2] He had previously raped the virgin daughter of Zopyros son of Megabyzos, for which reason King Xerxes intended to have him impaled. But Sataspes' mother, who was the sister of Darius, pleaded with him not to carry out this sentence, claiming that she would impose an even greater penalty: [3] she said she would compel him to sail from Egypt all the way around Libya until he came to the Arabian Gulf. Xerxes agreed to this condition, so Sataspes journeyed to Egypt, obtained a ship and sailors there, and sailed west toward the Pillars of Herakles. [4] After he passed through the Pillars, he rounded the cape of Libya called Soloeis[a] and then sailed south for many months, during which he traversed a long stretch of sea. Eventually, because there seemed to be nothing but more sea ahead, he turned around and sailed back to Egypt.

4.43
Herodotus' account of Sataspes' unsuccessful attempt to circumnavigate Africa.

4.42.2a Modern historians call this king Nechos II (610–595). On Nechos' uncompleted canal project, see 2.158–159.
4.42.2b Nile River: Map 4.39, locator.
4.42.2c Pillars of Herakles (modern Straits of Gibraltar): Map 4.39, locator.
4.42.2d Here Herodotus calls the Mediterranean "the northern sea" because he is adopting the perspective of the Egyptian pharaoh, who has told these Phoenicians to circumnavigate Africa clockwise, and to return through the Straits of Gibraltar and into what, for the Egyptians, is "the northern sea."
4.42.3a Erythraean Sea (in this case the modern Red Sea or Arabian Gulf): Map 4.39, locator.
4.42.4a Of course, this piece of information,

which Herodotus finds unbelievable, serves to support the veracity of their account for us, because as one rounded the Cape of Good Hope, deep into the Southern Hemisphere and sailing west, the sun would indeed be on their right, which it never is for someone facing west in the Northern Hemisphere. (Godley)
4.43.1a Carthage: Map 4.39, locator. This provocative sentence is left hanging. Although some scholars have interpreted it from the context to mean that the Carthaginians agree that Libya is surrounded by water, the fact is that Herodotus does not tell us what the Carthaginians say on this subject.
4.43.4a Cape Soloeis: Map 4.39, locator.

[5] From there he went to King Xerxes and described the short people he had seen while sailing along the coast of the most distant regions. He said they wore clothes made of palm leaves, and whenever he and his sailors came to land, they would flee to the mountains, forsaking their towns. Sataspes and his men refrained from attacking them and did them no harm, taking only their flocks. [6] And he said that the reason he did not complete the voyage around Libya was that it was impossible to sail any farther because the ship was held back and could not be made to move forward. Xerxes, however, was not convinced that Sataspes was telling the truth. And anyway, since he had not fulfilled the assigned task, Xerxes imposed the penalty of his original verdict and had him impaled. [7] A eunuch of Sataspes' ran off to Samos[a] with a large quantity of goods as soon as he learned of his master's death. These goods were seized by a Samian man whose name I know, but which I choose to forget here.

But as to Asia, most of it was discovered by Darius. There is a river, Indus,[a] the second of all rivers in the production of crocodiles. Darius, desiring to know where this Indus empties into the sea, sent ships manned by Skylax, a man of Karyanda,[b] and others whose word he trusted; [2] these set out from the city of Kaspatyros[a] and the Paktyikan country[b] and sailed down the river toward the east and the sunrise until they came to the sea; and voyaging over the sea westward, they came in the thirtieth month to that place from which the Egyptian king sent the above-mentioned Phoenicians to sail around Libya. [3] After this circumnavigation, Darius subjugated the Indians and made use of this sea. Thus it was discovered that Asia, except the parts toward the rising sun, was in other respects like Libya.

The boundaries of Europe, on the other hand, have not been ascertained by anyone at all, either in the areas toward the rising sun or toward the north, nor is it known whether or not it is surrounded by water. What is known is that its length extends along both of the other lands. [2] But I cannot understand why there are three names for a single landmass, with all these names representing women, nor why the boundaries set for them are the Nile River[a] in Egypt and the Colchian Phasis River,[b] though others say the boundaries are the Maeotic Tanais River[c] and the Cimmerian ferries.[d] And I have not even been able to find out who it was that established these boundaries or where they obtained these names. [3] Nowadays, many Hellenes say that Libya was named after a native Libyan woman, and that Asia was named after the wife of Prometheus.[a] The Lydians,[b] however, also lay claim to this name, asserting that Asia was named

4.44
Skylax sails from the Indus River to Egypt.

4.45
The boundaries of Europe are unknown, as is the reason that all three major lands are named afer women.

4.43.7a Samos: Map 4.39, BX.
4.44.1a Indus River: Map 4.39, locator.
4.44.1b Karyanda: Map 4.39, BX.
4.44.2a Kaspatyros, possible location: Map 4.39, locator.
4.44.2b Paktyikan country, possible location: Map 4.39, locator.
4.45.2a Nile River: Map 4.39, locator.
4.45.2b Phasis River, Colchis: Map 4.39, AY.

4.45.2c Tanais (modern Don) River, Lake Maeotis (modern Sea of Azov): Map 4.39, AY.
4.45.2d Cimmerian ferries, narrow straits within the Cimmerian Bosporus: Map 4.39, AY. See 4.12.
4.45.3a Prometheus is the Fire-giver celebrated by Aeschylus in his play *Prometheus Bound*.
4.45.3b Lydia: Map 4.39, BX.

after Asies son of Cotys son of Manes, not after Asia wife of Prometheus. And, they say, it was after Asies that the tribe called Asias in Sardis[c] was named. [4] No one in the world knows if Europe is surrounded by water, nor where its name came from or who really gave it this name, unless we shall say that the place got its name from Europa of Tyre[a] but had no name before that, just as the other lands once had no name. [5] This woman Europa, however, was evidently from Asia, and did not ever come to the land now called Europe by the Hellenes, but went from Phoenicia[a] to Crete[b] and from Crete to Lycia.[c] Let that be enough said about this, for we shall, after all, use the conventional boundaries and names for these places.

The Pontic region[a] to which Darius was leading his army is, except for the Scythians,[b] inhabited by the most ignorant peoples of all. For we cannot cite the wisdom of any nation there, other than the Scythian people, nor do we know of any man noted for wisdom in the Pontic region other than Anacharsis.[c] [2] The Scythians were more clever than any other people in making the most important discovery we know of concerning human affairs, though I do not admire them in other respects. They have discovered how to prevent any attacker from escaping them and how to make it impossible for anyone to overtake them against their will. [3] For instead of establishing towns or walls, they are all mounted archers who carry their homes along with them and derive their sustenance not from cultivated fields but from their herds. Since they make their homes on carts,[a] how could they not be invincible or impossible even to engage in battle?

They were helped in making this discovery by their land and their rivers, which foster and support this way of life. For their land is flat, grassy, and well watered, and the rivers running through it are not much fewer in number than the canals of Egypt.

[2] I shall now name all their rivers that are notable and navigable from the sea: the Ister, with its five mouths; next, the Tyras; the Hypanis; the Borysthenes; the Panticapes; the Hypakyris; the Gerros; and the Tanais. The courses of these rivers are as follows.

The Ister[a] is the largest of all rivers known to us, and it flows with equal volume in summer and winter. It is the first of the Scythian rivers one encounters coming from the west and is therefore the most voluminous, since many other rivers flow into it. [2] Adding to its volume are these five substantial rivers, which also flow through Scythian territory: the river

4.46
SCYTHIA
Brilliant discovery by the Scythians for military strategy: total mobility—no fixed towns or walls.

4.47
SCYTHIA
The rivers of Scythia.

4.48
SCYTHIA
The Ister (Danube) is the greatest of all rivers, and the westernmost river of Scythia.

4.45.3c   Sardis: Map 4.39, BX.
4.45.4a   Tyre: Map 4.39, BY. For the story of Europa of Tyre, see 1.2.1.
4.45.5a   Phoenicia: Map 4.39, BY.
4.45.5b   Crete (Creta): Map 4.39, BX.
4.45.5c   Lycia: Map 4.39, BX.
4.46.1a   Pontic region, the area around the Euxine (Black) Sea: Map 4.39, AX.
4.46.1b   Scythia: Map 4.39, AX, and locator.

4.46.1c   For more on Anacharsis, see 4.76–77.
4.46.3a   Not all Scythians were mobile nomads. See Appendix G, §5. Figure 4.46 shows two clay models of Scythian wagons.
4.48.1a   Ister (modern Danube) River: Map 4.53 AX.

FIGURE 4.46. CLAY MODELS OF SCYTHIAN WAGON TYPES FOUND IN SCYTHIAN TOMBS.

called Porata by the Scythians, but Pyretos[a] by the Hellenes; the Tiarantos,[b] the Araros,[c] the Naparis,[d] and the Ordessos.[e] [3] The first-mentioned river is quite large and shares its waters with the Ister as it flows in from the east. The second, the Tiarantos, is smaller and flows westward. The Araros, Naparis, and Ordessos flow between these and also empty into the Ister. [4] These are the rivers that help to fill it that have a genuine source in Scythia itself, while the Maris River,[a] which also mingles with the Ister, flows from the land of the Agathyrsoi.[b]

And from the peaks of Mount Haemus[a] flow three other rivers toward the north and then fall into it as well: the Atlas,[b] the Auras,[c] and the Tibiskos.[d] Through Thrace[e] and the land of the Thracian Krobyzians[f] flow the Athrys,[g] the Noas,[h] and the Artanes,[i] which then empty into the Ister.

4.49
SCYTHIA
Major tributaries of the Ister River.

4.48.2a   Pyretos River: Map 4.53, AX.
4.48.2b   Tiarantos River, possible location: Map 4.53, AX.
4.48.2c   Araros River: location unknown.
4.48.2d   Naparis River, possible location: Map 4.53, AX.
4.48.2e   Ordessos River: location unknown.
4.48.4a   Maris River: Map 4.53, AX. Herodotus probably means the modern Mures River, which some scholars feel he erroneously characterized as emptying directly into the Ister (modern Danube), whereas it actually flows into the Pathissus (modern Tisza), which then empties into the Ister. Pathissus and Ister Rivers: Map 4.53, AX. Of course the ancients may not always have adopted the modern relation between river and tributary. In this case, they might have identified the Pathissus as a tributary of the Maris, in which case it would lose its identity after joining the Maris River, which then continued to flow into the Ister.
4.48.4b   Agathyrsoi, approximate location of

territory: Map 4.53, Crimea inset. The Agathyrsoi can be archaeologically located on the banks of the Maris River: Map 4.53, AX. (Wheeler) See Appendix F, §3. However, the *Barrington Atlas* shows a label "Agathyrsoi" on its Map 23, A1, almost 200 miles to the east of the Maris River. Both identifications could be right, and refer to different time periods.
4.49.1a   Haemus Mountains: Map 4.53, BX.
4.49.1b   Atlas River: Ister system (modern Danube), location unknown.
4.49.1c   Auras River: Ister system, location unknown.
4.49.1d   Tibiskos River: Map 4.53, AX.
4.49.1e   Thrace: Map 4.53, BX.
4.49.1f   Thracian Krobyzians: location of territory unknown.
4.49.1g   Athrys River: Map 4.53, AX.
4.49.1h   Noas River: Ister system, location unknown.
4.49.1i   Artanes River: Ister system, location unknown.

The Oescus River[j] flows from the Paionians[k] and Mount Rhodope[l] and cuts through the middle of Haemus before flowing into the Ister. [2] And from the Illyrians,[a] the Angrus River[b] flows toward the north and empties into the Triballian Plain[c] and the Brongus River,[d] which then empties into the Ister. Thus the Ister receives large amounts of water from both these rivers. Further, out of the land above the Ombrikoi[e] flow the Carpis[f] as well as the Alpis,[g] flowing toward the north and then emptying into the Ister. [3] For the Ister itself actually flows through all of Europe, beginning at the land of the Celts, who, with the exception of the Kynetes, dwell at the farthest edge of Europe toward the setting sun; it then flows through the entire extent of Europe until it empties into the sea along Scythia's flank.

And so it is because of the rivers I have listed and many others, too, all contributing water to its volume, that the Ister becomes the greatest of all rivers, though if we compare one river to another by themselves, we find that the Nile[a] surpasses it in volume, since there is no river or spring which contributes to the size of the Nile. [2] It seems to me that the Ister maintains the same volume in summer and winter because in winter, when it may be slightly greater than its normal level, this land receives very little rain but there is a heavy snowfall everywhere. [3] In the summer, the heavy snows of the previous winter melt and flow into the Ister from all sides, and this melted snow combines with the rain that falls heavily and even violently during the summer, so that together they increase the volume of the river. [4] But the increase of the mingled waters is balanced by the summer sun, which draws up to itself more water than it does in winter, and thereby the river's volume appears to remain the same at all times.

But the Ister is just one of Scythia's rivers. After this one comes the Tyras,[a] which arises from the north, flowing out of a huge lake on the border between Scythian and Neurian territory.[b] At its mouth, Hellenes called the Tyritai[c] have established a colony.

The third river is the Hypanis.[a] This river begins in Scythia and flows out of a huge lake around which wild white horses graze. The lake is called Mother of Hypanis, and rightly so, [2] because it is from this lake that the Hypanis rises; from there it flows for a five-day journey in a swift stream and it is still sweet, but from this point on, and for a further four-day journey

4.50
SCYTHIA
The Nile may be greater in volume, but the Ister stays at the same height because it is regulated by snowmelt.

4.51
SCYTHIA
The Tyras River.

4.52
SCYTHIA
The Hypanis River.

4.49.1j Oescus River: Map 4.53, AX. Herodotus calls this the Scius River.
4.49.1k Paionians, location of territory: Map 4.53, BX.
4.49.1l Rhodope Mountains: Map 4.53, BX.
4.49.2a Illyria: Map 4.53, BX.
4.49.2b Angrus River, possible location: Map 4.53, AX.
4.49.2c Triballians, possible location of territory: Map 4.53, AX.
4.49.2d Brongus River, possible location: Map 4.53, AX.
4.49.2e Ombrikoi: location of territory unknown. For "Umbrians," see n. 1.94.6b.
4.49.2f Carpis River: Ister system, location unknown.

Its name could indicate that it originates in the Carpathian Mountains.
4.49.2g Alpis River: Ister system, location unknown. Its name could indicate that it originates in the Alps.
4.50.1a Nile River: Map 4.39, locator.
4.51.1a Tyras (modern Dniester) River: Map 4.53, Crimea inset.
4.51.1b Neurian territory, possible location: Map 4.118.
4.51.1c Tyritai, location of territory at the mouth of the Tyras River is unknown.
4.52.1a Hypanis (modern Bug) River: Map 4.53, Crimea inset.

toward the sea, its water is terribly brackish. [3] This change occurs because a brackish spring empties into it which is so bitter that, although it is rather small and the Hypanis is a great river surpassed in size by few others, as it mixes with the river, it renders its water brackish, too. This spring is located on the boundaries between the Scythian plowmen[a] and the Alazones.[b] It takes its name from the region in which it rises: this is called Exampaios[c] in the Scythian language, Hirai Hodoi[d] in Greek. [4] The Tyras and the Hypanis flow close to each other at the Alazones, but from there each turns away from the other, widening the distance between them.

4.53
SCYTHIA
The Borysthenes River.

The fourth river is the Borysthenes,[a] which is the largest after the Ister, and in our opinion the most productive, not only of Scythian rivers, but of all others as well—except of course for the Egyptian Nile, to which no other river can really be compared. [2] But of all the rest, the Borysthenes is most productive. It supplies the herds with the most beautiful and nurturing pastures and also provides by far the best and most numerous fish; its water is the sweetest for drinking and flows clear alongside others that are muddy; the seeds sown beside its waters grow the best, and where no seed is sown, the wild grass grows most thickly. [3] Salt deposits build up by themselves in abundant amounts at its mouth. And then there are the enormous invertebrate fish called *antakaioi*,[a] which are salted, and many other wondrous products from this river as well. [4] Now, the course of the river is known up to the land of the Gerroi[a] (a forty-day journey upstream to the north), but no one can describe the regions through which it flows above that point. It is clear, however, that it runs through an uninhabited region before entering the territory of the Scythian farmers,[b] who inhabit an area along the river for a ten-day journey. [5] Only this river and the Nile have sources which I cannot identify, but I don't believe any other Hellene can do so, either. When the Borysthenes nears the sea, the Hypanis River[a] joins it and then both empty into the same marsh. [6] Between these rivers lies a promontory called the Cape of Hippolaos[a] on which a sanctuary of Demeter has been built. The Borysthenites have established their settlement on the other side of the Hypanis, opposite the sanctuary.

4.54
SCYTHIA
The Panticapes River.

That is what can be said about these rivers, and after them we come to a fifth river, called the Panticapes.[a] This one also flows from a lake in the north, and between this river and the Borysthenes lies the land inhabited by the Scythian farmers. From there it flows into the land called Hylaia[b] and joins its waters with those of the Borysthenes.

4.52.3a Scythian plowmen, possible location of territory: Map 4.53, Crimea inset. See 4.17.
4.52.3b Alazones, approximate location of territory: Map 4.53, Crimea inset.
4.52.3c Exampaios: location unknown.
4.52.3d Hirai Hodoi translates as "Sacred Way."
4.52.1a Borysthenes (modern Dnieper) River: Map 4.53, Crimea inset.
4.53.3a *Antakaioi*: a type of sturgeon.
4.53.4a Gerroi: location of territory unknown.

4.53.4b Scythian farmers, possible location of territory: Map 4.53, Crimea inset.
4.53.5a The Hypanis (modern Bug) River does not join the Borysthenes, as Herodotus says here, although both rivers empty into the same estuary.
4.53.6a Cape of Hippolaos: Map 4.53, Hylaia inset.
4.54.1a Panticapes River, possible location: Map 4.53, Crimea inset.
4.54.1b Hylaia: Map 4.53, Hylaia inset.

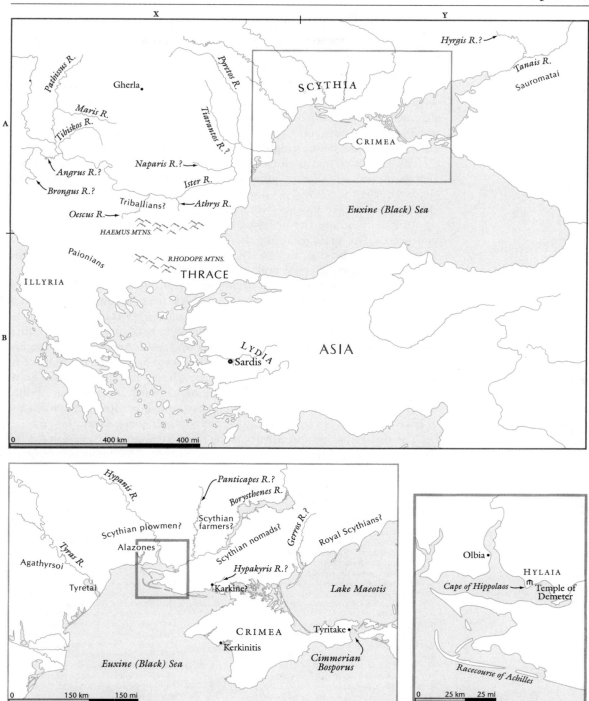

MAP 4.53

The sixth river is the Hypakyris,[a] whose source is a lake, from which it then flows right through the territory of the Scythian nomads[b] and empties out at the city of Karkine[c] with Hylaia and what is called the Racecourse of Achilles[d] to its right.

The seventh river, the Gerros,[a] splits off from the Borysthenes in the region where the Borysthenes is still known; from there it diverges into the region from which it gets its name, Gerros, then flows down toward the sea, forming the border between the land of the Scythian nomads and that of the Royal Scythians,[b] before emptying into the Hypakyris.

The eighth river, the Tanais,[a] has a great lake as its source, and from there it flows into an even greater lake called the Maeotis,[b] which divides the territory of the Royal Scythians from that of the Sauromatai.[c] And into the Tanais flows yet another river, called the Hyrgis.[d]

And so those are the noteworthy rivers with which the Scythians are endowed.[a] The grass growing there for the herds of cattle is the most bile-producing type known to us, which can be ascertained through the inspection of the dissected bodies of these animals.

Those, then, are their most important natural resources; it remains for me to describe the rest of their customs, which are as follows: the only gods they try to appease are Hestia, who is their most important divinity, Zeus, and Earth,[a] whom they consider to be the wife of Zeus; after these, they worship Apollo, Ourania Aphrodite, Herakles, and Ares. While these are the traditional gods of all the Scythians, the Royal Scythians also sacrifice to Poseidon. [2] In the Scythian language, Hestia is called Tabiti; Zeus, Papaios[a] (and most correctly so, in my opinion); Earth is called Api; Apollo, Goitosyros; Ourania Aphrodite, Argimpasa; and Poseidon, Thagimasadas. It is not their custom to erect statues, altars, or temples,[b] except for Ares.

The ritual they use for sacrifice is the same for all the gods except for the god Ares; it is performed as follows. The sacrificial victim stands by itself with its forefeet tied together in front of the sacrificer, who tugs on the end

4.55.1a　Hypakyris River, possible location: Map 4.53, Crimea inset.
4.55.1b　Scythian nomads, possible location of territory: Map 4.53, Crimea inset.
4.55.1c　Karkine: Map 4.53, Crimea inset. Herodotus is wrong about the site of Karkine and has probably misidentified the city Kerkinitis (Map 4.53, Crimea inset) on the coast of the Crimea. There are no remains of a city in the location indicated by Herodotus, and the land there is very hilly and not a good location for a city. (Wheeler)
4.55.1d　Racecourse of Achilles, a strip of land, now islands, about 80 miles long: Map 4.53, Hylaia inset.
4.56.1a　Gerros River, possible location: Map 4.53, Crimea inset. Scholars do not agree on the identification of this river or the region.
4.56.1b　Royal Scythians, possible location: Map 4.53, Crimea inset.
4.57.1a　Tanais (modern Don) River: Map 4.53, AY.

4.57.1b　Lake Maeotis (modern Sea of Azov): Map 4.53, Crimea inset.
4.57.1c　Sauromatai, approximate location of territory: Map 4.53, AY.
4.57.1d　Hyrgis River, possible location: Map 4.53, AY. Perhaps the Syrgis of 4.123; it may be the modern Donetz River.
4.58.1a　For an identification of the rivers of Herodotus with modern rivers, see Appendix F, §1. This description of Scythian territory as the land lying between the Ister (modern Danube) and the Tanais (modern Don) is not consistent with his later description (4.99–101) of Scythia as a square twenty-days' journey on each side, bounded on the south by the Black Sea and on the east by Lake Maeotis (modern Sea of Azov).
4.59.1a　Earth: Herodotus uses the name Ge (meaning "earth") from Greek mythology.
4.59.2a　Papaios: the name is similar to the Greek word for "father."
4.59.2b　Most unlike the Greek practices.

of a rope from behind the animal and thus brings it down. [2] As it falls, he invokes the god to whom he is sacrificing and then, casting a noose around its neck, inserts a stick into the noose which he proceeds to twist, thereby strangling the victim. He neither lights a fire, performs a preliminary rite of consecration, nor pours libations. Instead, after strangling the victim, he skins it and then begins to boil the meat.

Since the Scythian land has very little wood, the Scythians have devised their own way to boil their meat. After skinning the victim, they strip the meat from the bones and put it into a cauldron if they happen to have one; the cauldrons of Scythia are much like the mixing bowls of Lesbos, except far larger. Then they boil the meat in these cauldrons by burning the bones of the victim beneath the cauldron. If they do not happen to have a cauldron, they place all the meat inside the stomach of the victim, mix in some water, and then burn the bones beneath the stomach. [2] The bones produce a fine blazing fire, while the stomachs easily expand to enclose the meat stripped from the bones. In this way an ox and every other victim completely cooks itself. When the meat has finished cooking, the sacrificer makes an offering of some of the meat and entrails by tossing them before him. They sacrifice mostly horses, but all kinds of other animals as well.

That is how they sacrifice animals to all their gods except Ares, for whom their practice is different. A sanctuary for Ares is set up in each district of their provinces; they pile together bundles of sticks up to 580 yards[a] in length and width, and slightly less in height. The top of it is squared and flattened off, and three of the sides are steep, while the fourth can be climbed. [2] Each year an additional 150 wagonloads of sticks are heaped upon it, since the pile always settles and sinks due to storms in winter. On top of each pile is set an ancient iron sword,[a] which serves as the cult image of Ares. Every year they bring to the sword sacrifices of horses and other animals; and they also sacrifice another kind of victim to Ares more than they do for the other gods. [3] Of all the enemies they capture alive in war, they sacrifice one out of every hundred, but in a different manner than they sacrifice animals. They pour wine over the man's head, cut his throat over a jar, carry the jar up to the pile of sticks, and pour the blood upon the sword. [4] In addition to taking the blood up to the sword, down below, they cut off the right arms of all the men who have been slaughtered and they cast them up in the air. After the other victims have been sacrificed, they depart, leaving behind the arms to lie just where they have fallen, apart from the bodies.

Those, then, are the Scythians' sacrificial rituals. However, they do not sacrifice pigs and are unwilling even to raise them in their country at all.

4.61
SCYTHIA
How the Scythians cook their meat without wood.

4.62
SCYTHIA
How the Scythians sacrifice to Ares.

4.63
SCYTHIA
Pigs are not sacrificed.

4.62.1a Herodotus writes "3 stades." See Appendix J, §5–7, 19.
4.62.2a Herodotus uses the Persian word *akinakes*, a dagger or short sword. The Scythian practice of symbolizing the war god Ares by a sword stuck in the ground was also used by the Sarmatian Alans centuries later, one argument for the continuity of steppe culture.

4.64
SCYTHIA
Scythian treatment of
the bodies of enemies
taken in war.

Their customs concerning war are as follows. Whenever a Scythian slays his first man, he drinks some of his blood. He brings the heads of all those he slays in battle back to the king, and by bringing back a head, he receives a share of whatever plunder has been taken, but if he does not bring back a head, he receives nothing.[a] [2] He flays the head by first cutting in a circle around the ears and then, taking hold of it, shaking off the skin. He then scrapes it out with an ox's rib and works the skin in his hands until he has softened it, after which he uses it as a handkerchief, which he proudly attaches to the bridle of his horse. And he who displays the most skin handkerchiefs is esteemed as the best man. [3] Many Scythians make cloaks to wear from the skins by stitching the scalps together like shepherds' coats. Many also take the hands from the corpses of their enemies, skin them, and use them with the fingernails still intact as covers for their quivers. It turns out that human skin is both thick and translucent, in fact the most translucent of all types of skin because of its whiteness. [4] Many Scythians flay the skin from the entire bodies of men, stretch them over frames of wood, and carry them on their horses as they ride around.

4.65
SCYTHIA
Scythians make drinking
cups from the heads of
their bitterest enemies.

That is what they customarily do with the skins. They treat the skulls—not all of them, but those of their most hated enemies—in the following way. They saw off everything below the eyebrows and clean out everything that remains. If a poor man is doing this, he only stretches an untanned piece of oxhide around the outside and uses it as is. But if he is wealthy, he not only stretches an oxhide around the outside, but he gilds it on the inside as well, and the skull is then used as a drinking cup.[a] [2] They also do this to the skulls of their relatives if they have a dispute and one of them overpowers the other in the presence of the king. And when outsiders who are considered important come to visit a man, he brings out these heads and explains that, though these were his relatives, they brought war upon the family and he overpowered them. That is how they define a man's valor.

4.66
SCYTHIA
An honor for those
who have slain enemies.

Once every year in each district, the local governor mixes wine in a bowl and the Scythians who in that year have killed enemies drink from it. Those who have not managed to achieve this do not taste the wine, but instead sit apart in dishonor; indeed, this is the greatest disgrace among them. But any of them who have killed a very great number of men have two cups, and drink from them both.

The Scythians have many soothsayers, who practice their art with rods of willow as follows. They take huge bundles of rods, set them on the ground, and untie them. Then they set one rod upon another as they declare their prophecies and finally gather and bind them all up again one by one while still making their declaration. [2] That is their ancestral technique, but the

---

4.64.1a   Head hunting was also practiced by the
          Taurians of the Crimea and various
          Celtic peoples. Herodotus writes in
          1.214 that Tomyris, the queen of the
          Massagetai, cut off the head of the dead

Cyrus. See Appendix E, §11.
4.65.1a   Archaeologists have found skull cups in
          Scythian sites and skeletons which have
          shown distinct evidence of having been
          scalped. See Appendix E, §11.

Enarees,[a] the men-women, say that their own technique was given to them by Aphrodite. They prophesy by means of the bark of a linden tree: after splitting the bark into three strips, they braid and unbraid them with their fingers while giving their prophecies.

Whenever the king of the Scythians falls ill, he sends for three of the most distinguished soothsayers, and they perform prophecies in the first way that I described. What they generally report is that some person has sworn falsely by the royal hearth, and they accuse one of the townspeople by name. [2] In fact, it is the Scythian custom that when someone wants to swear the most solemn kind of oath, he most often does so by the royal hearth. The man named by these prophets is immediately apprehended and brought to the soothsayers, who charge that their prophecy has revealed him to be a perjurer on the royal hearth and thus to be the cause of the king's present pain. When the accused man protests vehemently and denies the charge, [3] the king responds by sending for twice as many soothsayers. If they, too, condemn the man as a perjurer through their prophecies, the man is immediately beheaded, and the first three prophets divide up his possessions by lot. [4] But if the recently summoned soothsayers in addition to the other three absolve him of the charge, then other soothsayers come, and again more besides. If the majority of all these acquit the man, it is decreed that the first three prophets themselves must die.

In that case, they are put to death as follows. The soothsayers, who have their feet bound, their hands tied behind their backs, and their mouths gagged, are thrust into the middle of a wagon that is filled with sticks and has oxen yoked to it. The sticks are then set on fire, and the oxen are released and put to flight. [2] Many of the oxen are burned up together with the prophets, while others are only scorched as they flee when their yoke pole catches fire. Prophets are burned in the same way for other reasons as well, when they are designated false prophets. [3] Moreover, those put to death by the king leave no sons behind, because the king kills all their male offspring, too, although he does no harm to the females.

This is how the Scythians swear oaths, no matter to whom they are swearing them. They pour wine mixed with their own blood—extracted from their bodies by stabbing themselves with awls or by making small knife cuts—into a large earthenware cup. They then dip a short sword,[a] some arrows, a battle-axe,[b] and a javelin into the cup. After this has been done, they declare their pledges and invoke many sanctions, and those directly involved in the pact together with their most worthy followers drink from the cup.

The kings of Scythia are buried in the land of the Gerroi[a] at the site where the Borysthenes[b] becomes navigable. Whenever one of their kings

4.68
SCYTHIA
When the Scythian king falls ill.

4.69
SCYTHIA
Scythian method of executing diviners.

4.70
SCYTHIA
How the Scythians make sworn pledges.

4.71
SCYTHIA
How the Scythians bury their kings.

4.67.2a Enarees: here Herodotus means impotent men, hermaphrodites. See 1.105 and n. 1.105.4a.
4.70.1a Herodotus uses the Persian word *akinakes*, a dagger or short sword.
4.70.1b For battle-axe, Herodotus here uses *sagaris*, as at 1.215.1 and 4.5.3.
4.71.1a Gerroi: location of territory unknown.
4.71.1b Borysthenes (modern Dnieper) River: Map 4.53, Crimea inset.

dies, they dig a large square pit in the ground there to receive the corpse, which has been prepared as follows. The belly is cut open, cleaned out, and filled with crushed galingale,[c] incense, celery seed, and aniseed. Then it is sewn up, and the entire body is coated with wax. From the Royal Scythians[d] it is carried in a wagon to another nation, [2] whose people receive the corpse brought to them and observe the same practice as has already been performed by the Royal Scythians: they cut off a piece from their ears, shear their hair all around their heads, make incisions all over their arms, scratch their faces and noses, and thrust arrows through their right hands. [3] Then these people take the king's corpse in the wagon to another people under Scythian rule, while those who have already received it follow along. When the corpse has made its rounds to all of them, it comes to the Gerroi, who dwell at the farthest boundary of the peoples under Scythian rule, in whose territory the royal graves are located. [4] They bring the corpse into the pit mentioned earlier, place it on a bed of rushes, and on both sides of it set up spears over which planks of wood have been extended and covered over with rushes to form a roof. Then they strangle one of the king's concubines and also his cupbearer, his cook, his groom, his principal servant, his courier, and his horses, and they bury them all in the remaining open space of the grave, along with the prized possessions dedicated by others and golden libation bowls (they use neither silver nor bronze). [5] After they have done all this, everyone enthusiastically joins in building up a huge mound, which they strive together to make as large as possible.[a]

4.72
SCYTHIA
More sacrifices at the king's grave one year later.

One year later, they attend to the rites once again. They first choose the most suitable of the surviving servants; these are native Scythians, for all whom the king orders to become his servants must do so, and servants are not bought and sold among the Scythians.[a] [2] Of these they strangle fifty males, and also fifty of the king's best horses. Then they remove the guts from both men and horses, clean them out, fill them with chaff, and stitch them up again. [3] Next, they set up half a wheel inverted on two pieces of wood, and the other half inverted on two other pieces, and repeat this process until they have erected many of these structures. They then drive thick shafts of wood lengthwise through the horses up to their necks, and mount them on the inverted half wheels. [4] The wheels in front hold up the horse's shoulders, while those in back support the belly alongside the thighs, and both legs hang in the air. Bridles and bits are fitted onto the horses, stretched down over the front and secured with pegs. [5] Then they mount each of the fifty strangled young men on a horse by driving a shaft of wood straight along his spine up to his neck, fixing the lower projecting

4.71.1c Galingale: a gingerlike plant.
4.71.1d Royal Scythians, possible location: Map 4.53, Crimea inset.
4.71.5a There are many large burial mounds in the former Scythian territory whose interiors, as exposed by archaeologists, support Herodotus' description, including the remains of animals and servants which were

slain and buried with the king. See Appendix E, §9, for a description of Scythian burial rites and Figure E.1 for a drawing of the contents of a Royal Scythian tomb.
4.72.1a This contrasts with slavery among the Hellenes, who bought, sold, and enslaved captives of war and did not often enslave, or think it right to enslave, their fellow Hellenes.

part of the shaft into a socket cut into the shaft driven through the horse. After arranging these horsemen in a circle around the burial site, they ride away.[a]

That is how they bury their kings, but when the other Scythians die, their closest relatives lay them out on a wagon and bring them around to each of their friends. The friends all welcome them and serve a feast to those accompanying the corpse, and they also set out before the corpse a portion of everything offered to the rest. The bodies of ordinary Scythians are carried around like this for forty days, and are then buried. [2] After a burial, Scythians purify themselves by washing their heads and cleansing their bodies as follows: they first lean three stakes of wood against one another and then stretch woolen cloth around them, securing it as tightly as possible. Then they throw red-hot stones into a trough set in between the stakes.

Now there is a plant called cannabis, which grows in their land and which most resembles flax, except that cannabis is far superior in its thickness and size. It grows both wild and cultivated, and from it the Thracians make clothing very much like garments of linen. Unless someone had real expertise, he would think they were made of linen and not cannabis; and if he had never seen cannabis at all, he would certainly think the cloth was linen.

Well, the Scythians take the seeds of this cannabis, creep beneath the wool covering the stakes, and throw the seeds onto the blazing-hot stones within. When the seeds hit the stones, they produce smoke and give off a vapor such as no steam bath in Hellas could surpass. [2] The Scythians howl, awed and elated by the vapor.[a] This takes the place of a bath for them, since they do not use any water at all to wash their bodies. [3] But the women pour water into a mixture of cypress, cedar, and frankincense wood, which they have ground on rough stone. They apply this thick substance all over their bodies and their faces, and thus become steeped in the fragrance; and in addition, when they remove the plaster the next day, they emerge from it sparkling clean.

The Scythians are another people who avoid foreign customs at all costs,[a] especially those of the Hellenes, as is clearly illustrated by the cases of Anacharsis and Skyles. [2] Anacharsis went abroad and saw a great deal of the world, demonstrating great wisdom along the way, and on his return home to Scythia, he sailed through the Hellespont[a] and put in at Cyzicus,[b] [3] where he discovered the citizens celebrating a splendid and magnificent

4.73
SCYTHIA
How the Scythians bury their nonroyal dead.

4.74
SCYTHIA
Hemp grows in Scythia and is made into cloth like linen.

4.75
SCYTHIA
The Scythians use the hemp seed to bathe.

4.76
SCYTHIA
Scythian attitudes toward foreign customs and toward Scythians who adopt them, as exemplified by the tale of Anacharsis.

4.72.5a The fourteenth-century Arab traveler Ibn Battutah reported the impaling of horses and servants at the burial of a Mongol chieftain, a practice recalling Scythian royal burials, and one which might argue for the continuity of steppe culture. (Wheeler)

4.75.1a For Scythian use of intoxicants, see Appendix E, §12. Figure 4.73 shows a Scythian kit for inhaling hemp, including poles, a brazier, and a scorching

vessel, used as Herodotus describes it. Opium and hashish have been found in some second- or third-century A.D. Sarmatian Alan tombs in the north Caucasus area, another instance of the continuity of steppe culture.

4.76.1a Herodotus alludes here to the Egyptians, who also resist foreign customs; see 2.91.
4.76.2a Hellespont: Map 4.81, inset.
4.76.2b Cyzicus: Map 4.81, inset.

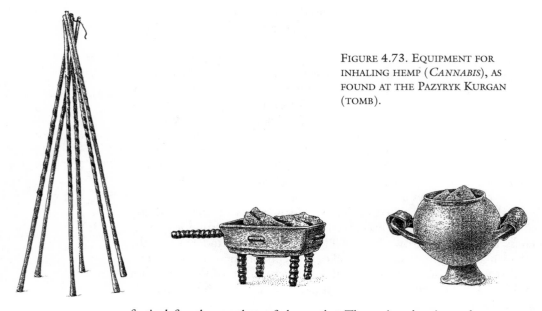

FIGURE 4.73. EQUIPMENT FOR INHALING HEMP (*CANNABIS*), AS FOUND AT THE PAZYRYK KURGAN (TOMB).

festival for the mother of the gods.[a] There Anacharsis made a vow to the mother that if he returned to his own land safe and sound, he would sacrifice just as he saw the Cyzicans doing and would also institute a nightlong festival for her. [4] And when he returned to Scythia, he retreated to the place called Hylaia[a] (which is next to the Racecourse of Achilles[b] and happens to be full of a great variety of trees), and here he celebrated the rites of the goddess in their entirety, with a drum and with images tied upon him. [5] But one of the Scythians saw him doing this and told the king, Saulios. The king himself then went to the same place, and when he saw Anacharsis performing these rites, he shot him with an arrow and killed him. And because Anacharsis had gone abroad, visited Hellas, and practiced foreign customs, if anyone even now asks the Scythians about him, they deny knowing about him at all. [6] I learned from Tymnes,[a] the chief official of Ariapeithes, that Anacharsis was the paternal uncle of Idanthyrsos king of the Scythians and the son of Gnouros son of Lykos, who was the son of Spargapeithes. And so if this was the family of Anacharsis, he should know that he died at the hand of his own brother, for Idanthyrsos was the son of Saulios, and it was Saulios who killed Anacharsis.[b]

I have heard yet another story about Anacharsis, told by the Peloponnesians, who claim that Anacharsis was sent away by the king of the Scythians to become an expert on Hellas, and that when he returned, he reported

4.77
SCYTHIA
The Peloponnesian story about Anacharsis.

4.76.3a   Mother of the gods: also known as Cybele or Kybele.
4.76.4a   Hylaia (the name means "woodlands"): Map 4.53, Hylaia inset.
4.76.4b   Racecourse of Achilles: Map 4.53, Crimea inset.
4.76.6a   Some scholars believe that Tymnus may be Herodotus' chief source for the geography and history of Scythia.
4.76.6b   The historicity of Anacharsis cannot be proved. He is probably a Greek invention.

to the king who sent him that all Hellenes were too busy to direct their attention to any kind of wisdom except for the Lacedaemonians,[a] and that it was possible to engage in a proper and sensible discussion only with them. [2] But this story is actually nothing more than a joke that Hellenes like to tell. And the man was really slain just as I described earlier. That, then, is how Anacharsis fared because of his close associations with foreign customs and Hellenes.

Many, many years later, something similar happened to Skyles son of Ariapeithes.[a] His mother was from Istria[b]—she was not Scythian at all—and she herself taught him both to speak and to read and write Greek. [2] Some time later, Ariapeithes met his end, betrayed by the treachery of Spargapeithes king of the Agathyrsoi,[a] and Skyles inherited the kingdom of his father and also his father's wife, whose name was Opoia. This Opoia was a local woman and had already borne a son, Orikos, to Ariapeithes. [3] Although he ruled as king of the Scythians, Skyles was not at all content to live as the Scythians did but, because of his education, was much more inclined to practice Hellenic customs. For example, whenever he led out the Scythian army and arrived at the village of the Borysthenites,[a] who claim to be Milesians,[b] he would leave his army outside the city [4] and would himself go within the town wall, having the gates locked behind him, and once rid of the presence of the Scythian army, he would put on Hellenic clothing and walk through the agora wearing it, with neither bodyguards nor anyone else attending him. Meanwhile, he had people guard the gates so that none of the Scythians would be able to see him wearing this apparel. In other respects, too, he practiced the Hellenic way of life, and he set up sanctuaries to the gods in accordance with Hellenic customs as well. [5] After spending a month or more among the Borysthenites, he would change back into his Scythian clothes and depart. He did this quite often; he even had a house built for himself in Borysthenes and brought a local woman home to it as his wife.

But it was fated that things would turn out badly for Skyles, and this is what led to his downfall. He had conceived a desire to be initiated into the rites of Bacchic Dionysos, but just as his initiation was at hand, the most

4.78
SCYTHIA
The story of Skyles, the Scythian king who took up Greek ways.

4.79
SCYTHIA
Some Scythians see Skyles cavorting with Bacchic worshipers.

4.77.1a Lacedaemon (Sparta): Map 4.81. Herodotus uses the names Spartans and Lacedaemonians interchangeably. "Spartans," however, often refers specifically to citizens of the state of Sparta, whereas any inhabitant of the territory of Lacedaemon is a Lacedaemonian. See Appendix B, The Spartan State in War and Peace, §5, 7, and n. B.7a.

4.78.1a The historicity of Skyles is thought to be confirmed by the gold signet ring shown in Figure 4.78 with an inscription identifying it as belonging to Skyles. It can be argued, however, that Skyles is a dynastic and not a personal name. Coins with the Greek legend "SK" and "SKUL" are known to be from the Dnieper River area.

4.78.1b Istria (Histria): Map 4.81.

4.78.2a Agathyrsoi, approximate location of territory: Map 4.81. The Agathyrsoi can be archaeologically located on the banks of the Ancient Maris (modern Mures) River: Map 4.53, AX. (Wheeler) See Appendix F, §3. However, the *Barrington Atlas* shows a label "Agathyrsoi" on its Map 23, A1, almost 200 miles to the east of the Maris. Both identifications could be right, and refer to different time periods. Although Herodotus says their customs were Thracian, their king Spargapeithes bears an Iranian name.

4.78.3a Village of the Borysthenites; also called Port of the Borysthenites (4.17), or just Borysthenes (4.78.5), or most frequently, Olbia: Map 4.81.

4.78.3b Miletus: Map 4.81.

FIGURE 4.78. A HEAVY GOLD
SCYTHIAN SIGNET RING WITH
THE GREEK INSCRIPTION
"SKYLEO," WHICH MEANS
"PROPERTY OF SKYLES."
FOUND SIX MILES SOUTH OF
ISTRIA AMONG COINS DATED
C. 450, IT BEARS ON ITS FACE
AN INSCRIPTION IN LETTER-
FORMS THAT CAN BE DATED
TO THE END OF THE SIXTH
OR EARLY FIFTH CENTURIES.

ominous portent occurred. [2] As I just mentioned, he had a house in the city of the Borysthenites. It was a vast and expensive property, surrounded by white stone statues of sphinxes and griffins. Well, the god hurled a thunderbolt at this house, which caused a fire that completely destroyed it. Nonetheless, Skyles went through with his initiation. [3] Now the Scythians reproach the Hellenes for their celebration of Bacchic rites because they say it is unfitting to seek out[a] a god who induces people to madness. [4] So when Skyles had been initiated into the Bacchic rites, one of the Borysthenites taunted the Scythians with these words: "You Scythians laugh at us because we celebrate Bacchus and the god takes possession of us. Well, now this same divinity has taken possession of your own king, and he is celebrating the Bacchic rites in a state of madness under the influence of the god. If you don't believe me, follow me and I will show you." [5] The leaders of the Scythians followed as the Borysthenite led them secretly to a tower and seated them there. When Skyles went past with his band of revelers, they observed him celebrating the Bacchic rites and, considering this to be a terrible disaster, left and told the whole army what they had seen.

4.80
SCYTHIA
Skyles flees but is turned over to the Scythians by the Thracians and is executed.

Afterward, Skyles marched back home, where the Scythians had revolted and had chosen his brother Octamasades, the son of Teras' daughter, to be their leader. [2] When Skyles learned what was happening and the reason for it, he fled to Thrace.[a] Upon hearing of this, Octamasades launched an expedition against Thrace, but when he reached the Ister, he found the Thracians there prepared to oppose him. Just as they were about to join battle, however, Sitalkes[b] sent this message to Octa-

4.79.3a Herodotus uses the Greek word
exeuriskein, which means "to seek out, to
try to find," but it also means "to
invent."
4.80.2a Thrace: Map 4.81, inset.

4.80.2b Sitalkes: the king of the Ordysian Thracians, who allied with the Athenians early
in the Peloponnesian War and would have
been well known to Herodotus' Athenian
audience. See *Thucydides* 2.29.

masades: [3] "Why should we make a trial of our strength in battle? After all, you are the son of my sister, and you hold my brother. Give my brother back to me, and I will hand over your brother Skyles to you. That way neither you nor I will endanger our troops." [4] That was the message Sitalkes sent and had proclaimed, for the brother of Sitalkes had in fact fled from him and had found refuge with Octamasades. Octamasades approved this suggestion and gave up his maternal uncle to Sitalkes, receiving his brother Skyles in return. [5] When Sitalkes got his brother back, he took him away with him, while Octamasades had Skyles beheaded on that very spot. So that is how protectively the Scythians uphold their own customs, and such are the penalties they exact on those who deviate from them by taking up foreign customs.

I have not been able to learn how many Scythians there are with certainty but have heard disparate accounts of their number. Some say that they are very numerous, while others claim they are few, particularly when counting only Scythians proper. [2] They did, however, present some evidence that I could see: there is a place between the Borysthenes River and the Hypanis River[a] called Exampaios,[b] which I mentioned a little earlier when I said its spring of brackish water runs into the Hypanis, making it undrinkable.[c] [3] At this site lies a bronze cauldron six times larger than the bowl dedicated by Pausanias son of Kleombrotos that is located at the mouth of the Pontus.[a] [4] In case someone has never seen that bowl, let me explain that the cauldron in Scythia easily holds 600 amphoras[a] and is six fingers thick. According to the local inhabitants, it was made out of arrowheads [5] when their king, whose name was Ariantas, seeking to determine the number of Scythians, ordered every Scythian to bring one arrowhead to him, and threatened death to anyone who failed to do so. [6] When a massive pile of arrowheads had been delivered to him, he decided to make something from all of them that he could leave behind as a memorial to his achievement. So he had this bronze cauldron made and dedicated at Exampaios. That, then, is what I heard concerning the number of the Scythians.[a]

Apart from the rivers of Scythia, which are larger and more numerous by far than those of any other country, this land does not contain marvels. I shall, however, mention one feature which, besides the rivers and the vastness of its plain, is truly marvelous and worthy of note. There is a footprint of Herakles that they show on a rock along the Tyras River,[a] resembling the

4.81
SCYTHIA
Scythian arrowheads gathered in a census are made into an immense vessel seen by Herodotus himself.

4.82
SCYTHIA
Many large rivers in Scythia, but no other marvels except Herakles' footprint.

4.81.2a Borysthenes and Hypanis Rivers: Map 4.81.
4.81.2b Exampaios: location unknown.
4.81.2c For the earlier mention of this brackish spring, see 4.52.3.
4.81.3a Pontus, or the Euxine (Black) Sea: Map 4.81. Pausanias, who led the Hellenes to victory over the Persians at the battle of Plataea in 479 (see 9.28–85), is said to have set up this cauldron in 478 or possibly 477 to commemorate the capture of Byzantium: Map 4.81, inset.

4.81.4a An amphora contained a little less than 9 gallons, so this bowl could hold more than 5,000 gallons.
4.81.6a Scholars cannot agree whether Herodotus' reference to having seen this bowl proves that he made a personal visit to Olbia (Map 4.81) and its environs. The cauldron he describes is larger than any bronze vessel known from ancient Greece or ancient China. See Appendix E, §5–7.
4.82.1a Tyras (modern Dniester) River: Map 4.81.

315

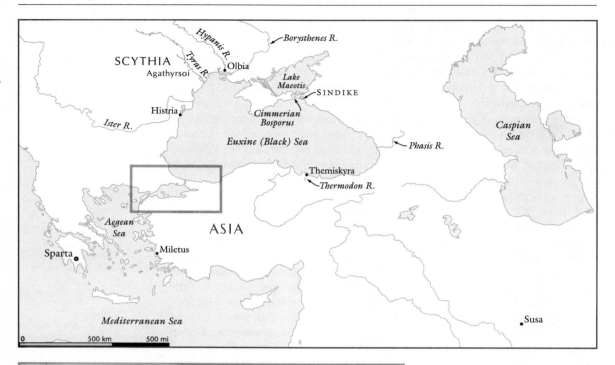

MAP 4.81

mark of a man's foot but three feet in length.[b] So much for all that; I shall now go back to the story I set out to tell at the beginning.[c]

In preparation for his campaign against Scythia, Darius sent messengers around his kingdom to order some of his subjects to provide troops for a land army, some to provide ships, and others to build a bridge across the Thracian Bosporus.[a] Darius' brother Artabanos son of Hystaspes pleaded with Darius not to lead an expedition against the Scythians, describing in detail how impossible it would be to deal with them.[b] [2] Although this was good advice, he could not persuade Darius to follow it, and so ceased his efforts. When Darius had completed his preparations, he led his army out of Susa.[a]

Just then one of the Persians, Oiobazos, asked Darius to leave behind one of his three sons who were serving in the army. Darius replied that he should leave all his sons behind, speaking to him as though to a friend making a moderate request. [2] Oiobazos was elated that his sons were released from military service. But Darius ordered those in charge of executions to put to death all three sons of Oiobazos, and indeed, after their throats had been cut, they were in fact left right there.[a]

Darius went on his way from Susa to Chalcedon[a] on the Bosporus, where the bridge had been built. There he embarked on a ship and sailed to what are called the Kyaneai Rocks,[b] which the Hellenes say were once floating. Sitting upon a height, Darius viewed the Pontus, which is really worth seeing, [2] for it is the most marvelous of all seas. Its length is 1,215 miles, and its width 365 miles at its widest point.[a] [3] Opening into this sea is a channel a little less than half a mile wide; the length of this entire strait, which is called the Bosporus,[a] and across which the bridge was built, is thirteen miles. The Bosporus extends to the Propontis, [4] which is fifty-five miles wide and 155 miles long;[a] It in turn flows into the Hellespont, a body of water which is, at its narrowest part, only eight-tenths of a mile wide although it is forty-four miles long;[b] the Hellespont empties into the vast expanse of the sea called the Aegean.[c]

4.83
513?
SUSA
Artabanos tries to dissuade Darius from attacking Scythia.

4.84
513?
SUSA
Darius executes all three sons of Oiobazos, who asked that one be released from military service.

4.85
CHALCEDON
Herodotus describes the dimensions and connections of the Pontus, Bosporus, Propontis, and Hellespont.

4.82.1b Herodotus writes "2 cubits," which equals approximately 36 inches. See Appendix J, §4, 5, 19.
4.82.1c Herodotus refers here to the story he began to tell back in 4.1.
4.83.1a Thracian Bosporus: Map 4.81, inset.
4.83.1b This Artabanos was later to attempt to persuade Xerxes not to attack Greece (7.10α–γ).
4.83.2a Susa: Map 4.81.
4.84.2a This story has clearly been inserted to illustrate the cruelty of Persian Kings and to contrast oriental despotism with Greek freedom—a motif of Herodotus' work.
4.85.1a Chalcedon: Map 4.81, inset.
4.85.1b Kyaneai Rocks (literally, blue-black or dark rocks): Map 4.81, inset. Located at the northwestern end of the Thracian Bosporus, these rocks were also known as the Symplegades (Clashing Rocks),

through which Jason and the Argonauts passed. See Glossary, Argonauts.
4.85.2a Herodotus gives these distances as "11,000 stades" long and "3,300 stades" wide. See Appendix J, §5–7, 19.
4.85.3a The Bosporus here is the Thracian Bosporus of Map 4.81, inset. Herodotus writes that it is "4 stades" wide and "120 stades" long. See Appendix J, §5–7, 19.
4.85.4a Propontis (modern Sea of Marmora): Map 4.81, inset. Herodotus writes these dimensions as "500 stades" wide and "1,400 stades long." See Appendix J, §6, 19.
4.85.4b The Hellespont (modern Dardanelles): Map 4.81, inset. Herodotus writes "7 stades" and "400 stades." See Appendix J, §5–7, 19.
4.85.4c Aegean Sea: Map 4.81.

4.86

PONTUS

How Herodotus measured
the dimensions of the
Pontus, the Bosporus,
and the Hellespont.

I arrived at these measurements in the following way. During the summer a ship usually traverses about 70,000 fathoms per day and 60,000 per night.[a] [2] And so, from the entrance to the Euxine (Black) Sea to Phasis,[a] which is the greatest extent of the Pontus lengthwise, a journey by boat takes nine days and eight nights, which adds up to 1,110,000 fathoms, or 1,220 miles.[b] [3] From Sindike[a] to Themiskyra[b] on the Thermodon River,[c] which is the widest part of the Pontus, it takes three days and two nights to cross by boat, adding up to 330,000 fathoms, or 363 miles.[d] [4] That is how I arrived at the measurements of the Pontus, the Bosporus, and the Hellespont, and they are in reality as I have described them.[a] The Pontus also contains a lake which flows out into it, not much smaller than the Pontus itself. This lake is called the Maeotis[b] and also Mother of the Pontus.

4.87

513

BOSPORUS

The numbers of men
and ships in the King's
expedition.

After Darius had gazed at the Pontus, he sailed back to the bridge, which had been planned and built under the supervision of Mandrokles of Samos.[a] Darius now viewed the Bosporus and set up on its shore two pillars of white stone, one engraved with Assyrian writing and the other with Greek, listing all the peoples who had contributed troops to the army that he was leading. He was in fact bringing with him peoples from all the nations he ruled; the army with its cavalry numbered 700,000, but that does not include the 600 ships of the navy which he had gathered there, too.[b] [2] Later, the people of Byzantium[a] took these pillars to their city and used them for their altar of Orthosia Artemis. They left one stone, however, which was covered with Assyrian writing, beside the temple of Dionysos in Byzantium. The site on the Bosporus at which King Darius built the bridge was, according to my own reckoning, halfway between Byzantium and the sanctuary[b] at the mouth of the Bosporus.

4.88

513

BOSPORUS

Darius rewards Mandrokles,
the Samian architect who
designed the bridge over the
Bosporus, and Mandrokles
dedicates an inscription.

Next, Darius expressed his delight with the bridge of boats by giving the engineer Mandrokles of Samos a multitude of gifts. Mandrokles reserved the first fruits of these and had a picture painted to portray the entire bridge over the Bosporus with King Darius sitting on his chair of state and the

4.86.1a   Herodotus uses the Greek fathom, equal
          to 6 Greek feet, which is the length of
          outstretched arms, to estimate that a ship
          travels 77 miles per day and 66 miles at
          night. See Appendix J, §2, 4–5, 19.
4.86.2a   Phasis: Map 4.81.
4.86.2b   Herodotus writes "11,100 stades." See
          Appendix J, §6, 19.
4.86.3a   Sindike: Map 4.81; Map 4.93, Scythia
          inset. This region is presumably the land
          of the Sindi of 4.28.1, bordering the
          Cimmerian Bosporus: Map 4.81; Map
          4.93, Scythia inset.
4.86.3b   Themiskyra: Map 4.81.
4.86.3c   Thermodon River: Map 4.81.
4.86.3d   Herodotus writes "3,300 stades."
4.86.4a   Herodotus overestimates the dimensions
          of the Black Sea, which, instead of being
          1,215 by 365 miles is actually 650 by
          270 miles; overestimates the length of
          the Hellespont (44 versus 33 actual

miles); and underestimates the length of
the Bosporus (his 13 miles versus 20
miles). See Appendix J, §2, 6, 19.
4.86.4b   Lake Maeotis (modern Sea of Azov):
          Map 4.81.
4.87.1a   Samos: Map 4.93, BY.
4.87.1b   With this brief account of the Scythian
          campaign, Herodotus is foreshadowing
          Xerxes' invasion of Hellas in Book 7.
          The numbers—an army of 700,000 and
          a fleet of 600 ships—are conventional
          figures, conveying a huge number, and
          not intended as an accurate estimate.
          Similarly, Herodotus says that the Persian
          fleet was 600 ships strong at the battles
          of both Lade (6.91) and Marathon
          (6.95.2).
4.87.2a   Byzantium: Map 4.93, AY.
4.87.2b   The sanctuary of Zeus Ourios, Zeus of
          the Fair Wind.

army crossing over the bridge. He dedicated it in the sanctuary of Hera,[a] with the following inscription engraved on it:

> [2] After spanning the Bosporus teeming with fish,
> To Hera Mandrokles dedicated this
> To commemorate his work on the bridge of boats,
> Winning a crown for himself, and glory for Samos,
> By fulfilling the will of Darius the King.

Those were the memorials of the man who built the bridge.

After having rewarded Mandrokles, Darius crossed the Hellespont.[a] He had earlier sent orders to the Ionians[b] to sail on the Pontus up to the Ister River,[c] and upon their arrival, to build a bridge over the river and wait for him, for the fleet was being led by the Ionians, Aeolians,[d] and the people of the Hellespont. [2] So the fleet sailed through the Kyaneai[a] directly to the Ister. After sailing up the river for two days from the sea, they reached the neck, where the Ister's mouths divide,[b] and here bridged the river. [3] Darius had crossed the Bosporus on the bridge of boats and was making his way through Thrace,[a] and when he arrived at the springs of the Tearos River,[b] he set up camp for three days.

The people who live near the Tearos River say that it is the best river for healing various ailments, but is especially effective as a cure for scabies for both men and horses. There are here thirty-eight springs which all flow from the same rock; some are cold, others hot. [2] The journey to these springs from the city of Heraion near Perinthus[a] is equal to the journey to them from Apollonia[b] on the Euxine Sea[c]—each takes two days. The Tearos empties into the Contadesdus River,[d] which flows into the Agrianes;[e] and the Agrianes flows into the Hebros,[f] which empties into the sea at the city of Ainos.[g]

And so it was to the Tearos River that Darius now came; and when he had set up camp, he expressed his delight with the river by erecting a pillar there, engraved with this inscription: [2] "The water springing from the sources of the Tearos River is the best and finest of all rivers. To these springs came Darius son of Hystaspes, King of Persia and the entire continent, the best and finest of all men, leading his army against the Scythians." Those are the words he had inscribed on the pillar.

4.89
513
THRACE
Darius crosses the
Bosporus into Europe.

4.90
513
THRACE
The Tearos River
heals mange.

4.91
513
THRACE
Darius leaves a
boastful inscription.

4.88.1a	The sanctuary of Hera (Heraion) on Samos (Map 4.93, BY) was one of the most important archaic Greek sanctuaries. See also 3.60.4, where Herodotus notes that it has the largest of all known temples.		contrast to the space enclosed by the spreading mouths." (How and Wells)
4.89.1a	Hellespont: Map 4.93, BY.	4.89.3a	Thrace: Map 4.93, AY.
4.89.1b	Ionia: Map 4.93, BY.	4.89.3b	Tearos River: Map 4.93, AY.
4.89.1c	Ister (modern Danube) River: Map 4.93, AY.	4.90.2a	Heraion near Perinthus: Map 4.93, AY.
4.89.1d	Aeolia (Aeolis): Map 4.93, BY.	4.90.2b	Apollonia: Map 4.93, AY.
4.89.2a	Kyaneai Rocks (islands): Map 4.93, AY.	4.90.2c	Euxine (Black) Sea: Map 4.93, AY, and Scythia inset.
4.89.2b	"The single stream is called 'neck' in	4.90.2d	Contadesdus River: location unknown.
		4.90.2e	Agrianes River: Map 4.93, AY.
		4.90.2f	Hebros River: Map 4.93, AY.
		4.90.2g	Ainos: Map 4.93, AY.

Setting out from there, Darius came to another river, called the Arteskos,[a] which flows through the territory of the Odrysians. When he reached this river, he designated a specific spot and ordered every man in the army to walk past it and to set one stone there. After his army had fulfilled this order, he led it away, leaving behind huge hills of stones.

Before Darius arrived at the Ister,[a] he made his first conquest in this region over the Getai,[b] who believe in immortality. Other peoples yielded to Darius without a fight: the Thracians who control Salmydessos,[c] as well as the inhabitants of the region above Apollonia[d] and the city of Mesembria,[e] called the Skyrmiadai and the Nipsaioi. The Getai, though they are the bravest and most just of the Thracians, adopted an attitude of foolish arrogance and were at once enslaved.

As to immortality, the Getai believe that they do not really die, but that when one of them passes away, he goes to Salmoxis, a sort of divinity whom some of them also call Gebeleizis. [2] Every fifth year they send off one of their number, who has been selected by lot to serve as a messenger to Salmoxis, with instructions as to what they want at that particular time. This is how they dispatch him. Three men who are appointed to the task each hold a javelin, while others seize the hands and feet of the man being sent to Salmoxis, swing him up in the air, and throw him onto the points of the javelins. [3] If the man dies from being impaled, they believe that the god is well disposed toward them; but if he does not die, they blame the messenger himself, accusing him of being a bad man, and seek another to send in his place. They give the messenger instructions while he is still alive. [4] These same Thracians shoot their arrows up into the sky, aiming at thunder and lightning as they shout threats at the god, and they believe that no other god exists but their own.

I have heard from the Hellenes who inhabit the Hellespont and the Pontus, however, that this Salmoxis was actually a human being who had been enslaved and served Pythagoras son of Mnesarchos on Samos.[a] [2] But he was eventually freed, and then he acquired abundant wealth there before returning to his own land. Now while the Thracians live a crude life and are rather stupid, Salmoxis knew the Ionian way of life and character, which is more profound than that of the Thracians, and he had associated with Hellenes, including Pythagoras, certainly not the feeblest thinker of the Hellenes. [3] And so he had a banqueting hall built where he hosted and entertained the leading men of the town, and he taught them that neither he nor they, his drinking companions, nor their descendants would die, but that they would come to a place where they would live on and have all good

4.92.1a Arteskos: site unknown.
4.93.1a Ister (modern Danube) River: Map
         4.93, AY.
4.93.1b Getai, approximate territory: Map
         4.93, AY.
4.93.1c Salmydessos: Map 4.93, AY.
4.93.1d Apollonia: Map 4.93, AY.
4.93.1e Mesembria: Map 4.93, AY.

4.95.1a Samos: Map 4.93, BY. Pythagoras was a
         famous Greek sophist and mathematician
         who emigrated from Samos to Italy, first
         to Croton (Map 4.93, BX) and then to
         Metapontum (Map 4.93, AX). He flour-
         ished c. 530 and founded a sect which
         believed in the power of numbers and the
         reincarnation of souls.

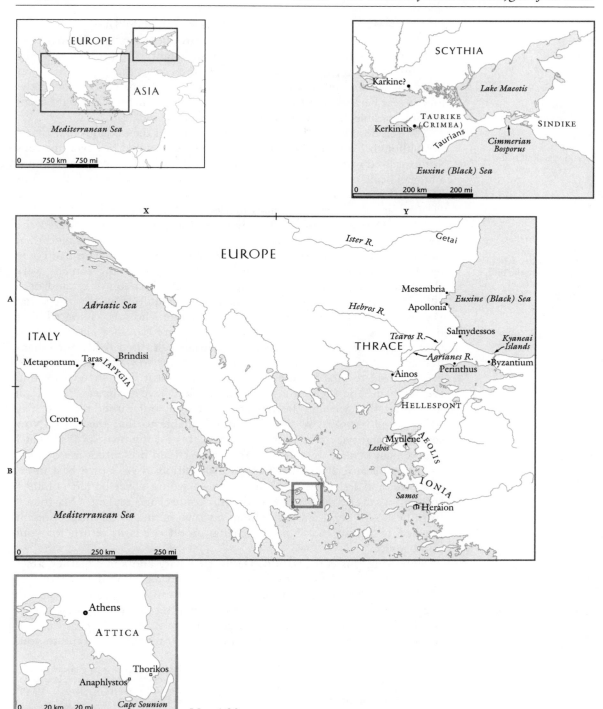

MAP 4.93

321

things. [4] And as he was composing these lessons and relating them to his guests, he was also constructing an underground chamber. When it was completely finished, he vanished from the sight of the Thracians, by descending into the chamber and spending three years there. [5] The Thracians missed him and grieved for him as though he had died, but in the fourth year he appeared to them, and thus what Salmoxis had taught them became credible. That, at least, is what they say he did.

4.96
THRACE
Herodotus doubts the story.

I myself do not believe this story about him and the underground chamber, although I do not discount it completely. I do think, however, that this Salmoxis lived many years before Pythagoras. But whether Salmoxis was born a human being or exists as some sort of native divinity among the Getai, let us bid him farewell. At any rate, that is how the Getai were subdued by the Persians, and they were now following along with the rest of the army.

4.97
513
ISTER RIVER
Koes of Lesbos advises Darius to leave the bridge intact so as to be able to return over it. Darius agrees and thanks him.

When Darius and his land army arrived at the Ister,[a] he ordered the Ionians to wait until everyone had crossed the bridge of boats, and then to take it apart; after that, they and the rest of the troops who had come by ship were to follow him on land. [2] But just as the Ionians were about to follow orders and break up the bridge, Koes son of Erxandros, a general of the Mytilenians[a] who had made inquiries and learned that Darius would welcome the opinion of someone who was willing to offer it to him, spoke to Darius as follows: [3] "Sire, you are about to lead your army over land where there are neither cultivated fields nor inhabited cities to be seen. So let your bridge continue to stand where it is and leave behind to guard it the very men who built it. [4] Then, if we find the Scythians and succeed in our plan, we shall have a safe way back. I am not afraid that we may be defeated in battle, but rather that we may suffer some harm as we wander around unable to find them. [5] Now someone might say that I am telling you this for my own sake, so that I may remain behind, but the real reason that I am presenting my opinion to you is because I found it to be a proposition in your own best interests, sire, and I shall in fact follow you—I would never be left behind." [6] Darius was extremely pleased by this counsel and replied, "My friend[a] from Lesbos, when I am back safe in my own home, by all means present yourself to me so that I may exchange good deeds in return for your good advice."

4.98
513
ISTER RIVER
Darius leaves the Ionians to guard the bridge for sixty days.

Following this conversation, Darius tied sixty knots in a leather strap, called the Ionian tyrants to a conference, and announced to them: [2] "Ionians, let my initial plan for the bridge be canceled. Instead, take this strap and follow these orders: as soon as you see me on my way against the Scythians, begin untying one knot each day. And if you go through all the knots and the days exceed them before my return, sail home to your

4.97.1a Ister (modern Danube) River: Map 4.93, AY.
4.97.2a Mytilene, Lesbos: Map 4.93, BY.
4.97.6a Herodotus uses *xein*, "guest-friend," here, but it is unlikely that the King of

Persia would have a guest-friend relationship of any kind with a Greek general from Mytilene. See Appendix T, Tyranny in Herodotus, §3.

own lands. [3] But until then, the new plan is for you to guard the bridge of boats and exert every effort to keep it safe and secure. If you follow these orders, you will do me a great favor." After saying this, Darius hurried off.[a]

Thrace, whose land juts out into the sea,[a] lies before Scythia, which begins where a bay curves back into the land; the Ister flows into this region and its mouth faces the east. [2] I shall now describe the coastal region of Scythian territory proper, as regards its measurements. Old Scythia[a] starts from the Ister and continues, facing the south and south wind, up to the city called Kerkinitis.[b] [3] From there, extending along the coast of the same sea, the land becomes mountainous and projects into the Pontus. This region is inhabited by the Taurians up to what is called the Rugged Peninsula,[a] which extends down into the sea toward the east.[b] [4] So two sides of Scythia's borders extend to the sea, one toward the south, the other toward the east, just as in Attica.[a] Since the Taurians inhabit part of Scythia, it would be nearly the same as if a people other than the Athenians inhabited the high ground of Sounion[b] and if Sounion extended farther into the sea, from Thorikos[c] up to the deme of Anaphlystos.[d] [5] I am of course comparing something small in proportion to something large. But that is what Taurike[a] is like. For those who have never sailed along this region of Attica, let me offer another example. It would be as if a people other than the Iapygians[b] had cut off for themselves the region from Brentesion[c] to Taras[d] and inhabited the cape. Although I have chosen these two places to compare, I assert that many other places, too, closely resemble Taurike.[e]

From Taurike to the north and toward the eastern sea[a] lies inhabited Scythia, which also extends from the Cimmerian Bosporus[b] to the west and from Lake Maeotis[c] to the Tanais River,[d] which flows into the [northern tip] of this lake. [2] From the Ister, the land of Scythia to the north and

4.99
SCYTHIA
Herodotus interrupts the narrative of the Persian invasion to describe the coast of Scythia, drawing analogies between the Tauric Peninsula and Attica or Iapygia. The narrative continues in 4.118.

4.100
SCYTHIA
Scythia beyond the Tauric country.

4.98.3a   A colorful anecdote, perhaps, but hardly a credible means for these sophisticates to measure time.

4.99.1a   The sea referred to here is the Euxine (Black) Sea: Map 4.93, AY, and Scythia inset.

4.99.2a   Old Scythia: Herodotus probably means the part of Scythia (Map 4.93, Scythia inset) first known to the Hellenes, which is southwestern Scythia. (How and Wells)

4.99.2b   Kerkinitis: Map 4.93, Scythia inset. It is situated on the modern Crimea.

4.99.3a   Rugged Peninsula (Trakheia Chersonese), the modern Crimea: Map 4.93, Scythia inset.

4.99.3b   This sea toward the east wind could be Lake Maeotis (modern Sea of Azov) (Map 4.93, Scythia inset) or the Euxine (Black) Sea (Map 4.93, AY, and Scythia inset), toward the southeast from the Crimea.

4.99.4a   Attica: Map 4.93, Attica inset. Herodotus' analogy is wrong. Scythia's southern border was on both land and sea and did not at all resemble Attica in shape or orientation.

4.99.4b   Sounion: Map 4.93, Attica inset.

4.99.4c   Thorikos; Map 4.93, Attica inset.

4.99.4d   Anaphlystos: Map 4.93, Attica inset.

4.99.5a   Taurike, the land of the Taurians: Map 4.93, Scythia inset.

4.99.5b   Iapygia, Italy: Map 4.93, AX.

4.99.5c   Brindisi (Brentesion): Map 4.93, AX.

4.99.5d   Taras: Map 4.93, AX.

4.99.5e   The Taurians live on a promontory (the Tauric Crimea), which is like the southeastern promontory of Attica (Sounion) or the heel of Italy (Iapygia). The difference, Herodotus says, is that the Taurians, while inhabiting a part of Scythia, are not Scythians, whereas the inhabitants of the Attic and Italian promontories are of the same stock as their neighbors. (Godley) See Map 4.93 and insets.

4.100.1a   Herodotus appears to mean the southeast area of the Euxine (Black) Sea: Map 4.93, AY, and Scythia inset.

4.100.1b   Cimmerian Bosporus: Map 4.93, Scythia inset.

4.100.1c   Lake Maeotis (modern Sea of Azov): Map 4.93, Scythia inset.

4.100.1d   Tanais River (modern Don): Map 4.110.

inland is bounded first by the Agathyrsoi,[a] then the Neurians;[b] after them, the Maneaters;[c] and last, the Black Cloaks.[d]

And so the shape of Scythia is square: two of its sides reach down to the sea, and these and its coastal and inland margins make it equal on all sides.[a] [2] For from the Ister[a] to the Borysthenes[b] is a ten-day journey, and from the Borysthenes to Lake Maeotis[c] is another ten days, while from the sea inland to the Black Cloaks, who live above the Scythians, is a journey of twenty days. [3] In my calculations, a day's journey is reckoned at twenty-two miles.[a] Thus, lengthwise Scythia measures 440 miles, and the distance inland at angles to the coast measures just as many miles.[b] That, then, is the extent of this land.

The Scythians deliberated together and concluded that by themselves they were incapable of repelling the army of Darius in a straightforward battle, so they sent messengers to their neighbors, whose kings had in fact already come together and were deliberating about how to deal with the huge army advancing toward them. [2] Those assembled here were the kings of the Taurians,[a] Agathyrsoi, Neurians, Maneaters, Black Cloaks, Gelonians,[b] Boudinoi,[c] and Sauromatai.[d]

Of these peoples, the Taurians practice the following customs. They sacrifice to the Virgin those who have been shipwrecked and any Hellenes they can take at sea. The sacrifice is carried out in the following way. [2] After the preliminary consecration rites, they strike the victim's head with a club. Then, some say, they impale the head upon a pole and push the body over a cliff (for it is at the top of the cliff that the sanctuary has been built). Others agree about what they do with the head but say that the body is buried in the ground, not pushed off the cliff. The Taurians themselves say that the divinity to whom they offer these sacrifices is Iphigenia, the daughter of Agamemnon. [3] When the Taurians overpower their adversaries, each man cuts off the head of an enemy, brings it to his home, fixes it on a tall wooden stake there, and sets it up so that it towers high over his

---

4.100.2a Agathyrsoi, approximate location of territory: Map 4.110. The Agathyrsoi can be archaeologically located on the banks of the Ancient Maris (modern Mures) River (Map 4.53, AX). (Wheeler) See Appendix F, §3.
4.100.2b Neurians, possible location of territory: Map 4.110.
4.100.2c Maneaters, possible location of territory: Map 4.110. For archaeological evidence of cannibalism in this area, see Appendix E, §10, Appendix F, §4.
4.100.2d Black Cloaks, possible location of territory: Map 4.110.
4.101.1a A typical ancient Greek attempt to find geometric shapes and symmetry in geography. See Appendix D, §1–3.
4.101.2a Ister (modern Danube) River: Map 4.110.
4.101.2b Borysthenes (modern Dnieper) River: Map 4.110.

4.101.2c Lake Maeotis (modern Sea of Azov): Map 4.110.
4.101.3a Herodotus writes "200 stades." See Appendix J, §6, 19.
4.101.3b Herodotus writes "4,000 stades." See Appendix J, §6, 19. This description of Scythian territory as a square twenty days' journey on each side bounded on the south by the Euxine (Black) Sea and on the east by Lake Maeotis is inconsistent with his earlier description of Scythia (4.17–20, 4.47–58) as the land lying between the Ister (modern Danube) and the Tanais (modern Don) Rivers.
4.102.2a Taurians, location of territory: Map 4.110.
4.102.2b Gelonians, possible location of territory: Map 4.110.
4.102.2c Boudinoi, possible location of territory: Map 4.110.
4.102.2d Sauromatai, approximate location of territory: Map 4.110.

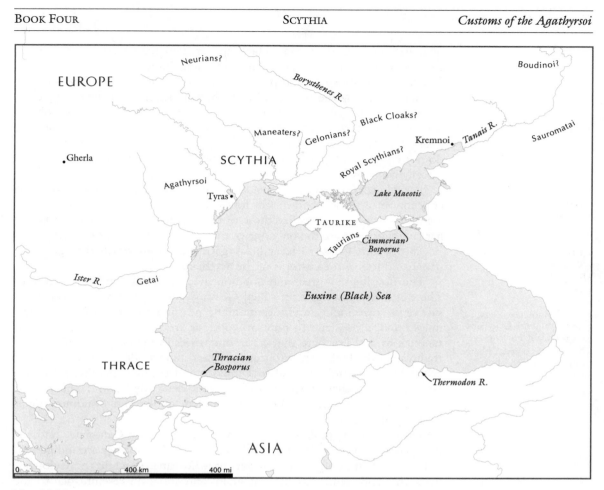

MAP 4.110

house—most of the time it is even higher than the chimney. They say that as these heads hang over the whole house, they serve as guardians of the household. These people live by plunder and war.

The males of the Agathyrsoi are most luxurious and wear gold more than other men. They share their women in common for the purposes of intercourse, in order that they will all be brothers to one another, and they thus eliminate envy and hatred among one another, since they are all related. The rest of their customs are like those of the Thracians.

The Neurians[a] follow the customs of the Scythians. One generation before the expedition of Darius, they were forced to leave their land because

4.104
SCYTHIA
The customs of
the Agathyrsoi.

4.105
SCYTHIA
The Neurians, who may
be wizards.

4.105.1a Neurians, possible location of territory:
Map 4.110.

325

of a great number of snakes which appeared in their territory, as well as many more that also assailed them from uninhabited regions to the north.[b] Finally, under the stress and pressure of this onslaught of snakes, they left and settled among the Boudinoi. It might well be true that these people are sorcerers, [2] for according to the Scythians and the Hellenes who inhabit Scythia, once each year every one of the Neurians turns into a wolf and, after a few days, changes back to himself again.[a] Those who make this claim do not convince me, but nonetheless, that is what they say, and they swear it really happens.

4.106
SCYTHIA
The savage Maneaters.

The Maneaters[a] have the most savage character of all men; they have no conception of justice, and in fact follow no civilized traditions at all. They are nomads, wear clothes like those of the Scythians, speak their own peculiar language, and are the only one of these peoples to eat human flesh.

4.107
SCYTHIA
The Black Cloaks.

The Black Cloaks[a] all wear black garments, from which they get their name, and follow the customs of the Scythians.

4.108
SCYTHIA
The Boudinoi have a city, Gelonos, and the Gelonians were originally Hellenes.

The Boudinoi,[a] a great and populous nation, are all blue-gray and red.[b] There is a city among them called Gelonos,[c] built entirely of wood. Each side of its surrounding wall is quite high, measures almost three and a third miles,[d] and is constructed only of wood, as are also the city's houses and sanctuaries. [2] For here they have sanctuaries of Greek gods, built in the tradition of the Hellenes, with statues, altars, and wooden temples; and they celebrate the biennial festival to Dionysos and conduct Bacchic rites. The Gelonians are actually Greek in their origins, descended from Hellenes who moved from their trading posts and settled among the Boudinoi. Their language is part Scythian, part Greek.

4.109
SCYTHIA
More on the Boudinoi and the Gelonians.

The Boudinoi speak a different language from the Gelonians, and the two peoples follow quite different ways of life. The former are indigenous nomads and the only people in Scythia who eat lice, while the Gelonians work the land, tend gardens, eat grain, and show no resemblance to the Boudinoi in complexion or general appearance. The Boudinoi are called Gelonians by Hellenes, who, however, are wrong in calling them by this name. [2] Their entire territory is wooded, with all kinds of trees. In their greatest forest lies an immense lake with a marsh surrounded by a bed of reeds. Otters and beavers are caught in this lake, as are other, square-faced animals[a] whose skins are sewn around the edges of their cloaks and whose testicles are useful for curing disorders of the womb.

4.105.1b   The area around Tyras (Map 4.110) had once been called Ophioussa, Snakeland.

4.105.2a   Herodotus' tale that Neurian men turn into wolves for a few days every year has parallels in the initiation rites to manhood of several Indo-European peoples. Such werewolves were said to exist among the Sarmatians and other Iranian peoples of Central Asia.

4.106.1a   Maneaters, possible location of territory: Map 4.110.

4.107.1a   Black Cloaks, possible location of territory: Map 4.110.

4.108.1a   Boudinoi, possible location of territory: Map 4.110.

4.108.1b   This has been interpreted in two different ways by both ancient and modern readers to mean that the Boudinoi either painted their bodies these colors or had blue-gray eyes and red hair.

4.108.1c   Gelonos: location unknown.

4.108.1d   Herodotus writes "30 stades." See Appendix J, §6, 19.

4.109.2a   Square-faced animals: may be elk, seals, or mink.

The following story is told about the Sauromatai.[a] The Hellenes fought with the Amazons,[b] whom the Scythians call Oiorpata (the equivalent of "man-slayers," since they use the word *oior* for "man" and *pata* for "slay"), and it is said that after the Hellenes defeated them in the battle at the Thermodon,[c] they sailed away on their three boats, taking with them as many Amazons as they could capture alive. But when they got out to sea, the Amazons attacked and massacred the men. [2] Now the Amazons knew nothing about boats or how to operate rudders, sails, and oars, so after they massacred the men, they drifted, borne along by wave and wind, until they came to Kremnoi,[a] which lies in the territory of the free Scythians[b] on Lake Maeotis.[c] There the Amazons disembarked and went on their way toward inhabited territory. They seized the first herd of horses they encountered, mounted them, and proceeded to plunder the land of the Scythians.

The Scythians could not comprehend what was happening. They recognized neither the language, clothing, nor nationality of these people but were struck with amazement when they wondered where these people might have come from. Believing that they were very young men, they engaged them in battle, and it was only after the battle, when the Scythians took possession of the corpses, that they discovered that they were in fact women. [2] After some deliberation, they resolved not to kill them anymore in any way, but instead to send off to them a number of their own young men, as many as they guessed to be the total number of the women. The young men were told to set up camp near the women and to act just as the women did. If the women tried to chase them away, they were not to fight, but to retreat before them until they stopped chasing, and then to go back and again camp nearby. The Scythians decided on this plan because they wanted to sire children by these women.

So the young men who were sent off followed their instructions, and when the Amazons realized they had not come to do them any harm, they let them be. Each day, the young men moved their camp closer and lived just as the Amazons did, having nothing except their weapons and horses, and living the same life of hunting and plundering.

Now what the Amazons used to do at about midday was to disperse in ones and twos, and once they had gone some distance from one another, to relieve themselves. When the Scythians noticed this, they did the same. And when one of them drew near to an Amazon who was all alone, she did not repulse him but allowed him to have his way with her. [2] Although she could not speak to him (since they did not understand each other's language), she communicated by hand gestures that he should come back the next day to the same place and bring along another man, gesturing that there should be two of them, and that

4.110
SCYTHIA
A tale of the Sauromatai, Amazons, and Scythians.

4.111
SCYTHIA
The Scythians and the Amazons.

4.112
SCYTHIA
The tale of the Scythians and the Amazons continues.

4.113
SCYTHIA
The tale of the Scythians and the Amazons continues.

4.110.1a Sauromatai, approximate location of territory: Map 4.110.
4.110.1b Amazons: legendary women warriors. See Appendix U, On Women and Marriage in Herodotus, §6.
4.110.1c Thermodon River: Map 4.110.
4.110.2a Kremnoi: Map 4.110.

4.110.2b Free Scythians are the Royal Scythians: possible location of territory, Map 4.110. See 4.20, where the Royal Scythians are said to consider all others their slaves.
4.110.2c Lake Maeotis (modern Sea of Azov): Map 4.110.

she would bring another woman. [3] The young man returned to camp and related all this to the others. And so the next day when he went back to the same place, he brought another man along and found there another Amazon waiting as well. When the rest of the young men heard this story, they all tamed the rest of the Amazons for themselves.

4.114
SCYTHIA
The tale of the Scythians and the Amazons continues.

Then, uniting their camps, they dwelled together, each man keeping the woman with whom he first had had intercourse. Although the men were unable to learn the language of the women, the women picked up that of the men, [2] and when they were able to understand each other, the men told the Amazons, "We have parents and possessions, so let us no longer live this kind of life, but instead, let us return to the greater part of our people and dwell among them together. We shall keep you as our wives and have no others." [3] The women replied, "We could not live among your women there, because our customs are not the same as theirs. We shoot arrows, throw javelins, and ride horses but have no knowledge of women's chores. Your women, on the other hand, do none of the things we just mentioned but stay in their wagons doing women's work, and they never leave them to hunt or to go anyplace at all. [4] We would not be able to get along with them. If you really want to keep us as your wives, and also wish to do what seems most just and fair, go to your parents, take away your share of possessions, and then return to us and let us live together but by ourselves."

4.115
SCYTHIA
The tale of the Scythians and the Amazons continues.

The young men were persuaded by what the Amazons said, and did what they had requested. When they had taken possession of the goods that were being handed down to them, they went back to the Amazons, who now said to them, [2] "We are afraid and anxious about having to live in this region, since we have both deprived you of your parents and laid waste to much of your land here. [3] But since you are resolved to have us as your wives, come away with us; let us move from this land, cross the Tanais River,[a] and live there." And the young men consented to this proprosal as well.

4.116
SCYTHIA
The tale of the Scythians and the Amazons concludes. They leave Scythia and become the Sauromatai

So they crossed the Tanais and traveled from the river toward the rising sun for three days, and then turned toward the north, away from Lake Maeotis, and traveled for another three days. Finally, they settled down in the region which they still inhabit today. [2] The Sauromatai women still practice their old way of life from that time, regularly riding out on horses to go hunting, both with and without their men, and going out to war,[a] wearing the same kind of clothing as do the men.

4.117
SCYTHIA
The language and marriage customs of the Sauromatai.

The Sauromatai customarily speak the Scythian language, though their usage of it has been incorrect from the beginning because the Amazons never did master it properly. Their marriage customs demand that no virgin ever gets married until she has slain a male enemy, and some of them actually grow old and die before they can marry because they are unable to fulfill this requirement.

4.115.3a Tanais (modern Don) River: Map 4.110.
4.116.2a Female warriors among the Sauromatai appear to be archaeologically attested by

weapons found in female burials. See Appendix F, §5.

And so the kings of the nations I have enumerated were all gathered together when the messengers from the Scythians arrived and informed them that the Persian had conquered all of the other continent,[a] built a bridge over the neck of the Bosporus,[b] crossed over to this continent,[c] subdued the Thracians,[d] and bridged the Ister River.[e] Now, they said, he wanted to make all this land, too, subject to himself. [2] "And so by no means should you take a neutral stance and allow us to be destroyed. Let us form the same resolve and together oppose the invader. Please do that; otherwise, if we are pressed by war, we shall either leave the country or come to an agreement with the enemy and remain. [3] What else could we do if you will not help us? And what happens to you at his hands will be no easier, for the Persian has come to attack you as well as us. He will not be satisfied with conquering us and leaving you alone. [4] We shall now give you substantial evidence for this assertion. If the Persian were advancing only against us because he wanted to punish us for the slavery we earlier imposed on his country,[a] then he should have left all the other peoples alone and proceeded directly to our land; by doing that, he would have shown everyone that he was marching only against Scythia,[b] and not against others here as well. [5] But as soon as he had crossed over to this continent, he began subjugating all the peoples he encountered along his way, one after the other, so that now he has all the Thracians subject to him, even the Getai,[a] our very own neighbors."[b]

When the Scythians had finished delivering their message, the kings who had gathered there from various nations considered what they had said and became divided in their opinions. The kings of the Gelonians,[a] Boudinoi,[b] and Sauromatai[c] were all in agreement to promise their support to the Scythians, while the kings of the Agathyrsoi, Neurians, Maneaters, Black Cloaks, and Taurians[d] gave the Scythians the following answer: [2] "If you had not been an unjust aggressor when you previously initiated hostilities against the Persians and were in that case making your present request, you would appear to us to

4.118
513
SCYTHIA
Herodotus rejoins and continues the narrative of the Persian invasion of Scythia. The Scythians ask their neighbors to resist the Persians, pointing out that the Persians come to conquer not only the Scythians, but all others with whom they come in contact.

4.119
513
SCYTHIA
Some agree to join the Scythians against the Persians; others decide to stand aside.

4.118.1a "The other continent" is Asia: Map 4.110.
4.118.1b Bosporus (Thracian): Map 4.110.
4.118.1c "This continent" is Europe: Map 4.110.
4.118.1d Thrace: Map 4.110.
4.118.1e Ister (modern Danube) River: Map 4.110.
4.118.4a See 1.104–106 on the Scythian invasion of Asia, defeat of the Medes, and subsequent rule over Asia; and 4.1, where Herodotus states that this is the reason Darius was invading Scythia now.
4.118.4b Scythia: Map 4.110.
4.118.5a Getai, approximate location of territory: Map 4.110.
4.118.5b Herodotus' account of Darius' Scythian campaign, which has a large Persian army marching from the Ister (modern Danube) River to the Tanais (modern Don) River and back in just over 60 days, is a logistical impossibility. The real aim of the campaign seems to have been to conquer Thrace and the Getai and to gain access to the gold-producing areas of Transylvania. A clay tablet written in Old Persian in cuneiform

(published 1954) was found at Gherla (Map 4.110) in northern Transylvania. The text records Darius' establishment of a palace or administrative building there.
4.119.1a Gelonians, possible location of territory: Map 4.110.
4.119.1b Boudinoi, possible location of territory: Map 4.110.
4.119.1c Sauromatai, approximate location of territory: Map 4.110.
4.119.1d Agathyrsoi and Taurians (approximate locations of their territories), Neurians, Maneaters, Black Cloaks (possible locations of their territories): Map 4.110. The Agathyrsoi can be archaeologically located on the banks of the Maris (modern Mures) River: Map 4.53, AX. (Wheeler) See Appendix F, §3. However, the *Barrington Atlas* shows a label "Agathyrsoi" on its Map 23, A1, almost 200 miles to the east of the Maris River. Both identifications could be right, and refer to different time periods.

be in the right, and we would be persuaded to do what you ask. [3] But as it is, you invaded their land without us and ruled over the Persians for as long as god granted you to do so; and now that the same god has aroused them, they are paying you back in kind. [4] We did not wrong these men in any way back then, and we will not try to wrong them now before they wrong us. If, however, their king invades our land and begins unjust aggression against us, we, too, will refuse to submit to him. But until that happens, we will keep to ourselves. For we think the Persians have come not against us but against those who were really responsible for the wrong done to them."

When these replies were reported to the Scythians they decided, now that these kings had refused to join them as allies, not to directly resist by giving battle, but instead to withdraw, and as they retreated, to destroy whatever wells and springs they passed and obliterate the grass from the earth. They also decided to divide themselves into two groups. [2] One of these, headed by King Skopasis and joined by the Sauromatai, was to retreat, and if the Persians turned in their direction, to flee along the coast of Lake Maeotis[a] and head straight for the Tanais River.[b] Then, if the Persians turned back, they were to pursue and attack them. That was the plan for one of the royal divisions. [3] Of the other two royal divisions, Idanthyrsos ruled the larger part, and Taxakis was king of the third. Both of these were to unite with the Gelonians and Boudinoi and were also to withdraw, but always to stay ahead of the Persians by one day's journey. [4] Their plan was to retreat directly toward the lands of those who had rejected the alliance and thus to provoke them to go to war. They thought that since these peoples were unwilling to take upon themselves a war against the Persians, they would have to be forced into it against their will. After that had been accomplished, they intended to turn back toward their own land and to attack if, by joint decision, that course seemed best to them.

When the Scythians had completed their plans, they dispatched an advance guard of their best cavalry and went out to confront the army of Darius. They also sent away the wagons in which all the women and children lived, along with all the livestock, except as much as would be needed for their own food, which they kept for themselves. All the rest they sent with the wagons, with instructions to travel continuously toward the north.

And so the wagons traveled on ahead. Meanwhile, the Scythians' advance guard discovered that the Persians were a three-days' journey from the Ister,[a] and once they had found them, they began to devastate all that was growing from the earth, keeping their camp one day ahead of the Persians. [2] When the Persians saw the Scythian horsemen appear in front of them, they tried to overtake them, following the path of their retreat. And so they raced after this one division of the Scythians, chasing it eastward toward the Tanais River; [3] and when the Scythians crossed the Tanais, the Persians crossed after them and continued their pursuit until

4.120.2a Lake Maeotis (modern Sea of Azov): Map 4.110.
4.120.2b Tanais (modern Don) River: Map 4.110.

4.122.1a Ister (modern Danube) River: Map 4.110.

they had passed entirely through the country of the Sauromatai and had arrived in the land of the Boudinoi.

As long as the Persians were passing through Scythian and Sauromatai territory, they were unable to inflict damage on the land, since it was dry and barren. But when they invaded the territory of the Boudinoi, they encountered the wooden wall around the city there,[a] which had been emptied of everything inside since the Boudinoi had left. The Persians burned down the wall [2] and continued in this area and arrived at the uninhabited region.[a] No men live here at all; the place lies above the land of the Boudinoi and extends the length of a seven-days' journey. [3] Beyond this uninhabited region live the Thyssagetai.[a] Four large rivers flow out of their territory through the land of the Maeotians and empty into the lake called Maeotis. The names of these rivers are the Lycus, the Oaros, the Tanais, and the Syrgis.[b]

When Darius reached this uninhabited region, he stopped the chase and encamped his army by the Oaros River. He then began to build eight huge forts, at equal intervals from each other, about six and a half miles[a] apart, whose remains were still standing in my time.[b] [2] But while he was working on these, the Scythians he had been chasing went inland on a roundabout course and turned back to Scythia. Since they had completely vanished and no trace of them could be found by Darius, he left his forts half finished and turned back toward the west, assuming that those he had pursued were all of the Scythians and that they had fled.[a]

Marching his army as swiftly as possible, he led it back to Scythia, where he encountered both of the Scythian divisions. He then pursued them, but they always managed to maintain their distance and remain a day's journey ahead of him. [2] As Darius did not give up the chase, the Scythians, in accordance with their plans, retreated into the lands of those who had rejected the alliance. The first of these was the land of the Black Cloaks.[a] [3] After the Scythians and Persians had invaded and wreaked havoc upon the Black Cloaks, both armies, with the Scythians leading the way, advanced into the country of the Maneaters[a] and, after harassing them, moved onward into the territory of the Neurians[b] and threw them into confusion,

---

4.123.1a This city and its wooden wall were mentioned in 4.108.1.
4.123.2a See 4.22, which mentions this deserted region.
4.123.3a Thyssagetai: also mentioned in 4.22.1.
4.123.3b The location of the Lycus River is unknown. The Oaros could be the Volga, the Dnieper, or even the Buzau in Moldavia. "Syrgis" seems to be a variant spelling for the Hyrgis River, mentioned at 4.57.
4.124.1a Herodotus writes "60 stades." See Appendix J, §6, 19.
4.124.1b No traces of these forts have been identified. See Appendix E, §5.
4.124.2a It is conceivable that Herodotus' account conflates two different "Scythian" campaigns: one of Darius in the western Pontic area against the Getai and Scythi-

ans and another associated with the area of Lake Maeotis (modern Sea of Azov) and the north Caucasus. Ctesias, a Greek physician at the court of Artaxerxes II (late-fifth/early-fourth century) and the author of a work called *Persica*, records that Darius ordered the satrap of Cappadocia to launch an expedition by sea against the Scythians. But the date and circumstances of this campaign are most obscure, and a naval expedition into the north Caucasus makes little sense.
4.125.2a Black Cloaks, possible location of territory: Map 4.110.
4.125.3a Maneaters, possible location of territory: Map 4.110. See 4.106; Appendix E, §10; and Appendix F, §4.
4.125.3b Neurians, possible location of territory: Map 4.110.

too. Finally they continued on toward the Agathyrsoi, [4] but the Agathyrsoi, who had already seen their neighbors harassed and put to flight by the Scythians, sent a herald to order the Scythians not to cross their borders, warning them that if they made any attempt to invade, they would have to fight it out with them first. [5] After issuing this threat, the Agathyrsoi rushed to defend their borders, intending to ward off the invaders. Now the Black Cloaks, Maneaters, and Neurians had not offered resistance when they had been invaded by the Scythians and Persians; indeed, they forgot their earlier promise[a] and instead fled in confusion and disorder toward the north without stopping until they reached the uninhabited area. [6] The Agathyrsoi, however, did not give way when the Scythians came, and so the Scythians led the Persians out of the land of the Neurians and back to their own land.

As there seemed to be no end to this pursuit, which had gone on for a long time, Darius sent a horseman to Idanthyrsos king of the Scythians with this message: "You extraordinary man! Why do you keep fleeing when you certainly could do otherwise? If you think you are able to challenge my power, then stop your wandering and stand to fight it out. Or, if you acknowledge that you are too weak for that course, then you should stop running away, bring gifts of earth and water to your master,[a] and enter into negotiations with him."

To this, Idanthyrsos king of the Scythians responded, "This is my situation, Persian. I have never yet fled from anyone out of fear before, and I am not fleeing from you now. What I have been doing is in fact no different from what I am accustomed to do in times of peace. [2] I will tell you why I do not engage you now: it is because we have neither towns nor cultivated land to worry about being captured or razed, which might induce us to engage you in battle sooner. But if you really must come to battle without further delay, know that we do have ancestral graves. [3] So come on, then; find them and try to destroy them, and you will know whether or not we shall fight for the graves. But before that we shall not engage you in battle, unless we see fit to do so. [4] So much for talk of battle, but as to my masters, the only ones I recognize are Zeus, my forefather, and Hestia queen of the Scythians. Instead of gifts of earth and water, I shall send you the kind of tokens you really merit. And in response to your claim to be my master, I tell you, 'Weep.' *That* is your answer from the Scythians."

The herald returned and announced this reply to Darius, while the Scythian kings became enraged when they heard the word "slavery."[a] [2] They sent the division commanded by Skopasis, which included the Sauromatai, to the Ionians guarding the bridge at the Ister, with orders to parley

4.125.5a At 4.119, these peoples as well as the Agathyrsoi had said they would offer resistance if directly confronted by the Persians.

4.126.1a Gifts of earth and water symbolized submission and surrender of land to a conqueror. See Darius at 6.48, Xerxes at

7.32, for Persian demands to the Greek cities to submit by giving earth and water.

4.128.1a Apparently, when Darius told the Scythians to recognize him as their master (4.126), the Scythians interpreted this as an assertion that they should be his slaves and became enraged.

with them. Those left behind resolved not to lead the Persians on a wandering course any longer, but to attack them every time they ventured out to forage for provisions. And so they watched for those times when Darius' men were out gathering food, and then they carried out their plan. [3] The Scythian cavalry always put to flight the Persian cavalry, and when the Persian horsemen, in their hasty retreat, would fall back on their own infantry, the infantry would come to their assistance.[a] Once the Scythians had driven the Persian cavalry back upon their infantry, they would withdraw, since they feared the infantry. The Scythians conducted attacks like this even at night.

But I shall now describe a most amazing phenomenon that worked for the Persians whenever the Scythians attacked Darius' army. This was the effect on the Scythian horses of the sounds made by the Persian donkeys and mules, as well as their appearance. [2] For as I have already explained, neither donkeys nor mules breed in Scythia; there are no donkeys or mules in any part of Scythia because of the intense cold. And so when these animals let out their clamorous braying, they would throw the Scythian horses into confusion and disorder;[a] [3] and often when the Scythians would be in the middle of an assault against the Persians, their horses would become agitated and turn about, pricking up their ears in astonishment when they heard the sound of the donkeys, since they had never heard such sounds nor seen such sights before. This had at least some effect on the outcome of the campaign.

However, when the Scythians observed that the Persians had become flustered and disconcerted, they developed a plan to induce them to remain longer in Scythia so that they would eventually suffer acute distress because of their lack of provisions. What the Scythians did was to leave some of their herds and herdsmen behind and stealthily go elsewhere. Then the Persians would go after the herds, seize them, and be encouraged by their success.

This happened over and over again until Darius at last found himself in an impossible situation. When the Scythian kings recognized this, they sent a herald to Darius bearing the following gifts: a bird, a mouse, a frog, and five arrows. [2] The Persians asked the herald bearing the gifts what the meaning of the gifts was, but he said he had received no orders other than to present the gifts and then to leave at once. He added, however, that the Persians would realize what the gifts meant if they were wise. Having heard this, the Persians considered the matter together.

Darius was of the opinion that the gifts meant that the Scythians were surrendering themselves to him with gifts of earth and water: a mouse, he thought, lives in the earth and eats the same crops as humans do; a frog

4.129
513
SCYTHIA
The braying of Persian mules and asses causes the Scythian horses to shy away.

4.130
513
SCYTHIA
The Scythians try to lure the Persians into staying longer.

4.131
513
SCYTHIA
The Scythians send Darius a riddle, which the Persians attempt to solve.

4.132
513
SCYTHIA
Darius interprets the gifts as a form of surrender, but Gobryas' view is the opposite.

4.128.3a Persian cavalry normally supported the infantry, protecting them in retreat and pursuing the foe after the infantry's archery or hand-to-hand combat had broken up the enemy formations or forced them into flight. Here the defeated Persian cavalry falls back upon,

and is protected by, the infantry formations. See Appendix O, The Persian Army in Herodotus, §6–8.
4.129.2a Cyrus the Great employed a similar stratagem with camels against the Lydian cavalry of Croesus at 1.80.4–5.

lives in the water; a bird is very much like a horse;[a] and arrows could represent the surrender of their prowess in battle. [2] That was the opinion Darius declared, but it conflicted with the view of Gobryas, one of the seven men who had deposed the Magus. He reasoned that the gifts had the following significance: [3] "Persians, unless you turn into birds and fly up into the sky, or mice and descend underground, or frogs and hop into the lakes, you will be shot by these arrows and never return home."

While the Persians were trying to guess the meaning of the gifts, the division of the Scythians which had earlier been appointed to keep watch along the coast of Lake Maeotis[a] but had then been sent to talk to the Ionians at the Ister,[b] now arrived at the bridge and addressed them. [2] "We have come here, Ionians, bringing you the gift of freedom, if only you are willing to follow our advice. We know that Darius instructed you to guard the bridge for just sixty days, and to leave and return home if he did not show up here within that time. [3] So now, if you will take our advice, you will escape his censure as well as ours by leaving this place as soon as you have waited this designated number of days." The Ionians promised to do this, and the Scythians immediately left and hurried back to their land.

After the gifts had been sent to the Persians, the Scythians who had stayed behind deployed their infantry and cavalry in preparation to give battle to Darius. The Scythians were assembled in their positions when a hare darted into the space between the armies. Now every Scythian, when he saw the hare, began to chase it.[a] Darius noticed that the Scythians were shouting and in disorder and asked what the uproar among his enemies was all about. When he learned that they were chasing a hare, he said to the men with whom he usually discussed everything, [2] "These men look on us with such contempt! I now believe that Gobryas' interpretation of the gifts from the Scythians was correct. And now that I, too, finally see things his way, we must form a good plan to ensure that our return journey home will be a safe one." In response to this, Gobryas said, "Sire, the reputation alone of these men had led me to a nearly perfect awareness of how impossible they would be to deal with, but since I have come here myself, and have watched them mock us, I have gained an even more profound understanding of them. [3] Here is a plan that seems best to me: as soon as night falls, let us light our campfires as usual, but then deceive those of our weakest soldiers who can least endure hardships and leave them behind. We should tie all the donkeys there with them and then immediately depart before the Scythians rush straight to the bridge and tear it down, or the Ionians decide to do something that could ruin us." That was the advice of Gobryas.

4.132.1a Apparently the analogy between the bird and the horse hinges on the swiftness of both.
4.133.1a Lake Maeotis (modern Sea of Azov): Map 4.110.
4.133.1b Ister (modern Danube) River: Map 4.110.
4.134.1a See Figure 4.134, a depiction of a Scythian hunting a hare.

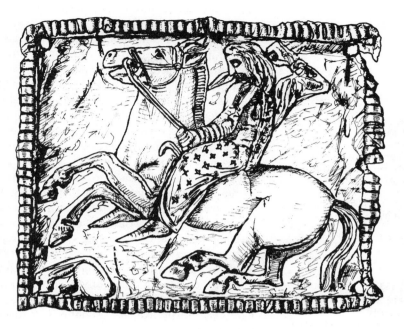

FIGURE 4.134. DRAWING OF A
GOLD PLAQUE DEPICTING A
MOUNTED SCYTHIAN HUNTING
A HARE, FROM THE KUL'-OBA
KURGAN (TOMB).

Night fell, and Darius carried out the plan. He left in the camp the men who were worn out and whose loss would matter least, together with all the donkeys, which had been tied there with them. [2] He left the donkeys behind so that they would make noise, and the men because of their weakness, although the pretext he gave to them was that he was going to attack the Scythians with his most fit troops, and that meanwhile, they were to guard the camp. [3] After thus informing the men being left there, Darius lit the fires and hurried toward the Ister. Left without the crowd of men, the donkeys brayed much more loudly than usual; and the Scythians heard them and remained confident that the Persians were there in their usual place.

When day came, the men who had been left behind realized that they had been betrayed by Darius. They stretched out their hands to the Scythians and told them about their predicament. When the Scythians had heard them out, they at once united the two divisions of Scythians with the single division that included the Sauromatai, Boudinoi, and Gelonians, and then went straight for the Ister in pursuit of the Persians. [2] Since most of the Persian force was infantry and unfamiliar with the roads (as in fact there were really no properly cleared roads), while the Scythian cavalry was familiar with shortcuts, the two forces failed to meet, and the Scythians reached

4.135
513
SCYTHIA
The Persians carry out
their plan.

4.136
513
ISTER RIVER
The Scythians reach the Ister
bridge ahead of the Persians
and ask the Ionians to break
up the bridge and depart.

the bridge long before the Persians. [3] Perceiving that the Persians had not yet arrived, the Scythians told the Ionians, who were in their ships, "Ionians, the appointed number of days has passed, and you do wrong to still remain here. [4] Before this you lingered on because of your fear, but now you could immediately tear down the bridge and depart with peace of mind: fare well in your freedom, and be grateful to the gods and the Scythians. As for your former master, we will deal with him in such a way that he will never wage war against anyone again."

4.137
513
ISTER RIVER
Histiaios argues that the Ionians, who ruled their cities at Darius' will, should stay and hold the bridge for him.

The Ionians then conferred about how they should respond to this advice. Miltiades of Athens,[a] the general and a tyrant of the Hellespontine Chersonese,[b] proposed that they obey the Scythians and thereby free Ionia.[c] [2] Histiaios of Miletus[a] was of the opposite opinion. He said that it was because of Darius that each of them now governed his city as tyrant, and if the power of Darius were destroyed, he himself would not be able to keep ruling Miletus, nor would anyone else be able to rule his own city, either. For, he said, all of their cities would prefer democracy to tyranny. [3] Although everyone had initially favored the opinion of Miltiades, as soon as Histiaios presented his view, they all redirected their support to his proposal.

4.138
513
ISTER RIVER
Herodotus lists those Hellenes who voted on Histiaios' proposal.

The men casting their votes—all of whom were respected by the King—included Daphnis of Abydos,[a] Hippoklos of Lampsacus,[b] Herophantos of Parium,[c] Metrodoros of Proconnesus,[d] Aristagoras of Cyzicus,[e] and Ariston of Byzantium.[f] [2] These were all tyrants from the Hellespont. The tyrants from Ionia were Strattis of Chios,[a] Aiakes of Samos,[b] Laodamas of Phocaea,[c] and Histiaios of Miletus, the man who had presented his proposal in opposition to Miltiades'. Of the Aeolians,[d] Aristagoras of Cyme[e] was the only one there worth mentioning.

4.139
513
ISTER RIVER
The Hellenes decide to deceive the Scythians, and break down the northern edge of the bridge.

So then, having favored the proposal of Histiaios, they decided to elaborate upon it in both word and deed: they would in fact tear down the bridge as the Scythians requested, but only as far as an arrow could be shot from the shore, so that the Scythians would think they were acting on their advice—though they would not actually be doing so—and in order to prevent the Scythians from attempting to cross the bridge over the Ister by force. And as they were tearing down the Scythian end of the bridge, they would tell the Scythians that they would continue to do everything they

4.137.1a Athens: Map 4.138, AX. This is the first appearance of Miltiades the younger, son of the elder Kimon, the Athenian general who is credited with the great victory at Marathon (6.109). He was the father of another Kimon, who also became a famous Athenian general. Since Darius let him remain in control of the Hellespontine Chersonese after the Scythian campaign, most scholars do not believe he took the anti-Persian stance at the bridge which Herodotus describes. See Appendix L, Aristocratic Families in Herodotus, §2 and 8 and Figure L, where the Philaid family (to which Miltiades belonged) is diagrammed.

4.137.1b Chersonese, Hellespont: Map 4.138, AX. See Appendix T.
4.137.1c Ionia: Map 4.138, BY.
4.137.2a Miletus: Map 4.138, BY.
4.138.1a Abydos: Map 4.138, AY.
4.138.1b Lampsacus: Map 4.138, AY.
4.138.1c Parium: Map 4.138, AY.
4.138.1d Proconnesus: Map 4.138, AY.
4.138.1e Cyzicus: Map 4.138, AY.
4.138.1f Byzantium: Map 4.138, AY.
4.138.2a Chios: Map 4.138, BX.
4.138.2b Samos: Map 4.138, BY.
4.138.2c Phocaea: Map 4.138, BY.
4.138.2d Aeolis: Map 4.138, BY.
4.138.2e Cyme: Map 4.138, BY.

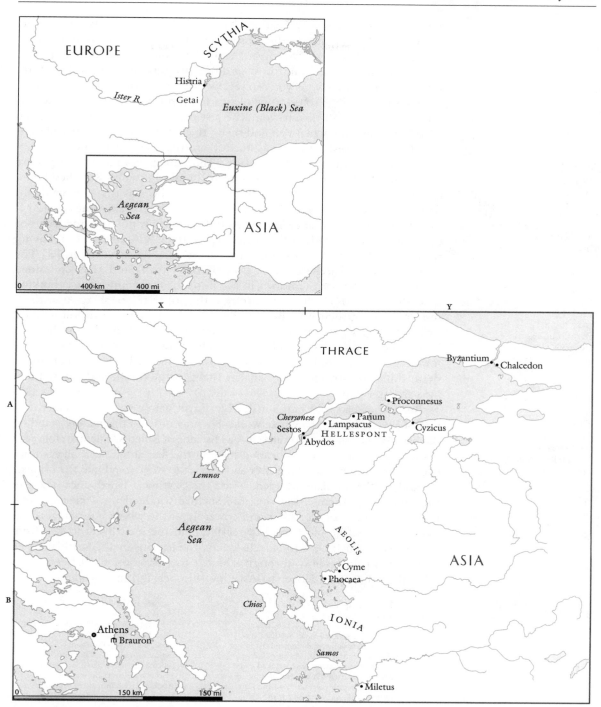

MAP 4.138

could to please them. [2] That is what they added to the plan. Of all the tyrants in this group, it was Histiaios who took the role of responding to the Scythians. He told them, "Scythians! You have come in haste in order to give us good advice. We are putting your advice to good use and will, in turn, serve you appropriately. As you can see, we are now tearing down the bridge, and we shall continue to do so wholeheartedly, since we wish to be free. [3] While we accomplish this, it would be just the right time for you to search for the Persians and, when you find them, to exact vengeance on behalf of us as well as yourselves, with a punishment that matches their offenses."

4.140
513
ISTER RIVER
The Scythians depart and fail to meet the Persians, who reach the bridge and are alarmed to find it apparently broken.

The Scythians trusted the Ionians again, and believing that they were telling the truth, turned back to search for the Persians. But they could find no signs of their path, and the reason for this was that the Scythians themselves had destroyed all the horse pastures and water sources. [2] If they had not done this earlier, it would have been possible for them to find the Persians with little effort when they wanted to. But having resolved that plan to be the best, they were now thwarted by it. [3] The Scythians next searched the region of their own land that contained water and fodder for the horses in the hunt for their opponents, thinking that they would be fleeing through this district so as to use these resources along their way. But the Persians had taken care to follow their earlier tracks, which, however, made it somewhat difficult for them to locate the bridge. [4] When they finally arrived there after dark, they found what appeared to them to be a torn-down bridge, which made them think that the Ionians had left them in the lurch, and threw them into an utter panic.

4.141
513
ISTER RIVER
The Hellenes rescue Darius' troops and repair the bridge.

But Darius had with him a man from Egypt whose voice was louder than that of anyone else in the whole world. He now ordered this man to stand on the bank of the Ister and to call out for Histiaios of Miletus. The man followed these orders, and Histiaios, hearing him on the first shout, sent all his ships over to ferry troops across the river and also set to work to rebuild the bridge.

4.142
513
SCYTHIA
The Persians escape; the Scythians taunt the Ionians as ideal slaves.

And so the Persians escaped, while the Scythians failed once again in their search for them. After this, the Scythians judged the Ionians as free men to be the most worthless and cowardly of the whole human race; but as slaves, to be the most fond of servility and the least likely to flee from their masters. Such were the insults cast at the Ionians by the Scythians.

4.143
513
ASIA
Darius crosses back to Asia, leaving Megabazos, whom he honors.

Darius made his way through Thrace[a] to Sestos on the Chersonese;[b] from there he crossed over to Asia[c] by ship, leaving in Europe a Persian

4.143.1a   Thrace: Map 4.138, AY.
4.143.1b   Sestos on the Chersonese: Map 4.138, AY.
4.143.1c   Asia (Asia Minor): Map 4.138, BY, and locator. Persian efforts in Scythia (Map 4.138, locator) were ephemeral. Istria (Histria on Map 4.138, locator, and in the *Barrington Atlas*) was attacked and partially destroyed at the end of the sixth century, probably a reaction of the Getai (Map 4.138, locator) and/or the Scythians to Darius' campaign. It is clear that at the time of the Persian invasion of 480 the Persians controlled only sites along the coast of Thrace. Miltiades was later chased out of the Thracian Chersonese by Scythians (5.40), but there is a chronological problem in dating this event: one scheme fits with a Scythian reaction to Darius' campaign, but another scheme would date it to the early 490s, thus too late to have a connection with Darius' expedition.

named Megabazos as his general. The King had already granted this man a mark of high esteem by a comment he had once made in the presence of other Persians. [2] It seems that Darius was about to eat some pomegranates, but just when he started on the first one, his brother Artabanos asked him what he would wish to have as many of as there were seeds in a pomegranate. Darius replied that he would rather have that many Megabazoses than to have Hellas subjected to his rule. [3] Darius thus paid him an honor by making this remark in front of other Persians, and he now left this man behind as the general of an army of 80,000 men.

This Megabazos once made a statement that will be remembered forever by the inhabitants of the Hellespont.[a] [2] Once when he was in Byzantium, he learned that the Chalcedonians[a] had settled their colony seventeen years earlier than the people of Byzantium had established theirs. Upon hearing this, he remarked that the Chalcedonians must have been blind at that time, for they would not have chosen such an inferior location when there was such a superior one available, unless they were blind. [3] And so this Megabazos was left to serve as general in the territory of the Hellespontines, and he subjugated those of them who were not medizing.[a]

While he was occupied with these conquests, another ambitious military expedition was taking place, this one against Libya. But before I explain the reason for it, there is something else to relate.

[2] When the grandsons of the crew of the *Argo*[a] were driven out of Lemnos[b] by the Pelasgians, the ones who had abducted Athenian[c] women from Brauron,[d] they sailed to Lacedaemon[e] and occupied Mount Taygetos,[f] where they kindled a fire. [3] When the Lacedaemonians noticed their presence, they sent a messenger to find out who they were and where they had come from. In response to the messenger's inquiries, they said that they were Minyans, sons of the heroes who had sailed on the *Argo* who had sired them after they had put in at Lemnos. [4] When the Lacedaemonians heard that they claimed to be of Minyan stock, they sent a second messenger to ask why they had come to their land and lit a fire; what did they want? They answered that, having been expelled by the Pelasgians, they had returned to the land of their fathers, which was certainly a just and equitable thing for them to do. Now what they wanted was to live there with them and to share in the government and in the allotments of land. [5] The Lacedaemonians accepted the Minyans and their conditions, and what especially induced them to do so was the fact that the sons of

4.144
513
HELLESPONT
Megabazos subjugates all the people of the Hellespont.

4.145
LACEDAEMON
The story of the reception of the descendants of the crew of the *Argo* in Lacedaemon.

4.144.1a   Hellespont: Map 4.138, AY.
4.144.2a   Chalcedon: Map 4.138, AY.
4.144.3a   To medize was to go over to the Persian side. Persians were often called Medes by the Hellenes.
4.145.2a   *Argo* and Argonauts: see Glossary.
4.145.2b   Lemnos: Map 4.138, AX.
4.145.2c   Athens: Map 4.138, BX.
4.145.2d   Brauron: Map 4.138, BX. On the Pelasgian abduction of Athenian women, see 6.137–138.

4.145.2e   Lacedaemon (Sparta, Laconia): Map 4.150, AX, BX. Herodotus uses the names Spartans and Lacedaemonians interchangeably. "Spartans," however, often refers specifically to citizens of the state of Sparta, whereas any inhabitant of the territory of Lacedaemon is a Lacedaemonian. See Appendix B, §5, 7, and n. B.7a.
4.145.2f   Mount Taygetos: Map 4.150, AX.

Tyndareos[a] had participated in the voyage of the *Argo*. So they welcomed the Minyans, giving them a share of land and distributing them among their tribes. The Minyans immediately began to intermarry with the Lacedaemonians and gave them the women they had brought from Lemnos to marry in exchange.

4.146
SPARTA
The Minyans escape from a Spartan prison.

Before long, however, the Minyans grew arrogant; they demanded a share of the kingship and committed impious infractions as well. [2] And so the Lacedaemonians decided to kill them; they arrested them all and put them in prison. Now when the Lacedaemonians put someone to death, they do so at night. They never execute anyone during the day. [3] So as they were waiting to execute them, the wives of the Minyans, who were natives of Sparta and daughters of the most prominent Spartans, came and begged permission to enter the prison so that each of them could talk to her husband. The men in charge let the women go in, since they could not imagine that these women could do anything deceitful. [4] But when the women gained entrance to the prison, they took off the clothes they were wearing, gave them to their husbands, and put on the men's garments instead. When the men had dressed themselves in their wives' clothes, they walked out in the guise of women and, thus having escaped, occupied Mount Taygetos again.

4.147
THERA
The tale of how Theras sailed to Calliste (now called Thera).

At the same time that this was happening, a colonial expedition was being organized by Theras son of Autesion, the son of Teisamenos, who was the son of Thersandros son of Polyneikes. [2] This Theras had a Kadmeian lineage and was the maternal uncle of the sons of Aristodemos, Eurythenes and Prokles. While they were still children, Theras wielded the royal power at Sparta when he acted as regent for them. [3] But when his nephews came of age, they took over the kingship, and Theras, who had now tasted supreme power, could not tolerate being ruled by others. Therefore, he announced that he would no longer remain in Lacedaemon but would sail away to join his kinsmen [4] who lived on the island now known as Thera,[a] but formerly called Calliste, and were descendants of the Phoenician[b] Membliaraos son of Poikiles. For Kadmos son of Agenor had put in at this island during his search for Europa, and whether it was because he found the island particularly pleasing or for some other reason, he left there some of the other Phoenicians—even his own relatives, including Membliaraos. [5] These then were the inhabitants of the island called Calliste for eight generations before the arrival of Theras from Lacedaemon.

4.148
THERA
The tale of Theras and the Minyans.

It was to the people on Calliste, then, that Theras was preparing to sail with a band of colonists he had gathered from the tribes of Lacedaemon. He had no intention of expelling them but planned rather to live there among them and to regard them as his kinsmen. [2] When the Minyans escaped

4.145.5a Sons of Tyndareos: Tyndareos was a mythical king of Sparta. His sons Castor and Pollux were legendary heroes famous for many exploits; they were also the brothers of Helen of Troy and of Clytemnestra of Argos, who murdered Agamemnon in the bath.

4.147.4a Thera Island: Map 4.150, BY.
4.147.4b Phoenicia: Map 4.150, locator.

from prison and reoccupied Taygetos, Theras begged the Lacedaemonians not to kill them; and in order to prevent their slaughter, he promised that he would take them out of the country. [3] The Lacedaemonians consented to his proposal, and Theras then sailed to the descendants of Membliaraos with three thirty-oared ships. He took along with him a few, but not all, of the Minyans, [4] for most of them went instead to the territories of the Paroreatai and Kaukones, and after they had driven them from their lands, they divided themselves into six groups and settled the following cities: Lepreon, Makistos, Phrixa, Pyrgoi, Epeion,[a] and Noudion.[b] Most of these cities had been taken and sacked by the Eleans[c] in my time.[d] And the island Calliste was named Thera after the leader of the colony.

When the son of Theras refused to sail with him, Theras remarked that he would therefore leave him behind as a sheep among wolves. It was because of this statement that the young man acquired the name Oiolykos,[a] which somehow prevailed over his original name. To Oiolykos was born a son named Aigeus, from whom the Aigeidai, a great tribe in Sparta, obtained their name. [2] At one time, all the children born to the men of this tribe died young until, on the advice of an oracle,[a] they founded a sanctuary to the Erinyes[b] of Laios and Oedipus. After that the children survived, as did the sons born of these men on Thera.

4.149
SPARTA
The Aegeidai at Sparta and Thera.

Up to this point, the Lacedaemonian and the Theraian versions of this story agree, but from here on the Theraians give the following account. [2] They say that Grinnos son of Aisanias, a descendant of Theras and king of the island of Thera, went to Delphi[a] bringing a hecatomb[b] from his city. He was attended by other citizens, in particular by Battos son of Polymnestos, a member of the tribe of the Euphemides, who were Minyans. [3] Although Grinnos king of the Theraians had come to consult the Pythia about other matters, she instructed him to found a city in Libya.[a] He replied, "But my lord, I am now too weighted down with age to pick up and settle elsewhere. Please command one of the younger men to go instead," and as he said this, he pointed to Battos. [4] That was all that happened at the time, and after they had returned home they ignored the oracular response. After all, they had no idea where Libya was and would not dare to lead a colonial expedition off into the unknown.

4.150
DELPHI
Delphi's role in the expedition of Battos to Libya.

But afterward, no rain fell on Thera for seven years, and all the trees on the island withered away except for one. So the Theraians again consulted the oracle, and the Pythia again urged them to colonize Libya. [2] Since they had obtained no solution to their problem, they sent messengers to Crete in search of a Cretan or resident alien who might have gone to Libya. The messengers wandered throughout Crete until they came to the city of

4.151
ISLAND OF PLATEIA
A Theran expedition to spy out the land of Libya.

4.148.4a   Lepreon, Makistos, Phrixa, Pyrgoi, Epeion: Map 4.150, AX.
4.148.4b   Noudion: location unknown.
4.148.4c   Elis: Map 4.150, AX.
4.148.4d   Approximately the second quarter of the fifth century (475–450).
4.149.1a   Oiolyko: the name means "sheep-wolf."

4.149.2a   See Appendix P, Oracles, Religion, and Politics in Herodotus, §9.
4.149.2b   Erinyes: often translated as "the Furies."
4.150.2a   Delphi: Map 4.150, AX.
4.150.2b   Hecatomb: a large number of animals offered for sacrifice. See Glossary.
4.150.3a   Libya: Map 4.150, locator.

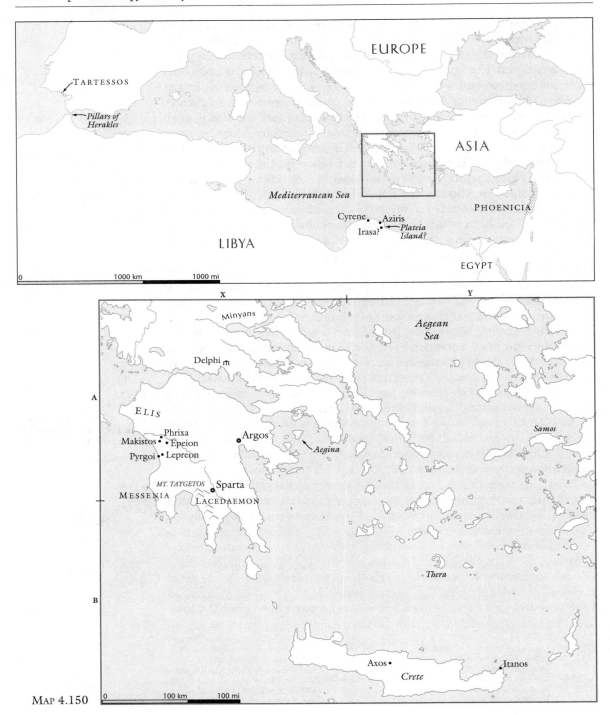

MAP 4.150

Itanos,[a] where they met a murex[b] fisherman named Korobios, who said he had once been blown off course by the wind and had come to the Libyan island called Plateia.[c] [3] They persuaded him to help them by offering him money and took him to Thera. From there, a small party sailed out on a scouting expedition. Korobios led them to the island of Plateia, and after leaving him there with provisions sufficient to last a designated number of months, they quickly sailed back to report to the Theraians about the island.

But they stayed away for longer than they had agreed upon, and when Korobios was running out of provisions, a Samian[a] ship arrived, whose captain was Kolaios. He had been driven off course to Plateia while headed for Egypt,[b] and when the Samians heard Korobios' whole story, they left him a year's supply of provisions. [2] Then they set sail from the island, intending to go to Egypt, but were again driven off course by an easterly wind, which did not abate until they had passed through the Pillars of Herakles[a] and by some divine guidance came to Tartessos.[b] [3] This trading post had not yet been exploited at this time, and so these men returned with a greater profit from their cargo than any other Hellenes of whom we have an accurate account, except for that of Sostratos son of Laodamas of Aegina,[a] since it is impossible for anyone to challenge his record! [4] The Samians took a tenth of their profits, six talents' worth, and had a bronze bowl made in the Argive[a] style, with griffin heads projecting around it.[b] They dedicated it in the sanctuary of Hera and set it upon three gigantic bronze kneeling statues, over ten feet[c] tall. It was the Samians' good deed to Korobios that first cemented the great friendship between the Cyrenaeans[d] and Theraians and the Samians.

So the Theraians left Korobios on the island and sailed back to Thera, where they announced that an island off Libya had now been settled by them. The Theraians resolved to send one out of every two brothers there, to be chosen by lot and accompanied by men from all seven districts, with Battos to be their leader and king. After manning two penteconters[a] in this way, they sent them off to Plateia.

That is what the Theraians say, and for the rest of the story, the Theraian and Cyrenaean accounts agree, except that the Cyrenaeans disagree completely with the Theraian version concerning Battos. This is how the Cyrenaeans tell the story. There is in Crete a city, Axos,[a] where Etearchos

4.152

TARTESSOS
The Samians on the island of Plateia and at Tartessos earn sixty talents and establish friendship with Cyrene and Thera.

4.153

ISLAND OF PLATEIA
The Theraians under Battos leave Thera for the island of Plateia off Libya.

4.154

CRETE
The Cyrenaean story of Phronime.

4.151.2a Itanos, Crete (Creta): Map 4.150, BY.
4.151.2b Murex: a mollusk from which a purple dye could be made. It was rare and expensive, and the color purple therefore became associated with high rank and wealth.
4.151.2c Plateia Island, Libya, possible location: Map 4.150, locator, and Map 4.165.
4.152.1a Samos: Map 4.150, AY.
4.152.1b Egypt: Map 4.150, locator.
4.152.2a Pillars of Herakles (modern Straits of Gibraltar): Map 4.150, locator.
4.152.2b Tartessos: Map 4.150, locator.
4.152.3a Aegina: Map 4.150, AX. See Figure 4.152a for a complete stone anchor and a

fragment of an anchor with an inscription that mentions Sostratos.
4.152.4a Argos: Map 4.150, AX.
4.152.4b See Figure 4.152b of a bronze griffin head which was once affixed to a bronze bowl.
4.152.4c Herodotus writes "7 cubits." See Appendix J, §4, 5, 19.
4.152.4d Cyrene, Libya: Map 4.150, locator.
4.153.1a Penteconters: ships powered by fifty oars; one line of twenty-five rowers on each side of the vessel. See Appendix S, Trireme Warfare in Herodotus, §4, 12.
4.154.1a Axos, Crete (Creta): Map 4.150, BY. Axos is also known as Oaxos; both spellings are found in manuscripts of Herodotus.

FIGURE 4.152A. A COMPLETE STONE ANCHOR FOUND AT ATHENS' PORT OF PEIRAIEUS (LEFT) AND A FRAGMENT OF AN ANCHOR FOUND AT GRAVISEA, THE PORT OF TARQUINIA IN ITALY (RIGHT). THE INSCRIPTION ON THE FRAGMENT SAYS THAT SOSTRATOS DEDICATED THE ANCHOR TO AEGINETAN APOLLO.

ruled as king. He had a daughter named Phronime whose mother had died, so he had married another woman who, [2] when she moved in, assumed the right to play the role of stepmother. She abused and harassed the girl, contriving all kinds of plots against her. Finally, she accused her of licentiousness and managed to persuade her husband to believe the charge. Convinced by his wife, he devised the following impious offense against his daughter. [3] There was in Axos a merchant, Themision of Thera, with whom Etearchos pledged guest-friendship[a] and whom he asked to swear to perform whatever service he would request. When Themision had sworn the oath, Etearchos brought forth his daughter and handed her over to him with instructions to take her away and throw her into the sea. [4] Infuriated at being deceived by the oath in this way, Themision renounced his pact of guest-friendship, and then, to release himself from obligation under the oath he had sworn to Etearchos, he sailed away with the girl, tied a rope around her, lowered her down into the sea, and then, after pulling her back up, took her with him back to Thera.[a]

4.154.3a Guest-friendship (*xenia*): a bond of ritualized friendship, usually between aristocrats or prominent men of different cities. It was passed down through generations and required hereditary privileges and obligations such as reciprocal hospitality

and assistance. See Appendix T, §3.

4.154.4a This is a sophistic interpretation of an oath, as it follows the letter, but not the intent, of the oath. Another example of this is at 4.201. The practice had to be guarded against even in Greek international treaties.

FIGURE 4.152B. A BRONZE GRIFFIN HEAD WHICH WAS ONCE AFFIXED TO A BRONZE BOWL IN THE ARGIVE STYLE, LIKE THE RARE VESSEL SHOWN BELOW, WHICH HAS ALL ITS GRIFFIN HEADS STILL IN PLACE.

There, Phronime was taken in by Polymnestos, a distinguished Theraian, to be his mistress. In the fullness of time, she bore to him a son who stuttered and spoke with a lisp. According to the Theraians and Cyrenaeans, the boy was named Battos.[a] I think, however, that he was initially given some other name, [2] since he changed his name after coming to Libya because of what the oracle at Delphi had told him, and also because of the honor he thereby acquired by taking this as his surname—for the Libyans call a king *battos*. Indeed, I believe the Pythia knew that he would be king in Libya when, in her prophecy, she called him by that title in the Libyan language. [3] When he grew to manhood, he went to Delphi to ask about his speech defect, and the Pythia gave this response to his question:

> Battos, you have come here for speech,
> and here is the speech of Lord Phoibos Apollo.
> He sends you to Libya, feeder of flocks, to found a colony.

4.155
BATTOS
The Cyrenaean story of Battos.

4.159.1a Battos I: see Appendix L, §9 and n. L.9b. Although Herodotus mentions a reign of 40 years, it is thought that Cyrene was founded c. 630, and that Battos I died c. 571.

As if the god had said in Greek, "O King, you have come here for speech," [4] Battos replied, "My lord, I did come for advice about my speech, but you have responded by presenting an irrelevant and impossible recommendation. You order me to colonize Libya, but how could I be capable of that? What men would I take along?" The god, however, was not persuaded to give him a different response, and as Battos realized that he was receiving the same prophecy as before, he left in the middle of it and returned to Thera.

But afterward, he and the rest of the Theraians suffered again from bad luck, and in their ignorance of the cause of their misfortunes, they consulted Delphi about their present troubles. [2] The Pythia responded that everything would go better for them if they would join Battos in settling Cyrene in Libya.[a] So the Theraians sent Battos off with two penteconters. He and his crew did sail to Libya, but since they did not know what to do when they got there, they returned to Thera. [3] As they were sailing in, however, the Theraians shot at them and would not allow them to land; they ordered them instead to sail back again. And so being forced to do so, they sailed back and settled an island off the coast of Libya, whose name, as I mentioned earlier, is Plateia.[a] This island is said to be equal in size to the present city of the Cyrenaeans.

For two years they lived on that island, but nothing went well for them there, so, leaving behind one man, the rest of them sailed for Delphi to consult the oracle. They announced that though they were now living in Libya, they were faring no better than before. [2] The Pythia replied:

> If you really know Libya feeder of flocks without having gone there
> better than I who have been to that place,
> Then I greatly admire your wisdom.

When Battos and his followers heard this, they realized that the god was not releasing them from their obligation to colonize until they moved into Libya itself, so they sailed back again. [3] They stopped at the island to pick up the man they had left there and then settled the region of Libya that lies on the mainland opposite the island, a place called Aziris.[a] It is bordered on either side by the most beautiful valleys, and a river flows along one side of it.

They lived here for six years, but in the seventh, some Libyans came to them and, offering to show them a better location, persuaded them to leave. [2] So when the Libyans had managed to move them out of their settlement, they led them to the west in such a way that the Hellenes would not be able to see the best district as they were passing through it. They calculated their timing so as to take them at night through that part of the country which is called Irasa,[a] [3] and leading them to what is said to be the spring of Apollo, they declared, "Hellenes, this is a suitable place for you to live, for here the sky is pierced with holes."

4.156.2a Cyrene, Libya: Map 4.150, locator.
4.156.3a Plateia Island, possible location: Map 4.150, locator, and Map 4.165.

4.157.3a Aziris, Libya: Map 4.150, locator.
4.158.2a Irasa, Libya, possible location: Map 4.150, locator.

Battos[a] the founder of the colony lived and ruled for forty years, and his son Arkesilaos[b] ruled for sixteen further years; and while they ruled, the number of the Cyrenaeans who lived there remained the same as the number of those who had originally joined the colonial expedition. [2] But in the reign of the third king, called Battos the Blessed,[a] the Pythia urged all Hellenes to sail to Libya and settle among the Cyrenaeans, since the Cyrenaeans had invited them to come and to share in the plots of land that they intended to divide and distribute among them.[b] [3] This is how the oracle went:

> He who comes to beloved Libya
> Too late for the division of land
> will, I predict, be sorry someday.

[4] When a great throng of people had gathered in Cyrene, the surrounding Libyan inhabitants found that they had been cut off from a large part of their lands. Infuriated at being thus deprived of their territory by the Cyrenaeans, these Libyans and their king, whose name was Adikran, sent a message to Egypt[a] offering to place themselves under the protection and rule of Apries king of Egypt. [5] Apries then assembled a large army and sent it against Cyrene,[a] but the Cyrenaeans marched out to Irasa, and at the spring called Theste engaged the Egyptians in battle and were victorious. [6] Egyptians, after all, had had no experience fighting Hellenes before this[a] and approached combat with them carelessly, and thereby suffered such devastating losses that few of them returned to Egypt. It was in response to this disaster that the Egyptians blamed Apries and revolted against him.[b]

When Arkesilaos, the son of this Battos,[a] became king, he quarreled with his brothers so that they left Cyrene and founded another city in Libya on their own—Barke[b]—and it is still called that today. While they were establishing their settlement, they led the Libyans in a revolt against the Cyrenaeans. [2] So Arkesilaos mobilized his troops and marched against the Libyans who had welcomed his brothers and revolted. At first, these Libyans feared the king and fled to eastern Libya. [3] Arkesilaos pursued them until he reached Leucon,[a] a site in Libya where the Libyans decided to turn and attack him. In the battle that followed, the Libyans won a great victory over the Cyrenaeans; indeed, 7,000 Cyrenaean hoplites fell there. [4] Following this calamity, Arkesilaos became ill and, after taking a drug,

4.159
c. 630–571?
CYRENE
Cyrene grows great, assisted by immigration that Delphi encourages. The Libyans apply to Egypt for help against Cyrene, but the army sent against it by the Egyptian king Apries (ruled from 589 to 570) is defeated with great loss.

4.160
?
LEUCON
King Arkesilaos quarrels with his brothers and is killed after being defeated by them in battle.

4.159.1a Battos I: see Appendix L, §9 and n. L.9b.
4.159.1b Arkesilaos I: see Appendix L, §9 and n. L.9b.
4.159.2a Battos II.
4.159.2b See Appendix P, §9.
4.159.4a Egypt: Map 4.150, locator.
4.159.5a The account of the expedition sent to Cyrene by Apries was promised by Herodotus at 2.161.3.
4.159.6a Herodotus' claim of Egyptian ignorance of Greek military methods c. 570 is curious, as Ionian and Carian mercenaries,

no doubt armed as hoplites, helped Psammetichos I secure his rule of Egypt in 663 (2.152–154) and Greek mercenaries served in Psammetichos II's Ethiopian campaign of 593. These Greek mercenaries scratched their names on the colossal statues of the temple at Abu Simbel in Upper Egypt.
4.159.6b This revolt against Apries took place in 570.
4.160.1a Arkesilaos II.
4.160.1b Barke: Map 4.165.
4.160.3a Leucon: location unknown.

was strangled by his brother Learchos, who, in turn, was treacherously killed by the wife of Arkesilaos, whose name was Eryxo.

Battos[a] son of Arkesilaos then inherited the kingship. He was lame and walked with a limp. In response to their overwhelming misfortune, the Cyrenaeans sent to Delphi[b] to inquire as to what institution they might create to assure themselves a better life there. [2] The Pythia ordered them to bring in a mediator from Mantineia.[a] And so the Cyrenaeans made this request, and the Mantineians responded by sending to them their most distinguished citizen, whose name was Demonax. [3] This man arrived in Cyrene, and after conducting a detailed investigation of the community, divided the people into three tribes: the first included the Theraians and the inhabitants of the surrounding area, the second was composed of the Peloponnesians and Cretans, and the third was made up of all the other islanders. In addition, Demonax set aside specific precincts and priesthoods for King Battos, but everything else that had earlier belonged to the kings he made public and placed in the hands of the people.[a]

During the reign of this Battos, these arrangements continued in force, but in the reign of his son Arkesilaos,[a] a great disturbance arose over rights and entitlements. [2] For this Arkesilaos, the son of Battos the Lame and Pheretime, refused to abide by the system prescribed by Demonax of Mantineia; he demanded the return of his ancestral privileges. In the civil strife that he created, Arkesilaos was defeated and fled in exile to Samos,[a] while his mother fled to Salamis on Cyprus.[b] [3] During this time the ruler of Salamis was Euelthon, the man who dedicated an incense burner at Delphi which is really worth seeing; it is set up in the treasury of the Corinthians. Pheretime came to Euelthon and asked for an army that would restore her to Cyrene.[a] [4] Euelthon offered her everything but an army, and while she said to him as she accepted his gifts that they were fine, she would add that it would be even better if he would grant her the army she had requested. She repeated this every time he offered her a gift, [5] until Euelthon finally sent her a golden spindle and distaff, with some wool to go along with them. When Pheretime recited the same complaint again, Euelthon replied that these were the sorts of gifts women should receive, not armies.

Meanwhile, Arkesilaos was on Samos collecting every man he could find with the prospect of sharing in a redistribution of land in Libya. When he had mustered a large army, he sent to Delphi to consult the oracle about his return. [2] The Pythia gave him this response:

4.161.1a   Battos III.
4.161.1b   Delphi: Map 4.150, AX.
4.161.2a   Mantineia: Map 4.165.
4.161.3a   Demonax of Mantineia belongs to an
           archaic Greek phenomenon of lawgivers:
           one man being given unlimited power
           to establish a just constitution in a trou-
           bled city. The Spartan Lykourgos and

the Athenian Solon are other examples.
Often the lawgiver establishes a constitution and immediately leaves town.
4.162.1a   Arkesilaos III.
4.162.2a   Samos: Map 4.165.
4.162.2b   Salamis on Cyprus: Map 4.165.
4.162.3a   Cyrene: Map 4.165.

To four kings named Battos and four named Arkesilaos,[a] for eight generations of men, does Loxias[b] grant the kingship of Cyrene. His advice is not to attempt to go beyond that. [3] As for you, return to your own land in peace, and if you find a kiln full of wine jars, do not fire them, but send them away with a fair wind. If you fire them, do not enter the place surrounded by water. If you do, both you and the prize bull will die.

That was the response given to Arkesilaos by the Pythia. So Arkesilaos picked up the men from Samos and returned from exile to Cyrene. But after he had taken control of the government, he forgot what the oracle had told him and instead sought to make his political opponents pay the penalty for his exile. [2] Some of them simply left the country for good; others were captured by Arkesilaos and sent away to be destroyed on Cyprus[a] but were blown off course to Cnidus,[b] where the Cnidians rescued them and sent them off to Thera.[c] Still other Cyrenaeans took refuge in a high tower which was the personal property of a man named Aglomachos. Arkesilaos piled up wood around the tower and set it on fire. [3] After the deed had been done, he realized that this corresponded to the Pythia's warning not to fire the wine jars in the kiln. So now, in dread of the death the god had prophesied, he purposely stayed out of the city of Cyrene, thinking that it was the place surrounded by water. [4] He had a wife (also his blood relative) who was the daughter of Alazeir the king of Barke,[a] so he now went to visit the king. But the men of Barke and some of the exiles from Cyrene noticed him in the agora and killed him there along with his father-in-law Alazeir. Thus Arkesilaos failed to understand the oracle, and whether intentionally or unwittingly, brought about the fulfillment of his own fate.

While Arkesilaos was living in Barke working out his own ruin, his mother Pheretime maintained his privileges in Cyrene, managing all things there and even sitting on the council. [2] When she found out that her son had been killed in Barke, she fled to Egypt,[a] for Arkesilaos her son had served Cambyses son of Cyrus well; indeed it was he who had given Cyrene over to Cambyses and had arranged for the payment of tribute to him.[b] [3] When she arrived in Egypt, Pheretime sat down before Aryandes as a suppliant and appealed to him to avenge her son, claiming that it was because of his medism[a] that her son was now dead.

This Aryandes had been appointed governor of Egypt by Cambyses; later he was put to death for trying to act like the equal of Darius. He had personally seen and heard how Darius had set his heart on leaving behind a

4.164
CYRENE
Arkesilaos forgets the oracle and unwittingly acts so as to fulfill it.

4.165
515–513?
EGYPT
Pheretime flees to Egypt and begs help from the Persians there.

4.166
497?
EGYPT-PERSIA
The viceroy of Egypt is executed by Darius for rebellion.

4.163.2a The House of Cyrene reigned from Battos I to Arkesilaos IV, c. 630 to 440.
4.163.2b Loxias is another name for Apollo.
4.164.2a Cyprus: Map 4.165.
4.164.2b Cnidus: Map 4.165.
4.164.2c Thera: Map 4.165.
4.164.4a Barke: Map 4.165.
4.165.2a Egypt: Map 4.165.

4.165.2b Compare this with 3.13.
4.165.3a The Hellenes used the word "medize" to characterize the policy or actions of anyone who submitted to, sided with, or showed friendliness to the Persians. This usage derives from the frequency with which the Hellenes used the term Medes for Persians.

349

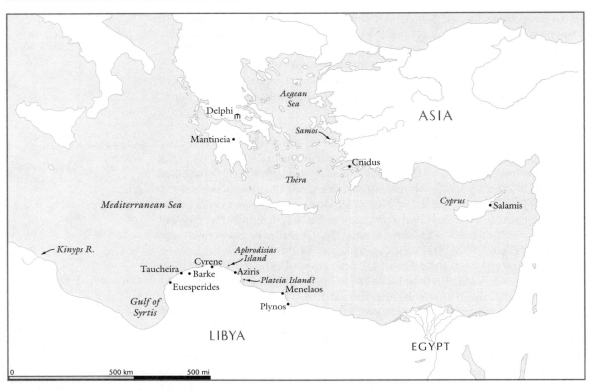

MAP 4.165

memorial to himself unlike any of those left by other kings, and Aryandes attempted to imitate the King in this until he received his just reward. [2] What happened was that after Darius refined a quantity of gold to its highest possible purity and struck the most valuable coins from this metal,[a] Aryandes, acting as the ruler of Egypt, did the same thing, but with silver. Even today, the purest silver coin is the Aryandic. But when Darius found out that Aryandes was doing this, he had him executed, although he did so on a different charge, accusing him of having revolted against him.

But now Aryandes pitied Pheretime and gave her his entire Egyptian military force, both the land army and the fleet. He appointed Amasis, a Maraphian,[a] as general of the army and Bardes, of the Pasargadae tribe,[b] to command the fleet. [2] Before dispatching the expedition to Barke, Aryandes sent a herald there to inquire about the identity of the man who had killed Arkesilaos. But the whole population of Barke assumed responsibility,

4.167
513
EGYPT
Aryandes of Egypt organizes an army and fleet to attack the Libyan Greeks.

4.166.2a   These coins were well known as gold Darics. See Appendix J, §14.
4.167.1a   The Maraphians were a leading Persian tribe: location unknown. See 1.125.

4.167.1b   Pasargadae (another important Persian tribe), location of territory: Map 1.142. See 1.125.3.

for they said they had suffered much abuse at his hands. When he learned of this, Aryandes sent forth the expedition with Pheretime.[a] [3] That, at least, was the ostensible reason he gave for sending his army against the Libyans, but it seems to me that he actually wanted to overthrow the Libyans, for the Libyans included many nations of all sorts, and few of them were subjects of the King. In fact, the majority of them couldn't have cared less about Darius.

The various Libyan nations inhabit their territories in the following order. Going west from Egypt, the first inhabitants of Libya one comes upon are the Adyrmachidians.[a] The customs they follow the most are those of the Egyptians, except that they dress like the rest of the Libyans. Their women wear a bronze ring around the calf of each leg and grow their hair long. Whenever they catch lice on themselves, they bite them back before throwing them away. [2] These are the only Libyans to practice this custom and also the only ones to display their virgins to their king just before they begin living with a man. Whichever of them pleases the king most must lose her virginity to him. The land of the Adyrmachidians extends from Egypt to a harbor by the name of Plynos.[a]

4.168
LIBYA
The Adyrmachidians, the Libyans who live nearest to Egypt.

From here the Giligamians[a] inhabit the land stretching to the west up to the island of Aphrodisias;[b] in between lies the island of Plateia,[c] on which the Cyrenaeans[d] settled, and on the mainland is the harbor of Menelaos and also Aziris,[e] where the Cyrenaeans subsequently lived. This is also the beginning of the region where silphium[f] grows, [2] which extends from the island of Plateia to the mouth of the Syrtis.[a] The customs of these people are very much like those of the other Libyans.

4.169
LIBYA
The Giligamians live to the west, where silphium cultivation begins.

To the west of the Giligamians are the Asbystaians,[a] who dwell to the south of Cyrene. They do not extend up to the coast, since the Cyrenaeans inhabit the region along the sea. The Asbystaians use four-horse chariots more than all the other Libyans and strive to imitate the Cyrenaeans in the greater part of their customs.

4.170
LIBYA
The Asbystaians live inland of Cyrene.

To the west of the Asbystaians live the Auschisians.[a] Their country lies south of Barke[b] and extends to the coast at Euesperides.[c] In the middle of the Auschisaian territory dwell the Bakalians,[d] a small nation that extends to the coast up to Taucheira,[e] a city in the territory of Barke. They follow the same customs as those who live south of Cyrene.

4.171
LIBYA
The Auschisians and the Bakales.

4.167.2a   The story of Pheretime's revenge continues at 4.200.1.
4.168.1a   Adyrmachidians: Map 4.175, BY.
4.168.2a   Plynos: Map 4.165; Map 4.175, BY.
4.169.1a   Giligamians: Map 4.175, BY.
4.169.1b   Aphrodisias Island: Map 4.165.
4.169.1c   Plateia Island, possible location: Map 4.165.
4.169.1d   Cyrene: Map 4.165; Map 4.175, BY.
4.169.1e   Menelaos and Aziris: Map 4.165.
4.169.1f   Silphium: a medicinal plant that was also used for food and fodder. It is now considered to be extinct, and its exact properties are unknown. It was such an important cash crop that export trade in it was strictly controlled as a Cyrenaean

royal monopoly. Figure 4.169 has a representation of the silphium plant on a Cyrenaean coin, and a scene painted on a plate from Sparta showing King Arkesilaos supervising the preparation of silphium for export.
4.169.2a   Gulf of Syrtis: Map 4.175, BY.
4.170.1a   Asbystaians: Map 4.175, BY.
4.171.1a   Auschisians, possible location: Map 4.175, BY.
4.171.1b   Barke: Map 4.165; Map 4.175, BY.
4.171.1c   Euesperides: Map 4.175, BY.
4.171.1d   Bakalians, possible location: Map 4.175, BY.
4.171.1e   Taucheira: Map 4.165.

FIGURE 4.169. THE EXPORT OF SILPHIUM, A TYPE OF THISTLE NOW EXTINCT THAT WAS THOUGHT TO HAVE MEDICINAL PROPERTIES, WAS A HIGHLY PROFITABLE ROYAL MONOPOLY. A CYRENAEAN COIN (LEFT) DEPICTS THE SILPHIUM PLANT. A PAINTED PLATE (TOP) SHOWS KING ARKESILAOS ON HIS THRONE, SUPERVISING THE WEIGHING AND LOADING OF SILPHIUM FOR EXPORT.

To the west of the Auschisians are the Nasamones,[a] a populous nation whose people leave their flocks on the coast in the summer and travel into the interior to Augila[b] to harvest dates. The palm trees grow prolifically and to a large size there, and all of them bear fruit. They hunt for locusts, and when they catch them, they leave them to dry in the sun and then grind them to powder and sprinkle it on milk before they drink it. [2] Although it is the custom for each Nasamonian man to have many wives, they consider them to be common property for the purposes of intercourse, very much like the Massagetai.[a] Whenever they have set up a staff outside, it means that they are having intercourse within. When a Nasamonian man marries for the first time, it is customary for his bride to have intercourse with all the guests at the feast in succession, and for each of these guests to then present a gift he has brought from home. [3] Their practices regarding oaths and prophecy are as follows. They swear oaths by the men of their country who are said to have been the best and most just, and as they do so, they place their hands upon the tombs of these men. They obtain prophecies by going to their own ancestors' tombs, saying a prayer, and then falling asleep upon the tombs. Whatever vision they receive in their sleep is regarded by them as the oracle's response. [4] When they make pledges to each other, each man drinks out of the other's hand, and if they have no water available, they take dust from the ground and lick it from each other's hands.

4.172
LIBYA
Customs and practices
of the Nasamones.

Adjacent to the Nasamones were the Psylloi,[a] who perished in the following way. The south wind blew through their land and dried up their reservoirs of water, so that their whole country, which is situated within the Syrtis,[b] became devoid of moisture. They discussed the problem and together agreed to make war on the south wind (I am repeating what the Libyans say). And when they reached the desert sand, the south wind blew upon them and buried them. Now that they are gone, the Nasamones have their land.

4.173
LIBYA
The Psylloi, and
how they perished.

Beyond this region and toward the south dwell the Garamantes[a] in an area full of wild animals. The Garamantes avoid all human contact and social interaction. They possess no weapons and have no knowledge of how to defend themselves in war.

4.174
LIBYA
The Garamantes.

While these people live inland of the Nasamones, the Makai[a] inhabit the coastal region to the west. They cut their hair so as to form a crest, letting it grow down the middle of their heads and shearing it down to the skin on each side. When they go to war, they hold ostrich skins in front of them for protection. [2] The Kinyps[a] River, which originates at what is called the Hill of the Graces, flows through their territory and empties into the sea. The Hill of the Graces has thick woods, although the rest of Libya that I have thus far described is bare of trees. It lies twenty-two miles[b] from the sea.

4.175
LIBYA
The Makai.

4.172.1a Nasamones, location of territory: Map
4.172.1b Augila: Map 4.175, BY.
4.172.2a Massagetai customs: see 1.216.
4.173.1a Psylloi: location of territory unknown.
4.173.1b Gulf of Syrtis: Map 4.175, BY.
4.174.1a Garamantes, possible location of terri-

tory: Map 4.175, BX.
4.175.1a Makai, location of territory: Map
           4.175, BX.
4.175.2a Kinyps River: Map 4.175, BX.
4.175.2b Herodotus writes "200 stades." See
           Appendix J, §6, 19.

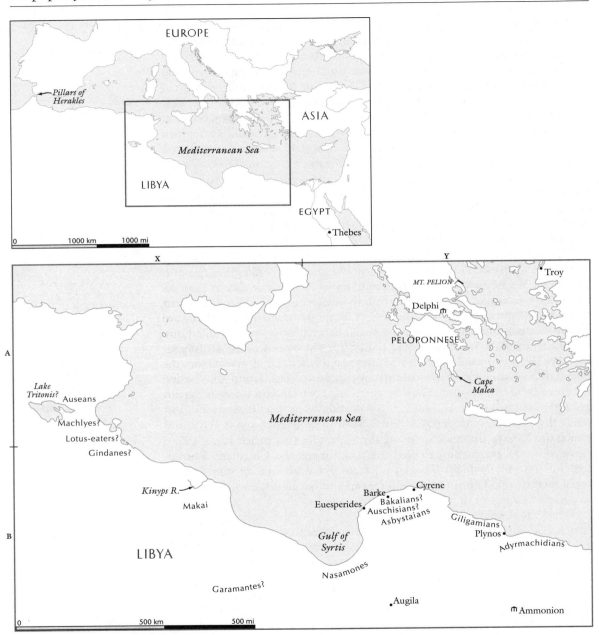

MAP 4.175

Next to the Makai are the Gindanes,[a] each of whose women wear many leather ankle bracelets. It is said that they put on one of these for every man with whom they have had intercourse, and the woman who wears the most is considered to be the best, since she has won affection from the most men.

From the land of the Gindanes, there extends a promontory into the open sea which is inhabited by the Lotus-eaters.[a] They live by chewing solely on the fruit of the lotus,[b] which is a fruit as big as that of the mastic berry,[c] and which has a sweet flavor, something like the fruit of the date palm. The Lotus-eaters also make wine from it.

After the Lotus-eaters, the Machlyes[a] live along the coast. They, too, use the lotus, though to a lesser extent than the people just described. They inhabit the region up to a large river by the name of Triton, which empties into a huge lake, Tritonis.[b] In this lake lies an island whose name is Phla.[c] They say there was a prophecy given to the Lacedaemonians, advising them to establish a settlement on this island.

The following is a story told about Jason. When he had completed the construction of the *Argo* beneath Mount Pelion,[a] he placed a hecatomb[b] and, most notably, a bronze tripod on board and began to sail around the Peloponnese,[c] intending to go to Delphi.[d] [2] But when he reached the cape at Malea,[a] the north wind caught him up and carried him off toward Libya.[b] Even before land had been sighted, he found that he had sailed into the shoals of Lake Tritonis and could find no way out. And the story goes that Triton appeared to Jason in his perplexity and told him to give him the tripod and in return he would show him the channel out and send him and his crew off safe and sound. [3] And indeed, after Jason was persuaded by his offer and gave him the tripod, Triton did show him how to navigate safely through the shallows. But before setting up the tripod within his own sanctuary, Triton prophesied over the tripod to Jason's companions, telling them of all the consequences that would occur whenever a certain descendant of the *Argo*'s crew carried off the tripod from the sanctuary to his home. When that happened, he said, then as a matter of fate and necessity,

4.176
LIBYA
The Gindanes.

4.177
LIBYA
The Lotus-eaters.

4.178
LIBYA
The Machlyes.

4.179
LIBYA
The story of Jason and the Argonauts in Libya: the tripod given to Triton.

4.176.1a Gindanes, possible location: Map 4.175, BX.
4.177.1a Lotus-eaters (Lotophagoi), possible location: Map 4.175, AX. The Lotus-eaters were described by Homer (*Odyssey* 9.84ff.).
4.177.1b This fruit of the lotus is also known as the jujube.
4.177.1c The mastic berry is about the size of an olive.
4.178.1a Machlyes (Machlyar?), possible location: Map 4.175, AX. This map follows the *Barrington Atlas*, which shows Machlyar? not on the coast, where Herodotus places the Machlyes, but inland by a depression called Tritonis Palus.
4.178.1b Lake Tritonis, possible location: Map

4.175, AX. No such lake or river as described by Herodotus exists today. The lake on Map 4.175 has no apparent outlet and is called Lake Tritonitis in the *Barrington Atlas*.
4.178.1c Phla Island: location unknown.
4.179.1a Mount Pelion: Map 4.175, AY. This Jason is the leader of the mythical Argonauts in their quest for the Golden Fleece. See Glossary, Argonauts.
4.179.1b Hecatomb: a large number of animals offered for sacrifice. See Glossary.
4.179.1c Peloponnese: Map 4.175, AY.
4.179.1d Delphi: Map 4.175, AY.
4.179.2a Cape Malea, Peloponnese: Map 4.175, AY.
4.179.2b Libya: Map 4.175, BX.

one hundred Greek cities would have to be built around Lake Tritonis. When the Libyan natives heard of this prediction, they hid the tripod.[a]

4.180
LIBYA
The customs of the Auseans.

Next to the Machlyes are the Auseans.[a] These people as well as the Machlyes inhabit the shores of Lake Tritonis, with the Triton River forming the boundary between them. The Machlyes let their hair grow long on the back of their heads; the Auseans, on the front. [2] At their annual festival for Athena, their maidens are divided into two groups, which fight each other with sticks and stones, claiming that they are thus fulfilling their ancestral obligations to their native goddess, whom we call Athena. If any maidens die from their wounds, they call them "false maidens." [3] Before they allow them to engage in battle, they dress up the most beautiful girl of that time in a Corinthian helmet and a Hellenic suit of armor and weapons; then they put her in a chariot and drive her around the circuit of the lake. [4] What they dressed the maidens in long ago before the Hellenes had settled nearby, I cannot say, though I suppose they dressed them in Egyptian armor. For I assert that it was from Egypt that the shield and the helmet came to the Hellenes.[a] [5] They say that Athena is the daughter of Poseidon and Lake Tritonis, but that she found some fault with her father and gave herself over to Zeus, who then made her his own daughter. Well, at least that is what they say. They share intercourse with their women in common, promiscuously like beasts, and do not dwell together as couples. [6] Whenever a woman's child has developed sufficiently, the men get together within three months, and whichever of them the child resembles most is acknowledged as his father.

4.181
LIBYA
Herodotus describes the inland people. First, the Ammonians and their fabulous spring.

The nomadic Libyans who live along the coast have now been described. Beyond their territory and toward the interior is the area of Libya that teems with wild beasts, and beyond that region lies a ridge of sand which stretches from Egyptian Thebes[a] to the Pillars of Herakles.[b] [2] On this ridge at intervals of approximately ten days' journey are hills topped with lumps of coarse salt, and on the crest of each of these hills, cool fresh water darts up from the middle of the salt. Around the water dwell people who are the most remote in distance from the region of the wild beasts and closest to the desert. The first of these peoples, at a ten-days' journey from Thebes, are the Ammonians.[a] They have a sanctuary of Zeus derived from that of Theban Zeus[b] which, as I mentioned earlier, has an image of Zeus with a ram's head. [3] They happen to have an additional source of water

4.179.3a There were no Greek cities around the lake, so this prophecy can be viewed as a justification for a future colony (if the tripod could be found) or as an explanation for failed attempts to settle there.
4.180.1a Auseans, location of territory: Map 4.175, AX.
4.180.4a This is another of Herodotus' efforts to find Egyptian origins for Greek practices. The hoplite shield was a Greek invention.
4.181.1a Thebes, Egypt: Map 4.175, locator.
4.181.1b Pillars of Herakles (modern Straits of Gibraltar): Map 4.175, locator.

Herodotus' description is true insofar as it points to the undoubted fact of a caravan route from Egypt to northwestern Africa, the starting point of which, however, should be Memphis (Map 4.195) and not Thebes (Map 4.195). But his distances between identifiable places are nearly always incorrect. (Godley)
4.181.2a Ammonion: Map 4.175, BY. The sanctuary of Ammonian Zeus has been located in the desert east of the Nile but many miles north of Egyptian Thebes.
4.181.2b On Theban Zeus, see 2.42.4.

from a spring which flows with warm water at dawn, but flows cooler at peak market hour,[a] and very cold by midday. [4] It is then that the Ammonians water their gardens. As the day declines toward evening the chill of the water abates until the sun sets, when the water becomes warm again. As midnight approaches, it increases in heat and then bubbles up into a boil. After midnight passes, it grows cooler until daybreak. This is called the Spring of the Sun.

After the Ammonians and an interval of another ten-days' journey along the ridge of sand lies a hill of salt like the Ammonian hill, also with water and people dwelling around it. The name of this place is Augila,[a] and it is here that the Nasamones[b] come to harvest their dates.

4.182
LIBYA
Augila.

From [there], another journey of ten days leads to another salt hill with water and many fruit-bearing date palms, just as there are in the places mentioned previously. The inhabitants here are called Garamantes,[a] a strong people who deposit soil over the salt and sow seeds into it. [2] This place lies at the shortest distance from the Lotus-eaters,[a] a journey of thirty days. In this area there are oxen that walk backward as they graze. The reason for this is that their horns bend forward [3] in such a way that they cannot graze going forward without their horns striking the ground in front of them. Other than that they are no different from other oxen, except for the thickness and firmness of their hides. [4] These Garamantes hunt the Ethiopian cave dwellers with four-horse chariots, for the Troglodytes are the swiftest runners of all humans about whom we have heard any reports. They eat snakes and lizards and other such reptiles. Their language is unlike any other: when they talk it sounds like the screeching of bats.

4.183
LIBYA
The Garamantes, whose cattle go backward as they graze.

From the Garamantes, another ten-days' journey brings one to another hill of salt with water and people living around it. These are called the Atarantes, and they are the only people we know of who have no names. Collectively, of course, they have the name Atarantes, but no name is assigned to each of them as an individual. [2] These people curse the sun when it is excessively hot and reproach it with all kinds of ugly insults, because it debilitates them as it burns, and it actually affects in this way both the people and their land.

4.184
LIBYA
The Atarantes and, farther on, the Atlantes.

[3] Then, after another ten-days' journey, there is yet another salt hill with water and people living around it, and next to this salt hill is a mountain called Atlas, which is narrow, rounded on all sides, and so high that its peak is said to be impossible to see, for it is covered by clouds in both summer and winter. [4] The native inhabitants say that this mountain is the Pillar of the Sky. The people living on it are known by a name derived from the mountain: they are called Atlantes. It is said that they eat no living thing and have no dreams in their sleep.

4.181.3a Peak market hour would be 9:00–
           10:00 a.m.
4.182.1a Augila: Map 4.175, BY.
4.182.1b Nasamones, location of territory: Map
           4.175, BY.

4.183.1a Garamantes, possible location of terri-
           tory: Map 4.175, BX.
4.183.2a Lotus-eaters, possible location of terri-
           tory: Map 4.175, AX.

I have been able to specify the names of the inhabitants along the ridge thus far up to the Atlantes, but I can no longer do so from here on. The ridge extends to the Pillars of Herakles,[a] and even beyond them. [2] There is a salt mine at the interval of a ten-days' journey with people living there who construct their houses out of lumps of salt. These regions of Libya receive no rain, for if they did, the walls of salt could not remain standing. [3] The salt excavated in this region is both white and purple in color. Beyond the ridge to the south and into the interior of Libya, the land is uninhabited desert, devoid of water, beasts, rain, and wood, without a drop of moisture at all.

And so from Egypt[a] to Lake Tritonis[b] live Libyan nomads who eat meat and drink milk, although they do not raise pigs and they abstain from eating cows for the same reason that constrains the Egyptians from doing so. [2] The women of Cyrene[a] also think it right to abstain from eating the meat of cows, on account of Isis in Egypt, for whom they fast and celebrate festivals. The women of Barke[b] abstain from the meat of pigs as well as cows.

That is what those regions are like. To the west of Lake Tritonis, the Libyans are no longer nomads, nor do they follow the same customs; and in particular the way they treat their children differs sharply from the practices of the nomads. [2] For the Libyan nomads have the following custom, though whether they all do this I cannot say with certainty, but a great number of them do. When their children reach the age of four, they singe the veins on their heads with an oily tuft of sheep's wool, though some of them sear the veins of the temples instead. They do this to prevent them from suffering for the rest of their lives from phlegm flowing out of their heads, [3] and they claim that this is why they are so healthy. Indeed, it is true that the Libyans are the healthiest of all peoples known to us, but whether it is because of this practice I cannot say with certainty; but surely they are the most healthy. If convulsions occur as they are burning the children, the remedy they have discovered is to revive them by sprinkling them with goat's urine. I am simply reporting here what the Libyans themselves say.

The sacrificial customs of the nomads are as follows. They begin by offering the ear of the animal to be sacrificed and throwing it over their house; only after doing this do they bend back the victim's neck. They sacrifice to the sun and the moon alone. But while all Libyans sacrifice to these gods, the inhabitants around Lake Tritonis perform sacrifices mostly to Athena, and after her, to Triton and to Poseidon.

It was from the women of Libya that the Hellenes adopted the garments and aegis of Athena's cult image.[a] For except for the fact that the Libyan women wear a garment made of leather and that from their aegises hang tassels made of thongs rather than snakes, they dress exactly the same as the image in all other respects. [2] Moreover, the very name of the apparel

4.185.1a　Pillars of Herakles (modern Straits of Gibraltar): Map 4.195, locator.
4.186.1a　Egypt: Map 4.195, locator.
4.186.1b　Lake Tritonis, possible location: Map 4.195.

4.186.2a　Cyrene: Map 4.195.
4.186.2b　Barke: Map 4.195.
4.189.1a　Athena's aegis was her shield and short cloak with a fringe of snakes and a Medusa's head.

worn by the statues of Pallas[a] discloses its Libyan origin. For the Libyan women put hairless goatskins with madder-dyed tassels[b] over their dresses, and it is from these goatskins (*aegeae*) that the Hellenes coined the term "aegis." [3] Further, it seems to me at least that the ritual cry *ololyge* at sacrifices also originated there, since the Libyan women quite often make this cry, and quite skilfully, too. In addition, it was from the Libyans that the Hellenes learned how to yoke four horses together.

The nomads care for the dead and dying just as the Hellenes do, except for the Nasamones,[a] who bury the corpse in a sitting position and take special care to ensure that people are sitting up as the life force is leaving them and that they are not lying down on their backs. They build their houses from asphodel stalks twined together around reeds, and carry them along with them. Such are the customs of these peoples.

4.190
LIBYA
Nasamone burial practices
and portable dwellings.

To the west of the Triton River[a] next to the Auseans dwell the Libyan plowmen, who possess permanent dwellings. They are called the Maxyes.[b] They wear their hair long on the right side of their heads, but shaved on the left, and they stain their bodies with red ochre pigment. These people claim to be descended from men who came from Troy.[c] [2] The land here, as well as what remains of Libya to the west, has more wild beasts and woods than the land of the nomads. [3] The eastern region of Libya where the nomads live is low-lying, sandy, flat land up to the Triton River, but west of this point, the land inhabited by the Libyan plowmen is very hilly, wooded, and teeming with wild beasts. [4] In fact, this is where the giant serpents and the lions live, and also the elephants, bears, asps, donkeys with horns, the dog-headed creatures and the headless beasts which have eyes on their chests—at least according to what the Libyans say—in addition to the wild men and women, and many other creatures which are not just fabulous inventions.

4.191
LIBYA
Farther west the Maxyes
cultivate the soil, and there
are fabulous men and beasts.

The land of the nomads contains none of these beasts but has other sorts of animals, such as white-rumped antelopes; gazelles; boubalies;[a] donkeys, though these do not have horns but are a different kind, the "nondrinking" donkeys (which in fact drink nothing); also oryes,[b] whose horns are used to construct the arms of the Phoenician lyre and whose size is that of an ox; [2] foxes; hyenas; porcupines; wild rams; dictyes; thoes;[a] panthers; boryes;[b] crocodiles up to four and a half feet[c] long that live on land and look very much like lizards; ostriches; and tiny snakes, each with one horn. Those are the creatures that are found here, in addition to those found elsewhere, except for deer and wild boar, which are not found in Libya at all. [3] There are three types of mice here: one type are those

4.192
LIBYA
The real animals of
Libya's nomad country.

4.189.2a　Pallas: Pallas Athena.
4.189.2b　Madder: a plant whose roots yield a red dye.
4.190.1a　Nasamones, location of territory: Map 4.195.
4.191.1a　Triton River: location unknown.
4.191.1b　Maxyes, location of territory: Map 4.195.
4.191.1c　Troy (Ilium/Ilion): Map 4.175, AY.
4.192.1a　Boubalies: a type of antelope. (How and Wells)

4.192.1b　Oryes: the antelope *leucoryx*. (How and Wells)
4.192.2a　Dictyes and thoes are thought to be kinds of jackals, but they have not been definitively identified. (How and Wells)
4.192.2b　Boryes have not been identified.
4.192.2c　Herodotus writes "3 cubits." See Appendix J, §4, 5, 19.

called dipodes,[a] another type are the *zegeries*[b] (which is the Libyan equivalent of hillock), and a third breed is the echinees.[c] There are also weasels which live in the silphium, very similar to the weasels at Tartessos.[d] Those, then, are as many beasts of the Libyan nomads' territory as we have been able to discover as far as our inquiries could reach.

Adjacent to the Libyan Maxyes are the Zauekes,[a] whose women serve as charioteers in war.

The Gyzantes[a] are neighbors to the Zauekes. Here bees produce a great quantity of honey, but skilled workmen[b] are said to produce a still much greater amount. All these people paint themselves with red ochre pigment, and they eat monkeys, which are quite abundant in the hills.

The Carthaginians[a] say that off the coast of this territory lies an island named Cyrauis,[b] twenty-two miles[c] long and narrow in width, which can be reached from the mainland on foot. The island is full of olive trees and grapevines, [2] and it contains a lake from which the native maidens draw gold dust out of the mud with bird feathers smeared with tar. Whether or not this is true I do not really know; I am only writing what is said. But this could be entirely true, since I myself have seen tar being drawn from the water of a lake on Zacynthus,[a] [3] where there are actually several lakes. The largest of these measures seventy feet in diameter and is twelve feet deep.[a] The Zacynthians lower a pole with myrtle tied to its tip into this lake, and with the myrtle, draw up the tar. Although this tar has the odor of bitumen, it is in all other respects superior to the pitch of Pieria.[b] Next they pour the pitch into a hollow they have dug beside the lake, and when they have collected a sufficient quantity of pitch, they transfer it from the hollow into wine jars. [4] Anything that falls into this lake sinks underground and then appears in the sea, which is about 2,330 feet[a] away from the lake. Thus it is likely that the report of the island off Libya is true.

The Carthaginians tell of a place in Libya outside the Pillars of Herakles[a] inhabited by people to whom they bring their cargoes. The Carthaginians unload their wares and arrange them on the beach; then they reboard their boats and light a smoky fire. When the native inhabitants see the smoke, they come to the shore and, after setting out gold in exchange for the goods, they withdraw. [2] The Carthaginians disembark and examine what the natives have left there, and if the gold appears to them a worthy price for their wares, they take it with them and depart; if not, they get back on

4.193
LIBYA
The Zauekes.

4.194
LIBYA
The Gyzantes.

4.195
LIBYA
The Carthaginian story of gathering pitch on the island of Cyrauis is plausible because Herodotus has seen it done on Zacynthus.

4.196
LIBYA
A Carthaginian story about trade with some people beyond the Pillars of Herakles.

4.192.3a   Dipodes: two-footed creatures.
4.192.3b   *Zegeries*: hill mouse For "hillock" Herodotus uses the word *bounoi*, specific to the dialects of Cyrene and Sicily; it is also used in 4.199.1.
4.192.3c   Echinees (the word means "stiff-haired"): this animal is unknown. (How and Wells)
4.192.3d   Tartessos: Map 4.195, locator.
4.193.1a   Zauekes, possible location of territory: Map 4.195.
4.194.1a   Gyzantes, possible location of territory: Map 4.195.
4.194.1b   See also 7.31, where men are said to make honey out of wheat and tamarisk.

4.195.1a   Carthage: Map 4.195.
4.195.1b   Cyrauis Island, possible location: Map 4.195.
4.195.1c   Herodotus writes "200 stades." See Appendix J, §6, 19.
4.195.2a   Zacynthus: Map 4.195.
4.195.3a   Herodotus writes "2 fathoms." See Appendix J, §4–5, 19.
4.195.3b   Pieria: Map 4.195.
4.195.4a   Herodotus writes "4 stades." See Appendix J, §6, 19.
4.196.1a   Pillars of Herakles (modern Straits of Gibraltar): Map 4.195, locator.

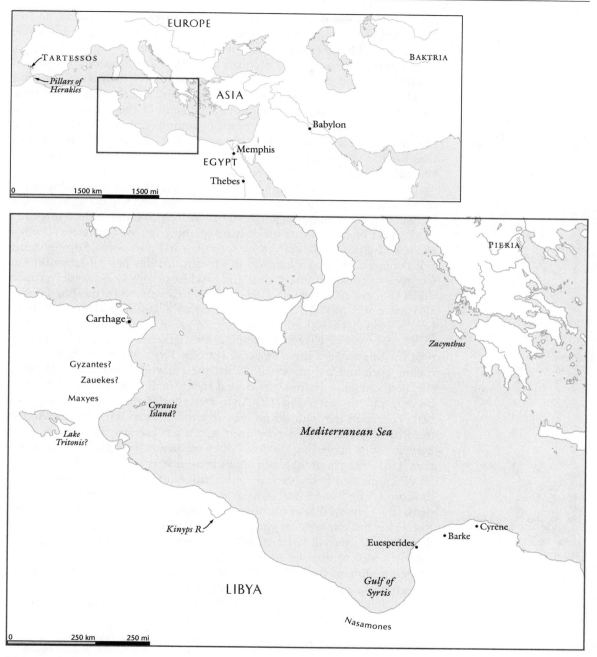

MAP 4.195

their boats and sit down to wait while the natives approach again and set out more gold, until they satisfy the Carthaginians that the amount is sufficient. [3] Neither side tries to wrong the other, for the Carthaginians do not touch the gold until it equals the value of their goods, nor do the natives touch the goods until the Carthaginians have taken away the gold.

Those, then, are all the Libyans we can name, and the majority of them then and now couldn't care less about the King of the Medes. [2] About the land of Libya I can say this much in summary: it is inhabited by only four nations as far as we know. Two of them are indigenous: the Libyans, who live in the northern region, and the Ethiopians, who live in the south. The Phoenicians and the Hellenes, however, are immigrants.

It seems to me that Libya cannot be compared with Asia or Europe in terms of good fertile soil, except for Kinyps (the land has the same name as its river).ᵃ [2] For Kinyps is not at all like the rest of Libya; indeed it is equal to the best of lands in its production of the crops of Demeter.ᵃ The soil there is black and well watered by springs; it has no worry of drought, nor is it damaged by drinking in too much rain, for this part of Libya does in fact receive rainfall. Indeed, this land produces crops in quantities proportional to those of Babylonia.ᵇ [3] The region inhabited by the Euesperidesᵃ also has good soil. At its best, it produces a 100-fold return, although Kinyps produces a 300-fold return.

The territory of Cyrene,ᵃ which is at the highest elevation of Libya occupied by nomads, has three amazing seasons. First, the crops of the coastal region ripen and are harvested. When these have been collected, those of the middle regions beyond the coastal area, which they call the "Hillocks," become ripe for gathering. [2] After the crops of the middle region have been collected, the high inland area ripens and bears its products. And so the first crops have been consumed just when the last ones are ready to harvest. Thus harvesting occupies the Cyrenaeans for eight months of the year. That, then, is enough said about these matters.

When the Persians whom Aryandes had sent from Egyptᵃ to assist Pheretime in taking vengeance arrived at Barke,ᵇ they laid siege to the city, demanding the surrender of those responsible for the murder of Arkesilaos. But since the majority of the populace was guilty of the murder, their demand was rejected. [2] And so they besieged Barke for nine months and launched violent assaults on the city, all the while digging underground tunnels leading to the wall. A blacksmith of Barke, however, discovered the tunnels using a bronze shield to detect their location. He did this by carrying the shield around within the wall and thrusting it against the ground

4.198.1a Kinyps River: Map 4.195. See 4.175.
4.198.2a Demeter is the goddess of grains.
4.198.2b Babylonia: Map 4.195, locator. For the astounding agricultural yields of Babylon, see 1.193.3–4.
4.198.3a Euesperides: Map 4.195. See also 4.171.

4.199.1a Cyrene: Map 4.195.
4.200.1a Egypt: Map 4.195, locator.
4.200.1b Barke: Map 4.195. Here the story of Pheretime's revenge, which was broken off in 4.167, is resumed.

inside the city. [3] When thrust on the ground at locations over the tunnels, the shield rang out with an echo, but at other locations the shield was mute. So the Barkaians, by digging countertunnels to reach the Persian miners, interrupted and killed them; that, then, is how the tunnels were dealt with. Moreover, the Barkaians repelled the other Persian assaults on the city.

For quite a long time they went on wearing each other out, and many men fell on both sides, though more on the Persian side. Then Amasis, the commander of the army, devised a plan, realizing that although the Barkaians could not be conquered by physical force, they might be taken by guile, so this is what he did. During the night he dug a wide trench and stretched over it fragile planks of wood, then spread over them the soil he had removed from the trench so as to make the area level with the rest of the ground. [2] When day came, he invited the Barkaians to negotiate with him. They were only too happy to comply, and so the two sides negotiated until they had reached an agreement, to which they swore over the hidden trench: "For as long as this earth stays in place here shall this our oath remain in force and binding upon us." The Barkaians promised that they would make a payment to the king, and the Persians, that they would refrain from any further disturbance of the status quo at Barke. [3] After swearing the oath, the Barkaians, now trusting the Persians, came outside of the city and opened their gates to let in any of the enemies who wished to come within the wall. The Persians ran inside the wall after breaking down the hidden planks in order to avoid violating their oath, since they had sworn it would remain in force as long as the earth remained in place. But now that they had broken through the hidden platform of planks and displaced the earth, the oath no longer remained in force or binding upon them.[a]

The people of Barke who were most responsible for the murder of Arkesilaos were turned over to Pheretime by the Persians. She had the men impaled in a circle around the wall and the women's breasts cut off and placed at intervals around the wall as well. [2] She told the Persians to regard the remaining Barkaians as their spoils of war, except for those of the clan of Battos or who had not been at all responsible for the murder. To them, Pheretime entrusted the city.

And so after enslaving the rest of the Barkaians, the Persians went on their way back to Egypt. [2] As the Persians were passing through Cyrene, the commander of their navy, Badres, ordered them to capture the city, but Amasis, the general of the army, would not permit it, since the only Greek city they had been sent to take was Barke. After passing through the city, they occupied the hill sacred to Zeus Lykaios, and at that moment regret-

4.201
513
BARKE
The Persians capture Barke by guile and deceit.

4.202
513
BARKE
Pheretime's revenge on the Barkaians.

4.203
513?
LIBYA
The Persians pass through Cyrene and are harassed by Libyans on their way back to Egypt.

4.201.3a This is another example of a sophistic interpretation of an oath, as it follows the letter, but not the intent, of the oath. See 4.154. The practice had to be guarded against even in Greek international treaties.

ted that they had not captured Cyrene. They tried to gain entrance into the city a second time, but the Cyrenaeans would not allow them to enter. [3] Then, although no battle was being fought, the Persians fell into a panic and fled to a site six and a half miles[a] away, but after they had set up camp there, a messenger came from Aryandes summoning them to return to Egypt. So the Persians asked the Cyrenaeans to give them provisions for the journey, and once they had obtained them, departed for Egypt. [4] The Libyans, however, caught up with and killed those who were straggling behind, taking their clothing and equipment, and continuing to do so until they reached Egypt.

4.204
BAKTRIA
The captive Barkaians are settled in Baktria.

The farthest point west this Persian army reached was Euesperides.[a] The enslaved Barkaians were sent as captives to King Darius, who gave them a village in the territory of Baktria[b] in which to settle. The name they gave to this village was Barke, which still exists as an inhabited region to this day.

4.205
EGYPT
Pheretime's awful death is a punishment from the gods.

The final strands in the life of Pheretime were woven with misery, for as soon as she had achieved her revenge on the Barkaians, she left Libya and returned to Egypt, where she died a miserable death from worms which teemed within her body and crawled out from it while she still lived. Thus the gods manifest their resentment against humans who execute vengeance violently and excessively. Such was the brutal vengeance wreaked by Pheretime, wife of Battos, against the Barkaians.[a]

4.203.3a Herodotus writes "60 stades." See
Appendix J, §6, 19.
4.204.1a Euesperides: Map 4.195.
4.204.1b Baktria (Bactria): Map 4.195, locator.

The location of a village here called
Barke is unknown.
4.205.1a A religious view of some significance.

BOOK FIVE

The Persians whom Darius had left in Europe under the command of Megabazos proceeded now to subdue the inhabitants of the Hellespont.[a] The first of these were the Perinthians,[b] since they would not willingly become the subjects of Darius. They had earlier suffered harsh treatment at the hands of the Paionians.[c] [2] For the Paionians from the Strymon River[a] had made war on the Perinthians, acting on the advice of an oracle from the god which said that if the Perinthians shouted out and called them by name as they were encamped opposite them, they were to attack, but if they did not do this, they were to refrain from attacking. And the Paionians followed this advice. The Paionians established their camp just ouside the town of Perinthus, and there challenged them to three duels: they pitted man against man, horse against horse, and dog against dog. [3] After the Perinthians had won two of the duels, they sang out a paean in joy.[a] The Paionians concluded that this must be what the oracle had predicted, and and must have said among themselves, "this could be the fulfilment of the oracle, therefore now is the time for us to act." And so because the Perinthians had sung a paean, the Paionians attacked them and won a great victory, leaving few of them alive.

That was what had happened earlier to the Perinthians at the hands of the Paionians, but now they proved themselves to be courageous men when fighting for their freedom. The Persians under Megabazos, however, overwhelmed them by their numbers. [2] And after Perinthus had come under his control, Megabazos led his army throughout Thrace, subduing for the King every city and every nation living there, for the conquest of Thrace was precisely what Darius had instructed him to accomplish.

The Thracians are the largest nation in all the world, at least after the Indians. If they could all be united under one ruler and think the same way, they would, in my opinion, be the most invincible and strongest of all

5.1
PERINTHUS
The tale of the Perinthians and the Paionians.

5.2
512?
PERINTHUS
Megabazos conquers the Perinthians and then marches through Thrace.

5.3
THRACE
Thracians are weak because they are not united.

5.1.1a Hellespont: Map 5.5.
5.1.1b Perinthus: Map 5.5.
5.1.1c Paionians, approximate territory of: Map 5.5.
5.1.2a Strymon River: Map 5.5.
5.1.3a The paean was a ritual chant that classical

Greek soldiers and sailors sang as they advanced into battle, rallied, or celebrated victory. In this case, they apparently sang a victory song consisting of the words "Ie Paian," which sounded much like the Paionians' name.

nations. But that is impossible; it will never happen, since their weakness is that they are incapable of uniting and agreeing. [2] They have many names corresponding to their specific locations, but the customs they follow are quite similar in all respects, except for those of the Getai,[a] the Trausians,[b] and those dwelling above the Krestonians.[c]

Of these, the Getai believe in immortality, as I have already described.[a] The Trausians do everything in the same way as the rest of the Thracians, except for the way they react to birth and death. [2] When a child is born to them, his relatives sit around him and grieve over all the evils he will have to endure later, recounting all things that humans must suffer. But when someone dies, they have fun and take pleasure in burying him in the ground, reciting over him all the evils he has escaped and how he is now in a state of complete bliss.

The customs of those who live above the Krestonians are as follows. Each man has many wives, and whenever a man dies, a great contest with fierce rivalry is held among his wives and their families concerning which of them was the wife whom he loved the most. The woman who is judged most worthy of this honor is eulogized by both the men and the women, after which her closest relative cuts her throat over the grave and she is buried with her husband. The other wives consider their rejection a terrible misfortune and the greatest possible disgrace.

The rest of the Thracians have the following customs. They sell their children for export abroad and do not keep watch over their unmarried daughters, but instead allow them to have intercourse with any man they want. They purchase their wives, however, from the women's parents for very high prices and then guard them quite strictly. [2] To have tattoos is a mark of nobility, while having none is a sign of baseness. The idle man of leisure is most admired, and the man who works the soil is most despised. The most honorable way to make a living is thought to be by war and plunder. Those are their most remarkable customs.

The only gods they worship are Ares, Dionysos, and Artemis.[a] Their kings, however, unlike the rest of the citizens, worship Hermes separately and more frequently than the other gods; they swear oaths only by this god alone and claim to be his descendants.

Burial rites of the more prosperous Thracians are as follows. They lay out the corpse for three days, and after slaughtering all kinds of victims, they have a feast. First, of course, they lament the dead, and after the feast they proceed to the funeral ceremony, either by burning the body or by burying it in the ground. Then they heap up a mound of earth and hold all kinds of contests with prizes, and the biggest prizes are offered in the category of single combat. That, then, is how the Thracians conduct their burial rites.

5.3.2a Getai, approximate territory of: Map 5.5.
5.3.2b Trausians, possible territory of: Map 5.5.
5.3.2c Krestonians (Erostonia), approximate loca-
        tion of territory: Map 5.5.

5.4.1a On the Getai's belief in immortality, see
        4.93.
5.7.1a Herodotus as usual identifies foreign with
        Greek deities. (Godley)

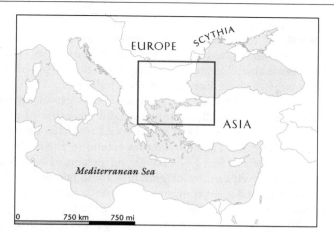

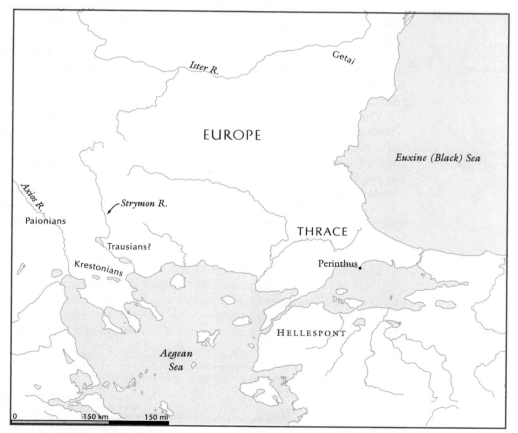

MAP 5.5

5.9
THRACE
The almost unknown
Sigynnai of the north.

5.10
512?
THRACE
Thracian tales of bees in the
north. Megabazos conquers
the Thracian coast.

5.11
512?
SARDIS
Darius rewards Histiaios
of Miletus and Koes
of Mytilene.

5.12
SARDIS
Darius and the Paionian
woman and her brothers
at Sardis.

What lies farther north of this country and who the inhabitants there might be no one can say for certain, but the region which extends beyond the Ister[a] is apparently uninhabited and has no known boundaries. The only inhabitants I have been able to learn of beyond the Ister are people called the Sigynnai, who wear clothing like that of the Medes.[b] [2] Their horses' bodies are completely covered with shaggy hair, which grows up to five fingers long; these horses are small, snub-nosed, and incapable of carrying men. They are, however, extremely swift when yoked to a chariot, which is why the natives drive chariots. Their boundaries extend to the region close to the Enetoi[a] on the Adriatic Sea. [3] The Sigynnai claim to be a Median colony, and although I myself cannot imagine how these people could have been colonists from the Medes, all things are possible in the long course of time. The word *Sigynna* means "shopkeeper" among the Ligurians who live above Massalia,[a] and "spear" in the language of the people of Cyprus.[b]

The Thracians say that bees occupy the region beyond the Ister and it is their presence that makes it impossible to travel through the land. But to me what they claim seems unlikely, since these creatures appear to be intolerant of frost. In fact, I think it is because of the cold that the regions under the constellation of the Bear[a] are devoid of settled habitations. That, then, is what is said about Thrace, and it was the coastal region of this land that Megabazos was making subject to the Persians.

Darius crossed the Hellespont, and as soon as he arrived in Sardis,[a] he recalled both the good service done for him by Histiaios and the sound advice of Koes of Mytilene.[b] He summoned both men to Sardis and offered them each a gift of their own choosing. [2] Histiaios, who was already tyrant of Miletus,[a] did not wish to have another tyranny, so he asked for Myrkinos[b] in the territory of the Edonians, as he wanted to found a city there. That was the choice of Histiaios, but Koes, who was not a tyrant at the time but only a private citizen, asked to be made tyrant of Mytilene. Both requests were granted, and so these men turned to the places they had chosen.

Meanwhile, Darius happened to see something that sparked an impulsive desire to order Megabazos to capture the Paionians,[a] uproot them from Europe, and compel them to move to Asia.[b] It so happened that there were two Paionians named Pigres and Mastyas who had come to Sardis after Darius had returned to Asia, because they wanted to rule as tyrants

---

5.9.1a   Ister (modern Danube) River: Map 5.5.
5.9.1b   Strabo (64/3 B.C.E.–21 C.E.) says much
      the same of the Sigynnai, according to him
      a Caucasian tribe. (*Geography, XV*)
      (Godley) On Median clothing, see 1.135,
      3.84, 5.49, 7.61, 9.1.
5.9.2a   Enetoi: precise location unknown. See
      1.196 and n. 1.196.1a. Adriatic Sea: Map
      5.14, locator.
5.9.3a   Ligurians, Massalia: Map 5.14, locator.
5.9.3b   Cyprus: Map 5.14, locator.
5.10.1a   Constellation of the Bear: the Big Dipper.

5.11.1a   Hellespont, Sardis: Map 5.14. For Darius'
      arrival at Sardis, see 4.143.
5.11.1b   Mytilene: Map 5.14. Darius promised to
      reward him in 4.97.6.
5.11.2a   Miletus: Map 5.14. For three tyrants who
      ruled there, see Appendix T, Tyranny in
      Herodotus, §2.
5.11.2b   Myrkinos, Edonia: Map 5.14, inset.
5.12.1a   Paionians, approximate territory of: Map
      5.14, inset.
5.12.1b   Europe, Asia: Map 5.14, locator.

over the Paionians. They had brought along their sister, a tall and attractive woman. [2] The two men watched for the time when Darius would be sitting at the entrance to the Lydian[a] city, and when they saw him there, this is what they did. First they dressed her up to look as beautiful as possible, and then they sent her out for water with a jug on her head, guiding a horse by a rein and spinning flax all at the same time. [3] When this woman walked past Darius, she roused his curiosity, for what she was doing was neither Persian nor Lydian practice, nor for that matter Asian at all. Once she had caught his attention, he sent out some of his bodyguards to serve as scouts and watch how this woman would manage her horse. [4] The bodyguards accordingly followed behind her, and when she came to the river, she first watered the horse and then filled the jug with water. Then she returned by the same road, carrying the jug of water on her head, guiding the horse by the rein hanging from her arm, and all the while twisting wool on her spindle.

Darius was so amazed at the account of his scouts (and in fact he had seen for himself just what they were reporting) that he ordered the woman to be brought into his presence. She arrived accompanied by her brothers, who had been close by, observing all that had occurred. When Darius inquired what country she had come from, the young men replied that she was their sister and that they were Paionians. [2] And Darius asked who the Paiaonians were, where in the world they lived, and what they wanted in coming to Sardis. They told him that Paionia was a land consisting of cities along the Strymon River[a] whose inhabitants were Teukrian, originally colonists from Troy,[b] and that they had come to offer themselves to him as his subjects. [3] After they told him this, Darius asked if all the women there were as hardworking as their sister, and since this was the very reason for what they had done there, they enthusiastically answered that this was indeed the case.

5.13
SARDIS
Darius questions the Paionian brothers.

Darius then wrote a letter to Megabazos, the general he had left in Thrace, instructing him to make all the Paionians, including their women and children, leave their homeland and to deliver them to him. [2] At once a horseman sped to the Hellespont and across it to deliver the scroll to Megabazos. After reading the letter, Megabazos obtained guides from Thrace[a] and proceeded to make war on Paionia.

5.14
511
PAIONIA
Darius orders Megabazos to send all the Paionians to him.

When the Paionians learned that the Persians were advancing against them, they mustered an army and marched out toward the sea, assuming that the Persians would make their attack from that quarter. [2] So the Paionians were quite prepared to repulse the invading army of Megabazos; but when the Persians learned that the Paionians had assembled an army and were watching for an attack from the coast, they turned inland with the help of guides and, unknown to the Paionians, fell upon their cities, and as

5.15
511
PAIONIA
Megabazos outwits the Paionians and captures their cities. They surrender and are taken to Asia.

5.12.2a Lydia: Map 5.14.
5.13.2a Strymon River: Map 5.14, inset.
5.13.2b Troy (Ilion/Ilium): Map 5.14.
5.14.2a Thrace: Map 5.14.

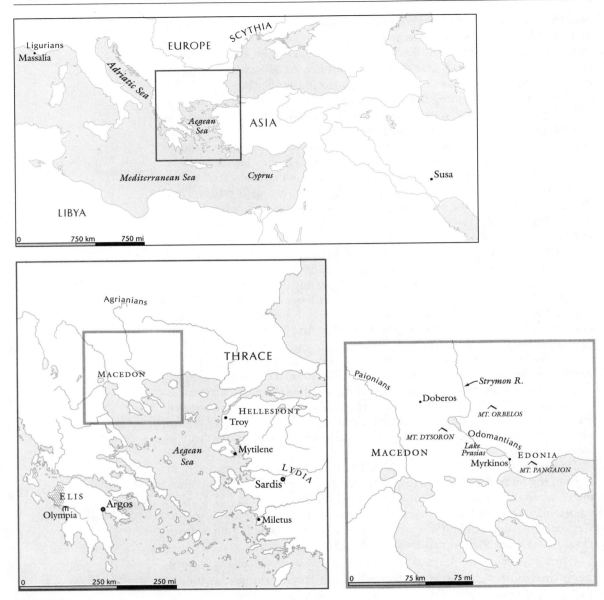

MAP 5.14

these were now devoid of fighting men, easily gained possession of them. [3] Upon learning that their cities had been taken, the Paionians immediately dispersed, each one of them returning to his own kin and then surrendering to the Persians. That is how the Paionians, the Siriopaiones, the Paioplai,ª and the people who live as far as Lake Prasiasᵇ were uprooted from their homeland and taken to Asia.

Those around Mount Pangaionª and near the Doberes,ᵇ Agrianians,ᶜ and Odomantians,ᵈ as well as around Lake Prasias itself, were not forced to submit to Persian rule by Megabazos. But Megabazos did try to conquer the people settled on this lake, who live there in homes built as follows. Broad planks of wood are fastened on top of high stakes set in the middle of the lake, to which a narrow path leads over a single bridge from the shore. [2] In the old days the stakes that supported the planks were set up by all the citizens jointly, but later on they adopted a different custom for erecting them. For every woman a man now marries—and each man weds many wives—he sets up three stakes, which are hauled from a mountain by the name of Orbelos.ª [3] Their manner of living is such that each man possesses a hut over the planks on which he dwells and has a trapdoor leading down through the planks into the lake. To avert the worry that their children may fall into the lake, they secure their babies by their feet with a rope. [4] Fish provide the fodder for their horses and beasts of burden. In fact, the fish are so plentiful here that whenever they open up the trapdoor and dip an empty basket by a rope into the lake, they do not have to wait for very long before they draw it back up full of fish. There are two types of fish here, which they call *paprakes* and *tilones*.

5.16
511
PAIONIA
Some of the Paionians are not subdued. How the lake dwellers live.

The Paionians who had been subjugated were taken to Asia, and after Megabazos had accomplished this, he sent seven Persians as messengers to Amyntas of Macedon.ª After Megabazos, these were the most distinguished men in the camp. They were sent to Amyntas to ask him for earth and waterᵇ for King Darius. [2] There is a short route straight to Macedon from Lake Prasias. Going this way from the lake, one comes first to the mine from which Alexandrosª of Macedon later derived income of a talent ᵇ of silver per day. And after passing this mine, one crosses the mountain called Dysoronᶜ and comes directly into Macedon.

5.17
510
MACEDON
Darius sends envoys to Macedon to demand earth and water.

5.15.3a Siriopaiones, Paioplai: locations unknown.
5.15.3b Lake Prasias: Map 5.14, inset.
5.16.1a Mount Pangaion, east of the Strymon River: Map 5.14, inset.
5.16.1b Doberes: location of territory unknown. Town of Doberes: Map 5.14, inset.
5.16.1c Agrianians, approximate location of territory: Map 5.14.
5.16.1d Odomantians, approximate location of territory: Map 5.14, inset.
5.16.2a Mount Orbelos: Map 5.14, inset.
5.17.1a Amyntas was then king of Macedon; he ruled from 540 to 498. Macedon: Map 5.14 and inset.
5.17.1b A Persian demand for earth and water was

a demand to recognize Persian authority and submit to Persian rule.
5.17.2a King Alexandros I of Macedon ruled from 495 to 452 (according to *Cambridge Ancient History* [Vol. 4, 2nd Edition], but *The Oxford Classical Dictionary* says from 498 to 454) and was prominent in the Persian Wars. See 7.173, 8.139–140, 9.44.
5.17.2b A talent was an ancient unit of weight whose value varied over time and place between 60 and 80 modern pounds. See Appendix J, Ancient Greek Units of Currency, Weight, and Distance, §11–13, 20.
5.17.2c Mount Dysoron: Map 5.14, inset.

5.18
510
MACEDON
Amyntas, king of Macedon,
agrees to submit to the
Persians. At the celebratory
banquet the Persians demand
Macedonian women.

And so when these Persians arrived at the court of Amyntas, they came into his presence and demanded that he give earth and water to King Darius. He, in fact, offered to do this and invited them to be his guests for dinner. Amyntas then had a magnificent feast prepared and entertained the Persians in a spirit of friendliness. [2] After dinner, as they lingered drinking, the Persians said, "Macedonian host, we Persians customarily bring our concubines and wedded wives to sit beside us whenever we serve a big feast. Now since you have welcomed us so warmly and are entertaining us so generously, as well as having agreed to offer earth and water to King Darius, we urge you to follow our custom." [3] To this Amyntas replied, "Persians, this is certainly not our custom here; indeed here we keep the men segregated from the women. But since you are now our masters and have made this additional request, we shall accommodate you in this also." Having said that, Amyntas sent for the women, who came when they were summoned, and one after the other they took their seats opposite the Persians. [4] But after the Persians took one look at these beautiful women, they told Amyntas that what he had done was not at all wise. For it would have been better for the women not to have come at all than to have them come and not seat them beside the men, but opposite to them instead, so that the men's eyes were painfully dazzled. [5] And so Amyntas, who felt compelled to do so, ordered the women to sit beside the men. The women obeyed, and immediately the Persians, now quite intoxicated, began to fondle their breasts and, every now and then, to try to kiss them.

5.19
MACEDON
Alexandros, angered by
the Persians' conduct, bids
his father Amyntas to leave
the banquet.

Amyntas looked on and found all this very hard to bear but made no move because of his fear of the Persians. However, his son Alexandros was also present and observed what was happening; since he was young and had never before been exposed to such evils, he could no longer contain himself and, overwhelmed with indignation, he blurted out to Amyntas, "Father, yield to your age: do not stay here and continue to drink, but go off and rest. I shall remain right here and supply your guests with everything they need." [2] To this, Amyntas replied in full awareness that Alexandros was intending to do something quite rash, "Son, you are almost on fire with anger, and I understand that you really wish to send me away so that you can do something radical. Now I want you to do nothing that will provoke these men, which might well lead to our destruction. Instead, you must just look on and endure it. But I agree that I should leave."

5.20
MACEDON
Alexandros' plot to kill the
rude Persians succeeds.

And after communicating these wishes to his son, Amyntas did indeed depart, and Alexandros then said to the Persians, "My guests, these women are at your disposition; you have only to decide whether you want to have intercourse with all or just some of them. [2] But right now, since it is nearly time for bed and I see that your wine has made you splendidly drunk, send these women away to bathe, and then, if you wish, welcome them back again after they have bathed." [3] When he had finished speaking, the Persians consented to his suggestion, and the women left. Alexandros sent them off to the women's quarters, while he himself found some smooth-chinned young men, enough to equal the prior number of the women, and dressed them up in the women's clothing. He then gave each of them a dagger and brought them in to the Persians, [4] to whom he now said, "Persians, it seems that your entertainment shall be a banquet complete to its last course. You have now received everything. We were already giving you everything we had when we discovered what we could provide in addition, so that now everything is yours; in particular, you get the greatest gift of all: we lavishly bestow upon you our own mothers and sisters. We do this so that you may realize how completely we honor you exactly as you deserve, and also so that you may report to the King who sent you that a Hellene, his governor of the Macedonians, has welcomed you warmly with both bed and board." [5] Having said this, Alexandros seated each Macedonian man in the guise of a woman beside a Persian. And when the Persians tried to touch them, they set about doing away with them.

And it was not only these men who suffered this fate, but all their servants as well. For they had brought with them carriages and attendants, and supplies for all their needs. All of these vanished, along with those who attended the banquet. [2] Not much later, the Persians launched an intensive search for these men, but Alexandros put a stop to it by his cleverness. He gave a large amount of money as well as his own sister, whose name was Gygaia, to a Persian called Boubares, the general in charge of those searching for the lost men. Thus repressed, the circumstances of the death of these Persians were kept secret.[a]

That these Macedonians, who are the descendants of Peridiccas, are Hellenes as they themselves say, I happen to know for myself and will demonstrate that in a later part of my account.[a] Furthermore, even those who preside over the Olympic games[b] of the Hellenes have come to recognize that this is the case. [2] For when Alexandros chose to compete in the games and entered the lists to do so, his Greek competitors tried to exclude him by claiming that the contest was for Greek contestants only, and barbarians were not allowed to participate. But when Alexandros proved that he was of Argive[a] ancestry, he was judged to be a Hellene, and proceeded to compete in the footrace, in which he tied for first place. That, then, is the story of what happened to the Persian envoys to Macedon.

Now Megabazos reached the Hellespont[a] with the Paionians he was leading to Darius, and from there he crossed over to Asia and came to Sardis.[b] He had learned that Histiaios of Miletus[c] was building fortifications

5.21
MACEDON
The Macedonians successfully keep secret the fate of these envoys and their retinues.

5.22
MACEDON
The Macedonians are Hellenes and have proved their Argive descent at Olympia.

5.23
SARDIS
Megabazos asks Darius to stop Histiaios from fortifying Myrkinos.

5.21.2a Scholars have found this story of the unavenged murder of the Persian envoys to be incredible. Some have speculated that the image of Persians reclining on couches with Macedonian women might prefigure a marriage ceremony not unlike the many mixed marriages organized by Alexander the Great at Susa in 324. It is much more likely that such marriages might later be disguised by Greeks than

that the murder of Persian envoys would go unavenged.
5.22.1a See 8.137–139.
5.22.1b Those who presided over the Olympic games were Elean citizens, usually ten in number. Elis, Olympia: Map 5.14.
5.22.2a Argos: Map 5.14.
5.23.1a Hellespont: Map 5.14.
5.23.1b Sardis: Map 5.14.
5.23.1c Miletus: Map 5.14.

at the site along the Strymon River[d] called Myrkinos,[e] which he had received from Darius after requesting it as his reward for guarding the bridge of boats.[f] And as soon as Megabazos arrived in Sardis with the Paionians, he spoke to Darius about this: [2] "Sire, just think of what you have done! You gave a dangerously clever Greek permission to found a city for himself in Thrace, where timber is abundant for construction of ships and oars, where there are also silver mines and multitudes of both Hellenes and barbarians. As soon as these people find a leader, they will follow his orders day and night. [3] So put an end to what this man is doing and thus avoid being afflicted by war within your own territory. Send for him and stop him, but treat him gently. And when you have him in your grasp, see to it that he never returns to the territory of the Hellenes."

Darius was easily persuaded by these words, and appreciated Megabazos' keen foresight, so he sent a messenger to Myrkinos to say, "Histiaios, King Darius sends you the following message: 'I have been thinking, and have made the discovery that there is no man more well disposed to me and my affairs than you. This I know not from reports, but from your own deeds. [2] Well, now I ask you to come to me by any and all means so that I may inform you of important projects which I am planning.'" Histiaios believed the message and considered it a great feat to become a counselor to the King, and so he went to Sardis. [3] When he arrived, Darius said to him, "Histiaios, I sent for you because as soon as I returned from Scythia[a] and you were no longer there before my eyes, I never missed anything so quickly and so much as I missed seeing and talking to you, knowing as I do that of all possessions the most valuable is a friend who is both intelligent and well intentioned. I am fully aware that you possess both of these qualities, which testifies to your commitment to my affairs. [4] And so now that you have done me the favor of coming here, I want to make you the following offer: leave Miletus[a] and your newly founded city in Thrace.[b] Follow me to Susa,[c] and share in everything I have. Be my table companion and my counselor."

After saying all this to Histiaios, Darius appointed Artaphrenes, his half brother by the same father, to be the governor of Sardis, and he himself rode off for Susa, taking Histiaios with him. He had also appointed Otanes to command the forces stationed along the coast. The father of this Otanes was Sisamnes,[a] one of the royal judges, whom King Cambyses had punished for accepting a bribe and giving an unjust verdict. The King had ordered that his throat be cut and his entire body flayed; and after his skin was removed, strips were cut from it and stretched on the throne on which he had sat while rendering judgments. [2] The judge whom Cambyses appointed to replace Sisamnes was actually the son of the very same Sisamnes he had executed and flayed, and Cambyses instructed this son to remember what throne he was sitting on whenever he was acting as judge.

5.23.1d Strymon River: Map 5.14, inset.   5.24.4a Miletus: Map 5.14.
5.23.1e Myrkinos: Map 5.14, inset.   5.24.4b Thrace: Map 5.14.
5.23.1f Guarding the bridge of boats: see 4.136–141. 5.24.4c Susa: Map 5.14, locator.
5.24.3a Scythia: Map 5.14, locator.   5.25.1a Sisamnes, father of Otanes: see 3.31.

And so it was the Otanes who was seated on this throne who now succeeded Megabazos as general. He proceeded to take Byzantium[a] and Chalcedon,[b] as well as Antandros[c] and Lamponia[d] in the Troad.[e] Then he obtained ships from the people of Lesbos[f] and took Lemnos[g] and Imbros,[h] which were both still inhabited by Pelasgians[i] at the time.

Although for a while the Lemnians fought well and bravely defended themselves, they were defeated in the end, and the Persians appointed Lykaretos the brother of Maiandrios, who had formerly ruled Samos,[a] to be governor over the survivors. [2] Lykaretos met his end while serving as governor of Lemnos, because he enslaved and subjugated everyone to himself, some on the charge of refusing to serve in the army against the Scythians, others for damages they had caused to the army of Darius as it returned from Scythia.[a]

That, then, was what Otanes achieved as general. After the Ionians[a] had enjoyed a rather brief reprieve from troubles, problems arose again for them from Naxos[b] and Miletus.[c] At this time, Naxos surpassed all the islands in its prosperity, while the affluence of Miletus, the pride of Ionia, was at its peak. Two generations before this it had been plagued mostly by factional strife until the Parians[d] reestablished order there, for the Milesians had chosen them out of all the Hellenes as their arbitrators, to restore order among them.

The Parians reconciled them in the following way. They sent their highest-ranking men to the city, who upon observing the Milesians living in a state of ruin, asked to tour the entire territory, which is what they did. As they journeyed throughout all the land belonging to Miletus, they noted each well-cultivated farm that they happened to see in the otherwise desolate landscape, and they wrote down the name of the farm's owner. [2] And after proceeding through the whole country and discovering only a few of these farms, they returned to the city, immediately called the people together, and appointed those whose farms they had found well tended to be managers of the city, for they believed that these men would take just as good care of public affairs as they did of their own. And they ordered the rest of the Milesians, who had formerly been at each other's throats in factional disputes, to obey these men from now on.

In this way, the Parians had restored order among the Milesians. But now trouble arose for the Ionians from these cities in the following way. Certain men of substance who were exiled from Naxos by the people had fled to Miletus. [2] Now the man actually in charge of Miletus at this time was Aristagoras son of Molpagoras, who was also the son-in-law as well as first cousin of Histiaios son of Lysagoras, whom Darius was keeping in

5.26.1a Byzantium: Map 5.31, AY.
5.26.1b Chalcedon: Map 5.31, AY.
5.26.1c Antandros: Map 5.31, AY.
5.26.1d Lamponia: Map 5.31, AY.
5.26.1e Troad: Map 5.31, AY.
5.26.1f Lesbos: Map 5.31, AY.
5.26.1g Lemnos: Map 5.31, AX.
5.26.1h Imbros: Map 5.31, AX.
5.26.1i Pelasgians, a people who the Hellenes

thought were the original inhabitants of parts of Hellas. See 1.56–57.
5.27.1a Samos: Map 5.31, BY.
5.27.2a Scythia: Map 5.31, locator.
5.28.1a Ionia: Map 5.31, BY.
5.28.1b Naxos (Aegean island): Map 5.31, BX.
5.28.1c Miletus: Map 5.31, BY.
5.28.1d Paros: Map 5.31, BX.

MAP 5.31

Susa. For although Histiaios was the official tyrant of Miletus and the Naxians were his former guest-friends,ᵃ he happened to be in Susa when the exiled Naxians went to Miletus. [3] So when they arrived, they asked Aristagoras if he could somehow provide them with the forces they would need in order to return to their homeland. And Aristagoras, thinking that he would obtain the rule over Naxos if the exiles succeeded in returning through his help, made a pretense of honoring their pact of guest-friendship with Histiaios and presented them with the following proposal: [4] "I myself do not have the power to provide you with a force great enough to restore you to your city against the will of the Naxians who now control it. For I hear that the Naxians have 8,000 men under arms and many warships. But I shall devote all my energy to solving your problem. What I have in mind involves [5] Artaphrenes, who happens to be a friend of mine, and who is also, as you may know, the son of Hystaspes and the brother of Darius the King. He rules over the entire coast of Asia and commands a large army and many ships." [6] After hearing this, the Naxians authorized Aristagoras to do his very best to obtain Artaphrenes' help. They told him to promise gifts and expenses for Artaphrenes' army, which they themselves would pay for, since they fully expected that when they appeared at Naxos, the Naxians would follow all their orders, and so would the rest of the islanders, for not one of the Cycladic islands had yet been conquered by Darius.

When Aristagoras arrived in Sardis,ᵃ he spoke with Artaphrenes, informing him that although Naxos was not a very large island, it was fair and fertile, and close to Ionia. Moreover, it contained abundant wealth and slaves. "Therefore," he said, "lead an army against this island and restore its exiles to it. [2] If you do this, I have a large sum of money ready for you in addition to the expenses of the army, since it is only right that we who are taking you there should furnish such funds. Further, you will acquire other islands to add to the territories of the King—not only Naxos itself but the islands connected with it, Paros, Andros,ᵃ and others called the Cyclades.ᵇ [3] And from there, you would be in a good position to attack Euboea,ᵃ a large and prosperous island no smaller than Cyprus,ᵇ which you could conquer with little effort. One hundred ships will suffice to subjugate these islands." And Artaphrenes answered, [4] "You do a great service to the house of the King by introducing this plan, and all your suggestions are good ones except for the number of ships. Instead of 100 ships, I will have 200 ready for you with the arrival of spring. But of course the King himself must grant approval of such a project."

5.31
c. 500?
SARDIS
Artaphrenes agrees to attack Naxos and conquer the Cyclades with 200 ships, if the King will approve the plan.

5.30.2a Guest-friendship (*xenia*): a bond of ritualized friendship, usually between aristocrats
or prominent men of different cities. It
was passed down through generations and
required hereditary privileges and obligations such as reciprocal hospitality and

assistance. See Appendix T, §3.
5.31.1a Sardis: Map 5.31, BY.
5.31.2a Paros, Andros: Map 5.31, BX.
5.31.2b Cyclades (islands): Map 5.31, BX.
5.31.3a Euboea: Map 5.31, BX.
5.31.3b Cyprus: Map 5.31, locator.

Aristagoras was delighted to hear this and returned to Miletus.[a] Artaphrenes sent to Susa[b] a report of what Aristagoras had said, and Darius himself approved the plan. So Artaphrenes equipped 200 triremes[c] and organized a vast multitude of Persians and their allies. Then he appointed Megabates, a Persian of the Achaimenid[d] clan who was a first cousin of his as well as of Darius, to command the expedition. Later on, if the story is true, the Lacedaemonian Pausanias son of Kleombrotos[e] arranged to marry Megabates' daughter because of his passionate desire to become tyrant over all of Hellas. After he appointed Megabates general, Artaphrenes dispatched the army to Aristagoras.

In Miletus, Megabates picked up Aristagoras, the Ionian army, and the Naxian exiles and sailed ostensibly for the Hellespont,[a] but when he reached Chios,[b] he halted the ships at Caucasa,[c] in order to use the north wind to take them across to Naxos. [2] But since this expedition was not destined to destroy the Naxians, what took place was the following. As Megabates was making his rounds of the watch on the ships, he happened to notice that no one was on guard duty on the ship from Myndos.[a] Infuriated by this, he ordered his bodyguards to find the man in charge of this ship, whose name was Skylax, and to tie him fast so that his head would project through an oar-hole of the ship and hang outside it while his body lay inside. [3] When Skylax had been bound in this position, someone reported to Aristagoras that Megabates had disgracefully abused his guest-friend from Myndos by tying him up. Aristagoras went straight to the Persian and pleaded with him, but when he could obtain nothing that he requested, he went to Skylax and freed the man himself. Megabates completely lost his temper at Aristagoras when he learned about this, [4] but Aristagoras said to him, "What business is this of yours? Were you not sent by Artaphrenes to obey me and to sail wherever I order you to go? Why are you being such a troublemaker?" This response by Aristagoras aggravated Megabates so much that after fuming over it until nightfall, he then sent some men by boat to Naxos to reveal to the Naxians the news of the impending assault against them.[a]

Now the Naxians had not at all expected that this expedition was going to sail against them, but when they learned this, they brought everything from their fields to within the city wall and prepared for a siege by stockpiling food, water, and wine and by reinforcing their wall. [2] As they were preparing for the war which they now expected, the expedition's fleet crossed from

5.32.1a   Miletus: Map 5.31, BY.
5.32.1b   Susa: Map 5.14, locator.
5.32.1c   Trireme: the most common ancient warship
          in the sixth and fifth centuries. See Appendix S, Trireme Warfare in Herodotus, §3–8.
5.32.1d   The Achaimenids were descendants of
          Achaimenes, who gave his name to the
          Persian royal family, whose members were
          eligible to become kings.
5.32.1e   Pausanias son of Kleombrotos: the Spartan king who commanded the victorious
          Greek army at Plataea. See Appendix B,
          The Spartan State in War and Peace, §23.
          Sparta: Map 5.31, BX.

5.33.1a   Hellespont: Map 5.31, AY. The misinformation given out here that the expedition's objective was the Hellespont was
          probably to keep the real purpose secret
          from its intended victims, the Naxians.
          Naxos: Map 5.31, BX.
5.33.1b   Chios: Map 5.31, BY.
5.33.1c   Caucasa: precise location unknown,
          evidently a harbor on the southwest coast
          of Chios.
5.33.2a   Myndos: Map 5.31, BY.
5.33.4a   For a critical view of this exchange and
          the entire Naxos episode, see Appendix
          H, The Ionian Revolt, §3.

Chios to Naxos and, when it had arrived, launched an attack on the Naxians, who were by then securely fortified. The Persians besieged the city for four months, [3] but then, when all the supplies that they had brought on the expedition had been exhausted, and Aristagoras had spent much of his own money in support of the siege, and yet still more supplies were needed to maintain it, they recognized that they were failing, and so they built a fortification for the Naxian exiles and departed for the mainland.

And so Aristagoras failed to fulfill his promise to Artaphrenes, and at the same time, the costs of the expedition had pressed him hard financially. Moreover, he also feared that because of the army's lack of success and the accusations of Megabates, his absolute rule over Miletus would be taken from him. [2] Plagued with anxiety, he began to plan a revolt, step by step; and by coincidence, the man with the tatooed head[a] arrived just then from Histiaios in Susa and delivered Histiaios' command that Aristagoras revolt from the King. [3] Histiaios had wanted to tell Aristagoras to revolt but could not safely send such an instruction to him, since the roads were guarded. And so he had chosen his most trustworthy slave, shaved his head, tattooed it with his message, and waited for the hair to grow back. As soon as it had done so, he sent the slave off with instructions to do nothing other than go to Miletus and, once there, to tell Aristagoras to shave off his hair and look at his head. As I mentioned earlier, the tattooed message ordered him to revolt. [4] Histiaios had made this move because he resented being detained at Susa and had high hopes that he would be released to go to the coast in the event of a revolt there; moreover, he thought that unless something to upset the prevailing system was done at Miletus, he would never return to the city again.[a]

So that was the intent of Histiaios when he sent his messenger, and it just so happened that all these circumstances converged at the same time. So Aristagoras deliberated with his supporters and revealed both his own opinion and the message that had arrived from Histiaios. [2] Everyone but Hekataios the author[a] declared their opinions in favor of a revolt; Hekataios, however, advised them not to take upon themselves a war with the King of Persia and reminded them of Darius' great power, reciting a list of all the peoples under his rule. When this failed to persuade them, he suggested as a second option that they should see to it that they gained control of the sea. [3] Declaring that he was well aware of how weak Miletus was, he stated that he could think of no other way to accomplish this than to seize the wealth that had been dedicated by Croesus the Lydian at the sanctuary at Branchidai.[a] He was quite confident that they would then

5.35
499
MILETUS
Aristagoras fears for his position and plans a revolt, particularly after a man arrives with a secret message from Histiaios urging Aristagoras to revolt.

5.36
499
MILETUS
The entire faction of Aristagoras favors revolt except for Hekataios, who advises them, in case they do revolt, to take command of the sea and use the treasure at the temple of Branchidai.

5.35.2a   The wording here indicates that the story of the man with the tattooed head, which follows, was well known to Herodotus' audience.
5.35.4a   For comment on Histiaios' role in the revolt and on this story, see Appendix H, §10.
5.36.2a   Hekataios was the author of geographical and historical accounts of Asia Minor and

the East who wrote in the late sixth century and was a source both used and criticized by Herodotus. He also plays a role in Herodotus' account of Ionian history. See 5.36, 5.125–126, and 6.137. See also Introduction, §3.1.
5.36.3a   Branchidai (Didyma): Map 5.31, BY. See also 1.46. For the treasure that Croesus gave to the temple there, see 1.92.2.

rule the sea and, moreover, that the money would be theirs to spend and not the enemies' to plunder. [4] This was indeed a large amount of treasure, which I have described in the first part of my work.[a] But this second suggestion did not win their approval either, and despite all he had said, they resolved that they would revolt and that one of them would sail to Myous,[b] where the fleet that had left Naxos was now docked, and attempt there to arrest the generals who were in command of the ships.

The man sent to do this was Iatragoras, and through guile he succeeded in arresting Oliatos son of Ibanollis of Mylasa,[a] Histiaios son of Tymnes of Termera,[b] Koes son of Erxandros, to whom Darius had given the rule over Mytilene[c] as a reward, Aristagoras son of Herakleides of Cyme,[d] and many others besides.[e] By this time Aristagoras of Miletus was in open revolt and devising every possible stratagem against Darius. [2] First of all, he claimed he was letting go of his tyranny, and he established isonomy[a] in Miletus, so that the Milesians would be willing to join him and support the revolt. Then he did the same in the rest of Ionia; he expelled some of the tyrants and surrendered to their own cities those others whom he had arrested from the ships that had sailed against Naxos, because he sought in this way to establish friendly relations with these cities.

As soon as the Mytilenians had control over Koes, they led him out in the open and stoned him to death. But the Cymaeans released the men given over to them, as did the majority of the others. [2] And now that the tyrants had been deposed in the Ionian cities, Aristagoras of Miletus ordered that generals be appointed in each city,[a] and he himself then sailed in a trireme to Lacedaemon,[b] for what he needed to find now was a powerful ally.

By this time, Anaxandridas son of Leon was no longer a king of Sparta, having died sometime earlier.[a] Kleomenes son of Anaxandridas now held the kingship; he had obtained it not by virtue of merit and valor, but rather by priority of birth.[b] For the wife of Anaxandridas, who was his sister's daughter, had borne him no children, though she was dear to his heart. [2] Because of this situation, the ephors[a] summoned him and said, "Even if you are not thinking of your future, we ourselves cannot look on and allow the line of Eurysthenes to die out. You do have a wife already, but since she has not given birth, divorce her now and marry another. By doing this you will please the Spartans." Anaxandridas replied that he would do neither of

5.36.4a　The "first part of my work" may refer to the history of Lydia, 1.6–94. The division of the work into nine books that we have now did not occur until later.
5.36.4b　Myous: Map 5.31, BY.
5.37.1a　Mylasa: Map 5.31, BY.
5.37.1b　Termera: Map 5.31, BY.
5.37.1c　Mytilene: Map 5.31, AY.
5.37.1d　Cyme: Map 5.31, AY.
5.37.1e　The implications of Iatragoras' success in arresting all these tyrants is explored in Appendix H, §4A.
5.37.2a　Isonomy: equality under the law (equal laws for all). See 3.80.6 and n. 3.80.6a.
5.38.2a　Apparently these generals were to be the

cities' chief magistrates.
5.38.2b　Lacedaemon (Sparta): Map 5.44. Herodotus uses the names Spartans and Lacedaemonians interchangeably. "Spartans," however, often refers specifically to citizens of the state of Sparta, whereas any inhabitant of the territory of Lacedaemon is a Lacedaemonian. See Appendix B, §5, 7, and n. B.7a.
5.39.1a　On Anaxandridas, see 1.67.1 and n. 1.67.1a.
5.39.1b　For a discussion of the Spartan dual kingship and succession, see Appendix B, The Spartan State in War and Peace, §10–11.
5.39.2a　Spartan ephors: a body of five magistrates with great powers. See Appendix B, §13.

these things, and that they had given him bad advice in telling him to throw away the wife he now had, who was faultless in his eyes, and to marry another. No, he said, he would not obey them.

In response to his refusal, the ephors discussed the matter with the Council of Elders[a] and then presented the following proposal to Anaxandridas: "Since we can see how fondly you cling to your present wife, this is what you must do—and you must not try to resist, lest the Spartans will find some other, less congenial way to deal with you. [2] We no longer ask that you divorce your present wife; continue providing all that you now provide for her. But marry another wife in addition, one who can give you children." To this Anaxandridas agreed, and afterward he had two wives and maintained two separate hearths, a practice that was not at all customary for a Spartan.[a]

Not much time passed before the new wife subsequently gave birth to Kleomenes. But now, just as she was showing off to the Spartans the heir to the throne that she had produced, by some coincidence the first wife, though childless before, became pregnant. [2] And although she was truly pregnant, the relatives of the new wife, when they heard about it, made things difficult for her, claiming that she was just making an empty boast, and that she intended to substitute another child and pretend it was her own. They expressed their indignation in that way, and when her time drew near, the ephors, who were suspicious, took seats around the woman to guard her as she gave birth. [3] And she did give birth, to Dorieus, and then at once conceived Leonidas, and immediately after he was born, she conceived Kleombrotos. Some say that Kleombrotos and Leonidas were actually twins. The second wife, who had borne Kleomenes and was the daughter of Prinetades son of Demarmenos, never gave birth to another child.

Because Kleomenes,[a] it is said, was not right in his mind and lived on the verge of madness, Dorieus, who was the leading youth among his peers, assumed that he would obtain the kingship by virtue of his manly excellence.[b] [2] And so with that attitude Dorieus became indignant when Anaxandridas died and the Lacedaemonians followed their tradition, and appointed the eldest son, Kleomenes, to be their king. Dorieus would not consent to be subject to his brother's rule, so he asked the Spartans for a group that he could lead out on an expedition to found a colony, but he neither consulted the Delphic[a] oracle about which land he should go to to build his colony, nor did he do anything else that was customary in these circumstances. But

5.40
SPARTA
Anaxandridas takes a second wife and maintains two households.

5.41
SPARTA
Anaxandridas fathers Kleomones by the second wife, and three more sons by his first wife.

5.42
520
SPARTA-LIBYA
When Kleomenes becomes king, Dorieus angrily leads an expedition to establish a colony in Africa, but he fails to consult the oracles, and after being driven away, he returns home.

5.40.1a Council of Elders, the Gerousia, at Sparta; established by Lykourgos, 1.65.4. See Appendix B, §12.

5.40.2a Bigamy was generally not allowed. A man might marry his half sister, but the Spartan practice differed from that of Athens. In Athens a man could marry his half sister if they were both descended from the same man; in Sparta a man could marry his stepsister if they both had the same mother (much more logical, given that Hellenes

thought of the woman as a seedbed). In addition, wife borrowing was allowed in Sparta, particularly for procreation.

5.42.1a See Kleomenes in Appendix B, §21–24.

5.42.1b Recall that Herodotus has just said in 5.39.1 that Kleomenes had become king but not by merit or valor, simply by virtue of his age.

5.42.2a Delphi: Map 5.44. For more on the Delphic Oracle, see Appendix P, Oracles, Religion, and Politics in Herodotus.

still bearing his bitter malice, he let his boats sail on until they reached Libya,[b] where some men from Thera[c] led them until [3] they reached the Kinyps River,[a] and there Dorieus established a settlement along the river at the most beautiful site in Libya. In the third year, however, Dorieus was driven out by the Makai,[b] the Libyans, and the Carthaginians,[c] and came back to the Peloponnese.[d]

5.43
DELPHI-ITALY
After Dorieus consults the oracle at Delphi, he sails to Italy.

There he was advised by Antichares, a man from Eleon,[a] who cited to him one of the oracles of Laios[b] that ordered the settlement of Herakleia in Sicily,[c] saying that the whole land of Eryx[d] in Sicily belonged to the Heraklids,[e] since Herakles himself had acquired it. When Dorieus heard this, he went to Delphi to consult the oracle about whether he really would be able to conquer the land to which he was about to sail, and the Pythia replied that he would. So Dorieus took along the same expeditionary force he had led to Libya, and eventually reached the coast of Italy.[f]

5.44
511? 510?
CROTON-SYBARIS
The Sybarites say that Dorieus helped Croton destroy them, but the Crotoniates deny receiving such help.

During this time, according to the Sybarites,[a] they and Telys their king were about to make war on Croton.[b] Frightened by this, the Crotoniates begged Dorieus to help defend them, and he granted their request. Together they fought the war against Sybaris, and together they conquered it. [2] Although the Sybarites say that Dorieus helped the Crotoniates do this, the Crotoniates say that no foreigner took part in the war against Sybaris, except for Kallias, a seer of the Iamidai clan from Elea,[a] who, they say, had fled from Telys, tyrant of the Sybarites, and had come to them because once when he had performed a sacrifice, the victims did not present good omens for any kind of hostilities against Croton. That, at least, is what the people of Croton say.

5.45
c. 510
CROTON-SYBARIS
The evidence from each city supporting its claim is cited.

Each of these peoples cite proofs of their claims. The Sybarites point to the precinct and temple beside the dry bed of the Crathis River,[a] which, they say, Dorieus established for Athena (with the epithet of Crathis) after he took part in capturing the city. But they consider their strongest evidence to be the death of Dorieus, since he perished while acting contrary to the advice of the oracle; for if he had just pursued the original goal of the expedition and had done nothing more than that, he would have conquered the land of Eryx and thus secured his possession of it, and in that case neither he nor his army would have been destroyed. [2] The people of Croton, for their part, point out that many plots of choice Crotonian land were set aside for Kallias of Elea, and it is a fact that his descendants still dwell on them in my time. But they say that no

5.42.2b	Libya (Africa): Map 5.44, locator.		See Appendix P, §4.
5.42.2c	Thera: Map 5.31, BX.	5.43.1c	Herakleia (Heraclea Minoa) in Sicily:
5.42.3a	Kinyps River: Map 5.44, locator.		Map 5.44.
5.42.3b	Makai: Map 5.44, locator.	5.43.1d	Eryx: Map 5.44.
5.42.3c	Carthage: Map 5.44, locator.	5.43.1e	Heraklids: descendants of Herakles.
5.42.3d	Peloponnese: Map 5.44, locator.	5.43.1f	Italy: Map 5.44.
5.43.1a	Eleon, in Boeotia, precise location unknown; near Tanagra: Map 5.44.	5.44.1a	Sybaris: Map 5.44.
		5.44.1b	Croton: Map 5.44.
5.43.1b	Laios: the father of Oedipus. The oracles collected under his name may have been those he received from the oracle or those given to others which he collected.	5.44.2a	Elea: Map 5.44. The Iamidai were descendants of Iamus, an Elean prophet who was the son of Apollo.
		5.45.1a	Crathis River, Italy: Map 5.44.

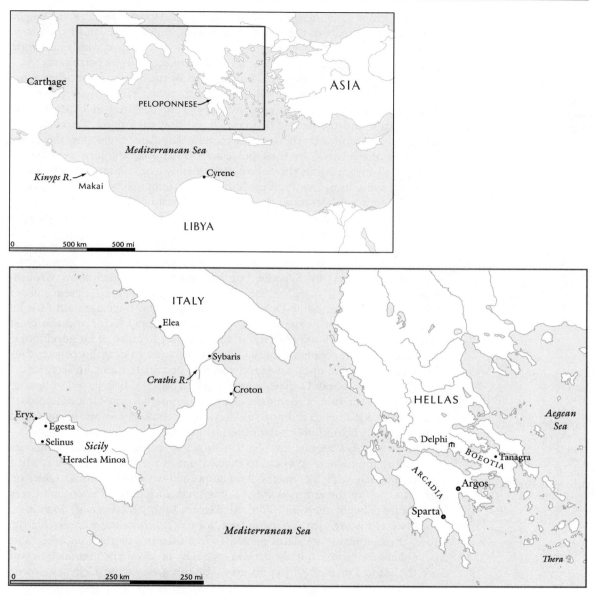

MAP 5.44

land was given to Dorieus or the descendants of Dorieus and that if Dorieus really had taken part in the war against Sybaris, much more land would have been given to him than to Kallias. So that is the evidence which each side presents, and one may believe whichever of them seems more persuasive.

5.46
SICILY
Other Spartan colonists are slain by Phoenicians, Egestans, and Selinuntines.

Sailing along with Dorieus as co-founders of the colony were other Spartans: Thessalos, Paraibates, Keleas, and Euryleon. When they arrived in Sicily with the rest of the company, they were defeated in battle by the Phoenicians[a] and the people of Egesta,[b] and they died there. Euryleon was the only co-founder to survive this tragedy. [2] After collecting the other survivors of the army, he took possession of Minoa, a colony of Selinus,[a] and joined in liberating the Selinuntines from their monarch Peithagoras. After deposing him, Euryleon made his own attempt to become tyrant, and he did succeed in becoming the sole ruler of Selinus, but he did not retain his power long, for the Selinuntines rose in revolt and killed him at the altar of Zeus of the Agora, where he had taken refuge.

5.47
c. 510
SICILY
The fate of Philip of Croton, victor at Olympia and the fairest Greek of his day.

Another man who had followed Dorieus and who died with him was Philip son of Boutakides of Croton. He had arranged a marriage with the daughter of Telys the Sybarite but had then been exiled from Croton. Cheated out of his marriage, he left Croton and sailed to Cyrene,[a] from which he set out to follow Dorieus in a trireme of his own and with men he supported at his own expense. Philip was an Olympic victor and the most handsome man of all the Hellenes in his time. [2] Because of his good looks, he won from the people of Egesta what no other man ever did before: they built a hero's shrine upon his grave, and they propitiate him with sacrifices.

5.48
490
SPARTA
Kleomenes dies without a male heir.

That, then, is how Dorieus met his end. Now if he had stayed in Sparta[a] and endured the rule of Kleomenes, he would have become king of Lacedaemon, since Kleomenes did not rule for long[b] but died without having sired a son. He left behind only a daughter, whose name was Gorgo.

5.49
499
SPARTA
Aristagoras describes the peoples, the great extent, and the wealth of the Persian Empire to Kleomenes and says that it is ripe for the taking.

But when Aristagoras, the tyrant of Miletus,[a] came to Sparta, Kleomenes was still ruling there. According to the account of the Lacedaemonians, when he went to talk with Kleomenes, Aristagoras had with him a bronze tablet on which a map of the entire world was engraved, including all rivers and every sea. [2] To begin the discussion, Aristagoras said, "Kleomenes, do not be surprised at my urgency in coming here, for this is how matters stand: that the sons of the Ionians[a] are slaves instead of free men is a disgrace and the most painful anguish to us, but also to you especially of all others, inasmuch as you are the leaders of Hellas.[b] [3] So now—by the gods of the Hellenes—come

5.46.1a Phoenicia: Map 5.52. There were Phoenician trading posts in Sicily since very early in the ninth century. In the eighth and seventh centuries, when the Hellenes arrived in Sicily to establish colonies, the Phoenicians withdrew to the western half of the island and formed an alliance with the Elimi, whose major city was Egesta. It was forces from this alliance who defeated Dorieus.
5.46.1b Egesta, Sicily: Map 5.44. The inhabitants of Egesta were non-Greek Sicels.

5.46.2a Selinus, Sicily: Map 5.44.
5.47.1a Cyrene: Map 5.44, locator.
5.48.1a Sparta: Map 5.44.
5.48.1b Kleomenes son of Anaxandridas is thought to have reigned as king from c. 520 to 491, some thirty years. We will hear more of his daughter Gorgo.
5.49.1a Miletus: Map 5.52, inset.
5.49.2a Ionia: Map 5.52, inset.
5.49.2b Is this statement the true reason for the Ionian Revolt? See Appendix H, §10–13.

rescue the Ionians from slavery; they are of the same blood as you, after all. This will be easy for you to accomplish, since the barbarians are not valiant, while you have attained the highest degree of excellence in war. Since they fight with bows and short spears, wearing trousers and turbans on their heads, [4] they are easily subdued. Further, the inhabitants of that continent possess more good things than all the other peoples of the world put together. To begin with, they have gold as well as silver, bronze, colorful clothing, beasts of burden, and slaves, all of which could be yours if you really desired them.

[5] "I shall now show you the sequence of the lands in which they live. Next to the Ionians dwell the Lydians;[a] their land is fertile and richest in silver." As Aristagoras said this, he pointed to the map engraved on the tablet he had brought along. "And next to the Lydians," Aristagoras continued, "the Phrygians[b] live here, to the east; they have the greatest abundance of flocks of anyone I know, as well as the most abundant crops. [6] Next to the Phrygians are the Cappadocians,[a] whom we call Syrians. Bordering them are the Cilicians,[b] whose land extends down right here to this sea in which lies the island of Cyprus;[c] the Cilicians pay the King an annual tribute of fifty talents. Next to the Cilicians are the Armenians,[d] who also have an abundance of flocks; and next to them the Matienians,[e] who dwell in this area here. [7] The land next to them belongs to the Kissians;[a] Susa[b] is located right here within it, along this River Choaspes.[c] It is here that the Great King makes his home, and where his stores of wealth are kept. Once you have taken this city, you can be confident that you will rival Zeus in wealth. [8] Well, then, would it not be advantageous for you to postpone your fight against the Messenians,[a] who are your equals in battle and whose land is neither so extensive nor fertile and is limited by confining boundaries, and to cease fighting against the Arcadians[b] and Argives,[c] who have no gold or silver, for which a man eagerly fights to the death? But when it is possible to so easily gain the rule over all of Asia, why would you choose to do anything else?" [9] That was what Aristagoras said, and Kleomenes replied, "My guest-friend of Miletus, I am going to delay giving you my answer until the day after tomorrow."

That was as far as they pushed the discussion on that day. When the day they had appointed for the answer arrived and they met at the place they had agreed upon, Kleomenes asked Aristagoras how many days the journey would take to go from the sea of the Ionians to the King. [2] Aristagoras, though he had cleverly misled Kleomenes in everything else, stumbled at this point. For he ought not to have told him the real distance if he wanted to bring the Spartans into Asia, but instead, he told them it was a journey of three months inland. [3] And at that, Aristagoras cut him short and, focusing on the jour-

5.50
499
SPARTA
When Kleomenes learns that it takes three months to journey from the sea to the King, he sends Aristagoras away.

5.49.5a Lydia: Map 5.52, inset.	Map 5.52.
5.49.5b Phrygia: Map 5.52.	5.49.7b Susa: Map 5.52.
5.49.6a Cappadocia: Map 5.52.	5.49.7c Choaspes River, possible location: Map
5.49.6b Cilicia: Map 5.52.	5.52.
5.49.6c Cyprus: Map 5.52.	5.49.8a Messenia: Map 5.52, inset.
5.49.6d Armenia: Map 5.52.	5.49.8b Arcadia: Map 5.52, inset.
5.49.6e Matienians (Matiane): Map 5.52.	5.49.8c Argos: Map 5.52, inset.
5.49.7a Kissians, possible location of territory:	

ney, said, "My guest-friend of Miletus, you must depart from Sparta before sunset. Your request will never be accepted by the Lacedaemonians if you intend to lead them on a three-month journey away from the sea."

Having said this, Kleomenes went home, but Aristagoras found an olive branch and, holding it as a suppliant,[a] went to the home of Kleomenes and entered, bidding him to listen, since he was now pleading in supplication. He first asked Kleomenes to send away the child there, for his daughter, whose name was Gorgo,[b] was standing beside the king. He happened to have only this one child, who at that time was about eight or nine years old. Kleomenes ordered Aristagoras to speak out and say what he wanted and not to hold back because of the presence of the child. [2] So Aristagoras began by promising him ten talents if he would fulfill his request. Kleomenes refused, and Aristagoras increased the sum step by step, until he had raised the offer to fifty talents. At this point the child blurted out, "Father, your guest-friend is going to corrupt you unless you leave and stay away from him." [3] Kleomenes was pleased with his child's advice, and he went to another room. Aristagoras departed and then left Sparta completely, losing the opportunity to explain the journey inland to the king any further.

Now the nature of the road on which one makes that journey is as follows. There are royal stations[a] and the most beautiful guesthouses along the entire length of the road, which passes through inhabited country and is safe for travel. There are twenty stations on that part of it which extends through Lydia and Phrygia[b]—a distance of about 330 miles.[c] [2] After Phrygia, the road approaches the Halys River, at which there is a huge guardhouse and gates[a] through which one must pass in order to cross over. Then, as one proceeds into Cappadocia and travels to the boundary of Cilicia, one passes altogether twenty-eight stations and covers a distance of 490 miles. At this border, you go through two gates and pass by two guardhouses. [3] Then there are three stations on the way through Cilicia, a distance of about 50 miles. The boundary between Cilicia and Armenia is formed by a navigable

5.51.1a No suppliant could be molested without causing an insult to the gods, particularly that god or gods in whose temple or at whose altar the suppliant had taken refuge.
5.51.1b Gorgo, daughter of Kleomenes: see Appendix B, §24.
5.52.1a On the Royal Road, stations were one day's journey apart; the distance varied somewhat depending on the difficulty or ease of traveling a particular section of the road.
5.52.1b Lydia, Phrygia, and all sites mentioned in this chapter 5.52, which describes the roads that probably became and were later known as the "Royal Road," are shown on Map 5.52, locator. This text is sometimes disputed; it is thought that Herodotus' description of this route may have been corrupted, especially since the geography does not always match what he appears to be saying and his sum total of parasangs is incorrect. There are at least two major routes (depicted in Map 5.52, locator) that have been identified—one going north

through Armenia, and another south through Cilicia. These two meet east of the Euphrates River and continue as one road across the Tigris River and south to Susa.
5.52.1c Herodotus gives all the distances in his description of the Royal Road in parasangs, which he says were each equal to 30 stades. If he meant the Attic stade equal to 583 feet, the parasang would equal about 3.3 miles. These factors produce the mile figures given in the text above (rounded to the nearest 10), and displayed, with ancient equivalent units, in the table below Map 5.52. Herodotus' calculation of the distance from the Sardis to Susa is short, as the actual measurement of that road is closer to 2,000 miles. See Distance Conversions, p. lxiv, and Appendix J, §2, 5–6, 19.
5.52.2a The word "gates" here may signify a defile or narrow pass through which the road passes, as in the famous Cilician Gates, but the word in this case may also mean actual gates (*pylai*), manned for traffic control.

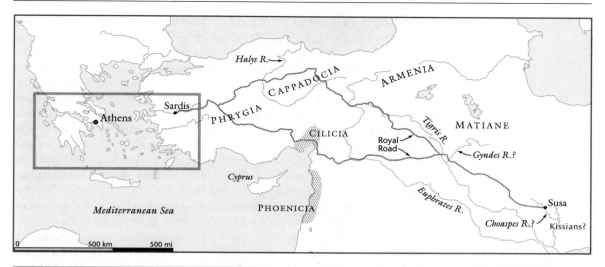

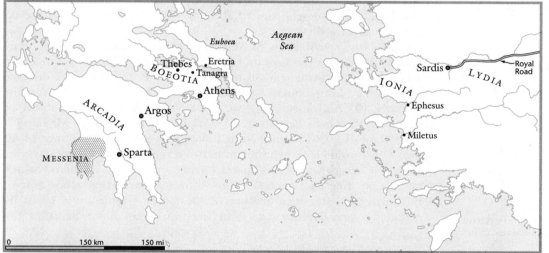

MAP 5.52

Distances Along the Royal Road

	parasangs	stades	miles	stations
Lydia to Phrygia	94.5	2,835	310	20
Phrygia to Cilicia border	140	4,200	460	28
Cilicia border to Cilicia	15.5	465	50	3
Cilicia to Armenia	56.5	1,695	190	15
Armenia to Matiane	137	4,110	450	34
Matiane to Kissia	42.5	1,275	140	11
Total	486	14,580	1,600	111

river named the Euphrates. The road in Armenia has fifteen stations which serve as rest stops and is about 200 miles long. There is a guardhouse along the way here, too. [4] Then there are four navigable rivers that one must cross which flow through this country: the first one is the Tigris; the second and third are both called Zabatos,[a] though they are not one and the same river and do not even flow from the same source—the former arises from Armenia and the latter from Matiane. [5] The fourth river bears the name Gyndes[a] and this is the one that Cyrus once divided into 360 channels.[b] On the way from Armenia to Matiane, the traveler passes thirty-four stations and covers a distance of 480 miles. [6] From here, one crosses into Kissia, and he passes eleven stations along a distance of 150 miles up to the Choaspes River, which is also navigable and on the banks of which the city of Susa is located. The total number of stations adds up to 111, and so that is how many rest stops there are along the inland journey from Sardis to Susa.

If the Royal Road has been correctly measured in parasangs, and a parasang equals 30 stades, which it does, then there are 13,500 stades, that is, 450 parasangs, from Sardis to what is called the palace of Memnon.[a] Thus those traveling at a pace of about 17 miles[b] per day would use up exactly 90 days for the journey.[c]

And so when Aristagoras of Miletus[a] told Kleomenes that the journey inland to the King took three months, he was correct. If anyone would like a more precise measurement, I can provide that as well, since the distance of the journey from Ephesus[b] to Sardis[c] should be added to the one just calculated. [2] And after doing so, I conclude that the total number of miles[a] from the Greek Sea[b] to Susa (for this is what the city of Memnon is called) comes to 1,615, since from Ephesus to Sardis is a distance of 60 miles, which would lengthen the journey of three months by three days.

After he was driven out of Sparta,[a] Aristagoras went to Athens,[b] which had become free of tyrants in the following way. Hipparchos son of Peisistratos, who was the brother of the tyrant Hippias, was killed by Aristogeiton and Harmodios,[c] who were in origin descendants of the

---

5.53
SUSA-SARDIS
A calculation of the Royal Road's length from Sardis to Susa.

5.54
EPHESUS-SUSA
A calculation of the distance from Ephesus on the coast to Susa.

5.55
514–499
ATHENS
Aristagoras goes to Athens (499), which had freed itself from tyrannical rule (510).

5.52.4a Zabatos (rivers): location unknown.
5.52.5a Gyndes River, possible location: Map 5.52, locator.
5.52.5b For the description of Cyrus dividing the Gyndes, see 1.189.
5.53.1a The palace of Memnon is in Susa: Map 5.52, locator.
5.53.1b Herodotus writes that a day's march is "150 stades" (16.6 miles). See Appendix J, §6, 19.
5.53.1c An army on foot might well require 90 days to cover 2,000 miles, but the Persians established a very efficient post service (described in 8.98), and historians estimate that such a courier service could deliver messages between Susa and Sardis in about a week's time.
5.54.1a Miletus: Map 5.52.
5.54.1b Ephesus: Map 5.52.
5.54.1c Sardis: Map 5.52 and locator.

5.54.2a Herodotus writes "540 stades" from Ephesus to Sardis which, when added to the 13,500 (*sic*) stades he has calculated in the previous chapter for the distance from Sardis to Susa, gives him a total from Ephesus to Susa of 14,040 stades, or approximately 1,615 miles. From his own list of distances from 5.52, he should have arrived at 15,120 stades, or 1,667 miles. See Appendix J, §6, 19.
5.54.2b The "Greek Sea" is the Aegean Sea: Map 5.52.
5.55.1a Sparta: Map 5.52.
5.55.1b Athens: Map 5.52.
5.55.1c Aristogeiton and Harmodios killed Hipparchos in 514. For another, more detailed version of how and why these famous tyrannicides, who were later lionized at Athens, assassinated Hipparchos, see *Thucydides* 1.20 and 6.54–59.

Gephyraians,[d] despite having seen quite clearly in a dream what was going to happen to him. But for four years afterward, the Athenians lived under an even harsher tyranny than before.

The dream of Hipparchos went as follows. On the eve of the Panathenaia,[a] he saw in his sleep a tall, good-looking man standing over him, reciting a riddle in verse:

> Be a Lion: endure, with a heart of endurance, unendurable suffering.
> There is no one on earth who will fail to pay for committing a crime.

[2] As soon as day came, Hipparchos is known to have communicated this vision to the interpreters of dreams, but then he dismissed it from his thoughts as he took part in the procession in which he met his end.[a]

The Gephyraians who murdered Hipparchos claim to have originally come from Eretria,[a] but I have discovered through my own inquiry that they were actually descended from Phoenicians, part of those who came with Kadmos[b] to the land now called Boeotia, and that they lived in this place after obtaining the region of Tanagra[c] by lot. [2] First the Kadmeians were expelled by the Argives,[a] and then the Gephyraians were driven out by the Boeotians. They made their way to Athens and were received by the Athenians on their own terms—admitted as citizens but excluded from a few privileges not worth mentioning.

So these Phoenicians, including the Gephyraians, came with Kadmos and settled this land, and they transmitted much lore to the Hellenes, and in particular, taught them the alphabet which, I believe, the Hellenes did not have previously, but which was originally used by all Phoenicians. With the passage of time, both the sound and the shape of the letters changed. [2] Because at this time it was mostly Ionians who lived around the Phoenicians, they were the ones who were first instructed in the use of the alphabet by them, and after making a few changes to the form of the letters, they put them to good use; but when they spoke of them, they called them "Phoenician" letters, which was only right since these letters had been introduced to Hellas by Phoenicians. [3] Furthermore, the Ionians have called papyrus scrolls "skins," since long ago, when papyrus was scarce, they used the skins of goats and sheep instead. In fact, even in my time many barbarians still write on such skins.[a]

5.56
514
ATHENS
The vision which Hipparchos had before he was killed.

5.57
ATHENS
The origins of the Gephyraian clan in Athens.

5.58
BOEOTIA
How the Phoenicians in Boeotia brought the alphabet which was revised and adopted by the Hellenes.

5.55.1d   Gephyraians: the name Gephyra means "bridge" or "dam" and is another name for Tanagra (Map 5.52). Perhaps Herodotus' theory of an eastern origin (5.57.1) is based on the fact that there was a place called Gephyrai in Syria. (Godley) For more on this family, see Appendix L, Aristocratic Families in Herodotus, §16.

5.56.1a   Panathenaia: a most important Athenian festival. See Appendix L, §16–17.

5.56.2a   Hipparchos was killed in 514.

5.57.1a   Eretria, Euboea: Map 5.52.

5.57.1b   Kadmos: the legendary Phoenician (Phoenicia: Map 5.52, locator) who founded Thebes in Boeotia: Map 5.52.

5.57.1c   Tanagra: Map 5.52.

5.57.2a   Argos: Map 5.52.

5.58.3a   Herodotus' account of the transmission of the alphabet to Hellas by Phoenicians is certainly correct. The first examples of writing in a Greek alphabet date from the second half of the eighth century.

5.59
BOEOTIA
Kadmeian writing in Boeotia
seen on tripod inscriptions.

I myself have seen Kadmeian letters at the sanctuary of Ismenian Apollo in Boeotian Thebes. These letters, which are engraved on three tripods, look for the most part like Ionian letters. One of the tripods bears the inscription:

> Amphitryon dedicated me, from the spoils that he took
> from the Teleboai.

5.60
BOEOTIA
A second tripod inscription.

This inscription would have to be contemporary with Laios son of Labdakos, whose grandfather was Polydoros son of Kadmos.
    Another tripod says in hexameter verse:

> Skaios the boxer, in return for his victory, dedicated me,
> An ornament of beauty, for you, Apollo Far-shooter.

5.61
BOEOTIA
A third tripod inscription.

Skaios would be the son of Hippokoon, if he actually made this dedication and not someone else by the same name. He would have been a contemporary of Oedipus son of Laios.
    The third tripod, also in hexameter, says:

> Laodamas himself dedicated this tripod during his reign;
> An ornament of beauty for you, Apollo Sharp-of-sight.

[2] In the reign of this Laodamas son of Eteokles, the Kadmeians were driven out by Argives and emigrated to the Encheles.[a] The Gephyraians, who were left behind, were later pressured by Boeotians and withdrew to Athens.[b] There they founded separate sanctuaries and rites of their own, in which the rest of the Athenians take no part, and which include the sanctuary of Achaean Demeter and her secret rites.

5.62
ATHENS
How the Alkmeonids
helped the Athenians to
free themselves of the
tyranny of Hippias.

    Now that I have described the dream of Hipparchos and the origin of the Gephyraians, the family to which his murderers belonged, I must resume the story I was beginning to tell[a]—namely, how the Athenians were freed from tyrants. [2] Hippias continued to rule as tyrant, now embittered against the Athenians because of the death of his brother Hipparchos, while the Alkmeonid clan,[a] who were Athenians in origin and had been exiled by the Peisistratids,[b] were trying, along with other Athenian exiles, to return and free Athens by force. They had built a fortification at Leipsydrion above Paionia,[c] but they not only failed to make progress in their attempts to return and liberate Athens; indeed, they suffered a severe defeat. As the Alkmeonids were considering every strategy they could think of against the

---

5.61.2a Encheles (Enchelei), a tribe of Illyria: Map
      5.63, locator. Also mentioned in 9.43.
5.61.2b Athens: Map 5.63.
5.62.1a Herodotus began to tell this story in 5.55.
5.62.2a Alkmeonids: Herodotus tells us more
      about this fascinating and influential
      Athenian family in 6.125–131. See
      Appendix L, §4, 9, 11, 15, 18. The fami-

ly's lineage from founder Alkmeon to
Pericles is shown in Figure L.
5.62.2b The Peisistratids were the ruling family,
      the Alkmeonids a rival family.
5.62.2c Leipsydrion is a fortress to the north of
      the general area of the deme of Paionidai
      (both sites are shown on Map 5.63), not
      Paionia as Herodotus has it.

Peisistratids, they accepted a contract from the Amphiktyones[d] to build the temple at Delphi,[e] the same one that is there now, but which had not yet been built at that time. [3] And since they were not only quite wealthy but also distinguished in their lineage, the temple they constructed turned out more beautiful in all respects than the original plan required; for example, whereas the agreement had called for them to use tufa as the building material, they built the façade of Parian marble[a] instead.

Now the Athenians say that these men established themselves at Delphi and bribed the Pythia to urge all Spartans who came to consult the oracle, whether on private or public missions, to liberate Athens. [2] After hearing the same instruction in their prophecies over and over again, the Lacedaemonians sent Anchimolios son of Aster, a man of distinction among them, with an army to drive the Peisistratids out of Athens, despite the very close ties of friendship between them, for they considered the concerns of the god to be of higher priority than those of men.[a] [3] And so the Spartans sent them by sea on boats, and the army came ashore at Phaleron.[a] Now the Peisistratids had already learned about this expedition and had summoned assistance from Thessaly, since they had made an alliance with the Thessalians[b] earlier. And the Thessalians had decided by joint resolution to respond to the summons. Once the Peisistratids had obtained them as allies, they employed the following strategy. [4] First, they cleared the plain of Phaleron, and after they had thus made the area suitable for cavalry maneuvers they sent the Thessalian horsemen in against the Spartan troops. In this attack they slaughtered many of the Lacedaemonians, including Anchimolios; those who survived were pushed back onto their ships, and that was how the first expedition from Lacedaemon turned out. The grave of Anchimolios is located in Attica,[a] at Alopeke,[b] next to the sanctuary of Herakles in Kynosarges.[c]

Afterward, the Lacedaemonians equipped a larger expedition and sent it against Athens, appointing King Kleomenes son of Anaxandridas[a] as general in command. This time they sent it not by sea, but by land. [2] And when they entered Attic territory, the Thessalian cavalry was the first to confront them in battle, but this time it was quickly routed, and over forty of its troops were killed. The survivors departed at once and went directly back to Thessaly. Kleomenes then went to the city with the Athenians who wanted their freedom, and besieged the tyrant and his supporters, who were shut up inside the fortress of the Pelargikon.[a]

5.63
c. 511
ATHENS
The Alkmeonids bribe the Delphic priestess to request those who visit her to free Athens. An initial Spartan attempt by sea is defeated by the Peisistratids with help from Thessalian cavalry.

5.64
510
ATTICA
A second Spartan army commanded by King Kleomenes defeats the Thessalians and besieges the Peisistratids.

5.62.2d Amphiktyones: a Greek league made up of representatives from mostly nearby who were selected to protect and oversee the sanctuary of Delphi. See also 2.180.1.
5.62.2e Delphi: Map 5.63.
5.62.3a Parian marble, from the island of Paros (Map 5.63), was considered a beautiful and expensive building stone.
5.63.2a See Appendix P, §14.
5.63.3a Phaleron: Map 5.63.
5.63.3b Thessaly: Map 5.63, locator.
5.63.4a Attica: Map 5.63.

5.63.4b Alopeke: Map 5.63.
5.63.4c Recent research places the site of Kynosarges south of the Ilissos River toward Phaleron (Map 5.63), though this issue is still debated among scholars.
5.64.1a For more on Kleomenes son of Anaxandridas, see Appendix B, §21.
5.64.2a Pelargikon: an ancient Mycenaean fortification wall on the Athenian Acropolis (Map 6.136, inset). Traces of it can still be seen today; see Figure 6.137a.

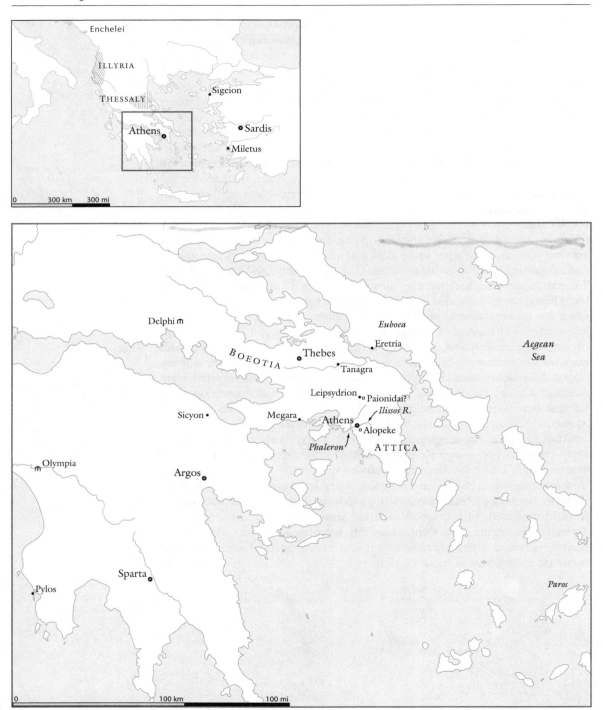

MAP 5.63

Now the Lacedaemonians would have had no success at all in forcing out the Peisistratids, since they had no intention to establish a long blockade, and the Peisistratids for their part were well supplied with food and drink; and so after a few days the Lacedaemonians would have lifted the siege and departed for Sparta. But then an incident occurred that happened to be a great help to one side and most injurious to the other. The children of the Peisistratids were captured while an attempt was being made to deliver them out of the country to a safer place. [2] This event threw all the Peisistratids' affairs into such confusion that they were forced to accept terms dictated by the Athenians in order to recover their children. The result was that they had to withdraw from Attica within five days.

[3] So after ruling the Athenians for thirty-six years,[a] the Peisistratids withdrew to Sigeion on the Scamander.[b] Their family was originally from Pylos,[c] and were descended from the Neleidai and of the same line as the followers of Kodros and Melanthos, who had earlier immigrated and become kings of the Athenians. [4] In memory of his ancestor, Hippocrates named his son Peisistratos after Peisistratos son of Nestor.[a] [5] That is how the Athenians were freed from their tyrants. Before the Ionians revolted from Darius and Aristagoras of Miletus[a] came to Athens to request their help, the Athenians performed noteworthy deeds and went through various experiences which I shall first describe in full.

Although Athens had been a great city before, it became even greater once rid of its tyrants. There were at that time two powerful men in Athens: Kleisthenes, an Alkmeonid who was said to have bribed the Pythia,[a] and Isagoras son of Teisandros, a man from a distinguished house; I cannot provide details on his origins, but his family sacrifices to Carian Zeus. [2] These two men competed for power, and when Kleisthenes found that he was facing defeat, he enlisted the common people into his association of supporters. Later, he organized the Athenians into ten tribes,[a] in place of their earlier division into four tribes, and he abolished the previous names of the tribes, which had been derived from the names of the sons of Ion—Gelaon, Aigikores, Argades, and Hoples—replacing them with names of local heroes that he discovered, and he also added Aias[b] to the list, who, although a foreigner, had been a neighbor and ally to the city.

I think that Kleisthenes, when he renamed the tribes, was imitating his maternal grandfather Kleisthenes of Sicyon.[a] For after Kleisthenes had made war on the Argives,[b] he stopped the bards from competing in Sicyon because the majority of the Homeric verses that they performed praised the

5.65
510
ATHENS-SIGEION
When their children are captured, the Peisistratids agree to leave Athens. They sail off to Sigeion.

5.66
508/07
ATHENS
Winning the political struggle that follows, Kleisthenes takes the common people into his faction and reforms the government, dividing the Athenians into ten tribes instead of four as previously.

5.67
c. 590
SICYON
How Kleisthenes of Sicyon diverted Argive devotion from the hero Adrastos to Melanippos.

5.65.3a From his last return to lead Athens, Peisistratos ruled from c. 546 to 510.
5.65.3b Sigeion: Map 5.63, locator, and Map 5.97, AY. Scamander River: Map 5.97, AY.
5.65.3c Pylos: Map 5.63.
5.65.4a Nestor son of Neleidai was well known from Homer's *Iliad*, as the king of Pylos.
5.65.5a Miletus: Map 5.63, locator.
5.66.1a Kleisthenes and the Alkmeonids were said to have bribed the Pythia to exhort the

5.66.2a For more about the nature of these ten new tribes, see Appendix A, The Athenian Government in Herodotus, §7.
5.66.2b Aias (Ajax) was the Homeric hero who came from Salamis.
5.67.1a Sicyon: Map 5.63. This Kleisthenes of Sicyon ruled that city as tyrant from c. 600 to 570.
5.67.1b Argos: Map 5.63.

Spartans to liberate Athens; see 5.63.1.

Argives and Argos. Further, there is a shrine to the hero Adrastos son of Talaos right in the agora of the Sicyonians, and because Adrastos was an Argive, Kleisthenes conceived a desire to expel him from the land. [2] So he went to Delphi[a] and consulted the oracle about whether he should expel Adrastos. But the Pythia answered that Adrastos was king of the Sicyonians, while he was just a stone-thrower.[b] Since the god did not grant him permission, Kleisthenes, while on his way home, devised a scheme to make Adrastos depart by his own volition, and when he thought he had discovered one, he sent a message to Boeotian Thebes,[c] saying that he wished to invite Melanippos son of Astakos[d] to come to Sicyon. The Thebans granted his request, [3] and so Kleisthenes brought Melanippos to Sicyon and assigned a precinct to him in the city hall itself and built it on the strongest site there. The reason Kleisthenes introduced this hero there (for this certainly requires an explanation) was that Melanippos was Adrastos' worst enemy; he had, after all, killed both Adrastos' brother Mekisteus and his son-in-law, Tydeus. [4] After designating the precinct for Melanippos, Kleisthenes deprived Adrastos of his sacrifices and festivals and gave them to Melanippos. The Sicyonians had been accustomed to worshiping Adrastos with very great honors, for Sicyon had once belonged to Polybos, whose grandson by his daughter was Adrastos. When Polybos died without having sired a son, he handed down the rule of Sicyon to Adrastos. [5] The Sicyonians honored Adrastos with a number of rites; in particular, they used to commemorate his sufferings with tragic choruses, honoring not Dionysos[a] but, rather, Adrastos by these performances. Kleisthenes rededicated the choruses to the honor of Dionysos and the remaining sacrificial ceremony to Melanippos.

So that is what Kleisthenes did to Adrastos. He also changed the names of the Dorian tribes so that they would not be the same for Sicyonians and Argives,[a] and on this occasion he heaped ridicule on the Sicyonians. For he gave them the names of the swine, the donkey, and the pig, changing these words only in their endings. To his own tribe, however, he gave a name derived from his office: the members of this tribe were called Archelaioi; the others were known as Hyatai, Oneatai, and Choireatai.[b] [2] The Sicyonians used these as the names of their tribes during the rule of Kleisthenes and for sixty years following his death. Then, however, after deliberating about the matter among themselves, they changed the names to Hyllees, Pamphyloi, and Dymanatai[a] and added a fourth tribal title, Aigialees, named after Aigaleos son of Adrastos.

5.68
c. 590
SICYON
Kleisthenes of Athens followed the policies of Kleisthenes of Sicyon, who had also changed the names of his city's tribes.

5.67.2a   Delphi: Map 5.63.
5.67.2b   This passage has been translated in a number of ways, but a king leads his army, and the stonethrowers would be the lowliest members of that army, without armor or civilized weapons.
5.67.2c   Thebes, Boeotia: Map 5.63.
5.67.2d   Melanippos had been a Theban hero; Kleisthenes apparently wanted to transfer his remains to Sicyon to gain this hero's allegiance and protection. See 1.68 on the bones of Orestes.

5.67.5a   Tragic choruses at Athens were performed in honor of Dionysos. These later developed into Athenian theater, which was also devoted to honoring Dionysos.
5.68.1a   All Dorian cities seem to have had the same four tribes with the same names.
5.68.1b   These names translate as follows: Archelaioi: Leaders of the People; Hyatai: Swinites (Swineans/Swine People); Oneatai: Donkeyites; Choireatai: Pigites.
5.68.2a   These are the traditional names of the Dorian tribes.

That is what Kleisthenes of Sicyon did with Dorian tribal names, and now Kleisthenes of Athens, the son of this Sicyonian's daughter who bore his name, imitated him, I think, in his attitude of contempt toward the Ionians and in his efforts to assure that the names of the Athenian tribes would not be the same as those of the Ionians. [2] For though the Athenian people had previously been spurned by their politicians, he now brought them into his own faction and increased the numbers of their tribes and gave them new names. He established ten tribal leaders to replace the previous four, and then distributed the demes[a] in ten parts throughout the tribes. By adding the people to his side, he gained the upper hand by far over his political opponents.

So now that Isagoras faced defeat, he in turn contrived the following counterstrategy. He invited Kleomenes the Lacedaemonian,[a] who had been his guest-friend[b] since the siege of the Peisistratids and who had also been accused of having relations with Isagoras' wife, to come to Athens.[c] [2] Kleomenes first sent a herald to Athens with a message which requested that the Athenians banish Kleisthenes and many other Athenians along with him, designating them as accursed. This message was worded according to the instructions of Isagoras, for long ago the Alkmeonids and their partisans had been charged with guilt for a certain murder in which neither Isagoras nor his friends and relatives had played any part.

The Athenians who were called accursed acquired this identification as follows. There was an Athenian named Kylon who had been victorious in the games at Olympia.[a] He preened himself with a view to becoming tyrant, and after enlisting a clique of supporters composed of young men his own age, he led them in an attempt to seize the Acropolis. When he found that he was unable to secure control of it, he sat down before the statue[b] as a suppliant.[c] [2] The presidents of the naval boards,[a] who were in charge of managing Athens at the time, had the suppliants rise and move away from their place of refuge, declaring that they would be liable to any punishment except death. Nevertheless, they were all slain, and the Alkmeonids were accused of having murdered them.[b] These events had occurred before the time of Peisistratos.[c]

5.69
508/07
ATHENS
Kleisthenes sets up ten new tribes with new names, distributes demes to the tribes, and gains ascendancy over his political rivals.

5.70
508/07
ATHENS-SPARTA
Isagoras plots with Kleomenes of Sparta to defeat Kleisthenes by seeking his banishment as an accursed Alkmeonid.

5.71
632
ATHENS
The conspiracy of Kylon, and the guilt attributed to the Alkmeonids for the death of the conspirators.

5.69.2a Prior to this reform of Kleisthenes, Attic demes had been just townships, villages, or regions. Now they were official political units of the Athenian state, and every Athenian citizen was identified by his name and the deme in which he was born.
5.70.1a Lacedaemon (Sparta): Map 5.63.
5.70.1b Guest-friendship (*xenia*): a bond of ritualized friendship, usually between aristocrats or prominent men of different cities. It was passed down through generations and required hereditary privileges and obligations such as reciprocal hospitality and assistance. See Appendix T, §3.
5.70.1c Athens: Map 5.63.
5.71.1a Olympia: Map 5.63. Kylon's name appears in the Olympic victor lists in the thirty-fifth of the quadrennial Olympiads, or in the year 640. His attempt to set up a tyranny was therefore made in either 636

or 632. See Appendix I, Classical Greek Religious Festivals, §6.
5.71.1b Probably the statue of Athena on the Acropolis.
5.71.1c No suppliant could be molested without insult to the gods, particularly the god or gods in whose temple or at whose altar the suppliant had taken refuge.
5.71.2a "The naval boards (nauraries) were local districts whose presidents were responsible for levying money and contingents for the army and ships for the fleet." (How and Wells) But the statement that they "were in charge of managing Athens" appears to be inaccurate.
5.71.2b For the curse on the Alkmeonids, see Appendix L, §11, 15.
5.71.2c See Thucydides' version of Kylon's coup and the resulting curse in *Thucydides* 1.126.

5.72
507
ATHENS
Kleomenes attempts to
put Isagoras in power but
is thwarted by an Athenian
uprising and forced to
leave Athens.

While Kleomenes was sending the herald to cast out Kleisthenes and all those who were accursed, Kleisthenes retired from the city on his own accord. Nonetheless, Kleomenes marched to Athens with a small force and, upon his arrival, endeavored to drive out the pollution[a] by banishing the 700 Athenian households that had been specified by Isagoras. Having accomplished this, he next attempted to dissolve the Council and to place power in the hands of 300 partisans of Isagoras. [2] But when the Council refused to obey and resisted this measure, Kleomenes and Isagoras with his partisans seized the Acropolis.[a] The rest of the Athenians united in their resolve and besieged them for two days. On the third day, all the Lacedaemonians departed from the place under a truce. [3] Thus a divine utterance was fulfilled, for when Kleomenes had climbed up to the Acropolis with the intent of taking possession of it, he went to the inner chamber of the goddess to address her. But before he could pass through the doors, the priestess stood up from her throne and said, "Foreigner from Lacedaemon: go back, and do not come into the shrine. For it is not lawful for Dorians to enter here." He replied, "But woman, I am not a Dorian; I am an Achaean."[a] [4] And so now he made his attempt, heedless of the words of omen, and again was evicted with the Lacedaemonians. The Athenians bound and confined the rest to await their death. Among them was Timesitheos of Delphi, whose mighty deeds of strength and will I could recount at great length.

5.73
507
ATHENS-SARDIS
The Athenians recall
Kleisthenes and send an
embassy to Sardis seeking
an alliance with Persia.

After those who had been taken into custody met their end, the Athenians sent for Kleisthenes and the 700 households previously banished by Kleomenes. They then sent envoys to Sardis,[a] wanting to form an alliance with the Persians, since they realized that the Lacedaemonians and Kleomenes had now clearly become their enemies. [2] When the envoys arrived in Sardis and spoke according to their instructions, Artaphrenes son of Hystaspes, the governor of Sardis, inquired who were these people who asked to become allies of the Persians, and where in the world did they live?[a] When he had heard the answer from the envoys, he gave them the brief answer that if the Athenians offered earth and water[b] to King Darius, they would have their alliance, but if they did not do so, he ordered them to leave. [3] The envoys, wanting to bring about the alliance, took the responsibility on themselves and consented to offering earth and water, for which they faced serious charges when they returned to their own land.

5.72.1a   Drive out the "pollution" caused by the sacrilegious act for which the Alkmeonids and others were cursed. In ancient Hellas, a city which harbored such criminals would incur the anger of the gods, which might endanger the entire body of citizens.
5.72.2a   The Acropolis of Athens was a steep hill on the top of which stood the city's most ancient religious shrines and temples. At one time it constituted the entire city (*Thucydides* 2.15.3–6), which Kleomenes had briefly occupied with Isagoras in 506. See 5.72.2.

5.72.3a   The Spartan kings were said to be descended from the Heraklids, representing the pre-Dorian population of the Peloponnese, later restored to power over the more recently settled Dorians.
5.73.1a   Sardis: Map 5.63, locator.
5.73.2a   Another instance of Persian ignorance of basic geography west of Asia.
5.73.2b   To give the Persians "earth and water" was to subject oneself to Persian rule. See Appendix M, Herodotus on Persia and the Persian Empire, §7.

Now Kleomenes, who felt that the Athenians had insulted him terribly in both word and deed, mustered an army from the entire Peloponnese[a] without stating his purpose, but wishing to punish the Athenian people and to establish Isagoras as tyrant, for Isagoras had left the Acropolis with him. [2] So with a large army, Kleomenes invaded Eleusis.[a] Meanwhile, by a prearranged agreement, the Boeotians captured Oinoe[b] and Hysiai,[c] the demes on the frontiers of Attica, and the Chalcidians[d] invaded and plundered other areas of Attica. The Athenians were being attacked from two sides, so they decided to postpone taking action against the Boeotians and Chalcidians until later and now deployed their troops against the Peloponnesians in Eleusis.

But as they were about to engage their forces in battle, the Corinthians,[a] after considering among themselves and concluding that they were becoming involved in unjust acts, were the first to do an about-face and leave. And next to leave was Demaratos son of Ariston,[b] the other king of the Spartans, who had joined Kleomenes in leading the army out of Lacedaemon and had not disagreed with him before. [2] After this dissension between the two kings, a policy was established at Sparta that prohibited both kings from going out and together accompanying the army when it left the country on campaign, as had been the practice up until then. With this rule exempting one of the kings from the campaign, they also made a rule that one of the sons of Tyndareos[a] was to be left behind in Sparta as well; previously, both of these had been called on to accompany them into battle. [3] So at that time in Eleusis, when the rest of the allies observed that the kings of the Lacedaemonians were not in agreement and that the Corinthians had deserted their post, they, too, left and disappeared from sight.

This was the fourth time that the Dorians had marched against Attica. They had invaded on two occasions before in order to make war, and twice more for the benefit of the Athenian majority. The first occasion was when they established the settlement of Megara[a] (and this expedition would correctly be dated to the reign of the Athenian King Kodros);[b] the second and third times occurred when they marched out of Sparta in order to expel the Peisistratids; and the fourth time was when Kleomenes led the Peloponnesians in this invasion of Eleusis. Therefore, this was the fourth time that the Dorians had invaded Athens.[a]

5.74
506
ATTICA
Kleomenes returns with a large army. The Boeotians and Chalcidians attack Attica also.

5.75
506
SPARTA
The Spartan army breaks up when King Demaratos leaves it, which leads to a new Spartan law.

5.76
ATTICA
The four Dorian invasions of Attica.

5.74.1a Peloponnese: Map 5.82, BX.
5.74.2a Eleusis, Attica: Map 5.82, AY.
5.74.2b Oinoe: Map 5.82, AY.
5.74.2c Hysiai: Map 5.82, AY.
5.74.2d Chalcis, Euboea: Map 5.82, AY.
5.75.1a Corinth: Map 5.82, BX.
5.75.1b Demaratos son of Ariston was to play a
         major role in Herodotus' narrative.
5.75.2a Apparently this refers to one of the
         images or statues of the twin sons of
         Tyndareos, Castor and Pollux.
5.76.1a Megara: Map 5.82, AY.
5.76.1b There is a clear tradition that this
         happened soon after the Dorian invasion
         of the Peloponnese. (Godley)
5.76.1c The first Dorian invasions of Attica listed by

Herodotus occurred in the distant past at the time of King Kodros. The second and third invasions took place in 511 and 510 and were described in 5.63 and 5.64–5. Apparently Herodotus did not consider the next ignominious incursion by Kleomenes (in 507, described in 5.72) to rank as a Dorian "invasion" because of the small forces involved. So it was in the following year, 506, that his fourth and final invasion took place when a large allied army broke up in dissension at Eleusis (5.74–75). This list was undoubtedly written down after the Dorian invasion of Attica of 446, and possibly after the later invasions of 431, 430, and 428.

The Athenians defeat the Boeotians and the Chalcidians in battle on the same day.

Now that this expedition had ingloriously fallen apart, the Athenians wanted vengeance, so they first launched an expedition against the Chalcidians. The Boeotians rushed to aid their allies at the Euripos,[a] and when the Athenians saw this, they resolved to attack the Boeotians before the Chalcidians. [2] Thus the Athenians joined battle with the Boeotians, and decisively overwhelmed them, slaughtering vast numbers and capturing 700 of them alive. Then, on the same day, the Athenians crossed over to Euboea[a] and engaged the Chalcidians in battle as well. Winning another victory there, they left behind 4,000 klerouchs[b] on the land of the horse-breeders,[c] which is what the Chalcidian men of substance were called. [3] And all the captives they had taken there, together with the Boeotian captives, they bound in shackles and kept under guard. But in time they released them for a price they fixed at two minas[a] each. They hung up the shackles with which they had been bound on the Acropolis, where they remained even in my time, suspended from the walls that had been scorched with fire by the Mede,[b] opposite the megaron[c] facing west. [4] They dedicated a tenth of the ransom by having a bronze four-horse chariot constructed. This stands to the left as one enters the gateway to the Acropolis, and bears the inscription:

> The Boeotian and Chalcidian peoples were tamed
> by the sons of Athenians in works of war,
> Who quelled their arrogance in dark bonds of iron,
> And set up these horses as a tithe for Pallas.[a]

Herodotus says that equality made the Athenians strong in war.

So the Athenians had increased in strength, which demonstrates that an equal voice in government has beneficial impact not merely in one way, but in every way: the Athenians, while ruled by tyrants, were no better in war than any of the peoples living around them, but once they were rid of tyrants, they became by far the best of all. Thus it is clear that they were deliberately slack while repressed, since they were working for a master, but that after they were freed, they became ardently devoted to working hard so as to win achievements for themselves as individuals.[a]

The Thebans appeal to Delphi for advice on how to seek revenge against the Athenians.

So that is what the Athenians did. Afterward, the Thebans, wanting to take revenge on the Athenians, sent a mission to the god at Delphi. The Pythia told them that they would not be the ones to achieve the revenge they sought, and ordered them to report the matter to the "many voiced"[a]

5.77.1a   Euripos (the narrowest point in the channel between Euboea and the mainland): Map 5.82, AY. The channel there is 120 feet wide. Strong and unpredictable currents run through it.
5.77.2a   Euboea: Map 5.82, AY.
5.77.2b   Klerouchs: Athenian citizens settled as lotholders/allottees on confiscated lands. The Klerouchs turned their new properties into virtual extensions of Athenian territory and served, if only by their presence, as Athenian garrisons overseeing the local citizens.
5.77.2c   Chalcidian horse-breeders: *hippobotai*, also mentioned in 6.100.1.

5.77.3a   A mina was 100 drachmas, or one sixtieth of a talent (6,000 drachmas). See Appendix J, §11–13, 20.
5.77.3b   This is another instance where, like many of his Greek contemporaries, Herodotus uses the term "Medes" for Persians.
5.77.3c   Megaron: a rectangular building with an entrance porch and usually a hearth.
5.77.4a   Pallas is Athena.
5.78.1a   Herodotus here states his emphatic approval of democracy and its superiority to a tyrannical form of government.
5.79.1a   The "many-voiced" must refer here to the assembly.

and to "ask those who are closest." [2] The sacred delegates returned home, called an assembly, and reported the oracular response. When the Thebans heard them saying, "Ask those who are closest," they said, "Don't the Tanagraians,[a] Coronaeans,[b] and Thespiai[c] live closest to us? But they *always* fight together with us zealously and help us to wage our wars. Why then should we ask them? Surely that is not what the oracle meant."

They continued to consider factors such as these, until someone figured it out and said, "I think I understand what the prophecy is trying to tell us: Thebe and Aegina are said to be the daughters of Asopos. Since they are sisters, I believe the god has advised us to ask the Aeginetans[a] to become our avengers." [2] They decided that no other explanation appeared to be better than this one, and so they at once sent to the Aeginetans, calling upon them to rush to their assistance in accordance with the oracular instructions and on the grounds that they were "closest." The Aeginetans replied to those asking for their help that they would send the Aiakidai[a] back with them.

Because the Aiakidai were now allied with them, the Thebans attempted an attack but suffered rough treatment at the hands of the Athenians. So once again they sent envoys to Aegina, this time to return the Aiakidai and to ask for men. [2] The Aeginetans, both elated by their present prosperity and mindful of their ancient enmity toward the Athenians, now responded to the Theban request by waging an undeclared war[a] against the Athenians. [3] So while the Athenians were occupied with their attack on Boeotia, the Aeginetans sailed in warships to Attica and laid waste to Phaleron,[a] as well as to many demes along the rest of the coast, and thus inflicted great damage on the Athenians.

This is how the long-standing enmity felt by the Aeginetans for the Athenians first developed. At one time when the land of the Epidaurians[a] was producing no crops, they consulted the oracle at Delphi about their misfortune. The Pythia told them to set up statues of Damia and Auxesia,[b] and that once they had done this, their fortunes would improve. [2] The Epidaurians then inquired whether they should have the statues made of bronze or of stone. The Pythia authorized neither of these but recommended the wood of a domesticated olive tree instead. The Epidaurians asked the Athenians to grant them permission to cut down one of their olive trees, since they considered these to be the most sacred. Actually, it is said that at the time, no olive trees grew in any territory other than that of Athens.[a] [3] The Athenians granted their request on the condition that each year the Epidaurians would bring sacred offerings for Athena Polias[a] and for Erechtheus.[b] The Epidaurians agreed to these terms, obtained approval of their request, made the statues out of the wood of olive trees,

5.80
THEBES
The Thebans interpret the Delphic oracle to mean they should seek to ally with Aegina against Athens.

5.81
505?
ATTICA
The Thebans are defeated again by the Athenians, but the Aeginetans make a successful surprise raid on the coasts of Attica.

5.82
EPIDAUROS
How the Epidaurians obtained olive wood from the Athenians to make images suggested by the Delphic oracle.

5.79.2a Tanagra: Map 5.82, AY.
5.79.2b Coronea: Map 5.82, AX.
5.79.2c Thespiai: Map 5.82, AY.
5.80.1a Aegina: Map 5.82, BY.
5.80.2a By Aiakidai, they probably meant "images of Aiakos and his sons," heroes especially connected with Aegina. (How and Wells)
5.81.2a "Undeclared war" here means they started hostilities without first sending a

herald to announce their intentions.
5.81.3a Phaleron: Map 5.82, BY.
5.82.1a Epidauros: Map 5.82, BY.
5.82.1b Damia and Auxesia were goddesses of increase and fertility. (Godley)
5.82.2a Athens: Map 5.82, AY.
5.82.3a Athena Polias: Athena in her role as guardian of the city.
5.82.3b Erechtheus: a mythical king of Athens.

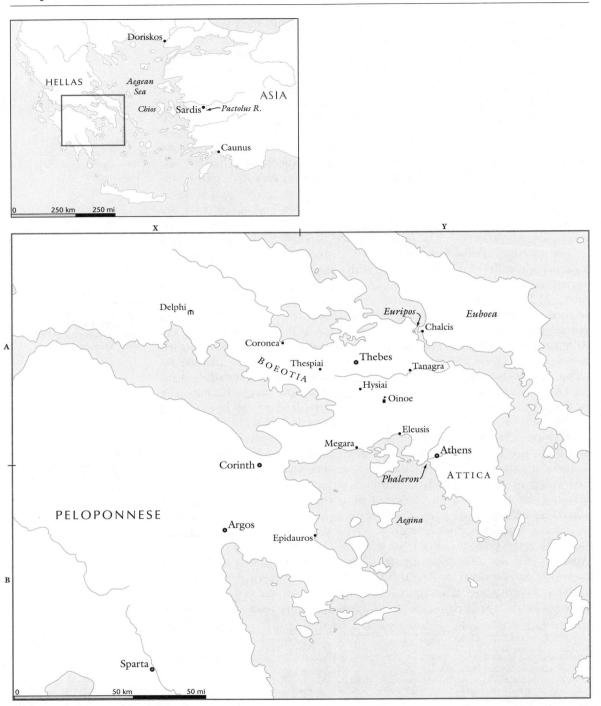

MAP 5.82

402

and erected them. After this, their land produced crops, and they fulfilled their agreement with the Athenians.

Now at this time, as well as earlier, the Aeginetans followed the dictates of the Epidaurians in judicial and other matters, crossing over to Epidauros to have their lawsuits judged there. But then they began to construct ships for themselves, and from that time on, they adopted an attitude of disdain toward the Epidaurians, and revolted from them. [2] Now that they were at odds, the Aeginetans attempted to harm the Epidaurians so as to gain control over the sea. In particular, they stole their statues of Damia and Auxesia, brought them home, and set them up at an inland location of their own called Oia,[a] which lies a little more than two miles[b] from the city. [3] After erecting the statues here, they tried to appease them with sacrifices and scurrilous choruses of women, and they appointed ten men to be responsible for the chorus of each of the divinities. The choruses uttered no abuse against any man, only against local women. These were the same sacred rites that the Epidaurians had observed as well. They also conduct other sacred rites about which one must remain silent.

After these statues had been stolen, the Epidaurians ceased to fulfill the terms of their agreement with the Athenians, who then sent a message expressing their anger. The Epidaurians responded to their complaint with the logical argument that they were doing nothing wrong, since they had fulfilled the agreement as long as they had kept the statues in their territory, but now that they had been deprived of them, it was not right and just for them to continue to pay the Athenians for them. They told the Athenians to exact payment from the Aeginetans instead. [2] The Athenians then sent to Aegina a demand for the return of the statues, but the Aeginetans replied that they and the Athenians had nothing to do with each other.

Now the Athenians say that after they had asserted their demand and had been refused, they dispatched a single trireme manned with citizens sent by the authority of the state, and when they arrived in Aegina, they attempted to tear the statues from their bases, on the grounds that they were made of their own wood. [2] When they found themselves unable to gain possession of the statues in this way, they tied ropes around the statues and began to drag them off, but as they were doing so, peals of thunder and an earthquake occurred at the same time. The crew of the trireme lost their minds as they tugged on the ropes, and in this state began to kill one another as though they were enemies, until only one was left, and he alone was conveyed back to Phaleron.

That is how the Athenians describe what happened, but the Aeginetans say that the Athenians did not come in a single ship, for if there had been only one or even a few ships more than that, the Aeginetans would have easily driven them away even if they did not then happen to have ships of their own. In fact, they say, the Athenians who sailed against their land

5.83
AEGINA
The Aeginetans build ships and revolt from Epidauros, stealing the images and organizing sacrifices and satirical choruses in their honor.

5.84
AEGINA
The Athenians apply to the Aeginetans for the annual payment connected with the images.

5.85
AEGINA
The tale of the failed Athenian attempt to steal the images from Aegina.

5.86
AEGINA
The Aeginetan version of the Athenian attempt to steal the images.

5.83.2a Oia, Aegina: precise location unknown.
5.83.2b Herodotus writes "20 stades" from the

city, which would equal about 2.2 miles. See Appendix J, §6, 19.

came with many ships, and that the Aeginetans yielded and would not engage them in a naval battle. [2] They cannot reveal precisely whether they yielded in acknowledgment of their inferiority in sea-fighting or whether they did so because that was in accord with the plan which they eventually carried out. [3] So when no one ventured out to do battle with them, the Athenians disembarked from their ships and turned their attention to the statues; when they found themselves unable to tear them away from their bases, they tied ropes around them and began to drag them off until both statues did the same thing. What the Aeginetans say happened next—which I cannot believe, although some may do so—is that as the statues were being dragged off, both of them fell to their knees, and from then on remained in that position. [4] Moreover, the Aeginetans say that when they learned that the Athenians intended to wage war against them, they secured the assistance of the Argives,[a] so that after the Athenians had disembarked and were present on Aegina, the Argives came to the aid of the Aeginetans, secretly crossing over to the island from Epidauros. They fell upon the Athenians, who had no advance warning of their arrival, and cut them off from their ships just as the thunder and earthquake struck.

5.87
ATHENS
How the Athenian
women came to dress
in the Ionian fashion.

That is the account told by the Argives and Aeginetans, and they agree with the Athenians that only one Athenian returned home to Attica safe and sound, [2] except that the Argives say that it was they who destroyed the Attic army from which the one man survived, while the Athenians attribute the loss of the army to a divine force. Actually that one man did not survive long either, but perished in the following way. After he had returned to Athens he reported the disaster, and when the wives of the men who had served with him against Aegina heard of it, they became outraged that of all the men, he alone had come back safely. They took hold of him on all sides and, as they all asked him where their own husbands were, they stabbed him with the pins of their cloaks; [3] and so that is how he, too, died.[a] To the Athenians, what the women had done seemed an even more terrible disaster than the loss of the army. They could find no other penalty to impose upon the women except to make them change their style of dress to the Ionian fashion. Prior to this, the Athenian women had worn Dorian clothing, which most resembles the Corinthian[b] style, but now they changed to wearing a linen tunic, so that they would have no pins to use.

5.88
CARIA
The true origin of
"Ionian" dress is Carian.

The truth is that this style of dress was originally not Ionian, but Carian,[a] since long ago all Greek women dressed in the fashion that we now call Dorian. [2] The following customs were also established by both the Argives and the Aeginetans: in each country the size of the cloak pins was increased by half their former size, and these pins became the objects most frequently dedicated by women to the sanctuary of these goddesses.[a] In

---

5.86.4a Argos: Map 5.82, BX.
5.87.3a Women as killers: see Appendix U, On Women and Marriage in Herodotus.
5.87.3b Ionian and Dorian dress: see Appendix K, Dialect and Ethnic Groups in Herodotus,

§2–9. Corinth: Map 5.82, AX.
5.88.1a Caria: Map 5.97, BY.
5.88.2a These goddesses are not identified by Herodotus.

addition, neither Attic pottery nor any other Attic product was permitted to be brought into the sanctuary; from then on, they were to drink only from vessels made in their own land. And so ever since that time, even down to my own day, the Argive and Aeginetan women have been wearing larger pins than they had earlier, all because of the strife with the Athenians.

So that is how the enmity of the Athenians toward the Aeginetans began. And at this time,[a] when the Thebans[b] called on the Aeginetans for help, the Aeginetans resolutely invoked the controversy over the statues and the events surrounding them and rushed to the aid of the Boeotians. [2] They began laying waste to the coastal regions of Attica, but just as the Athenians were setting out to wage war against them, an oracle from Delphi came to them which advised them to refrain from responding to the crime of the Aeginetans for the next thirty years, but that in the thirty-first year they should assign a precinct to the hero Aiakos[a] and begin the war against Aegina. In this way they would attain their goals. If, on the other hand, they began a war immediately, they would both suffer and accomplish a great deal in the intervening years, but they would nevertheless prevail in the end. [3] When the Athenians had heard the report of this oracle, they appointed a precinct for Aiakos, the one which is now set up in the agora,[a] but they could not endure hearing the advice that they should wait thirty years to start the war because of the injuries they had suffered at the hands of the Aeginetans.

But while they were making preparations to exact vengeance, the Lacedaemonians[a] posed a problem for them which stood in their way. The Lacedaemonians had found out how the Alkmeonids had connived with the Pythia and about her resulting policy toward them and the Peisistratids. They now felt that they had been doubly unfortunate, since the Peisistratids, whom they had driven out of their own land, were their guest-friends, and the Athenians had never shown them any gratitude for having done so. [2] In addition, they were provoked by oracles that predicted that the Athenians would inflict many terrible injuries on them. They had been unaware of the existence of these oracles earlier, but they found out about them when Kleomenes brought them to Sparta after he had taken possession of them from the Athenian Acropolis.[a] These oracles had belonged to the Peisistratids, but when they were being driven out, they had left them in the sanctuary, and Kleomenes took what was left behind.

So the Lacedaemonians had taken possession of the oracles, and as they observed the Athenians growing in strength and by no means ready or willing to obey the Lacedaemonians, they recognized that in freedom, the Attic race would equally match their own, but that when repressed by tyranny, it would be weaker and willing to submit to the authority of others. After

5.89
498?
ATHENS
The Athenians receive a Delphic oracle advising them to wait thirty years for vengeance against Aegina.

5.90
505?
SPARTA
The Spartans learn of the Alkmeonid plot and receive Attic oracles predicting enmity between Athens and Sparta.

5.91
504
SPARTA
The Spartans wish to restore the Athenian tyranny. They assemble their allies and explain their previous error.

5.89.1a Herodotus here refers back to 5.80–81.
5.89.1b Thebes, Boeotia: Map 5.82, AY.
5.89.2a Aiakos: in mythology he was the son of Zeus and Aegina (daughter of the river god Asopos) and the eponymous founder

of the clan of Aiakidai.
5.89.3a Agora: the central marketplace of an ancient Greek city. See Glossary.
5.90.1a Lacedaemon (Sparta): Map 5.82, BX.
5.90.2a Acropolis of Athens: see 5.72.2.

coming to this realization, they sent for Hippias son of Peisistratos in order to bring him from Sigeion on the Hellespont,[a] where the Peisistratids had taken refuge. [2] Hippias came at their summons, and the Spartans then sent for envoys from their other allies and spoke to them as follows: "We admit to you that we have not done the right thing. We were induced by counterfeit oracles[a] into driving men who were our special guest-friends out of their own country, although they had taken it upon themselves to subjugate the Athenians. After we had done so, we handed over the city to its thankless people who, once they had been liberated by us, raised their heads high and committed a grave insult against us by expelling us from their land with our king. Their growth in power inflates them with pride, as their neighbors—especially the Boeotians and Chalcidians—have learned so well from their own mistakes, and as others may learn soon enough, too. [3] But since we have erred in what we did, we shall now, with your assistance, attempt to remedy our past mistake. That is why we sent for Hippias and summoned you to come here from your cities, so that by a common resolution and a shared mission we can bring him back to Athens and restore to him what we took away."

That was the speech of the Spartans, and the majority of the allies did not approve of it. While the others held their peace, Sokleas of Corinth[a] said:

"Well, heaven will be under the earth, and the earth above heaven; human beings will dwell in the sea, and fish will take over the former abodes of men, when you, Lacedaemonians, destroy systems of political equality[a] and prepare to restore tyrannies to the cities—there is nothing among men more unjust or bloodstained than tyranny. [2] If you really believe it to be a good policy to have cities ruled under tyrannies, then *you* should be the first to install a tyrant among yourselves before seeking to do so for everyone else. But as it is, you have no experience of tyrants, and in fact take the most dire precautions to prevent them from arising in Sparta, while you mistreat your allies. If you had experienced tyranny the way we have,[a] you would be able to come up with better policies concerning it than you have now.[b]

"Just listen to what conditions have been like in the city of the Corinthians. It used to be ruled under an oligarchy, by men called the Bacchiads,[a] who intermarried among themselves. One of them, Amphion, had a daughter who was lame, and her name was Labda.[b] Since none of the Bacchiads wanted to marry her, Eetion son of Echekrates took her as

5.92
504
SPARTA
Allies reject Spartan speech.
5.92.α*
504
SPARTA
The speech of Sokleas, the Corinthian.

5.92.β
504
CORINTH
The speech of Sokleas continues: how the oracle foretold the role of Eetion's son by Labda in bringing down the Corinthian oligarchs called the Bacchiads.

5.91.1a   Sigeion on the Hellespont: Map 5.97, AY.
5.91.2a   For more on false oracles, see Appendix P, §14.
5.92.1a   Corinth: Map 5.97, BX.
5.92.α*   This chapter in the *Histories* has subdivisions indicated by Greek letters in alphabetic sequence. That sequence (with the letters' Latin equivalents) is as follows: α (a), β (b), γ (g), δ (d), ε (e), ζ (z), η (h).
5.92.α.1a Civic equality (*isocratia*) meant equality of power, equal access to political powers.

5.92.α.2a Corinth was ruled by the tyrants Kypselos from 655 to 625 and his son Periandros from 625 to 587.
5.92.α.2b The Spartan policy of putting down tyrannies in Hellas is discussed in Appendix B, §20–21.
5.92.β.1a Bacchiads: ruling family at Corinth until replaced by the Kypselids; see Appendix L, §12.
5.92.β.1b The name Labda is a reference to the Greek letter λ (lambda), apparently based on its resemblance to her deformity.

his wife. He was from the deme of Petra,[c] but in origin a Lapith and a Caenid.[d] [2] Since he had no children from this woman nor from any other, he went to Delphi[a] to inquire about having offspring. As he was entering, the Pythia spontaneously addressed him with these verses:

> You, Eetion, are quite worthy of honor, yet you are honored by no one.
> Labda will conceive and give birth to a stone,
> Which will fall upon monarchs and impose justice on Corinth.

[3] "This oracular response to Eetion was somehow reported to the Bacchiads. They had obtained an earlier oracle given to Corinth, but they had not understood it then; however, it hinted at much the same thing as the one given to Eetion, saying:

> An eagle is breeding among the rocks,[a] and it will sire a lion
> Strong and savage, the undoer of many whose knees will give way;
> So, you who dwell around lovely Peirene[b] and the height of Corinth,
> Consider this well.

"This oracle had at first baffled the Bacchiads,[a] but when they heard the one that Eetion had received, they saw how it harmonized with his and realized its meaning. They kept quiet about it, however, intending to destroy the child of Eetion which was about to be born. And so, as soon as Eetion's wife gave birth, they sent ten of their number to the deme in which Eetion lived in order to kill the child. [2] When they arrived at Petra, they entered the courtyard and asked for the child. Labda, knowing nothing of the real reason for their visit, supposed they had come out of friendliness toward the father, fetched the child, and handed him to one of the men. The men had agreed along the way that the first to hold the child was to cast him down on the ground. [3] But when Labda gave the child to one of the men, the child, by divine luck, smiled up at him, and the man felt constrained by a sort of pity from killing him. Moved by compassion, he gave the child to the second man, and then he to the third, and so on, until the infant had passed through the hands of all ten, and not one of them was willing to kill him. [4] And so they gave the child back to his mother and went outside, where they stood by the doors and assailed one another with reproaches, especially against the man who had held the child first, since he had not acted according to their decision. They berated one another until they finally decided to go inside again, and this time all of them were to participate in the murder.

5.92.γ
CORINTH
The speech of Sokleas continues: how the Bacchiads failed to kill the child of Eetion and Labda.

5.92.β.1c   Petra: location unknown.
5.92.β.1d   The Lapiths were thought to be a pre-Hellenic people of Thessaly, and the Caenids were the descendants of the fabled Lapith Caeneus, who took part in the battle against the Centaurs.
5.92.β.2a   Delphi: Map 5.97, BX.

5.92.β.3a   The Greek word for "eagle" is a pun on Eetion's name; the word for "rocks" is a pun on the name of his deme, Petra.
5.92.β.3b   Peirene: location unknown.
5.92.γ.1a   Mysterious oracles: see Appendix P, §9.

5.92.δ
CORINTH
The speech of Sokleas continues: the Bacchiads try again but fail to find the child.

"But it was fated that evils for Corinth would germinate from this offspring of Eetion. For Labda had been standing at those very doors listening and had heard everything they had said. Terrified that they would change their minds and that if they held the child again they would certainly kill him this time, she took the boy and hid him in what she thought was the place they would least expect—a chest—knowing that if they came back in to look for him, they would search everywhere, which indeed they did. [2] But after they had entered and searched, and could find no sign of the child, they decided to leave and to tell those who had sent them that they had carried out all their orders.

5.92.ε
CORINTH
The speech of Sokleas continues: Kypselos grows up and, spurred by an oracle, takes over the government of Corinth. He kills many, confiscates much wealth, and drives other Corinthians into exile. He rules from 655 to 625.

"After that, the son of Eetion grew and was given the name Kypselos in reference to the chest[a] in which he had escaped danger. When he reached adulthood, Kypselos received a two-edged oracular response at Delphi, which instilled confidence in him to make an attempt on Corinth and to take it. [2] The oracle ran as follows:

> Prosperous he will be, this man now entering my house,
> Kypselos son of Eetion, king of illustrious Corinth,
> He and his sons will prosper, but the sons of his sons, no longer.

"That was the oracular response, and it proved to be an accurate description of Kypselos, since he did in fact become tyrant. He banished many Corinthians, deprived many others of their possessions, but the greatest number by far were deprived of their lives.[a]

5.92.ζ
MILETUS-CORINTH
The speech of Sokleas continues: Kypselos dies and is succeeded by his son Periandros (625–587). How Thrasyboulos advised Periandros on the best way to rule at Corinth.

"After he had ruled for thirty years and had woven out the final strands of his life, his son Periandros succeeded to the tyranny. In the beginning, Periandros was certainly a more gentle ruler than his father, but after communicating with Thrasyboulos tyrant of Miletus[a] through messengers, he became far more bloodthirsty than Kypselos had ever been. [2] What happened was that he sent a herald to Thrasyboulos to ask advice about how he could best administer the city so as to make his rule as secure as possible. Thrasyboulos led the man who had come from Periandros outside the town and into a field planted with grain. While they walked together through the grain crop, Thrasyboulos kept questioning the herald about why he had come from Corinth, the reason for his arrival from Corinth, and all the while, whenever he saw one of the stalks extending above the others, he would cut it off and throw it away, until the finest and tallest of the grain had been destroyed. [3] Although they went through the entire field in this manner, he never offered a single word of advice, but sent the herald back. When the herald returned to Corinth, Periandros was eager to hear the advice he had requested, but the herald said that Thrasyboulos had given no advice at all, and that he was amazed that he had been sent to a man who was clearly not in his right mind and who

---

5.92.ε.1a　*Kypselos* means "chest" in Greek.
5.92.ε.2a　See Figure 5.92.
5.92.ζ.1a　Miletus: Map 5.97, BY.

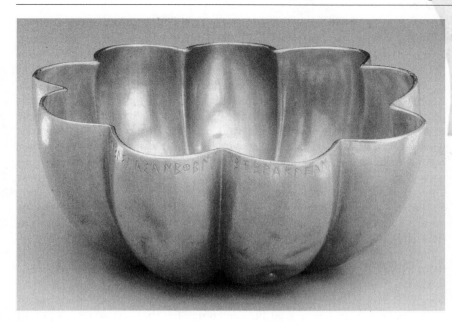

FIGURE 5.92. A GOLD DISH WITH AN INSCRIPTION ON ITS LIP WHICH IDENTIFIES IT AS AN OFFERING DEDICATED TO ZEUS AT OLYMPIA BY A DESCENDANT OF KYPSELOS. THE LETTERING DATES THE BOWL TO ABOUT 600.

[handwritten note: melissa: killed by Periandros.]

destroyed his own possessions; and then he reported everything that Thrasyboulos had done.

"Periandros understood the meaning of what Thrasyboulos had done and perceived that he was advising him to murder the prominent men of the city. It was then that he exhibited every kind of evil to the citizens. For Periandros completed all that Kypselos had left undone in his killing and banishing of the Corinthians. And on one day, he had all the Corinthian women stripped of their clothing, for the sake of his own wife, Melissa.[a] [2] He had sent messengers to the Thesprotians on the Acheron River[a] to consult the oracle of the dead there concerning a deposit of treasure belonging to a guest-friend. When Melissa appeared, she refused to tell him about it and said that she would not disclose where it was buried because she was cold and naked and could make no use of the clothes that had been buried with her since they had not been consumed by the fire. She said that the evidence for the truth of her claim was that Periandros had placed his loaves in a cold oven. [3] When her response was reported to Periandros, he found her token of its truth credible, for he had engaged in intercourse with Melissa's corpse. As soon as he heard the message, he made a proclamation announcing that all Corinthian women were to go to the sanctuary of Hera; and so they went there dressed in their finest clothes as though to attend a festival. Periandros had posted his bodyguards in ambush, and now he had

5.92.η
504
CORINTH
The speech of Sokleas concludes: he tells of the outrage the tyrant Periandros committed on the Corinthian women. He appeals to the Spartans not to establish tyrants in any cities.

[handwritten note: not highly developed super Ego. Primal desire.]

5.92.η.1a Melissa was killed by her husband, Periandros, perhaps accidentally; see also 3.50.

5.92.η.2a Acheron River, Thesprotia: Map 5.97, locator.

the women stripped, both the free women and the servants alike. Then he gathered their clothes together and, taking them to a pit in the ground, said a prayer to Melissa and burned all the clothes completely. [4] After doing that, he sent to consult Melissa a second time, and her ghost now told him the place where his guest-friend had deposited the treasure. This, then, Lacedaemonians, is what tyranny is like, and that is the sort of deeds it produces.[a] [5] And so we Corinthians were struck with wonder when we saw that you were sending for Hippias, and now we are even more amazed at what you are saying here. We call to witness the gods of the Hellenes: do not establish tyrannies in the cities! If you will not cease these efforts to bring back Hippias, which are contrary to what is right and just, then you must know that the Corinthians are not in agreement with you."

That was what Sokleas the ambassador from Corinth said, and Hippias replied to him by summoning the same gods and declaring that surely more than any others, the Corinthians would yearn for the presence of the Peisistratids when the days appointed for the Athenians to give *them* grief had arrived. [2] In this reply, Hippias was relying on his thorough and unrivaled knowledge of oracles. Now, although the rest of the allies had held their peace for a time, when they heard Sokleas speaking freely, every one of them spoke out and expressed his preference for the Corinthian's opinion and appealed to the Lacedaemonians not to impose such radical changes on a Greek city.

So that is how the restoration of Hippias was thwarted. Hippias was forced to leave Lacedaemon and on his way home was offered Anthemous[a] by Amyntas of Macedon, and Iolkos[b] by the Thessalians; but he accepted neither of these. Instead he returned to Sigeion,[c] which Peisistratos had seized by force from the Mytilenians,[d] and once he had secured control of it, he installed as tyrant over it his illegitimate son by an Argive[e] woman, Hegesistratos. But Hegesistratos could not hold on to what he had received from Peisistratos without fighting for it, [2] for the Mytilenians, demanding the return of their land, made incursions from the citadel of Achilleion[a] and waged a long war against the Athenians of Sigeion.[b] But the Athenians refused to acknowledge their claim, arguing that a share in the land of Ilium[c] belonged no more to the Aeolians[d] than to themselves or any other Hellenes who had joined Menelaos in avenging the abduction of Helen.[e]

Incidents of all kinds occurred in this war; for example, Alkaios the poet[a] fled and escaped during a battle against the Athenians, who were prevailing

5.93
504
SPARTA
Hippias speaks to the assembly, but most there side with the Corinthians.

5.94
504?
SIGEION
Hippias departs for Sigeion, where his half brother rules as tyrant.

5.95
SIGEION
The anecdote about the lost armor of the poet Alkaios. Periandros makes peace between the Athenians at Sigeion and the Mytilenians.

5.92.η.4a A powerful denunciation of tyranny. See Appendix T, §4.
5.94.1a Anthemous: Map 5.97, AX.
5.94.1b Iolkos, Thessaly: Map 5.97, AX.
5.94.1c Sigeion: Map 5.97, AY.
5.94.1d Mytilene, Lesbos: Map 5.97, AY.
5.94.1e Argos: Map 5.97, BX.
5.94.2a Achilleion: Map 5.97, AY. A fortification built around the grave of Achilles.
5.94.2b Herodotus, whose sixth-century chronology is often inaccurate, appears to be

wrong in assigning this war to the period of Peisistratos; its date cannot be later than 600. (Godley)
5.94.2c Ilium (Troy/Ilion): Map 5.97, AY.
5.94.2d Aeolis: Map 5.97, AY.
5.94.2e Note the use of Homer in establishing legitimacy to claims against others.
5.95.1a Alkaios: an aristocrat from Mytilene on Lesbos who wrote lyric poetry c. 620–600; the poem mentioned in 5.95.2 has survived (Fragment 401B, West).

in this battle, and the Athenians kept his weapons and hung them up in the sanctuary of Athena at Sigeion. [2] Alkaios then composed a lyric poem about this and sent it off to Mytilene to inform his friend Melanippos of his experience. The Mytilenians and the Athenians were finally reconciled by Periandros son of Kypselos, to whom they had entrusted the task of mediation. He reconciled them by ordering that each side would retain possession of the land that it then occupied. And so that is how Sigeion came to be controlled by the Athenians.

When Hippias returned to Asia[a] from Lacedaemon,[b] he missed no opportunity to slander the Athenians to Artaphrenes[c] and did all he could to bring about Athens' submission to himself and Darius. [2] The Athenians found out what Hippias was doing and sent messengers to Sardis[a] to dissuade the Persians from giving credence to exiles from Athens. But Artaphrenes ordered them to take Hippias back if they wished to remain secure. The Athenians, however, when his command was reported to them, refused to consent to it, and by this refusal their posture as enemies of the Persians became public.

It was just at this juncture, when they were feeling quite antagonistic toward the Persians, that Aristagoras of Miletus[a] arrived in Athens[b] after his expulsion from Sparta by Kleomenes of Lacedaemon.[c] For after Sparta, Athens was the next most powerful state. When Aristagoras appeared before the Athenian people, he repeated the same things that he had said in Sparta about the good things in Asia and about Persian warfare—that they used neither shields nor spears and how easy it would be to subdue them. [2] In addition, he told them that Miletus was originally an Athenian colony, and therefore, since the Athenians were a great power, it was only fair and reasonable for them to offer protection to the Milesians. There was nothing he failed to promise them, since he was now in dire need, and at last he managed to win them over. For it would seem to be easier to deceive and impose upon a whole throng of people than to do so to just one individual, since he had failed with Kleomenes of Lacedaemon, who was alone, but then succeeded with 30,000 Athenians.[a] [3] After the Athenians had been won over, they voted to dispatch twenty ships to help the Ionians[a] and appointed Melanthion, a man of the city who was distinguished in every respect, as commander over them. These ships turned out to be the beginning of evils for both Hellenes and barbarians.

Aristagoras sailed on ahead and arrived at Miletus before the others. He had devised a plan that would not result in a single benefit for the Ionians,

5.96
504?
SARDIS
Hippias seeks and receives support from the local Persian governor, who advises the Athenians to take him back.

5.97
500/499
ATHENS
Athens and Persia are already on bad terms when Aristagoras arrives. He persuades the Athenians to help Ionia.

5.98
?
PHRYGIA-CHIOS
To anger Darius, Aristagoras incites the Paionians to leave Phrygia and return home to Paionia.

5.96.1a   Asia: Map 5.97, locator.
5.96.1b   Lacedaemon (Sparta, Spartan territory):
          Map 5.97, BX. Herodotus uses the names
          Spartans and Lacedaemonians inter-
          changeably. "Spartans," however, often
          refers specifically to citizens of the state
          of Sparta, whereas any inhabitant of the
          territory of Lacedaemon is a Lacedae-
          monian. See Appendix B, §5, 7, and n.
          B.7a.
5.96.1c   Artaphrenes: half brother to King Darius,

          appointed by him to be governor of
          Sardis. See 5.25.1.
5.96.2a   Sardis: Map 5.97, BY.
5.97.1a   Miletus: Map 5.97, BY.
5.97.1b   Athens: Map 5.97, BX.
5.97.1c   For the expulsion of Aristagoras, see
          5.50–51.
5.97.2a   Scholars have wondered if this statement
          is a reliable indication of the number of
          Athenian citizens. See Appendix A.
5.97.3a   Ionia: Map 5.97, BY.

411

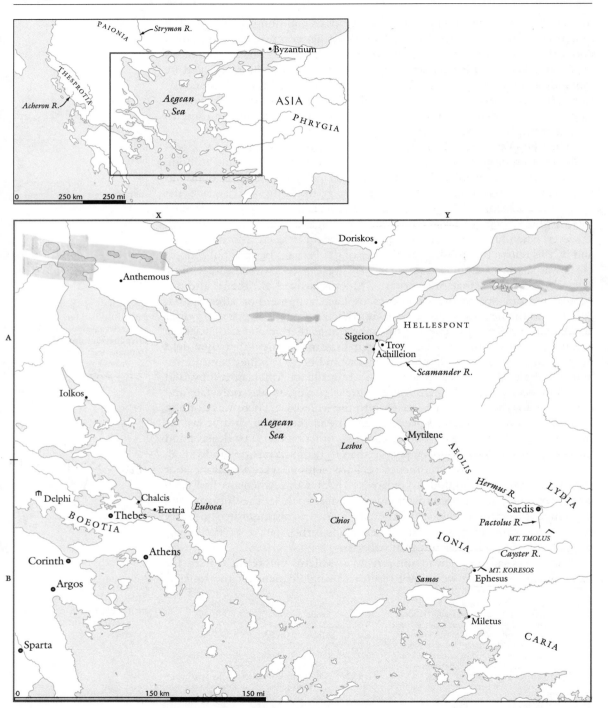

MAP 5.97

412

but after all, that was not his goal; his efforts were really aimed at disturbing Darius. He now sent a man to Phrygia,[a] to the Paionians whom Megabazos had captured as prisoners of war at the Strymon River[b] and who were at this time inhabiting a village by themselves in Phrygian territory. When the man arrived there, he announced to them, [2] "Paionians, Aristagoras tyrant of Miletus sent me to advise you about your deliverance, which you will achieve only if you are willing to obey. For now that all Ionia has revolted from the King, you have an opportunity to go back to your own land safe and sound. Your journey to the sea is your own responsibility, but after that we will take care of you." [3] The Paionians welcomed this advice enthusiastically and, after retrieving their women and children, began to hurry toward the sea, though some of them remained behind out of fear. When the Paionians who had departed arrived at the sea, they crossed over to Chios.[a] [4] A large cavalry force of Persians had pursued them closely, but now that the Paionians had reached Chios and the Persians had failed to overtake them, they sent an order to Chios demanding that the Paionians return. The Paionians refused to accept the order, and the Chians brought them to Lesbos,[a] whose people conveyed them to Doriskos,[b] from where they returned on foot to Paionia.[c]

The Athenians came to Miletus with their twenty ships and brought along with them five triremes of the Eretrians.[a] The Eretrians participated in this war not for the sake of the Athenians, but in order to repay a debt they owed to the Milesians, who had earlier helped the Eretrians wage war against Chalcis[b] at the very time when the Samians[c] had rushed to the aid of the Chalcidians. When the Athenians, the Eretrians, and the rest of the allies had arrived and were present in Miletus, Aristagoras organized an expedition against Sardis.[d] [2] He himself did not accompany the troops but stayed in Miletus; he appointed his own brother Charopinos and one of the other citizens, Hermophantos, to serve as generals over the Milesians.

With this army, the Ionians came first to Ephesus,[a] from where, after leaving their boats at Koresos,[b] they journeyed inland in massive force, with Ephesians as their guides. They traveled along the Cayster River,[c] crossed over Mount Tmolus,[d] and came to Sardis, where they captured the city without resistance from anyone whatsoever. They took control of everything there except for the acropolis. For Artaphrenes himself defended the acropolis with a rather large force of men.

5.99
MILETUS
Why Eretria joined the Ionians. Aristagoras organizes an expedition against Sardis.

5.100
498
EPHESUS-SARDIS
The Ionian army captures all of Sardis except the citadel.

5.98.1a Phrygia: Map 5.97, locator.
5.98.1b Strymon River: Map 5.97, locator. On these Paionians, see 5.15 and 5.23.1.
5.98.3a Chios: Map 5.97, BY.
5.98.4a Lesbos: Map 5.97, AY.
5.98.4b Doriskos: Map 5.97, AY.
5.98.4c Paionia: Map 5.97, locator.
5.99.1a Eretria, Euboea: Map 5.97, BX.
5.99.1b Chalcis, Euboea: Map 5.97, BX. These "alliances" took place during the Lelantine war, between the Euboean cities of Eretria and Chalcis over the agricultural

land of the Lelantine Plain. Its dates are uncertain, but it took place in the seventh century and was a long and costly struggle, involving a number of Greek states on one side or the other.
5.99.1c Samos: Map 5.97, BY.
5.99.1d Sardis: Map 5.97, BY.
5.100.1a Ephesus: Map 5.97, BY.
5.100.1b Mount Koresos: Map 5.97, BY.
5.100.1c Cayster River: Map 5.97, BY.
5.100.1d Mount Tmolus: Map 5.97, BY.

5.101
498
SARDIS
The Ionians burn the city of Sardis and retire.

Although they had taken the city, they were unable to plunder it because most of the houses in Sardis were constructed of reeds, and even those made of bricks had roofs made of reeds; and when a soldier set one of these houses on fire, the flames spread rapidly from house to house until they engulfed the entire city. [2] As the city burned, the Lydians[a] and all the Persians there were cut off from every direction, and as the fire consumed the outer edges of the town, they could find no way out. And so they fled together into the agora and to the Pactolus River,[b] the same river which brings gold dust to them from Mount Tmolus and flows through the center of the agora before emptying into the Hermus River,[c] which flows into the sea. So at the Pactolus River in the agora the Lydians and Persians crowded together and were compelled to act in their own defense. [3] When the Ionians saw some of them attempting to defend themselves and others in great numbers approaching as in an assault, they withdrew in fear to Mount Tmolus, and then, under the cover of night, left for their ships.

5.102
498
EPHESUS
A temple burned at Sardis is a pretext for later Persian destruction of Hellenic temples. The Persians rout the Ionians at Ephesus.

So Sardis had been burned, and in the fire a sanctuary of the local goddess Kybele[a] had also gone up in flames. The Persians later relied on this incident as their pretext for burning divine sanctuaries in Hellas. But when the Persians who dwelled in the districts west of the Halys River[b] heard about these events, they gathered together and rushed to the aid of the Lydians. [2] Discovering that the Ionians were not in Sardis any longer, they followed their tracks and caught up with them at Ephesus. The Ionians deployed their troops to oppose them, but in the battle that followed they suffered a severe defeat. [3] Many of them were slaughtered by the Persians, including several famous men, especially Eualkides, who was serving as general of the Eretrians and had won crowns in the games, for which he had received much praise from Simonides of Keos.[a] Those who escaped from the battle dispersed as each one fled to his own city.

5.103
498?
HELLESPONT-CARIA
The Ionians bring over to their side the cities of the Hellespont and Caria. The Athenians withdraw from the fight.

Thus ended that round of fighting. From then on, the Athenians completely abandoned the Ionians, and although Aristagoras sent many messengers with appeals to the Athenians, they refused to help the Ionians any further. But even deprived of the Athenian alliance, the Ionians nonetheless prepared for war against the King, since they had gone so deeply into the conflict already. [2] First they sailed to the Hellespont[a] and made Byzantium[b] and all the other cities there subject to themselves. Then, sailing out from the Hellespont, they secured the greater part of Caria[c] as their ally. For although Caunus[d] had previously refused to enter into an alliance with them, once Sardis had been burned, the Caunians now joined in their alliance.

5.101.2a Lydia: Map 5.97, BY.
5.101.2b Pactolus River: Map 5.97, BY. See Figure 5.101.
5.101.2c Hermus River: Map 5.97, BY.
5.102.1a Kybele (or Cybele) is the great "Mother of the Gods," goddess of the Phrygians and Lydians.
5.102.1b Halys River: Map 5.108.
5.102.3a Simonides of Keos (556–468), a famous fifth-century poet. Keos: Map 5.108. See Appendix Q, Herodotus and the Poets, §3, 5.
5.103.2a Hellespont: Map 5.97, AY; Map 5.108, Hellespont inset.
5.103.2b Byzantium: Map 5.97, locator; Map 5.108.
5.103.2c Caria: Map 5.97, BY; Map 5.108.
5.103.2d Caunus: Map 5.108.

FIGURE 5.101. A VIEW OF THE AGORA OF SARDIS, LOOKING ACROSS THE REMAINS OF THE TEMPLE OF ARTEMIS NORTH TOWARD THE ACROPOLIS FROM THE PACTOLUS RIVER.

All the Cyprians voluntarily joined them except for the Amathousians,[a] for the Cyprians, too, had revolted from the Mede,[b] and in the following way. The younger brother of Gorgos king of Salamis[c] was Onesilos son of Chersis, who was the son of Siromos son of Euelthon.[d] [2] Onesilos tried to persuade Gorgos to revolt from the King even before, and now when he learned that the Ionians had revolted, he exerted the utmost pressure on his brother to rebel. But once he saw that he was not succeeding, he watched for an occasion when Gorgos went outside the city of Salamis, and then Onesilos together with his partisans locked the gates and shut Gorgos out. [3] Thus deprived of his city, Gorgos fled to the Medes, while Onesilos took over the rule of Salamis and tried to persuade all the Cyprians to join him in revolt. He won over all but the Amathousians, who refused to comply with him, so he set up a blockade and laid siege to their city.

While Onesilos was besieging Amathous, word reached Darius that Sardis[a] had been burned by the Athenians[b] and Ionians[c] and that the man who led these combined forces and had designed its course of action was Aristagoras of Miletus.[d] It is said that when Darius first heard this report, he disregarded the Ionians, since he knew that they at least would not escape

5.104
497
CYPRUS
How the revolt against the Persians took place in Cyprus.

5.105
SUSA
Darius resolves to take revenge against the Athenians.

5.104.1a   Cyprus and Amathous: Map 5.108,
                Cyprus inset.
5.104.1b   "Mede" means "Persian" here.
                Hellenes used the terms interchangeably.
5.104.1c   Salamis: Map 5.108, Cyprus inset.

5.104.1d   On Euelthon, see 4.162.
5.105.1a   Sardis: Map 5.108.
5.105.1b   Athens: Map 5.108.
5.105.1c   Ionia: Map 5.108.
5.105.1d   Miletus: Map 5.108.

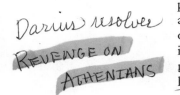

Darius resolves
REVENGE ON
ATHENIANS

5.106
SUSA-IONIA
Darius calls on Histiaios
to quell the rebellion, and
Histiaos promises to do so
if the King will send him
to Ionia.

5.107
497?
IONIA
The King sends
Histiaios to Ionia.

punishment for their revolt; but he inquired who the Athenians were, and after he had been told, he asked for a bow. He took the bow, set an arrow on its string, and shot the arrow toward the heavens. And as it flew high into the air, he said: [2] "Zeus, let it be granted to me to punish the Athenians." After saying this, he appointed one of his attendants to repeat to him three times whenever his dinner was served: "My lord, remember the Athenians."

After giving these orders, Darius summoned into his presence Histiaios of Miletus, whom he had been detaining by now for a long time, and said to him, "I hear, Histiaios, that the governor to whom you entrusted Miletus has fomented a revolution against me. He led men from the other continent to join the Ionians—who will pay their penalty to me for what they have done—and after persuading both the Ionians and the Athenians to follow him, he has now deprived me of Sardis. [2] Well, then, do these events seem good in any way to you? How could such an act have been committed without your counsel and advice? You had better watch that you do not have cause to blame yourself later." [3] "Sire," Histiaios replied, "what an allegation for you to assert! To think that I would plan or advise doing anything that could cause you great sorrow—or even the slightest pain. What could I want in addition to what I have that would lead me to do such a thing? Do I lack anything? I have everything, as much as you have, and besides, you deem me worthy to hear your deliberations and plans. [4] If my governor is acting as you have described, know that he bears the responsibility for it himself. But I actually do not believe the claim that the Milesians and my governor are involved in a revolt against your authority. If, however, what you have heard is true and they are revolting, then you, sire, should understand that you have caused the problem for me by wrenching me away from the coast. [5] For it is probably because of my absence that the Ionians are now doing what they have for a long time yearned to do. If I had been there in Ionia, not a single city would have made such a move. Therefore, permit me now to make the journey to Ionia immediately; once there, I shall restore everything to its former order and deliver into your hands the governor of Miletus, who has engineered this plot. [6] And after I have carried out your will, I swear by the gods—your royal gods[a]—that I shall not take off the tunic that I am wearing when I arrive in Ionia until I make Sardo,[b] the largest island of all, a tribute-paying subject of yours."

With this speech, Histiaios successfully misled the King, and Darius, convinced by his arguments, gave him leave to go, with the injunction to come back to his side in Susa[a] after he had fulfilled his promises.

5.106.6a   See also 3.65. In the inscription at
　　　　　Persepolis (Map 5.122, locator), Darius
　　　　　invokes Ormazd and the "gods of his
　　　　　race." (Godley)

5.106.6b   Sardinia (Sardo in Greek): Map 5.122,
　　　　　locator.
5.107.1a   Susa: Map 5.122, locator.

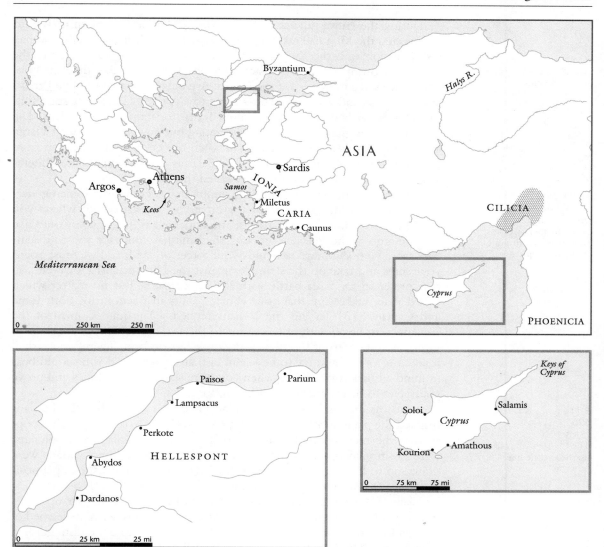

MAP 5.108

417

5.108
497
CYPRUS
A Persian sea and
land assault is launched
against Salamis.

5.109
496
CYPRUS
Given their choice, the
Ionians decide to fight
the Phoenicians at sea.

5.110
496
CYPRUS
The Cyprian kings draw
up their battle line.

5.111
CYPRUS
Onesilos and his attendant
decide how best to attack
Artybios and his vicious
horse.

During the entire time that the message about Sardis was on its way to Darius, and the King had taken up his bow as I related, and Histiaios had had his discussion with the King, had been released, and was journeying to the sea, the following events took place. Onesilos, while besieging the Amathousians,[a] received a message that the Persian Artybios was leading a huge Persian army on ships and was expected to come to Cyprus. [2] Upon hearing this, Onesilos dispatched heralds throughout Ionia[a] to summon the Ionians. The Ionians did not spend much time deliberating but quickly arrived with a large army. They had just arrived at Cyprus when the Persians crossed over from Cilicia[b] in their ships and proceeded to Salamis[c] on foot, while the Phoenicians[d] sailed around the promontory called the Keys of Cyprus.[e]

Meanwhile, the tyrants of Cyprus summoned together the Ionian generals and said: "Ionians, we Cyprians offer you the choice of whom you would prefer to face, the Persians or the Phoenicians. [2] If you would like to have a go at the Persians on land, the time has come for you to disembark from your ships and to deploy your forces on land, and we must board your ships and take up the struggle against the Phoenicians. However, you may prefer to try a sea battle with the Phoenicians. But no matter which you decide, make sure that your choice results in freedom for both Ionia and Cyprus." [3] To this the Ionians replied, "The joint council of the Ionians[a] sent us off with orders to guard the sea, not to deliver our ships to Cyprians and confront the Persians by ourselves on land. Therefore we shall follow our orders and try to be useful in that capacity, and you should bear in mind all that you suffered when you were slaves to the Medes and prove yourselves to be brave and valiant men."

That was the response of the Ionians; and afterward, when the Persians reached the plain of Salamis, the kings[a] of the Cyprians drew up their troops so that the men selected from the best of the Salaminians and Soloians[b] were positioned opposite the Persians, and the rest of the Cyprians were drawn up to face the rest of their army. Onesilos voluntarily took up a position opposite Artybios, general of the Persians.

Now Artybios was riding a horse that had been trained to rear up on its hind legs when directly in front of a hoplite; and Onesilos, when he learned of this, said to his shield bearer—a Carian[a] by race who was quite distinguished in warfare and daring in other respects as well—[2] "I hear that the horse of Artybios stands on its hind legs and with its hooves and its mouth destroys anyone in front of it. So think for a moment and then tell me which of the two do you want to watch for and strike, the horse or Artybios himself?" [3] The attendant answered, "Sire, I am ready and willing to do both or either, or anything else you order me to do, but allow me to tell you what I think

5.108.1a Amathous: Map 5.108, Cyprus inset.
5.108.2a Ionia: Map 5.108.
5.108.2b Cilicia: Map 5.108.
5.108.2c Salamis: Map 5.108, Cyprus inset.
5.108.2d Phoenicia: Map 5.108.
5.108.2e Keys of Cyprus (Kleides): Map 5.108,

Cyprus inset.
5.109.3a On this council of the Ionians, see 1.141ff.
5.110.1a Called "tyrants" in 5.109.1.
5.110.1b Soloi: Map 5.108, Cyprus inset.
5.111.1a Caria: Map 5.108.

would serve you better. [4] I say that a king and general ought to confront a king and general, since if you bring a general down, it will be a great achievement for you, and second, should he bring you down—perish the thought—then to die in this way would be only half a misfortune, for you would die thus at the hands of a worthy man. But we who serve under you ought to challenge other underlings and the horse. Do not fear that horse's skills, for I will take it upon myself to ensure that it will never rear up before anyone again."

Thus spoke the shield bearer, and just after that, the two sides engaged in battle on land and on sea. Now with their fleet, the Ionians proved themselves superior on this day and overcame the Phoenicians; and of the Ionians, the Samians[a] especially distinguished themselves. Meanwhile, the armies on land had met and were fighting each other. [2] As for the two generals, when Artybios rode up on his horse and approached, Onesilos struck him in accordance with the shield bearer's plan. And as the horse cast its hooves upon the shield of Onesilos, the Carian struck the horse with a scythe and cut off its forelegs. And so Artybios general of the Persians fell there, together with his horse.

While the rest of the troops continued to fight, Stesenor, the tyrant of Kourion,[a] turned traitor with a considerable force of men around him (these Kouriees are said to be colonists from Argos[b]), and as soon as they had deserted, the Salaminians' war chariots did the same; when this happened, the Persians gained the upper hand over the Cyprians. [2] The Cyprian army was thus routed, and among the many who fell were Onesilos son of Chersis, who had brought about the revolt, and Aristokypros son of Philokypros, king of Soloi, whom Solon of Athens,[a] when he came to Cyprus, praised above all other tyrants in his verses.

Because Onesilos had besieged the Amathousians, they cut off his head and took it to Amathous, where they hung it up over the city gates. The head eventually became hollow as it hung there, and then swarms of bees entered it and filled it with honeycombs. [2] This phenomenon led the Amathousians to consult an oracle, which advised them to take down the head, bury it, and sacrifice to Onesilos as a hero every year. If they did this, the oracle said, things would turn out better for them.

The Amathousians have carried out the oracle's command even up to my time. Now the Ionians in Cyprus who had been fighting at sea learned that Onesilos was dead and that all the Cyprian cities were now under siege except for Salamis, whose inhabitants had handed it back to its former king, Gorgos. As soon as the Ionians heard this news, they sailed back to Ionia. [2] Of all the Cyprian cities under siege, Soloi resisted for the longest period of time, until in the fifth month the Persians dug a tunnel beneath its outer wall and captured it.

5.112
496
CYPRUS
The battle is joined on land and sea.

5.113
496
CYPRUS
The Persians finally defeat the Cyprians on land.

5.114
496
CYPRUS
The fate of Onesilos.

5.115
496
CYPRUS-IONIA
Learning of the Persian victory on land, the Ionians sail off without delay.

5.112.1a   Samos: Map 5.122.
5.113.1a   Kourion: Map 5.108, Cyprus inset.
5.113.1b   Argos: Map 5.108.
5.113.2a   Solon of Athens: see 1.29–33.

Thus after one year of freedom, the Cyprians were reduced to slavery all over again. Now Daurises, whose wife was a daughter of Darius, along with Hymaees and Otanes (other Persian generals also married to daughters of Darius), pursued the Ionians who had attacked Sardis,[a] and when they found them, they drove them toward their ships and overcame them in battle. After they had done that, they divided the cities among themselves and laid waste to them.

Daurises then headed for the Hellespont,[a] where he captured Dardanos,[b] and then also Abydos, Perkote, Lampsacus, and Paisos,[c] one city each day. While proceeding from Paisos to the city of Parium,[d] he received a message that the Carians had joined the side of the Ionians and had revolted from the Persians. So turning back, he left the Hellespont and led his army to Caria.

But before Daurises arrived, the Carians somehow learned of his approach, and upon hearing the news, they gathered at what are called the White Pillars[a] at the Marsyas River,[b] which flows out of the territory of Idrias[c] and empties into the Maeander.[d] [2] Once the Carians were assembled there, many plans were considered, but the best, it seems to me, was that of Pixodaros son of Mausolos of Kindye,[a] who was married to the daughter of Syennesis, king of the Cilicians.[b] This man proposed that the Carians should cross the Maeander and join battle there, with the river at their backs, so that they would have no escape route behind them and they would be forced to stand their ground and prove themselves superior to their natural instincts. [3] But this opinion did not prevail; they decided that instead of themselves, it should be the Persians who would cross and would have the river at their backs during the fight, presuming that if the Perisans were defeated and tried to flee, they would be forced into the river to drown, and they would never return to their homes again.

And so the Persians came and crossed the Maeander, and the Carians joined battle with them on the banks of the Marsyas River, fighting fiercely and for a long time, but because they were outnumbered, they were defeated in the end. About 2,000 Persians fell there and 10,000 Carians. [2] Some Carians managed to escape and fled to Labraunda, where they were trapped in the sanctuary of Zeus Stratios,[a] a large sacred grove of plane trees; the Carians are indeed the only people we know of to conduct sacrifices to Zeus Stratios. When the Carians found themselves trapped there, they deliberated about how they could save themselves, whether they would fare better by surrendering to the Persians or by leaving Asia[b] altogether.

5.116.1a Sardis: Map 5.108.
5.117.1a Hellespont: Map 5.108, Hellespont inset.
5.117.1b Dardanos: Map 5.108, Hellespont inset.
5.117.1c Abydos, Perkote, Lampsacus, Paisos: Map 5.108, Hellespont inset.
5.117.1d Parium: Map 5.108, Hellespont inset.
5.118.1a White Pillars: location unknown.

5.118.1b Marsyas River: Map 5.122, BY.
5.118.1c Idrias: Map 5.122, BY.
5.118.1d Maeander River: Map 5.122, BY.
5.118.2a Kindye: Map 5.122, BY.
5.118.2b Cilicia: Map 5.122, locator.
5.119.2a Labraunda, sanctuary of Zeus Stratios (Zeus as god of war): Map 5.122, BY.
5.119.2b Asia: Map 5.122, locator.

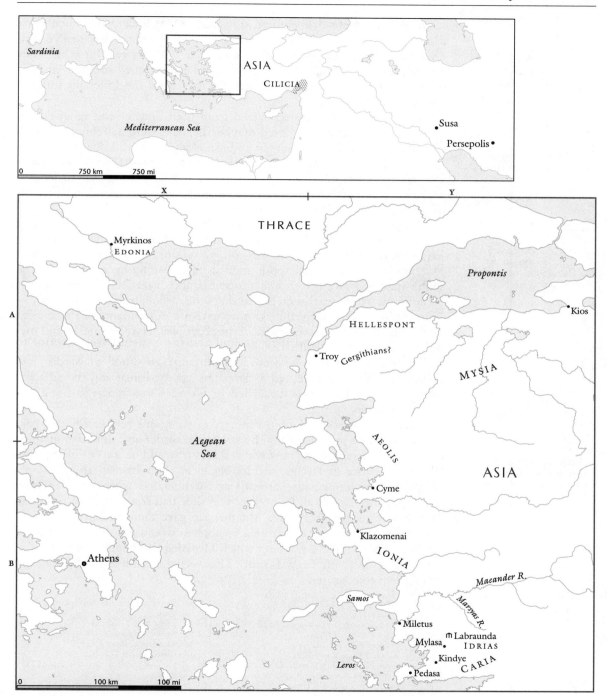

MAP 5.122

5.120
496–495
CARIA
Joined by the Milesians, the Carians fight again but are again badly defeated.

5.121
496–495
PEDASA
The Carians ambush the Persian army and destroy it.

5.122
497?
HELLESPONT-PROPONTIS
The Persians reconquer the Hellespont and Propontis regions.

5.123
497?
IONIA-AEOLIS
The Persians retake Klazomenai and Cyme.

5.124
497
MILETUS?
Aristagoras considers whether to flee to Sardinia or Myrkinos.

While they were deliberating, however, the Milesians[a] and their allies came to their assistance, so the Carians gave up the plans they had considered earlier and now prepared to wage war once more. But when they attacked and again joined battle with the Persians, they suffered an even worse defeat than before. Many men fell there, but the Milesians suffered the greatest losses of all.

Afterward, the Carians recovered from their disaster and renewed the struggle. For when they learned that the Persians were marching to attack their cities, they set themselves in ambush along the road in Pedasa,[a] and at night the Persians stumbled into their trap and perished—even the generals Daurises, Amorges, and Sisimakes were killed, and with them also Myrsos son of Gyges.[b] The ambush was led by Herakleides son of Ibanollis of Mylasa.[c] And so those Persians died.

Hymaees, also one of the Persian generals who had pursued the Ionians for their attack on Sardis, had advanced to the Propontis,[a] where he took Mysian Kios.[b] [2] But after he had conquered this territory, he learned that Daurises had left the Hellespont and was now leading his troops to Caria; so he marched away from the Propontis and brought his army to the Hellespont, where he conquered all the Aeolians inhabiting the territory of Ilium,[a] and also the Gergithians,[b] the surviving descendants of the ancient Teukrians. But after his conquest of these peoples, Hymaees fell ill and met his own end in the Troad.[c]

So now Hymaees was dead. Artaphrenes, governor of Sardis, and Otanes, the third general, led a campaign against Ionia[a] and the adjacent territory of Aeolis.[b] They succeeded in taking Klazomenai[c] in Ionia and Cyme[d] in Aeolis.

After these cities had been captured, Aristagoras revealed how weak-spirited he really was; for when he saw the disorder and upheaval in Ionia that he had stirred up, he now realized that it would be impossible for him to get the better of Darius, and he began to think instead about escape. [2] So he summoned his partisans and deliberated with them, advising them that they would all be better off if they had some place of refuge in case they were forced to leave Miletus. He gave them the choice that he would lead them either to Sardinia,[a] where he would found a colony, or to the city of Myrkinos in Edonia,[b] which Histiaios had begun to fortify after receiving it as a gift from Darius. This was the choice that Aristagoras asked them to consider.

5.120.1a Miletus: Map 5.122, BY.
5.121.1a Pedasa: Map 5.122, BY.
5.121.1b On Myrsos son of Gyges, see 3.122.
5.121.1c Mylasa: Map 5.122, BY.
5.122.1a Propontis: Map 5.122, AY.
5.122.1b Kios in Mysia: Map 5.122, AY.
5.122.2a Ilium (Troy/Ilion): Map 5.122, AY.
5.122.2b Gergithians, possible location of territory: Map 5.122, AY. These Gergithians are also mentioned at 7.43.2.

5.122.2c Troad: the territory in the vicinity of Troy.
5.123.1a Ionia: Map 5.122, BY.
5.123.1b Aeolis: Map 5.122, BY.
5.123.1c Klazomenai: Map 5.122, BY.
5.123.1d Cyme: Map 5.122, BY.
5.124.2a Sardinia (Sardo in Greek): Map 5.122, locator.
5.124.2b Myrkinos in Edonia: Map 5.122, AX.

Hekataios[a] the author, son of Hegesandros, proposed that they should not journey to either of these places, but rather that Aristagoras, if he were banished from Miletus, should fortify the island of Leros[b] but cause no trouble from there so that he might later return from Leros to Miletus.

That was the advice of Hekataios, but Aristagoras himself preferred the proposal that he should lead them to Myrkinos. After he had entrusted Miletus to Pythagoras, a distinguished citizen, he enlisted every man willing to accompany him and sailed with them to Thrace,[a] where he took possession of the site he had set out to obtain. [2] Using this as his base, he surrounded and laid siege to a Thracian city and, although the Thracians were willing to leave the place under a truce, it was here in the fighting that occurred that Aristagoras and his army perished at the hands of the Thracians.

5.125
497
MILETUS?
Hekataios urges Aristagoras to go to Leros.

5.126
497–496?
THRACE
Aristagoras departs for Myrkinos in Edonia but is killed there besieging another Thracian city.

5.125.1a Hekataios was the author of geographical and historical accounts of Asia Minor and the East who wrote in the late sixth century and was a source both used and criticized by Herodotus. He also plays a role in Herodotus' account of Ionian history. See 5.36, 5.125–126, 6.137, and Introduction, §3.1.
5.125.1b Leros: Map 5.122, BY.
5.126.1a Thrace: Map 5.122, AX.

BOOK SIX

Thus Aristagoras met his end after inciting Ionia to revolt. And now Histiaios, the tyrant of Miletus,[a] came to Sardis[b] following his release from Susa[c] by Darius. Upon his arrival, Artaphrenes, governor of Sardis, asked him what he thought had been the reason for the Ionians' revolt, and Histiaios not only denied knowledge of the reason, he even acted as though he was astonished at what had happened and was completely unaware of what was going on there. [2] But Artaphrenes, knowing the full details of the revolt, saw right through his cunning deceit and said, "Well, then, let me tell you how and why it happened, Histiaios: you stitched up the shoe, and Aristagoras put it on."

6.1
496–495?
SARDIS
Artaphrenes accuses Histiaios of having instigated the Ionian Revolt.

That is what Artaphrenes said about the revolt, and Histiaios, in fear because Artaphrenes knew and understood so much, ran away toward the coast as soon as night fell. He had thoroughly deceived Darius when he promised to conquer Sardinia,[a] the largest of all islands, and had instead attempted to insinuate himself into the leadership of the Ionians in a war against Darius. [2] Now he crossed over to Chios,[a] but there the Chians bound and confined him, suspecting that he had been sent by Darius to overturn their government. But when the Chians learned the whole story and knew that he was really hostile to the King, they released him.

6.2
496–495?
CHIOS
Histiaios flees to Chios.

Then the Ionians asked Histiaios why he had been so eager to command Aristagoras to revolt from the King and had caused so much trouble for the Ionians. He would not disclose the real reason to them at all, but said that he had acted because he had learned that King Darius had planned to uproot the Phoenicians[a] and settle them in Ionia[b] and to move the Ionians to Phoenicia. He told this to the Ionians in order to frighten them, for the King had never made such plans at all.

6.3
496–495?
CHIOS
Histiaios lies to the Ionians as to the intentions of Darius.

6.1.1a Miletus: Map 6.8. For comment on Histiaios' role in the revolt, see Appendix H, The Ionian Revolt, §10.
6.1.1b Sardis: Map 6.8.
6.1.1c Susa: Map 6.8, locator.

6.2.1a Sardinia (Sardo in Greek): Map 6.8, locator. See 5.106.6 and 1.170.2.
6.2.2a Chios: Map 6.8.
6.3.1a Phoenicia: Map 6.8, locator.
6.3.1b Ionia: Map 6.8.

6.4
496–495?
SARDIS
The messages he sends to Persian co-conspirators in Sardis are disclosed to Artaphrenes.

6.5
494?
LESBOS
Repulsed by the Milesians, Histiaios obtains ships from Lesbos and sails to Byzantium, where he seizes ships coming out from the Pontus.

6.6
494
MILETUS
The Persians concentrate their army and fleet against Miletus.

6.7
494
LADE
The Ionians decide to defend Miletus by fighting the Persian fleet at sea.

After this, Histiaios appointed Hermippos, a man from Atarneus,[a] as a messenger to deliver letters to Persians in Sardis with whom he had previously communicated about a revolt. But Hermippos did not give the letters to their intended recipients; instead, he brought them to Artaphrenes and placed them in his hands. [2] Once Artaphrenes became aware of all that was going on, he ordered Hermippos to deliver the letters from Histiaios to the designated Persians as he had been ordered, but to bring back their replies to Artaphrenes himself. And so when Artaphrenes eventually found out what was happening, he executed many Persians.

So trouble had now come to Sardis. And Histiaios, who was thus thwarted in his hopes, begged the Chians to restore him to his rule over Miletus, which they attempted to do. But the Milesians, who now had tasted liberty, were so happy to be rid of Aristagoras that they had no desire whatsoever to accept another tyrant into their land. [2] So Histiaios came back at night and tried to take Miletus by force, but he was driven away from his own city by force, and one of the Milesians even wounded him in the thigh. After that repulse, he went back to Chios, but because he could not persuade the Chians to give him ships, he crossed over from Chios to Mytilene[a] on Lesbos, where he succeeded in convincing the people of Lesbos to do so. [3] After he manned eight triremes, he took them to Byzantium,[a] where they lay in wait and seized the ships that were sailing out of the Pontus,[b] except for those whose crews asserted that they were willing to follow the commands of Histiaios.

While Histiaios and the Mytilenians were doing this, a large navy and army were expected to be approaching Miletus; for the generals of the Persians had concentrated their forces into one large army and were marching toward Miletus, regarding the rest of the cities as less important. Of the naval force, the Phoenicians were the most ardent for battle, and serving with them were the recently subjugated Cyprians,[a] as well as the Cilicians[b] and Egyptians.[c]

So they were going to wage war on Miletus and the rest of Ionia,[a] and when the Ionians learned of their plans, they sent representatives from their cities to meet at the Panionion.[b] After the representatives had arrived and deliberated there, they decided not to assemble a land army to oppose the Persians, but instead to have the Milesians defend their own walls and for the rest to assemble a naval force that would include every one of their ships, without exception. They agreed to concentrate this fleet as soon as possible at Lade,[c] a small island lying off the coast of Miletus, and to fight for Miletus from there.

6.4.1a   Atarneus: Map 6.8.
6.5.2a   Mytilene, Lesbos: Map 6.8.
6.5.3a   Byzantium: Map 6.8, locator.
6.5.3b   Pontus, the Euxine (Black) Sea: Map 6.8, locator. In 6.26.1, Herodotus says that Histiaios was seizing Ionian merchant ships, which were probably carrying grain from the Black Sea region.

6.6.1a   Cyprus: Map 6.8, locator. Recently subjugated: see 5.115–117.
6.6.1b   Cilicia: Map 6.8, locator.
6.6.1c   Egypt: Map 6.8, locator.
6.7.1a   Ionia: Map 6.8.
6.7.1b   Panionion: Map 6.8. On the Panionion, see 1.141–142 and 1.170.
6.7.1c   Lade: Map 6.8.

And so the Ionians came with their ships fully manned, and with them came the Aeolians[a] from Lesbos,[b] and they drew up their ships in the following formation. The Milesians themselves in 80 ships took a position on the eastern wing. Next to them in order were the 12 ships from Priene,[c] the 3 ships from Myous,[d] the 17 ships from Teos,[e] 100 ships from Chios,[f] [2] and beyond these were posted the 8 ships from Erythrai,[a] the 3 ships from Phocaea,[b] the 70 ships from Lesbos, and finally, on the western wing 60 from Samos.[c] The sum of all these together was 353 triremes.

These were the Ionian ships. The barbarian fleet numbered 600 ships. When it arrived at Miletus, where the Persian army was also stationed, and the Persian generals learned how large the Ionian fleet was, they became frightened that they would be unable to prevail over it, and that having thus failed to become masters of the sea, they would not be able to capture Miletus and would be subject to punishment by Darius. [2] In light of these considerations, they assembled the former tyrants of the Ionians who had been deposed from their offices by Aristagoras of Miletus and who had fled to the Medes. These former tyrants now happened to be accompanying the expedition against Miletus, and the Persian generals called all of them together and said, [3] "Ionians, now is the time for you to prove yourselves to be benefactors to the house of the King. We ask each of you to try to detach your former citizens from the rest of the allied Ionian force. Tell them that they will suffer no unpleasant consequence because of their revolt; that no harm will come to them, nor will their sacred or private property be set afire; and that they will experience no more force than they did previously. [4] But if they refuse to follow this advice and still prefer to engage us in battle despite our offer, then issue the following threat to them, which is exactly what will befall them: we shall lead them into captivity as slaves, and we shall turn their sons into eunuchs and drag their virgin daughters away to Baktria[a] and give over their land to others."

Thus spoke the Persian generals, and that very night the tyrants of the Ionians sent out, each to his own camp, this same proclamation. The Ionians who received this message maintained a stubborn disdain and refused to turn traitor, each group supposing that the Persians had sent this announcement to themselves alone. So that is what happened immediately after the arrival of the Persians at Miletus.[a]

After the Ionians had united their ships off Lade, they held assemblies at which I suppose other speakers addressed them, but one among them was certainly the Phocaean general Dionysios, who said, [2] "Our welfare, Ionians, now balances on a razor's edge, whether we shall be free men or

6.8
494
LADE
The number and battle order of the combined Greek fleet off Lade.

6.9
494
MILETUS
The Persians gather the former Ionian tyrants and instruct them to promise good treatment to their former subjects if they surrender, and cruel treatment if they persist in the rebellion.

6.10
494
MILETUS
The Ionians reject the Persian offer.

6.11
494
LADE
Dionysios, the Phocaean general, addresses the Greek fleet.

6.8.1a   Aeolis: Map 6.8.
6.8.1b   Lesbos: Map 6.8.
6.8.1c   Priene: Map 6.8.
6.8.1d   Myous: Map 6.8.
6.8.1e   Teos: Map 6.8.
6.8.1f   Chios: Map 6.8.
6.8.2a   Erythrai: Map 6.8.

6.8.2b   Phocaea: Map 6.8.
6.8.2c   Samos: Map 6.8.
6.9.4a   Baktria (Greek text says Bactra): Map 4.195, locator. In 4.204, the enslaved Barkaians were settled by Darius in Baktria.
6.10.1a   Miletus: Map 6.8.

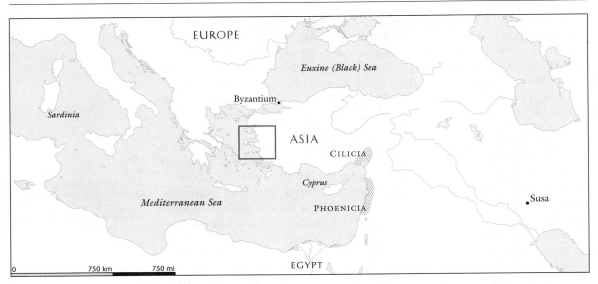

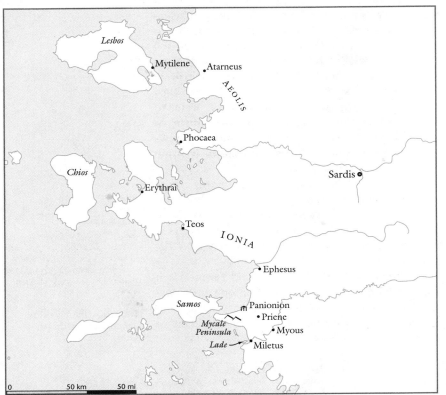

MAP 6.8

Ionians v. Persians: LADE
FREE MEN OR SLAVES?

slaves—runaway slaves, that is. So if you are willing to endure hardships in the present, you must set to work right now; only thus will you be able to prevail over your opponents and be free. On the other hand, if you remain feeble and undisciplined, I have every expectation that you will pay the penalty to the King for your revolt. [3] So obey and entrust yourselves to me, and I promise you that as long as the gods grant equal treatment to both sides, our enemies will either not join battle with us at all or, if they do, they will suffer a decisive defeat."

Upon hearing this speech, the Ionians committed themselves to Dionysios. And every time he led out their ships, he had them form up in column formation. And when he trained the rowers, he had them practice the breakthrough maneuver[a] of sailing through a line of the enemy's ships, and he armed the marines[b] who fought from the deck. Then for the remainder of the day he would keep the ships at anchor, but he gave the Ionians work to do all day long. [2] For seven days they followed him and obeyed his orders, but on the eighth, the Ionians, since they were unaccustomed to such hard labor and were worn out by both their exertions and the sun, spoke to one another as follows: [3] "What divine power have we offended, that we must suffer in this way? We have lost our wits and have sailed away from our senses in committing ourselves to this Phocaean braggart. He provides only three ships, and yet we entrust ourselves to his command! And after he enlisted us, he has insulted and injured us so severely that we will never recover; many of us have fallen ill, and many more are likely to do so as well. We would be better off suffering anything rather than these evils; even to endure future slavery, whatever that may be like, would be better than to continue as we are at present. Come on, then, let's not follow his orders any longer." [4] And as soon as they had spoken to this effect, no one would obey Dionysios any longer, and, as though they were an army, they pitched tents on the island and remained in their shade, refusing to board the ships or to practice their maneuvers.

The Samian[a] generals had just learned of what the Ionians were doing when Aiakes son of Syloson, from whom they had previously received messages by order of the Persians, sent word to them again, asking them to abandon the alliance of the Ionians. Having observed the Ionians' extreme lack of discipline, the Samians now became receptive to his request. Besides, they clearly recognized that it would be impossible for them to prevail over the King's power, since even if they were to defeat the fleet that now opposed them, they knew that they would certainly have to face another one five times as large. [2] So as soon as they saw the Ionians shirking their duties, they found this to be a good excuse to desert their cause, and

6.12
494
LADE
Dionysios drills the fleet with long and arduous exercises. After seven days, the Ionians complain and refuse to obey him further.

6.13
494
SAMOS
Learning of the Ionian insubordination, the Samians decide to accept the Persian offer transmitted to them via their former tyrant, Aiakes.

6.12.1a In the breakthrough maneuver—in Greek, *diekplous* ("sailing out through")—ships rowed through a line of enemy ships, then turned back to ram their sterns or sides. See *Thucydides* 2.83, 2.89. See also Appendix S, Trireme Warfare in Herodotus, §13, n. S13a.

6.12.1b Marines: a trireme usually carried a contingent of soldiers on board who were armed as hoplites or archers but trained to fight from a moving and tilting deck. They could board enemy ships or repel enemy marines who tried to board theirs. See Appendix S, §3–7.

6.13.1a Samos: Map 6.8.

431

regarded that step as advantageous to themselves for preserving their own sacred and private property. It was this Aiakes, who was the son of Syloson son of Aiakes, from whom they had received the message. He had once been tyrant of Samos, but Aristagoras of Miletus had deprived him of his office, just as he had removed the other Ionian tyrants.[a]

Now when the Phoenicians[a] sailed against them, the Ionians took their ships out to sea to oppose them in a column formation. The two sides closed and joined battle, but I am unable to record precisely which Ionians proved themselves to be cowards or brave and valiant men in this encounter, for now they all reproach one another. [2] It is said that just as the battle began, the Samians, in accord with their agreement with Aiakes, raised their sails, abandoned their posts in the line, and sailed away to Samos—all of them, that is, except for eleven ships whose trierarchs[a] refused to listen to their generals and remained to fight in the sea battle. [3] And because of what these eleven did, the Samian government awarded them a pillar inscribed with their full names and patronymics[a] proclaiming that they had proved themselves to be brave and valiant men. This pillar still stands in the agora of Samos. The Lesbians[b] saw the men beside them turning to flee and did the same, and indeed, so did the majority of the Ionians.

Of those who stayed to fight at sea, the Chians[a] received the roughest treatment, as they performed brilliant feats and refused to behave like cowards. They had provided 100 ships, as I mentioned earlier, and on each trireme they had stationed forty men selected from their citizenry to fight as marines.[b] [2] When they saw that most of the allies were betraying the alliance, they did not think it right to act like such cowards, so instead, although left alone with just a few allies, they proceeded to fight by performing the breakthrough maneuver until they had taken many of their enemies' ships but had lost most of their own. Finally, the Chians fled back to their own land in the ships that were left intact.[a]

Those Chians who were aboard the ships that had been damaged and rendered useless were pursued but managed to flee to Mycale[a] for refuge. There they beached and left their ships and set out to travel through the mainland on foot. [2] But when these Chians entered the territory of Ephesus,[a] they happened to arrive on the same night as the women's Thesmophoria.[b] The Ephesians had not received any advance word about the Chians' situation, but now when they saw that an army had already entered their territory, they

---

As the battle begins, the Samians flee, and seeing this, the Lesbians do the same, and many Ionians follow.

Although abandoned by most of their allies, the Chians decide to fight and bravely take many enemy ships while losing most of their own. The survivors flee back to Chios in the ships that remained intact.

Thinking the crews of the disabled Chian ships are pirates when they enter Ephesian territory by night, the Ephesians attack and kill them.

6.13.2a   For Aristagoras' removal of the Ionian tyrants, see 5.37.
6.14.1a   Phoenicia: Map 6.8, locator.
6.14.2a   Trierarch: a commander of a trireme.
6.14.3a   A patronymic is a name derived from one's father, for example, Aiakes son of Syloson. This statement illustrates Herodotus' intimate knowledge of Samos. See also 3.60.
6.14.3b   Lesbos: Map 6.8.
6.15.1a   Chios: Map 6.8.
6.15.1b   Marines: see n. 6.12.1b. Forty marines is a much larger complement than is typical

for Greek triremes. See Appendix S, §7.
6.15.2a   See Figures 8.10 and S.5a–c, photographs and drawings of triremes.
6.16.1a   Mycale (mountain, peninsula, and district): Map 6.8.
6.16.2a   Ephesus: Map 6.8.
6.16.2b   Thesmophoria: a women's ritual honoring Demeter. These rites, some taking place at night, were conducted outside the city's walls, and excluded men. See 2.171.2 and 6.138. See also Appendix U, On Women and Marriage in Herodotus, §7.

suspected that these men were going to pursue and steal their women. So they marched out in full force and proceeded to kill the Chians.

When Dionysios of Phocaea[a] realized that the cause of the Ionians was now completely lost, he seized three of the enemies' ships and sailed off, but not to Phocaea, because he knew that it would soon be enslaved with the rest of Ionia. Instead he sailed, just as he was, straight for Phoenicia. There, after he had sunk some merchant ships and amassed a large sum of money, he sailed to Sicily[b] and established himself as a pirate, though he did not sail against any of the Hellenes, only against Carthaginians[c] and Tyrrhenians.[d]

When the Persians had won the naval battle against the Ionians, they besieged Miletus[a] by land and sea, dug beneath the walls, and used every kind of siege engine against it. In the sixth year after the revolt of Aristagoras, they conquered the city completely and enslaved its people. This disaster confirmed an oracle that had come to Miletus earlier.

Once when the Argives[a] were consulting the Delphic oracle[b] concerning the survival of their own city, they received an unusual double oracle which was not only directed toward the Argives themselves but which also had an appendix adding advice regarding the Milesians. [2] I shall mention that part of the oracle bearing on the Argives when I come to that episode in my history,[a] but what the oracle advised the Milesians, even though they were not present, was as follows:

> The time will come, Milesians, devisers of evil deeds,
> When many will feast on you: a splendid gift for them;
> Your wives will wash the feet of many long-haired men,
> And others will assume the care of my own temple at Didyma.[b]

[3] That is just what happened now to the Milesians, when the majority of their men were killed by the long-haired Persians and their women and children became their captive slaves.[a] And at the sanctuary of Didyma, both the temple and the oracle were plundered and set on fire. I have often mentioned the wealth of this sanctuary elsewhere in my history.[b]

The Milesians who had been captured alive were taken to Susa.[a] King Darius inflicted no further harm on them, but settled them on the sea called the Erythraean[b] in the city of Ampe[c] past which the Tigris River[d] flows and empties into the sea. Of Milesian territory the Persians kept the regions

6.17
494
PHOENICIA-SICILY
Dionysios of Phocaea becomes a pirate, sails to Phoenicia and Sicily to rob non-Greeks.

6.18
494
MILETUS
The Persians besiege and capture Miletus.

6.19
ARGOS-DELPHI
Herodotus quotes a Delphic oracle which had predicted doom for Miletus and which has now come true.

6.20
494–?
MILETUS–PERSIAN GULF
The fate of the captive Milesians at Susa and of the Milesian lands.

6.17.1a Phocaea: Map 6.8.
6.17.1b Sicily: Map 6.20 and locator.
6.17.1c Carthage: Map 6.20, locator.
6.17.1d Tyrrhenia (Etruria): Map 6.20, locator.
6.18.1a Miletus: Map 6.20.
6.19.1a Argos: Map 6.20.
6.19.1b Delphi: Map 6.20.
6.19.2a The other half of this double oracle can be found at 6.77.2.
6.19.2b Didyma (Branchidai): Map 6.20. Located near Miletus, the temple, like Delphi, was dedicated to Apollo. Compare with 1.46.2, 1.92.2.

6.19.3a On conquered women and children enslaved as booty, see Appendix U, §4.
6.19.3b Herodotus refers here to 1.92.2 and 5.36.3.
6.20.1a Susa: Map 6.20, locator.
6.20.1b Erythraean Sea (not the modern Red Sea in this instance, but the Persian Gulf): Map 6.20, locator.
6.20.1c Ampe: precise location unknown.
6.20.1d Tigris River: Map 6.20, locator. Today the Tigris and Euphrates (Map 6.20, locator) join to form the Shatt al Arab Channel before entering the Persian Gulf (Erythraean Sea).

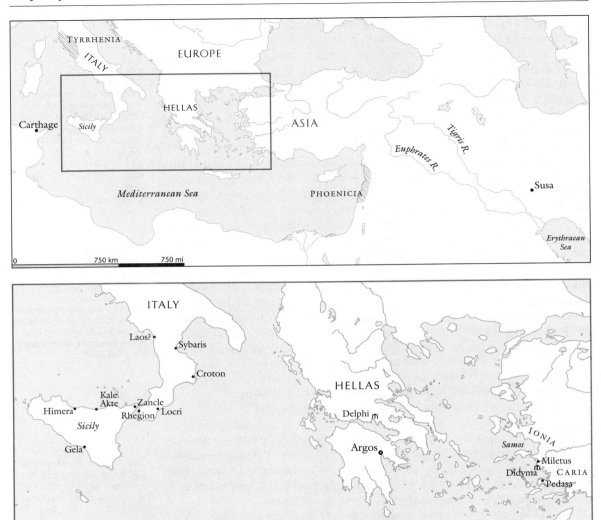

MAP 6.20

around the city and the plain for themselves,[e] but gave the hill country to the Carians[f] of Pedasa.[g]

Now the people of Sybaris[a] did not respond to what the Milesians suffered at the hands of the Persians with an intensity that in any way equaled the Milesian reaction to the disaster inflicted upon the Sybarites when they, too, were deprived of their city and had to live in Laos[b] and Skidros.[c] For after the capture of Sybaris by Croton,[d] all the Milesians, from the youth on upward, cut off their hair and imposed upon themselves a period of mourning. In fact, of all cities known to us, these two had the closest ties of friendship with each other. [2] The Athenians reacted differently than the Sybarites, for the Athenians clearly expressed their profound grief over the capture of Miletus in many ways, but one in particular deserves mention: when Phrynikos[a] composed his play on the capture of Miletus and produced it on stage, the audience burst into tears, fined him 1,000 drachmas for reminding them of their own evils, and ordered that no one should ever perform this play again.

So now there were no Milesians in Miletus.[a] The property owners of Samos[b] were very displeased at how their generals had dealt with the Medes, and immediately after the naval battle they deliberated and decided that before the tyrant Aiakes returned to their land, they would sail away to settle a colony rather than remain and become slaves of Aiakes and the Medes. [2] For during this time, the people of Zancle[a] were sending messengers from Sicily[b] to Ionia[c] and inviting the Ionians to found a city at a site called Fair Point.[d] This site lay in the territory of the Sicels in the part of Sicily that faces Tyrrhenia.[e] Of the Ionians who had been invited here, only the Samians and the Milesian fugitives set out on the journey.

But on their way to Sicily, the Samians reached the Epizephyrian Locrians[a] just at the time when the Zanclaeans and their king, whose name was Skythes, were surrounding and besieging a city of the Sicels, intending to destroy it. [2] The tyrant of Rhegion,[a] Anaxilaos, was hostile to the Zanclaeans at this time, and when he learned of the presence of the Samians, he established communications with them and tried to persuade them to forget about Fair Point, to which they had been sailing, and to take possession

6.20.1e   The one instance in which Herodotus mentions Persians taking for themselves what had been Greek properties. See Appendix H, §8.
6.20.1f   Caria: Map 6.20.
6.20.1g   Pedasa: Map 6.20. The map shows the most important site of that name, but Herodotus probably refers here to another place with the same name close to Miletus.
6.21.1a   Sybaris, Italy: Map 6.20.
6.21.1b   Laos, Italy, possible location: Map 6.20.
6.21.1c   Skidros: location unknown.
6.21.1d   Croton, Italy: Map 6.20. Croton is supposed to have destroyed Sybaris in 510.
6.21.2a   Phrynikos: Athenian tragedian of the late

sixth and early fifth centuries, a rival of Aeschylus.
6.22.1a   Miletus: Map 6.20.
6.22.1b   Samos: Map 6.20.
6.22.2a   Zancle, the later Messana (modern Messina), Sicily: Map 6.20.
6.22.2b   Sicily: Map 6.20.
6.22.2c   Ionia: Map 6.20.
6.22.2d   Fair Point (in Greek, Kale Akte), Sicily: Map 6.20, on the north coast of Sicily.
6.22.2e   Tyrrhenia (Etruria): Map 6.20, locator.
6.23.1a   Epizephyrian Locri, Italy: Map 6.20. The epithet "Epizephyrian" distinguishes the Italian Locrians from the Opuntian and Ozolian Locrians of Hellas. See Map 9.93.
6.23.2a   Rhegion, Italy: Map 6.20.

of Zancle instead, since it was now empty of men. [3] The Samians consented to this and did seize Zancle, but when the Zanclaeans learned that their city was being occupied, they hastily returned to defend it and called on their ally Hippocrates, the tyrant of Gela,[a] to assist them. [4] When Hippocrates arrived with his army, he placed Skythes the monarch in shackles, on the grounds that he had thrown away his city, and he did the same to Skythes' brother Pythogenes and sent them both off to the city of Inyx.[a] He betrayed the rest of the Zanclaeans by negotiating with the Samians and exchanging oaths with them, [5] and they agreed to the price he demanded: Hippocrates was to have all the moveable property in the city, plus half of the captive slaves in the city, and all of those in the rural districts. [6] He kept most of the Zanclaeans himself and had them bound and confined as slaves, but gave 300 of the leading men to the Samians so that they could cut their throats. The Samians, however, did not do so.

Scythes, the monarch of the Zanclaeans, escaped from Inyx and fled to Himera;[a] from there, he went to Asia[b] and then inland to King Darius. And Darius became convinced that he was the most righteous of all the Hellenes who had ever come to him. [2] For after the King granted his request and he returned to Sicily, he left Sicily once again and came back to the King, with whom he stayed until he ended his life in old age and great prosperity. And so that is how the Samians escaped from the Medes and acquired the most beautiful city with no effort at all.

After the sea battle over Miletus, the Phoenicians, at the orders of the Persians, restored Aiakes son of Syloson to Samos, for they felt that what he had accomplished was much to their advantage and was worth a great deal to them. [2] As for the Samians, they were the only ones involved in the revolt against Darius whose city and sanctuaries were not set on fire, because their ships had deserted during the naval battle. Immediately following the capture of Miletus, the Persians took possession of Caria,[a] and while some of the cities there submitted voluntarily to them, others resisted and were taken by force.

So that is the account of those events. Now, when all that had happened to Miletus was reported to Histiaios of Miletus, who was at that time in Byzantium,[a] seizing Ionian merchant ships that were sailing out of the Pontus,[b] he entrusted his affairs in the Hellespont[c] to Bisaltes son of Apollophanes of Abydos[d] and sailed to Chios[e] with his troops from Lesbos.[f] And when a body of Chian guards refused to admit him, he gave battle at the site in Chian territory called the Hollows.[g] [2] Then, using Polichna[a] in Chian territory as his base, he and his troops from Lesbos slaughtered many Chians and overcame those that were left, since they had suffered greatly in the sea battle.

6.23.3a Gela, Sicily: Map 6.20.
6.23.4a Inyx: location unknown.
6.24.1a Himera: Map 6.20.
6.24.1b Asia: Map 6.20, locator.
6.25.2a Caria: Map 6.20.
6.26.1a Byzantium: Map 6.30, AY.
6.26.1b Pontus, the Euxine (Black) Sea: Map 6.30, AY.

6.26.1c Hellespont region: Map 6.30, AX.
6.26.1d Abydos: Map 6.30, AX.
6.26.1e Chios: Map 6.30, BX.
6.26.1f Lesbos: Map 6.30, BX. Histiaios had convinced the Lesbians to support him; see 6.5.2.
6.26.1g Hollows of Chios: location unknown.
6.26.2a Polichna: Map 6.30, BX.

It often happens that signs are given whenever great evils are about to fall upon a city or nation. And in fact remarkable signs had appeared to the Chians before these events occurred. [2] First, they had sent a chorus of 100 youths to Delphi, and only two of them returned home; the other ninety-eight were struck down and carried off by plague. Secondly and simultaneously, just a short time before the naval battle, a roof in the city collapsed on a group of boys as they were learning their letters, with the result that out of 120 children, only one escaped with his life. [3] Those were the signs sent by the god in advance. Then the naval battle overcame the city and brought it to its knees, and in addition to that, after the naval battle, Histiaios came leading his Lesbian troops, and as the Chians had recently been badly mauled, he vanquished them quite easily.

From there, Histiaios moved against Thasos[a] with a large force of Ionians[b] and Aeolians.[c] But as he was besieging Thasos, word reached him that the Phoenicians[d] were sailing out from Miletus[e] and were heading for the rest of Ionia, so he left Thasos unconquered and hurried to Lesbos, taking his entire army there with him. [2] But because his army was suffering from hunger, he crossed over from Lesbos to Atarneus[a] to reap the harvest of grain there and from the plain of the Caicus River[b] in the territory of the Mysians.[c] Harpagos, a Persian general commanding a considerable army, happened to be in this region at the time, and after Histiaios disembarked, Harpagos launched an attack and, in the battle that followed, captured Histiaios alive and destroyed most of his army.

This is how Histiaios was taken alive. The Hellenes were fighting the Persians at Malene[a] in the territory of Atarneus; and they stood their ground for a long time, until the cavalry charged and overwhelmed them. This feat of the cavalry was decisive, and now that the Hellenes had been routed, Histiaios, expecting that his present transgression would not lead to his execution at the hands of the King succumbed to such a cowardly desire to survive that [2] he fled for his life. But then, when he was overtaken by a Persian and just about to be stabbed, he blurted out some words in Persian and informed his assailant that he was Histiaios of Miletus.

Now if, after being captured alive, Histiaios had been taken to King Darius, I suppose that Darius would have forgiven him for his offense and that he would have suffered no harm. But Artaphrenes, the governor of Sardis, and Harpagos, the general who had captured him, also thought this was likely to happen; and in order to prevent Histiaios from escaping and again attaining prominence with the King, they took him to Sardis and there hanged him from a stake. But they embalmed his head and brought it to King Darius in Susa.[a] [2] When Darius learned what had happened, he rep-

6.27
494?
CHIOS
Herodotus describes disasters that happened to the Chians before their defeat that should have warned them that a god was angry at them.

6.28
494?
MYSIA
Seeking grain for his troops, Histiaios lands at Mysia, where he is attacked by Harpagos, defeated, and captured.

6.29
494?
ATARNEUS
Where and how the battle was fought. How Histiaios permitted himself to be taken alive.

6.30
494?
SARDIS
Histiaios is immediately executed by Harpagos at Sardis.

6.28.1a Thasos: Map 6.30, AX.
6.28.1b Ionia: Map 6.30, BX.
6.28.1c Aeolis: Map 6.30, BX.
6.28.1d Phoenicia: Map 6.20, locator. The Phoenician ships were the strongest contingent of the Persian fleet.
6.28.1e Miletus: Map 6.30, BX.
6.28.2a Atarneus: Map 6.30, BX.
6.28.2b Caicus River: Map 6.30, BY.
6.28.2c Mysia: Map 6.30, BY.
6.29.1a Malene: Map 6.30, BX.
6.30.1a Susa: Map 6.20, locator.

rimanded them for having done that rather than bringing Histiaios into his presence alive; he ordered them to wash the head, to wrap it up tightly, and to bury it, since Histiaios had been a great benefactor to himself and to the Persians. So that is what happened to Histiaios.

6.31
494/93
CHIOS-LESBOS-TENEDOS
The Persian fleet winters at Miletus but the next year captures Chios, Lesbos, and Tenedos.

After wintering in the vicinity of Miletus, the Persian fleet sailed off the next year and with little effort took control of the islands close to the mainland—Chios,[a] Lesbos,[b] and Tenedos.[c] Whenever they conquered one of the islands, the barbarians would net its people,[d] [2] which means that each man takes hold of another man's hand until they form a line stretching from the sea on the north to the sea on the south, and they then go through the entire island hunting out the people. The cities on the Ionian mainland were likewise taken, except that the people there were not netted, since that was impossible.

6.32
493
IONIA
The Persian generals capture the Greek cities and carry out their earlier threats.

At this point the Persians made good on the threats that they had voiced earlier against the Ionians when they were camped opposite them.[a] For after they had completed their conquest of the cities, they picked out the most handsome boys and castrated them, making them eunuchs instead of males with testicles. And they dragged off the most beautiful of the virgins to the King. After they had carried out these threats, they also set fire to the cities and to their sanctuaries, too. Thus the Ionians were reduced to slavery for the third time, the first being at the hands of the Lydians, and then twice in succession by the Persians.

[handwritten marginal note: 3RD TIME IONIANS ARE ENSLAVED]

6.33
493
HELLESPONT-THRACE-PROPONTIS
The Persian fleet conquers more cities in the Hellespont region in Thrace and the Propontis.

The Phoenician fleet now left Ionia and sailed up the Hellespont, capturing everything along the left bank, for the Persians had already subjugated by land everything on the right bank. The Hellespont on the European side consists of the Chersonese,[a] in which there are numerous cities: Perinthus,[b] the fortifications on the coast of Thrace,[c] Selymbria,[d] and Byzantium.[e] [2] Now the Byzantians and the Chalcedonians,[a] who live beyond the Byzantians, did not wait for the Phoenicians to sail against them but left their land behind and went in along the shores of the Euxine Sea,[b] where they settled down in Mesembria.[c] After the Phoenicians had burned down the places mentioned earlier, they turned to Proconnesus[d] and Artace,[e] which they also consigned to flames before sailing back to the Chersonese again in order to destroy the remaining cities that they had landed at but not ravaged earlier. [3] Against Cyzicus,[a] however, they did not sail at all, because before the Phoenicians sailed in, the people of Cyzicus had become subjects of the King, after having come to an agreement with Oibares son of Megabazos, the governor in Daskyleion.[b] But the Phoenicians did subdue all the other cities of the Chersonese except for the city of Kardia.[c]

6.31.1a Chios: Map 6.30, BX.
6.31.1b Lesbos: Map 6.30, BX.
6.31.1c Tenedos: Map 6.30, BX.
6.31.1d Net the inhabitants: as at Samos in 3.149
         and n. 3.149.1a.
6.32.1a For these threats, see 6.9.4.
6.33.1a Chersonese, Hellespont: Map 6.30, AX.
         The name means "peninsula."
6.33.1b Perinthus: Map 6.30, AY.
6.33.1c Thrace: Map 6.30, AX.

6.33.1d Selymbria: Map 6.30, AY.
6.33.1e Byzantium: Map 6.30, AY.
6.33.2a Chalcedon: Map 6.30, AY.
6.33.2b Euxine (Black) Sea: Map 6.30, AY.
6.33.2c Mesembria: Map 6.30, AY.
6.33.2d Proconnesus: Map 6.30, AY.
6.33.2e Artace (the port of Cyzicus): Map 6.30, AY.
6.33.3a Cyzicus: Map 6.30, AY.
6.33.3b Daskyleion: Map 6.30, AY.
6.33.3c Kardia: Map 6.30, AX.

EUROPE

ASIA

0   750 km   750 mi

X   Y

Mesembria

Euxine (Black) Sea

THRACE

A

Mesambria   Selymbria   Byzantium
                              Perinthus   Chalcedon
Thasos   APSINTHIS
                          Proconnesus
              Kardia Paktye
Chersonese   Artace
          Lampsacus   Cyzicus
          HELLESPONT
          Abydos   Daskyleion

Tenedos   MYSIA

                    Malene   Caicus R.
Lesbos   Atarneus

                          AEOLIS

B
Chios   Polichna   Sardis

          IONIA

                    Miletus

                    CARIA

MAP 6.30

0   100 km   100 mi

At this time, the cities in the Chersonese were ruled by the tyrant Miltiades son of Kimon son of Stesagoras. Miltiades son of Kypselos[a] had earlier acquired this office in the following way. The Thracian Dolonci were then in possession of the Chersonese, and because the Apsinthians[b] were pressuring them with war, they sent their kings to Delphi[c] to consult the oracle about the war. [2] The Pythia[a] told them that after they left the sanctuary, the first man they met on their journey home who offered them hospitality should be invited by them to come to their land as leader of their settlement. So the Dolonci left and traveled down the Sacred Way[b] through Phocis[c] and Boeotia,[d] but since they received no invitation from anyone, they turned off the road toward Athens.[e]

This occurred during the period when Peisistratos had complete political control over Athens. Miltiades son of Kypselos, however, did command a degree of influence and prestige there; his household was wealthy enough to race four-horse chariots, and he was descended from Aiakos and Aegina, but he was Athenian by a more recent ancestor—Philaios son of Ajax—who was the first of this family to have become an Athenian. [2] Now this Miltiades was sitting on his front porch when he saw the Dolonci passing by. He noticed that they were wearing clothes that had not been made locally and were carrying spears.[a] He called out to them, and when they drew near, offered them lodging and hospitality. They accepted, and after they had been fed and entertained by him, they revealed everything the oracle had said and asked him to obey the god. [3] As soon as he heard their story, Miltiades consented to their request, since the rule of Peisistratos irritated him and he wanted to get away from it. So he immediately sent an inquiry to the oracle at Delphi, asking whether he should do what the Dolonci had asked of him.

The Pythia ordered him to do so, and thus Miltiades son of Kypselos, who had previously achieved a victory at Olympia in the four-horse chariot race,[a] now took with him every Athenian who wanted to participate in his expedition, sailed with the Dolonci to their land, and took possession of it, whereupon the Dolonci who had brought him there established him as

6.34.1a Miltiades son of Kimon was the future victor at Marathon and the younger nephew of Miltiades son of Kypselos, who was the brother of Kimon. See Appendix L, Aristocratic Families in Herodotus, §2, 8, and Figure L, which diagrams the somewhat confusing family of the Philaids, to which Miltiades, Kimon, and Stesagoras all belonged.
6.34.1b Apsinthis: Map 6.30, AX.
6.34.1c Delphi: Map 6.34.
6.34.2a The Pythia was the priestess at Delphi who recited the oracles, the god's responses. See Appendix P, Oracles, Religion, and Politics in Herodotus, §9.
6.34.2b The Sacred Way seems to have led east from Daulis, by Panopeos, and Chaeronea, then southeast by Coronea, Haliartos, and

Thebes, then south over Mount Cithaeron to Eleusis, whence it continued to Athens by the best-known *hodos hiera* ("holy road," "sacred way"). (How and Wells; Godley) For all these locations, see Map 6.34.
6.34.2c Phocis: Map 6.34.
6.34.2d Boeotia: Map 6.34.
6.34.2e Athens: Map 6.34.
6.35.2a By carrying spears, they revealed themselves to be "foreigners," since the Greeks of that region did not carry arms on an everyday basis anymore.
6.36.1a Olympic victor: see Appendix I, Classical Greek Religious Festivals, §5–9, on Panhellenic games and ceremonies. Olympia: Map 6.34, locator.

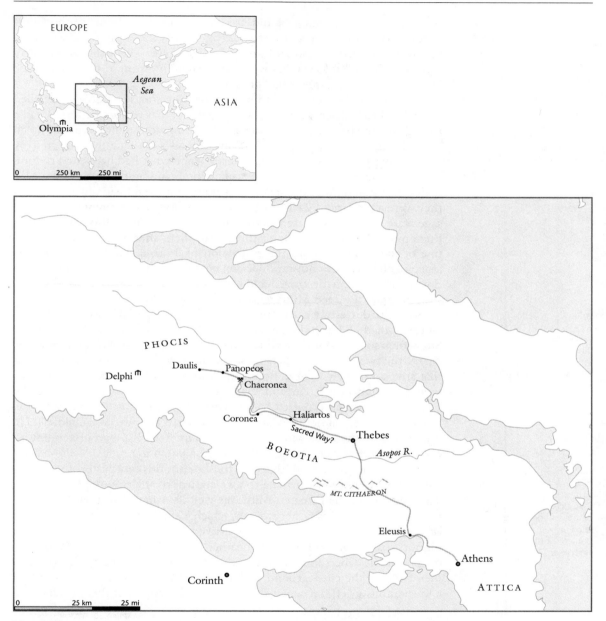

MAP 6.34

tyrant. [2] The first thing he did was to wall off the isthmus of the Chersonese[a] from the city of Kardia[b] to Paktye,[c] so that the Apsinthians would be unable to invade the land and cause damage there. This isthmus measures somewhat less than four miles wide, and extending from it, the Chersonese measures something more than 46 miles.[d]

6.37
c. 555
LAMPSACUS
Miltiades is captured by the Lampsacenes, but they release him when commanded to do so by Croesus.

Thus, by walling off the isthmus of the Chersonese, Miltiades repelled the Apsinthians. Then, among all the peoples in that region, he first began a war against the people of Lampsacus.[a] The Lampsacenes, however, set up an ambush and captured him alive. Now Miltiades was highly respected by Croesus the Lydian, and when Croesus learned what had happened to him, he sent a declaration to the Lampsacenes commanding them to release Miltiades, threatening that if they did not do so, he would wipe them out as if they were a pine tree. [2] The Lampsacenes who tried to interpret this message were at first bewildered as to why Croesus had used the phrase "wipe them out like a pine tree" in his threat, but then, after much hard thinking, one of the elders came to the realization of its true significance: the pine alone of all trees does not produce any new shoot once it has been chopped down, but is utterly destroyed and gone forever. So now in fear of Croesus, the Lampsacenes freed Miltiades and let him go.

6.38
519?
CHERSONESE
The elder Miltiades dies and is honored in the Chersonese. Stesagoras, his successor, is assassinated.

So Miltiades escaped this peril through the aid of Croesus, and later, when he died childless, he handed down both his office and his wealth to Stesagoras son of Kimon, who was his maternal half brother. And after his death, the people of the Chersonese sacrificed to him with the same rituals that are traditionally used to honor the leaders and founders of settlements: they instituted equestrian and gymnastic contests in which none of the Lampsacenes were permitted to compete. [2] During the war against the Lampsacenes, Stesagoras was overtaken by death and was also childless. He was struck on the head with an axe in the city hall by a man pretending to be a deserter, but who was actually a hot-tempered foe.

6.39
516
CHERSONESE
The Peisistratids send Miltiades son of Kimon to the Chersonese. He takes control of the region and marries a Thracian princess.

After Stesagoras died in this way, the Peisistratids sent his brother Miltiades son of Kimon[a] in a trireme to take control of affairs in the Chersonese. The Peisistratids had treated Miltiades well in Athens,[b] just as if they had not been guilty of his father's death, which I shall describe in another part of my history.[c] [2] After Miltiades arrived in the Chersonese, he stayed indoors, ostensibly to honor his brother by mourning for him. When the people of the Chersonese learned what he was doing, the most powerful men from all the cities around assembled and set out together to join him and share his grief; but when they arrived, Miltiades had them bound and

6.36.2a Chersonese: Map 6.30, AX.
6.36.2b Kardia: Map 6.30, AX.
6.36.2c Paktye: Map 6.30, AX.
6.36.2d Herodotus says the isthmus is "36 stades" wide and that the peninsula extends "420 stades" to its cape. See Distance Conversions, p. lxiv, and Appendix J, Ancient Greek Units of Currency, Weight, and Distance, §6, 19.

6.37.1a Lampsacus: Map 6.30, AX.
6.39.1a Miltiades son of Kimon served as eponymous archon (see Appendix A, The Athenian Government in Herodotus, §3) in 524/23 under the tyrannical Peisistratid regime.
6.39.1b Athens: Map 6.34.
6.39.1c The Peisistratids and the death of Kimon son of Stesagoras are described in 6.103.

confined. Miltiades now seized control over the Chersonese, took on the support of 500 mercenaries, and married Hegesipyle daughter of Oloros king of the Thracians.[a]

Miltiades son of Kimon had only recently come back to the Chersonese, but he was now[a] overtaken by more difficult problems than he had faced two years before this return. Then he had fled to avoid the Scythian nomads, who, after having been provoked by King Darius, united their forces and advanced against the Chersonese. [2] Miltiades had not waited for their attack but had fled the Chersonese and stayed away for three years until the Scythians had departed and the Dolonci had brought him back.

He then learned, however, that the Phoenician fleet was at Tenedos, so he filled five triremes with all his wealth and sailed away to Athens, setting out from the city of Kardia[a] and going through the Black Gulf.[b] But as he was passing the Chersonese, he encountered the Phoenician fleet, [2] and although Miltiades himself and four of his ships managed to escape to Imbros,[a] his fifth ship was pursued and taken by the Phoenicians. It happened that the commander of this ship was Miltiades' eldest son, Metiochos, whose mother was not the daughter of Oloros of Thrace, but another woman. [3] The Phoenicians captured him along with his ship, and when they learned that he was the son of Miltiades, they took him inland to the King, thinking that they would thereby gain great favor, since they assumed that this man's father was the Miltiades who had proposed that the Ionians[a] should, in compliance with Scythian[b] advice, tear down the bridge and sail away to their own lands.[c] [4] However, when the Phoenicians brought Metiochos son of Miltiades to the King, Darius not only did him no harm but indeed much good instead. For he gave him a house and possessions as well as a Persian wife, who bore him children who were to be regarded as Persians. Meanwhile, Miltiades left Imbros and sailed to Athens.

The Persians caused no further strife with the Ionians that year. Indeed, they instituted some policies that actually served them well. Artaphrenes, the governor of Sardis, summoned envoys from the Ionian cities and through them compelled the Ionians to make compacts with one another

6.40
510?
CHERSONESE
Miltiades flees from the Scythians, but later returns (496) after they leave.

6.41
493
IMBROS-ATHENS
Miltiades flees from the Phoenicians, but they capture Metiochos, his son, and send him to Darius, who treats him well.

6.42
493
IONIA
The Persians force the Ionians to agree to live in lawful peace and, measuring the land, establish an equitable annual tribute for them to pay to the King.

6.39.2a Since the full name of the Athenian historian Thucydides was Thucydides son of Olorus, (*Thucydides* 4.104.4) and he described himself as possessing the right to work certain gold mines (*Thucydides* 4.105.1), and thus enjoying great influence with the inhabitants of the mainland, it is thought that he was possibly related to Miltiades through his mother, or at least to a Thracian royal house. See Figure L, which diagrams the family of the Philaids, to which Miltiades belonged, and which shows that Miltiades' mother, Hegesipyle, was the daughter of someone named Olorus.
6.40.1a Herodotus refers to the time of his main

narrative, 493, when the Phoenicians were to encounter Miltiades, which he left off at 6.34 and will resume at 6.41, after giving a brief account here of Miltiades' flight from the Scythians about two years earlier. However, the text is unclear, and alternative interpretations (without the emendation adding the word "before," as in this translation) are possible.
6.41.1a Kardia: Map 6.43, AY.
6.41.1b Black Gulf (Melas Kolpos): Map 6.43, AY.
6.41.2a Imbros: Map 6.43, AY.
6.41.3a Ionia: Map 6.43, BY.
6.41.3b Scythia: Map 6.43, locator.
6.41.3c For this incident of Scythian advice and Miltiades' proposal, see 4.136–137.

so that they would submit their disputes to legal arbitration and refrain from pillaging and plundering one another. [2] Not only did he enforce these procedures; he also measured out their land in parasangs, the Persians' term for distances of thirty stades,[a] and according to these divisions, he assessed tribute for each district. And Artaphrenes' assessments on the basis of land, which did not differ very much from the previous ones, have continued to be observed from that time to my own day.[b]

These policies contributed to peace. With the coming of spring,[a] Mardonios son of Gobryas, a young man who had recently married Artozostre, the daughter of King Darius, and who was the one general left after the King had discharged the others, went down to the coast,[b] commanding both a very large army and a large fleet. [2] He led his army as far as Cilicia,[a] where he embarked on a ship and continued his journey with the rest of the fleet, while other commanders marched the land army toward the Hellespont.[b] [3] Mardonios sailed along the coast of Asia,[a] and when he came to Ionia,[b] something happened that I shall now relate and which will greatly surprise those Hellenes who do not believe that Otanes, one of the seven Persians,[c] presented the proposal that the government of the Persians should be a democracy.[d] For what Mardonios now did was to depose all the tyrants of the Ionians and establish democracies in their cities. [4] After doing that, he hurried to the Hellespont, and when a vast fleet as well as a huge land army had gathered there, they crossed the Hellespont on their ships and then proceeded to march through Europe, advancing toward Eretria[a] and Athens.[b]

Those two cities were the professed goals of the expedition, but what the Persians really intended was to subjugate as many Greek cities as they could. And with their fleet they subjugated the island of Thasos,[a] whose

6.42.2a Using the Attic stade of 583 feet, the parasang of 30 stades would be 3.3 miles long. See Appendix J, §2, 5–6, 19.
6.42.2b If these Ionians were paying tribute in the mid-fifth century, when Herodotus presumably wrote this, they were probably paying it to the Athenians, not the Persians, but the text makes it possible that they were paying tribute to the Persians as well. It is most likely that the Athenians adopted the tax system designed by the Persians, and so their assessments—based on land—could have been very similar in amount to that determined and imposed by Artaphrenes and the Persians. See Appendix M, Herodotus on Persia and the Persian Empire, §7.
6.43.1a The year was 492.
6.43.1b Apparently his march originated in Media or Mesopotamia, since "the coast" he arrived at was in Cilicia, and the army marched from there toward the Hellespont.
6.43.2a Cilicia: Map 6.43, locator.
6.43.2b Hellespont: Map 6.43, AY.

6.43.3a Asia: Map 6.43, locator.
6.43.3b Ionia: Map 6.43, BY.
6.43.3c Otanes was one of the seven Persians who overthrew the Magus and debated what would be the best form of government for Persia. They selected Darius to be King; see 3.70–88.
6.43.3d On Otanes' argument in favor of democracy, see 3.80. By this remark, Herodotus reveals that a number of Greeks had already expressed their disbelief that any Persian ever argued for a democratic form of government, or that such a debate among Persians about alternate forms of government ever took place. How and to whom Herodotus' version of this debate was disseminated prior to the publication of his *Histories*, and how they voiced their skepticism, are interesting, unresolvable questions.
6.43.4a Eretria, Euboea: Map 6.43, AX.
6.43.4b Athens: Map 6.43, BX.
6.44.1a Thasos: Map 6.43, AY.

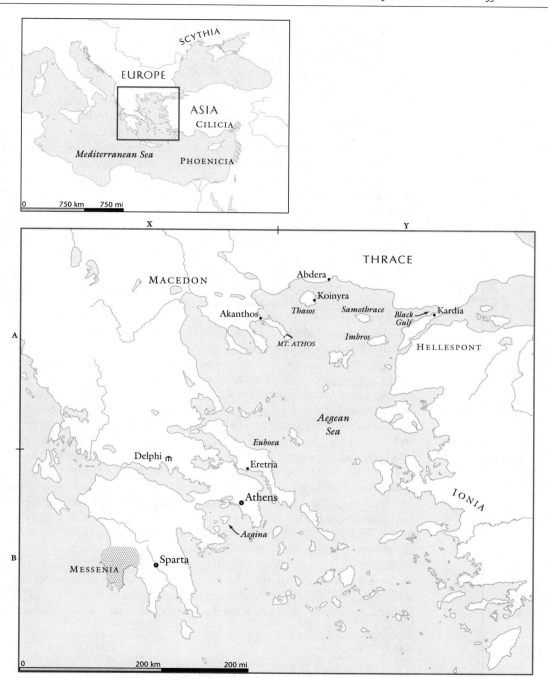

Map 6.43

inhabitants did not even lift a finger to oppose them, while with their army they added the Macedonians[b] to their already existing host of slaves, for all the peoples east of Macedon had already become Persian subjects. [2] From Thasos the fleet crossed over and sailed close to the shore of the mainland up to Akanthos,[a] from which they set out in an attempt to round Mount Athos.[b] But as they were sailing around it, a strong north wind came up on them, which was so impossible to deal with that it battered them badly and wrecked many of their ships against the shore of Mount Athos. [3] In fact it is said that about 300 of their ships were destroyed with more than 20,000 men. And since this sea is full of savage creatures, some were snatched up and killed by them, while others were dashed against the sharp rocks; some men perished because they did not know how to swim, and still others died from the cold. So that is what happened to the fleet there.

Meanwhile, as Mardonios and the army were making their camp in Macedon, they were attacked one night by the Thracian Byrgoi, who slaughtered many of them and wounded Mardonios himself. However, not even they escaped being enslaved by the Persians, for Mardonios did not leave these regions until he had made them Persian subjects. [2] After subduing them, he led his forces back, since both the land army, in its encounter with the Byrgoi, and the navy, in its wreck around Athos, had suffered severe damages. So after these disgraceful failures the expedition withdrew and headed for Asia.

In the next year, the first thing Darius did regarding the Hellenes was to send a messenger to the Thasians, whose neighbors had slandered them by accusing them of plotting a revolt. Darius now ordered them to tear down their city wall and to bring their ships to Abdera.[a] [2] For the Thasians, who had earlier been besieged by Histiaios of Miletus,[a] possessed large revenues, and were using their wealth to build warships and to enclose their city in a stronger wall to better protect themselves. They derived their revenues from the mainland and from their mines on their own island. [3] From the gold mines of Skaptesyle[a] they usually collected a total of eighty talents,[b] and from those in Thasos somewhat less but still such a great amount that the Thasians, who do not even pay taxes on their crops, regularly derive 200 talents annually from the mainland and the mines, and when revenues are at their highest, they obtain 300 talents.

I have seen these mines myself, and by far the most amazing are those that were discovered by the Phoenicians[a] who, under their leader Thasos, settled this island, which thereafter received its name from him. [2] These Phoenician mines of Thasos are between the place called Ainyra[a] and

6.44.1b   Macedon: Map 6.43, AX.
6.44.2a   Akanthos: Map 6.43, AX.
6.44.2b   Mount Athos: Map 6.43, AY.
6.46.1a   Abdera: Map 6.43, AY.
6.46.2a   This siege was mentioned in 6.28.1.
6.46.3a   Skaptesyle: precise location unknown.
6.46.3b   The talent is a unit of weight whose value varied over time and place between 60

and 80 pounds; when measuring an amount of gold, it represented a huge sum. See Appendix J, §11–13, 20.
6.47.1a   Phoenicia: Map 6.43, locator.
6.47.2a   Ainyra, precise location unknown but clearly located on Thasos' east coast, facing Samothrace: Map 6.43, AY.

Koinyra,[b] facing Samothrace, on the site of a huge mountain they overturned in their search. So much for their mines.

At the King's command, the Thasians tore down their wall and brought all their ships to Abdera. After this, Darius tried to test the Hellenes to find out whether they intended to wage war against him or to surrender to him. [2] He sent out heralds in all directions throughout Hellas and ordered them to ask for earth and water for the King.[a] And while he sent some heralds to Hellas, he sent others to his tribute-paying cities along the coast with orders to build warships and vessels to transport horses.

So the cities began to construct these ships. On the mainland, many of the Hellenes visited by the heralds gave what the Persian asked, as did all of the islanders to whom the heralds had come with the request. Included among the islanders who gave earth and water to Darius were the Aeginetans.[a] [2] And as soon as they had done so, the Athenians assailed them, thinking that the Aeginetans had granted the King's request out of hostility to themselves, in order to march with the Persians. Happily exploiting this pretext, they went to Sparta,[a] where they accused the Aeginetans of betraying Hellas.

In response to this accusation against them, the Spartan king Kleomenes son of Anaxandridas[a] crossed over to Aegina intending to arrest the most guilty Aeginetans. [2] But when he tried to arrest them, other Aeginetans showed up to oppose him, foremost among them one Krios son of Polykritos, who said that Kleomenes would not get away with seizing even one Aeginetan, for he had no authority from the Spartan government for doing this, but had been swayed by Athenian money; otherwise, his fellow king of the Spartans would have accompanied him to make the arrests. [3] The source of Krios' assertion was a letter from Demaratos.[a] As Kleomenes was being driven out of Aegina, he asked Krios what his name was, and Krios told him. Kleomenes then said to him, "Well, then, Krios, cover your horns in bronze, since you are about to encounter great trouble."[b]

Meanwhile, Demaratos son of Ariston remained behind in Sparta, maligning Kleomenes. He was the other king of the Spartans, but from the inferior house, though not inferior in all respects, since the origin of their ancestry was actually the same, but the house of Eurysthenes received somewhat more esteem because of seniority of birth.

6.48
491
HELLAS
Darius sends heralds throughout Hellas demanding submission.

6.49
491
ATHENS-AEGINA
The Athenians appeal to Sparta against the Aeginetans, accusing them of submitting to Persia out of enmity to Athens.

6.50
491
AEGINA
Kleomenes, king of Sparta, goes to Aegina to arrest the medizers among them, but is driven off.

6.51
491
SPARTA
Demaratos criticizes Kleomenes, both being kings of Sparta.

6.47.2b   Koinyra, Thasos: Map 6.43, AY.
6.48.2a   Gifts of earth and water symbolized submission and surrender to a conqueror. See Appendix M, §7.
6.49.1a   Aegina: Map 6.43, BX.
6.49.2a   Sparta: Map 6.43, BX.
6.50.1a   Kleomenes son of Anaxandridas: see Appendix B, The Spartan State in War and Peace, §21.
6.50.3a   Demaratos son of Ariston was the other (Eurypontid) king of Sparta. He held that office from 515 to 491 and was

driven from office by Kleomenes and others on the ground of illegitimacy. He finally fled to Persia and accompanied King Xerxes on his invasion of Hellas, giving good predictions and advice, which were not believed or heeded by his royal host.

6.50.3b   In Greek, *krios* means "ram." Kleomenes' remark refers to the practice of placing a small amount of bronze or gold on the horns of an animal that was about to be sacrificed.

447

6.52

SPARTA

The Spartan version of
how the early Spartans
determined which of the
royal twins was the firstborn.

For according to the Lacedaemonians[a]—though no poet agrees with them in this—it was not the sons of Aristodemos, but Aristodemos himself, the son of Aristomachos son of Kleodaios who was the son of Hyllos, who had, during his reign, led them to the land they now possess. [2] And not much time had passed before the wife of Aristodemos, whose name was Argeia, gave birth. They say that she was the daughter of Autesion son of Teisamenos the son of Thersandros, who was the son of Polynices, and that she gave birth to twins, and that Aristodemos lived to see his infant sons, but then died of an illness. [3] So the Lacedaemonians of that time followed their custom and resolved to make the elder son king. But they did not know which to choose, because the boys were so much alike and they were, in fact, identical. Since they were incapable of distinguishing between them, they asked the boys' mother (or perhaps had done so even before this). [4] But she said that not even she could tell them apart. Now she was actually well able to distinguish between them but denied that she could because she wanted both of them to be kings if possible. So the Lacedaemonians, now at a complete loss, sent to Delphi[a] asking what they should do about this problem. [5] The Pythia ordered them to regard both children as kings, but to award the senior brother greater honor. This response by the Pythia left the Lacedaemonians no less bewildered than they had been before, because they had no way to determine which of the boys was the elder. Finally a Messenian[a] man by the name of Panites suggested [6] that the Lacedaemonians watch the mother carefully to see which of the boys she would bathe and feed first. And if she clearly and consistently followed the same sequence, they would obtain the object of their search and find out what they were seeking to discover. But if she alternated between the two, then it would be obvious that she knew no more than they did, in which case they would have to try another method of investigation. [7] The Spartans followed the Messenian's advice, and as they watched the mother of the sons of Aristodemos (who did not know why she was being watched), they indeed saw her consistently picking up and honoring one of the boys by bathing and feeding him before the other. So they took the child that they had found to be more highly honored by its mother, on the grounds that it must be the firstborn, and raised it at public expense. The name given to this boy was Eurysthenes; that given to the other was Prokles. [8] And they say that even though they were brothers, after they grew up they disagreed with each other throughout their entire lives, just as their descendants continue to do.

6.53

SPARTA

The Greek version of
this story, with proofs
of its correctness.

Of the Hellenes, the Lacedaemonians are the only ones who tell that version of the story. Now I shall put in writing what other Hellenes report. They correctly list the Dorian kings as far back as Perseus son of Danae,

6.52.1a   Lacedaemon (Sparta): Map 6.43, BX. Herodotus uses the names Spartans and Lacedaemonians interchangeably. "Spartans," however, often refers specifically to citizens of the state of Sparta, whereas any inhabitant of the territory of Lacedaemon

is a Lacedaemonian. See Appendix B, The Spartan State in War and Peace, §5, 7, and n. B.7a.

6.52.4a   Delphi: Map 6.43, BX.

6.52.5a   Messenia: Map 6.43, BX.

omitting the god[a] and showing that these kings were Hellenes, and that even in those early days they were classified as Hellenes. [2] I said "as far back as Perseus" since I cannot trace the lineage back any further than that because no one is named as the mortal father of Perseus—as Amphitryon, for example, is named the father of Herakles. Therefore I was correct to say "as far back as Perseus." But if someone were to recount the ancestors of Danae daughter of Akrisios and trace them all the way back in a continuous sequence, it would become obvious that the leaders of the Dorians are actually genuine Egyptians by direct descent.

That, then, is the genealogy of the Spartan kings according to the Hellenes. The account of the Persians is that Perseus was an Assyrian who became a Hellene, and that his ancestors did not. The forefathers of Akrisios, they say, were not related to Perseus at all but were, as the Hellenes also say, Egyptians.

6.54
Persians say Perseus was originally Assyrian.

Let that be the extent of what is said on this topic. For others have told of the deeds they performed to obtain their positions as kings over the Dorians,[a] even though they were Egyptians, so I shall leave that subject alone. I shall, however, record what the accounts of others have not already covered.

6.55
Herodotus finishes with this subject.

The Spartans have granted the following privileges to their kings: two priesthoods, one of Zeus Lacedaemon, the other of Zeus of Heaven;[a] the prerogative to wage war against any land they wish, and no Spartan can hinder them from doing so; if anyone tries, he is subject to a curse; and when they wage war, the kings go out first and return last.[b] On their expeditions, the kings have 100 picked men to serve as their guards, and as they depart for war, they may sacrifice as many flocks as they wish and take all the hides and backs of the victims for themselves.

6.56
SPARTA
Privileges of the Spartan kings in war.

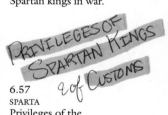

Those are their privileges in war. Their privileges in peace are as follows: whenever someone performs a sacrifice at public expense, the kings are the first to sit down and the first to be served at the feast, and they are given a portion twice as large as any other person dining there. They also begin the libations and receive the hides of the sacrificial victims. [2] At every new moon, as well as on the seventh day of every month, they are provided from the public treasury with a full-grown sacrificial victim for the sanctuary of Apollo, a medimnos of barley meal, and a Laconian fourth[a] of wine. They receive special seats up front at all the contests. The kings also have the prerogative of appointing whomever of the citizens they want as *proxenoi,*[b] and they are empowered to choose two *Pythioi* as well. The *Pythioi* are sacred delegates who are sent to Delphi, and who eat their meals with the kings at public expense. [3] If the kings do not come to

6.57
SPARTA
Privileges of the Spartan kings in peace.

6.53.1a The god: Zeus. According to one legend, Perseus is the son of Zeus and Danae. (Godley)
6.55.1a Dorians: see Appendix K, Dialect and Ethnic Groups in Herodotus, §7–9.
6.56.1a In Greek, Zeus Ouranios.
6.56.1b Herodotus says this now, but in 5.75.2 he asserted that after Kleomenes' invasion of Attica in 506, which failed due to dissension between the two kings, the Spartans adopted a policy that one of their kings was

always to remain at home while the other campaigned abroad with the army. See Appendix B, §11.
6.57.2a A medimnos and Laconian fourth: see Appendix J, §17, 18, 21, 22.
6.57.2b *Proxenoi* were representatives of a city other than their own who provided assistance and protected the interests of citizens of that city. At Sparta they were appointed by the kings. See Appendix B, §11.

dinner, they receive two choinikes of barley meal and a kotyle[a] of wine sent to their homes. And when the kings do attend dinner, they receive double portions of everything. If they are invited to dine with private citizens, they receive the same honors from them. [4] The kings are in charge of keeping the oracles received that pertain to the state, and the *Pythioi* share their knowledge of the contents of these oracles. The kings act as sole judges only in the following cases: they decide who will marry a girl possessing an inheritance if her deceased father has not arranged a marriage for her; and they also judge cases concerning public roads. [5] In addition, anyone who wants to adopt a child must do so in the presence of the kings. The kings sit with the Council of Elders,[a] who number twenty-eight, during their meetings, and if the kings do not attend, the Elders most closely related to the kings assume their prerogatives and cast two votes for the kings and a third for themselves.[b]

Those are the privileges granted by the Spartan community to the kings while they live; after their death they receive the following honors. Horsemen carry the news of the king's death throughout all of Laconia, and in every city, women walk about beating on cauldrons; and whenever this occurs, two free people from each household, a man and a woman, must defile themselves,[a] otherwise they incur large fines. [2] One custom observed by the Lacedaemonians at the death of their kings is the same as that practiced by a majority of the barbarians in Asia when their kings die: whenever a king of the Lacedaemonians dies, a fixed number of the *perioikoi*[a] from all of Lacedaemon, in addition to the Spartans, must attend the funeral to grieve. [3] And when many thousands of people have gathered there—*perioikoi*, helots,[a] and Spartans—men mingling together with women, all beating their heads vigorously, they wail continuously and loudly, proclaiming that this king who has just died had proved himself to be the best. If one of the kings should die in war, they make an image of him and carry it out on a bier with sumptuous coverings. After the king is buried, all business in the agora as well as meetings to elect officials are suspended for ten days, during which they mourn.

The customs they follow when a king dies also resemble those of the Persians. Whenever a Spartan king dies and a new king is installed, the new king forgives the debt of every Spartan who owes anything to the king or the state; in the same way, among the Persians, a new king releases all the cities from their obligation to pay back-tribute.

6.58
SPARTA
Spartan customs and ceremonies when the king dies.

6.59
SPARTA
Debts to the king or state are forgiven when the king dies.

6.57.3a Laconian choinix and kotyle: see Appendix J, §17, 18, 21, 22.
6.57.5a Council of Elders, the Gerousia: see Appendix B, §12.
6.57.5b Herodotus' language is ambiguous as to whether each king had one or two votes. Thucydides says that the Greeks hold many uninformed notions, one of them being that the Spartan kings have two votes each, whereas they actually have only one each. (*Thucydides* 1.20.3)

6.58.1a Defile themselves: this tradition of mourning involved tearing garments and throwing dirt on one's hair and clothing.
6.58.2a The *perioikoi*, literally, "dwellers-around," ranked between the Spartan citizens and the helots in their obligations to the state and their degree of freedom. For more on the *perioikoi*, see Appendix B, §7, 17–18.
6.58.3a Helots: serfs who were forced to till the land for the Spartans.

Lacedaemonian practices also conform to the following customs of the Egyptians. Their heralds, flute players, and cooks inherit their professions from their father, so that a flute player is the son of a flute player, a cook the son of a cook, a herald the son of a herald; and others do not apply themselves to these skills. One cannot become a herald on the strength of one's voice and thus try to take the place of hereditary heralds; instead, these occupations are performed only by those who have inherited them from their ancestors.[a] Those, then, are their customs.

So while Kleomenes was in Aegina trying to work for the common good of Hellas, Demaratos was maligning him, not because he cared much about the Aeginetans, but from jealousy and malice. After Kleomenes returned home from Aegina, he considered how to depose Demaratos from the kingship, and when the following circumstances provided him with an opportunity, he moved against him.

While Ariston had reigned in Sparta, he had married twice, but neither of his wives had borne him any children. [2] And because he knew that he was not the cause of this problem, he married a third wife, and this is how that marriage came about. There was a Spartan man who was a close friend of Ariston's; in fact, of all citizens, Ariston was attached to him the most. This man happened to have a wife who was by far the most beautiful woman in Sparta, and who in fact had become the most beautiful only after having been the ugliest. [3] For her appearance was once quite homely. Her nurse, however, realizing that the unattractive girl was the daughter of wealthy people who regarded her appearance as a disaster, developed the following plan. Every day she took the girl to the sanctuary of Helen, which is located in the district called Therapne above the sanctuary of Phoibos. Whenever the nurse brought her here she would stand her at the statue and pray that the goddess would deliver the child from her ugliness. [4] And it is said that once, while the nurse was leaving the sanctuary, a woman appeared before her and asked what she was carrying in her arms, to which the nurse replied that she was carrying a child. The woman then requested that the nurse show her the child, which the nurse refused to do, since the parents had forbidden her to show the child to anyone. But the woman ordered her to reveal it anyway. [5] And because the woman kept trying to see the child and was making a huge fuss about viewing it, the nurse finally showed it to her. The woman then touched the child's head, and said that she would be the most beautiful of all the women in Sparta. From that day on her appearance changed, and when she reached marriageable age, Agetos son of Alkeides, the man who was the friend of Ariston, married her.

But it turned out that Ariston began to be disturbed by passion for this woman, and so he devised the following strategy. He promised Agetos, his good friend and the husband of this woman, that he would give to him any

6.60
SPARTA
Like the Egyptians, Spartans inherit their crafts from their fathers.

6.61
SPARTA
The story of how King Ariston's third wife went from being very ugly to becoming the most beautiful woman in Sparta.

6.62
SPARTA
How King Ariston outwitted his friend so that he could marry this woman.

6.60.1a   Some of the same practices among the Egyptians are described in 2.67.3 and 2.166.2.

object from his possessions that he would select, and he asked his friend to grant the same favor to himself. Agetos had no fear for his wife, since he could see that Ariston already had a wife, and so he consented to the terms of this agreement, and they confirmed it by exchanging strong and binding oaths. [2] Then Ariston gave Agetos what he chose to take from his store of treasures, and when the time came for Ariston himself to seek a gift of equal value, he attempted to take away his friend's wife. Agetos argued that he had agreed to give anything except for this; but because he was compelled by his oath, after his friend had thoroughly misled and deceived him, he allowed Ariston to take his wife away.

So that is how Ariston came to divorce his second wife and married a third. But in less than a ten-month interval,[a] this wife gave birth to Demaratos. [2] Ariston was sitting in council with the ephors when one of his household servants announced that a son had been born to him. And he, after remembering when he had married the woman and counting out the months on his fingers, swore an oath: "He could not be my own son!" The ephors heard this, but for the moment, thought nothing of it. As the child grew, Ariston repented these words, for he indeed came to regard Demaratos as his very own son. [3] He named him Demaratos because before he was born, the entire population of Sparta had said a prayer that a son would be born to Ariston, since of all the kings of Sparta, he was held in the highest esteem. So that is how Demaratos received his name.[a]

In the course of time, Ariston died, and Demaratos succeeded him as king. But it seems that what had happened was destined to become known, and would bring the reign of Demaratos to an end. This occurred as a consequence of the hostility between the two kings. Demaratos and Kleomenes had been antagonistic toward each other before, when Demaratos had led the army out of Eleusis,[a] and the hostility between them grew more intense now, when Kleomenes crossed over to Aegina to oppose the Aeginetans who were medizing.[b]

Kleomenes now ardently sought revenge, and entered into a pact with Leotychidas son of Menares son of Agis, who belonged to the same branch of the royal family as Demaratos. The terms of the agreement were that if Kleomenes were to make Leotychidas king in place of Demaratos, then Leotychidas would join him against the medizing Aeginetans. [2] Leotychidas was already a personal enemy of Demaratos, particularly because when Leotychidas had arranged to marry Perkalos, the daughter of Chilon son of Demarmenos, Demaratos had conspired to rob Leotychidas of his marriage by seizing Perkalos and making her his own wife. [3] That is how Leotychidas' hatred of Demaratos had begun, and now, following the

6.63
SPARTA
Demaratos is born a bit too soon after the marriage of his mother with King Ariston, creating doubt that he is Ariston's son.

6.64
495–491?
SPARTA
Demaratos became king, but Kleomenes questions the legitimacy of his royal birth.

6.65
SPARTA
Kleomenes joins with Leotychidas—who hates Demaratos for having robbed him of his betrothed—and now declares that Demaratos is not Ariston's son and therefore cannot be king.

6.63.1a   The Greeks counted inclusively; we would say "nine-month interval."
6.63.3a   In Greek, *demos* means "people" and *aratos* means "prayed for"; thus Demaratos means "prayed for by the people."
6.64.1a   Eleusis: Map 6.75, AY. For Kleomenes' invasion of Attica in 506 and his advance to Eleusis, see 5.74–77.
6.64.1b   To "medize" was to go over to the Persian side. Persians were often called Medes by the Greeks.

desire of Kleomenes, Leotychidas swore an oath accusing Demaratos of not rightfully ruling as king of the Spartans, since he was not the son of Ariston. And after swearing this oath, he prosecuted Demaratos in court and resurrected what Ariston had said when the household servant had announced the birth of a son to him, and he had counted the months and had declared the child was not his own. [4] Resting his case on this statement, Leotychidas tried to demonstrate over and over again that Demaratos was not the son of Ariston and therefore did not rightfully reign as king of Sparta, and he provided as witnesses the ephors who had happened to be sitting in council with Ariston at the time and who had heard what he said.

The controversy continued until finally the Spartans decided to ask the oracle at Delphi[a] whether Demaratos was or was not the son of Ariston. [2] It was Kleomenes who had come up with the idea to refer this question to the Pythia,[a] and he next gained the support of Kobon son of Aristophantos, who wielded the greatest influence at Delphi and who then persuaded Periallos the Pythia to proclaim what Kleomenes wanted her to say. [3] And thus, when the sacred delegates presented their question, the Pythia asserted that Demaratos was not the son of Ariston. Later, however, these intrigues became known, and as a result, Kobon was exiled from Delphi, while Periallos the Pythia was ousted from her position of honor.[a]

So that is how Demaratos was deposed from his kingship. He subsequently fled from Sparta to the Medes because of the following affront. After his kingship had come to an end, Demaratos was elected to a certain magistracy. [2] Now Demaratos was in the audience watching the events at the Gymnopaidiai[a] when Leotychidas, now king in his place, sent a servant to ridicule and insult Demaratos by asking him how it felt to be a magistrate after having been king. [3] Grievously offended by this question, Demaratos answered by saying that while he himself was now experienced in both, Leotychidas was not, adding that the asking of this question would be the beginning of either a multitude of evils or a multitude of blessings for the Lacedaemonians. After saying this, Demaratos covered his head, left the theater, and returned home, where he immediately prepared and performed the sacrifice of an ox to Zeus. Then he summoned his mother.

When his mother came to him, he placed some of the entrails in her hands and entreated her, saying, "Mother, I appeal to the other gods and especially to Zeus Protector of Our Household right here,[a] and I beseech you to tell me the truth: who is my real father? [2] For Leotychidas said during our disputes that you were pregnant from your former husband when you came to Ariston, while others tell an even more insulting story, that one of the stableboys visited you and that I am his son. [3] Now I implore you by the gods: tell me

6.66
DELPHI
The Delphic priestess is secretly persuaded to rule against Demaratos and declare that he is not the son of Ariston.

6.67
SPARTA
Leotychidas, who takes Demaratos' place as king, insults Demaratos in public.

6.68
SPARTA
Demaratos asks his mother for the truth about his paternity.

6.66.1a Delphi: Map 6.75, AY.
6.66.2a The Pythia was the priestess at Delphi who recited the oracles, the god's responses. See Appendix P, Oracles, Religion, and Politics in Herodotus, §9.
6.66.3a See Appendix P, §12, 14, 16.
6.67.2a Gymnopaidiai: a festival of Apollo that

included singing, dancing, and gymnastic contests of boys and men.
6.68.1a Zeus Protector of the Household: in the Greek, Zeus Herkeios, literally Zeus of the Enclosure, referring to his shrine set up in the front court of a house, between the house and the wall facing the street.

the truth! Even if you have done anything like what is rumored, you are not alone; many women have done such things. And besides, there is much talk in Sparta about how Ariston lacked the seed to produce offspring; otherwise, they say, his earlier wives would have given him children."

6.69
SPARTA
His mother tells Demaratos the truth, that he is the son either of the hero Astrabakos or of Ariston, and that she had carried him only seven months, a short term which was not all that unusual.

After he had appealed to her in this way, she replied, "My son, you have implored me with prayers to tell you the truth, and that is what I will tell you, and in detail. On the third night after the night on which Ariston had brought me to his home, an apparition in the likeness of Ariston came to me, and after lying with me, put the garlands it had been wearing on me. [2] The apparition left, and then Ariston came; when he saw me wearing the garlands, he asked who had given them to me. I told him it was he himself, but he refused to admit it. Then I swore an oath and said that it was not right for him to deny it, since only a short time before, he had come in and given me the garlands after lying with me. [3] Seeing that I had sworn to it on oath, Ariston realized that this had been the act of a divinity. For the garlands had evidently come from the shrine of the hero called Astrabakos which is set up at the doors of the courtyard, and the prophets had proclaimed this very Astrabakos to be a hero. [4] So now I have told you the whole story, my son, all that you wanted to know: either your father is the hero Astrabakos, or else your father is Ariston. For that was the night I conceived you. As to your enemies' exploiting the story that Ariston denied that you could have been his son when your birth was announced because ten months had not yet passed, it was his ignorance regarding these matters that led him to blurt out such a comment. [5] For some women give birth at nine months, or even seven; not all of them carry a full ten months of pregnancy, and I, my son, gave birth to you in the seventh month. Not long afterward, Ariston himself recognized that he had uttered these words out of stupidity. So do not believe other stories about your birth, for you have now heard the whole truth, and may it be Leotychidas and those who say such things whose wives will bear the children of stableboys."[a]

6.70
491
SPARTA-PERSIA
Demaratos escapes from the Spartans and goes into exile in Persia, where King Darius treats him well.

Those were the words of his mother, and now that Demaratos had found out what he wanted to know, he took provisions for a journey and made his way to Elis,[a] after giving as a pretext that he was going to Delphi to consult the oracle. But the Lacedaemonians suspected that Demaratos was trying to run away, and they pursued him. [2] Demaratos somehow managed to cross over from Elis to the island of Zacynthus[a] before they caught up with him. But then the Lacedaemonians crossed over in pursuit, took away his servants, and tried to apprehend him. The Zacynthians, however, refused to give him up, so he was then able to cross over to Asia[b] and travel to the court of King Darius.

6.69.5a　It is interesting to note that the variations in human gestation terms seem to have been unknown to ancient Spartans (or at least to Herodotus, his Spartans, and perhaps his contemporary audience), and that no one thought

to call the mother of Demaratos to testify at the hearing on his legitimacy. See Appendix B, §1, 24–25.
6.70.1a　Elis: Map 6.75, AX.
6.70.2a　Zacynthus: Map 6.75, BX.
6.70.2b　Asia: Map 6.93, locator.

The King gave him a lavish welcome and furnished him with both land and cities. [3] Such was the fortune of Demaratos, and that is the story of how he came to Asia. He was famous among the Lacedaemonians for his brilliant deeds and good judgment on many occasions, and in particular for having conferred on them an Olympic[a] victory when he won in the four-horse chariot race; he was the only one of all the kings in Sparta who had ever done this.

After Demaratos had been deposed, Leotychidas son of Menares succeeded to his kingship. Now Leotychidas had a son named Zeuxidemos, who was called Kyniskos[a] by some of the Spartans. But this Zeuxidemos did not become a king of Sparta, because he died before Leotychidas did, leaving behind a son of his own, Archidamos. [2] After Leotychidas had lost Zeuxidemos, he married a second wife, Eurydame, the sister of Menios and daughter of Diactoridas. She bore him no sons, but she did bear a daughter named Lampito, who was given in marriage by Leotychidas to Archidamos son of Zeuxidemos.[a]

Leotychidas did not grow old in Sparta but paid the penalty for what he had done to Demaratos in the following way. He had led the army of the Lacedaemonians into Thessaly, and although it would have been possible for him to subjugate all of that land, he accepted a large bribe instead [2] and was caught in the act, sitting in camp on a glove full of money. For this, Leotychidas was put on trial, with the result that he was exiled from Sparta and his house was demolished. He then fled to Tegea,[a] where he died.

But all that happened much later. Now, after Kleomenes' plot against Demaratos had succeeded, he at once took Leotychidas with him and advanced on the Aeginetans,[a] against whom he bore a a bitter grudge for their having treated him so contemptuously before. [2] Now that both kings had come against them, the Aeginetans decided not to offer any further resistance, so the Spartan kings selected ten Aeginetans of the highest value in terms of wealth and lineage and took them away. Among them were the most powerful Aeginetans, Krios son of Polykritos and Kasambos son of Aristokrates. The kings brought these men to Attica[a] and deposited them as hostages with the Athenians,[b] who were the most hostile enemies of the Aeginetans.

After that, Kleomenes' evil plot against Demaratos became known and so, in fear of the Spartans, he slipped away secretly to Thessaly.[a] From there, he went to Arcadia[b] and tried to instigate a revolt by uniting the Arcadians against Sparta and having them swear oaths that they would follow wherever he would lead them. In particular, he was eager to bring the leading men of Arcadia to the city of Nonakris[c] and make them swear that oath by the waters of the River Styx,[d] [2] for the Arcadians say that the waters of the

6.71
SPARTA
The offspring of King Leotychidas.

6.72
SPARTA
Much later, Leotychidas is banished for having accepted a bribe.

6.73
491
AEGINA
Kleomenes and the new king, Leotychidas, now punish the Aeginetans, sending ten of the most prominent of them as hostages to Athens.

6.74
491
ARCADIA
Later Kleomenes' plot against Demaratos becomes known, and he flees to the Arcadians, whom he attempts to unite against Sparta.

6.70.3a Olympia: Map 6.75, BX. See Appendix I, §5–6, on the prestige that accrued to cities and individuals who gained victory in the Olympic festival games.
6.71.1a *Kyniskos* in Greek means "puppy."
6.71.2a Leotychidas gave his daughter in marriage to his grandson. They were of different mothers, so she married her half-nephew.

6.72.2a Tegea: Map 6.75, BX.
6.73.1a Aegina: Map 6.75, BY.
6.73.2a Attica: Map 6.75, BY.
6.73.2b Athens: Map 6.75, BY.
6.74.1a Thessaly: Map 6.75, AX.
6.74.1b Arcadia: Map 6.75, BX.
6.74.1c Nonakris: Map 6.75, AX.
6.75.1d Styx River: Map 6.75, AX.

Styx lie in this city[a] and that a small stream of water emerges from a rock and drips into a hollow surrounded by a circular enclosure of stones. This spring happens to be located in Nonakris, a city of Arcadia near Pheneos.[b]

6.75
491
SPARTA
The Spartans bring Kleomenes home, but he goes mad, abuses others, and kills himself. The Athenians and Argives each have their explanations for his downfall.

When the Lacedaemonians learned what Kleomenes was up to, they became afraid and brought him back to Sparta, where he resumed ruling on the same terms as he had before. But as soon as he had returned, he was stricken by madness (although he had been somewhat deranged even before this). For now, whenever he encountered a Spartan, he would thrust his staff into his face. [2] Because he was doing this and not in his right mind, his relatives confined him in a wooden pillory,[a] and while he was thus confined, he noticed that one of the guards had been left alone with him, and he asked the guard to give him a knife. The guard refused him at first, but when Kleomenes threatened what he would do to him when he was released, the frightened guard, who was a helot,[b] gave him a knife. [3] Kleomenes then took the weapon and started to mutilate himself, beginning from his shins. Cutting his flesh lengthwise, he proceeded to his thighs, and from his thighs, his hips, and then his sides, until he reached his abdomen, which he thoroughly shredded and then died. Many of the Hellenes say this happened because he had bribed the Pythia to give those responses concerning Demaratos;[a] but according to the Athenians, it was because when he had invaded Eleusis,[b] he had ravaged the precinct of the goddesses. The Argives, however, say it was because he had brought the fugitives out of the sanctuary of Argos[c] and executed them, and had no regard for the grove itself, but had burned it down.[d]

6.76
494
ARGOLID
Kleomenes withdraws from the Erasinos when the omens are unfavorable, and approaches Argos by sea via Nauplia and Tiryns.

For Kleomenes had once received an oracle at Delphi,[a] predicting that he would capture Argos. On his way to Argos, he came to the Erasinos River, which is said to flow out of the Stymphalian Lake[b] and to disappear into an invisible chasm, only to reappear in Argos, where the river is called the Erasinos by the Argives. Upon his arrival at these waters, he performed a sacrifice, [2] but the omens were not favorable for his crossing of the river. Kleomenes then commented that while he admired the Erasinos for not betraying its local citizens, the Argives would not escape unharmed.

6.74.2a   The River Styx was imagined to run undergound to the underworld.
6.74.2b   Pheneos: Map 6.75, AX.
6.75.2a   Apparently some wooden device much like the stocks, which held the legs fast but left the hands free, used to punish wrongdoers among the American Pilgrims.
6.75.2b   Helots were the lowest class in Spartan society and were treated with great harshness. They were hereditary serfs owned by the state, which assigned them to cultivate land for the benefit of Spartans, who were thus free to pursue military excellence. See Appendix B, §8–9, 17, 23.
6.75.3a   For Kleomenes' bribery of the Pythia, see 6.66.

6.75.3b   Eleusis: Map 6.75, AY. For Kleomenes' invasion of Attica (Map 6.75, BY) and advance to Eleusis, see 5.74–77.
6.75.3c   Argos: Map 6.75, AY.
6.75.3d   Herodotus hasn't yet told us of Kleomenes' massacre of the Argives, but he is about to do so. Argos: Map 6.75, BY.
6.76.1a   Delphi: Map 6.75, AY.
6.76.1b   Stymphalian Lake, near the base of Mount Kyllene in the northeast Peloponnese: Map 6.75, AX, BX, for all locations. The lake discharges into a cavern at the foot of a cliff, and the river, which reappears near Argos, has generally been identified as the Erasinos River. (Godley)

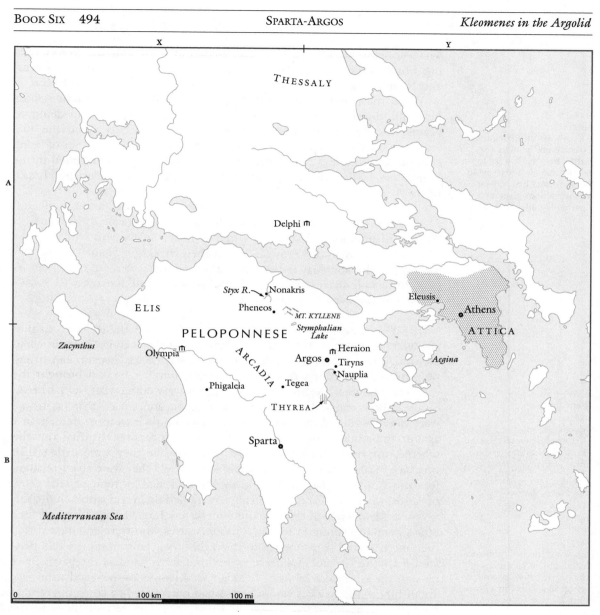

MAP 6.75

Then he retreated and led his army down to Thyrea,[a] where, after sacrificing a bull to the sea, he took his army on boats to the territory of Tiryns[b] and Nauplia.[c]

When the Argives learned of this, they rushed to the coast to oppose him, and, drawing near to Tiryns, at the place called Sepeia,[a] they deployed against the Lacedaemonians, leaving very little space between the two armies. Now the Argives were not afraid of open battle, but rather of being conquered by guile, [2] for that was what the Pythia had indicated in the double oracle[a] that she had given to the Argives and the Milesians.[b] It said to the Argives:

> When the female conquers and drives out the male,[c]
> And among the Argives is exalted in glory,
> Many women of Argos will tear at their cheeks,
> And thus someday in the future a mortal will say:
> "A terrible snake, triple in coils, was subdued and destroyed
>   by the spear."

[3] The concurrence of all the omens frightened the Argives, so they resolved to protect themselves by making use of the enemies' herald:[a] whatever the Lacedaemonian herald announced to the Lacedaemonians, they, the Argives, would carry out the same instructions.

When Kleomenes realized that the Argives were doing whatever his herald ordered, he commanded that when the herald announced that his troops were to eat breakfast, they should instead pick up their weapons and advance against the Argives. [2] The Lacedaemonians successfully carried out this scheme, for their attack caught the Argives while they were eating their breakfast in accordance with the herald's order, and they were able to slaughter many of them. Many more Argives, however, fled for refuge to the grove of Argos, where the Lacedaemonians surrounded them and stood on guard.

Next Kleomenes questioned some deserters he had with him and then sent a herald to summon by name those Argives who were confined within the sanctuary and to announce to them that their ransom money had been paid. (Among the Peloponnesians,[a] two minas[b] is fixed as the payment of ransom for a prisoner of war.) ~~In this way, Kleomenes managed to induce about fifty of the Argives whose names had been called to come out, and as they did so he killed every one of them.~~[c] [2] The rest of those in the precinct remained unaware of what was happening outside, since the foliage

6.77
494
SEPEIA
The Argives approach the Spartans and prepare for battle, but, made wary by an oracle, they decide to avoid being tricked by carrying out all instructions given by the Spartan herald.

6.78
494
SEPEIA
Kleomenes sees the Argives perform his herald's instructions and uses this to rout them in a surprise attack.

6.79
494
SEPEIA
Speaking falsely, Kleomenes lures out and kills many of the Argives who have taken refuge in a shrine in a grove, until his ruse is discovered.

6.76.2a   Thyrea: Map 6.75, BY.
6.76.2b   Tiryns: Map 6.75, BY.
6.76.2c   Nauplia: Map 6.75, BY.
6.77.1a   Sepeia: location unknown except near Tiryns.
6.77.2a   The double oracle: see 6.19 and Appendix P, §9.
6.77.2b   Miletus: Map 6.93, BY.
6.77.2c   Scholars have come up with several possible interpretations for the oracle's predicted victory of the female over the male, but

none of them are convincing.
6.77.3a   On the role of heralds in warfare, see Appendix N, Hoplite Warfare in Herodotus, §11.
6.79.1a   Peloponnese: Map 6.75, BX.
6.79.1b   Two minas equaled 200 drachmas. See Appendix J, §10–13, 15, 20.
6.79.1c   Kleomenes lures them out of the sacred precinct in the grove because to attack and kill them there would be sacrilege.

of the grove was thick and they could not see what was happening to the men outside it until finally one of them climbed a tree and, looking down, discovered what was happening. After that, the Argives no longer went out when they were summoned.

At that point, Kleomenes ordered the helots with the army to pile up wood around the grove, and after they had obeyed this command, he set the entire grove on fire. As it burned, he asked one of the deserters which of the gods this grove belonged to and was told that it was the grove of Argos. When he heard this, Kleomenes heaved a great sigh and said, "Apollo god of prophecy, you certainly deceived me when you told me that I would capture Argos; I assume your prophecy has now been fulfilled."

Kleomenes then sent the greater part of the army back to Sparta,[a] but he himself took 1,000 of his best men to the sanctuary of Hera,[b] where he wanted to perform a sacrifice at the altar. The priest, however, forbade him from doing so, saying that it was a sacrilege for an outsider to sacrifice there. Kleomenes ordered the helots to lead the priest away from the altar and to whip him, and then performed the sacrifice by himself; then he, too, went back to Sparta.

After his return, his enemies brought him to trial before the ephors, claiming that he had accepted bribes to refrain from taking Argos when he could easily have captured it. In his reply to this charge—which I cannot judge if it was a lie or the truth—he said that when he had taken the sanctuary of Argos, he supposed that the god's oracle had been fulfilled, and thus he had not thought it right to make an attempt on the city until he had performed a sacrifice and learned whether the god would surrender Argos to him or stand in his way. [2] But while he was hoping to obtain favorable omens in the sanctuary of Hera, a flame of fire blazed from the chest of the statue of the goddess, which convinced him that he would not take Argos. For if it had been the head of the statue that had blazed, he would have taken over the city from top to bottom, but since the fire had blazed out of the chest, he knew that he had already done all that the god willed for him to do. What he said was both plausible and credible to the Spartans, and so his judges voted by a large margin to acquit him.[a]

Argos was now so bereft of its male citizens that their slaves took control of affairs there, governing and managing the city until the sons of those who had perished reached maturity. When that happened, the sons regained control over Argos for themselves and threw out the slaves, who, being compelled to leave, took possession of Tiryns by force. [2] These two cities were on good terms with each other for some time, but then a prophet Kleandros, a man of Arcadian Phigaleia[a] by origin, came to the slaves and persuaded them to attack their masters. This gave rise to a long war between them until finally the Argives prevailed, though with much difficulty.

6.80
494
SEPEIA
Kleomenes burns down the grove and discovers that this fulfills his own prophecy.

6.81
494
ARGOS-SPARTA
After worshiping at the sanctuary of Hera, Kleomenes returns to Sparta.

6.82
494?
SPARTA
Kleomenes successfully defends himself against a suit brought by his enemies that he accepted bribes to spare Argos.

6.83
ARGOS
Argos is ruled by slaves until the sons of those slain grow up. The cast-out slaves capture Tiryns.

6.81.1a Sparta: Map 6.75, BX.
6.81.1b Sanctuary of Hera (Heraion): Map 6.75, BY.

6.82.2a See Appendix P.
6.83.2a Phigaleia, Arcadia: Map 6.75, BX.

6.84
SPARTA
The Spartans say that Kleomenes went mad from an addiction to strong drink he had acquired by keeping company with the Scythians.

According to the Argives, then, that is why Kleomenes went mad and died an evil death. The Spartans, however, say that Kleomenes became deranged not because of any divine force, but because he had become, through his association with Scythians,[a] a drinker of undiluted[b] wine. [2] For the Scythian nomads, eager to punish Darius for having invaded their land, had sent an embassy to Sparta to form an alliance and to organize a plan whereby they themselves would attempt to invade Media[a] from the Phasis River,[b] and they wanted to arrange that the Spartans would march inland from Ephesus[c] and meet them at the same place. [3] They say that when the Scythians had come to Sparta for this purpose, Kleomenes spent a great deal of time in their company, and in fact associated with them more than was appropriate; and it was from them that he learned to drink unmixed wine, which the Spartans believe was the cause of his madness. And they claim that ever since then, whenever they wish to drink stronger wine, they call for a "Scythian" drink.[a] So that is what the Spartans tell about Kleomenes. For myself, I think that the best explanation is that Kleomenes was punished for his treatment of Demaratos.

6.85
490
SPARTA
At the instigation of the Aeginetans after the death of Kleomenes, a Spartan court condemns Leotychidas, but the Aeginetans refrain from punishing him and agree that he will accompany them to Athens to ask for the Aeginetan hostages.

When the Aeginetans[a] found out that Kleomenes had died, they sent messengers to Sparta to denounce Leotychidas for the hostages being held in Athens.[b] The Lacedaemonians organized a trial and decided that the Aeginetans had suffered an egregious insult at the hands of Leotychidas and sentenced him to be surrendered to the Aeginetans as compensation for the hostages held in Athens. [2] But just as the Aeginetans were about to lead Leotychidas away, Theasides son of Leoprepes, a man of some distinction in Sparta, spoke up: "What are you planning to do, Aeginetans? Will you really seize the king of the Spartans now being surrendered by his own citizens? Even if the Spartans have made this decision now out of anger, you, if you do this, will have to worry that they will later invade and utterly destroy your land." [3] Upon hearing this warning, the Aeginetans halted their abduction of Leotychidas and instead negotiated an agreement whereby he would accompany them to Athens, where he would make sure that their hostages were returned to them.

6.86
490
ATHENS
The Athenians at first refuse to give back the Aeginetan hostages.

When Leotychidas came to Athens, he asked for the return of the hostages that he had deposited with them,[a] but the Athenians were unwilling to give them back. They spun out excuses, claiming that since two kings had deposited them, it would not be right if the Athenians should now return the hostages to just one king without the other.

6.84.1a   Scythia: Map 6.93, locator.
6.84.1b   The Greek custom was to dilute wine with some proportion of water to reduce the potency of its alcohol content.
6.84.2a   Media: Map 6.93, locator. Darius' invasion of Scythia is described throughout Book 4, particularly 4.97–142.
6.84.2b   Phasis River: Map 6.93, locator.

6.84.2c   Ephesus: Map 6.93, BY.
6.84.3a   For evidence of the Scythian love of wine, see Appendix E, Herodotus and the Black Sea Region, §12.
6.85.1a   Aegina: Map 6.93, BX.
6.85.1b   Athens: Map 6.93, BX.
6.86.1a   The delivery of these hostages was described in 6.73.3ff.

Leotychidas replied to their refusal, "Athenians, you may do whatever you wish; either return them, which would be the pious thing to do, or not, which would be the opposite. I would like to tell you, however, about a certain deposit that once was made in Sparta. [2] We Spartans tell the story of Glaukos son of Epikydas, who lived in Lacedaemon in about the third generation before my own. We tell how this man was preeminent in all respects, and especially in his reputation for justice; he was the best among all who dwelled in Lacedaemon at this time. [3] And we tell what happened to him in the fullness of time, how a certain Milesian[a] who wanted to talk to him once came to Sparta and presented him with the following proposition: 'I am a Milesian, but I have come to your land, Glaukos, because I would like to benefit from your justice, [4] which is much talked of throughout all Hellas, and especially in Ionia.[a] I have been thinking about how Ionia is always in danger, while the Peloponnese is secure, established, and stable; in my land, it is impossible for one to see wealth remaining in the hands of the same people continuously. [5] After I had considered all this and thought it through, I decided to convert half of all my property into silver and to deposit the money with you, because I am absolutely certain that what I deposit with you will be safe and secure. So accept my money and take also these tokens to keep safe with it; restore the silver to whoever comes to you with the same tokens and asks you for it.'

"When the visitor from Miletus had said just that and no more than that, Glaukos accepted the deposit and the stated conditions. And after a great deal of time had passed, the sons of the man who had made the deposit came to Sparta, arranged to talk to Glaukos, and, showing him the tokens, asked for the return of the money. [2] But Glaukos tried to put them off, saying: 'I really do not remember this matter, and I can't think of anything that would help me recall what you are talking about. Of course, if I do come to remember something of it, I would do only what is just; if I did take the money, I shall do the right thing and return it, but if I never took it in the first place, I shall abide by the customs of the Hellenes in my dealings with you. I shall postpone my decision until the fourth month from this one.'

"The Milesians thought themselves most unfortunate and departed under the impression that they had been robbed of their money. Glaukos then journeyed to Delphi to consult the oracle. He inquired whether he could seize the money for himself by swearing a solemn oath,[a] and the Pythia attacked him with these verses:

6.86.α*
490
ATHENS
Leotychidas speaks to the Athenians, telling them the tale of the Spartan Glaukos, known everywhere for justice, who accepted money for safekeeping from a Milesian stranger.

6.86.β
ATHENS
When asked for the return of the money by the stranger's sons, Glaukos procrastinates.

6.86.γ
ATHENS
But the Delphic oracle, although acknowledging the immediate profit of his taking the money, threatens his entire family with long-term ruin.

6.86.α*   This chapter in the *Histories* has subdivisions indicated by Greek letters in alphabetic sequence. That sequence (with the letters' Latin equivalents) is as follows: α (a), β (b), γ (g), δ (d).
6.86.α.3a   Miletus: Map 6.93, BY.

6.86.α.4a   Ionia: Map 6.93, BY.
6.86.γ.1a   Glaukos was asking whether by swearing a solemn (but false) oath that the money was his, he could get away with keeping it for himself.

[2] Glaukos son of Epikydas, right now you will gain the
     greater advantage
To plunder and win the money by oath.
Then swear, since even the trustworthy man meets death
     in the end.
But the child of oath is a nameless force, with no hands
And no feet, yet swiftly pursues and destroys with its grasp
All his kin, his whole house will afterward perish,
While the line of the trustworthy man will fare better.

"After hearing this response, Glaukos begged the god to grant him forgiveness for what he had said. But the Pythia replied that the testing of the
god and the commission of the crime were one and the same thing.

"Glaukos then sent for the Milesian visitors and returned the money to
them. But I tell this story to you, Athenians, because no descendant of
Glaukos exists today, and not a single hearth is acknowledged to belong to
his family; his line has been wiped out root and branch from Sparta. Therefore, when it comes to a deposit, it is best to think only of returning it to
those who ask for its return." That was what Leotychidas said, but the
Athenians still did not heed his words, so he left them.

Now the Aeginetans had not yet paid the penalty for the crimes which
they committed earlier against the Athenians in order to please the Thebans.[a]
Nevertheless, they now prepared to punish the Athenians, claiming that it
was they themselves who had suffered injustice and that the Athenians were
to blame. At that time the Athenians were celebrating their quadrennial festival[b] off Cape Sounion,[c] so the Aeginetans set up an ambush and seized the
ship carrying the sacred officials, with many of the leading men of Athens on
board. After capturing these men, they bound them in chains.

Having suffered this insult at the hands of the Aeginetans, the Athenians
no longer postponed developing every conceivable scheme against them.
Now there lived on Aegina a distinguished man called Nikodromos son of
Knoithos, who resented the Aeginetans for having exiled him from the
island earlier and who now, when he learned that the Athenians were
preparing to harm the Aeginetans, arranged to betray Aegina to the Athenians, designating a certain day on which he would make his attempt and
when they should come to his assistance. To fulfill his part of this arrangement, Nikodromos seized what is called the Old City, but the Athenians did
not appear at the appointed time.[a]

It so happened that they did not then have enough battleworthy ships to
engage the Aeginetan fleet, so they asked the Corinthians to lend them

6.86.δ
ATHENS
Glaukos returns the money,
but his house is extirpated
anyway, proving it unsafe to
think of violating a trust.

6.87
490
AEGINA
The Athenians refuse to
release the hostages, so the
Aeginetans capture a sacred
ship with many leading
Athenians aboard.

6.88
490
ATHENS
The Athenians plot to attack
Aegina, and Nikodromos,
an Aeginetan exile, offers to
betray the island for them.

6.89
490
AEGINA-CORINTH
The Athenians "buy" twenty
ships from Corinth, but they
attack Aegina too late for
Nikodromos' plot.

6.87.1a Thebes, Boeotia: Map 6.93, BX. For
         these crimes, see the episode in 5.79–81.
6.87.1b This festival, probably in honor of Posei-
         don, was held every four years.
6.87.1c Cape Sounion: Map 6.93, BX.
6.88.1a Herodotus does not make clear whether

these hostilities took place before or after
the battle of Marathon in 490 (see
6.107–114). There is some indication
later in his text that they were still at war
in the late 480s (7.144–145).

ships, but by the time they obtained them, the project was ruined. The Corinthians and the Athenians were the best of friends at this time, so the Corinthians did give twenty ships in response to the Athenian request, but they had to charge five drachmas[a] each for them, since the law did not permit them to give the ships as a gift. Adding these ships to their own, the Athenians manned a total of seventy ships when they left for Aegina, but they sailed one day after the agreed-upon date.

When the Athenians did not show up on time, Nikodromos went on board a boat and fled from Aegina, accompanied by other Aeginetans; the Athenians permitted them to settle at Cape Sounion, from where they raided and plundered the Aeginetans on the island.

That, however, is what happened afterward.[a] But at this time, Nikodromos led the common people in an attempted revolt, which was put down by the affluent Aeginetans. The victors led out the captive rebels in order to execute them, and because of what happened next, they came under a curse that they were unable to counter through sacrifice, since they were driven off the island before they could appease the goddess. [2] They had taken 700 of the people alive, and while they were leading them out to be executed, one of the captives broke out of his bonds and fled to the porch of Demeter Thesmophoros.[a] There he grasped the door handles and clung to them so tightly that, although they tried to drag him away, they were unable to loosen his grip on the doors, so they cut off his hands and took him like that, with his hands still clinging fast to the door handles.

So that is what the Aeginetans had done to their own people. And when the Athenians arrived with the fleet of seventy ships, the Aeginetans fought a sea battle against them but were defeated. The Aeginetans then called for assistance from the Argives,[a] the same people to whom they had appealed before, but this time the Argives did not rush to their aid, since they were angry that the Aeginetan ships that Kleomenes had seized by force[b] had put in to shore on Argive territory and that the ships' crews had disembarked with the Lacedaemonians and invaded their territory; in addition, the men from Sicyonian[c] ships had also participated in this invasion. [2] So the Argives imposed a fine of 1,000 talents,[a] 500 to be paid by each of the two peoples. But while the Sicyonians admitted that they had done wrong and agreed to be freed from further expense by paying 100 talents now, the Aeginetans would not admit their guilt and in fact were rather perversely

6.90
490
SOUNION
Nikodromos escapes to Athenian territory.

6.91
490
AEGINA
Class warfare in Aegina leads to massacres and sacrilege.

6.92
490
AEGINA-ARGOS
The Athenians defeat the Aeginetans in a sea fight. Argos refuses to help Aegina as before, but 1,000 volunteers come anyway, most of whom are killed by the Athenians on Aegina.

6.89.1a Drachma: a common unit of currency. There were 100 drachmas in a mina and 6,000 in a talent, so this was a very low token price for the rental of a trireme, which could cost a talent to build. One drachma was the standard daily wage for a skilled laborer in fifth-century Athens. See Appendix J, §15, 16, 20.
6.91.1a Scholars do not agree on when all of these events occurred. In particular, the dates for Nikodromos' actions are unknown but are put by scholars sometime before

Marathon, anywhere from 494 to 491.
6.91.2a Demeter Thesmophoros is thought to mean Demeter the Lawgiver, referring to the establishment of agriculture and settled law.
6.92.1a Argos: Map 6.93, BX.
6.92.1b Kleomenes' seizure of Aeginetan ships was described in 6.76.2.
6.92.1c Sicyon: Map 6.93, BX.
6.92.2a A talent was an ancient Greek unit of weight and currency. See Appendix J, §11–13, 20.

stubborn and remorseless about the whole thing. As a result, when they now requested the Argive state to help them, not a single Argive was officially sent to assist them, although about 1,000 of them did volunteer to go. The general leading these volunteers was a man by the name of Eurybates, who had trained for the pentathlon.[b] [3] The majority of these volunteers never returned home again but were killed by the Athenians on Aegina. The general himself, Eurybates, showed his skill in single combat by killing three men, but he then died at the hands of the fourth, one Sophanes of Dekeleia.[a]

Sometime later, when the Aeginetans spotted the Athenian ships floundering in disorder, they attacked and this time won the battle, taking four Athenian ships with all their crews.

So the Athenians waged war against the Aeginetans. Meanwhile, the Persian was attending to his own concerns, as he was constantly being reminded by his servant to remember the Athenians,[a] and the Peisistratids were at his side maligning the Athenians; moreover, Darius himself wanted to seize this pretext[b] to subjugate all those Hellenes who had refused to give him earth and water.[c] [2] Since Mardonios had failed on his expedition,[a] Darius relieved him of his command and appointed other generals: Datis, a Mede by race, and Artaphrenes son of his brother Artaphrenes. Darius sent these generals off, instructing them to enslave Athens[b] and Eretria[c] and to bring back the captive slaves into his presence.

So the newly appointed generals left the King and set out on their journey. They went first to the plain of Aleion in Cilicia,[a] bringing along a huge and well-equipped land army. As they camped there, all the ships that had been levied from the various districts arrived to join their forces, as well as the horse-transport ships, which Darius had ordered his tribute-paying peoples to prepare the year before. [2] After putting the horses on board these ships, the land army embarked, and the expedition sailed to Ionia[a] with a fleet of 600 triremes. From there, instead of keeping their ships close to the mainland and sailing toward the Hellespont[b] and Thrace,[c] they set out from Samos,[d] went past Ikaros,[e] and made their voyage through the islands. I suppose they took this route because they were afraid to sail around Mount Athos,[f] since the year before they had suffered catastrophic losses on this route. Moreover, the fact that Naxos[g] had not yet been conquered provided another compelling reason for them to go this way.

6.92.2b The pentathlon consisted of jumping, discus-throwing, spear-throwing, running, and wrestling. (Godley) That Herodotus would mention this about Eurybates is an example of an individual's athletic prowess leading to fame. See Appendix I, §5–6.

6.92.3a Sophanes of Dekeleia (Map 6.93, BX) is mentioned again in 9.75.

6.94.1a See Darius' admonition to his servant after the burning of Sardis, in 5.105.2.

6.94.1b Apparently the burning of Sardis would justify his attack on the Hellenes who had defied him.

6.94.1c Darius had previously sent heralds to Hellas demanding earth and water. See 6.48–49.

6.94.2a Mardonios failed when his fleet was destroyed in a storm off Mount Athos (Map 6.93, AX) in 492. See 6.44.

6.94.2b Athens: Map 6.93, BX.

6.94.2c Eretria, Euboea: Map 6.93, BX, and Map 6.105, AY.

6.95.1a Aleion Plain (Aleion Pedon) of Cilicia: Map 6.93, locator.

6.95.2a Ionia: Map 6.93, BY.

6.95.2b Hellespont: Map 6.93, AY.

6.95.2c Thrace: Map 6.93, AY.

6.95.2d Samos: Map 6.93, BY.

6.95.2e Ikaros: Map 6.93, BY.

6.95.2f Mount Athos: Map 6.93, AX.

6.95.2g Naxos: Map 6.93, BY.

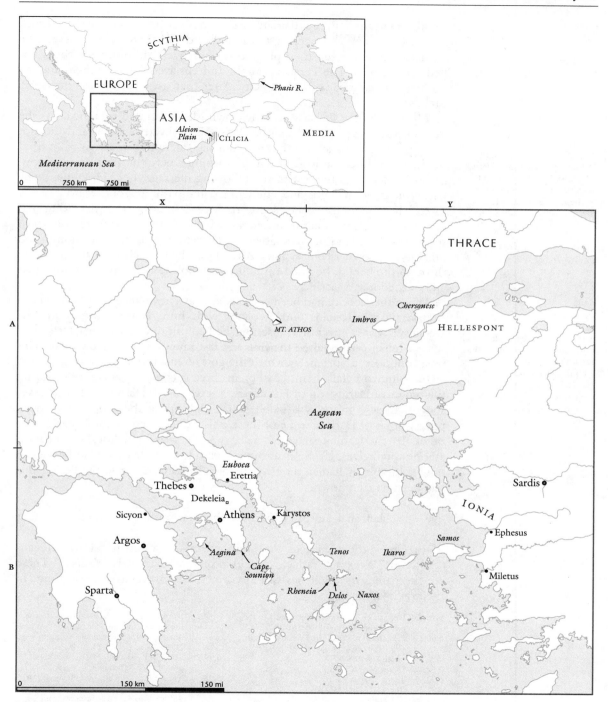

Map 6.93

6.96
490
NAXOS
The Persians conquer
Naxos, enslaving all those
they catch.

6.97
490
DELOS
The Delians flee before the
Persian approach, but Datis,
the Persian general, promises
good treatment and honor
to the holy place and bids
them to return.

6.98
490
DELOS
After Datis leaves, Delos
suffers an earthquake, its first
according to Herodotus,
who thinks it a portent from
the gods of all the evils the
Hellenes were to suffer in
the ensuing years.

The Persians left the Ikarian Sea,[a] and since they intended to attack Naxos first, they approached the island and put in to shore there. The Naxians, remembering their previous experience,[b] did not await them but fled for the hills. The Persians caught and enslaved some of them and set fire to their sanctuaries and the city. After that, they set sail for the other islands.

Meanwhile, the Delians[a] left their own island and fled to Tenos.[b] As the Persian forces approached Delos, Datis sailed ahead of them and did not allow the ships to anchor off Delos, but had them put in across from it, at the island of Rheneia[c] instead. Upon learning where the Delians were now, he sent a herald to them with the following message: [2] "Holy men, why have you gone in flight and condemned me without good reason? For I myself have enough good sense to know, and besides the King has instructed me, not to harm the site on which the two gods were born,[a] nor the rest of the island or its inhabitants. Therefore return to your homes and inhabit your own island again." After Datis had proclaimed this message through the herald, he piled up 300 talents[b] of frankincense upon the altar and burned it as a sacrifice.

When the sacrifice had been completed, Datis next sailed with his forces to Eretria, taking Ionians and Aeolians with him. And according to the Delians, it was at this point, just after he had put out to sea, that Delos was shaken by an earthquake—the first and last one up until my own day. This was, I suppose, a portent by which the god revealed to mortals the evils that were going to befall them. [2] For in three successive generations, during the reigns of Darius son of Hystaspes, Xerxes son of Darius, and Artaxerxes son of Xerxes,[a] more evils befell Hellas than in all the other generations prior to that of Darius. Some of these evils were caused by the Persians, but others by the leading states of Hellas waging war for political domination among themselves. [3] So it was not at all odd that Delos should be shaken now, although it had never been before. In fact an oracle predicting this had been written down:

I shall shake even Delos, though it was unshaken before.

In Greek the names of the kings mean the following: Darius means "Achiever," Xerxes "Warlike," and Artaxerxes "Extremely Warlike." These are the names the Hellenes would correctly use to refer to these Kings in their own language.

6.96.1a Ikarian Sea, presumably the waters to the west of the island of Ikaros: Map 6.93, BY.
6.96.1b Herodotus refers to the Persian attack in 499 led by Aristagoras and Megabates, which failed. See 5.34.
6.97.1a Delos: Map 6.93, BY.
6.97.1b Tenos: Map 6.93, BY.
6.97.1c Rheneia: Map 6.93, BY.
6.97.2a The gods Apollo and Artemis were supposed to have been born on Delos. This

pious announcement must have surprised the Greeks, coming from a force that had recently burned all the sanctuaries of Naxos (Map 6.93, BY).
6.97.2b The talent was a unit of weight of about 57 pounds. See Appendix J, §11–13, 20.
6.98.2a Their reigns span almost 100 years: Darius reigned from 521 to 480, Xerxes from 480 to 465/4, and Artaxerxes from 465/4 to 425/4.

After the barbarians sailed from Delos, they put in at the islands, where they enlisted men to join their forces and took sons of the islanders as hostages. [2] But when, as they made their rounds of the islands, they put in at Karystos,[a] the inhabitants there refused to give them hostages or to march against their neighbors, by whom they meant the Eretrians and Athenians.[b] So the Persians besieged the city and ravaged the land until the Karystians adopted the Persian way of thinking and came over to their side.

When the Eretrians learned that Persian forces were sailing against them, they appealed to the Athenians to come to their assistance, and the Athenians, not wishing to refuse them military aid, offered them as allies their 4,000 klerouchs who had taken over the land of the Chalcidian horse-breeders.[a] The planning of the Eretrians, however, was not at all sound, for although they had sent for Athenian assistance, they were divided among themselves over what they should do. [2] Some of them considered leaving the place and heading for the rough headlands of Euboea, while others, expecting to win personal gains from the Persians, were preparing to betray their city. [3] When Aischines son of Nothon, the leading man of Eretria, became aware of this situation, he informed those Athenians who had arrived about the present state of affairs and begged them to depart for their own land so that they would not perish along with the Eretrians. The Athenians followed his advice, [6.101] and by crossing over to Oropos,[a] they saved themselves. Now the Persians put in their ships at Tamynai,[b] Choereai,[c] and Aigilia[d] in Eretrian territory, and as soon as they landed, they disembarked the horses and prepared to attack their enemies. [2] The Eretrians had no intention of marching out to meet them in battle, so now their prevailing plan was to stay in the city, and their main concern was to defend its walls if they possibly could. The assault on the walls was fierce and lasted for six days, and many fell on both sides. On the seventh day, two prominent citizens, Euphorbos son of Alkimachos and Philagros son of Kyneas, betrayed their city and surrendered it to the Persians. [3] After entering the city, the Persians plundered and set fire to the sanctuaries, exacting vengeance for the sanctuaries burned down in Sardis,[a] and as Darius had instructed, they enslaved the people.

After their conquest of Eretria, the Persians lingered for a few days and then sailed for Attica,[a] thus applying pressure on the Athenians and fully expecting that they would do to the Athenians what they had done to the Eretrians.

6.99
490
KARYSTOS
The Persians recruit soldiers from the islands. Karystos at first refuses them, but then gives in.

6.100
490
ERETRIA
When the Eretrians ask Athens for help, she sends 4,000 klerouchs from Chalcis, but finding divisions among the Eretrians, these go away.

6.101
490
ERETRIA
After resisting Persian assaults for six days, the Eretrians are betrayed by two of their own citizens, the city is taken, and they are enslaved.

6.102
490
MARATHON
Hippias then leads the Persians to Marathon.

6.99.2a   Karystos, Euboea: Map 6.93, BX.
6.99.2b   Athens: Map 6.93, BX.
6.100.1a In 506, after defeating the Chalcidians
          (Chalcis, Euboea: Map 6.105, AY),
          Athens had settled her own citizens
          as klerouchs, lot-holders on Euboean
          land confiscated from the wealthier
          Chalcidians, known as the *hippobotai*, or
          horse breeders. See 5.77.
6.101.1a Oropos: Map 6.105, AY.

6.101.1b Tamynai, Euboea: Map 6.105, AY.
6.101.1c Choereai, in the territory of Eritrea,
          Euboea: precise location unknown.
6.101.1d Aigilia: location unknown.
6.101.3a Sardis: Map 6.93, BY. This refers to the
          fire that burned down the sanctuaries at
          Sardis when the Greek captured the city
          in 498. See 5.101.
6.102.1a Attica: Map 6.105, AY.

Since Marathon[b] was the region of Attica most suitable for cavalry as well as the one closest to Eretria, that is where Hippias son of Peisistratos led them.

As soon as they heard about this, the Athenians rushed to Marathon to defend it themselves, led by the ten generals, of whom Miltiades was the tenth. His father, Kimon son of Stesagoras,[a] had been driven into exile from Athens by Peisistratos son of Hippocrates. [2] And during his exile he won a race with his four-horse team at Olympia,[a] achieving the same victory that had been won by Miltiades, his half brother by the same mother. At the next Olympiad, Kimon won again with the same mares, but this time gave up his victory so that it could be proclaimed in the name of Peisistratos. By relinquishing his victory, he was able to return from exile to his own land. [3] But when he had won with the same mares yet again, it was his fate to die at the hands of the sons of Peisistratos after Peisistratos was no longer alive. They killed him by placing men at the Prytaneion[a] at night to ambush him; he now lies buried at the entrance to the city, across the road called "Through the Hollow,"[b] and the horses that won his three Olympic victories are buried opposite him. [4] The horses of Euagoras of Laconia[a] accomplished this same feat, but no others have ever done so. Kimon's elder son Stesagoras was at the time being raised in the Chersonese with his uncle Miltiades, while the younger son was with Kimon himself in Athens. He was named Miltiades after the Miltiades who had settled the Chersonese.

This was the Miltiades who had escaped death twice and who had left the Chersonese and was now a general of the Athenians. For the Phoenicians, judging his capture and delivery to the King to be of great importance, had pursued him as far as Imbros.[a] [2] But he escaped them and returned to his own land, thinking he was now safe. There, however, his enemies caught up with him and prosecuted him in court for having behaved like a tyrant in the Chersonese. But he was acquitted and escaped them, too, and thus came to be a general of the Athenians, elected by the people.[a]

The first thing the generals did, while still in the city, was to send a message to Sparta by dispatching a herald named Philippides,[a] who was an Athenian long-distance runner and a professional in this work. Now Philippides himself reported to the Athenians afterward that when he was running in the vicinity of Mount Parthenion overlooking Tegea,[b] the god Pan fell in with him [2] and, shouting out his name, "Philippides," ordered him to ask

6.102.1b   Marathon: Map 6.105, AY. Marathon was indeed a plain suitable for cavalry (see Figure 6.102), but it was also a beach and a sheltered anchorage for a fleet landing, which would have been important to the expedition.

6.103.1a   See Appendix L, §2, 8, and Figure L which diagrams the family of the Philaids, to which Miltiades, Kimon, and Stesagoras all belonged.

6.103.2a   Olympia: Map 6.105, AX.

6.103.3a   Prytaneion (the town hall of Athens at the end of the sixth century): Map 6.105, inset.

6.103.3b   "Through the Hollow road" (in Greek, Dia Koiles), possible location: Map 6.105, inset.

6.103.4a   Laconia: Map 6.105, BX.

6.104.1a   Imbros: Map 6.93, AY. For the Phoenician pursuit of Miltiades from the Chersonese, see 6.41.1–2.

6.104.2a   The ten generals of Athens were almost the only officials elected to office; the others were selected by lot.

6.105.1a   Philippides is written as Pheidippides in some of the manuscripts.

6.105.1b   Mount Parthenion, Tegea: Map 6.105, BX.

FIGURE 6.102. AERIAL VIEW OF THE PLAIN OF MARATHON, WHERE THE BATTLE TOOK PLACE. IT IS THOUGHT THAT THE PERSIAN FLEET WAS ANCHORED OFF THE BEACH NEAR THE NARROW PENINSULA AT THE TOP LEFT.

the Athenians why they were paying no attention to him, although he was well disposed toward them, had already and often been of service to them, and would serve them further in the future. [3] The Athenians believed this report was true, and once their affairs were settled and stable again, they set up a shrine to Pan below the Acropolis,[a] and in response to his message to them, they propitiate Pan with sacrifices and a torch race every year.

So after Philippides had been sent off by the generals and, as he claimed, Pan had appeared to him, he arrived in Sparta on the day after he had left Athens.[a] There he said to the magistrates, [2] "Lacedaemonians, the Athenians beg you to rush to their defense and not look on passively as the most ancient city in Hellas falls into slavery imposed by barbarians. For in fact Ere-

6.106
490
SPARTA
Philippides arrives in Sparta the day after leaving Athens. The Spartans promise to help, but in accordance with their law, must wait for the full moon before sending troops.

6.105.3a   Shrine to Pan (Pandion) below the Acropolis in Athens, probable location: Map 6.105, inset.

6.106.1a   The distance between Athens and Sparta is approximately 150 miles.

469

tria has already been enslaved, and thus Hellas has become weaker by one important city." [3] When he had announced this as he had been instructed, the Spartans resolved to help the Athenians, but it was impossible for them to do so at that moment, since they did not wish to break their law. For that day was the ninth of the month, and on the ninth, they said, they could not march out to war, but must instead wait until the moon was full.[a]

So they waited for the full moon while Hippias son of Peisistratos was leading the barbarians to Marathon.[a] During the previous night Hippias dreamt that he was sleeping with his own mother.[b] [2] He interpreted this vision to mean that he would return to Athens, recover his rule, and die as an old man there in his native land; at least that was his interpretation of his dream at the time. After Hippias led the captive slaves from Eretria to the island of the Styrians, which is called Aigilia,[a] and had them disembark there, he directed the ships to put in at Marathon. When the barbarians had come ashore, he set about assigning them to their various positions. [3] In the midst of this work, however, he was seized by an unusually severe fit of sneezing and coughing, and since he was getting on in age, most of his teeth were loose, and one of them fell out with the force of his coughing and landed on the sand. Hippias tried very hard to find it, [4] but the tooth was nowhere to be seen. He then groaned to those standing nearby, "This land is not ours, and we shall not make it subject to us, either, for my tooth now holds all that was to be my share."[a]

In this way, then, Hippias concluded that his vision had been fulfilled.

Now just when the Athenians had taken up their positions in the precinct of Herakles,[a] the Plataeans[b] arrived in full force to assist them. They had earlier placed themselves under the protection of the Athenians,[c] who had then exerted much effort on their behalf. [2] This had happened in the following way. Once, when the Plataeans were being hard pressed by the Thebans,[a] they had offered themselves to Kleomenes son of Anaxandridas and the Lacedaemonians, since the Lacedaemonians happened to be

6.107
490
MARATHON
While the Spartans wait for the full moon, Hippias guides the Persians to Marathon and establishes them there. Herodotus recounts the tales of Hippias' dream and the loss of his tooth.

6.108
490
PLATAEA
The Plataeans arrive at Marathon to fight alongside the Athenians. Herodotus tells how thirty years earlier, following Spartan advice, they allied themselves with Athens for protection against Thebes.

6.106.3a This statement probably applies only to the month of Karneios (Attic Metageitnion), when the Karneia was celebrated at Sparta in honor of Apollo from the seventh to the fifteenth of the month. (Godley) Plato writes in *Laws* 693 and 698 that Spartans were prevented from sending timely assistance to the Athenians at Marathon because they were at that time fighting the Messenians. Perhaps another helot revolt had taken place and required Spartan forces to remain in Messenia (Map 6.105, BX) or at least close to home. See Appendix B, §19.
6.107.1a Marathon: Map 6.105, AY.
6.107.1b Significant dreams were thought to be communications from the gods warning of threats and dangers, advising on cures for illness, imposing policies, or answering pressing questions, but Herodotus

has Artabanos give a surprisingly rational explanation for them when (at 7.16 .β.2) he advises Xerxes that "most of the visions visiting our dreams tend to be what one is thinking about during the day."
6.107.2a Styra, Euboea, and the possible location of Aigilia: Map 6.105, AY.
6.107.4a See Appendix P, §2, 14.
6.108.1a Precinct of Herakles: precise location unknown.
6.108.1b Plataea: Map 6.105, AY.
6.108.1c In the year 519 (*Thucydides* 3.68). Herodotus here uses a Greek expression which signifies that the Plataeans had given themselves over to the Athenians, allying themselves in a subordinate position to receive protection, as well as to assist the senior partner against its enemies.
6.108.2a Thebes: Map 6.105, AY.

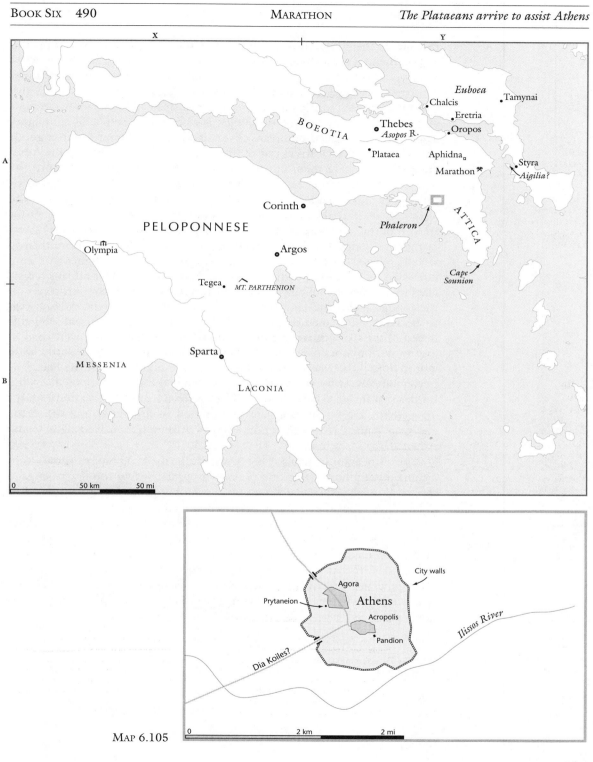

X   Y

Euboea
Chalcis   • Tamynai
Thebes ○   • Eretria
Asopos R.   Oropos
A   Plataea •   Aphidna ▫
Aphidna

B O E O T I A

Marathon ✳   • Styra
Aigilia?

Corinth ○
Phaleron
A T T I C A

PELOPONNESE

Olympia ⛩
Argos ○

Tegea •   ⌃ *MT. PARTHENION*

Cape Sounion

B   M E S S E N I A   Sparta ○

L A C O N I A

0   50 km   50 mi

City walls
Agora
Prytaneion   **Athens**
Acropolis
• Pandion
Ilissos River
Dia Koiles?

0   2 km   2 mi

MAP 6.105

471

present in their region at the time. But the Lacedaemonians refused to accept them, saying, "We live too far away, and any assistance we could offer you would be cold and remote. You could be enslaved many times over before we ever heard anything about it. [3] So we advise you to give yourselves to the Athenians for protection instead; they not only are your close neighbors, but also are no sluggards when it comes to lending military assistance." The Lacedaemonians gave this advice not so much out of goodwill toward the Plataeans as out of their wish to create trouble for the Athenians by provoking them into active hostilities against the Boeotians.[a] [4] The Plataeans did not reject their advice, so while the Athenians were conducting their sacrifices to the twelve gods,[a] the Plataeans sat down at the altar and offered themselves to the Athenians. As soon as the Thebans learned of this, they marched against the Plataeans, and the Athenians rushed to their assistance. [5] Battle was about to be joined when the Corinthians,[a] who happened to be present, would not allow them to fight, and were entrusted by both sides with the task of arbitration. The Corinthians reconciled the parties by defining the boundaries of their respective territories on the condition that the Thebans should leave anyone alone who did not wish to be classified as members of the Boeotian League. After rendering this decision, the Corinthians departed, but as the Athenians, too, were marching away, the Boeotians attacked them, and in the ensuing battle were defeated. [6] The Athenians then extended the boundaries of the Plataeans beyond those set by the Corinthians, making the River Asopos[a] itself the border that divided the territory of Thebes from that of Plataea and Hysiai.[b] That, then, is how the Plataeans had offered themselves to the Athenians and thus gained their protection. And now they had arrived to help the Athenians at Marathon.

The Athenian generals were divided in their opinions: some were against joining battle, thinking their own numbers were too few to engage the forces of the Medes, while others, including Miltiades, urged that they fight. [2] So they disagreed, and the worst of the two proposals seemed to be prevailing when Miltiades went up to the polemarch at that time, one Kallimachos of Aphidna,[a] who had been selected by lot for his office as polemarch of the Athenians. It was he who had the eleventh vote, for in the old days the Athenians used to grant the polemarch an equal vote with their generals.[b] [3] Miltiades said to Kallimachos, "It is now up to you, Kallimachos, whether you will reduce Athens to slavery or ensure its freedom and thus leave to all posterity a memorial for yourself which will

6.108.3a   Boeotia: Map 6.105, AY.
6.108.4a   The twelve gods—Zeus, Hera, Poseidon, Demeter, Apollo, Artemis, Hephaistos, Athena, Ares, Aphrodite, Hermes, and Hestia—shared a central altar in the agora, from which distances to other sites were reckoned.
6.108.5a   Corinth: Map 6.105, AY.

6.108.6a   Asopos River: Map 6.105, AY.
6.108.6b   Hysiai, a settlement very near Plataea. Plataea: Map 6.105, AY.
6.109.2a   Aphidna (an Athenian deme): Map 6.105, AY. The polemarch was one of the nine archons, magistrates of Athens; see Glossary.
6.109.2b   See Appendix N, §4.

exceed even that of Harmodios and Aristogeiton.[a] For from the time Athenians first came into existence up until the present, this is the greatest danger they have ever confronted. If they bow down before the Medes, it is clear from our past experience what they will suffer when handed over to Hippias; but if this city prevails, it can become the first among all Greek cities. [4] I shall explain to you how matters really stand and how the authority to decide this matter has come to rest with you. We ten generals are evenly divided in our opinions, some urging that we join battle, others that we do not. [5] If we fail to fight now, I expect that intense factional strife will fall upon the Athenians and shake their resolve so violently that they will medize.[a] But if we join battle before any rot can infect some of the Athenians, then, as long as the gods grant both sides equal treatment, we can prevail in this engagement. [6] All this is now in your hands and depends on you. If you add your vote for my proposal, your ancestral land can be free and your city the first of Greek cities. But if you choose the side of those eager to prevent a battle, you will have the opposite of all the good things I have described."

Miltiades' arguments persuaded Kallimachos, and when the polemarch's vote was added to the tally, the decision was made to join battle. And afterward, the generals in favor of the battle each in their turn ceded their day of command[a] to Miltiades when the day came around for each to be in charge. But while Miltiades accepted this, he would not make the attack until it was his day to preside.

When his turn came, he deployed the Athenians for battle with the polemarch Kallimachos leading the right wing, for at that time the Athenians observed a custom that the polemarch was always to command the right wing. Once Kallimachos had taken his position there as their leader, the tribes[a] were posted next to one another in succession according to their numerical order,[b] and the Plataeans were posted at the end of the line, holding the extreme left wing. [2] In fact, as a consequence of this battle, whenever the Athenians perform sacrifices at their quadrennial festivals,[a] the Athenian herald prays that both the Athenians and the Plataeans together will be blessed with good fortune. [3] The result of the Athenians' deployment at Marathon was that the line of the Athenian army was equal in length to that of the Medes, but the center of the Athenian line was only a

6.110
490
MARATHON
Kallimachos votes to attack, and leadership of the army is granted by all to Miltiades.

6.111
490
MARATHON
Miltiades arrays the army in line, with more strength in the wings than in the center.

6.109.3a Harmodios and Aristogeiton: legendary tyrant slayers of Athens, whose plot in 514 to kill Hippias, the son of Peisistratos and reigning tyrant at the time, failed. They did assassinate Hipparchos, the brother of Hippias. See 5.55–56.

6.109.5a To "medize" was to go over to the Persian side. Persians were often called Medes by the Greeks.

6.110.1a Each day, a new general seems to have taken his turn to preside as head commander. See Appendix A, §9.

6.111.1a The Athenian army was organized into ten hoplite units, one for each of the political tribes set up by Kleisthenes in 508/7. See 5.66.2; Appendix A, §7; and Appendix N, §4.

6.111.1b The tribal units were posted either in the order of the ten tribes established by the reforms of Kleisthenes, or in an order determined by lot. (How and Wells)

6.111.2a The most important quadrennial festival was the Panathenaia. See Appendix I, §3, 12.

few rows deep and thus the army was at its weakest there; each wing, however, was strong in numbers.

6.112
490
MARATHON
After the sacrifices prove favorable, the Athenians charge at the run, the first Hellenes to do so and not fear the sight of the Medes.

After the troops were in position and the sacrifices had proven favorable,[a] when the Athenians were let loose and allowed to advance, they charged at a run toward the barbarians.[b] The space between the two armies was about a mile,[c] [2] and the Persians, who saw the Athenians advancing toward them on the double, prepared to meet their attack; they assumed that the Athenians were seized by some utterly self-destructive madness, as they observed how few the Athenians were in number and how they were charging toward them with neither cavalry nor archers in support.[a] [3] So the barbarians suspected that the Athenians had gone mad, but when the Athenians closed with them in combat, they fought remarkably well. For they were the first of all Hellenes we know of to use the running charge against their enemies, as well as the first to endure the sight of the Medes' clothing and the men wearing it. In fact, until then, even to hear the name "Medes" spoken would strike terror into Hellenes.

6.113
490
MARATHON
The Athenian wings prevail and then unite to defeat the initially victorious Persian center, driving the enemy to their ships.

They fought in the battle at Marathon for a long time. The barbarians prevailed in the center of the line, where the Persians themselves and the Sakai[a] were deployed, and as the barbarians were winning here, they broke through the line of the Hellenes and chased them inland; but at the same time, the Athenians and Plataeans were prevailing on the wings. [2] In their victory there, they allowed the barbarian troops that they had routed to flee and then, drawing both of their wings together, they fought those enemy troops who had broken through the center; in this encounter, too, the Athenians were victorious, and as the Persians fled, the Athenians pursued them and cut them down until they reached the sea, where they called for fire and started to seize the ships.

6.114
490
MARATHON
Some of the famous Athenians who fell in the fighting.

It was in this struggle that the polemarch Kallimachos perished, having proven himself a noble and courageous warrior; Stesilaos son of Thrasylaos, one of the generals, also died. In addition, Kynegeiros son of Euphorion fell, for while seizing the sternpost of a ship, his hand was chopped off by an axe. Many other famous Athenians died in this conflict as well.

6.112.1a   Sacrifices were always performed before troops went into battle. See Appendix N, §11.
6.112.1b   It was highly unorthodox for phalanxes of hoplites to break ranks and charge on the run against their foes, although it makes sense as a tactic to reduce the effect of archery on an approaching formation. See Appendix O, The Persian Army in Herodotus, §4; and Appendix N, §8.
6.112.1c   Herodotus writes "8 stades." See Appendix J, §6, 19.
6.112.2a   It should be noted that in Herodotus' narrative of the battle of Marathon (6.112–115), there is no mention of participation of cavalry by either side. Some scholars have speculated that the Persian cavalry had been loaded on board their

ships in preparation for a move to somewhere else (perhaps to Phaleron, near Athens, where they sailed after the battle), and that the Athenians decided to attack when they did in order to exploit the absence of the Persian horse. It is also possible that the small force of cavalry that could be transported by ship, which might have been useful for scouting and reconnaissance, was not numerous enough to play a significant role in the battle itself. See Appendix O, §6–7; Appendix N, §7.
6.113.1a   Sakai, location of territory: Map 6.125, locator. The Sakai were probably serving as marines; they are mentioned in that capacity in 7.96.1.

In their attempts, the Athenians gained possession of seven ships. The barbarians pushed off from shore with their fleet and, after picking up the captive slaves from Eretria[a] whom they had left on the island,[b] sailed around Sounion,[c] hoping to arrive at the city of Athens[d] before the Athenians could march there. At Athens, the Alkmeonids were later blamed for having contrived a scheme whereby a shield would be displayed to send a signal to the Persians aboard their ships.[e]

Now while the Persians were sailing around Sounion, the Athenians were marching back as fast as they could to defend their city, and they managed to arrive there in advance of the barbarian fleet. Coming from the sanctuary of Herakles in Marathon, they arrived and set up their camp in another sanctuary of Herakles, the one in Kynosarges.[a] The barbarians anchored their ships off Phaleron[b] (for that was the harbor of the Athenians at the time), held their ships there for a while, and then sailed back to Asia.

In the battle of Marathon, about 6,400 of the barbarians died, and of the Athenians, 192. Those were the casualties from both sides.[a] [2] It happened that an amazing occurrence took place there, when Epizelus son of Cuphagoras, an Athenian who was fighting in the battle and proving himself to be a noble and courageous warrior, was stricken with blindness, though he had not been struck or hit on any part of his body. But from this time on and for the rest of his life, he continued to be blind. [3] I have heard that the story he told about it went something like this: he thought he saw a huge hoplite whose beard overshadowed his entire shield and who was standing opposite him; but this phantom passed by Epizelus and killed the man standing next to him. At least that is what I have heard that Epizelus said.

Datis was well on his way to Asia with his forces when he came to Mykonos,[a] where he had a vision in his sleep. What he saw is not reported, but as soon as the light of day arrived, he made a search of his ships and found in a Phoenician vessel a gilded statue of Apollo. Upon inquiring about the site from which it had been looted, he learned the name of the sanctuary

6.115
490
MARATHON
The Persians sail off and head for Athens, hoping to find the city undefended.

6.116
490
ATHENS
The Athenians march home in time to confront the enemy fleet when it arrives.

6.117
490
MARATHON
Herodotus notes the very unequal number of casualties suffered by each side in the battle. The tale of Epizelus.

6.118
DELOS
The story of Datis' dream and the image of Apollo he left at Delos.

6.115.1a Eretria, Euboea: Map 6.105, AY.
6.115.1b The island was Aigilia, possible location: Map 6.105, AY.
6.115.1c Cape Sounion: Map 6.105, BY.
6.115.1d Athens: Map 6.105, inset.
6.115.1e Herodotus seems to have been convinced that a shield was used to signal the Persians (see also 6.124.2). He also appears anxious to exonerate the Alkmeonids (6.125–131), suggesting that the family into which the great Pericles' father was to marry would not have been involved in treachery. But this whole story, although apparently believed by enough Athenians to provoke Herodotus' denial, is questioned by scholars. Certainly no message of any complexity could have been conveyed, and whether from high ground or by the shore, a signal would hardly have been visible from half a mile or more out

at sea. Perhaps it was a slanderous tale concocted to discredit the family.
6.116.1a Kynosarges, Athens: precise site unknown. It is mentioned in 5.63.4c.
6.116.1b Phaleron: Map 6.105, AY. Phaleron was a long beach near Athens which served as the city's port prior to the development of Peiraieus.
6.117.1a Normally the Athenians' practice was to bring their battle dead home and hold a funeral in Athens, but on this occasion they buried their dead on the battlefield and erected a mound over their bones that can still be seen today. See Figure 6.117c. The number of Athenian casualties would have been well known, and their names may have been inscribed in stone; the number of Persian casualties was probably a wild guess.
6.118.1a Mykonos: Map 6.125, BY.

FIGURE 6.117A. TWO HELMETS FOUND AT OLYMPIA. THE INSCRIPTION ON THE ASSYRIAN ONE (LEFT) SAYS THAT IT WAS TAKEN FROM THE MEDES (PERSIANS) BY THE ATHENIANS AND DEDICATED TO ZEUS. THE OTHER HELMET'S INSCRIPTION SAYS THAT IT WAS DEDICATED TO ZEUS BY MILTIADES.

FIGURE 6.117B. THESE WEAPONS—AN IRON SWORD, ARROWHEADS, AND TWO LEAD SLING BULLETS—WERE ALL FOUND ON THE BATTLEFIELD OF MARATHON.

FIGURE 6.117C. THE SOROS, THE EXTRAORDINARY BURIAL MOUND BUILT OVER THE GRAVES OF THE ATHENIAN TROOPS WHO DIED AT MARATHON. THE BONES OF ATHENIAN MILITARY DEAD WERE NORMALLY RETURNED TO ATHENS AND, AFTER PROPER CEREMONY, INTERRED OUTSIDE THE CITY. ITS ORIGINAL HEIGHT IS THOUGHT TO HAVE BEEN MORE THAN 45 FEET. OVER TIME, EROSION HAS REDUCED IT TO ITS CURRENT DIMENSIONS— ROUGHLY 100 FEET IN DIAMETER AND JUST UNDER 30 FEET HIGH.

from which it had come and sailed to Delos[b] in his own ship. [2] Datis deposited the statue in the sanctuary there and instructed the Delians, who had by now returned to their island, to take the statue to Delion[a] in Thebes, which lies on the coast opposite Chalcis.[b] [3] After giving these orders, Datis sailed away. The Delians, however, did not deliver the image; but twenty years later, the Thebans brought it to Delion because of a prophecy.

Datis and Artaphrenes sailed to Asia[a] and brought the captive Eretrian slaves to Susa.[b] Darius the King had been nursing a bitter grudge against the Eretrians before they were brought to him as slaves, because they had struck first and been the aggressors.[c] [2] But when he saw them delivered up to him as his subjects, he did them no further harm but instead settled them at his royal station[a] in the land of the Kissians[b] called Arderikka, about twenty-three miles from Susa, and almost four and a half miles[c] from the well which supplies three types of products. For bitumen, salt, and oil are

6.119
490–?
ERETRIA-KISSIA
Darius settles the Eretrians near a well that produces asphalt, salt, and oil.

6.118.1b Delos: Map 6.125, BY.
6.118.2a Delion: Map 6.125, AY.
6.118.2b Chalcis, Euboea: Map 6.125, AY.
6.119.1a Asia (Asia Minor): Map 6.125, locator.
6.119.1b Susa: Map 6.125, locator.
6.119.1c For the Eretrian aggression against the King, see 5.99.

6.119.2a The King's royal station: see 5.52.
6.119.2b Kissians, possible location of territory: Map 6.125, locator. Arderikka: location unknown.
6.119.2c Herodotus writes "210 stades" from Susa and "40 stades" from the well. See Appendix J, §6, 19.

drawn from this well in the following way. [3] A shadoof[a] is used, to which is fastened half a wineskin to serve as a bucket. They dip this into the well and draw up the liquid and pour it into a container, from which it is then poured into another, where it is diverted into three separate channels. The bitumen and salt immediately congeal, while the oil [. . .][b] The Persians call this oil *rhadinake*. It is black and has a heavy acrid odor. [4] So the Eretrians were settled in this place by King Darius, and they continue to inhabit this land up to my own time, still speaking their original language.

That, then, is what happened to the Eretrians. After the full moon, 2,000 Lacedaemonians marched to Athens[a] in such great haste that they arrived in Attica[b] on the third day out of Sparta.[c] They were too late to engage in battle, but nevertheless wished to see the Medes, which they did when they reached Marathon.[d] Then they praised the Athenians for their achievement and went home.

I am astonished by that story about the Alkmeonids.[a] I do not believe that they could ever have displayed a shield to the Persians pursuant to an agreement that was motivated by any desire on their part to subject the Athenians to Hippias and the barbarians. For the Alkmeonids are obviously more vehement tyrant haters than even Kallias son of Phainippos and father of Hipponikos. [2] Kallias was the only one of all the Athenians, after Peisistratos had been exiled, who dared to buy the tyrant's property when it was put up for sale by the public auctioneer, and he devised every other kind of hostile act against him as well.

This Kallias is worth recalling for many reasons by everyone. First of all, as has already been mentioned, he was a man who gave excellent service in the liberation of his native land. Then he also won a victory with his horse at Olympia[a] and came in second with his four-horse team; he had earlier won at the Pythian games,[b] and became famous among all the Hellenes for his lavish expenditures. [2] Furthermore, he treated his daughters in the following exceptional way: when they came of age, he generously granted them the most extravagant gift by giving them in marriage to the man whom each of them had selected for herself from among all Athenian men.

The Alkmeonids were tyrant haters every bit as much as Kallias. To me the accusation that they displayed the shield[a] is simply fantastic, and I refuse

6.119.3a   Shadoof: see 1.193.1, n. 1.193.1a, and Figure 1.193.
6.119.3b   There is a lacuna in the text here. One manuscript fills the gap with the phrase "is collected into vessels."
6.120.1a   Athens: Map 6.125, BY.
6.120.1b   Attica: Map 6.125, BY.
6.120.1c   Sparta: Map 6.125, BX.
6.120.1d   Marathon: Map 6.125, BY.
6.121.1a   For the Alkmeonids, see Appendix L and Figure L, which diagrams the famous men of the family.
6.122.1a   Olympia: Map 6.125, BX. On the

Olympic games, see Appendix I.
6.122.1b   The Pythian games were held at Delphi (Map 6.125, AX). See Appendix I, §5, and Appendix P, §10.
6.123.1a   Herodotus returns here to the question first raised in 6.115, of the shield signal to the Persians and who might have done it. He defends the Alkmeonids vigorously and at length. Did a large number of Athenians suspect that the Alkmeonids had pro-Perrsian sentiments?

to accept it, since they were exiled by the tyrants during all the years of the tyranny, and it was through their scheme that the Peisistratids abandoned the tyranny. [2] So in my judgment, they were far more the liberators of Athens than were Harmodios and Aristogeiton, who, by killing Hipparchos, did not put an end to the tyranny but only drove the surviving Peisistratids to savagery. The Alkmeonids, on the other hand, if they were truly the ones who bribed the Pythia to proclaim in her prophecies that the Lacedaemonians should free Athens (as I indicated earlier),[a] were the real liberators of Athens.

One might object that they betrayed their native land because they found fault with the Athenian people, but in fact, among the Athenians, no other men were more esteemed or more highly honored than the Alkmeonids. [2] Thus it contradicts all logic to assert that they could have displayed the shield for any such reason. A shield was certainly displayed—that is a fact that it is impossible to deny, since it did happen—but as to who was responsible, I can say no more than I already have.

6.124
490
ATHENS
A signal was sent by shield, but Herodotus does not know who did it.

The Alkmeonids were illustrious among the Athenians from their very beginnings, but became even more so because of Alkmeon[a] and later Megakles. [2] For Alkmeon son of Megakles enthusiastically assisted and proved himself an avid supporter of those Lydians[a] who used to come from Sardis,[b] being sent by Croesus to the oracle at Delphi.[c] When Croesus learned from the Lydians who regularly visited the oracle that Alkmeon was serving him well, he sent a message for him to come to Sardis; and when Alkmeon arrived there, Croesus offered him a gift of as much gold as he could carry away on his person at one time. [3] So Alkmeon devised and carried out an effective way to deal with such a gift. He put on a large tunic, leaving a deep fold hanging down from it, and high boots, the widest he could find, then entered the treasury to which he was led. [4] Diving into the heap of gold dust, he first packed as much gold along his shins as his boots could hold; next, he filled the entire fold forming a pocket with gold, sprinkled the hair on his head with gold dust, put some more into his mouth, and finally left the treasury, barely able to drag his boots along with him, resembling anything but a human being, with his mouth full and puffed out! [5] When Croesus saw him, he was overcome with laughter and offered to give Alkmeon not only all that he had with him but an additional amount equal to that which he was now carrying.[a] That is how the house of the Alkmeonids became extremely wealthy, and in this way Alkmeon

6.125
LYDIA
Alkmeon helps Croesus' envoys at Delphi, so Croesus rewards him by letting him take away as much gold as he can carry away at one time.

6.123.2a   Herodotus is referring to his account in 5.63.
6.125.1a   Alkmeon flourished about 590. Croesus' reign was from 560 to 546. It was Megakles son of Alkmeon, and not Alkmeon himself, who was Croesus' contemporary. (Godley)
6.125.2a   Lydia: Map 6.125, locator.
6.125.2b   Sardis: Map 6.125, locator.
6.125.2c   Delphi: Map 6.125, AX.
6.125.5a   Does this fanciful anecdote contain a kernel of truth? Did some relationship with Lydia and perhaps Croesus lie behind the later great wealth of the Alkmeonids? The family's links with Delphi have already been mentioned in 5.62. See Appendix L, §4.

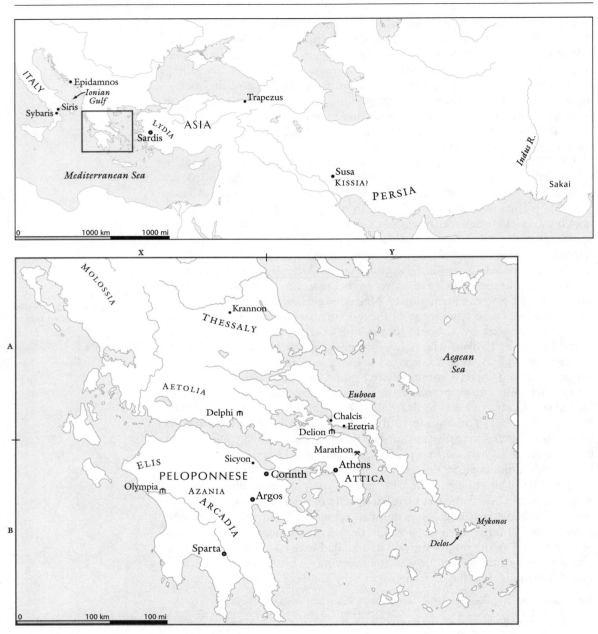

Map 6.125

became rich enough to keep a four-horse chariot and team, with which he won an Olympic victory.[b]

Afterward, in the next generation, Kleisthenes the tyrant of Sicyon[a] supported the rise of the Alkmeonid family, so that it became even much more famous among the Hellenes than it had been previously. This Kleisthenes, who was the son of Aristonymos son of Myron, the son of Andreas, had a daughter by the name of Agariste, and he wished to find the best man of all the Hellenes and to make him her husband. [2] So at the Olympic games, after having won a victory with his four-horse team,[a] Kleisthenes made a proclamation that any Hellene who thought himself worthy to become the son-in-law of Kleisthenes should come to Sicyon on the sixtieth day from this one, or earlier, so that Kleisthenes could validate the marriage within one year. [3] So all Hellenes who were inflated with pride in themselves and their native communities made the journey to compete as suitors. Meanwhile, Kleisthenes had a racecourse and a wrestling ground constructed, and he kept them ready for this purpose.

From Italy[a] came Smindyrides of Sybaris,[b] son of Hippocrates, who had attained a life of the highest luxury possible for one man (Sybaris during this time was at its peak of prosperity), and from Siris[c] came Damasos, the son of a man named Amyris, who was also called "the wise." [2] Those were the men who came from Italy. From Epidamnos[a] came Amphimnestos son of Epistrophos, the only man to arrive from the Ionian Gulf; and from Aetolia[b] came Males, the brother of that Titormos who surpassed all Hellenes in physical strength and who had fled human contact to live on the frontiers of Aetolian territory. [3] From the Peloponnese[a] came Leokedes son of Pheidon[b] the tyrant of Argos.[c] Pheidon is the one who established the standard measures for the Peloponnesians and who committed the greatest act of arrogance of all Hellenes when he forced the Elean[d] commissioners of the Olympic games to leave and put himself in charge of them; this man's son now came as one of the suitors. From Arcadia[e] came Amiantos son of Lykourgos of Trapezus,[f] and from Azania,[g] Laphanes son

6.126
?
SICYON
Kleisthenes tyrant of Sicyon (600–556) offers a challenge to all who would compete for the hand of his daughter.

6.127
?
SICYON
A list of the eminent suitors who responded to the challenge of Kleisthenes of Sicyon.

6.125.5b   Horses in ancient Greece were the property of rich men, and were used for racing only, not for agriculture. Winning the horse-racing events in the great religious games brought high prestige for those individuals who entered the teams, and honor and fame for their cities. See Appendix I, §6.

6.126.1a   Sicyon: Map 6.125, BX. Kleisthenes (ruled from c. 600 to 556) was contemporary with Alkmeon.

6.126.2a   Kleisthenes won the four-horse chariot race at Olympia in the year 582.

6.127.1a   Italy: Map 6.125, locator.
6.127.1b   Sybaris: Map 6.125, locator.
6.127.1c   Siris: Map 6.125, locator.
6.127.2a   Epidamnos, Ionian Gulf: Map 6.125, locator.

6.127.2b   Aetolia: Map 6.125, AX.
6.127.3a   Peloponnese: Map 6.125, BX.
6.127.3b   Pheidon was an early king of Argos who is said to have changed his kingship into a tyranny. The date of his reign is debated by scholars, as there are a number of anecdotes about him, some of them undoubtedly legendary, which make dating quite arbitrary. If Herodotus is correct that a son of his was among the suitors for Kleisthenes' daughter, then he would have reigned from the late seventh into the early sixth century.

6.127.3c   Argos: Map 6.125, BX.
6.127.3d   Elis: Map 6.125, BX.
6.127.3e   Arcadia: Map 6.125, BX.
6.127.3f   Trapezus: Map 6.125, locator.
6.127.3g   Azania: Map 6.125, BX.

of Euphorion, of the city of Paion.[h] According to the story told in Arcadia, Euphorion received the Dioskouroi[i] into his home and from that time on offered hospitality to all men. From Elis came Onomasous son of Agaios. [4] Those were the men from the Peloponnese. From Athens came Megakles son of the Alkmeon who had visited Croesus, and also another man, Hippokleides son of Teisandros, who was preeminent among the Athenians in both wealth and good looks. From Eretria,[a] which was flourishing during this period, came Lysanias. He was the only suitor from Euboea. From Thessaly[b] came Diaktorides of Krannon,[c] who was a Skopad,[d] and also Alkon, a Molossian.[e]

6.128
?
SICYON
Kleisthenes keeps the suitors with him for a year to observe them. He favors those from Athens, particularly Hippokleides.

Those were all the suitors who came, and when they arrived on the appointed day, Kleisthenes first questioned each one about his native land and lineage. Then he kept them there for a year, testing them each on their merit, valor, disposition, education, and character. He did this by keeping company with each one individually as well as observing them together with all the others. And he took the younger men outside to participate in gymnastic contests, too. But his greatest test of all was in their social gatherings. For during the entire period that he detained them, he not only did all this, but at the same time entertained them extravagantly. [2] The suitors who pleased him most were the ones from Athens, and of these he tended to prefer Hippokleides son of Teisandros, for both his merit and his valor, and because he was related to the Kypselids[a] of Corinth by his distant ancestry.

6.129
?
SICYON
On the day of the marriage, the favored suitor, Hippokleides, dances so shamelessly that Kleisthenes rejects him, but he responds with indifference, originating thereby a well-known proverb.

When the day came that had been appointed for the wedding feast and for Kleisthenes to declare which man he had chosen out of all of them, Kleisthenes sacrificed 100 cattle and served a feast to the suitors and to all the people of Sicyon. [2] After the meal, the suitors participated in a competition in music and in speeches delivered to everyone there. As the drinking progressed, Hippokleides, who was already commanding much attention from the others, ordered the flute player to play a dance tune for him. The flute player complied, and while I suppose Hippokleides pleased himself with his dancing, Kleisthenes, as he watched, was annoyed at everything he saw. [3] After pausing for a moment, Hippokleides ordered that a table be brought to him; then he stepped up on the table and first danced some Laconian steps, and then some Attic ones, too. But the third thing he did was to turn upside down and, with his head resting on the table, gesticulate

6.127.3h Paion: location unknown.
6.127.3i Dioskouroi: the twins Castor and Pollux. Dioskouroi means "sons of Zeus."
6.127.4a Eretria, Euboea: Map 6.125, AY.
6.127.4b Thessaly: Map 6.125, AX.
6.127.4c Krannon: Map 6.125, AX.
6.127.4d Skopad: a member of an aristocratic family who ruled Krannon and were rivals of another leading Thessalian family, the Aleuadai, until c. 515; named

after Skopas, who was the first to impose a war tax on the surrounding communities (see also Xenophon's *Hellenica* 6.1.19).
6.127.4e Molossia: Map 6.125, AX.
6.128.2a Kypselids of Corinth: the line of Kypselos son of Eetion and Periandros son of Kypselos (see 1.14.2 and 1.23), who were tyrants of that city. Corinth: Map 6.125, BY.

with his legs waving in the air. [4] Now during the first and second of these dances, Kleisthenes restrained himself and did not blurt out his thoughts, although he felt somewhat disgusted at the thought that Hippokleides might still become his son-in-law, but when he saw him waving his legs around, he could no longer contain himself and said, "Son of Teisandros, you have just danced away your marriage!" And the young man replied, "For Hippokleides, no problem!"

And that is where this saying came from.[a] Kleisthenes then silenced the crowd and spoke: "Suitors of my daughter, I praise you all, and if it were possible, I would gratify you all by not singling out one of you as my choice and rejecting the rest. [2] But since it is impossible to fulfill the wishes of all while planning for the marriage of only one daughter, I offer to each of you who will be rejected a silver talent as a gift in return for your willingness to marry into my family and to be absent from your own homes. It is to Megakles son of Alkmeon that I shall give my daughter Agariste in marriage, in compliance with the laws of the Athenians." Megakles then accepted the betrothal, and the marriage was validated by Kleisthenes.[a]

So that is the story of the judgment of the suitors, which made the fame of the Alkmeonids resound throughout Hellas. From the union of this couple was born that Kleisthenes who established the tribes and the democracy of the Athenians,[a] taking his name from his mother's father, Kleisthenes of Sicyon.[b] [2] This son was born to Megakles, and so was Hippocrates, who himself had two children, another Megakles and another Agariste, named after Agariste daughter of Kleisthenes.[a] This Agariste married Xanthippos son of Ariphron, and during her pregnancy she had a vision in her sleep: she dreamed she saw herself giving birth to a lion, and a few days later, she gave birth to Pericles son of Xanthippos.

Though previously Miltiades had been held in high esteem by the Athenians, after the defeat of the Persians at Marathon he gained even more power and influence.[a] Thus the Athenians were thrilled to grant his request when he asked them for seventy ships, an army, and some money, without revealing against what country he would lead these forces; he claimed, however, that he would make them all rich if they followed him, because they were certain to gain much gold from the land to which he would lead them—at least that's the sort of thing he told them as he asked for the ships.

6.130
?
SICYON
Kleisthenes selects Megakles son of Alkmeon to marry his daughter Agariste.

6.131
ATHENS
The illustrious progeny of Megakles and Agariste culminates in Pericles.

6.132
490
ATHENS
Miltiades' great fame permits him to seek and receive command of an Athenian fleet without disclosing where he intends to use it.

6.130.1a   The saying by Hippokleides (which appears only here in Greek literature) apparently was used when the speaker meant to say that he couldn't care less about something, that it made no difference at all to him.

6.130.2a   A marriage was not valid without the sanction of the bride's father, who gave her to the groom and his family. See

1.46.3a, and n. 1.96.2a.

6.131.1a   Herodotus tells how Kleisthenes established the new Athenian tribes and demes in 5.69.2.

6.131.1b   Sicyon: Map 6.136.

6.131.2a   Agariste: on the naming of women, see Appendix L, §13.

6.132.1a   See Figure 6.117a (right), a helmet dedicated by Miltiades to Zeus at Olympia.

FIGURE 6.132. PLATE WITH
PAINTING OF A WARRIOR ON
HORSEBACK IN PERSIAN ATTIRE.
AN INSCRIPTION ON THE PLATE
IN PRAISE OF MILTIADES HAS
LED TO MUCH SCHOLARLY
DISCUSSION AND DISAGREEMENT
AS TO EXACTLY WHO OR WHAT IS
REPRESENTED.

6.133
489
PAROS
Miltiades attacks Paros
because of a personal grudge,
and besieges the city.

So Miltiades took command of the army and sailed for Paros,[a] on the pretext that the Parians had initiated a conflict by earlier contributing a trireme to the Persian forces at Marathon.[b] That was his excuse, but actually he bore a grudge against the Parians because Lysagoras son of Teisias, a Parian by birth, had maligned him to Hydarnes the Persian. [2] And so Miltiades sailed out, and when he arrived at Paros, he laid siege to the city while the Parians confined themselves within their city walls. Then he sent a herald to demand 100 talents[a] from them, saying that if they did not give him the money, he would not permit his army to withdraw until it had completely destroyed them. [3] The Parians had no intention of giving any money to Miltiades, and instead began to devise strategies to protect their city; in particular, they set to work at night to double the original height of their wall wherever it had recently proven to be vulnerable.

6.133.1a   Paros: Map 6.136.
6.133.1b   Marathon: Map 6.136.
6.133.2a   The talent was a unit of weight and money. One hundred talents was a

very large sum to ancient Greeks. It amounted to 600,000 drachmas, when a skilled workman earned a drachma a day. See Appendix J, §11–13, 20.

That much of the story is related by all the Hellenes, but from here on, the Parians say that what happened is the following. Miltiades was at a loss as to what to do next; but then a captive slave woman named Timo, who was a Parian by birth and a temple servant of the goddesses of the underworld,[a] met with him and told him that if the capture of Paros was of great importance to him, he should follow her advice. [2] After hearing her counsel, Miltiades went to the hill that lies in front of the city and, since he was unable to open the doors, leapt over the wall enclosing the sanctuary of Demeter Thesmophoros.[a] Then, once he had jumped to the inside, he went toward the hall of the temple in order to do whatever he intended within, perhaps to remove some object that was not supposed to be moved or maybe to do something else. As he approached the doors, however, he was suddenly overcome with trembling and ran back the way he had come, but as he jumped down from the wall, he badly twisted his thigh, though others say he injured his knee.

So Miltiades sailed home in a sorry state; he was bringing no money for the Athenians, nor had he added Paros to their territory, despite the fact that he had besieged it for twenty-six days and had laid waste to the island. [2] When the Parians found out that Timo the temple servant had provided guidance to Miltiades, they wished to punish her for it, so they sent sacred delegates to Delphi[a] as soon as they had obtained a respite from the siege. The question they sent to Delphi was whether they should put to death the temple servant of the goddesses because she had instructed their enemies on how to capture her native land and had revealed sacred matters to Miltiades that were not to be disclosed to any male. [3] The Pythia would not permit them to do this, saying that it was not Timo who was at fault for what happened; that Miltiades was destined to end his life unhappily and that Timo had appeared in order to start him down the path to its bad ending.

That was the Pythia's response to the Parians. Now when Miltiades returned home from Paros, he was the subject of much discussion among the Athenians. One in particular, Xanthippos son of Ariphron, brought him to court to be tried by the people on the capital charge of having deceived the Athenians. [2] Miltiades, though present, did not speak in his own defense, for he was incapacitated by his thigh, which was now infected. So as he lay there on a couch, his friends and relatives spoke on his behalf, recounting at length the battle of Marathon and how Miltiades had conquered Lemnos[a] and given it over to the Athenians to punish the Pelasgians.[b] [3] The people sided with him to the extent that they released him from the death penalty, but they fined him fifty talents[a] for his offense. After

6.134
489
PAROS
The Parians say that Miltiades injured himself when leaving the shrine of Demeter, which he entered on the advice of a captive Parian woman.

6.135
489
ATHENS
Miltiades returns home defeated, and the Parians are prevented from punishing the woman who guided him by the Delphic oracle.

6.136
489
ATHENS
Miltiades is prosecuted and convicted in Athens and forced to pay a huge fine, which is paid by Kimon his son after Miltiades dies from the injury he suffered at Paros.

6.134.1a   The goddesses of the underworld were Demeter and Kore.
6.134.2a   Demeter Thesmophoros is thought to mean Demeter the Lawgiver, referring to the establishment of agriculture and settled law.
6.135.2a   Delphi: Map 6.136.
6.136.2a   Lemnos: Map 6.136.

6.136.2b   Pelasgians: Herodotus and later classical authors use the term to describe the pre-Hellenic populations in general throughout the Aegean and Mediterranean regions.
6.136.3a   Fifty talents was an immense sum to be assessed against a private individual. See Appendix J, §11–13, 20.

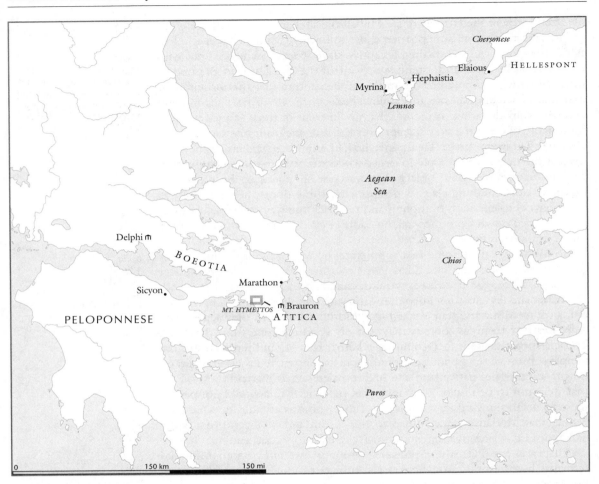

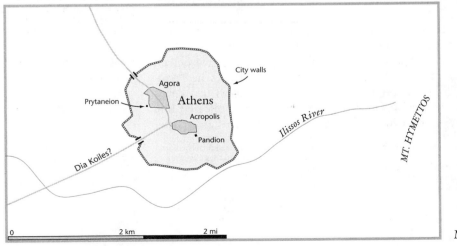

MAP 6.136

the trial, <u>gangrene developed in Miltiades' already infected thigh, and ended his life</u>. His son Kimon[b] subsequently paid off the fifty talents.

Miltiades son of Kimon had taken possession of Lemnos in the following way. The Pelasgians[a] had been expelled from Attica[b] by the Athenians, whether justly or unjustly I cannot say, I merely recount what others have told me: Hekataios son of Hegesandros[c] said in his works that they did so unjustly. [2] For he claimed that the Athenians had given the land below Mount Hymettos[a] to the Pelasgians to reside in as their payment for the wall that had once surrounded the Acropolis.[b] But later, when the Athenians saw how well cultivated this land had become after having been infertile and worthless before, they were seized with envy and a desire to have it back for themselves again. So without offering any pretext, they drove the Pelasgians out. [3] According to the Athenians, however, the expulsion was just, for the Pelasgians inhabiting the area under Hymettos used this land as their base for unjust acts. At that time the daughters and sons of the Athenians used to frequent the Nine Springs[a] to fetch water, since neither they nor any other Hellenes had servants yet. And whenever the daughters would go there, the Pelasgians would insult and show their contempt for the Athenians by violating them. And they did not rest with that offense, but were finally caught in the act of plotting to attack Athens. [4] The Athenians say they proved themselves to be so much better men than the Pelasgians that though they could have killed them when they caught them plotting, they instead simply ordered them to depart from their territory. Thus the Pelasgians withdrew and took possession of various places, Lemnos in particular. Those, then, are the contrasting accounts given by Hekataios and by the Athenians.

So now these Pelasgians who inhabited Lemnos wanted to take revenge upon the Athenians. They knew all about the calendar and rituals of the Athenian festivals, so they obtained some penteconters[a] and ambushed the Athenian women during their celebration of the festival of Artemis at Brauron.[b] The Pelasgians seized many of the women and disappeared, sail-

6.137
ATTICA-LEMNOS
The different accounts of Hekataios the historian and of the Athenians as to how and why the Athenians drove the Pelasgians out of Attica to Lemnos.

6.138
ATTICA-LEMNOS
After abducting many Athenian women and taking them to Lemnos, the Pelasgians decide to kill the women and their sons, providing the basis for the saying "a Lemnian crime."

6.136.3b Kimon son of Miltiades had an illustrious career leading the Athenians against the Persians. See Appendix L, §2, 8, and Figure L, a diagram of the Philaid family, to which Kimon belonged.
6.137.1a According to the legend, the Pelasgians were said to have been driven into Attica from Boeotia (Map 6.136) by the immigration of the Dorians, about sixty years after the Trojan War.
6.137.1b Attica: Map 6.136.
6.137.1c For more on Hekataios son of Hegesandros, see 2.143.1, 2.143.4, 5.36.2, 5.125–6. See also Introduction, §3.1.
6.137.2a Mount Hymettos: Map 6.136 and inset.
6.137.2b Acropolis at Athens: Map 6.136, inset. See Figure 6.137a for remains of the wall circling the top of the Acropolis. It was built in the cyclopean manner and was then believed to be the remnant of

the original Acropolis wall built by the Pelasgians.
6.137.3a Nine Springs (*Enneakrounos*), situated southeast of Athens near the Ilissos River: Map 6.136, inset. See Figure 6.137b.
6.138.1a Pentecenter: a ship like a trireme but of a simpler design, with one line of rowers instead of three, and a total of fifty oars. See Appendix S, §4, 8, 12.
6.138.1b Brauron: Map 6.136. The ritual of the Festival of Artemis was performed by women with few or no men present, which would have facilitated the Pelasgian kidnapping or added verisimilitude to the myth. See Appendix I, §12, for other examples of how knowledge of local festivals could be used for political gain. See Appendix U, §7, about women's role in religious ritual.

FIGURE 6.137A. REMAINS OF CYCLOPAEAN (MYCENAEAN) WALLS AT THE WEST END OF THE ATHENIAN ACROPOLIS. "CYCLOPAEAN" IS THE TERM NORMALLY APPLIED TO THE MASONRY STYLE CHARACTERISTIC OF MYCENAEAN FORTIFICATION, NAMELY WALLS BUILT OF HUGE, UNWORKED IRREGULAR BOULDERS WHICH ARE ROUGHLY FITTED TOGETHER.

ing away and taking the women with them to Lemnos, where they kept them as their concubines. [2] These women gave birth to many children and taught them the language of Attica and the way of life of the Athenians. Their children were unwilling to mingle with the children of the Pelasgian women, and if any of them were struck by the children of the Pelasgian women, they would all rush to help and defend one another. Moreover, these boys deemed it their right to rule over the others and to dominate them. [3] When the Pelasgians recognized this, they discussed it, and as they deliberated, they were struck by a dreadful thought, that if these boys were so determined now to help one another in opposition to the sons of their wedded wives, what, then, would they do as grown men? [4] After they had considered this awhile, they resolved to kill the sons of the Attic women, and that is what they did, and they slew their Attic mothers, too. It was because of this act as well as the earlier one, when the women killed their husbands along with Thoas, that throughout Hellas, all savage deeds are customarily called "Lemnian."[a]

6.138.4a Lemnos: Map 6.136. For more on the
Pelasgians of Lemnos and the crimes
there, see 4.145.2 and Appendix U, §6.

FIGURE 6.137B.
A FIFTH-CENTURY
VASE PAINTING OF
WOMEN FETCHING
WATER FROM THE
NINE SPRINGS
FOUNTAIN IN
ATHENS.

After the Pelasgians had killed their own sons and these women, the Lemnian earth no longer brought forth crops, and neither their wives nor their flocks bore offspring to the same extent as before. Afflicted by hunger and the failure to produce children, they sent to Delphi[a] to ask for a release from their present troubles. [2] The Pythia ordered them to pay a penalty to the Athenians of whatever the Athenians should decide was just. So the Pelasgians went to Athens and announced that they were willing to pay them a just penalty for all their wrongdoing. [3] The Athenians then set up a couch in their city hall[a] and covered it with the finest blankets they could find and placed beside it a table filled with all good things and ordered the Pelasgians to deliver their land to them in the same fine condition. [4] The Pelasgians replied, "Whenever a ship sails with the north wind and completes the journey from your land to ours on the same day, then we shall give it over." Of course the Pelasgians knew this was impossible, for Attica[a] lies far to the south of Lemnos.

6.139
LEMNOS
When their land and women prove barren, the Pelasgians apply to Delphi and are told to pay the Athenians whatever penalty the Athenians think just. The Pelasgians in turn require the Athenians to sail to Lemnos in one day while a north wind is blowing.

6.139.1a   Delphi: Map 6.136.
6.139.3a   The city hall of Athens, the Prytaneion:
           Map 6.136, inset.
6.139.4a   Attica: Map 6.136.

6.140
496
LEMNOS
Many years later Miltiades sails south with a north wind from Athenian territory in the Chersonese and forces the Pelasgians to leave Lemnos.

That is as far as things went at that time. But many years later, after the Chersonese in the Hellespont[a] had come under Athenian control,[b] Miltiades son of Kimon sailed while the Etesian winds[c] were prevailing and accomplished the voyage from Elaious[d] in the Chersonese to Lemnos on the same day. Once there, he made a public proclamation that the Pelasgians were to leave the island, reminding them of the oracle which the Pelasgians had thought would never be fulfilled. [2] The people of Hephaistia[a] obeyed, but those of Myrina[b] refused to concede that the Chersonese was Attica, and they were besieged until they too submitted. So that is how Miltiades and the Athenians acquired possession of Lemnos.

6.140.1a Chersonese, Hellespont: Map 6.136.
6.140.1b Athens: Map 6.136, inset. For when and how the Chersonese in the Hellespont fell under Athenian rule, see 6.34–37.
6.140.1c Etesian winds: the northeast winds that blow in July, August, and September. (Godley)
6.140.1d Elaious: Map 6.136.
6.140.2a Hephaistia, Lemnos: Map 6.136.
6.140.2b Myrina, Lemnos: Map 6.136.

BOOK SEVEN

$\mathbf{W}$hen the report of the battle of Marathon[a] reached Darius son of Hystaspes, who had already been thoroughly exasperated by the Athenians' attack on Sardis,[b] he now reacted with a much more intense fury and became even more determined to make war on Hellas[c] than he had been before. [2] At once he began to issue commands and to send messengers throughout the cities of the empire with instructions to each of them to provide a great deal more than they had provided previously, including horses, food, warships, and transport boats. The announcement of these orders threw Asia[a] into commotion for three years,[b] as the best men were enlisted to serve in the army and to make preparations for war against Hellas. [3] Then in the fourth year the Egyptians,[a] who had been enslaved by Cambyses, revolted from the Persians, which only increased Darius' desire to go to war, but now against both peoples.

While Darius was still making arrangements for these expeditions against Egypt and Athens,[a] his sons began a fierce dispute over which of them should hold supreme power, since according to the Persian custom, the King always appointed his successor before marching out to war. [2] Before he had become King, Darius had had three sons by an earlier wife, the daughter of Gobryas; and after becoming King, he had four others by Atossa daughter of Cyrus. Artobazanes was the eldest of the three he had sired earlier, and Xerxes the eldest of those born later. [3] These two sons, since they did not share the same mother, now entered into a hostile rivalry with each other. Artobazanes asserted that he was the eldest of all Darius' offspring, and that it was the custom among all peoples for the eldest to hold the power, while Xerxes countered that he should rule, since he was the son of Atossa, who was the daughter of Cyrus, the King who had won freedom for the Persians.

7.1
489–486
SUSA-EGYPT
Darius organizes another expedition against Hellas, but his preparations are interrupted by a revolt in Egypt.

7.2
486
SUSA
The three sons of Darius demand that he formally decide and announce which of them should succeed him.

7.1.1a   Marathon: Map 7.10, BX.
7.1.1b   Sardis: Map 7.10, BY.
7.1.1c   Hellas: Map 7.10, BX.
7.1.2a   Asia: Map 7.10, locator.

7.1.2b   The three years 489–487.
7.1.3a   The year 486. Egypt: Map 7.10, locator.
7.2.1a   Athens: Map 7.10, BX.

7.3
486
SUSA
Demaratos provides arguments from Spartan tradition to support Xerxes' claim, and Darius selects Xerxes. Herodotus suspects that the influence of Xerxes' mother, Atossa, would have been sufficient to gain the succession for Xerxes.

Darius had not yet revealed his decision when Demaratos son of Ariston, who had been deprived of the kingship in Sparta[a] and had willingly exiled himself from Lacedaemon, happened to arrive in Susa.[b] [2] The story goes that, upon hearing about the disagreement between the sons of Darius, he went to Xerxes and advised him to strengthen his argument by pointing out that he had been born while Darius was King and held power over the Persians, whereas Artobazanes had been born while Darius was still just a private citizen.[a] [3] Therefore, he argued, it was neither reasonable nor just for anyone else to assume the royal prerogative before him. In Sparta, at any rate, so Demaratos advised him, they followed this custom: if sons were born before their father had become king, and another son was born during his father's reign, it was this younger son who succeeded to the kingship. [4] Xerxes followed Demaratos' advice, and Darius, realizing that his argument was just, appointed him King. But I suppose that even without this advice, Xerxes would have become King, since it was Atossa who really held all the power.

7.4
486
SUSA
Darius dies after a reign of thirty-six years.

Having appointed Xerxes as King of the Persians, Darius then directed his thoughts to war. But after this appointment and the revolt of the Egyptians in the following year, Darius was fated to die in the midst of his preparations and was thus deprived of the opportunity to punish the Egyptians and Athenians. He had reigned a total of thirty-six years,[a] and at his death the kingship was assumed by his son Xerxes.

7.5
485
SUSA
Mardonios advises Xerxes to attack and conquer Hellas after subduing Egypt.

Now at first, Xerxes had no desire at all to march on Hellas,[a] but he did muster an army against Egypt.[b] Mardonios son of Gobryas, however—who was present at court, and who as the son of Darius' sister was first cousin to Xerxes and had more influence with the King than all other Persians—persistently made speeches to Xerxes like this: [2] "My lord, it is unreasonable that the Athenians have inflicted great evils upon the Persians but have paid no penalty for it. Since you have enough on your hands right now, by all means, do subdue and punish Egypt first for its outrageous offense, but then you must march against Athens in order to gain a good reputation among men and to ensure that others will beware of making war on your land afterward." [3] That was how Mardonios argued for revenge, and he would add that Europe[a] was a very beautiful place; that it produced all sorts of cultivated trees, was unsurpassed in fertility, and was worthy of being possessed by the King alone among mortals.

7.6
485
SUSA
Mardonios wanted adventure and to be governor of Hellas. Thessalian princes invite Xerxes to invade Hellas. The Peisistratids also try to persuade Xerxes to invade Hellas.

He spoke this way because he loved to stir things up and because he wanted to become governor of Hellas himself; in time he succeeded in persuading Xerxes to follow his advice. And indeed, there were other factors

7.3.1a Sparta: Map 7.10, BX. For Herodotus' account of how Demaratos lost the kingship of Sparta, see 6.63–70.
7.3.1b Susa: Map 7.10, locator.
7.3.2a According to Plutarch, *Life of Artaxerxes*, this same argument was advanced upon Darius' death by the mother of his younger son Cyrus in her efforts to gain the succession for him, but on this occasion the argument did not prevail. Artax-

erxes II, Darius' elder son, was proclaimed King in 404. Cyrus' attempt to gain the throne ended when he died at the battle of Cunaxa in 401, and Artaxerxes went on to reign for forty-three more years until 358.
7.4.1a The years 521–486.
7.5.1a Hellas: Map 7.10, BX.
7.5.1b Egypt: Map 7.10, locator. See Figure 7.5, a coin of Xerxes' reign.
7.5.3a Europe: Map 7.10, locator.

FIGURE 7.5. A COIN OF XERXES'
REIGN, PROBABLY REPRESENTING
KING XERXES HIMSELF, WITH
CROWN, BOW, AND ROYAL SCEPTER.

which proved most helpful to him in his efforts to convince Xerxes: [2] messages were arriving from the Aleuadai of Thessaly inviting the King to invade
Hellas with the assurance of their full support and allegiance to him (the
Aleuadai were the kings of Thessaly);[a] and the Peisistratids, who had come to
Susa, expressed the same sentiments as the Aleuadai and sought to entice
him with further arguments as well. [3] They had with them Onomakritos,
an Athenian oraclemonger[a] and a compiler of the oracles of Mousaios, with
whom they had earlier reconciled their differences. Hipparchos son of Peisistratos had once expelled Onomakritos from Athens after Lasos of
Hermione[b] had caught him in the act of inserting words into an oracle by
Mousaios which said that the islands lying off the coast of Lemnos[c] would
disappear into the sea. [4] Hipparchos drove him out for that forgery,
although he had previously treated him as his closest friend. But now he
accompanied the Peisistratids inland, and they would speak of Onomakritos
with solemn respect whenever he came with them into the King's presence,
where he would quote oracles. But if some oracles portended failure for the
barbarian, he did not mention them. He recited only those that predicted
the most fortunate outcomes. He told how the Hellespont[a] was fated to be
bridged by a man of Persia, and expounded upon the route of the expedition. [5] And while he constantly presented himself and recited oracles, the
Peisistratids and the Aleuadai persisted in declaring their opinions.

   Thus Xerxes was finally persuaded to march against Hellas; but first, in
the year following the death of Darius, he sent an army against those who
had revolted in Egypt. He led the expedition against those who had
revolted, and once he had subjugated them, he imposed a more oppressive

7.7
485
EGYPT
Xerxes first conquers Egypt.

7.6.2a	Thessaly: Map 7.10, AX. The Aleuadai were not kings but, rather, a very powerful family in Thessaly.	
7.6.3a	The Greek word used here sometimes means "diviner"; here it probably has more the sense of a selector and publisher	

of existing oracles. (Godley)
7.6.3b Lasos of Hermione: a poet and musician, Pindar's teacher. (Godley) Hermione: Map 7.10, BX.
7.6.3c Lemnos: Map 7.10, AY.
7.6.4a Hellespont: Map 7.10, AY.

slavery upon Egypt than had been enforced during the reign of Darius. Then he handed the rule of the country over to his brother Achaimenes, who was also a son of Darius. Afterward, while Achaimenes was acting as governor of Egypt, he was murdered by a Libyan, Inaros son of Psammetichos.[a]

After conquering Egypt, Xerxes intended to undertake the expedition against Athens, but first he summoned a special assembly of the Persian nobility in order to hear their opinions and to express his own wishes in person to all of them. When they had assembled, Xerxes addressed them as follows:

"Persians, I am not about to introduce a new custom to you; instead I shall follow the tradition handed down to me. For as I hear from our elders, we have never been at rest or idle since Cyrus deposed Astyages[a] and we assumed the sovereignty from the Medes. Thus the god guides us as we pursue our many goals, and things turn out the better for us. Now the achievements of Cyrus, Cambyses, and my father, Darius, along with the peoples they added to our empire, are well known and unnecessary for me to recount. [2] But after I assumed the throne, I pondered how I could avoid proving inferior to my predecessors in this honorable position, and how I could increase the power of Persia no less than they had. As I pondered this, I was struck by the realization that we could gain glory; take possession of lands fully as extensive, productive, and fertile as those which we have now; and at the same time obtain vengeance and retribution, too. That is why I have assembled you here to communicate my thoughts to you.

"I intend to bridge the Hellespont and lead my army through Europe to Hellas, so that we can punish the Athenians for all that they did to the Persians and to my father. [2] Now you saw how even Darius had his mind set on marching against these men, but that he died and did not have the opportunity to exact vengeance upon them. I, however, on his behalf and that of the rest of the Persians, shall not give up until I conquer Athens and set it on fire, since it is they who began the offenses against me and my father. [3] First of all, they went to Sardis[a] in the company of our slave Aristagoras of Miletus[b] and set fire to the groves and sanctuaries there. Next, I suppose you know what they did to us when our troops under the command of Datis and Artaphrenes disembarked onto their land.[c]

"Well, that is why I am preparing to march against them. And I find as I work out the details of this project that there will be many good things in store for us if we subdue them and their neighbors who inhabit the land of

7.7.1a In 460; the victory of Inaros over Achaimenes at the battle of Papremis is mentioned at 3.12.4.

7.8.α* This chapter (like 7.9, 7.10, and 7.16) in the *Histories* has subdivisions indicated by Greek letters in alphabetic sequence. That sequence (with the letters' Latin equivalents) is as follows: α (a), β (b), γ (g), δ (d), ε (e), ζ (z), η (h), θ (th).

7.8.α.1a For Cyrus' deposition of Astyages, see 1.123–130.

7.8.β.3a Sardis: Map 7.10, BY. For the Ionian expedition against Sardis and Athens' participation in it, see 5.99–101.

7.8.β.3b When Herodotus has Xerxes refer to Aristagoras as a "slave," he is following the Greek custom of rendering the Persian term *bandake* as "slave," but more properly it bore the flavor of our phrase "your humble servant."

7.8.β.3c This refers to the Persian landings at Marathon (Map 7.10, BX). See 6.107–117.

Pelops[a] the Phrygian as well. By this step we shall make the boundary of the land of Persia border on the lofty realm of Zeus. [2] The sun will not look down on any territory bordering our own, because after I, together with you, have passed through all of Europe,[a] we shall have made them all one single territory. [3] I make this claim because I have learned that there could be no city of men nor race of humans left who would be capable of doing battle with us once we have done away with the ones I have mentioned. Thus those we regard as guilty as well as those who are innocent will bear the yoke of slavery.

"Well, then, you would please me greatly by doing what I shall now ask of you. Whenever I declare that it is time for you to come, then every one of you should come to me promptly and eagerly. And whoever arrives with the army that is best prepared and equipped, to him I shall give the gifts that we regard as most valuable in our land. [2] That, then, is how we must proceed. But so that I should not seem to be the kind of man who makes plans all by himself, I now set the matter before you for open discussion, and bid any of you who wishes to do so to reveal his own opinion."

Thus he ended his speech, and now Mardonios spoke up: "My lord, you are the best of all Persians, not only of those who came before you, but even of those yet to be born, since everything you said was right on the mark, especially your refusal to allow the Ionians who dwell in Europe to laugh at us when they have no right to do so. [2] For we have conquered and made slaves of the Sacae, Indians, Ethiopians, Assyrians, and many other great nations, not because they had committed injustices against Persia, but only to increase our own power through them; so it would indeed be dreadful if after doing that to them, we do not punish the Hellenes, who began the wrongdoing against us.

"What have we to fear? The number of men they could assemble? The amount of money they could collect? We know what they are like in battle, and we know that their power and influence is quite feeble. We have subjugated their sons who inhabit our own land and are called Ionians, Aeolians, and Dorians.[a] [2] I myself, under orders from your father, have already attempted to march against these men, and I advanced as far as Macedon,[a] just a short distance away from Athens,[b] and no one came out to face us in battle.

"As a matter of fact, according to what I hear, the Hellenes are in the habit of starting wars without the slightest forethought, out of obstinacy and stupidity. For whenever they declare war on one another, they seek out

7.8.δ
484?
SUSA
Xerxes solicits opinions on his plan from the assembled Persian nobles.

7.9
484?
SUSA
Mardonios responds to Xerxes by arguing in favor of the attack on Hellas.

7.9.α
484?
SUSA
Mardonios argues that he knows from experience that the Hellenes are weak.

7.9.β
484?
SUSA
Mardonios argues that the Hellenes wage war in a foolish manner.

7.8.γ.1a The legendary Phrygian Pelops, who conquered and gave his name to the Peloponnese: Map 7.10, BX.
7.8.γ.2a Europe: Map 7.10, locator. Xerxes seems to vastly underestimate the size of Europe, its geographic complexity, and its population, which would certainly be no easy conquest and too large to hold. Of course it is also possible that Xerxes never said anything like this, and that Herodotus is here tainting him with wildly extravagant

ambitions and delusions of power. See Appendix M, Herodotus on Persia and the Persian Empire, §6.
7.9.α.1a Territories of the Ionians, Aeolians, and Dorians in Asia: Map 7.10, AY, BY. See Appendix K, Dialect and Ethnic Groups in Herodotus.
7.9.α.2a Macedon: Map 7.10, AX. Mardonios alludes here to his successful campaign to incorporate Macedon into the empire (6.44–45).
7.9.α.2b Athens: Map 7.10, BX.

the finest and most level land and go there to fight, so that the victors depart from the field only after great damage has been done, and I won't say anything at all of the defeated, for they are completely destroyed. [2] What they ought to do, since they speak the same language and use heralds and messengers, is to thus put an end to their differences and employ any means other than battles to become reconciled. And if they absolutely must wage war against one another, they should seek out the place where either of the two sides would be the most difficult to subdue and then try to fight there. Thus the Hellenes do not employ intelligent strategies, and when I had marched as far as Macedon they never even came out to offer battle.

"And so who, sire, would ever be likely to declare war and oppose you when you lead the vast numbers of Asia and all of its ships? My thought is that the Hellenes can never be so bold as to do so, but even if I should be mistaken in this opinion and they, inspired by recklessness, should come out to do battle with us, they would find out that when it comes to war, we are the greatest people on earth. So let nothing go untried. For nothing is gained without effort, but all things come only to those who try to achieve them."

Having said so much in his efforts to polish and refine the proposal of Xerxes, Mardonios ended his speech. Now the rest of the Persians remained silent and did not dare to express an opinion in opposition to the one that had been offered; but then Artabanos son of Hystaspes, confident because he was the uncle of Xerxes, spoke as follows:

"Sire, if no opposing opinions are expressed in the course of a discussion, it becomes impossible to try to choose and to finally select the better one. Instead, one will have to make do with the proposal that has been stated. But when a different opinion is set forth, it is just like comparing two grades of gold: we cannot distinguish gold that is pure in isolation, but when we rub it next to another piece of gold,[a] we can then pick out the better of the two. [2] I, in fact, told your father, my brother Darius, not to march against the Scythians,[a] who have no settled communities anywhere in their land. But since he hoped to subjugate the Scythian nomads, he did not listen to me; he marched against them and returned only after throwing away many noble and courageous men of his army. [3] But you, sire, are about to march against men who are said to be the best both on land and at sea, men far better than the Scythians. So it is only right and just that I inform you of the terrible danger inherent in your plan.

"You say that after bridging the Hellespont[a] you will lead the army through Europe to Hellas. But suppose it happens that you are defeated on land or sea, or even both: their men are said to be strong and warlike, and we can estimate their strength when we consider that the Athenians alone destroyed as large an army as went to Attica[b] with Datis and Artaphrenes.

7.9.γ
484?
SUSA
Mardonios boasts that the Persians and their Asian allies will overwhelm the Hellenes easily.

7.10
484?
SUSA
Mardonios having finished, Artabanos rises to speak.

7.10.α
484?
SUSA
Artabanos warns Xerxes of the dangers of such expeditions, reminding him of the disaster that occurred to his father, Darius, in Scythia.

7.10.β
484?
SUSA
Artabanos reminds Darius of the peril of advancing the army into Europe with a vulnerable bridge at its rear.

7.10.α.1a　Purer gold, when rubbed on a touchstone, would leave a darker stain than an alloyed sample.
7.10.α.2a　For Herodotus' account of Darius' invasion of Scythia (Map 7.10, locator),　see 4.83–143.
7.10.β.1a　Hellespont: Map 7.10, AY.
7.10.β.1b　Attica: Map 7.10, BX. Referring to the Persian defeat at Marathon; see 6.11–17.

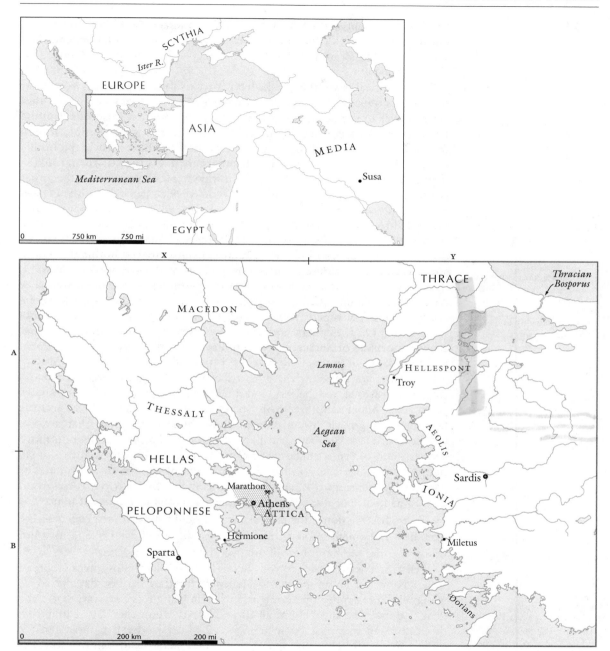

MAP 7.10

[2] Or even suppose they do not succeed completely on either land or sea, but if they were to attack us with their ships and win a sea battle, and then sail to the Hellespont and destroy the bridge—that, sire, would indeed be terrible!

"I do not calculate these risks from any wisdom of my own, but rather from my knowledge of what almost happened to us once when your father crossed over to the Scythians after bridging the Thracian Bosporus[a] and the Ister River.[b] That is when the Scythians used every means possible to beg the Ionians to tear down his way to return home, which was via the bridge over the Ister that the Ionians had been assigned to guard.[c] [2] And if Histiaios, the tyrant of Miletus,[a] had conformed to the opinion of the other tyrants instead of opposing them, that would have been the end of Persian power. Indeed, even to hear it reported that all the King's power once depended upon one man is certainly a terrible experience.

"So please do not willfully incur such risks when nothing compels you to do so, but instead listen to me. Dismiss this assembly now and then later, after you have considered the matter yourself and have made a decision, declare whatever you think best. [2] For I find that the greatest profit comes from planning with care and deliberation. Then, if you should be impeded by any adversity, your plan is still a good one but fails only because of bad luck. On the other hand, one who has done a poor job of planning, even if good luck attends him, nonetheless eventually discovers that his plan was a bad one.

"Further, you see how the god strikes with his thunderbolt those creatures that tower above the rest, and does not permit them to be so conspicuous, while those who are small do not at all provoke him. And you see how he always hurls his missiles at those houses and trees that are the largest and tallest. For the god likes to lop off whatever stands out above the rest; and so, on a similar principle, a huge army is destroyed by a small one; for whenever the god has become resentful toward an army, he casts panic or lightning into it, and it is thus completely destroyed through no fault of its own. For the god will not tolerate pride in anyone but himself.

"Now, hasty action is the father of failure, and failure in turn begets severe penalties. But much good comes from restraint, and even if one may not think so at the moment, he will discover, in time, that it is so.

"That, sire, is my advice to you. But as for you, Mardonios son of Gobryas, stop talking nonsense about the Hellenes, for they do not deserve to be maligned. You slander them only to incite the King to go to war; that is the goal, I think, that lies behind all these zealous arguments. But I pray that this campaign may not come to pass. [2] For slander is a most terrible crime, one in which two people commit the injustice and a third is the victim of it. The one who slanders commits an injustice against the one who is

7.10.γ.1a　Thracian Bosporus: Map 7.10, AY.
7.10.γ.1b　Ister (modern Danube) River: Map 7.10, locator.
7.10.γ.1c　For Herodotus' own narrative of these events, see 4.136ff.
7.10.γ.2a　Miletus: Map 7.10, BY.

not present, while the person who listens to him does wrong by believing him before learning if his claims are accurate. And the man who is absent from their talk is wronged, being slandered by the one and assumed to be bad by the other.

"But if it is absolutely necessary to march against these men, then let the King himself remain in the homeland of the Persians while we risk our children; and you, Mardonios, select the men you want yourself and take the army, leading it as far as you like. [2] If things turn out as you claim they will for the King, then let my children be killed, and me along with them. But if it goes as I predict, then let that happen to your children, and you along with them, if you succeed in returning. [3] If, however, you prefer not to assume the burden of an agreement such as this, and yet would still wish to lead the army against Hellas, then I declare that those left behind in Persia will hear that you, Mardonios, after doing great harm to the Persians, were torn to pieces by dogs and birds somewhere in the land of the Athenians or Lacedaemonians, if not even earlier on your way there, but only after realizing what sort of men you had tried to persuade the King to attack."

Thus Artabanos ended his speech; and Xerxes, enraged at what he had said, replied, "Artabanos, you are the brother of my father, and that will protect you from paying the penalty your foolish words deserve, though for your cowardice and lack of nerve I shall impose upon you the disgrace of not accompanying me on my campaign against Hellas. No, you will remain here with the women instead, and I shall accomplish all that I said that I would without you! [2] If I fail to punish the Athenians, may I be disowned as the son of Darius son of Hystaspes, the son of Arsames son of Ariaramnes, the son of Teispes son of Cyrus, the son of Cambyses son of Teispes, the son of Achaimenes,[a] since I know well that if we abide in peace, the Athenians will not do the same, but will even lead an army against our country, judging by how they began it all by marching into Asia and setting Sardis on fire. [3] And so neither side can possibly back down from a conflict now. Whether we actively engage in it or passively suffer what it may bring, we are facing a struggle to determine whether our entire land will come under Greek control or theirs will come under Persian control. For there is no middle ground in our hatred for each other. [4] But since we Persians were the first to be wronged, it is right and fitting that we now punish them, so that I may indeed learn of this terrible thing that I shall suffer when I march against these 'men' whom Pelops the Phrygian, a slave of my forefathers, conquered so decisively that even to this day these people and their land bear the name of their conqueror."

7.10.θ
484?
SUSA
Artabanos advises Xerxes to stay in Persia and let him and Mardonios wager their children's lives against the quality of their respective advice.

7.11
484?
SUSA
Xerxes denounces Artabanos as a coward and refuses his advice, insisting that honor demands that he punish the Athenians.

7.11.2a   The first seven names represent two parallel lines of descent from Teispes son of Achaimenes (except that the first "Teispes" is a fiction), which Herodotus has apparently fused into one direct line. Xerxes could claim descent from both by virtue of his mother, Atossa, Cyrus' daughter; hence perhaps the confusion.

For a complete discussion, see How and Wells, Appendix IV. It may be remembered that Herodotus probably deals with Egyptian chronology in the same way, making a sequence out of lists of kings, some of whom were contemporaries. (Godley)

7.12
484?
SUSA
Xerxes changes his mind that evening but is visited by a vision in his sleep which tells him to march against Hellas.

That was as far as the discussion went at the time, but afterward, when night had fallen, the arguments of Artabanos kept vexing Xerxes. And in the quiet of the night as he pondered what Artabanos had said, he realized that marching against Hellas would not be a good thing for him to do. After he had reached this conclusion, he fell asleep, and it was perhaps on this night that he had the following vision, as the Persians describe it. Xerxes thought he saw a tall handsome man standing over him and saying, [2] "Are you really revising your plans, Persian, so that you will not lead an expedition against Hellas, after having already ordered the Persians to muster an army? If so, you do yourself no favor by changing your mind, and you will not be forgiven by anyone here with you. Instead, take the path you decided to follow during the day." After Xerxes heard him saying this, he thought he saw him fly away.

7.13
484?
SUSA
Xerxes ignores the advice of the vision and announces in the morning that he has changed his mind and will not march against Hellas.

When day dawned, Xerxes paid no attention to this dream. He reassembled the Persians he had gathered together before and said to them, [2] "Persians, please pardon me for completely reversing my plans, for my mental faculties have not yet reached their prime. Those urging me to take that other course of action have not given me a moment's peace, and when I heard the opinion of Artabanos, my youth boiled over, so that I blurted out words too unseemly to be addressed to an older man. But now I agree with him and shall follow his judgment. [3] So since my new decision is not to march against Hellas, you may all relax." Upon hearing this, the Persians rejoiced and prostrated themselves before him.

7.14
484?
SUSA
The vision returns to Xerxes that night and demands once again that he press on against Hellas.

But during the night, the same vision appeared to Xerxes while he was fast asleep, standing over him again and saying, "Son of Darius, have you actually appeared before the Persians, renouncing your military campaign and paying no attention to my words, as though you had heard them from a nobody? Well, then, you can be sure of this: if you do not lead this campaign at once, then here is what will happen as a result: as high and mighty as you have become in a short time, so low will you fall again and just as quickly."

7.15
484?
SUSA
Xerxes asks Artabanos to take his place to see if the vision will visit him.

Terrified by this vision, Xerxes jumped up from his bed and sent a messenger to summon Artabanos. When he arrived, Xerxes said, "Artabanos, I was not in my right mind for a moment when I spoke foolish words to you in response to your good counsel. [2] But not long afterward I changed my mind and realized that I should do as you advised. I find that I am not capable, however, of carrying this out, even though I want to. For ever since I changed my mind and turned to your plan, a dream vision has visited and appeared to me, and it totally opposes my carrying out your plan. Just now it threatened me before it disappeared. [3] Now, if a god is sending this dream and it is his strong pleasure that I should undertake this campaign against

Hellas, the same dream will come to you and give orders to you as it has to me. I am most likely to ascertain that this is the true explanation for what is happening if, after our meeting here, you take all of my clothing, put it on, sit upon my throne, and then sleep in my bed."

Thus spoke Xerxes; but Artabanos would not at first obey his order, since he did not deem himself worthy to sit upon the royal throne. In the end, however, he did so when he was compelled, after saying,

"In my judgment, sire, good sense is every bit as valuable as the willingness to heed someone's good advice. Although you possess both of these, they are being thwarted by your associations with evil people, just as they say that the sea can be the most beneficial thing of all to mortals, but the force of the winds that fall upon it prevent it from being true to its nature. [2] Now the pain of hearing your harsh criticism of me was not as sharp as the fact that when two proposals were presented to the Persians, one that would increase their arrogance and another that would put an end to it because it would be evil to teach the heart to always pursue more than it already has—that of these two proposals, you chose the one more perilous both to yourself and to the Persians.

"But now, when you have converted to the better of the two, you claim that since giving up your expedition against Hellas you are are being visited by a dream sent by some god, which will not allow you to disband the army. [2] But this, my son, is not really a divine phenomenon. I, being much older than you, shall teach you what sorts of things these dreams which make their way to humans actually are. Most of the visions visiting our dreams tend to be what one is thinking about during the day. During the days before this dream our minds have been engaged in dealing with this military campaign more than anything else.

"Now, if this dream is not what I judge it to be after all, but something divine whose meaning you yourself have found and summarized, then let it appear and instruct me as it has you. But if it really wants to appear, it should not be more likely to appear to me just because I am wearing your clothes rather than my own, or resting in your bed instead of mine. [2] For whatever it is that appears to you in your sleep could not possibly be so stupid as to see me and think that I am you on the evidence of clothing. Whether I wear my own clothes or yours, it may consider me of no importance and not deem me worthy of its appearance, but what we must really find out is whether it will come back to visit you again. For if it does continue to visit you, even I myself would say that it is divine. [3] So if you are firmly resolved and there is no way to divert you from your decision that I must soon sleep in your bed, then fine: let it appear to me as I sleep. But until it does, I shall maintain my present opinion."

7.16
484?
SUSA
Artabanos agrees to do as he is asked.

7.16.α
484?
SUSA
Artabanos tells Xerxes that the company of bad men led him away from good advice.

7.16.β
484?
SUSA
Artabanos says that such visions do not come from the gods but from our thoughts of the day.

7.16.γ
484?
SUSA
Artabanos agrees that if the vision visits him, it will be evidence of its divine provenance.

Artabanos is visited in his sleep by the vision, which threatens him for dissuading Xerxes from attacking Hellas.

That is what Artabanos said, and he then proceeded to carry out his orders, hoping to prove that Xerxes had been talking nonsense. He put on Xerxes' clothes, sat upon the royal throne, and went to the King's bed. And as he slept, the same vision that had visited Xerxes came to Artabanos, and standing above him, it said, [2] "Are you the one who has been so forcefully dissuading Xerxes from marching against Hellas, as though you are so worried about him? Well, neither in the immediate present nor in the future will you escape punishment for trying to avert what is destined to happen. As for Xerxes, he has already been enlightened as to what he must suffer if he refuses to obey." TRYING TO AVERT DESTINY

Artabanos now changes his mind and agrees that the god's message is clear: the Persians must destroy Hellas.

After hearing these threats in his dream, Artabanos saw the figure about to burn out his eyes with hot irons. With a loud shriek he jumped out of bed; then he sat down beside Xerxes and described his dream vision in full. When he had finished, he said, [2] "Sire, I, being a person who has already seen many great powers fall to lesser ones, was unwilling to permit you to give up everything you have to the impetuosity of your youth, knowing as I do how evil it is to desire too many things. I remembered how Cyrus' attack on the Massagetai turned out, and I remembered also the expedition of Cambyses against the Ethiopians, and when I accompanied Darius on his campaign against the Scythians. [3] Because I was aware of all this, I held the opinion that as long as you stayed still, you would be the most blessed of all mortals. But since some sort of supernatural impulse has arisen and, as it seems, some god-driven destruction is to overtake the Hellenes, I will change my mind and retract my opinion. You should now reveal to the Persians this guidance sent to us by the god, and order them to make their preparations just as you first commanded. And you must make every effort so that, as long as the god permits it, you do not fail in your responsibility." [4] Those were the words of Artabanos, and both men were now aroused by the vision. As soon as day came, Xerxes communicated all this to the Persians, while Artabanos, who before had been the only one to publicly oppose Xerxes, now openly and eagerly encouraged him.

The Magi interpret Xerxes' third vision to predict his rule over all men.

After this, as Xerxes eagerly focused on the expedition, a third vision came to him in his sleep, which the Magi interpreted as having significance for the whole earth, indicating that everyone in the world would become the slaves of Xerxes. The vision was as follows. Xerxes thought he saw himself being crowned with an olive bough from which branches extended over the entire earth, and then the crown set upon his head seemed to vanish. [2] As soon as the Magi had interpreted this dream, each of the Persians who had been assembled rode back to his own province in eager anticipation of what had been promised, every one of them desiring to take for himself the gifts that Xerxes had offered. Meanwhile, Xerxes searched throughout the entire continent to muster his forces.

During four full years[a] following the conquest of Egypt,[b] Xerxes prepared his army and gathered provisions for it. Then, in the course of the fifth year, he set out on his campaign with an enormous body of troops. [2] In fact, of all the expeditions we know of, this was by far the largest. Darius' expedition against the Scythians[a] looks like nothing in comparison with that of Xerxes, and the same is true of the Scythian expedition when the Scythians chased the Cimmerians into Media[b] and then subjugated and occupied almost the whole interior of Asia,[c] which was the reason Darius later attempted to punish them. Nor can we compare the expedition of the sons of Atreus against Troy,[d] according to the traditional account, nor that of the Mysians and Teukrians[e] before the Trojan War, when they had crossed over to Europe[f] at the Bosporus,[g] subjugated all the Thracians,[h] advanced down to the Ionian Sea,[i] and marched as far south as the Peneios River.[j]

All these expeditions combined, even with others added to them, could not possibly equal the size of this expedition of Xerxes, for what nation of Asia did Xerxes not lead to Hellas? What body of water did his forces not drink dry except for the greatest rivers? [2] Some of his subjects furnished ships, and others were appointed to serve in the army; some were assigned to provide cavalry, others supplied both horse-transport vessels and men to serve in the army; some contributed the longboats for the bridges while still others provided food and additional ships.[a]

Since terrible shipwreck had thwarted the first Persians to attempt a voyage around Mount Athos,[a] Xerxes had begun to prepare for this danger at least three years earlier. He had anchored triremes off Elaious[b] in the Chersonese[c] and sent troops there from every nation to use this as their base for digging a canal, which they did, laboring under the whip and working in relays. The inhabitants settled around Athos also worked on the canal. [2] Two Persians, Boubares son of Megabazos and Artachaias son of Artaios, supervised the project. Athos is a large and well-known mountain extending

7.20
483–480
PERSIAN EMPIRE
Xerxes' preparations go on for four years after the conquest of Egypt.

7.21
PERSIAN EMPIRE
Xerxes' expedition is greater than all the others combined.

7.22
483
MOUNT ATHOS
To avoid the disaster that befell the last Persian fleet that tried to sail around Mount Athos, Xerxes orders a canal cut through its isthmus. Herodotus lists the names of the towns on Mount Athos.

7.20.1a Presumably, the years 484–481, immediately prior to the invasion of 480.
7.20.1b Egypt: Map 7.24, locator.
7.20.2a Scythia: Map 7.10, locator.
7.20.2b Media: Map 7.10, locator. For more on Herodotus' description of this Scythian "invasion" of Media, see 1.103; 4.11–13; nn. 1.105.1a, 1.106.1a, 1.106.1b.
7.20.2c Asia: Map 7.24, locator.
7.20.2d Troy (Ilion/Ilium): Map 7.10, AY.
7.20.2e Teukrians is another name for Trojans.
7.20.2f Europe: Map 7.10, locator.
7.20.2g Bosporus (Thracian): Map 7.10, AY.
7.20.2h Thrace: Map 7.10, AY.
7.20.2i Ionian Sea: Map 7.24, locator.
7.20.2j Peneios River: Map 7.24.
7.21.2a See Appendix R, The Size of Xerxes' Expeditionary Force, §1–4.
7.22.1a Mount Athos: Map 7.24, inset. In 6.44, Herodotus mentions the disaster suffered

by the previous Persian attempt to sail a fleet around Mount Athos, by Mardonios in 493/2.
7.22.1b Elaious: Map 7.24. Many commentators on Herodotus find the designation of Elaious as the base for the force that excavated the canal at Mount Athos to be quite reasonable, particularly as a location from which to gather workers from Asia, who would be shipped to Sane (Map 7.24, inset) to join workers from that region. (Macan) But the fact that Elaious is almost 100 miles from Mount Athos and that several other adequate and closer sites for such a base can easily be found has led some scholars to believe that there is an error in the manuscript or that Herodotus was simply mistaken here. See Figure 7.22, a striking aerial view of the canal site and the entire Mount Athos Peninsula.
7.22.1c Chersonese, Hellespont: Map 7.24.

FIGURE 7.22. AERIAL VIEW OF THE MOUNT ATHOS PENINSULA, SHOWING XERXES' CANAL SITE, IN THE PLAIN AT THE BOTTOM, AND THE LONG COAST AGAINST WHICH THE STORM DESTROYED MARDONIOS' FLEET IN 493/92.

into the sea and supporting a number of human settlements. Where the mountain joins the mainland it forms a peninsula with an isthmus less than a mile and a half[a] wide. This region contains flat land and some low hills, and extends from the Sea of the Akanthians[b] to the sea opposite Torone.[c] [3] On this isthmus at the top end of Athos the Greek city of Sane[a] was founded. Beyond Sane, the other cities within Athos which the Persian now sought to make island rather than mainland towns are Dion, Olophyxos, Akrothooi, Thyssos, and Kleonai.[b]

7.22.2a Herodotus writes "12 stades." See Distance Conversions, p. lxiv, and Appendix J, Ancient Greek Units of Currency, Weight, and Distance, §6, 19.
7.22.2b The sea to the east, toward Akanthos: Map 7.24, inset.
7.22.2c The sea to the west, toward Torone: Map 7.24, inset.
7.22.3a Sane (Mount Athos): Map 7.24, inset.
7.22.3b Dion, Olophyxos, Akrothooi, Thyssos, Kleonai: Map 7.24, inset.

Those are the inhabited cities of Athos. Now the barbarians divided up the ground along the canal route among their nations and dug the channel as follows. They drew a straight line along the border of the city of Sane, and when they had dug the trench deep enough, some of them kept digging at the bottom of the channel while others continuously carried the excavated soil up to another group of men standing on scaffolds above; these in turn passed it up to yet others, until it reached those at the very top, who carried it away and deposited it elsewhere. [2] At the sites assigned to all except the Phoenicians,[a] the banks of the trench kept caving in, doubling their work. This was sure to happen, since they made the width of the trench the same at both its top and its bottom. [3] But the Phoenicians, whose expertise is evident in many situations, displayed it here in particular, for on all the land that fell to them to dig, they made the top of the trench twice as wide as it was supposed to be and reduced the width as they dug farther down, so that when they reached the bottom, the trench was equal in width to what had been dug by the others. [4] At this site there is a meadow where they had an agora and market; here a large quantity of grain already ground into flour was delivered to them from Asia.

From what I can gather, Xerxes ordered the canal to be dug because of his arrogant pride. He wanted to display his power and leave behind a memorial to himself. For they could easily have drawn the ships across the isthmus, but instead he ordered that this canal be dug to connect with the sea sufficiently wide for two triremes to row side by side on it. The same men who excavated the canal were assigned also to bridge the Strymon River.[a]

While these projects were being carried out, Xerxes ordered Phoenicians and Egyptians to make cables of papyrus and white flax for the bridges and to establish reserves of food for the army to prevent it and the pack animals from starving on their way to Hellas. [2] After investigating the various territories they were to pass through, he ordered deposits of food to be established in the most suitable locations, to be transported on merchant ships and ferryboats from all parts of Asia.[a] The greatest quantity was taken to what is called the White Point in Thrace.[b] Other places designated for the storage of food were: Tyrodiza in the territory of the Perinthians, Doriskos, Eion on the Strymon River, and Macedon.[c]

While these people were carrying out the work assigned to them, the entire land army had gathered together and, with Xerxes, was making its way to Sardis; it began its march in Critalla in Cappadocia,[a] where the whole mainland army had been told to assemble. [2] Now I cannot say which of the governors received the gifts offered by the King for bringing the best-equipped

7.23
483–481
MOUNT ATHOS
Herodotus describes how the canal was dug in sections by nation. He praises the superior skill of the Phoenicians.

7.24
MOUNT ATHOS
Herodotus believes the canal was dug to display Xerxes' power, as the ships could have been dragged across the isthmus.

7.25
483–481
HELLESPONT
Xerxes orders the Phoenicians and Egyptians to make ropes for the bridge, and to send supplies to various places along the expedition's route.

7.26
481
CAPPADOCIA-PHRYGIA
The land forces had mustered and were marching with Xerxes to Sardis from Critalla in Cappadocia.

7.23.2a Phoenicia: Map 7.24, locator.
7.24.1a Strymon River: Map 7.24.
7.25.2a Asia: Map 7.24, locator.
7.25.2b Thrace: Map 7.24. The location of the White Point, White Headland, or White or Fair Coast (as Leuke Akte is variously

translated) is unknown.
7.25.2c Tyrodiza, Perinthus, Doriskos, Eion, Macedon: Map 7.24.
7.26.1a Cappadocia: Map 7.33, locator. Critalla's location is unknown.

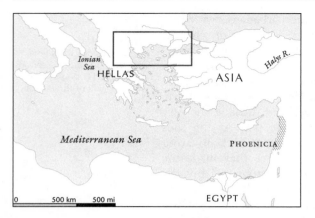

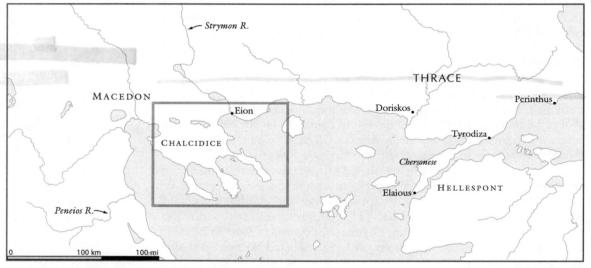

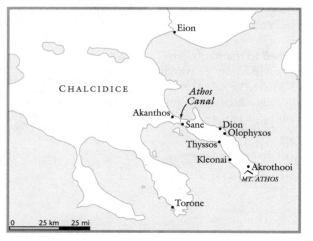

MAP 7.24

contingent. In fact, I do not even know whether a decision was reached about this at all. [3] In any case, after crossing the Halys River,[a] they entered Phrygia,[b] and on their way through that country they arrived at Kelainai,[c] the location of the sources of the Maeander River[d] and of another river just as big as the Maeander, which happens to be called Catarractes;[e] this one rises from Kelainai's agora itself and flows into the Maeander. It is in this city that the skin of Marsyas the silenus is suspended; according to the story told by the Phrygians, it was hung there after Marsyas was flayed by Apollo.

In this city, a Lydian man, Pythios son of Atys, had been awaiting the army, and now he hosted all the troops of the King as well as Xerxes himself with the most lavish hospitality and announced that he wanted to provide money for the war. [2] When Xerxes heard that Pythios had offered money, he asked the Persians with him who in the world this Pythios was, and how much money he possessed that he could make this offer. They told him, "Sire, this is the man who gave the gifts of the golden plane tree and grapevine to your father, Darius. And even now he is the richest of all people we know of after you."

Xerxes was amazed at the last of these statements, and so he took it upon himself to ask Pythios how much money he had. Pythios replied, "Sire, I shall not conceal nor pretend that I don't know the extent of my riches, since I do know it and shall tell you the precise amount. [2] For as soon as I learned that you were marching down to the Greek Sea,[a] I investigated this matter because I wanted to give you money for the war, and I found, after some calculation, that I possess 2,000 talents of silver[b] and just 7,000 short of 4,000,000 Daric staters of gold.[c] [3] All this I present to you as a gift. For myself, a sufficient livelihood is provided by my slaves and estates." Those were the words of Pythios, and Xerxes was delighted with them and replied as follows:

"My Lydian host, ever since I left Persian territory, I have encountered no man besides yourself who wished to give hospitality to my army, nor anyone who has in my presence and of his own will volunteered to contribute money to me for the war. You have offered both lavish hospitality to my troops and a generous amount of money to me. [2] So in return I shall reward you: I now count you as my guest-friend,[a] and I shall give you 7,000 staters of my own to make yours equal a full 4,000,000, so that your 4,000,000 will no longer be lacking 7,000, and that I may round off the full amount for you. [3] Keep what you have already acquired for yourself,

7.27
481?
KELAINAI
Pythios, a wealthy Lydian entertains Xerxes and offers money for the war.

7.28
481?
KELAINAI
In response to Xerxes' query, Pythios admits his great wealth in money and offers it all to Xerxes for his war.

7.29
481?
KELAINAI
Xerxes praises and thanks Pythios, gives him money, and makes him his guest-friend.

7.26.3a   Halys River: Map 7.24, locator.
7.26.3b   Phrygia: Map 7.33.
7.26.3c   Kelainai: Map 7.33. To pass through
            Kelainai requires a divergence off the Royal
            Road (see 5.52ff.) to the south, perhaps
            to pass through country capable of sup-
            plying additional provisions and troops.
7.26.3d   Maeander River: Map 7.33.
7.26.3e   Catarractes River: location unknown.
7.28.2a   Greek (Aegean) Sea: Map 7.33, locator.
7.28.2b   The talent was a unit of weight and mone-
            tary value that varied from place to place

in the ancient world. See Appendix J,
§11–13, 20.
7.28.2c   The Daric stater of gold was a unit of cur-
            rency used throughout the Persian
            Empire. See Appendix J, §14.
7.29.2a   Guest-friendship (*xenia*): a bond of ritual-
            ized friendship, usually between aristocrats
            or prominent men of different cities. It
            was passed down through generations and
            required hereditary privileges and obliga-
            tions such as reciprocal hospitality and
            assistance. See Appendix T, §3.

and know always how to be the man you are today. For you will not regret your present actions, neither now nor hereafter."

After Xerxes said this and fulfilled his promise to Pythios, he resumed his journey and continued his advance. Passing by the Phrygian city called Anaua[a] and a lake that yields salt, he came to Colossae,[b] a great Phrygian city where the Lycus River[c] empties and disappears into a chasm of the earth but then reappears about half a mile[d] away. This river also flows into the Maeander. [2] From Colossae, the army went toward the boundary between Phrygia and Lydia, and came to the city of Cydrara,[a] where there still stands the stele that Croesus erected with an inscription to indicate the boundaries.

So Xerxes marched from Phrygia and entered Lydia.[a] Here the road divides, so that the way to the left leads toward Caria,[b] while the one to the right leads to Sardis.[c] Along the road to the right, one must cross the Maeander River and pass by the city of Callatebus,[d] where there are men who manufacture a honeylike syrup made of tamarisk and wheat. While Xerxes was traveling along this road he discovered a plane tree that so impressed him with its beauty that he endowed it with golden ornaments and entrusted it to one of the Immortals[e] as its guardian. On the next day, Xerxes reached the capital of Lydia.

Upon his arrival at Sardis, he first sent heralds to Hellas to ask for earth and water and to order the Hellenes to prepare feasts for the King; he sent them everywhere except Athens[a] and Lacedaemon[b] to ask for earth. Xerxes' reason for making this second request for earth and water was that he fully expected that all those who had refused to give it before when Darius had sent heralds[c] would now give it out of fear. So he sent these heralds, hoping to find out for certain whether that would be the case.

After this, he prepared to march to Abydos.[a] At this time, bridges were being built across the Hellespont[b] from Asia[c] to Europe.[d] On the Chersonese[e] at the Hellespont, between the cities of Sestos[f] and Madytos,[g] there is a rocky promontory extending into the sea opposite Abydos. It was here that not long after this, when Xanthippos son of Ariphron was general of the Athenians, they[h] took Artayktes, a Persian serving as governor of Sestos, and nailed him alive to a wooden plank because he had committed the unlawful deeds of bringing women into the sanctuary of Protesilaos at Elaious.[i]

7.30.1a Anaua: Map 7.33.
7.30.1b Colossae: Map 7.33.
7.30.1c Lycus River: Map 7.33. The Lycus here flows through a narrow gorge, but there is no indication of its ever having flowed underground, except for a few yards. (Godley)
7.30.1d Herodotus writes "5 stades." See Appendix J, §6, 19.
7.30.2a Cydrara: location unknown.
7.31.1a Lydia: Map 7.33.
7.31.1b Caria: Map 7.33.
7.31.1c Sardis: Map 7.33.
7.31.1d Callatebus: location unknown.
7.31.1e The Immortals were an elite corps of Persian troops in Xerxes' army. See 7.83.1 and

Appendix O, The Persian Army in Herodotus.
7.32.1a Athens: Map 7.33, locator.
7.32.1b Lacedaemon (Sparta): Map 7.33, locator.
7.32.1c See 6.48.2 for the dispatch of heralds to Hellas by Darius in the year 491.
7.33.1a Abydos: Map 7.33.
7.33.1b Hellespont: Map 7.33 and locator.
7.33.1c Asia: Map 7.33, locator.
7.33.1d Europe: Map 7.33, locator.
7.33.1e Chersonese, Hellespontine: Map 7.33.
7.33.1f Sestos: Map 7.33.
7.33.1g Madytos: Map 7.33.
7.33.1h "They" refers to the Athenians serving in this region. See 9.116–120, where Herodotus tells this story at greater length.
7.33.1i Elaious: Map 7.33.

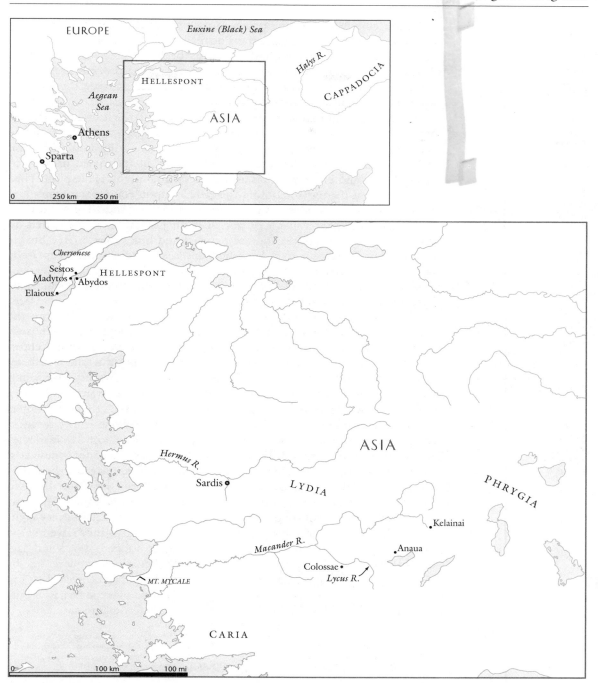

MAP 7.33

Handwritten margin note: XERXES PUNISHES RIVER?

7.34
482? 481?
HELLESPONT
The first pair of bridges, which stretches from Abydos, is broken up by a storm

7.35
482? 481?
HELLESPONT
Xerxes orders that the Hellespont waters be whipped, fettered, and branded as punishment, and that the overseers of the bridge be executed.

7.36
481?
HELLESPONT
Herodotus describes how new bridges across the Hellespont were constructed.

Handwritten margin note: How two Bridge is Built

It was from Abydos to this promontory, then, that the bridges were built by those assigned to this task, the Phoenicians working on the white flax bridge and the Egyptians on the papyrus bridge. The distance between Abydos and the opposite shore here is about 1,350 yards.[a] But in fact after these bridges had been built, a violent storm descended upon them, broke them up, and tore apart all that work.

Xerxes was infuriated when he learned of this; he ordered that the Hellespont was to receive 300 lashes under the whip, and that a pair of shackles was to be dropped into the sea. And I have also heard that he sent others to brand the Hellespont. [2] In any case, he instructed his men to say barbarian and insolent things as they were striking the Hellespont: "Bitter water, your master is imposing this penalty upon you for wronging him even though you had suffered no injustice from him. And King Xerxes will cross you whether you like it or not. It is for just cause, after all, that no human offers you sacrifice: you are a turbid and briny river!" [3] Thus he ordered that the sea was to be punished, and also that the supervisors of the bridge over the Hellespont were to be beheaded.

And so those assigned to this joyless office went to work on it, while other engineers were building new bridges as follows. They set together penteconters and triremes, 360 as support for a bridge on the side toward the Euxine Sea,[a] and 314 as support on the other side. These ships were positioned at right angles to the Pontus and parallel to the current of the Hellespont[b] in order to keep the cables taut. [2] After doing this, they let down very large anchors, some on the side toward the Pontus, to offset the winds blowing out of that sea, and others, on the western side toward the Aegean, to offset the west and south winds. They left a gap between the penteconters and triremes[a] large enough to sail through, so that anyone who wanted to sail on small boats into and out of the Pontus could do so. [3] Next, they stretched the cables from the shore, twisting them with wooden windlasses. But they did not separate the types of cables as before; instead they apportioned two white flax cables and four papyrus cables to each of the two bridges. The thickness and quality of the cables were the same, but those made of flax were proportionally heavier, weighing one talent every eighteen inches.[a] [4] When the straits had thus been bridged, they sawed wood into planks whose length matched the width of the bridge of boats and, laying them out over the stretched cables, they tied them down in place, side by side. [5] Next, they placed brushwood on top and stamped down soil on top of it. Finally, they extended a fence along each side so that the beasts of burden and the horses would not look out to the sea below and panic.

7.34.1a　Herodotus says the distance is "7 stades." See Appendix J, §6, 19.	7.36.2a　Adopting the anonymous conjecture "triremes" (*triereon*) instead of the manuscripts' "in three places." (Purvis, trans.)
7.36.1a　Pontus, the Euxine (Black) Sea: Map 7.33, locator. The side "toward the Euxine" means the northern bridge. "The other side" was the southern bridge.	7.36.3a　Herodotus writes "1 talent per cubit." the talent was a unit of weight that varied from place to place in the ancient world. See Appendix J, §11–13, 20.
7.36.1b　Hellespont: Map 7.33. See also Appendix O, §10.	

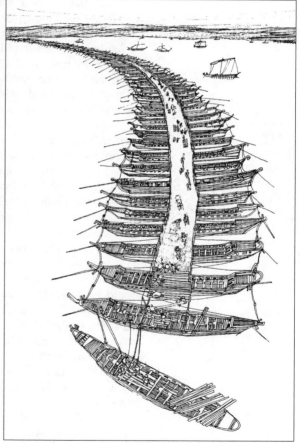

FIGURE 7.36. A PHOTOGRAPH OF A MODERN
BRIDGE OF BOATS ON THE KABUL RIVER (LEFT),
AND AN ARTIST'S DRAWING OF A BRIDGE OF BOATS
BEING ASSEMBLED.

So the bridges were completed, and the work around Mount Athos[a] was also done: mounds of earth had been heaped up around both entrances to the channel to act as breakwaters against the flood tide and to prevent them from filling up, and it was reported that the channel had been completely finished. The army waited for the winter to pass and, with the coming of spring, set out from Sardis, now fully prepared, and began the march to Abydos. [2] At the very beginning of its journey, the sun left its seat in the heavens and disappeared; and although the sky had been especially clear and cloudless, day was now eclipsed into night.[a] Xerxes himself observed this and grew concerned. He asked the Magi what this portent meant. [3] They told him that the god[a] was showing the Hellenes in advance that he would abandon[b] their cities, since the sun is the prophetic symbol for the Hellenes, while for the Persians it is the moon. When Xerxes had heard this, he rejoiced and continued his march.

But as he was marching away with the army, Pythios the Lydian, terrified by the portent that had appeared from the heavens but encouraged because of the gifts presented to him by the King, went to Xerxes and said, "My lord, I would like to obtain a certain favor from you, one which would be trivial for you to grant me, but would be of great importance to me were you to grant it." [2] Xerxes thought Pythios would ask for anything but what he actually requested, so he told him he would grant this favor and bade him to say what he wanted. Hearing this, Pythios was emboldened and said, "My lord, I happen to have five sons, and as it happens, they have all been drafted to march with you to Hellas. [3] Please, sire, have pity on me at this time of my life and release one of my sons from the army, the eldest one, so that he may take care of me and my property, but do take the other four along with you; and may you return after having accomplished all your goals."

Xerxes became enraged at this and replied, "You despicable wretch. How dare you even mention your own son when you are my slave and should be following me with your entire household, even with your wife, while I myself am marching along with my own sons, brothers, servants, and friends? Well, listen and take heed of this: a person's feelings dwell in his ears, and when this seat of the emotions hears something good, the body fills up with delight, but when it hears the opposite, it swells with rage. [2] You once did me a good turn and promised more of the same, but you will not boast that your good services surpassed those of your King. And now that you have veered to a shameful course, you will receive less than your former actions deserved. Your hospitality will save you and four of your sons, but that one son to whom you cling the most will have to surrender his life as your punishment." [3] Such was Xerxes' reply to Pythios.

7.37.1a   Mount Athos: Map 7.24, inset.
7.37.2a   This eclipse cannot be confirmed from astronomical calculations.
7.37.3a   The god in this case is Helios, the Sun.
7.37.3b   The Greek word *eklepsis* (hence "eclipse") means "abandonment."

Then he immediately ordered his men assigned to such tasks to find the eldest son of Pythios, cut him in two, and place one half of the body on the right side of the road and the other half on the left so that the army would march between them.

They carried out these orders, and the army marched between. First in line were the baggage carriers and the beasts of burden; next came a mixed body of troops of many nationalities, all marching together without distinct divisions. These comprised more than half of the army, and then there was a gap which separated them from the King. [2] Riding before the King were 1,000 horsemen, chosen from all the Persians. Then came 1,000 spear bearers[a] carrying their spears pointed toward the ground; they, too, had been selected from all the Persians. After them came ten sacred horses called the Nesaian horses, adorned with magnificent equipment. [3] They are called "Nesaian" after a vast plain in Median territory of that name[a] from which these horses come. [4] Then, in its appointed position behind these ten horses, came the sacred chariot of Zeus, pulled by eight white horses and followed by the charioteer holding the reins; he marched on foot, since no human ever mounts this throne. After him rode Xerxes himself in a chariot pulled by Nesaian horses, and walking beside the King was his charioteer, whose name was Patiramphes, the son of a Persian named Otanes.

That is how Xerxes rode out of Sardis, but whenever he thought it prudent to do so, he would get out of his chariot and move into a covered wagon.[a] Behind the King marched 1,000 spear bearers, who were the best and most noble of all the Persians; these held their spears in the usual position.[b] After them came another 1,000 horsemen, who were also all elite Persians. And following this unit of cavalry were 10,000 picked men from the rest of the Persians,[c] serving as infantry. [2] Of these troops, 1,000 carried spears with golden pomegranates instead of spikes at the tips,[a] and they surrounded the rest. The 9,000 men within this formation carried spears with silver pomegranates. The troops marching with their spears pointed toward the ground also had golden pomegranates on their spears, while those following Xerxes most closely had apples. Riding in order after these 10,000 troops were 10,000 Persian horsemen. Then, after a gap of as much as 400 yards,[b] followed the rest of the army, a jumbled multitude.

7.40
480
THE MARCH FROM LYDIA
The army marches with its divisions mixed together. In the center is Xerxes and a special Persian bodyguard.

7.41
480
THE MARCH FROM LYDIA
Herodotus describes the special Persian units that accompany the King as his guard.

7.40.2a Some scholars believe that this body of spear bearers was a special unit of royal bodyguards.
7.40.3a The location of the Nesaian Plain is not known.
7.41.1a Covered wagons were associated with travel by women and children.
7.41.1b The "usual" position was with spear pointed upward, rather than toward the ground, as Herodotus describes the spears held by the 1,000 infantry who marched in front of the King.

7.41.1c These were the band of so-called Immortals. See 7.83.1.
7.41.2a Greek spears usually were armed with a large spear-head blade at the top and a short utilitarian spike at the other end. See Appendix N, Hoplite Warfare in Herodotus, §3. At 7.211.2 Herodotus says Persian spears were shorter than Greek ones, which left the Persians at a disadvantage in close combat.
7.41.2b Herodotus writes "2 stades." See Appendix J, §6, 19.

From Lydia[a] the army advanced to the Caicus River[b] and into Mysian[c] territory. Then, proceeding from the Caicus and keeping Mount Kane[d] on its left, it went through Atarneus[e] and to the city of Karene.[f] From there it marched over the plain of Thebe,[g] passing by the cities of Adramyttium[h] and Pelasgian Antandros.[i] [2] Then, keeping Mount Ida[a] always to its left, it entered the territory of Ilium.[b] And the first event that befell the army was that thunder and tornadoes descended upon the troops as they stayed the night below Mount Ida. These storms destroyed a rather large number of them right there on the spot.

The army then went to the Scamander,[a] which was the first river it had encountered on its journey from Sardis that failed to provide enough water for the troops and the pack animals attempting to drink from it. After Xerxes arrived at this river, he climbed up to the Pergamon of Priam,[b] which he longed to behold. [2] After viewing the site and inquiring into its particulars and past, he sacrificed 1,000 head of cattle to Athena of Ilium, and the Magi poured libations to the heroes.[a] During the night a panic fell upon the camp, but at the break of day the troops resumed their march, keeping the cities of Rhoiteion[b] and Ophryneion[c] and Dardanos,[d] which borders Abydos,[e] on their left, and the Teukrian Gergithians[f] on their right.

When they reached Abydos, Xerxes wanted to review his entire army. He had deliberately ordered an elevated throne of marble to be made and set up on a hill[a] in advance, and the people of Abydos had built it according to the King's instructions. And so there he sat, gazing down at the shore, viewing his army and his ships. And as he looked down upon them, he felt a longing to see the ships compete in a race. This was duly carried out; the Phoenicians of Sidon[b] won the contest, and Xerxes was delighted with both the race and his forces.

~~As he looked out over the whole Helle~~spont, whose water was completely hidden by all his ships, and at all the shores and the plains of Abydos, now so full of people, ~~Xerxes congratulated himself for being so blessed.~~ But then he suddenly burst into tears and wept.

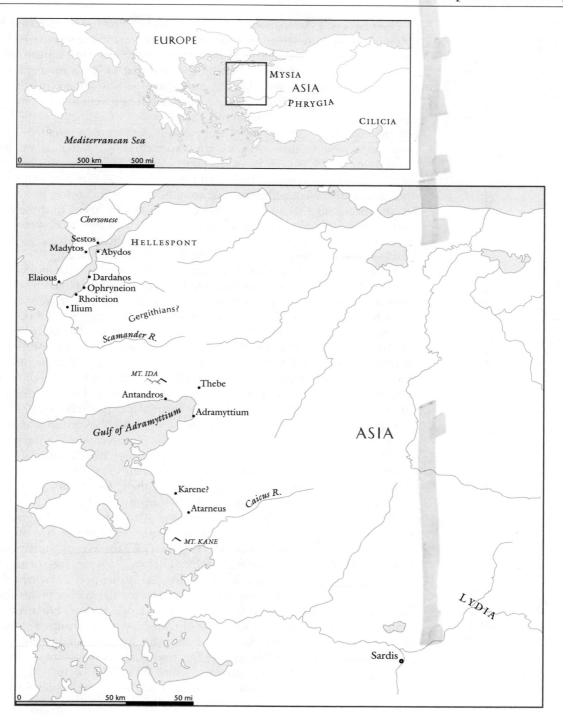

MAP 7.42

7.46
480
ABYDOS
Xerxes mourns the shortness of human life, realizing that not one of all that multitude would be alive 100 years from now. Artabanos comments on the bitter misfortunes men suffer during their lives.

Now his uncle Artabanos, the one who had at first freely expressed his opinion as he attempted to dissuade Xerxes from marching against Hellas, noticed that Xerxes was weeping and said to him, "Sire, what a great divergence there is between your behavior now and that of just a moment ago: then you deemed yourself a blessed man, but now you are weeping!" [2] And Xerxes replied, "That is because I was suddenly overcome by pity as I considered the brevity of human life, since not one of all these people here will be alive one hundred years from now." Artabanos responded, "But even more pitiable than that are the experiences we suffer as we pass through life. [3] For even in such a short span of life, no human being is born so fortunate—neither these men nor any others—that the wish to be dead rather than alive will not occur to him, and not just once, but often. For the misfortunes that befall us and the illnesses that harass us make even a short life seem long. [4] And so because life is a hardship, death proves to be a human being's most welcome escape, and the god, who gives us merely a taste of sweetness in life, is revealed to be a jealous deity."

7.47
480
ABYDOS
Artabanos still fears that the expedition may fail, given Xerxes' two greatest enemies.

Xerxes then said, "Artabanos, let us leave the topic of human life, since it is indeed just as you have defined it, and let us not bring to mind evil things when we have so many good things at hand. But tell me, if your dream vision had not been so vivid, would you have held to your original opinion and still have tried to prevent me from marching against Hellas, or would you have changed your mind? Come now, tell me truly." [2] Artabanos answered him, "Sire, may the vision that appeared in that dream be fulfilled in accordance with what we both want. However, I am still quite out of my mind with fear as I consider many things, but especially as I foresee that you will have to fight against two of the most formidable adversaries of all."

7.48
480
ABYDOS
Thinking Artabanos felt his forces were insufficient, Xerxes offers to increase its size.

Xerxes said, "What in the world has gotten into you? What can you mean when you say that? You think I have two of the most formidable adversaries? Would you find fault with the size of my land army? Would you think the Greek army is likely to be many times larger than ours? Or will our navy prove inferior to theirs? Or both together? Well, then, if it appears to you that our forces are insufficient, another army could be mustered at once."

7.49
480
ABYDOS
Artabanos explains that the two enemies are the land and the sea; that there will be few harbors able to shelter such a great fleet, and that advancing the army ever farther into unknown lands risks famine.

Artabanos then answered, "Sire, anyone with an ounce of common sense could find no fault with your present army, nor with the size of your fleet. And if you did gather more forces, those two adversaries I mentioned would only become still more formidable. The two I am speaking of are the land and the sea. [2] For the sea, I believe, has no harbors anywhere that are large enough to receive your fleet and guarantee the safety of your ships should a storm arise. And you require not just one harbor, but many of them, located all along the entire coast of your expedition's route. [3] Since there are no ample harbors, you must realize that fortune will now rule over the affairs of men instead of men ruling over their own fortunes. Having thus explained one of two adveraries, I shall now describe the other. [4] The land has also become your adversary, in that if no one comes forth to oppose you, the land itself will become more and more hostile to you the farther you advance and are lured into going ever farther, since human beings never have their fill of success. [5] So what I am saying is that by taking more and more land and spending more and more time, you will generate famine. The mark of a superior man would be to feel fear as he makes his plans, considering everything that could happen to him, and yet be able to act boldly when the time for action arrives."

To this, Xerxes replied, "Artabanos, you have been fair and reasonable in your judgment of all these concerns, but do not be afraid of everything, and do not, in your considerations, give every factor equal weight. For if you gave every matter that confronts you equal weight, you would never act at all. It is better to confidently confront all eventualities and suffer half of what we dread than to fear every single event before it happens and never to suffer at all. [2] If you dispute every proposed course but will not point the way to a safe and secure one, then you ought to fail in your argument just as much as the man who argues for the contrary course, since both suggestions for and against thus turn out to be of equal value. How could any human being accurately discern the safe and secure course? I think it can never be done. But for the most part, success tends to come to those who are willing to take action rather than to those who hesitate and consider every detail. [3] You see how far the power of the Persian Empire has advanced. Well, if the Kings who preceded me had held opinions such as yours, or even if they did not hold them but had followed other advisors such as you, you would never have seen us come as far as we have. As it is, we have reached this point because we have been led by those who were willing to play a dangerous game, for it is by taking great risks that great power will be won. [4] And so let us try to be like them; we are making our journey during the best season of the year, and after we conquer all of Europe,[a] we shall return home without encountering famine anywhere, or suffering any other unpleasant experience. For not only are we bringing plenty of food with us on our journey, but we shall also have the food of any land and nation on which we set foot: after all, it is against farmers, not nomads, that we are marching."

After hearing this response, Artabanos said, "Since you will not allow for fear of anything, sire, please at least accept some advice from me, for one absolutely must prolong a discussion when so many factors are involved. Cyrus son of Cambyses subjugated all of the Ionians[a]—all except for the Athenians[b]—and made them tribute-paying subjects of Persia. [2] My advice to you is that you should not lead these men against their fathers. For we can defeat our enemies without them; and if they follow us, they must either turn out to be the most unjust of men by enslaving their

7.50
480
ABYDOS
Xerxes replies that it is better to act boldly and suffer half of what you dread than to fear everything and never suffer anything; that the great successes of past Persian Kings were not won except by taking great risks.

7.51
480
ABYDOS
Artabanos points out the dangers of requiring the conquered Ionians to assist in the conquest of Athens, their mother city.

7.50.4a Europe: Map 7.58, locator. This exhorta-
       tion is another indication of the Persians'
       appalling ignorance of Europe's geogra-
       phy. See Appendix M, §6; and Appendix

       D, Herodotean Geography, §4.
7.51.1a Ionia: Map 7.58, locator.
7.51.1b Athens: Map 7.58, locator.

mother city, or the most just, by assisting it to be free. [3] And if they do turn out to be the most unjust, they will still not contribute very much to our advantage, while if they turn out to be the most just, they would be capable of doing great damage to your army. And so keep in mind and think hard on that old saying which is so well expressed: the end of every matter is not revealed in perfect clarity at the beginning."

Xerxes then said, "Artabanos, of all the points you have made, it is in this last one, your fear that the Ionians will transfer their loyalties, that you are most mistaken. We have the strongest proof against this, which you yourself witnessed, as did the others on the campaign with Darius against the Scythians: the destruction or survival of the whole Persian army depended on the Ionians, and they dealt with us justly and faithfully and caused us no grief at all.[a] [2] Besides, they could not possibly defy our authority after having left behind their women, children, and property in our land. So have no fear of that, but with good courage keep my house and my tyranny safe. For it is to you alone among the Persians that I have chosen to entrust my scepter."

Having said that, and sending Artabanos off to Susa,[a] Xerxes then summoned the most eminent of the Persians and, when they had come into his presence, said to them, "I have assembled you, Persians, to make a request of you. I ask you to prove yourselves to be noble and courageous men and to not disgrace the earlier achievements of the Persians, which are great and very worthy indeed. Let us all, both as individuals and as a group together, maintain our zeal. For the goal toward which we are striving is the common good of all. [2] I command you, therefore, to persevere in this war with all your might, because I hear that we are marching against men who are noble and courageous, and that if we conquer them, no other army in the world will ever oppose us. And so, after praying to the gods who hold Persia in their charge, let us cross over to them."

That day they prepared for the crossing, and on the next they waited, wanting to see the sun rise first, and meanwhile burning incense of all kinds on the bridges and strewing myrtle branches along the road. [2] Then, as the sun was rising, Xerxes poured a libation from a golden cup into the sea as he faced the sun and prayed that nothing unexpected would happen to stop him from subjugating Europe before he reached the very ends of that land. After his prayer, he threw the libation cup into the Hellespont,[a] along with a golden mixing bowl and a Persian sword, which they call an *akinakes*.[b] [3] But I cannot judge for certain whether he let these sink into the water as offerings to the sun, or whether he presented them to the sea in repentance, to compensate for his earlier whipping of the Hellespont.

7.52
480
ABYDOS
Xerxes disagrees, recalling the loyalty of the Ionians in the Scythian campaign, and that Ionian wives and children are hostages for their good conduct.

7.53
480
ABYDOS
Xerxes sends Artabanos home and exhorts the remaining Persian notables to conduct themselves bravely.

7.54
480
HELLESPONT
The Persians prepare to cross the Hellespont. Xerxes pours a libation and prays to the sun to be allowed to conquer all of Europe.

7.52.1a Xerxes' remark refers to the faithfulness of the Ionians at the Danube bridge, for by destroying it, they could have marooned the Persian army on the northern (Scythian) bank and left them to die of starvation and/or attack by the

Scythians. See 4.98, 4.136–142.
7.53.1a Susa: Map 7.58, locator.
7.54.2a Hellespont: Map 7.58.
7.54.2b *Akinakes*: Herodotus here uses the Persian word for a dagger or short sword.

After that they all crossed over, the infantry and all the cavalry, via the bridge toward the Pontus,[a] the beasts of burden and the train of servants via the bridge toward the Aegean.[b] [2] The first to go over were the 10,000 Persians, all wearing garlands, and after them came the troops that included all sorts of peoples mixed together. It took the whole day for these men to make the crossing, and the first to go over on the next day were the horsemen and the troops who were holding their spears pointed downward. These too wore garlands. [3] Then came the sacred horses and the sacred chariot, followed by Xerxes himself, his spear bearers, and the thousand horsemen, and after these, the rest of the army marched over. At the same time, the ships were sailing for the opposite shore. I have also heard it said that the King crossed last of all.

After Xerxes had passed over into Europe, he watched his army cross under the lash. It took the army seven days and seven nights without pause to cross the bridges, [2] and it is reported that just as Xerxes had completed the crossing, a man who lived there in the Hellespont region said, "Zeus, why do you assume the appearance of a Persian man and call yourself Xerxes instead of Zeus? Why do you bring all the peoples of the world with you to remove the Hellenes from their land? Surely you could have done it without them!"

When all of them had crossed over and they were setting out on their journey, a great portent appeared to them. Xerxes paid no attention to it, however, although it was quite easy to interpret. A horse gave birth to a hare, which clearly symbolized the fact that Xerxes was about to lead an expedition against Hellas with the greatest pride and magnificence, but would return to the same place running for his life. [2] Another portent had occurred earlier while he was still in Sardis;[a] there a mule had given birth to a mule with two kinds of genitals, both male and female, with the male genitals above the female.

But Xerxes paid no attention to either of these portents and continued his advance with the land army. The fleet sailed out of the Hellespont and made its voyage along the shore, just the opposite of the direction taken by the land forces, [2] for while the ships sailed westward to arrive at Cape Sarpedon,[a] where they had been ordered to await Xerxes' arrival, the army on land first made its way eastward toward the rising sun and up through the Chersonese,[b] marching so that the grave of Helle, the daughter of Athamas, was on their right and the city of Kardia[c] was on their left, and passing right through the center of the city that happens to have the name Agora.[d] [3] Then they rounded what is called the Black Gulf[a] and crossed the Black River, which has the same name as the gulf. This river did not

---

7.55
480
HELLESPONT
The army and its service train cross the Hellespont by separate bridges. Elite Persian units wear garlands.

7.56
480
HELLESPONT
Xerxes crosses over and watches his army do the same, which takes seven days and nights.

7.57
480
HELLESPONT
Great portents at Sardis and the Hellespont were ignored by Xerxes.

7.58
480
HELLESPONT-DORISKOS
Herodotus describes the route of march of both the army and the fleet.

7.55.1a Pontus, the Euxine (Black) Sea: Map 7.58, locator. The bridge toward the Pontus was the more northerly one.
7.55.1b Aegean Sea: Map 7.58. The southern bridge of the two.
7.57.2a Sardis: Map 7.58, locator.
7.58.2a Cape Sarpedon (Sarpedon Promontory): Map 7.58.

7.58.2b Chersonese, Hellespontine: Map 7.58.
7.58.2c Kardia: Map 7.58.
7.58.2d Agora: Map 7.58.
7.58.3a Black Gulf (in Greek, Melas Kolpos), Black River: Map 7.58. On the Black Gulf, see also 6.41.

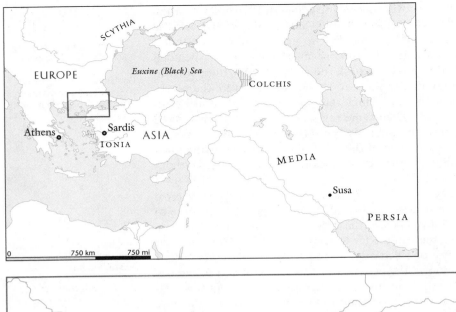

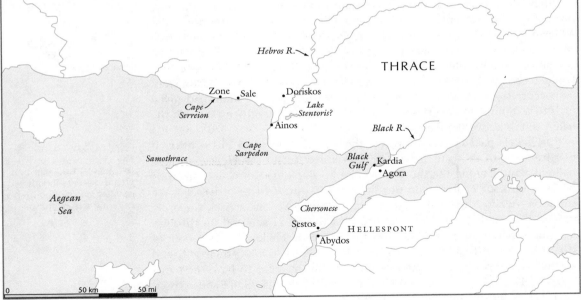

MAP 7.58

hold out against the army as the troops drank its waters dry. Next they went westward, passing by the Aeolian city of Ainos[b] and Lake Stentoris,[c] until they reached Doriskos.[d]

Doriskos is a vast coastal plain in Thrace[a] through which flows the great River Hebros;[b] and in Doriskos is the royal fort which is also called Doriskos, where a garrison of Persians was established by Darius at the time when he was marching against the Scythians.[c] [2] And so Xerxes, finding this place a perfect site for drawing up and counting his troops, now required that this be done. And as all the ships reached Doriskos, the captains beached them, as Xerxes had ordered, adjacent to Doriskos in the region which in ancient times had belonged to the Cicones, along the shore between Zone[a] and the Samothracian[b] city of Sale,[c] at the end of which lies the well-known Cape Serreion.[d] [3] So they landed their ships and dragged them up on the beach there to dry.[a] And while they did all this, Xerxes was counting up his troops in Doriskos.

Now I cannot say for certain how many men each contingent contributed to the total number, since nobody can report that, but the number of troops in the whole land army added together was found to be 1,700,000.[a] [2] This is how they managed to count them. They gathered groups of 10,000 men together at one spot, packed them in as closely as they could, and then drew a circle around them from the outside. After delineating the circle and dismissing those 10,000, they erected a dry wall on the edge of the circle high enough to reach a man's navel. [3] When that was done, they had others go into the enclosure they had built, until they had counted them all in this manner. After the count had been completed, the army was drawn up into units according to their various nationalities.

The following peoples were serving in the army. There were the Persians,[a] who were dressed and equipped in this manner: they wore soft felt caps on their heads, which they call *tiaras*, and multicolored tunics with sleeves, covering their bodies, and they had breastplates of iron fashioned to look like fish scales. On their legs they wore trousers, and instead of shields they carried pieces of wicker, which had quivers hung below them. They were armed with short spears, long bows, and arrows made of reeds. From their belts they fastened daggers, which hung down along the right thigh. [2] The Persians were commanded by Otanes, the father of Xerxes' wife Amastris. In ancient times the Persians were called Kephenes by the Hellenes, but Artaioi by themselves and their neighbors. [3] Then Perseus son of Danae and Zeus came to Kepheus son of Belos and obtained Kepheus'

7.59
480
DORISKOS
Xerxes decides that Doriskos is a suitable place to number his army.

7.60
480
DORISKOS
XERXES' ARMY
The Persians count their troops in an unusual way.

7.61
480
DORISKOS
XERXES' ARMY
Herodotus begins to describe the Persian army. First he tells of the Persians, their arms, their commander, and their mythical origins.

7.58.3b	Ainos: Map 7.58.	7.59.2b	Samothrace: Map 7.58.
7.58.3c	Lake Stentoris, possible location: Map 7.58.	7.59.2c	Sale: Map 7.58.
		7.59.2d	Cape Serreion: Map 7.58.
7.58.3d	Doriskos: Map 7.58.	7.59.3a	Dragging ships out of the water to dry: see Appendix S, Trireme Warfare in Herodotus, §8.
7.59.1a	Thrace: Map 7.58.		
7.59.1b	Hebros River: Map 7.58.		
7.59.1c	Scythia: Map 7.58, locator. Darius invaded Scythia in the year 513.	7.60.1a	For a discussion of this number, see Appendix R, §7.
7.59.2a	Zone: Map 7.58.	7.61.1a	Persia: Map 7.58, locator.

daughter Andromeda as his wife, and she bore him a son who was given the name Perses. This son was left behind by Perseus, since Kepheus had no male heir; and so it was from this Perses that the Persians got their name.[a]

7.62
480
XERXES' ARMY
The Medes, Kissians, and Hyrcanians.

The Medes[a] on the expedition were dressed and equipped in the same way, for this attire is actually Median, not Persian. They had brought Tigranes, an Achaimenid, as their commander. Long ago the Medes had been called Arians by everyone, until Medeia of Colchis[b] came to them from Athens, and then, at least according to what the Medes themselves say, they, too, changed their name. [2] The Kissians[a] who had joined the expedition were dressed and equipped just as the Persians were in everything, except that they wore turbans instead of felt caps; they were commanded by Anaphes son of Otanes. The Hyrcanians[b] were dressed and equipped just as the Persians were, and brought as their commander Megapanos, who was later entrusted with the governorship of Babylon.[c]

7.63
480
XERXES' ARMY
The Assyrians.

The Assyrians[a] on the expedition wore helmets of bronze on their heads and also plaited helmets[b] made by a certain barbarian method that is not easy to describe. They carried shields, spears, and daggers similar to those of the Egyptians, and in addition, wooden clubs with knobs of iron; they wore breastplates of linen. These people are called Syrians by the Hellenes, but Assyrians by the barbarians. Among them were the Chaldaeans.[c] Leading them was Otaspes son of Artachaias.

7.64
480
XERXES' ARMY
The Baktrians and Scythians.

The Baktrians[a] in the army wore caps on their heads that were almost exactly like those of the Medes, and they carried native bows made of reeds, and also short spears. [2] The Scythian Sacae[a] wore on their heads stiff turbans sticking straight up in a point. They were dressed in trousers and wielded native bows and daggers; in addition, they carried battle-axes, known as *sagareis*.[b] Though these people are actually Scythians of Amyrgion,[c] they were called Sacae because the Persians call all Scythians Sacae. The Baktrians and the Sacae were commanded by Hystaspes son of Darius and Atossa the daughter of Cyrus.

7.65
480
XERXES' ARMY
The Indians.

The Indians[a] wore clothing made of cotton[b] and carried bows made of reeds and arrows also made of reeds, but tipped with iron. That is how the Indians were equipped, and they had been ordered to march under the command of Pharnazathres son of Artabates.

7.66
480
XERXES' ARMY
The Areians, Parthians, Sogdians, Dadikai, Gandarians, and Chorasmians.

The Areians[a] carried Median bows, but in all other respects were dressed and equipped exactly like the Baktrians. Commanding the Areians was

7.61.3a   Herodotus is always prone to base ethnological conclusions on Greek legends and the similarity of names, as in 7.62. Medea supplies the name of the Medes. (Godley)
7.62.1a   Media: Map 7.58, locator.
7.62.1b   Colchis: Map 7.58, locator.
7.62.2a   Kissians, possible location of territory: Map 7.66, BX.
7.62.2b   Hyrcania: Map 7.66, AY.
7.62.2c   Babylon: Map 7.66, BX.
7.63.1a   Assyria: Map 7.66, AX.
7.63.1b   Plaited helmets were probably made of leather thongs. (How and Wells)

7.63.1c   This sentence may be an interpolation. The Chaldaeans are mentioned at 1.181.5, 183.1–3, and 3.155.5.
7.64.1a   Baktrians (Baktrianoi): Map 7.66, AY.
7.64.2a   Scythian Sacae (the Scythians living in East Sogdiana near Baktria): Map 3.94, AY.
7.64.2b   The Scythian word *sagareis* (singular, *sagaris*) also appears at 1.215.1 and 5.4.3.
7.64.2c   Amyrgion: location unknown.
7.65.1a   India: Map 7.66, AY.
7.65.1b   Literally, "of wood," as at 3.47.2.
7.66.1a   Areians (Areia): Map 7.66, AY.

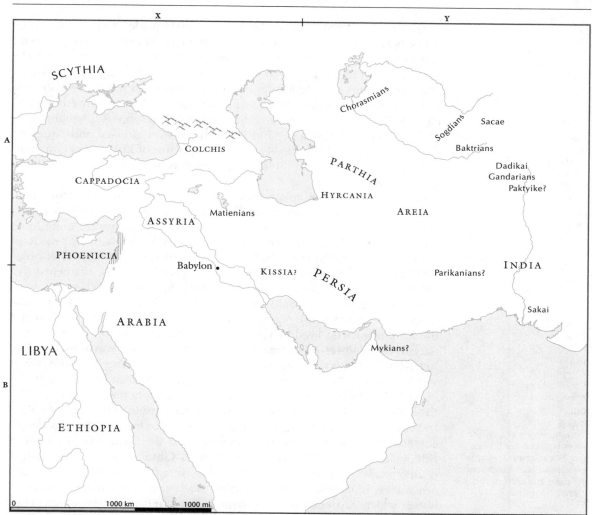

MAP 7.66

Sisamnes son of Hydarnes. The Parthians,[b] Chorasmians,[c] Sogdians,[d] Gandarians,[e] and Dadikai[f] in the army also dressed and equipped themselves like the Baktrians. [2] They were commanded by Artabazos son of Pharnakes, general of the Parthians and Chorasmians; Azanes son of Artaios, general of the Sogdians; and Artyphios son of Artabanos, general of the Gandarians and Dadikai.

7.66.1b Parthia: Map 7.66, AY.
7.66.1c Chorasmians, location of territory: Map
         7.66, AY.
7.66.1d Sogdians, location of territory: Map
         7.66, AY.

7.66.1e Gandarians (Gandaris): Map 7.66, AY.
7.66.1f Dadikai, location of territory: Map
         7.66, AY.

525

7.67
480
XERXES' ARMY
The Caspians, Sarangians,
and Paktyes.

The Caspians[a] on the expedition wore cloaks made of skins and carried native bows made of reeds and swords.[b] That was their dress and equipment, and they brought as their leader Ariomardos the brother of Artyphios. The Sarangians[c] wore brightly dyed clothing and boots reaching to their knees, and carried bows and Median spears. Their commander was Pherendates son of Megabazos. [2] The Paktyes[a] wore hide cloaks and had native bows and daggers. They brought as their commander Artayntes son of Ithamitras.

7.68
480
XERXES' ARMY
The Outians, Mykians,
and Parikanians.

The Outians,[a] Mykians,[b] and Parikanians[c] were dressed and equipped the very same way as the Paktyes. Arsamenes son of Darius was commander of the Outians and Mykians; Siromitras son of Oiobazos, of the Parikanians.

7.69
480
XERXES' ARMY
The Arabians and Ethiopians.

The Arabians[a] wore *zeiras*[b] bound up with belts, and they carried long concave bows on their right sides. The Ethiopians[c] were clad in leopard and lion skins; they carried bows made of palm blades which were quite long, no less than six feet.[d] And they had small reed arrows with tips made of sharp stone instead of iron, the kind of stone used for carving signet rings. They also carried spears with tips made of gazelles' horns, sharpened like the tips of a lance. And they carried knobbed clubs as well. When they were going into battle, they would smear half of their bodies with chalk and the other half with red-ochre pigment. [2] The commander of the Arabians and the Ethiopians who lived in Upper Egypt[a] was Arsames son of Darius and Artystone daughter of Cyrus; of all his wives, Darius was most fond of Artystone and had an image of her crafted out of beaten gold. So Arsames was in command of the Arabians and the Ethiopians from Upper Egypt.

7.70
480
XERXES' ARMY
Herodotus says the differences between the Libyan
and Asian Ethiopians are in
speech and hair. He describes
the dress and arms of the
Asian Ethiopians.

But two different groups of Ethiopians were on this expedition. The Ethiopians who live toward the sunrise had been assigned to march with the Indians; they were not at all different in appearance from the other Ethiopians, but they did differ in their language and their hair. For the Eastern Ethiopians[a] have straight hair, while those of Libya[b] have the wooliest hair of all humans. [2] The Ethiopians from Asia were for the most part equipped just as the Indians were, but on their heads they wore the foreheads of horses which had been skinned, with the ears and mane left intact. They wore the mane as a crest, with horse's ears pointing up straight. And instead of shields they carried cranes' skins in front of them for protection.

7.71
XERXES' ARMY
The Libyans.

The Libyans came dressed in leather and wielded javelins sharpened by burning. They brought as their commander Massages son of Oarizos.

7.67.1a Caspians, probably of the Eleventh
Province: location of territory unknown.
7.67.1b Herodotus uses the Persian word
akinakes, a dagger or short sword.
7.67.1c Sarangians: location of territory unknown.
7.67.2a Paktyes of Paktyike in Thirteenth
Province: location unknown.
7.68.1a Outians: location of territory unknown.
7.68.1b Mykians, possible location of territory:
Map 7.66, BY.
7.68.1c Parikanians, possible location of territory:
Map 7.66, BY. Presumably, those who
lived in the south near the Mykians.
7.69.1a Arabia: Map 7.66, BX.

7.69.1b The *zeiras* was a type of long robe worn
also by Thracians.
7.69.1c Ethiopia: Map 7.66, BX.
7.69.1d Herodotus writes that these bows were
"4 cubits" high. There were several
standard measures for the cubit in the
ancient world, but the cubit probably
referred to here equaled approximately
1.5 feet. See Appendix J, §4, 5, 19.
7.69.2a Egypt: Map 7.86, BX.
7.70.1a Eastern or Asian Ethiopians: location of
territory unknown.
7.70.1b Libya: Map 7.66, BX.

The Paphlagonians[a] in the expedition wore plaited helmets on their heads and had small shields and short spears. They also carried javelins and daggers. On their feet they wore native boots reaching to the middle of their calves. The dress and equipment of the Ligyeans,[b] Matienians,[c] Mariandynians,[d] and Syrians was the same as that of the Paphlagonians. These Syrians are called Cappadocians[e] by the Persians. [2] Now the commander of the Paphlagonians and Matienians was Dotos son of Megasidraos; leading the Mariandynians, Ligyeans, and Syrians was Gobryas son of Darius and Artystone.

The Phrygians[a] were dressed and equipped very much like the Paphlagonians, with just a few differences. According to what the Macedonians[b] say, the Phrygians used to be called Briges when they lived in Europe as neighbors to the Macedonians, but when they crossed over into Asia, they changed their name to Phrygians. The Armenians[c] were dressed and equipped just as the Phrygians were, since they were colonists of the Phrygians. In command of both these contingents was Artochmes, who had married a daughter of Darius.

The Lydians[a] were armed very much like the Hellenes. In ancient times, the Lydians were called the Meiones, but they gave up their old name and took a new name from Lydos son of Atys. The Mysians[b] wore native helmets and carried small shields and javelins sharpened by burning. [2] These people were colonists of the Lydians, and are called Olympienians, named after Mount Olympus.[a] The Lydians and Mysians were commanded by Artaphrenes son of Artaphrenes, who had invaded Marathon[b] together with Datis.

The Thracians[a] who marched with the army wore fox-skin caps, and tunics with colorful *zeiras* thrown over them; on their feet and shins they wore fawn-skin boots. They carried javelins, small light shields, and small daggers. [2] They came to be called Bithynians[a] only after they had crossed over from Europe into Asia. Before that, according to their own account, they were called Strymonians, since they lived along the Strymon;[b] but then, they say, they were forced out of their homeland by the Teukrians[c] and Mysians. The commander of the Thracians of Asia was Bassakes son of Artabanos.

[. . .][a] carried small shields of untanned ox hide, and each had two Lycian-made hunting spears.[b] On their heads they wore bronze helmets, to

7.72.1a Paphlagonia: Map 7.75.
7.72.1b Ligyeans: location of territory unknown. Scholars are not sure who these people were, but they were certainly not the Ligurians from the coast of France mentioned at 5.9.3 and 7.165.
7.72.1c Matienians (Matiane): Map 7.66, AX.
7.72.1d Mariandynia: Map 7.75.
7.72.1e Cappadocia: Map 7.75.
7.73.1a Phrygia: Map 7.75.
7.73.1b Macedon: Map 7.75.
7.73.1c Armenia: Map 7.75.
7.74.1a Lydia: Map 7.75.
7.74.1b Mysia: Map 7.75.
7.74.2a Mount Olympus (the one near Mysia, not

the one in Thessaly): Map 7.75.
7.74.2b Marathon: Map 7.86, inset. For Herodotus' account of the Persian invasion at Marathon, see 6.102–121 passim.
7.75.1a Thrace: Map 7.75.
7.75.2a Bithynia: Map 7.75.
7.75.2b Strymon River: Map 7.75.
7.75.2c Teukrians is another name for Trojans.
7.76.1a The name of this contingent is missing in the manuscript. Scholars have speculated that the subject could be the Pisidians and/or the Chalybes (both on Map 7.75).
7.76.1b An alternative reading given by some manuscripts is "wolf-hunting spears."

MAP 7.75

which were attached the ears and horns of an ox, fashioned in bronze, and a crest on the top. Their shins were covered with red pieces of cloth. These people have an oracle of Ares.

7.77
480
XERXES' ARMY
The Meiones and Milyans.

The Meionian Kabales,[a] who are called Lasonians, had the same equipment as the Cilicians;[b] I shall describe it when I reach my account of the Cilician contingent. The Milyans[c] carried short spears and had their garments fastened with brooches. Some of them carried Lycian bows, and they wore helmets made of hides. Badres son of Hystanes was in command of all of them.

7.78
480
XERXES' ARMY
The Moschians, Tibarenoi, Makrones, and Mossynoikians.

The Moschians[a] wore wooden helmets and carried shields and small spears with huge spear points. The Tibarenoi,[b] Makrones,[c] and Mossynoikians[d] who came on the expedition were dressed and equipped just as the Moschians were. The following commanders were jointly assigned to marshall these contingents: Ariomardos son of Darius and Parmys (who was the daughter of

7.77.1a Kabalis: Map 7.75.
7.77.1b Cilicia: Map 7.75.
7.77.1c Milyas: Map 7.75.
7.78.1a Moschians, location of territory: Map 7.86, AY.
7.78.1b Tibarenoi, location of territory: Map 7.86, AX.
7.78.1c Makrones, location of territory: Map 7.86, AY.
7.78.1d Mossynoikians, location of territory: Map 7.86, AX.

Smerdis son of Cyrus) was in charge of the Moschians and Tibarenoi; and Artayktes, who was acting governor of Sestos in the Hellespont[e] and the son of Cherasmis, was in command of the Makrones and Mossynoikians.

The Mares[a] wore native plaited helmets on their heads and carried small leather shields and javelins. The Colchians[b] wore wooden helmets and carried small shields of untanned ox hide, short spears, and also knives. The commander of the Mares and Colchians was Pharandates son of Teaspis. The Alarodians[c] and Saspeires[d] were equipped with the same armor as the Colchians; their commander was Masistios son of Siromitras.

7.79
480
XERXES' ARMY
The Mares and Colchians.

The island peoples from the Erythraean Sea[a] were also accompanying this expedition; they came from the islands inhabited by those called "the Deported," who had been settled there by the King. They had clothing and weapons most closely resembling those of the Medes. Mardontes son of Bagaios was in command of these islanders; in the next year he served as general at Mycale[b] and died in battle there.

7.80
480
XERXES' ARMY
The island tribes from the Erythraean Sea.

Those, then, were the nations enrolled in the infantry and marching on land; their commanders, who have already been named, were also in charge of marshalling and counting the troops. In addition, these commanders appointed the *chiliarchs* (captains of 1,000 troops) and the *myriarchs* (captains of 10,000 troops), while the latter appointed the *hekatonarchs* (captains of 100) and *dekarchs* (captains of 10). There were other officers in charge of communicating orders to the various units and national contingents.[a] So the commanding officers were as I have enumerated.

7.81
480
XERXES' ARMY
How the contingents from many nations were numbered and officered.

The generals holding supreme authority over them and the entire land army were as follows: Mardonios son of Gobryas, Tritantaichmes son of Artabanos (the Artabanos who had expressed his opposition to the war against the Hellenes), Smerdomenes son of Otanes (both of the last two generals were sons of Darius' brothers, and so cousins of Xerxes), Masistes son of Darius and Atossa, Gergis son of Ariazos, and Megabyzos son of Zopyros.

7.82
480
XERXES' ARMY
The chief generals and commanders of the army are listed.

These generals were in charge of the entire land army, except for the 10,000 who were selected from all the Persians; they were commanded by Hydarnes son of Hydarnes. The Persians call these 10,000 "the Immortals," because if any of them leaves their number, forced out by either death or illness, another man is chosen, so that their number is never higher or lower than 10,000. [2] The most impressive dress and equipment were displayed by the Persians, and the Persian troops themselves were the best in the army. Their dress and arms have already been described, but in addition, they were conspicuous because of the lavish amounts of gold that they wore. And they had brought along covered wagons which carried their con-

7.83
480
XERXES' ARMY
Hydarnes led the picked and favored force of 10,000 Persians called Immortals.

7.78.1e Sestos in the Hellespont: Map 7.98, AY.
7.79.1a Mares: location of territory unknown.
7.79.1b Colchis: Map 7.86, AY.
7.79.1c Alarodians, location of territory: Map 7.86, AY.
7.79.1d Saspeires, location of territory: Map 7.86, AY.
7.80.1a Erythraean Sea, in this case the entire "Southern Sea," represented here by both

the modern Red Sea (Map 7.86, BX) and the Persian Gulf (Map 7.86, BY).
7.80.1b Mycale Peninsula: Map 7.75. Site of a great Greek victory over the Persians in 479; see 9.99–105.
7.81.1a That is, native leaders, not the regular officers of the army. (Godley) See Appendix R, §8.

cubines and large retinues of well-dressed servants. Camels and beasts of burden carried their food supply separate from that of the rest of the army.

Although these people were horsemen, not all of them supplied cavalry to the expedition; only the following ones did so. The Persian[a] cavalry were dressed and equipped the same as the infantry, except that on their heads, some of the horsemen wore helmets forged from bronze and iron.

Then there were the nomads called the Sagartians,[a] whose people speak the Persian language but whose equipment and dress fell in style midway between that of the Persians and that of the Paktyikans;[b] they supplied 8,000 horsemen. It is not their custom to carry weapons made of bronze or iron, with the exception of their daggers. Instead they wield lassos of plaited thongs. [2] And when they go to war, they use these lassos in battle in the following way. As they engage their enemies, they cast their lassos, which have a noose at the end, and whatever the noose catches, whether a horse or a man, they drag in toward themselves. Then they kill the victim entangled in the coils of the noose. So that is the way they fight in battle; they were assigned to the Persian contingent on this expedition.

The Medes[a] and the horsemen of the Kissians[b] had equipment and dress just like that of their foot soldiers. The Indian[c] cavalry was also equipped and dressed the same as their infantry, but some rode horses and others drove chariots drawn by horses as well as wild donkeys. The Baktrians[d] and Caspians[e] were likewise equipped and dressed the same way as their infantry. [2] The cavalry of the Libyans[a] wore the same clothes and armor as their infantry, but all drove chariots. And in the same manner, the Parikanians,[b] the Caspians, and the Arabians[c] all had clothes and equipment similar to that of their infantry, but they all drove camels that were just as swift as horses.

Those were the only peoples who rode horses on the expedition, and they added up to a total of 80,000, not counting the camels and chariots. These horsemen were all marshaled to ride with their various national units except for the Arabians, who were assigned to bring up the rear, since none of the horses could endure the presence of the camels; so they were posted last in order to avoid frightening the horses.[a]

The commanders of the cavalry were Harmamithres and Tithaios, both sons of Datis.[a] The third cavalry commander who had been appointed to serve with them jointly was Pharnuches, but he had become ill and was left behind in Sardis.[b] A dreadful accident had happened to him just as the army

7.84.1a   Persia: Map 7.86, BY.
7.85.1a   Sagartians: location of territory unknown.
7.85.1b   Paktyikans (Paktyike), possible location of territory: Map 7.66, AY.
7.86.1a   Media: Map 7.86, AY.
7.86.1b   Kissians, possible location of territory: Map 7.86, BY.
7.86.1c   India: Map 7.66, AY.
7.86.1d   Baktrians (Baktrianoi), location of territory: Map 7.66, AY.
7.86.1e   Caspians, probably of the Fifteenth Province: location of territory unknown.

7.86.2a   Libya (modern Africa): Map 7.86, BX.
7.86.2b   Parikanians, possible location of territory: Map 7.66, BY.
7.86.2c   Arabia: Map 7.86, BX.
7.87.1a   For an interesting comment on why Xerxes would have included such a large number of ethnic contingents in this army, see Appendix R, §12.
7.88.1a   Datis: the Median commander who led, with Artaphrenes, the Persian expedition that was defeated by the Athenians at Marathon in 490. See 6.94.2.
7.88.1b   Sardis: Map 7.86, AX.

MAP 7.86

was setting out from Sardis: as he was riding out, a dog ran beneath his horse's feet, and the horse, who had not seen it coming, panicked and, standing up on its hind legs, threw Pharnuches to the ground. When he fell, he began to vomit blood, and after that his illness developed into consumption. [2] As soon as the accident happened, his household servants carried out their master's orders: they brought the horse to the spot where he had been thrown and there cut off its legs at the knees. So that is how Pharnuches was discharged from his position as leader.

The total number of triremes came to 1,207,[a] and they were furnished by the following peoples: the Phoenicians[b] with the Syrians of Palestine[c] provided 300; they were equipped with helmets made very much in the Greek style and wore linen breastplates. They carried rimless shields and javelins. [2] The Phoenicians, according to their own account, used to live along the shores of the Erythraean Sea[a] in ancient times, but from there they crossed over to Syria, where they now dwell along the coast. This region of Syria, together with all the land extending as far as Egypt,[b] is called Palestine. The Egyptians furnished 200 ships. [3] On their heads they wore knitted helmets; they carried hollow shields with broad rims, naval spears, and large battle-axes. The majority of them wore breastplates and carried huge knives.

That is how they were armed. The Cyprians[a] provided 150 ships and were dressed as follows. Their kings wore turbans wrapped around their heads, but the rest wore felt caps; otherwise they were dressed and equipped like the Hellenes. The Cyprians themselves say that some of them came from Salamis[b] and Athens,[c] others came from Arcadia,[d] Kythnos,[e] Phoenicia, and Ethiopia.[f]

The Cilicians,[a] who contributed 100 ships, wore native helmets and woolen tunics; they carried rawhide ox skins to serve as shields, and each of them wielded two javelins and a sword made very much like the Egyptian knives. In ancient times these people were called Hypachaioi, but then obtained their current name from Kilix son of Agenor, a Phoenician.

The Pamphylians[b] provided 30 ships and were equipped with Greek arms and weapons. The Pamphylians are descended from those who were scattered abroad from Troy and went with Amphilochos and Calchas.

The Lycians[a] supplied 50 ships; they wore breastplates and greaves, and carried bows made of cornel wood, featherless reed arrows, and javelins. They wore goatskins hanging from their shoulders, and on their heads, felt caps wreathed with feathers. And they also carried daggers and scythes. The Lycians came from Crete. They used to be called Termilai but later took their name from an Athenian, Lykos son of Pandion.

7.89
480
XERXES' FLEET
Herodotus lists the nations supplying triremes—describing the number of ships, their weapons, and their origins—starting with the Phoenicians, Syrians, and Egyptians.

7.90
480
XERXES' FLEET
The Cyprians.

7.91
480
XERXES' FLEET
The Cilicians and the Pamphylians.

7.92
480
XERXES' FLEET
The Lycians.

7.89.1a The number 1,207 arouses suspicion among scholars. See Appendix R, §13–14.
7.89.1b Phoenicia: Map 7.86, AX.
7.89.1c Palestine: Map 7.86, BX.
7.89.2a Erythraean Sea: Map 7.86, BX, BY.
7.89.2b Egypt: Map 7.86, BX.
7.90.1a Cyprus: Map 7.86, AX.
7.90.1b Salamis: Map 7.86, inset. The Cyprians

must mean that their population contains contingents from these various locations.
7.90.1c Athens: Map 7.86, inset.
7.90.1d Arcadia: Map 7.86, inset.
7.90.1e Kythnos: Map 7.86, inset.
7.90.1f Ethiopia: Map 7.86, BX.
7.91.1a Cilicia: Map 7.86, AX.
7.91.1b Pamphylia: Map 7.86, AX.
7.92.1a Lycia: Map 7.86, AX.

The Dorians from Asia,[a] who originally came from the Peloponnese,[b] provided 30 ships and had Greek weapons. The Carians[c] contributed 70 ships and had Greek equipment and dress, except that they carried scythes and daggers. What they used to be called has already been mentioned in the first part of my work.[d]

The Ionians[a] supplied 100 ships, and their equipment and dress were like that of the Hellenes. The Hellenes say that as long as this people lived in the Peloponnese, in what is now known as Achaea,[b] they were called Pelasgian Aigialees.[c] Then, after Danaos and Xouthos arrived in the Peloponnese, they took the name "Ionians" from Ion son of Xouthos.

The islanders provided 17 ships and had Greek arms and armor. They, too, were of the Pelasgian race, and were later called Ionians for the same reason as the Ionians of the twelve cities[a]—who came from Athens—are called Ionians. The Aeolians[b] furnished 60 ships and were supplied with Greek equipment and dress. According to what the Hellenes say, they also were anciently called Pelasgians. [2] All of the Hellespontines[a] took part in the expedition except the men of Abydos,[b] who had been assigned by the king to stay where they were and to guard the bridges. The others from the Pontic region[c] on the expedition provided 100 ships, and had Greek equipment and dress; they were colonists of the Ionians and Dorians.

Persians,[a] Medes,[b] and Sakai[c] served as marines on board all the ships, of which the best were furnished by the Phoenicians, and of the Phoenicians, the Sidonians.[d] Native leaders were appointed over each of these naval contingents and infantry divisions, but I shall not mention them, since no necessity compels me to include them in my narrative. [2] After all, the leaders of each national contingent are not really worthy of mention, and within every contingent there were as many leaders as there were cities represented. Besides, they followed the army not as generals, but as slaves, just as the rest did, since the generals who held the real power and ruling authority over all the national contingents were really those Persians I have already named.

The commanders of the fleet were Ariabignes son of Darius, Prexaspes son of Aspathines, Megabazos son of Megabates, and Achaimenes son of Darius. The Ionian and Carian ships were under the command of Ariabignes son of Darius by Gobryas' daughter; the Egyptian ships were commanded by Achaimenes, who was a full brother of Xerxes. The rest of the fleet was commanded by the other two. The total number of triaconters, pentaconters, light boats, and horse-transport boats came to 3,000.[a]

7.93
480
XERXES' FLEET
The Dorians and Carians.

7.94
480
XERXES' FLEET
The Ionians.

7.95
480
XERXES' FLEET
The Ionian islanders, Aeolians, and Greek settlers from Pontus.

7.96
480
XERXES' FLEET
Persians, Medes, and Sakai serve as soldiers on the ships.

7.97
480
XERXES' FLEET
Herodotus lists the Persian admirals of the fleet and estimates that there were 3,000 triaconters, penteconters, light boats, and horse transports.

7.93.1a   Dorians of Asia, location of territory:
          Map 7.98, BY.
7.93.1b   Peloponnese: Map 7.98, BX.
7.93.1c   Caria: Map 7.98, BY.
7.93.1d   Herodotus said they were called Leleges
          in 1.171.2.
7.94.1a   Ionia: Map 7.98, BY.
7.94.1b   Achaea: Map 7.98, BX.
7.94.1c   Herodotus generally uses the name
          "Pelasgian" for the oldest known popula-
          tion of Hellas; see 1.146, 2.171. (Godley)
7.95.1a   The twelve cities (Dodekapolis) of the

          Ionians: see 1.143, 1.145, 1.147–148.
7.95.1b   Aeolis: Map 7.98, AY.
7.95.2a   Hellespont: Map 7.98, AY.
7.95.2b   Abydos: Map 7.98, AY.
7.95.2c   Pontus, the Euxine (Black) Sea: Map
          7.98, AY, and locator.
7.96.1a   Persia: Map 7.98, locator.
7.96.1b   Media: Map 7.98, locator.
7.96.1c   Sakai, location of territory: Map 7.66, BY.
7.96.1d   Sidon: Map 7.98, locator.
7.97.1a   For an analysis of the probable actual size
          of Xerxes' navy, see Appendix R, §13–14.

7.98
480
DORISKOS
XERXES' FLEET
He names the non-Persian
admirals of the fleet.

After these commanders, the most famous men on board the ships were Tetramnestos of Sidon son of Anysos, Matten of Tyre[a] son of Siromos, Merbalos of Arados[b] son of Agbalos, Syennesis of Cilicia son of Oromedon, and Kyberniskos of Lycia son of Sikas; of the Cyprians, Gorgos son of Chersis and Timonax son of Timagoras; of the Carians, Histiaios son of Tymnes, Pigres son of Hysseldomos, and Damasithymos son of Kandaules.

7.99
480
HALICARNASSUS
XERXES' FLEET
Artemisia of Halicarnassus
commands the ships from
several islands and Dorian
cities of Asia.

Although I am not mentioning the other subordinate commanders because I am not compelled to do so, I shall mention Artemisia. I find it absolutely amazing that she, a woman, should join the expedition against Hellas. After her husband died, she held the tyranny, and then, though her son was a young man of military age and she was not forced to do so at all, she went to war, roused by her own determination and courage. [2] Now the name of this woman was Artemisia; she was the daughter of Lygdamos, by race part Halicarnassian[a] on her father's side, and part Cretan[b] on her mother's side. She led the men of Halicarnassus, Kos,[c] Nisyros,[d] and Kalymna,[e] and provided five ships for the expedition. [3] Of the entire navy, the ships she furnished were the most highly esteemed after those of the Sidonians, and of all the counsel offered to the king by the allies, hers was the best. I can prove that all the cities under her leadership which I have just mentioned were Dorian, since the Halicarnassians came from Troizen[a] and all the rest came from Epidauros.[b]

That concludes my description of the fleet.

7.100
480
DORISKOS
Xerxes reviews his
assembled army and fleet.

After his forces had been numbered and marshaled, Xerxes felt a desire to ride through their ranks and view the troops for himself, and so he rode among them in his chariot, and as he did so, he inquired about each and every national division that he passed while his scribes recorded all the information, until he had come to the very last ranks of the cavalry and the infantry.[a] [2] When he had finished his review and the ships had been hauled back out to sea, Xerxes stepped down from his chariot and boarded a Sidonian ship. Seated under a golden awning, he sailed past the prows of the ships, asking about each and having the information recorded just as he had done while viewing the land army. [3] The admirals had sailed out about four hundred feet[a] offshore and arranged all their ships in line so that their prows faced the land: they had the marines armed as though for battle. Xerxes viewed them all as he sailed between their prows and the shore.

7.101
480
DORISKOS
Xerxes asks Demaratos, the
exiled Spartan king, whether
the Hellenes will actually
fight the overwhelming
Persian army.

After sailing through them, he disembarked from the ship and sent for Demaratos[a] son of Ariston, who had joined him in the expedition against Hellas, and when he had answered the summons, Xerxes said, "Demaratos,

7.98.1a   Tyre: Map 7.98, locator.
7.98.1b   Arados: Map 7.98, locator.
7.99.2a   Halicarnassus: Map 7.98, BY.
7.99.2b   Crete (Creta): Map 7.98, locator.
7.99.2c   Kos: Map 7.98, BY.
7.99.2d   Nisyros: Map 7.98, BY.
7.99.2e   Kalymna: Map 7.98. BY. Herodotus here
          uses the spelling Kalydna.
7.99.3a   Troizen: Map 7.98, BX.

7.99.3b   Epidauros: Map 7.98, BX.
7.100.3a Herodotus writes "4 plethra." The
          plethron equaled 100 feet. See Appendix
          J, §5–6, 19.
7.101.1a Demaratos, the exiled king of Sparta,
          appeared last at 7.3. For an account of
          how his enemies obtained his exile, see
          6.63–70. Sparta: Map 7.98, BX.

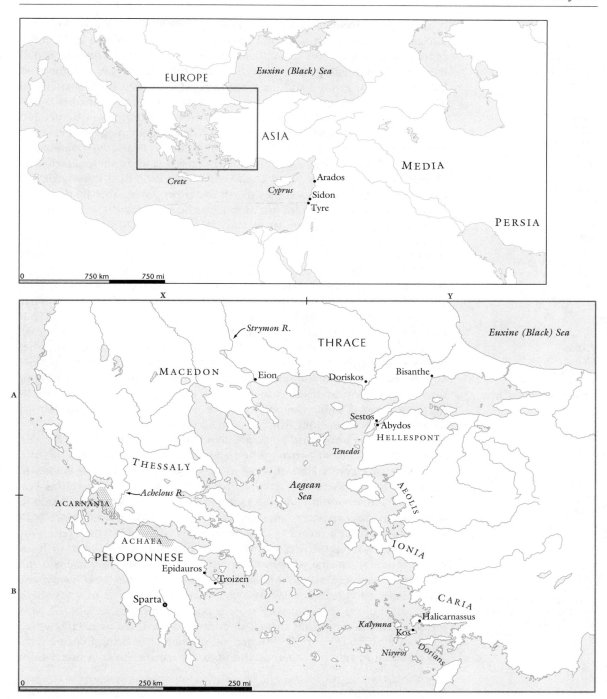

MAP 7.98

it is now my pleasure to ask you something that I wish to know. You are a Hellene, and according to what I have heard from you as well as from the other Hellenes who have spoken with me, you come from a city that is neither one of the smallest nor one of the weakest. [2] So tell me, will the Hellenes stand their ground and use force to resist me? For I think that even if all the Hellenes were assembled together, and even if they joined the peoples who dwell west of them, they still could not match me in battle, and therefore they will not stand their ground when I attack them—unless, that is, they should unite. [3] However, I would like to hear your opinion; do tell me anything you can say about them." That was what Xerxes asked, and Demaratos replied, "Sire, shall I tell you the truth or shall I say what will please you?" Xerxes ordered him to tell the truth, saying that by doing so, Demaratos would please him just as much as he had before.

Upon hearing this, Demaratos said, "Sire, since you insist that I speak the truth and say nothing for which you could later accuse me of falsehood, here it is: in Hellas, poverty is always and forever a native resident, while excellence is something acquired through intelligence and the force of strict law. It is through the exercise of this excellence that Hellas wards off both poverty and despotism. [2] Now while I commend all the Hellenes who live in the Dorian lands, what I shall next tell you applies not to all of them, but only to the Lacedaemonians. First of all, there is no way that they will accept your stated intention to enslave Hellas; next, even if all the other Hellenes come to see things your way, the Spartans will certainly oppose you in battle. [3] And you need not ask as to their number in order to consider how they could possibly do this, for if there are 1,000 of them marching out, they will fight you, and if they number more or less than that—it makes no difference—they will fight you all the same."

When Xerxes heard this, he laughed and said, "Demaratos, how can you make such a statement—that 1,000 men will fight my troops! Tell me, you claim that you were a king of these men, so would you then be willing to fight against ten men on the spot? Yet if your citizens are at all as you describe them, it would be fitting that you as their king should be ready to stand up to twice as many antagonists as they would, in accordance with your own laws and customs.[a] [2] So if each one of them is worth ten of my troops, then I would expect you to be the equal of twenty. That, at least, would square with what you have told me. But if these men are like you and about the same size as you and similar to the other men who have come from Hellas to visit and speak with me, then you Hellenes may go ahead and boast, but see to it that your story is not just empty bragging. [3] Now please allow me to look at this in an entirely rational manner. How could 1,000 or even 10,000 or 50,000 men, all of them alike being free and lacking one man to rule over them, stand up to an army as great as mine? Even

7.103.1a This remark no doubt alludes to the
double portion given to a Spartan king
at feasts; see 6.57.1. (Godley)

if there are 5,000 of them, we will outnumber them by more than 1,000 to one. [4] Now if they were under the rule of one man, as is our way, they would fear that man and be better able, in spite of their natural inclinations, to go out and confront larger forces, despite their being outnumbered, because they would then be compelled by the lash. But they would never dare to do such a thing if they were allowed their freedom! I myself think that even if the Hellenes were equal in numbers to us, they would have difficulty fighting just us, the Persians, alone. [5] I must admit that among our men, the kind of courage you described is rare rather than common, but I do have Persian spearmen who would gladly fight three Hellenes at once. So you are simply talking nonsense and are clearly ignorant concerning these matters."

To that, Demaratos replied, "Sire, from the beginning of this conversation I knew that if I told you the truth you would not like it. But since you compelled me to speak the absolute truth, I have told you how things stand with the Spartans. [2] You yourself, however, are well aware of how I happen to love them right now, given my circumstances: they have deprived me of my office and ancestral privileges and have rendered me an exile belonging to no city. It was your father who took me in, supported me, and gave me a home. Now surely it would be unreasonable for a prudent man to turn away goodwill when it appears to him. On the contrary, he should welcome it with open arms. [3] I do not claim to have the ability myself to fight ten men at once, nor even two, and I would not fight even one in a duel if I had the choice. But if I were compelled or urged on by some great challenge, I would indeed take the utmost pleasure in fighting one of those men who says that he by himself is equal to three Hellenes. [4] The Lacedaemonians are in fact no worse than any other men when they fight individually, but when they unite and fight together, they are the best warriors of all. For though they are free, they are not free in all respects, for they are actually ruled by a lord and master: law is their master, and it is the law that they inwardly fear—much more so than your men fear you. [5] They do whatever it commands, which is always the same: it forbids them to flee from battle, and no matter how many men they are fighting, it orders them to remain in their rank and either prevail or perish. Now if I appear to you to be talking nonsense when I say this, I am quite willing to hold my tongue from now on; I said all this because you compelled me to do so. Nevertheless, sire, I hope that everything turns out in accord with your wishes."

That was the reply of Demaratos. Xerxes expressed no anger at all; in fact he made a joke of it and sent him away gently. After concluding his talk with Demaratos, Xerxes appointed a new governor for Doriskos,[a] Maskames son of Megadostes, ousting the man that had been appointed by Darius. Then he proceeded on his way toward Hellas, leading the army through Thrace.[b]

7.104
480
DORISKOS
Demaratos replies that he only speaks what he believes to be the truth: that the Spartans are the best warriors on earth, that they fear their law more than the Persians fear Xerxes and will obey it and fight bravely.

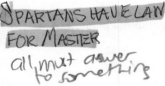

7.105
480
DORISKOS
Xerxes sends Demaratos away without anger.

7.105.1a Doriskos: Map 7.98, AY.
7.105.1b Thrace: Map 7.98, AY.

7.106

DORISKOS

How Maskames, governor of Doriskos, and his descendants successfully fought off the Hellenes and earned many gifts from the Persian Kings.

Maskames, the man Xerxes had left behind, proved to be the only governor to whom Xerxes would send gifts, on the grounds that he was the best of all of those that had been appointed by either Xerxes or Darius. Xerxes continued to send this man gifts each and every year, just as his son Artaxerxes later sent them to the descendants of Maskames. Previous to this expedition, governors had been appointed to serve in all parts of Thrace and the Hellespont,[a] [2] but after this campaign, the Hellenes ousted all of these governors except for the one in Doriskos, since no one was ever able to evict a governor from there, though many made the attempt. And that is why gifts are still sent to the governor of Doriskos by whoever is reigning as King of the Persians at the time.

7.107

EION

The Persians also praise Boges, who defended Eion against the Hellenes, and killed his family and himself rather than surrender.

Xerxes did not consider any of the governors who were evicted by the Hellenes to be noble and courageous men except for Boges, the governor of Eion.[a] This man he never ceased praising, and he even awarded special honors to his surviving children in Persia. Boges certainly proved himself worthy of high praise, for when he was being besieged by the Athenians under Kimon son of Miltiades and he could have left under a truce and returned home to Asia,[b] he did not go, lest the King were to believe that it was through cowardice that he had survived; instead he endured the siege to the bitter end. [2] And when there was no longer anything left to eat within the walls, he lit a huge pyre, cut the throats of his children, wife, concubines, and servants, and threw them all into the fire. Next, he took all the gold and silver from the city and cast it down from the wall into the River Strymon.[a] And after he had done all that, he threw himself into the fire. Thus it is for good reason that this man is praised by the Persians even to this day.

7.108

480

MESAMBRIA-STRYME

Xerxes and his army continue their advance toward Hellas.

As Xerxes journeyed from Doriskos to Hellas, he compelled everyone along his way to join his forces. For as I explained earlier,[a] all the peoples as far as Thessaly had been enslaved and forced to pay tribute as subjects of the King after the conquests of Megabazos and, later, Mardonios. [2] On the journey from Doriskos, Xerxes first passed by the fortifications belonging to Samothrace,[a] of which the last, situated the farthest to the west, is a city by the name of Mesambria.[b] After Mesambria lies Stryme,[c] a city belonging to Thasos,[d] and flowing between these two cities is the Lisos River,[e] whose waters proved insufficient for the troops of Xerxes' army, who drank its waters dry. [3] Long ago this country was called Gallaike, but it is now known as Briantike. It would be most precise, however, to call it the land of the Kikones.

7.109

480

THRACE

The route of the army takes them by various Thracian lakes, rivers, and cities.

After crossing the now dried-up channel of the Lisos River, Xerxes passed the Greek cities of Maroneia,[a] Dikaia,[b] and Abdera,[c] and two well-known lakes, Ismaris[d] (which lies between Maroneia and Stryme) and Bistonis[e] (sit-

7.106.1a	Hellespont: Map 7.98, AY.
7.107.1a	Eion: Map 7.98, AX.
7.107.1b	Asia: Map 7.98, locator.
7.107.2a	Strymon River: Map 7.98, AX.
7.108.1a	For that earlier explanation of how Xerxes added local forces on his route to his army, see 5.1–2; 6.43–45.
7.108.2a	The fortifications were erected by the Samothracians on the mainland to protect their possessions there. Samothrace: Map. 7.111, BY.

7.108.2b	Mesambria: Map 7.111, AY.
7.108.2c	Stryme: Map 7.111, AY. On the mainland, although belonging to the people of Thasos.
7.108.2d	Thasos: Map 7.111, BY.
7.108.2e	Lisos River: Map 7.111, AY.
7.109.1a	Maroneia: Map 7.111, AY.
7.109.1b	Dikaia: Map 7.111, AY.
7.109.1c	Abdera: Map 7.111, AY.
7.109.1d	Lake Ismaris: Map 7.111, AY.
7.109.1e	Lake Bistonis: Map 7.111, AY.

uated near Dikaia), into which flow the waters of two rivers, the Trauos and the Kompsatos.[f] At Abdera there was no well-known lake that Xerxes passed, but he did cross the Nestos River[h] near where it flows into the sea. [2] Next, Xerxes went past the cities on the mainland that are in the territory belonging to Thasos. In one of these cities there happens to be a lake of approximately three and a third miles[a] in circumference, which is full of fish and whose water is quite salty; this lake was drained dry after only the beasts of burden had drunk from it. The name of the city is Pistyros.[b] These, then, were the Greek cities along the coast that Xerxes passed, keeping them to his left.

Xerxes next made his way through the territories of the following Thracian peoples: the Paitians, Kikones, Bistones, Sapaians, Dersaians, Edonians, and Satraians.[a] Of all the peoples he passed, those settled along the coast followed Xerxes in their ships, while all those living inland whom I have enumerated were forced to follow on foot, except for the Satraians.

The Satraians have never become subject to anyone at all, as far as we know, and they continue up to my time to be the only Thracians who are free. They dwell high up in mountains that are completely covered with snow and all kinds of trees, and they are extremely skillful warriors. [2] These are the people who possess the oracle of Dionysos; it is situated on the loftiest part of the mountains, and of the Satraians, the Bessans[a] serve as the spokesmen of the sanctuary. The prophetess there delivers oracles just as the one at Delphi does, in a manner no more complicated than the one used there.

After passing this region, Xerxes next went by the forts of the Pieres,[a] of which one is called Phagres,[b] the other Pergamos.[c] So he made his way past these walls, with Mount Pangaion[d] to his right. This is a massive and high mountain range which contains gold and silver mines controlled by the Pieres, the Odomantians,[e] and especially the Satraians.

Xerxes continued his journey westward, past the people who dwell north of Mount Pangaion—the Paionians,[a] Doberes,[b] and Paioplaians,[c]—until he

---

7.110
480
THRACE
Xerxes marches inland through lands of Thracian tribes, not those of Greek coastal cities.

7.111
480
THRACE
Unlike the other tribes, the Satraians do not join Xerxes but remain independent.

7.112
480
MOUNT PANGAION
Xerxes marches along Mount Pangaion with its gold and silver mines.

7.113
480
EION
Xerxes continues the march westward south of Mount Pangaion to the Strymon River and Eion.

7.109.1f   Trauos and Kompsatos (or Kompsantos) Rivers: locations unknown.
7.109.1g   Nestos River: Map 7.111, AY.
7.109.2a   Herodotus writes that it is "30 stades" in circumference. See Appendix J, §6, 19.
7.109.2b   Pistyros, possible location: Map 7.111, AY.
7.110.1a   All these are tribes of the Nestos and Strymon valleys or the intervening hill country. (Godley) They are shown on Map 7.111: approximate locations of the territories of the Paitians (AY), Kikones (AY), Bistones (AY), Sapaians (AY), and Edonians (AX). The locations of the territories of the Dersaians and Satraians are unknown.
7.111.2a   Bessans: location of territory unknown.
7.112.1a   Pieres, approximate location of territory: Map 7.111, AX.
7.112.1b   Phagres, city of: Map 7.111, AX.
7.112.1c   Pergamos: location unknown.
7.112.1d   Mount Pangaion: Map 7.111, AX.
7.112.1e   Odomantians: Map 7.111, AX.
7.113.1a   Paionians, location of territory: Map

7.111, AX. This location, based on the *Barrington Atlas* makes Herodotus' description of the Paionians as among those dwelling "north of Mount Pangaion" seem way off the mark. Perhaps the *Atlas* is showing a position occupied by the Paionians at some other time than the early fifth century, or Herodotus is here revealing the limitations of his geographical knowledge of Xerxes' route of march. It is also possible that both sources are correct, that the Paionian territory was centered about seventy-five miles north and west of Mount Pangaion, but that some tribes or groups of Paionians lived far to the southeast of that homeland, closer to Bisaltia, the Strymon River, and Mount Pangaion.
7.113.1b   Doberes, location of territory presumably near Doberos: Map 7.111, AX.
7.113.1c   Paioplaians: precise location of territory unknown.

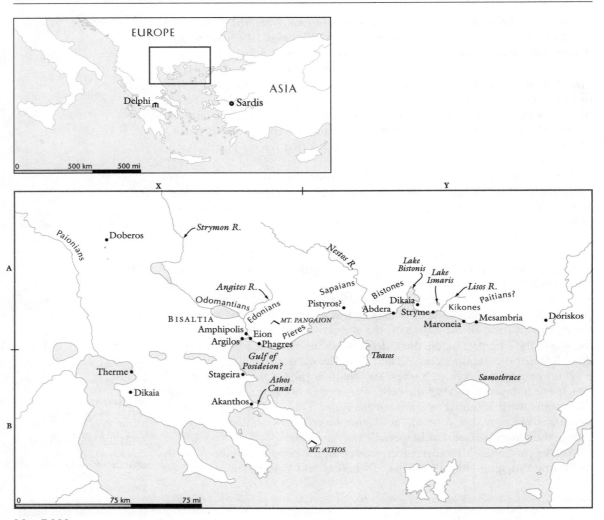

MAP 7.111

reached the River Strymon[d] and the city of Eion,[e] where Boges, whose story I recently told, was still alive and in charge.[f] [2] This land in the vicinity of Mount Pangaion is called Phyllis;[a] it extends to the west as far as the River Angites,[b] which flows into the Strymon, and to the south as far as the Strymon itself. It was into this river that the Magi sacrificed white horses to obtain favorable omens.

7.113.1d   Strymon River: Map 7.111, AX.
7.113.1e   Eion: Map 7.111, AX.
7.113.1f   The story of Boges' heroic defense of
           Eion was told in 7.107.

7.113.2a   Phyllis: location unknown
7.113.2b   Angites River: Map 7.111, AX.

After using this charm upon the river and performing many others as well, they discovered that the Strymon had been spanned and made their way across the bridges at Nine Roads[a] in the territory of the Edonians.[b] When they heard that this place was called Nine Roads, they buried alive there that many sons and daughters of the local inhabitants. [2] The burial of the living is a Persian practice, as I heard that Xerxes' wife Amastris, when she reached old age, caused fourteen children of prominent men to be buried alive, presenting them in place of herself as a gift to the deity they call the god of the netherworld.

When the army had left the Strymon, it marched in the direction of the setting sun along the coast where Argilos,[a] a Greek city, is situated. This place together with the region above it is called Bisaltia.[b] [2] From there, keeping the Gulf of Posideion,[a] on its left, it advanced through the plain called Syleos[b] past the Greek city of Stageira[c] and came to Akanthos.[d] Meanwhile, Xerxes had recruited men from each and every one of the peoples he encountered, including those dwelling around Mount Pangaion. As I said earlier, he had those who were living along the coast join the expedition in ships, and those who dwelled inland from the sea follow him on foot. [3] The Thracians do not disturb or sow with seed the road on which King Xerxes marched with his army; they treat it with great reverence even now in my time.

When Xerxes arrived at Akanthos, he proclaimed a pact of guest-friendship[a] with the people of that city, gave them gifts of Median garments, and praised them, since he observed their eager desire for the war and had heard about their zeal for the canal.[b]

While Xerxes was in Akanthos, it happened that Artachaias, the man who had been in charge of digging the canal, died of an illness. He was an Achaimenid who had been highly esteemed by Xerxes; he was the tallest of Persians, about eight feet tall,[a] and had the loudest voice of any human being. Xerxes considered his death a great misfortune and gave him a most splendid funeral and burial. The entire army worked to pile up his grave mound. [2] On the advice of an oracle, Akanthians still sacrifice to this Artachaias as a hero, invoking him by name as they do so. Indeed, the loss of Artachaias was considered a great calamity by Xerxes.

7.114
480
STRYMON RIVER
When crossing the Strymon River, the Persians bury alive nine local boys and nine maidens.

7.115
480
CHALCIDICE
Xerxes marches into Chalcidice, compelling the local men to join his own forces.

7.116
480
AKANTHOS
The Akanthians are treated well by Xerxes.

7.117
480
AKANTHOS
Artachaias, the overseer of the canal construction, dies at Akanthos, and is honored by Xerxes, the army, and the Akanthians.

7.114.1a   Nine Roads (Ennea Hodoi in Greek), about three miles above Eion on the Strymon, where the Athenians later founded Amphipolis (Map 7.111, AX). For more about Nine Roads or Amphipolis, see *Thucydides* 4.102.
7.114.1b   Edonians, approximate location of territory: Map 7.111, AX.
7.115.1a   Argilos: Map 7.111, AX.
7.115.1b   Bisaltia: Map 7.111, AX.
7.115.2a   Gulf of Posideion, possible location: Map 7.111, BX.
7.115.2b   Syleos: precise location unknown.

7.115.2c   Stageira: Map 7.111, BX.
7.115.2d   Akanthos: Map 7.111, BX.
7.116.1a   Guest-friendship (*xenia*): a bond of ritualized friendship, usually between aristocrats or prominent men of different cities. It was passed down through generations and required hereditary privileges and obligations such as reciprocal hospitality and assistance. See Appendix T, §3.
7.116.1b   The Mount Athos Peninsula Canal: Map 7.111, BX. See 7.22–24.
7.117.1a   Herodotus writes "four fingers short of 5 royal cubits." See Appendix J, §4, 5, 19.

Those Hellenes who received the army into their territory and who provided feasts for Xerxes were reduced to the utmost hardship; they were even driven from house and home. For example, after the Thasians[a] received and fed the army of Xerxes on behalf of their mainland cities, Antipatros son of Orgeus, a prominent citizen equal to their best, whom they had elected[b] to oversee the affair, rendered them an account for the feasting that came to 400 talents of silver.[c]

And the accounts submitted by those in charge of the feasts in the other cities were similar to that one. For these feasts had been ordered long in advance and were considered to be of great importance. [2] As soon as the citizens of a town heard the announcement proclaimed by the heralds,[a] they all divided up their grain and then for many months ground it into wheat flour and barley meal. Furthermore, they fattened the finest livestock that money could buy and raised birds, both land birds in pens and waterfowl in reservoirs, all for the entertainment of the troops. Then they had golden and silver cups and mixing bowls made, along with everything else needed to set a proper table [3] for the King and those who dined with him; whereas, for the rest of the army, they had been assigned to provide only food. Whenever the troops arrived at a place, they would always find there a tent pitched and ready for Xerxes to use as his quarters, while the rest of the army camped out in the open air. [4] When dinnertime came, the hosts were kept busy with their work, and when the guests were full, they would spend the night there on the spot. The next day, they would march away, but only after pulling up the tent and taking all moveable property along with them. They left nothing behind.

It was at this point that a witty remark was made by Megakreon of Abdera.[a] For he advised all the men and women of that city to go to their sanctuaries, sit down there as suppliants, and entreat the gods to ward off half of the evils still to befall them in the future, while acknowledging their gratitude for avoiding those evils that had just passed them by, namely that King Xerxes did not make it his custom to take food twice each day. [2] For if the King had ordered the Abderitans to provide lunch as well as dinner, either they would not have been able to wait for Xerxes' arrival, or, if they had stayed for it, they would have been more utterly ruined than any other people.[a]

And in this way all the citizens were placed under intense pressure, but they nevertheless fulfilled the commands imposed upon them. After Akanthos, Xerxes dismissed the ships, instructing his commanders to have the navy go ahead and wait for him at Therme,[a] a settlement on the Thermaic

---

7.118.1a   Thasos: Map 7.111, BY.
7.118.1b   It is uncertain and disputed whether Antipatros (Antipater) was elected to provide the feast or to render the account of it or both.
7.118.1c   An enormous sum for a Greek city. The "Attic" talent had a weight of about 58 pounds; the "Aeginetan," of about 82.

See Appendix J, §11–13, 20.
7.119.2a   These may have been the heralds that Xerxes had sent out while at Sardis (Map 7.111, locator). See 7.32.1.
7.120.1a   Abdera: Map 7.111, AY.
7.120.2a   For a discussion of the size of Xerxes' army, see Appendix R, §1–2.
7.121.1a   Therme: Map 7.111, BX.

Gulf (which is named after this town), because he had learned that this was the shortest and most direct route. [2] From Doriskos[a] to Akanthos, the entire army had been organized by Xerxes into three columns and assigned separate routes. One of them marched on the coast alongside the navy, [3] led by Mardonios and Masistes. Another column, led by Tritantaichmes and Gergis, was assigned to march farther inland. The last of the three, with which Xerxes himself traveled, went between the other two and had as its commanders Smerdomenes and Megabyzos.

When the fleet had been dismissed by Xerxes, it sailed through the canal at Athos,[a] which had been excavated as far as the gulf on which the cities of Assa,[b] Piloros,[c] Singos,[d] and Sarte[e] are located. After collecting troops from these cities, too, it left that region and sailed for the Thermaic Gulf. As it rounded Ampelos, the promontory at Torone,[f] it passed by the following Greek cities from which additional ships and troops were recruited: Torone, Galepsos,[g] Sermylia,[h] Mekyberna,[i] and Olynthos.[j] This country is called Sithonia.[k]

Next the fleet of Xerxes sailed directly across from the promontory of Ampelos to that of Kanastraion,[a] the point of Pallene[b] that extends the farthest into the sea. Both ships and troops were added to the expedition from Poteidaia,[c] Aphytis,[d] Neapolis,[e] Aige,[f] Therambos,[g] Skione,[h] Mende,[i] and Sane.[j] These cities are part of what is now considered Pallene but was once called Phlegra. [2] Sailing on past this region, the fleet headed for its destination while picking up forces from the adjacent cities on Pallene and from those situated along the Thermaic Gulf,[a] which are called Lipaxos, Kombreia,[b] Aisa,[c] Gigonos,[d] Kampsa, Smila,[e] and Aineia.[f] The territory of these cities was and is still to this day called Krossaia. [3] From Aineia, the last of the cities in my list, the fleet proceeded on its voyage directly to the Thermaic Gulf proper, and to the land of Mygdonia.[a] It arrived at its appointed destination cities of Therme, Sindos,[b] and Chalastra[c] on the Axios River.[d]

7.122
480
MOUNT ATHOS
The fleet sails through the Athos Canal.

7.123
480
CHALCIDICE
The fleet sails around the Pallene Peninsula, recruiting men and ships as it proceeds. Entering the Thermaic Gulf, it anchors off Therme. Xerxes' army marches through Chalcidice.

7.121.2a Doriskos: Map 7.111, AY.
7.122.1a Athos Canal, located at the isthmus of Mount Athos Peninsula: Map 7.123, BY.
7.122.1b Assa, possible location: Map 7.123, BY.
7.122.1c Piloros: Map 7.123, BY.
7.122.1d Singos: Map 7.123, BY.
7.122.1e Sarte: Map 7.123, BY.
7.122.1f Ampelos Promontory at Torone: Map 7.123, BY.
7.122.1g Galepsos: Map 7.123, BY, AY. The *Barrington Atlas* shows two sites with that name in this vicinity. The context would imply that Herodotus here means the one located on Sithonia at BY.
7.122.1h Sermylia: Map 7.123, BX. Herodotus spells this city Sermyle.
7.122.1i Mekyberna: Map 7.123, BX.
7.122.1j Olynthos: Map 7.123, BX.
7.122.1k Sithonia Peninsula: Map 7.123, BY.
7.123.1a Kanastraion Promontory: Map 7.123, BY.
7.123.1b Pallene Peninsula: Map 7.123, BX.
7.123.1c Poteidaia: Map 7.123, BX.

7.123.1d Aphytis: Map 7.123, BX.
7.123.1e Neapolis: Map 7.123, BX.
7.123.1f Aige: Map 7.123, BX.
7.123.1g Therambos: Map 7.123, BY.
7.123.1h Skione: Map 7.123, BX.
7.123.1i Mende: Map 7.123, BX.
7.123.1j Sane (Pallene): Map 7.123, BX.
7.123.2a Thermaic Gulf: Map 7.123, BX.
7.123.2b Lipaxos and Kombreia, possible locations: Map 7.123, BX. Not found in the *Barrington Atlas*.
7.123.2c Aisa: Map 7.123, BX. Herodotus spells this city Lisai.
7.123.2d Gigonos: Map 7.123, BX.
7.123.2e Kampsa and Smila, possible locations: Map 7.123, BX. Not found in the *Barrington Atlas*.
7.123.2f Aineia: Map 7.123, BX.
7.123.3a Mygdonia: Map 7.123, AX.
7.123.3b Sindos: Map 7.123, AX.
7.123.3c Chalastra: Map 7.123, AX.
7.123.3d Axios River: Map 7.123, AX.

MAP 7.123

That river is the boundary between Mygdonian[e] territory and Bottiaia,[f] where a narrow strip of land belonging to the cities of Ichnai[g] and Pella[h] extends down to the coast.

There around the Axios River, the city of Therme, and the cities in between, the navy made its camp as it awaited the King. Meanwhile, Xerxes and the land army were advancing to Therme from Akanthos by the inland route. Along the way, they went through Paionian[a] and Krestonian[b] territory toward the Echeidoros River,[c] which begins in the land of the Krestonians, flows through Mygdonian territory, and empties into the marsh near the Axios River.

As they were making their way on this route, lions attacked the camels that were carrying provisions. During the night, the lions would wander down from their normal habitats and would ravage only the camels, touching nothing else, neither men nor other beasts of burden. Whatever reason it was that compelled the lions to attack the camels but to stay away from the rest is a wonder to me, as the camel was a creature they had neither seen nor experienced in any way before this.

In these parts there are many lions, and wild oxen as well, whose immense horns are imported by the Hellenes. The boundaries of these lions' territory are the Nestos River,[a] flowing through Abdera,[b] and the Achelous,[c] flowing through Acarnania.[d] For east of the Nestos and on that entire side of Europe, one would never see a lion anywhere, nor are lions found west of the Achelous on the rest of the mainland, but only in the region between these two rivers.

When Xerxes arrived at Therme, he ordered his army to camp there. The army's camp, once it was set up, extended along the coast from the city of Therme[a] through Mygdonia, all the way to the rivers of Loudias[b] and Haliakmon,[c] whose waters flow together[d] and form the boundary between the lands of Bottiaia and Macedon.[e] [2] While the barbarians camped in this area, the only river of all those I mentioned that failed and was drunk dry by the army was the Echeidoros,[a] which flows out of Krestonia.

From Therme, Xerxes saw the Thessalian mountains Olympus[a] and Ossa,[b] and observed how extraordinarily high they were. When he learned that between them lies a narrow gorge through which the Peneios River[c]

7.123.3e   Mygdonia: Map 7.128, AY.
7.123.3f   Bottiaia: Map 7.123, AX; Map 7.128, AY. Herodotus calls this Botiaiis.
7.123.3g   Ichnai: Map 7.123, AX.
7.123.3h   Pella: Map 7.123, AX.
7.124.1a   Once again, Herodotus places the Paionians (Map 7.123, AX) far south of where the *Barrington Atlas* (and our Map 7.123) shows them to be. For possible explanations of this discrepancy, see n. 7.113.1a.
7.124.1b   Krestonia: Map 7.123, AX.
7.124.1c   Echeidoros River: Map 7.123, AX.
7.126.1a   Nestos River: Map 7.123, AY.
7.126.1b   Abdera: Map 7.123, AY.
7.126.1c   Achelous River: Map 7.98, AX,
7.126.1d   Acarnania: Map 7.98, BX.
7.127.1a   Therme: Map 7.128, AY.

7.127.1b   Loudias River: Map 7.128, AY. Herodotus calls it Lydias, as does Euripides. Much later, Strabo uses Loudias.
7.127.1c   Haliakmon River: Map 7.128, AX.
7.127.1d   The Loudias and Haliakmon rivers do not flow together at any point. Each river had its own distinct mouth. This error, like his confusion about the location of Paionia, seems another instance which reveals limits of Herodotus' knowledge of the geography of Xerxes' route of march.
7.127.1e   Macedon: Map 7.128, AY.
7.127.2a   Echeidoros River: Map 7.128, AY.
7.128.1a   Mount Olympus (Thessaly): Map 7.128, AY.
7.128.1b   Mount Ossa: Map 7.128, BY.
7.128.1c   Peneios River: Map 7.128, BX.

flows, and heard also that there was a road leading into Thessaly[d] there, he desired to sail out and observe the mouth of the Peneios, although he intended to take an inland road through the settlements in northern Macedon to those of the Perraibians[e] and past the city of Gonnoi,[f] for this, he was told, was the safest route. [2] Having conceived this desire, he immediately embarked on the Sidonian ship that he always boarded whenever he wished to do something like this, and giving a signal for the rest of the fleet to set sail as well, he left his land army there. When Xerxes reached the mouth of the Peneios and inspected it, he was struck with amazement. Summoning his guides, he asked whether it would be possible to divert the course of the river so that it would flow into the sea at a different place.

There is an account that long ago Thessaly was a lake, since it is bounded on all sides by high mountains. On its eastern side, it is enclosed by the mountains Pelion[a] and Ossa, which join at their foothills. Toward the north it is shut in by Mount Olympus,[b] as it is by the Pindus[c] range on the west, and toward the south by the Othrys.[d] In the center of all these mountains that I have mentioned lies the hollow of Thessaly. [2] Of the many rivers that flow into it, the five most important are the Peneios, Apidanos,[a] Onochonos,[b] Enipeus,[c] and Pamisos.[d] These rivers, which bear their separate names as they flow down from the mountains encircling Thessaly, join together on the plain into a single, quite narrow channel, and flow out toward the sea. [3] As soon as the rivers mingle their waters into a single stream, the name Peneios prevails and renders the rest nameless. It is said that long ago, when the current channel and outlet did not yet exist, these rivers and Lake Boebeis[a] were not named as they are now, but their waters flowed no less powerfully than they do today, so that they turned all of Thessaly into a sea of water. [4] The Thessalians say that it was Poseidon who made the channel through which the Peneios flows, which is a reasonable idea, for whoever believes that Poseidon shakes the earth and that the gaps formed by earthquakes are the works of the god would surely say that what he saw here was the work of Poseidon. It certainly seems to me that the cleft through these mountains was caused by the force of an earthquake.[a]

When Xerxes asked his guides whether the Peneios had any other outlet to the sea, they answered him with certainty, "Sire, this river has no other passage by which it can reach the sea, for all of Thessaly is ringed by mountains." Xerxes is reported to have said in response to this, "The Thessalians are indeed wise. [2] That is the reason they were on their guard long before now, and also why they decided to yield to us: they recognized that their

7.128.1d	Thessaly: Map 7.128, BY.	7.129.1d	Pamisos River: Map 7.128, BX.
7.128.1e	Perraibia: Map 7.128, AX.	7.129.3a	Lake Boebeis: Map 7.128, BY.
7.128.1f	Gonnoi: Map 7.128, BY.	7.129.4a	The correspondence in formation of
7.129.1a	Mount Pelion: Map 7.128, BY.		the two sides of the pass (salients on
7.129.1b	Mount Olympus: Map 7.128, AY.		one side answering to recesses on the
7.129.1c	Pindus Mountains: Map 7.128, AX.		other) gives the impression that they
7.129.1d	Mount Othrys: Map 7.128, BY.		were once united and have been vio-
7.129.2a	Apidanos River: Map 7.128, BX.		lently separated. (Godley) Figure 7.129
7.129.2b	Onochonos River: Map 7.128, BX.		shows the canyon of the Peneios River.
7.129.2c	Enipeus River: Map 7.128, BY.		

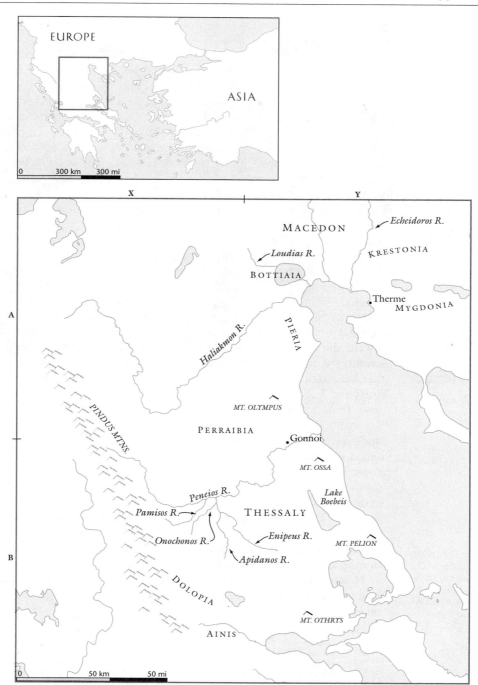

MAP 7.128

FIGURE 7.129. THE CANYON OF THE PENEIOS RIVER, THESSALY, ALSO KNOWN AS THE VALE OF TEMPI.

7.131
480
PIERIA
The army clears a
road to Perraibia.

land was really very easy to take and could be quickly conquered. For one would only have to divert the river from the channel through which it now flows, turning it aside by means of a dam and letting it flood their land, so that all of Thessaly except for the mountains would be submerged in water." [3] In saying this, Xerxes was referring to the sons of Aleuas.[a] They were the Thessalians who had been the first of the Hellenes to surrender themselves to the King, and he assumed that they were thereby declaring friendship with him on behalf of their entire nation. After saying this and viewing the site, Xerxes sailed back to Therme.

He lingered at Pieria[a] while one-third of the army cleared the Macedonian mountain so that the entire army could pass through there to reach the Perraibians.[b] And now the heralds who had been sent off to Hellas to ask for earth and water arrived,[c] some empty-handed, others bringing earth and water.

7.130.3a   Sons of Aleuas: the Aleuadai, a powerful family in Thessaly (Map 7.128, BX), also appeared in 7.6.5.
7.131.1a   Pieria: Map 7.128, AY.
7.131.1b   Perraibia: Map 7.128, AX.
7.131.1c   These heralds were sent out while Xerxes was still in Sardis (Map 7.137, locator). See 7.132.1.

Those Hellenes who gave earth and water were the Thessalians,[a] Dolopians,[b] Ainianes,[c] Perraibians, Locrians,[d] Magnesians,[e] Malians,[f] Achaeans of Phthiotis,[g] Thebans,[h] and all the Boeotians[i] except for the Thespians[j] and the Plataeans.[k] [2] Concerning these peoples, the Hellenes who were undertaking war against the barbarians swore a solemn oath, vowing that all the Hellenes who had surrendered themselves to the Persian without being forced to do so would have to pay the tithe[a] to the god at Delphi once they had succeeded and their affairs were settled. That, then, was the oath sworn by the Hellenes.

Xerxes did not send heralds to Athens[a] and Sparta[b] to ask for earth and water, because when Darius had sent heralds to these cities some years before,[c] the Athenians had cast these heralds, when they made their request, down into a pit,[d] and the Spartans had thrown theirs into a well; and the heralds were told to take their earth and water to the King from there! [2] So that is why Xerxes did not send anyone to Athens or Sparta to make the request. Now I cannot say whether it was because the Athenians had dealt with the heralds in this way that they later suffered the disaster of having their land and city laid waste, but in my opinion it was not on account of what they had done to the heralds.[a]

In any case, the wrath of Talthybios, the herald of Agamemnon, struck the Lacedaemonians. There is a sanctuary of Talthybios in Sparta where his descendants, who are called Talthybiads, are granted the office and honor of serving on all embassies sent out by Sparta. [2] Now after the incident of the heralds, the Spartans were unable to obtain good omens when they sacrificed, and as they found this to be the case for a long time, the Lacedaemonians became troubled and vexed that this kept happening; and so they held frequent assemblies and made a proclamation asking whether any Lacedaemonian was willing to die on behalf of Sparta. The men who volunteered to undertake the punishment imposed by Xerxes for the loss of Darius' heralds were Sperthias son of Aneristos and Boulis son of Nikolaos, Spartans of noble birth who had also attained the first rank in wealth. [3] And so the Spartans sent them off to the Medes[a] to die.

7.132
480
PIERIA
A list of those Hellenes who gave earth and water to Xerxes' heralds and thus submitted.

7.133
491
ATHENS-SPARTA
Athens and Sparta were guilty of having sacrilegiously killed heralds sent by Darius.

7.134
480
SPARTA
To atone for the murder of Darius' heralds, the Spartans sent two volunteers to Persia to face death or any punishment imposed by Xerxes.

7.132.1a Thessaly: Map 7.128, BY.
7.132.1b Dolopia: Map 7.128, BX.
7.132.1c Ainis (territory of the Ainianes): Map 7.128, BX. Herodotus uses the Ionic Enienes.
7.132.1d Locris (Opuntian): Map 7.137, AY.
7.132.1e Magnesia, Hellas: Map 7.137, AY.
7.132.1f Malis: Map 7.137, AX.
7.132.1g Phthiotis (Achaea Phthiotis): Map 7.137, AX.
7.132.1h Thebes: Map 7.137, BY.
7.132.1i Boeotia: Map 7.137, BY.
7.132.1j Thespiai: Map 7.137, BY.
7.132.1k Plataea: Map 7.137, BY.
7.132.2a While "pay the tithe" usually means to give a tenth of one's property or profits, it

may here imply that all the property of these people was to be confiscated and one tenth would serve as the tithe to the god.
7.133.1a Athens: Map 7.137, BY.
7.133.1b Sparta: Map 7.137, BX.
7.133.1c For Darius' dispatch of heralds throughout Hellas, see 6.48.
7.133.1d In Athens, criminals condemned to death were thrown into a pit.
7.133.2a It is possible that Herodotus believes the burning of the temple at Sardis (Map 7.137, locator; see 5.102) would have been a stronger cause for divine retribution.
7.134.3a Media (Persia in this case): Map 7.137, locator.

7.135
480
ASIA
Herodotus tells the anecdote
of these men's sharp reply to
Hydarnes the Persian, who
talked of the advantages of
the King's friendship.

The courage of these men is certainly worthy of awe, as are also the words they spoke. For along their journey to Susa,[a] they came to Hydarnes, a Persian by race, who was general of the peoples along the coast of Asia.[b] He entertained them by serving them a feast during which he asked them, [2] "Lacedaemonians, why are you trying to avoid becoming the King's friends? You can see that the King knows how to honor good men when you look at me and the state of my affairs. This could be the same for you if only you would surrender yourselves to the King, since he would surely think you to be good men and allow each of you Greek territory to rule over." [3] To this they replied, "Hydarnes, you offer us this advice only because you do not have a fair and proper perspective. For you counsel us based on your experience of only one way of life, but you have had no experience of the other: you know well how to be a slave but have not yet experienced freedom, nor have you felt whether it is sweet or not. But if you could try freedom, you would advise us to fight for it, and not only with spears, but with axes!"

7.136
480
SUSA
The Spartans nobly tell
Xerxes their mission, but
he refuses to execute them
and thus imitate the
Spartan blasphemy.

After giving that answer to Hydarnes, they traveled inland to Susa and gained an audience with the King. At first the King's bodyguards ordered them and actually tried to force them to prostrate themselves before the King;[a] but they refused to do so, saying that they would never do that, even if the bodyguards should try to push them down to the ground headfirst, since it was not their custom to prostrate themselves before any human being, and besides, that was not the reason for which they had come. So they succeeded in fighting off this command, and next made a speech with words to this effect: [2] "King of the Medes, the Lacedaemonians have sent us here to make up for the heralds you lost in Sparta, so that we may bear the punishment for what happened to them." Xerxes responded to their speech with proud magnanimity. He said he would not act like the Lacedaemonians, who had violated laws observed by all humanity when they killed the heralds; no, he himself would not do the kind of thing for which he was reproaching them: he would not kill these two men to release the Lacedaemonians from their guilt.

7.137
430
ATHENS
The two Spartans return
home safe, but their sons,
while on their way to Persia
as envoys from Sparta, are
captured by Thracians friendly
to Athens and sent to Athens,
where they are executed.
Herodotus considers this
divine retribution for the
killing of the envoys of Darius.

So Sperthias and Boulis returned home, but the Spartans had nevertheless managed for the time being to stop the wrath of Talthybios. Much later, however, as the Lacedaemonians say, this wrath was reawakened during the war between the Peloponnesians and the Athenians. And it is apparent to me that this phenomenon was especially divine, [2] for this wrath of Talthybios struck messengers in particular, and did not stop until it had been vented completely, which implies the idea of justice. Moreover, it fell upon the very sons of those men who had gone to the King to placate it earlier—Nikolas son of Boulis and Aneristos son of Sperthios. Aneristos was the man who took Halieis,[a] an offshoot of Tiryns,[b] after sailing there in a

7.135.1a   Susa: Map 7.137, locator.
7.135.1b   Asia: Map 7.137, locator.
7.136.1a   The Persian custom of *proskynesis* was a
           gesture of obeisance, sometimes involv-

ing prostration, when approaching a
superior. See Appendix M, §3.
7.137.2a   Halieis: Map 7.137, BY.
7.137.2b   Tiryns: Map 7.137, BY.

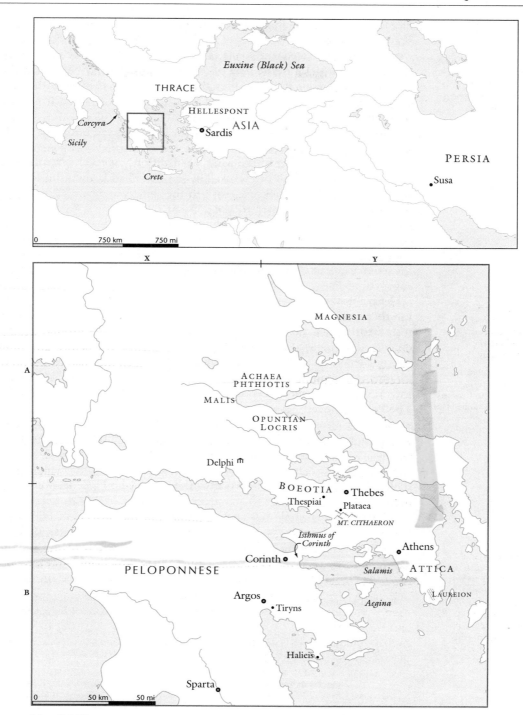

MAP 7.137

551

merchant ship full of men.[c] In any case, it is quite clear to me that what occurred was divine and a result of this wrath. [3] For when these men were sent by the Lacedaemonians as messengers to Asia, they were betrayed by Sitalkes son of Teras, the king of the Thracians,[a] and by Nymphodoros of Abdera,[b] the son of Pytheas; after they were captured in Bisanthe on the Hellespont,[c] they were carried off to Attica,[d] where the Athenians executed both of them along with Aristeas of Corinth,[e] son of Adeimantos.

But that happened many years after the King's expedition, and so I shall now return to my earlier account.

The proclaimed goal of the King's expedition was to attack Athens, but his real objective was all of Hellas. The Hellenes had known this for a long time, but they did not all react to it in the same way now. [2] Those who had given earth and water to the Persian felt confident that they would come to no harm at the hands of the barbarian, but others, who had refused to give earth and water, were now absolutely terrified that there were not enough battleworthy ships in Hellas to face the invader, and that most of the men were unwilling to engage in the war actively, but were instead eager to medize.

I have now reached a point at which I am compelled to declare an opinion that will cause offense to many people, but which nevertheless appears to me to be true, so I shall not restrain myself. [2] If the Athenians had evacuated their land in terror of the danger approaching them, or if they had not left their land but remained and surrendered themselves to Xerxes, no one at all would have tried to oppose the King at sea. And if no one had then opposed Xerxes at sea, this is what would have happened on land. [3] The Peloponnesians, even if they had covered over their isthmus[a] with walls, would have been abandoned by their allies, who, seeing their cities conquered one by one by the barbarian fleet, would have been forced to submit against their will. Finally those thus deserted, now all alone, would have performed great feats and died honorably. [4] Of course that might not be their fate if they had earlier seen how the rest of the Hellenes were medizing and would have come to an agreement of their own with Xerxes. Thus, either way, Hellas would have been conquered by the Persians. For I cannot discern what advantage could have been derived from walls extended across the isthmus if the King had control of the sea. [5] So anyone who said that the Athenians proved to be the saviors of Hellas would not have strayed from the truth. For whichever course they chose to follow was certain to tip

7.138
480
THRACE
The King's intent to conquer all of Hellas is clear. Many Hellenes are afraid and unwilling to go to war.

7.139
480
ATHENS
Herodotus declares that Athens saved Hellas, although this might be a displeasing statement to many Hellenes, for if Athens had submitted, the Persians would have been supreme at sea, and no land defense by the Peloponnesians could have succeeded.

7.137.2c	The capture of Halieis probably took place between 461 and 450, when Athens and Argos (Map 7.137, BY) were allied against Sparta (Map 7.137, BX). (Godley)	summer of 430, the second year of the Peloponnesian War, and is recorded in *Thucydides* 2.67.2. It is one of the latest incidents mentioned by Herodotus, and it thus sets a date certain after which Herodotus completed at least this part of his text.
7.137.3a	Thrace: Map 7.137, locator.	
7.137.3b	Abdera: Map 7.123, AY.	
7.137.3c	Bisanthe on the Hellespont: Map 7.98, AY.	
7.137.3d	Attica: Map 7.137, BY. The ignominious death of these men took place in the	7.137.3e Corinth: Map 7.137, BY.
		7.139.3a Isthmus of Corinth: Map 7.137, BY.

FIGURE 7.139. THE TREASURY OF THE ATHENIANS AT DELPHI (RESTORED), BUILT AFTER THE BATTLE OF MARATHON.

the scales of war. They chose that Hellas should survive in freedom; and after rousing to that cause all the other Hellenes who had not medized, they repelled the King with the help of the gods. [6] Indeed, not even the frightening oracles they received from Delphi[a] threw them into a panic or persuaded them to abandon Hellas. Instead, they stood fast and had the courage to confront the invader of their land.[b]

For the Athenians had prepared to consult the oracle by sending sacred delegates to Delphi, who, after performing the usual preliminaries at the sanctuary, entered the inner shrine and took their seats. The Pythia, whose name was Aristonike, gave them the following oracular response: [2]

7.140
480
DELPHI
Herodotus recounts an oracle predicting disaster and ruin for the Athenians at the hands of the Persians.

7.139.6a   Delphi: Map 7.137, AX. See Figure 7.139, the restored Treasury of the Athenians at Delphi.
7.139.6b   In this extraordinary paragraph, Herodotus, who lived and wrote in the mid-fifth century, reveals a profound pro-Athenian bias that apparently was not shared by many other Hellenes. He has elsewhere displayed his approval of democracy and the superiority of its citizens to those who live under tyrants (5.78). See Appendix A, The Athenian Government in Herodotus, §10.

Why sit so idle, you poor wretched men? To the ends of the land
    you should flee.
Leave your homes, leave the heights of your circular fortress,
For neither the head nor the body remains in its place,
Nor the feet underneath, nor the hands nor the middle
Is left as it was, but now all is obscure. For casting it down
Is fire and Ares so sharp on the heels of a Syrian chariot
[3] And he will destroy many cities with towers, and not yours alone;
And into the devouring fire he will give the temples of eternal gods,
Which now drip with sweat and shake in their fear
As blood gushes darkly from the tops of their roofs,
Foreseeing the force of compelling disaster.
Now step out of this shrine, and shroud over your heart with the
    evils to come.

7.141
480
DELPHI
The Athenians return to
Delphi as suppliants for a
better answer. The priestess
now says that wooden
walls may save them and
mentions Salamis.

When the sacred delegates of the Athenians heard this, they felt that they had met with the greatest disaster; and as they were giving themselves up for lost over the evils predicted by the oracle, Timon son of Androboulos, a man of Delphi and a prominent citizen equal to their best, advised them to take olive branches and to consult the oracle a second time, this time as suppliants. [2] Following his advice, the Athenians went again and said to the god, "Lord, deliver to us a better oracle concerning our fatherland out of respect for these branches which we carry, coming here as suppliants, or else we shall not leave your shrine but shall remain here until we die." After they said this, the prophetess gave them a second oracle, as follows:

[3] Unable is Pallas[a] to appease Zeus Olympian
With copious prayers, with counsel quite cunning.
Now to you once again my word I shall speak, making it adamantine:
The rest will be taken, all lying within the boundary of Kekrops[b]
And that of the hollow of sacred Cithaeron.[c]
But a wall made of wood does farsighted Zeus to Tritogenes[d] grant
Alone and unravaged, to help you and your children.
[4] Do not await peacefully the horse and the foot,
The army gigantic that comes from the mainland;
Withdraw, turn your backs, though someday you still will meet
    face to face.
O Salamis[a] Divine, the children of women you will yet destroy
While Demeter[b] is scattered or while she is gathered.

7.141.3a Pallas refers here to Athena, a patron
         goddess of Athens.
7.141.3b Kekrops: a mythical first king of Athens.
7.141.3c Mount Cithaeron, which forms
         roughly the northwestern boundary of

Attica: Map 7.137, BY.
7.141.3d Tritogenes: an epithet for Athena.
7.141.4a Salamis (Attic), the Athenian island just
         west of Athens: Map 7.137, BY.
7.141.4b Demeter symbolizes grain.

FIGURE 7.143. A BUST
WHICH PURPORTS TO BE,
AND PERHAPS ACTUALLY IS
OR WAS COPIED FROM, A
TRUE PORTRAIT OF
THEMISTOKLES.

Since this oracle seemed, and really was, less harsh to them than the earlier one, they copied it down and departed for Athens.[a] When they arrived, the sacred delegates proclaimed the oracle to the assembly of the people, and many sought to interpret what it meant, but the following two interpretations were particularly contradictory. Some of the elders said that in their opinion, the god was prophesying that the Acropolis would be preserved; for in ancient times the Acropolis of the Athenians had been enclosed by a thorn hedge, [2] so they concluded that this oracle's "wall made of wood" corresponded to the enclosing fence. Others in turn said that the god was referring to their ships, and they urged them to abandon everything else and to make their ships ready. But those who said that the wooden wall referred to ships were perplexed by the last two lines spoken by the Pythia:

> O Salamis Divine, the children of women you will yet destroy
> While Demeter is scattered or while she is gathered.

[3] These verses thwarted the proposal of those who interpreted the oracle's wooden wall to represent ships, for the oracle interpreters took these

7.142
480
ATHENS
The Athenians could not
agree whether the oracle's
"wooden walls" were the
ancient walls of the Acropolis
or Athens' new fleet of
triremes.

7.142.1a For a discussion of this "reversal" on the
         part of the Pythia, see Appendix P, Oracles,
         Religion, and Politics in Herodotus, §16.

lines to mean that once they had made preparations for a sea battle, they were destined to be defeated around Salamis.

But among the Athenians was a certain man who had just recently come into the highest prominence; his name was Themistokles,[a] and he was called the son of Neokles. Now this man asserted that the explanation of the oracle interpreters was not entirely correct. He said that if the real import of these verses to the Athenians was that the inhabitants were to end their lives around Salamis, then he did not think it would have used such mild language, but would have said something like "O Salamis Cruel" rather than "O Salamis Divine." [2] But if, in fact, one understood the oracle properly, this part of it was directed by the god not to the Athenians but to their enemies. And so the god had advised them to prepare for a sea battle, and their fleet was what he meant by the wooden wall. [3] When Themistokles proclaimed this opinion, the Athenians decided that his interpretation was preferable to that of the oracle experts, who would not have allowed them to prepare for a sea battle and who said, in a word, that they should abandon Attica and settle in some other land.

There was an earlier occasion on which Themistokles proposed a measure that proved to be optimal for the predicament of that moment. At the time when the Athenians were receiving large revenues into their public treasury from the silver mines at Laureion,[a] and they were intending to apportion it so that each one of them would individually receive ten drachmas,[b] Themistokles stopped this plan to divide the money by persuading the Athenians to use it instead to build 200 ships for the war, by which he meant the war against the Aeginetans.[c] [2] It was actually the onset of this war that saved Hellas by forcing the Athenians to take to the sea. For although the ships were not after all used for the purpose for which they had been constructed, they were there for the benefit of all of Hellas when they were needed. These ships, then, had been built in advance and were therefore ready for the Athe-

7.143
480
ATHENS
Themistokles persuades the Athenians that the wooden walls means their navy and that they should prepare to fight at sea.

7.144
483
ATHENS
Themistokles had earlier persuaded the Athenians to use a sudden increase in the production of the Laureion silver mines for the construction of a fleet of 200 triremes.

7.143.1a   This is the first appearance of Themistokles, certainly one of the most extraordinary Athenian politicians and leaders in Herodotus' narrative. Themistokles was from an old and distinguished family, the Lycomids, but was politically a "new" man, since the Lycomids were not one of the aristocratic families which dominated Athenian politics at the time. Some scholars have speculated that Herodotus is sneering that Themistokles' origins were lowly; certainly his attitude toward Themistokles is a complicated one. See n. 7.144.1c and Appendix L, Aristocratic Families in Herodotus, §5. See Figure 7.143, thought to be a portrait bust of Themistokles.

7.144.1a   Laureion: Map 7.137, BY. The site in Attica of silver mines, from which the state drew an annual revenue. Apparently a rich vein of the metal had recently been discovered, which so greatly increased the public revenue that a distribution to the citizenry was contemplated.

7.144.1b   Ten drachmas: see Appendix J, §10–11, 14–16, 20.

7.144.1c   Aegina: Map 7.137, BY. It seems as though Herodotus would have us think that Themistokles had enjoyed good luck, or employed successful duplicity, when he persuaded the Athenians to use the newfound wealth to finance the construction of a fleet "against the Aeginetans." Athens had been at war with Aegina ever since that island had offered earth and water to Xerxes, and Themistokles must have known full well that the fleet would really be needed against the Persians. Thucydides writes that the fleet was prepared during the war with Aegina "when at that very time the coming of the barbarian was expected." (*Thucydides* 1.14.3) It should be noted, however, that hostilities between Athens and Aegina continued until 481 (7.145.1), the year after these 200 triremes were built, and one year before open hostilities with Persia began.

nians to use, although they now had to build others in addition. [3] After their deliberations concerning the oracle, they resolved to confront the barbarian's invasion of Hellas with all their people and their ships in obedience to the god, together with those of the Hellenes who wished to join them.

So those were the oracles that had been delivered to the Athenians. And now those Hellenes who wanted what was best for Hellas gathered together, engaged in discussions, and exchanged pledges. As they deliberated, the first of the matters they decided was that all existing hostilities and wars between one another were to be brought to an end. For wars had been stirred up between some Hellenes and others—the most serious of them being that between the Athenians and the Aeginetans. [2] Then, after learning that Xerxes and his army were in Sardis,[a] they agreed to send men as spies to Asia to determine the extent of the King's power. They also resolved to send some messengers to Argos[b] to attempt to establish a military alliance with the Argives against the Persian, and they decided to dispatch other envoys to Gelon son of Deinomenes in Sicily,[c] to Corcyra,[d] and to Crete[e] to urge them all to come to the aid of Hellas. They did this in the hope that if they put their heads together and worked toward a common goal, Hellas could then somehow unite into a single state, since the invasion threatened all Hellenes alike. Gelon's power was said to be great, and of all the other Greek states, none had power greater than his.

Having made these decisions, they resolved their differences and sent off the spies to Asia first. These men arrived at Sardis and closely observed the forces of the King, but they were discovered and tried by the generals of the army and led away to be executed. [2] However, when Xerxes heard that they had received the death sentence, he reproached the generals for their judgment and sent for some of his bodyguards, whom he ordered to bring the spies to him if they found them still alive. [3] They did find the spies still living, and when they led them into the presence of the King and he learned why they had come, he ordered his bodyguards to take them around to show them all of his infantry and cavalry and, after they had seen all they wanted to see, to send them back to wherever they wished to go.

Xerxes explained that if the spies had been executed, the Hellenes could not have learned in advance that his power was greater than words could describe, whereas the execution of three men would not cause any significant harm to his enemies. But he thought it likely that if these spies did return to Hellas, the Hellenes would learn of the magnitude of his power before the expedition took place and give up their distinctive freedom so that there would be no need to take the trouble of marching against them. [2] This was similar to another opinion that Xerxes had once expressed when he was in Abydos and he saw boats carrying provisions sailing from

7.145
481? 480?
ISTHMUS OF CORINTH
The Hellenes who oppose Persia meet to resolve their current quarrels, to send spies to Asia, and to send envoys to other Hellenes inviting them to join in the common defense.

7.146
480
SARDIS
The spies are discovered at Sardis. Instead of executing them, Xerxes shows them the whole army and sends them away unharmed.

7.147
480
SARDIS
Xerxes treated the spies thus in the hope that their information would intimidate the Hellenes and persuade them to submit. He also permitted grain ships to sail through the Hellespont to his Greek enemies.

7.145.2a   Sardis: Map 7.137, locator.
7.145.2b   Argos: Map 7.137, BY.
7.145.2c   Sicily: Map 7.137, locator.
7.145.2d   Corcyra: Map 7.137, locator.
7.145.2e   Crete (Creta): Map 7.137, locator.

the Pontus[a] through the Hellespont[b] on their way to Aegina[c] and the Peloponnese.[d] Those sitting beside him learned that these were enemy ships, and were only waiting for the King to give his command to seize them. [3] But instead, Xerxes asked them where these ships were headed. They answered, "To your enemies, my lord, carrying grain." And to this, Xerxes responded, "And are we not also sailing to the very same place that they are, equipped with grain as well as everything else? Then how can they be doing wrong by taking grain there for us?"

So after the spies had seen everything and were sent away, they returned to Europe. Now after they had dispatched the spies, the Hellenes who had sworn an oath of alliance against the Persian had next sent messengers to Argos. [2] The Argives have their own version of what happened, and this is what they say. They had learned from the very beginning about what the barbarian was stirring up against Hellas and, realizing that the Hellenes would try to recruit them to their side against the Persian, they had sent sacred delegates to Delphi to ask the god what their best course of action would be. For just recently, 6,000 of them had died[a] at the hands of the Lacedaemonians under Kleomenes son of Anaxandridas, and for that reason they had decided to send delegates to Delphi. [3] When they put their question to the Pythia, she gave them this response:

> Hated by your neighbors, but dear to the gods immortal,
> Hold your spear withdrawn, and on your guard, sit still.
> Keep your head well guarded, and it will save the body.

That, they say, was the response from the Pythia that the delegates brought back to them. Afterward, when the messengers from the Hellenes arrived at Argos, they came forward in the council chamber and said what they had been instructed to say. [4] The Argives responded that they were ready to do what had been requested, but they would do so only after concluding a treaty for thirty years of peace with the Lacedaemonians, and only if they themselves could assume the leadership over half of the entire alliance. They said that even though the principle of justice entitled them to the leadership over the entire alliance, they would nevertheless be content with half of it.

That, the Argives say, was the reply of their council, even though the oracle had earlier advised them against forming an alliance with the Hellenes. For despite their fear of the oracle, they were quite anxious to conclude a thirty-year treaty with the Lacedaemonians so that during those years their sons could grow into manhood. They were worried that without such a treaty, another defeat—this time at the hands of the Persians—following the affliction they had recently suffered, would leave them as subjects of the

7.148
480
ARGOS-DELPHI
Argos, having recently suffered high casualties in a battle with Sparta (c. 494), seeks counsel from the Delphic oracle. It tells them to remain on the defensive, but they offer to join the united effort against Persia if they are allowed a thirty-year truce with Sparta and permitted to share the command with Sparta.

7.149
ARGOS
When told by Spartan envoys that the two Spartan kings would never cede control over the command, the Argives sent the envoys away angrily.

7.147.2a   Pontus, the Euxine (Black) Sea: Map 7.137, locator.
7.147.2b   Hellespont: Map 7.137, locator.
7.147.2c   Aegina: Map 7.137, BY.
7.147.2d   Peloponnese: Map 7.137, BX.
7.148.2a   The 6,000 Argives were slain at the battle of Sepeia near Tiryns (Map 7.137, BY) in 494. See 6.77–80.

Lacedaemonians forever. [2] Of all the messengers, the ones from Sparta answered the council's statement. The matter of the treaty, they said, would be referred to the Spartan majority, but concerning the leadership, they had been instructed to answer, and indeed to assert, that Sparta had two kings, but Argos only one; and while neither of the Spartan kings could possibly be deprived of his command, nothing need prevent the Argive king from having a vote equal in weight to either of the two of theirs. [3] As a result, the Argives say, they decided that they could not endure the greed of the Spartans and would rather be ruled by barbarians than to yield anything to the Lacedaemonians. They proclaimed that the messengers must leave Argive territory before the sun set or else they would be treated as enemies.

Well, that is the Argive account of these events, but there is another one told throughout Hellas, that Xerxes had sent a herald to Argos before he set out to make war on Hellas. [2] It is reported that upon his arrival, the herald said, "Men of Argos, King Xerxes has this to say to you: 'It is our traditional belief that we are descended from Perses, whose father was Danae's son Perseus and whose mother was Andromeda daughter of Kepheus. If that is so, we would be your own descendants and it would be improper for us to march against our own ancestors or for you to become our opponents by helping others against us; instead, you should remain at ease by yourselves and at peace. For if matters turn out as I intend, no people will be greater in my esteem than the Argives.'" [3] It is said that this made a great impression upon the Argives, and for the time being, they made no offers or demands; but that when the Hellenes tried to win them over, they asked for a share of the command because they knew that the Lacedaemonians would not give it and they wanted to have a pretext for being left in peace.

Supporting this version is an account told by certain Hellenes about something that happened many years later. Some Athenian envoys—Kallias son of Hipponikos and those who went up-country with him—happened to be in Memnonian Susa[a] on some business or other at the same time that some Argive envoys had also been sent to Susa.[b] The Argives had come to ask Artaxerxes son of Xerxes whether the close friendship they had established with Xerxes still remained firm, as they wished, or whether he now considered them to be enemies. King Artaxerxes replied that the relationship certainly did remain firm and that no city was more dear to him than Argos.

Now I cannot say for certain if Xerxes really sent a herald to Argos who said these things, or whether Argive messengers went to Susa and asked Artaxerxes about their friendship, nor will I even express an opinion about that other than what the Argives themselves say. [2] This much I do know: if every human being should collect his afflictions and bring them together in public, intending to exchange them for those of his neighbors, each one

---

7.150
ARGOS
That is the Argive account of the affair, but it is also said that Xerxes offered them friendship, so that their request to share the command was a cunning move, as they knew they would be refused.

7.151
462?
ARGOS-SUSA
In support of this story, some Hellenes cite the mission of the Argive envoys discovered at Susa many years afterward.

7.152
c. 450
ARGOS
Citing conflicting versions of this story, Herodotus does not condemn the Argives.

7.151.1a Susa: Map 7.158. For the adjective Memnonian, see 5.53.
7.151.1b Various dates have been proposed for Argive and Athenian embassies to coincide at Susa, but by far the most probable

is 462, just after Athens had left the league led by Sparta against Persia and allied with Argos, the King's best friend in Greece. (*Thucydides* 1.102.4)

would stoop down to examine the afflictions of others, but would then gladly carry away the ones he had brought there himself. [3] And so the deeds of the Argives were not the most shameful.[a] I may be obliged to tell what is said, but I am not at all obliged to believe it. And you may consider this statement to be valid for my entire work. For example, it is also said that it was actually the Argives who summoned the Persian against Hellas because, after their battle against the Lacedaemonians had turned out badly, they preferred anything to their present distress.

That, then, is what is said about the Argives.

The other envoys sent out by the allies arrived in Sicily[a] to make contact with Gelon;[b] of particular importance among them was a man named Syagros, who was sent by the Lacedaemonians. An ancestor of Gelon had come from the island of Telos,[c] which lies off Triopion,[d] and he settled at Gela,[e] for he was not left behind when Gela was colonized by Antiphemos and the Lindians[f] who had set out from Rhodos.[g] [2] Over time, his descendants became priests of the goddesses of the underworld[a] and continued to fill this position afterward. Telines was the ancestor of Gelon who acquired this office, and this is how he did so. After some Geloans had been defeated in factional strife and had fled to Maktorion,[b] a city inland of Gela, [3] Telines restored them to Gela, not with a company of men but with the sacred objects of the goddesses. Now I cannot say where he obtained them or whether they were already in his possession at the time; but it was by relying on them that he brought back the exiles, on the condition that his own descendants would preside as the priests of the goddesses. [4] From what I have been told, I am amazed that Telines was able to accomplish such a feat, for I really believe that deeds like this cannot be performed by just any ordinary man, but only by one who possesses a brave spirit and manly strength. The inhabitants of Sicily, however, say that Telines was actually quite the opposite; he was effeminate and rather weak.

In any case, that is how he acquired this position of honor. After Kleandros son of Pantares had ruled as tyrant of Gela for seven years, he died at

7.153
480
GELA
In telling of the envoys sent to Gelon in Sicily, Herodotus recounts the story of Gelon's ancestor Telines, who settled in Gela and won for his descendants the office of priests of the goddesses of the underworld.

7.154
498–491
GELA
How Hippocrates became tyrant of Gela and how, with Gelon as his commander of cavalry, he conquered many Sicilian cities except for Syracuse, which was rescued by Corinthians and Corcyrians.

7.152.3a Argive medism (siding with the Persians) was a touchy subject, and Herodotus is saying simply that the medism of Argos was not as reprehensible as that of others. It has been suggested that Herodotus here may have been thinking of the Athenians' own peace agreement with Persia (the Peace of Kallias, which was probably the business of Kallias alluded to here) and which—if it took place—was probably concluded sometime in the mid-fifth century. But conclusive evidence for this agreement is lacking, and Herodotus may have had other targets in mind.

7.153.1a Sicily: Map 7.158, Sicily inset.
7.153.1b Gelon (c. 540–478) became tyrant of Syracuse in a manner described by Herodotus in 7.154–156. Under his rule the city grew and prospered until it was considered the most powerful of Greek cities anywhere. By

demanding to lead the Greek forces against Persia, he intentionally avoided service in the east, perhaps because he was fully occupied with the Carthaginian menace to Sicily. In fact, a Carthaginian invasion of Sicily took place at the same time as the Persian attack on Hellas. He defeated the Carthaginians and died two years later.

7.153.1c Telos: Map 7.158, Hellas inset.
7.153.1d Cape Triopion: Map 7.158, Hellas inset.
7.153.1e Gela: Map 7.158, Sicily inset.
7.153.1f Lindos, Rhodos: Map 7.158, Hellas inset.
7.153.1g The traditionally accepted date for the founding of Gela is 688.
7.153.2a The priests were in charge of the sacred objects and rites of the chthonian goddesses of the underworld, Demeter and Persephone; see also 6.137.1.
7.153.2b Maktorion, possible location: Map 7.158, Sicily inset.

the hands of Sabyllos, a man of Gela, and the monarchy was taken over by Hippocrates, the brother of Kleandros. While Hippocrates held the tyranny, Gelon, a descendant of Telines the priest, along with many others, including Ainesidemos son of Pataikos, who was a bodyguard of Hippocrates [. . .][a] [2] Before very long, Gelon was appointed as commander of the whole cavalry because of his valor and competence. For when Hippocrates besieged Kallipolis,[a] Naxos, Zancle, Leontini, Syracuse,[b] and many barbarian communities, it was Gelon who clearly emerged as the most brilliant of military men. Of all those that I mentioned who had been besieged, only the Syracusans escaped enslavement by Hippocrates. [3] For when the Syracusans were defeated in battle at the River Helorus,[a] the Corinthians[b] and Corcyrians[c] saved them by reconciling the parties on the condition that the Syracusans would turn over to Hippocrates the city of Camarina[d] (which had originally belonged to Syracuse).

After Hippocrates had reigned for the same number of years as his brother Kleandros, death overtook him at the city of Hybla,[a] where he was campaigning against the Sikels. Gelon now ostensibly helped the sons of Hippocrates, Eukleides and Kleandros, against the citizens of Gela, who no longer wished to be ruled as subjects. But in fact, when he had defeated the Geloans in battle, he dispossessed the sons of Hippocrates and seized the rule for himself. [2] This stroke of fortune was followed by another when the class of Syracusans who were called the landowners[a] were ousted by the people and their own slaves, who were known as the Kyllyrians. Gelon brought these people back to Syracuse from their exile in Kasmenai[b] and took control of Syracuse, too, when upon his approach the people of Syracuse surrendered to him both their city and themselves.

Once Gelon had taken control over Syracuse, he thought little of ruling Gela, and entrusted it to his brother Hieron while he governed Syracuse himself; indeed, Syracuse now meant everything to him. [2] And at once it grew like a sapling and flourished, for he brought all the inhabitants of Camarina to Syracuse and made them citizens there, and razed the town of Camarina to the ground. Then he did the same for more than half of the Geloans. Moreover, when he besieged the Megarians[a] in Sicily and they agreed to his terms, he brought their men of substance to Syracuse and made them citizens, too, though they had begun the war against him and for that reason were expecting to be killed. As for the Megarian people, though they had taken no part in the war and so did not expect to suffer any harm, he brought them also to Syracuse and then sold them into slav-

7.155
491?
SYRACUSE
Hippocrates is slain in battle, and Gelon, after deposing Hippocrates' sons, takes over as tyrant and wins possession of Syracuse.

7.156
SYRACUSE
How Gelon made Syracuse his seat of power and increased its size and greatness. He treated the wealthy well but not the common people, whom he disliked.

7.154.1a Some information may have dropped out from the text of this sentence.
7.154.2a Kallipolis, Sicily: location unknown.
7.154.2b Naxos, Zancle (Messana), Leontini, Syracuse: Map 7.158, Sicily inset.
7.154.3a Helorus River: Map 7.158, Sicily inset. Herodotus spells it Elorus.
7.154.3b Corinth: Map 7.158, Hellas inset.
7.154.3c Corcyra: Map 7.158, Hellas inset.

7.154.3d Camarina: Map 7.158, Sicily inset.
7.155.1a Hybla: Map 7.158, Sicily inset.
7.155.2a The "landowners" were the aristocrats or at least the wealthier, upper class of Syracuse.
7.155.2b Kasmenai: Map 7.158, Sicily inset.
7.156.2a The Megarians of the city of Hyblaia (also known as Megara Hyblaia): Map 7.158, Sicily inset.

ery for export from Sicily. [3] And he made the same distinction in his treatment of the Euboeans in Sicily,[a] for in both cases he was motivated by the belief that living with the people was most difficult and unpleasant. So that is how Gelon became a great tyrant.

Now, when the messengers of the Hellenes arrived at Syracuse,[a] they spoke to him as follows: "The Lacedaemonians[b] and their allies have sent us to recruit you to our side against the barbarian. For surely you have heard of his invasion of Hellas: how the Persian has bridged the Hellespont[c] and is bringing the whole army of the east out of Asia[d] to lead a campaign against Hellas. His pretext is that he is marching against Athens,[e] but he actually plans to subject all of Hellas to himself. [2] You yourself have attained great power, and your share of Hellas is hardly insignificant, since you rule over Sicily. So help us to defend the freedom of Hellas, and join us in keeping it free. With all the men of Hellas joined together, a great force will be assembled, and with it we can match the invaders in battle. If, however, some of us turn traitor and others refuse to help defend Hellas, the health of Hellas will be much diminished, and therein lies the danger that all of Hellas will fall. [3] For you should not expect that if the Persian defeats us in battle and subjects us to his rule, that he will not then march against you. No, you should try to prevent this from happening in advance. Therefore, we say that by coming to our aid, you will actually be defending yourself; for sensible planning generally produces a good result."

Gelon answered with great vehemence: "Men of Hellas, you have been so bold as to come here and present your self-seeking request, summoning me to become your ally against the barbarian. [2] A while ago, however, when I was waging war with the Carthaginians,[a] I asked you then to join me in attacking a barbarian army, I urged you to exact vengeance from the Egestaians for the murder of Dorieus[b] son of Anaxandridas, and I offered to join you in defending the freedom of the trading posts which have provided you with great profits and benefits.[c] But then you refused to come for my sake to help against the barbarian, or to participate in avenging the murder of Dorieus. So it would seem that for all it matters to you, everything here already belongs to barbarians! [3] Well, in spite of all that, things have worked out well, even, in fact, to my advantage. But now that it is your turn and war has come to you, you recall Gelon and have come to court him! [4] Though I have received dishonorable treatment from you, I shall not behave the same way. Instead I am ready and willing to come to your aid by supplying you with

7.156.3a Euboeans at Leontini: Map 7.158, Sicily inset. This was a colony of Chalcis, Euboea (Map 7.158, Hellas inset).
7.157.1a Syracuse: Map 7.158, Sicily inset.
7.157.1b Some manuscripts add "and the Athenians." Herodotus uses the names Spartans and Lacedaemonians interchangeably. "Spartans," however, often refers specifically to citizens of the state of Sparta, whereas any inhabitant of the territory of Lacedaemon is a Lacedaemonian. See Appendix B, The Spartan State in War and Peace, §5, 7, and n. B.7.a. Sparta:

Map 7.158, Hellas inset.
7.157.1c Hellespont: Map 7.158, Hellas inset.
7.157.1d Asia: Map 7.158.
7.157.1e Athens: Map 7.158, Hellas inset.
7.158.2a Carthage: Map 7.158. The Carthaginians were as influential in the west of Sicily as Gelon in the east; Hellenes and Phoenicians constantly competed for commercial and political supremacy. (Godley)
7.158.2b For the murder of Dorieus, see 5.42–46.
7.158.2c Scholars are not sure what Gelon (or Herodotus) is referring to here as "the freedom of the trading posts."

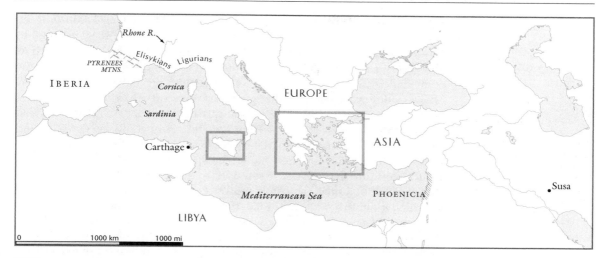

MAP 7.158

200 triremes, 20,000 hoplites, 2,000 cavalry, 2,000 archers, 2,000 slingers, and 2,000 lightly armed troops to serve among the cavalry. I also promise to provide food for the entire army of the Hellenes until we bring the war to its end. [5] But I promise to do all this only on the condition that I shall be the commander and leader of the Hellenes against the barbarian. Under any other conditions, I would neither go myself nor send others."

Now Syagros could not bear to hear this and replied, "Well, I am sure that Agamemnon the descendant of Pelops would turn over in his grave in loud lament if he heard that the Spartans were being robbed of their command by Gelon and the Syracusans! You can forget all about the condition that we surrender our leadership to you. If you want to come to the aid of Hellas, know that you will be under the command of the Lacedaemonians. Or, if you do not think it right to be commanded, then do not come or help at all."

Recognizing the hostility in Syagros' words, Gelon declared his final conditions: "Spartan visitor, an onslaught of reproaches tends to provoke one's temper, but although your speech to me was blatantly insulting, you have not persuaded me to become impolite in my reply to you. [2] Inasmuch as you cling so tightly to the command, it is only reasonable that I am even more attached to it, since I command an army and a fleet of ships many times larger than yours. But since my condition has proved so onerous to you, I shall yield somewhat from my original proposition. Let us agree that you will lead the land army while I command the fleet, or, if it is your pleasure to lead at sea, then I would command the army. Now you must either be satisfied with these terms or go away, without any kind of alliance at all."

So that was the offer extended by Gelon. And now the envoy sent by the Athenians interjected before the one from the Lacedaemonians could reply: "King of the Syracusans, Hellas did not send us to you because it needed a leader, but rather because it required an army. But you have given us no indication that you would send an army unless you were to become the leader of Hellas; to command its forces is what strongly attracts you. [2] Now as long as you were asking to lead the entire force of the Hellenes, we Athenians were content to keep quiet, knowing that the Laconian would be capable of answering for us both. But now that your leadership over the whole force has been ruled out and you ask to command the fleet, you should know that this is the situation: even if the Laconian yields the command of the fleet to you, we shall not yield it to you. For that command belongs to us, unless the Lacedaemonians want it. Now if they want to lead the fleet, we shall not oppose them, but we shall allow no one else to command it. [3] For if we yield our leadership to the Syracusans, it would then be all for nothing that we have acquired the greatest naval force of all the Hellenes—we, the Athenians, who represent the most ancient nation of the Hellenes and are the only ones who did not migrate. Even Homer the epic poet said that the best man to go to Troy[a]

7.159
480
SYRACUSE
Syagros of Sparta refuses Gelon's condition, saying Sparta must lead the Hellenes.

7.160
480
SYRACUSE
Despite the Spartan arrogance, Gelon offers to divide the command, having Sparta lead at sea or on land, but ceding to himself the other command.

7.161
480
SYRACUSE
The Athenians reply to Gelon that while their fleet will serve under Spartan leadership, it will not fight under the command of anyone else, including Gelon.

7.161.3a   Troy (Ilion/Ilium): Map 7.158, Hellas
        inset.

and to draw up and marshal the troops was one of ours,[b] so we cannot be reproached for asserting this claim."

Gelon replied, "Visitor from Athens, it appears that you have commanders who will not have men under their command. And so, since you want everything and will give up nothing, you could not leave here soon enough: go back and announce to Hellas that spring has been taken away from its year." [2] The sense and meaning of this expression is clearly that as spring is considered the best of the year, so his army would have been the best of the Greek forces; thus he equated Hellas deprived of its alliance with him to a year whose spring had been taken from it.

After these negotiations with Gelon, the Greek envoys sailed away, and although Gelon feared that the Hellenes might not be able to prevail over the barbarian, he thought that for himself, the tyrant of Sicily, to go to the Peloponnese and submit to the command of the Lacedaemonians would be dreadful and even unbearable. So he disregarded that course and adopted a different one. [2] As soon as he learned that the Persian had crossed the Hellespont,[a] he sent Kadmos son of Skythes[b] (a man from Cos[c]) to Delphi[d] with three penteconters,[e] a large amount of money, and professions of friendship. Kadmos was instructed to wait and see which way the battle would turn out, and if the barbarian won, Kadmos was to present him with the money, along with earth and water on behalf of all the people ruled by Gelon, but if the Hellenes won, he was to return and bring the money back to Gelon.

Earlier, this Kadmos had inherited the tyranny over Cos from his father. And although the tyranny there was firmly established, he handed over control of the government to the Coan people; this he did of his own free will, motivated not by pressure from any danger, but rather by a sense of justice. He then had gone to Sicily and there obtained from the Samians[a] the city of Zancle (which changed its name to Messana[b]), where he settled. [2] That is how Kadmos had come to Sicily, but now Gelon sent him because he knew and valued the man's sense of justice, evidence of which he had personally seen on several other occasions. And among the many deeds which Kadmos left as proof of his righteousness, the one concerning this large sum of money was among the most significant. The money with which Gelon had entrusted him was completely under his control, and he could easily have taken it for himself, but he refused to do so. Instead, when the Hellenes prevailed in the naval battle[a] and Xerxes had gone and was marching back to Asia, Kadmos returned to Sicily, bringing all of the money back with him.

7.162
480?
SYRACUSE
Gelon replies that in that case the Greek envoys should return home empty-handed.

7.163
480
DELPHI
Gelon sends Kadmos to Delphi with instructions to submit to the Persians if the Persians win the battle, but to sail back again if the Hellenes are victorious.

7.164
479?
COS-ZANCLE
Kadmos tyrant of Cos had freely given the government to the Coans. He then went to Sicily, colonized Zancle, and renamed it Messana. He returned all the money with which Gelon had entrusted him.

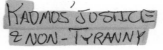

KADMOS JUSTICE & NON-TYRANNY

7.161.3b The reference is to the Athenian, Menestheus (*Iliad* 2.552–554). Here is an example of how the Greeks used quotations from their epic poems to support their arguments. Herodotus, who employs the same technique on occasion, here puts it in the mouth of the Athenian envoy (not the Spartan envoy). See Appendix Q, Herodotus and the Poets, §4.

7.163.2a Hellespont: Map 7.158, Hellas inset.

7.163.2b This Kadmos was probably the expelled ruler of Zancle; see also 7.164 and 6.23.

7.163.2c Cos: Map 7.158, Hellas inset.

7.163.2d Delphi: Map 7.158, Hellas inset.

7.163.2e Penteconters were 50-oared ships as against triremes, which were 170-oared. See Appendix S, §4.

7.164.1a Samos: Map 7.158, Hellas inset.

7.164.1b Zancle (Messana): Map 7.158, Sicily inset.

7.164.2a The naval battle mentioned here must be the decisive one at Salamis (Map 7.158, Hellas inset) in 480.

7.165
480
SICILY
Another tale told by the Sicilians is that Gelon could not assist the Hellenes because of a major attack by the Carthaginians instigated by Terillos, tyrant of Himera.

7.166
480
SICILY
Gelon is said to have defeated the Carthaginians on the same day that the Hellenes won at Salamis.

7.167
480
SICILY
The Carthaginians say that Hamilcar cast himself into a great pyre upon seeing his army routed.

The inhabitants of Sicily claim that Gelon would have gone to assist the Hellenes even if he would have had to submit to the command of the Lacedaemonians, had it not been for what was done by Terillos son of Krinippos. This man, the tyrant of Himera,[a] who had been expelled from that city by Theron son of Ainesidemos, monarch of Akragas,[b] brought to Sicily at this time an army of 300,000 Phoenicians,[c] Libyans,[d] Iberians,[e] Ligyes,[f] Elisykians,[g] Sardinians,[h] and Kyrnians (Corsicans),[i] led by their general Hamilcar son of Hanno. Hamilcar was the king of the Carthaginians[j] and had been persuaded to lead this army by Terillos to honor their pact of guest-friendship,[k] but he had mainly done this because of the desire of Anaxilaos son of Kretines, the tyrant of Rhegion.[l] Anaxilaos had given his own children to Hamilcar as hostages and had brought him to Sicily to assist Terillos, his father-in-law, for Anaxilaos had married Kydippe, the daughter of Terillos. And so, since it was impossible for Gelon to leave to help the Hellenes directly, he sent money to Delphi instead.

Furthermore, they say that on the very same day that the Hellenes won their victory over the Persian at Salamis, Gelon and Theron won their battle against Hamilcar the Carthaginian. I have heard that Hamilcar's mother was Syracusan, so that he was only half Carthaginian, on his father's side, and also that he became king of the Carthaginians because of his valor; yet when battle was joined and he was defeated, he vanished from sight and, although Gelon searched for him everywhere, he was never seen again anywhere in this world, living or dead.

The Carthaginians themselves offer a logical explanation: they say that the barbarians on that day fought against the Hellenes in Sicily from dawn until late afternoon (for that is how long they say this battle went on), and that during this time, Hamilcar remained in his camp and made sacrifices to obtain omens, burning a holocaust of whole carcasses on a pyre. Then, as he happened to be pouring libations on the sacrificial victims, he saw his troops being routed, and he threw himself into the fire. Thus he disappeared because his body was completely consumed by the fire. [2] Whether

7.165.1a   Himera: Map 7.158, Sicily inset.
7.165.1b   Akragas: Map 7.158, Sicily inset.
7.165.1c   Phoenicia: Map 7.158.
7.165.1d   Libya: Map 7.158.
7.165.1e   Iberia: Map 7.158.
7.165.1f   Ligyes (thought to be Ligurians), location of territory: Map 7.158.
7.165.1g   Elisykians (Iberians living on the coast between the Pyrenees and the Rhone), location of territory: Map 7.158.
7.165.1h   Sardinia: Map 7.158.
7.165.1i   Kyrnians (inhabitants of the island later known as Corsica): Map 7.158. The Carthaginians (Carthage: Map 7.158) invaded Sicily with forces drawn from Africa and the western Mediterranean. According to a statement quoted by the historian Ephorus (in Diodorus Siculus *Histories*, Vol. XI. 20.1), this Carthaginian expedition was part of a plan whereby

the Greek world was to be attacked simultaneously by the Carthaginians in the west and the Persians in the east. (Godley)
7.165.1j   Herodotus is in error here, for the government of Carthage was not a monarchy. Its highest magistrates, called suffetes, were elected annually and were not at all hereditary. This Hamilcar may have been a suffete, although later they are not known to have served as generals of the armed forces in the field.
7.165.1k   Guest-friendship (*xenia*): a bond of ritualized friendship, usually between aristocrats or prominent men of different cities. It was passed down through generations and required hereditary privileges and obligations such as reciprocal hospitality and assistance. See Appendix T, §3.
7.165.1l   Rhegion, Italy: Map 7.158, Sicily inset.

Hamilcar vanished in this manner, as told by the Phoenicians, or perhaps in another way, such as that related by the Carthaginians and Syracusans, they sacrifice to him and have erected monuments in his memory in all the cities of Carthaginian colonists, and the greatest memorial to him stands in Carthage. That is enough about what happened in Sicily.

The same envoys that had gone to Sicily also went to the Corcyrians[a] and tried to recruit them, too, making the same request of them as they had of Gelon. The Corcyrians immediately promised to send help and come to their defense, declaring that they could not stand by as Hellas was being destroyed. For they knew that if Hellas fell, they would have no choice but to become slaves, too, and on the very next day after the Greek defeat. Therefore, they would have to help defend Hellas to the best of their ability. [2] Now this answer seemed fair enough, but when their help was needed, they were inclined to act differently. They did man sixty ships and set out to sea in them, though with much reluctance; but then they put in to the shore of the Peloponnese[a] and beached their ships along the coast of Pylos[b] and Tainaron[c] in Lacedaemonian[d] territory. For they, too, had decided to wait and see how the war would turn out, particularly since they had no hope that the Hellenes would prevail and expected rather that the Persian would win a decisive victory and would rule over all of Hellas. [3] So they deliberately hung back in this way in order to be able to say something to the Persian to this effect: "Sire, the Hellenes tried to recruit us for this war, since we are hardly the least powerful among the Hellenes and the number of our ships is such that we could have furnished more of them than any other Greek state except Athens; but we refused to oppose you or to do anything to displease you." They hoped that by saying something like this they would gain some advantage for themselves over the other Hellenes, [4] and I suppose that is exactly what would have happened. But they also had prepared a pretext for the Hellenes, which they actually did employ. For when the Hellenes asked why they had not come to help them, they claimed that they had manned sixty triremes, but because of the Etesian winds[a] they had been unable to get past Cape Malea,[b] and for that reason they did not reach Salamis;[c] so it was not due to cowardice that they were absent from the sea battle. That, then, is how they dodged the Hellenes.

7.168
480
CORCYRA
The Corcyrians respond positively to the envoys, but they beach their ships on the Peloponnesian coast to wait and see whether the Hellenes or Persians are victorious, with a suitable story ready for either alternative.

7.168.1a Corcyra: Map 7.169, AY.
7.168.2a Peloponnese: Map 7.169, BY.
7.168.2b Pylos: Map 7.169, BY.
7.168.2c Tainaron: Map 7.169, BY.
7.168.2d Lacedaemon (Sparta): Map 7.169, BY. Herodotus uses the names Spartans and Lacedaemonians interchangeably. "Spartans,"however, often refers specifically to citizens of the state of Sparta, whereas any inhabitant of the territory of Lacedaemon is a Lacedaemonian. See Appendix B, §5, 7, and n. B.7a.
7.168.4a The Etesian winds are said to blow

hard from the northeast during the summer (the battle of Salamis took place in late September) and often prevented ships from passing by the cape from west to east. There are other instances in the history of ancient Hellas in which fleets were unable to pass the cape from east to west due to frequent storms and strong contrary winds. See Appendix S, §16.
7.168.4b Cape Malea, Peloponnese: Map 7.169, BY.
7.168.4c Salamis: Map 7.169, BY.

As for the Cretans,[a] when the envoys of the Hellenes appointed to deal with them tried to recruit them, they responded by sending a joint sacred delegation to Delphi[b] to ask the god if the better course of action for them would be to help defend Hellas. [2] The Pythia answered, "You foolish men, who complain of all the tears of wrath that Minos sent to you when the Hellenes failed to join you in avenging his death at Kamikos,[a] although you had joined the Hellenes and helped to defend Menelaos for the sake of the woman abducted from Sparta by a barbarian." When this oracle was reported to the Cretans, they refrained from aiding the Hellenes

For it is said that Minos came to Sikania, which is now called Sicily,[a] in his search for Daidalos, and that he died a violent death there. In time, all the Cretans except for the people of Polichna[b] and Praisos[c] came to Sikania, urged on by a god, and they brought a large army with which they besieged the city of Kamikos for five years. This city is inhabited in my time by people who came from Akragas.[d] [2] At last, unable to capture the city or remain and endure hunger any longer, they abandoned the siege and left. But as they sailed by Iapygia,[a] a violent storm overtook them and drove them against the shore. Since their boats had been smashed and they could find no way to return to Crete, they founded the city of Hyria[b] and remained there, changing their name from Cretans to Messapian Iapygians, and became mainlanders instead of islanders. [3] Using the city of Hyria as their base, they settled other cities. Much later, the Tarantines[a] attempted to expel them from these but were badly defeated. In fact, the men of both Taras and Rhegion[b] suffered such a crippling disaster here that this was the greatest slaughter of Hellenes that is known to us. The citizens of Rhegion had been forced by Mikythos son of Choiros to go to the aid of the Tarantines, and 3,000 of them died. Under such circumstances, there was no count taken of Tarantine losses. [4] This Mikythos was a servant of Anaxilaos, who had left him behind and entrusted Rhegion to him, and he is also the same man who, after being exiled from Rhegion, settled in Arcadian Tegea[a] and dedicated those numerous statues at Olympia.[b]

What happened to the Rhegines and Tarantines, however, is parenthetical to my narrative. According to the Praisians, when Crete had been deserted, other peoples went there and settled it, including the Hellenes. In the third generation after Minos had passed away, the Trojan War was waged, in which the Cretans were clearly not the least of those who avenged Menelaos. [2] But as their reward, when they returned home from Troy, both they and their cattle were afflicted with famine and plague, until

7.169.1a Crete (Creta): Map 7.169, BY.	7.170.1d Akragas, Sicily: Map 7.169, BX.
7.169.1b Delphi: Map 7.169, AY.	7.170.2a Iapygia: Map 7.169, AX. A name used by
7.169.2a Kamikos, possible location: Map 7.169,	the Greeks imprecisely to denote the
AX.	southeast or "heel" of Italy.
7.170.1a Sicily: Map 7.169, AX.	7.170.2b Hyria: location unknown.
7.170.1b Polichna, Crete: Map 7.169, BY. There	7.170.3a Taras (modern Taranto): Map 7.169, AX.
are two cities called Polichna on Crete,	7.170.3b Rhegion: Map 7.169, AX.
and it is not known to which of these	7.170.4a Tegea: Map 7.169, BY.
Herodotus is referring.	7.170.4b Olympia: Map 7.169, BY.
7.170.1c Praisos, Crete: Map 7.169, BY.	

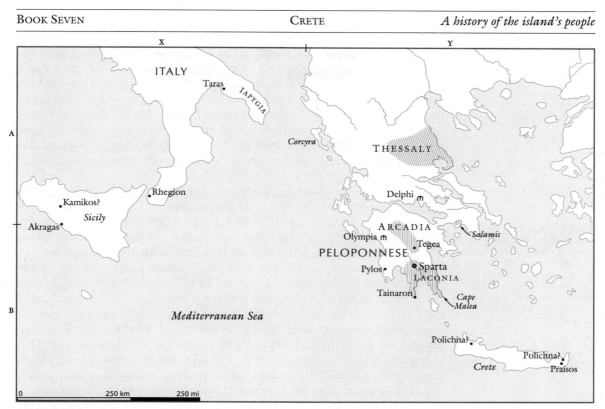

MAP 7.169

Crete was once again depopulated. Those who survived were then joined by a third set of Cretans who came there and who still inhabit the place. And so by recalling these events, the Pythia restrained the Cretans from assisting the Hellenes, though they had been willing to do so.

The Thessalians[a] did medize, but only in response to pressure, since they made it clear that they were displeased with the intrigues of the Aleuadai.[b] For as soon as they learned that the Persian was about to cross over into Europe,[c] they sent messengers to the meeting of Greek representatives then taking place at the isthmus.[d] These representatives were men chosen from the cities that were supporting what was best for Hellas. [2] The messengers from the Thessalians came to them and said, "Men of Hellas, the pass at Mount Olympus[a] must be defended so that Thessaly and all of Hellas

7.172
480
ISTHMUS OF CORINTH
The Thessalians meet with the Hellenes at the isthmus and bid them send a force to hold the pass of Olympus, threatening to make terms with the Persians if the Hellenes fail to defend the pass with them.

7.172.1a Thessaly: Map 7.169, AY.
7.172.1b The Aleuadai were then the leading aristocratic family of Thessaly. Their intrigues with the Persian King were mentioned by Herodotus in 7.6.5.
7.172.1c Europe: Map 7.158.
7.172.1d Isthmus of Corinth: Map 7.176, locator.
7.172.2a Mount Olympus (Thessaly): Map 7.176, AX. By "the pass at Mount Olympus" here, the Thessalians must mean the

canyon through which flows the Peneios River near Tempe (Map 7.176, AX). It is narrow and easily defended, to be sure, but the issue is still puzzling, since other paths over the shoulder of Mount Olympus were not lacking and, indeed, it was one of those that the Persians planned to follow and did eventually use. See 7.128 and 7.173.

569

may be sheltered from this war. Now we are ready and willing to join you in protecting it, but you must send a large army; and you should know that if you fail to do so, we shall come to terms with the Persian, for it would not be right for us to die before you, and for you, just because our land lies so far before the rest of Hellas in the path of the invader. [3] And should you refuse to come to our aid, do not think you can exert pressure on us, since no pressure can be stronger than a lack of power. But you can be sure that we shall make our own effort to devise some means to save ourselves." Those were the words of the Thessalians.

7.173
480
TEMPE
The Hellenes send 10,000 men to guard the pass between Olympus and Ossa, but these retreat, Herodotus believes, when they learn that the Persians are marching to Thessaly by another pass over the hill country through Perraibia.

In response, the Hellenes resolved to send an army by sea in order to guard the pass; and after this army had assembled, it sailed through the channel of the Euripos[a] to Halos in Achaea,[b] where the the troops disembarked and, leaving the ships, set out on the journey to Thessaly. They marched to Tempe[c] and reached the pass that leads from Macedon[d] into Thessaly. It runs along the River Peneios,[e] which flows between Mount Olympus and Mount Ossa.[f] [2] About 10,000 Greek hoplites made their camp there, along with the cavalry of the Thessalians. The commander of the Lacedaemonians was Euainetos son of Karenos, who had been selected from the polemarchs[a] even though he was not of royal lineage. The commander of the Athenians was Themistokles son of Neokles. [3] They remained there for only a few days, however, for messengers soon arrived from the Macedonian Alexandros son of Amyntas, telling them of the number of troops and ships the enemy had and advising them to depart, lest by remaining at the pass, they would be trampled under by the invading army. The Hellenes thought this was sound advice and, recognizing that the Macedonian was thus displaying his goodwill toward them, they followed it. [4] But in my opinion, what really convinced them to leave was fear, which arose when they learned that another pass into Thessaly led from northern Macedon through Perraibia,[a] by the city of Gonnoi,[b] which was the pass that the army of Xerxes actually did take. So the Hellenes returned to their ships and sailed back to the isthmus.[c]

7.173.1a	Euripos, the narrowest channel between Euboea and the mainland, near Chalcis: Map 7.176, BY. The channel there is 120 feet wide. Strong and unpredictable currents run through it.	7.173.1f	Mount Olympus, Mount Ossa: Map 7.176, AX.
		7.173.2a	The Spartan polemarchs: see Appendix B, §16, and Glossary.
		7.173.4a	Perraibia: Map 7.176, AX.
7.173.1b	Halos in Achaea Phthiotis: Map 7.176, BX. Herodotus spells this site Alos. This Achaea is not the one in the north Peloponnese but Achaea Phthiotis, north of the Malian Gulf (Map 7.176, inset) and south of Thessaly (Map 7.176, AX).	7.173.4b	Gonnoi: Map 7.176, AX.
		7.173.4c	It is most unlikely that this force sent to Thessaly was intended to block the advance of the Persian army, for they would have had to remain in that position for a very long time before the Persians arrived, and they would need to be supplied. That is the sort of campaign the Greeks could not sustain. Perhaps this was never more than a show of force intended to dissuade the Thessalians from medizing.
7.173.1c	Pass (or Valley) of Tempe: Map 7.176, AX.		
7.173.1d	Macedon: Map 7.176, locator.		
7.173.1e	Peneios River: Map 7.176, AX.		

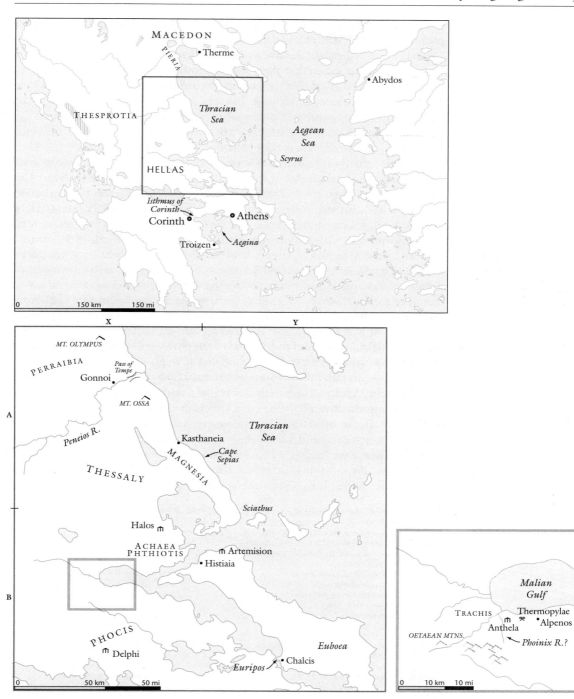

MAP 7.176

This army had gone to Thessaly while the King was about to cross over to Europe from Asia and was already at Abydos.[a] And so the Thessalians, now that their allies had deserted them, medized with no further hesitation, and indeed so zealously that they proved most useful to the King in the war.

When the Hellenes arrived back at the isthmus, they deliberated about how and where they would wage the war in view of what Alexandros had told them. The opinion that prevailed over all the others was to defend the pass at Thermopylae,[a] since they saw that it was narrower than the pass into Thessaly and closer to their own territory. [2] The path by which the Hellenes were actually defeated at Thermopylae was not known to them until they arrived at Thermopylae and learned of it from the men of Trachis.[a] The Hellenes planned to defend this pass in an attempt to keep the barbarian out of Hellas, and also to have their fleet sail to Artemision[b] in the territory of Histiaiotis,[c] so that their land and sea forces would be close enough to keep informed about each other's status. The lay of the land is as follows.

First, near Artemision, the expanse of the Thracian Sea[a] narrows into a channel between the island of Sciathus[b] and Magnesia[c] on the mainland. From this channel one next reaches Artemision, which is located on a beach of Euboea[d] where there is a sanctuary dedicated to Artemis. [2] Now while the road leading through Trachis into Hellas[a] tapers down to where it is only about fifty feet[b] wide, it is narrower still on either side of Thermopylae. At both Alpenos[c] and the Phoinix River[d] close to the city of Anthela,[e] the track is wide enough for only a single wagon. [3] To the south[a]—inland—there is an impassable mountain which extends all the way to Mount Oeta,[b] and to the north lies the sea with its shoals. There are hot springs along this stretch of the road which the local residents call Chytroi,[c] and beside them stands an altar dedicated to Herakles. A wall had been built across this pass, and a long time ago gates were added to it. [4] It was the Phocians[a] who built this wall, having done so out of fear when the Thessalians came from Thesprotia[b] to dwell in Aeolian land[c] which they now possess. Indeed, the Thessalians were trying to conquer them, so the

7.174.1a Abydos: Map 7.176, locator.
7.175.1a Thermopylae: Map 7.176, inset.
          This inset map is based entirely on
          Herodotus' description of the topogra-
          phy, which might be quite inaccurate;
          see n. 7.176.3a.
7.175.2a Trachis: Map 7.176, inset.
7.175.2b Artemision: Map 7.176, BY.
7.175.2c Histiaiotis was another name for Perraibia.
7.176.1a Thracian Sea: Map 7.176, AY.
7.176.1b Sciathus: Map 7.176, BY.
7.176.1c Magnesia, Hellas: Map 7.176, AX.
7.176.1d Euboea: Map 7.176, BY.
7.176.2a Hellas in the narrower sense, not includ-
          ing Thessaly (Map 7.176, AX).
7.176.2b Herodotus writes that the road is only
          "a half-plethron" wide. The plethron is
          about 100 Greek feet. See Appendix J,
          §2, 5–6, 19.
7.176.2c Alpenos: Map 7.176, inset.

7.176.2d Phoinix River, possible location: Map
          7.176, inset.
7.176.2e Anthela: Map 7.176, inset.
7.176.3a Herodotus' points of the compass are
          wrong throughout in his description of
          Thermopylae. The road runs east–west,
          not north–south as he supposes; so his
          "west" has been changed in this text to
          "south," and "east" to "north." (Godley)
7.176.3b Mount Oeta (Oetaean Mountains): Map
          7.176, inset.
7.176.3c *Chytroi* is Greek for "pots" or "cauldrons."
7.176.4a Phocis: Map 7.176, BX. In 480 the pass
          of Thermopylae was no longer in Phocian
          territory.
7.176.4b Thesprotia: Map 7.176, locator.
7.176.4c This remark may reflect the early expul-
          sion from Hellas and the migration of
          the Aeolian Hellenes to their lands in
          Asia Minor.

Phocians contrived every means they could think of to guard against this, and to prevent the Thessalians from invading their land, they even let the hot water overflow out onto the road so that the ground would be carved up by ravines. [5] This ancient wall had suffered all the ravages of time and now lay mostly in ruins. So the Hellenes decided to rebuild it in order to prevent the barbarian from entering Hellas. The village closest to this road is called Alpenos, and it was from here that the Hellenes planned to obtain provisions.

This, then, was the region that appeared to the Hellenes to suit their purpose. For they had thoroughly investigated it in advance and concluded that the barbarians would not be able to exploit the great number of their infantry or cavalry on this terrain. Therefore they resolved to confront the invader of Hellas here; and when they learned that the Persian had reached Pieria,[a] they dispersed from their meeting at the isthmus and set out to do battle, some traveling on foot to Thermopylae, and others by sea to Artemision.

7.177
480
THERMOPYLAE
After careful survey, the Hellenes found the position advantageous, and set off to occupy it.

While the Hellenes divided into two groups[a] and hastened to their own defense, the citizens of Delphi[b] were completely terrified, and consulted the god on behalf of themselves and Hellas. The oracle advised them to pray to the winds, because they would prove to be great allies of Hellas. [2] The first thing the Delphians did upon receiving this oracle was to report what it said to those Hellenes who wanted to be free, at a time when they, too, were terrified of the barbarians, and "the Delphians, by reporting it, won from them eternal thanks."[a] After that, the Delphians erected an altar to the winds at the very location of the precinct of Thyia daughter of Kephisos, from whom this place gets its name.[b] There they sought to win the goodwill of the winds by offering them sacrifices, and they follow the instructions of the oracle by continuing to propitiate the winds even to this day.

7.178
480
DELPHI
The Delphians consult the god and are advised to pray to the winds, which they and their allies do, and still do today.

Before the fleet of Xerxes sailed out from the city of Therme,[a] it sent forth ten of its best ships to sail straight for Sciathus, where three Greek ships were keeping watch. These ships were from Troizen,[b] Aegina,[c] and Attica,[d] and they quickly fled when they saw the ships approaching.

7.179
480
SCIATHUS
The Persian fleet arrives.

The ship from Troizen, which was under the command of Praxinos, was promptly pursued by the barbarians and captured. Then the barbarians took its most handsome marine to the prow of the ship and cut his throat, securing a good omen by taking the most handsome as the first of their Greek

7.180
480
SCIATHUS
After taking a Greek trireme, the Persians sacrifice one of the captured sailors.

7.177.1a Pieria: Map 7.176, locator.
7.178.1a Two groups: one traveling by land, the other by sea.
7.178.1b Delphi: Map 7.176, BX.
7.178.2a Herodotus quotes a metrical phrase here which is probably part of a poem praising the Delphians or recounting the events of the war. The Hellenes were eternally grateful that the Delphians had found out and revealed to them what the Pythia had said—namely which gods to propitiate—since the Delphians could have kept it to themselves and saved themselves alone. For more about the Delphic oracle, see Appendix P, §2, 5, 9, 12.
7.178.2b Thyia: location unknown.
7.179.1a Therme: Map 7.176, locator.
7.179.1b Troizen: Map 7.176, locator.
7.179.1c Aegina: Map 7.176, locator.
7.179.1d A ship from Attica would be an Athenian ship. Athens: Map 7.176, locator.

captives.[a] The name of the man whose throat was cut was Leon, and perhaps his name had something to do with what happened to him.

The ship from Aegina, whose trierarch[a] was Asonides, created quite a stir among the barbarians because one of its marines, Pytheas son of Ischenoos, proved himself the most valiant man on that day. During the capture of the ship, he continued to fight until he had been almost completely butchered. [2] And when he did fall, he did not die but still had breath left in him. The Persians who served as marines on the ships took great care to assure his survival out of respect for his valor; they treated his wounds with myrrh and wrapped them in bandages of fine linen.[a] [3] And when they came back to their own camp, they expressed their amazement and admiration for him as they showed him off before the whole army. They treated him quite well but they treated the rest of the men captured on this ship as slaves.

So that is what happened when two of the ships were overtaken and subdued. The third, whose trierarch was Phormos, an Athenian, fled to the mouth of the Peneios,[a] where it ran aground. There the barbarians captured the hull of the ship but not its men, for as soon as they had run the ship aground, the Athenians leapt ashore and then made their way through Thessaly[b] until they reached Athens.[c]

The Hellenes who were making their camp at Artemision[a] learned of all this through fire beacons from Sciathus.[b] They were frightened by this news and transferred their anchorage from Artemision to Chalcis[c] in order to guard the Euripos,[d] but they left lookouts on the heights of Euboea to keep watch by day. [2] Of the ten ships of the barbarian squadron, three went aground at the reef called Myrmex,[a] between Sciathus and Magnesia.[b] The barbarians had brought a stone pillar with them, which they erected there upon the reef.[c] And now that their route was clear, all the ships set sail from Therme,[d] eleven days after the King had begun his march from there. [3] It was Pammon of Scyrus[a] who had pointed out to them the general location of the reef within the strait. After sailing all day, the barbarians arrived at Sepias[b] in Magnesian territory and at the beach situated between the city of Kasthaneia[c] and Cape Sepias.

Until the barbarian forces came to this region and to Thermopylae, they had suffered no harm, and according to my estimates, their number remained the same. The ships that had come from Asia numbered 1,207,[a] and the orig-

7.180.1a   This type of ritual human sacrifice is not known to have been carried out elsewhere by the Persians. Herodotus clearly believed it took place, and in 7.114 he writes that the burial of the living is a Persian practice and gives examples.

7.181.1a   A trierarch was the commander of a trireme.

7.181.2a   Fine linen, the same material the Egyptians used to wrap their most expensively prepared mummies; see 2.86.6.

7.182.1a   Peneios River: Map 7.176, AX.
7.182.1b   Thessaly: Map 7.176, AX.
7.182.1c   Athens: Map 7.176, locator.
7.183.1a   Artemision: Map 7.176, BY.
7.183.1b   The mountains of Sciathus are clearly visible

from Euboea (both, Map 7.176, BY).
7.183.1c   Chalcis, Euboea: Map 7.176, BY.
7.183.1d   Euripos (strait): Map 7.176, BY.
7.183.2a   In Greek this reef was called Myrmex, which means "the ant."
7.183.2b   Magnesia, Hellas: Map 7.176, AX.
7.183.2c   They had gone to find the reef and erect the pillar to mark it so that other ships of their fleet could avoid it later on.
7.183.2d   Therme: Map 7.176, locator.
7.183.3a   Scyrus: Map 7.176, locator.
7.183.3b   Cape Sepias: Map 7.176, AY.
7.183.3c   Kasthaneia: Map 7.176, AX.
7.184.1a   As previously mentioned in n. 7.89.1a, the number 1,207 arouses suspicion among scholars. See Appendix R, §13–14.

inal complement of men from each national contingent were still on board; if we estimate that there were 200 men per ship,[b] they totaled 241,400. [2] Serving as marines on each of these ships, in addition to the usual units of the crew's own nationality, were units made up of 30 Persians, Medes, or Sakai. This additional force adds up to a total of 36,210. [3] And let me add to this and to the earlier count the crews from the penteconters, assuming there was an average of 80 men on each of them. As I said before,[a] 3,000 of these vessels had been gathered, which would mean that the total number of men on board would come to 240,000. [4] Therefore the naval forces from Asia added up to 517,610 men in all. The number of the infantry came to 1,700,000, and that of the cavalry amounted to 80,000. But let me add also to these the Arabians[a] who drove the camels and the Libyans[b] who drove the chariots; altogether, they added up to 20,000 men. [5] And so now, the numbers from the fleet combined with the land army come to a total of 2,317,610. That, then, was the number of the armed forces that had set out from Asia. I have not yet added in the train of servants which accompanied the expedition, nor the crews of the boats that carried provisions.

For I must add to the total which I have calculated the men in the forces that were recruited from Europe.[a] About these, however, I can offer only a guess. The Hellenes from Thrace[b] and from the islands lying off its coast provided 120 ships, and on board these would be 24,000 men. [2] Land forces were provided by the Thracians, Paionians,[a] Eordians,[b] Bottiaians,[c] the nation of Chalcidians,[d] Brygoi,[e] Pierians,[f] Macedonians,[g] Perraibians,[h] Ainianes,[i] Dolopians,[j] Magnesians, Achaeans,[k] and all who inhabited the coastal region of Thrace. I would estimate that the number of all these peoples totaled 300,000. [3] When these tens of thousands are added to those from Asia, the total number of fighting men comes to 2,641,610.[a]

Now, since the fighting force was so large, I would guess that the number of servants who followed the troops, as well as of the men on the light vessels that carried provisions, and of course those in the other boats that sailed with the army, was not less but probably even greater than the number of those who made up this fighting force. [2] But if I should estimate their number to be not greater or smaller but the same, it would equal the same

7.185
480
CAPE SEPIAS
Then Herodotus adds
the forces brought from
Europe and the total climbs
to 2,641,610.

7.186
480
CAPE SEPIAS
Estimating that the service
and supply troops were equal
in number to the fighting
men, Herodotus calculates
the total Persian force at
5,283,220.

7.184.1b For the number and composition of crews of triremes, see Appendix S, §5–7.
7.184.3a Herodotus did not say there were 3,000 penteconters with the fleet. At 7.97, he said that there were 3,000 triaconters, penteconters, light boats, and horse transports attached to the fleet.
7.184.4a Arabia: Map 7.186, locator.
7.184.4b Libya: Map 7.186, locator.
7.185.1a Europe: Map 7.186, locator.
7.185.1b Thrace: Map 7.186, AY.
7.185.2a Paionia: Map 7.186, AX.
7.185.2b Eordaia: Map 7.186, AX.
7.185.2c Bottiaia: Map 7.186, AX.
7.185.2d Chalcidice: Map 7.186, AX.
7.185.2e Brygoi, possible location of territory:

Map 7.186, AX.
7.185.2f Pieria: Map 7.186, AX.
7.185.2g Macedon: Map 7.186, AX.
7.185.2h Perraibia: Map 7.186, BX.
7.185.2i Ainis (territory of the Ainianes): Map 7.186, BX. Herodotus uses the Ionic Enienes.
7.185.2j Dolopia: Map 7.186, BX.
7.185.2k Achaea Phthiotis: Map 7.186, BX.
7.184.5a Herodotus attempts to be methodical and exact in his calculations here. He does err on the number of penteconters and their crews, although this hardly matters since the total he arrives at is generally regarded as incredibly high. For a discussion of these numbers, see Appendix R, §1–2.

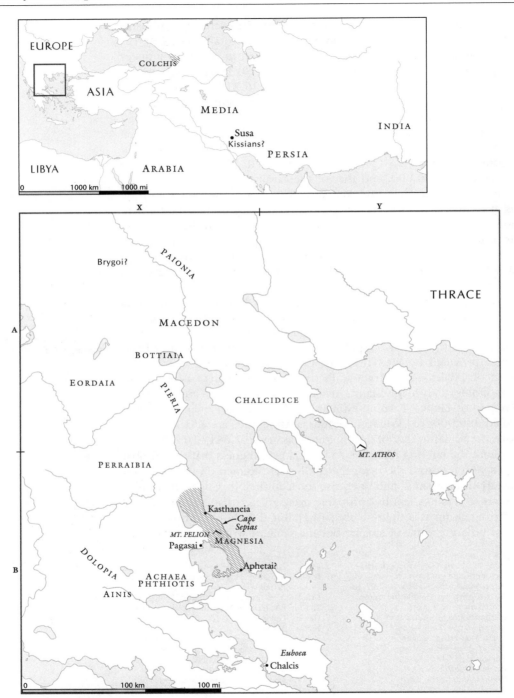

MAP 7.186

number of tens of thousands in the fighting force, so until Xerxes son of Darius reached Sepias and Thermopylae, he was leading 5,283,220 men.[a]

While that is the total number of men in the military forces under Xerxes, no one could calculate the precise number of those others who followed along—the women who prepared the food, the concubines,[a] the eunuchs, or of the yoke animals and other beasts of burden and the Indian dogs; indeed, the number of all these was so great that no one could possibly express it. And so it is no wonder to me that some of the rivers ran dry, but it is a wonder to me that there were enough provisions for so many tens of thousands. [2] For my calculations reveal that if each person received one choinix of wheat per day and no more than that, then 110,340 medimnoi would be consumed daily,[a] though I have not counted in this calculation anything for the women, eunuchs, beasts of burden, and dogs. And of so many tens of thousands of men, not one of them was, by reason of his good looks and stature, more worthy of holding this power than Xerxes.

The Persian fleet set out to sea and sailed to the beach of Magnesia,[a] which lies between the city of Kasthaneia[b] and Cape Sepias.[c] The first ships to arrive there moored close to the beach while the others lay at anchor farther offshore. Since the beach was not long, they rode at anchor in a formation eight rows deep, with their prows pointing out to sea. [2] That is how they remained during that entire night, but at daybreak, out of a clear and windless sky, the sea suddenly began to seethe and a violent storm with a strong east wind fell upon them; it was the wind that the inhabitants of this region call the Hellespontian. [3] Those who realized that the wind was rising, and who had a mooring that made it possible, drew their ships up onto the shore before the storm could hit them, and so both these men and their ships survived. But of the ships caught out on the high sea, some were carried to shore at the rocks called the Ovens of Pelion[a] while others were thrown onto the beach, or were wrecked around Sepias itself or at the city of Meliboia.[b] Still others were dashed against the shore at Kasthaneia. This storm was indeed an overwhelming disaster.

It is said that the Athenians had summoned Boreas[a] on the advice of a prophecy, and that another oracle they received had told them they should call on their son-in-law as their ally. According to the story told by the Hellenes, Boreas had a wife from Attica,[b] Oreithyia daughter of Erechtheus.[c]

7.187
480
CAPE SEPIAS
When Herodotus adds the number of camp followers with the army, he wonders how provisions could have been supplied to so many, calculating the huge amount of wheat required each day.

7.188
480
MAGNESIA
The beach where the fleet puts in is too small for all but a few of the ships. The rest anchor offshore, and many are wrecked when a terrible storm occurs.

7.189
480
ATHENS
Without committing himself to it, Herodotus recounts the Athenian story that their sacrifice to Boreas led the wind to destroy so many Persian ships.

7.186.2a This huge number is, of course, quite impossible. See Appendix R, §1–3.
7.187.1a Women camp followers were essential to ancient armies.
7.187.2a The numbers would indeed be staggering. From the equivalents table of Appendix J, §21, and assuming with Herodotus that each person requires a choinix of wheat per day, one can calculate that 5,000,000 people would consume 104,167 medimnoi per day (close to but not exactly the figure 110,340 that Herodotus arrives at). Applying some U.S. government data, one can translate those medimnoi into 157,235 bushels, or 4,700 tons, of wheat per day! See Appendix R, §7.
7.188.1a Magnesia, Hellas: Map 7.186, BX.
7.188.1b Kasthaneia: Map 7.186, BX.
7.188.1c Cape Sepias: Map 7.186, BX.
7.188.3a Mount Pelion: Map 7.186, BX. Herodotus writes *ipnoi*, which means "ovens" in Greek.
7.188.3b Meliboia: precise location on the Magnesian coast unknown.
7.189.1a Boreas was the god of the North Wind.
7.189.1b Attica: Map 7.197.
7.189.1c Erechtheus was an early, mythical king of Athens.

[2] In view of this connection by marriage, so the story goes, the Athenians concluded that Boreas was their son-in-law. And when their fleet was stationed at Chalcis[a] in Euboea[b] and they realized that a storm was rising, or perhaps before this, they sacrificed and summoned Boreas and Oreithyia to help them and to destroy the ships of the barbarians, as had happened once earlier, around Athos.[c] [3] I cannot say whether it was really because of their prayers and sacrifices that Boreas fell upon the barbarians as they were lying at anchor. But in any case, the Athenians claim that Boreas had helped them before, and that it was he who was responsible for what had happened now. So after they left this place and returned home to Athens, they dedicated a sanctuary to Boreas beside the River Ilissos.[a]

It is reported that in the Persians' encounter with this storm, no fewer than 400 ships were destroyed, and that it was impossible to count the men or estimate the immense quantity of material goods lost. And so it happened that these shipwrecks came to greatly benefit Ameinokles son of Kretines, a Magnesian who owned land in the vicinity of Sepias. For afterward, he picked up many golden drinking vessels that had been dashed ashore, and many silver ones as well, and he found the Persians' treasure stores, too, thereby obtaining for himself untold amounts of money. But although he became very wealthy through this windfall, he was not lucky in all other respects. For even he was afflicted by a painful misfortune—the murder of his son.

The number of merchant ships carrying provisions and other vessels that were destroyed was incalculable. Because the commanders of the fleet feared that the Thessalians would attack them now that they had suffered severe damages, they surrounded themselves with a tall palisade constructed from material salvaged from the wrecked ships. [2] The storm continued for three days, but at last the Magi, by offering sacrificial victims and singing incantations to the wind in addition to performing sacrifices to Thetis and the Nereids, brought about an end to the storm on the fourth day—or perhaps it abated of its own accord. The reason they sacrificed to Thetis was that they had heard from the Ionians that she had been abducted from this region by Peleus, and thus all of Cape Sepias belonged to her and the rest of the Nereids.

So the storm ceased on the fourth day. As for the Hellenes, their lookouts descended from the heights of Euboea on the second day after the storm began and informed them all about the details of the shipwrecks. [2] When the Hellenes learned what was happening, they prayed to Poseidon the Savior and poured libations; then immediately after that, they quickly sailed back to Artemision,[a] expecting to find there only a few enemy ships to oppose them. So they sailed to Artemision for the second time and lay at

7.189.2a	Chalcis: Map 7.186, BY.	
7.189.2b	Euboea: Map 7.186, BY.	
7.189.2c	Mount Athos: Map 7.186, AY. An earlier Persian fleet was destroyed off	

	Mount Athos in 482. See 6.44.2–3.
7.189.3a	Ilissos River: Map 6.136.
7.192.2a	Artemision: Map 7.197, inset.

FIGURE 7.193. THE BEACH AT PLATANIA BAY, THOUGHT TO BE APHETAI (MAP 7.197, INSET), WHERE A SIGNIFICANT PART OF THE PERSIAN FLEET IS THOUGHT TO HAVE BEEN BASED BEFORE THE BATTLE OF ARTEMISION, WHICH TOOK PLACE JUST A SHORT DISTANCE TO THE SOUTH.

anchor there. From that time on, even to this day, they invoke the god by the name "Poseidon the Savior."

When the wind had ceased and the sea had become smooth, the barbarians hauled their ships into the water and sailed along the mainland, rounding the Cape of Magnesia[a] and continuing directly to the gulf that leads to Pagasai.[b] [2] In the Gulf of Magnesia[a] lies the site where Herakles is said to have been left behind when he had been sent to fetch water by Jason and his companions on the ship *Argo*. This happened when they were sailing to Aia in Colchis for the fleece.[b] They intended to leave for the open sea from there after obtaining water, and for this reason the name of the place came to be Aphetai.[c] In any case, it was at this place that Xerxes' fleet now made its anchorage.

7.193
480
APHETAI
When the storm ends, the Persians sail into the Gulf of Pagasai and anchor at Aphetai.

7.193.1a   Cape of Magnesia: Map 7.197, inset.
7.193.1b   Pagasai: Map 7.197, inset.
7.193.2a   Gulf of Magnesia: Map 7.197, inset.
7.193.2b   Aia: site unknown. Colchis: Map 7.186, locator. In the Greek tale of the Golden Fleece, the fleece or sheepskin was the prize stolen by the legendary Argonauts, who were commanded by Jason and assisted by Medea, the daughter of the king of Colchis. The tale formed the basis for several poems and plays. See Glossary, Argonauts.
7.193.2c   Aphetai, probable location: Map 7.197, inset. More probably, the name gave rise to the legend, as it derives from the verb *aphiemi*, meaning "to leave, let go, send off." (Godley) See Figure 7.193.

7.194
480
ARTEMISION
Fifteen Persian ships at sea mistook the Greek ships off Artemision for their own, and sailed into their midst and were captured.

7.195
480
ARTEMISION
After interrogating the prisoners, the Hellenes send them away to the Isthmus of Corinth in bonds.

7.196
480
MALIS
The Persians march through Thessaly, conduct horse races, and find the rivers there unable to sustain the army's thirst.

7.197
480
ACHAEA PHTHIOTIS
When Xerxes is informed of the ancient tale of Athamas, he refrains from entering the temple grove, holding Athamas and his descendants in reverence.

But a squadron of fifteen barbarian ships had put out to sea much later than the others and, as it happened, their crews sighted the Greek fleet at Artemision. Assuming that these were their own ships, the barbarians actually sailed into the midst of the enemy fleet. This squadron was commanded by Sandokes of Cyme,[a] son of Thamasios, who was the governor of Aeolis.[b] Before this, when Sandokes was serving as one of the royal judges, King Darius had had him arrested and hung suspended from a stake on the charge of having rendered an unjust verdict for a bribe. [2] But then, after Sandokes had been hung up on the stake, Darius thought it over and realized that this man's good deeds toward the royal household outweighed his faults. When Darius realized this, he recognized that he had acted with more haste than wisdom, and he ordered that Sandokes be released. [3] So Sandokes escaped death at the hands of Darius the King and survived on that occasion, but now, as he sailed into the Greek fleet, he was not to escape a second time. For when the Hellenes saw his ships sailing toward them, they realized the error the barbarians were making and swiftly put out to sea and captured them all.

On one of these ships, they captured Aridolis, the tyrant of Alabanda in Caria,[a] and on another, the commander Penthylos of Paphos,[b] son of Demonoos. He had commanded twelve ships which had sailed from Paphos, but eleven of them had been lost to the storm at Sepias. Now, as he was sailing on his one surviving ship, he was captured at Artemision. The Hellenes interrogated their captives and, after learning what they wanted to know about the forces of Xerxes, sent them away in bonds to the isthmus of the Corinthians.[c]

Except for those fifteen ships I mentioned, which had been commanded by Sandokes, the rest of the barbarian fleet arrived at Aphetai.[a] Three days before, Xerxes with his land army had passed through Thessaly[b] and Achaea[c] and had entered Malis.[d] Having heard that the horses of Thessaly were the best in Hellas, he had held a race there to test his own horses against those of the Thessalians. The Greek horses were left far behind. Of the rivers in Thessaly, only the Onochonos[e] failed to supply enough drinking water for the army. Of those in Achaea, not even the greatest of them, the Apidanos,[f] proved really sufficient, barely supplying the water they needed.

When Xerxes arrived at Halos in Achaea,[a] his guides, wanting to convey to him everything they knew, told him a local story about the sanctuary of Laphystian Zeus, and how Athamas son of Aiolos, in a plot with Ino, contrived the doom of Phrixos; and how, afterward, the Achaeans imposed upon his descendants the following trials and tribulations. [2] The eldest member of the family was ordered to stay out of the public hall (for the Achaeans call the Prytaneion the "public hall"), but to guard it himself. And if he did once

7.194.1a   Cyme: Map 7.197.
7.194.1b   Aeolis: Map 7.197.
7.195.1a   Alabanda in Caria: Map 7.197.
7.195.1b   Paphos, Cyprus: Map 7.213, locator.
7.195.1c   Isthmus of Corinth: Map 7.197.
7.196.1a   Aphetai, probable location: Map 7.197, inset.
7.196.1b   Thessaly: Map 7.197.
7.196.1c   Achaea Phthiotis: Map 7.197, inset.

7.196.1d   Malis: Map 7.197, inset.
7.196.1e   Onochonos River: Map 7.197.
7.196.1f   Apidanos River: Map 7.197, inset. Herodotus spells this river Epidanos here, and Apidanos in 7.129.2. Some scholars suggest this may reflect a different source of information.
7.197.1a   Halos in Achaea Phthiotis: Map 7.197, inset.

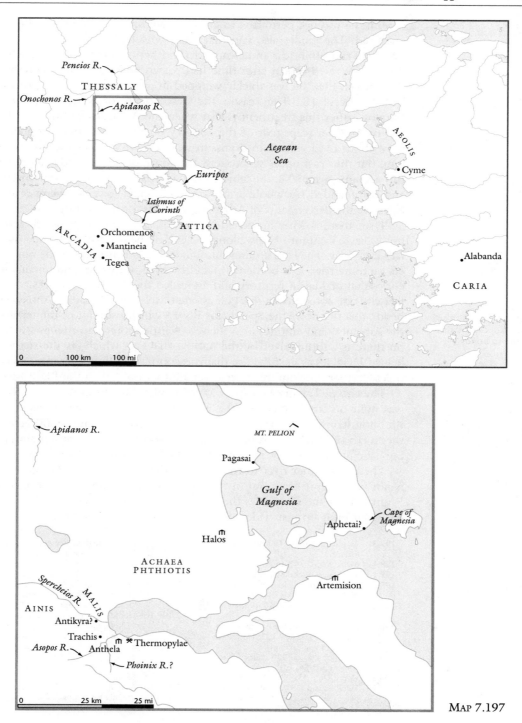

MAP 7.197

581

enter it, he was not permitted to go out again until it was time for him to be sacrificed. The guides also said that many who had been about to be sacrificed had run off in fear and escaped to another country. But if one who had done so were to return after time had passed and was caught entering the Prytaneion, then he was thickly wrapped in garlands, led out in procession, and sacrificed. [3] The reason the descendants of Kytissoros, a son of Phrixos, suffer this treatment is that when the Achaeans had made Athamas son of Aiolos a scapegoat of the country on the advice of a prophecy and were about to sacrifice him, Kytissoros came from Aia in Colchis[a] and saved him, but thus cast upon his progeny the wrath of the god. [4] After hearing this account, when Xerxes came to the grove, he refrained from entering it and commanded his whole army to do the same, out of reverence for the house of the descendants of Athamas as well as for the god's precinct.

That, then, is what happened in Thessaly and Achaea. From these countries, Xerxes went into Malis[a] along the gulf of the sea, where the tide rises and falls every day. The land around this gulf is flat, in some parts wide but in others quite narrow; it is bordered inland by high, impassable mountains which enclose all of Malian territory and are called the Trachinian Rocks.[b] [2] The first city one comes to on this gulf as one travels from Achaea is Antikyra,[a] and beside this city flows the Spercheios River,[b] which rises out of the territory of the Ainianes[c] and empties into the sea. A little more than two miles[d] farther on there is another river by the name of Dyras,[e] which, as the story goes, helped Herakles against the fire that was consuming him;[f] a bit more than two miles[g] farther on from this river is yet another one called the Black River.[h]

The city of Trachis[a] lies about a half a mile[b] away from the Black River. It was built on land which has the widest expanse of the entire region from the mountains to the sea, for the plain here covers some 5,500 acres.[c] To the north of Trachis, cutting through the foothills of the mountain enclosing Trachinian territory, is a ravine in which the Asopos River[d] flows.

There is another river to the south of the Asopos—the Phoinix[a]—which is not very big; it flows out of the mountains and empties into the Asopos. Right here at the Phoinix is the narrowest part of the region, where a path has been built up just wide enough for a single wagon. From the Phoinix

7.197.3a　Aia: site unknown. Colchis: Map 7.186,
　　　　　locator.
7.198.1a　Malis: Map 7.197, inset.
7.198.1b　Trachinian Rocks: Map 7.213, inset.
7.198.2a　Antikyra, possible location: Map 7.197,
　　　　　inset.
7.198.2b　Spercheios River: Map 7.197, inset; Map
　　　　　7.213, inset.
7.198.2c　Ainis (territory of the Ainianes): Map
　　　　　7.197, inset. As at 7.132, Herodotus
　　　　　uses the Ionic Enienes.
7.198.2d　Herodotus writes "20 stades." See
　　　　　Appendix J, §6, 19.
7.198.2e　Dyras River: Map 7.213, inset.
7.198.2f　Herakles had thrown himself onto a
　　　　　pyre; see Sophocles' *Trachiniai.*
7.198.2g　Herodotus writes that this distance was

　　　　　also "20 stades." See Appendix J, §6, 19.
7.198.2h　Black River: site unknown. This river is
　　　　　spelled the same as the one mentioned
　　　　　in 7.58.3, but it is not the same one.
7.199.1a　Trachis: Map 7.197, inset.
7.199.1b　Herodotus describes this distance as
　　　　　"5 stades." See Appendix J, §6, 19.
7.199.1c　Herodotus writes that the plain covers
　　　　　"22,000 plethra." Assuming he means
　　　　　square plethra, a unit of surface area
　　　　　equal to about 100 square Attic feet, or
　　　　　one quarter of an acre, this plain would
　　　　　measure 5,500 acres. See Appendix J,
　　　　　§5–6, 19.
7.199.1d　Asopos River: Map 7.197, inset.
7.200.1a　Phoinix River, possible location: Map
　　　　　7.197, inset; Map 7.213, inset.

River it is a little less than one and three-quarter miles[b] to Thermopylae,[c] [2] and between the Phoinix River and Thermopylae lies a village by the name of Anthela.[a] The Asopos flows beside this village and from there continues on until it empties into the sea. The plain around Anthela is broader, and on it stands the sanctuary of Demeter[b] Amphiktyonis. Here are the seats of the Amphiktyones[c] and the sanctuary of Amphiktyon himself.

Now King Xerxes made his base in the Trachinian part of Malis, while the Hellenes were camped at the pass. Most of the Hellenes call this place Thermopylae, but the inhabitants dwelling here called it Pylae.[a] So that is where each army made its camp, one controlling everything toward the north down to Trachis, the other in control of the regions toward the south on that side of the Greek mainland.

The Hellenes who were waiting for the Persian in this region were 300 Spartan hoplites, 1,000 men from Tegea[a] and Mantineia[b] (each providing 500), 120 from Orchomenos in Arcadia,[c] and 1,000 from the rest of Arcadia. These were all the troops that came from Arcadia. From Corinth[d] there were 400 hoplites, from Phleious[e] 200; and there were also 80 Mycenaeans.[f] Those, then, were the troops that had come from the Peloponnese.[g] From Boeotia[h] there were 700 Thespians[i] and 400 Thebans.[j]

In addition to these, both the Opuntian Locrians,[a] who had come in full force, and 1,000 Phocians[b] had responded to the Greek call for assistance. For the Hellenes had sent messengers to summon their help, saying to them that those who had come to Thermopylae were merely an advance guard of the rest of the allies who were expected to arrive any day now; moreover, they said, the sea was being guarded by the Athenians,[c] Aeginetans,[d] and those others who had been assigned to the fleet, so that they had nothing to fear; [2] for it was not a god but a human being who was invading Hellas, and no mortal existed now, nor would ever exist, who did not have a mixture of adversity in his life from the moment of his birth; indeed the greatest men encountered the greatest adversities. Therefore it was

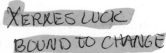

XERXES LUCK BOUND TO CHANGE

7.200.1b Herodotus writes this distance as "15 stades." See Appendix J, §6, 19.
7.200.1c Thermopylae: Map 7.197, inset; Map 7.213.
7.200.2a Anthela: Map 7.197, inset; Map 7.213, inset.
7.200.2b Demeter, the goddess who governs the fruits of the earth, in particular grains for bread. She was worshiped all over the Greek world, with local variations. The most famous rites in her honor were the Great Mysteries of Eleusis, secret ceremonies celebrated in the early autumn. Worshipers were initiated into the cult and swore never to reveal the ritual to the uninitiated. Herodotus appears to have been an initiate.
7.200.2c Amphiktyones: a league of neighbors to an important sanctuary, in this case that of Demeter at Anthela, called the sanctuary of Demeter Amphiktyonis. This league later became associated with the

sanctuary of Apollo at Delphi. It administered the temple and its property and managed the Pythian games.
7.201.1a *Pylae* in Greek means "gates," and the place was called Thermopylae because hot springs were located there, and because although it was a narrow pass, it was the best entrance into Hellas from the north.
7.202.1a Tegea: Map 7.197.
7.202.1b Mantineia: Map 7.197.
7.202.1c Orchomenos, Arcadia: Map 7.197.
7.202.1d Corinth: Map 7.213, BY.
7.202.1e Phleious: Map 7.213, BX.
7.202.1f Mycenae: Map 7.213, BY.
7.202.1g Peloponnese: Map 7.213, BX.
7.202.1h Boeotia: Map 7.213, AY.
7.202.1i Thespiai: Map 7.213, AY.
7.202.1j Thebes: Map 7.213, AY.
7.203.1a Locris (Opuntian): Map 7.213, AY.
7.203.1b Phocis: Map 7.213, AX.
7.203.1c Athens: Map 7.213, BY.
7.203.1d Aegina: Map 7.213, BY.

bound to happen that the one who was marching against them, since he was mortal, would fail in his glorious expectations. When they heard this, ·the Locrians and Phocians hurried to Trachis[a] to help.

Each contingent of these troops was under the command of generals assigned by their individual cities, but the most admired and the leader of the whole army was a Lacedaemonian: Leonidas son of Anaxandridas, the son of Leon son of Eurykratides, the son of Anaxandros son of Eurykrates, the son of Polydoros son of Alkamenes, the son of Teleklos son of Archelaos, the son of Hrgesilaos son of Doryssos, the son of Leobotas son of Echestratos, the son of Agis son of Eurysthenes, the son of Aristodemos son of Aristomachos, the son of Kleodaios son of Hyllos, who was the son of Herakles. Leonidas had become a king of Sparta unexpectedly.

For since he had two older brothers, Kleomenes and Dorieus, he had long before cleared his mind of any thoughts that he might become king. But then Kleomenes died without a male heir, and Dorieus, who had met his end in Sicily,[a] was no longer in the picture either. Since Leonidas was older than Kleombrotos, the youngest son of Anaxandridas, and, moreover, because he had married the daughter of Kleomenes, the kingship came to devolve upon him. [2] So Leonidas arrived at Thermopylae[a] with his assigned force of 300 men, whom he had selected from those who had sons living at the time. He took with him also the Thebans I mentioned when I listed the number of Greek troops; they were under the command of Leontiades son of Eurymachos. [3] Leonidas had made a special effort to bring the Thebans from among all of the Hellenes, because they had been strongly accused of medizing. So he had summoned them to come to war with him, wanting to find out whether they would send men to go with him or whether they would publicly refuse to endorse the alliance of the Hellenes. And though their hearts were not in it, they did send men.

The Spartans sent Leonidas with his men first so that their allies would see them and join in the war, since if they learned that the Spartans were delaying, they too might medize. The rest of the Spartans were held back to celebrate the festival of the Karneia,[a] but they intended to go as soon as they had concluded it. They planned to leave some men behind to guard Sparta, but for the rest of them to march out immediately afterward with all speed and in full force. [2] The rest of the allies had similar intentions for themselves, since the Olympic festival[a] also coincided with these events. And as they did not expect that the battle at Thermopylae would be decided so swiftly, they sent only their advance guards.

7.204
480
THERMOPYLAE
The most admired leader of the Hellenes was the Spartan king Leonidas, who became king unexpectedly.

7.205
480
THERMOPYLAE
Leonidas became king after his two older brothers died. He now leads his picked force of 300 Spartans to Thermopylae. He also brought the Thebans with him because they were accused of medizing.

7.206
480
THERMOPYLAE
Leonidas was sent out to show other Hellenes that Sparta would be there, although their main force was delayed by the Karneia.

7.203.2a Trachis: Map 7.213, inset.
7.205.1a Sicily: Map 7.213, locator. For the story of Dorieus, see 5.42–48.
7.205.2a Thermopylae: Map 7.213, inset.
7.206.1a The Karneia was the Doric festival in honor of Apollo, held in September. A whole month was named for this festival in most Doric calendars, and the entire month was considered holy. The Spartans

had delayed coming to the assistance of the Athenians at Marathon ten years earlier because of the requirement to celebrate the Karneia (6.106.3).
7.206.2a The Olympic festival was the great quadrennial festival conducted in honor of Zeus at Olympia: Map 7.213, BX. See Appendix I, Classical Greek Religious Festivals, for more on the role of such festivals.

That, then, was what the allies intended, but the Hellenes at Thermopylae became terrified when the Persian drew near the pass, and began to discuss whether or not they should leave. The rest of the Peloponnesians thought it best to return to the Peloponnese to protect the isthmus,[a] but this proposal infuriated the Phocians[b] and Locrians,[c] and Leonidas voted to remain where they were and to dispatch messengers to the cities asking them to send help because their numbers were too few to repel the army of the Medes by themselves.

As they deliberated, Xerxes sent a mounted scout to see how many of them there were and what they were doing. While still in Thessaly,[a] the King had heard that a small army was gathered here, and that its leaders were the Lacedaemonians and Leonidas, who traced his lineage to Herakles. [2] When the scout rode up to the camp, he looked around and watched, but could not see the whole army, since some men were posted within the wall that they had rebuilt[a] and were now guarding it, so that it was impossible for the spy to see them. But he did see those outside, whose arms were lying in front of the wall, and it just so happened that at the moment, the Lacedaemonians were the ones posted outside. [2] The scout saw some of these men exercising and others combing their hair, which astonished him. After he had ascertained their number and every other detail, he rode back undisturbed, for no one pursued him; in fact he was practically ignored. When he returned, he reported all that he had seen to Xerxes.

Xerxes listened but could not understand: that the Lacedaemonians were really preparing to kill or be killed, to fight as much as was in their power, seemed to him to be the height of folly, the action of fools. So he sent for Demaratos[a] son of Ariston, who was in the camp, and [2] when Demaratos arrived, Xerxes questioned him about everything he had been told, trying to understand the meaning behind what the Lacedaemonians were doing. Demaratos answered, "You heard what I said about these men before, when we were just setting out against Hellas,[a] and you made me a laughingstock when you heard my view of how these matters would turn out. But it is my greatest goal to tell the truth in your presence, [3] so hear me now once again. These men have come to fight us for control of the road, and that is really what they are preparing to do. For it is their tradition that they groom their hair whenever they are about to put their lives in danger. [4] Now know this: if you subjugate these men and those who have remained behind in Sparta, there is no other race of human beings that will be left to raise their hands against you. For you are now attacking the most noble kingdom

COMBING HAIR

7.207
480
THERMOPYLAE
As the Persians approach Thermopylae, the Hellenes deliberate about whether to retire.

7.208
480
THERMOPYLAE
When Xerxes learns of the Greek forces at Thermopylae, he sends a scout to spy on them.

7.209
480
THERMOPYLAE
Amazed at the small size of the army opposing him, Xerxes asks the Spartan Demaratos what they are about, and cannot believe it when told that they are preparing to hold the pass and fight the Persians for it.

7.207.1a Isthmus of Corinth: Map 7.213, BY.
7.207.1b Phocis: Map 7.213, AX.
7.207.1c Locris (Opuntian): Map 7.213, AY.
7.208.1a Thessaly: Map 7.197.
7.208.2a For the wall thus rebuilt, see 7.176.
7.209.1a Demaratos, the exiled king of Sparta,

appeared last at 7.3. For an account of how his enemies obtained his exile, see 6.63–70.
7.209.2a For the conversation Demaratos refers to here, see 7.101–104.

of all the Hellenes, and the best of men." [5] What Demaratos said seemed quite incredible to Xerxes, and he asked for the second time how they could possibly intend to fight his whole army, since there were so few of them. Demaratos replied, "Sire, if things do not turn out just as I claim they will, treat me like a liar." But even by saying this he did not convince Xerxes.

Xerxes let four whole days elapse, all the while expecting that the Hellenes would run away. But when, on the fifth day, they had still not gone away but were instead holding their positions in what seemed to him a display of reckless impudence, he lost his temper and ordered the Medes[a] and the Kissians[b] out against them, with instructions to bring them back alive and to conduct them into his presence. [2] The Medes charged headlong into the Hellenes, and great numbers of them fell. Although others rushed forth to replace them, even they could not drive the Hellenes away, though they, too, suffered great losses in the attempt. Indeed, the Hellenes made it clear to everyone, and especially to the King himself, that although there were many in his army, there were few real men. The fighting went on all day.

Since the Medes were suffering extremely rough treatment, they now withdrew, and the Persians under the command of Hydarnes, whom the King called the Immortals,[a] came forth to take their place. There was every expectation that they, at least, would easily prevail, [2] but when they joined battle with the Hellenes, they fared no better than the Medes, and indeed they suffered the very same setbacks. The fighting continued to take place in a confined space, with the Persians using shorter spears than those of the Hellenes and unable to derive any advantage from their superior numbers. [3] The Lacedaemonians fought remarkably well, proving that they were experts in battle who were fighting among men who were not, especially whenever they would turn their backs and feign flight all together, and the barbarians, seeing this, would pursue them with much clatter and shouting; the Lacedaemonians would allow the barbarians to catch up with them and then suddenly turn around to face them, at which point they would slay countless numbers of them. Of the Spartans themselves, however, only a few fell there.[a] Finally the Persians retreated, since despite all their efforts to attack by regiments or by any other means, they could not gain any ground in the pass.

It is said that during these assaults, the King, who was watching, leapt up from his throne three times in fear for his army. Thus ended the contest that day, and on the next, the barbarians did no better. They attacked with the expectation that such a small number of Hellenes would be covered with wounds and unable to lift a hand against them. [2] But the Hellenes had formed ranks in their national contingents, and each group fought in its turn except for the Phocians, who had been posted to guard the path on the mountain. When the Persians found that nothing had changed from what they had seen the day before, they retreated again.

7.210
480
THERMOPYLAE
After waiting four days for the Hellenes to withdraw, Xerxes orders his army to attack.

7.211
480
THERMOPYLAE
After the Medes fail, Xerxes orders the Persians to attack, but they, too, fail to exploit their superior number and fare no better. The Spartans show themselves to be superior in training, skill, and arms.

7.212
480
THERMOPYLAE
The Persians continue the assault the next day but withdraw after failing to move the Hellenes.

7.210.1a Media: Map 7.186, locator.
7.210.1b Kissians, possible location of territory: Map 7.186, locator.

7.211.1a The Immortals were an elite corps of Persian troops in Xerxes' army. See 7.83 and Appendix O, §3.

FIGURE 7.211. A SMALL BRONZE STATUETTE OF A SPARTAN
WARRIOR (LEFT) WHICH DISPLAYS THE LONG HAIR SPARTAN
SOLDIERS FREQUENTLY COMBED BEFORE BATTLE, A SIGHT
WHICH ASTONISHED THE PERSIAN SCOUT AT THERMOPYLAE.
THE WARRIOR IS WRAPPED IN HIS RED CLOAK, FOR WHICH
THE SPARTAN HOPLITES WERE FAMOUS; THE UNUSUAL
TRANSVERSE HELMET CREST MAY SUGGEST THAT HE IS MEANT
TO BE A GENERAL OR PERHAPS EVEN A KING. BELOW, A SMALL
BRONZE STATUETTE DEPICTS THE COSTUME OF A CLASSICAL
HOPLITE: SHIELD, HELMET WITH CREST, BRONZE CUIRASS,
GREAVES, AND (MISSING) SPEAR.

The King was at a loss about how to deal with this impasse, but just then Ephialtes of Malis,[a] son of Eurydemos, came to speak with him, expecting to win some great reward for telling the King of the path that led through the mountain to Thermopylae.[b] By so doing, he caused the destruction of the Hellenes stationed there. [2] This man later fled to Thessaly[a] in fear of the Lacedaemonians, and during his exile a price was set on his head by the Pylagoroi during a meeting of the Amphiktyones[b] at Pylaia. After a while he went back to Antikyra,[c] where he died at the hands of Athenades, a man of Trachis.[d] [3] This Athenades killed Ephialtes for another reason, which I shall explain in a later section of my story,[a] but Athenades was honored nonetheless by the Lacedaemonians. That is how Ephialtes was later killed.

Another version of these events is that Onetes of Karystos,[a] son of Phanagoras, and Korydallos of Antikyra were the ones who gave this information to the King and who guided the Persians around the mountain, but I find this version to be completely inconceivable. [2] For on balance, the weight of consideration should be given to the fact that the Hellenes, that is the Pylagoroi, set a price of silver on the head of Ephialtes of Trachis, not on Onetes and Korydallos, and they would certainly have done so only after finding out exactly what had happened. Moreover, we know that it was for this reason that Ephialtes went into exile. [3] Now Onetes could indeed have known about this path, even though he was not a Malian, since he may have been familiar with this area anyway, but in fact it was Ephialtes who guided the Persians around the mountain along the path, and so I am recording in writing that he is the guilty one.

Xerxes was pleased and exhilarated by what Ephialtes promised to accomplish, and he at once sent off Hydarnes and those under his command,[a] who set out from camp at the time the lamps were being lit. This path[b] had been discovered by the local Malians, who had led the Thessalians along it against the Phocians[c] at the time when the Phocians had

---

7.213.1a Malis: Map 7.213, inset. Ephialtes is the
more common current spelling of the
name Herodotus wrote as Epialtes.
There may well have been a traitor
named Ephialtes who told the Persians
about the path, but there is no mention
of the great rewards that Xerxes would
normally give to someone who provided such crucial assistance. The reason is not difficult to find. The
Thessalians, who were allied to Persia
and actively helping them, had used
that path years earlier in one of their
wars with Phocis; see 7.215.
7.213.1b Thermopylae: Map 7.213, inset.
7.213.2a Thessaly: Map 7.197.
7.213.2b The Pylagoroi were the delegates of the
member states of the Amphiktyony,
who met at the Pylaia, originally in the
area of Thermopylae and later at Delphi. The Amphiktyones were a league

of state who originally were neighbors
to an important sanctuary, in this case
that of Demeter at Anthela. This league
later became associated with the sanctuary of Apollo at Delphi. It administered
the temple and its property and managed the Pythian games.
7.213.2c Antikyra, possible location: Map 7.213,
inset.
7.213.2d Trachis: Map 7.213, inset.
7.213.3a Herodotus never does explain the other
reason why Athenades killed Ephialtes.
7.214.1a Karystos: Map 7.213, BY.
7.215.1a Hydarnes commanded the regiment of
Persian Immortals. See 7.211.1.
7.215.1b A likely location of the Anopaia Path
(so called because it crosses a mountain
named Anopaia; see 7.216) is shown on
Map 7.213, inset.
7.215.1c Phocis: Map 7.213, AX.

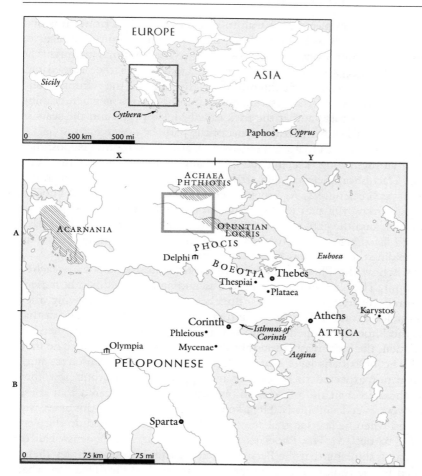

The Anopaia Path

This inset is actually a diagram in map form of Herodotus' description of the topography of the area. It was necessary to represent it this way because, over the past 2,500 years, the sea has receded a great deal, the rivers have altered their course significantly, and towns and other features have disappeared. Scholars have walked the ground and made many attempts to reconstruct the landscape and locate the features he describes, but all their maps are quite speculative, as is this one. Moreover, there is the possibility that Herodotus' account may not be accurate in some or many respects; his list of inscriptions on the monuments erected on the site, however, would indicate that he visited the site himself.

MAP 7.213

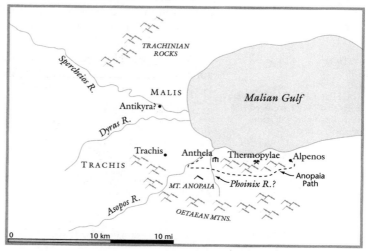

barricaded the main pass with a wall to protect themselves from invasion.[d] So long ago the Malians had found that this path could be put to ill use.

The path begins from the Asopos River[a] where it flows through the ravine; both the path and the mountain it crosses have the same name: Anopaia.[b] This Anopaia Path extends along the ridge of the mountain and ends both at Alpenos[c] (the first Locrian[d] city one arrives at when coming from Malian[e] territory) and at the rock called Melampygos and the seats of the Kerkopes; this is the narrowest part of the path.

So this was the path that the Persians took after crossing the Asopos; they marched all night long, keeping the mountains of Oeta[a] on their right and those of Trachis[b] on their left, and arrived at the summit of the mountain just as dawn was breaking. [2] As I mentioned earlier,[a] there were 1,000 Phocian hoplites guarding this part of the mountain to protect their own country as well as to defend the path here. For while the pass below[b] was being guarded by those I listed before, the Phocians had volunteered to guard this mountain path,[c] holding themselves responsible to Leonidas for this task.

This is how the Phocians became aware that the Persians had reached the summit. They had not noticed them ascending the mountain because it was entirely covered with oak trees. But then, as no wind was blowing, they heard the loud sound of leaves being trampled under many feet, and at that point, the Phocians jumped up and began to arm themselves, but then, all of a sudden, the barbarians were right there in front of them.

[2] The barbarians were amazed to see men arming themselves, since they had not expected to encounter any opposition at all, but now they found themselves in the presence of an army. Hydarnes feared that these troops were Lacedaemonians. He asked exactly what country this army was from, and when he learned that they were Phocians, he formed up the Persians for battle. [3] The Phocians were at once hit with a dense hail of arrows, and, thinking that the Persians had originally set out to attack them, they fled to the peak of the mountain and prepared to die. That was what they thought, but the Persians with Ephialtes and Hydarnes were now paying no attention to the Phocians; they were descending the mountain as fast as they could go.

As for the Hellenes at Thermopylae, the first news of the enemy's approach came from the prophet Megistias; he had inspected the sacrificial victims and now predicted that they would face death at dawn. After that,

7.216
480
THERMOPYLAE
The nature of the Anopaia Path is described.

7.217
480
ANOPAIA
The Persians march to the summit, where they are detected by the Phocians sent by Leonidas to guard the path.

7.218
480
ANOPAIA
The Persians encounter the Phocians as they climb the mountain and, brushing them aside, continue their advance.

7.219
480
THERMOPYLAE
The Hellenes at Thermopylae learn that they have been outflanked and will soon be surrounded.

7.215.1d The construction of a wall by the Phocians in the past is also mentioned in 7.176.3–4.
7.216.1a Asopos River: Map 7.213, inset.
7.216.1b Mount Anopaia: Map 7.213, inset.
7.216.1c Alpenos: Map 7.213, inset.
7.216.1d Locris (Opuntian): Map 7.213, AY.
7.216.1e Malis: Map 7.213, inset.
7.217.1a Oetaean Mountains: Map 7.213, inset.
7.217.1b Trachinian Rocks (mountains): Map 7.213, inset.
7.217.2a Herodotus mentioned that 1,000 Phocians joined the Greek forces at Ther-

mopylae at 7.203.1. At 7.212, he says the Phocians had been sent to guard the path on the mountain.
7.217.2b "The pass below": the one by Thermopylae and the sea.
7.217.2c At 7.175.2 Herodotus writes that the Greeks did not know about the path before they arrived. Yet the Phocians, who were allied with the Greeks, must have known about it, having fought the Thessalians who used it in years past; see 7.215.

deserters came while it was still dark and reported that the Persians were making their way around the mountain toward them. And finally, as day dawned, their lookouts ran down from the heights and told them the same news. [2] At that point the Hellenes discussed what to do and found that they were divided in their opinions: some advised against deserting their post, while others argued the opposite course. After these deliberations they split up: some departed and scattered to their several cities, while the rest prepared to remain there with Leonidas.

It is also said, however, that Leonidas himself sent most of them away as he was worried that all of them might otherwise be killed. But he felt that for himself and the Spartans with him, it would not be decent to leave the post that they had originally come to guard. [2] I myself am most inclined to this opinion and think that when Leonidas perceived the allies' lack of zeal and their reluctance to share with him in the danger ahead, he ordered them to leave. He perceived that it would be ignoble for him to leave the pass, and that if he were to remain, he would secure lasting glory and assure that the prosperity of Sparta would not be obliterated. [3] For the Spartans had consulted the oracle about the war at its very outset, and the Pythia had told them that either Lacedaemon would be depopulated by the barbarians or their king would die. She answered them in these hexameter verses:

> [4] As for you who dwell in the vast land of Sparta,
> Either your city of glory will perish, sacked by the Perseids,[a]
> Or else the boundaries of Lacedaemon will grieve for the death of
>   a king born of Herakles,
> Since neither bulls nor lions have enough might
> to oppose him, for the power of Zeus is his possession.
> And he, I declare, will not be restrained until one or the other
>   is torn apart.

Bearing in mind this oracle, and wanting to gain future glory for the Spartans alone, Leonidas sent the allies away, rather than have them leave. That is why they left, rather than because of a difference of opinion.

One of the most significant proofs that I can assert in order to support this claim has to do with Megistias of Acarnania,[a] who is said to have been descended from Melampous.[b] He was the prophet accompanying this army and had predicted what was going to happen from his inspection of the sacrificial victims. It is clear that Leonidas tried to send him away to prevent him from being killed with those who remained. But though Megistias was dismissed, he refused to leave, and instead sent away his son, who was serving in the army and was his only child.

7.220
480
THERMOPYLAE
Leonidas tells his allies to depart, but he decides to remain with his Spartans, spurred by the prospect of fame and by an oracle predicting that Sparta would be saved if a Spartan king were to die.

7.221
480
THERMOPYLAE
Leonidas sends away the seer Megistias, but he will not leave.

7.220.4a   There is a pun here in the Greek
            between "perish" and "Perseids," the
            descendants of Perseus.

7.221.1a   Acarnania: Map 7.213, AX.
7.221.1b   This Melampous was mentioned by
            Herodotus in 2.49.

7.222
480
THERMOPYLAE
Leonidas keeps the Thebans
there as hostages. The
Thespians remain gladly.

7.223
480
THERMOPYLAE
Battle is joined again at
midmorning. The Hellenes
fight recklessly and
desperately, knowing they
are to die, and inflict high
casualties on the enemy.

7.224
480
THERMOPYLAE
Finally Leonidas and many
famous Spartans fall there
(Herodotus has learned all
their names), and many
eminent Persians.

7.225
480
THERMOPYLAE
The Hellenes rout the
Persians four times and retire
to the narrow pass for a last
stand when the men with
Ephialtes arrive.

Now those allies who had been dismissed left in obedience to Leonidas, and only the Thespians[a] and the Thebans[b] stayed behind with the Lacedaemonians. The Thebans did not want to be there, but Leonidas held them back, treating them as hostages and keeping them there against their will. The Thespians, however, were quite willing to stay; they refused to go away and to abandon Leonidas and his men; instead, they remained there to die with them. Their commander was Demophilos son of Diadromes.

At sunrise, Xerxes poured libations and then waited until about the time of peak market hour to make his attack. That is what Ephialtes had told him to do, since the way down the mountain was quicker and the ground they had to cover much shorter than the climb up and around the mountain. [2] Xerxes' men advanced, but so did the Hellenes with Leonidas, and since the latter were marching to their death, they now ventured much farther than they had at first onto the wider part of the strip of land, for on the preceding days they had been guarding the defensive wall[a] and had kept back to fight at the narrower part. [3] Now, however, they joined battle beyond that sector. Many of the barbarians fell, for the leaders of the regiments were behind them with whips, flogging each and every man and urging them ever forward. Many fell into the sea and died, but even more were trampled alive by one another. There was no counting the number of the dead. [4] The Hellenes knew they were about to face death at the hands of the men who had come around the mountain, and so they exerted their utmost strength against the barbarians, with reckless desperation and no regard for their own lives.

By this time most of their spears had broken, so they were slaying the Persians with their swords. And it was during this struggle that Leonidas fell, the man who had proved himself the most valiant of all, and with him those other famous Spartans whose names I have learned because I think they also proved themselves to be worthy men; indeed, I have learned the names of all 300 of them.[a] [2] Many Persians fell there, too, including some famous ones; in particular, two sons of Darius, Abrokomes and Hyperanthes, who had been born to Darius by Phratagoune daughter of Artanes. This Artanes was the brother of King Darius and the son of Hystaspes son of Arsames. After giving his daughter in marriage to Darius, he had given him also his whole estate, since she was his only child.

Two brothers of Xerxes also fell there, while they were fighting in the melée over the body of Leonidas, for the Persians and Lacedaemonians

7.222.1a   Thespiai: Map 7.213, AY.
7.222.1b   Thebes: Map 7.213, AY.
7.223.2a   How had the Hellenes used the wall? As
     a base from which to deploy? As
     shelter against Persian arrows? Herodotus does
     not say, although he mentions the wall
     three times (7.176.3–5, 7.208.2,

     7.215). See Appendix N, §10.
7.224.1a   Leonidas' body was brought to Sparta
     and buried there in 440; a column bearing
     the names of the 300 was erected on
     his grave, which was probably seen by
     Herodotus. (Godley)

engaged in a violent struggle over the corpse until the Hellenes, after rout-
ing their opponents four times, managed with great valor to drag it out and
away from the crowd. The fighting continued until the forces with Ephialtes
arrived. [2] When the Hellenes learned that they had come, the contest took
a different turn, as they retreated back to the narrow part of the road, and
after passing the wall, all of them except for the Thebans stationed themselves together upon the hill that is located at the place on the road where
the stone lion in honor of Leonidas now stands. [3] On this spot they tried
to defend themselves with their daggers if they still had them, or if not, with
their hands and their teeth. The barbarians pelted them with missiles, some
running up to face the Hellenes directly and demolishing the defensive wall,
and others coming to surround them on all sides.

Though the Lacedaemonians and the Thespians alike proved themselves
to be brave in this battle, it is said that the Spartan Dienekes proved himself to
be the most valiant man of all. It is reported that before the Hellenes engaged
the Medes in battle, one of the Trachinians said that there were so many barbarians that whenever they shot their arrows, the sun was blocked by their
number. [2] Dienekes was not alarmed to hear this but rather, in total disre-
gard for the vast numbers of Medes, said that what his Trachinian friend had
reported was in fact good news, since it meant that while the Medes were
blocking the sun, they would fight them in the shade.[a] This saying and others
like it have been left as memorials of Dienekes the Lacedaemonian.

After Dienekes, the most outstanding men in this battle are said to be
two Lacedaemonian brothers, Alpheos and Maron, sons of Orsiphantos. Of
the Thespians, the man who earned the highest distinction was named
Dithyrambos son of Harmatides.

They were buried just where they had fallen, and for these men as well as
for those who had met their end before Leonidas could send them away, an
inscription was erected which says:

> Three million foes were once fought right here
> By four thousand men from the Peloponnese.

[2] That inscription applied to them all, but the Spartans have one of
their own:

> Tell this, passerby, to the Lacedaemonians:
> It is here that we lie, their commands we obey.

7.226
480
THERMOPYLAE
The anecdote of Dienekes,
who, hearing that the huge
number of enemy missiles
would darken the sun, said
that he would prefer to fight
in the shade.

7.227
480
THERMOPYLAE
Other Hellenes who
gained renown.

7.228
480
THERMOPYLAE
Herodotus recounts some
epitaphs that were later
inscribed at Thermopylae
over the graves of Hellenes
who fell there to memorial-
ize them and the battle.

7.226.2a   Perhaps this anecdote reveals some-   fronting the Greek hoplite phalanx. See
thing about the Persian method of con-   Appendix O, §4–7.

[3] That inscription is for the Lacedaemonians, and this one, for the prophet:

> This is the monument of the famous Megistias,
> Slain by the Medes when they crossed the Sperchias.
> A prophet knowing for certain that Doom was approaching,
> Yet he could not endure to forsake Sparta's leaders.

[4] The first two of these inscriptions and pillars were set up in honor of these men by the Amphiktyones. Simonides son of Leoprepes had the monument to the prophet Megistias inscribed for the sake of friendship.[a]

It is said that two of the 300 men, Eurytos and Aristodemos, had the opportunity to return safely to Sparta[a] if only they had come to an agreement, since they had been released from the camp by Leonidas and were laid up in Alpenos[b] with the most serious cases of eye disease. Or, if they had not wanted to return home, they could die together with the others. Though it was possible for both of them to take either of these courses of action, they made different decisions about what to do. When Eurytos learned of the Persian advance around the mountain, he asked for his arms, put them on, and ordered his helot[c] to lead him to those who were fighting. After leading him to the fighting, the helot fled and disappeared from sight, while Eurytos charged into the raging battle and was killed. But Aristodemos was left behind, faint and feeble. [2] Now if it had been only Aristodemos who became ill and returned to Sparta, or if both of them alike had taken the journey home together, I do not think the Spartans would have been provoked to any wrath at all against them. When, however, one of them was slain and the other had the same excuse but was unwilling to die, it became inevitable that the Spartans would be stirred to great wrath against Aristodemos.

While some say that Aristodemos returned safely to Sparta and report the illness as his excuse, others say that he had been sent from the camp as a messenger; and that although he could have come back in time for the battle, he was unwilling to do so and instead lagged behind on his journey and thus survived, while his fellow messenger came back for the battle and died in it.

So after returning to Lacedaemon, Aristodemos met with disgrace and dishonor. The dishonor he suffered was that not a single Spartan would give him fire or speak to him, and his disgrace was that he was called "Aristodemos the Trembler." But at the battle of Plataea[a] he acquitted himself of all blame that had been cast upon him.

7.228.4a   Simonides son of Leoprepes, from Keos
        (556–468). Simonides is supposed to
        have composed all three inscriptions,
        but the epitaph of Megistias was the
        only one which he made at his own
        expense.
7.229.1a   Sparta: Map 7.213, BX.

7.229.1b   Alpenos: Map 7.213, inset.
7.229.1c   Spartiate hoplites were normally accompanied to war by helot servants. See Appendix B, §8.
7.231.1a   Plataea: Map 7.213, AY.

It is also said that another of these 300 men was sent away as a messenger to Thessaly and that he survived as well; his name was Pantites, and when he returned to Sparta, he suffered such dishonor that he hanged himself.

Now the Thebans, whose commander was Leontiades, fought alongside the Hellenes against the army of the King for a while, since they were being compelled to do so. But when they saw the Persian side prevailing and the Hellenes with Leonidas hurrying to the hill, the Thebans broke away and approached the barbarians with their hands outstretched, saying most truthfully that they had medized and had been among the first to give earth and water to the King, but had been compelled to come to Thermopylae, and were guiltless of inflicting any damages on the King. [2] By saying all this they survived, since they had the Thessalians as witnesses to their claims; they were not entirely fortunate, however. Some of them were seized and killed by the barbarians as they approached, and Xerxes ordered that a majority of the rest be branded with the royal marks, beginning with the commander Leontiades. The son of this Leontiades, Eurymachos, was murdered long after this by the Plataeans after he had taken the city of Plataea with 400 Thebans under his command.

That, then, is how the Hellenes fought at Thermopylae. Now Xerxes summoned Demaratos and questioned him, beginning, "Demaratos, you are a good man. My evidence for this is your past truthfulness, for everything has turned out just as you said it would. But now tell me how many Lacedaemonians are left, and how many of them are warriors like these men were, or are they all like this?" [2] Demaratos replied, "Sire, the total number of Lacedaemonians is quite large, and they have many cities. But I will tell you now what you really want to know. In Lacedaemon there is a city called Sparta, with about 8,000 men living in it,[a] and these men are all the equals of those who fought here, while the other Lacedaemonians are not, though they are good men." [3] Xerxes responded, asking, "Demaratos, what would be the easiest way for us to conquer these men? Come now, give me your expert advice, for you know the details of how they plan their strategies, since you were once their king."

Demaratos replied, "Sire, if you really are seeking my advice in earnest, it is only right that I should give you the best counsel that I can. Suppose you were to send 300 ships from your fleet to Laconian territory. [2] Well, lying off the coast of that land is an island by the name of Cythera.[a] And Chilon,[b] the wisest man among our people, once said that the Spartans could profit

---

7.232
480
SPARTA
Another Spartan who survived dishonored.

7.233
480
THERMOPYLAE
The Thebans surrendered when they could, saying they had been forced to fight against the Persians. Some were killed, and many of the rest were branded by the Persians.

7.234
480
THERMOPYLAE
Xerxes questions Demaratos, admitting that what he had said had proved true, asking him for advice on how to overcome the Spartans at least cost to the Persians.

7.235
480
THERMOPYLAE
Demaratos advises Xerxes to send a naval force to occupy Cythera and to carry the war from there directly against Sparta to embroil the Spartans at home. He predicts that if the Persians do not do this, they will face harder and more costly battles than Thermopylae at the Isthmus of Corinth.

7.234.2a   For the significance of this number of men and the precipitous decline in Spartan manpower after 480, see Appendix B, §17.
7.235.2a   Cythera: Map 7.213, locator.
7.235.2b   Chilon was almost certainly the ephor of 556/55 regarded in antiquity as one of the seven wise men, who were accorded divine honors in Sparta. (Pau-

sanias 3.16.4) This remark about Cythera was astonishingly prophetic, for one could hardly suppose that the island was a source of danger to Sparta in the mid-sixth century. Perhaps Herodotus wrote it down after the Athenians seized the island in 424 in the Archidamian War (431–421). (*Thucydides* 4.53)

more if this island would sink into the sea than they could if it continued to remain above water. He said this because he always expected that something like what I am now advising you to do would happen someday. He, of course, had no advance knowledge of your expedition, but he feared any and all such expeditions conducted by men. [3] My advice is that you should use this island as your base to frighten the Lacedaemonians. If they have a war of their own at home, you will then be able to conquer the rest of Hellas with your land army and not have to fear that they will come to the assistance of the other Hellenes. Then, when the rest of Hellas has been enslaved, Laconia will be the only land left to oppose you, and it will be a weakened one at that.

[4] "If you do not follow this advice, however, this is what you should expect. There is, at the entrance to the Peloponnese, a narrow isthmus[a] where all the Peloponnesians who will form a solemn league against you will join forces. There you may expect to face more difficult battles than those that have been fought so far. But if you do as I say, this isthmus and the cities will surrender to you without a fight."

After these words of Demaratos, Achaimenes, a brother of Xerxes and a commander of the fleet, spoke up. He had happened to be present and was afraid that Xerxes would be persuaded to take Demaratos' advice. "Sire," he said, "I can see that you approve of the words of this man who envies your success or perhaps is even acting treacherously against you and your interests. For these are exactly the sorts of things that Hellenes delight in doing. They envy prosperity and hate whoever is better and stronger than themselves. [2] Now in our present situation, having lost 400 ships wrecked in the storm, if you were to send 300 more ships from our fleet to sail around the Peloponnese, your adversary's fleet will certainly be a match for you in battle. But if our fleet stays concentrated, it will be very difficult for them to deal with it, and they will be no match for you at all. By keeping your entire fleet together, it can then assist your army, and the army can travel with the support of your fleet. But if you divide your fleet, you will not be able to help the separated forces, nor will they be able to help you. [3] So decide on a course that well serves your own interests instead of concerning yourself with your enemies: where they will take a stand to fight you, or what they will do, or how many of them there are. For they are quite capable of thinking for themselves, just as we are for ourselves. And even if the Lacedaemonians do advance against the Persians for battle, they will in no way be able to heal the injuries they have now suffered."

7.235.4a   Isthmus of Corinth: Map 7.213, BY.

7.236
480
THERMOPYLAE
Achaimenes advises Xerxes not to follow Demaratos' advice. He asserts that all Hellenes hate power and are jealous of success. He advises that the Persians keep their forces concentrated as they advance, and predicts that Sparta will not recover from recent losses.

DEMARATOS = Like Croesus

Xerxes replied, "Achaimenes, I think that you have given good advice, and I shall certainly follow it. Although Demaratos advised me to do what he thinks would be the best plan for me, his judgment has proved inferior to yours. [2] But I do not accept at all your assertion that he is antagonistic to my interests when I weigh what he said before, as well as the fact that a citizen normally envies another citizen who is successful and shows his hostility by his silence; he refuses to give good advice when consulted by someone from his own community unless he has attained a high degree of virtue—but men like this are rare. [3] And a guest-friend[a] is the most benevolent of all toward his guest-friend when the latter succeeds, and will give him the best advice when consulted; so since Demaratos is my guest-friend, I forbid anyone to utter any slander against him ever again."

After having said this, Xerxes made his way among the corpses, including that of Leonidas. Having heard that Leonidas was a king and the commander of the Lacedaemonians, he ordered that his head be cut off and impaled on a stake. [2] For me this is the clearest of many proofs that King Xerxes felt greater animosity for Leonidas while he was still alive than he felt for any other man. Otherwise he would not have treated the corpse so outrageously, since of all the peoples I know of, the Persians especially honor men who are good at waging war. So now, those to whom he had given these orders duly carried them out.

I shall now go back to a detail of my account that I left unexplained before. The Lacedaemonians had been the first to learn that the King would lead an expedition against Hellas, and so had sent to consult the oracle at Delphi,[a] to which they received the response I quoted a little earlier.[b] But the way in which they received this news is quite extraordinary. [2] When Demaratos son of Ariston was in exile among the Medes, I do not believe—and here reason is my ally—that he had goodwill toward the Lacedaemonians, though one may conjecture whether he acted out of benevolence or out of spiteful satisfaction. For when Xerxes resolved to lead an expedition against Hellas, Demaratos was in Susa,[a] and upon learning Xerxes' plans, immediately wanted to communicate this information to the Lacedaemonians. [3] There was a risk that he would be caught, so there was no other way he could inform them except by the following scheme. Taking a double writing tablet, he scraped off the wax and inscribed the plan of the King onto the wood of the tablet. After doing this, he melted some wax back over what he had written, so that the tablet would be apparently blank and thus cause no trouble from the guards as it was conveyed to

7.237
480
THERMOPYLAE
Xerxes decides to follow Achaimenes' advice, but praises Demaratos as a friend and trustworthy adviser.

7.238
480
THERMOPYLAE
Xerxes orders that the head of Leonidas should be cut off and impaled.

7.239
485?
SUSA
How Demaratos used a clever trick to send a message of warning to the Spartans of the aggressive plans of the Persians, and how Gorgo, Kleomenes' daughter, discovered the message.

7.237.3a   Guest-friendship (*xenia*): a bond of ritualized friendship, usually between aristocrats or prominent men of different cities. It was passed down through generations and required hereditary privileges and obligations such as reciprocal hospitality and assistance. See Appendix T, §3.
7.239.1a   Delphi: Map 7.213, AX.
7.239.1b   Herodotus refers here to 7.220, where he mentioned that the Spartans received early

intelligence of Xerxes' plans against Hellas. Only now does he tell us that the warning came from the exiled Spartan king Demaratos, whose hidden message was perceived by Kleomenes' daughter Gorgo. As a child she warned her father against the corrupting bribery of Aristagoras (5.51.3); as an adult, she became the wife of King Leonidas. See Appendix B, §24.
7.239.2a   Susa: Map 7.186, locator.

its destination. [4] When it arrived at Lacedaemon, the Lacedaemonians could not understand what it meant until, according to what I have heard, Gorgo the daughter of Kleomenes[a] and wife of Leonidas deduced the answer herself. She ordered them to scrape off the wax, and said that they would then discover a message written on the wood. When they followed her advice, they did discover the message and, after reading it, dispatched the news to the rest of the Hellenes. That, then, is how this is said to have happened.

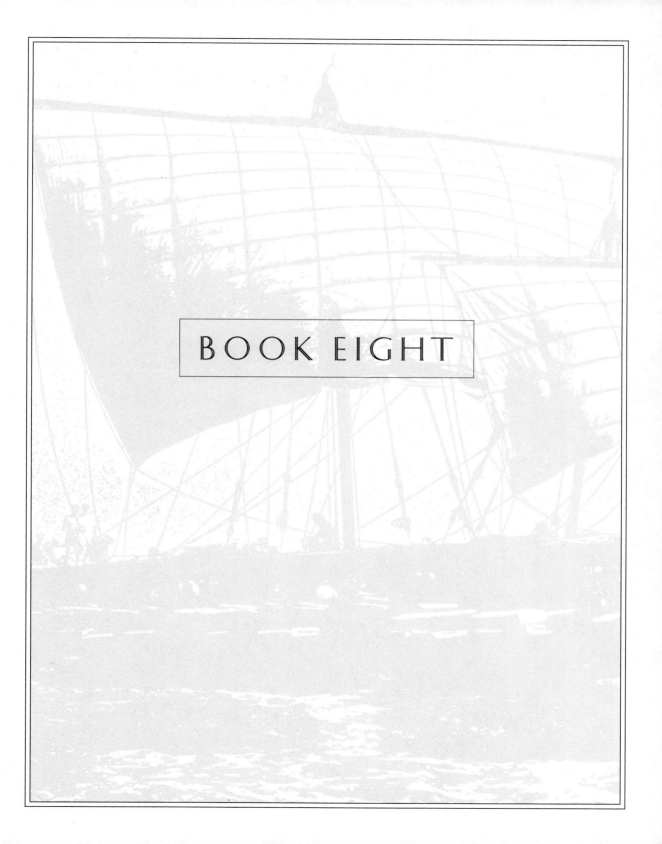

BOOK EIGHT

Those are the Hellenes who were
assigned to the fleet. The Athenians[a] provided 127 ships, to which the
Plataeans[b] contributed men, serving eagerly and valorously despite their
inexperience at sea. The Corinthians[c] supplied forty ships, and the Megarians[d] twenty. [2] The Chalcidians[a] manned twenty ships that the Athenians
provided to them; the Aeginetans[b] furnished eighteen; the Sicyonians,[c]
twelve; the Lacedaemonians,[d] ten; the Epidaurians,[e] eight; the Eretrians,[f]
seven; the Troizenians,[g] five; the Styrians[h] two; and the Keans,[i] two ships
and two penteconters. The Opuntian Locrians[j] also came to help, adding
seven penteconters to the fleet.

Those were the forces serving at Artemision,[a] and I have listed them in
the order of the number of ships each provided. The total number of ships
gathered at Artemision was 271, not counting the penteconters. [2] The
Spartans provided the commander who had supreme authority over them
all, Eurybiades son of Eurykleides. For the allies had refused to follow
Athenian leaders and had asserted that unless a Laconian led them, they
would call off the anticipated assembly of their armed forces.

In fact, at the very beginning, even before they had sent envoys to Sicily,[a]
to seek an alliance, there had been talk that the Athenians should be placed
in charge of the fleet. But the allies resisted this proposal, and the Athenians
yielded to them because they considered the survival of Hellas of paramount
importance, and they knew that if they quarreled over the leadership, Hellas

8.1
480
ARTEMISION
The composition by city
of the Greek fleet.

8.2
480
ARTEMISION
Athens provides almost
half the ships, but the allies
insist that a Spartan must
command the fleet.

8.3
480
ISTHMUS OF CORINTH?
When the allies resist
Athens' claim to lead the
fleet, the Athenians give
way, in the interest of the
safety of Hellas.

8.1.1a Athens: Map 8.3, BY. Scholars agree that
Herodotus means warships—specifically,
triremes—in this list as against merchant or
cargo ships, but he employs the general
word for "ships." For descriptions of warships such as triremes and penteconters, see
Appendix S, Trireme Warfare in Herodotus,
§4–7.
8.1.1b Plataea: Map 8.3, BX.
8.1.1c Corinth: Map 8.3, BX.
8.1.1d Megara: Map 8.3, BX.
8.1.2a Chalcis (Euboea): Map 8.3, BY.
8.1.2b Aegina: Map 8.3, BX.
8.1.2c Sicyon: Map 8.3, BX.
8.1.2d Lacedaemon (Sparta): Map 8.3, BX.

Herodotus uses the names Spartans and
Lacedaemonians interchangeably. "Spartans,"
however, often refers specifically to citizens of
the state of Sparta, whereas any inhabitant of
the territory of Lacedaemon is a Lacedaemonian. See Appendix B, The Spartan State
in War and Peace, §5, 7, and n. B.7a.
8.1.2e Epidauros: Map 8.3, BX.
8.1.2f Eretria, Euboea: Map 8.3, BY.
8.1.2g Troizen: Map 8.3, BX.
8.1.2h Styra: Map 8.3, BY.
8.1.2i Keos: Map 8.3, BY.
8.1.2j Locris (Opuntian): Map 8.3, AX.
8.2.1a Artemision: Map 8.3, AX.
8.3.1a Sicily: Map 8.3, locator.

would be destroyed. They were indeed quite right in this, for compared to a united war effort, internal quarrels are as bad as war itself is when compared to peace. [2] And so, because they were well aware of this, they yielded and did not resist, but they did so only for as long as they really needed the allies, as they later demonstrated. For after the Persian had been repulsed, when they were then fighting over his lands, they took the leadership from the Lacedaemonians—their pretext being the arrogance of Pausanias. But of course, all that happened later.

8.4
480
ARTEMISION
Seeing the size of the enemy fleet, the Hellenes lose heart and consider flight. Failing to persuade Eurybiades to stay and fight, the Euboeans offer a bribe to Themistokles.

At this time, the Hellenes who had come to Artemision saw the many ships that had put in at Aphetai[a] and the whole place packed full of troops, and since the current condition of the barbarians was quite contrary to their expectations, they grew frightened and deliberated about fleeing from Artemision back toward mainland Hellas. [2] When the Euboeans[a] realized what was being planned, they petitioned Eurybiades to wait for a little while until they could rescue their children and the other members of their households. But when they were unable to persuade him to wait, they changed their tactics and offered Themistokles, the commander of the Athenians, a bribe of thirty talents[a] to make the Hellenes remain there and fight a sea battle in defense of Euboea.

8.5
480
ARTEMISION
Themistokles bribes the Spartan and Corinthian commanders to stay. They assume that Athens has supplied his funds, but he actually uses a small part of the Euboean money he received to persuade him to stay.

Themistokles managed to prevent the Hellenes from leaving by giving over five talents of his bribe to Eurybiades, pretending that he was giving it out of his own funds. And after he had thus persuaded Eurybiades, the only remaining commander who put up a struggle was Adeimantos son of Okytos, the commander of the Corinthian ships, who asserted that he would refuse to stay there and was going to sail away from Artemision. Themistokles said to him, and swore it on oath, [2] "Surely you will not leave us, since I shall give you a gift more generous than that which the king of the Medes would send to you if you deserted the allies." And without a moment's delay, he sent three talents of silver to the ship of Adeimantos. [3] These men were both overwhelmed by the bribes and were thus persuaded, which pleased the Euboeans, while Themistokles made a good profit for himself, keeping the rest of the money without anyone's knowing; for those who had received a share of this money were convinced that it had come from Athens for this very purpose.

8.6
480
ARTEMISION
The Persians are eager to bring on a battle, but fear that the Hellenes will flee from a direct attack.

And so they stayed at Euboea and fought a battle at sea. What happened was this. The barbarians had arrived at Aphetai early in the afternoon already knowing that a few Greek ships were stationed at Artemision. And when they actually saw them there, they became eager to attack in an attempt to capture them. [2] But they thought it best not to sail straight for them head on, lest the Hellenes would see them coming and hurry to escape while evening fell and sheltered them in their flight. They were certain that the Hellenes would try to escape, but in their plans the Persians hoped that not even a torchbearer would escape and survive.[a]

8.4.1a   Aphetai, possible location: Map 8.3, AX.
8.4.2a   Euboea: Map 8.3, AY.
8.4.2b   A talent was a unit of weight and a large amount of money. See Appendix J, Ancient Greek Units of Currency,

    Weight, and Distance, §11–13, 20.
8.6.2a   The torchbearer's duty was to carry fire to the altar, and he was therefore considered inviolable.

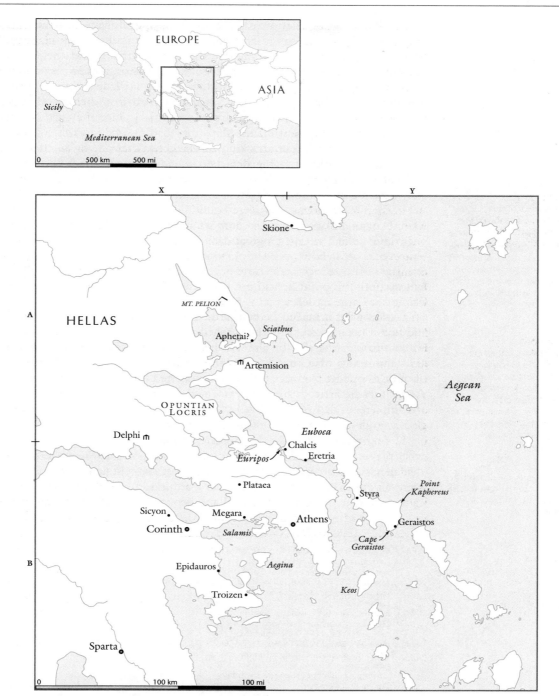

MAP 8.3

8.7
480
EUBOEA
The Persians send 200 ships to sail around Euboea and cut off the Greek retreat.

8.8
480
ARTEMISION
Skyllias from Skione escapes to the Hellenes and informs them of the shipwreck and of the fleet that the Persians have sent around Euboea to trap them.

8.9
480
ARTEMISION
The Hellenes decide to offer battle late in the day, to test their enemy's methods of fighting.

In view of this situation, they contrived the following scheme. They detached 200 ships from the fleet and sent them to sail around the outside of Sciathus[a] so that the Hellenes would not see them, and then to sail around Euboea past Kaphereus[b] and around Geraistos[c] and up through the Euripos.[d] That way the Persians could trap the Hellenes, since the ships coming by this route would block off their retreat from behind while the rest of the fleet attacked them from the front. [2] Once they had decided on this strategy, they sent off the ships they had assigned to this squadron. They had no intention of attacking the Hellenes that day or any day until the signal appeared from the detached squadron to let them know of its arrival.[a] And while they were sending these ships off to sail around Euboea, they took a count of their ships that remained at Aphetai.

In the meantime, as they were counting their ships, there was a man of Skione[a] named Skyllias in their camp who was the best diver in the world at that time; he had salvaged a great deal of property for the Persians from the shipwrecks off Pelion[b] and had obtained a lot of it for himself, too. Skyllias, it turned out, had for some time been intending to desert to the Hellenes, but up until this point he had not been given an opportunity to do so. [2] I cannot say for certain exactly how he came to the Hellenes, but I am amazed at what is said to be true: that he dived into the sea at Aphetai and did not come up again until he reached Artemision, after swimming underwater through the sea for almost nine miles.[a] [3] There are other stories told about this man that also sound like lies, though some are true, but about this one let me voice the opinion that he came to Artemision by boat. As soon as he arrived there, he informed the commanding generals about the shipwrecks that had occurred in the storm and also about the ships that had been detached and sent off to sail around Euboea.

Upon hearing this news, the Hellenes began to discuss among themselves what they should do. Of all that was said, the proposal that won the day was that they should remain there until it was past the middle of the night, and then sail out to confront the ships sailing around Euboea. But since no ships came to threaten them, they stayed and kept watch until the late afternoon

8.7.1a Sciathus: Map 8.3, AX.
8.7.1b Point Kaphereus: Map 8.3, BY.
8.7.1c Geraistos (city and cape): Map 8.3, BY.
8.7.1d Euripos (the narrow straits between Euboea and the mainland near Chalcis): Map 8.3, BX. The channel there is 120 feet wide. Strong and unpredictable currents run through it.
8.7..2a Many scholars have seriously questioned Herodotus' story of the abortive circumnavigation of Euboea. This would have involved a voyage of 250 nautical miles by a fleet not significantly larger than the Greek fleet in the area, which, if it were attacked, could not be supported by other Persian fleet elements, and which would be entirely out of contact with Persian headquarters. Moreover, if the circumnaviga-

tion had an important part to play in the action against the Greek fleet, its voyage would have had to go entirely on schedule—which is rare in war. Since Herodotus reports that this squadron was completely destroyed by a storm (8.13), it is possible that the story was invented to reduce the wildly improbable total of ships in the Persian fleet to a more sensible figure. See n. 8.13.1b.
8.8.1a Skione: Map 8.3, AY.
8.8.1b Mount Pelion: Map 8.3, AX. The storm that wrecked these ships was described in 7.188.
8.8.2a Herodotus writes the distance as "80 stades." See Distance Conversions, p. lxiv, and Appendix J, Ancient Greek Units of Currency, Weight, and Distance, §6, 19.

FIGURE 8.10. THE MODERN TRIREME *OLYMPIAS* UNDER SAIL. IT WAS FIRST LAUNCHED IN 1987 AND SAILED AS A SHIP OF THE GREEK NAVY.

of the day before sailing out against the barbarians. They hoped to test their enemies in battle and in their use of the breakthrough maneuver.[a]

When Xerxes' soldiers and commanders saw the Hellenes sailing at them in their few ships, they assumed they were utterly mad. They now brought their own ships out to sea, expecting to capture the Greek ships easily, which was a very reasonable expectation, as they could see that the Hellenes had only a small number of ships and that they had many times more, and that their own were in better sailing condition, too. So it was with pride and contempt that they surrounded the Hellenes in a circle of their ships.[a] [2] Now the Ionians[a] who were benevolent toward the Hellenes were unwilling to join in the fight and thought it a grave misfortune to watch them being encircled and to realize that not one of them was ever going to return home again—so weak did the cause of the Hellenes appear to them at the time. [3] But other Ionians were delighted by what was happening and competed with one another to see who could be the first to capture a ship from Attica and thus receive rewards from the King. For throughout their camps most of the talk centered on the Athenians.

8.10
480
ARTEMISION
The Persians eagerly advance and surround the Hellenes with their superior numbers. Some Ionians sailing with the Persians are distressed to see the Hellenes in such peril.

8.9.1a   The breakthrough maneuver: *diekplous*; see 6.12.1 with note and Appendix S, §13. Herodotus is vague about the day or days on which these events took place.

8.10.1a   See Figure 8.10. For more on triremes and the trireme *Olympias*, see Appendix S, §3–8, 15.
8.10.2a   Ionia in Asia Minor: Map 8.16, locator.

8.11
480
ARTEMISION
After adopting a hedgehog defense, the Hellenes attack and acquit themselves well before nightfall ends the engagement.

When the Hellenes got the signal, the first thing they did was to turn the prows of their ships outward to face the barbarians, drawing their sterns close together toward a central point. At the second signal, they applied themselves to the work at hand, though hemmed within a confined space and facing the enemy ships head on. [2] In the battle that ensued, they took thirty of the barbarians' ships, and captured a man of great importance in the barbarian forces, Philaon son of Chersis, the brother of Gorgos, the king of the Salaminians.[a] The first of the Hellenes to capture an enemy ship was an Athenian, Lykomedes son of Aischraios, and it was he who won the prize for valor. [3] The contest was still undecided when night fell and parted the two sides. After a struggle that had thus turned out quite contrary to their expectations, the Hellenes sailed back to Artemision,[a] and the barbarians to Aphetai.[b] In this battle, Antidoros of Lemnos[c] was the only one of the Hellenes accompanying the King who deserted to the Greek side, and in reward for this feat, the Athenians gave him land on Salamis.[d]

8.12
480
APHETAI
A storm from Pelion drives the dead and wrecks toward the dismayed Persians at Aphetai.

Evening fell, and although it was the season of midsummer, heavy rains poured down without stopping throughout the entire night, and violent thunder boomed off Mount Pelion.[a] Corpses and wreckage were carried to shore at Aphetai, collecting around the prows of the ships and chaotically tumbling into and becoming tangled in the blades of the oars. [2] When the Persian troops heard this, they began to panic, expecting that they would be utterly destroyed, so terrible were the adversities that they had by now encountered, for even before they could catch their breath from the shipwrecks and the storm raging off Pelion, they were confronted by a fierce sea battle and after that by torrential rains and mighty torrents that teemed into the sea with violent thunder.

8.13
480
EUBOEA
~~The same storm drives the Persian fleet sailing around Euboea onto the rocks and destroys it.~~

That is how they passed the night, but for those who had been detached to sail around Euboea, this same night was much more savage still, as it fell upon them while they were sailing out on the open sea, and their end was grim indeed. The tempest and the rain descended upon them as they were sailing off the Hollows of Euboea;[a] they were carried along by the wind without being able to see where they were going, and were wrecked on the rocks along the coast. All this was the god's doing, so that the Persian side would be equal to instead of much greater than the Greek side.[b]

8.14
480
ARTEMISION
The Hellenes are encouraged by the further Persian losses and by the arrival of reinforcements from Athens. Late in the day they attack again, successfully.

Thus these men perished at the Hollows of Euboea.

As for the barbarians at Aphetai, they were glad when day dawned, and made no move with their ships, content for the moment to remain at ease after having fared so badly before this. And now fifty-three ships from Attica came to the aid of the Hellenes, [2] who were encouraged by their

8.11.2a   Gorgos was king of the city of Salamis on Cyprus: Map 8.16, locator. See 5.104.
8.11.3a   Artemision: Map 8.16.
8.11.3b   Aphetai, possible location: Map 8.16.
8.11.3c   Lemnos: Map 8.16.
8.11.3d   Salamis (Attic), the Athenian island just west of Athens: Map 8.16.
8.12.1a   Mount Pelion: Map 8.16. Heavy rainstorms are extremely rare in summer in Greece.

8.13.1a   Hollows of Euboea: location unknown; probably on the southwestern coast of Euboea (Map 8.16), which is rocky and dangerous for ships.
8.13.1b   This remarkable statement deserves attention! Despite Herodotus' totals elsewhere, he seems here to be saying that the two naval forces were equal when it came to a battle.

arrival as well as by news they received at the same time, that all the barbarians sailing around Euboea had perished in the storm that had fallen upon them. So after waiting most of the day, they sailed out at the same hour as they had before and attacked some Cilician[a] ships and destroyed them. Then, when evening fell, they sailed back to Artemision.

By the third day, however, the commanders of the barbarians, thinking it terrible to have incurred such disgrace in an engagement with so few ships, and fearing what Xerxes might do, no longer waited for the Hellenes to initiate battle, but prepared for it themselves and put out to sea in their ships at midday. It just so happened that these sea battles were waged during the very same days as the land battles at Thermopylae.[a] [2] For the Hellenes at sea, the whole struggle was to maintain control of the Euripos, just as for those on land with Leonidas, it was to block the pass. The battle cry of the Hellenes was to prevent the barbarians from entering Hellas, while that of the barbarians was to destroy the Greek forces and secure a passage into Hellas.

Xerxes' men drew up their ships for battle and advanced to attack, while the Hellenes, making no move, remained in position off Artemision. But when the barbarians formed a crescent with their ships and began to encircle them in order to trap them, the Hellenes sailed out and engaged them in battle. In this fight, the two sides turned out to be just about an even match for each other. [2] For Xerxes' forces failed by reason of their own size and numbers; their ships chaotically crashed into one another and were wrecked. Nevertheless, they held out and would not give way, since they thought it would be terrible to be put to flight by such a small force. [3] Many Greek ships and men were lost there, but many more of the barbarians' ships and men were destroyed. The fight continued until the two sides broke off the engagement and parted from each other.

In this sea battle, the Egyptians distinguished themselves as the best of Xerxes' forces; they performed several great feats, and in particular, they captured five Greek ships with their crews. As for the Hellenes, the Athenians performed the best on this day, and of them the best was Kleinias son of Alkibiades, who was serving in their forces at his own private expense, providing 200 men and his own ship.

When the two sides parted, each gladly hurried to its anchorage. After the Hellenes had disengaged from the battle and were done with fighting, they secured control over the corpses and the wrecked ships. They had suffered rough treatment—especially the Athenians, who had half of their ships disabled in the battle. They now made plans to escape back into the inner waters of mainland Hellas.

8.14.2a   Cilicia: Map 8.16, locator.
8.15.1a   Thermopylae: Map 8.16.
8.15.2a   Euripos: Map 8.16.

8.15
480
ARTEMISION
After three days, the Persian commanders order their fleet to attack, simultaneously with their land assaults.

8.16
480
ARTEMISION
The naval battle off Artemision is indecisive. Both sides have successes and losses.

8.17
480
ARTEMISION
Of the combatants, the Egyptians and Athenians fought best.

8.18
480
ARTEMISION
Both sides retire with losses. The Hellenes decide to retreat.

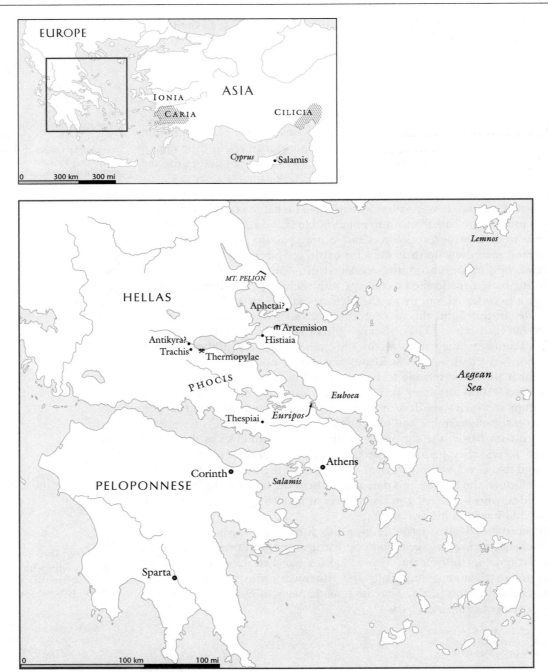

MAP 8.16

Now Themistokles perceived that if the Ionians[a] and Carians[b] could be detached from the barbarian forces, the Hellenes might then prevail over the rest. As the Euboeans were driving their flocks toward the sea, he convened a meeting of the commanders and told them that he had a scheme which he hoped would induce the best of the King's allies to desert. [2] That is all he would reveal of his plan, but he did tell them that, given their current circumstances, they should kill as many of the flocks as they wanted, since it was better that they, rather than their enemies, should have them. He advised all of them to order their men to light fires, and said that he would arrange the time of their departure to assure their safe return to Hellas unharmed. They were happy to do as he said, and at once they started fires and turned their attention to the flocks.

The Euboeans had earlier disregarded an oracle of Bakis,[a] thinking it had no significance, and had neither carried away any belongings nor laid up any provisions in preparation for the coming war.[b] Thus they themselves were responsible for the reversal of their fortunes, [2] for this oracle of Bakis had said:

> When he who speaks a barbarian tongue
> casts into the brine a yoke of papyrus,
> See to it then that loud-bleating goats are away from Euboea.

In their circumstances at the time, they had paid no attention to these verses, nor did they heed them in view of future evils, and it turned out that, having ignored them, they now had to pay all the more attention to their present misfortune.

While the Hellenes were doing this, the lookout from Trachis[a] arrived. Polyas of Antikyra[b] had been stationed as a lookout at Artemision.[c] He had a boat already fitted out and ready to go so that if the Greek fleet should be beaten, he could convey this news to those at Thermopylae. In the same way, the Athenian Abronichos son of Lysikles stood by with Leonidas, having a triaconter[d] ready to bring news to those at Artemision in case anything happened to the army on land. [2] Now at this point, Abronichos arrived and informed them of what had happened to Leonidas and his troops, and when they heard this news, they no longer considered whether to delay their departure but set out on their voyage, each contingent in its assigned position, with the Corinthians[a] first and the Athenians last.

Themistokles next picked out the most seaworthy ships of the Athenians and, making his way to the coastal sites that had drinking water, carved a message into the rocks for the Ionians to read the next day when they came to Artemision. The message said, "Men of Ionia, you do not do what is right

8.19
480
EUBOEA
Themistokles hopes to neutralize the Ionian and Carian allies of the Persians. He orders his men to slaughter what they can of the Euboean flocks and to light fires to hide their departure.

8.20
480
EUBOEA
How the Euboeans ignored the oracle of Bakis, to their cost.

8.21
480
ARTEMISION
The Greek fleet learns by messenger of the annihilation of the Hellenes at Thermopylae and departs immediately.

8.22
480
EUBOEA
Themistokles leaves messages engraved on rocks asking the Ionians and Carians to desert, or at least to hang back, if they cannot desert.

8.19.1a   Ionia: Map 8.16, locator.
8.19.1b   Caria: Map 8.16, locator.
8.20.1a   Herodotus writes about Bakis as if that was the name of a writer of oracles. *The Oxford Classical Dictionary* asserts that it was a generic name of a class of inspired prophets.
8.20.1b   This error by the Euboeans was not unusual. See Appendix P, Oracles, Religion, and Politics in Herodotus, §13.
8.21.1a   Trachis: Map 8.16.
8.21.1b   Antikyra, possible location: Map 8.16.
8.21.1c   Artemision: Map 8.16.
8.21.1d   Triaconter: old-fashioned warship rowed by thirty oarsmen, fifteen on a side.
8.21.2a   Corinth: Map 8.16.

[handwritten annotation in top margin: UNJUST TO REDUCE OTHERS TO SLAVERY]

and just by going to war against your fathers and reducing Hellas to slavery. [2] The best thing for you to do would be to come over to our side, but if that is impossible for you, then you should even now at this point assume a posture of neutrality and ask the Carians to do the same. If neither of these options is possible and you are constrained by a yoke so tight that you cannot revolt from it, then when the forces are engaged and you are in the midst of the action, you should deliberately fight like cowards, remembering that you have been born of us and that from the very beginning, you have been the source of the hostility between us and the barbarian."[a] [3] That is what Themistokles wrote, and I suppose he had two possibilities in mind: either the message would go unnoticed by the King and would induce the Ionians to change sides and come over to the Hellenes, or, if someone reported it and complained to Xerxes, it would render the Ionians untrustworthy in his judgment and ensure that he kept them from participating in the sea battles.

So that was the message Themistokles inscribed, and immediately afterward a man of Histiaia[a] in a boat came to the barbarians and told them that the Hellenes had fled from Artemision. In disbelief, they kept him under guard and dispatched swift ships to look around. The crews of the ships reported the truth of the matter, and then, just as the sun was beginning to diffuse through the sky, the whole fleet sailed together to Artemision. [2] The Persian forces lingered there until midday and then sailed off to Histiaia. When they arrived there, they took possession of the city of the Histiaians and the territory of Hellopia,[a] overrunning all the coastal villages of the land of Histiaiotis.

While they were in Histiaia, Xerxes arranged the bodies of the dead and sent a herald to his fleet. Of all the corpses from his own army at Thermopylae (and there were actually about 20,000 of them), he left about 1,000 on the battlefield and buried the rest in a trench he had excavated, heaping earth over them and throwing leaves on top so that they would not be visible to the men of his fleet. [2] When the herald had crossed over to Histiaia, he convened an assembly of the entire camp and addressed the men, saying, "Allies, Xerxes grants leave to anyone who would like to do so to quit his post and come see how he does battle against ignorant people who had hoped to surpass the power of the King."

When he made this announcement, there were so many who wished to view the battlefield that nothing was harder to find than a boat. After they were conveyed across, they viewed the corpses as they made their way through them. And everyone was certain that those lying there were all Lacedaemonians[a] and Thespians,[b] though they were also looking at

8.22.2a Herodotus has Themistokles assert that the Ionian Revolt led to the Persian invasion of the Greek mainland, since the Athenians had helped the Ionians and so provoked the King to retaliate. This view is again expressed by the Spartan messengers sent to the Athenians in 479 (8.142), by Mardonios in the debate at the Persian court (7.5.2), and by Xerxes himself (7.8.β.1). It is, of course, highly unlikely

that Herodotus had any real information about what went on in the King's inner councils. He is here reflecting what some Greeks said among themselves about the cause of the war. (Cawkwell)
8.23.1a Histiaia: Map 8.16.
8.23.2a Hellopia: an older term for the northern half of the island of Euboea (Map 8.16).
8.25.1a Lacedaemon (Sparta): Map 8.16.
8.25.1b Thespiai: Map 8.16.

helots.[c] [2] But those who had crossed over were well aware of what Xerxes had done with the corpses of his own troops, for that really was quite absurd. Of their own side, they could see 1,000 bodies lying dead there, while all those from the enemy's side had been brought together and were lying in the same place—4,000 bodies in all. [3] So they spent all of this day viewing the battlefield, but on the next day some sailed off to rejoin their ships at Histiaia, while others set out on the land route with Xerxes.

Now a few deserters from Arcadia[a] had come to them who needed to make a living and wanted employment.[b] The Persians led them into the presence of the King and inquired of them what the Hellenes were doing, there being one Persian who asked the question on behalf of them all. [2] The Arcadians told them that the Hellenes were celebrating the Olympic[a] festival and watching an athletic competition and an equestrian contest. When he asked what prize they were competing for, they told him that the winner would receive an olive wreath. At that, Tritantaichmes son of Artabanos expressed a most noble insight which, however, made the King consider him a coward from that day on, [3] for when he heard that their prize was an olive wreath rather than money, he could not bear to keep quiet, but cried out to them all, "Good grief, Mardonios, what kind of men did you lead us here to fight, who compete not for money but for excellence alone?"

That was his reaction to the Hellenes' response. Meanwhile, right after the defeat at Thermopylae, the Thessalians[a] sent a herald to the Phocians,[b] because they had always felt bitter anger toward them, and it was at this moment extremely intense due to the recent disaster. [2] For not many years before this expedition of the King, the Thessalians and their allies had invaded Phocian territory in full force and had suffered rough treatment by them, and indeed were defeated. [3] The Phocians had taken refuge on Mount Parnassus,[a] and they had with them the prophet Tellias of Elis,[b] who devised a clever stratagem for them. He made 600 of the best Phocian men completely white with chalk, did the same to their weapons, and had them attack the Thessalians at night, with the order that they should kill anyone they saw who was not chalky white like they were. [4] The Thessalian sentries were the first to see them, and they immediately panicked, supposing that they were seeing some strange portent. After the sentries, the troops themselves saw them and panicked as well, so the result was that the Phocians took possession of 4,000 corpses and shields, half of which they dedicated at Abai[a] and the rest at Delphi.[b] [5] The tithe of their profits from this battle was the huge statues standing together around the tripod in front of the temple at Delphi, and another group like those set up at Abai.

8.26
480
THERMOPYLAE
Questioned by the Persians, Arcadian deserters say that the Hellenes are celebrating the Olympic festival, where they contend in sport for olive-wreath crowns, which amazes Tritantaichmes son of Artabanos.

GREEKS COMPETE FOR EXCELLENCE ALONE

8.27
480
PHOCIS
How the Phocians defeated and panicked the Thessalian infantry several years earlier in a night assault, from the spoils of which they dedicated great statues at Delphi and Abai.

8.25.1c Helots often accompanied Spartiate hoplites on campaign as servants; see Appendix B, §8.
8.26.1a Arcadia: Map 8.32, locator.
8.26.1b On mercenaries, see Appendix N, Hoplite Warfare in Herodotus, §9.
8.26.2a Olympia: Map 8.32, locator.
8.27.1a Thessaly: Map 8.32, locator.

8.27.1b Phocis: Map 8.32, BX.
8.27.3a Mount Parnassus: Map 8.32, AX.
8.27.3b Elis: Map 8.32, locator.
8.27.4a Abai: Map 8.32, AY.
8.27.4b Delphi: Map 8.32, BX. The tithe was one-tenth of a gain or revenue, the portion set aside for the god as a thanks offering.

8.28
480
PHOCIS
How the Phocians defeated the Thessalian cavalry with a concealed pit.

8.29
480
PHOCIS
The Thessalians demand fifty talents from the Phocians in recompense for these past defeats.

8.30
480
PHOCIS
The Phocians refuse the Thessalian offer and remain allied to the Hellenes, due to their hatred for the Thessalians.

8.31
480
DORIS-PHOCIS
The Thessalians guide the Persian advance from Trachis into Doris and then to Phocis.

8.32
480
PHOCIS
The Phocians flee to Mount Parnassus and to Amphissa while the Persians lay waste to their lands, towns, and temples.

The Phocians did this to the Thessalian infantry while they were being besieged by them, and they also inflicted irremediable damages on the Thessalian cavalry when it invaded Phocian territory. For at the pass near Hyampolis[a] the Phocians dug a huge trench and, after filling it with empty wine jars, covered it over with earth and made it look just like the rest of the ground. They then awaited the attack of the Thessalians. The Thessalians, thinking that they would quickly take the Phocians by storm, charged right onto the wine jars on which their horses' legs were broken.

Those were the two recent reasons for the grudge that the Thessalians bore against the Phocians, and they now sent a herald to them with this proclamation: "Phocians, the time has come for you to recognize that you are no match for us. [2] Even in the past, we always carried more weight with the Hellenes than you did, as long as we favored their side. Now our influence with the King is so great that we have the power to determine whether or not you will be deprived of your land and be enslaved. But though we could be mindful of all the wrongs done to us, we choose to forget them. Give fifty talents of silver[a] to us, and we promise that, in exchange, we shall turn away the invasion from your country."

That was what the Thessalians told them. For the Phocians were the only people in this region who had not medized, and they did this for no reason that I can logically infer other than their hatred of the Thessalians. [2] If the Thessalians had supported the Hellenes, I suppose that the Phocians would then have medized. In response to the proclamation of the Thessalians, the Phocians not only refused to give them any money but declared that they could medize just as well as the Thessalians, if they were so inclined, but in fact there was no way they would willingly betray Hellas.

When the words of the Phocians were reported to them, the Thessalians, out of bitter hatred for the Phocians, took it upon themselves to guide the barbarians as they advanced. From Trachinian[a] territory they marched into the country of Doris,[b] for in Dorian territory there extends a strip of land a little less than three and a half miles wide,[c] lying between the countries of Malis[d] and Phocis. Doris was called Dryopis in ancient times and was the motherland of the Dorians who now live in the Peloponnese.[e] In any case, the barbarians did no harm to the land of Doris when they invaded, since its inhabitants were already medizing and the Thessalians were against their being harmed.

When the barbarians marched out of Doris and invaded Phocis, they did not take any Phocians themselves, because a number of the Phocians had climbed to the heights of Parnassus,[a] where there is a suitable haven for many people on an isolated peak called Tithorea, overlooking the city of Neon.[b] Those who climbed this peak brought their belongings along with them. [2]

8.28.1a Hyampolis (pass): Map 8.32, AY.
8.29.2a Fifty talents of silver was an immense sum.
         See Appendix J, §11–13, 20.
8.31.1a Trachis: Map 8.32, AX.
8.31.1b Doris: Map 8.32, AX.
8.31.1c Herodotus writes that the territory was
         "30 stades" wide. See Appendix J, §6, 19.

8.31.1d Malis: Map 8.32, AX.
8.31.1e Peloponnese: Map 8.43.
8.32.1a Mount Parnassus: Map 8.32, AX.
8.32.1b Tithorea, a peak of Mount Parnassus,
         perhaps a peak near the town of
         Tithorea/Neon: Map 8.32, AX.

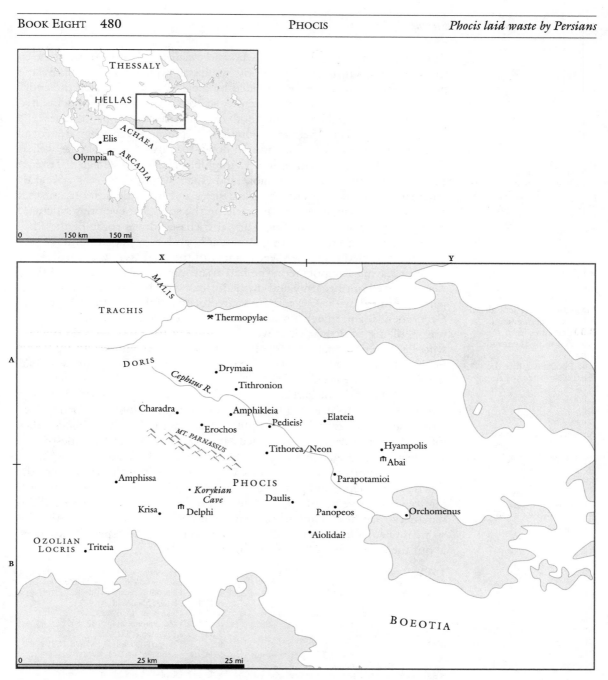

MAP 8.32

But the majority of the Phocians who had evacuated their land had gone to the Ozolian Locrians,[a] to the city of Amphissa,[b] which is located above the plain of Krisa.[c] The barbarians, guided by the Thessalians, overran the entire country of Phocis, and in every place they set foot, they cut down or devastated with fire all that was there, sending both cities and sanctuaries up in flames.

For as they made their way along the Cephisus River,[a] they destroyed everything in their path: they burned down the city of Drymaia,[b] as well as Charadra,[c] Erochos,[d] Tithronion,[e] Amphikleia,[f] Neon, Pedieis,[g] Triteia,[h] Elateia,[i] Hyampolis,[j] Parapotamioi,[k] and Abai,[l] where there was a wealthy sanctuary of Apollo, adorned with treasures and many dedications. At that time and still today there was an oracle on the spot. But even this sanctuary they plundered and set on fire. They also chased down some of the Phocians, catching them near the mountains, and they raped some of the women, who died from the sheer number of the men assaulting them.

After leaving Parapotamioi, the barbarians came to Panopeos,[a] and there Xerxes sorted out his army and divided it in two. The largest and strongest part continued with Xerxes to invade Boeotia[b] through the territory of Orchomenus[c] and march toward Athens. The entire population of Boeotia was medizing, and their cities were being protected by some Macedonians who had been appointed and sent to them by Alexandros. The purpose behind this move was to make clear to Xerxes that the Boeotians were taking the side of the Medes.

While this force of barbarians was taking this course, the other one set out with guides to march toward the sanctuary at Delphi[a] by skirting Parnassus and keeping it on their right. Wherever they went in Phocis, they inflicted wanton damage, and indeed they even set fire to the cities of the Panopeans, the Daulians,[b] and the Aiolians.[c] [2] The reason they split off from the rest of the army and took this route was in order to plunder the sanctuary at Delphi and to display its wealth to King Xerxes. Now, according to what I have heard, Xerxes knew more about the notable items in this sanctuary than he did about the items that he had left at home, what with so many people constantly talking about them; and he especially knew all about the dedications of Croesus son of Alyattes.[a]

8.33
480
PHOCIS
The Persians ravage and burn twelve towns in Phocis, plunder and burn the temple at Abai, and kill some Phocian women by multiple rape.

8.34
480
BOEOTIA
Macedonians are sent ahead to protect the medizing Boeotian cities from destruction by the invaders.

8.35
480
DELPHI
Another force of Persians heads for Delphi, intending to plunder the temple there.

8.32.2a Locris (Ozolian): Map 8.32, BX.
8.32.2b Amphissa: Map 8.32, BX.
8.32.2c Krisa: Map 8.32, BX.
8.33.1a Cephisus River: Map 8.32, AX.
8.32.1b Drymaia: Map 8.32, AX. Herodotus spells it Drymos.
8.33.1c Charadra: Map 8.32, AX.
8.33.1d Erochos: Map 8.32, AX.
8.33.1e Tithronion: Map 8.32, AX. Herodotus spells it Tethronion.
8.33.1f Amphikleia: Map 8.32, AX. Herodotus spells it Ampikaia.
8.33.1g Pedieis, possible location: Map 8.32, AX.
8.33.1h Triteia: the location of this Triteia in the Cephisos valley is unknown. There is another city of that name in Ozolian Locris (Map 8.32, BX), but this one,

lying south and west of Delphi, which was not sacked, cannot be the one that Herodotus means in this list.
8.33.1i Elateia: Map 8.32, AY.
8.33.1j Hyampolis: Map 8.32, AY.
8.33.1k Parapotamioi: Map 8.32, BY.
8.33.1l Abai: Map 8.32, AY.
8.34.1a Panopeos (Phanotis): Map 8.32, BY.
8.34.1b Boeotia: Map 8.32. BY.
8.34.1c Orchomenus, Boeotia: Map 8.32, BY.
8.35.1a Delphi: Map 8.32, BX.
8.35.1b Daulis, Phocis: Map 8.32, BX.
8.35.1c Aiolians (Aiolidai), possible location of territory: Map 8.32, BY.
8.35.2a For the gifts to Delphi of the Lydian king Croesus, see 1.50–51.

When the Delphians learned of the approach of the barbarians, they were completely terrified, and in their terror they consulted the oracle about what they should do with the sacred property: bury it underground or carry it off to some other land? But the god forbade them to move it, claiming that he was quite capable of protecting and presiding over his own property. [2] After they heard this reply, the Delphians began to take thought for themselves. They sent their women and children over to Achaea,[a] while most of their men climbed to the peaks of Parnassus and took their belongings into the Korykian Cave;[b] others retreated to Amphissa in Locris. And so now all the Delphians had left the city except for sixty men and a prophet.

When the barbarians had advanced so close to the sanctuary that they could see it, the prophet, whose name was Akeratos, saw the armor and weapons—the sacred arms which no human being can touch without committing sacrilege—lying in front of the temple, having been removed from the inner shrine. [2] While he went to tell the remaining Delphians about this amazing portent, the barbarians advanced quickly, but as they came near the sanctuary of Athena Pronaia,[a] they met with portents even greater than the one that had already occurred. For although it is certainly very amazing for armor and weapons of war to appear spontaneously, lying outside in front of the temple, the next thing that happened was actually the most marvelous sign of all. [3] For just as the barbarians approached near the sanctuary of Athena Pronaia, thunderbolts out of the heavens struck down among them, and from Parnassus two peaks broke away, falling upon them with a deafening crash and overwhelming many of them, while out of the sanctuary of Pronaia arose a great shout and battle cry.

All these marvels happening together struck panic into the hearts of the barbarians, who turned to flee, and the men of Delphi, realizing this, ran down and killed a number of them. The survivors fled straight for Boeotia. I have heard that the barbarians from this group who returned home said that they saw other divine signs in addition to these: two hoplites of more than human stature pursued them, chasing them down and killing some of them.

The people of Delphi say that these two figures were local heroes, Phylakos and Autonoos, whose precincts lie in the vicinity of the sanctuary. The precinct of Phylakos is situated beside the road beneath the sanctuary of Pronaia, while that of Autonoos is near Kastalia[a] under the peak of Hyampeia.[b] [2] The stones that fell from Parnassus were still extant in my time, lying in the precinct of Pronaia, where they had landed after crashing through the barbarian ranks. That, then, was how these men withdrew from the sanctuary.

8.36
480
DELPHI
The frightened Delphians flee, but following the counsel of the oracle, they leave the treasures in place.

8.37
480
DELPHI
The miraculous appearance of sacred arms, thunderbolts, and rockfalls saves Delphi from the invaders.

8.38
480
DELPHI
The barbarians panic and flee, pursued by the Delphians.

8.39
480
DELPHI
The fleeing Persians later tell of yet more fearful apparitions.

8.36.2a   Achaea: Map 8.32, locator.
8.36.2b   Korykian Cave: Map 8.32, BX.

8.39.1a   Kastalian Spring at Delphi: Map 8.43, BX.
8.39.1b   Hyampeian Peak: location unknown.

8.40
480
SALAMIS
Learning that the Peloponnesians are fortifying the isthmus, the Athenians request that the fleet put in at Salamis to assist their evacuation and to consult on future strategy.

8.41
480
ATHENS
The Athenians, believing the oracle and that the goddess had deserted the Acropolis, evacuate their households to Troizen, Aegina and Salamis.

8.42
480
SALAMIS
The Greek fleet concentrates at Salamis rather than Troizen under the command of the Spartan Eurybiades.

8.43
480
SALAMIS
The Peloponnesian contingents of ships in the combined Greek fleet are listed.

The Greek fleet left Artemision and, at the Athenians' request, put in at Salamis.[a] The Athenians made this request so that they would be able to convey their women and children out of Attica[b] to safety and, in addition, so that they could all confer about what they were going to do next. They intended to hold a council meeting to discuss their present situation, because they felt that they had been deceived, [2] for they had expected to find the Peloponnesians in Boeotia[a] waiting in full force for the barbarian but they had found nothing of the sort. Instead, they discovered that the Peloponnesians were at the isthmus[b] building a wall, making the protection and survival of the Peloponnese[c] their highest priority while giving up on everything else. It was after the Athenians had learned this that they requested the fleet to put in at Salamis.

While the allies brought their ships to Salamis, the Athenians put in at their own shore[a] and made a proclamation that every Athenian should try to save his children and other members of his household in any way that he could. Most of them dispatched their households to Troizen,[b] though some sent them to Aegina[c] and others to Salamis. [2] They made a tremendous effort to evacuate everything, not only because they wanted to comply with the oracle,[a] but especially because of the following reason: the Athenians say that a huge snake guards the Acropolis and dwells in the sanctuary, but more to the point, they say that they celebrate a ritual in which they set out an offering of a honey cake every month for it as though it were a real snake. [3] Now before this, the honey cake had always been consumed, but this last time it was left untouched. When the priestess revealed this to the Athenians, they became even more eager to leave their city, believing that the goddess[a] had abandoned the Acropolis. And when they had removed everything to safety, they sailed off to join the naval forces at Salamis.

After the ships from Artemision had put in and anchored at Salamis, the rest of the Greek fleet, at Troizen, learned of their arrival, and they all streamed in together to join them. This part of the fleet had been ordered earlier to gather at Pogon,[a] the harbor of Troizen. So now there were assembled far more ships than had fought at Artemision, and from many more cities. [2] Their commander was the very same man who had commanded them at Artemision, Eurybiades son of Eurykleides; he was a Spartan, though not of royal lineage. The most numerous ships by far, and also the best,[a] were furnished by the Athenians.

Serving in these forces were the following peoples. From the Peloponnese, the Lacedaemonians[a] furnished sixteen ships; the Corinthians,[b] the

8.40.1a Salamis (Attic): Map 8.43, BY.
8.40.1b Attica: Map 8.43, BY.
8.40.2a Boeotia: Map 8.43, BY.
8.40.2b Isthmus of Corinth: Map 8.43, BY.
8.40.2c Peloponnese: Map 8.43, BX.
8.41.1a Athens: Map 8.43, BY.
8.41.1b Troizen: Map 8.43, BY.
8.41.1c Aegina: Map 8.43, BY.
8.41.2a The oracle referred to here could be either the first one, of 7.140, which advises the Athenians to leave their homes; or the second one, of 7.141, which tells them that all of Attica

will be taken and counsels them to withdraw.
8.41.3a The goddess referred to by Herodotus is Athena, the protector of Athens.
8.42.1a Pogon: Map 8.43, BY.
8.42.2a The word "best" here means that the Athenian ships were the best built and best maintained in the fleet and were manned by the best-trained and most skillful crews.
8.43.1a Lacedaemon (Sparta): Map 8.43, BX.
8.43.1b Corinth: Map 8.43, BY. The Corinthians brought forty ships to Artemision (Map 8.43, AY). See 8.1.1.

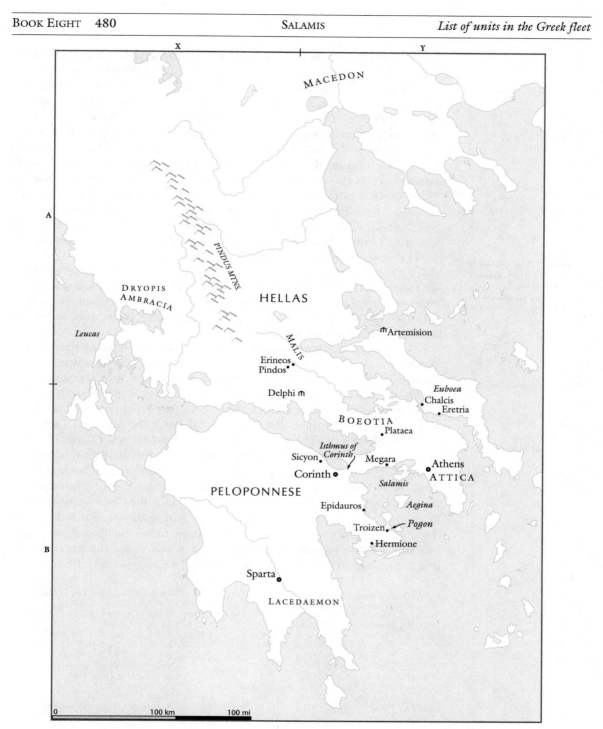

MAP 8.43

full number of those they had brought to Artemision;[c] the Sicyonians,[d] fifteen; the Epidaurians,[e] ten; the Troizenians, five; and the Hermionians,[f] three. Except for the Hermionians, these men belonged to the Dorian[g] and Macedonian[h] races; their people had been the last to set out for the Peloponnese from Erineos,[i] Pindos,[j] and Dryopis.[k] The Hermionians are Dryopes; they were forced to leave the country now called Dryopis by Herakles and the Malians.[l]

Those were the Peloponnesians serving in the fleet. Those listed next came from outside the mainland of the Peloponnese. The Athenians, in contrast to all the others, furnished 180 ships all by themselves, for the Plataeans[a] did not join the Athenians to fight the naval battle at Salamis because when the Hellenes were on their way back from Artemision and were just off Chalcis,[b] the Plataeans disembarked on the opposite shore, in Boeotian territory, and attended to the evacuation of their households. And so, as they were saving their families, they were left behind.

[2] The Athenians were originally Pelasgians, and at the time when the Pelasgians held what is now called Hellas, they were called Kranaoi. In the time of King Kekrops they were called Kekropids; and when Erechtheus inherited the rule, the Athenians' name changed to Ionians, after Ion son of Xouthos, who commanded their army.

The Megarians[a] supplied the same number of ships as they had at Artemision, while the Ambraciots[b] came to help with seven ships, and the Leucadians[c] three; these people were Dorian in race, from Corinth.

Of the islanders, the Aeginetans supplied thirty ships. They had other ships already manned with which they were guarding their own land, but it was their thirty best ships that fought at Salamis.[a] The Aeginetans are Dorians from Epidauros. The former name of their island was Oione. [2] After the Aeginetans come the Chalcidians, who provided the twenty ships they had brought to Artemision, and the Eretrians[a] with seven. Those were the Ionians[b] present. Next came the Keians,[c] also with the same ships; they are an Ionian people from Athens. [3] The Naxians[a] furnished four ships; they had been sent off to the Medes by their citizens, just as the other islanders were, but they disregarded their commands and came to the Hellenes at the urging of Demokritos, a prominent man among the people of the city who was serving as trierarch[b] at the time. The Naxians are Ionians who came from Athens.

8.43.1c Artemision: Map 8.43, AY.
8.43.1d Sicyon: Map 8.43, BY.
8.43.1e Epidauros: Map 8.43, BY.
8.43.1f Hermione: Map 8.43, BY.
8.43.1g Dorians: See Appendix K, Dialect and Ethnic Groups in Herodotus, §7–9.
8.43.1h Macedon: Map 8.43, AY.
8.43.1i Erineos: Map 8.43, AX.
8.43.1j Pindos: Map 8.43, AX.
8.43.1k Dryopis: Map 8.43, AX.
8.43.1l Malis: Map 8.43, AX.
8.44.1a Plataea: Map 8.43, BY.
8.44.1b Chalcis, Euboea: Map 8.43, BY.
8.45.1a Megara: Map 8.43, BY. The Megarians

furnished twenty triremes at Artemision.
8.45.1b Ambracia: Map 8.43, AX.
8.45.1c Leucas: Map 8.43, AX.
8.46.1a Salamis: Map 8.43, BY.
8.46.2a Eretria, Euboea: Map 8.43, BY.
8.46.2b Ionians: see Appendix K, §2–9.
8.46.2c Keos: Map 8.47, BY. The Keians furnished two triremes and two pentecontors to the Greek fleet at Artemision.
8.46.3a Naxos: Map 8.47, BY.
8.46.3b A trierarch was the commander of a trireme. See 6.14.2.

[4] The Styrians[a] furnished the same ships as they had at Artemision; the Kythnians,[b] one ship plus a penteconter. Both of these peoples are Dryopes. The Seriphians,[c] Siphnians,[d] and Melians[e] also joined the forces, for they alone of the islanders did not give earth and water to the barbarian.

Those are all the members of the forces who inhabit the areas east of Thesprotia[a] and the Acheron River.[b] For the Thesprotians share boundaries with the Ambraciots and Leucadians, who were coming from the most distant lands of all those in the forces. Outside of these, the Crotonians[c] alone came to help Hellas when it was endangered, with one ship commanded by Phayllos, a three-time Pythian victor.[d] The Crotonians are of Achaean[e] lineage.

All those who served in the fleet provided triremes except for the Melians, Siphnians, and Seriphians, who furnished pentecounters.[a] The Melians, whose lineage originated in Lacedaemon,[b] supplied two; the Siphnians and Seriphians, both of whom are Ionians from Athens, one each. The total number of ships, not counting the pentecounters, came to 378.

When the commanders from the cities I have mentioned came together at Salamis, they held a council to discuss plans, and Eurybiades proposed that whoever so wished should express his opinion about which of all the places remaining under their control would seem most suitable for a naval engagement; for since Attica[a] had now been given up for lost, he was inquiring about their other territories. [2] The majority of those voicing opinions favored sailing to the isthmus and fighting there in defense of the Peloponnese, arguing that should they be defeated in battle at Salamis, they would find themselves besieged on an island where no one would appear to help them, but if they were defeated at the isthmus, they could go ashore to their own people.

While the commanders from the Peloponnese were speaking to this effect, an Athenian arrived with the message that the barbarian had come to Attica and that it was now being completely devastated by fire. [2] For after the army with Xerxes had made its way through Boeotia, it had set fire to the city of the Thespians, who had already left it for the Peloponnese[c] and likewise to the city of the Plataeans; ~~then it had come to Athens and was now destroying everything there.~~ The army had burned down

8.47
480
SALAMIS
A few distant states send forces to fight with the Hellenes.

8.48
480
SALAMIS
A few islands send pentecounters, but the rest provide triremes.

8.49
480
SALAMIS
The generals hold a council at Salamis at which most advise that they sail to the Isthmus of Corinth and give battle to the Persians there.

8.50
480
SALAMIS
An Athenian informs the generals that the Persians burned Thespiai and Plataea and were now entering and destroying Attica.

8.46.4a   Styra, Euboea: Map 8.47, AY. The Styrians furnished two triremes to the Greek fleet at Artemision (8.1.2).
8.46.4b   Kythnos: Map 8.47, BY.
8.46.4c   Seriphos: Map 8.47, BY.
8.46.4d   Siphnos: Map 8.47, BY.
8.46.4e   Melos: Map 8.47, BY.
8.47.1a   Thesprotia: Map 8.47, AX.
8.47.1b   Acheron River: Map 8.47, AX.
8.47.1c   Croton, Italy: Map 8.47, locator.
8.47.1d   Phayllos was a three-time victor in the Pythian games celebrated at Delphi. See Appendix P, §10.
8.47.1e   The Achaeans, who inhabited the north coast of the Peloponnese, were one of the ethnic groups into which the Hellenes were divided. They spoke the Aeolian dialect. See Appendix K, §7–9.
8.48.1a   A triremes had 170 rowers; 85 were deployed on each side of the vessel in three tiers. Pentecounters had 50 rowers in one tier, 25 on each side of the vessel. See Figure 8.10, Appendix S, and Figures S.1–3.
8.48.1b   Lacedaemon (Sparta): Map 8.47, BX. Coming from Lacedaemon, they were Dorians.
8.49.1a   Attica: Map 8.47, BY.

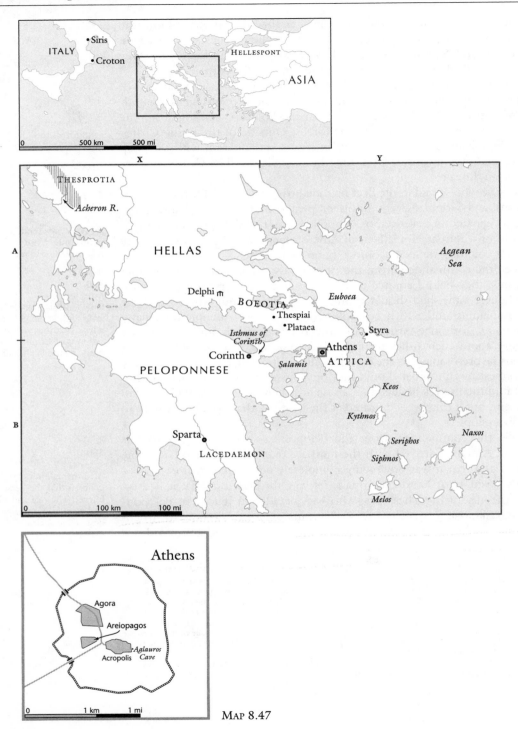

MAP 8.47

Thespiai and Plataea after learning from the Thebans that these cities had refused to medize.

From the passage of the Hellespont,[a] where the barbarians began their journey, they spent one month crossing over to Europe, and another three months on their march to Attica, arriving during the archonship of Kallias.[b] [2] Once there, they captured the city and found it deserted, although they subsequently discovered a few Athenians in the sanctuary; these were the treasurers of the temple and some indigent people who, in an effort to ward off the invaders, had barricaded themselves on the Acropolis[a] with a rampart of doors and planks of wood. They had refused to withdraw from their country to Salamis not only because of their poverty but also because of their conviction that they had discovered the true significance of the oracle delivered by the Pythia: the prophecy that the wooden wall would be impregnable[b] was interpreted by them to mean that this very place and not the ships was to be their refuge.

The Persians took up their position upon the hill which the Athenians call the Areiopagos[a] and which faces the Acropolis, and then began their siege of the place in this way. They wrapped their arrows with hemp fiber and, after setting them on fire, shot them at the barricade. The besieged Athenians tried to defend themselves, although they now confronted the worst of evils as their barricade failed them. [2] When the Peisistratids[a] tried to propose terms of surrender, they would not even listen to them and instead contrived various means of defense, such as rolling boulders down at the barbarians when they approached the gates, so that for quite a while, Xerxes found himself at an impasse and unable to capture them.

In time, however, a way out of this impasse appeared to the barbarians, for the prophecy had ordained that all of Attica on the mainland was to fall under the control of the Persians. Now in front of the Acropolis, but behind the gates and the ascending path, there was an area which no one was guarding, since no one would ever have imagined that a human being could climb up there; but although this was a precipitous cliff, some Persians managed to ascend it up to the sanctuary of Aglauros the daughter of Kekrops.[a] [2] When the Athenians saw that they had climbed onto the Acropolis, some threw themselves down from the wall and perished, while others took refuge inside the megaron[a] there. Upon reaching the summit, the Persians went first of all to the gates and opened them; then they mur-

8.51
480
ATHENS
When the Persians take Athens, they find a few Athenians barricaded on the Acropolis, believing that the Acropolis' barrier, not Athens' fleet, is the true meaning of the oracle about wooden walls.

8.52
480
ATHENS
Although the Persians destroy the barricade, they fail to defeat the defenders.

8.53
480
ATHENS
Finally, by climbing where the Acropolis is a sheer and undefended cliff, the Persians take the place. They kill its defenders and, after plundering the sacred precinct, set fire to it.

8.51.1a Hellespont: Map 8.47, locator.
8.51.1b The archon was at that time the chief magistrate of Athens. The naming of the year after the current archon was a common method of dating events. See Appendix A, The Athenian Government in Herodotus, §3. See also Glossary.
8.51.2a Acropolis of Athens: Map 8.47, inset.
8.51.2b See 7.141.3 for the prophecy that mentioned a a wall made of wood.
8.52.1a Areiopagos, Athens: Map 8.47, inset. *Areiopagos* means "rocky hill of Ares."

8.52.2a Naturally the Peisistratids accompanied Xerxes to Athens, having incited and persuaded him to undertake the expedition against Greece; see 7.6.
8.53.1a The sanctuary of Aglauros is at the east end of the Acropolis of Athens.
8.53.2a A megaron is a rectangular building with an entrance porch and usually a hearth. It is certain that this building on the Acropolis was part of a holy sanctuary or a shrine, but scholars are not sure which building is meant here.

FIGURE 8.53. THESE PHOTOS SHOW UNFINISHED COLUMN DRUMS INTENDED FOR A TEMPLE UNDER CONSTRUCTION ON THE ATHENIAN ACROPOLIS WHEN THE PERSIANS CAPTURED IT. THE PERSIANS DESTROYED THE WORK, AND RATHER THAN USE THE DRUMS ON ANOTHER BUILDING, THE ATHENIANS PLACED THEM IN THE NORTH OUTER WALL OF THE ACROPOLIS FACING THE AGORA, SO ATHENIANS GOING ABOUT THEIR EVERYDAY BUSINESS WOULD NEVER LOSE SIGHT OF THE SACRILEGIOUS INJURY DONE TO THEM BY THE PERSIANS.

dered the suppliants within. When everyone there had been cut down, they plundered the sanctuary and set the whole Acropolis on fire.

8.54
480
ATHENS
Xerxes orders the Athenian exiles to perform sacrifices on the Acropolis, which they do.

Having taken complete possession of Athens, Xerxes now sent off a mounted messenger to Artabanos to announce his present success, and the day after sending the messenger, he summoned the exiles from Athens who had accompanied him and ordered them to climb to the Acropolis and sacrifice according to their tradition. Perhaps he gave this command after seeing a vision in his sleep, or maybe his conscience was troubled by the burning of the sanctuary. In any case, the Athenian exiles carried out his command.

Allow me to explain why I have recounted this episode. On this Acropolis is a temple of Erechtheus, who is called Earth-born, and inside it there is an olive tree and a pool of salt water.[a] According to the Athenians, Poseidon and Athena placed these here as witnesses to their dispute over Attica. Well, this olive tree happened to be burned down together with the rest of the sanctuary by the barbarians; but on the day after it had burned, the Athenians who had been ordered by the King to sacrifice climbed up to the sanctuary and saw a fresh shoot sprouting up from the stump, already about one and a half feet[b] tall, and they reported what they had seen.

When the news of what had happened to the Athenian Acropolis was announced to the Hellenes assembled at Salamis,[a] they became so deeply disturbed that some of the commanders did not even wait for the business under discussion to be resolved, but dashed to their ships and hoisted their sails to take flight. Those left behind ratified the decision to fight a sea battle in defense of the isthmus,[b] and when night fell, they all dispersed from the conference and boarded their ships.

At that point, Themistokles returned to his ship, and Mnesiphilos, an Athenian, asked him what had been discussed at their meeting. When he learned that they had resolved to sail to the isthmus and fight a sea battle in defense of the Peloponnese, he said, [2] "Well, then, if they launch their ships to sail away from Salamis, you can be sure that there will no longer be a united fatherland to fight for at sea, because each man will turn to his own city and Eurybiades will not be able to hold them back, nor will anyone else in the world be able to prevent the army from scattering completely; Hellas will be destroyed by this bad counsel. So if there is any way you can do it, go back and try to confound their decision and to somehow persuade Eurybiades to change his mind and remain here."

Themistokles was delighted to hear this suggestion, and without even replying, he went to Eurybiades' ship, and when he had reached it, said that he wished to converse with him about a matter of common concern. Eurybiades told him that if there was something Themistokles wanted, he should board his ship. [2] So Themistokles came and sat beside him and recited every word he had heard from Mnesiphilos as though it were his own speech, and added much to it as well, until he had persuaded him by his entreaties to disembark from the ship and have the commanders reassemble for another conference.

When they had all assembled, but before Eurybiades could explain why he had brought the commanders together, Themistokles spoke out with great urgency, since he was now quite desperate. But as he was speaking, Adeimantos son of Okytos, the Corinthian commander, said, "Themistokles, in the games, those who start off before the signal are beaten with a stick," to

8.55	
480	
ATHENS	
The exiles on the Acropolis find a new shoot sprung from the burnt sacred olive tree.	
8.56	
480	
SALAMIS	
News of he ruin of Athens alarms the Hellenes at Salamis, who decide to flee.	
8.57	
480	
SALAMIS	
The Athenian Mnesiphilos predicts disaster if the fleet leaves Salamis and advises Themistokles to persuade the Hellenes to stay.	
8.58	
480	
SALAMIS	
Themistokles persuades Eurybiades to disembark and gather the generals for a council of war.	
8.59	
480	
SALAMIS	
The repartee between Adeimantos of Corinth and Themistokles.	

8.55.1a   Herodotus refers to this spring as a "sea." Perhaps it was a well of salt water which gave off a sound like waves when the wind blew over it.

8.55.1b   Herodotus writes that the "shoot was already as tall as a cubit." The cubit he probably had in mind would have equaled about 1.5 feet. See Appendix J, §4, 5, 19.

8.56.1a   Salamis: Map 8.47, BY.

8.56.1b   Isthmus of Corinth: Map 8.47, BX.

which Themistokles replied, "Yes, but those left behind are never crowned with the victor's wreath."

So on this occasion, Themistokles was gentle in his reply to the Corinthian.[a] Now to Eurybiades he said nothing of what he had argued before—about how they would all flee in different directions if they once launched their ships to sail away from Salamis—for it would not be at all appropriate for him to make such accusations in the presence of the allies.

So he adopted a different argument, saying, "It is in your power to save Hellas, if only you will follow my advice: stay and fight a sea battle here instead of heeding the words of these men and moving the fleet to the isthmus.[a] Just listen and compare the two sides of the argument.

"If you engage the enemy at the isthmus, you will be fighting on the open sea, which is least to our advantage as our ships are heavier and our fleet inferior in number to theirs. Besides, by doing this, you will lose Salamis,[b] Megara,[c] and Aegina,[d] even if we should meet with good fortune elsewhere. Furthermore, the land army of the enemy will follow its fleet, and thus you yourself will be leading them to the Peloponnese[e] and so endanger all of Hellas.

"On the other hand, if you do as I advise, you will find many advantages: first, if we engage the enemy in a narrow strait with our few ships against their many, then, if we can expect the laws of probability to govern the battle's outcome, I believe we shall achieve a great victory; for fighting in a narrow strait is best for us, while fighting on the open sea is best for them. And besides, then Salamis will survive, the very place to which we have conveyed to safety our wives and children. And there is also the following point, which speaks to your greatest concern: by remaining here, your men will be fighting in defense of the Peloponnese just as much as if they were fighting at the isthmus, so if you are in your right mind, you certainly will not lead the Persians to the Peloponnese.

"And if things turn out as I expect and we win the victory with our ships, the barbarians will not be there at your isthmus; in fact, not only will they advance no farther than Attica, but they will depart in complete disarray, while we will reap the benefit of the survival of Megara, Aegina, and Salamis, where, according to the prophecy, we are to prevail over our foes. When men plan according to what is probable, events usually turn out according to their wishes; but when their plans are improbable, not even god is willing to support their intentions."

As Themistokles was saying this, Adeimantos the Corinthian again attacked him, ordering him to be silent since he had no fatherland, and forbidding Eurybiades to allow any man who had no city to propose a motion for a vote. He told Themistokles that when he could demonstrate that he

---

8.60
480
SALAMIS
Themistokles addresses the Greek commanders.

8.60.α*
480
SALAMIS
Themistokles argues that sailing to the isthmus will lose Salamis, Megara, and Aegina and force the Hellenes to fight at a disadvantage in open sea.

8.60.β
480
SALAMIS
Themistokles says that by giving battle here, the Hellenes would fight in a narrow strait, save Salamis and their families, and still defend the Peloponnese.

8.60.γ
480
SALAMIS
Themistokles points out that a victory at Salamis will stop the Persian advance.

8.61
480
SALAMIS
When Adeimantos attacks Themistokles as a man without a city, he replies that the Athenians still have 200 triremes deployed, more than all the rest.

8.60.1a   Corinth: Map 8.65, AX.
8.60.α*   This chapter in the *Histories* (as well as
            8.68 and 8.140) has subdivisions indi-
            cated by Greek letters in alphabetic
            sequence. That sequence (with the letters'
            Latin equivalents) is as follows: α (a), β
            (b), γ (g).

8.60.α.1a   Isthmus of Corinth: Map 8.65, AX.
8.60.α.1b   Salamis: Map 8.65, inset.
8.60.α.1c   Megara: Map 8.43, BY.
8.60.α.1d   Aegina: Map 8.65, BY.
8.60.α.1e   Peloponnese: Map 8.65, BX.

had a city, then he should contribute his opinions. This reproach against Themistokles referred to the enemy's capture and current occupation of Athens. [2] This time Themistokles replied at length, and with venom directed against Adeimantos and the Corinthians; he declared that in fact the Athenians' city and land were greater than theirs, as long as they had 200 ships of their own, fully manned, for none of the Hellenes could repulse them if they were to launch an assault.

After this retort he turned to address Eurybiades, and now he spoke to him with greater vehemence than before: "As for you, if you remain here, you will be a good and noble man simply by remaining. But if you do not, you will be the ruin of Hellas, for the whole outcome of this war hangs on the ships. [2] Now, if you refuse to do as I say, we shall pick up and leave with our families, and without further ado go off to Siris in Italy,[a] which is still ours from ancient times, and which the prophecies say we are destined to colonize. Then, when you find yourself left alone without allies like us, you will remember my words."

Eurybiades was converted by what Themistokles said, chiefly, I suppose, out of fear that the Athenians would leave them if they transferred the fleet to the isthmus, since if the Athenians left, the rest of them would no longer be a match for the enemy. So he chose to follow the proposal of Themistokles to remain and wage the decisive naval battle there.

And so once the Hellenes at Salamis had concluded this verbal skirmish, they then prepared to fight a naval battle there, as Eurybiades had resolved. When day broke and the sun was rising, an earthquake occurred on land and sea, at which point they decided to pray to the gods and invoke Aiakos and his descendants as their allies, and they carried out that decision. First they prayed to all the gods and then, after invoking the aid of Ajax and Telamon[a] from Salamis, they sent a ship to Aegina to fetch Aiakos and the rest of his descendants.[b]

Now, an Athenian exile named Dikaios son of Theokydes, who had attained some respect among the Medes, said that during this time when the land of Attica was being laid waste by the army of Xerxes after Athens had been deserted by the Athenians, he happened to be on the Thriasian Plain[a] with Demaratos the Lacedaemonian, and they saw dust coming from Eleusis[b] as though raised by a force of about 30,000 men on the march. As they marveled at this dust and wondered who in the world could be causing it, they suddenly heard a voice which seemed to Dikaios like the Iakhos cry of the mysteries.[c] [2] Knowing nothing of the rites at Eleusis, Demaratos asked him what this sound was. Dikaios replied, "Demaratos, there is no way that great disaster will not befall the army of the King, for it is perfectly clear that since Attica has been deserted by its people, that cry is divine, and comes

8.62
480
SALAMIS
Themistokles threatens that the Athenians will sail to Italy if the Peloponnesians leave Salamis.

8.63
480
SALAMIS
Frightened by this threat, Eurybiades decides to stay.

8.64
480
SALAMIS
In response to an earthquake, the Hellenes pray to their gods and heroes to assist them.

8.65
480
THRIASIAN PLAIN
Herodotus recounts the story of the dust cloud and the cry of Iakhos from the rites of Eleusis that foretold the destruction of the Persian fleet at Salamis to Dikaios and Demaratos.

8.62.2a   Siris in Italy: Map 8.47, locator.
8.64.1a   Ajax (Aias) and Telamon were Homeric heroes.
8.64.1b   They sent a ship to Aegina to bring the images of the heroes from Aegina to Salamis.
8.65.1a   Thriasian Plain: Map 8.65, inset.

8.65.1b   Eleusis: Map 8.65, inset.
8.65.1c   The Iakhos cry was made by the initiates into the mysteries celebrated at Eleusis, the site of the famous shrine to Demeter, the goddess who governs the fruits of the earth, in particular grains for bread.

625

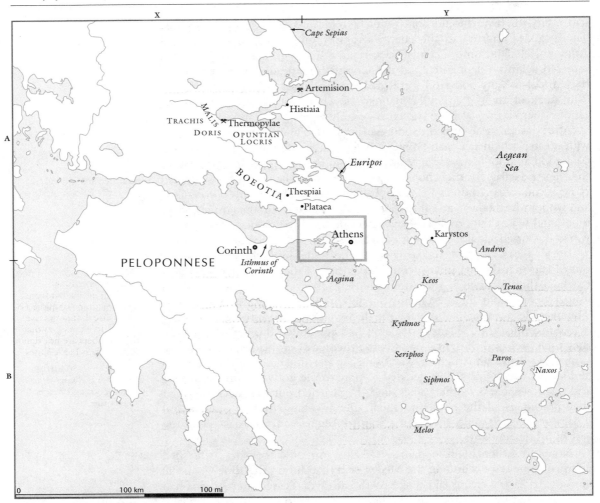

MAP 8.65

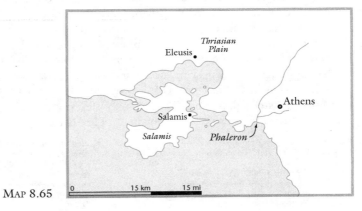

from Eleusis to the aid of the Athenians and their allies. [3] If this phenomenon strikes the Peloponnese, the King himself and the army on the mainland will be in danger, but if it should turn toward the ships at Salamis, the King will risk losing his fleet. [4] The Athenians celebrate a festival each and every year in honor of the Mother and Kore,[a] and any of the Athenians or other Hellenes who want to are initiated. The sound you hear is the Iakhos hymn they sing at this festival." To this, Demaratos responded, "Be silent and tell no one else what you have just told me, [5] for if your words are reported to the King, you will lose your head; neither I nor any human being on this earth will have the power to save you. So keep quiet, and the gods will take care of the army." [6] That was the advice of Demaratos, and now, out of the dust and after the voice there arose a cloud high up in the sky, and it moved toward Salamis to the camp of the Hellenes. Thus they realized that Xerxes' fleet would be destroyed. So that is what Dikaios son of Theokydes said had happened, and he cited Demaratos and others as witnesses.

After viewing the disaster of the Laconians,[a] the men assigned to Xerxes' fleet crossed from Trachis[b] to Histiaia,[c] where they stopped for three days before sailing through the Euripos,[d] and three days later they arrived at Phaleron.[e] It seems to me that the number of them invading Athenian territory by land and by sea was no less than the number of the troops who had arrived at Sepias[f] and Thermopylae.[g] [2] For I would offset all those who perished in the storm, at Thermopylae, and in the sea battles off Artemision[a] with those who joined the King after these events:[b] namely, the Malians,[c] Dorians,[d] and Locrians,[e] and the whole force of the Boeotians[f] except for the Thespians[g] and Plataeans;[h] and one must also add the Karystians,[i] Andrians,[j] Tenians,[k] and all the rest of the islanders—except for the five cities whose names I mentioned earlier[l]—for the farther the Persian advanced into the interior of Hellas, the more peoples there were who joined and followed him.

8.66
480
HISTIAIA-PHALERON
The Persians are reinforced by forces from conquered or cowed Greek states as they advance to Athens, so that their numbers are not diminished by their battle losses.

8.65.4a The Mother and Kore are Demeter and her daughter Persephone, whose worship was central to the Eleusinian Mysteries. The festival was a secret ceremony. Witnesses were initiated and swore never to reveal the rituals. Although there were thousands of initiates over almost a thousand years, little is known today about these ceremonies.

8.66.1a Herodotus returns here to the movements of the Persian fleet, last mentioned at 8.25, where the sailors had gone at Xerxes' invitation to Thermopylae (Map 8.65, AX) to view the battlefield and the Spartan dead there.

8.66.1b Trachis: Map 8.65, AX.
8.66.1c Histiaia, Euboea: Map 8.65, AX.
8.66.1d Euripos: Map 8.65, AY. The narrowest point in the straits between Boeotia and Euboea.
8.66.1e Phaleron: Map 8.65, inset. Phaleron was a long beach near Athens which served as the port of Athens prior to the development of Peiraeus.

8.66.1f Cape Sepias: Map 8.65, AX.
8.66.1g Themopylae: Map 8.65, AX.
8.66.2a Artemision: Map 8.65, AX.
8.66.2b See Appendix R, The Size of Xerxes' Expeditionary Force, §14.
8.66.2c Malis: Map 8.65, AX.
8.66.2d Doris: Map 8.65, AX.
8.66.2e Locris (Opuntian): Map 8.65, AX.
8.66.2f Boeotia: Map 8.65, AX.
8.66.2g Thespiai: Map 8.65, AX.
8.66.2h Plataea: Map 8.65, AX.
8.66.2i Karystos: Map 8.65, AY.
8.66.2j Andros: Map 8.65, AY.
8.66.2k Tenos: Map 8.65, BY.
8.66.2l In 8.46, Herodotus mentions six island states: Keos, Naxos, Kythnos, Seriphos, Siphnos, and Melos (all shown on Map 8.65, BY). Seriphos is not inscribed on the victory tripod offered at Delphi which is mentioned by both Herodotus (9.81) and Thucydides (*Thucydides* 1.132.2–3), and which is still visible today in Istanbul. See Figure 9.81a.

8.67
480
ATHENS
When all naval forces
under Persian control are
concentrated at Athens,
Xerxes visits the ships to
consult with the sailors.

So all of these troops came to Athens except for the Parians,[a] who had stayed behind on Kythnos,[b] watching to see how the war would turn out. When the rest had arrived at Phaleron, Xerxes himself came down to the ships, wishing to converse and to hear the opinions of the men on board. [2] When he arrived, he sat before them, and those he had summoned, the tyrants of their nations and subordinate commanders of their ships, came to him and sat as the King granted honor to each: first, the king of Sidon[a] and after him the king of Tyre,[b] followed by the others. When they had seated themselves in their order of precedence, Xerxes sent Mardonios to question them and to put the question to each one about whether or not he should wage a naval battle.

8.68
480
ATHENS
The tyrants and commanders
want a sea battle.
8.68.α
480
ATHENS
Artemisia advises Xerxes not
to risk battle at sea, but to
hold his present conquests
and wait.

So Mardonios made his way around and questioned them, beginning with the Sidonian. They all expressed the same opinion, urgng him to initiate a battle at sea, except for Artemisia, who said:

"Speak to the King for me, Mardonios, and tell him what I say, since I have not proven to be the worst fighter in his naval battles off Euboea,[a] nor have I performed the least significant of feats. Tell him, 'My lord, it is right and just that I express my opinion, and what I think is best regarding your interests. Here is what I think you should do: spare your fleet; do not wage a battle at sea. For their men surpass yours in strength at sea to the same degree that men surpass women. [2] And why is it necessary for you to risk another sea battle? Do you not already hold Athens, the very reason for which you set out on this campaign? And do you not have the rest of Hellas, too? No one is standing in your way; those who have stood against you have ended up as they deserved.

8.68.β
480
ATHENS
Artemisia predicts that the
Greek fleet will not remain
together, but will soon disperse to their repective cities.

" 'Let me tell you what I think your foes will end up doing. If you do not rush into waging a sea battle, but instead wait and keep your ships near land, or even if you advance to the Peloponnese, then, my lord, you will easily achieve what you intended by coming here. [2] The Hellenes are incapable of holding out against you for very long; you will scatter them, and each one will flee to his own city. For I hear that they have no food with them on this island, and if you lead your army to the Peloponnese, it is unlikely that those who came from there will remain where they are now and concern themselves with fighting at sea for the Athenians.

8.68.γ
480
ATHENS
Artemisia points out that
Xerxes' allies at sea are of
no use at all.

" 'But if you rush into a sea battle immediately, I fear that your fleet will be badly mauled, which would cause the ruin of your land army as well. And there is one more thing that you should think about, sire, and keep in mind: bad slaves tend to belong to good people, while good slaves belong to bad people. And you, the best of all men, have the worst slaves, who are said to be included among your allies, namely, the Egyptians, Cyprians, Cilicians, and Pamphylians:[a] they are absolutely worthless.'"

8.67.1a   Paros: Map 8.65, BY.
8.67.1b   Kythnos: Map 8.65, BY.
8.67.2a   Sidon: Map 8.72, locator.
8.67.2b   Tyre: Map 8.72, locator.
8.68.α.1a Artemisia, queen of Halicarnassus
          (Map 8.72, locator); see Appendix U,
          On Women and Marriage in Herodotus,

§2, 5, 8. She is referring here to the
battles described in 8.9–10, 8.14, and
8.16 near Artemision. Euboea: Map
8.72, AY.
8.68.γ.1a Egypt, Cyprus, Cilicia, Pamphylia: Map
8.72, locator.

As Artemisia was speaking to Mardonios, all those who were well-disposed toward her thought her words most unfortunate, since they believed she would suffer some punishment from the King for telling him not to wage a battle at sea. On the other hand, those who were envious and jealous of her, because she was honored as one of the most prominent of the allies, were delighted by her response to the question, thinking that she would perish for it. [2] When these opinions were reported to Xerxes, however, he was quite pleased with Artemisia's answer. Even prior to this, he had considered her worthy of his serious attention, but now he held her in even higher regard. Nevertheless, his orders were to obey the majority; he strongly suspected that off Euboea they had behaved like cowards because he was not present, but now he was fully prepared to watch them fight at sea.

When the command to put out to sea was given to the Persian fleet, the crews launched their ships and sailed for Salamis.[a] They deployed into their battle lines in a leisurely fashion, and since the day was too far advanced for them to fight a battle and night was coming on, they prepared to do battle on the following day. [2] Now fear and terror overcame the Hellenes, especially those from the Peloponnese, who were terrified because there they were, stationed at Salamis, about to fight at sea for the land of the Athenians, and they felt sure that after their defeat they would be trapped and besieged on an island while leaving their own land unprotected.

In fact, that very night, the army of the barbarians was on the march to the Peloponnese, although the Hellenes had contrived everything in their power to prevent the barbarian from invading it by land. For as soon as the Peloponnesians had learned that Leonidas and his troops had lost their lives at Thermopylae, they hastily left their cities and gathered together at the isthmus, where they established their camp; their commander was the brother of Leonidas, Kleombrotos son of Anaxandridas. [2] Taking their positions at the isthmus, they blocked the Skironian road,[a] and then, as they had resolved in council, they built a wall across the isthmus. And since many tens of thousands of men were present and every one of them was working on this project, they were making substantial progress on the work. Stones, bricks, wood, and baskets full of sand were carried to the site, and those who had come to help never ceased from their labor, day or night.

The Hellenes who had come to help at the isthmus were the Lacedaemonians,[a] all the Arcadians,[b] the Eleans,[c] the Corinthians,[d] Sicyonians,[e] Epidaurians,[f] Phleiasians,[g] Troizenians,[h] and Hermionians.[i] These were the men

Marginal notes

8.69
480
ATHENS
Many believe that Artemisia wil be punished for voicing her negative sentiments, but Xerxes is pleased, although he sides with the majority against her opinion.

8.70
480
SALAMIS
The Persians sail to Salamis, causing fear among the Hellenes that if defeated they might be besieged.

8.71
480
ISTHMUS OF CORINTH
The Persian army advances to the Peloponnese, which is defended by the recent construction of a wall across the isthmus by the Peloponnesians.

8.72
480
ISTHMUS OF CORINTH
Herodotus lists those states which manned the wall to defend the Peloponnese.

Footnotes

8.70.1a Salamis: Map 8.65, inset.
8.71.2a The Skironian road was a very difficult path that by Megarian legend had been made by a hero named Skiron. It is thought to have had precarious sections of narrow ledges high up over the sea on the face of an almost sheer cliff, which would make it quite easy to destroy or block.

8.72.1a Lacedaemon (Sparta): Map 8.72, BX.
8.72.1b Arcadia: Map 8.72, BX.
8.72.1c Elis: Map 8.72, AX.
8.72.1d Corinth: Map 8.72, AX.
8.72.1e Sicyon: Map 8.72, AX.
8.72.1f Epidauros: Map 8.72, BY.
8.72.1g Phleious: Map 8.72, AX.
8.72.1h Troizen: Map 8.72, BY.
8.72.1i Hermione: Map 8.72, BY.

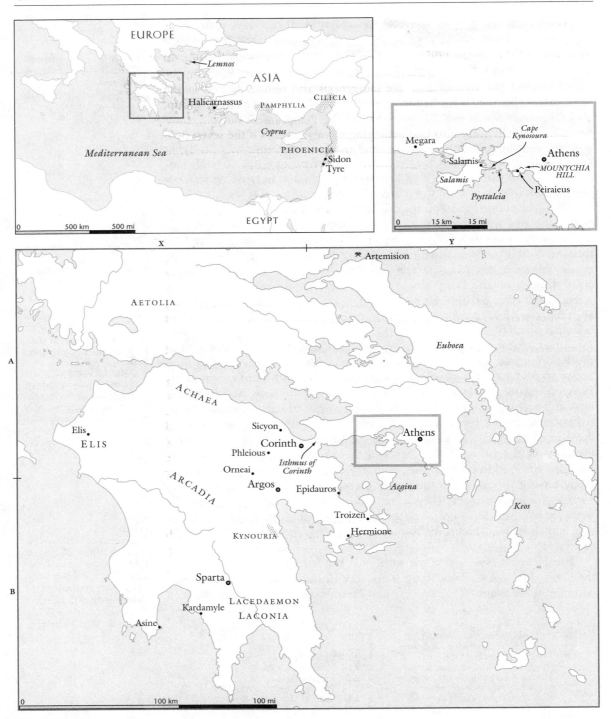

EUROPE

ASIA

→ *Lemnos*

Halicarnassus

PAMPHYLIA   CILICIA

Cyprus

PHOENICIA

•Sidon
•Tyre

Mediterranean Sea

EGYPT

0   500 km   500 mi

Megara

*Cape
Kynosoura*

Salamis

Athens
○
*MOUNYCHIA
HILL*

Salamis

Psyttaleia   Peiraieus

0   15 km   15 mi

X   Y

⁜ Artemision

AETOLIA

Euboea

A

ACHAEA

Sicyon

Elis•
ELIS

Corinth ○

Athens
○

Phleious •

*Isthmus of
Corinth*

Orneai •

ARCADIA

Argos ○

Epidauros •

Aegina

Keos

Troizen •

KYNOURIA

Hermione •

Sparta •

B

LACEDAEMON
LACONIA

Kardamyle •

Asine •

0   100 km   100 mi

MAP 8.72

who rushed to the defense of Hellas in fear of the danger it was in, while the rest of the Peloponnesians cared not at all, even though the festivals of Olympia and Karneia[j] had by now been concluded.

Seven peoples inhabit the Peloponnese, and of these, two of them, the Arcadians and the Kynourians,[a] are indigenous and remain settled in the same places that they inhabited in ancient times. There is one ethnic group, the Achaeans,[b] which never migrated from the Peloponnese but did move out of its own territory into one belonging to others. [2] Of the seven peoples, the remaining four have immigrated to where they now live: the Dorians, Aetolians,[a] Dryopes,[b] and Lemnians.[c] The Dorians have many notable cities; the Aetolians only one, Elis; the Dryopes have Hermione and Asine,[d] which lies near Kardamyle[e] in Laconia; the Lemnians have all the land of the Paroreatai.[f] [3] The Kynourians, being indigenous, seem to be the only Ionians, but they became thoroughly Dorian under the rule of the Argives[a] and with the passage of time; they are inhabitants of Orneai[b] and its surrounding territory. The rest of the cities belonging to these seven peoples, apart from those I mentioned, assumed a neutral stance; but if I may speak freely, they were in effect medizing by remaining neutral.

Those at the isthmus took on such hard work as they did because they knew they were now running a race with everything at stake, and they did not expect the fleet to distinguish itself. Those at Salamis heard of what the others were doing at the isthmus, but they were terrified nonetheless, afraid not so much for themselves as for the Peloponnese. [2] For a while, they stood side by side, speaking only in whispers, one man to the next at his side, expressing amazement at Eurybiades' foolish decision. But finally the tension burst out into the open. A meeting was convened, and many of the earlier debates were repeated, some of them arguing that they should sail for the Peloponnese and undertake the risk of battle for that land instead of staying to fight for a land that had already been taken by the spear. On the other hand, the Athenians,[a] Aeginetans,[b] and Megarians[c] asserted that they should stay here and defend themselves where they were.

When it became clear that Themistokles was losing the dispute with the Peloponnesians, he withdrew from the conference without being noticed and, after going outside, sent a man by boat to the camp of the Medes with precise instructions as to what he should say. This man's name was Sikinnos;[a]

8.73
PELOPONNESE
Herodotus lists the seven nations which inhabit the Peloponnese.

8.74
480
SALAMIS
As work progresses at the isthmus, the Peloponnesians at Salamis call another assembly to debate whether to stay and fight or retreat to the isthmus.

8.75
480
SALAMIS
Themistokles, finding himself outvoted, sends a trusted servant to the Persians to advise them to prevent the Greek fleet from escaping from Salamis.

8.72.1j Olympian and Karneian festivals: these festivals might have served as pretexts for Dorian inaction, but not at this time of year (September). See Appendix I, Classical Greek Religious Festivals, §5–12.
8.73.1a Kynouria: Map 8.72, BX.
8.73.1b Achaea: Map 8.72, AX. The Achaeans are said to have moved from Laconia (Map 8.72, BX) to Achaea, which at that time was inhabited by Ionians.
8.73.2a Aetolia: Map 8.72, AX.
8.73.2b Dryopis: Map 8.43, AX.
8.73.2c Lemnos: Map 8.72, locator.
8.73.2d Asine: Map 8.72, BX.
8.73.2e Kardamyle, Laconia: Map 8.72, BX.

8.73.2f Paroreatai: location of this group's territory is unknown, but these Lemnians are the Minyans who came from Lemnos; see 4.145–146, 4.148.
8.73.3a Argos: Map 8.72, BX.
8.73.3b Orneai: Map 8.72, AX.
8.74.2a Athens: Map 8.72, AY, and inset.
8.74.2b Aegina: Map 8.72, BY.
8.74.2c Megara: Map 8.72, inset.
8.75.1a Some have doubted this story of Sikinnos' mission before the battle, but more accept it, reserving their skepticism for Sikinnos' second mission (8.110.2), which, despite what Greeks thought, probably did not in any way influence what Xerxes ordered.

[who] was a household servant of Themistokles' who looked after his children. After these events had passed, and at a time when the Thespians were accepting new citizens, Themistokles made this man a Thespian and also made him wealthy. [2] When Sikinnos arrived by boat at the camp, he said to the commanders of the barbarians, "I have been sent here by the commander of the Athenians without the knowledge of the other Hellenes, for he happens to favor the cause of the King and wants your side to prevail over that of the Hellenes. I have come to tell you that the Hellenes are utterly terrified and are planning to flee, and that you now have the opportunity to perform the most glorious of all feats if you do not stand by and watch them escape, [3] for they are in great disagreement with one another and will not stand up to you; indeed you will see them fighting a naval battle against themselves, those favoring your side opposing those who do not." Having conveyed this message, he left them alone and departed.

[margin note: Sikinnos' message]

The commanders, thinking the message credible, responded by first landing many Persians on the islet of Psyttaleia,[a] which lies between Salamis[b] and the mainland. Then, when the middle of the night had come, they directed the western wing of the fleet to encircle Salamis, while those who had been posted around Keos[c] and Kynosoura[d] deployed their ships so that they now occupied the entire strait from Salamis to Mounychia.[e] [2] They did this in order to prevent the Hellenes from escaping; they intended to trap them at Salamis, where they would make them pay for their encounters at Artemision.[a] And the reason they landed Persian troops on the islet of Psyttaleia was so that when the battle took place, the men on the islet would be able to save their compatriots and destroy their enemies, since the island was located in the very path of the battle about to be fought, and most of the men and wreckage would be cast ashore there. [3] All these steps were carried out quietly so that their opponents would not learn of them, but because of all these preparations, the fleet's crews were unable to catch any sleep at all that night.

[margin note: credited by Xerxes' hubristic message]

Now I cannot refute the truth of oracles, since I refuse to reject prophecies that speak quite plainly when I consider words like these:

[margin note: ORACLE: XERXES' HUBRIS]

When with their ships they bridge the sacred coast
of Artemis, who wields a sword of gold, with Kynosoura by the sea
In madness from their hopes after sacking lustrous Athens,
Justice the Divine will then smother mighty Greed, ravenous
    son of Hubris

8.76
480
SALAMIS
The Persians find this message credible, and send troops to occupy the island of Psyttaleia and deploy their fleet so as to prevent the Greek ships from escaping.

8.77
Herodotus cites an oracle he considers both clear and irrefutable.

8.76.1a   Psyttaleia: Map 8.72, inset. Some scholars have wanted to identify Psyttaleia with the island now called St. George (Hagia Georgios), which is well inside the strait between Salamis and Attica, but most of them agree that Psyttaleia was modern Lipsokoutali, at the entrance to the strait. It is also identified in Figure 8.84.

8.76.1b   Salamis: Map 8.72, inset.

8.76.1c   Keos: the location of Keos on Salamis is unknown.

8.76.1d   Cape Kynosoura (the word means "dog's tail"), the easternmost peninsula of Salamis island: Map 8.72, inset.

8.76.1e   Mounychia Hill (Peiraieus): Map 8.72, inset.

8.76.2a   Artemision: Map 8.72, AY.

Raging in his lust, he thinks to drink and swallow all.
[2] Bronze against bronze will then engage closely,
and Ares will color the open sea red.
At that time will Hellas see the day of its freedom,
brought by far-seeing Kronides and the Lady of Victory.[a]

I do not dare to refute oracles such as these, expressed so plainly by Bakis,[b] nor do I listen to others who do so.

Meanwhile, the commanders at Salamis were now engaged in fierce wrangling. They were not yet aware that the barbarian ships had encircled them on the island; they assumed that they were all still in the same positions in which they had been observed on the day before.

Then, as the commanders were in the midst of their dispute, Aristeides[a] son of Lysimachos crossed over from Aegina.[b] He was an Athenian who had been ostracized[c] by the people, but I have come to believe through my inquiries into his character that he was actually the best and most just of all the Athenians.[d] [2] This man stood at the door of the council and summoned Themistokles to come out, though he was no friend of his but in fact had been his worst enemy. Because of the magnitude of their present evils, however, he forced himself to forget the past and summoned Themistokles, wishing to converse with him, for he had heard that those who had come from the Peloponnese were eager to sail to the isthmus.[a] [3] And when Themistokles emerged, Aristeides said to him: "In any crisis, Themistokles, but especially in this one, it is we who should strive to see which of us can do more for our fatherland. Let me tell you that as far as the Peloponnesians are concerned, it makes no difference whether there is much or little talk about sailing away, for I have seen with my own eyes that even if the Corinthians and Eurybiades himself wanted to sail out of here, they could not possibly do so, because we are encircled by our enemies. Well, then, go in and tell them this news."

Themistokles replied, "The appeal that you make is as worthy as the news that you bring is welcome. For you are an eyewitness to just what I wanted to have happen. You should know that what the Medes are doing is all because of me. Since the Hellenes were unwilling to go into battle, it proved necessary to lead them to it against their will. So since you have such

8.78
480
SALAMIS
The Greek generals argue in ignorance.

8.79
480
SALAMIS
Aristeides returns from ostracized exile and, calling out his rival Themistokles, tells him to inform the other commanders that the Greek fleet is now surrounded and cannot flee.

8.80
480
SALAMIS
Themistokles tells Aristeides that he is pleased, having caused the Persians to move to cut them off, and asks Aristeides to tell the others the news himself.

8.77.2a   Kronides: Zeus son of Kronos. Lady of
              Victory: Nike.
8.77.2b   Bakis, a famous source of prophecies. See
              n. 8.20.1a.
8.79.1a   Aristeides was an Athenian statesman and
              general of the early fifth century. He sup-
              ported Militiades' decision to fight at
              Marathon, and although he was ostracized
              in 482, he was recalled in the general
              amnesty that was declared as Xerxes' forces
              neared Attica. He commanded the Greek
              forces at Psyttaleia, and when the anti-
              Persian Delian League was formed under
              Athenian leadership in 478, he fixed the
              tribute quota of each contributory state.
8.79.1b   Aegina: Map 8.86, inset.
8.79.1c   Ostracism was a procedure by which an
              Athenian citizen could be honorably ban-
              ished from Athens and her possessions
              for ten years without loss of property or
              citizenship if, after the Athenians chose to
              hold such a vote, he received the most
              votes out of a total of at least 6,000 cast
              (votes were noted on shards of pottery
              called *ostraka*). See Appendix A, §8, and
              Figure 8.79, which shows *ostraka* that
              were used in ostracism votes.
8.79.1d   He was known in Athens as "Aristeides
              the Just."
8.79.2a   Isthmus of Corinth: Map 8.86.

FIGURE 8.79. POTTERY FRAGMENTS (*OSTRAKA*) FOUND IN THE ARCHAEOLOGICAL EXCAVATIONS OF THE ATHENIAN AGORA WHICH WERE USED TO REGISTER OSTRACISM VOTES. THE NAMES SCRATCHED ON THE *OSTRAKA* ARE (CLOCKWISE FROM UPPER LEFT) MEGAKLES, ARISTEIDES (MISSPELLED ARISSTEIDES), KIMON, THEMISTOKLES, PERICLES, AND HIPPOCRATES.

good news to report, go tell them yourself. [2] For if I were to tell them, I would appear to have made it up and I would fail to persuade them; no, they will not believe that the barbarians are really doing this. So then, go in yourself and describe the situation to them, and when you have delivered the news, the best thing that could happen would be that they are convinced, but if they do not believe you, it will be all the same for us, because if, as you say, we are surrounded on all sides, they will no longer be able to run away."

So Aristeides went to meet with the commanders and told them the news, saying that he had just come from Aegina and had experienced great difficulty in trying to sail here and elude those who were now blockading them, because the entire camp of the Hellenes was now encircled by the ships of Xerxes. He then counseled them to prepare to defend themselves, and after saying this, he withdrew. And once again a dispute arose, for the majority of the commanders did not believe him.

They continued to distrust his report until a trireme of Tenian[a] deserters arrived, commanded by Panaitios son of Sosimenes, which now, indeed, brought the whole truth. It was in reward for this feat that the Tenians were honored with an inscription, as among those who had assured the destruction of the barbarian, on a tripod at Delphi.[b] [2] With the addition of this ship that had deserted to join the fleet at Salamis[a] and with the Lemnian[b] ship that had earlier joined it at Artemision,[c] the Greek fleet was now filled out to 380 ships; it had previously fallen short of this number by two ships.

Since the words of the Tenians were quite convincing to the Hellenes, they made preparations for a naval battle. As dawn was breaking, they convened a meeting of the marines, and of all the commanders, Themistokles issued the most effective orders. Everything he said communicated a contrast between the better and the worse in human nature and circumstances, [2] and he encouraged them to choose the better of these for themselves; and then, after winding up his speech, he ordered them to their ships. Now, just as they were going on board, the trireme that had gone off to fetch the descendants of Aiakos arrived back from Aegina.

The Hellenes set sail with all their ships, and as they moved offshore, they were immediately attacked by the barbarians.

The rest of the Hellenes began to back water and turn their ships toward the beach, but an Athenian, Ameinias of Pallene,[a] had advanced his ship farther out, and he rammed one of the enemy's vessels. The two ships became entangled and could not be separated, so it was in that manner, when the others came to help Ameinias, that the battle started. [2] That is how the Atheni-

8.81
480
SALAMIS
Aristeides informs the Peloponnesian generals but is not believed.

8.82
480
SALAMIS
A ship of Tenos deserts from the Persian fleet, confirms the news, and brings the number of Greek ships to 380.

8.83
480
SALAMIS
The Hellenes hold an assembly. Themistokles addresses them, and they prepare to fight.

8.84
480
SALAMIS
The Persian fleet attacks, and although some Hellenes retreat, an Athenian ship charges and begins the fighting, but some say it was an Aeginetan ship that began the battle.

8.82.1a Tenos: Map 8.86.
8.82.1b Delphi: Map 8.86. This may be a reference to the tripod commemorating the victory of the Hellenes over the Persians which is described in 9.81.1. The base and shaft of this tripod can still be seen today in Istanbul on the site of the ancient hippodrome. See Figure 9.81a.
8.82.2a Salamis: Map 8.86, inset.
8.82.2b Lemnos: Map 8.86.
8.82.2c Artemision: Map 8.86.
8.84.1a Pallene, Attic deme: Map 8.86 inset. Attic demes may have originally been just townships, villages, or regions in Attica. After the reforms of Kleisthenes in 508/07 (see 5.69), they became official political units of the Athenian state, and every Athenian citizen was identified by his name and the deme in which he had been born.

FIGURE 8.84. AN AERIAL VIEW OF THE ISLAND OF SALAMIS AND THE NEARBY MAINLAND (NORTH IS AT THE BOTTOM). THE ISLAND MOST SCHOLARS BELIEVE TO BE PSYTTALEIA, THE CHANNEL THROUGH WHICH THE PERSIAN FLEET ENTERED THE STRAITS, AND MOUNT AIGALEOS (FROM WHICH XERXES WATCHED THE BATTLE) ARE SHOWN IN THE LOWER LEFT QUADRANT OF THE PHOTOGRAPH.

ans claim the sea fight began, but the Aeginetans say it was the ship that had gone to Aegina for the descendants of Aiakos that started it. And it is also said that an apparition of a woman appeared and urged them on so loudly that the entire force of the Hellenes could hear her, beginning with the reproach, "What has gotten into you! How long will you continue to back water?"

The Athenians were facing the Phoenicians,[a] whose ships held the west wing of the Persian line toward Eleusis;[b] and opposite the Lacedaemonians[c] were the Ionian[d] ships, who formed the east wing of the Persian line over toward Peiraieus.[e] Few of the Ionians, however, deliberately fought like cowards as Themistokles had told them to do;[f] in fact, the majority did not. [2] While I could list the names of many trierarchs who captured Greek ships, I will deal with none of them except Theomestor son of Androdamas and Phylakos son of Histiaios, both of whom were Samians.[a] [3] The reason

8.85
480
SALAMIS
How most of the Ionians fight well for the Persians, and two of them are well rewarded.

8.85.1a Phoenicia: Map 8.72, locator.
8.85.1b Eleusis: Map 8.86, inset.
8.85.1c Lacedaemon (Sparta): Map 8.86.
8.85.1d Ionia: Map 8.86, locator.
8.85.1e Peiraieus: Map 8.86, inset.
8.85.1f Themistokles' tactical instructions to the Ionians were described in 8.22.2.
8.85.2a Samos: Map 8.86.

why I mention these alone is that Theomestor, on account of this feat, was installed as tyrant of Samos by the Persians, while Phylakos was recorded as benefactor of the King and granted much land. The benefactors of the King are called *orosangai* in Persian.

That, then, is how these men fared. Most of Xerxes' ships at Salamis were disabled, some being ruined by the Athenians, others by the Aeginetans. For since the Hellenes fought the naval battle in disciplined order and remained in their ranks, while the barbarians failed to hold their positions and made no moves that might have followed a sensible plan, the battle was bound to turn out as it did. The men in Xerxes' fleet did, however, prove themselves better men by far on this day than they had off Euboea, since each man fought eagerly and in fear of Xerxes, thinking that the King was watching him.

I cannot speak with certainty about the rest of them, how each specific group of barbarians and Hellenes performed in the fighting, but this is what happened to Artemisia, which resulted in her winning still higher esteem from the King. [2] The King's fleet had reached a state of mass confusion, and it was during this crisis that Artemisia's ship was pursued by one from Attica. She was unable to escape it because there were so many other friendly ships in front of her, and since her own ship was closest to those of the enemy, she made a decision which turned out to be very much to her advantage. While she was still being chased by the Attic ship, she rammed at full speed a friendly ship manned by Kalyndians[a] and the king of the Kalyndians himself, Damasithymos. [3] Now I cannot say if there was some quarrel she had with him that had arisen while they were still near the Hellespont,[a] or even whether, when she ran into the Kalyndian ship, the deed was premeditated or accidental. [4] But when she rammed it, the good she accomplished for herself was twofold. For when the trierarch of the Attic ship saw that she was ramming a ship of the barbarians, he assumed that Artemisia's vessel was either a Greek ship or one that was deserting from the barbarians and now fighting for the Hellenes, so he turned away from her ship to attack others.

That was one result to her advantage: she escaped and was not destroyed. But another outcome was that, even though she was doing harm to her own side, she won the highest possible praise from Xerxes. [2] For it is said that as the King was watching, he noticed the one ship ramming the other, and one of the men with him said, "My lord, do you see how well Artemisia is fighting, and how she has sunk an enemy ship?" Xerxes inquired if it was truly Artemisia who had accomplished this feat, and they confirmed that it was, clearly recognizing the ensign of her vessel, and believing that the one she had destroyed belonged to the enemy. [3] So all that, as I have explained, brought her good fortune. And in addition, no one from the Kalyndian ship survived to become her accuser. In response to what he had heard, Xerxes is reported to have said, "My men have become women, and my women, men!"

8.86
480
SALAMIS
The Persians are disorganized, but they fight bravely, out of fear of Xerxes, who observes the battle.

8.87
480
SALAMIS
The story of Artemisia, and how she cleverly evades pursuit by ramming a friendly ship and sinking it, leading her pursuer to think her a friendly ship or a defector.

8.88
480
SALAMIS
Xerxes, thinking Artemisia had sunk a Greek ship, praises her and remarks that his women have become men, and his men, women.

8.87.2a   Kalynda: Map 8.86.   8.87.3a   Hellespont: Map 8.86.

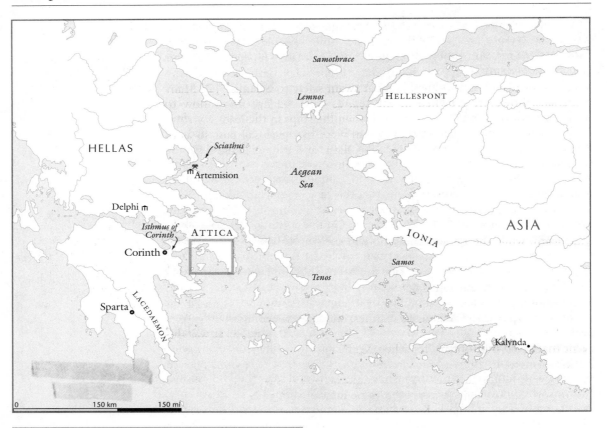

MAP 8.86

In this struggle the commander Ariabignes, the son of Darius and brother of Xerxes, lost his life, as did many other notable men of the Persians, the Medes, and their other allies; but few of the Hellenes died, for they knew how to swim, so those whose ships were destroyed and who were not killed in hand-to-hand combat swam safely to Salamis.[a] [2] Many barbarians, however, drowned in the sea, as they did not know how to swim. Most of their fleet was destroyed when the ships in the lead turned to flee, because those deployed behind them were trying to sail past so as to perform some spectacular feat before the King, and they collided with the leading ships from their own side who were in flight.

In this state of confusion, some of the Phoenicians[a] whose ships had been destroyed went to the King and slandered the Ionians, saying that it was because of them that their ships had been lost and that they were traitors. But it so happened that Xerxes did not punish the Ionian commanders with death, while the Phoenicians who had slandered them were repaid for doing so in the following way. [2] While they were still speaking to this effect, a Samothracian[a] ship rammed an Attic[b] ship, and as the Attic ship began to sink, an Aeginetan[c] ship attacked and sunk the Samothracian ship. The Samothracians, being javelin fighters, threw their weapons from their own sinking ship at the Aeginetan marines; and after sweeping them off the deck, they boarded the enemy ship and took possession of it. [3] It was this event that saved the Ionians, for when Xerxes saw them achieving this great feat, he turned to the Phoenicians and, in his extreme vexation, blamed them for everything that had happened, and he ordered that their heads be cut off so that those who had proved to be inferior should never again slander their betters. [4] In fact, Xerxes was constantly watching to see if any of his men performed some remarkable feat. He observed the fighting as he sat at the foot of the mountain called Aigaleos,[a] facing Salamis, and whenever he saw one of his commanders carry out an extraordinary deed, he would immediately inquire who was doing it, and had his scribes write down the name of the trierarch, his patronymic,[b] and the city from which he came. The presence of Ariaramnes, a Persian who was a friend of the Ionians, also contributed to the sufferings of the Phoenicians.

The King's men now dealt with the Phoenicians.

Those barbarians who had taken flight and were trying to sail out toward Phaleron[a] were met by the Aeginetans, who were lying in ambush in the strait and who there performed noteworthy deeds. For while the Athenians in the midst of the melée disabled those ships that resisted or that attempted to flee, the Aeginetans did the same to those who were trying to sail out. So those ships which escaped from the Athenians ran right into the Aeginetans.

8.89
480
SALAMIS
Many Persians drown because they cannot swim, but few Hellenes, who can.

8.90
480
SALAMIS
The Phoenicians go to Xerxes and accuse the Ionians of treason; but he, who in his vexation blames everyone, seeing a heroic Samothracian ship defeat its foes, condemns the Phoenicians instead.

8.91
480
SALAMIS
Aeginetan ships attack those Persian ships who try to flee to Phaleron.

8.89.1a	Salamis: Map 8.86, inset.	8.90.4a	Mount Aigaleos: Map 8.86, inset.
8.90.1a	Phoenicia: Map 8.72, locator.	8.90.4b	A person's patronymic was derived from
8.90.2a	Samothrace: Map 8.86.		his father's name, as in Themistokles son
8.90.2b	Attic here means Athenian. Attica: Map		of Neokles.
	8.86 and inset.	8.91.1a	Phaleron: Map 8.86, inset.
8.90.2c	Aegina: Map 8.86, inset.		

8.92
480
SALAMIS
Herodotus recounts the anecdotes of Polykritos mocking Themistokles and of the safe return of Pytheas. The remaining Persian ships reach Phaleron and the protection of their army.

At that point, the ship of Themistokles, which was chasing another ship, met with the ship of an Aeginetan, Polykritos son of Krios, which had rammed a Sidonian[a] ship. Now this Sidonian ship was the same one that captured the Aeginetan ship that had been keeping watch off Sciathus[b] and on which Pytheas son of Ischenoos had been sailing. He was the man whom the Persians had greatly admired after he had been nearly chopped to pieces in the fighting. They still had him on their ship, keeping him there because they respected his valor,[c] and now this Sidonian ship conveying him along with some Persians was captured, so that Pytheas in this way survived to return safely to Aegina. [2] When Polykritos looked at the Attic ship and recognized the ensign as belonging to the Athenian flagship, he shouted to Themistokles, taunting him with the charge of "medism"[a] that had been brought against the Aeginetans. Such were the insults that Polykritos cast at Themistokles as he rammed the ship. The surviving barbarian ships fled to Phaleron, where they came under the protection of their army.

8.93
480
SALAMIS
The Hellenes credited most courageous conduct in the fighting to first the Aeginetans and then the Athenians.

Of the Hellenes who fought in this naval battle at Salamis, praise for the greatest valor went to the Aeginetans, and after them to the Athenians; of individual men, to Polykritos of Aegina and the Athenians Eumenes of Anagyrous[a] and Ameinias of Pallene.[b] It was Ameinias who had pursued Artemisia; if he had realized that she was sailing on that ship, he would not have stopped before capturing her or being taken himself, [2] for orders to capture her had been given to the Athenian trierarchs, and a prize of 10,000 drachmas had been offered to whoever captured her alive, since they considered it a disgrace that a woman should wage war on Athens. But as I described earlier, she managed to escape, and there were others whose ships had survived also who were all now at Phaleron.

8.94
480
SALAMIS
Herodotus recounts a nasty rumor spread by the Athenians that the Corinthians fled in terror, but the other Hellenes agree that the Corinthians were foremost in the battle.

The Athenians say that at the beginning of the battle, just as the ships first clashed, the Corinthian[a] commander Adeimantos became utterly terrified. He panicked, raised his sails, and fled from the scene. The rest of the Corinthians, seeing their flagship in flight, did the same and also disappeared. [2] But during their flight, when they had reached the region of Salamis near the sanctuary of Athena Skiras,[a] they encountered a small ship sent by some god (it never became apparent who had sent it), and at the time when it came up to the Corinthians, they knew nothing of what was happening to the rest of the fleet. They came to believe that this was a divine occurrence because when this ship drew near to theirs, the men on board said, [3] "Adeimantos, by turning your ships around and fleeing in such haste you have utterly betrayed the Hellenes, who now are winning a victory over their enemies every bit as great as the one they had prayed for."

8.92.1a   Sidon: Map 8.72, locator.
8.92.1b   Sciathus: Map 8.86.
8.92.1c   The capture of Pytheas son of Ischenoos was described in 7.181.
8.92.2a   The Athenians must have accused the Aeginetans of favoring the Persian side, which was now belied

by their conduct in this battle.
8.93.1a   Anagyrous, Attic deme: Map 8.86, inset.
8.93.1b   Pallene, Attic deme: Map 8.86, inset.
8.94.1a   Corinth: Map 8.86.
8.94.2a   Precinct of Athena Skiras on Salamis: Map 8.86, inset.

When Adeimantos did not believe what they said, they spoke again, and told him that they were willing to be treated as hostages and to be put to death if the Hellenes did not prove to be victorious. [4] So it was then that he turned his ships around and, with the rest of the Corinthians, sailed back to the camp, but he arrived after the battle had been concluded. That, at least, is the story told by the Athenians. The Corinthians themselves, however, disagree, and think of themselves as among the first in the battle, and the rest of Hellas testifies to the validity of their claim.[a]

During the confusion at Salamis, the Athenian Aristeides son of Lysimachos, whom I recently mentioned as the best of men,[a] performed the following deed. Picking up many hoplites of Athenian origin, who had been stationed along the coast of Salaminian territory, he brought them to the island of Psyttaleia[b] and had them disembark there, and these hoplites then proceeded to murder all the Persians who were occupying the island.

When the battle at sea had broken off, the Hellenes hauled up on the shore of Salamis as much of the wreckage as still remained afloat. They were prepared for another naval battle, expecting the King to use those of his ships that had survived intact. [2] Much of the wreckage was carried by the west wind and driven to the beach of Attica called Kolias,[a] and thus was fulfilled every oracle, not only those about the sea battle spoken by Bakis and Mousaios, but also the one concerning the wreckage carried to shore. This oracle had been given many years earlier and belonged to those of the oraclemonger[b] Lysistratos of Athens, but it had escaped the notice of all the Hellenes. The oracle said, "The women of Kolias will do their roasting on oars." This prophecy was to be fulfilled after the King had gone away.[c]

When Xerxes realized the severity of the disaster that had occurred, he became afraid that one of the Ionians would advise the Hellenes (if they did not think of it themselves) to sail to the Hellespont[a] and break apart the bridges, so that he would be trapped in Europe and in danger of perishing there. And so he made plans to flee. But because he did not want his plan to be detected by either the Hellenes or his own men, he began the attempt to construct a causeway[b] to Salamis by tying together Phoenician

8.95
480
PSYTTALEIA
Aristeides lands soldiers on Psyttaleia, who kill all the Persians there.

8.96
480
SALAMIS
As the Hellenes prepare for further battle, many wrecks are blown onto the Kolian shore, fulfilling oracles.

8.97
480
ATHENS
Xerxes decides privately to return to Persia, although he orders further moves to threaten Salamis. All are deceived except Mardonios.

8.94.4a   The role of the Corinthians in the battle is mysterious. Herodotus gives the Athenian story of the Corinthians starting to run away as soon as the battle was joined, but adds that the Greeks generally accept that the Corinthians did play the part they claim. A fragmentary inscription of which Plutarch ("On the Malice of Herodotus." *Moralia*, 870E) gives the full version supports the Corinthian claim. But what were they doing? Was their role, as some have speculated, to feign flight and thus draw the Persian fleet into the straits? Did they "capture Persians and Medes" as the inscription declares? There are awkward holes in Herodotus' account of the battle.

8.95.1a   Aristeides was mentioned in 8.79.1.

8.95.1b   Psyttaleia: Map 8.86, inset.
8.96.2a   Cape Kolias: Map 8.86, inset.
8.96.2b   On oraclemongers, see 7.6.3 and n. 7.6.3a.
8.96.2c   There must have been a vast body of oracular predictions, from which one could draw a few that proved to be genuinely prophetic. See Appendix P, §13, 14.
8.97.1a   Hellespont: Map 8.86.
8.97.1b   Ctesias, an ancient historian of whose work only fragments remain, says that the Persians began to build the causeway before the battle, which would have been pointless. Herodotus' version is even more improbable, for after the battle had been lost, building the causeway would have been both pointless and hardly possible. Very few modern scholars take Herodotus' story here seriously.

merchant ships to serve as a pontoon bridge and a wall. In addition, he made preparations as though he was actually determined to wage another naval battle. [2] When the others saw him doing these things, they were convinced that he was firmly committed to staying there to fight, but he did not deceive Mardonios, who was especially experienced in the way Xerxes' mind worked.

As Xerxes was doing all this, he also sent a courier to Persia to report his present misfortune. There is nothing that travels faster, and yet is mortal, than these couriers; the Persians invented this system, which works as follows. It is said that there are as many horses and men posted at intervals as there are days required for the entire journey, so that one horse and one man are assigned to each day. And neither snow nor rain nor heat nor dark of night keeps them from completing their appointed course as swiftly as possible.[a] [2] The first courier passes on the instructions to the second, the second to the third, and from there they are transmitted from one to another all the way through, just as the torchbearing relay is celebrated by the Hellenes in honor of Hephaistos. The Persians call this horse-posting system the *angareion*.

The first message had arrived at Susa[a] while Xerxes was in possession of Athens, and the news so delighted the Persians who had stayed behind that they scattered myrtle on all the roads, burned incense, and gave themselves over to sacrifices and pleasure. [2] The second message, following closely as it did on the first, so disturbed them that everyone tore their tunics to shreds, with endless crying and wailing, and placed the blame on Mardonios. The Persians behaved this way not so much because they were upset about the ships lost as out of fear for Xerxes himself. *SLAVE BEHAVIOR*

That remained the situation in Persia for the whole time that passed between the arrival of the message and that of Xerxes himself, whose presence put an end to their distress. Now Mardonios could see that Xerxes considered the outcome of the naval battle a great disaster, and he suspected that the King was planning to flee from Athens. So now, fearing that he would pay the penalty for having persuaded the King to make war on Hellas, he decided that it would be better to take the risk of either conquering Hellas or ending his life nobly after risking it for high stakes (although he was inclined to think that he would succeed in conquering Hellas). And so after he had carefully calculated all the factors, he made the following speech to Xerxes: [2] "My lord, do not be distressed or consider what has happened a great misfortune. For our whole contest depends not on wooden things but on men and horses. None of the men who suppose that they are now complete victors will step off their ships

8.98
480
PERSIA
A message is sent to Persia to announce the disaster. Herodotus praises the Persian courier system, whose couriers are not stopped by weather or darkness from their appointed course.

8.99
480
SUSA
While the Persians are celebrating the capture of Athens, they are confounded by news of the battle of Salamis.

8.100
480
ATHENS?
Mardonios advises Xerxes not to be discouraged, as only allies at sea have been defeated, not Persians on land. Fearing blame for his earlier aggressive counsel, he offers, should Xerxes decide to return to Persia, to continue the advance and to conquer the Hellenes with just a part of the Persian army.

american postal service motto

8.98.1a   This sentence, has long served as an unofficial motto of the U.S. Postal Service. Historians estimate that a courier system as described by Herodotus could cover the 2,000 miles between Sardis and Susa (Map 8.107, AY, and locator) in about a week. An army on foot might well require

three months for the journey, as Aristagoras told Kleomenes (5.50.2).
8.99.1a   Susa: Map 8.107, locator.
8.100.2a   Mardonios is undoubtedly referring to the Greeks who died at Thermopylae, which the Persians considered to be their victory.
8.100.3a   Peloponnese: Map 8.107, BX.

and try to oppose you, nor will anyone from the mainland. Those who have already done so have paid the penalty.[a] [3] So if you think it best, we can make an attempt on the Peloponnese[a] immediately; or, if it seems better to wait, we can do that, too. But do not be disheartened, for the Hellenes can have no escape from being called to account for what they have done both just now and earlier, and from becoming your slaves. So whichever of these courses you follow will turn out for the best. But if instead you have made plans to lead your army back, then go and return with it, since in that event I have another strategy to suggest. [4] But whatever you do, sire, do not make the Persians a laughingstock to the Hellenes. For no harm has been done to you by the actions of the Persians, and you could not cite an occasion on which we proved to be cowards. It may be that the Phoenicians, Egyptians, Cypriots, and Cilicians[a] have proved themselves to be cowards, but this disaster can in no way be attributed to Persians. [5] And since you cannot blame the Persians, do follow my advice. If it is your decision not to remain here, then go back to your homeland and lead back the larger part of your army, but what I must do is select 300,000 troops from the army and deliver Hellas to you when it has been completely enslaved."

Xerxes felt as much joy and pleasure in hearing this as he could, considering his adversities. He told Mardonios that he would first consult with others about the two courses before giving him an answer. And while he was deliberating with his specially chosen counselors, he decided to summon Artemisia to join the consultation, because she had obviously been the only one before who had correctly perceived what should be done. [2] When Artemisia arrived, Xerxes sent away all the others, his counselors as well as his bodyguards, and said to her, "Mardonios bids me to stay and make an attempt on the Peloponnese, claiming that the Persians—the land army, that is—are not to blame for the disaster, and that they want to display proof of that. [3] In any case, he bids me to do that, or if not, he wants to pick out 300,000 troops from the army and completely enslave Hellas, and bids me to lead the rest of the army back to my homeland. [4] Well, then, since you counseled me well by trying to prevent me from waging the naval battle that has taken place, please tell me now how I can prosper through your good advice."

Thus he requested her advice, and this is what she told him: "Sire, it is difficult for me to give the best advice to you, as you are seeking the best possible course of action, but in view of the present situation, it seems to me that you should go back home, and if Mardonios wants and promises to do what he has suggested, leave him behind here with the men of his choice. For if he does subjugate this land as he claims he would like to do and thus succeeds in this plan, the success will be yours, my lord, since the

8.100.4a   Phoenicia, Egypt, Cyprus, Cilicia: Map
              8.107, locator. It is interesting to note
              that Mardonios does not include the
              Ionian Hellenes in his list of cowards.

8.101
480
ATHENS
Xerxes thanks Mardonios and considers what he should do, asking the advice of Persians and of Artemisia whether he should persevere or return and leave Mardonios with the pick of the army.

8.102
480
ATHENS
Artemisia advises Xerxes to return home, arguing that as King, he will still have credit for any victory that Mardonios gains, but will at home be safe from any disaster that Mardonios might suffer.

conquest will be performed by your slaves. On the other hand, if the outcome is the opposite of what Mardonios thinks will happen, it will be no great misfortune, since you will survive and so will your power in Asia[a] as far as your own house is concerned. [3] And if you and your house survive, the Hellenes will have to run many races for their lives. Besides, if something happens to Mardonios, it is of no great consequence. And even if the Hellenes win, they will not win anything substantial by destroying your slave, while you will march home after you have burned Athens,[a] and thus will have achieved the goal of your expedition."

Xerxes was delighted with this advice, for she had succeeded in telling him exactly what he was thinking himself. But I suppose that even if all the men and women in the world had advised him to stay, he would not have done so, such was his state of utter terror. After praising Artemisia, he sent her off to take his sons to Ephesus,[a] for some of his illegitimate sons had accompanied him.

And along with his sons he sent a guardian, Hermotimos, a Pedasian[a] by birth who had won a place second to none among the eunuchs serving the King. The Pedasians live above Halicarnassus, and among the Pedasians, whenever some difficulty is about to beset those who dwell around that city, then within a certain amount of time the current priestess of Athena grows a long beard. This has already happened twice before.[b]

So it was from these Pedasians that Hermotimos had come, and of all the people we know of, it was he who managed to get the greatest revenge for an injustice done to him. Having been captured by his enemies and offered up for sale, he was bought by Panionios of Chios,[a] who made a living off the most ungodly practice: whenever he acquired boys endowed with beauty, he would castrate them and then take them to Sardis[b] or Ephesus and sell them for large sums of money, [2] for among the barbarians, eunuchs are more valuable than males with testicles because of their trustworthiness and fidelity. So Panionios castrated this man as well as many others, since that is how he made his living. But Hermotimos did not encounter bad fortune in everything; for from Sardis he went to the King's court along with other gifts being sent there, and as time went on he became the most honored of all the eunuchs in the court of Xerxes.

Now when the King sent the Persian army to Athens, and while he was still at Sardis, Hermotimos went down to the coast on some business to the Mysian[a] territory that is inhabited by Chians and called Atarneus.[b] And it was there that he found Panionios. [2] Hermotimos recognized him, and spoke to him amicably and at length, first telling him about all the benefits

8.102.2a   Asia: Map 8.107, locator.
8.102.3a   Athens: Map 8.107, BX.
8.103.1a   Ephesus: Map 8.107, BY.
8.104.1a   Pedasa: Map 8.107, BY.
8.104.1b   The reader might wish to compare this passage about the Pedasian priestess of

Athena's beard with that of 1.175, of which it is almost a paraphrase.
8.105.1a   Chios: Map 8.107, BY.
8.105.1b   Sardis: Map 8.107, AY.
8.106.1a   Mysia: Map 8.107, AY.
8.106.1b   Atarneus: Map 8.107, AY.

he now possessed thanks to him, and next promising that in return he would provide just as many benefits for him, if Panionios would bring the members of his household to Atarneus and live there.ᵃ And so Panionios gladly accepted what he was told and brought his wife and children there. [3] When Hermotimos had him there with his whole family, he said, "Of all men up to this time you are the most impious in your livelihood, which you earn by the most ungodly deeds! What evil did I—myself or any of my people—do to you or yours that you would render me a neuter instead of a man? You thought that the gods would not notice your practice, but they do observe justice, and they have surreptitiously led you, the performer of ungodly deeds, right into my hands; and so you cannot find fault with the just penalty you will receive from me." [4] After he had cast these reproaches at him, he had Panionios' sons—all four of them—brought before them, and then compelled Panionios to cut off the private parts of his sons; and because he was forced, he did it. Then, when he had finished, his sons were forced to castrate him. So it was that vengeance at the hands of Hermotimos came to Panionios.

GODS SEE TO JUSTICE

After Xerxes had entrusted his sons to Artemisia for her to take them to Ephesus, he summoned Mardonios and ordered him to sort through his army and select those troops he wanted, and to try to perform deeds that would live up to his promises. That is all that happened that day. But that night the commanders, at the King's order, put out to sea from Phaleronᵃ to sail back to the Hellespont,ᵇ each as quickly as he could, in order to protect the bridges of boats in preparation for the King's journey back home. [2] While the barbarians were sailing close to Cape Zoster,ᵃ they thought they saw ships—though these objects were actually small promontories extending out from the mainland—and they fled for quite some distance. But then after a while they realized that these were not ships but capes, and so they gathered together again and resumed their journey.

8.107
480
HELLESPONT
Xerxes leaves Mardonios and his army of picked troops and orders his navy to sail to the Hellespont to guard the bridges there.

When day came, the Hellenes could see that the army still remained where it had been before, and they therefore expected that the fleet was still off Phaleron as well. Thinking that they would have to fight another sea battle, they made preparations to defend themselves. But then, when they learned that the ships were gone, they immediately decided to pursue them. With that in mind, they sailed as far as Androsᵃ in pursuit of Xerxes' fleet but did not catch sight of any ships, so upon reaching that island, they held a council. [2] Themistokles proposed that they should make their way through the islands, pursue the ships, and sail straight for the Hellespont in order to break apart the bridges. But Eurybiades opposed

8.108
480
ANDROS
The next day the Hellenes discover that the Persian fleet has gone. They give chase, and Themistokles advises them to cut the bridges at the Hellespont. Eurybiades rejects this, arguing that it is better to allow the Persians a way to leave Hellas.

8.106.2a Herodotus' text is vague about where exactly Hermotimos asked Panionios to settle. It might have been Atarneus, or perhaps Sardis (Map 8.107, AY). Scholars do not agree.

8.107.1a Phaleron: Map 8.107, BX; for better

scale, Map 8.86, inset.
8.107.1b Hellespont: Map 8.107, AY.
8.107.2a Cape Zoster, Attica (the "Girdle"): Map 8.107, BX; for better scale, Map 8.86, inset.
8.108.1a Andros: Map 8.107, BY.

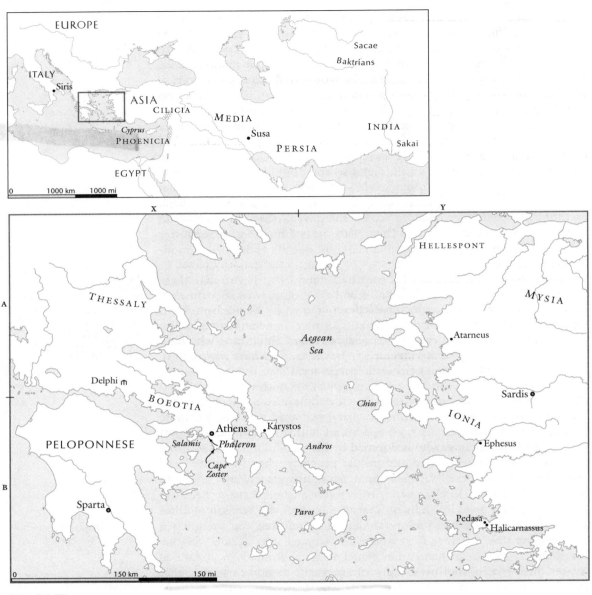

MAP 8.107

this, pointing out that if they broke apart the bridges of boats, they would inflict upon Hellas the greatest evil of all. [3] He explained that if the Persian was trapped and forced to remain in Europe, he would try his best to stir up trouble, since, if he remained inactive, it would be impossible for him to achieve anything at all; besides, he would have no apparent means of returning, and his army would perish from starvation. But if he set his hand to it and worked diligently at it, everyone in Europe would go over to him—city by city and nation by nation—whether they were captured or because they came to an agreement with him before they were taken. And all this time, his troops would rely on the annual crops of the Hellenes for their food. [4] Eurybiades thought that the Persian, now that he had been defeated in the naval battle, would not want to stay in Europe and therefore he should be allowed to flee until he reached his own land; from then on, Eurybiades told them, the contest should be fought in and over Xerxes' territory. The other Peloponnesian commanders agreed with this opinion.

Realizing that he would not be able to persuade the majority to sail to the Hellespont, Themistokles turned his attention to the Athenians, for the enemy's escape infuriated them more than all the others, and they were all dead set on sailing to the Hellespont even by themselves, if the others refused to go. He said to them, [2] "I have seen for myself on many occasions and have even far more often heard about men who have been defeated and driven to extremes by necessity, who have managed to renew the fight and recover from their former weakness. But we are lucky, and so is Hellas, that we found a way to repulse such a huge and ominous multitude, so let us not pursue men who are fleeing from us. [3] For it is not we who have achieved all this, but the gods and heroes; they were jealous that one man should become king of both Asia and Europe, particularly an ungodly man who is doomed by his own folly. This man made no distinction between sacred and private property when he burned and demolished the statues of the gods; he whipped the sea violently and then sank shackles into it. [4] But since we are doing well for the present, let us stay in Hellas for now and take care of ourselves and our households. Let each one of us rebuild his home and diligently tend to his sowing, now that we have successfully driven away the barbarian. Then, with the coming of spring, let us sail to the Hellespont and Ionia."[a] [5] Now the reason Themistokles said this was in order to secure a reserve of credit with the King, so that in case he were to suffer some calamity at the hands of the Athenians, he would have a refuge to run to, which of course is exactly what did happen.

8.109.4a   Ionia: Map 8.107, BY.

8.109
480
ANDROS
Themistokles now advises the Athenians to let the Persians escape, but does so to curry future favor with the Persians should he ever need to flee Athens.

[handwritten margin notes] WHY XERXES = DEFEATED

THEM'S MOTIVES

This speech of Themistokles both misled the Athenians and successfully persuaded them. For if prior to this he had seemed to them to be a shrewd and clever man, events had shown him to be truly wise and prudent in his counsel, so they were entirely willing to follow his advice now. [2] And as soon as Themistokles had convinced them, he sent off a boat with some men in it whom he trusted to keep silent—even under any torture—about the message they were to deliver to the King. Among these, he once again sent his household servant Sikinnos. When they had arrived off Attica, the rest stayed behind on the boat while Sikinnos went to Xerxes and said, [3] "I have been sent by Themistokles son of Neokles, the commander of the Athenians and the best and wisest man of all the allies, to convey this message to you: 'Themistokles the Athenian wishes to do you a favor, and has held back the Hellenes from pursuing your fleet with their ships and breaking apart the bridges at the Hellespont, since that is what they wanted to do. So now go on your way and be at ease.'"

Once the message had been delivered, the men sailed back again. And the Hellenes, after resolving not to pursue the barbarians' ships any farther or to sail to the Hellespont to break apart the passageway across it, mounted a siege against Andros, as they wanted to destroy it. [2] For the Andrians were the first of the islanders from whom Themistokles had demanded money and who had refused to pay him. Themistokles had presented his demand in these terms: since the Athenians had come with two great gods, Persuasion and Necessity, the Andrians certainly had to give them money. To this the Andrians replied that it made sense for Athens to be so great and prosperous, since she had the good fortune that came with useful gods; [3] but the Andrians had come to a point of extreme deficiency in land, and they had two useless gods—Poverty and Helplessness—who apparently wished to remain on their island forever and refused to leave it. So since the Andrians had come into the possession of these gods, they would not give any money, for the power of the Athenians could never be stronger than their own utter powerlessness. It was after this reply and their refusal to pay any money that they were besieged.

There was no satisfying the greed of Themistokles. He sent threatening requests for money to the other islands through the same messengers that he had sent to the King, warning them that if they did not give what was asked, he would lead the Greek forces against them and destroy them by siege if necessary. [2] By warning them in this way he collected large sums of money from the Karystians[a] and the Parians,[b] who had heard both that Andros was being besieged because it had medized, and that Themistokles was the most highly reputed of all the commanders; so they sent the money out of fear. I

8.112.2a　Karystos: Map 8.107, BX.
8.112.2b　Paros: Map 8.107, BY.

cannot say whether any of the other islanders paid; I suppose some of them did, and not these alone. [3] The Karystians failed to defer misfortune by having paid, but the Parians managed to escape the army by appeasing Themistokles with bribes. Using Andros as his base, Themistokles acquired this money from the islanders, unknown to the other commanders.

The troops with Xerxes lingered a few days after the naval battle, and then marched off to Boeotia[a] along the same route by which they had come. For Mardonios had decided it was best for him to escort the King, thinking that this was an unseasonable time of year to wage war, so it was better to spend the winter in Thessaly[b] and then, when spring arrived, to make an attempt on the Peloponnese.[c] [2] When they reached Thessaly, Mardonios picked out his troops. The first were all the Persians known as the Immortals, except for Hydarnes the commander, since he refused to be separated from the King. Next he chose from the rest of the Persians the troops who wore breastplates, and 1,000 horsemen; he also took the Medes,[a] Sacae,[b] Baktrians,[c] and Indians,[d] both infantry and cavalry. [3] While he chose these as entire national contingents, he also picked out troops from the rest of the allies in lesser numbers, selecting them for their appearance or for some good service he knew that they had performed. The greatest national contingent he chose was that of the Persians, men who wore necklaces and bracelets, and after them, the Medes, whose numbers were no fewer than those of the Persians, but who were inferior in physical strength. Altogether he collected an army of 300,000 troops, including the cavalry.

While Mardonios was selecting his forces and Xerxes was still in Thessaly, the Lacedaemonians[a] received an oracle from Delphi[b] advising them to demand satisfaction for the murder of Leonidas and to accept whatever he gave them. So as quickly as they could, the Spartans sent off a herald, who managed to overtake all the forces while they were still in Thessaly. When he came into the presence of Xerxes, he said to him, [2] "King of the Medes, the Lacedaemonians and the Heraklids from Sparta demand satisfaction for murder, because you killed their king as he was trying to protect Hellas." At this, Xerxes burst into laughter, but refrained from answering for quite some time. Then, as Mardonios happened to be standing close by, he pointed at him and said, "Well, then, Mardonios here will give them the sort of satisfaction they deserve."

Accepting this reply, the herald departed. Xerxes then left Mardonios in Thessaly and made a swift journey to the Hellespont.[a] He arrived at the passage leading across it in forty-five days, but did not bring back even a fraction of his army intact, if I can put it that way. [2] Because they were starving, wherever his troops went and no matter what peoples they

8.113
480/79
THESSALY
Mardonios marches the army back to Thessaly to winter quarters and selects the best soldiers to stay with him in Hellas.

8.114
480
THESSALY
The Spartans send a herald to Xerxes demanding compensation for his slaying of Leonidas. He laughs and says Mardonios will take care of it appropriately.

8.115
480
THRACE
Xerxes leaves Mardonios and journeys to the Hellespont. Many with him suffer hunger and disease on the retreat.

8.113.1a   Boeotia: Map 8.107, BX.
8.113.1b   Thessaly: Map 8.107, AX.
8.113.1c   Peloponnese: Map 8.107, BX.
8.113.2a   Media: Map 8.107, locator.
8.113.2b   Sacae, location of territory: Map 8.107, locator.
8.113.2c   Baktrians (Baktrianoi), location of territory: Map 8.107, locator.
8.113.2d   India: Map 8.107, locator.
8.114.1a   Lacedaemon (Sparta): Map 8.107, BX.
8.114.1b   Delphi: Map 8.107, AX.
8.115.1a   Hellespont: Map 8.107, AY.

encountered along the journey, they seized all the crops and consumed them, but if they could find no crops, they would devour the grass growing from the ground, and they stripped the bark and plucked the foliage from trees both cultivated and wild alike, eating everything and leaving nothing at all behind. [3] Moreover, a plague descended upon the army, and dysentery wasted the troops along their way. Those who fell sick were left behind, and Xerxes commanded the cities they passed by along their march to feed and care for them, some in Thessaly, and others at Siris,[a] in Paionia,[b] and in Macedon.[c] [4] It was there that he had left the sacred chariot of Zeus on his march to Hellas, but upon his return he did not receive it back again, because the Paionians had given it to the Thracians,[a] and when Xerxes asked for it, they said that its mares had been seized while they were grazing by the inland Thracians who dwell around the sources of the Strymon.[b]

There an extraordinary deed was performed by the Thracian king of the Bisaltai[a] and the Krestonian[b] territory. He had told Xerxes that he himself would not willingly become his slave and, forbidding his sons to participate in the war against Hellas, he himself withdrew to Mount Rhodope.[c] [2] But his sons paid no attention to his orders, or perhaps they had their hearts set on seeing the war, and they joined the Persian on his expedition. For this reason, when all six of them now returned unharmed, their father gouged out their eyes.

That was their reward for what they had done. When the Persians had come out of Thrace and reached the passage, they were impatient to cross over the Hellespont to Abydos[a] in ships, for they did not find the bridges of boats still intact, since they had been broken apart by a storm. [2] While they were detained there, they obtained more food than they had found along the way, but because of their immoderate gorging and the change of water, many of the troops who had survived now died. The rest managed to reach Sardis[a] with Xerxes.

There is another version of the story that is also told: that when Xerxes marched out of Athens,[a] he came to Eion[b] on the Strymon, and once there, he no longer continued the journey by land, but entrusted his army to Hydarnes to lead to the Hellespont while he himself boarded a Phoenician ship and went on his way to Asia[c] by sea. [2] As he was sailing along, however, he was overtaken by a violent wind from the Strymon, which created surging waves. As the storm grew more violent and the ship became endangered, as it was heavily laden with the many Persians who were traveling with Xerxes and who were now on deck, the King fell into a panic and shouted to the helmsman, asking if there was any way they could be saved.

8.116
480
THRACE
How the Thracian king punished his disobedient sons, who had joined Xerxes.

8.117
480
HELLESPONT
The army crosses the Hellespont in boats, as the bridges were broken by a storm.

8.118
480
THRACIAN SEA
Herodotus recounts another version of Xerxes' return, in which a storm at sea forces many Persians to demonstrate their loyalty to the King by leaping overboard to lighten the ship.

8.115.3a   Siris, Italy: Map 8.121, locator.
8.115.3b   Paionia: Map 8.121, AX.
8.115.3c   Macedon: Map 8.121, AY.
8.115.4a   Thrace: Map 8.121, AY.
8.115.4b   Strymon River: Map 8.121, AX.
8.116.1a   Bisaltia: Map 8.121, AX.
8.116.1b   Krestonia: Map 8.121, AX.

8.116.1c   Rhodope Mountains: Map 8.121, AX.
8.117.1a   Abydos: Map 8.121, AY.
8.117.2a   Sardis: Map 8.121, BY.
8.118.1a   Athens: Map 8.121, BX.
8.118.1b   Eion: Map 8.121, AX.
8.118.1c   Asia: Map 8.121, BY, and locator.

[3] The helmsman replied, "My lord, there is none, unless we rid ourselves of these many men on board." Upon hearing this, Xerxes said, "Men of Persia, it is now time for you to prove your care for your king. For in you, it seems, lies my safety." [4] After he said this, his men prostrated themselves, leapt out into the sea, and the now lightened ship sailed safely to Asia. As soon as Xerxes stepped onto shore, he gave the helmsman a gift of a golden crown in return for saving his life, but then, because he had been responsible for the death of many Persians, he had his head cut off.

XERXES 'Z HELMSMAN

So that is another story told about the return of Xerxes, but to me at least this one is completely incredible for several reasons, but especially because of what it says happened to the Persians. For if the helmsman really did say this to Xerxes, I think there is not one in ten thousand people who would oppose my opinion that the King would have done something rather like this: he would have sent the Persians, including the most prominent of them, from the deck down to the ship's hold, and would have had Phoenicians in numbers equal to those Persians thrown overboard into the sea. In any case, I am sure that he returned to Asia with the rest of the army via the land route, as I described earlier.

And here is convincing proof of this claim. It is evident that on his way back, Xerxes came to Abdera,[a] since he at that time made an alliance of friendship with its people and gave them gifts of a golden sword[b] and a *tiara*[c] ornamented with gold. And the Abderitans themselves say (though I for my part find it completely incredible) that in his flight from Athens back to Asia, the first time Xerxes took off his belt was when he reached Abdera, because he felt safe there. And besides, Abdera is closer to the Hellespont than are the Strymon and Eion, where they say he had embarked on the ship.

The Hellenes proved unable to take Andros,[a] so they turned to Karystos[b] and, after laying waste to its land, departed for Salamis.[c] The first thing they did there was to set aside from their spoils victory offerings for the gods, of which the most significant were three Phoenician[d] triremes. One of these they dedicated at the isthmus,[e] and it was still there in my time; another they sent to Sounion,[f] and the third they dedicated to Ajax[g] right there on Salamis. [2] After that, they divided the spoils and sent off victory offerings to Delphi[a] from which were made a statue eighteen feet[b] tall, holding the beak of a ship in its hand. This statue was placed where the golden statue of Alexandros of Macedon[c] stands.

8.119
480
THRACIAN SEA
Herodotus does not believe this version, because he thinks they would have thrown the rowers overboard, not the highborn Persians.

8.120
480
ABDERA
That Xerxes came to Abdera also argues against the second version of his return.

8.121
480
SALAMIS-DELPHI
The Hellenes return to Salamis to divide the spoils and give the gods their due.

8.120.1a   Abdera: Map 8.121, AX.
8.120.1b   Herodotus here uses the Persian word *akinakes*, a dagger or short sword.
8.120.1c   The *tiara* was a kind of Persian headgear.
8.121.1a   Andros: Map 8.121, BX.
8.121.1b   Karystos: Map 8.121, BX.
8.121.1c   Salamis: Map 8.121, BX.
8.121.1d   Phoenicia: Map 8.121, locator.
8.121.1e   Isthmus of Corinth: Map 8.121, BX.
8.121.1f   Cape Sounion: Map 8.121, BX.
8.121.1g   Ajax (Aias) was the Homeric hero who came from Salamis.

8.121.2a   Delphi: Map 8.121, BX.
8.121.2b   Herodotus writes that the statue was "12 cubits" tall. The cubit equaled about 1.5 feet. See Appendix J, §4, 5, 19.
8.121.2c   Alexandros I, king of Macedon (Map 8.121, AX), who reigned from 495 to 450, not Alexander III (The Great—Megalexandros) of Macedon, who reigned from 333 to 323 and who conquered both Greece and Persia about a century after Herodotus' death.

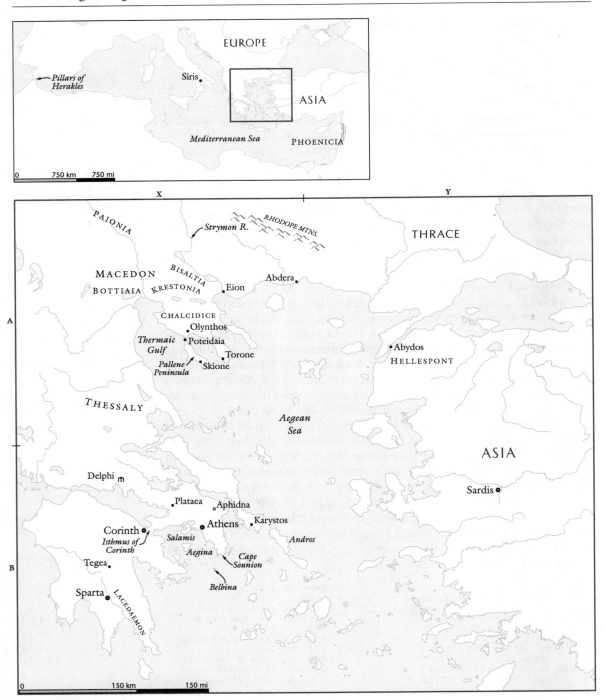

MAP 8.121

After they sent the victory offerings to Delphi, they made a joint inquiry to the god concerning whether the offerings he had received seemed sufficient and pleasing to him. He answered that he had received what he wanted from all the Hellenes except for the Aeginetans,[a] from whom he demanded the prize for valor they had won for their role in the sea battle at Salamis. Upon learning this, the Aeginetans dedicated three golden stars, which are on a bronze mast standing in the corner of the temple entrance next to the bowl of Croesus.[b]

Following the division of the spoils, the Hellenes sailed to the isthmus[a] to present the prize of valor to the Hellene who had proved himself the most worthy throughout this war. [2] When they arrived, the commanders cast their votes at the altar of Poseidon to choose the first and second men out of them all. Every one of them placed his first vote for himself, since each thought that he himself had proved to be the most valorous. But for second place, the majority of them voted for Themistokles. So while they were all left with one vote each for first place, Themistokles surpassed them all by far with the most votes for second place.

After the Hellenes proved unwilling to choose the winner because of jealousy, they sailed away, each to this own land, without reaching a decision. Nevertheless, the fame of Themistokles resounded throughout all of Hellas, and he was reputed to be by far the wisest of Hellenes. [2] But because he received no prize for his victory from those who had fought at Salamis, he went straight to Lacedaemon,[a] wishing to be rewarded there, and the Lacedaemonians welcomed him graciously and showed him great honor indeed; although they gave the prize for valor—an olive wreath—to Eurybiades, they presented another olive wreath to Themistokles as the prize for wisdom and shrewdness, and they also gave him the gift of the most magnificent chariot in Sparta. [3] After honoring him with celebrations of praise, they sent him off to the border of Tegea[a] with an escort of 300 Spartans called "the Knights."[b] He is actually the only person in the world that we know of to whom the Spartans ever gave this escort.

When Themistokles had left the Lacedaemonians and arrived back at Athens, an Athenian named Timodemos of the deme of Aphidna,[a] who was an enemy of Themistokles but otherwise not a prominent man, rebuked him out of insane jealousy about his trip to Lacedaemon, asserting that he had been awarded all those honors because of Athens and not because of

---

8.122
480
DELPHI
The god at Delphi demands the victor's prize from the Aeginetans.

8.123
480
ISTHMUS OF CORINTH
In awarding the prize for worthiness, each general votes for himself, but all pick Themistokles for second place.

8.124
480
SPARTA
The Hellenes are too jealous to assign the prize, but all laud Themistokles. He goes to Sparta, where he is awarded a crown of olive, a fine chariot, and an escort by the Knights out of the country.

8.125
480
ATHENS
The anecdote of Themistokles and Timodemos.

8.122.1a   Aegina: Map 8.121, BX.
8.122.1b   For the dedication of this bowl by
            Croesus, see 1.51.1.
8.123.1a   Isthmus of Corinth: Map 8.121, BX.
8.124.2a   Lacedaemon (Sparta): Map 8.121, BX.
8.124.3a   Tegea: Map 8.121, BX.
8.124.3b   Knights: thought to have been Spartan
            royal bodyguards who, despite their
            name, definitely fought as infantry in
            Herodotus' day and later.

8.125.1a   Aphidna: Map 8.121, BX. Attic demes
            had originally been just townships,
            villages, or regions in Attica. After the
            reforms of Kleisthenes in 508/07 (see
            5.69), they became official political
            units of the Athenian state, and every
            Athenian citizen was identified by his
            name and the deme in which he had
            been born.

himself. [2] Timodemos continued to say this without cease until Themistokles retorted, "The fact is that if I were from Belbina,[a] I would not have been honored this way by the Spartans, but neither would you, my friend, even even though you are an Athenian."

That was the end of this incident. Now even before all this, Artabazos son of Pharnakes had been an important man among the Persians, and he became even more distinguished because of what later happened at Plataea.[a] It was he who, along with 60,000 troops from among the men chosen by Mardonios, escorted the king as far as the passage at the Hellespont.[b] [2] And after the King had reached Asia, Artabazos turned back and, feeling no urgency to rejoin Mardonios and the rest of the army wintering in Thessaly[a] and Macedon,[b] he went to the vicinity of Pallene,[c] where he found that the Poteidaians[d] had risen in revolt. Now, to his thinking, it seemed only right and just that he should enslave them, [3] for after the King had marched by as he withdrew, and the Persian navy had fled from Salamis[a] and disappeared, the Poteidaians and all the others who lived in Pallene had openly revolted from the King.

So Artabazos laid siege to Poteidaia. And he did the same to Olynthos,[a] suspecting that the Olynthians too were involved in the revolt against the King. Olynthos had been in the possession of the Bottiaians,[b] who had been driven out from the Thermaic Gulf[c] by the Macedonians. After Artabazos had captured them by siege, he took them to a lake and there slaughtered them. Then he handed their city over to Kritoboulos of Torone[d] to be its governor, and to people of Chalcidian[e] descent; so it was in that way that the Chalcidians gained possession of Olynthos.

After Artabazos had taken Olynthos, he ambitiously turned his thoughts to Poteidaia, and as he did, he found that Timoxeinos, the general of the Skionaians,[a] was more than willing to arrange for the betrayal of the place to him. How this started, I cannot say, since no one speaks of this. But in the end it happened like this. Timoxeinos would write a letter to Artabazos, or Artabazos would write one to him, and they would wrap the message around an arrow beneath the point, tie it to the feathers, then shoot it to an agreed-upon place. [2] But the plan of Timoxeinos to betray Poteidaia was detected, for on one occasion when Artabazos shot an arrow to the assigned location, he missed his aim and hit a man of Poteidaia in the shoulder instead. A crowd of people gathered around this wounded man, as tends to happen in war; they at once pulled out the arrow, and when they perceived the letter, they brought it to their generals. At this time the other allies of Pallene were there with them, [3] and when the generals read the letter and learned who was betraying them, they decided

8.126
480
HELLESPONT-POTEIDAIA
Artabazos escorts the King out of Europe and finds Poteidaia in revolt.

8.127
480
OLYNTHOS
Artabazos besieges and captures Olynthos and gives possession of it to the Chalcidians.

8.128
480
POTEIDAIA
Artabazos lays siege to Poteidaia and negotiates with Timoxeinos, general of Skione, to betray the place. Their correspondence is discovered, although not generally revealed, out of deference to the Skionaians.

8.125.2a	Belbina: Map 8.121, BX.	8.126.2d	Poteidaia: Map 8.121, AX.
8.126.1a	Plataea: Map 8.121, BX. The "later" event referred to here is the battle of Plataea.	8.126.3a	Salamis: Map 8.121, BX.
		8.127.1a	Olynthos: Map 8.121, AX.
8.126.1b	Hellespont: Map 8.121, AY.	8.127.1b	Bottiaia: Map 8.121, AX.
8.126.2a	Thessaly: Map 8.121, AX.	8.127.1c	Thermaic Gulf: Map 8.121, AX.
8.126.2b	Macedon: Map 8.121, AX.	8.127.1d	Torone: Map 8.121, AX.
8.126.2c	Pallene Peninsula: Map 8.121, AX.	8.127.1e	Chalcidice: Map 8.121, AX.
		8.128.1a	Skione: Map 8.121, AX.

not to strike Timoxeinos with the charge of treason for the sake of the city of Skione, so that its people would not be considered traitors afterward and for all time.

8.129 480 POTEIDAIA The Persians attempt to take Poteidaia by crossing to it during an unusual ebb tide, but are destroyed in midpassage by a great high tide. Herodotus agrees that this disaster was punishment for having profaned a nearby temple of Poseidon.

Artabazos' siege had gone on for three months when an extreme ebb tide occurred, which continued for quite a long time. Seeing that the sea there had become shallow, the barbarians began to make their way across to Pallene. [2] But when they had advanced two-fifths of the way across—not even half the distance they needed to cover in order to reach Pallene—a huge flood tide came upon them. According to the local inhabitants, these flood tides occur often, but none before had ever been quite so high as this one. Those who did not know how to swim perished in the sea, while those who did know how to swim were killed by the Poteidaians, who sailed out after them in their boats. [3] The Poteidaians say that the reason for the high flood tide and for the calamity of the Persians was that the temple and statue of Poseidon situated just outside the city were profaned by the very Persians who drowned in the sea, and this reason seems like a good one to me. Those who survived were led by Artabazos to Mardonios in Thessaly.

DIVINE REASON
GOOD FOR HERODO

8.130 480/79 SAMOS The Persian fleet, after having ferried the King and his army over the Hellespont, winters off Samos, to guard against a revolt in Ionia. Their own morale is low, but they expect Mardonios and his army to prevail, and they wait for news from him.

So that is what happened to those who had escorted the King. When what was left of Xerxes' fleet reached Asia[a] in its flight from Salamis, it conveyed the king and the army from the Chersonese[b] to Abydos[c] and then wintered at Cyme.[d] With the arrival of spring it gathered at Samos,[e] where some of its ships had spent the winter. The majority of Persians and Medes in the fleet were serving as marines, [2] and they now received new commanders who joined them there: Mardontes son of Bagaios and Artayntes son of Artachaias. Artayntes had also chosen his nephew Ithamitras to serve with them as joint commander. Since their fleet had been badly mauled, it advanced no farther westward, and besides, no one was pressuring them to do so. Instead, the troops settled down at Samos and tried to guard against a revolt of Ionia; they had 300 ships, including some from Ionia. [3] They did not expect that the mainland Hellenes would go to Ionia but thought rather that they would be content to guard their own land, particularly in light of the fact that the Hellenes had not pursued Xerxes' ships as they fled from Salamis, but had been happy to be rid of them. And though their defeat at sea had depressed their spirits, they expected that in the end Mardonios would prevail on land. [4] They spent the time they were at Samos discussing how they could inflict harm on their enemies, but all the while they were there, they waited to hear how things would turn out for Mardonios.

8.131 479 AEGINA With the coming of spring, the Greek fleet mobilizes at Aegina, led by the Spartan Leotychidas.

The Hellenes were roused by the arrival of spring and challenged to action by the presence of Mardonios in Thessaly. Their army had not yet assembled when their fleet arrived at Aegina[a] to the number of 110 ships.

8.130.1a Asia: Map 8.134, BY.
8.130.1b Chersonese, Hellespont: Map 8.134, AY.
8.130.1c Abydos: Map 8.134, AY.
8.130.1d Cyme: Map 8.134, BY.
8.130.1e Samos: Map 8.134, BY.
8.131.1a Aegina: Map 8.134, BX.

[2] Commanding both the army and the navy was Leotychidas son of Menares, the son of Hegisilaos[a] son of Hippokratides, the son of Leotichydas son of Anaxilaos, the son of Archidamos son of Anaxandridas, the son of Theopompos son of Nikandros, the son of Charilaos son of Eunomos, the son of Polydektes son of Prytanis, the son of Euryphon son of Prokles, the son of Aristodemos son of Aristomachos, the son of Kleodaios son of Hyllas, who was the son of Herakles. Leotychidas belonged to the second of the two houses of the kings of Sparta.[b] [3] All of these except for the first seven listed after Leotychidas had been kings of Sparta. The commander of the Athenians was Xanthippos son of Ariphron.

8.132
479
AEGINA-SPARTA
Ionian messengers come to Sparta and Aegina to beg the Hellenes to free Ionia. The Hellenes, frightened of the Persians and ignorant of Aegean geography, refuse to sail beyond Delos.

When all the ships had reached Aegina, Ionian messengers arrived at the Hellenes' camp. Just prior to this, they had gone to Sparta,[a] where they had pleaded with the Lacedaemonians to free Ionia. [2] Herodotos son of Basileides was among these men, who had united as conspirators to plot the death of Strattis the tyrant of Chios.[a] There had been seven of them at that time, but in the midst of their intrigues, they were exposed when one of the conspirators betrayed them. And so the six who were left slipped away from Chios and went to Sparta and now to Aegina, asking the Hellenes to send their fleet to Ionia. But they managed to persuade the Hellenes to sail only as far as Delos,[b] and that far only with some difficulty, [3] for the Hellenes were terrified of everything that lay beyond that point, since they were not familiar with that territory and they feared that the whole region was garrisoned by enemy forces. Besides, they firmly believed that Samos was as far away from them as the Pillars of Herakles.[a] And so it turned out that while the barbarians did not dare to sail farther west than Samos because they were completely terrified, the Hellenes would sail no farther east than Delos, despite all the entreaties by the Chians for them to do so. And thus the space in between them was preserved by fear.[b]

8.133
480/479
THESSALY
Mardonios, wintering in Thessaly, sends a messenger to visit the oracle shrines.

While the Hellenes were sailing to Delos, Mardonios, who was wintering in Thessaly,[a] sent off from there a man of Europos[b] by birth whose name was Mys, with orders to go everywhere and to consult all the oracles that he could. I cannot be certain what he wanted to learn from the oracles when he gave these instructions, for that has not been reported, but I for my part think he sent to inquire about his current situation and for no other reason.

8.131.2a   Hegesilaos, used here by Herodotus, is the Ionic (and less familiar) form of Agesileos, the Doric form. See 6.65 and 7.204. (At 6.65, Herodotus lists Agis as the grandfather of Leotychidas, which probably reflects his use there of different sources.)

8.131.2b   The two ruling house of Sparta traced their ancestry back to Agis and Eurypon, both descended from Herakles. Leotychidas was a Eurypontid, and Leonidas (see 7.204) was an Agiad. See Appendix B, §10, 11.

8.32.1a   Sparta: Map 8.134, BX.
8.132.2a   Chios: Map 8.134, BY.
8.132.2b   Delos: Map 8.134, BY.
8.132.3a   Pillars of Herakles (modern Straits of Gibraltar): Map 8.121, locator.

8.132.3b   One must assume that these remarks are an example of Herodotean sarcasm. Fifth-century Hellenes were quite knowledgeable about the Aegean and the Mediterranean, and they would certainly have known that the distance to Samos from Hellas was only a small fraction of that between Hellas and the Pillars of Herakles. See Appendix D, Herodotean Geography, §1.

8.133.1a   Thessaly: Map 8.134, AX.
8.133.1b   Europos: Map 8.134, AX. Two sites quite close together are both named Europos in the *Barrington Atlas*.

It is clear that Mys came to Lebadeia[a] and bribed a local man to go down into the cave of Trophonios, and that he also came to Abai,[b] the oracle of the Phocians.[c] But he went first to Thebes[d] to question Ismenian Apollo, where the oracle is consulted through sacrifices, just as it is at Olympia,[e] and he also paid a certain visitor to Thebes—not a Theban—to sleep in the sanctuary of Amphiareios.[f] [2] None of the Thebans are permitted to consult the oracle here, because Amphiareios gave them a choice through his oracles to select one of two options: they could have him either as their prophet or as their ally, but they had to forfeit one of the two roles. They chose to have him as their ally, and so for that reason no Theban is allowed to sleep in this sanctuary.

According to the Thebans, an event took place at this time which to me is most amazing. As Mys of Europos was visiting all of the oracles, he came also to the precinct of Ptoian Apollo, the sanctuary called the Ptoios,[a] which belongs to the Thebans and, being situated near a mountain and next to the city of Akraiphiai,[b] overlooks Lake Copais.[c] [2] So when this man called Mys came to this sanctuary, three men who had been selected by the state to write down the expected prophecy accompanied him, but all of a sudden, the prophet began to speak in a barbarian tongue. [3] The Thebans accompanying Mys were struck with wonder at hearing barbarian speech instead of Greek, and had no idea how to deal with it. Mys, however, snatched away from them the tablet they had brought along and wrote down what the prophet was saying. He then told them that the oracle was spoken in the Carian[a] tongue, and once he had written down what it had said, he left and returned to Thessaly.

After Mardonios had read the oracles, he sent Alexandros of Macedon,[a] the son of Amyntas, as a messenger to Athens,[b] because the Persians were related to Alexandros by marriage; Gygaia, who was the daughter of Amyntas and Alexandros' sister, was the wife of Boubares of Persia. She had given birth to Amyntas of Asia,[c] who bore the name of his maternal grandfather and to whom the King had given the large Phrygian city of Alabanda[d] from which to draw revenues. Moreover, since Mardonios had heard that Alexandros was a *proxenos*[e] and a benefactor of Athens, [2] he thought that by this move he could best succeed in winning over the Athenians to his side. Because he had learned that they were a populous and warlike people, and he knew that the

8.134
479
HELLAS
The messenger visits shrines at Thebes, Lebadeia, and Abai in Phocis, and hires a non-Theban to sleep at the Amphiareion.

8.135
BOEOTIA
Herodotus recounts the story of Mys and the Thebans at the Ptoios, where the prophecy was given in Carian, not Greek.

8.136
479
ATHENS
Mardonios sends Alexandros of Macedon to Athens to persuade the Athenians to abandon the other Hellenes and ally with the Persians, as the oracle of the Ptoios has counseled.

8.134.1a Lebadeia: Map 8.134, inset. Site of the oracle of Trophonios mentioned earlier at 1.46.
8.134.1b Abai: Map 8.134, inset.
8.134.1c Phocis: Map 8.134, inset.
8.134.1d Thebes: Map 8.134, inset.
8.134.1e Olympia: Map 8.134, BX.
8.134.1f Amphiareion (shrine of Amphiareios): Map 8.134, inset. The hero of this shrine answered questions or gave advice through dreams as the suppliant slept in the sanctuary. It was a healing shrine and oracle: see Appendix P, §4, and Figure 1.52.
8.135.1a Ptoios: Map 8.134, inset. Shrine of

Ptoian Apollo, shown in the *Barrington Atlas* as Apollo.
8.135.1b Akraiphiai: Map 8.134, inset.
8.135.1c Lake Copais: Map 8.134, inset.
8.135.3a Caria: Map 8.134, BY.
8.136.1a Macedon: Map 8.134, AX.
8.136.1b Athens: Map 8.134, inset.
8.136.1c Asia: Map 8.134, BY.
8.136.1d Alabanda: Map 8.134, BY.
8.136.1e A *proxenos* was a representative of a city other than his own, who provided assistance and protected the interests of its citizens.

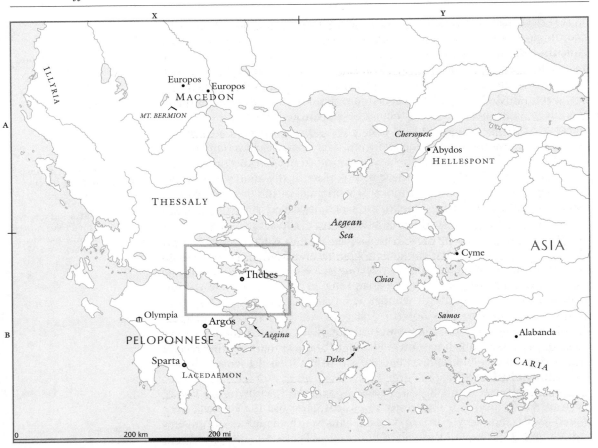

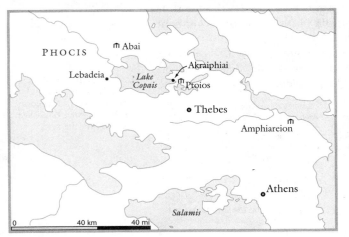

MAP 8.134

disaster that had befallen the Persians at sea had been accomplished mainly by the Athenians, [3] he fully anticipated that if they were on his side, he would easily gain control over the sea, which was certainly a correct assumption. He considered his army to be far stronger on land than theirs. Thus, he reasoned, he would be able to prevail over the Hellenes. Perhaps the oracles had predicted this outcome to him and advised him to form an alliance with Athens, and it was in obedience to their advice that he now sent off Alexandros.

Now Alexandros' ancestor who lived six generations before him[a] was named Perdikkas, and this is the story of how he established a tyranny over the Macedonians.[b] He was one of three brothers, Gayannes, Aeropos, and Perdikkas, who were descended from Temenos and who fled from Argos[c] into exile to Illyria,[d] crossed over to inland Macedon, and came to the city of Lebaia.[e] [2] There they worked as menial laborers for the king, one tending the horses, another the cattle, and Perdikkas, the youngest of them, the sheep and goats. Now in the old days even tyrants were poor, not only common people, so the wife of the king used to prepare their food for them herself. [3] And whenever she baked bread, the loaf she made for the youngest worker, Perdikkas, would rise to twice its normal size. Since this happened over and over again, she told her husband about it and he, upon hearing of it, immediately grasped the fact that this was a portent of great significance. He summoned the three laborers and ordered them to leave his land. [4] They replied that it was only right and just that they first receive their wages, so they would not depart until then. When the king, who was apparently unbalanced by some god, heard them speak of wages, he pointed to the sun, which was shining through an opening in the roof of his house, and said, "I shall pay you that as the wages you deserve." [5] Upon hearing this response, Gayannes and Aeropos, the elder brothers, just stood there as if struck dumb, but the boy (who happened to have a knife) said, "We accept what you give us, sire." And with his knife he traced a circle around the sunshine on the floor of the house and drew its light into the fold of his garment three times. He then left, and the other two went with him.

And when they had gone away, one of the king's counselors explained what the boy had done and how this youngest of the brothers had been clever to take what he had been offered; these comments provoked the king to send out horsemen to kill them. Now in this country there is a river to which the descendants of the men who came from Argos sacrifice as their savior. [2] And after the Temenids had crossed it, its waters began to surge so violently that the horsemen could not cross it in pursuit of them. The brothers then went to another region of Macedon, and settled down near the gardens which are called the gardens of Midas son of Gordias, where roses grow wild, each with sixty petals and a fragrance superior to all other roses. [3] According to the Macedonians, it was in these gardens that

[handwritten: Alexandros related to tyrant]

8.137
MACEDON
Herodotus tells the tale of how the Temenids, originally from Argos, came to rule over Macedon.

8.138
MACEDON
How the Temenid brothers escape from the king and settle in a part of Macedon from which, once established, they conquer the rest.

[handwritten: ROSES]

8.137.1a   Herodotus says seven generations because the Hellenes counted inclusively and he included Alexandros himself in the number of generations.
8.137.1b   Macedon: Map 8.134, AX.
8.137.1c   Argos: Map 8.134, BX.
8.137.1d   Illyria: Map 8.134, AX.
8.137.1e   Lebaia: location unknown.

Silenos was captured.[a] Above these gardens lies a mountain by the name of Bermion,[b] which is inaccessible because of its cold climate. So it was from here that the brothers, after gaining control over this land, went forth to conquer the rest of the territory of Macedon.

And it was from this Perdikkas that Alexandros was descended; for Alexandros was the son of Amyntas, who was the son of Alketes, whose father was Aeropos son of Philippos, the son of Argaios, who was the son of that Perdikkas who acquired the rule of this land.

That, then, is the lineage of Alexandros the son of Amyntas. And so after Alexandros had been sent off by Mardonios, he arrived at Athens[a] and said to the Athenians, "Men of Athens, Mardonios has this to tell you: 'A message has arrived from the King, saying: "I will forget all the wrongs done to me by the Athenians [2] so now, Mardonios, you must do as I say. First, give them back their land, and then let them have another land of their choice in addition, which they may govern independently. And if they wish to come to an agreement with me, you are to rebuild all the sanctuaries that I burned down." These are my orders, and I have no choice but to carry them out unless you yourselves should prevent me from doing so. [3] But here is what I myself would say to you: Why are you so insanely driven to wage war against the King? You could not possibly prevail, nor could you hold out against him forever. Surely you have seen the size of Xerxes' expedition and what it has already achieved, and you have heard about the forces that I now have with me, so that even if you should prevail over us and win a victory (though you will abandon all hope for that if you have any sense), you will then still have to encounter another force many times larger. [4] Therefore I tell you, do not be deprived of your country and have to run for your lives forever all because you want to prove yourselves a match for the King. I advise you to make peace, which you can now achieve on the most favorable terms, since the King is so inclined; live in freedom and join us without guile or deceit in a military alliance.'

"That, Athenians, is what Mardonios instructed me to tell you. As for myself, I shall say nothing of my own goodwill toward you (since now would not be the first time you could recognize that), but I do entreat you to follow the advice of Mardonios. [2] For I can see that you will not be able to wage war against Xerxes forever—if I had observed that you were capable of doing so, I would never have come to you with this advice. The fact is, the King's power is superhuman, and his reach extends far and wide. [3] And so if you do not immediately come to an agreement with the Persians while they are offering you such generous conditions, then I fear for you indeed, because you alone of all the allies dwell along the most beaten

8.139
c. 650
MACEDON
Perdikkas begins the Temenid rule.

8.140.α
479
ATHENS
Alexandros delivers Mardonios' message to the Athenians as if it were from the King, offering to give the Athenians their lands and autonomy, and to rebuild their temples, if they will ally with Persia. Mardonios adds that sensible Hellenes must realize that their struggle against the King's power is hopeless.

8.140.β
479
ATHENS
Alexandros expresses his goodwill to Athens and advises them to accept the offer, given the King's tremendous power and their vulnerable location.

8.138.3a   Midas is a legendary king known for his wealth and his golden touch (which would explain the luxuriance of the roses here). Wishing to know the secret of life, Midas captured the satyr Silenos, who was then compelled to reveal it. Herodotus is our earliest witness to the tradition that

Midas' gardens were in Macedon. He is probably not the Phrygian king Midas mentioned at 1.14.2, though the two figures may have been frequently conflated in early Greek literature.

8.138.3b   Mount Bermion: Map 8.134, AX.
8.140.α.1a   Athens: Map 8.134, inset.

track of this war and constantly suffer devastation, and the land you possess is often chosen as the disputed ground on which battles are waged. [4] So, then, do heed my advice, since you have such a precious opportunity, insofar as the great King wishes to become your friend and to forgive you alone of all the Hellenes for the wrongs done to him."

Those were the words of Alexandros. Now when the Lacedaemonians[a] learned that Alexandros had come to Athens to bring the Athenians into an agreement with the barbarian, they remembered the prophecies predicting that they, together with the rest of the Dorians, were destined to be expelled from the Peloponnese by the Medes and the Athenians. And so now they became quite frightened that the Athenians might actually reach an agreement with the Persians, and they at once resolved to send messengers to Athens. [2] And in fact it turned out that they obtained an audience there during the visit of Alexandros, which was no accident, for the Athenians were waiting and delaying, well aware that the Lacedaemonians would find out that a messenger from the barbarian had come to negotiate an agreement with them, and that upon learning this, the Lacedaemonians would hastily send messengers of their own. Thus they delayed the proceedings on purpose, so as to make a public declaration of their stance before the Lacedaemonians.

So when Alexandros had ended his speech, the messengers from Sparta took their turn. "The Lacedaemonians have sent us here," they said, "to ask that you do nothing to upset the status quo of Hellas, and that you refuse to accept any proposals from the barbarian. [2] For that would in no way be just or decent for any of the other Hellenes to do, but least of all for you, for many reasons: you are the ones who incited this war, while we, for our part, had no desire for it, and from the very start, the conflict concerned your land. But now it affects all of Hellas. [3] And aside from that, it would be completely unbearable if the Athenians, who have always and of old been seen as the liberators of many peoples, should now prove responsible for the enslavement of Hellas. We do, however, sympathize with you for the pressures that you currently bear, for you have already been deprived of two harvests and have been for a long time now in a state of economic ruin. [4] So to compensate you for your troubles, the Lacedaemonians and their allies offer to support and maintain your women and all other members of your household who cannot serve in the military for as long as the war continues. Do not let Alexandros of Macedon win you over with his polished version of Mardonios' message. [5] For he really must act this way: he is, after all, a tyrant who is assisting another tyrant. But if you have any sense at all, you must not follow the advice of barbarians, knowing as you do that they are neither trustworthy nor truthful." That was the speech of the Lacedaemonian messengers.

8.141.1a Lacedaemon (Sparta): Map 8.134, BX.

[handwritten note:] Persians value truth

[handwritten margin note:] SPARTANS RE: OFFER

The Athenians first answered Alexandros as follows: "We ourselves are already well aware that the forces of the Mede are many times greater than our own, so there is no need to admonish us about that. Nevertheless, we shall defend ourselves however we can in our devotion to freedom. So do not attempt to seduce us into an agreement with the barbarian, since we shall not be persuaded. [2] Report back to Mardonios that the Athenians say: 'As long as the sun continues on the same course as it now travels, we shall never come to an agreement with Xerxes. Trusting in the gods and heroes as our allies (for whom he showed no respect when he burned their homes and images), we shall advance against him and defend ourselves.' [3] As for you, Alexandros, in the future, do not appear before the Athenians with speeches such as this one, nor pretend to be doing us a favor while encouraging us to commit deeds that violate all tradition. For we would not want you, our *proxenos* and friend, to suffer anything unpleasant at the hands of the Athenians."

After giving this answer to Alexandros, they turned to address the messengers from Sparta: "It was quite natural for the Lacedaemonians to fear we would come to an agreement with the barbarian, but nevertheless, we think it disgraceful that you became so frightened, since you are well aware of the Athenians' disposition, namely, that there is no amount of gold anywhere on earth so great, nor any country that surpasses others so much in beauty and fertility, that we would accept it as a reward for medizing and enslaving Hellas. [2] Besides, even if we were willing to act that way, there are many serious considerations which would prevent us from doing so. First and foremost of these is that the images and buildings of the gods have been burned and demolished,[a] so that we are bound by necessity to exact the greatest revenge on the man who performed these deeds, rather than to make agreements with him. And second, it would not be fitting for the Athenians to prove traitors to the the Greek people, with whom we are united in sharing the same kinship and language, with whom we have established shrines and conduct sacrifices to the gods together, and with whom we also share the same way of life. [3] So understand this now, if you have not learned it before: as long as even one Athenian still survives, we shall make no agreement with Xerxes. But we do commend your foresight and appreciate your consideration for us, especially in recognizing that we are in such a state of ruin that you have volunteered to support and maintain the members of our households. [4] Your kindness has been more than sufficient. We, however, will persevere in whatever way we can, without troubling you. But now, since the situation is as it is, do send out an army as quickly as possible, [5] for it is our conjecture that before long, indeed, as soon as the barbarian hears that we have refused to do as he asked, he will be here invading our land again. And so now, before he reaches Attica, is the time for you to hasten to battle in Boeotia." When they had received this answer from the Athenians, the messengers departed to return to Sparta.

8.144.2a   For evidence of the demolished temples,
               see Figure 8.53.

BOOK NINE

When Alexandros returned and conveyed to Mardonios the response of the Athenians, Mardonios set out from Thessaly[a] and swiftly led his army toward Athens.[b] And he took men to add to his army from each place through which he passed.

Far from repenting for what they had done before, the leading men of Thessaly now provided even more encouragement for the Persians; and Thorax of Larissa,[c] who had helped to escort Xerxes in his flight, openly allowed Mardonios to pass by and advance against Hellas.[d]

When the army on its march came to Boeotia,[a] the Thebans[b] tried to halt Mardonios there, advising him that there was no more suitable place in which to make his camp; they tried to dissuade him from advancing any farther, telling him that he should instead make his base there, where he could achieve the subjugation of all Hellas without a battle. [2] They explained that to prevail over the Hellenes by force of arms would be a difficult task for even the whole world, as long as the Hellenes were united in their determination to resist, as they had been previously. "But if you follow our recommendation," they said, "you will know all their intentions and thereby gain the power to master and control them with ease. [3] Just send some money to the most powerful men in their cities. You will thus divide Hellas against itself, and from then on, with the aid of your partisans, you will easily subjugate any who oppose you."

That was the advice of the Thebans, but Mardonios did not follow it. Instead, he was pervaded by a fierce desire to capture Athens again, both out of foolish pride, and because he fancied the idea of notifying the King in Sardis[a] by means of signal beacons located throughout the islands that he had Athens in his grasp. [2] But even now, when he arrived in Attica,[a] there

9.1
479
THESSALY
After receiving the Athenian refusal, Mardonios leads his army forth.

9.2
479
THEBES
The Thebans advise Mardonios to halt in their territory and try to divide the Hellenes by bribing their leaders.

9.3
479
ATHENS
Mardonios, however, advances to occupy a still-deserted Athens to impress the King.

9.1.1a Thessaly: Map 9.8.
9.1.1b In July 479. Mardonios occupied Athens (Map 9.8).
9.1.1c Larissa, Thessaly: Map 9.8.
9.1.1d Although Herodotus doesn't say so, the Persians must have held on to the Thermopylae (Map 9.8) choke point with some sort of garrison (just as Philip of Macedon did between 346 and 340). They would

surely not have given the Hellenes a second chance to prevent them from entering Hellas, especially when the Persian fleet had gone back to Asia.

9.2.1a Boeotia: Map 9.8.
9.2.1b Thebes: Map 9.8.
9.3.1a Sardis: Map 9.8.
9.3.2a Attica: Map 9.8.

665

were no Athenians to be found. He learned that most of them were on their ships at Salamis,[b] so he was capturing a city that was deserted. Mardonios' expedition took place in the tenth month after the capture of Athens by the King.

When he reached Athens, he sent a man from the Hellespont[a] called Mourychides to Salamis with the same message to the Athenians that Alexandros of Macedon[b] had conveyed. [2] Though he knew in advance of the Athenians' unfriendly attitude, he dispatched this message a second time because he hoped, now that all of Attic territory had been taken by the spear and was under his control, that they would give up their foolish pride. That, then, was why he sent Mourychides off to Salamis.

Upon his arrival, Mourychides went before the council and relayed the message from Mardonios. One of the members of the council, Lykidas, declared his opinion that the better course would be to accept the offer of Mourychides and present it to the people.[a] [2] Whether he had received money from Mardonios or actually liked the idea, this, at least, was the proposal that he publicly expressed. The Athenians, both those in attendance at the council and others outside, at once grew so indignant when they found out about this proposal that they surrounded Lykidas and stoned him until he died. But they sent Mourychides of the Hellespont away unharmed. [3] Now with all the commotion going on at Salamis concerning Lykidas, the Athenian women found out about what had happened, and word of it passed from one woman to the next as they recruited one another, until, on their own initiative, they all went to the home of Lykidas and there stoned to death his wife and children.[a]

The reason why the Athenians had crossed over to Salamis was that they had waited in Attica as long as they could for an army to come from the Peloponnese[a] to assist them. But since the Peloponnesians seemed to be moving at a slow and leisurely pace, and they received reports that the invader was even now in Boeotia, they decided to convey everything to safety and crossed over to Salamis. They also sent messengers to Lacedaemon[b] to reproach the Lacedaemonians for having allowed the barbarian to invade Attica rather than having joined with the Athenians to oppose him in Boeotia, and to remind them of how much the Persian had promised to give them if they changed sides. The messengers were told to proclaim that if the Lacedaemonians did not help defend the Athenians, then the Athenians would find some way to save themselves without such assistance.

9.3.2b Salamis: Map 9.8.
9.4.1a Hellespont: Map 9.8.
9.4.1b This is King Alexandros I of Macedon who ruled from 495–454 or 452, not Alexander the Great (Megalexandros) who reigned from 333–323. Macedon: Map 9.8. Macedon: Map 9.8.
9.5.1a So that the people could debate it and vote on it in the Assembly. See Appendix A, The Athenian Government in Herodotus, §7, 10.
9.5.3a Women as killers: see Appendix U, On Women and Marriage in Herodotus, §5, 8.
9.6.1a Peloponnese: Map 9.8.
9.6.1b Lacedaemon (Sparta): Map 9.8. Herodotus uses the names Spartans and Lacedaemonians interchangeably. "Spartans," however, often refers specifically to citizens of the state of Sparta, whereas any inhabitant of the territory of Lacedaemon is a Lacedaemonian. See Appendix B, The Spartan State in War and Peace, §5, 7, and n. B.7a.

During all this time the Lacedaemonians, who considered the care of the god to be of the utmost importance, were celebrating their festival called the Hyakinthia;[a] and at the same time, the wall being built at the isthmus[b] was now receiving its parapets. So when the messengers from Athens arrived in Lacedaemon, bringing along messengers from Megara[c] and Plataea[d] as well, they came before the ephors and said:

"The Athenians have sent us here to tell you that the King of the Medes is offering to give us back our land and wants to consider us his allies on fair and equal terms, without guile or deceit; he also wishes to give us another land in addition to our own, whichever one we choose. [2] But out of respect for Zeus Hellenios,[a] and because we think it would be dreadful to betray Hellas, we did not accept his terms, but have refused him, even though we feel that we have been wronged and forsaken by the Hellenes and we know that it would be more profitable to come to an agreement with the Persian than it would be to wage war against him. And if we have a choice, we shall not make an agreement with him in the future either. So our policy toward the Hellenes has been sincere and unambiguous.

"You, on the other hand, came to us utterly terrified that we would make an agreement with the Persian, but now, when you are well aware of our determination and have learned that we would never betray Hellas, and now just as the wall you are extending across the isthmus is nearing completion, we find that you pay no attention to the Athenians. You made an agreement with us to oppose the barbarian in Boeotia, but you have betrayed us and have allowed him to invade Attica. [2] So you have provoked and enraged the Athenians by your improper conduct. But at this time they urge you to send out your army as quickly as possible to join ours, so that together we may face the barbarian in Attica. For now that we have lost Boeotia, the most suitable place to fight is in our territory, on the Thriasian Plain.[a]"

When the ephors had heard the end of this speech, they postponed their reply until the following day, on which they again put it off until the next. And they continued to delay from day to day in this manner for ten days in all. Meanwhile all the Peloponnesians were working as hard as they could on the wall, and they were almost finished. [2] I cannot explain why the Lacedaemonians, who took such great pains to prevent the Athenians from medizing[a] when Alexandros of Macedon came to Athens,[b] now seemed not to care whether they did so or not; perhaps the fact that they had by this time completed the fortification of the isthmus led them to feel that they no longer needed the Athenians, while during Alexandros' visit to Attica, the wall was not yet finished and they were still working on it in great fear of the Persians.

9.7
479
SPARTA
The Spartans celebrate a festival and finish their wall at the isthmus.

9.7.α*
479
SPARTA
The Athenians describe to the Spartans the offer that they received and refused from the Persians, and promise to remain faithful to the Greek cause.

9.7.β
479
SPARTA
The Athenians contrast their conduct with the delay of the Spartans, and ask the Spartans to send their army north immediately.

9.8
479
SPARTA
The Spartans continue to delay. They do not send their army north but work to fortify the isthmus.

9.7.1a   The Hyakinthia was a festival said to be of pre-Dorian origin, commemorating the killing of Hyakinthos by Apollo. (Godley)
9.7.1b   Isthmus of Corinth: Map 9.8.
9.7.1c   Megara: Map 9.8.
9.7.1d   Plataea: Map 9.8.
9.7.α*   This chapter in the *Histories* has two subdivisions indicated by Greek letters in alphabetic sequence. That sequence (with the

letters' Latin equivalents) is as follows: α (a), β (b).
9.7.α.1a   Zeus, god of the Hellenes.
9.7.β.2a   Thriasian Plain: Map 9.8.
9.8.2a   To "medize" was to go over to the Persian side. Persians were often called Medes by the Hellenes.
9.8.2b   For the Spartan response to Alexandros' mission to the Athenians, see 8.141–142.

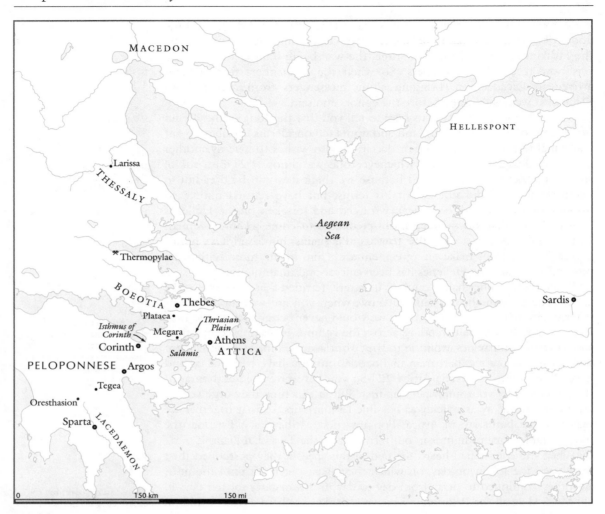

Map 9.8

9.9
479
SPARTA
Chileos of Tegea points out
to the Spartans that their
wall at the isthmus would be
worthless if the Athenians
defect to the Persians.

The way the Spartans finally answered the messengers and marched out to
war was as follows. On the day before the one designated as the last for a
hearing with the Athenians, Chileos, a man from Tegea[a] who had the greatest
influence of all outsiders in Lacedaemon, learned from the ephors what the
Athenians had told them, [2] and after he had heard it, he assessed the situation for them in this way, saying, "Honorable ephors, if the Athenians are not
united with us, but become allies of the barbarian instead, then no matter

9.9.1a   Tegea: Map 9.8.

how strong a wall is extended across the Isthmus, there will be gates flung wide open for the Persian to enter the Peloponnese. So take heed before the Athenians decide to do something that would bring disaster to Hellas."

That was his advice, and the ephors at once grasped the import of what he had said. They spoke not a word to the messengers who had come from the cities, but while it was still dark, they sent out 5,000 Spartans, with seven helots appointed to accompany each one, and assigned Pausanias son of Kleombrotos to lead them into battle. [2] By right the supreme command actually belonged to Pleistarchos son of Leonidas, but he was still a child, and Pausanias was his guardian and first cousin. For Kleombrotos, the father of Pausanias and son of Anaxandridas, was no longer alive, having died shortly after he brought back from the isthmus the army that had been working on the wall. [3] Kleombrotos had led the army back from the isthmus because as he was sacrificing to determine what to do about the Persian, the sun was darkened in the heavens.[a] Pausanias chose Euryanax son of Dorieus, who belonged to his own family,[b] to share the command. The troops with Pausanias then marched out of Sparta.

When day had dawned, the messengers came before the ephors, knowing nothing about the departure of the troops, but intending to go back themselves, each one returning to his own city. They addressed the ephors as follows: "Lacedaemonians, you may remain here, celebrating the Hyakinthia and amusing yourselves while betraying your allies. The Athenians, since they have been wronged by you and are destitute of allies, will give up and make peace with the Persian in whatever way they can. [2] And once we have done that, it is quite clear that we shall become the King's allies, and we shall join him in marching against any land to which the Persians direct us. From that point on you will learn the results of your policy." In response to these words from the messengers, the ephors spoke on oath, telling them that they believed that their troops were already at Orestheion,[a] as they marched against the outsiders (for they used to call the barbarians "outsiders"). [3] Knowing nothing of all this, the messengers questioned the ephors and soon learned the whole truth. And so after expressing their great astonishment at this, they went off by the quickest route to overtake them. And 5,000 hoplites picked from the Lacedaemonian *perioikoi*[a] accompanied them to do the same.

While the messengers were hurrying toward the isthmus,[a] the Argives[b] heard that Pausanias and his troops had marched out of Sparta,[c] and they at once sent a herald, the best long-distance runner they could find, to

9.10
479
SPARTA
The Spartans now send their army north under Pausanias, cousin and guardian to Pleistarchos the king, who was still a boy.

9.11
479
SPARTA
The Athenian envoys now threaten to ally with the Persians, but are pleased to find out that the Spartans have already marched north to assist them.

9.12
479
ARGOS
The Argives warn Mardonios that the Spartans are marching north, and that the Argives cannot prevent their advance.

9.10.3a   There was a partial solar eclipse in that part of Greece on October 2, 480.
9.10.3b   Euryanax was his cousin, the son of Dorieus, who was a brother of Pausanias' father Kleombrotos.
9.11.2a   Other references place Orestheion (Oresthasion) northwest of Sparta (Map 9.8).
9.11.3a   *Perioikoi* were the inhabitants of the country districts of Laconia, another

name for Lacedaemon and Spartan territory. They were Spartan citizens but did not have the full rights and privileges of Spartiates. See Appendix B, §7, 17–18.
9.12.1a   Isthmus of Corinth: Map 9.8.
9.12.1b   Argos: Map 9.8.
9.12.1c   Sparta: Map 9.8.

Attica[d] because they had earlier promised Mardonios that they would prevent the Spartans from marching out. [2] When the herald arrived at Athens, he said, "Mardonios, the Argives have sent me to tell you that the men of military age have marched out from Lacedaemon, and that the Argives are unable to stop them. You must now form your own plan for dealing with this situation."

After relaying this message, the herald returned to Argos.

Now after hearing this news, Mardonios had no further desire to remain in Attica. Prior to this, he had hoped that the Athenians would make an agreement with him, and wanting to see what they would do, he had held off and done no violence or harm to Attic territory. [2] But since he had had no success in persuading them to do so, and he had now learned the whole truth, he demolished all walls, buildings, and sanctuaries still standing, leaving everything in a heap of ruins, and then set Athens on fire and retreated before Pausanias and his troops arrived at the isthmus. [3] He marched away both because Attica was unsuitable for cavalry, and because he knew that if he were defeated in battle there, he would have only one route by which to get away, and that was by a narrow road on which his troops could be blocked by even a small force.[a] Therefore he decided to retreat to Thebes,[b] where he could join battle near a friendly city and on land suitable for cavalry.

As Mardonios began his retreat, he received a message that an advance guard of 1,000 Lacedaemonians had arrived at Megara,[a] and when he heard this, he modified his plan in an attempt to first destroy these troops. So he now turned his army around and led it toward Megara, while his cavalry rode on ahead and trampled over the Megarian land. This was the farthest point toward the setting sun in Europe that this Persian army ever reached.

Soon after this, however, Mardonios received another report that the Hellenes had united their forces at the isthmus, so he turned around again and made his way back through Dekeleia.[a] From there he was guided through Sphendale[b] and Tanagra[c] by some neighboring Asopians[d] who had been sent for that purpose by the Boeotarchs.[d] [2] After passing the night in Tanagra, he went on the next day to Skolos[a] in Theban territory, where he cleared the land of trees. He did this not because of any animosity toward the Thebans, but because of the absolute necessity to build a fortification as a place of refuge for his army if the battle did not turn out as he hoped. [3] His troops were stationed along the Asopos River, from Ery-

9.13
479
ATHENS-BOEOTIA
When Mardonios becomes convinced that the Athenians will not retreat with him, he burns and demolishes Athens and retreats to Boeotia, whose terrain is more favorable to his cavalry.

9.14
479
MEGARA
Mardonios sends a force to Megara, the farthest Persian advance into Europe.

9.15
479
BOEOTIA
Learning that the Hellenes had concentrated at the isthmus, Mardonios withdraws from Attica and establishes a permanent base camp in Theban territory in Boeotia.

9.12.1d	Attica: Map 9.8.		location is unknown.
9.13.3a	Mardonios would have to retreat into Boeotia (Map 9.17) by way of the pass over Mount Cithaeron (Map 9.17 and inset). (Godley)	9.15.1c	Tanagra: Map 9.17.
		9.15.1d	Asopians presumably were inhabitants of the Asopos River valley who would know the route from Dekeleia to Tanagra. See Map 9.17.
9.13.3b	Thebes: Map 9.17.		
9.14.1a	Megara: Map 9.17.	9.15.1d	The Boeotarchs were the chief magistrates of the government of Boeotia (Map 9.17).
9.15.1a	Dekeleia: Map 9.17.		
9.15.1b	Sphendale: an Attic deme whose precise	9.15.2a	Skolos: Map 9.17, inset.

thrai[a] through Hysiai[b] and all the way to Plataean[c] territory. The fort, however, was not that extensive, being a little less than 2,000 yards[d] on each side. [4] While the barbarians were engaged in this work, a Theban named Attaginos son of Phrynon, after making elaborate preparations, invited Mardonios himself along with fifty of the most noteworthy Persians to be his guests at a feast, and they accepted his invitation. This dinner was held in Thebes.

The rest of the story that follows was told to me by Thersandros of Orchomenus,[a] a man held in the highest esteem in Orchomenus. Thersandros said that he himself was invited to this dinner by Attaginos, along with fifty Theban men, and that Attaginos did not have them recline separately from each other, but had a Persian and a Theban sharing each couch.[b] [2] After dinner, as they lingered drinking, the Persian on the couch with Thersandros asked him in Greek what country he came from, to which he replied, "Orchomenus." The Persian then said, "Since you have shared with me a meal and libations, I would like to leave you with this insight of mine to remember me by, so that being informed in advance, you will be able to make plans to secure a favorable outcome for yourself. [3] Do you see these Persians dining here, and did you see the army we left camping by the river? Well, of all these men, you will see only a few surviving within a short time." And as the Persian said this, he began to sob and weep profusely. [4] In amazement at what he had said, Thersandros asked, "But should you not tell this to Mardonios and to the other Persians who rank just below him in esteem?" The Persian then replied, "My friend, what has been destined to happen by the god is impossible for a mortal to avert by any contrivance, for no one believes even what trustworthy people say. [5] And though many Persians know that this is true, we are bound by necessity to follow our orders. The most painful anguish that mortals suffer is to understand a great deal but to have no power at all." That is what I heard from Thersandros of Orchomenus, and also that he told this to others just before the battle at Plataea took place.

And so as Mardonios set up his camp in Boeotia, most of the Hellenes who inhabited this region who were medizing had contributed troops to his army and had participated in the invasion of Athens;[a] the Phocians[b] were the only ones who had not taken part in the invasion. They definitely were medizing, but they did so under compulsion and against their will. [2] And not many days after the arrival of Mardonios' army at Thebes, 1,000 Phocian hoplites went there under the command of Harmokydes, one of the

9.16
479
THEBES
The anecdote of the Persian who predicted the defeat and destruction of the Persians and told Thersandros the Hellene at a banquet that many Persians feared the outcome of their expedition, but were powerless to do anything about it.

9.17
479
BOEOTIA
How Mardonios ordered the Phocians who had joined him at Thebes to form up in the plain, and then surrounded and threatened them with the entire corps of Persian cavalry.

9.15.3a   Erythrai: Map 9.17, inset.
9.15.3b   Hysiai: Map 9.17, inset.
9.15.3c   Plataea: Map 9.17, inset.
9.15.3d   Herodotus writes this distance as "about 10 stades on a side." See Distance Conversions, p. lxiv, and Appendix J, Ancient Greek Units of Currency, Weight, and Distance, §6, 19. These dimensions have been used by some scholars to estimate

the size of Mardonios' forces. See Appendix R, The Size of Xerxes' Expeditionary Force, §11.
9.16.1a   Orchomenus, Boeotia: Map 9.17.
9.16.1b   Greeks dined while reclining on couches.
9.17.1a   Athens: Map 9.17.
9.17.1b   Phocis: Map 9.17.

most prominent Phocian citizens. After their arrival at Thebes, Mardonios sent horsemen to order them to take up a position out on the plain by themselves, [3] and as soon as they had done so, the entire force of Persian cavalry appeared before them. Then a rumor spread through the camp of the Hellenes who had taken the side of the Mede, and through that of the Phocians as well, that the Persians intended to shoot down the Phocians with javelins. [4] At that point, Harmokydes, the Phocian general, exhorted his troops as follows: "Phocians, it is quite obvious that these people are about to put us to death and have planned to do so in advance, and it is my guess that we have been slandered by the Thessalians. So it is now time for each one of you to prove himself a noble and courageous man. For it is better to end your lives honorably, fighting to defend yourselves, than to yield and thus perish in the most disgraceful way of all. But above all, let them learn that they are mere barbarians who have contrived to murder Hellenes who are *men*." BARBARIANS ≠ MEN

9.18
479
BOEOTIA
When the Phocians prepare to defend themselves, the charging cavalry turns and rides away, whether from fear of the Phocians or because they were ordered to retire, as Mardonios later says.

That was how he exhorted his troops. So when the cavalry that had surrounded them charged as though about to kill them, and the horsemen raised their weapons as though they were going to throw them (and perhaps someone among them even did throw one), the Phocians stood firm in opposition, deploying themselves into densely packed ranks as they faced their foes in every direction. [2] At that point, however, the horsemen suddenly turned and rode away. Now I cannot say for certain whether they had initially intended to destroy the Phocians at the request of the Thessalians and that then, when they saw the Phocians adopt a firm defensive stance, they became frightened of suffering losses themselves and for that reason turned away, and in doing so had followed the orders of Mardonios, or whether Mardonios had wanted merely to test their valor. [3] But when the horsemen returned, Mardonios sent a herald to the Phocians with this message: "Have no fear, Phocians, for you have clearly proven yourselves to be noble and courageous men, contrary to what I have heard. And now I tell you to wage this war wholeheartedly, for if you do, the value of your service will be far surpassed by the benefits that both the King and I will render back to you." That is the end of my account of the Phocians.

9.19
479
ELEUSIS
The Spartans and the Peloponnesians who accompanied them march north to Eleusis, where the Athenians join them.

After the Lacedaemonians reached the isthmus,[a] they set up their camp there. And when those other Peloponnesians who wanted what was best for Hellas learned of this—and some of them had even witnessed the Spartans marching out—they thought it would be wrong to be left behind. [2] And so, after obtaining favorable omens in sacrifice, they all set out together from the isthmus and made their way to Eleusis.[a] They performed sacrifices there as well, and when they found the omens favorable, they continued their march, now in the company of the Athenians who had crossed over from Salamis[b] and joined them at Eleusis. [3] And so they came to Erythrai[a]

9.19.1a Isthmus of Corinth: Map 9.17.
9.19.2a Eleusis: Map 9.17.
9.19.2b Salamis: Map 9.17.
9.19.3a Erythrai: Map 9.17, inset.

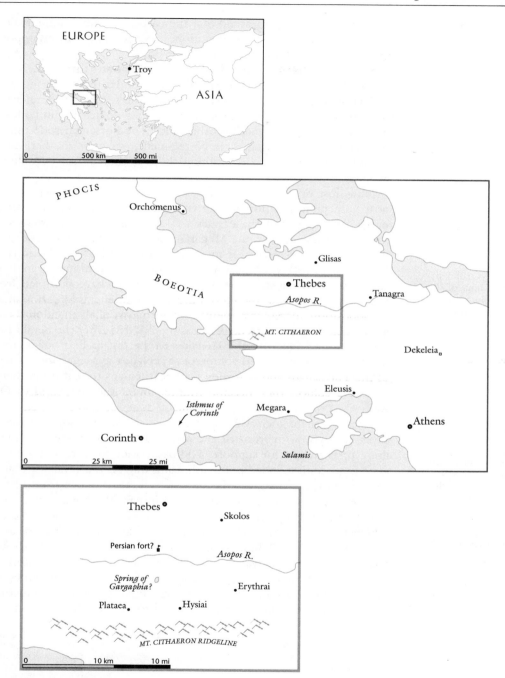

MAP 9.17

in Boeotia, where they learned that the barbarians were camping along the Asopos River.[b] After some deliberation, they took up positions opposite the enemy on the foothills of Mount Cithaeron.[c]

Since the Hellenes refused to come down onto the plain, Mardonios sent against them his entire corps of cavalry under the command of Masistios, whom the Hellenes call Makistios and who was very prominent among the Persians. He rode a Nesaian[a] horse with a golden bit and adorned by many other kinds of beautiful ornaments. The horsemen rode out against the Hellenes and charged them by regiment, one after another, doing significant harm to them and insulting them as they did so by calling them "women."[b]

Now, just by chance, the Megarians[a] happened to be deployed in the most vulnerable position of the entire battlefield, and it was they who received the brunt of the cavalry's assaults. Because they were so hard-pressed by these attacks, the Megarians sent a herald to the generals of the Hellenes who conveyed this message to them: [2] "The Megarians have this to tell you: 'We who are your allies cannot continue to confront the cavalry of the Persians alone in the position we have occupied from the beginning. So far, we are resisting by tenacity and valor, though we are hard-pressed. But now you should know that we shall abandon this post if you do not send others to replace us there.'" [3] After the herald had told them this, Pausanias put the Hellenes to the test to find out if any of the others would be willing to volunteer to replace the Megarians at their position. When all the rest had refused, the Athenians took it upon themselves to send a company of 300 picked men under the command of Olympiodoros son of Lampon.

These were the men who undertook this task, and they stationed themselves at Erythrai in front of the other Hellenes who were there, taking along their archers for support. The battle they fought there went on for some time, until it ended in the following way. As the cavalry was attacking by regiments, the horse of Masistios, which stood out in front of the rest, was pierced in its ribs by an arrow, and in pain the horse reared up on its hind legs and threw Masistios to the ground. [2] As soon as he fell, the Athenians attacked him. They took his horse and killed Masistios as he was struggling to defend himself. But at first they were unable to kill him because of the way he was armed. Since he was wearing a breastplate made of golden scales next to his skin, and over it a crimson tunic, they accomplished nothing as they struck against the breastplate. Then someone realized the reason for this and jabbed him through the eye, at which point he

9.20
479
ERYTHRAI
When the Hellenes refuse to descend onto the plain, Mardonios harasses them with his cavalry.

9.21
479
ERYTHRAI
The Megarians, hard-pressed by the Persians in their exposed position, ask the Greek generals for help, threatening to abandon their post. A force of 300 Athenians volunteers to relieve the Megarians.

9.22
479
ERYTHRAI
The Athenians hold their own against the Persian cavalry's attacks. Finally, after they wound the horse of Masistios, the enemy commander is thrown and killed. The Persians charge to recover his body.

9.19.3b   Asopos River: Map 9.17 and inset.
9.19.3c   Mount Cithaeron: Map 9.17 and inset.
9.20.1a   In 7.40.2, Herodotus writes that there is a large plain in Media called the Nesaian Plain, presumably the location from which these horses came, but its location is not now known.

9.20.1b   The Persian cavalry attack. The insults were probably a tactic to provoke the Hellenes into breaking ranks for a counterattack or at least advancing into the plain in pursuit of their harassing foes. See Appendix O, The Persian Army in Herodotus, §6–7.
9.21.1a   Megara: Map 9.17.

collapsed and died. [3] The rest of the cavalry was at first ignorant of all this, because as they had turned around and were riding away in retreat, no one had seen how he fell from his horse and subsequently died fighting. But they immediately missed him after they stopped, for no one was there to command them. Once they realized what had happened, they cried out and rallied one another, and then charged back to retrieve the corpse.

When the Athenians saw that the cavalry was no longer charging them in regiments, but was now in a mass formation, they shouted to the rest of the army for help. And as all the infantry there rushed to assist them, a bitter struggle was fought over the corpse. [2] Now, for as long as the 300 Athenians were there alone, they were in danger of being badly beaten; indeed, they were beginning to abandon the corpse when the main body of infantry came to their aid. Then it was the horsemen who could no longer stand their ground. Not only did they fail to retrieve the corpse, but they now lost other horsemen in addition to their commander. And so they drew back about 400 yards[a] and discussed what they should do. In view of the fact that they had no leader, they decided to ride back to Mardonios.

Upon the arrival of the cavalry at their camp, the whole army, and Mardonios most of all, went into mourning for Masistios, and in boundless grief they shaved their heads and also their horses and pack animals. All Boeotia echoed with their laments as they mourned the death of the man who had been, next to Mardonios, the most esteemed by the Persians and by the King himself. So it was that the barbarians honored Masistios in death according to their custom.

The Hellenes gained much courage from the fact that they had stood up to the attack of the cavalry and had repelled it. The first thing they did was to place the corpse on a wagon and have it drawn past the army's various units in their assigned positions. They displayed it this way because the body of Masistios was worth seeing for its size and its beauty, and the men left their ranks in order to see it. [2] Next, the Hellenes decided to advance down into Plataea,[a] for they could see that the Plataean land was much more suitable for their camp than that of Erythrai; among other advantages, it had a better supply of water. So they decided to advance to the Spring of Gargaphia[b] located there, and to establish their camps in that location after deploying into their various separate units. [3] And so, taking up their arms, they advanced through the foothills of Cithaeron, past Hysiai[a] and into Plataean territory. There they deployed in their national contingents near the Spring of Gargaphia and the precinct of the hero Androkrates.[b] Their forces extended across the low hills and the level land there.

9.23
479
ERYTHRAI
In a desperate struggle over Masistios' body, the Athenians call for help, which, when it arrives, drives off the Persian cavalry.

9.24
479
ERYTHRAI
Mardonios and the whole army mourn for the loss of Masistios.

9.25
479
ERYTHRAI
The Hellenes are encouraged by their victory over the enemy cavalry, and decide to move their positions from Erythrai down to Plataea, where water is more plentiful.

9.23.2a Herodotus writes this distance as "2 stades." See Appendix J, §6, 19.
9.25.2a Plataea: Map 9.17, inset.
9.25.2b Some authorities think the Spring of Gargaphia is the spring now called Retsi, possible location: Map 9.17 inset.
9.25.3a Hysiai: Map 9.17, inset.

9.25.3b Androkrates, a legendary hero who founded Plataea. His shrine is thought to be located in the vicinity of the Spring of Gargaphia.

9.26
479
ERYTHRAI
There is a dispute between the Tegeans and the Athenians as to who should hold the left wing in the battle order. The Tegeans give their argument why they should have that honorific position.

But while they were drawing up in their ranks, fierce wrangling arose between the Tegeans[a] and the Athenians;[b] for both thought it only right that they should occupy the other wing of the army,[c] and both of them justified their claims by citing both recent and ancient deeds. The Tegeans said, [2] "Of all the allies, we have always been worthy of this position in every previous joint expedition of the Peloponnesians—both long ago and recently—ever since the Heraklids tried to return to the Peloponnese[a] after the death of Eurystheus. [3] We gained this position because of what happened at that time. We had gone to help in the fight at the isthmus[a] together with the Achaeans[b] and the Ionians who then lived in the Peloponnese, and we took up our positions against the returning exiles. But then, the story goes, Hyllos[c] proclaimed that it was unnecessary for the armies to risk an engagement, but instead, the Peloponnesians should select the best man in their camp, and he would then fight Hyllos in single combat on agreed-upon terms. [4] The Peloponnesians decided that they had to carry out his proposal, and they swore a solemn oath with Hyllos on these conditions: if Hyllos won the victory over the leader of the Peloponnesians, the Heraklids should return to the land of their father, but if he lost, then the opposite would happen; the Heraklids would depart and Hyllos would lead their army away, and they would not seek to return to the Peloponnese for 100 years. [5] Out of all the allies, our general and king, Echemos son of Aeropos, the son of Phegeus, volunteered and was chosen. He fought Hyllos in single combat and killed him. And because of that feat we obtained several important privileges from the Peloponnesians, and we continue to hold them today. In particular, we always lead one of the two wings on a joint expedition. [6] We do not oppose you, men of Lacedaemon;[a] we offer you the choice of whichever wing you want, and we yield the command of it to you. But we claim the other wing, which belongs under our command, just as it has in times past. And apart from the achievement just described, we are more worthy to win a victory in this position than the Athenians, for we have been successful in many battles fought against you as well as against many others. And so it is only right and just that we, rather than the Athenians, should hold the other wing, for they have not accomplished such feats as we have, neither in recent nor ancient times."

9.27
479
ERYTHRAI
The Athenians give their arguments about why they deserve to hold the left wing, but state that they will take any position chosen for them by the Spartans and endeavor to acquit themselves valiantly there.

That was the speech of the Tegeans, and the Athenians responded to it as follows: "We know that this meeting has been convened to prepare for battle against the barbarians and not for speeches, but since this man from Tegea has put before you accounts of valiant deeds that each of us has accomplished in both ancient and recent times, we are forced to demonstrate to you that the most prominent positions belong to us as our ances-

9.26.1a Tegea: Map 9.27, BX.
9.26.1b Athens: Map 9.27, BY.
9.26.1c The other wing of the army in this case is the left wing, as the Spartans took the more honorable right wing.
9.26.2a Peloponnese: Map 9.27, BX.
9.26.3a Isthmus of Corinth: Map 9.27, BY.
9.26.3b Achaea: Map 9.27, BX.
9.26.3c Hyllos, the son of Herakles.
9.26.6a Lacedaemon (Sparta): Map 9.27, BX.

tral right rather than to the Arcadians,[a] because we are truly valiant. [2] Now the Heraklids, whose leader they claim to have killed at the isthmus, had earlier fled enslavement by the Mycenaeans,[a] and were driven away by all the Hellenes wherever they sought refuge, until we alone received them and subdued the arrogance of Eurystheus;[b] and with them we won the victory in battle over those who held the Peloponnese at that time. [3] Secondly, when the Argives[a] who marched against Thebes[b] with Polyneikes[c] met their end, they lay unburied until we fought the Kadmeians,[d] and it is our claim to fame that we picked up their bodies and buried them in our own territory of Eleusis.[e] [4] We also did well against the Amazons who at one time invaded from the Thermodon River[a] into Attica;[b] and in the struggles at Troy[c] we were inferior to none. But there is no profit in recalling all this, for the same men who were valiant back then could now be inferior, and those who are inferior now could have been superior then. [5] So let that be enough talk about deeds performed long ago. And even if there were nothing else for us to show as our achievement—as if any of the other Hellenes had as many successes as we have had—our accomplishment at Marathon[a] certainly makes us worthy to hold this privilege and others besides: there we alone of the Hellenes fought the Persian all by ourselves and not only survived such a remarkable endeavor, but won a victory over forty-six nations.[b] [6] Well, then, should we not justly be entitled to hold this post because of this one feat alone? But since it is not really appropriate to engage in such disputes at a time like this, we are ready and willing to obey you, Lacedaemonians, and we shall take our position in the line wherever, and opposite whomever, you decide is most suitable. We shall try to be valiant in any post we occupy."

That was how the Athenians replied, and the whole camp of Lacedaemonians shouted out that the Athenians were more worthy than the Arcadians to win the glory of victory holding this wing. And thus the Athenians prevailed over the Tegeans and obtained the post. [2] After this, the Hellenes, both those who had come there first and those who were joining the army now, took up their positions in the following order. Ten thousand Lacedaemonians held the right wing, and of these there were 5,000 Spartans with 35,000 light-armed troops of helots guarding them, seven posted

9.28
479
PLATAEA
The whole army awards the wing position to the Athenians by acclamation. Herodotus describes the Greek order of battle from the Spartans on the right to the Athenians on the left, citing their numbers by city as well as by their position.

9.27.1a   The Tegeans were Arcadians. Arcadia: Map 9.27, BX.
9.27.2a   Mycenae: Map 9.27, BY.
9.27.2b   Hyllos, pursued by his enemy Eurystheus, took refuge with the Athenians, and with their aid defeated and killed Eurystheus and his sons. (Godley)
9.27.3a   Argos: Map 9.27, BY.
9.27.3b   Thebes: Map 9.27, BY.
9.27.3c   When Polyneikes tried to recover Thebes from his brother Eteocles: see Aeschylos *Seven Against Thebes*. (Godley)
9.27.3d   Kadmeians (sons of Kadmos) was an archaic name for the inhabitants of Thebes.
9.27.3e   Eleusis: Map 9.27, BY.
9.27.4a   Thermodon River, Boeotia: location

unknown, although Herodotus says at 9.43.2 that the river flows between Tanagra and Glisas (for both, see Map 9.17 or 9.46, inset).
9.27.4b   Attica: Map 9.27, BY.
9.27.4c   Troy (Ilion/Ilium): Map 9.17, locator. The reference is to the legendary Trojan War.
9.27.5a   Marathon: Map 9.27, BY.
9.27.5b   The Spartans had also fought valiantly against the Persians at Thermopylae (Map 9.27, AY) but were ultimately defeated there. "Forty-six nations" assumes that all the ethnic groups represented in Xerxes' army of invasion were present with the force at Marathon ten years earlier.

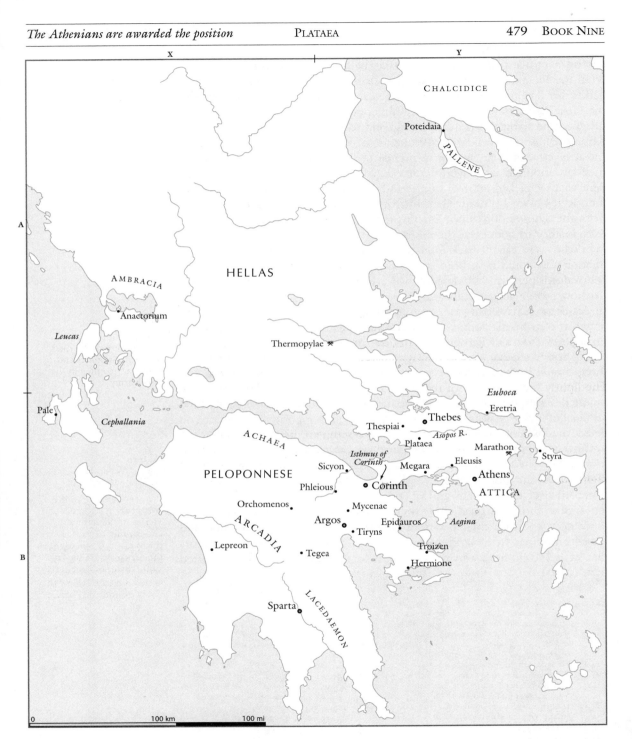

MAP 9.27

around each man. [3] The Spartans chose the Tegeans to stand next to them in line to show them honor and because of their valor. There were 1,500 Tegeans who served as hoplites. After them stood 5,000 Corinthians,[a] and Pausanias gave them the 300 Poteidaians[b] from Pallene[c] who were there to join them in their ranks. [4] Next to them stood 600 Arcadians of Orchomenos,[a] followed by 3,000 men of Sicyon.[b] After these were 800 Epidaurians,[c] and next to them were posted 1,000 Troizenians,[d] then 200 men of Lepreon,[e] followed by 400 men of Mycenae and Tiryns;[f] then 1,000 Phleiasians,[g] next to whom stood 3,000 troops from Hermione.[h] [5] After the Hermionians 600 Eretrians[a] and Styrians,[b] were posted, and they were followed by 400 Chalcidians,[c] and next to them, 500 Ambraciots.[d] Next came 800 Leucadians[e] and Anactorians,[f] then 200 Palees[g] from Cephallania. [6] Posted after them were 500 Aeginetans,[a] and next to them stood 3,000 Megarians,[b] followed by 600 Plataeans.[c] Finally, leading the ranks were the Athenians, 8,000 of them holding the left wing, and their commander was Aristeides son of Lysimachos.

All these (except for the seven helots posted with each Spartan) were hoplites, and added together their number was 38,700.[a] That is the number of hoplites that had gathered to oppose the barbarians. The numbers of lightly armed troops were as follows: posted with the Spartans were 35,000, seven for each hoplite, and every one of these was equipped for war. [2] The lightly armed troops of the other Lacedaemonians and Hellenes were assigned one to each hoplite, and they numbered 34,500, bringing the total number of lightly armed troops to 69,500.

So the sum of the entire Greek force assembled at Plataea, including both the hoplites and the lightly armed troops, was 1,800 less than 110,000, but when the Thespians[a] who had survived and were now in the camp, although not wearing armor, are added to the total, their number comes to a full 110,000.

Deployed in these positions, they camped beside the Asopos River.

After the barbarians under the command of Mardonios had finished their mourning for Masistios, they learned that the Hellenes were at Plataea, so they also advanced to where the Asopos[a] flowed nearby. When they arrived there, Mardonios arranged them opposite the Hellenes in the following manner. He placed the Persians so that they faced the Lacedaemonians; [2] but since the Persians actually far outnumbered the Lacedae-

9.29
479
PLATAEA
Herodotus lists the total number of hoplites and lightly armed men in the Greek army.

9.30
479
PLATAEA
The Greek forces number 110,000.

9.31
479
PLATAEA
Herodotus lists by nationality Mardonios' order of battle of the Persian forces as they advance against the Greek position at Plataea.

9.28.3a Corinth: Map 9.27, BY.
9.28.3b Poteidaia: Map 9.27, AY. Poteidaia had been colonized by Corinth.
9.28.3c Pallene: Map 9.27, AY.
9.28.4a Orchomenos, Arcadia: Map 9.27, BX.
9.28.4b Sicyon: Map 9.27, BY.
9.28.4c Epidaurus: Map 9.27, BY.
9.28.4d Troizen: Map 9.27, BY.
9.28.4e Lepreon: Map 9.27, BX.
9.28.4f Tiryns: Map 9.27, BY.
9.28.4g Phleious: Map 9.27, BY.
9.28.4h Hermione: Map 9.27, BY.
9.28.5a Eretria, Euboea: Map 9.27, BY.
9.28.5b Styra, Euboea: Map 9.27, BY.
9.28.5c Chalcidice: Map 9.27, AY.
9.28.5d Ambracia: Map 9.27, AX.
9.28.5e Leucas: Map 9.27, AX.
9.28.5f Anactorium: Map 9.27, AX.
9.28.5g Pale, Cephallania: Map 9.27, BX.
9.28.6a Aegina: Map 9.27, BY.
9.28.6b Megara: Map 9.27, BY.
9.28.6c Plataea: Map 9.27, BY.
9.29.1a See Appendix R, §6.
9.30.1a Thespiai: Map 9.27, BY.
9.31.1a Asopos River: Map 9.27, BY.

monians, they faced the Tegeans also, and they were deployed in more ranks than usual. That was the position of the Persians. As the Thebans had informed and instructed him, Mardonios chose the most powerful part of his forces to stand opposite the Lacedaemonians and deployed the weaker units against the Tegeans. [3] Next to the Persians he posted the Medes[a] to stand opposite the Corinthians, Poteidaians, Orchomenians, and Sicyonians. And next to the Medes he marshaled the Baktrians,[b] who faced the Epidaurians, Troizenians, Lepreans, Mycenaeans,[c] and Phleiasians. [4] After the Baktrians he posted the Indians[a] to stand opposite the Hermionians, Eretrians, Styrians, and Chalcidians. Next to the Indians he had the Sakai[b] stand to face the Ambraciots, Anaktorians, Leucadians, Palees, and Aeginetans. [5] Opposite the Athenians,[a] Plataeans,[b] and Megarians, he deployed the Boeotians,[c] Locrians,[d] Malians,[e] Thessalians,[f] and the 1,000 troops from Phocis;[g] Not all of the Phocians were medizing; some of them were supporting the Greek cause by taking refuge around Parnassus[h] and using this as their base from which to plunder and rob the army of Mardonios and the Hellenes who were with him. Mardonios also positioned the Macedonians[i] and the inhabitants of the region surrounding Thessaly so that they faced the Athenians.

These ethnic contingents just listed were the greatest of those deployed by Mardonios, in that they were the most noteworthy and most important. But there were men of other nations mingled among them: Phrygians, Thracians, Mysians, Paionians, and the rest, including Ethiopians and Egyptians[a]—namely, the Ermotybians and those called the Kalasiries,[b] who bear knives and are the only Egyptians classed as warriors. [2] These Egyptians were really marines, but Mardonios had ordered them to disembark at Phaleron,[a] for they had not been originally assigned to the army that went with Xerxes to Athens. So as I mentioned earlier, there were 300,000 barbarians.[b] There is no number reported for the Hellenes allied with Mardonios, but if I may venture a guess, I would estimate that up to 50,000 of them had assembled there and were drawn up as infantry; the cavalry was stationed apart from them.

On the day after they had all been marshaled into their ethnic contingents and units, both sides conducted sacrifices. The man who performed

9.32
479
PLATAEA
Herodotus lists other ethnic units fighting with the Persians, including their Greek allies. He says the barbarians number 300,000, and estimates the number of Greek allies as 50,000.

9.33
479
PLATAEA
How Teisamenos, the army diviner, almost wins the pentathlon at Olympia, gains the freedom of Sparta, and asks for citizenship for himself and his brother.

9.31.3a Media: Map 9.33, locator.
9.31.3b Baktrians (Baktrianoi), location of territory: Map 9.33, locator.
9.31.3c Mycenae: Map 9.33, BX.
9.31.4a India: Map 9.33, locator.
9.31.4b Sakai, location of territory: Map 9.33, locator. These might have been the Sakai cavalry mentioned later, but they are here in a list of infantry, and placed in the line next to their geographic neighbors, the Indians, so it is assumed they are the Sakai marines, not infantry and not the Sacae (Scythian) cavalry. Herodotus does not otherwise indicate which Sacae or Sakai he is citing.
9.31.5a Athens: Map 9.33, BY.

9.31.5b Plataea: Map 9.33, AY.
9.31.5c Boeotia: Map 9.33, AX.
9.31.5d Locris (presumably in this instance both Opuntian and Ozolian): Map 9.33, AX.
9.31.5e Malis: Map 9.33, AX.
9.31.5f Thessaly: Map 9.33, AX.
9.31.5g Phocis: Map 9.33, AX.
9.31.5h Mount Parnassus: Map 9.33, AX.
9.31.5i Macedon: Map 9.46.
9.32.1a Phrygia, Thrace, Mysia, Paionia, Ethiopia, Egypt: Map 9.33, locator.
9 32.1b The Egyptian military classes were mentioned at 2.164. (Godley)
9.32.2a Phaleron: Map 9.33, BY.
9.32.2b For a discussion of these numbers, see Appendix R, §6–12.

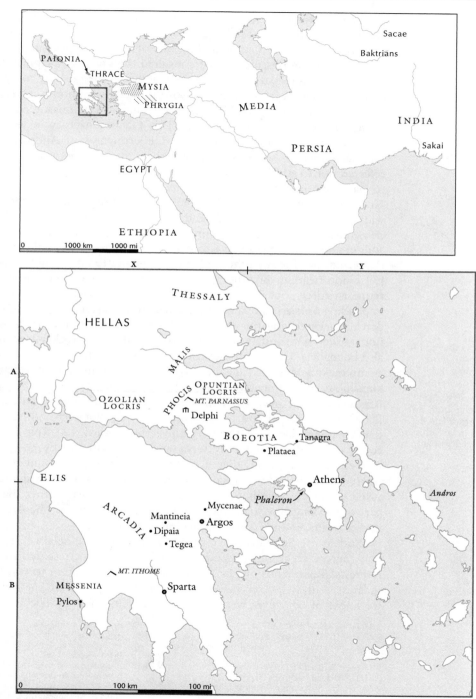

MAP 9.33

the sacrifice for the Hellenes was Teisamenos son of Antiochos, who had accompanied this army as its seer. He was an Elean[a] of the Iamid clan,[b] but the Lacedaemonians[c] had made him one of their own people. [2] It seems that once, when Teisamenos had consulted the oracle at Delphi[a] about offspring, the Pythia had replied that he would win the greatest contests—five of them, in fact. Missing the point of the oracular response, he turned his attention to athletics, thinking that he would win gymnastic contests. He practiced the pentathlon[b] and missed an Olympic victory in wrestling by just one fall in a competition against Hieronymos of Andros.[c] [3] The Lacedaemonians, however, realized that the prophecy to Teisamenos referred not to athletic but to military contests, and they tried to bribe him to lead them in war together with the Heraklids who were their kings. [4] Now, Teisamenos could see that the Spartans thought it very important to win him over as their friend, and because he realized this, he began to demand a higher price, stipulating that if they made him a Spartan citizen and granted him his share of all their privileges, he would do as they requested, but for any other or lesser compensation he would refuse them. [5] Upon hearing this, the Spartans became outraged and withdrew their request entirely; but in the end, when they grew very frightened due to the impending Persian campaign, they pursued him again and consented to his demands. Perceiving the change in their attitude, he said that he was now not satisfied with just these conditions, but that his brother Hegias should also be made a Spartan on the same terms as himself.

By making this demand, he was imitating Melampous, if a demand for kingship can be compared with one for citizenship. For when the women of Argos[a] had gone mad, the Argives tried to pay Melampous to come from Pylos[b] and bring an end to the illness of their women,[c] and he proposed that they give him half the kingship as his reward. [2] This the Argives could not endure, and they went away. But after many more of their women had gone mad, they accepted his demand, and went to him and offered what he had proposed. But then, seeing their change in attitude, he asked for more, claiming that unless they gave to his brother Bias a third part of the kingship, he would not do what they wanted. The Argives were in dire straits, so they consented to this demand also.

And so the Spartans, since they were in desparate need of Teisamenos' help, agreed to all his demands. And after they had consented to both his requests, Teisamenos of Elis, now a Spartan, helped them to win their five greatest contests by serving as their seer. These two were the only people we know of who ever were made Spartan citizens. [2] The five contests

9.33.1a	Elis: Map 9.33, AX.
9.33.1b	The Iamidai were a priestly family whose members were found in all parts of Greece. (Godley)
9.33.1c	Lacedaemon (Sparta): Map 9.33, BX.
9.33.2a	Delphi: Map 9.33, AX.
9.33.2b	The five events of the pentathlon were running, jumping, wrestling, and spear and discus throwing. (Godley)
9.33.2c	Andros: Map 9.33, BY.
9.34.1a	Argos: Map 9.33, BX. Women gone mad: see Appendix U, §4, 7.
9.34.1b	Pylos: Map 9.33, BX.
9.34.1c	According to the legend, the Argive women were driven mad by Dionysos for refusing to take part in his orgies, and were cured by Melampous the seer. Many Greek authors refer to it, with varying details.

were, first, the one at Plataea;[a] next, one at Tegea[b] against the Tegeans and Argives; after that, at Dipaia[c] against all the Arcadians[d] except for the Mantineians;[e] then against the Messenians near Ithome;[f] and finally, in Tanagra[g] against the Athenians and Argives, and the last one completed the series of five contests.

This was the Teisamenos whom the Spartans led to Plataea to be a seer for the Hellenes. The sacrificial omens for the Hellenes were favorable if they fought to defend themselves, but not if they crossed the Asopos[a] and initiated battle.

The sacrifices conducted for Mardonios also turned out to be adverse if he were eager to initiate battle, but favorable if he fought in self-defense. He too obtained sacrificial omens in the Greek way; his seer was Hegesistratos of Elis, the most noteworthy of the Telliads.[a] Earlier, the Spartans had arrested, imprisoned, and condemned Hegesistratos to death for the many and terrible damages they had suffered because of him. [2] Caught in this dire situation, Hegesistratos, recognizing that he was in a race against death, resolved to suffer severe pain rather than to die, and he then performed a feat that beggars description. Although he was confined in wooden stocks rimmed with iron, he gained possession of an iron implement that had somehow been brought there. As soon as he obtained it, he devised the bravest of all deeds that we know of: he first measured how much of his foot could be freed from the stocks, and then proceeded to cut it off between the toes and the heel. [3] After he had done this, he still had to evade his guards, so he tunneled through the wall and fled to Tegea, traveling during the nights and hiding in the woods to rest during the days until, on the third night, he arrived in Tegea. Meanwhile, the Lacedaemonians, who were struck with amazement when they saw half of his foot lying in the stocks, were out searching for him in full force, but they could not find him. [4] Thus he escaped the Lacedaemonians on that occasion and took refuge in Tegea, which was not on friendly terms with the Lacedaemonians at that time. When he had recovered his health and had a wooden foot made for himself, he became openly hostile to the Lacedaemonians. In the end, however, his enmity toward them brought him no good, for while he was serving as a seer on Zacynthus,[a] they captured and killed him.

9.36
479
PLATAEA
Teisamenos is the diviner at Plataea.

9.37
479
PLATAEA
Mardonios' sacrifices predict a bad outcome if he should attack first. The story of his diviner, Hegesistratos of Elis, and how he escapes from the Spartans and is their enemy until they capture and kill him.

9.35.2a Plataea: Map 9.33, AY. The battle of Plataea in 479, described in 9.58–70.
9.35.2b Tegea: Map 9.33, BX. The date of this battle of the Spartans against the Tegeans and the Argives is uncertain, but it is thought to have occurred sometime between 479 and 450.
9.35.2c Dipaia: Map 9.33, BX. This battle by the Spartans against all the Arcadians is thought to have taken place sometime after 465, but possibly still during the helot revolt.
9.35.2d Arcadia: Map 9.33, BX.
9.35.2e Mantineia: Map 9.33, BX.
9.35.2f Mount Ithome, Messenia: Map 9.33, BX. Although the Greek text says this battle took place at "Isthmus," the lack of any location called that between Sparta and Messenia has led most scholars to assume that it should read "Ithome," where the Spartans and their allies did successfully lay siege to the Messenians during the helot revolt, around 465.
9.35.2g Tanagra: Map 9.33, AY. A battle fought by the Spartans against the Athenians and Argives in 458, an engagement of the "first" Peloponnesian War.
9.36.1a Asopus River: Map 9.27, BY.
9.37.1a The Telliads were a reknowned family of Elean seers.
9.37.4a Zacynthus: Map 9.46.

9.38
479
PLATAEA
The omens remain
unfavorable as the Greek
army grows more numerous.
A man from Thebes advises
Mardonios to guard the pass
over Mount Cithaeron.

9.39
479
MOUNT CITHAERON
Mardonios sends his cavalry
on a successful raid against
supply trains coming over
the Cithaeron pass.

9.40
479
PLATAEA
Neither side will begin
the battle, but Mardonios'
cavalry, aided by the Thebans,
harass the Hellenes.

9.41
479
PLATAEA
After many days of skirmishing,
Artabazos and the Thebans
counsel Mardonios to withdraw inside the walls of Thebes
and attempt to break the unity
of the Hellenes by bribing the
chief men of the various cities.
Mardonios, however, wants to
bring about a battle immediately, before the Greek army
grows stronger.

But of course the death of Hegesistratos occurred after the events at Plataea.[a] At this time he was serving by the Asopos,[b] receiving no small payment from Mardonios for performing sacrifice, which he carried out enthusiastically both because of his hatred for the Lacedaemonians and because of the profit he was making. [2] Now the omens concerning battle were unfavorable not only for the Persians themselves but also for the Hellenes who were allied with them (since they had a seer of their own, Hippomachos of Leucas).[a]

But as time passed, and the Greek army grew larger as more and more Hellenes streamed in to join it, a Theban named Timagenides son of Herpys advised Mardonios to occupy the pass at Cithaeron,[b] telling him that the Hellenes were pouring through it every day and that great numbers of them could be intercepted there.

Eight days had already passed since the two sides had been camping opposite each other when Timagenides counseled Mardonios to do this. Realizing that this was good advice, Mardonios waited until night fell and then sent his cavalry to the pass of Cithaeron, which opens toward Plataea and is called Three Heads by the Boeotians[a] and Oaks Heads by the Athenians.[b] [2] And these horsemen did not go there in vain, for as they raided the plain,[a] they captured 500 beasts of burden carrying food from the Peloponnese[b] toward the Greek camp, and the people tending the wagons as well. After they had taken this quarry, the Persians proceeded to slaughter everything without mercy, sparing neither man nor beast. When they had their fill of killing, they surrounded what was left and drove them back to Mardonios and his camp.

Two more days elapsed after they had done this deed, as neither side wanted to initiate battle. The barbarians tested the Hellenes by going as far as the Asopos, but neither side crossed the river. Mardonios' cavalry, however, continually harassed the Hellenes and pressed them hard. For the Thebans, who were staunch medizers and eager participants in the war, always led the way until the actual battle, at which point the Persians and the Medes took over and were the ones who performed feats of great valor.

But for the first ten days nothing happened other than what I have related. Then, with the arrival of the eleventh day after the armies had camped opposite each other at Plataea, by which time the Greeks had indeed greatly increased their numbers, Mardonios son of Gobryas grew exasperated at the continued standoff; at that point he held a conference with Artabazos son of Pharnakes, one of the few Persian men highly esteemed by Xerxes. [2] During their discussion, Artabazos expressed the opinion that they should have the whole army pack up as quickly as possible and retreat behind the walls of Thebes, where much food for them and fod-

9.38.1a   Plataea: Map 9.46, inset.
9.38.1b   Asopos River: Map 9.46, inset.
9.38.2a   Leucas: Map 9.46.
9.38.2b   Mount Cithaeron: Map 9.46, inset. The
          location of this pass is unknown.

9.39.1a   Boeotia: Map 9.46, inset.
9.39.1b   Athens: Map 9.46 and inset.
9.39.2a   For Persian cavalry tactics against hoplites,
          see Appendix O, §7, and Figure 9.39.
9.39.2b   Peloponnese: Map 9.46.

FIGURE 9.39. AN ATTIC VASE PAINTING DATED TO 425, SHOWING A GREEK HOPLITE
FIGHTING A PERSIAN CAVALRYMAN. A GREEK ARCHER ON THE LEFT AIMS HIS BOW AT THE
ENEMY.

der for the pack animals had been taken, and where they could accomplish their goals at their leisure; [3] for they had there a great store of gold, both coined and uncoined, and much silver and many drinking vessels as well. They should spare none of this, he said, but send it off to be distributed among the Hellenes, especially among those who were prominent in their cities; if they did this, the Hellenes would quickly surrender their freedom and the Persians would not have to be exposed to the risks of battle. [4] This proposal of Artabazos was really the same advice as that which the Thebans had given, as he also had more foresight than the Persian commander. Indeed, Mardonios' attitude was the more forceful and competitive of the two, and in no way submissive, for he believed that his army was much stronger than that of the Hellenes, and that it should engage in battle as quickly as possible rather than allow the Hellenes to marshal still more men than they had already assembled. As for the pre-battle sacrifices of Hegesistratos, he said they should forget about them rather than try to force them to become favorable. Instead, he thought that they should join battle in the Persian tradition.

That is what Mardonios thought was the right course of action, and since no one opposed him, his opinion prevailed. For it was he, and not Artabazos, who had received control over the army from the King. He sent for the subordinate commanders of the regiments and the generals of the Hellenes serving with them and asked them if they knew of any prophecy predicting that the Persians would be destroyed in Hellas. [2] These specially summoned men responded with silence, some of them because they did not know the oracles, others knowing them but thinking that it was unsafe to speak about them. So Mardonios himself said, "Well, then, since you either know nothing or do not dare to speak up, I shall tell you, because I am quite knowledgeable about this matter. [3] There is an oracle that the Persians are destined to come to Hellas and that they will all die, but only after they plunder the sanctuary at Delphi. So since we know this, we shall not go to this sanctuary or try to plunder it, and for that reason we shall not die. [4] All of you who happen to be well disposed toward the Persians may take pleasure in this, since it means that we shall prevail over the Hellenes." After saying this, he gave the signal for the second time to make all the preparations and put everything in good order for the battle to be joined on the following day.

As to the oracle that Mardonios said applied to the Persians, I know that it was not composed about the Persians but actually about the Illyrians and the army of the Encheles.[a] But there is another one composed by Bakis[b] which does refer to this battle:

9.42
479
PLATAEA
Mardonios is the commander, so his view prevails. Steps are ordered to prepare the army for battle the next day.

9.43
479
PLATAEA
Herodotus says that the oracle quoted by Mardonios really refers to the Illyrians, and not the Persians.

9.43.1a   The oracle refers to a legendary expedition of Illyrian tribes directed against Hellas and Delphi. (Godley) Illyria: Map 9.46. See Appendix P, Oracles, Religion, and Politics in Herodotus, §2–4, 8–9.

9.43.1b   Herodotus writes about Bakis as if that was the name of a writer of oracles. *The Oxford Classical Dictionary* asserts that it was a generic name of a class of inspired prophets.

[2] Beside the River Thermodon and grassy banks of Asopos,[a]
Greek armies will assemble; barbarian tongues will shriek;
Medes who wield bows will fall here in great numbers,
Before their time allotted, when this day of death arrives.

I also know other prophecies referring to the Persians similar to this one, by Mousaios. The Thermodon River flows between Tanagra and Glisas.[b]

After this inquiry about the oracles and the exhortation offered by Mardonios, night fell, and men were stationed at the guard posts. The night was well advanced; all was quiet throughout the camp, and most of the men were fast asleep when Alexandros son of Amyntas[a] rode up on horseback to a guard post of the Athenians, seeking to speak to their generals. [2] While most of the guards remained at their posts, some ran to their generals, and when they found them they told them that someone on horseback had arrived from the camp of the Medes, and that he would say nothing more than that he wished to speak to some of their generals, whom he named.

As soon as they heard this, the generals followed the guards back to their post, and when they arrived there, Alexandros said to them, "Men of Athens, I entrust you with what I am about to say, charging you to keep it an absolute secret and to tell no one but Pausanias, lest you utterly destroy me. You must know that I would not be speaking to you if I did not care greatly about all of Hellas, [2] for I myself am a Hellene of ancient lineage and would not wish to see Hellas exchange its freedom for slavery. And so I am here to tell you that Mardonios and his army are unable to obtain from their sacrifices the omens they desire. Otherwise you would have fought a long time ago. Now, however, Mardonios has resolved to dismiss the oracles and to engage in battle beginning at the break of day; my guess is that he is very worried that more men will come here to join you. So you should prepare yourselves for this. If it turns out that Mardonios delays the encounter and does nothing, you should remain and persevere, for they have enough food left for only a few days. [3] And if this war ends in your favor, then you must remember me and my own quest for liberation, for it is on my own initiative that I have performed this dangerous feat as a service to the Hellenes; I wish to reveal the intent of Mardonios to you so that the barbarians will not be able to fall upon you suddenly and unexpectedly. I am Alexandros of Macedon." After saying this he rode away, back to his camp and his own post.

9.44
479
PLATAEA
Late in the night, Alexandros of Macedon rides to the Athenian lines and asks to speak to the generals.

9.45
479
PLATAEA
Alexandros warns the Hellenes that although Mardonios has not received favorable omens, he plans to attack at dawn, having only enough food to hold his position for a few days more. He asks that the Hellenes, if successful, remember to liberate Macedon, too, from Persian rule.

9.43.2a   Asopos River: Map 9.46, inset.
9.43.2b   The Thermedon River's precise location in Boeotia is unknown. For Glisas, Tana- gra, and Thebes, see Map 9.46, inset.
9.44.1a   Alexandros son of Amyntas, king of Macedon: Map 9.46.

When Pausanias is told of the Persian plans, he suggests that the Athenians and Spartans exchange positions in the Greek line, so each will oppose a familiar foe—the Athenians against the Persians, the Spartans against the Boeotians.

The Persians counter the Greek maneuver, which leads Pausanias to return the Spartans to the right wing.

Mardonios sends a message to the Spartans, mocking them for attempting to avoid battle with the Persians and challenging them to a decisive encounter of equal numbers.

The Athenian generals went to the right wing and told Pausanias exactly what they had heard from Alexandros. With the report of this news, Pausanias grew frightened at the very thought of the Persians and said, [2] "Well, then, since the battle will begin at dawn, it would be best for you, the Athenians, to oppose the Persians, and for us to face the Boeotians[a] and the Hellenes now posted opposite you. After all, you are familiar with the Medes and how they fight, since you fought them at Marathon,[b] while not a single one of us, the men of Sparta, has any experience or knowledge of the Medes in battle,[c] although we are quite familiar with the Boeotians and Thessalians.[d] [3] Therefore you should take up your arms and come over to this wing, and we shall go to the left." To this the Athenians replied, "Actually, for a long time now, indeed from the very beginning when we saw you deployed opposite the Persians, we ourselves have been thinking about suggesting just what you have now proposed, but we feared that our advice would displease you. Now that you have suggested it, we are pleased with your proposal and are most ready and willing to carry it out."

Since this plan satisfied both parties, they exchanged positions as dawn was breaking. But when the Boeotians found out what was happening and reported it to Mardonios, he immediately tried to shift positions, too, so as to again place the Persians opposite the Lacedaemonians. Then, when Pausanias learned what was going on and realized that his maneuver had been detected and countered, he brought the Spartans back to the right wing, and Mardonios, in the same way, brought the Persians back to the left.

When everyone had settled back into their original positions, Mardonios sent a herald to the Spartans with this message: "Lacedaemonians, you are *said* to be the best and bravest of men by the people of these parts; they are overcome with awe for you because, so they say, you neither flee from battle nor desert your posts, but stand fast and either destroy your foes or are destroyed yourselves. [2] But it turns out that none of this is true. For even before we have joined battle and come to close combat, we have seen you flee and abandon your assigned positions to make the Athenians test us first, while you deploy yourselves opposite our slaves. [3] These are certainly not the deeds of noble and courageous men! We have been altogether deceived about you, for we expected that you, given your glorious reputation, would send a herald to challenge us, and that you would want to fight only the Persians; and we were ready to act accordingly. Now we find that you are making no such proposal but are cringing before us instead. Well, then, since you have not initiated the challenge, we shall do so ourselves. [4] Why don't you fight for the Hellenes, since you are reputed to be the most valiant of them, and we shall fight for the barbarians, with equal numbers on each side. If you think the others should fight, too, fine: let them fight afterward. Or if not, and if you should think we alone are enough, we

9.46.2a Boeotia: Map 9.46, inset.
9.46.2b Marathon: Map 9.46, inset. The battle of
Marathon took place in 490, eleven years
earlier. See 6.107–113.
9.46.2c Spartan hoplites had fought the Persians

at Thermopylae (Map 9.46) in the previous year, but none of them survived that battle.
9.46.2d Thessaly: Map 9.46.

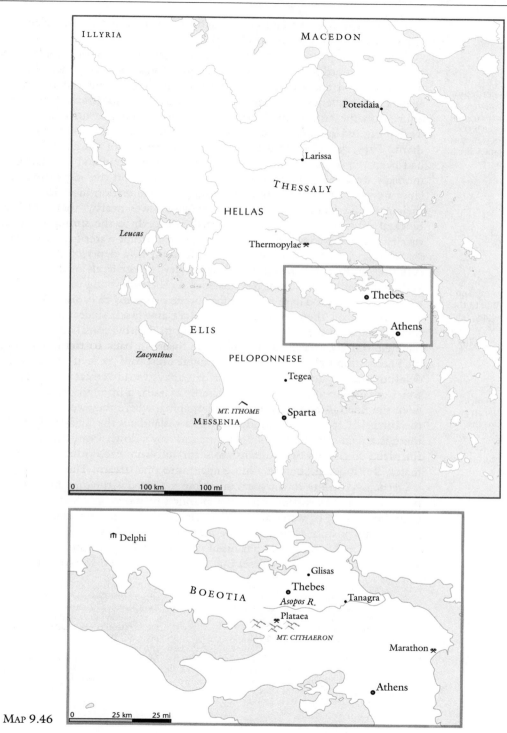

MAP 9.46

shall fight it out to the end, and whichever of us wins will then claim the victory over the entire army of the other."

The herald paused after saying this, and when no one replied, he returned to Mardonios and informed him of what had happened. Mardonios, overjoyed and exalted by this phantom victory, sent out his cavalry against the Hellenes. [2] The horsemen rode out and attacked, inflicting injuries on the entire Greek army with their javelins and arrows, for they were mounted archers and it was impossible for the Hellenes to close with them. They also blocked and destroyed the Spring of Gargaphia,[a] which had been the source of water for the whole Greek army. [3] The Lacedaemonians were the only ones posted at the spring, and the rest of the Hellenes were farther away from it, according to the position in which each of their units was stationed. Though the Asopos was nearby, they had been blocked off from it and had to go back and forth to the spring, since the cavalry and archers prevented them from transporting water from the river.

So that was their situation; and with the army now deprived of water and suffering under the harassment of the cavalry, the generals of the Hellenes gathered together and went to Pausanias on the right wing to discuss these and other matters. There were in fact other problems that distressed them even more than these: they no longer had any food, since the auxiliaries they had sent to the Peloponnese[a] to bring back provisions had been completely blocked by the enemy's cavalry and were unable to reach their camp.

Taking counsel together, the generals resolved that if the Persians delayed and did not give battle that day, they would retreat to the island[a] which was situated in front of the city of Plataea, a little more than a mile from the Asopos[b] and the Spring of Gargaphia, where they were camping at the time. [2] It could be thought of as an island on the mainland, in that there is a river which divides upstream and flows down from Cithaeron[a] to the plain, so that its two streams are separated from each other by approximately 2,000 yards[b] before joining again into one stream. The river's name is Oëroë;[c] according to the local inhabitants, Oëroë is the daughter of Asopos. [3] So it was to this place they planned to move, in order to have an unlimited supply of water and so that the cavalry could not inflict harm on them from positions directly opposite them, as it was doing now. They decided to make the move that night during the second watch, so that the Persians would not see them set out and their horsemen would not be able

9.49.2a   Spring of Gargaphia, possible location: Map 9.17, inset. Some authorities think it is the spring today called Retsi near the existing church of St. Demetrius.
9.50.1a   Peloponnese: Map 9.46.
9.51.1a   Scholars have not been able to identify this "island" with any certainty. Some believe that it may be a long strip of land—now not actually surrounded by water, and 2.2 miles from the Asopos River rather than "a little more than a mile" (10 stades), as Herodotus figures

it—that lies between two of several streams that flow north or northwest from Mount Cithaeron (Map 9.46, inset), uniting to form the small river Oëroë. (Godley) For stades, see Appendix J, §6, 19.
9.51.1b   Asopos River: Map 9.46, inset.
9.51.2a   Mount Cithaeron: Map 9.46, inset.
9.51.2b   Herodotus writes this distance as "10 stades." See Appendix J, §6, 19.
9.51.2c   Oëroë stream: location unknown.

to harass them in pursuit. [4] They also decided that during the same night, upon their arrival at the island around which Oëroë daughter of Asopos flows from Cithaeron, they would dispatch half the army to Cithaeron to rescue the auxiliaries who were supposed to be transporting their provisions, since they were stranded there on Cithaeron.

After they had discussed and planned this move, they suffered throughout the whole day from attacks by the Persian cavalry; and it was not until the day was drawing to a close that the horsemen finally ceased their assaults. After night fell and the hour they had arranged to leave arrived, most of them departed, though they had no intention of going to the destination upon which they had previously agreed. For once they were in motion, they were so happy to flee from the cavalry that they continued their flight toward the city of Plataea[a] until they arrived at the sanctuary of Hera, which lies in front of the city and is a little more than two miles[b] from the Spring of Gargaphia. Upon their arrival there they set down their arms in front of the sanctuary.

Thus they made their camp around the sanctuary of Hera. Now when Pausanias saw them departing from their previous camp, he gave orders to the Lacedaemonians to take up their arms and follow the others who had gone before them and who he assumed were on their way to the place upon which they had previously agreed. [2] The other subordinate commanders were all ready to obey Pausanias, but Amompharetos son of Poliades, the commander of the Pitana brigade,[a] would not move, saying that he was unwilling to flee from the outsiders[b] and bring disgrace upon Sparta; he was amazed by what was happening, because he had not been present at the earlier conference. [3] Pausanias and Euryanax were infuriated at his disobedience, but they were even more upset by the fact that they would have to leave the Pitana brigade behind if he persisted in his refusal. They feared that by carrying out the agreement they had made with the other Hellenes, they would have to desert Amompharetos and his men, who, being left behind there, would surely be destroyed. [4] As they were reasoning this through, they kept the Laconian[a] army from moving off, and tried to persuade Amompharetos that he was wrong to act this way.

And while they were thus urging Amompharetos, who was the only one of the Lacedaemonians and Tegeans who was about to be left behind, the Athenians also refused to move, but stayed where they had been originally posted, firmly believing that the Lacedaemonians' disposition was to say one thing while intending to do another. [2] So when the army had started

9.52
479
PLATAEA
The Hellenes suffer attacks all day from the Persian cavalry, so that when they depart for their assigned places, most of them go instead to Plataea.

9.53
479
PLATAEA
Pausanias gives orders to the Spartans to move to their assigned position, but one captain, Amompharetos, refuses. Rather than abandon his unit, the Spartans remain there while Pausanias and others try to persuade Amompharetos to go with the rest.

9.54
479
PLATAEA
The Athenians ask Pausanias whether the Spartans are marching and what the Athenians should do.

9.52.1a Plataea: Map 9.46, inset.
9.52.1b Herodotus writes this distance as "20 stades." See Appendix J, §6, 9.
9.53.2a Pitana brigade: it is not clear what Herodotus means here. See Appendix B, §15. In 3.55.2, Herodotus mentions a district or village of Sparta called Pitane. Thucydides (*Thucydides* 1.20) denies the existence of a Pitana brigade or regiment

(Greek transliteration, *ths lo-xos*) as a formal part of the Spartan army. (Godley)
9.53.2b The "outsiders" mentioned by Amompharetos are the Persians. See 9.11.2, where Herodotus explains that the Spartans used to call all barbarians (non-Greeks) outsiders.
9.53.4a The Laconian army is the Spartan army.

to move, they had sent one of their horsemen to see whether the Spartans were making an attempt to leave or whether they actually did not intend to depart at all, and also to ask Pausanias what they themselves should do.

When the herald reached the Lacedaemonians, he saw that they were deployed in their original positions and that their most prominent men were involved in a quarrel. For Euryanax and Pausanias had no success at all in persuading Amompharetos not to risk leaving himself and his men isolated as the only Lacedaemonians to remain there, and their discussion had finally developed into an open quarrel, just as the Athenian herald arrived and stood next to them. [2] During this argument Amompharetos picked up a rock with both hands and, placing it before the feet of Pausanias, said that with this voting pebble he was casting his vote not to flee from the outsiders. Pausanias then called him a madman and said he was out of his mind. The Athenians' herald inquired as he had been instructed, and in reply, Pausanias ordered him to tell the Athenians about his current situation, and to request that they come now to join his troops; as for what to do about retreating, he said they should follow the lead of the Lacedaemonians.

The herald then returned to the Athenians. When dawn came, the Spartans were still bickering. Pausanias had not moved all this time, but now, thinking that Amompharetos would not really stay behind if the rest of the Lacedaemonians marched away (which is just what happened), he gave the signal and led off all the rest of the troops through the hills, while the Tegeans[a] followed. [2] The Athenians marched in the opposite direction, as they had been assigned, for while the Lacedaemonians kept close to the ridges and the foothills of Cithaeron in fear of the cavalry, the Athenians turned down toward the plain.

At first Amompharetos had expected that Pausanias would not dare to leave him and his men behind, and he remained determined to stay and not to abandon his post. But then, as Pausanias and his troops continued to march away, he concluded that they were quite clearly abandoning him. At this point he had his brigade take up their arms, and he led them forth at a walking pace toward the main body of troops. [2] The latter had gone ahead a little less than half a mile,[a] but then had stopped to wait for the brigade of Amompharetos around the River Moloeis at the place called Argiopion,[b] where there is a sanctuary of Eleusinian Demeter. Pausanias and his men waited there so that if Amompharetos and his company remained at their formerly appointed post, they would be able to hurry back to help them. [3] Now, just as Amompharetos and his men reached Pausanias and his troops, the entire cavalry of the barbarians pressed hard upon them. For the horsemen were acting as they usually did: when they saw empty space where the Hellenes had been in position on the previous days, they rode forward and, as soon as they caught up with the Hellenes, they attacked them.

9.55
479
PLATAEA
The Athenian messenger arrives during the argument with Amompharetos, and Pausanias asks the Athenians to join the Spartans and to follow their lead.

9.56
479
PLATAEA
The Spartans march off, keeping to the hills to avoid Persian cavalry. The Athenians march down into the plain.

9.57
479
PLATAEA
After the rest of the Spartans marched off, Amompharetos follows, and finds them waiting for him not far away. Then they are attacked by the Persian cavalry.

9.56.1a Tegea: Map 9.46.
9.57.2a Herodotus writes this distance as "4 stades." See Appendix J, §6, 9.

9.57.2b Moloeis River and Argiopion: locations unknown.

When Mardonios learned that the Hellenes had gone away during the night and he saw that the place where they had been was deserted, he summoned Thorax of Larissa[a] and his brothers Eurypylos and Thrasydaios and said to them, [2] "So, sons of Aleuas,[a] will you still talk as you did, now that you see this place is deserted? For you who are neighbors[b] of the Lacedaemonians used to say that they do not flee from battle. You claimed that they are the best of all warriors, but earlier you saw them leave their battle positions, and now we can all see that during the night just past, they have scattered and fled, just when they would have had to contend in battle against people who are indisputably the best. Thus they have made it plain that they are people of no account, trying to distinguish themselves among Hellenes, who are also people of no account. [3] Now I at least shall certainly pardon you, since you had no experience of the Persians before and were praising those about whom you had some knowledge. But I am rather amazed at how Artabazos was utterly terrified of the Lacedaemonians, and how because of his fear he declared that most cowardly proposal, namely, that we should break up our camp and retreat to the city of Thebes, where we would have been besieged. The King will hear about this from me, [4] but the accounting for all that will take place elsewhere. As for now, the Hellenes must not be permitted to get away from us; they must be pursued until they are overtaken and made to pay the penalty for all that they have inflicted on the Persians."

After saying this, he led the Persians at a run across the Asopos[a] and along what he assumed was the path of the fleeing Hellenes. He was actually directing his troops toward the Lacedaemonians and Tegeans alone, for because of the ridges, he had not perceived the Athenians turning toward the plain. [2] When the rest of the barbarian regiments saw the Persians setting out to pursue the Hellenes, their commanders immediately raised the signal and joined in the chase as fast as they could, without marshaling the troops into any order or assigned positions. They rushed against the Hellenes in a mass, shouting the battle cry and determined to take them by storm.

As the enemy cavalry approached, Pausanias sent a horseman to the Athenians with this message: "Men of Athens, as our greatest contest, one which will determine the freedom or enslavement of Hellas, lies before us, we Lacedaemonians and you Athenians have been betrayed during the past night by our allies, who have run away. [2] So now it is obvious what we must do from this point on: we must defend and protect each other to the best of our abilities. If the enemy cavalry had rushed out against you first,

9.58
479
PLATAEA
Mardonios, seeing the Spartans had retreated during the night, mocks them as cowards who are afraid to face the braver Persians. He orders an immediate pursuit.

9.59
479
PLATAEA
Thinking the Hellenes are fleeing, the Persians charge the Spartans at top speed and without order.

9.60
479
PLATAEA
Pausanias sends a message to the Athenians asking them to assist the Spartans, who bear the full brunt of the Persian attack. Should they be unable to march to his aid, he asks them to at least send their archers.

9.58.1a   Larissa, Thessaly: Map 9.46.
9.58.2a   By calling them "sons of Aleuas," Mardonios identifies them as Thessalian Aleuadai, the leading aristocratic family of Thessaly.
9.58.2b   When Mardonios calls the Thessalians "neighbors" of the Lacedaemonians, he is either revealing an ignorance of Greek

geography (unlikely in this case) or perhaps indicating that, in Persian terms, the distance between Thessaly and Sparta (for both, see Map 9.66) was small, or perhaps he is just sarcastically exaggerating their proximity to each other.
9.59.1a   Asopos River: Map 9.66.

then we along with the Tegeans, who have refused to betray Hellas, would have been obliged to come to your aid. But as it is, their whole cavalry[a] has advanced against us, and so it is only right and just that you come to defend the division that is being pressed the hardest. [3] But if some circumstance makes it impossible for you to come to our aid, you will gain our gratitude by sending us your archers. We know, because you have shown such great zeal throughout this war, that you will certainly comply with this request."

When the Athenians heard this, they set out to assist the Lacedaemonians and to support them as best they could; but along the way they were attacked by Greek allies of the King who were posted opposite them, and this attack caused them such distress that they were no longer able to go to their aid. [2] Thus the Lacedaemonians and Tegeans were left to stand alone; the number of the Lacedaemonians, including the lightly armed troops, came to 50,000, and of the Tegeans (who had never left the Lacedaemonians), 3,000. Since they were about to engage in combat with Mardonios and his army before them, they performed pre-battle sacrifices, [3] but the omens turned out to be unfavorable for them. And during all this time, many of them fell to their deaths and many more by far were wounded. The Persians had set up a barricade of their wicker shields and were relentlessly shooting volleys of arrows at them, so that, as the Spartans were being pressed hard and the sacrifices continued to prove unfavorable, Pausanias turned to gaze toward the Plataeans' sanctuary of Hera and called upon the goddess, entreating her that they would not be cheated of their hope for victory.

While he was still invoking the aid of the goddess with this prayer, the Tegeans[a] took up a position against the barbarians in the front line ahead of the others and began to advance toward them. And just then, as Pausanias concluded his prayer, the Lacedaemonians' sacrifices yielded favorable omens. Now that this had finally happened, the Lacedaemonians also advanced against the Persians, who threw down their bows as they confronted them. [2] They fought their first battle around the wicker shields, and when these had fallen over, they waged a fierce struggle beside the sanctuary of Demeter[a] itself, which went on for a long time, until they reached the point of close-quarters pushing and shoving, for the barbarians seized the Hellenes' spears and broke them. [3] The Persians were not inferior in courage or strength, but they did not have hoplite arms,[a] and besides, they were untrained and no match for their opponents in tactical skill. They were dashing out beyond the front lines individually or in groups

9.61
479
PLATAEA
The Athenians are attacked by the enemy Hellenes, and cannot send assistance to the Spartans. The Spartans stand their ground and suffer many casualties from Persian archers shooting from behind a shield wall. Spartan sacrifices do not prove favorable.

9.62
479
PLATAEA
As the Tegeans suddenly charge, the sacrifices prove favorable, and the Spartans charge also. Now the Persian lack of armor and skill in close-quarters fighting proves decisive.

9.60.2a　Herodotus does not mention Persian cavalry in his narrative of the battle of Plataea until 9.68, when he says the cavalry gave vital support to cover the fleeing Persian infantry. Thus, according to him, this battle, like Marathon, was essentially an infantry conflict. Did Mardonios permit the battle to take place where cavalry could not be effective? Were the horses worn down by their strenuous actions in the previous days? Did lower morale prevent a more effective intervention on their

part? Alas, Herodotus sheds no light on these questions. See Appendix O, §8.
9.62.1a　Tegea: Map 9.66.
9.62.2a　Clearly there were sanctuaries to both Hera and Demeter at and near Plataea. That of Hera was close to the city and not touched by the battle, that of Demeter was in the valley where the battle took place.
9.62.3a　The Persians were armed, but they did not have the heavy armor of hoplite equipment. See Figure 9.62.

FIGURE 9.62A.
A PAINTING FOUND IN
THE TONDO (ROUND
INNER BOTTOM SURFACE)
OF A CUP, SHOWING A
GREEK HOPLITE (RIGHT),
AND A PERSIAN FIGHTING
AT CLOSE QUARTERS
WITH SWORDS.

FIGURE 9.62B. THE IMPRESSION
OF A CYLINDER SEAL, SHOWING A
PERSIAN SLAYING A GREEK HOPLITE.

of ten, joining together in larger or smaller bands, and charging right into the Spartan ranks, where they perished.

The place where the Lacedaemonians pressed their opponents the hardest was at the spot where Mardonios was fighting. He was mounted on a white horse and surrounded by 1,000 picked men, the best of the Persians, and for as long as he survived, the Persians maintained their resistance; and as they defended themselves, they struck down many of the Lacedaemonians. [2] But when Mardonios was killed and the troops posted around him, who made up the most formidable division of the army, had also fallen, the others turned to flee and gave way to the Lacedaemonians. They were hurt the most by how they were equipped, namely by their lack of armor, for they were fighting as unarmed soldiers in a contest against well-equipped hoplites.[a]

Thus, in accordance with the oracle,[a] Mardonios paid a just and full retribution to the Spartans for the murder of Leonidas, and Pausanias son of Kleombrotos, the son of Anaxandridas, achieved the finest victory of all those known to us. [2] The names of his earlier ancestors have been listed with reference to Leonidas, since they happen to be the same for both. Mardonios died at the hands of a notable Spartan named Arimnestos, who later, after the wars of the Medes, led a troop of 300 men against the entire army of the Messenians[a] in the war at Stenykleros,[b] where he himself and all his men were killed.

But at Plataea, when the Persians were routed by the Lacedaemonians, they fled in disorder to their camp and the wooden wall they had built in Theban[a] territory. What really amazes me is that, though they were fighting beside the grove of Demeter, not one of the Persians was seen entering the precinct or dying there; for the majority of the Persians who fell that day died on the unconsecrated ground immediately surrounding the sanctuary. I assume, if it is necessary to assume anything about matters of the divine, that the goddess herself refused to admit them because they had set fire to her inner hall at Eleusis.[b]

That was what happened in the battle. Now, Artabazos son of Pharnakes had from the very beginning disapproved of the King's having placed Mardonios in charge; and after that he had repeatedly tried to dissuade Mardonios from joining battle, but had accomplished nothing. So it was his displeasure with Mardonios' direction of their affairs that motivated what he did now. [2] Artabazos was the commander of no small force, having up

Sidebar

9.63
479
PLATAEA
The Persians hold their ground, although fighting without armor against armored Hellenes, until Mardonios and his guards fall.

9.64
479
PLATAEA
Herodotus praises the victory over Mardonios as the finest "of all those known to us."

9.65
479
PLATAEA
The Persians flee in disorder to their camp.

9.66
479
PLATAEA
Artabazos, whose advice not to engage had been ignored by Mardonios, leads his forces away from the battle to Phocis and toward the Hellespont.

Footnotes

9.63.2a A hoplite's minimal equipment consisted of a large shield and a helmet, but very often they would also wear a metal cuirass to protect their chests and back, and sometimes metal greaves on their lower legs. See Appendix N, Hoplite Warfare in Herodotus, §2–3.

9.64.1a The oracle cited here came to the Spartans from Delphi. See 8.114.

9.64.2a Messenia: Map 9.66.

9.64.2b Stenykleros: Map 9.66. This Spartan defeat occurred during the helot revolt, also called the Third Messenian War, 465–464, although dates are uncertain; see *Thucydides* 1.101–103.

9.65.1a Thebes: Map 9.66.

9.65.1b Eleusis: Map 9.66. Presumably they had burned the inner hall down at Eleusis when they occupied Attica the year before. See 8.50.1

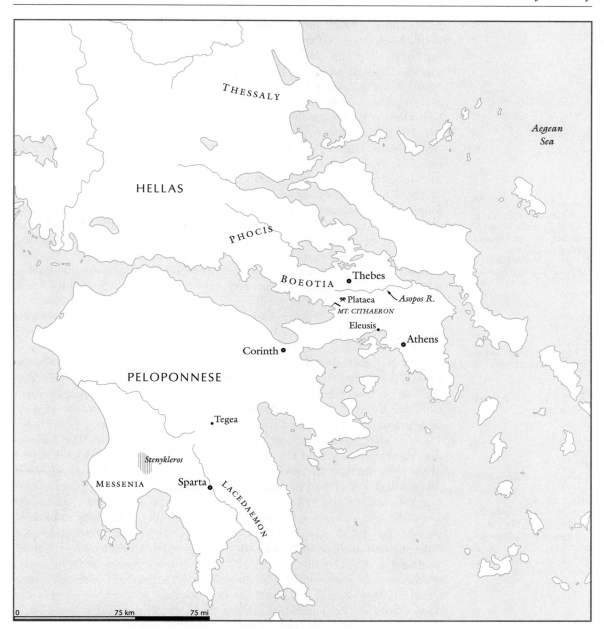

Map 9.66

to 40,000 men with him. When the battle was joined, he knew very well what the outcome of the fight would be, and as he led his men out, he deployed them in close formation and commanded them all to stay together and go wherever he led them at the same pace as his own. [3] After giving this order, he led his force as though to take it into battle, but as he advanced farther along the road and saw the Persians already in flight, he no longer kept his men in the same good order as before, but took off at a run by the quickest route—not to the wooden wall of their camp or to the city walls of Thebes, but directly toward Phocis[a]—because he wanted to reach the Hellespont[b] as soon as possible.

So they turned in that direction, and meanwhile, most of the Greek allies of the King were behaving like cowards, but not the Boeotians,[a] who fought the Athenians a long time, for those Thebans[b] who had medized were so keen to fight and not play the coward that 300 of the best and most prominent of them fell there at the hands of the Athenians. But finally, when they too had been routed, they fled to Thebes, though not along the path taken in flight by the Persians and the whole throng of the other allies, who had neither fought to the end with anyone nor accomplished any remarkable feats.

It is clear to me that the barbarians depended entirely for their success on the Persians, since it was because they saw that the other Persians were fleeing that Artabazos and his troops fled from the enemy, though they had not yet even joined in the battle. Thus they were all in flight except for the cavalry, particularly the Boeotian division, which provided vital assistance to the fleeing troops by riding up close to the Hellenes and blocking them from the fleeing allies; the Hellenes, now that they had won the victory, were intent on pursuing and slaughtering the troops of Xerxes.

Now while this rout was well under way, the other Hellenes who had stationed themselves around the sanctuary of Hera[a] and who had not taken part in the fight received the news that the battle was over and that Pausanias and his men had won. Upon hearing this, they set off without bothering to organize themselves into any battle order or assigned positions; the Corinthians[b] and those with them took the route leading through the foothills and knolls, straight up to the sanctuary of Demeter,[c] while the Megarians,[d] the Phleiasians,[e] and those with them advanced through the plain along the most level of the roads in this region. [2] When the Megarians and Phleiasians drew near their enemies, the Theban horsemen caught sight of them rushing ahead in disorder, and charged them on horseback, under the command of Asopodoros son of Timandros. Falling upon them, they cut down 600 of them and drove the rest back all the way to Cithaeron.[a]

9.66.3a　Phocis: Map 9.66.
9.66.3b　Hellespont: Map 9.80.
9.67.1a　Boeotia: Map 9.66.
9.67.1b　Thebes: Map 9.66.
9.69.1a　Temple of Hera: in the vicinity of Plataea (Map 9.66), but precise location unknown.

9.69.1b　Corinth: Map 9.66.
9.69.1c　Sanctuary of Demeter: precise location unknown.
9.69.1d　Megara: Map 9.80, inset.
9.69.1e　Phleious: Map 9.80, inset.
9.69.2a　Mount Cithaeron: Map 9.66.

These troops perished without accomplishing anything noteworthy at all. Meanwhile, the Persians and the crowd of allies that were with them had taken refuge within the wooden wall and climbed the towers before the Lacedaemonians[a] could get there, and ascending the wall, they strengthened it as well as they could. When the Lacedaemonians arrived and began their assault, the battle at the wall grew increasingly fierce, [2] for as long as the Athenians[a] were absent, the Persian troops defended themselves effectively and had the advantage over the Lacedaemonians, since the latter had little experience of siege warfare. But when the Athenians arrived and joined the attack, the assaults intensified and went on for quite some time. Finally, by their valor and perseverance, the Athenians mounted the wall and tore it down, and the Hellenes streamed in. [3] The Tegeans,[a] who were the first to enter inside the wall, were the ones who plundered the tent of Mardonios; among the various items they took from it was a feeding trough for horses made entirely of bronze, which is certainly worth seeing. Later, the Tegeans dedicated this feeding trough of Mardonios at the temple of Athena Alea,[b] but everything else they had taken they contributed to the common stockpile of spoils collected by all the Hellenes. [4] Once the wall had been torn down, the barbarians no longer formed up in military order. Not one of them any longer thought of resistance; they had fallen into a state of panic, as tens of thousands of people were trapped there in a confined space. [5] The Hellenes were thus provided with such a great opportunity for slaughter that out of an army numbering 300,000, not counting the 40,000 troops with whom Artabazos had fled, not even 3,000 survived. Of the Lacedaemonians from Sparta, in all ninety-one died in this encounter; of the Tegeans, sixteen; and of the Athenians, fifty-two.[a]

The barbarians who proved the best and bravest were the Persian infantry and the cavalry of the Sacae,[a] while Mardonios is said to have been the best and bravest of individual men. Of the Hellenes, the Tegeans and Athenians proved noble and courageous, but the Lacedaemonians surpassed them in valor. [2] I can present no proof of this judgment, since they all shared in the victory against their opponents, except that the Lacedaemonians attacked the strongest division and conquered it. And in my opinion, the man who proved the best and bravest by far was Aristodemos, the only one of the 300 to have survived Thermopylae, for which he had met with disgrace and dishonor.[a] After him, the best were the Spartans Poseidonios, Philokyon, and Amompharetos. [3] When the question of which man had proven himself the best came up for discussion, however, the surviving Spartans recognized that Aristodemos had wanted to die in front of every-

9.70
479
PLATAEA
The Persians defend their walled camp successfully against the Spartans, but the Athenians, after a long struggle, finally breach the wall. The Hellenes enter and plunder the camp, slaughtering all but 3,000 Persians. Herodotus lists Greek losses from the battle.

SPARTANS MOST VALOROUS

9.71
479
PLATAEA
Herodotus describes the post-battle discussion of who was the bravest and deserves the most praise. Among themselves, the Spartans select Poseidonios over Aristodemos, because the latter clearly wished to die.

9.70.1a   Lacedaemon (Sparta): Map 9.66.
9.70.2a   Athens: Map 9.66.
9.70.3a   Tegea: Map 9.66.
9.70.3b   The temple of Athena Alea was located in Tegea.
9.70.5a   These extremely low Greek casualty figures for such a large engagement must be taken with a healthy dose of skepticism.

Perhaps they refer to the losses of Spartiates alone, not counting the *perioikoi* and helots who fell.
9.71.1a   Sacae, location of territory: Map 9.33, locator.
9.71.2a   Aristodemos' disgrace was described in 7.229–231.

one because of the charge against him, and so had left his post in a rage and displayed great feats, while Poseidonios did not want to die, but proved himself a noble and courageous man all the same, and was therefore much the better man for it. [4] But perhaps it was jealousy that motivated them to render this judgment. Of those who died in this battle, all the men I have listed except for Aristodemos were awarded official honors, while Aristodemos was not because he had wanted to die for the reason I have just mentioned.

Those were the men who won the greatest fame at Plataea.[a] For Kallikrates died away from the battle; he had come to the camp as the most handsome man of the Hellenes at that time, not only among the Lacedaemonians, but among all the other Hellenes, too. What happened was that while Pausanias was conducting the pre-battle sacrifices, Kallikrates was sitting at his assigned post when he was wounded in his side by an arrow. [2] So as the others fought, he had been carried out of the ranks, and while he struggled against death he said to Arimnestos, a Plataean, that he did not mind dying for Hellas, but regretted that he had not struck a blow or performed any feats to show his worth, though he had been eager to do so.

It is said that of the Athenians, Sophanes son of Eutychides, from the deme of Dekeleia,[a] distinguished himself in the battle. According to the Athenians, the Dekeleians had once performed a deed whose worth endures forever. [2] A long time ago, the sons of Tyndareos invaded Attica[a] with a large army to recover Helen,[b] and ravaged the demes, since they did not know where Helen, for her own safety, had been hidden. Some say that it was the Dekeleians, others say that it was Dekelos himself, who, annoyed by the arrogance of Theseus and fearing for all of the Athenian territory, guided the sons of Tyndareos in this matter and led them to Aphidna,[c] which Titakos, who was born of this land, then betrayed by handing it over to them. [3] Because of this deed, when the Dekeleians are in Sparta, they are exempt from payments and are provided front-row seats, and these privileges still continue without interruption to this day, so that even in the war many years later between the Athenians and Lacedaemonians, the Lacedaemonians spoiled the rest of Attica but stayed away from Dekeleia.[a]

Sophanes had come from this deme, and it was he who proved to be the best and bravest of the Athenians at that time. Two different stories are told about him: one, that from the belt of his breastplate he carried an iron anchor slung from a bronze chain, which he would throw whenever he drew near his enemies so that when they broke out of their position in the

9.72
479
PLATAEA
Herodotus describes the sad fate of Kallikrates, who was killed by an arrow before he could strike a blow for Hellas.

9.73
479
PLATAEA
The Athenian Sophanes of Dekeleia wins renown. Herodotus tells the tale of how the Dekeleians helped the Spartan Tyndaridae to locate Helen at Aphidna.

9.74
479
PLATAEA
Herodotus recounts two tales about Sophanes' bravery and his "anchor" in the battle.

9.72.1a Plataea: Map 9.80, inset.
9.73.1a Dekeleia: Map 9.80, inset. Attic demes had originally been just townships, villages, or regions in Attica. After the reforms of Kleisthenes in 508/07 (5.69), they became official political units of the Athenian state, and every Athenian citizen was identified by his name and the deme in which he was born.
9.73.2a Attica: Map 9.80, inset.
9.73.2b According to legend, the Dioskouri came

to recover their sister Helen, who had been carried off to Aphidna in Attica by Theseus and Pirithous. (Godley)
9.73.2c Aphidna: Map 9.80, inset.
9.73.3a But in the later part of that "Peloponnesian" war (413) the Lacedaemonians fortified and established themselves at Dekeleia and held it as a base from which to continuously menace and harass the Athenians. (Godley) See *Thucydides* 7.19.

ranks to assault him, they would be unable to budge him; then, when his opponents were in flight, his tactic was to pick up the anchor and chase them with it. [2] That is one of the stories; according to the other, which conflicts with the first, he did not actually wear an anchor attached to his breastplate but instead had an anchor as an emblem on his shield, which never ceased moving and was always in swift motion.

And there is another illustrious deed that Sophanes performed: when the Athenians were blockading Aegina,[a] on a challenge he fought and killed Eurybates of Argos, a victor in the pentathlon. Much later, it happened that Sophanes, while proving himself noble and courageous as general of the Athenians in joint command with Leagros son of Glaukon, died at the hands of the Edonians[b] as he was fighting for the gold mines at Daton.[c]

After the Hellenes had overwhelmed the barbarians at Plataea, a woman came to them of her own accord; she had been a concubine of a Persian named Pharandates son of Teaspis, and when she realized that the Persians had been destroyed and the Hellenes victorious, she adorned herself lavishly with gold and dressed herself and her servants in the finest clothes they had with them; then she stepped down from her carriage and went to the Lacedaemonians, who were still in the midst of the slaughter. She was already quite familiar with the name of Pausanias and his homeland, since she had often heard them mentioned, and when she saw that Pausanias was in charge of everything, she knew who he was. Clasping his knees, she said to him, [2] "King of Sparta, save me, your suppliant, from captive slavery. For you have helped me even before this by destroying these men who respect neither divinities nor gods. I am from Cos[a] by birth, the daughter of Hegetorides son of Antagoras, and the Persian took me by force from Cos and kept me against my will." Pausanias answered her, [3] "Woman, you are a suppliant, and if indeed you are telling the truth and really are the daughter of Hegetorides of Cos, then have no fear. Hegetorides happens to be my closest guest-friend[a] of all the people who live in that region." After saying this, he entrusted her to the ephors who were with him and later sent her to Aegina in accord with her own wishes.

Immediately following the appearance of this woman, the Mantineians[a] arrived, but the battle was now over. When they found out that they had come too late for the engagement, they thought it a terrible calamity and said that they deserved to be punished. [2] And then, when they heard that

9.75
479
PLATAEA
Herodotus describes another glorious deed by Sophanes, and how he met his death.

9.76
479
PLATAEA
A woman of Cos deserts the Persians and, as a suppliant, begs Pausanias to protect her. He proves to be a friend of her father's and promises to treat her well.

9.77
479
PLATAEA
The Mantineians and the Eleans arrive after the battle is over, and are so upset to have missed it that they banish their leaders.

9.75.1a Aegina: Map 9.80, inset. This incident presumably took place during either the War of Nikodromos (491) or hostilities that took place in the 480s. See 6.92.3.
9.75.1b Edonians, location of territory: Map 9.80.
9.75.1c Sophanes was killed by the Edonians while attempting to establish an Athenian settlement at Amphipolis in 465 (*Thucydides* 1.100–102). Daton was the valley north of Mount Pangaion, which lies near the coast opposite Thasos. Mount Pangaion was long famous for the gold

extracted from it. Amphipolis, Daton, Mount Pangaion, Thasos: Map 9.80.
9.76.2a Cos: Map 9.80.
9.76.3a Guest-friendship (*xenia*): a bond of ritualized friendship, usually between aristocrats or prominent men of different cities. It was passed down through generations and required hereditary privileges and obligations such as reciprocal hospitality and in many cases, assistance. See Appendix T, §3.
9.77.1a Mantineia: Map 9.80, inset.

the Medes with Artabazos were fleeing, they were about to set out to pursue and drive them as far as Thessaly,[a] but the Lacedaemonians[b] would not allow them to chase down the fleeing enemy. So they went back to their own land, where they drove their military leader out of their country. [3] After the Mantineians, the Eleans[a] arrived, and they likewise thought it a terrible calamity to have missed the battle and departed, and when they returned home, they also drove out their leaders. So much for the Mantineians and the Eleans.

Back at Plataea[a] there was in the camp of the Aeginetans one Lampon son of Pytheas, one of the most prominent men of Aegina, who now rushed to Pausanias and, speaking with great zeal, made this most ungodly proposal: [2] "Son of Kleombrotos, you have accomplished a feat that is extraordinary in both its magnitude and its nobility; god granted that you should be the one to protect Hellas and gain the greatest glory of all Hellenes known to us. But now you should carry out what still remains to be done so that you will have an even greater reputation and so that in the future, every barbarian will beware of initiating reckless acts against the Hellenes. [3] For after Leonidas died at Thermopylae,[a] Mardonios and Xerxes cut off his head and suspended it from a stake;[b] and if you now pay back Mardonios by treating him in the same fashion, you will win praise first from all the Spartans, and then from the rest of the Hellenes, since by impaling Mardonios, you will have vengeance for what happened to your uncle Leonidas." Though he thought he would please Pausanias by saying this, Pausanias replied as follows:

"My friend from Aegina, I commend and appreciate that you mean well and are trying to look out for my future interests, but this idea of yours falls short of good judgment. After you have raised me up on high, together with exalting my homeland and my achievement, you cast me down to nothing by encouraging me to abuse a corpse, claiming that if I did so, I would have a better reputation. But this is a deed more appropriate to barbarians than to Hellenes, though we resent them for it all the same. [2] In any case, because of this, I could hardly please the Aeginetans or anyone else who approves of such deeds as this. It is quite enough for me to please the Spartans by committing no sacrilege and by speaking with respect for what is lawful and sacred. As for Leonidas, whom you urge me to avenge, I tell you that he and the others who met their ends at Thermopylae have already achieved great vengeance by the countless souls of those who lie here dead. As for you, do not ever again approach me with such a suggestion or try to advise me, and be thankful to leave here without suffering harm."

9.78
479
PLATAEA
Lampon of Aegina advises Pausanias to take revenge for the Persians' ill-treatment of the body of Leonidas at Thermopylae by impaling the corpse of Mardonios.

9.79
479
PLATAEA
Pausanias rejects the advice of Lampon as unworthy of a Greek and a Spartan, and sends him away, warning him not to return with such counsel.

[handwritten margin note: ABUSING CORPSE = GODLESS]

9.77.2a　Thessaly: Map 9.80.
9.77.2b　Lacedaemon (Sparta): Map 9.80.
9.77.3a　Elis: Map 9.80.
9.78.1a　Plataea: Map 9.80, inset.

9.78.3a　Thermopylae: Map 9.80, inset.
9.78.3b　The mutilation of Leonidas' body was described at 7.238.

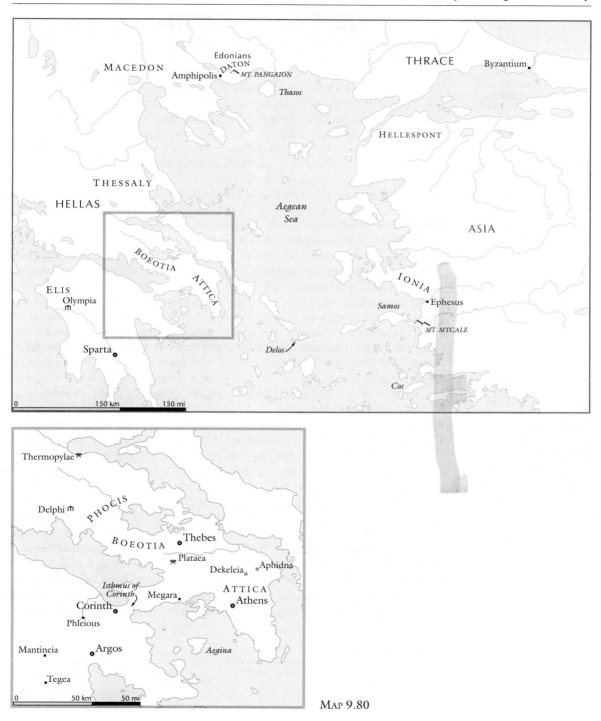

Map 9.80

9.80
479
PLATAEA
At Pausanias' order, the helots gather the spoils, but they sell some of the gold secretly to the Aeginetans as though it were bronze, thereby making many Aeginetan fortunes.

After hearing this reply, Lampon departed. Pausanias now issued a proclamation that no one should touch the spoils, and he ordered the helots to gather all the goods together in one place. They scattered throughout the camp and found tents adorned with gold and silver, couches gilded with gold and silver, golden mixing bowls, libation bowls, and other drinking vessels. [2] On the wagons they discovered sacks in which they saw cauldrons of gold and silver. And they stripped the bodies lying there of their bracelets, necklaces, and golden daggers,[a] but they paid no attention at all to the embroidered clothing. [3] The helots presented and accounted for much of these spoils—as much as they were unable to hide—but they stole quite a bit and sold it to the Aeginetans. And so it was from this time on that the Aeginetans became very wealthy, as they were buying gold from the helots as though it were bronze.

9.81
479
PLATAEA
After one-tenth of the loot is dedicated to each of three gods, Apollo, Zeus, and Poseidon, the rest—gold, silver, women, horses, camels, and other goods—is distributed to the soldiers, with ten of each category set apart for Pausanias.

After bringing all the goods together, the Hellenes took out a tenth for the god at Delphi,[a] and from this they dedicated a golden tripod[b] set upon a three-headed serpent of bronze, which stands next to the altar. They removed another tenth for the god at Olympia,[c] and from it dedicated a bronze statue of Zeus fifteen feet tall, and another for the god at the isthmus,[d] from which was made a bronze Poseidon seven feet[e] tall. After taking out these tithes, they divided the rest, and each took what he deserved of the Persians' concubines, gold, silver, other goods, and the pack animals. [2] There are no reports about everything that was taken and distributed to those who proved the best at Plataea, but I for my part suppose that of what remained, ten of every type of spoil were separated out and given to Pausanias—women, horses, talents, camels,[a] as well as the other types of goods in the same proportion.

9.82
479
PLATAEA
Herodotus tells the anecdote of Pausanias' comparison of the sumptuous Persian dinner to that of the Spartans.

It is also reported that Xerxes had left his tent to Mardonios when he fled from Hellas, and that when Pausanias saw these quarters of Mardonios and how they were furnished with embroidered draperies, he ordered the bread bakers and the cooks to prepare a meal for him like those they had made for Mardonios. [2] When they had carried out their orders and Pausanias saw the golden and silver couches with sumptuous coverings and the tables, also of gold and silver, all set out with a magnificent feast, he was struck with wonder at the good things lying before him,[a] and then, as a joke, ordered his servants to prepare a Laconian meal. [3] When the banquet was ready, the difference between the two was great indeed, and Pausanias laughed, and then sent for the generals of the Hellenes. When they had all come to him, Pausanias, as he pointed to each of the meals that had been served, said, "Men of Hellas, I have brought you here together, because I wanted to show you what an idiot

9.80.2a Herodotus here uses the Persian word *akinakes*, meaning a dagger or short sword.
9.81.1a Delphi: Map 9.80, inset.
9.81.1b This tripod was intended to commemorate the victory of the Greek alliance over Persia. See Figure 9.81a.
9.81.1c Olympia: Map 9.80.
9.81.1d Isthmus of Corinth: Map 9.80, inset.
9.81.1e Herodotus writes that the statue of Zeus was "10 cubits" high and the statue of Poseidon was "7 cubits" high. There were several standard measures for the cubit in the ancient world, but the cubit probably referred to here was approximately 1.5 feet. See Appendix J, §4, 5, 19.
9.81.2a See Figure 9.81b, a painting of a camel with a Persian rider and attendants.
9.82.2a See Figure 9.82.

FIGURE 9.81A. THE COLUMN OF THE COMMEMORATIVE VICTORY TRIPOD ERECTED BY THE GREEKS TO CELEBRATE THEIR VICTORY OVER THE PERSIANS. IT WAS DEDICATED TO APOLLO AT DELPHI AND MOVED FROM THERE TO CONSTANTINOPLE (NOW ISTANBUL) SOME 800 YEARS LATER BY THE EMPEROR CONSTANTINE TO ADORN THE HIPPODROME OF THE CITY. IT STILL CAN BE SEEN TODAY; THE STILL-LEGIBLE INSCRIPTION READS, "THESE FOUGHT IN THE WAR," AND LISTS THIRTY-ONE GREEK STATES THAT UNITED TO FIGHT AGAINST THE PERSIANS. ABOVE RIGHT IS THE UPPER HALF OF ONE OF THREE SNAKE HEADS WHICH ORIGINALLY ADORNED THE TOP OF THE COLUMN.

FIGURE 9.81B. LATE-FIFTH-CENTURY VASE PAINTING OF A CAMEL. THE MEN SHOWN ON AND AROUND THE CAMEL ARE WEARING PERSIAN CLOTHES. IT IS POSSIBLE THAT A DESCENDANT OF ONE OF THE CAMELS THAT ACCOMPANIED XERXES' ARMY, WHICH HERODOTUS SAYS WERE CAPTURED AND DISTRIBUTED AS SPOILS, MAY HAVE SERVED THE ARTIST AS A MODEL FROM WHICH HE DREW SUCH A GOOD LIKENESS OF WHAT OTHERWISE MUST HAVE BEEN A STRANGE AND EXOTIC BEAST TO MAINLAND GREEKS.

the leader of the Medes was. This was his lifestyle, but he came to us, who have this miserable way of life, in order to deprive us of it." That is what Pausanias is reported to have said to the generals of the Hellenes.

But later, well after these events, the Plataeans found chests made of gold and silver as well as other goods. And still later, something else appeared among the corpses, now bare of their flesh (for the Plataeans had collected all the bones in one place): a skull was found which had not a single suture, but was apparently all of one bone. And the jaw on its upper part apparently had teeth all joined in one piece, also a single bone, both the front teeth and the molars. The skeleton of this man measured seven and a half feet long.[a]

9.83
479
PLATAEA
For long after, the Plataeans find chests of gold and silver and amazing skeletal remains.

9.83.1a   Herodotus writes that the man's skeleton was "5 cubits" long. See Appendix J, §4, 5, 19.

FIGURE 9.82. A SET OF PERSIAN LUXURY TABLEWARE WITH CRYSTAL, SILVER, AND GOLD CUPS, PLATES, AND BOWLS, PROBABLY MUCH LIKE THOSE FOUND BY PAUSANIAS IN MARDONIOS' TENT.

The corpse of Mardonios had disappeared by the day after the battle, and I cannot say for certain who might have been responsible for its disappearance, but I have heard of many people from various places who allegedly buried Mardonios, and I know that many by now have received large rewards from Artontes, the son of Mardonios, in return for this deed. Although I am unable to tell for certain who secretly took the corpse of Mardonios and buried it, there is a rumor about that the one who did it was Dionysophanes, a man from Ephesus.[a]

In any case, it seems that Mardonios was buried in some way or other. When the Hellenes at Plataea had finished dividing up the spoils, each group buried their own dead separately. The Lacedaemonians made three different tombs: [2] in one they buried the priests, who included Poseidonios, Amompharetos, Philokyon, and Kallikrates. So the priests were buried in one grave, and in another were the rest of the Spartiates, and in the third were the helots.[a] That is how the Lacedaemonians buried their men. The Tegeans[b] buried all their men together in a separate place, the Athenians[c] had graves of their own, and the Megarians[d] and Phleiasians[e] also separately

9.84
479
PLATAEA
Many people claim to have buried Mardonios, and collect rewards for having done so.

9.85
479
PLATAEA
The Spartans bury their dead by class in three separate tombs. Each Greek city whose men fought at Plataea bury their dead in single tombs. Many cities erect empty sepulchers, out of embarrassment that their men were not engaged in the fight.

9.84.1a   Ephesus: Map 9.80.
9.85.2a   Herodotus fails to mention an casualties among the Spartan *perioikoi*, who were, literally, "dwellers around," and who ranked between the Spartiates (full Spartan citizens) and the helots (Spartan serfs) in their rights, priveleges, and obligations to the state. For more on these three classes of Spartans, see Appendix B, §7–9, 17–18.
9.85.2b   Tegea: Map 9.80, inset.
9.85.2c   Athens: Map 9.80, inset.
9.85.2d   Megara: Map 9.80, inset.
9.85.2e   Phleious: Map 9.80, inset.

buried their men who had been killed by the cavalry. [3] The graves of all these were full of bodies, but according to what I have heard about all the other graves that are seen at Plataea, each of the peoples who felt disgraced by their absence from the battle piled up empty mounds for the sake of posterity, and even the so-called grave of the Aeginetans[a] there, so I have been told, was heaped up ten years later at the request of the Aeginetans by Kleades son of Autodikos, a Plataean and their *proxenos*.[b]

9.86
479
THEBES
The Hellenes now march against Thebes, demanding that the city hand over its pro-Persian leaders.

After the Hellenes buried their dead at Plataea, they at once held a conference at which they resolved to wage war on the Thebans[a] and to demand from them the surrender of those who had medized. The most prominent of these were Timagenides and Attaginos, who were the leaders among their chief men. And if the Thebans refused to give up these men, the Hellenes would not withdraw from assaulting the city until they had destroyed it. [2] That was their decision, and so, on the eleventh day after the battle, they approached Thebes and prepared to lay siege to it, ordering the Thebans to give up the men. When the Thebans would not do so, the Hellenes devastated their land and launched assaults against their walls.

9.87
479
THEBES
After nineteen days of siege, the Theban leaders say they will give themselves up to the Hellenes for trial.

And in fact the Hellenes continued to inflict damages on the Thebans, so that on the twentieth day, Timagenides addressed them as follows: "Men of Thebes, since the Hellenes have resolved that they will not withdraw from this siege until either they destroy Thebes or you surrender us to them, do not now allow our land of Boeotia to suffer more harm for our sake, [2] but if what they really want is money, and they are asking you to surrender us to them as a pretext, then let us give them money from our public treasury, for we medized not as individuals, but as part of the community. Or, if it is true that they are besieging our city because they want us, then we shall give ourselves up to answer the charge against us." The Thebans decided that this was very sound and timely advice, and they immediately sent a herald to Pausanias, announcing their willingness to surrender the men.

9.88
479
THEBES
One Theban leader escapes. The rest surrender, are taken to Corinth, and executed.

But after everyone had agreed upon these conditions, Attaginos fled from the town. His sons were taken and brought before Pausanias, but he absolved them of all guilt, saying that the sons bore no responsibility for the medizing of the father. The rest of the men whom the Thebans gave over assumed that they would receive the opportunity to answer the charges against them and were quite confident that they would be able to get off by means of bribes. But when Pausanias received them, he suspected that this was their thinking, and so, after sending the entire allied army home, he took the Thebans to Corinth[a] and put them to death. That, then, was what happened at Plataea and Thebes.

9.85.3a	Aegina: Map 9.80, inset.	9.86.1a	Thebes: Map 9.80, inset.
9.85.3b	A *proxenos* was a representative of a city other than his own who provided assistance to, and protected the interests of, the citizens of the foreign city. See Appendix B, §11.	9.88.1a	Corinth: Map 9.80, inset.

Meanwhile, Artabazos son of Pharnakes had gone some distance by now in his flight from Plataea.[a] When he arrived in Thessaly,[b] the Thessalians invited him to be their guest at a feast, and inquired about the rest of the army, since they were unaware of what had happened at Plataea. [2] Artabazos realized that if he revealed the whole truth about their fight against the Hellenes, he himself as well as his troops would run the risk of being killed (for he thought everyone would attack them once they learned what had happened). Following this line of reasoning, he had earlier reported nothing to the Phocians[a] either, and he now said to the Thessalians, [3] "Men of Thessaly, as you can see, I am marching with all haste by the quickest route to Thrace,[a] and I am eager to reach my destination, since I was sent from the camp with these men here to deal with a certain matter. Mardonios himself and his army are marching right behind me and are expected to arrive here shortly. Extend your hospitality to him as well, and prove yourselves his benefactors; you will not regret it in the long run." [4] After saying this, he hurried off with his army through Thessaly and Macedon,[a] making a straight line toward Thrace, for if truth be told, he really was in a great hurry. By the time he arrived at Byzantium,[b] he had left behind many of his troops, who had been cut down by the Thracians along the road or had been overcome by hunger and fatigue. From Byzantium he crossed over the strait in boats. That is how Artabazos returned to Asia.[a]

Now on the very same day as the disaster at Plataea, it happened that another one was also inflicted on the Persians at Mycale in Ionia.[b] For after the Hellenes had arrived at Delos[c] and stationed themselves on the island with Leotychidas the Lacedaemonian,[d] three messengers came to them from Samos:[e] Lampon son of Thrasykles, Athenagoras son of Archestratides, and Hegesistratos son of Aristagoras. The Samians had sent them secretly, unknown to both the Persians and the tyrant whom the Persians had installed at Samos, Theomestor son of Androdamas. [2] When these messengers came forward to address the generals, Hegesistratos spoke at great length, saying all sorts of things: how if the Ionians merely caught sight of the Hellenes, they would immediately revolt from the Persians; how the barbarians would not stand their ground, and if they did, the Hellenes would find no easier prey to catch than them. Invoking their common gods, he urged them to deliver the Ionian Hellenes from slavery and to drive off the barbarian. [3] That, he said, would be easy for them to accomplish, since the Persians' ships were in poor sailing condition and their men were no match for the Hellenes in battle. And if anyone should suspect that they, the messengers, were trying to lead them on by some trick, they were ready and willing to be taken on board the ships of the Hellenes as hostages.

9.89
479
THESSALY-ASIA
Artabazos crosses Thessaly, arrives at Byzantium, and crosses into Asia. He conceals the truth, fearing attack if Mardonios' defeat were known.

9.90
479
DELOS-SAMOS
Herodotus begins the story of the battle of Mycale with the dispatch of anti-Persian Samian envoys to the Greek fleet, who urge the Greeks to attack the Persians and lead an Ionian revolt. He also says that the battles of Mycale and Plataea took place on the same day.

9.89.1a   Plataea: Map 9.80, inset.
9.89.1b   Thessaly: Map 9.80.
9.89.2a   Phocis: Map 9.80, inset.
9.89.3a   Thrace: Map 9.80.
9.89.4a   Macedon: Map 9.80.
9.89.4b   Byzantium: Map 9.80.

9.90.1a   Asia: Map 9.80.
9.90.1b   Mount Mycale, Ionia: Map 9.80.
9.90.1c   Delos: Map 9.80.
9.90.1d   Lacedaemon (Sparta): Map 9.80.
9.90.1e   Samos: Map 9.80.

9.91
479
DELOS
The Spartan commander is inspired to accept the Samian envoy's name as a good omen.

9.92
479
DELOS
The Samians depart, and the sacrifices performed by the Hellenes turn out well.

9.93
479
APOLLONIA
Herodotus recounts the tale of Euenios the diviner for the Greek fleet; how he was blinded for failing as a guardian of the sacred flock of the sun at Apollonia.

While the visitor from Samos was pleading so fervently, Leotychidas asked him a question, perhaps wishing to hear him speak an omen, or else to utter something fortuitously, by the act of a god. "Visitor from Samos," he said, "what is your name?" And when the man replied, "Hegesistratos,"[a] [2] Leotychidas then cut him short, preventing him from saying anything further, and said: "I accept this omen, visitor from Samos. Now give us your pledge and then sail away with these men who have accompanied you; but swear that the Samians will be zealous allies to us."

And no sooner had Leotychidas spoken these words than the deed was done. The Samians gave their pledges and swore their oaths concerning their alliance with the Hellenes, [2] and having done this, they sailed away. But Leotychidas ordered Hegesistratos to sail with the Hellenes because he considered his name an omen. The Hellenes lingered there that day, and on the next they sought omens through sacrifices. Serving as their seer was Deiphonos son of Euenios, a man from that Apollonia[a] which is on the Ionian Gulf.[b] And there is a story about what once happened to Euenios, his father, which I will now relate.

In this Apollonia there are flocks sacred to Helios, which graze during the day beside the river that flows from Mount Lakmon[a] through Apollonian territory and down to the sea past the harbor of Orikon.[b] These flocks are guarded by men chosen as the most distinguished among the citizens in terms of wealth and lineage, and each man serves for a year. The people of Apollonia consider these flocks very important because of a prophecy. The flocks spend the night in a cave far from the city, [2] and it was there that Euenios was guarding them, as he had been chosen to do. But one night he fell asleep during his watch, and some wolves got past him and entered the cave, where they killed about sixty of the flock. When Euenios perceived what had happened, he kept quiet about it and told no one, intending to buy others to replace them. [3] But the Apollonians noticed what had happened, and having discovered it, they brought him before a court, which condemned him to be deprived of his sight for falling asleep on his watch. As soon as Euenios was blinded, the flocks ceased to give birth and the earth did not bear crops as it had before. [4] At Dodona[a] and Delphi[b] the Apollonians asked about the cause of their current evils and received word from the gods in response that Euenios, the guard of their sacred flocks, had been unjustly deprived of his sight, for it was the gods themselves who had set the wolves on their flocks, and they would continue to seek vengeance for Euenios until the Apollonians paid the penalty for what they had done, which would be whatever Euenios chose and thought was just. And when the penalty was paid, the gods would give Euenios a gift that would make many people consider him blessed.

9.91.1a   Hegesistratos means "leader of the army."
9.92.2a   Apollonia: Map 9.97, AX.
9.92.2b   Ionian Gulf: Map 9.97, locator.
9.93.1a   Mount Lakmon: Map 9.97, AX.
9.93.1b   Orikon: Map 9.97, AX.

9.93.4a   Dodona: Map 9.97, AX. See Appendix P, §5, 11.
9.93.4b   Delphi: Map 9.97, BX.

That was the response the oracles gave to the Apollonians, who considered it an absolute secret and commanded some men among their citizens to carry out the oracle's advice. They did so as follows. Coming up to Euenios as he was sitting on a bench, they sat down beside him and made conversation about various topics, until they came around to expressing sympathy for his suffering. They gradually led him on this way until they asked what penalty he would choose if the Apollonians should wish to take it upon themselves to pay a penalty for what they had done. [2] Euenios, who knew nothing of the prophecy, replied by naming citizens who he knew possessed the two finest estates in all of Apollonia and said that if he was given their land—and in addition, a house he had seen which was the finest in the city—then, once in possession of these properties, he would let go of his wrath in the future and be satisfied that they had paid the proper penalty. [3] That is what he said, and the men seated beside him spoke in response: "Euenios, the Apollonians will pay you all this as their penalty for blinding you, in obedience to prophecies they received." Euenios was infuriated when he heard this, feeling, as he learned the whole story, that he had been thoroughly deceived. So the Apollonians bought the properties he had chosen and gave them to him. And afterward he immediately became possessed of the power of innate divination, so that he became very famous.

9.94
APOLLONIA
Herodotus concludes the tale of Euenios, and tells how he acquired his powers of divination.

The son of this Euenios was Deiphonos, who had been brought by the Corinthians[a] and was serving as seer for the army. I have also heard, however, that Deiphonos was not really the son of Euenios, but had appropriated the name of Euenios as his father as he procured work throughout Hellas.

9.95
479
DELOS
Deiphonos was the army's prophet.

After the Hellenes had obtained favorable omens in their sacrifices, they left Delos[a] and set sail for Samos.[b] When they reached the area near Kalamoi[c] on Samos, they dropped anchor off this region's sanctuary of Hera[d] and prepared for a sea battle. When the Persians learned of their approach, they sailed toward the mainland with all of their ships except those of the Phoenicians,[e] which they sent away, [2] for in the course of their deliberations, the Persians had decided not to engage in a battle at sea, since they thought they were no match for their opponents. They were sailing to the mainland in order to secure the protection of their army at Mycale,[a] which Xerxes had ordered to stay behind, separate from his expeditionary force, so as to guard Ionia.[b] These troops numbered 60,000, and their general was Tigranes, who surpassed the other Persians in good looks and stature. [3] So the commanders of the fleet planned to take refuge under the protection of this army. They intended to beach their ships and surround them with a palisade as a defensive wall to serve both as a shelter for the ships and as a refuge for themselves.

9.96
479
SAMOS-MYCALE
The Hellenes put out to sea, seeking battle. The Persians, learning of their approach and thinking their fleet not strong enough, retreat to Mycale on the mainland in order to gain the support of their land army.

9.95.1a   Corinth: Map 9.97, BX.
9.96.1a   Delos: Map 9.97, BY.
9.96.1b   Samos: Map 9.97, BY.
9.96.1c   Kalamoi (Greek for "the reeds"): precise location unknown.
9.96.1d   Heraion, temple of Hera (if Herodotus

means the famous one on Samos): Map 9.97, BY.
9.96.1e   Phoenicia: Map 9.97, locator.
9.96.2a   Mycale Peninsula: Map 9.97, BY.
9.96.2b   Ionia: Map 9.97, BY.

Having made these plans, they put out to sea, and after they passed the sanctuary of the Venerable Goddesses[a] on Mycale, they went on to the Gaison and Skolopoeis,[b] where there is the sanctuary of Eleusinian[c] Demeter which was established by Philistos son of Pasikles when he accompanied Neilaos son of Kodros during the foundation of Miletus.[d] There they hauled their ships ashore and, after cutting down cultivated trees that were nearby, surrounded themselves with a wall built of stone and wood. Then they fixed stakes into the ground as an outer palisade around it. They were ready to stand a siege or win a victory, and had considered both possibilities in their preparations.

When the Hellenes found out that the barbarians had gone to the mainland, they were angry that the enemy had managed to escape, and were at a loss as to whether they should return home or sail on toward the Hellespont.[a] Finally they decided to do neither, but to sail instead to the mainland; [2] and so they prepared boarding gangways and everything else they would need to fight a battle at sea, and then set sail for Mycale. When they drew near to the enemy's camp, no one appeared to sail out against them, and they saw both that the enemy's ships were beached within the wall and that a large army was deployed in line along the shore. First of all, Leotychidas sailed past in his ship, skirting the shore as closely as possible while he proclaimed to the Ionians through a herald: [3] "Men of Ionia,[a] all of you who can hear my voice, heed what I am about to say, for the Persians, in any case, will understand nothing of my commands to you. When we join battle, each of you should remember freedom first and foremost, and after that, recall the password 'Hera,'[b] and make sure that those of you within the sound of my voice inform all the others who cannot hear me." [4] His intention here was the same as that of Themistokles at Artemision:[a] either his words would go unnoticed by the barbarians and he would persuade the Ionians to follow his advice, or, if what he had said was reported to the barbarians, it would make them distrust their Greek allies.

After Leotychidas had instructed the Ionians in this way, the Hellenes beached their ships and disembarked on the shore. There they deployed for battle while the Persians, seeing that the Hellenes were preparing to fight and that they had made an appeal to the Ionians, stripped the Samians[a] of their arms, as they suspected that the men of that island would favor the Hellenes; [2] for indeed, when the barbarian ships had brought in some Athenian[a] prisoners of war who had been captured after being left behind by Xerxes in Attica,[b] the Samians had released them all and sent them back

9.97.1a Sanctuary of the Venerable Goddesses: location unknown. The venerable goddesses were Demeter and Kore (Persephone).
9.97.1b The Gaison was probably a stream running south of Mount Mycale, and Skolopoeis, a place on its east bank. (How and Wells; Godley) Mount Mycale occupies a large part of the Mycale Peninsula: Map 9.97, BY.
9.97.1c Eleusis: Map 9.97, BX.
9.97.1d Miletus: Map 9.97, BY.
9.98.1a Hellespont: Map 9.97, AY.
9.98.3a Ionia: Map 9.97, BY.
9.98.3b Some scholars believe the text says "Hebe," not "Hera." Both are plausible passwords.
9.98.4a Artemision: Map 9.97, AX. See 8.22.
9.99.1a Samos: Map 9.97, BY.
9.99.2a Athens: Map 9.97, BX.
9.92.2b Attica: Map 9.80 and inset.

MAP 9.97

to Athens after equipping them for the journey. So the Samians were suspected mostly because they had released 500 of Xerxes' enemies. [3] Next, they assigned the Milesians[a] to guard the passes leading to the peaks of Mycale on the pretext that they knew this region better than anyone else. Of course the real reason they did this was to ensure that the Milesians were far away from their camp. Of all the Ionians, these were the ones they felt certain would turn against them if they found an opportunity to do it. So that was how the Persians took precautions against them. Then they placed their wicker shields close together to form a defensive wall to protect themselves.

After the Hellenes had made all their preparations, they advanced against the barbarians, and as they marched forth, they found a herald's staff lying on the beach. There was also a rumor that flew through the whole army that the Hellenes fighting in Boeotia[a] had won a victory over Mardonios there. [2] Now there are indeed many clear proofs that the divine is present in what happens, and certainly one would be that on the day of the defeat at Plataea[a] and on which the defeat at Mycale was about to occur, a rumor of the earlier victory reached the Hellenes at Mycale and greatly encouraged them, increasing their confidence and their willingness to undergo the dangers of battle with greater zeal than before.

And in addition there was another coincidence: both battles were fought near precincts of Eleusinian Demeter: the fight at Plataea took place beside the sanctuary of Demeter itself, as I mentioned earlier,[a] while the battle about to be fought at Mycale was close to a sanctuary of Demeter as well. [2] And the arrival of the rumor corresponded correctly with the occurrence of the victory of the Hellenes fighting under Pausanias. For the battle at Plataea took place early in the day, while the battle at Mycale occurred in the afternoon. The fact that these events occurred on the same day of the same month became clear not long afterward, when they investigated the matter in detail. [3] The troops at Mycale had been frightened before the rumor arrived, not so much for themselves as for all the Hellenes, that Hellas might suffer catastrophe at the hands of Mardonios. But after these tidings had flown to them, they advanced against the enemy with a lighter and swifter step. Both the Hellenes and the barbarians were eager to fight this battle, because the prizes set before them were the islands as well as the Hellespont.[a]

The Athenians[a] and those posted with them—which amounted to about half of the forces—advanced along the beach on level ground, while the route taken by the Lacedaemonians[b] and those posted with them went through a ravine and hills. As the Lacedaemonians were still making their way around by this path, the troops of the other wing had engaged and were already fighting. [2] Now as long as the Persians' wicker shields were standing, the Persians defended themselves and were not at all inferior to their

9.100
479
MYCALE
Herodotus sees divine intervention in the fact that although the battles of Plataea and Mycale took place on the same day and were separated by great distance, yet the news of the victory at Plataea arrived at Mycale in time to affect the outcome of the battle there.

9.101
479
MYCALE
There is another coincidence about the two battles. How the rumor of victory at Plataea encourages the Hellenes at Mycale.

9.102
479
MYCALE
The battle is fierce. While the Spartans march around the enemy flank, the Athenians and the other Hellenes in their part of the line break through the Persians' line and successfully assault the palisade of the enemy camp.

9.99.3a   Miletus: Map 9.97, BY.
9.100.1a Boeotia: Map 9.97, BX.
9.100.2a Plataea: Map 9.97, BX.
9.101.1a Fighting at sanctuaries of Demeter: at
          Mycale, see 9.97.1; at Plataea, see 9.62.2.

9.101.3a Hellespont: Map 9.97, AY.
9.102.1a Athens: Map 9.97, BX.
9.102.1b Lacedaemon (Sparta): Map 9.97, BX.

opponents in the battle. But when the army of the Athenians and the troops with them shouted encouragement to one another and set to work with greater zeal so that the feat would be their own rather than the Lacedaemonians', the situation changed. [3] They charged forward and pushed their way through the wicker shields, falling upon the Persians in a mass. The Persians received the attack and defended themselves for quite some time, but in the end they began to flee within the wall. The Athenians, Corinthians,[a] Sicyonians,[b] and Troizenians[c] (posted next to each other in that order) pursued them closely and rushed inside the wall with them. Once the wall had been breached, all the barbarians except for the Persians lost their will to fight and attempted only to escape. [4] The Persians, however, formed up into small groups and fought the Hellenes, who continued to rush inside the wall. Of the Persian generals, two managed to escape and two met their end there: Artayntes and Ithamitras, the commanders of the fleet, escaped, while Mardontes and Tigranes, the generals of the land army, died fighting.

While the Persians were still fighting, the Lacedaemonians and the troops with them arrived and helped to finish off what was left of the resistance. Many Hellenes also fell in this battle, including some Sicyonians, and in particular, their general Perilaos. [2] The Samians[a] who were serving in the camp of the Medes and who had been deprived of their arms saw from the very beginning that the battle could go either way and did as much as they could in their desire to help the Hellenes. Upon seeing the Samians take the lead in this, the other Ionians also revolted from the Persians and turned on the barbarians.

The Persians had appointed the Milesians to watch over the passes for the sake of their own safety, so that in case something happened to them like what was happening now, they would have guides to help them reach safety on the heights of Mycale.[a] In addition to performing that task, another reason the Milesians had been posted there was to prevent them from turning against the Persians, as they would have been able to do if they had stayed with the army. But what they did was completely contrary to their assignment, for they guided the fleeing Persians along paths which took them directly into the midst of their foes, and finally, when the Milesians turned on them and killed them, they proved themselves to be the Persians' worst enemies. Thus for the second time Ionia revolted from the Persians.[b]

Of all the Hellenes who fought in this battle, the Athenians proved to be the best and bravest, and of the Athenians, Hermolykos son of Euthoinos, who had practiced the pankration.[a] Later, after these events and during the war between the Athenians and the Karystians,[b] it befell Hermolykos to die in a battle at Kyrnos[c] in Karystian territory and to be laid to rest at

9.103
479
MYCALE
The Spartans arrive for the end of the battle. The Ionians, following the Samians, attack the Persians.

9.104
479
MYCALE
The Milesians, whom the Persians had posted at the passes to prevent them from harming their cause, now misguide the fleeing Persians and then attack them.

9.105
479
MYCALE
Herodotus cites those who fought best at the battle of Mycale.

9.102.3a   Corinth: Map 9.97, BX.
9.102.3b   Sicyon: Map 9.97, BX.
9.102.3c   Troizen: Map 9.97, BX.
9.103.2a   Samos: Map 9.97, BY.
9.104.1a   Mycale Peninsula: Map 9.97, BY.
9.104.1b   Ionia: Map 9.97, BY. The first Ionian revolt took place twenty years earlier in

499 and ended ignominiously in 495. See 5.30–6.33 and Appendix H.
9.105.1a   The pankration was a mixture of boxing and wrestling. (Godley)
9.105.1b   Karystos, Euboea: Map 9.107.
9.105.1c   Kyrnos, Euboea: location unknown.

Geraistos.[d] After the Athenians, the Corinthians, Troizenians, and Sicyonians proved the best and bravest.

When the Hellenes had destroyed the majority of the barbarians, both those fighting and those fleeing, they set fire to the enemy ships and to the entire wall. But before they did that, they collected and removed all the spoils to the beach, and there discovered that among the items they had siezed were some treasure chests full of riches. After setting fire to the wall, they sailed away in their ships.

[2] When they arrived at Samos,[a] the Hellenes held a conference to discuss the evacuation of the Ionians[b] and in which part of Hellas under Greek control they might be settled, because they were considering the abandonment of Ionia to the barbarians. On the one hand, it seemed impossible for them to protect the Ionians by guarding their land forever, but on the other, they knew that if they did not somehow protect the Ionians, the latter would have no hope of escaping punishment at the hands of the Persians. [3] In view of these considerations, the Peloponnesians[a] in office at the time thought it best to depopulate the trading centers of those Greek peoples who had medized and to allow the Ionians to inhabit those lands.

But the Athenians believed that Ionia should not be evacuated at all, and that the Peloponnesians should not determine what would happen to Athenian colonists. In the face of their vehement opposition, the Peloponnesians yielded to them. [4] And so it was in this way that the Hellenes admitted into their alliance[a] the Samians, Chians,[b] Lesbians,[c] and the other islanders who had joined the Greek side in the fight, and they obliged them with pledges and oaths to remain faithful to the alliance and not to desert it. After binding them to the alliance with sworn oaths, they sailed off to break up the bridges,[d] which they thought would still be intact.

So they sailed toward the Hellespont. The few barbarians who had escaped had at first taken refuge on the peaks of Mycale,[a] and they now made their way toward Sardis.[b] Along their journey, Masistes son of Darius, who had happened to be present at the calamity of the Persians, insulted the commander Artayntes at length, saying among other things that he was worse than a woman in the way he had led the troops, and that he deserved to suffer every kind of harm for having harmed the house of the King. Now, to be called worse than a woman is the most terrible reproach of all among the Persians, [2] and Artayntes was so outraged at receiving so many insults that he drew his sword[a] on Masistes, intending to kill him. But Xeinagoras son of Praxilaos of Halicarnassus[b] saw him running at Masistes and, as he

9.106
479
SAMOS
After the battle the Hellenes sail to Samos and debate what policy to follow vis-à-vis the Ionian Hellenes. The Peloponnesians wish to evacuate them to Hellas, but the Athenians object. Finally, the Athenians win the debate, and the islanders are accepted as allies of the Hellenes. The fleet departs to attack the bridges at the Hellespont.

9.107
479
MYCALE-SARDIS
During the Persian retreat to Sardis, Masistes criticizes and insults Artayntes so fiercely that Artayntes attacks him. Artayntes is thwarted, however, by Xeinagoras, and Xerxes later rewards Xeinagoras by granting him the rule over all of Cilicia.

9.105.1d Geraistos, Euboea: Map 9.107.
9.106.2a Samos: Map 9.107.
9.106.2b Ionia: Map 9.97, BY.
9.106.3a Peloponnese: Map 9.107.
9.106.4a This alliance is known as the Hellenic League.
9.106.4b Chios: Map 9.107.
9.106.4c Lesbos: Map 9.107.

9.106.4d The Persian bridges of boats at the Hellespont: Map 9.107, inset.
9.107.1a Mycale Peninsula: Map 9.107.
9.107.1b Sardis: Map 9.107.
9.107.2a Herodotus here uses the Persian word *akinakes*, a dagger or short sword.
9.107.2b Halicarnassus: Map 9.107.

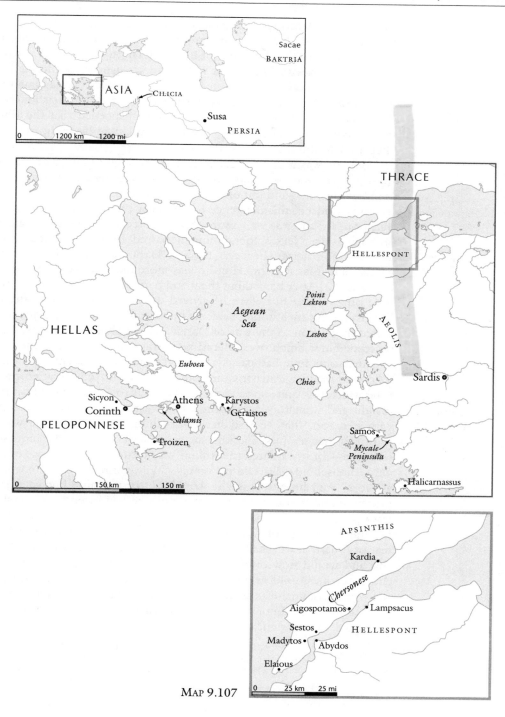

MAP 9.107

stood behind Artayntes, he grabbed him by the waist, lifted him up, and then threw him down on the ground. Meanwhile, the bodyguards of Masistes came to stand in front of him. [3] Through this deed, Xeinagoras stored up favor with Masistes as well as Xerxes, whose brother he had rescued. And on account of this feat, the King granted Xeinagoras the rule over all of Cilicia.[a] There was no further incident along their journey, and they finally arrived at Sardis. Now, it just so happened that the King had been in Sardis ever since he had come to that city in his flight from Athens after his defeat in the naval battle.[b]

While he was in Sardis at that time, Xerxes fell in love with the wife of Masistes, who was also there. But though he kept sending her messages, he could not win her, and out of respect for his brother Masistes, he would not use force; indeed, this deference to him kept the woman safe in her determination, for she was well aware that no force would be used against her. So then, since Xerxes found himself barred from other alternatives, he arranged a marriage between his son Darius and the daughter of this woman and Masistes, thinking he was more likely to succeed with her by doing so. [2] After betrothing them and performing the customary rites, he rode off to Susa.[a] But when he arrived there and had brought the wife of Darius into his own home, he ceased to love the wife of Masistes and redirected his passion to the wife of Darius and daughter of Masistes, whom he succeeded in winning over. The name of this woman was Artaynte.

After some time had passed, however, their affair became known, in the following manner. Amastris the wife of Xerxes wove a great embroidered robe which was quite spectacular, and gave it to Xerxes. He put it on with delight and went to see Artaynte while wearing it. [2] He was so pleased with her, too, that he told her to ask him for whatever she wanted in return for her services, and said she could have anything she requested. In response—for it was fated that things would turn out badly for her and her entire household—she said to Xerxes: "Will you really give me whatever I ask for?" And he, thinking she would ask for anything but what she did, promised and swore to do so. Then, once he had given his oath, she fearlessly asked for the robe. [3] Xerxes did all he could to make her change her mind; he did not want to give it to her for no other reason than his fear of Amastris, who had begun to suspect what was going on even before this and would now discover for certain what was going on. He offered Artaynte cities, gold in great abundance, and an army which no one but she would command (and an army is a very generous gift for a Persian to give), but he could not persuade her. Finally he gave her the robe and she, overjoyed with this gift, put it on and gloried in it.

9.108
479
SARDIS
At Sardis Xerxes courts Masistes' wife but without success. He arranges a marriage between his son and Masistes' daughter, but then, at Susa, forgets the mother and woos and wins the daughter.

9.109
479
SUSA
Xerxes' intrigue ends badly when, to fulfill a grateful but careless oath, he gives a mantle especially embroidered for him by his wife Amastris to his new mistress.

9.107.3a   Cilicia: Map 9.107, locator.
9.107.3b   In 480 at Salamis: Map 9.107.
9.108.2a   Susa: Map 9.107, locator.

When Amastris learned that she had the robe and realized what was going on, she bore no grudge against this woman, for she supposed that her mother was at fault and had arranged this. So now Amastris planned a violent death for the wife of Masistes. [2] She waited for Xerxes, her husband, to serve the royal feast which is prepared once a year on the King's birthday. In Persian, the name of this feast is *tykta*, which means "complete" or "perfect." This is the only time when the King anoints his head with oil and gives gifts to the Persians. After waiting for this day, Amastris asked Xerxes to give her the wife of Masistes as her gift. [3] Xerxes thought it would be terrible and shocking to hand over the wife of his brother to her, and besides, the wife of Masistes was not to blame for this, for he realized why his wife was asking this of him.

Finally, however, since she persevered and because he was compelled by the tradition that he could not possibly deny someone's request when the royal banquet was served, he granted her wish, though much against his will, and gave over the woman in the following way. After telling his wife to do whatever she liked, he sent for his brother, to whom he said, [2] "Masistes, you are my brother and the son of Darius, and in addition, you are a good man. Now do not continue to live with your present wife; I offer you my own daughter to take her place. It is with her you should live, for I do not think it good for you to keep the wife you have now." [3] Astounded by these words, Masistes replied, "My lord, what do you mean by speaking these improper words, saying that I should abandon my wife, from whom I have young sons and daughters, including one to whom you married your own son? She happens to be very agreeable to my taste, yet you order me to put her aside and marry your own daughter! [4] I do consider it a great honor, sire, to be deemed worthy of your daughter, but I shall carry out neither of your orders. Please do not resort to force for what you are asking. Surely another man no worse than I will be found for your daughter, so permit me to continue to live with my own wife." [5] Such was his reply, at which Xerxes was enraged, and said, "Look at what you have done, Masistes: now I would no longer give you my daughter to marry, and you will no longer live with your wife either, so that you may learn how to accept what you are offered." When Masistes heard this, he went away, saying only, "My lord, you have not destroyed me yet."

During the time that Xerxes was conversing with his brother, Amastris sent for Xerxes' bodyguards and had the wife of Masistes badly mutilated. She cut off her breasts and threw them to the dogs, then cut out her nose, ears, lips, and tongue and sent her back home horribly mutilated.

9.110
479?
SUSA
Amastris, who believes Masistes' wife, the girl's mother, is responsible for the affair, plots to destroy the mother.

9.111
479?
SUSA
When Xerxes asks Masistes to put his wife aside and marry one of Xerxes' daughters, Masistes refuses.

9.112
479?
SUSA
Amastris cruelly mutilates Masistes' wife.

Though Masistes had as yet heard no word of this, he expected that he would now encounter some sort of evil, and so he rushed home at a run. When he saw his wife utterly destroyed, he immediately consulted his children, and then set out for Baktria[a] with his sons and, I suppose, others as well, so that he could incite the Baktrian province to revolt and cause the King as much harm as possible. [2] And I believe that would have happened if he had managed to complete the inland journey to the Baktrians and the Sacae[a] in time, for they were fond of him and he was the governor of the Baktrians. But Xerxes learned what he was doing and sent an army in pursuit of him, which killed him, his sons, and his army while they were on their way. So that is the story of Xerxes' passion and the death of Masistes.

The Hellenes who had sailed for the Hellespont[a] from Mycale[b] anchored first at Lekton,[c] having been driven off their course by contrary winds; and from there they went to Abydos[d] and discovered that the bridges, which were their chief reason for coming to the Hellespont, and which they had expected to find still intact, had already been broken apart. [2] The Peloponnesians[a] with Leotychidas decided to sail back to Hellas, but the Athenians[b] and their commander Xanthippos resolved to stay and make an attempt on the Chersonese.[c] So while the Peloponnesians sailed off, the Athenians crossed from Abydos to the Chersonese and began siege operations against Sestos.[d]

When the people who lived in this region heard that the Hellenes were at the Hellespont, they gathered at Sestos, since the fortifications there were the strongest of those in the area. Among the other local inhabitants there was a Persian named Oiobazos, who was from the city of Kardia,[a] and who had earlier removed the cables that had been used for the bridges and brought them to Sestos. This place was inhabited by the native Aeolians,[b] but the Persians and a large group of their allies had joined them here as well.

Ruling as a tyrant over this province was a Persian named Artayktes, whom Xerxes had appointed to be its governor; he was a terrible man doomed by his own folly, for he stole from Elaious[a] the wealth of Protesilaos[b] son of Iphiklos, and he thoroughly deceived Xerxes about it while the King was marching against Athens. [2] At Elaious on the Chersonese there is a tomb and a precinct surrounding it dedicated to Protesilaos, where there used to be an abundance of wealth: libation bowls of gold, silver, and bronze, clothing, and other offerings, all of which Artayktes carried off with the King's permission. But he had deceived Xerxes by saying, [3] "My lord, there is here a house of a Greek man who waged war against your land and died, thus paying his just penalty. Give his house to me, so that all may learn not to wage war on your land." This statement was an easy way to persuade Xerxes to give him the house of this man, since Xerxes suspected nothing of what his real intentions were. For by saying that Protesilaos made war on the land of the King, he had in mind the fact that the Persians think that all Asia belongs to them and lives under the rule of the King in power at the time. And then, after Artayktes had been given this property, he removed its treasure from Elaious and brought it to Sestos. He also cultivated and farmed the precinct at Elaious for profit, and whenever he came there, he would have intercourse with women in the inner shrine. Now he was under siege by the Athenians, and he had made no preparations for it, since he had not anticipated the arrival of the Hellenes, and therefore was off his guard when they attacked him.

Nonetheless, the Athenians found themselves still conducting siege operations when autumn arrived. Frustrated at their inability to take the city's wall, and losing patience at being away from their homes, they asked their generals when they could return, but were told that they could not leave until they either took the city's wall or the government of the Athenians recalled them. So they had to accept their present circumstances.

Within the city wall, the people were by now reduced to utter misery, even to the point of boiling the leather straps of their beds and eating them. At last, when they had no more of these, the Persians, with Artayktes and Oiobazos, ran off under the cover of night and disappeared from the site by climbing down the wall at the rear of the city where their enemies were fewest. [2] When day came, the people of the Chersonese signaled to the Athenians in order to tell them what had happened, and opened their gates. The majority of the Athenians pursued the Persians, while others occupied the city.

Oiobazos escaped to Thrace[a] where the Apsinthian[b] Thracians seized him and sacrificed him in their own fashion to the local god, Pleistoros; they murdered those who had accompanied Oiobazos, however, in a different manner. [2] Artayktes and those with him had set out to escape later than Oiobazos, and they were overtaken a short distance beyond Aigospotamoi.[a] Although they tried to defend themselves for a while, many of them were killed, and those who survived were captured. The Hellenes shackled them together and led them to Sestos, and among the prisoners they had shackled were Artayktes himself and his son.

9.119.1a Thrace: Map 9.107.
9.119.1b Apsinthians (Apsinthis), location of territory: Map 9.107, inset.
9.119.2a Aigospotamoi (Aigospotamos): Map 9.107, inset.

Moved by a strange portent, Artayktes offers to make a rich donation to Protesilaos and to pay a great sum to the Athenians for his and his son's freedom, but the Athenians refuse it and execute him and his son.

According to the people of the Chersonese, a portent occurred while one of the guards was roasting his salted fish: as the fish were lying over the fire, they began to dart about and wriggle, behaving as if they had just been caught. [2] A crowd gathered around the fire and watched in amazement, and when Artayktes saw the portent, he called out to the man roasting the fish, "My friend from Athens, have no fear of this portent; it is not being revealed for your sake, but for mine. Protesilaos in Elaious is showing me that even though he is as dead and dry as a salted fish, he has power from the gods to pay back the person who wrongs him. [3] And so now I would like to impose a penalty and a ransom on myself: I shall deposit 100 talents[a] for the god in return for the riches I took from his sanctuary, and I shall pay 200 talents to the Athenians for myself and my son, provided that I survive." [4] But these promises failed to persuade the general Xanthippos, for the people of Elaious[a] wanted to avenge Protesilaos and were demanding that Artayktes be executed, and the general himself was inclined to the same opinion. So the Athenians led Artayktes to the promontory where Xerxes had bridged the strait, though some say they led him to the hill overlooking the city of Madytos.[b] There they fastened him to a wooden plank, and hung him up on it, and then they stoned his son to death before his very eyes.

The Athenians sail home with spoils.

Having done this, they sailed back to Hellas, taking spoils along with them, and in particular they took the cables of the bridges in order to dedicate them in their sanctuaries. Nothing else of consequence happened in that year.

Years earlier, wise Cyrus reproved Persians who wish to move to a richer country by pointing out that from there they will cease to be rulers because soft lands breed soft men.

The ancestor of this Artayktes who was hung on the plank was Artembares,[a] who spelled out for the Persians a proposal that they adopted and brought before Cyrus. This proposal was as follows: [2] "Since Zeus is granting hegemony to the Persians, and of all men, to you Cyrus, who have destroyed Astyages, here is our proposal: since this land we possess is small and what is here is rough, let us move out of it and take a better land. There are many neighboring lands, and many farther away, and by taking one of these, more people will regard us with greater wonder. It is only reasonable for rulers to act this way. And indeed, when will there be a finer opportunity to do this than now, while we are ruling over many peoples and all of Asia?" [3] Cyrus did not regard this as a wonderful proposal; he did tell them to carry it out, however, with the recommendation that as they did so they should prepare to be rulers no longer, but rather to become subjects under the rule of others. This was so, he said, because soft places tend to produce soft men; for the same land cannot yield both wonderful crops and men who are noble and courageous in war. [4] And so the Persians agreed with him and departed, leaving him alone. They had lost the argument with Cyrus, and chose to dwell in a poor land rather than to be slaves to others and to cultivate the plains.

[handwritten marginal note: SOFT LANDS = SOFT MEN]

9.120.3a 300 talents would have been an immense fortune for a private individual. It was worth 18,000 drachmas when something close to one drachma was a day's wages for a skilled laborer. See Appendix J,

§10–16, 20.
9.120.4a Elaious: Map 9.107, inset.
9.120.4b Madytos: Map 9.107, inset.
9.122.1a There is an Artembares at 1.114, but he is a Mede and so can hardly be meant here.

APPENDIX A

The Athenian Government in Herodotus

§1. Attica, the triangular peninsula of ancient Athens, has a number of plains in addition to the one around Athens itself: the Plain of Marathon beyond Mount Pentelikon to the northeast, the Plain of the Mesogaia beyond Mount Hymettos to the east, and the Thriasian Plain beyond Mount Aigaleos to the west.[a] These plains might have supported numerous independent city-states (poleis) of a typical size. According to Athenian tradition, the legendary Bronze Age hero Theseus had united the twelve poleis of Attica long ago, although many scholars today place the unification later, some as late as the end of the sixth century. Certainly Athens in the archaic period played only a limited role on the broader Greek stage, struggling even to keep its neighbor Megara[b] from annexing the island of Salamis,[c] just off the west coast of Attica.

§2. At the time of the Persian Wars, the Athenians had a democratic government in which every adult male citizen was entitled to vote in the Assembly. King Theseus himself was said to have made a "democratic" proclamation reducing the powers of Athens' traditional kings in some way, perhaps by recognizing certain families as Eupatrid ("well-born") and creating the Council of the Areiopagos as an advisory body. But the man Athenians generally credited with creating their democracy was Solon, archon in 594/93,[a] who was given extraordinary powers to write laws, not necessarily in 594/93 but certainly within the first four decades of the sixth century.

§3. Legend said that centuries before Solon, Eupatrid archons (leaders or magistrates) replaced the kings, at first archons ruling for life, later for ten-year terms, and finally for a single year. The *basileus* (king), the *polemarchos* or polemarch (war leader), and the eponymous archon (who gave his name to the year) were the first to be created. Later six *thesmothetai* (lawgivers) were also named annually, for a total of nine archons, who became life members of the Council of the Areiopagos after they left office. The archons had the authority to give final judgments in legal disputes, and the Council of the Areiopagos supervised the city's affairs.

§4. Solon's special appointment grew out of increasing tension between rich and poor. Poor Athenians had fallen into debt, some being sold into slavery when they

A.1a Attica, Athens, Marathon Plain, Mount Pente-
      likon, Mesogaia Plain, Mount Hymettos, Thriasian
      Plain, Mount Aigaleos: Map A, inset.
A.1b Megara: Map A, inset.
A.1c Salamis: Map a, inset.
A.2a Solon appears at 1.29–33. See n. 1.29.1a.

could not pay. Solon saw himself as a mediator. In his surviving poems, he describes himself as a boundary stone between the two sides, and as a wolf among dogs. Herodotus says that he found it expedient to leave town for ten years after completing his legislation (1.29). To solve the immediate crisis, he canceled debts by a measure known as the *seisachtheia* ("shaking-off of burdens"). He also decreed that people could no longer use their persons as security for loans.

§5. Solon divided the Athenians into four economic classes based on annual income: the *pentakosiomedimnoi* (producers of 500 measures a year), the *hippeis* ("horsemen," who produced 300 measures a year), *zeugitai* ("yoked men," perhaps meaning those who could afford oxen, who produced 200 measures), and *thetes* (hired men). Solon made eligibility for government offices dependent on membership in these classes, rather than birth. Treasurers came from the top class only, archons probably from the top two. *Thetes* were allowed membership only in the Assembly and the Eliaia, the Assembly meeting as a court. Solon created a distinction between private cases (*dikai*), in which the victim (or a member of his family in the case of homicide) brought the charges, and public cases (*graphai*), in which he allowed any citizen to prosecute. He also allowed appeals to the Eliaia, a change that the author of the Aristotelian *Constitution of Athens* regarded as the one that most increased the power of the people (9.1).[a] Scholars continue to debate whether Solon created a new Council of Four Hundred to prepare business for the Assembly (*Constitution of Athens* 8.4). This step would have made sense if he had wished to trim the powers of the Eupatrids, who would dominate the Council of the Areiopagos for years to come, but there is no indisputable evidence of the Council of Four Hundred's actually doing anything, and it may be an invention of the oligarchs of 411 as a precedent for their own Council of Four Hundred when they overthrew the democracy almost 200 years later.

§6. Important as they were, Solon's laws neither solved the underlying problems of the poor nor ended political squabbling among the rich. In 561/60, Peisistratos, whose family claimed descent from Neleus of Pylos (5.65), father of the Homeric hero Nestor, made himself tyrant by persuading the people that his enemies had attacked him. When the people granted him a bodyguard, he used it to help him seize the Acropolis (1.59). Peisistratos apparently made no changes to the constitution. He just made sure that his friends held the important offices. His political enemies, however, soon forced him into exile, from which he returned by a trick Herodotus thought the silliest one he had ever heard of (1.60). He made a deal with the Alkmeonid politician Megakles, whose daughter he agreed to marry. They dressed up a young woman to look like Athena in armor, put her with Peisistratos in a chariot, and brought her into the city, with heralds announcing that the goddess was bringing Peisistratos back. Later sources make it clear that Peisistratos played the subordinate role of chariot driver, and the story is better interpreted as a staged return of Athena to the Acropolis. In any case, Peisistratos soon went into exile

A.5a The philosopher Aristotle (384–322) collected more than 150 constitutions of Greek states. The Constitution of Athens, discovered in Egypt in 1890, is the only one to survive. It contains a historical survey of the development of Athenian democracy, followed by a description of the constitution as it operated in Aristotle's day. It may have been written by one of Aristotle's students, rather than by the philosopher himself.

again, not to return for ten years. In 546/45, backed by foreign aid and mercenaries, he landed at Marathon, won a battle against the Athenians from the city, and regained the tyranny that he was to hold until his death in 528/27 (1.60–61). His son Hippias succeeded him as tyrant, and an inscription shows that Hippias' relations with other prominent Athenian families were good at first: Kleisthenes, a member of the Alkmeonid family that had been in exile (1.64), was archon in 525/24 (disproving Herodotus' claim at 6.123 that the Alkmeonids were in exile throughout the tyranny), and Miltiades, a member of the prominent Philaid family, was archon in 524/23 (supporting Herodotus' comment at 6.39.1 that the tyrants treated him well).ᵃ But Hippias became more oppressive after the assassination of his brother Hipparchos in 514 (5.55–56). Herodotus writes that the exiled Alkmeonids bribed the Delphic oracle to encourage the Spartans to drive Hippias out, which, after one unsuccessful attempt by sea, they finally did with a land invasion led by King Kleomenes in 510 (5.62–65, 6.123).

§7. Kleisthenes returned from exile, only to find himself losing in a power struggle with Isagoras, who was elected archon for 508/07. He responded to this reverse by "enlisting the common people into his association of supporters" (5.66.2), and with their help, he passed important new legislation. Later sources agree that Kleisthenes wanted to "mix up" the Athenians. He did so by dividing the citizens into ten new tribes. These tribes were theoretically equal in population and were based on geography rather than kinship: each tribe comprised three *trittyes* (thirds), one made up of men from the city, one of men from the coast, one of men the inland regions. Each *trittys*, in turn, comprised one or more demes (villages), some previously existing and some newly created. There were 139 demes in all. Kleisthenes then created a Council of Five Hundred, consisting of fifty representatives from each tribe, determined by the population of the deme in proportion to the population of the tribe. Much remains unclear about Kleisthenes' innovations, such as who was eligible for the council and whether its members were originally elected or chosen by lot, but Herodotus firmly credits him with establishing "democracy" (6.131.1) and credits *isegoria* (the equal right of all citizens to speak in the assembly) and freedom with making the Athenians better fighters (5.78). Herodotus' emphasis on the new tribes is understandable, since the Athenian army was now organized into ten tribal units (*taxeis*), and tribal choruses of fifty men and fifty boys competed at the festival of Dionysos. The tribes played a critical role in developing a community consciousness that transcended particular regions in Attica.

§8. Kleisthenes also passed the famous ostracism law. Once a year, the Athenians voted on whether or not to conduct an ostracism. If the vote was in the affirmative, they reassembled about two months later for the voting. Each citizen scratched a man's name on a broken piece of pottery (*ostrakon*). These ballots were counted and, provided that at least 6,000 people voted, the man with the most votes was exiled from Attica for ten years, after which he was free to return and would be

A.6a For more information on these important
      Athenian families, see Appendix L, Aristocratic
      Families in Herodotus.

restored to the full possession of his civic rights. Kleisthenes was said to have intended this curious procedure to prevent a future tyranny, and if such was his intent, he succeeded. Later, ostracism seems to have been used to settle disputes among rival politicians. Five men were ostracized in the 480s, the last of whom was Aristeides son of Lysimachos[a] (8.79.1). In the face of Xerxes' impending invasion, all these men were recalled in 481/80.

§9. According to the Aristotelian *Constitution of Athens* (22.2), it was not until 501/00 that the Athenians began to elect ten generals, one from each tribe, for annual terms. Earlier generals there undoubtedly were, but they were probably chosen for particular campaigns. In 490, all ten generals went to Marathon, and Herodotus says the polemarch Kallimachos had an equal vote and held the position of honor on the right wing (6.109.1). Herodotus' understanding of the Athenian command structure has been criticized because he says that Kallimachos "had been selected by lot for his office as polemarch," while Aristotle's Constitution of Athens says the archons began to be chosen by lot in 487/86 (*Constitution of Athens* 22.5). Perhaps Kallimachos was first elected one of the archons, then chosen by a lottery among the archons to be polemarch, a nominal commander in chief, since the ten generals rotated the leadership day by day and fought on Miltiades' day (6.110.1).

§10. The constitution became much more democratic in the years to come. By the middle of the fifth century, most officials served on committees chosen by lot, and eligibility was opened up to the third class. The Council of Five Hundred, rather than the Council of the Areiopagos, reviewed the performances of officials. The old Eliaia, the Assembly meeting as a law court, was divided into jury courts with jurors chosen from a pool of 6,000, thought of as representing the people as a whole. Pay was introduced for counselors and jurors so that even poor citizens could attend. Yet Herodotus has it essentially right when he says that Kleisthenes established a democracy at Athens. By means of resolutions passed by the assembly, the Athenians decided not to take Hippias back, to aid the Ionian Revolt, to march out to Marathon, to use the silver found at Laureion to build a large fleet, and to evacuate the city and defend themselves at sea against Xerxes.

Peter Krentz
Department of Classics
Davidson College
Davidson, NC

A.8a Aristeides was an Athenian statesman and general of the early fifth century. He supported Miltiades' decision to fight at Marathon, and although he was ostracized in 482, he was recalled in the general amnesty that occurred as Xerxes' forces neared Attica. In the battle of Salamis, he commanded the Greek forces at Psyttaleia. When the anti-Persian Delian League was formed under Athenian leadership in 478, Aristeides determined the tribute quota of each contributory state. In contrast to Themistokles, he had a reputation for honesty. In Athens he was known as Aristeides the Just.

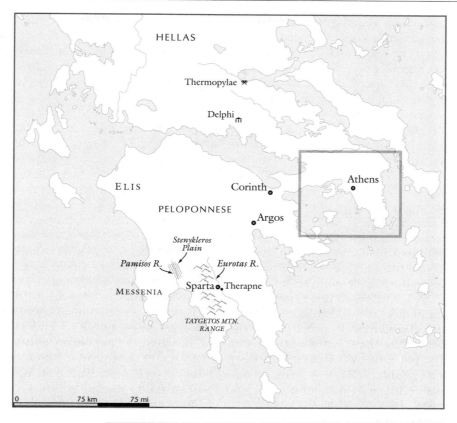

HELLAS

Thermopylae ✼

Delphi

ELIS

Corinth

PELOPONNESE

Argos

Stenykleros
Plain

Pamisos R.

Eurotas R.

MESSENIA

Sparta • Therapne

TAYGETOS MTN.
RANGE

Athens

| 0 | 75 km | 75 mi |

✼ Plataea

Marathon
✼

Thriasian
Plain

Mesogaia Plain

MT. PENTELIKON

Megara •

MT. AIGALEOS

Athens

Salamis

MT. HYMETTOS

ATTICA

Aegina

MAP A

| 0 | 25 km | 25 mi |

APPENDIX B

The Spartan State in War and Peace

Herodotus as Ethnographer of the Spartans

§1. Herodotus the "father of history" (Cicero's *pater historiae*) is also the father of comparative ethnography. He is a generally fair-minded and balanced ethnographer not only of non-Greek "others" but of the Greeks, too. He explicitly describes the ethnicity, customs, and beliefs of many "barbarian" peoples in elaborate, if not always entirely accurate, detail. By contrast, his discourse on Greek ethnicity, customs, and beliefs is for the most part implicit, with one huge exception: his treatment of the Spartans. In Book 6, between his descriptions of the Ionian Revolt (499–494) and the battle of Marathon[a] (490), Herodotus provides a long excursus on the prerogatives of the odd dual kingship of the Spartans (6.51–60). This is followed not long after by a story of the birth of a Spartan king, Demaratos, who was to play a key role in Herodotus' version of Xerxes' invasion of Greece (6.63–69). Part of that story (6.69) is told, moreover, from the point of view of a woman—Demaratos' mother.

§2. These two extended passages in Book 6 convey two important messages, as forcefully as narrative skill can. First, that the Spartans, though they are of course Hellenes, are also, in some vital respects, "other"—in their political arrangements and their social customs they depart significantly from Greek norms. Second, that not the least important way in which they differ from other Greeks is in the role they allocated to, or that was assumed by, Spartan women, at any rate royal women. There is a growing consensus among scholars that Herodotus was a master of the art of historiography as embedded narrative. Herodotus' account—or rather multiple accounts—of Sparta and Spartans are an excellent illustration of his narrative mastery.

Lykourgos

§3. The chronological starting point of the *Histories* in our terms would be somewhere about the year 550, roughly three generations before Herodotus' birth. At that time, the two most powerful mainland Greek cities were Sparta[a] and Athens.[b] Herodotus is quite conventional in ascribing most of Sparta's basic political and military institutions to the reforms of the famed lawgiver Lykourgos (1.65). He writes of

B.1a   Marathon: Map A, inset.
B.3a   Sparta: Map A.
B.3b   Athens: Map A and inset.

Lykourgos as a human being, though he records a Delphic[a] oracle which suggests that he was to be paid divine, not heroic, cult honors after his death. He does not date Lykourgos precisely; later writers dated him variously within a huge span of several centuries. That was only one of many such disagreements as to the details of Lykourgos' life and achievement; other sources differed on, for example, whether or not he played a role in the origins of the ephorate. So great indeed was the disagreement surrounding him that Plutarch (c. C.E. 100) begins his "biography" of Lykourgos by saying that there is nothing that is asserted of him by one writer that has not been contradicted by another. It is very noticeable that Herodotus does not mention Lykourgos again, not even when he comes to describe in detail what is supposed to have been Lykourgos' arrangement for the prerogatives of the two joint kings (6.56–60).

The Names for Sparta, the Spartans and Their Territory

§4. Herodotus comments sharply on the Spartans' own local tradition about their original settlement of their territory, saying that in one respect they contradicted "all the poets" (6.52.1). From this we would have been likely to infer not only that Herodotus was very learned but also that he had gained direct access to local Spartan genealogical and mythical history. That inference is explicitly confirmed elsewhere (§15 below). Here I concentrate on one reflection of his local knowledge, namely his use of the Spartans' own terminology for themselves, their city, and their city-state territory. Unfortunately, Herodotus was not always rigorously consistent in applying his undoubted firsthand knowledge.

§5. The strict technical term for Spartan citizens of full status was Spartiatai (which Herodotus spells in the Ionic way, with an ēta instead of a long alpha in the third syllable, Spartiētai, 9.85.2). Lakōn (7.161.1; feminine Lakaina, 3.134.5) was an alternative form; it is from the adjectival form of *lakōn*, *lakōnikos*, that we get our word "laconic" (see also 3.46 for a classic anecdote illustrating this quintessentially Spartan mode of speech). But Herodotus, like other authors, more usually calls them Lakedaimonioi, meaning either inhabitants of or citizens of Lakedaimōn.[a] For Lakedaimōn could mean either the entire territory of the Spartan state, for which Lakonikē (sc. *gē*, "land," 1.69, 6.58, 7.235) or "*gē* of the Lakedaimonioi" (7.158.2) were alternative usages, or just specifically the city—or town, more correctly—of Sparta (which might also be called Spartē).

§6. The entire civic territory of Sparta consisted of pretty much the southern portion of the Peloponnese,[a] some 8,000 square kilometers (3,000 square miles) in all, easily the largest city-state territory in the entire Greek world. It may be divided into two roughly equal halves separated by the Taygetos[b] mountain range (rising to more than 2,400 meters or 8,000 feet). On the west lay Messenia,[c] the ancient term. This was territory that the Spartans had acquired by conquest beginning in the late eighth century, not without fierce resistance from the Messenians. Spartan control was firmly established by 550, but Messenian recalcitrance (alluded to at 5.49.8) remained high; and in the 460s a major revolt broke out (§9 below), mentioned at 9.64.2

B.3c Delphi: Map A.
B.5a This volume uses the spellings Lacedaemon and Lacedaemonians in accordance with the *Barrington Atlas*.
B.6a Peloponnese: Map A.
B.6b Taygetos Mountains: Map A.
B.6c Messenia: Map A.

(Stenykleros[d] is in the main river valley of the Pamisos[e]). On the east, where the town of Sparta lies toward the head of the valley of the River Eurotas,[f] is what we call anachronistically Laconia (which is in fact the late Roman, not a classical Greek, name).

Other Inhabitants of *Lakedaimōn*: *Perioikoi* and Helots

§7. The problem with the term Lakedaimonioi, for us rather than for them, is that it could also encompass inhabitants of Lakedaimōn who were not full citizens of Sparta, namely the *perioikoi* or "outdwellers." There were perhaps as many as eighty communities of *perioikoi*, situated on the periphery of the two great riverine valleys of Laconia and Messenia and all around the very long and indented coastline. Within these communities there was clear class differentiation: the wealthier *perioikoi* served the Spartans either as hoplites or as cavalrymen, and some even rose to hold positions of command in the fleet. It was when *perioikoi* served in Spartan or larger allied armies together with Spartan citizens that they were most naturally called Lakedaimonioi.[a]

§8. Apart from the status and behavior of women (§25 below), the other great social oddity of Sparta was the helots. These were local Greek natives of Laconia and Messenia whom the Spartans reduced to a serflike status and exploited mainly for performing agricultural functions but also several other tasks, for instance on campaign as body-servants (7.229) and even as lightly armed fighters (9.29). The helots who died at Thermopylae[a] (8.25.1) may have been both.

§9. Herodotus does justice to them in a number of ways. Apart from a variety of individual helots featured, such as the one who was set to guard King Kleomenes and was persuaded with fatal consequences to hand the king his knife (6.75.2), Herodotus also mentions the Messenian helots collectively, not least in the context of his tale of Teisamenos the seer and his five "contests" (9.33–36). Teisamenos was originally from Elis,[a] but he and his brother were made a unique grant of Spartan citizenship, for the sake of their indispensable gift of prophecy. Teisamenos had said that, if the Spartans accepted him and his brother as citizens, he would help them to be successful in five "contests," as predicted by a Delphic oracle (9.33, 9.35). The fourth of the "contests" won by the Spartans with his aid was against the Messenian helots, when they revolted en masse in the 460s, taking advantage of the Great Earthquake of c. 464.[b] The development of Sparta as a peculiarly military society (a mere armed camp to critics like Isokrates[c]) was necessitated as much as anything by the helot enemy within.

Political System

§10. As a military society, Sparta predictably ordered its political arrangements from the top down. At the very pinnacle of the hierarchy were the two kings, each from a different aristocratic house and claiming divine descent ultimately from Zeus via Herakles and his descendants Agis and Eurypon. Herodotus quite rightly appre-

B.6d The Stenykleros Plain (Map A), was the site of a battle between a small Spartan force and Messenian rebels during the revolt of the 460s.

B.6e Pamisos River: Map A.

B.6f Eurotas River: Map A.

B.7a The corresponding anglicized terms used in this volume are Spartiate (for full-status citizens); Laconia, Laconian, Laconians; Lacedaemon, Lacedaemonian, Lacedaemonians; and Sparta, Spartan, Spartans.

B.8a Thermopylae: Map A.

B.9a Elis: Map A.

B.9b This helot revolt began when a strong earthquake struck Sparta and environs. See *Thucydides* 1.101.

B.9c Isokrates was a Greek writer of the early fourth century, best known for advocating that the Greeks should unite, even under Philip of Macedon, and wage an aggressive war of reprisal against Persia.

ciated the uniqueness of the Spartan dyarchy and devoted several pages to setting out his understanding of the two kings' special privileges and prerogatives (*gerea*: 6.51–60). These included lavish funeral rituals that were the very opposite of the austerely restrained burial practices prescribed for nonroyal Spartans, and indeed they recalled "barbarian" (Egyptian, Scythian) rather than normal Greek funerary customs. The importance and oddity of the Spartan kingship are further brought out by Herodotus' dwelling on succession crises (e.g., 5.39–40) and dynastic marriage practices (e.g., 6.63–69) more redolent of an oriental court than of a Greek citizen-state.

§11. Not all the details of the kings' powers are absolutely clear. For example, Thucydides (1.20.3) perhaps unfairly accused Herodotus (without mentioning him by name) of foolishly believing that kings had two votes each in the thirty-member senate called the Gerousia (§12), whereas in fact they had only one. It is anomalous, moreover, that the kings allegedly appointed diplomatic representatives (*proxenoi*) of other Greek cities from among the citizens of Sparta: normally, that was the prerogative of the partner city itself. Thus Athens would appoint its own *proxenos* or multiple *proxenoi* from among the Spartan citizens, and so forth. And although Herodotus says (6.56) it was the kings' prerogative to declare and wage war on whom they wished, it is clear that the Spartan Assembly would have to vote affirmatively for war for it to become official (§14).

§12. The Gerousia (1.65, 5.40.1, 6.57.5) was a tiny permanent body of thirty senior citizens who—except for the two kings, who were members ex officio and by birthright—were elected for life by the Spartan citizenry as a whole. Candidates had to be over sixty, that is, beyond active-service military age, and probably also aristocrats, members of families that, like those of the two kings, called themselves collectively "descendants of Herakles" (Herakleidai). The election was carried out by votes delivered in the same manner as for other decisions, by the members of the Assembly shouting out loud. Aristotle considered this procedure "childish." The Gerousia acted as a probouleutic (pre-deliberative) body for the Assembly and also functioned as Sparta's supreme court. Even Spartan kings might be tried before the Gerousia, on which occasions it would probably be joined by the members of the Board of Ephors (§13). At 6.82 Herodotus gives his untechnical account of the trial of Kleomenes in about 494. Voting in such cases was open, each member having one vote, but trials took place in camera. There were no truly popular courts at Sparta, as there were in Athens.

§13. The Board of Five Ephors ("overseers," "supervisors") was elected annually by the Assembly (§14). All Spartan citizens were eligible for election, which was conducted according to the same "childish" procedure as elections for the Gerousia. Even quite poor Spartans might stand and be elected. Re-election was banned, so ephors might be very powerful for a year but unheard of before or after. The board constituted the effective day-to-day government of Sparta. Among their many powers, the ephors supervised a king's behavior, even in the most intimate matter of dynastic marriage (5.39.1–2, 5.42.1), and it was their responsibility when need arose to decide, by majority, whether or not a king should be required to stand trial. Besides supervising the kings, ephors were also responsible for military mobilization and in peacetime for the conduct of the Agōgē ("upbringing"), the unique state education system through whose carefully defined stages all Spartan boys, except the two heirs apparent, were required to pass between the ages of seven and eighteen. The military character and purposes of this education (*paideia*) were explicit.

§14. The Assembly (Ekklesia) consisted of all Spartan citizens in good standing—that is, males aged twenty or over who had passed successfully through the compulsory educational system and been duly elected members of a dining society, or "mess." The Assembly met statutorily once a month on the feast day of Apollo but could be summoned to extraordinary sessions if need be (as at 7.134.2, where the Assembly is given the generic name *haliē*, or "gathering"). Meetings were presided over by the senior member of the Board of Ephors, who would invite ephors, members of the Gerousia, and perhaps other senior office-holders to speak to the issue at hand. The matter would then be put to the popular vote of the Assembly, which would be registered by shouting in the usual Spartan way (*Thucydides* 1.87.2). The outcome would depend on the presiding ephor's judgment as to which shout—for or against the motion—had been the louder. Scope for manipulation seems manifest. The Assembly decided mainly matters of peace and war. Occasionally, that involved legislation. At 5.75.2 Herodotus cites the "law" introduced in about 505 decreeing that only one of the two kings might at any one time be in command of a particular Spartan or Spartan-led combined force. The passage of that law would have been the outcome of a complicated legislative procedure, the details of which are again hugely disputed among scholars (Herodotus himself, in his usual way, simply takes the process for granted). According to what I consider the most probable reconstruction, any new legislation would have to originate within the elite Gerousia. Presumably, except in the cases where it acted as a supreme court, it would operate by consensus rather than by formally registering votes. If a proposal commanded majority support in the Gerousia, a motion would then be put before a meeting of the Assembly for its final decision.

Army Organization

§15. Herodotus states that he personally visited Sparta. Indeed, he names Archias, a leading Spartan, as one of his informants there (3.55), and this is one of only three cases in the entire *Histories* where he cites an individual informant by name. Moreover, he also names the village from which Archias came, namely Pitana, one of the four that together constituted the town of Sparta. Thereby hangs an intriguing historiographical tale. In his account of the battle of Plataea, Herodotus mentions a "Pitanate *lokhos*" (9.53.2), or "Pitanate brigade," a detail about which he was presumably informed by Archias. Yet Thucydides, in one of his opening methodological chapters (1.20.3), pours scorn on a benighted predecessor who was naïve enough to believe there had once been a Pitanate *lokhos* when in fact no such unit had ever existed. The unnamed predecessor he had in his sights was of course Herodotus. Presumably the reason Thucydides was so sure Herodotus was wrong was that in his own day such a regiment did not exist, and he seems to have been one of those who held the view—widespread but false (see §14, on 5.75.2)—that all Spartan political and military institutions were of timeless antiquity.

§16. It is far more plausible to infer that a major military reform was enacted sometime between the battle of Plataea (479) and Thucydides' Atheno-Peloponnesian War (431–404), in which the Spartan army of the early fifth century, described by Herodotus and based on regiments called *lokhoi*, was replaced by one based on regiments called "divisions" (*morai*), as described by Xenophon, who fought with a Spartan army in the early fourth century. Regimental commanders in both cases were known as polemarchs (7.173.2), which may further account for Thucydides' confusion. The chief reason for such a major organizational reform is not hard to find: namely, the growing shortage or shrinkage of adult Spartan military manpower (what Aristotle was to call *oliganthrōpia*).

§17. In 480 there were reportedly some 8,000 Spartan citizens of military age and capacity (7.234.2), but by 371 there were only about 1,000. Between 480 and 371 there had been a major loss of life among young as well as mature Spartans caused by a massive earthquake in about 464 whose epicenter was near Sparta itself. The Atheno-Peloponnesian War had also taken its toll, but to these natural and military causes must be added certain social factors, including the increasing concentration of privately owned land in ever fewer and ever richer hands. Spartiate citizen-soldiers were required to feed themselves from foodstuffs produced by helots on land they themselves owned. Thus the concentration of land ownership directly reduced the number of men able to contribute food to the common messes that were at the basis of the political and military systems. One vital purpose of the postulated army reform (which I would date to the later 440s, during a brief interlude of peace with Athens) was therefore to compensate for the decrease in the number of frontline citizen-status hoplites by incorporating selected *perioikoi* into the new mixed "divisions." There is no sign that the inclusion of *perioikoi* hoplites in what had formerly been exclusively Spartiate regiments had any deleterious effect on Sparta's military capacity or efficiency. Rather the opposite, as the battle of Mantiniea in 418 proved.

§18. *Perioikoi* had been regarded as a necessary complement to Spartan citizen troops since at least the Plataea campaign of 479, when an equal number (5,000) of *perioikoi* hoplites was sent out alongside the Spartiate contingent (9.11.3). They presumably fought separately in the line of battle, and when it came to burying their dead, the Spartans interred them in three separate mounds. However, Herodotus fails to mention the *perioikoi* dead at all, though he does mention the mound given exclusively to the helot corpses.

B.16a   Plataea: Map A, inset.

Religion

§19. Herodotus' treatment of the Spartans' religious beliefs and practices is evenhanded. He makes it quite clear that the Spartans were perceived to be exceptionally pious. On several major occasions—not least the battles of Marathon and Thermopylae—he reports without comment that the Spartans felt unable to act immediately or in full force because they had prior religious obligations to perform. For the Spartans, as he twice puts it (5.63.2, 9.7), "considered the things of the gods more weighty than the things of men." More skeptical modern historians have inferred that the Spartans were merely using religion as a self-serving pretext. But if the manuscript reading at 9.85.2 is correct, the Spartans erected a special mound at Plataea for those dead Spartiates who were priests. Likewise Herodotus is careful to point out that Spartan kings were themselves priests and maintained close connections with the holiest of all Greek shrines, that of Apollo at Delphi (6.56–57). The perceived importance to Sparta both of Delphi and of military divination is apparent not least from the special grant of citizenship to the seer Teisamenos of Elis (§9). The conduct of Regent Pausanias at Plataea, refusing to order the Greek advance until the sacrificial omens were right (9.61–62), is another telling illustration. The Spartans earned from Xenophon the title of "craftsmen of war" precisely because of the minute attention they paid to the conduct of pre-battle sacrifices and other divinatory signs.

The Peloponnesian League and King Kleomenes I

§20. The Spartan history that Herodotus wanted to discuss with Archias undoubtedly included the expansion of Sparta into the eastern Mediterranean about 525. He believed that the Spartans already had brought most of the Peloponnese under their control as early as 550 (1.68). This, as we can see with hindsight, was part of the process that many of us refer to now as the establishment of the Peloponnesian League (a modern term). The league in fact extended outside the Peloponnese, although it never included all Peloponnesian cities—most notably not Argos.[a] This alliance devised and led by Sparta was a privileged system of separate offensive and defensive military treaties between Sparta and several other states. It mainly benefited Sparta, which was protected by it against hostile invasion and whose relatively few hoplites were transformed by it into an army of formidable proportions. One propaganda claim that Sparta seems regularly to have used in order to legitimate its alliance was an alleged principled opposition to tyrannies—one-man dictatorships (5.92.α.2). But Sparta's foreign relations took a new and more expansive turn in the reign of King Kleomenes I (c. 520–490).

§21. Herodotus' description of Kleomenes and his reign is one of the most puzzling, even contradictory, accounts in the whole *Histories*. On the one hand, Kleomenes was a great and powerful king who—at any rate in the late 490s—had the best interests of Hellas at heart (6.61.1). On the other hand, Kleomenes was at

B.20a   Argos: Map A.

least a bit of a madman (5.39.1), who died horribly by self-mutilation (6.75) in divinely just retribution, according to Herodotus, for an act of gross sacrilege (6.84; here once again Herodotus explicitly contradicts the official local Spartan explanation). He certainly was instrumental in ending the tyranny of the Peisistratid family led by Hippias at Athens in 510 (5.64–65), but Herodotus was probably right that in the long run the major impact of his clumsy interventions here (again in the years 508 and 506; 5.70, 5.72–76) was to prompt Athens to implement the reforms of Kleisthenes and become a democracy (6.131; see also 5.78). A direct consequence of the failure of the 506 expedition was the calling of the first Peloponnesian League congress in about 504 (5.91–93). Sparta proposed to reinstate Hippias as tyrant of Athens, but Sparta's allies had now secured a collective right of veto on the decisions of the alliance's leader, and in this first case, led by Corinth,[a] they rejected Sparta's proposal.

Other Great Spartan Men—and Women

§22. When it came to choosing between Athens and Sparta as to which of those two states contributed most to saving mainland Greece from total Persian conquest in 480–479, Herodotus delivers what he knows will be to many an objectionable judgment, but the one that he considers to be true: namely, that it was the Athenians who—above all by their conduct at the battle of Salamis[a]—were the principal saviors of Greece (7.139.1, 7.139.5). Yet that does not mean that he (unlike some modern historians, perhaps) in any way downplays the almost equally critical and decisive contribution of the Spartans to the Persians' eventual defeat in the battle of Plataea in 479.

§23. The Spartan who led the Greeks to victory in that battle was Regent Pausanias, another hugely controversial character like Kleomenes, both in Sparta and outside, and both in his own lifetime and after his death. Like Kleomenes he came to a bad end (near murder by the Spartan authorities for his alleged treason). But unlike Kleomenes, Pausanias predominantly earns plaudits from Herodotus. After victory has been won at Plataea, "the most splendid of all those we know" (9.64.1), Herodotus relates two telling episodes in which Pausanias is featured as an exemplar of the best Spartan—and Greek—values. A hotheaded Greek from Aegina urges Pausanias to mutilate the corpse of Mardonios in revenge for the mutilation of the corpse of Leonidas by Mardonios and Xerxes at Thermopylae the previous year. Pausanias sharply rebukes the man and tells him that such barbarity is not the Greek way (9.78–79). Then, when Pausanias is shown the rampant luxuriousness of Mardonios' tent and the vast amounts of lavish food prepared for the Persian commander, Pausanias quietly orders his helot attendants to prepare a Spartan—indeed, as we say, a "spartan," meaning frugal—meal in order to demonstrate the superior virtue of Greek self-restraint (9.82).

§24. Leonidas, a half brother of Kleomenes, was also Kleomenes' son-in-law, since his wife Gorgo was Kleomenes' only daughter. Unusually, Gorgo is named by Herodotus—whereas the mother of Demaratos remains anonymous (§1). And

B.21a Corinth: Map A.
B.22a Salamis: Map A, inset.

whenever Gorgo gets a mention by Herodotus, she cuts a fine figure. She warns her father not to be taken in by a plausible Greek suitor from Samos[a] (5.50–51), and it is she alone who can figure out how to read the vital message concealed beneath an apparently blank wax tablet (7.239).

§25. These two Spartan women are, admittedly, not ordinary, everyday Spartan women and wives. Indeed, the anonymous mother of Demaratos was not just a queen but had had what can only be called a magical experience: as an unprepossessing infant she had been graced by the presence of the legendary Helen in her shrine at Therapne[a] and thereafter grew up to be a great beauty herself (6.61). Yet behind these two exceptional figures we sense the perception widespread in the rest of Greece that Spartan women were not as other Greek women were. They had something to say and were not afraid to say it, even in public in front of other, unrelated men. Many centuries later, Plutarch was to collect a number of these "apophthegmata" in his *Sayings of Spartan Women*. Their formidable presence was based ultimately on legal entitlement: unlike almost all other Greek women, they were allowed to own landed property in their own right, and as such were quite properly referred to by Herodotus as "heiresses" (*patroukhoi*: 6.57.4).

§26. It is doubtful therefore that Persian Great King Darius I's wife Atossa (daughter of Cyrus the Great) would have found the Spartan maids she professed to desire (3.134.5) to be altogether amenable and docile. But whether their relatively enhanced social status amounts to the existence of a certain feminism in Sparta is another matter. At any rate, the treatment of the anonymous mother of Demaratos as a political pawn in a game of dynastic matchmaking suggests otherwise. Her testimony in a key royal succession dispute was not deemed worthy of delivery or public record.

Paul Cartledge
Professor of Greek History
University of Cambridge
Cambridge, UK

Bibliography

Bakker, E. J., I. J. F. de Jong, and H. van Wees, eds. *Brill's Companion to Herodotus* (Leiden, 2002).

Cartledge, P. A., "Herodotus and 'the Other': A meditation on empire." *Echos du Monde Classique/Classical Views* 9 (1990), 27–40.

_____. *The Greeks. A Portrait of Self and Others* (2nd ed., Oxford, 2002).

_____. *The Spartans. The World of the Warrior Heroes of Ancient Greece* (rev. ed., New York, 2003).

Derow, P., and R. Parker, eds. *Herodotus and His World* (Oxford, 2003).

Dewald, C., and J. Marincola. "A Selective Introduction to Herodotean Studies." *Arethusa* 20 (1987), 9–40.

Evans, J. A. S. "Father of History or Father of Lies: The Reputation of Herodotus." *Classical Journal* 64, 1 (1968), 11–17.

Hartog, F. *The Mirror of Herodotus: The Representation of the Other in the Writing of History* (Berkeley, Los Angeles, and London, 1988 [French original, *Le Miroir d'Hérodote. Essai sur la représentation de l'autre*, Paris, 1980, repr. with new intro., 1991]).

Luraghi, N., ed. *The Historian's Craft in the Age of Herodotus* (Oxford, 2001).

Momigliano, A. D. "The Place of Herodotus in the History of Historiography" (1st pub. 1958), in his *Studies in Historiography* (London, 1966), 127–142.

Pritchett, W. K. *The Liar School of Herodotus* (Amsterdam, 1993).

Romm, J. S. *Herodotus* (New Haven, 1998).

B.24a   Samos: Map H.
B.25a   Therapne: Map A.

APPENDIX C

The Account of Egypt: Herodotus Right and Wrong

§1. Book 2 is much the longest and most self-indulgent excursus in Herodotus' *Histories*, and it gives the author the opportunity to discuss a wide range of aspects of ancient Egypt, including the antiquity of its civilization, geology, geography, ethnography, zoology, botany, history, and building works. In this survey we are always clearly located in the physical and cultural context of ancient Egypt, but the accuracy of the information is extremely variable, and the data can be distorted by a number of factors, including faulty memory, inaccurate source material, Greek cultural and historical preoccupations, fallacious thinking, a marked tendency to impose a rigid order on Egyptian practice where none existed, Herodotus' personal historical agenda, and the sheer difficulty which he must sometimes have encountered in acquiring accurate information.

§2. The antiquity issue is addressed in Book 2 where Herodotus describes an experiment set up by Psammetichos I to determine which was the oldest civilization. This narrative is quite unhistorical, though it does reflect current and earlier Greek research into genealogies and related phenomena, and the solution which emerges, that is, that Phrygian civilization was the oldest, could hardly be more wrong. Herodotus then proceeds to list the areas in which Egypt had scored a series of cultural "firsts," an example of the widely current Greek concern with the *protos heuretes* ("the first inventor") of cultural phenomena (2.4). These include astronomy (where he provides an accurate account of the structure of the Egyptian civil year); the naming of the twelve gods which he alleges was subsequently taken over by the Greeks (a notion which forms part of his basic thinking about the origins of Greek religion but which is quite incorrect); and the invention of altars, images, temples, and statues, activities in which the Egyptians were certainly early starters but equally certainly not originators for all men. In all these areas the basis of the assertion is simply that Egypt presented Herodotus with the oldest examples which he knew, that is, they exhibit a view of human cultural evolution based ultimately on the *post hoc, ergo propter hoc* fallacy: if *a* is equal to or the same as *b* and earlier than *b*, then *b* must be the result of *a*.

§3. The discussion of geography and geology is strongly influenced by earlier Ionian studies and speculation, and Herodotus not infrequently takes issue with this research and backs up his comments with an impressive array of arguments, including geological observation, again very much in line with earlier and current Greek scientific inquiry. He is very much aware of the alluvial nature of Egypt, though he dates the creation of the Delta[a] from Nile silt far too late, and he is somewhat restrictive in his claims on how much of the country was created in this way (2.4ff.). His grasp of the physiognomy of Egypt is generally sound, but accuracy of measurement is not a strong point, and dimensions are frequently incorrect simply because of the sheer difficulty of getting them right. He also engages in the long-running debate about how many continents there were, impelled by a determination to prove the Ionians wrong (2.5ff.), but he does provide a definition of Egypt with which the Egyptians would have had no difficulty agreeing (2.18). He then moves on to discuss the hydrography of the Nile, devoting much attention to the cause of the inundation, another topic on which there had been much previous speculation (2.19–28). His review of the debate concludes with his own opinion, which is incorrect (the true cause being monsoon rains in central Africa), but his erroneous position is most cleverly argued, and he also manages to get access to an old Egyptian tradition on the topic (2.28). At 2.97 he provides a most vivid account of the freedom of navigation created by the inundation of the Nile, which has been echoed in a host of later accounts down to modern times. His comments on the Upper Nile are vague and speculative (2.29–34), a situation which reflects the standard phenomenon whereby his information becomes thinner, and often more fanciful, the further he moves from areas with which the Greeks had long familiarity. Nevertheless, his observations can sometimes be related to genuine geographical features.

§4. Herodotus' account of Egyptian culture spreads far and wide but is fundamentally superficial in that it shows no understanding of its ideological underpinning and concentrates entirely on external observable phenomena, which he describes with variable accuracy. He does less than justice to Egyptian agriculture in claiming that it was the least laborious in the world because there was no need to plow or hoe (2.14), missing completely the enormous effort required to set up and maintain the irrigation system which was the prerequisite for successful agriculture in Egypt. He was aware, however, of the pervasive presence of the canal network, which he ascribes to the pharaoh Sesostris (2.108). The ethnographical excursus at 2.35–36 is dominated by the conviction that everything in Egypt is done the opposite way from how the rest of the world does it. There is some truth in much that is said in this section, but Herodotus demonstrably goes way too far and produces a far too schematized picture. The long account of Egyptian religious practices (2.37ff.) is largely sound, but this section contains a discussion of the origins of Greek religion which argues that nearly all Greek deities have been imported from Egypt (2.49–58), a notion which is incorrect in every single case but which resurfaces at a number of points later in the book (2.144–146, 2.153; see also 2.156). His comments on the ethnography of the Upper Nile again can be related to genuine phenomena but cannot be endorsed in their entirety (2.29–32). His lengthy

C.3a   Nile Delta: Map C.

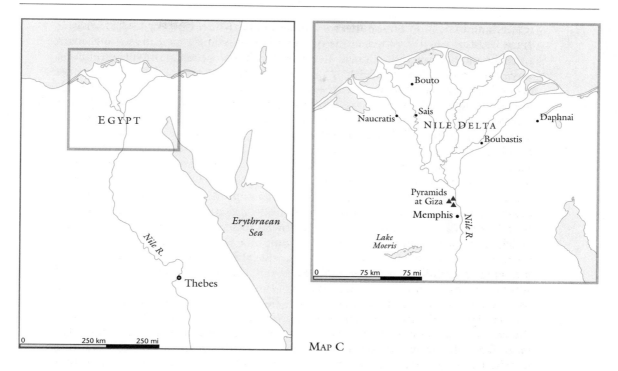

MAP C

discussion of mummification has merit on technological aspects, though it is not infallible, but misses completely its religious dimension (2.86–89). The account of the subdivisions in Egyptian society has some basis in reality (2.164–168) but is greatly oversimplified and sometimes distorted by the erroneous conviction that some Greek social structures, like the Spartan military system, were modeled on Egyptian prototypes.

§5. Herodotus' discussion of the religious role of animals leads him on to describe their zoology, and here his taste for the marvelous is given full rein. This is particularly true of the account of the cat (2.66), an animal largely unknown to Greeks, and here he makes some extraordinary statements which have no basis at all in fact. His discussion of the crocodile is much better (2.68–70), but he lets himself down again with the hippopotamus, which he describes in most bizarre terms (2.71). At 2.74 he gives a brief account of the horned viper, or *cerastes*, but he certainly errs in claiming that it is harmless. The account of the phoenix (2.73) and that of the winged snakes (2.75–76) belong in a different world. Although he regards and treats the first as a genuine animal, it was, in fact, a mythical creature, albeit based ultimately on the Egyptian concept of the heron as an agent of creation, while the winged serpents belong to the world of fantasy, though for some as yet unaccountable reason Herodotus was convinced of their reality. At 2.93 Herodotus is led by his discussion of fish in the diet of marsh-dwelling Egyptians to an account of the zoology of the Nile bream. In addition to some peculiar and incorrect comments on the bruising of the fish as a result of their swimming practices, he provides an oddly confused account of their breeding habits which combines a surprisingly accurate description of what the fish actually do with a total misunderstanding of their method of procreation. His speculation on the origin of fish in pools created by the inundation is equally untenable.

§6. Herodotus' first excursions into botany arise from his discussion of the eating habits of Egyptians living in the marshes. He describes both the *Nymphaea* lotus and the rose lotus (2.92). The account of the first is accurate, but his comments on the second err in that he regards the seed vessel as growing on a separate stalk from the flower, whereas it is part of the flower itself. Presumably he, or his source, had seen these lotuses in clumps where some flowers had lost their petals and others had retained them. His brief comments in the same chapter on the papyrus are sound, as far as they go. In all cases he is right to state that the plants in question were used as a food source, though he is intriguingly unaware of the use to which the upper section of the papyrus plant is put, that is, the manufacture of paper. Some comment is made on the castor-oil plant (2.94), but there is little detail, because Herodotus is more interested in its use as a source of oil.

§7. The historical section is much the longest single component of the book and is complemented by references in other parts of the *Histories*. The discussion in Book 2 breaks down into two segments: the history from Min to Sethos (2.99–141) and that from the Dodecarchs (the Twelve Kings) to Amasis (2.147–182), though the narrative continues into Book 3 with the accession of Psammetichos III (Psammenitos) and the conquest of Egypt by Cambyses. This narrative gives Herodotus an opportunity to describe public works for which these kings had been responsible, above all pyramids and temples (see §8), and also to visit themes such as the origins of Greek religion (see §4). Herodotus recognizes explicitly that his sources for the second section are better than the first because he has Greek material to work with from the time of Psammetichos (2.154), and the first section is indeed a curious mixture of historical fact and very dubious tradition. Nearly all the rulers mentioned can be identified with historical figures or, at least, figures who appear in Egyptian historical tradition, and all the major periods of Egyptian history are featured, even the dynasty of the gods (2.144), but there are major errors and distortions: the Colchians were certainly not descendants of the ancient Egyptians (2.103–105)—a notion based on certain points of cultural similarity—and no Egyptian pharaoh invaded Europe, as Sesostris is alleged to have done (2.103); Proteus and the narrative surrounding him have been imported from Homeric tradition and owe next to nothing to an Egyptian archetype (2.112–120); and the pyramid builders are located far too late in the sequence of kings (2.124). The narratives themselves are mainly the product of an Egyptian oral tradition which is an amalgam of vague historical reminiscence, the propaganda of kingship, and folk motifs, and this farrago, in turn, gets overlaid from time to time with Greek ethical and historical preoccupations and the demands of Greek narrative tradition. The upshot is that the student of Egyptian history, in the strict sense, has little to learn from this section of Herodotus' account, but there is much information here both on the nature of the tradition which was current in Egypt from the seventh century onward and on the ways in which this material was customized for Greek consumption. The second section of the history (2.147ff.) focuses on the Saite or XXVI Dynasty (664–525). It has a much stronger purchase on historical reality and can, at many points, be confirmed from Egyptian and Near Eastern sources, but we should not ignore three crucial facts. First, Herodotus' choice of subject matter is determined largely by events in which Greek mercenaries and other expatriates were involved and is not in the least concerned with providing a balanced overall picture; there may have been many important issues in Egypt at this period which he completely ignored simply because Greeks did not participate in them. Second, even when Greeks were deeply involved, we may obtain a narrative which we can show to be seriously distorted, and that means that there may be others which are misleading but which we do not have the evidence to control. Finally, contamination of the historical tradition with folk elements, popular tradition, Greek moral thinking, and the imperatives of Greek narratology is again demonstrably a pervasive presence. This all means that, although this section of the narrative is the earliest and best consecutive account of Saite history from any source and has no Egyptian counterpart, we must proceed with circumspection if we intend to extract history from it. Not infrequently we can confirm what Herodotus says, but all too often we cannot.

§8. Book 2 contains numerous accounts of buildings or public works, but it is important to remember that Herodotus does not normally insert them for their own sake. Nearly all are there because they form part of a discussion of the career of a major historical figure. The one significant exception is the description of Lake Moeris[a] (2.149), which is strictly irrelevant but has crept in by association with the labyrinth allegedly constructed by the Twelve Kings (2.148). It follows that we cannot use the absence of an account of a temple or any other building as an argument that Herodotus never saw it. One of the great merits of these descriptions is that the buildings have sometimes survived in whole or in part, or when they have not, we have parallel structures; so that it becomes possible to get a sense of how accurate the descriptions are and what is likely to go wrong when Herodotus deals with them to a degree which is impossible in other aspects of his work. Temples and their monuments feature prominently, such as those of Memphis,[b] above all that of Hephaistos (Egyptian Ptah), which appears frequently, and correctly, as a focus of royal building and monumental activity,[c] but other sacred enclosures on the site are also described; here the broad outlines can be accepted, though detail is often impossible to verify. The account of the temple of Bastet at Boubastis,[d] though difficult to control on the

C.8a   Lake Moeris: Map C, inset.
C.8b   Memphis: Map C, inset.
C.8c   The Temple of Hephaistos (Egyptian Ptah) is
        mentioned at 2.99, 2.101, 2.108, 2.110, 2.112,
        2.121, 2.136, 2.141, 2.153, and 2.176.
C.8d   Boubastis: Map C, inset.

basis of modern observations and work on this much ruined site, creates few qualms (2.137–138). Herodotus knows of the existence of a great hall in a temple at Thebes,[e] which is presumably that of Karnak (2.143). The account of the labyrinth is difficult to control in detail (2.148), but he is talking of a real building whose site is known, though its attribution to the Twelve Kings is much too late and he is unaware of its real function. We can be cautiously optimistic about what he says of the temples of Bouto[f] (2.155–156), except for the floating island, which belongs firmly in the area of Egyptian myth. And we can be equally optimistic about his comments on the temples and temple monuments of Sais[g] (2.170–171, 2.175–176). As for tombs, pride of place belongs to the pyramids of Giza,[h] where we are informed on builders, dimensions, technology, and motivation in a complex amalgam of fact and fiction which must be treated with extreme caution (2.124–135). Herodotus is also aware that pyramids could be made of brick, though the detail is patently quite unhistorical (2.136). What is said on the royal necropolis at Sais cannot be verified on the ground, but it causes few qualms (2.169). On nonreligious public works his claims are sometimes wrong but compatible to some degree with Egyptian tradition, as with Min (Menes) and Memphis at 2.99 and Sesostris and the canal system at 2.108. What little is said of the palace of Sais looks plausible but cannot be confirmed in detail from the site (2.163). The camps built by Psammetichos for his mercenaries have in part been identified by the discovery of the fort at Tell Defenneh (Daphnai),[i] but Herodotus' notion of the chronological evolution of the site is incorrect, despite the fact that Greeks had been involved in the camps since their creation (2.154). In the same general context we should note that much of what is said about the city of Naucratis[j] can be verified, though again Herodotus falls victim to his besetting sin of overschematization and presents an altogether simpler picture of its evolution than is justified by other evidence (2.178–179). There is no reason to doubt the claim that Necho began a canal to link the Nile with the Red Sea[k] (2.158), but some of his other comments must be dismissed out of hand: the assertion that Rhampsinitos built a treasury of stone is quite unacceptable (2.121.α), and the insistence that Lake Moeris was an artificial creation is completely erroneous (2.149), though this strange notion may well reflect Egyptian efforts to manage the water supply of the area during the XII Dynasty.

§9. To conclude: Herodotus' account of Egypt is the oldest and longest classical discussion of the subject to have survived from any source, but we must never forget that it is written to a Greek agenda and for a Greek audience. It therefore inevitably reflects Greek experience, interests, and preoccupations, and there is no attempt whatsoever to present an objective description of what was there or of the country's historical evolution. Not surprisingly, Herodotus shows no ability to get inside the minds of the ancient Egyptians, and he shows no understanding of the conceptual basis of their culture, though in this respect he is typical of all Greek and Roman writers on alien peoples. Nevertheless, his account contains rich nuggets of informa-

C.8e   Thebes: Map C.
C.8f   Bouto: Map C, inset.
C.8g   Sais: Map C, inset.
C.8h   Giza: Map C, inset.

C.8i   Daphnai: Map C, inset.
C.8j   Naucratis: Map C, inset.
C.8k   Nile River, Red (Erythraean) Sea: Map C.

tion on both Egyptian history and culture, and it has, in particular, an enormous value as the record of the reaction of a European to the culture of pharaonic Egypt when that culture was still a going concern, and if its agendas are borne firmly in mind, his account is still capable of yielding much of value to the discriminating reader.

Alan B. Lloyd
Department of Classics, Ancient History, and Egyptology
University of Wales
Swansea, UK

APPENDIX D

Herodotean Geography

§1. Study of the earth, in particular the configuration of its lands and waters, was a well-established tradition in the Greek world long before Herodotus began to write, though this pursuit would not get the name "geography" until later centuries. Herodotus refers to his predecessors in this tradition at several points in his *Histories*, identifying them generally as "Ionians" in his discussion of Egyptian geography (2.15, 2.16) and elsewhere as "[the] many people . . . drawing maps of the earth" (4.36). All these passages, interestingly enough, refer to geographic suppositions which Herodotus thought to be wrong: the separation of Libya from Asia by the Nile (2.15–16), the reasons for the Nile floods (2.21–22), the existence of a river Ocean flowing around what Herodotus terms the *oikoumenē*—the known world (2.23, 4.8, 4.36), and the circularity of the *oikoumenē* and symmetry of its continents (4.36). Ionian science, with its love of polarities, symmetries, and neat geometric constructs, had in the sixth century established a theoretical map of the earth; Herodotus, who lived at the dawn of the age of empiricism, sought to reform that map on the basis of personal knowledge and eyewitness reports. His efforts may seem crude by modern standards, but they are certainly long strides ahead of his known predecessors, in particular Anaximander and Hekataios, the two great Milesian thinkers who had published geographic treatises before him.

§2. The question of Ocean's existence brought Herodotus into conflict not only with his fellow geographers but with a mythic tradition dominated by Homer and Hesiod. These two great poets had both "drawn" symbolic maps of the earth in their verses, by way of the decorations on the shield of Achilles in Homer's *Iliad* and on the shield of Herakles in a short poem which was attributed in antiquity (perhaps incorrectly) to Hesiod. In both cases the world is conceived as a disk, surrounded on all sides by the circular "river" called Ocean. Herodotus, however, mistrusted the Ocean scheme as an overly geometric construct unsupported by eyewitness evidence, especially in the far north and east (4.8). His critique of that construct includes what must be the earliest known assertion of the concept of poetic license: "I have no certain knowledge that . . . a river Ocean exists; I think, rather, that Homer or one of the poets before him invented the name and introduced it into his poetry." Such an assertion, in a culture that regarded the epic bards as divinely inspired preservers of historical memory, required extraordinary confidence in the value of the scientific method.

§3. Herodotus was not a systematic thinker, however, and at times one finds him relying on the same sort of symmetries and polarities he derides in the work of "the Ionians."[a] When his attempt to trace the upper course of the Nile reaches a dead end, for example, he assumes that this southern river must run parallel to its northern "twin," the Ister (modern Danube) (2.34). In a passage discussing the Hyperboreans, whose name seems to mean "men beyond the north wind," he asserts that if such a race exists, then there must also be Hypernotians or "men beyond the south wind" (4.36). The thinking behind this assertion is so baldly speculative that some scholars have taken it to be a sarcastic reductio ad absurdum, mocking the idea that either race exists, even though the tone seems perfectly earnest and sincere. It is unclear how such a statement could come from the same man who exploded the myth of Ocean, except to say that the polarity of north and south, rooted as it is in the empirical phenomenon of extreme cold and heat, struck Herodotus as inherently more plausible than the circular geometry of the Ocean construct.

§4. The parallel Herodotus draws between the Ister and the Nile partly determined his selection of the regions defined by these rivers, Egypt and Scythia, as the subjects of his two longest geographic excursuses, occupying all of Book 2 and the first half of Book 4. Herodotus visited both places, according to his own testimony (which is doubted by some);[a] in each of them he seems to have undertaken extensive research, both by way of personal observation and by the questioning of local informants. In his accounts of these places Herodotus seems especially concerned with determining the outer limits of the *oikoumenē*, exploring the far south by way of a journey up the Nile (2.29–34) and the far north by way of various obscure, secondhand reports (4.13–31). Elsewhere in the *Histories* he takes an interest in the "farthest reaches of the earth," a ring of semi-legendary lands said to possess the most valuable of natural resources but also the harshest climates (3.106–116). In his most ambitious geographic discussion, 4.36–44, Herodotus constructs a verbal map of the entire known world, summarizing the highly imperfect but nonetheless impressive mass of knowledge he gleaned over many years of geographic investigation.

§5. Much of that knowledge came from the voyages of exploration which the Greeks, Phoenicians, and Egyptians had begun undertaking, both within the Mediterranean and outside it, starting shortly before Herodotus' time. Indeed, Herodotus lived in a golden age of geographic discovery, though because the means by which explorers published their finds were not far advanced, he was not always aware of what had been learned. The naval expedition of Scylax, a Greek sea captain hired in the sixth century by the Persians to explore the rivers of South Asia, seems to have entirely escaped his notice, since in his vague accounts of India he makes no

D.3a   Witness his description of Scythia as a square, 4.101.
D.4a   See Appendix C on Egypt in Herodotus for an
       assessment of Herodotus' information on Egypt,

and Appendix E, §4, for an opinion on how much
and whether he ever visited the Black Sea region.

reference to it. And the voyage of Hanno the Carthaginian down the west coast of Africa may have taken place too late for Herodotus to have learned of it. He does, however, know of a different West African voyage led by Sataspes, a Persian, who discovered a race of dwarfish men wearing palm-frond clothing before he turned back out of fear of the unknown (4.43). He also recounts the tale of a Phoenician crew, dispatched by the Egyptian pharaoh Nechos, which claimed to have made a three-year circumnavigation of Africa from east to west (4.42). Herodotus disbelieves their account of the voyage because they mentioned that the sun appeared on their right as they rounded the Cape of Good Hope; not conceiving that Africa might extend south of the equatorial line, he rejects the very datum which modern historians find most convincing.

§6. Herodotus evidently cast a wide net in his search for voyage accounts and other empirical knowledge of the earth's distant spaces. The inquiry into the sources of the Nile in Book 2 (2.28–34) is a good case in point. Herodotus reports questioning many inhabitants of Egypt and North Africa about this most enduring of terrestrial riddles (finally solved only in the late nineteenth century).[a] In the end the best information he can record comes to him at *fifth* hand, from Cyrenaean Greeks, who heard it from the ruler of the Egyptian oasis of Ammon, who heard it from some visitors to his town called Nasamonians, who heard it from some adventurous youths of their own tribe. On a lark these young Nasamonian men had set out across the Sahara and into the heart of Africa, ultimately to be taken prisoner by dwarfish black-skinned men living beside a river filled with crocodiles (2.32). Herodotus inclines to the view that this river was an upper stretch of the Nile, since he believes for other reasons (see §3 above) that the Nile ought to flow east–west in this region. In fact, this passage may well contain the first European report of the Niger River and of the tribe known to later Greeks, and hence to us, as Pygmies— perhaps the same people as the palm-wearing dwarfs encountered by Sataspes the Persian. All this came to light only because Herodotus asked enough questions during his visit to Cyrene to uncover *someone* who knew *something*.

§7. None of the geographic discussions of the *Histories*, however, can be understood as purely scientific researches; all are subordinated to the main theme of the work, the conflict between Greece and Persia, in that all of them help explain the global expansion of the Persian Empire and its eventual defeat at the hands of the Greeks. Though he may not have subscribed to a strict notion of geography as cultural destiny, as did a near-contemporary who authored the treatise *Airs Waters Places*,[a] Herodotus certainly regarded climate, topography, and access to resources as major determinants of social development and, in particular, military strength. The chapter with which he closed the *Histories* highlights this idea: in Cyrus' view the Persians would remain powerful only so long as they stayed on the rugged slopes of their mountainous homeland. Similarly, the military prowess of the Spartans is described by their exiled king Demaratos as a virtue born of the poverty native to

---

D.6a   The basic cause of the annual flooding of the Nile is the monsoon rains on the mountains of Ethiopia.

D.7a   *Airs Waters Place* is a fifth-century text normally ascribed to Hippocrates, or included as part of a collection of medical treatises known as the Hippocratic writings.

Greece (7.102). In the contrasting excursuses on Egypt and Scythia, Herodotus portrays a south-dwelling people with rich farmlands, on the one hand, and a north-dwelling race of hardy nomads on the other; it accords well with the patterns of his text that, in their successive conflicts with the Persians, the former suffers quick defeat and humiliating occupation while the latter manages a bold victory by stalemate.

§8. Indeed, the north–south antithesis can be regarded as the essential framework governing all of Persia's wars, if we understand that Herodotus loosely correlated the north with Europe and the south with Asia. Unlike modern geographers, who split these two continents along the axis of the Ural Mountains, Herodotus followed Greek tradition by using the Euxine (Black) Sea, Lake Maeotis (modern Sea of Azov), and the river he knew as the Araxes[a] (perhaps the modern Syr-Darya) to form their boundary. This meant that for Herodotus, Europe occupied the northern half of the *oikoumenē*, stretching from the Pillars of Herakles (Straits of Gibraltar) in the west to unknown parts in the east; the southern half was made up of Asia, or Asia and Libya together, since Herodotus leaves unresolved the question of whether or how those two landmasses were to be distinguished (see 2.16). If the *Histories* portrays a continuing conflict between Europe and Asia, as its first five chapters might suggest, then Herodotus conceived that battle as being fought along north–south, not east–west, lines of demarcation.

§9. The most prominent synapses between Europe and Asia, in Greek eyes, were the Hellespont (modern Dardanelles) and the Bosporus, and these straits figure prominently in some of the most important episodes of the *Histories*. Darius spans the Bosporus with a pontoon bridge (4.87–89) to invade Scythia, and Xerxes more famously bridges the Hellespont (7.33–37) to invade Greece. Both campaigns turn out badly for the Persians, a pattern perhaps leading the reader to the conclusion drawn by Themistokles, that "the gods and heroes take it ill that one man should rule over both Europe and Asia" (8.109). But Herodotus does not permit us to make such formulations easily or without complication. Indeed in one geographic discussion he calls into question the very notion of continental divisions, "since all the earth is one land" (4.45)—so why should it not have one ruler? Such are the complexities and internal contradictions one needs to confront when entering the vast treasure-house of the *Histories*.

James Romm
James H. Ottaway Jr. Associate Professor of Classics
Bard College
Annandale-on-Hudson, NY

D.8a Herodotus uses the name Araxes for both the Armenian river, which flows into the Caspian Sea, and probably also the Jaxartes (modern Syr-Darya), which flows into the Aral Sea. Since later ancient writers frequently confused the Tanais (modern Don) River with the Jaxartes, it is possible that Herodotus refers here to the Tanais River.

APPENDIX E
Herodotus and the Black Sea Region

Greeks on the Black Sea

§1. Herodotus' fifth-century account of Scythia[a] (4.1–144) provides the earliest (preserved) detailed treatment of the geography and peoples of the present Bulgaria, Romania, Ukraine, south Russia, and Georgia, but Greeks since the late eighth century had been aware of the Black Sea area, including some items in Herodotus' account. The Cimmerians[b] and the voyage of Jason's *Argo* through the Clashing Rocks at the mouth of the Euxine (Black) Sea[c] appear in Homer's *Odyssey*. Hesiod (c. 700) mentions both the Ister (modern Danube)[d] and a Phasis River,[e] and the Corinthian[f] poet Eumelus (c. 700) names a land called Colchis,[g] although it is debatable whether these poets already knew the precise locations later associated with these names. Indeed the Spartan poet Alkman (late seventh century) referred to the horse of the Scythian Colaxaïs (4.4) and to the Issedones (4.13, 4.16, 4.25–27).

§2. Although eighth-century Greek exploration and trade in the Black Sea region cannot be ruled out, verifiable Greek colonization there belongs to the larger phenomenon of new settlements that were established in Chalcidice, Thrace,[a] and the Propontis (modern Sea of Marmara)[b] in the seventh and sixth centuries. Pottery finds suggest that the first settlements in both the Propontis and the Black Sea were roughly simultaneous in the second half of the seventh century. Miletus,[c] an Ionian city, established the greatest number of these colonies, initially as trading centers at the mouths of major rivers.[d] Then, during the first forty years of the sixth century, Miletus expanded her existing colonies and created new ones on the western Black Sea coast, on the eastern coast of the Crimea,[e] and on the eastern coast of Lake Maeotis (modern

E.1a Scythia: Map E.2, AX.
E.1b Cimmerians, possible location of territory: Map E.2, AY.
E.1c Euxine (Black) Sea: Map E.2.
E.1d Ister (modern Danube) River: Map E.2, AX.
E.1e Phasis River: Map E.2, BY.
E.1f Corinth: Map E.1.
E.1g Colchis: Map E.2, BY.
E.1h Issedones: possibly a mythical group of nomads, located in ancient writings somewhere in what is now Kazakhstan.
E.2a Chalcidice, Thrace: Map E.1.
E.2b Propontis: Map E.2, BX.
E.2c Miletus: Map E.1.
E.2d These Milesian colonies (with coordinates for Map

E.2 and approximate dates) are: Borysthenes (Olbia?) (675–650), AX, on the estuary of the Hypanis and Borysthenes (modern Bug and Dnieper) Rivers; Histria (c. 630), AX, south of the Ister's mouth; and Kremnoi (Taganrog, now submerged; 650–625), AY, west of the Tanais (modern Don) River's mouth. Apollonia (Sozopol, Bulgaria), BX, is slightly later. On the Turkish coast Sinope, BY, and Amisus (Samsun), BY, also Milesian foundations, yield pottery dated just after 600. Trapezus (Trabzon), BY, 250 miles east of Sinope and according to Xenophon a Sinopean foundation, has produced no Archaic Greek pottery despite a foundation date of 756 in a late literary source.
E.2e Crimea: Map E.2, AX.

Sea of Azov).[f] Milesian expansion waned in the second half of the sixth century, only to be supplemented by new settlements from other cities.[g] By Herodotus' time Greek cities and trade both between them and with native populations were well established on all shores of the Black Sea. Some of these trade routes were quite extensive.[h]

§3. Athenian familiarity with the Black Sea world came from Athens' activities in the Hellespont, Thrace, and the Thracian Chersonese[a] beginning in the mid-sixth century. The motif of Scythian archers on Athenian pottery in this period reached the peak of its popularity around 510–500. Whether such "Scythians" depict real Scythians as Athenian mercenaries or constitute a common "uniform" of archers in contemporary colonial warfare can be debated, but at some point after the Persian Wars, Athens did establish a police force of Scythian archers, which functioned into the early fourth century.[b] In addition, references to the Hyperboreans, somewhere north or northeast of the Scythians in Herodotus' account, appear in fifth-century Athenian comedies. But Pericles' Pontic expedition (c. 437), known to Plutarch and ignored by Thucydides, prefaced further Athenian ventures in the Black Sea (mid-420s). Herodotus (7.147.2) reports grain shipments through the Bosporus[c] in 480 headed for Aegina and the Peloponnese.[d] A date for the beginning of similar Athenian imports of Black Sea grain, evident at the end of the Peloponnesian War, is still debated. From all this activity, we can be sure that Herodotus' account of Scythia hardly exposed an area totally unknown to Athenians and other Greeks.

Herodotus' Autopsy of the Black Sea?

§4. Many believe that Herodotus visited Olbia[a] c. 450 or slightly later, but no scholarly consensus exists on the question, and Herodotus himself left the matter ambiguous. Clearly his detailed knowledge decreases the farther his narratives depart from Olbia. For example, specific tribal names (Kallipidai, Alazones) eventually yield to generic ethnic descriptions (Maneaters, Black Cloaks). Herodotus concedes as much (4.13–15, 416) when, for data on the interior and farther reaches of Scythia, he cites Aristeas of Proconnesus' poem *Armiaspea* (variously dated c. 475 or c. 550) and certain accounts of Greek traders who had journeyed as far as "the bald men"

E.2f New colonies on the western Black Sea coast (all shown on, and with coordinates for, Map E.2) are: Olbia, AX; Tyras (earlier called Ophioussa [?]; Belogorod-Dnestrovsky), AX, at the mouth of the Tyras (modern Dniester) River; Tomis (Constantia), AX; and Odessus (Varna), BX. On the eastern Crimean coast (all shown on Map E.2, inset): Pantikapaion (Kerch), Myrmekion, Tyritake, Nymphaion, and Theodosia. And on the eastern coast of Lake Maeotis, on and near the Taman peninsula, Kepoi and Hermonassa (Taman), Map E.2, inset, a joint foundation with Mytilene (Map E.1). Milesian contacts with Colchis from the mid-sixth century eventually produced fifth-century colonies at Dioscurias (Suchumi), Gyenos, and Phasis (Poti), all at Map E.2, BY.

E.2g Later colonies not founded by Miletus (with dates and coordinates for Map E.2): Kerkinitis (later Eupatoria), AX, on the western Crimean coast, also originally Ionian (mother-city unknown), Phanagoria, on the Taman Peninsula, was founded c. 542 by Teos (Map E.1). Peloponnesian Megara, (Map E.1),

founder of Byzantium, BX, c. 600 and Mesembria (Nesebur, Bulgaria; sixth century), BX, introduced a Doric element to Black Sea settlements. The Megarian colony Heraclea Pontica (Eregli, Turkey), BX, established in 554, in turn became the mother-city of Callatis (Romania), BX, south of Tomis, c. 525–500? and re-founded Chersonese, BX, (the sixth-century Ionian settlement of) on the southwestern Black Sea coast in the late 420s.

E.2h For example, Olbia marked the terminus of a Greek-Scythian trade route that ran up the Ingul River (the southernmost tributary of the Bug [ancient Hypanis]), then east across the middle Dnieper (ancient Borysthenes), Don (ancient Tanais), and Volga to the Urals and on into Central Asia.

E.3a Hellespont, Thrace, Thracian Chersonese: Map E.1.

E.3b See Figure N.3, a depiction of a Scythian archer.

E.3c Bosporus: Map E.2.

E.3d Aegina, Peloponnese: Map E.1.

E.4a Olbia: Map E.2, AX.

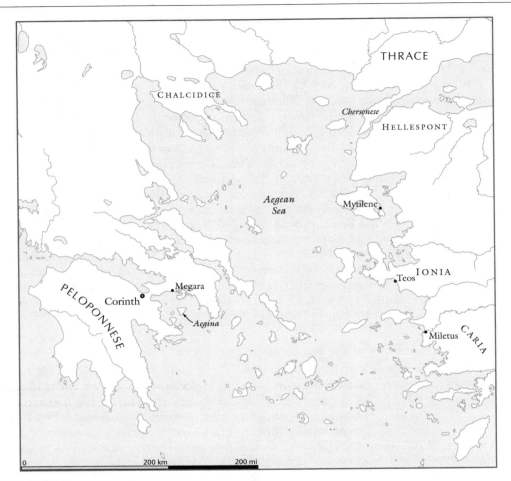

MAP E.1

(4.24.1). The navigability of the Borysthenes upstream for ten (4.53.4) or eleven (4.18.2) days' sail probably reflects what he learned from traders rather than Herodotus' personal experience. Indeed Herodotus' notions of the Black Sea's measurements, including his much exaggerated Lake Maeotis (4.85), and of Negroid Colchians, connected to the Egyptian conquests of the legendary pharaoh Sesostris (2.102–105) can be easily assailed, although these accounts need not be tied to autopsy. Inconsistencies between his two overviews of Scythia (4.16–58, 4.99–117) surely indicate the use of different sources. Nevertheless, the frequent criticism that Herodotus ignored the Greek cities of the Black Sea can be excused in part, as these settlements did not figure significantly in his major theme of east–west conflict. He was aware of other Greek trading posts with the Scythians (4.24.1) besides Olbia,

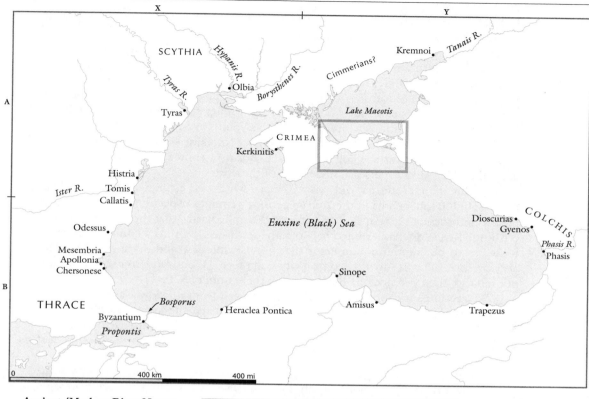

Map E.2

Ancient/Modern River Names

Ister River = modern Danube
Tyras River = modern Dniester
Hypanis River = modern Bug
Borysthenes River = modern Dnieper
Tanais River = modern Don

and mentioned the Black Sea cities of Histria,[b] Sinope,[c] and even Kremnoi[d] west of the Tanais (modern Don) River's mouth.[e]

§5. Traces of autopsy such as Herodotus' description of Herakles' footprint at the Tyras (modern Dniester) River[a] (4.82) or the Cimmerian tomb still visible in his time beside the Tyras (4.11.4) can be deceptive, since these eyewitness observations may belong to Herodotus' source(s). Even more problematic are the supposed remains of Darius I's eight forts built about eight miles apart along the Oaros River (4.124.1), a stream variously interpreted as the Volga River, the Borysthenes (modern Dnieper), or the Buzau, a tributary of the Ister (modern Danube); see also Araros River, 4.48.2, a variant spelling of Oaros?). Again, a source's report seems more likely than Herodotus' personal inspection of these sites.

§6. But if Herodotus did visit Olbia, which is estimated to have had 5,000–10,000 inhabitants in the archaic period, we might expect him to give a more precise and accurate description of this city. When he writes that the Hypanis (modern Bug) River[a] discharges into the Borysthenes instead of into a common estuary, he seems to be committing an error that no eyewitness would make (4.53.5). He also says that Olbia is surrounded by a city wall (4.78.4), but modern excavations do not indicate the existence of a defensive wall there until c. 370.

§7. Herodotus mentions information he received from a fellow Carian,[a] Tymnes (a fairly common Carian name), who formerly had been the agent at Olbia of the Scythian king Ariapeithes (d. 475–460), but their meeting need not have occurred at Olbia (4.76.6). Tymnes, whom many scholars consider Herodotus' chief source for Scythians and Scythia, is probably responsible for the tales of fifth-century Scythian regal history (4.78–80); if so, Tymnes also told Herodotus about both the city wall at Olbia, which is not archaeologically attested, and also a story about the Scythian sage Anacharsis (4.76–77), who is certainly a mythical figure. Herodotus describes a salty spring at Exampaios (site uncertain) between the Hypanis and Borysthenes, which allegedly turned the whole lower Hypanis River brackish (4.52.3, 4.81.2). At 4.81.2—a statement whose validity is much disputed among commentators—he also seems to say that he saw a cauldron of incredible size and impossible manufacture. But this supposed proof of autopsy is compromised by the final sentence of 4.81.6, where he writes that he reports what he *heard*. Herodotus had good sources for Scythian customs, as is reported below, but the evidence is inconclusive, if not negative, that he ever actually visited Olbia or other areas of the Black Sea.

Herodotus on Scythian Customs

§8. Archaeology illustrates, often dramatically, Herodotus' general accuracy about many Scythian customs, even if the material evidence does not always derive from the area he called Scythia.

§9. *Burial Customs.* Embalming corpses (4.71.1) to preserve the deceased's remains in the forty-day period before interment finds confirmation in one of the "frozen" burials at Pazyryk in the Altai Mountains (fifth to third centuries). The "royal" burial in

E.4b	Histria: Map E.2, AX. See 2.33.4, 4.78.1.
E.4c	Sinope: Map E.2, BY. See 1.76.1, 2.34.2, 4.12.2.
E.4d	Kremnoi: Map E.2, AY. See 4.20.2, 4.110.2.
E.4e	Tanais River: Map E.2, AY.
E.5a	Tyras River: Map E.2, AX.
E.6a	Hypanis River: Map E.2, AX.
E.7a	Caria: Map E.1.

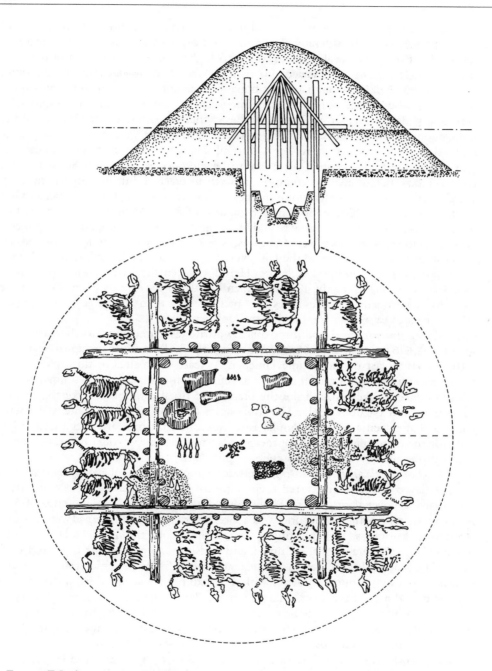

FIGURE E.1. AN ARCHAEOLOGICAL DIAGRAM OF THE ROYAL SCYTHIAN KURGAN (TOMB MOUND) AT KOSTROMSKAYA STANICA, ILLUSTRATING THE BURIAL OF MANY HORSES.

kurgan #5 contains a female whose skull has been trepanned, and both the male and female bodies reveal the stitching after removal of organs and muscles.[a] Excavations in the 1980s at the huge royal kurgan (20 meters high) at Chertomlyk, west of the large bend of the lower Dnieper (ancient Borysthenes), revealed a foundation fence around the exterior base of the mound and the bones of nine horses and human remains along the edge of the mound. These remains suggested to the excavators confirmation of Herodotus' description, at 4.72, of how the Scythians surrounded the exterior of the burial mound with fifty horses and fifty servants, all strangled, gutted, and subsequently impaled to appear as erect riders. The Chertomlyk kurgan, however, belongs to the second half of the fourth century—too late to be Herodotus' model for Scythian royal burials. Horse burials are also common in Scythian practice, but the large number of slaughtered horses which Herodotus implies do not occur in the Tiasmin (ancient Gerros?) River region, which some consider the area of Royal Scythian burials in the first half of the fifth century. For the sixth and fifth centuries massive horse burials in princely kurgans belong to the northwest Caucasus, where sixteen to twenty-four horse skeletons appear in some burials and the Ulski kurgan (15 meters high), south of the Kuban River, features over 400 horse skeletons. Herodotus seems to have transferred a northwest Caucasus practice to the Royal Scythian burials on the Gerros River. Only in the late fifth and fourth centuries does this practice appear in the huge royal kurgans erected in the area of the great bend of the Dnieper River.

§10. *Cannibalism.* Herodotus explicitly attributes cannibalism to the Maneaters (4.18.3, 4.106), a people that some identify with the Sula River group of Scythian-related culture east of the middle Dnieper. At least seven sites of this group show unbroken human bones mixed in kitchen refuse with cut and broken animal bones. This evidence is taken to indicate the practice of ritual cannibalism like that of the Massagetai and Issedones, who Herodotus says (1.216.2–3, 4.26.1) ate males who had reached extreme old age. Similar ritualistic cannibalism is attested archaeologically for the Sauromatai of the southern Urals and the lower Volga River, as well as Iranian tribes in the Kazakhstan steppe.

§11. *Scalping and Headhunting.* Herodotus reports (4.64) that Scythians scalped and/or flayed enemies, converted their skin into handkerchiefs or cloaks, and used fingernails to cover their quivers. Skulls could be molded into drinking cups (4.65). Scythian scalping achieved notoriety, as a Greek verb for scalping, *aposkythizo*, is first attested in Euripides. Headhunting is also attributed to the Tauri (4.103.3), who inhabited the mountains of the Crimea, and is also found among the Celts and Germans. The practice is also seen in Scythian art. A belt from the cemetery at Tli in the Caucasus[a] shows a mounted warrior with a human head suspended from the reins of his horse, and a gold cap from a kurgan at Kurdzhips, near a southern tributary of the Kuban River, depicts a Scythian carrying a head to another Scythian.[b] Indeed, at Belsk on the Vorskla River, which some believe is Herodotus' joint city of the Boudini and Geloni (4.108–109), the remains of a workshop for converting skulls into drinking bowls was found. Use of enemy skulls as drinking vessels can be seen as a steppe tradition. The practice is also attributed to the Bulgars in Byzantine sources.

E.9a   Rolle 31, figures 13–14; see Appendix E Bibliography.
E.11a Rolle 81, figure 58; see Appendix E Bibliography.
E.11b Minns 223, figure 126; Rolle 82, figure 59. See Appendix E Bibliography.

§12. *Scythian Use of Intoxicants.* Herodotus describes (4.75.1–2) Scythians "getting high" from the vapor of burning hemp inside a small tent. Again, the frozen tombs of the eastern Scythian culture at Pazyryk in the Altai confirm his account. Sets of portable hash parlors occur in the tombs: a frame of six poles (about four feet) tied at the top, to be covered with felt or leather rugs, bronze cauldrons, and bags of hemp seeds or melilot seeds, which also have intoxicating properties. Occurrence of this paraphernalia in tombs alongside other grave goods of daily life suggests that hemp use was not limited to funerary ritual. A certain continuity of steppe culture is also evident, as hashish and opium are found in Sarmatian Alan tombs north of the Caucasus. A Scythian passion for wine, which, unlike the Greeks, they consumed without diluting it with water (6.84), finds confirmation in the number of Greek amphorae found at Scythian sites. A Scythian reputation for drunkenness appears already in the lyric poet Anacreon (fl. 550).

§13. *Rabbit Hunt on Horseback.* The impromptu Scythian pursuit of a rabbit when Persian and Scythian armies were in proximity to each other during Darius I's Scythian campaign (4.134) is more than a curious tale. A Scythian rabbit hunt on horseback is illustrated on a fourth-century gold plaque[a] from the kurgan at Kul'-Oba near Kerch in the Crimea and may indicate a favorite Scythian sport, resembling somewhat the furious equestrian game called *buskashi* still played among riders in Central Asia today.

Everett L. Wheeler
Department of Classical Studies
Duke University
Durham, NC

Bibliography

Greeks on the Black Sea

Bäbler, B. "Bobbies or Boobies? The Scythian Police Force in Classical Athens." In D. Braund, ed., *Scythians and Greeks* (2005), 114–122.

Boardman, J. *The Greeks Overseas* (1999).

Braund, D. "Pericles, Cleon and the Pontus: The Black Sea at Athens c. 440–421." In D. Braund, ed., *Scythians and Greeks* (2005), 80–99.

Grammenos, D., and E. Petropoulos, eds. *Ancient Greek Colonies in the Black Sea.* 2 vols. (2003).

Ivanchik, I. "Who Were the 'Scythian' Archers on Archaic Attic Vases?" In D. Braund, ed., *Scythians and Greeks* (2005), 100–113.

Tsetskhladze, G. "Greek Penetration of the Black Sea." In G. Tsetskhladze and F. De Angelis, eds., *The Archaeology of Greek Colonisation: Essays Dedicated to Sir John Boardman* (1994), 111–135.

Herodotus' Autopsy of the Black Sea?

Armayor, O. K. "Did Herodotus Ever Go to the Black Sea?" *Harvard Studies in Classical Philology* 82 (1978), 45–62.

_____. "Sesostris and Herodotus' Autopsy of Thrace, Colchis, Inland Asia Minor and the Levant." *Harvard Studies in Classical Philology* 84 (1980), 51–74.

Kryzhitskiy, S. "Olbia and the Scythians in the Fifth Century: The Scythian 'Protectorate.'" In D. Braund, ed., *Scythians and Greeks* (2005), 123–130.

Herodotus on Scythian Customs

Alekeyev, A. "Scythian Kings and 'Royal' Burial-Mounds of the Fifth and Fourth Centuries." In D. Braund, ed., *Scythians and Greeks* (2005), 39–55.

Chernenko, E. "Investigations of the Scythian Tumuli in the Northern Pontic Steppe." *Ancient Civilizations Scythia to Siberia* 1 (1994), 45–53.

Knauer, E. "Observations on the 'Barbarian' Custom of Suspending the Heads of Vanquished Enemies from the Neck of Horses." *Archäologische Mitteilungen aus Iran und Turan* 33 (2001), 283–332.

Minns, E. H. *Scythians and Greeks.* 2 vols. (1913).

Murphy, E., I. Gorkhman, Y. Christov, and L. Barkova. "Prehistoric Old World Scalping: New Cases from the Cemetery of Aymyrlyg, South Siberia." *American Journal of Archaeology* 106 (2002), 1–10.

Rolle, R. *The World of the Scythians,* tr. F. Walls (1989).

Pritchett, W. K. *The Liar School of Herodotus* (1993), 191–226.

Riedlberger, P. "Skalpieren bei den Skythen. Zu Herodot IV 64." *Klio* 78 (1996), 53–60.

Thordarson, F. "The Scythian Funeral Customs. Some Notes on Herodotus IV, 71–75." In *Barq-i Sabz (A Green Leaf): Papers in honour of Professor Jes P. Asmussen* (1988), 539–548.

E.13a This gold plaque is shown in the text as Figure 4.134 (Rolle 99, figure 71).

APPENDIX F

Rivers and Peoples of Scythia

§1. Rivers in Herodotus' account serve both as boundaries between peoples and as reference points for the location of various populations. Five of his eight Scythian rivers can be identified: the Ister is the modern Danube, the Tyras is the modern Dniester, the Hypanis is the modern Bug, the Borysthenes is the modern Dnieper, and the Tanais is the modern Don.[a] The Panticapes and Hypakyris Rivers cannot be convincingly situated on a modern map. A theory that Herodotus' Gerros is the Tiasmin River, a western tributary joining the Dnieper near Kremenchug, Ukraine, derives more from a concentration of Scythian settlements and finds in this area on the border of the forest and treeless steppe than from Herodotus' vague descriptions. His placement of the burial ground of Scythian kings in the land of the Gerroi (4.71.3) coincides with some princely burials in the area of what archaeologists identify as the "Tiasmin group" of Scythian culture, particularly the kurgan (burial mound) at Litoi-Melgunov (dated 575–500), the earliest known Scythian burial in the region Herodotus called Scythia. Yet a cultural mix in the area of the Tiasmin group is clear from a variance in burial practices: Scythians proper practiced inhumation, whereas cremation in the area is assigned to the group Herodotus called Scythian plowmen.

§2. Identification of material remains with peoples named in literary sources is a vexing problem for all archaeologists. Scythians belonged to that complex of Iranian-speaking peoples inhabiting the vast expanse of Central Asia between the Ural Mountains of Russia and Kazakhstan and the Altai Mountains of southern Siberia in the third and second millennia, including the ancestors of the Medes and the Persians and the forebears of the various tribes of Sacae (also Scythians) around the Aral Sea and the Jaxartes (modern Syr-Darya) and Oxus (modern Amu-Darya) rivers. Many of these peoples shared some common cultural traits, particularly the building of subterranean burial chambers topped by large mounds for members of their elite. But in the sixth century, Scythians chiefly inhabited the northern Cauca-

F.1a   These five rivers are shown on Map E.2.

756

sus, particularly around the Kuban River, and the migration of Scythians into southern Russia and the Ukraine was thus simultaneous with Greek settlements on the northern coasts of the Euxine (Black) Sea in the seventh and sixth centuries.

§3. In the tenth and ninth centuries, much of the treeless steppe of southern Russia and the northern Crimea seems to have been unoccupied. West of the Dnieper (ancient Borysthenes) River and south into Romanian Transylvania, the majority of the population in the ninth to fifth centuries was Thracian. The Agathyrsoi, whose territory lay west of Herodotus' Scythia and whose existence was first archaeologically attested in the sixth century, can be situated securely by their association with the Mures River (Herodotus' Maris: 4.48.1)[a] of northern Transylvania. Locations and cultural identities of Herodotus' Kallipidai, Alazones, and Scythian farmers are less archaeologically secure, but some believe them to be Thracians or a mixed Thracian-Scythian population tributary to the Royal Scythians. A cluster of settlements on the middle Dniester River (called the West Podolian group) shows affinities with the Tiasmin group, and the destruction of many West Podolian sites near the end of the sixth century may be related to Darius' Scythian campaign.

§4. Two eastern tributaries of the Dnieper featured other groups with ties to Scythian culture. The largest group, formed in the sixth century along the Ukraine's Sula River, constructed up to 450 kurgans and practiced ritualized cannibalism, so the Sula group must surely represent Herodotus' Maneaters. Farther south, along another eastern tributary of the Dnieper, the Vorskla River, a second group (or groups) likewise emerging in the sixth century created a massive settlement at Belsk, which was clearly a major trade and industrial center where Greek imports account for 20 percent of the pottery and about 2,000 burials are known. Some equate Belsk with the joint city of the Boudini and Geloni (4.108–109), although Darius' destruction of the city (4.123) is so far not part of the archaeological record there.

§5. East of the Vorskla group, in the basin of the Donets River near modern Kharkov, Ukraine, another "Scythian" group with some cultural affinities to the Maneaters of the Sula River resided from the sixth century. Some scholars have suggested, because of their location north of Herodotus' Royal Scythians, that this group was the Black Cloaks, but there can be no certainty. Beyond this point identification of cultural groups with Herodotus' various peoples east or north of Scythia becomes extremely hazardous. The only secure identification is that of the Sauromatai, a different Iranian group from the Scythians and first attested archaeologically in the sixth century. The Sauromatai extended from the area east of Lake Maeotis (modern Sea of Azov) and the lower Don (ancient Tanais) across the Volga River to the southern Urals in the fifth century. They had close cultural ties to the Scythians, whose burial mounds they often reused. The unique Sauromatian employment of female warriors, attested by arms and equipment in women's graves, suggests the mixture of the Iranian Sauromatai with a non-Iranian people tied to a matriarchal

F.3a The *Barrington Atlas* shows a label "Agathyrsoi" on Map 23, A1, almost 200 miles to the east of the Maris (modern Mures) River. The maps of this edition of the *Histories* that show the Agathyrsoi (Map 4.53, Crimea inset; Map 4.81; and Map 4.110, AX) have followed that atlas' identification. The Maris River is shown on Map 4.53, AX.

society. Stories of female Sauromatian warriors probably reinforced Greek tales about Amazons. Nevertheless, Herodotus' one-eyed Arimaspians (4.27), goat-footed men (4.25.1), and androgynous Enarees (4.67.2) may not be pure fabrications, as the severe physical deformities in 800 skeletons from a cemetery at Aimyrlyg[a] in southern Siberia (dated c. third to second centuries) demonstrate.

Everett L. Wheeler
Department of Classical Studies
Duke University
Durham, NC

Bibliography

Davis-Kimball, J., V. A. Bashilov, L.T. Yablonsky, eds. *Nomads of the Eurasian Steppes in the Early Iron Age* (1995).

Georges, P. "Darius in Scythia." *American Journal of Ancient History* 12 (1987 [1995]), 97–147.

Minns, E. H. *Scythians and Greeks*, 2 vols. (1913).

Murphy, E. "Herodotus and the Amazons Meet the Cyclops: Philology, Osteoarchaeology and the Eurasian Iron Age." In E. Sauer, ed., *Archaeology and Ancient History: Breaking Down the Boundaries* (2004), 169–184.

Murzin, V. "Key Points in Scythian History," in D. Braund, ed., *Scythians and Greeks* (2005), 33–38.

Sulimirski, T. "The Scyths." In *Cambridge History of Iran II* (1985), 149–199.

F.5a Aymyrlyg (also spelled Aimyrlyg) is on a southern tributary of the Khemchek River in the Tuva Republic (south Siberia) of the Russian Confederation. This general area contains many kurgans and Scythian cemeteries, which only over the past decade or two have attracted archaeologists.

APPENDIX G
The Continuity of Steppe Culture

§1. Herodotus had a vague notion of a general Scythian nation inhabiting the area from the Ister (modern Danube) River deep into Central Asia. His Scythians of Amyrium,[a] brigaded with the Baktrians in Xerxes' army in 480, were named Sacae because the Persians called all Scythians Sacae (7.64.2). Herodotus' view reflects rival generic ethnic terms: Greeks called the Iranians north of the Euxine (Black) Sea and in the Aral Sea area Scythians, whereas for the Persians they were Sacae. According to Herodotus (4.6.1), the Scythians called themselves Scoloti. References to Scythians in Akkadian and Hebrew sources complement the Greek and permit reconstruction of the original ethnic as Skuda. The root appears in various Scythian names: Skuka, Scyles, Scilurus, and Scolopitus.

§2. Darius I's trilingual inscription at Behistun (in modern Iran)[a] describing his rise to power and early campaigns includes an expedition (520/19) against the "Saka haumavarga" (*hauma*- or *haoma*-drinking Sacae) and the "Saka tigraxauda" (Sacae wearing pointed caps). The latter, with their king Skukam, are depicted on the Behistun monument. *Hauma* was an intoxicating beverage of debated origin, possibly used to increase a warrior's ferocity in battle, but also consumed in the religious rituals of the Persian Magi. A much later inscription of Darius' from Persepolis refers to the "Saka paradarya" (Sacae beyond the sea), the Scythians north of the Black Sea. Scythians/Sacae east of the Aral Sea and along the Oxus (modern Amu-Darya) and Jaxartes (modern Syr-Darya) rivers represented a security threat to the Persian empire's northeastern frontier. Here Cyrus the Great died fighting the Massagetai (1.201–214), whose name, like Scythians and Sacae, is a generic term for barbarian peoples of northern Asia. Herodotus described them (1.215–216) as non-Scythians with Scythian customs.

§3. The unity of Scythian culture for tribes in the area between the western Ukraine and southern Siberia has been much debated. It would seem that a common Scythian culture binding together tribes from the Danube to the Altai over

G.1a Amyrium (Amyrgion): location of territory unknown. But since these Scythians are brigaded with the Baktrians, we have to assume a location east of the Aral Sea or in the obscurities of Central Asia. Herodotus mentions the Sacae of Amyrgion at 7.64.2.

G.2a For more on the Behistun inscriptions, see Appendix M, Herodotus on Persia and the Persian Empire, §2 and n. M.2b.

many centuries is neither likely nor realistic. Geographic locations, interaction of Scythian newcomers with native peoples and their traditions, and changes in technological and artistic preferences over time speak against any unified Scythian culture. A search for the origin of the so-called Scythian animal style in art has only complicated the issue. The dramatic discoveries in southern Siberia since the 1970s, of the royal burial mound at Arzhan (Tuva Republic, Russian Federation; c. ninth to eighth centuries) and the frozen burials 300 miles west at Pazyryk in the Altai Mountains (c. fifth to third centuries), reinforce the case for a common origin of many Scythian customs. The many specific and local variations do not refute some commonalities regardless of ethnicity. For example, Scythians practiced inhumation of the dead with weapons in a central subterranean chamber topped by a mound (kurgan), although structural details and rites could vary in different areas of Scythian culture and change over time. The eighth-century royal burial at Arzhan featuring a low stone-covered mound differs dramatically from the lofty royal kurgans of the fourth century north of the Black Sea, which could be 20 meters high and covered exclusively with rich black soil often imported from elsewhere.

§4. With due caution, one can construct an Iranian thought-world, of which the Scythians formed a part. The modern Ossetians of the central Caucasus, direct descendants of the Sarmatian Alans, speak an Iranian dialect. Their customs and folklore provide some insights into Scythian practices. Likewise, the Avesta, the holy book of Zoroastrianism (despite the sixth-century A.D. date of its earliest extant written form), reflects early Iranian thought and religious concepts, which can be further supplemented by fragments of religious texts in northeastern Iranian dialects. Herodotus' Scythian account of their origin (4.5–7), rather than pure fiction, is related to material in the Avesta, and the Greek account of the Scythians as the offspring of Herakles and a snake goddess (4.8–10) combines Greek myth with a legged snake goddess prominent in Scythian art.[a]

§5. From the Scythians to the Mongols, steppe culture was based on the horse. Scythian sacrifice of horses (4.61.2)—as well as their consumption of horse meat at funerary feasts—had a limited parallel in Persian sacrifice of horses annually at the tomb of Cyrus the Great. The pastoralism practiced by the Scythians and later peoples involved herds of horses, cattle, and sheep, supplemented by agriculture in river valleys. Scythians knew bronze and iron working, produced their own pottery, and could develop settlements. To view them as nomads constantly on the move is a gross and incorrect generalization. Political alliances and confederations of tribes tended to be quite fluid. Bad harvests, exhausted grazing lands, increases in population, drought, and pressure from other steppe peoples all influenced stability.

G.4a   See Figure 4.9 for a representation of the Scythian
         snake goddess.

§6. Perhaps the most that can be said is that there are scattered parallels between certain practices of Scythian culture as reported by Herodotus and/or attested by archaeology, and practices of some of the later cultures that inhabited the same region,[a] but any concept of a unified Scythian culture, or of the continuity of steppe culture, must allow for numerous differences in detail both geographically and chronologically.

Everett L. Wheeler
Department of Classical Studies
Duke University
Durham, NC

Bibliography

Bokovenko, N. "Asian Influence on European Scythia." *Ancient Civilizations from Scythia to Siberia* 3 (1996), 97–122.

Ivantchik, A. "Une légend sur l'origine des Scythes (*Herodotus* IV, 5–7) et le problème des sources du Scythicos logos d'Hérodote." *Revue des études grecques* 112 (1999), 141–192.

Maenchen-Helfen, O. *The World of the Huns* (1973).

Ustinova, Y. "Lycanthropy in Sarmatian Warrior Societies: the Kobyakovo torque," *Ancient West & East* 1 (2002), 102–123.

G.6a   See nn. 4.61.2a, 4.72.5a, 4.75.1a, and 4.105.2a.

APPENDIX H

The Ionian Revolt

§1. The Persian Empire was vast, and not surprisingly, when one considers the distances and the means of communication, there were frequent revolts, especially on the periphery. The most notable example is the satrapy of Egypt[a] incorporated in the 520s but in revolt for about 80 of its 190 years of Persian rule. India[b] (that is, the valley of the River Indus), incorporated by Darius (4.44), disappeared from the lists of subject peoples at some time unknown to us. From 499 to 494 the Greeks of Asia Minor were in revolt. This, the so-called Ionian Revolt, was by comparison dealt with easily enough and was in itself of no great importance to the Persians, though it had a very important consequence for the Greeks of mainland Greece: it delayed the Persian invasion of Greece, giving the Greeks precious time.

§2. Herodotus is our only full source for this revolt. Thucydides (*Thucydides* 4.102.2) mentions the attempt of Aristagoras, the leader of the revolt, to found a city in Thrace when it was clear to him that further resistance would be of no avail, and a fragment of Diodorus (*Histories* 10.25.4) provides valuable information about the role of Hekataios[a] at the end of the revolt; the fragment of a late historian provided by Plutarch[b] is generally, and rightly, discounted. We have to make what we can out of Herodotus, whose reception by scholars has been varied, ranging from despairing acceptance to blatant disbelief, especially with regard to his account of the start of the revolt (5.28–38).

§3. The revolt was, he claims, due to Aristagoras, the ruler of Miletus,[a] who, having failed in his attempt to restore exiles to the island of Naxos[b] despite Persian assistance, and so being afraid that the Persians would take reprisals against him, set Ionia[c] in revolt. The whole story is quite unsatisfactory.

A. The commander of the Persian force, Megabates, was a first cousin of King Darius. Yet at 5.33.4 Herodotus has Aristagoras address him in a wholly incredible fashion and not suffer punishment: "Were you not sent by Artaphrenes to obey me and to sail wherever I order you to go?" Speaking in

H.1a Egypt: Map H, locator.
H.1b India: Map H, locator.
H.2a Hekataios: author in the late sixth century of geographical and historical accounts of Asia Minor and the East, and a source used by Herodotus. He also plays a role in Herodotus' account of Ionian history. See 5.36, 5.125–126, and 6.137.
H.2b Plutarch, "On the Malice of Herodotus," *Moralia* 861 B and C.
H.3a Miletus: Map H, BY.
H.3b Naxos: Map H, BY.
H.3c Ionia: Map H, BY.

Map H

that manner to such a high-ranking Persian would have led immediately to severe punishment; yet Herodotus would have us believe that Aristagoras did so and got away with it.

B. Then, to spite Aristagoras, Megabates seeks to sabotage the whole campaign against Naxos by sending a message forewarning the Naxians of the impending attack, whereupon they bring their animals and other possessions into the city from the countryside, lay up stores of food and drink, and strengthen the walls. Thus the city is able to endure a siege of four months. This is a wildly unsatisfactory story. The sabotaging message was sent to Naxos from Chios,[a] a distance of about eighty miles, thus, a voyage of not many hours, far too little time for the Naxians to get themselves into a condition to withstand a four-month siege. But the main difficulty in Herodotus' story lies in the conduct of Megabates. The King had at the very least given his blessing to the expedition and the employment of Persian forces, and anyone who sabotaged such an operation had nothing to expect other than the most severe punishment. If Megabates wanted to deal with Aristagoras, the action attributed to him in Herodotus' account could not have been taken with impunity. Megabates had other ways of getting back at Aristagoras.

§4. Herodotus' description of the start of the revolt does not stand up to scrutiny, and his whole account of the revolt is open to three main lines of attack.

A. It is far too personal. Aristagoras was the leader, and his motives may have been self-seeking, but there must have been some organization involving a large number of people. Herodotus speaks of Aristagoras' taking council with "supporters" (5.36.1). These may or may not have been only his supporters within Miletus, but Herodotus says that after the decision to revolt was made, a man was sent to the fleet still assembled at Myous,[a] where by trickery he succeeded in arresting a number of the Greek commanders; and that after that various tyrants throughout Ionia were expelled or arrested. All this must have been part of a wide conspiracy which would have been carefully planned and prepared well in advance.[b] There certainly was much more to the revolt than Herodotus lets on. Aristagoras may or may not have been a self-seeking adventurer, but what of the rest? They were risking their lives and the peace of their cities. What were their motives? Herodotus does not discuss the question.

B. Herodotus knew a lot about the Persians, and without the information he provides we would be sadly in the dark. However, he fails to understand the institutions and spirit of this oriental monarchy. For instance, he has Darius come to the throne through a bit of horseplay (3.85–6)—a nice story, but that was not how a bearer of the blood royal acceded to the throne. Most remarkably, in connection with the end of the Ionian Revolt—the settlement

H.3.Ba Chios: Map H, BY.
H.4.Aa Myous: Map H, BY.

H.4.Ab The decision to revolt: see 5.36.4, 5.37, and 5.38.

of 492—Herodotus writes, "what Mardonios now did was to depose all the tyrants of the Ionians and establish democracies in their cities" (6.43.3, 6.43.4), adding that this report would come as a very great surprise to those Greeks who did not accept that Otanes had expressed the opinion that it was necessary for the Persians to be ruled in a democracy. He refers to the debate on forms of government held, he claimed, by the Seven Persian Conspirators (3.80–2). It is true that the debate is of great interest to us as the earliest recorded formal discussion of such a topic, but it was evidently received with skepticism by some Greeks, and rightly so. A debate of that sort in such circumstances is quite improbable and indeed ludicrous. But Herodotus evidently found it all perfectly credible in a kingdom where the blood of King Cyrus was essential in a claimant, and where the Persians were dispersed over vast distances and elections and assemblies were impossible. Apparently, he thought of this oriental world as if it were a Greek city-state; he did not understand what he was talking about. No wonder he could talk as he did about Megabates and the attack on Naxos.

C. Herodotus' attitude toward the revolt is curious. He constantly treats it as a hopeless venture. Instead of seeing it as a wonderful opportunity for the Greeks of Asia to be free of Persian rule, an opportunity missed at least in part because the mainland Greeks failed to give proper support, he sees it as the start of evils for the Ionians;[a] the Spartans had the sense to stay clear of the whole business, whereas the Athenians[b] let themselves be gulled by Aristagoras and were drawn into a mess (5.97.2).

Now, it must be conceded that the revolt could never have succeeded. History shows that the defense of Ionia depended on naval power. The Athenian navy kept Ionia free through much of the fifth century, and Persia regained control only when Athenian naval power was greatly diminished. However, in 499 the leading part in any fleet assembled by the Persians was played by Phoenicians,[c] and the Phoenicians, despite having heavier ships, could at that date outrow and outmaneuver the best of Greeks. The battle of Lade[d] in 494 (6.8–17) proved it; the Greeks had been specially trained to confront the Phoenician methods of naval battle, but they were not equal to either the training or the actual conflict. Not until the Athenians had practiced and developed their skills were they a match for the Phoenicians. In that way the revolt was indeed a hopeless venture.

Herodotus, however, was in no position to make this sober appraisal. His accounts of the naval engagements of the invasion of Greece in 480 show that he had an inadequate grasp of naval warfare. The Athenian tactic of the *diekplous* ("sailing through") was not fully developed until the Peloponnesian War, for when the Athenian general Kimon went out on the Eurymedon campaign (469?), he imitated the Phoenician battle tactic and crowded his ships

H.4.Ca The revolt as the start of evils for the Ionians: see 5.28, 5.30.1; 6.3.
H.4.Cb Sparta and Athens: Map H, BX.
H.4.Cc Phoenicia: Map H, locator. The superior Phoenician rowing skills: 8.10.1; 7.179–82
H.4.Cd Lade: Map H, BY.

with marines.[c] Herodotus showed no understanding of how and why the battle of Salamis[f] was a freak. With his insistence on "ramming," we are left thinking that the tactics of 480 were much the same as those of 431, and Herodotus could have seen no reason why Greek naval forces should not have succeeded during the Ionian Revolt.

Why, then, did Herodotus treat the Ionian Revolt as hopeless? He was not alone. Hekataios of Miletus had taken a pessimistic view (5.36), and Herodotus may have been influenced by that. Also his native city, Halicarnassus,[g] is conspicuously absent from his account of the revolt. It must have declined to join in, and Halicarnassians may have sought to justify themselves by treating the revolt as a hopeless venture. So might the Samians,[h] in whom Herodotus seems to have been especially interested, who ran away and may have sought to excuse their conduct by arguing that the revolt could never have succeeded. Others also, among the Ionian cities, no doubt had much to say that may have impressed Herodotus.

But there was perhaps another influence on Herodotus' thinking, namely, isolationist opinion in mainland Greece, especially in Athens. When Herodotus speaks of Persian motives for invading Greece, two strands are discernible. On the one hand, the Persians are moved by a desire for universal conquest (see also 7.11.3, 7.19.1), the common motive of imperial power. On the other, the view is constantly represented that if only the Athenians had not sent ships to assist the Ionians in revolt, Persia would not have attacked mainland Greece;[i] for those who took this view, Sparta had the good sense to keep out, while the Athenians had been deceived into supporting the Ionians (5.97.2). As to who among the Athenians took this view and influenced Herodotus, one could conjecture that it was the Alkmeonid family, for whom Herodotus displays some partiality (see also his notice of the parentage of Pericles "the lion" at 6.131) when at 6.121 he gives his oblique answer to the question of whether the Alkmeonids were in treacherous communication with the Persians at Marathon.

H.4.Ce	See Plutarch, *Kimon*, 12.2.
H.4.Cf	Salamis: Map H, BX. In the Persian Wars the Phoenicians fought their sea battles by packing their ships with marines (7.184.2), sailing through the enemy line (the *diekplous* maneuver), turning quickly, and by superior oarsmanship coming alongside, tying up to the enemy ship, then boarding and fighting it out on deck. By this tactic, fighting ships were captured, and it is clear that the Ionians tried to imitate the Phoenicians at the battle of Lade in 4.94 (6.15). Ramming was also not employed at the battles off Artemision in 480, as can be seen from the accounts of those engagements (8.11, 8.16–18).

At Salamis, however, both Greek and Persian ships (at least Artemisia's) are found ramming each other and ships were sunk or at least holed and rendered helplessly unmaneuverable if they remained afloat—but they were not captured (8.84.1, 8.87.4, 8.90.2, 8.92). This change of tactics was perhaps imposed on the combatants because so many ships were deployed in the constricted waters of the Salamis channel that traditional maneuvers became impossible. Later, possibly not long before the Peloponnesian War broke out in 431, the Athenians developed their own form of *diekplous* with ramming. Thucydides' account of the battle of Sybota (*Thucydides* 1.49) shows that most Greek states were still fighting in the "old-fashioned way." The success of ramming at the battle of Salamis may have pointed the way to the future, but from Kimon's tactics at the Eurymedon in 469 (?), it is clear that no one realized it until later. The battle of Salamis was, and long remained, a unique example of naval tactics until perhaps the battles in Syracuse Harbor of 413.

H.4.Cg	Halicarnassus: Map H, BY.
H.4.Ch	Samos: Map H, BY. Herodotus' interest in the Samians: 3.60, 6.13.1, and 6.14.2–3.
H.4.Ci	The argument that Athenian support for the Ionion Revolt led to Persian retaliation is expressed at 5.105, 6.94.1, 8.142.

§5. Much, of course, is debatable, but it is not to be denied that Herodotus' account is highly unsatisfactory, and one is encouraged to try to stand, as far as one can, outside Herodotus and pose important questions about the revolt.

§6. First, what was the cause of the revolt? What moved not just Aristagoras but a large number of Greeks to risk the appalling vengeance of the Great King? Three answers have been given: first, that the tyrants in the Ionian cities who counted on Persian support had by 499 become intolerable; second, that Persian rule had seriously affected the economy and the prosperity of the cities; third, that the uprising was a revolt against Persian domination in general and sought liberty for the Greeks.

§7. The case for supposing that it was the tyrannies that were especially hated rests largely on Herodotus' account of a debate about the breaking up of the bridge over the Ister (modern Danube) River[a] (4.137), wherein the tyrants who were with the expedition argued against the destruction of the bridge and leaving Darius and his army to the tender mercies of the Scythians, for if that were to happen, the tyrants themselves would not have much of a future. It is highly questionable whether such a debate ever took place, but the presumption of the story is that the rule of tyrants depended on Persian power. It is true that when the revolt began, the initial step taken by the Ionians was to remove their tyrants (5.37, 5.38), and when the revolt had ended, the Persians did not restore the tyrants but instead installed democracies in the cities (6.43.3), as if they considered the tyrannies to have been the root of the disaffection. However, one must note that the revolt involved not only Greeks but also peoples of Caria[b] and Cyprus,[c] who were probably quite differently minded about tyranny and tyrants. Nor did all the tyrants in Greek cities suffer expulsion (see also 5.103, where there is no mention of expelling tyrants when the cities of the Hellespontine[d] area are won over to the cause). As to the Persian establishment of democracies after the revolt, it may be that their having permitted tyrants to resume power right after the end of the revolt was seen by the Persians as a mistake. Perhaps Hekataios played an influential part in this.[e] All in all, the case for supposing that the real reason why the Ionians revolted was their hatred of tyranny as a political system is not strong.

§8. Nor is the case strong that the Greek states were feeling the economic pinch of Persian empire. The revolt originated in Miletus, which Herodotus declared to be in prime condition in 499 (5.28). It is true that in the course of time Persians are found more and more in occupation of substantial estates, as Xenophon's account of an attempt to kidnap a Persian estate owner shows.[a] Perhaps this sort of colonization had begun in the sixth century, though there is no evidence that it had done so, but even if it had, it is to be doubted that it affected more than a relatively small number of individual Greeks.

§9. What does seem in general likely, and what emerges in the terms in which Aristagoras made his appeal to Sparta (5.49), is that the root of the trouble was that the Greeks of Asia[a] were "subjects and not free" (5.49.2) and hated having to live

H.7a   Ister River: Map E.2, AX..
H.7b   Caria: Map H, BY.
H.7c   Cyprus: Map H, locator. For Caria and Cyprus in revolt, see 5.103, 5.104.3, and 5.117.
H.7d   Hellespont: Map H, AY.
H.7e   For Hekataios in the revolt, see Diodorus *Histories* 10.25.
H.8a   See Xenophon's *Anabasis*, 7.8–9, 7.23.
H.9a   Asia (Asia Minor): Map H, locator.

under foreign rule. What brought it to a head in 499 was that the failure of the attack on Naxos gave the leaders of the revolt an excellent opportunity to gain the support of the states of mainland Greece in the effort to throw off the Persian yoke. When the forces that had failed at Naxos returned to Asia but were kept together (5.36.4) to renew the attack, Sparta, the leading power of Greece itself, could be appealed to for help; Naxos and the other islands of the Cyclades[a] could be persuasively represented as stepping-stones to Euboea[b] and the Greek mainland (5.31.2–3). Aristagoras could argue that Sparta and Greece generally could now see what was coming if the Persians were not stopped, and that the best place for stopping them was in Ionia itself, where the forces of the Greek mainland and the Greek states of Asia could fight side by side. Sparta declined the challenge. To their glory, the Athenians, despite the disapproval of Herodotus (5.97.2), took it up, and the raid on Sardis[c] ensued (5.99–102).

§10. Whether Aristagoras was privately urged by Histiaios (5.35) to begin the revolt is questionable. Histiaios appears to have been in the King's circle (5.24, 5.106); and may well have been aware of the King's grand strategy. He may actually have sent a message to Aristagoras apprising him of an intended western expansion by the Persians. (The story of the tattooed slave at 5.35.2, in itself improbable, may be an embroidery of truth.) If the message counseling revolt did arrive at the time indicated by Herodotus, it would have given Aristagoras a sense of urgency. However, the whole story of Histiaios in Herodotus may deserve skepticism. Histiaios may have been a man who greatly embroidered the truth.

§11. In view of Herodotus' extreme prejudice against Aristagoras, one may be right to see him as a man who made a desperate attempt to rescue the Greeks of Asia from Persian domination. He did not get the wholehearted support of the Greeks of mainland Greece and so failed, as heroes in the cause of liberty so often have. History should think better of him than Herodotus did.

[For a fuller discussion, the reader is referred to George Cawkwell, *The Greek Wars*, Oxford University Press, 2005, pp. 61–86.]

George L. Cawkwell
University College
Oxford, UK

H.9a Cyclades (islands): Map H, BY.
H.9b Euboea: Map H, BX.
H.9c Sardis: Map H, BY.

APPENDIX I

Classical Greek Religious Festivals

§1. The Athenians[a] executed Socrates for impiety, while vandalism of statues sacred to Hermes and profanation of the Eleusinian mysteries (detailed in Book 6 of Thucydides) brought down sentences of exile and death.[b] Even in the late fifth century, an eclipse of the moon frightened the Athenians into delaying their retreat from Syracuse[c] and led to the annihilation of the entire expedition (*Thucydides* 7.50). The average twentieth-first-century American would have been appalled at the high level of superstition in fifth-century Greece, even in the most sophisticated city of Athens.

§2. Herodotus quotes more than thirty oracles in the *Histories*, and each plays a substantive role in affecting events. But if oracles in Herodotus have meaning, that meaning can be hard to decipher. Thus, when the Lydian[a] king Croesus, whose prosperity and misfortune foreshadows the fate of the Persian Kings who follow him, turns to the Greek oracle at Delphi,[b] he learns (1.53.3) that if he crosses the frontier that separates his kingdom from the expanding Persian Empire, he will "destroy a great empire." Ever the optimist, Croesus launches the expedition, only to discover that the empire he thereby destroys is his own.

§3. It is important to bear in mind two key aspects of Greek religion. First, Greeks had no religious texts comparable to the Bible or the Koran. Their religion centered on ritual practice rather than doctrine: participation in the communal activities was the heart of Greek religion, while belief was less important. Second, all Greek religious actions were, in some measure, exclusive: some religious cults were restricted to kinship groups, others were open only to citizens of a particular city-state, while the great "Panhellenic" events were restricted to those who could prove themselves to be Greek. Participation in any Greek religious activity was a sign of membership in an exclusive group, whether large or small.

§4. Scattered as they were among more than 700 small city-states from the Crimea to Spain, the Greeks desperately needed a small number of central locations where they could gather, exchange information, establish and strengthen personal contacts, and compete for prestige that would transcend their own city-states. In his

I.1a Athens: Map H, BX.
I.1b In ancient Greece, blasphemous behavior on the part of one's fellow citizens could bring down the offended gods' wrath upon the entire community, so it was no trivial or even personal matter but, rather, a critical communal one. Hence violators were subject to the most extreme punishments.
I.1c Syracuse: Map H, locator.
I.2a Lydia: Map H, BY.
I.2b Delphi: Map H, BX.

history, Thucydides stressed that Homer has no word for the Greeks as a whole (*Thucydides* 1.3): the idea of Greece and common Greek identity gained force only as Greeks founded colonies throughout the Mediterranean world and came into contact with a number of different, often unfriendly, cultures. The Persian Wars were just the most traumatic of such encounters and did much to solidify centuries of cultural formation.

§5. In the eighth century, the local athletic contests at Olympia[a] began to acquire an international character, as Greeks from outside the Peloponnese[b] started competing for prizes and to gain the admiration of their peers. The oracle of Apollo at Delphi also evolved into an international Greek institution: those who wished to found a new colony regularly consulted the god, and the oracle could, at the least, prevent two expeditions from accidentally setting off to colonize the same location. The popularity of the athletic contests at Olympia grew so great that in the first half of the sixth century similar games were added to the festival at Delphi (the so-called Pythian games), as well as to those celebrated at Nemea and the Isthmus of Corinth.[c] There were Panhellenic games each year, with those at Olympia remaining the most prestigious.

§6. Greek states took pride in the achievements of their citizens, and individuals who won victories at these games enjoyed economic and other privileges in reward for the glory they brought to their city. They could also convert their athletic prestige into political power (see also the attempt by the Athenian Kylon at 5.71 to make himself tyrant after becoming an Olympic victor). Croesus sought to enhance his own standing in the Greek world by lavishly endowing the sanctuary of Apollo at Delphi with spectacular gifts (1.50). The Peisistratids found the prestige of Kimon son of Stesagoras so threatening after he won the four-horse chariot race for the third time that they had him ambushed and killed (6.103.2–3).[a]

§7. The Panhellenic sanctuaries became destinations for tourists and travelers. When Euripides portrays visitors of the heroic age spending three days seeing the sights at Delphi (*Andromache* 1085), he gives us an idea of how his contemporaries would have behaved: the Panhellenic sanctuaries were in effect museums of art, wealth, and power. Croesus' story was thus of interest in no small part because many Greeks had seen and more had heard stories of his offerings at Delphi; Herodotus tells them (and us) precisely where they stood (1.51). In return, the people of Delphi gave Croesus and all Lydians the right to be first when consulting the oracle, exemption from all charges, the chief seats at festivals, and perpetual right to obtain Delphian citizenship if they should want it (1.54).

§8. Such privileges for non-Greeks were extraordinary: Panhellenic centers helped the Greeks define their national identity. When Alexander king of Macedon,[a] an ancestor of Alexander the Great, attempted to compete at Olympia (5.22), the

I.5a Olympia: Map H, BX.
I.5b Peloponnese: Map H, BX.
I.5c Nemea and Corinth: Map H, BX.
I.6a Nine other winners in the games appear in Herodotus' narrative: Philip son of Boutakides of Croton, 5.47.1; Alexander of Macedon, who ties for first place in the footrace, 5.22.2; Euagoras of Laconia, 6.103.4; Alkmeon, 6.125; Kallias son of Phaenippus, a runner-up, 6.122.1; Demaratos, 6.70.3; Miltiades son of Kypselos, 6.36; Phayllos, a three-time Pythian victor, 8.47.1; Teisamenos son of Antiochos, who missed an Olympic victory in wrestling by just one fall in a competition against Hieronymos of Andros, 9.33.2.
I.8a Macedon: Map H, AX.

Greeks who were to run against him wanted to bar him from the race, saying that the contest should be for Greeks and not for foreigners. Alexander, however, proving himself to be an Argive[b] by descent, was judged to be a Greek.

§9. As important as the splendor of the offerings may have been and as significant as wealth may have seemed for attracting people to Delphi and other sanctuaries, the Greeks simultaneously maintained a theatrical disdain for explicit monetary rewards at the Panhellenic games—a phenomenon that shocked non-Greeks. For example, Herodotus, at 8.26.2–3, writes that the Persians, upon learning that the Greeks are celebrating "the Olympic festival and viewing sports matches and horse races, ask what is the prize offered to the contestants, and are told that what the victor receives is a crown of olive leaves. At that, Tritantaichmes son of Artabanos expressed a most noble insight which, however, made the King consider him a coward from that day on, for when he heard that their prize was an olive wreath rather than money, he could not bear to keep quiet, but cried out to them all, 'Good grief, Mardonios, what kind of men did you lead us here to fight, who compete not for money but for excellence alone?'"

§10. The Greeks were extremely jealous of their independence and suspicious of any entity that acquired too much power. Panhellenic religious centers badly needed at least the appearance of neutrality if they were to maintain their authority. The religious center of the classical Greek world was unquestionably the sanctuary of Apollo at Delphi. Located in the virtual center of the Greek world (it was, in fact, called the "navel of the world"), Delphi played a crucial role: it was militarily weak and thus could not translate any cultural prestige or moral authority into imperial power.

§11. At these festivals, members of the Greek elite from different cities could exchange hospitality and establish "international" guest-friendships.[a] Trade was probably also promoted, and negotiations between quarreling states could be facilitated. Widespread truces for the duration of the ceremonies were established so that even citizens of states at war could meet in what had to be peaceful circumstances. Cities probably funded the training of their star athletes, and wealthy men put together horse teams and compete in races for their respective cities. The festivals must have been financially successful for the host cities and for the shrines, too.

§12. Access to religious events often helped define social identity: religious action was exclusive, and participation defined membership in some larger entity. Thus, the Ionian Greek city-states of Asia Minor established the Panionion[a] to maintain their corporate identity (1.148). Similarly Herodotus mentions local religious festivals at cities such as Athens (1.56, 6.87, 6.111, 6.138), Smyrna (1.150), Samos (3.48), Sicyon (5.67), and Sparta[b] (6.67, 7.206). Such festivals appear in the history not just as testimony to Greek piety but because they provide opportunities to describe political manipulation and power plays: the people of Aegina ambush the

---

I.8b Argos: Map H, BX.

I.11a Guest-friendship (*xenia*): a bond of ritualized friendship, usually between aristocrats or prominent men of different cities. It was passed down through generations and required hereditary privileges and obligations, such as reciprocal hospitality and in many cases, assistance.

I.12a Ionia, Panionion shrine: Map H, BY. Asia Minor (Asia): Map H, locator.

I.12b Smyrna, Samos: Map H, BY. Sicyon, Sparta: Map H, BX.

Athenians during a festival at Sounion[c] (6.87); exiles from a nearby city-state seize control of Smyrna when its proper citizens are outside the city celebrating a festival (1.150); a festival in honor of Apollo conveniently prevents the main Spartan army from arriving in time to be annihilated along with Leonidas and his advance force at Thermopylae[d] (7.206).

§13. Born in Halicarnassus[a] on the edge of what was then the vast cultural space of the ancient Near East, Herodotus was a cosmopolitan observer with broad knowledge not only of many Greek city-states but of the cultures that bordered the Greek world in his day. In a famous passage (3.38.3–4), he provides a relativist view of cultural practices that seems to contrast with the more provincial views of Greeks and non-Greeks of the time: "During his reign, Darius summoned the Hellenes at his court and asked them how much money they would accept for eating the bodies of their dead fathers. They answered that they would not do that for any amount of money. Later, Darius summoned some Indians[b] called Kallatiai, who do eat their dead parents. In the presence of the Hellenes, with an interpreter to inform them of what was said, he asked the Indians how much money they would accept to burn the bodies of their dead fathers. They responded with an outcry, ordering him to shut his mouth lest he offend the gods. Well, then, that is how people think, and so it seems to me that Pindar was right when he said in his poetry that custom is king of all."[c]

§14. But if Herodotus calls into question the authority of particular practices and institutions, he does not deny the role of super-human forces, more mysterious than those which we can observe. In the remarkable prelude to Xerxes' invasion (7.1–19), when the young Persian King decides against invading Greece, a vision in a dream visits him twice to prod him on his way and then visits his heretofore wise uncle, Artabanos, who had counseled against the invasion. Artabanos had applied a surprisingly modern critique (7.16.β: "we dream about what has occupied our minds during the day"), but the dream vision visits Artabanos and in turn forces the older man to change his mind and support the invasion. The results confirm Artabanos' earlier observation that divine force brings down the powerful (7.10.ε). Forces greater than human are at play and help shape the grand narrative that Herodotus presents.

Gregory Crane
Professor of Classics
Tufts University
Medford, MA

I.12c   Aegina, Sounion: Map H, BX.
I.12d   Thermopylae: Map H, BX.
I.13a   Halicarnassus (modern Bodrum, Turkey): Map H, BY.
I.13b   India: Map H, locator.
I.13c   Pindar, Fragment 169. Pindar (518–438) was a lyric poet active in the first half of the fifth century until c. 446. He was especially known for the victory odes he composed for victorious athletes throughout the Greek world.

APPENDIX J

Ancient Greek Units of Currency, Weight, and Distance

§1. No universal standards for units of distance, currency, or capacity existed in Herodotus' time. Ancient Greeks in different locales used different-sized units, as did the diverse peoples living in the many parts of the non-Greek world about which Herodotus wrote. Ancient peoples understood very clearly the importance of maintaining standard units of measurement, especially weights, measures, and capacities necessary to ensure fair and reliable commercial and official transactions, and we have ample evidence of the care and expense that communities such as Athens expended to maintain such standards, by appointing officials to oversee their use and by making available publicly accessible specimens of relevant units.[a]

§2. Units of distance were probably the most difficult standards to establish and publicize. Units of currency, which indicated weights, and of capacity (liquid and dry) were easier to standardize. It is essential to recognize that all modern equivalences for ancient units of measurement, which themselves existed in a bewildering diversity, can only be approximations, as precision is impossible to attain. For this reason, different modern reference works often give somewhat different absolute values for the same ancient units; the table of equivalences at the end of this appendix should be consulted with this limitation in mind.

§3. Greek (and other Mediterranean and Near Eastern) units for measuring distance were originally based on notional lengths of parts of the human body, as the famous Roman architect and engineer Vitruvius says (*On Architecture* 3.1.5).[a] The length of units varied according to the local standard in use, but there seems to have been an effort to publicize the ratios existing between the more widely recognized standards, especially the Attic foot, the Doric foot, and the Egyptian royal cubit.[b]

J.1a See Aristotle *Athenaion Politeia* 10.1–2, 51.1–2, on classical Athens' officials; the long Athenian inscription specifying procedures for overseeing weights and measures from the third century, *Inscriptiones Graecae* 2 (2nd ed., no. 1013, translated in Austin, no. 111); the two relief sculptures displaying standard units of length discussed by Wilson Jones, 2000; and the official weights and measures found in the agora of ancient Athens catalogued in Lang and Crosby, 1964, and conveniently illustrated on plates 102–106 in Camp, 1986.

J.3a The depiction of length standards related to the male body carved on two surviving metrological relief sculptures, one preserved in the Ashmolean Museum in Oxford (see www.ashmol.ox.ac.uk/ash/faqs/q002) and the other, the so-called "Salamis relief," in the Archaeological Museum at Piraeus, the port of Athens (see Wilson Jones, 2000 and Vickers, 2006; and www.ajaonline.org/archive/104.1/wilson_jones_mark.html).

J.3b For more information on these three units, see §19–22. See Neal, 2000, for a detailed argument that ancient standards were numerically interrelated.

FIGURE J.1. THIS METROLOGICAL TRIANGULAR STONE SLAB CARVED IN RELIEF SHOWS STANDARD DIMENSIONS FOR MEASUREMENT OF THE FOOT, THE PALM, THE FINGER (INCH), A FATHOM (OUT-STRETCHED ARMS), AND THE CUBIT (ELBOW TO FINGERTIP). SCHOLARS AGREE THAT IT WAS PROBABLY CARVED SOMETIME BETWEEN 460 AND 430. ITS PROVENANCE IS UNKNOWN.

Scholars have calculated absolute values for Greek units by studying the dimensions and construction marks of surviving buildings, the length of the distance between the start and finish lines in running tracks of ancient Greek athletic stadiums, and two wooden measuring instruments found in a shipwreck of about 400.[c]

§4. The units of distance found in Herodotus related to parts of the body are finger (*daktylos*), palm (*palaste*, also spelled *palaiste*), span of all fingers (*spithame*), foot (*pous*), elbow to first knuckle (*pygon*), elbow to tip of middle finger (*pechys*, also known in translation, from the Latin, as a cubit), and the outstretched arms (*orgyia*, also known in translation as a fathom because it was six feet long). In addition to the "normal" or "common" (*metrios*) cubit, Herodotus mentions the royal cubit (which he says at 1.178 is three fingers longer than a normal cubit), the Egyptian cubit, and the "Samian cubit." The last two cubits are the same, Herodotus says at 2.168, in reporting that an aroura of land equaled 100 square Egyptian cubits; he does not record this cubit's absolute length. The Egyptians had two different such units, but the one to which Herodotus refers was probably their royal cubit of 52.3 centimeters, making an aroura equal to 2,735.29 square meters.[a]

§5. Scholars calculate that the length of the foot in use at ancient Athens, the so-called Attic standard, equaled approximately 11.65 inches (29.6 centimeters), while

J.3c   These measuring instruments are shown in
       Stieglitz, 2006.
J.4a   Lloyd, 1988, p. 200.

on the Olympic standard a foot equaled approximately 12.60 inches, and on the Doric standard approximately 12.87 inches. Since a Greek foot equaled sixteen fingers, the length of the finger unit on the Attic standard was 0.73 inches. Scholars usually assume that Herodotus is referring to the Attic standard when he gives Greek units of distance; Alan B. Lloyd, however, flatly states that "[w]e know neither the length of the Herodotean foot nor that of the Herodotean cubit and can never possibly know."[a] This being said, Herodotus remains a vitally important source for our knowledge of ancient units of distance, not only because he gives explicit numerical ratios for the relationship of the royal cubit to the normal cubit, but also provides the information that allows us to deduce the relationships of the foot to the palm, the cubit, the fathom, the plethron, the stade, the parasang, and the schoinos (2.6, 2.9, 2.149, 4.41, 4.86, 5.53, 6.42).

§6. By far the most commonly mentioned longer unit of distance in Herodotus is that known in English as a stade, which apparently equaled 600 Greek feet (equivalent to approximately 583 English feet on the Attic standard, or approximately 630 feet on the Olympic standard). The term "stade" is derived from the ancient Greek word for "stadium" (*stadion*), and it was a standard distance for a footrace in Greek athletic competitions. The plethron, parasang, and schoinos were, like the stade, units to indicate longer distances. The plethron was equal to 100 Greek feet. Much longer was the parasang, a Persian unit of distance that is said to have indicated the distance that infantry could walk in an hour, about three and a third miles. (This measuring of distance by time spent walking is also known, for example, from modern Greece, where rural dwellers commonly expressed distances in units of "cigarettes," meaning the number of cigarettes a person would smoke while walking that distance.) Herodotus says the parasang equaled 30 stades (2.6, 5.53, 6.42), but the later geographical author Strabo reports[a] that people variously equated the parasang with 30, 40, or 60 stades.

§7. Most problematic of all these longer units is the schoinos. In Greek, the word literally means "reed" or "rush," and therefore, by extension, "a rope made from plaited rushes," but Greeks also used it to designate an Egyptian unit of distance. Herodotus in fact employs the term as a unit of distance only in Book 2, his extended description of Egypt. In discussing the geographical extent of that land, he reports that a schoinos equals 60 stades (the length of the unit used in the Thebaid region of Egypt) (2.6, 2.9). This would equate to about six and two-thirds miles. Strabo, however, records that, from his own research, including a visit to Egypt, he discovered that the schoinos could vary from 30 to 120 stades;[a] this information on varying lengths for the schoinos unit corresponds to the remark of the Roman encyclopedia writer Pliny the Elder that even Persians gave different lengths for the schoinos (and the parasang as well).[b] The astonishing degree of variation recorded

J.5a   Lloyd, 1988, p. 43.
J.6a   Strabo 11.11.5, C 518.
J.7a   Strabo 17.1.24, C 804; see also 11.11.5, C 518.

J.7b   Pliny the Elder, *Natural History* 6, 30, 124.

in the sources for the schoinos gives a sense of the scope of the innate uncertainty that comes into play when trying to give specific quantities to any and all ancient units of distance.

§8. Currency in Herodotus' time meant coins (there were no bills), which were minted in bronze, silver, or (rarely in the Greek world) gold. Greek mints identified their coinages by designs and inscriptions, but they did not usually include an indication of a coin's value as money. Consumers were expected to know how much a particular coin was worth. Greek silver and gold coinages derived perhaps as much as 95 percent of their monetary value from the intrinsic bullion value of the precious metal contained in each coin. For this reason, plated coins such as those mentioned by Herodotus at 3.56 would be worthless unless they were issued as an official token coinage for strictly local or temporary circulation. In this passage Herodotus reports what he calls a "very foolish story": that Polykrates, tyrant of Samos[a] in the later sixth century, plated lead slugs with gold (which at the time probably would have meant electrum, a naturally occurring gold-silver alloy) to pay off the Spartans to lift their blockade of his island, and that the Spartans then sailed away, content with these plated coins. Herodotus judges the story to be foolish, we can guess, because he thought that not even the allegedly currency-deprived Spartans[b] would likely have been naïve enough not to test such coins by using a touchstone or cutting into them to verify their bullion content before accepting them in payment. Some example of lead coins from Samos that may have been part of this scheme, whether it was a fraud or was in fact some sort of token coinage arrangement, have actually been found.[c]

§9. The remaining value of officially minted precious-metal coinage was added by the implicit guarantee that the authority issuing an official coinage would enforce its coins' acceptance as legal tender in its home region. That authority was identified by the pictures (called "types") and sometimes words (called "legends") stamped onto officially minted coins. For ordinary transactions, Greeks assumed that the purity of the precious metal in coins issued by different mints was essentially the same.

§10. The weight of silver and gold coins mattered because their value came primarily from the amount of precious metal that they represented. (Bronze coins, the small change of the ancient Greek world, circulated in their region of origin at nominal, agreed-upon values.) The only Greek denomination specifically mentioned by Herodotus (6.21, 7.144, 8.93) is the drachma of Athens, which on the Attic currency standard weighed about 4.3 grams on average.[a]

§11. For calculating large sums of money, Greeks used units of accounting called minas and talents that, strictly speaking, designated weights. For our purposes, these units are most easily understood as numbers of drachmas. A mina was a unit of 100 drachmas, which on the Attic standard would amount to about 15 ounces (approxi-

J.8a   Samos: Map H, BY.
J.8b   Plutarch, *Life of Lykourgos* 9. Sparta: Map H, BX.
J.8c   Barron, 1966, pp. 17–18.
J.10a   For conveniently presented information with information on additional units, see Colin Kraay,

Archaic and Classical Greek Coins (1976), "Appendix I: Weight Standards," pp. 329–330, and *The Oxford Classical Dictionary*, 3rd ed. (1996), "measures," pp. 942–943, and "weights," pp. 1620–1621.

mately 430 grams). A talent was a unit of 6,000 drachmas or 60 minas, which on the Attic standard would amount to about 57 pounds (a bit less than 26 kilograms). As with all standards in antiquity, local variations in the weights of these accounting units could be significant. Herodotus specifically mentions the Babylonian and Euboean[a] talents (3.89), reporting that the former equates to 70 Euboean minas (or 78, according to the emendation of the text accepted by some scholars, based on the ratio implied at 3.95). The Euboean talent he mentions apparently had the same weight as the Athenian talent. If the Babylonian talent was equal to 70 Euboean (Attic) minas, then it probably weighed about 30 to 31 kilograms.

§12. The terms "minas" and "talents" were frequently used to indicate amounts of precious metal still in bullion form, or the weight of substantial amounts of other materials. See, for example, Herodotus' references to the weights of the gifts in precious metal that King Croesus of Lydia[a] sent to the oracle of Apollo at Delphi[b] in Greece (1.50–51), such as the enormous bowl made of gold weighing "eight and a half talents and twelve minas"; or his references to minas of grain and beef (2.168), to a boat that could carry a cargo weighing 5,000 talents (1.194), and to a cable made of woven flax so thick that it weighed a talent per cubit (7.36).

§13. Another well-known currency standard besides the Attic was named after the civic mint on the island of Aegina,[a] not far from Athens. Therefore, when at 3.131 Herodotus reports that the Aeginetans paid the renowned physician Democedes a talent for a year of service and then the Athenians hired him the following year for 100 minas, it may be that the talent was on the Aeginetan standard, while the minas were on the Attic standard. Coins minted on the Aeginetan standard weighed about 40 percent more than coins on the Attic standard and were correspondingly more valuable in each denomination. The standard exchange rate between the two standards was seven Aeginetan coins to ten Athenian.

§14. The Greek term "stater" ("weight" or "standard"), designated the largest denomination in a currency standard. Herodotus mentions gold staters of King Croesus of Lydia (1.54.1) and of the Persians, specifically those that the Greeks called "Darics," after King Darius I (3.130.5, 4.166.2, 7.28.2, 7.29.2). As Herodotus tells us (1.94), the coins of the Lydians were the earliest ever minted. Most scholars believe that Croesus did in fact mint gold (and silver) coins; the gold coins, called "Croesids," seem to have been minted on two different standards, with a stater weighing approximately either 10.9 grams or 8.2 grams. Darics weighed about 8.35 grams.[a] Herodotus calculates the ratio of value between gold and silver as 13:1 (3.95), which helps give some idea of the value of these staters compared to, say, an Attic drachma weighing about 4.3 grams.

§15. The only meaningful way to measure the value of ancient money in its own time is to study wages and prices. Since wages and prices in antiquity were as variable as they are today, generalizations about them cannot be authoritative.[a] There

J.11a Euboea: Map H, BX.
J.12a Lydia: Map H, BY.
J.12b Delphi: Map H, BX.
J.13a Aegina: Map H, BX.

J.14a On the chronology of Croesids and Darics, see Carradice, 1987.
J.15a Loomis, 1998, pp. 261–340, conveniently tabulates the specific evidence from classical Athens.

was no standard or mandatory wage scale; before the inflation that came during the Peloponnesian War (431–404), a laborer at Athens could perhaps hope to earn a third of a drachma per day. Toward the end of the fifth century, that amount had risen to a drachma a day, which is what a rower on a warship in the Athenian navy earned. A talent (equal to 6,000 drachmas) was therefore a huge sum, enough to pay the wages of a crew of a 200-man warship for a month, or twenty years' wages for an individual worker making a drachma per day for 300 days each year.

§16. By about 425, an Athenian citizen received half a drachma for each day spent on jury duty. This payment seems to have been enough to make jury service attractive for men who could use the money to supplement other income, but it was not enough to replace a day's pay for most workers. Food and clothing could be expensive by modern Western standards. Enough barley to provide a day's porridge, the dietary staple, for a family of five cost only $\frac{1}{48}$ of a drachma, but a gallon of olive oil, another staple, cost three drachmas. A woolen cloak cost from five to twenty drachmas, a pair of shoes from six to eight drachmas.

§17. Units of capacity, like units of currency, appear only rarely in Herodotus. Despite the discovery by archaeologists of some ancient examples of capacity standards, uncertainty remains over the exact absolute values to be assigned to various units.[a] Herodotus mentions the Greek dry measures the medimnos (about 52 liters); by comparison, an American bushel is about 35 liters)[b] and the choinix ($\frac{1}{48}$ of a medimnos, approximately 1.08 liters), which was regarded as a usual day's ration of grain for a soldier. He also mentions the Persian measure called an artabe, explaining (1.192) that it equaled one Attic medimnos plus three choinikes, which would make it about 55 liters. (For Persian evidence for an artabe of about half that capacity, see Bivar, 1985, pp. 631–634.)

§18. As for liquid measures, Herodotus mentions the amphora,[a] the kotyle (which can also be a dry measure), the aryster, and the "Laconian (Spartan) fourth." There were 144 kotyles in an amphora, making a kotyle about 270 milliliters. The aryster, mentioned only once, at 2.168, as a fourth of a day's wine ration for the Egyptian kings' personal guards, is said by the later lexicographer Hesychius[b] to have held the same amount as a kotyle. The size of a Laconian fourth, which Herodotus says was the amount of wine given at regular intervals to a Spartan king at public expense, is uncertain; Hultsch[c] asserts that it was a quarter of the measure called a metretes, which was itself equivalent to an amphora, and that the Spartan standard was equivalent to the Aeginetan standard, which had a metretes of 56.4 liters; on this calculation, a Laconian fourth would be 13.65 liters. Oxé,[d] 1941, by contrast, argues that the Spartan metretes was equal to 29 liters, which would yield a Laconian fourth of 7.25 liters.

J.17a See tables, §21–22, for metric and U.S. equivalents.
J.17b 35 liters = 32 U.S. dry measure quarts.
J.18a The amphora is said by Hultsch, 1882, p. 703, to be 39.39 liters, or about 10.4 U.S. liquid measure gallons.
J.18b Hyesychius, probably of the fifth century C.E.
J.18c Hultsch, 1882, p. 500.
J.18d Oxé, 1941.

§19. Table of Units of Distance in Herodotus (Attic Standard)*

This table assumes that Herodotus consistently referred to the units of distance in use in ancient Athens (the Attic standard), which is far from certain.

finger ($\frac{1}{16}$ foot) = 0.73 inch
palm ($\frac{1}{4}$ foot) = 2.91 inches
span ($\frac{3}{4}$ foot) = 8.74 inches
foot (1 foot) = 11.65 inches
pygon ($1\frac{1}{4}$ feet) = 14.56 inches
cubit ($1\frac{1}{2}$ feet) = 17.46 inches
Royal cubit (27 fingers) = 19.66 inches
fathom (6 feet) = 5 feet 9.9 inches
plethron (100 feet) = 97 feet
stade (600 feet) = 583 feet
parasang (30 stades) = 5,830 yards (a little less than $3\frac{1}{3}$ miles)
schoinos (60 stades) = 11,660 yards (a little less than $6\frac{2}{3}$ miles)

§20. Table of Greek Currency Units in Herodotus (Attic Standard)*

drachma = 0.15 ounces
mina (100 drachmas) = 15 ounces
talent (6,000 drachmas or 60 minas) = 57 pounds[a]

§21. Table of Units of Capacity in Herodotus—Dry Measures*

medimnos (Attic standard) = 52 liters
choinix ($\frac{1}{48}$ medimnos) = 1.08 liters
artabe (1 Attic medimnos + 3 choinikes) = 55 liters[a]

§22. Table of Units of Capacity in Herodotus—Liquid Measures*

amphora (144 koytles) = 39.39 liters
kotyle or aryster = 270 milliliters
Laconian (Spartan) fourth = estimates range from 7.25 to 13.65 liters[a]

Thomas R. Martin
Department of Classics
College of the Holy Cross
Worcester, MA

---

*All equivalences are approximate.
J.20.a The metric equivalents are:
    drachma = 4.3 grams
    mina = 430 grams
    talent = 25.9 kilograms
J.21.a The original sources for these measures are metric.
    The U.S. dry measure equivalents are:
      medimnos = 47.22 quarts
        (assuming 1.101 liters = 1 quart)

    choinix = 0.98 quart
    artabe = 49.95 quarts.
J.22.a The original sources for these measures are metric.
    The U.S. liquid measure equivalents are:
      amphora = 10.4 gallons
        (assuming 3.785 liters = 1 gallon)
      kotyle, aryster = 0.57 pint
      "Laconian (Spartan) fourth" = 1.9 to 3.6 gallons.

Bibliography

Austin, M. M. *The Hellenistic World from Alexander to the Roman Conquest* (Cambridge: Cambridge University Press, 1981).

Barron, John. *The Silver Coins of Samos* (London: Athlone Press, 1966).

Ben-Menahem, H., and N. S. Hecht. "A Modest Addendum to 'The Greek metrological relief in Oxford.'" *Antiquaries Journal* 65 (1985), 139–140.

Bivar, A. D. H. "Achaemenid Coins, Weights and Measures." In *The Cambridge History of Iran*. Vol. 2, *The Median and Achaemenian Periods*, ed. Ilya Gerschevitch (Cambridge: Cambridge University Press, 1985), 610–639.

Camp, John M. *The Athenian Agora. Excavations in the Heart of Classical Athens* (London: Thames and Hudson, 1986).

Carradice, Ian. "The 'Regal' Coinage of the Persian Empire." In *Coinage and Administration in the Athenian and Persian Empires. The Ninth Oxford Symposium on Coinage and Monetary History*, ed. Ian Carradice (Oxford: BAR International Series, 343, 1987), 73–107.

Chantraine, H. "Gewichte." In *Der Kleine Pauly. Lexikon der Antike in fünf Bänden*, ed. K. Ziegler and W. Sontheimer (Munich: Deutscher Taschenbuch Verlag, 1979), vol. 2, cols. 791–793.

_____. "Talent." In *Der Kleine Pauly. Lexikon der Antike in fünf Bänden*, ed. K. Ziegler and W. Sontheimer (Munich: Deutscher Taschenbuch Verlag, 1979), vol. 5, cols. 502–503.

Fernie, Eric. "The Greek Metrological Relief in Oxford." *Antiquaries Journal* 61 (1981), 256–263.

Hitzel, Konrad. "Gewichte. III. Griechenland." In *Der Neue Pauly* (Stuttgart and Weimar: Verlag J. B. Metzler, 1998), vol. 4, cols. 1050–1053.

Hultsch, Friedrich. *Griechische und Römische Metrologie.* 2nd ed. (Berlin: Weidmannsche Buchhandlung, 1882).

Lang, Mabel, and Margaret Crosby. *Athenian Agora.* Vol. 10. *Weights, Measures, Tokens* (Princeton, New Jersey: American School of Classical Studies at Athens, 1964).

Lloyd, Alan B. *Herodotus. Book II. Commentary* (Leiden: E. J. Brill, 1976), 1–98.

_____. *Herodotus. Book II. Commentary* (Leiden: E. J. Brill, 1988), 99–182.

Loomis, William T. *Wages, Welfare Costs and Inflation in Classical Athens* (Ann Arbor: University of Michigan Press, 1998).

Lorenzen, Eivind. *Technological Studies in Ancient Metrology* (Copenhagen, 1966).

Morrison, John. "Ancient Greek measures of length in nautical contexts." *Antiquity* 65 (1991), 298–305.

Neal, John. *All Done with Mirrors: An Exploration of Measure, Proportion, Ratio and Number* (London: The Secret Academy, 2000).

Oxé, A. "Das spartanisch-dorische Hohlmasssystem." *Rheinisches Museum* 90 (1941), 334–341.

Rhodes, P. J. *A Commentary on the Aristotelian Athenaion Politeia* (Oxford: Clarendon Press, 1981).

Schulzki, Heinz-Joachim. "Hohlmasse. III. Griechenland." In *Der Neue Pauly* (Stuttgart and Weimar: Verlag J. B. Metzler, 1998), vol. 5, cols. 673–674.

_____. "Masse. II. Klassische Antike," in *Der Neue Pauly* (Verlag J. B. Metzler: Stuttgart and Weimar: 1999), vol. 7, cols. 988–989.

Stieglitz, Robert R. "Classical Greek Measures and the Builder's Instruments from the Ma'agan Mikhael Shipwreck." *American Journal of Archaeology* 110 (2006), 195–203.

Vickers, Michael. *The Arundel and Pomfret Marbles in Oxford. Ashmolean Handbooks* (Oxford: Ashmolean Museum, 2006).

Wilson Jones, Mark. "Doric Measure and Architectural Design 1: The Evidence of the Relief from Salamis." *American Journal of Archaeology* 104 (2000), 73–93.

APPENDIX K

Dialect and Ethnic Groups in Herodotus

§1. Herodotus, the "father of history," was much interested in ethnography, and could equally well be called the "father of ethnography." He provides lists of peoples and their habits, sometimes, it would appear, simply for the joy of the sound of their names. He lists Persian tribes (1.125), the tribes of Libya (North Africa; 4.168–196), and the peoples of the Peloponnese[a] (8.73). His catalog of tribes and peoples, together with the amount of tribute paid the Persian King (3.90–94), is important to his theme, as is his list of Persian forces (7.61–86). It is perhaps surprising that in his catalog (1.28) of those subdued by Croesus west of the Halys River,[b] along with peoples like Lydians, Phrygians, Mysians, and Carians he includes Ionians, Dorians, and Aeolians,[c] groups that we would probably subsume under the heading "Greeks"; he here makes no distinction between peoples speaking different languages and those speaking forms of Greek. Of course he knew that the Aeolians, Ionians, and Dorians of Asia Minor[d] spoke Greek (7.9), and in other passages (3.1) he separates these Greeks out from other nations.

§2. As the reader will have abundantly observed, Herodotus was fascinated by foreign customs. He refers to "dress, speech, and nationality" as determinants of racial or tribal affinities (4.111), and to these categories we can add religious and funerary beliefs (compare with 1.131–140) and descent from a common ancestor (Persians from Perseus, 7.180; Hellenes from Hellēn, 1.56). He describes Persian customs (9.14) and Persian dress (8.113); in 2.35–98 he discusses Egyptians and their customs; and in 4.59–80 he deals with those of the Scythians.[a] The Greeks receive their (smaller) due in 8.144 and 9.7. He does contrast Ionian and Dorian dress (5.87), but unlike, for example, Thucydides, he does not assign different moral categories to these tribes, because he is more concerned with the opposition between Greeks and Persians. He remarks, however, that the Ionians were thought—at least by the Persians—to be unreliable (7.50–52), and he does describe general characteristics of the Ionians (1.142–148) and the Dorians (1.56).

§3. Herodotus was also very interested in language, though clearly in a nonsystematic manner. He remarks on the similarity in language between Colchian[a] and

K.1a Persia, Libya: Map K, locator. Peloponnese: Map K, BX.
K.1b Halys River: Map K, locator.
K.1c Lydia, Phrygia, Caria, Ionia, territory of the Dori-

ans: Map K, BY. Aeolia, Mysia: Map K, AY.
K.1d Asia Minor (Asia): Map K, locator.
K.2a Egypt, Scythia: Map K, locator.
K.3a Colchis: Map K, locator.

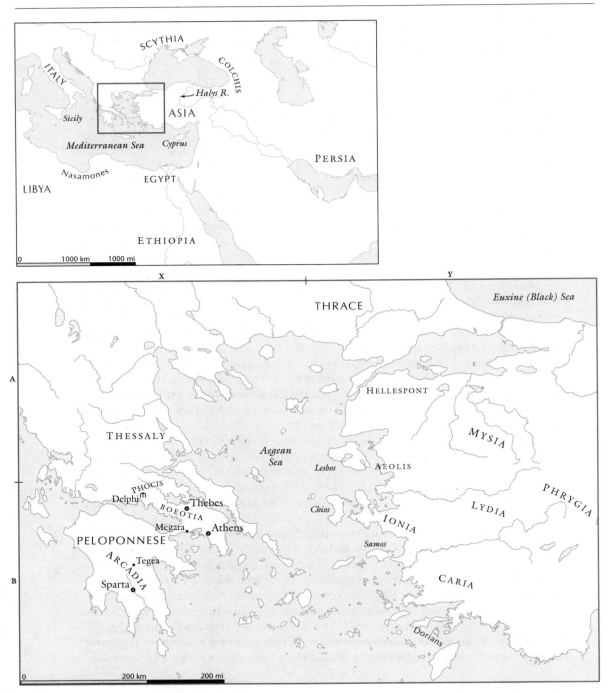

MAP K

Egyptian (2.105), and occasionally records foreign words with their meanings (for example, the Egyptian word for "crocodile" at 2.69). He states (incorrectly) that all Persian names of nobility end in the letter "s" (1.139), noting in the same breath that the Ionians call this letter sigma, the Dorians san. He observes that the language of the pygmies was unknown to the Nasamonians (2.32), and that the cave-dwelling Ethiopians speak a language unlike any other, squeaking like bats (4.183; see also 2.57 and twittering like birds). He speculates on the language spoken by the Pelasgians (1.57), and maintains that the Athenians,[b] themselves once Pelasgian, changed language when they became Greeks (see also 2.51–52 where he incidentally proposes an etymology of the Greek *theoi*, "gods"). His most celebrated report of linguistic matters is Psammetichos' attempt by controlled experiment to identify the oldest language, which he determined to be Phrygian (2.2).

§4. "Hellas," as the Greeks did and continue to refer to their land, was not a unified nation in Herodotus' time, but rather a country composed of many independent city-states, most of them very small. The citizens of these states all spoke Greek, but the Greek of each city-state was at least slightly different from the Greek speech of all other city-states. Athenian speech, for example, differed greatly from the Aeolic speech of neighboring Boeotian Thebes,[a] less so from the Ionic spoken in Ionia of Asia Minor; and Spartan (Lacedaemonian) speech differed from both of these and also from that of neighboring Tegea in Arcadia (9.46).[b] Herodotus does, to be sure, recognize that there was a distinct Hellenic entity (*to Ellēnikon ethnos*) speaking the same language (1.58).

§5. In general, Greeks made little comment about dialects. There was no ancient, common, standard Greek, as there is (more or less) a modern standard English; it seemed natural to them that the people of different city-states had different patterns of speech, and every Greek could understand every other Greek regardless of dialect. Greek authors only occasionally took notice of dialectal differences. The Athenian comic poet Aristophanes brings Spartan, Megarian,[a] and Boeotian characters on stage, each speaking in his native dialect, to achieve comic effects; and Aeschylus, the tragic poet, has one character in the drama *The Libation Bearers* refer to speaking "in the Phocian manner"—the dialect spoken in the vicinity of Delphi.[b]

§6. Herodotus is no exception to this neglect of dialectal matters and does not comment on differences between, for example, Spartan and Athenian speech, but he does note that there are four varieties of Ionic: that of the cities of Caria, that of the cities of Lydia, the speech of Chios and the coast opposite, and the variety spoken on Samos.[a] He is undoubtedly right about this, himself being a speaker of Asia Minor Greek, for the Carian and Lydian varieties can be expected to differ, if only slightly, because in these cases Greek was imposed on a substrate of Lydian and Carian language: speakers of these languages will have imported into Greek certain of their native patterns of speech. Samos may be distinct because it was repopulated after the Persians had slain the men and boys (3.147, 3.149), and from inscriptions we can detect features of the Chian dialect that set it apart from the rest of Ionic.

K.3b   Athens: Map K, BX.
K.4a   Boeotia, Thebes: Map K, BX.
K.4b   Sparta, Tegea in Arcadia: Map K, BX.

K.5a   Megara: Map K, BX.
K.5b   Phocis, Delphi: Map K, BX.
K.6a   Chios, Samos: Map K, BY.

Herodotus also (correctly) maintains that the Athenians, though speaking their own language (6.138), were nonetheless Ionians (7.51), and that the Ionians originated as Athenian colonists (9.106). It is interesting that, while using legendary criteria, he nonetheless isolates the four major dialects that modern scholars customarily identify—partly, to be sure, because the ancients divided these areas in the same way. Although he does not name the Arcado-Cypriote dialect as such, he does distinguish Tegean (Arcadian) from surrounding Doric (2.171), and speaks of Arcadian settlements in Cyprus[b] (7.90; compare with 8.73 for Arcadian autochthony).

§7. Throughout antiquity the Greeks thought all their local dialects arose from three main roots: Doric, Ionic, Aeolic. This concept must be an ancient one, for it is found in the work of the early epic poet Hesiod, who says (Fragment 9) that from King Hellēn (meaning Greek) were born three sons, Dōros, Xouthos, and Aiolos. These three are the ancestors of the later Dorians, Ionians, and Aeolians; Xouthos had a son Ion, who settled in Athens and was regarded as the ancestor of the Ionians. Modern scholars accept the ancient classification, but add a fourth grouping, the Arcado-Cypriote, a dialect spoken over much of the Peloponnese before the arrival there of the Dorians. It is to be noted that modern scholars point to linguistic similarities and differences, whereas the ancients point rather to genetic origins and descent; for them, Ionic, for example, was an ethnic designation, not a linguistic one.

§8. The origin of these dialectal differences is of course lost to us by time. Some scholars used to feel that the Greeks migrated into Greece in three distinct waves: first the Ionians, then the Aeolians, and finally the Dorians. And it is true at least that the Aeolic and Ionic dialects must have become differentiated long before they crossed over to Asia Minor, perhaps around 1000. The Dorian "invasion" was thought to have taken place at the very end of the Bronze Age (c. 1200) or later, and this date, at least for the Dorian settlement of the Peloponnese and elsewhere, must be about right. A later wave of Greek colonization (750–600) took speakers of the various dialects to Sicily, southern Italy, and the Black Sea region.[a]

§9. Scholars today no longer believe in this three-wave hypothesis of the arrival of the Greeks; they assume rather that the attested dialectal differences arose within Greece during the Bronze Age (2200–1200). There are, however, a number of cultural differences that argue for some period of independent development of Dorians and Ionians, at least. The names of the Dorian tribes—Hylleis, Dumanes, Pamphyloi (5.68)—are common to all states whose citizens speak the Doric dialect, but are found in no others. Each of the main dialectal groups celebrates at least a few religious festivals that are peculiar to themselves and different from those of other groups. The Karneia (7.206, 8.72) was a uniquely Lacedaemonian festival, just as the Panionia (1.148) was uniquely Ionian. Their calendars also differ in characteristic ways, as in the names of the months. Herakles, the protagonist of many tales, was the Dorian hero par excellence, and the Ionians developed myths involving the Athenian Theseus in part so as to have a native hero as powerful as Herakles.

K.6b   Cyprus: Map K, locator.
K.8a   Sicily, Italy: Map K, locator. Euxine (Black) Sea:
       Map K, AY.

§10. The linguistic differences between the dialect groups were clear. Where all Dorian (and hence Lacedaemonian) cities said *dāmos*, meaning "people"—as in the name of the Spartan king Archidamos—Ionians (and hence Athenians) said *dēmos*; and when a Dorian said, "he gives," he would say *didōti*, while an Ionian would say *didōsi*. These differences were slight, but did serve to distinguish these dialect groups. Aeolic, the dialect spoken in Boeotia, Thessaly, Lesbos, and a small portion of the northern Asia Minor coast,[a] differs only slightly from the other dialects, most notably in its treatment of the ancient labiovelar consonants. When Herodotus refers to Aeolians, he always means the Aeolians of Asia Minor, and they are often grouped either with the Ionians or with the Ionians and the Dorians as being all under Persian domination prior to the Persian Wars. He knew nothing of the Arcado-Cypriote dialect, though he did know of Arcadian connections with Cyprus (§6).

§11. Herodotus himself spoke and wrote Ionic, though of a peculiar sort, a sort that displayed general Ionic characteristics, but with a few distinctive features not shared by most Ionic authors and inscriptions. In addition, there are forms and locutions clearly derived from the Homeric poems, and other forms that seem to bespeak the influence of the dialect of Athens. He was linguistically as well as thematically unique.

William F. Wyatt
Emeritus Professor of Classics
Brown University
Providence, RI

K.10a Thessaly: Map K, AX. Lesbos: Map K, AY.
Asia Minor (Asia): Map K, locator.

APPENDIX L

Aristocratic Families in Herodotus

§1. Before the fifth century, political power in the Greek world was concentrated in families. Certain families amassed land, wealth, religious offices and privileges, and power, which was then passed on to generation after generation if all went well. Men in each generation might be endowed with political, military, or oratorical skills which, in combination with the power of their family and other sources of strength such as marriage alliances, could increase the might and standing of the family.

§2. Particularly prominent families were those who could trace their origins back to a legendary founder, someone who had participated in any of the mythological adventures, such as the Trojan War, the adventures of Herakles, the Argonautica, or the stories of Thebes and Corinth. Herodotus mentions that the Peisistratids, the tyrants of Athens, were originally from Pylos and were descended not only from Neleus, the father of Nestor, who fought in the Trojan War, but also from two early, mythical kings of Athens (5.65.3). Similarly, we learn from Herodotus that a son of the Trojan War hero Ajax, Philaios, was the founder of another prominent Athenian family, the Philaids, to which several famous Athenians such as Miltiades and Kimon belonged (6.35).

§3. From the founder's name would be formed a clan or family name, originally a patronymic,[a] which then acquired a broader meaning and referred to all of the founder's descendants. The Heraklids claimed descent from Herakles, just as the Peisistratids identified Peisistratos as their ancestor and the Philaids so honored Philaios.

§4. At a potential disadvantage were families like the Alkmeonids who did not trace themselves back to a founder from the days of Herakles and the Trojan War, but only to a more recent figure, someone from the seventh or sixth century. Herodotus comments that the Alkmeonids were an old family, but that not until the sixth century and the lifetime of Alkmeon, who was enriched by Croesus, did the family come to the forefront of Athenian political life (6.125) and thus acquire a political identity as Alkmeonids. This suggests that they were without certain traditional bases of power in the Athenian world and so had to compensate by using other methods in order to stay in the forefront.

L.3a   One's patronymic was based on the name of
       one's father: Hyllos Heraklides was Hyllos son of
       Herakles.

§5. Also without a traditional base of power in a family was Themistokles, whom Herodotus introduces into his story as "a certain man who had just recently come into the highest prominence; his name was Themistokles, and he was called the son of Neokles" (7.143). Although Themistokles seems to have belonged to a junior branch of an old Attic family, the Lykomidai, Herodotus does not mention this. We might speculate from this that Themistokles began his career as something of an outsider in Athenian politics, that he came from a family long resident in the Attic countryside, but one which had not previously played any role in city life.

§6. So important was family that even certain professions, such as seers, heralds, and epic poets, created for themselves fictitious clan names and descent from a mythological figure, who came to be regarded essentially as the founder of a guild. The adoption of this sort of family name signaled one's line of work or skills. When Herodotus reports on the aftermath of the Spartan murder of Xerxes' heralds, he adds this story: "the wrath of Talthybios, the herald of Agamemnon, struck the Lacedaemonians. There is a sanctuary of Talthybios in Sparta where his descendants, who are called Talthybiads, are granted the office and honor of serving on all embassies sent out by Sparta" (7.134.1). Seers, often attached to armies in Herodotus' narrative, were similarly associated with either real or fictive families, as is clear from the identification of the prophet who accompanies the Greek troops at Plataea. Tisamenos is said to be one of the Iamidai, descendants of Iamos the son of Apollo, a family of seers (9.33). Although Herodotus does not happen to use the term, epic poets often claimed to belong to the Homeridai, the sons of Homer.

§7. A sixth- or fifth-century Greek could not typically trace all of the generations which came between himself and the legendary founder of his house; the important thing was to know the hero who had established the family. He would be able to identify his father, his grandfather, and perhaps his great-grandfather, but then he would skip back in time to the founder. Exceptions to this included some royal families who claimed to be able to do all of the intervening generations in patterns which sound quite biblical to us. Herodotus gives such genealogies for the two Spartan royal houses, both of which traced themselves back to the Heraklids, the sons of Herakles. The Spartan king who earned immortality at Thermopylae (7.204) was "Leonidas son of Anaxandridas, the son of Leon son of Eurykratides, the son of Anaxandros son of Eurykrates, the son of Polydoros son of Alkamenes, the son of Teleklos son of Archelaos, the son of Agesilaos son of Doryssos, the son of Leobotas son of Echestratos, the son of Agis son of Eurysthenes, the son of Aristodemos son of Aristomachos, the son of Kleodaios son of Hyllos, who was the son of Herakles."

§8. Genealogies preserved in oral memory often confused generations which shared the same name and reduced one's ancestry to a series of fathers succeeded by sons when the truth was much more complex, frequently involving many different branches of a family tree, multiple marriages, and adoption of a male relative (nephew, cousin, etc.) as one's heir. Herodotus provides evidence for a series of complicated relations within the Philaid family: according to him, Miltiades III and Kimon I were half brothers who shared a mother, and when this Miltiades died without a son, Kimon's son, Stesagoras II, was his heir (6.38); two generations later, Metiochos I and Kimon II were half brothers sharing a father, Miltiades IV, who had fought at Marathon (6.39, 6.41, 6.103). The genealogy for the earlier generations of this family, as preserved in Marcellinus' life of Thucydides, is much simpler, suspiciously so, since son succeeds father in a neat and orderly fashion, without any of the complications known from other sources.

§9. Greek naming patterns for boys reinforced this particular kind of simplifying memory. In general, in Greek cities from Sparta to Athens and even Macedonia, a son was named after his paternal grandfather or his maternal grandfather. The pattern is so ubiquitous that Herodotus does not pause to comment on it. Kleisthenes of Athens was named for his maternal grandfather, Kleisthenes the tyrant of Sicyon, and Herodotus suggests that he even imitated that grandfather in some of the political changes which he instituted in Athens (5.67.1). The last member of the family who ruled Athens in the sixth century, Peisistratos was named after his paternal grandfather, the tyrant, who had been named by his father not for someone in the previous generation, but after Peisistratos the son of the Trojan War hero Nestor (5.65.4). Perhaps the most extreme example of this pattern is the family which ruled Cyrene and which claimed descent from Euphemus, one of the Argonauts[a] (4.150): the founder Battos was succeeded by his son Arkesilaos, who was succeeded by his son Battos, who was succeeded by his son Arkesilaos . . . for eight generations, just as the Delphic oracle had foretold (4.163). To distinguish one ruler from another with the same name, descriptive adjectives might be added, and so Herodotus refers to Battus the Prosperous (4.159), grandfather of Battus the Lame (4.161–62).[b]

§10. Herodotus distinguishes the men who come into his narrative by a combination of these naming patterns. He may give them their personal name, their patronymic, their family name, and their city. He might then add some detail which further characterizes the man: he was an Olympic victor, tyrant of a city, a seer, or held some civic or religious office. Thus, we read about: "an Athenian called Kylon, who had been victorious in the games at Olympia" (5.71.1); "Stesagoras son of Kimon, who was his maternal half-brother" (6.38.1); and "Eetion son of Echekrates . . . from the deme of Petra, but in origin a Lapith and Caeneid" (5.92).

§11. Such prominent men and families strengthened their position in the world in many ways, but frequently through marriage alliances. The Alkmeonids made use of this technique more than once. As Herodotus reports, Kleisthenes of Sicyon held a year-long competition to find a suitor for his daughter Agariste. The Alkmeonid Megakles was chosen, which "made the fame of the Alkmeonids resound throughout Hellas" (6.131). Then, in the struggles for control of Athens in the first half of the sixth century, this same Megakles, the head of one political faction, offered Peisistratos, leader of another faction, his daughter in marriage and his support for Peisistratos' tyranny. Presumably, Megakles anticipated that a son might be born

L.9a   For the ship *Argo* and its crew the Argonauts, see the entry for Argonauts in the Glossary.
L.9b   In footnotes to the text, the alternate Battos-

Arkesilaos generations are identified by Roman numerals: Battos, Battos II, Arkesilaos III, etc.

from this marriage who might come to power in his own turn. Peisistratos accepted, and for a time, the combined power of the two groups enabled him to rule Athens; but there were no offspring from the marriage, and Megakles withdrew his support from Peisistratos, causing him to lose power for the second time. Herodotus' version of the story includes references to a curse on the Alkmeonids, which was one of the reasons that prompted Peisistratos not to father children with Megakles' daughter (1.61.1–2).

§12. Stories like the alliance between the Alkmeonids and the Peisistratids also reveal the fragility of such marriage alliances between families. These might not last even one generation or might be broken in subsequent ones. Some families seem to have tried to avoid such problems altogether: Herodotus reports that the Bacchiads, the oligarchs who controlled Corinth for many generations before Kypselos, chose marriage partners from within their family only (5.92.1). The downfall of the Bacchiads came about, according to Herodotus, from not following this policy: when a lame girl was born to one of them, none of her clansmen wanted to marry her, so she was given to a husband of a different family. She bore a son who grew up to be Kypselos, who took control of Corinth and established a brutal regime (5.92).

§13. Women in Herodotus' narrative are not as frequently identified by their personal names as the men are, but are often referred to simply as someone's daughter or someone's wife. This pattern demonstrates, however, just how important women were as links between families. Herodotus never gives, for instance, the name of the Alkmeonid girl unhappily married to Peisistratos, but merely refers to her as "the daughter of Megakles" (1.61). Occasionally, we do get a glimpse of naming patterns for women, however, and they seem to parallel those of men: Agariste daughter of Kleisthenes of Sicyon (6.127) has a granddaughter named Agariste (6.131).

§14. Although the paternal line might be of primary importance in Greek society, the maternal line was not overlooked when it was useful to one side or another. Thus, Kleisthenes of Athens was related to the tyrant of Sicyon through his mother, as Herodotus notes (6.131), and Pericles was also part of the Alkmeonids through his mother (6.131). The maternal line was particularly useful if one claimed a divine ancestor, since usually (though there were a few exceptions) a god fathered a child on a human mother.

§15. Alliance with the Alkmeonids reveals another potential drawback of power gained through political marriages. In a family's past might lie an ancestral curse which would not be of any significance until a political enemy chose to make it so. The Alkmeonids, part of the Athenian government in the late seventh century, had suppressed the attempt of Kylon to set up a tyranny. They were remembered for having murdered the Kylonian conspirators despite having promised them a safe exit from the sanctuaries on the Athenian Acropolis (5.71). At least twice in later years, political enemies used this curse to attack the Alkmeonids. In the aftermath of the Peisistratid tyranny, when Kleisthenes and Isagoras were struggling for control of the city, there was an attempt to banish Kleisthenes because he was an Alkmeonid and thus cursed (5.70–71). A similar charge was brought against Pericles, as Thucydides reports (*Thucydides* 1.126–127), in the political maneuvering before the Peloponnesian War.

§16. Just as religion could be used against a family, a family could also gain power through control of religious sites and festivals. When the Gephyraians came to Athens, they founded their own sanctuaries and established their own rites, including those of Achaean Demeter, in which no one else was allowed to participate (5.61.2). Herodotus notes that they were "excluded from a few privileges not worth mentioning" (5.57.2–3), but their prominence allowed them to participate in other Athenian festivals, including the Panathenaia, which under the Peisistratids had become the most important. One of the Gephyraian girls, a sister of the tyrannicide Harmodios, was chosen to be a basket-carrier in the Panathenaic procession when her brother and Aristogeiton, also Gephyraian, killed Hipparchos, the younger brother of the tyrant (see *Thucydides* 6.56).

§17. The power of religious sites and festivals might also be glimpsed in the efforts of some politicians either to break the link between a family and a shrine or to create a new festival to enhance their own power. Historical and archaeological evidence suggests that the Panathenaic festival in honor of Athena grew in importance during Peisistratid control of Athens. Perhaps the tyrants encouraged these rites because they had no important family religious center from which to draw power and because, by developing the Panathenaia, they could reduce the power which other important Athenian families drew from their ancestral shrines.

§18. Like the Peisistratids, the Alkmeonids, too, seem not to have had any connection with a Athenian cult. Their name is also derived not from a mythological founder, but from an historical figure. These two weaknesses in their status may be partly responsible for Kleisthenes' decision to replace the four traditional tribes of Athens with ten new ones. The old tribes had all been named after the sons of Ion, a mythical war-leader of Athens (8.44), while the ten new tribes were local heroes, including Ajax, who was from Salamis but was identified as a friend to Athens (5.66, 5.69.1). Herodotus remarks that Kleisthenes did, in fact, broaden his base of power by doing this (5.69.2).

§19. In surveying the evidence for the power of families in sixth- and fifth-century Greek cities, we must always remember that family traditions were shaped purposely by family members and others, and that Herodotus had his own reasons for giving the genealogies he did and for rejecting others. We should not simply accept the versions we are given, nor reject them out of hand, but understand that Greek patterns of thought, their understanding of their place in the world, and Herodotus' own perspective have all shaped the portraits of families which emerge from his text.

Carolyn Higbie
Professor of Classics
State University of New York
Buffalo, NY

The Lineage of Three Important Athenian Families

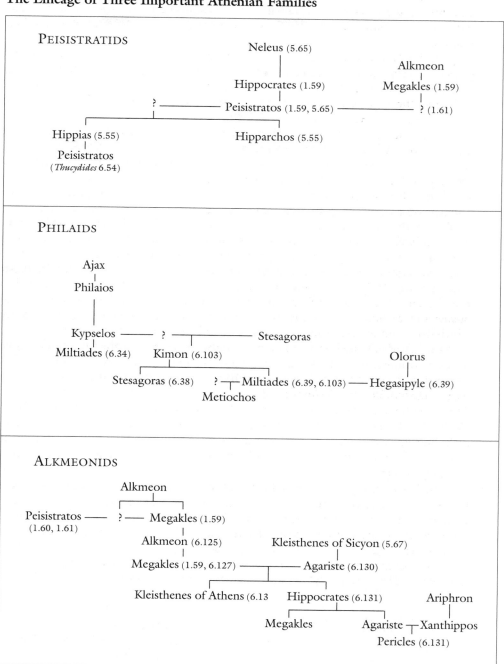

FIGURE L

APPENDIX M

Herodotus on Persia and the Persian Empire

§1. About half of Herodotus' text deals with Persian history. No preserved author but Xenophon can compete as a contemporary source on the empire; and, even if Ctesias[a] or the first-generation Alexander historians[b] had survived in full, Herodotus would still claim a special place. Still, there is more to Achaimenid history than Greco-Roman authors, and authors other than Herodotus have much to contribute.

§2. Persian sources are occasionally envisaged,[a] notably in a discussion of the cause of the Greco-Persian conflict (1.1.5), but the process of data collection is mostly a matter for speculation. The lists of tribute payers in 3.89–95 and military units in 7.61–97 are not authentic documents but amalgamations of Persian and Greek information (see §4); the account of Darius' accession has important points of contact with Darius' own account in the Behistun text[b]—notably the claim that the ruler whom he displaced was not Cambyses' brother Smerdis but an impostor—but does not depend directly upon it (too much is missing) and greatly elaborates on the shared elements. Herodotus admits several Old Persian words to his text, though few that were not naturalized in Greek, but his etymologies of royal names (6.98.3) and observation that all Persian proper names end in "s" (1.139) prove his limited linguistic expertise, and he could certainly have gathered Persian information from Greek speakers. Megabazos' complaint that the Myrkinians will do what Histiaios commands night and day (5.23.2) recalls Darius' "what has been said to them by me either by night or by day that they used to bring about,"[c] so genuine Persian turns of phrase may sometimes reach Herodotus. The King's house[d] is a more banal example of the phenomenon.

§3. Herodotus presents Persia and its empire in four ways. First, there's a ten-

M.1a Ctesias: a late-fifth-century doctor at the Persian court, author of a history of Persia, a geographical treatise, and the first separate work on India, now all lost except for a few fragments.

M.1b First-generation Alexander historians: men who accompanied Alexander of Macedon on his conquest of Persia, and who wrote histories or accounts containing sections on Persian history. None of these works, which apparently varied greatly in quality, have survived.

M.2a Citations of Persian sources: 1.95, 3.1.5, 3.87, 3.89.3, 3.105.1, 7.12.1.

M.2b The original text (in Old Persian, Akkadian, and Elamite) forms part of the monument carved into a mountainside at Behistun (in modern Turkey) above the high road from Babylon to Ecbatana. Copies were distributed through the empire, and part of an Aramaic version is preserved on a papyrus from Egypt.

M.2c This appears in the Behistun text (Darius *Behistun*, §7).

M.2d The King's house: 5.31.4, 7.52.2, 8.102.2, 9.107.1.

chapter passage on Persian religious and social customs (1.131–140). Much of this is probably accurate so far as it goes (though the apparent identification of Mitra as a goddess in 1.131.3 is a startling error, and the assertion that Persians did not anthropomorphize gods is not wholly true), but it is a scrappy collection, and we know enough to see that it oversimplifies the Iranian religious landscape. One notable problem is that, although the Magi (the only relevant priests Herodotus knows about) are important elsewhere as omen and dream interpreters (7.19, 7.37.2) and ritual officiants (1.132.3, 7.43.2, 7.113, 7.191.2), Herodotus does not seem to see the need to explain why a group associated with the Medes (1.101, 3.65), who have alien funerary customs, was so important among Persians. Herodotus knows that it was a polytheist environment and that "foreign" gods could be acknowledged,[a] but his mention of Xerxes' "Chariot of Zeus" (7.40.4, 8.115.4) does not prove he grasped Ahura Mazda's central role in royal ideology, and there were other sacrifice procedures than just the one he describes. Any treatment of Persian religion (the hardest topic in Achaimenid studies) must take into account (and make sense of) Herodotus' information, but it will be far more complex than his version. As for social customs, independent contemporary evidence is consistent with his reports of hatred of lies, rewards for producing male children, and dislike for pollution of rivers, but elsewhere—for example, the claim about debating matters both sober and drunk, or the summary of Persian education (ride, shoot, and speak the truth)—Herodotus is on his own. The depiction of *proskynesis*[b] as a social practice is important, as Greek authors (and Herodotus, too) tend to show it only in relation to the King. The Greek aversion to this practice, which they associated with worship of gods (although it was not common even in that context), is already visible (7.136). On debt (1.138) and disdain for marketplace practices (1.153), Herodotus postulates a quasi-moral economic primitivism that is ill-matched with the complexities of the Persepolis documents,[c] not to mention the market set up for the Mount Athos canal workers (7.23). But description of Darius' gold coins as a "memorial" (4.166) may not be unfair.

§4. Second, Herodotus offers lists of tribute districts (3.89–95) and military contingents (7.61–97). These largely identical sets of nations, arranged in the twenty satrapies reputedly established by Darius and the forty-one military units (twenty-nine terrestrial, twelve naval) of Xerxes' army, raise many questions. Some believe the tribute figures can be used to illuminate imperial economics (others disagree strongly); many feel that the roll call of military commanders (some of whom appear in Persepolis documents, as do persons from other parts of Herodotus' text) is good evidence about the

M.3a Foreign gods in Persian religious environment: 7.43.2, 7.191.2, 8.54, 9.37.1.

M.3b *Proskynesis*: a gesture of obeisance, sometimes involving prostration, when approaching a superior. See 3.86.2, 7.13.3, 7.136.1, 8.118.4.

M.3c There are two archives of Elamite documents from Persepolis, Treasury and Fortification. The latter in particular (currently still only half published) reveals a complex system for the management of worker groups and the collection, disbursement, and occasional sale of natural produce in a large administrative area stretching from Susa to Persepolis and beyond.

pinnacle of Persian society. But the lists are not authentic Persian documents, and almost no one thinks all twenty-nine terrestrial units marched against Greece. They are better seen as the components of a review army: see also 7.44, 7.100.1–2.

§5. Third, there's a narrative of the origins and growth of Persian power up to the unsuccessful attacks on Greece (some later events are also mentioned).[a] On one level this tells how the Persians surrendered their tribal character (1.125, 4.167) to the dominance of the Achaimenids, a clan ("phratry") of the Pasargadai tribe (1.125), and at the same time exchanged their original austerity for the enjoyment of luxuriant prosperity—a theme that is highlighted at the start and end of the narrative (1.71, 1.89, 1.126, 9.122) and recurs at many points in between.[b] On another level it is a complex politico-military story spanning seventy years, in which the main focus is on the Persians' liberation from Median control, their conquest of Lydia, Babylon, and Egypt, their defeat at the hands of the Scythians, and their ultimate failure in Greece. By contrast, the eastward extension of the empire to India is barely mentioned, and the Persian advances into Thrace and Macedonia are only sketched. The general lineaments of this story are reliable, but some specific components are suspect: for example, Cyrus' origins are saga, and his onetime subjection to the Medes debatable; Darius' Scythian campaign is geographically outrageous; and Persian relations with Macedonia are misrepresented. Surviving non-Greek sources tend to be either non-narrative royal inscriptions or administrative or business documents—quite different in nature and purpose from Herodotus' narrative history—and only rarely is there the sort of overlap that allows Herodotus' stories to be directly compared with a more local version. On Darius' accession (see §2) there *is* some agreement, although this does not prove that Darius' claim about the identity of his displaced predecessor was true. Egyptian material does not depict a mad Cambyses, but not all of it is entirely objective in character, and Herodotean distortion may be informed by Egyptian ill will. Babylonian narrative texts[c] provide an un-Herodotean (if not entirely neutral) depiction of Cyrus' capture of Babylon, while other documents do not even confirm the existence of Darius' satrap Zopyrus, let alone his heroic self-mutilation (3.160).

§6. One important narrative issue for Herodotus is what lay behind the culminating Greco-Persian conflict of 480–479. He highlights (a) the long-term implications of Croesus' subjection of Asiatic Greeks and his disastrous provocation of Persia, and (b) the chain of misfortunes that flowed from Athens' involvement in the Ionian Revolt. The Asiatic Greeks are a common factor, and successive Persian actions are variously seen in terms of self-defense, revenge, and the King's need to prove himself, to distract potential dissidents or match his own or his predecessors' successes. The resulting combination of specific casus belli with a pattern of aggression that increasingly takes on a life of its own answers the question posed in Herodotus' first sentence, "concerning the causes that led them to make war upon each other," and may

M.5a   Herodotus mentions later events at 3.15.3, 3.160.2, 7.7, 7.106–107, 7.134–137, 7.151.
M.5b   Persian wealth and luxury: 1.207.6–7, 3.22.1–4, 3.130.5, 3.139.2, 4.1.1, 5.21.2, 7.69.2, 7.83.2, 7.100.2, 7.190, 9.20, 9.22.2, 9.41.3, 9.70.3, 9.80–83.
M.5c   There are two relevant Babylonian texts: 1) The Nabonidus Chronicle, a succinct and ostensibly

neutral year-by-year account of major events in the reign of Nabonidus (555–539), the last part of which covers the Persian conquest in September–October 539. 2) The Cyrus Cylinder, a specially created propaganda text criticizing Nabonidus' impiety and representing Cyrus' "peaceful" conquest of Babylon as a fulfillment of the will of the Babylonian god Marduk.

encapsulate a view that the Achaimenid state acquired a structural need for imperial expansion. The dream's insistence on war in 7.12–18 frames this in quasi-epic form— it is not for the King to abandon the *nomos* of conquest that he himself has articulated (7.8)—and territorial extension is even represented as a satrapal imperative (3.120.3, 5.31.2–4). Neither this nor Xerxes' talk of equating his realm with the entire world (7.8.γ.2) is unequivocally justified by genuine royal utterances. The Persians of Herodotus display a strange mixture of exploratory zeal (4.43–44) and geographical ignorance (5.31.3, 5.106.6, 7.50.4, 7.54.2).

§7. Finally there is the information on the character and institutions of the Achaimenid state that is embedded in the narrative. For Herodotus, the empire's capital is Susa: Persepolis is unknown, Pasargadai appears only as a tribe name, Ecbatana only as the Median capital, and the King's regular movement between capitals is thus missing (1.188 might be a hint, though). Susa is joined to the west by a well-guarded Royal Road and a courier system,[a] though dependable independent testimony for the latter is lacking. The empire's extent (with the slight fuzziness at the northern and southern edges) is well caught in the tribute and army lists, but Herodotus' narrative of Persian history, like the Greek tradition in general, is heavily skewed to the west. That royal power was exercised through governors (never called "satraps" in Herodotus) controlling areas of the magnitude of tribute-list "satrapies" is a reasonably accurate proposition. People with an apparently larger sphere of authority appear occasionally (5.25.1, 5.30.5, 7.135.1). The space between satrap and more local areas of authority (exemplified by native rulers in Phoenicia, client-kings in Egypt, and tyrants in Greek cities[b]) is not systematically mapped, though Herodotus does associate indirect rule through a chain of intermediaries with Media, not Persia (1.134.2–3). To speak, as Herodotus does, of Persia's "allies" (5.32, 8.113) misapplies a Greek template, as does sending messages "to the cities" (7.1.2). Prospective subjects offer earth and water,[c] a symbolic ritual of debated import known only from Herodotus. Actual subjects offer precious-metal tribute, payment in kind, gifts[d] and corvée service. This is a broadly accurate picture, but the local systems are beyond Herodotus' ken (though 3.117.5 shows awareness of other possible income streams), and the Persepolis documents show that the claim that Persia was tax-exempt (3.97.1) is only partly true. (In the same way there is no Persian delegation among the subjects bringing gifts to the King on the Apadana frieze.[e]) Individuals hold land or cities by royal grant,[f] a whole city can receive extra territory (1.160), populations are deported across the empire,[g] terrain is measured and water exploited to generate tribute (3.117.5, 6.42.2). Roads are created (3.7–9, 7.115.3, 7.131), dikes mended (2.99.3), and garrisons installed (2.30.3, 3.90.3, 3.91.3). Otherwise Herodotus

M.7a The Royal Road: 5.35.3, 5.50.2, 5.52–54, 7.239.3. Courier system: 3.126, 5.14, 8.98.

M.7b Phoenicia: 8.67.2. Egypt: 3.15. Greek tyrants: 4.137, 5.11, 6.43.3, 7.130.3, 8.85.3.

M.7c Earth and water: 4.126, 5.17.1, 5.73.2, 6.48, 7.32, 7.131, 7.133, 7.138.1, 7.163.2.

M.7d Precious-metal tribute of Persian subjects: 3.89–95; see also 1.196.5, 3.13.3–4, 3.67.3, 4.165. Payment in kind: 1.192; 2.98.1, 2.149.5, 3.90.3, 3.91.3, 3.92.1, 7.32.1, 7.119.1–4. Gifts: 3.97.4–5. Corvée service: 7.23.

M.7e The monumental stairways to the Persepolis Apadana (palace complex) originally bore a cycle of carved images in which the enthroned king was surrounded by courtiers and gift-bearing delegations from subject peoples.

M7f Holding land by royal grant: 5.102.1, 6.20, 6.41.4, 6.70.2, 8.85.3, 8.136, 9.109.3.

M7g Forced movement of populations by Persians: 3.93.2, 4.204, 5.12.1, 6.3.3, 6.9.4, 6.20, 6.32, 6.119.1–4, 7.80.

conveys little sense of the empire's institutional occupation of territory, but one might mention large, labor-intensive projects[h]—of which the Red Sea canal is authenticated by contemporary records, and the Athos canal by its lasting topographic effect—as well as the Kings' marking of the landscape with inscribed monuments.[i] With the exception of the Victory Tripod (see Figure 9.81a), none of Herodotus' items reproduces a surviving monument, but the statue *not* erected at Heliopolis (2.110) does evoke a celebrated hieroglyph-adorned statue of Darius in Egyptian stone found at Susa. Darius set up a pillar to mark a beautiful spring (4.91), and Xerxes adorned a fine plane tree with gold (7.31), but the famous Persian gardens (*paradeisoi*) familiar from other sources are not found in Herodotus.

§8. Aside from army commanders and governors, we meet few nonmilitary office-holders in Herodotus, and all those whom we do encounter have direct royal connections: cupbearer (3.34), charioteer (7.40), household overseer (3.61), controllers of access (3.34.1, 3.77.2, 3.118.2), the satrap's royal secretary (3.128), royal judges (3.14.5, 3.31.2–4, 5.25, 7.194), and the King's Eye (1.114.2)—although some Greeks held that there was no such official because anyone could be a "king's eye" by turning informer. Greek comment on royal judges reflects a consciousness that regulation (the Old Persian word is *data*) mattered in the Persian scheme, but the judges' supposed declaration that law is whatever the King wants (3.31) reveals a Greek conviction that it was all a sham, as was only to be expected in a system where everyone, however exalted, was the King's slave.[a] More generally the King is served by an elite Persian society, with relatives by blood or marriage at the top and privileges for the families of Darius' co-conspirators (3.84.2; some doubt this)—an elite that supplies not only his governors and army commanders but also the core of his advisors.[b] (Apart from Harpagos, Mazares, and Datis, however, Medes are entirely absent. This is a *Persian* empire: see 1.134.) But such advisors, though they may share the King's dinner, cannot be sure he wants honesty and open debate,[c] and 7.8–18 pictures Persian decision-making as a strange drama of self-seeking flattery, rejected rationality, and supernatural intervention. Royal power is the central fact: no primus inter pares—though no god either (Herodotus does not make the mistake of later authors). And, despite the cordon sanitaire in 7.40, not really a secluded figure (see also 3.65, 5.12), the King dominates the political process, while the administrative process (which embraced numerous officials and managed a ration-based system wholly unknown to Herodotus, as to most Greeks) is simply ignored. It is a culture of lavish gifts and rewards,[d] with formally recognized benefactors,[e] but also one of fear of punishment for failure (6.9.1, 8.15, 8.100)—punishment that is often brutal[f]

M7h Labor-intensive projects: 1.189.3–4, 2.158, 3.117, 4.87.1, 4.89, 4.124.1, 7.22–25, 7.34–36, 7.130.2, 8.97.1.

M7i Inscribed monuments: 2.110.2, 3.88.3, 4.88.2, 4.91.2.

M8a Everyone but the King is a slave: 7.8.β.2, 7.11.4, 7.39.1, 7.135.3, 8.102. In Greece men are slaves only of law: 7.102–104.

M8b A core of advisors which can be joined by Greeks (3.133, 4.97.6, 5.24, 5.106, 7.3.1–4, 7.101–104, 7.209, 7.234–7), Lydians (1.155, 1.207, 3.34–36), and women (3.134, 8.69).

M8c Sharing the King's dinner: 3.132, 5.24.4, 7.119.3. The problem of honesty and debate: 1.88.2,

3.154.1, 4.97.2, 7.8.δ.2, 7.10.1, 7.10.α.1–2, 7.11.1, 7.101, 7.105, 7.209.

M8d Royal gifts: 3.84.1, 3.130.3–4, 3.160.2, 4.88.1, 6.70.2, 7.106.1, 7.116, 7.135.2, 8.5, 8.85.3, 8.120, 8.136.1, 9.18.3, 9.41.3, 9.107.3, 9.109.3, 9.110–11. Rewards: 1.84.1, 1.162, 3.138.1, 3.154.1, 4.88.1, 4.143, 5.11, 6.30.2, 6.100.2, 7.19.2, 7.26.2, 7.106.1, 8.10.3, 8.85.3, 9.18.3.

M8e Recognized benefactors: 3.140.1, 6.9.3, 6.30.2, 8.85.3, 8.90.4.

M8f Persian brutality: 3.35, 3.69.5, 3.125.3, 3.130.1, 3.132.2, 3.155.4, 3.159.1, 4.43.1–6, 5.25, 6.9.4, 6.30.1, 6.32, 7.194.1, 7.238.1, 8.90.3, 8.118.4, 9.112.

and wide-ranging (3.119, 9.113.2). The King's advantage is what matters (1.132.2), so the assessment of a person's record is pragmatic and calculating (1.137); a man can be crucified but then rescued when Xerxes realizes he has done his sums wrong (7.194), and no one, however generous to the King, can rely upon him to be generous in turn in his demand for service (4.84, 7.27–28, 7.39).

§9. Around the King (who is supposed to be as handsome as he is powerful: 4.91.2, 7.187.2) are eunuchs, concubines, and polygamous queens; it is a world of conspiracy and erotic intrigue, hunting and lavish eating.[a] But Herodotus eschews garish depiction of oriental decadence: there is no strong sense of harem—rightly, judging from the Persepolis archive—and the King's dinner is evoked only in its campaign version (7.118), as is large-scale ceremonial (7.40). Xerxes' womenfolk do produce a classic tale of court debauchery and violence (9.108–113). But Atossa's involvement with plans for imperial conquest (3.134) and Xerxes' succession (7.2) are presented in matter-of-fact terms, and Herodotus evidently found no juicy stories prompted by the fact that, while Atossa was the powerful wife (7.3), Artystone was the favorite one (7.69.2). (Ironically only Artystone appears in the Persepolis archives.) Atossa was one of Cambyses' sister-brides (3.31), but Herodotus' treatment of sister-marriage (to be seen as pragmatic endogamy, not Mazdaean injunction) concentrates on royal judges and the King's madness, and it does not cast the other sister-bride as a royal harridan.

§10. Apart from the army list, with its record of clothing and weapons, and the implications of a story full of warfare (though battle-narrative occupies a small proportion of the whole), Herodotus' record of the military aspect of the Persian state is modest. At sea Persia is entirely dependent upon subject peoples. On land cavalry is important (and generals enter battle on horseback), but it is by no means dominant: infantrymen with bow, spear, sword, scale armor (barely armor at all to a Greek: 9.62.3), and wicker shield[a] were crucial to Persian success and failure—such were the famous 10,000 "Immortals," with their gold-adorned clothing (7.83.2), and all the troops immediately around the King (7.40). Labor-intensive siege works (of the sort still visible at Old Paphos), slaughter, and destruction[b] marked the progress of Persian armies, whose scale prompted absurd estimates of numbers, peddled by Herodotus tongue-in-cheek (7.184–186). Bravery is a privileged virtue (1.136) and Mardonios calls it the Persian *nomos* to win by fighting, not bribery (9.41); but Herodotus makes no particular effort to represent Persia as a militarist power, and palatial royal iconography certainly eschews such a representation. Herodotus' text culminates in comprehensive Persian defeat on land and sea, but the empire survived another 150 years.

Christopher Tuplin
Department of Classics and Ancient History
School of Archaeology, Classics, and Egyptology
University of Liverpool, UK

M.9a   Eunuchs: 3.92.1, 3.130.4, 6.32, 7.187.2, 8.104–106. Concubines: 1.135, 5.18.2, 6.32, 7.83.2, 7.187.1, 9.76, 9.81.1. Polygamous queens: 3.68, 3.88.2–3, 3.130.4, 7.2, 7.69.2, 7.78, 7.224.2. Conspiracy: 1.209–210, 3.30.3, 3.119.1, 9.113. Erotic intrigue: 9.108–113. Hunting: 3.30.3, 3.129.1. Lavish eating: 1.133, 7.32, 7.118–119, 9.82, 9.110.2.

M.10a Wicker shields: 7.61.1, 9.62.2, 9.99.3, 9.102.2–3.

M.10b Labor-intensive siege works: 1.163, 4.200, 5.115, 6.18. Slaughter: 1.176, 3.147, 6.19, 8.127, 9.39. Destruction: 1.154, 6.19, 6.25, 6.31–33, 6.95–96, 6.102, 8.32, 8.35, 8.50, 8.53, 8.109, 9.13, 9.66.

APPENDIX N

Hoplite Warfare in Herodotus

§1. Herodotus' *Histories*, our major source for Archaic Greek history and especially the era of the Greek-Persian Wars, provide a frustratingly incomplete picture of Greek warfare. When it came to war, Herodotus was concerned more with the moral than the technical, more with the influence of gods than of generals, more with the illustrious or cowardly deeds of individuals than with the overall course of an engagement. To the modern reader, Herodotus' descriptions of the great land battles—Marathon, Thermopylae, Plataea—of the Greek-Persian Wars can thus be confusing and elliptical. He omits crucial details, notably the strength of the Athenian army at Marathon and the precise positioning of the Greek army at Plataea. The Persian troop figures he offers are fantastically exaggerated.[a] Elsewhere he presents contradictory (1.171, 4.180) or misleading (6.112) information about military affairs. Only by examining Herodotus in conjunction with later written sources and the evidence of archaeology and art history can we fill in the gaps in his account.

§2. Armored spearmen called hoplites dominated the armies of Archaic Greece. The essential component of hoplite equipment was a concave round shield of bronze-faced wood, about three feet in diameter and weighing some twelve to sixteen pounds. The shield was supported on its bearer's left arm by a distinctive double grip, said to be a Carian innovation (1.171) but probably borrowed from the Near East. Most hoplites also wore armor, usually a bronze breastplate or cuirass along with a bronze helmet and bronze greaves or shin guards (2.152, 4.180). By the time of the Persian Wars, composite armor of leather or laminated cloth reinforced with bronze was also available, as were linen corselets, light and durable but expensive (3.47). Complete hoplite panoply might weigh up to sixty pounds. While cumbersome and uncomfortable, it provided excellent protection against missile and melée attacks (9.62). Fit and trained soldiers could move nimbly, even run, while wearing hoplite gear (6.112).

§3. For offense, the hoplite relied on his bronze-tipped thrusting spear, some

N.1a   See Appendix R, The Size of Xerxes' Expedi-
       tionary Force, for a discussion of this issue.

seven or eight feet long. The spear was fitted with a bronze end-spike, enabling it to remain a serviceable weapon even if its shaft broke in battle. A short, straight iron sword, typically less than two feet long, served as a secondary weapon (7.224). Vase paintings reveal that a few hoplites, following old-fashioned Homeric style, still carried a pair of lighter throwing spears in place of a single thrusting spear.[a]

§4. Most hoplites were citizen-soldiers who furnished their own armor and weapons. Outside Sparta, few of them underwent organized military training.[a] Several states did deploy elite hoplite units, typically 300 strong.[b] At the time of the Persian Wars, tactical organization remained fairly simple. The Spartan army was composed of an uncertain number of *lochoi*, or regiments (9.53), each divided into *enomotiai*, "sworn bands" or platoons (1.65). There were regimental and platoon officers, with Sparta's kings holding overall command (5.74–76). The Athenians mustered their hoplites in ten regiments, one for each of the ten democratic tribes established by Kleisthenes in 508/07 (5.66). A polemarch, or war leader, once headed the Athenian military, but in the early fifth century was superseded by a board of ten elected generals[c] (6.103, 6.109). Discipline in citizen armies could be lax: men might play dice or nap in the afternoon (1.63), refuse to drill (6.14), or sit down to lunch without posting sentries (6.78). Even in the strictly trained Spartan army, orders were not always orders: at Plataea one Spartan regiment caused considerable confusion by refusing to obey what it considered a dishonorable command to withdraw to a new position (9.53).

§5. The standard hoplite battle formation, the phalanx, developed gradually over the centuries. In classical times the phalanx was a densely packed arrangement, typically eight ranks deep,[a] optimized for mass shock combat. While Herodotus sometimes anachronistically portrays hoplites fighting in classical fashion, the Archaic phalanx was in reality looser and less structured. Armies did form up in close-ordered lines, but contingents were able to advance or withdraw on their own initiative (5.75, 5.113, 9.62). Battles could proceed in seesaw fashion, with troops repeatedly charging and falling back (7.225, 9.21, 9.74). Archers[b] and other light troops occasionally fought mixed in with hoplites (9.22, 9.29–30). Though Herodotus presents hoplite war as ritualized, head-on combat (7.9), night ambushes (5.121) and surprise attacks (6.78) were not unheard of. The Spartans at Thermopylae even used feigned flight to lure their enemies to destruction (7.211). Hoplites also fought outside the phalanx: in single combat (1.82, 6.92), as marines at sea (6.12), and as amphibious raiders (3.45, 6.28).

§6. Although the Greeks also deployed light infantry in their wars with Persia, Herodotus virtually writes them out of his story. He highlights the absence of Athenian archers at Marathon (6.112), but a unit of Athenian archers that played a vital role at Plataea (9.22) receives only passing mention. The 70,000 other light

N.3a See Figure N.1, statues of hoplites from the temple of Aphaia on Aegina.

N.4a See Figure N.4, a vase painting of a hoplite putting on his armor as his wife stands by, holding two spears and his shield; an archer in a Scythian cap is just behind him (early fifth century).

N.4b Some 300 Spartan Knights, 8.124; 300 picked Athenians, 9.21–23; 300 of the best and most prominent Thebans, 9.67.

N.4c Polemarch, Board of Generals at Athens: see Appendix A, The Athenian Government in Herodotus, §9.

N.5a See *Thucydides* 5.68 and Xenophon's *Hellenica* 3.2.16.

N.5b See Figures N.2 and N.3, early fifth-century statues of archers, from the west pediment of the temple of Aphaia on Aegina.

FIGURE N.1. STATUES OF HOPLITES—
ONE IN COMBAT, ANOTHER DYING—
FROM THE WEST PEDIMENT OF THE
TEMPLE OF APHAIA ON AEGINA. LATE
SIXTH OR EARLY FIFTH CENTURY.

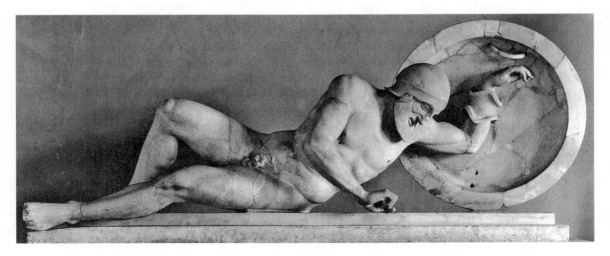

troops, including some 35,000 helots,[a] alleged to have fought at Plataea (9.28–30) play no discernible role in Herodotus' account. The helots who fought with the Spartans at Thermopylae are likewise barely mentioned (7.229).

§7. Most Greek states fielded little cavalry; the Syracusans and Thessalians were notable exceptions.[a] A few wealthier hoplites still served as mounted infantry, riding to the battlefield but fighting on foot (1.63). Some Greeks, notably on Cyprus, employed war chariots as well as cavalry (5.113). Horsemen were most dangerous to infantry on open ground (5.63, 6.102) or if they stood off and launched missile attacks (9.49, 9.60). They could also turn the tide after a long infantry struggle (6.29) and were very effective for screening friendly hoplites in retreat or for pursuing routed and disordered foes. Hoplites, though, could counter cavalry by taking up positions on high or difficult terrain (6.108, 9.20), by closing ranks to form a defensive hedgehog (9.18), or by attacking in tandem with missile troops (9.22–23). At Marathon, some have hypothesized that the Athenians, lacking cavalry, waited to attack until the horsemen in the Persian landing force had re-embarked on their transports and were no longer a threat. Herodotus, however, never explicitly mentions the Persian cavalry in his narrative, and it is also possible that there were simply not enough of them in the landing force to play a decisive role in the battle.

§8. Traditional hoplite generalship involved little beyond pointing an army toward the enemy; generals fought, and sometimes died, in ranks with their troops (6.92, 6.114). The Greek-Persian Wars, though, required more than that, and Greek leadership rose to the occasion. At Marathon, the Athenian commanders skillfully chose the proper moment to attack and devised a new formation to defeat an enemy using unfamiliar tactics and equipment. By advancing quickly during the last stage of their attack—although certainly not the eight stades (about 4,800 yards) of Herodotus' account—they also minimized the danger from Persian archery. Leonidas at Thermopylae made cunning use of terrain to offset his numerical inferiority and shelter his troops (7.208–225). At Plataea the allied Greek commanders under Pausanias overcame the triple challenges of holding together a coalition army, coping with terrain, and keeping supplies flowing from distant bases.

§9. Not all Greeks fought in defense of their homelands. The more civilized states of the Near East had long sought mercenary soldiers, and by the mid-seventh century thousands of hoplites were serving abroad for pay. Ionian and Carian hoplites established permanent camps in Egypt (2.152–154), from which Egyptian kings could recruit up to 30,000 mercenaries; these "bronze men" (2.163) played a major role in the unsuccessful Egyptian resistance to Persian invasion (3.11). The Samians employed mercenaries against the Spartans (3.54), and Argive "volunteers" helped Aegina against Athens (6.92). Although they were not strictly speaking mercenaries, Greek hoplites, both conscripts (3.1, 4.97–98, 6.99) and willing allies (9.31, 9.67), fought alongside the Persians in numerous campaigns.

§10. While the Archaic Greeks lagged behind the Persians in offensive siege technology, they did develop effective defenses, including stone city fortifications with

---

N.6a Helots: see Appendix B, The Spartan State in War and Peace.

N.7a For Thessalian cavalry, see 5.63, 7.196, 8.28; for Syracusan cavalry, 7.158.3.

FIGURE N.2. STATUE OF A GREEK ARCHER FROM THE PEDIMENT OF THE TEMPLE OF APHAIA ON AEGINA, DATED FROM THE LATE SIXTH OR EARLY FIFTH CENTURY.

towers (1.163, 3.54), deep ditches (1.174), rural strongholds (5.62), and border walls (6.36, 7.176). The Spartans at Thermopylae used one such rural wall to good effect (7.223). Direct assaults on fortified cities were costly (6.101), and could lead to intense street fighting (3.55–56, 5.101–102). Sometimes attackers were able to breach defenses by stealth (1.84), but often the best way to gain entry was to enlist the aid of traitors within (1.150, 3.147). Otherwise the only option was to invest a city and wait until the defenders exhausted their food (5.65).

§11. Religion held an important place in Archaic Greek warfare. Religious scruples shaped military decisions: the Spartans, for instance, were prevented from reinforcing the Athenians at Marathon because of a religious festival (6.105–107). Before joining battle, commanders performed sacrifices, invoked the gods (6.112, 9.61), and consulted soothsayers (1.62, 7.219–221, 9.33). Soldiers advanced to the fray singing their paean, or war hymn. The psychological traumas of battlefield violence were interpreted as manifestations of the divine (6.117). In battles between Greeks, victory customarily went to the side that held the field at day's end, although there was still dispute about this at the end of the sixth century. Stripping the bodies

FIGURE N.3. STATUE OF A SCYTHIAN ARCHER FROM THE PEDIMENT OF THE TEMPLE OF APHAIA ON AEGINA, DATED FROM THE LATE SIXTH OR EARLY FIFTH CENTURY.

of the enemy was the victor's prerogative. Along with it came the obligation to hand over the bodies of the dead for burial under truce (1.82). Professional messengers called heralds carried messages between armies, made public announcements, and mediated truces (1.83, 6.77). To harm a herald was sacrilege. Victors consecrated a tithe of their spoils to the gods, leaving temples across Greece adorned with captured arms and armor, or with statues bought from the sale of war booty (8.27). Setting up a *tropaion*, or trophy, to mark possession of the field, once thought a traditional religious element of war, did not in fact become common until after the Persian Wars.

§12. The triumph of heavy-armed hoplites over light infantry and cavalry at Marathon and Plataea proved, or so it seemed, the superiority of Hellenic methods on the battlefield (9.62–63). Persian archery, galling as it may have been, seemed ultimately to have been unable to stop Greeks relying on close combat (6.113). Even the defeat at Thermopylae could be held up as an example of superior Greek courage and better weaponry (7.211) triumphing over impossible odds. To Greeks who had served in the Persian Wars, the hoplite phalanx thus came to represent the

FIGURE N.4. AN EARLY-FIFTH-CENTURY VASE PAINTING OF A HOPLITE PUTTING ON HIS ARMOR AS HIS WIFE STANDS BY, HOLDING TWO SPEARS AND HIS SHIELD. AN ARCHER WEARING A SCYTHIAN CAP IS JUST BEHIND HIM.

truest and best way of war. Such was the power of this idea that the playwright Aeschylus, a veteran of Marathon, inflated a minor hoplite skirmish that accompanied the naval engagement of Salamis (8.95) into the decisive moment of the battle (Aeschylus *Persae* 435–471). Only in the Peloponnesian War would the grandsons of Aeschylus' generation learn the limits of hoplite warfare.

John W. I. Lee
Department of History
University of California
Santa Barbara, CA

APPENDIX O

The Persian Army in Herodotus

§1. The Persian army of Herodotus' *Histories* presents a paradox. On the one hand there are the swift, powerful warriors of Cyrus and Cambyses, capable of creating the greatest empire the world had yet seen. On the other, there are the lumbering and inept troops of Darius and Xerxes that invaded Greece in 490 and 480–479. Herodotus' depiction of the latter is plainly skewed to present a picture of heroic Greek resistance against overwhelming odds. Little if any of the information he offers on the size, equipment, tactics, and leadership of Persian armies during the Greek-Persian Wars, therefore, can be taken at face value. On rare occasions, evidence from archaeology and the few surviving Achaimenid documents allow us to make more realistic assessments of Persian military capabilities. For the most part, however, we have no option but to rely on Herodotus and attempt to correct for his biases. Even so, his narrative is sometimes so selective that no more than educated guesses about what actually happened are possible.

§2. Determining the size of Persian armies is exceedingly difficult. No reliable figures are available for the expedition of Datis and Artaphrenes in 490, despite Herodotus' claim that the Persians suffered 6,400 casualties at Marathon[a] (6.117). It is possible that Datis and Artaphrenes led a force equal or inferior in numbers to the Athenians and Plataeans who faced them there. Xerxes' army in 480 is said to have mustered 1,700,000 infantry and 80,000 cavalry (7.60, 7.184), divided into twenty-nine national contingents under the command of six generals (7.61–88). These figures are impossibly exaggerated.[b] Comparisons with other ancient armies operating in the eastern Mediterranean, along with analysis of the practical constraints of supply and movement, suggest that Xerxes actually fielded perhaps 75,000 to 100,000 men. The next year at Plataea,[c] Mardonios allegedly deployed a force of 300,000 (8.100, 9.32). Less than half this number, though, could have fit into the palisaded camp Herodotus describes (9.15). Indeed, his narrative of Greek and Persian deployments at Plataea implies that the two sides had battle lines of roughly equal length. Some modern scholars estimate that the Persian army at

O.2a   Marathon: Map O, inset.
O.2b   For a more detailed discussion of the size of Xerxes'   O.2c   Plataea: Map O, inset.

expeditionary force in 480, see Appendix R.

805

Plataea numbered about 30,000 Persians and 20,000 Greek allies, compared to the 40,000 hoplites Herodotus reports for the combined Greek army (9.29).

§3. Persian units were organized on a decimal basis: squads of ten, companies of 100, regiments of 1,000, and brigades of 10,000 (7.81). There were also picked units of 1,000 men for special missions (9.63). Achaimenid ration tablets from Egypt and Babylonia[a] reveal that the actual strength of a unit could fall well below its official complement. A notable exception was the elite infantry brigade of 10,000 Immortals (7.31, 7.83), so called because its casualties were always immediately replaced.

§4. The Persian "Army List" of Herodotus (7.61–88) details the equipment of the various national contingents of the army, but troops armed in the Persian style dominate Herodotus' battle narratives. Persian infantry wore little armor, often consisting of no more than a reinforced fabric tunic and trousers, and carried large rectangular shields of wicker and leather (7.61, 9.63). They had swords or daggers and short spears (7.41, 7.211) for close combat, but relied primarily on their large bows (7.61). On the battlefield, Persian troops could use their shields to form a protective barricade from behind which they could shoot their bows (9.61–62, 9.102). After loosing volleys of arrows to soften up an enemy, they could follow up with a hand-to-hand assault (1.214, 9.62) or let their cavalry charge the enemy's now disorganized ranks (6.29).

§5. In his account of Plataea, Herodotus stresses the inability of lightly armored Persian infantry to withstand well-protected Greek hoplites in melée combat (9.63). Despite their inferior equipment, though, Persian infantry displayed great bravery (7.210, 9.62); Herodotus' tale of their being driven forward with whips at Thermopylae[a] has the ring of Greek propaganda (7.223). The reluctant troops in the Persian army tended to be Greeks, especially Ionians (4.97–98, 4.136, 6.99). Persian infantry were also tough and capable fighters. At Marathon they withstood a hoplite charge and held their own for a long time before the Athenians gained the upper hand (6.113). Herodotus' own narrative, moreover, reveals that Persian infantry had repeatedly defeated more heavily armored opponents, including hoplites, in Egypt and Ionia[b] (3.11, 5.119–122, 6.28–30).

§6. It comes as no surprise that the Persians, who prized the ability to ride, shoot a bow, and tell the truth (1.136), excelled as horsemen. Their mounts were of the highest quality (7.196) and sometimes received special combat training (5.109–113). Persian cavalry typically wore metal breastplates and helmets. An uncertain proportion possessed additional armor, and in some cases their horses too may have been armored (Xenophon, *Anabasis* 1.8.6). The general Masistios wore a particularly splendid and heavy cuirass at Plataea (9.22). Like infantry, cavalry was organized on a decimal basis, with regiments of 1,000 maneuvering independently in battle (7.41).

§7. The main weapons of the Persian cavalry were spears and bows (9.49). Rather than closing immediately with an enemy, they preferred to begin a battle by hurling missiles from a distance, often attacking in unit relays (9.18–22, 9.52, 9.57,

O.3a   Egypt, Babylon: Map O, locator.   O.5b   Ionia: Map O.
O.5a   Thermopylae: Map O.

MAP O

9.71). Once this harassment had broken the enemy's formation, the cavalry could pursue and ride down fleeing fugitives. These tactics required open, level ground to work effectively (9.21). Datis and Artaphrenes are said to have landed at Marathon for exactly this reason (6.102), and Mardonios in 479 apparently left Attica for Boeotia[a] because the latter region was more suited for cavalry (9.13). Cavalry was useful in protecting retreating infantry against hostile pursuit (9.68) and could inflict severe losses on disordered hoplites (9.69). Sometimes it was employed to ride behind the enemy's army to capture or at least disrupt the flow of supplies (9.50). The Persians also conducted some of the first known experiments in the long-range seaborne transport of cavalry (6.95).

§8. While Persian troops were skilled and courageous, their leadership was often deficient. To be sure, on some occasions Persian commanders did display tactical brilliance. At Thermopylae, for example, Xerxes and his officers skillfully pinned the defending Greeks with what may well have been a series of diversionary frontal assaults while they scouted for a way around the narrow pass. After locating a flanking route, they then executed a swift and well-coordinated night march to turn Leonidas' position (7.214–218). Elsewhere, though, Persian leadership in the Greek-Persian Wars failed. With rare exceptions (6.29), infantry and cavalry attacks were never properly combined for mutual support[a] (9.23). This lack of coordination may explain the notable absence of Persian horsemen from Herodotus' account of Marathon. Some have surmised that Datis and Artaphrenes re-embarked their cavalry in preparation to transport their force elsewhere without considering how this withdrawal would leave their infantry vulnerable to a sudden Greek hoplite attack. At Plataea, Mardonios led both infantry and cavalry, but was unable to keep his units in proper formation (9.59). While earlier Persian leaders had been famous for their use of stratagems and trickery (1.79–80, 4.201), the commanders during the wars with the Greeks were, at least as Herodotus portrays them, easy prey to Greek ruses (7.211).

§9. Persian commanders drew on a Near Eastern tradition of siege technology that had long been unsurpassed. Their engineers expertly used siege mounds, rams, and mines to capture fortified towns (1.162, 4.200, 6.18). Cyrus even dug channels to divert the Euphrates River during his siege of Babylon, enabling his troops to enter the city (1.190–191). Occasionally the Persians conducted direct assaults on fortifications (6.101). More often they relied on careful reconnaissance before using stealth (1.84), deceit (3.152–158), or traitors (6.101) to breach enemy defenses. They also excelled in constructing city walls (1.98–99, 1.177–181) and palisaded army camps (4.124, 9.65), and were tenacious in defending both (5.101–102, 9.70).

§10. The Persians also displayed their extraordinary engineering skills on campaign. They were capable of laying long pontoon bridges across major water obsta-

O.7a Attica, Boeotia: Map O.
O.8a Although the Persian and Boeotian cavalry did support and assist their infantry when the latter were fleeing from the enemy at the end of the pitched battle.

cles, including the Bosporus[a] (4.83–88) and the Ister (modern Danube) River (4.97–98). In 480, to avoid the delay, the labor and the risk of ferrying men, horses, and supplies by boat, they constructed not one but two bridges across the Hellespont[b] (7.36). To forestall the dangers of a rough sea passage, they cut a canal through the peninsula of Mount Athos,[c] complete with breakwaters at both ends to protect the entrances and prevent the canal from silting up (7.22–23, 7.37).

§11. Persian logistical services were similarly advanced. A system of pipelines and camel convoys carrying water enabled Cambyses to traverse the Arabian[a] desert on his way to conquer Egypt (3.9). For Xerxes' expedition, a carefully sited series of supply depots enabled the army to march swiftly across Thrace and Macedon and into Thessaly[b] (7.25). In some cases, supplies were requisitioned from towns along the route (7.118–121). After that, the army was efficiently supplied by sea. Mardonios in 479 prepared Thebes[c] as a base, with ample provisions and fodder (9.41). Herodotus harps on the rivers that Xerxes' force supposedly drank dry, but even he admits the overall effectiveness of Persia's quartermasters (7.43, 7.109, 7.187). The Persians also exploited the logistical vulnerabilities of their enemies. During the Plataea campaign they raided Greek supply convoys (9.39) and fouled vital water sources (9.49). Methodical preparation was the key to Persian logistics (7.20–21). On the rare instances when their system failed (3.25), it was the result of hasty and insufficient planning.

§12. The Persians who invaded Greece in 490 and 480–479 were trained, brave soldiers, not an unwilling rabble. Even Herodotus' slanted narrative reveals that Greek victory did not come easily. If the Persian center at Marathon had been able to follow up its success (6.113), or if Masistios and Mardonios had not been killed at Plataea (9.22, 9.63), these decisive battles might easily have gone the other way. A realistic appreciation of the Persian army thus enhances, rather than detracts from, our appreciation of the Greek accomplishment in the Greek-Persian Wars.

John W. I. Lee
Department of History
University of California
Santa Barbara, CA

O.10a Bosporus: Map O.
O.10b Hellespont: Map O.
O.10c Mount Athos: Map O.

O.11a Arabia: Map O, locator.
O.11b Thrace, Macedon, Thessaly: Map O.
O.11c Thebes, Boeotia: Map O, inset.

APPENDIX P

Oracles, Religion, and Politics in Herodotus

§1. Many cultures, both advanced and more primitive, recognize institutions at fixed locations that claim to have immediate channels to divinities. So too did the Greeks, and indeed divination was central to Greek religion. Live human beings in human-built edifices managed the Hellenic oracles. These people claimed communication with the supernatural realm since the indefinite past, often with the prophetic god Apollo, but also with certain chthonian, that is, presently buried, heroes—great men who once roamed the earth. Solemn communications from privileged sources help puzzled people cope with life's confounding problems like crop failure and choices such as marriage. Like other human institutions, these operations can lie, become greedy (9.38), or adjust their announcements to the way the wind is blowing. Oracles and oraclemongers were not automatically trusted; Lydian[a] Croesus famously tested many (1.46); the upstart Egyptian Amasis credited only some in Egypt[b]—namely, those that correctly identified him as a thief (2.174)!

§2. Divination in ancient Greece could be public or private, could travel through mediums human and nonhuman (acolytes, birds, leaves), and be conveyed through media both verbal and nonverbal.[a] The gods could guide, warn, or encourage their creatures. Delphi's[b] familiar chanting priestess reported divine guidance, the most familiar modus operandi, but the Greeks recognized other forms of revelation. For example, they found divine communication in unexpected animal appearances, in birthmarks, and in sneezes; in inadvertent remarks or utterances or in chance verbal connections, such as a name (9.91: Hegesistratos, "leader of the force"). They interpreted an old man's lost tooth (6.107.3–4) and such prodigies as the birth of monsters or blood-red rains. Many perceived as significant portents for the future random, spontaneous events, as well as signs and wonders at critical moments—

P.1a Lydia: Map O.
P.1b Egypt: Map O, locator.
P.2a One can find contextualizing information on Hellenic religion in Burkert and Raffan's book, the basics on Hellenic oracles in Parker's entry in *The Oxford Classical Dictionary*, 3rd edition. Mikalson's 1983 book surveys Athenian religion and cults. The works by Parke and Wormell and by Fontenrose examine the rich evidence for the Delphic oracle. For examinations of Herodotus' treatment of both Greek and barbarian oracles and the gods' involve-

ment in human affairs, see Crahay's book; Lateiner's Chapter 9, portraying a skeptical Herodotus; and for a different, credulous Herodotus, compare Harrison's Chapter 5 and Mikalson's 2003 book. Gould's essay discusses Herodotus' treatment of oracular and other rituals. He considers Herodotus more conventional in his treatment of divine interference in human affairs than this writer does; his reading finds freaky supernatural hands often meddling in human affairs.

P.2b Delphi: Map O, inset.

810

natural phenomena like thunder and earthquakes. These cosmic signs were sometimes solicited and sometimes not.

§3. Divination by sacrifice—an entirely non-Homeric form of taking the divine temperature—allowed anyone, such as the later historian Xenophon, to take a read on divine sympathy on the fly, wherever he was. The many Greek modes of divination (the "mancies" such as necromancy) developed often from older, Near Eastern "Magi" methods. They testify to a common human intuition that the gods who run the universe want their inferiors to have some intimation about their whims and policies.

§4. In addition to the prestigious fixed oracular shrines, there were floating or traveling oraclemongers who attached themselves somehow to the inspired wandering men of yore, like Bakis, Laios, Mousaios, Lysistratos, Orpheus, and camp-following seers like Amphilytos, and Onomakritos.[a] These noninstitutional *manteis* usually offered advice to private parties. So did the healing oracles, mostly associated with Aisklepios, such as the healing shrines at Epidauros[b] or the Amphiareion.[c] Both these destinations supplied special dormitories where wounded and ill people sought dream oracles and other therapies.

§5. Delphic Apollo's shrine appears five times as often in Herodotus as in Thucydides. This frequency of reports of divine consultation reflects Herodotus' more comprehensive concept of history and the springs of human action. Further, it probably reflects the historical fact that human communities invoked, supplicated, and visited divine shrines blessed with the capacity to receive divine communiqués more often in the archaic period than in the classical (although we lack appropriate statistics). Further, the Persian threat to a weak national Hellenic identity provoked greater anxiety than even deadly inter-polis rivalries.

§6. Herodotus the comprehensive historian is interested in Greek and barbarian religious personnel, practices, beliefs, possessions, and institutions. Parochial, ethnic, and universal forms of prayer, image, and cult attracted his amused and awed responses. Pausanias, the later, imperial travel writer of the second century C.E., inventoried more particularly various towns' bizarre examples of religious high art and schlock. Some cults were exclusive and allowed only relatives of the priests, or only men, or Greeks, or initiates, to participate in the rites; but much, indeed most, Greek cult practice was civic, open-air, and public.

§7. Herodotus mentions eight mainland oracles: Delphi, Dodona, Abai (Phocis), Trophonios (Boeotia), Olympia, the Amphiareion, Ptoion Apollo, and Ismenian Apollo at Thebes[a] (8.134: Mys' multiple consultations; see also Croesus 1.46–49). Beyond old Greece, he also specifies Apollo's oracle at Didyma (Branchidai) near Miletus (1.46), the Telmessian shrine, and that at Patara[b] (1.78, 182), the Egyptian oracle of Ammon at the oasis of Siwa (2.18 et al.), the oracle of Leto (Wadjet) at Bouto (2.83), and the Satrians' Thracian mountain shrine[d] (7.111). Herodotus does not identify particular shrines for all the oracles he mentions (for example, 5.1), and he

P.4a   Bakis, 8.20, 8.77, 8.96, 9.43; Laios, 5.43; Mousaios. 7.6, 8.96, 9.43; Lysistratos, 8.96; Amphilytos, 1.62; Onomakritos, 7.6.
P.4a   Epidauros: Map O.
P.4b   Amphiareion: Map O, inset.
P.7a   Dodona, Olympia, Delphi, Abai, Boeotia, Ptoios,

Thebes: Map O, inset. The cave of Trophonios is located at Lebadeia: Map O, inset.
P.7c   Didyma (Branchidai), Miletus, Telmessos, Patara: Map O.
P.7d   Ammonion, Bouto: Map O, locator. The location of the Satrians' Thracian mountain shrine is unknown.

prefers to report rituals, barbarian and Greek, rather than beliefs or spiritual states. Nevertheless, he consistently refuses to describe ceremonies that one is forbidden to reveal (2.51, 2.171, 5.61, 8.65). By contrast, oracle delivery systems did not work under conditions of secrecy; they provided an interface between religious rituals and the public politics of the polis and poleis. Although from his text one may tentatively infer the personal beliefs and practices of Herodotus the individual, one cannot know them, because the historian had no motive or interest in describing his own spiritual convictions and practices connected to the supernatural realm.

§8. One finds oracles mentioned in all nine books of the text, with particular concentrations in Books 1, 5, and 6—which describe many prominent Greeks and Greek-influenced decision-makers who are uncertain about what to do next. But the oracles that Herodotus records are often sufficiently obscure or ambiguous to mislead—intentionally or not—the rulers, communities, or individuals traveling or delegating others to consult them.[a] Another commonly reported type of oracle confirmed (or not) a dynasty or person in its or his rule (e.g., 1.7, 1.13, 4.163). The Herodotean theme of realizing a truth too late for one's own good often verifies hitherto mocked or misconstrued oracles (such as Cambyses' realization at 3.64).

§9. Oracles responded to questions concerning health, spiritual or ritual pollution, colonization opportunities, and any other problem (business risks) that might confront anxious human beings. At Delphi, the most prestigious shrine, inquirers followed prescribed procedures (the detailed description at 7.140 acknowledges this fact). The patrons paid a fee, had a preliminary sacrifice performed for them, entered the temple, sacrificed again before the *adyton*, or sacred room, and, finally— accompanied by the male *prophetai*, or interpreters—approached the chaste, purified, and somehow possessed Pythia. The Pythian priestess experienced some peculiar inspiration (psychotropic trance or otherwise induced ecstasies).[a] She, basing her behavior on signs and visions, pronounced something in Greek, usually in some way responsive to the inquirer's query, an answer that the older if not wiser interpreters further shaped, while almost always leaving some ambiguous phrases. Answers were probably not in verse as Herodotus often reports them (e.g., 1.47). Gods, after all, cannot be expected to speak straightforwardly, and fallible humans often misinterpret, while wishful suppliants hear what they want, as Croesus so memorably illustrates. Inquirers could be turned away (1.19). Some answers were notably impenetrable (e.g., 6.77) or palpably beyond any human test (7.178).

§10. Delphi's Panhellenic Pythian contests (athletics, poetry, music, speech) clearly and intentionally imitated Olympia's older and more famous ones. Delphi's oracles, however, were supreme. Cities pondering war (7.148, 7.220) or colonial ventures sent for Delphic responses. Individuals seeking specific answers contemplating revolution and counterrevolution (5.67, 5.93) or enlistment in get-rich-quick military junkets (such as Xenophon, the Athenian friend of Socrates, who spoke with unfailing respect for the oracle) could and did request Delphic reaction to their

P.8a For misleading or misinterpreted examples, see Croesus, the Lacedaemonians, the Cymaeans, the Persian King Cambyses, the Spartan Kleomenes, and Xerxes (1.56, 1.90, 1.66, 1.158–159, 3.64, 6.80, 7.6).

P.9a A recent theory argues that the shrine was built over a geologic fault and that the Pythia might have been affected by emitted ethylene vapors.

schemes. Delphic responses occasionally directed cities where to settle their excess citizens, or to establish an *emporion*, or trading post, in the wide Mediterranean (4.150, 4.157, 4.159, 5.43), but the practice has been misconceived as common.

§11. Zeus at Dodona[a] (see also 2.54–57) answered questions posed on lead tablets (of which many survive). Most of them concern cult practices, such as sacrifice, but here too some concern travel, marriage, and reproductive quandaries (5.92.β, 6.66). Political inquiries were rarer than mundane questions about physical infirmities (4.149, 4.155), lending and banking money (6.86), taking a trip by boat, and so forth. Zeus at Olympia communicated through pyromancy (interpretation of flames on the altar). Consultation of the hero Trophonios at Lebadeia required visitors to descend into an underground cave (8.134).

§12. Oracular centers favored glamorous donors, those who cultivated the resident god with gifts of gold, silver, and the like (1.54, 9.81). The shrines tried to stay neutral among warring Hellenic states (7.148, 7.169). Peculiar pressures in the archaic age shook Delphi's moral authority and prestige more than once. The Spartans, in particular, ingratiated themselves repeatedly with the oracular establishment at Delphi (even the hero Lykourgos, at least in legend: 1.65). The quirky Attic clan the Alkmeonids reportedly was successful in bribing the Pythia to pressure the Lacedaemonians (by incessantly repeating the same message) to liberate the Athenians from the Peisistratids, the Spartans' tyrannical associates and friends (5.63, 5.91).

§13. Herodotus records the significant historical foibles and pratfalls of revered institutions and persons more than the arcane procedures of cult or the unknowable divine communicators (9.100 is a quite exceptional endorsement of "signs and wonders"). He happily acknowledges an occasional "correct" prophecy of an oracular source, and even the more skeptical Thucydides notes one instance of this (*Thucydides* 5.26). The Euboeans[a] at 8.20 are guilty of ignoring a potentially helpful Bakis oracle (see also 8.96, 9.43), and Bakis' victory oracle is emphatically affirmed at 8.77 (although the passage may be a later scribe's insertion). He admires human ingenuity that is engaged in disentangling apparent oracular obscurity (1.68, 1.159, 7.142). He deemed some oracles and shrines to be more trustworthy than others (1.53, 2.174); for example, he grudgingly described the one at Bouto as "the least false" in Egypt[b] (2.152; see also its judgment at 2.18). He clearly thought that some prophets deserve more credit than others (Melampos, 2.49; Euenios, 9.94), and his characters regard some shrines and shamans as more reliable than the rest. We read that some men referred issues to oracles; that must strike recent readers as most unlikely to be historical (such as a Pelasgian question about the names of the gods, 2.52).

§14. Herodotus also gamely reports examples of oracular sources that were bribed[a] whose oracles were false (9.95), recycled or falsely applied (9.43), fabricated (1.78, post-eventum), and partisan. He mentions "incorrect" prophets and prophe-

---

P.13a Euboea: Map O, inset.
P.13b Egypt: Map O, locator.
P.14a Bribed or influenced oracles: 5.62–63, 5.90, 6.123; Alkmeonids bribe the Pythia to persuade the Spartans to oust the Peisistratids from Athens:

6.66, 6.75; Kleomenes influences the Pythia to say that Demaratos is not the son of Ariston: 6.84.

cies and exposes charlatans and frauds, although the practice of unmasking shams does not seem to affect whether he believed that other channeling sources and institutions were dependable. Onomakritos provides him with a paradigm of the false prophet and his methods (7.6), and Greek informants describe Salmoxis as a preposterous pretender (4.95–96). But, "incorrect" human interpretations do not prove a specific oracle shrine or response wrong. Therefore, some prophecies are salvageable, and "let out" clauses explain some faulty invalid answers or non-responses (1.19, 84; see also the Magi's ad hoc rationalizations at 1.120). Moreover, an oracle's fulfillment can be indefinitely delayed (Gyges, 1.13; Colian women's cooking, 8.96) or lie dormant to the present day (4.178; see also 4.179). Believers may ascribe any oracular "failure" to a "mistaken" human "reader." Herodotus distances himself from some oracle tales as well as from other narratives (for example, Boreas at 7.189).

§15. This brief appendix cannot consider one by one all the Herodotean passages that mention oracles. A rough and rapid collection discovers more than eighty different oracular events, some of them brief, but others extended and significant. The early catastrophic story of Croesus hinges on his confidence in and generosity to the Delphic shrine, and on the paradigmatically ambiguous oracle that he received about destroying a great empire (1.53) if he attacked the Persians. The entire Croesus saga may be Delphic confirmatory propaganda. Apollo eventually saves his unworthy and distrustful Lydian consulter (1.91). The origin of the Corinthian[a] tyranny involves Eetion's and others' consultation of the Delphic oracle (5.92.β). The long story of Glaukos the perjuring Corinthian (6.86), and of his abuse of the Delphic oracle's services, contains one of the central themes of Herodotus: "mind your own and restore to others their own."

§16. Delphi's role in discouraging Hellenic resistance to the mighty Persian juggernaut may have permanently harmed its prestige. You did not need an oracle to know which way the odds tilted. The Athenian public debate over the Delphic pronouncement concerning their protection by "wooden walls" (7.140–143) occurs at the climax of Hellenic uncertainty about whether and how the Greeks will face the armed forces of Persia. First, the Pythian priestess Aristonike gave them a notably unambiguous, dire, and negative oracle. Timon the Delphian advised the visiting Athenian[a] embassy to ask again. They supplicated Apollo and his apparatus for "some better oracle," and they did subsequently obtain another response that offered more optimistic possibilities for Athenian survival. We may only conjecture why the second try worked some charm, but Herodotus remains mum on the subject. When the messengers brought it home to the Athenian assembly, the Athenians wrestled with its possible political and strategic meanings. Some suggested the fence around the Acropolis, and others the naval fleet, to be the Delphic referent for a bulwark of wood. Themistokles, an upstart politician and certainly no religious official, produced a strained but definitely welcome exegesis favoring a showdown fight to the finish in Salamis Straits.

§17. He prevailed over the usual explicators of oracles—further evidence of the

P.15a   Corinth: Map O, inset.   P.16a   Athens: Map O and inset.

weak authority of prophets (see also 9.33) and religious consultants, if not of the oracles themselves, in ancient Greece. To some readers, Herodotus seems to be querulously defending traditional practices (including a confidence in oracles) against contemporary skepticism, and not least against the destructive attacks launched on primitive religion and its human apparatus by the Sophists. To others, Herodotus as a cultural critic is exposing the malleability and fallibility of a most peculiar, if popular, ancient "religious" institution.

Donald Lateiner
John R. Wright Professor of Humanities-Classics
Ohio Wesleyan University
Delaware, OH

Bibliography

Burkert, Walter, and John Raffan. *Greek Religion* (Cambridge, MA: Harvard University Press, 1985 [orig. 1977; Eng. tr. John Raffan]).

Crahay, Roland. *La littérature oraculaire chez Hérodote* (Paris: Les Belles Lettres, 1956).

Fontenrose, Joseph Edward. *The Delphic Oracle: Its Responses and Operations* (Berkeley: University of California Press, 1978).

Gould, John. "Herodotus and Religion." In S. Hornblower, ed. *Greek Historiography*. (Oxford: 1994), 91–106.

Harrison, Thomas. "Oracles and Divination." *Divinity and History: The Religion of Herodotus.* Oxford Classical Monographs (Oxford: Clarendon Press, 2000).

Lateiner, Donald. "Event and Explanation." *The Historical Method of Herodotus* (Toronto: University of Toronto Press, 1989), 189–210.

Mikalson, Jon D. *Athenian Popular Religion* (Chapel Hill: University of North Carolina Press, 1983).

_____. *Herodotus and Religion in the Persian Wars* (Chapel Hill: University of North Carolina Press, 2003).

Parke, Herbert William, and Donald Ernest Wilson Wormell. *The Delphic Oracle* (Oxford: Blackwell, 1956).

APPENDIX Q

Herodotus and the Poets

§1. In the centuries before Herodotus took up his "inquiry" (*historiē*) into the past, poets had provided the Greeks with stories about their origins and the great achievements of long ago. The earliest such poems preserved for us are by Homer and Hesiod, long epics that are dated to the late eighth or early seventh century; but Homer and Hesiod were clearly carrying on much older poetic traditions that reached back for centuries to the Bronze Age. As entertainers and as preservers of oral traditions, rather than critical and well-equipped researchers, epic singers welcomed myths of all kinds into their stories, which they located in a long-lost heroic age, peopled by "godlike men, a race of demigods" (Hesiod, *Works and Days* 159–165). But epic singers were not completely fancy-free: as memorizers of old stories and versifiers of good new ones, they functioned in a society without writing as an important repository of stories about the past, whether it be in Thebes or Troy; singers also knew that heroic traditions, what Homer calls "the fames [*klea*] of men of former times, the heroes" (*Iliad* 9.524–525), had always inspired ambitious spirits to attempt great things. Hence they would find much to agree with in Herodotus' opening declaration that the purpose of history is "that what has happened may not be lost to men through the agency of time, and so the great and marvelous deeds of men, whether Greek or foreigner, may not become without fame [*a-klea*]" (1.1). The development of history was undoubtedly a major intellectual advance of the fifth century, but Herodotus and his colleagues were also developing a form of storytelling as old as that word *kleos*, ancient source of the name Clio, the Muse of history, as well as of the English word "listen."

§2. When Herodotus follows up his statement of purpose by promising to disclose "on account of what cause they came to fight against each other," this also suggests the way epic poets asked the Muse to tell them their stories from the beginning (see, for example, the opening lines of the *Iliad*). Such affinities, along with Herodotus' easy narrative style, fondness for speeches, and Ionic dialect, have led him to be regarded sometimes as writing a sort of prose epic of the Persian Wars. But this would be an inadequate description of Herodotus' complex relationship to

Greek poetic traditions, in which he was deeply versed but which he also could appraise quite coolly.

§3. An ancient report says that Herodotus was closely related to Panyasis, a fifth-century poet whose works include an epic on Herakles. This may be a fiction inspired by the fact that Panyasis came from the same hometown, Halicarnassus. But it usefully points to Herodotus' rich familiarity with Greek poetry. Doubtless well educated, Herodotus could hear poetry everywhere when he was growing up: Homer, Hesiod, and many other epics were widely performed, and a good many short songs from the sixth and early fifth centuries (what scholars call "archaic lyric poetry") were in the air. Apart from Homer and Hesiod, Herodotus exhibits knowledge of Athenian tragedy and of a number of lyrics by the likes of Sappho, Alkaios, Solon, Arion, Simonides, and Pindar.[a] He also quotes (some suspect composed) numerous oracles in verse as well as epigrams commemorating a person or place. His devotion to poetic culture is also evident in his excursuses into literary history: he looked into such difficult questions as the date of Homer and Hesiod (whom he places around 400 years before his own time, not a bad estimate at all) and when the cult song called the dithyramb was invented.[b] He knows something of the lives of such figures as the fable composer Aesop or the love poet Anakreon.

§4. A number of Herodotus' poetic references serve no historical purpose but seem designed to show his broad and sophisticated culture, as when he quotes with approval some words of Pindar (the opening of a famous poem) on the power of convention (3.38). In a similar way, speakers in Herodotus can sometimes drop a poetic tag into an oration, as when an Athenian envoy to Syracuse pulls a line out of Homer in praise of Athens to convince Gelon of his city's greatness (8.161). Herodotus sometimes cites poets to help locate a historical figure in time, such as Archilochus' reference to Gyges (1.12, if genuine), Solon's to a contemporary tyrant (5.113), or Sappho's to a famous courtesan who left a display at Delphi (2.135).

§5. Herodotus is far from naïve in citing these poets, who, he suggests on more than one occasion, were primarily concerned to please their audiences. It was already proverbial in his day that poets often lied, and as an inveterate collector of sources he knew that even eyewitnesses could be unreliable. This seems to be the reason why Herodotus does not go to the poets for information when other sources are available. He quotes the famous Simonides several times, but apparently did not seek out his long elegiac poem (which has only recently come to light) retelling the battle of Plataea. Again, he knows the work of the tragic poet Aeschylus in some detail (2.156), but does not refer explicitly to *The Persians*, Aeschylus' great meditation on the meaning of the Persian wars. So, too, he knows that the Athenian Phrynikos caused a sensation with his historical drama on the fall of Miletus (6.21), but gives no evidence of having consulted it for the Ionian Revolt.

§6. In some cases, however, Herodotus interprets poetic texts closely. Especially when dealing with prehistory, he can subject the oldest writings he knows—the

---

Q.3a Sappho: 2.135.1. Archilochus: 1.12.2, n. 1.12.2a. Alkaios: 5.95.1. Solon: 1.29–33. Arion: 1.23–24. Simonides: 5.102.3. Pindar: 3.38.4.

Q.3b The dithyramb, supposedly created and named by Arion (1.23).

poetry of Homer and Hesiod—to acute scrutiny. Such passages show that Herodotus went beyond urbane skepticism toward poetry and developed a studious and reasonable method for getting information from old songs. The great example is his long speculative discussion of what actually happened at Troy (2.50–60). Here he has appeared to some readers as a bit of a fool for ending up believing a fantastic story he claims to have got out of Egypt—that Helen never went to Troy (the gods having duped Paris with a phantom), but was spirited away to a welcoming Egypt. To an enlightened fifth-century thinker, however, Homer's story was really no better, and in dismantling this, Herodotus shows extraordinary skill and resourcefulness as a reader. He can point to, and quote, the exact lines in the *Iliad* that prove the "Egyptian" account is earlier than Homer, and shows such a thorough knowledge of old poems that he anticipates modern Homerists in discerning that some of the epics ascribed to Homer or Heisod could not have been composed by them (4.32). It was once common to contrast Herodotus as a poetic tale-teller with Thucydides as scientific historian. But both are careful in using poets as sources: like any informant, poets may be attended to on subjects they were in a position to know about, but one must bear in mind that, being poets, they did not feel bound to record historical truth.

§7. Herodotus, then, not only was deeply interested in the Muses' arts but, when necessary, he was a scrupulous and intelligent reader of poetry. His complex stance can be summed up by returning to the opening of the *Histories* and noticing precisely where the story begins (1.2–6). Having promised to tell "what caused" the Greeks and Persians to fight, Herodotus begins by surveying a series of legends in which Eastern women were stolen by Greeks and vice versa. Phoenicians started everything, "they say," when they kidnapped Io, a young woman from Argos in the Peloponnese and ran off to Egypt. The story of Europa is then introduced as the Greek response, portraying her not on the back of a tauriform Zeus, but as a maid from Phoenician Tyre snatched away by Greeks. The story of Jason and Medea is told next, as the tale of a kidnapped princess from the Black Sea. Finally comes Paris, who carried the Greek beauty Helen off to Troy and so sparked the first war between East and West. Herodotus is noncommittal on the veracity of these traditions, many of which, despite being attributed to "learned Persians" and others, were surely circulating in Greek poems. As an ensemble, as a tit-for-tat series of narratives, their source is ultimately Herodotus' talent for comparing traditions and arranging them in patterns, along with his pleasure in telling the tales he collected. But he was also a critical collector, and Herodotus breaks off this dip into the mythic past to ask who "actually" first attacked Greece. This he professes to be able to answer from his own knowledge: it was Croesus of Lydia (c. 560–546). With this decidedly nonpoetic figure, history has begun.

Andrew Ford
Department of Classics
Princeton University
Princeton, NJ

APPENDIX R

The Size of Xerxes' Expeditionary Force

§1. Herodotus invites his readers to imagine an army so large that it drank rivers dry and bankrupted cities that attempted to provide it with food even for a single day. So it was that Megakreon of Abdera advised his fellow countrymen to give thanks to the gods that Xerxes was not in the habit of taking *two* meals a day, because it would have ruined them to provide both breakfast as well as dinner (7.118–120). Herodotus emphatically states that the forces in all previous military expeditions taken together, including that of the Greeks against Troy, were not the equal of Xerxes' (7.20–21).

§2. The numbers claimed by Herodotus are indeed astounding (7.184–187). The fleet and land army that Xerxes brought over from Asia consisted of 1,207 triremes (warships), 1,700,000 infantry, 80,000 cavalry, and 20,000 camel riders and charioteers. The total number of fighting men, including the crews and marines on the ships, was 2,317,610. When one adds the troops that Xerxes collected as he passed through Thrace into Greece (24,000 sailors and 300,000 infantry), as well as male noncombatants, the army that eventually reached Thermopylae numbered 5,283,220 men. The infantry divisions that set out with Xerxes from Sardis in 480 contained contingents from forty-three different ethnic groups, all dressed in their own native costume (7.61–88). The whole of Asia, it would seem, had descended upon Greece.

§3. The modern reader will not be surprised, even if a bit disappointed, that the grand army of Xerxes could not have been on anything near the scale that Herodotus describes. Although his method of calculation gives the impression of care and precision, Herodotus' figures must be grossly exaggerated. The requirements of supply, maneuverability, logistics, finance, and command and control would have made it impossible for Xerxes to have led an army even a quarter of the size of the one that Herodotus has given him. The German scholar Hans Delbrück calculated that if Xerxes' army really was as large as Herodotus says, then the column of march would have been 2,000 miles long, with the head of the column reaching Thermopylae in Greece at the same time as the end of the column was marching out of Susa in Iran.

§4. Dismissing Herodotus' figures is one thing, but estimating the actual size of the Persian army is an altogether more difficult endeavor. Modern scholars are unanimous that the figure of 1,700,000 infantry is impossibly high, but there is little agreement about how to approximate the actual number. Estimates generally range from as high as 300,000 to as low as 30,000. Two questions need to be asked. First of all, if Herodotus' figures are too big, is there any method that can be used to approximate the actual size of Xerxes' land forces and fleet? And second, if Herodotus has exaggerated, did he do so knowingly or inadvertently? The question of numbers is important because it is impossible to assess strategy and tactics without having some concrete and realistic idea of the sizes of the forces that were involved in the various battles.

§5. Let us take the second question first. All historians, whether ancient or modern, are inclined to stress the importance of their subject. The war that is being narrated must be more important, bigger, more critical, more worth writing about, than any struggle that had come before. So the historian Thucydides, who wrote about the twenty-seven-year Peloponnesian War between Athens and Sparta (432–405), emphasizes at the beginning of his history that the Peloponnesian War was much longer and more catastrophic for Greece than the Persian War of 480, which was quickly decided in two sea battles and two land battles (2.23). At the same time, the greater the size of the enemy, the more glorious is the achievement in repulsing them. In this, the great and heroic struggle of Greek liberty against oriental despotism, the glory of the Greek victory was enhanced in direct proportion to the odds that were against them. That fact alone required that the Greeks imagine Xerxes' army to be by far the largest that the world had ever seen.

§6. It may seem natural to suppose that the number of Xerxes' soldiers and ships has to be big enough to allow for the possibility of exaggeration by the Greeks. Although it may sound counterintuitive, his army did not actually have to be any larger than that of the Greek opposition (38,700 Greek hoplites opposed Mardonios at Plataea in 479)[a] for Greek contemporaries to have turned it into a cast of millions. To give one stark example, in 1476 Charles the Bold fought unsuccessfully against the Swiss with about 14,000 men; but his Swiss adversaries, whose own army was on the order of 25,000, estimated Charles' force at 100,000 to 120,000 men. One could cite other examples of relatively small armies that have been imaginatively transformed into countless masses.

§7. The presence of exaggeration does not mean that Herodotus is deliberately intending to deceive his readers. Very large numbers probably meant very little to Herodotus and his contemporaries in the sense that it was difficult to comprehend them, just as numbers in the billions, or even in the millions, can be difficult for us to conceptualize. The epitaph that was written for those who were buried on the battlefield of Thermopylae claimed that 4,000 from the Peloponnese had fought with 3,000,000 (7.228). It is probably in reaction to such claims, as well as rhetorically to bolster confidence in his own narrative, that Herodotus attempts to be precise in his calculations (7.184–187). He even describes the method by which Xerxes himself numbered his troops: that is, by packing 10,000 into one place, marking that space off with a low fence, and then having his whole army fill the same space in turns (7.60). It is impossible to say whether this procedure was a fantasy either of Herodotus

R.6a Herodotus lists the various Greek hoplite contingents in 9.28, describes the lightly armed troops   in 9.29, and provides the sum total of both in 9.30.

or of his Greek informants (who may have tried to guess how Xerxes could have counted such large numbers), or indeed was employed by Xerxes as a check on the figures handed in by his officers. In any case, Herodotus was well aware that it would not have been easy to feed an army of some 5,000,000 soldiers and support personnel: he calculates that each day they would have consumed a minimum of 110,340 medimnoi of wheat, or, in our terms, 157,235 bushels (just over 20,000,000 cups!). Writers later than Herodotus seem to have realized that his figures were too high. Thus Ctesias of Cnidus, who in the early fourth century was a Greek doctor at the court of the Persian King Artaxerxes II, put the number at 800,000 infantry. The lowest total for fighting men, 700,000, is given by the Athenian orator Isocrates (*Archidamus* 100 and *Panathenaicus* 49, published in 366 and 339, respectively), although he nonetheless accepts a grand total of 5,000,000 for the land forces.

§8. How can we arrive at a more realistic figure? One very simple solution has been suggested. It is to suppose that the Greeks consistently misinterpreted a Persian chiliad (a unit of 1,000 men) as a myriad (a unit of 10,000 men), and thus one should divide Persian numbers by ten. That would give an original invasion force of 170,000 infantry. But even that is too large an army, given the inevitable problems of logistics, supply, and command. Other solutions must be sought.

§9. Comparison with other battles, both modern and ancient, can put Herodotus' figures into better perspective. At the battle of Ipsus in 321, in which all of Alexander the Great's successors participated, Antigonus took the field with 70,000 infantry and 10,000 cavalry, while his opponents had 64,000 infantry and 10,500 cavalry. This same Antigonus invaded Egypt in 306 with an army of 80,000 infantry and 8,000 cavalry. More recent battles give figures in the same range. Waterloo in 1815 involved 73,000 French soldiers against an allied army from Britain and other European countries of approximately 93,000. At Gettysburg in 1863 the Union forces numbered 90,000 men and the Confederate forces 75,000. And finally, during the invasion of Normandy in 1944, one of the greatest assaults in history, 100,000 American and British fighting men took part in the landing.

§10. Herodotus' account of the battle of Plataea in 479 provides an important clue that confirms the result of such comparisons. The Persian commander Mardonios is said to have selected 300,000 from the forces of Xerxes before the King left Greece after his defeat at Salamis. He picked out the Persians, Medes, Sacae, Baktrians, and Indians, both foot and horse, in their entirety (8.113.3). It is highly likely that this selection actually comprised the bulk of Xerxes' original land force. Thus if we could calculate the size of Mardonios' army that fought at the battle of Plataea, we would have a good estimation of the size of the army that left Sardis in 480.

§11. Herodotus claims that Mardonios built a stockade as a place of refuge for his army, in case he got into difficulties. This was a square with sides 10 stades (about 1,943 yards) long, containing an area just over one square mile. By using a comparison with much smaller Roman legionary camps, one scholar has calculated that this could hold an army of 60,000 to 70,000 men, of whom not more than

10,000 were cavalry. I think, therefore, that, as an upper limit, one could estimate the original land army that Xerxes brought from Asia as numbering 80,000 infantry and 10,000 cavalry. A lower limit, however, of 40,000 to 50,000 infantry is certainly conceivable, and perhaps even probable, since it is confirmed by our only other independent fifth-century source for the size of Xerxes' army. The historian Thucydides has Hermocrates exhort the Syracusans to resist the Athenian invaders in 415 by drawing a parallel with the Persian invasion of Greece, in which he suggests that Persian mistakes and lack of provisions were the primary cause of their failure and that the Persian army was not larger than that of the united Greek forces (6.33.5). These claims, of course, nicely support Hermocrates' rhetorical purpose, which is to bolster the confidence of his countrymen. Nonetheless, it is possible that his words reflect Thucydides' own personal beliefs about the Persian invasion of 480.

§12. The core of Xerxes' army was probably composed of Persians and Medes, who were the best fighters. Nonetheless, it would be rash to dismiss as unhistorical Herodotus' description of the forty-three ethnic groups who contributed infantry, cavalry, horse-drawn chariots, or camels (7.61–88). It would have served both an ideological and a practical purpose for Xerxes to bring with him contingents, however small, from all of the peoples subject to Persia. Ideologically, participation in the expedition was a demonstration both of loyalty to the King and of the King's power; politically, the presence of representatives from every subject people were so many hostages to guarantee that revolts did not take place in the King's absence. The power and ethnic diversity of the Persian Empire, the largest empire the world had yet seen, was on display for the world to see.

§13. It is rather more difficult to estimate the size of Xerxes' fleet. Herodotus claims that it originally comprised 1,207 triremes and 3,000 smaller boats of various types (7.89–97, 7.184). This has seemed credible to some modern scholars because Aeschylus' *The Persians*, a tragedy performed in 472 on the theme of the Persian reaction to the battle of Salamis, also specifies 1,207 triremes.[a] If nothing else, this correspondence at least shows that Herodotus did not make up the number himself. Yet some 4,000 vessels would make this one of the largest naval armadas in history, whether ancient or modern, and would have required, according to Herodotus' own calculations, crews and marines to the number of 517,610. Although the sizes of the ships involved are not comparable, it is worth noting that the naval force that took part in the invasion of Normandy on June 6, 1944, consisted of 5,000 ships of various types and was the largest armada ever assembled. But in terms of numbers of ships, Xerxes' fleet, if we believe Herodotus, was a close second. Sending a large fleet far from home presents considerable challenges of supply and maintenance. It is striking that the Athenians and their allies sent a total of 207 triremes to Syracuse between 415 and 413 and that the famous Spanish Armada that sailed against England in 1588 had only 130 ships and 30,000 men. Various considerations suggest that Xerxes' fleet numbered no more than 600 triremes at an absolute maximum. Yet

R.13a   Aeschylus is believed to have taken part in the battle of Salamis, so his description of the battle in the tragedy is therefore an eyewitness account, and there must have been many fellow eyewitnesses in his Athenian audience. Yet even if they realized that his numbers were inaccurate, they may well have been pleased by the exaggeration.

even 600 ships would require 138,00 men, if Herodotus is indeed correct that each trireme in the Persian fleet had a standard crew of 200 and 30 extra marines. Even if we suppose that the marines were drawn from the land forces and only embarked just before a battle, each ship would still require 170 rowers. It is worth considering the possibility that the fleet numbered only in the range of 300 to 400 triremes (requiring between 51,000 and 68,000 rowers), and thus was actually about the same size as the Greek fleet of 380 ships that fought at Salamis.

§14. Quite apart from the number of mouths to feed, two things should arouse our suspicions about Herodotus' numbers. First of all, 1,200 was the number of ships that Homer says sailed against Troy, and thus Xerxes' fleet was just enough bigger than the one commanded by Agamemnon to make the Persian War of 480 more important than the Trojan War. Second, Aeschylus specifies that 207 of the Persian ships were "exceptionally fast." It is unclear just what Aeschylus means by that, but one possibility is that the Phoenician ships, which were the fastest sailing ships in the Persian fleet (7.44, 7.96), numbered only 207 at Salamis. Or, more radically, he may even mean that Phoenician-style ships (which were lighter and more maneuverable than the Greek triremes: 8.60) contributed by the Phoenicians, Egyptians, and Cyprians numbered only 207 by the time of that battle. In either case, it is probable that the fleet which set sail from Asia originally numbered 300 to 600 triremes, including ships from the Levant as well as from the Greek cities of Asia Minor that were subject to Persia. Herodotus seems aware that he needed to pare down the size of Xerxes' original fleet, and thus implausibly claims that about half of his triremes, some 600 ships, were destroyed by storms before the battle of Salamis (7.190, 8.7, 8.13); but he later unrealistically asserts that these losses were made up by the arrival of Greek ships from the Aegean islands (8.66). Perhaps he wanted to make his own number match that of Aeschylus. Much is uncertain, but one thing should be taken as a given: Xerxes did not depart from Asia with a fleet of anything near 1,207 triremes.

§15. It is easy for us to criticize Herodotus or to scoff at his numbers. But it is well to remember how difficult it has proved to be even in modern times to estimate the size either of armies or of any large body of people. Herodotus himself recognized the difficulty of the task when he conceded, perhaps with a touch of humor, that no one would be able to give the exact number of female cooks, concubines, eunuchs, pack animals, and Indian dogs that followed Xerxes' army (7.187). Despite his errors, Herodotus should at least be given credit for attempting to give an enumeration of the enemy forces that was both accurate and precise.

Michael A. Flower
Department of Classics
Princeton University
Princeton, NJ

APPENDIX S

Trireme Warfare in Herodotus

§1. Herodotus describes a vigorous era in the history of the maritime traffic and warfare in the Mediterranean. Greek[a] and Phoenician colonies anchored far-flung trading networks north to the Black Sea and west along the African and European coasts to Spain and even beyond the Straits of Gibraltar.[b] Sea lanes had to be policed, colonies protected, parochial navies developed and increased. Furthermore, naval strength, always a prerogative of coastal and island states, became an important factor in the expanding domains of inland powers such as Sparta[c] and Persia. The jostling of all these escalating commercial and political interests in the seas of the Mediterranean fostered developments in ship design, construction, and handling.

§2. Herodotus is one of our primary sources for these developments. But he assumes a firsthand familiarity with seagoing ships of the Greeks and Persians, and so his abbreviated references do not provide us with the complete manual of ancient seafaring in the archaic Aegean[a] that we would have liked. It is not easy to complete the picture. There are images of ships, primarily on Attic pottery, but they are difficult to interpret. Underwater explorations have yielded only cargo ships; ancient warships have left few traces. Men jumped off sinking ships, and without the weight of human ballast, the empty wooden hulls floated just below the surface and were often salvaged before they sank completely. Those hulls that did sink to the seafloor had no cargo to protect them from marine predators and deterioration, and so there is now little or nothing left for underwater archaeologists to discover. Especially conspicuous is the lack of Phoenician testimony; we know of the ships and maritime achievements of these most excellent seafarers and sea fighters mostly through secondhand, often hostile accounts. Thus Herodotus' story remains the essential account of archaic maritime history.

S.1a Greece (Hellas): Map S, AX.
S.1b Europe, Phoenicia, Euxine (Black) Sea, Africa (Libya), Spain (Iberia), Straits of Gibraltar (Pillars of Herakles): Map S, locator.

S.1c Sparta: Map S, BX.
S.2a Aegean Sea: Map S.

Warships

§3. He recounts the age of the development of the *triereis* (anglicized as "trireme"), the oared vessel that would become the premier warship of the classical world. In the centuries between Homer and Thucydides, warships evolved from transports that carried warriors to the battlegrounds where they disembarked and fought on land, to fighting machines designed to ram and sink opponents on the seas. During the long transitional period before triremes achieved their classical form and purpose (and even then), many navies relied on a third option: using ships to carry troops on deck for launching missiles at the enemy and engaging in pirate-style boarding at sea. Whether the battle plan depended on boarding or ramming, successful maneuvers against the enemy depended on the rowers (sailing and wind being too variable to be counted on in battle), and thus developments in warship design focused on increasing the number of oars, and thereby power, without sacrificing efficiency. There came a point beyond which it was not feasible to lengthen wooden hulls for the purpose of adding rowers—the increased length made the hulls either fragile or too cumbersome—and the most significant change in warship design thereafter, in the centuries preceding the Persian War, was the incorporation of a second and eventually a third level of oarsmen. There is no unambiguous evidence for where and when these advances were made or how quickly they spread. Scholarly debate on these topics is lively.

§4. Herodotus' narrative portrays a general adoption of triremes over the course of the sixth century, but the specific dynamics of that shift are difficult to define, partly because Herodotus so often uses vague vocabulary. The term that he uses most frequently in his catalogs of fleets and descriptions of naval maneuvers is *neus* (the Ionic form of *naus*, whence "nautical" and "naval"), a word that simply means ship. Context is the indication that *neus* means a warship (rather than a merchant ship),[a] and sometimes it is clear that Herodotus is referring specifically to triremes. But there are many instances when the reference cannot be defined. His narrative does indicate that the changeover was gradual, for the fleets of the early fifth century are still an amalgam of older and new-model warships. The old-fashioned vessels were triaconters (thirty-oared) and penteconters (fifty-oared, with either one or two levels of rowers). Triaconters are listed in the catalog of Xerxes' fleet (7.97), and a triaconter served as messenger ship to the Greek navy stationed at Artemision (8.21.1).[b] Penteconters were still substantial elements of the navies mustered in 480.

§5. Probably during the tyranny of Polykrates of Samos[a] (533–522), and certainly by the time of the Ionian Revolt (499), the trireme had become the cutting edge of naval power. The trireme is thought to have taken its name from the arrangement of

S.4a Herodotus occasionally modifies *neus* with *makre* ("long") to specify a warship; a *neus strongule* ("round") means specifically a cargo ship. The term *ploia* usually signifies vessels other than warships.

S.4b Artemision: Map S, AX. Triaconters in the Persian fleet, 7.97; among Gelon's ships, 7.163.1; among the Greeks at Artemision, 8.12; at Salamis, 8.48.

S.5a Samos: Map S, BY.

rowers. In its classical form, the hull enclosed two levels of rowers, and a third row of oarsmen sat in outriggers mounted along the topsides of the hull. Only the topmost rowers were in a position to see the oar blades enter the water, and each rower in the upper bank was responsible for guiding the two rowers below him to adjust their stroke to fit the general cadence. Thus the trireme crew worked in teams of three, and this is why the Greeks referred to these warships as *triereis*, "three-fitted." This configuration packed 170 rowers into a hull about 120 feet long and 15 feet wide, and optimized the balance of power, speed, and maneuverability: a longer boat with more rowers would have been heavier and more difficult to maneuver without gaining much in the way of increased speed, while a smaller boat with fewer rowers would have lacked sufficient speed and striking power. During the classical period, since ramming was the primary offensive technique, and since lightness and speed were paramount, the rest of the crew was pared down to a bare minimum. In addition to the rowers, the standard complement for an Athenian trireme during the Peloponnesian War consisted of only ten marines, four archers, and about sixteen other crew to sail the boat.[b]

§6. At what point the trireme attained its classical specifications is a matter of debate. There is likely to have been significant variability among the earliest models. Certain fleets of archaic triremes had a reputation for better performance. Herodotus praises especially the ships of the Sidonians among the Phoenicians, and the Samians, Athenians, and Aeginetans[a] among the Greek fleets. But he does not specify whether this is a matter of construction, crew, or condition; his stock praise is simply that the ships "moved best in the water." If this was a matter of design, the differences cannot have been conspicuous, since there are several incidents of confusion between enemy and friendly ships in the *Histories* (for example, 7.194.1, 8.87.4). Herodotus does mention that Phoenician triremes could be distinguished by the figureheads on their prows[b] (3.37.2), and at least some ships carried individual insignia (8.88.2, 8.92.2), but in general and at least externally all triremes must have looked essentially alike.[c]

§7. The number of marines on the decks of these early fleets of triremes did vary,[a] and scholars debate whether these differences in the number of fighting men are indicative of substantive differences in ship design and/or battle tactics. Essentially the question is whether marines played a primary or auxiliary role in offensive tactics. Or, put another way, at what point did ramming strategies supersede the old-fashioned conception of warships as troop carriers? How one understands Herodotus is the linchpin to this debate. Can Herodotus' descriptions of certain ships/fleets as "better at sailing" or "heavier" (8.60.α) be understood in terms of number of marines on board and/or modified designs? How many marines would necessitate modifications to ship design (added deck space, for example)? Does a report by Herodotus of an increased number of marines indicate a fleet built for

S.5b   See Figure S.1 for a photograph of the *Olympias*, a full-scale trireme constructed in Greece and sailed, rowed, and tested in the 1990s; and Figure S.2 for a construction and manning diagram of the ship.

S.6a   Sidon: Map S, locator. Athens, Aegina: Map S, BX.

S.6b   See also Samian ships (not triremes) with boars' heads on their prows (3.59.3).

S.6c   In the catalog of Xerxes' fleet (8.89–95), the differ-

ent contingents are described in terms of their armor, weapons, and dress, but not by distinctive triremes.

S.7a   The Chians at Lade fought with a complement of 40 marines (6.15.1). (Chios, Lade: Map S, BY.) Xerxes sailed with an additional 30 marines on deck (7.184.2). Kleinias' crews of 200 conform to the classical standard, namely, 10 marines (8.17).

FIGURE S.1. THE MODERN TRIREME *OLYMPIAS*, BEING ROWED BY STUDENTS.

boarding tactics, or does a small number of marines suggest a battle strategy reliant on ramming?

§8. One indirect indication of an increased emphasis on ship handling might be the existence of facilities for hull maintenance. Hull speed would have become a vital factor with the advent of ramming tactics. Thucydides records that the naval commanders of the Peloponnesian Wars, when ramming warfare reached its apogee, were concerned with keeping their hulls from becoming waterlogged while on campaign,[a] and archaeologists have uncovered the foundations of the shipsheds in which classical Athenian triremes were berthed in Peiraieus, their home port.[b] Herodotus also mentions such concerns in connection with triremes. He states it clearly when he specifies that Xerxes' fleet (powered by triremes) halted at Zone[c] to "dry out" (7.59.2). The connection is not made explicit in his passing reference to Polykrates' boathouses, but perhaps it is not chance that this is the same ruler whom he records making the transition from penteconters to triremes.[d] Whether or not Herodotus' description of Nechos' (610–594) fleet of triremes is anachronistic, it is perhaps not coincidental that he mentions gear for pulling ships out of the water (*holkos*) in the same sentence (2.159.1).

S.8a   *Thucydides* 7.12.3–5.
S.8b   The size of these trireme shipshed berths has helped scholars and marine designers determine at least the maximum dimensions of triremes. See Figure S.4.
S.8c   Zone: Map S, AY.
S.8d   The term which Herodotus uses for "shipshed" in 3.45.4, *neosoikoi*, is a general one, and it is possible that these boathouses had been built for the penteconter fleet, or even for nonmilitary use.

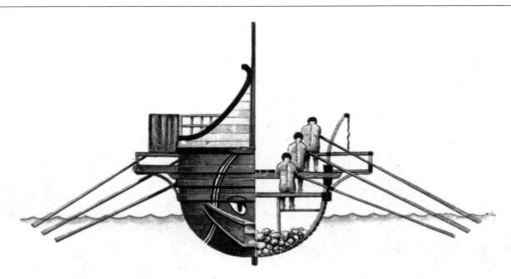

FIGURE S.2. CROSS-SECTIONAL DIAGRAM OF A TRIREME, SHOWING PLACEMENT OF ROWING STATIONS.

Sea Battles

§9. Herodotus' account of the battle of Salamis[a] is his most detailed description of a naval engagement; he was a boy when the battle took place, and as a native of Halicarnassus,[b] he must have heard about it—and especially Artemisia's role—directly from participants on the Persian side. There exists a second contemporary source, the Athenian tragedian Aeschylus, who probably took part in the battle. His drama *The Persians* played before an audience that undoubtedly included many who had fought at Salamis eight years earlier. The two authors disagree about the numbers of ships on each side[c] and the locations of their ships and tactics at the initial attack.[d] These discrepancies highlight the uncertainties of Herodotus' method, reliant primarily upon oral and, most often, secondary or even tertiary sources.

§10. It should be remembered, too, that literary considerations influenced his narrative. So, for example, the figure of Artemisia, who certainly existed and whose reported actions may well reflect reality, also serves to illustrate the themes of inversion[a] and transgression[b] and resulting confusion that pervade this history. Herodotus'

S.9a   Salamis: Map S, BX.
S.9b   Halicarnassus: Map S, BY.
S.9c   Herodotus: 1,207 Persian vs. 380 Greek.
        Aeschylus: 1,000 Persian vs. 300 Greek.
S.9d   For detailed discussions, see J. S. Morrison and
        J. F. Coates, *The Athenian Trireme* (1986), 59–60,
        and, most recently, D. Potter, *Bryn Mawr Classical
        Review* 2006.03.29 (a review of R. T. Wallinga,
        *Xerxes' Greek Adventure: The naval perspective.
        Mnemosyne supplement 265* [Leiden: Brill, 2005]).
S.10a   A common theme of Herodotus' ethnographic

accounts is the depiction of foreign customs as an inversion of the normal order. So, for example, Egyptian women urinate standing up, but the men sit down.

S.10b   Boundary crossings and boundary violations, physical and behavioral, are a central theme of the *Histories*. Herodotus characterizes especially the Persian Kings with such actions, as, for example, Xerxes' crossing of the Hellespont (Map S, AY) or his treatment of the son of the Lydian Pythios (Lydia: Map S, BY).

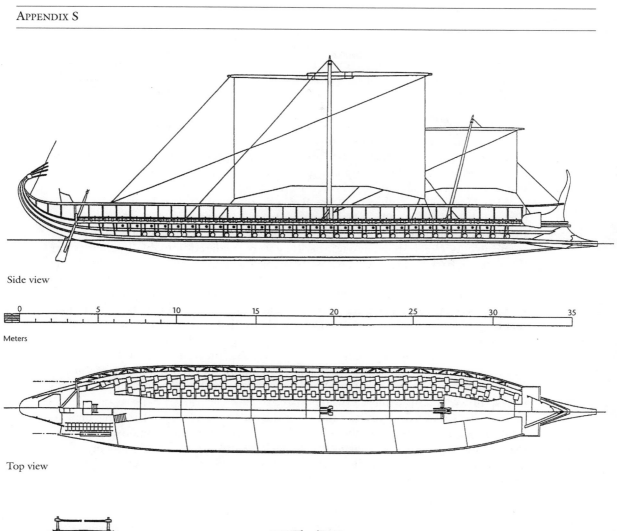

Side view

Meters

Top view

Cross-sections

Stern

Midship

Bow

FIGURE S.3. DIAGRAM OF THE MODERN TRIREME *OLYMPIAS*.

829

description of Artemisia ramming a Persian ship is an excellent example of this combination of historical report and literary topos.[c] In assessing Herodotus' historical narrative, it is important to realize that this is first of all a work of literature, in which imagery is manipulated and "facts" are tools used to advance the themes of his history.

§11. Even so, it is possible to detect in Herodotus' narrative an increasing emphasis on naval warfare (and skills) in its implementation over the course of the sixth and early fifth centuries. Fleets grow ever larger, and coalitions become increasingly broad in scope. Battle strategy grows more reliant on rowing tactics and perhaps incorporates ramming as an offensive weapon.

§12. Herodotus reports only the barest outlines of the battle at Alalie (535), between a fleet of sixty Phocaean ships (probably penteconters) and a Carthaginian-Etruscan coalition double that size.[a] Of special interest is his description of the damage to twenty Greek ships: he says that they were rendered unusable by their "rams being 'bent back'"[b] (1.166). This is the earliest extant mention of rams in battle (although there are earlier depictions) and, as discussed above, it is possible that this awkward image of damage is indicative of newly emergent technology and tactics.

§13. Less than half a century later (494), at Lade,[a] ramming may have been integral to battle strategy. It is perhaps no coincidence that here, too, the primary role is played by a Phocaean commander (Dionysius), in spite of the fact that he heads one of the smallest contingents (only three ships!) of the Ionian fleet. Dionysius concentrates especially on two maneuvers: sailing in column (*epi keras*) and the *diekplous*,[b] which in classical times consisted of breaking through an enemy line and then turning rapidly to ram his defenseless side or stern.

§14. By 480, at Artemision,[a] the Greeks have become adept at rowing maneuvers. The significantly outnumbered Greek fleet successfully defended itself by drawing up into a tight circle (*kuklos*), bows facing outward against the enemy. They were able to maintain formation and fight successfully until nightfall put a halt to the action.

Dangers on the Waters

§15. The greatest danger to ships was not battle but storm, and no ancient naval expedition ever set sail in the Mediterranean during winter months. The Persian disasters at Athos (6.44.2) and along the coasts of Magnesia (7.168) and Euboea[a] (8.13) vividly confirmed Artabanos' caution to Xerxes: the greatest threat to a large-scale naval expedition against Greece lay in the lack of adequate havens from storms

S.10c For more on Artemisia, see R. V. Munson, "Artemisia in Herodotus," *Classical Antiquity* 7 (1988), 91–106.

S.12a Alalie (Corsica), Carthage: Map S, locator. Phocaea: Map S, BY.

S.12b Literally, "They were bent back as to their beaks." Other suggested translations: their rams were "buckled," "twisted off," "badly bent."

S.13a Lade: Map S, BY.

S.13b Literally, "to sail through and out." Later sources associate this maneuver specifically with ramming, but Cawkwell argues that the fully developed *diekplous* was not employed until the Peloponnesian War and that Herodotus' use of the word indicates only a maneuver used to bring the marines into fighting range. See Appendix H, The Ionian Revolt, n. 4Cf, and G. Cawkwell, *The Greek Wars. The Failure of Persia* (Oxford: Oxford University Press, 2005).

S.14a Artemision: Map S, AX.

S.15a Mount Athos, Magnesia: Map S, AX. Euboea: Map S, BX.

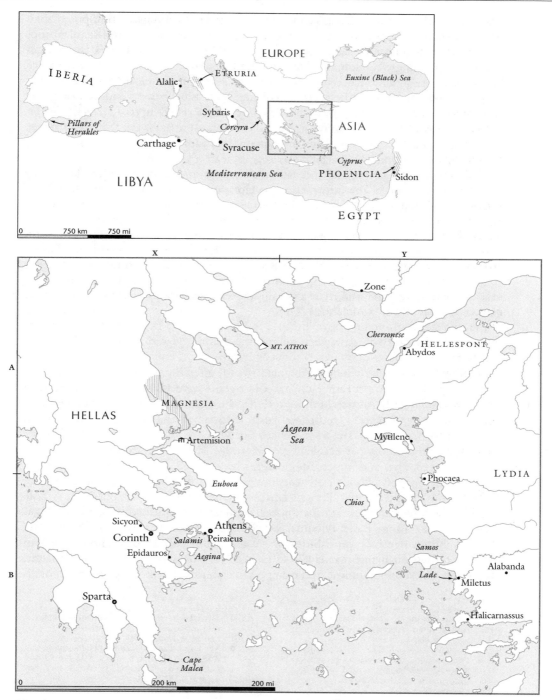

(7.49.2–3). Ancient naval fleets by necessity hugged the very coasts that posed their most imminent danger, for the cramped quarters of warships required regular stops for the crew to eat and sleep. Even in good weather, long stretches in triremes became exceedingly uncomfortable for the oarsmen. Rowers on the modern *Olympias*[b] were much bothered by the heat and stench that quickly permeated their close wooden quarters; in the prelude to Lade, Dionysius' rowers endured only one week of daylong training regimes on shipboard before rebelling (6.12.2–4).

§16. Ships also stayed within sight of coasts because these were their guideposts. Stars were no aid to navigation in the narrow latitudes of the Mediterranean; preserved ancient "admiralty charts" (*periploi*) indicate that mariners set their courses primarily by coastal landmarks and estimated speeds and distances. Herodotus may have obtained some of the information he cites for the areas of seas and lengths of rivers from such mariners' handbooks. Apparently Darius could not get his hands on such a guide, and so his first step in the invasion of Greece was to send ahead an expedition to reconnoiter the Greek coastline (3.136.1). In fact, Herodotus notes several instances in which lack of detailed knowledge of the Aegean coastline caused troubles for the Persian fleet (7.183.2, 8.107). The Corcyrians,[a] on the other hand, used local knowledge of geography and weather to their advantage, citing the well-known storms off Cape Malea[b] as a plausible excuse for not joining the Greek coalition at Salamis (7.168.4, 4.179.2).

Seafaring Nations

§17. Herodotus says that the Aeginetans and, after them, the Athenians fought best at Salamis (8.93.1).[a] Other Greek contingents have their moment in the sun: the Milesians[b] during Alyattes' reign (1.17.3), the Chians at Lade (6.15.1), and several times the Samians.[c] Herodotus also recognizes the wide-ranging Samian (4.152) and Phocaean (1.163.1) merchant fleets.

§18. But the sailors par excellence of Herodotus' account are the Phoenicians.[a] Phoenician colonists and merchants open his narrative (1.1.1) and Phoenician ships permeate its entirety. Phoenician warships were the backbone, the heart, and the stars of the Persian fleets,[b] Phoenician merchant ships (*gauloi*) plied the whole sweep of the Mediterranean, and a Phoenician fleet accomplished the circumnavigation of Africa.[c] Among the Phoenicians, the Sidonians had special pride of place: Xerxes' chosen flagship was a Sidonian vessel (7.100.2, 7.128.2), and a Sidonian warship won the rowing match (7.44; especially 7.96) at Abydos.[d] Unfortunately, archaeological, iconographical, and other textual sources for the ships of the Phoenicians are sparse.

S.15b The keel of the *Olympias* was laid down in 1985 and the ship was launched in 1987.

S.16a Corcyra: Map S, locator.

S.16b Cape Malea: Map S, BX.

S.17a See also 5.83.2 for Aeginetan superiority at sea (shortly thereafter contradicted by 5.86.2). Aegina, Athens, Salamis: Map S.

S.17b Miletus: Map S, BY.

S.17c The Samians are mentioned on four occasions; 3.44.2, 3.122.2, 5.117, 6.14.3.

S.18a Phoenicia: Map S, locator.

S.18b The Phoenicians are mentioned in this capacity at 3.19.2–3, 5.109.3, 6.6, 6.28.1, 6.31.1, 6.33.

S.18c Phoenician circumnavigation of Africa: 4.42; also, perhaps 2.102.2, 4.43.

S.18d Abydos: Map S, AY.

Figure S.4. A late-nineteenth-century photograph of the remains of foundations and column supports of the Athenian shipsheds at Peiraieus.

§19. It makes sense that Xerxes turned to his expert Phoenician sailors to provide the cables that spanned the Hellespont.[a] He turns also to the Egyptians (7.25, 7.34.2). Egypt was, of course, the source of papyrus.[b] But there are hints in Herodotus' narrative that the Egyptian facility with cables was due to more than their being the source of the raw materials. It is possible that these people of the Nile were also premier builders and sailors of seafaring vessels. Herodotus associates triremes with Nechos (2.159.1), which would be the earliest appearance of these ships. Further indication of Egyptian seamanship may perhaps underlie the reports (2.102.2, 4.43) that "Sesostris" and Sataspes started their voyages of exploration in Egypt.[c]

§20. In contrast to the seafarers, there are those who are not so inclined: Amazons, the Lydians, and the Persians.[a]

S.19a Hellespont: Map S, AY.
S.19b Egypt: Map S, locator. Papyrus was normally used in place of paper in the ancient Mediterranean, but in this case it was used to create some of the immense cables which were used to hold Xerxes' boat bridges in place (7.25.1, 7.34, 7.36.3).
S.19c It is likely, however, that they hired Phoenician vessels there (4.42).
S.20a The Lydians under Croesus (1.27); the Persians at 1.143.2 (although Persian troops served on ships as marines), and the Amazons (4.110.1–2).

Merchants and Colonists

§21. Herodotus' enumeration of fleets only occasionally makes reference to the supply ships that accompanied and outnumbered the warships. In contrast to the sleek lines of the oared ships designed for speed, cargo ships[a] were built for capacity, and thus their profiles were rounded and full. Merchant traffic through the Hellespont was particularly important, for the fertile fields of the Greek colonies in the Black Sea provided vital resources of grain to their homelands. Thus, control of these straits was strategically important for both sides. But Dionysius' acts of piracy against Carthaginian and Tyrrhenian[b] merchant shipping in Sicily illustrate that dangers beset merchant shipping throughout the Mediterranean (6.17). It is perhaps because of such dangers that oared warships are regularly associated with colonization movements.[c]

"Other" Watercraft

§22. It is only when he discusses foreign watercraft, such as the Armenian boats or the baris of the Nile, that Herodotus provides details. In both instances, archaeological, iconographic, and/or ethnographic evidence corroborates his descriptions. Round, skin-covered boats (Arabic: *kufah*) were sailed down the lower Euphrates into the early twentieth century, and just as in Herodotus' account (1.149), they were broken up at the end of the journey, their skins carried back upstream and refitted for another trip downstream. Herodotus also accurately describes the construction of Nile riverboats;[a] the use of short lengths of acacia wood and a construction technique reliant upon beams at deck level for the hull were foreign to Greek shipbuilding. His descriptions of the mechanics of towing the Nile boats upstream and keeping them on course downstream also ring true.

Nicolle Hirschfeld
Assistant Professor
Department of Classical Studies
Trinity University
San Antonio, TX

S.21a   Greek merchant ship: *holkas*; Phoenician: *gaulos*.
S.21b   Carthage, Tyrrhenia (Etruria): Map S, locator.
S.21c   Warships associated with colonization: triaconters, 4.148.3; penteconters, 1.163.1, 4.153, 4.156.2; triremes, 5.47.1.
S.22a   C. Haldane and C. W. Shelmerdine. "Herodotus 2.96.1–2 Again." *Classical Quarterly* 40 (1990), 535–539, with references.

APPENDIX T

Tyranny in Herodotus

§1. In the seventh- and sixth-century Greek-speaking world, city-states were customarily ruled by competing groups of powerful aristocratic families. The *tyrannos*, or tyrant, was a powerful individual, usually at least connected to an aristocratic family by birth, who rose to autocratic power within his city with the help of military and sometimes popular support; while he ruled, he controlled the competitive excesses of the men who would otherwise have been his peers, and so of course was disliked and envied by them, as the archaic poets Alkaios and Simonides testify. A Greek tyranny rarely lasted more than one or two generations; ordinarily, after the death of the tyrant or his sons, the government again reverted to the hands of local aristocrats, although in Athens and Syracuse institutions set in place during the tyranny gave rise to democratic forms of rule instead. In the hands of the fourth-century political theorists (one classic text is Plato's *Gorgias*), tyranny became defined as the lowest form of government, and the tyrant the model of the man ruthlessly oppressing his city but himself driven by his own basest and uncontrollable desires.

§2. Herodotus is our richest early source for historical information on the great Greek tyrannies of the late archaic and early classical age, and the most important witness to the details of their rule. He gives us vivid sketches of the tyrannies of Kypselos and Periandros of Corinth; Polykrates of Samos; Peisistratos, Hippias, and Hipparchos of Athens; the Miltiades family in the Chersonese; Thrasyboulos, Histiaios, and Aristagoras of Miletus; Kleisthenes of Sicyon; Gelon of Syracuse; and brief mentions of other tyrannical rulers, like Koes of Mytilene, the tyrants of Cyprus, Prokles of Epidaurus, Telys of Sybaris, and Aridolis of Alabanda.[a]

T.2a Kypselos and Periandros of Corinth: 1.20–24, 3.48–53, 5.92, 5.95.
Polykrates of Samos: 3.39–45, 3.120–125.
Peisistratos, Hippias, and Hipparchos of Athens: 1.59–64, 5.55–65, 5.93–96, 6.102–107, 7.6.
Miltiades family in the Chersonese: 4.137–138, 6.34–41, 6.103–104, 6.109–110, 6.132–137, 6.140.
Thrasyboulos, Histiaios, and Aristagoras of Miletus: 1.20–22, 4.137–139, 4.141, 5.11, 5.23–25, 5.30–38, 5.49–51, 5.54–55, 5.97–98, 5.103–107, 5.124–126, 6.1–6, 6.9, 6.13, 6.26–30, 7.10.
Kleisthenes of Sicyon: 5.67–69, 6.126–131.
Gelon of Syracuse: 7.145, 7.153–167.
Koes of Mytilene (Lesbos): 5.37–38.
tyrants of Cyprus: 5.108–109, 113.
Prokles of Epidaurus: 3.50.
Telys of Sybaris: 5.44.
Aridolis of Alabanda: 7.195.
See Map S and locator for the locations of these tyrannies.

§3. A number of these tyrants, according to Herodotus, were linked to each other and other powerful aristocratic families as well by *xenia*, ties of aristocratic guest-friendship and marriage. The most vivid picture of tyrannical *xenia* in Herodotus links Thrasyboulos of Miletus to Periandros of Corinth, especially in Book 5, where Thrasyboulos lops off the ears of grain silently for Periandros' messenger, in response to Periandros' request for information about what to do in order to maintain his tyrannical power. The messenger reports to Periandros that Thrasyboulos must be mad, but Periandros gets the message: to stay in power, destroy the strongest of your subjects (5.92.ζ–η; see 1.20 as well for the importance of this guest-friendship). Another picture of tyrannical *xenia* occurs when Kleisthenes tyrant of Sicyon throws his famous yearlong house party to select a son-in-law, and invites most of the rich and famous eligible young bachelors of Greece to participate (6.126–131). The front-runner, Hippokleides of Athens (probably from the Philaid family), cracks under the strain—or perhaps decides the honor of being Kleisthenes' son-in-law is not worth the bother—and does a headstand, drunk, waving his feet about in time to the music, at the tyrant's final festive dinner party. The girl, Agariste, marries an Alkmeonid from Athens instead and becomes the great-grandmother of Pericles.[a]

§4. Herodotus' picture of these tyrannies is complex. On the one hand, he sprinkles throughout the *Histories* comments concerning the perils and disadvantages of autocratic government. Three passages in particular are lengthy and very striking, and together they construct the outlines of Herodotus' critique of autocratic tyranny. In two of them, though the word "tyranny" is used, the topic is large-scale Eastern autocracy and not the rule of individual Greek cities. In Book 1, Deiokes, the founder of Median rule, *erastheis tyrannos*—in love with tyranny—is chosen as an autocratic ruler because he has already successfully imposed law and order on his people as a judge. He builds himself a palace with seven layers of walls and becomes a harsh and increasingly inaccessible autocratic ruler (1.96–103). In Book 3, after the expansionist Persian reigns of Cyrus and Cambyses, the seven co-conspirators take back the rule of Persia from its Median usurpers and debate among themselves what kind of rule should be instituted. Otanes develops a highly critical picture of autocratic monarchy, arguing that the single ruler is unconstrained (*aneuthunos*) and therefore a dangerously outrageous, jealous, and violent oppressor of his subjects (3.80). The one lengthy Greek description of a tyranny is delivered by Sokleas the Corinthian in Book 5, when the Spartans try to convince their Peloponnesian allies to reinstate tyranny in Athens. Sokleas thinks that although a tyrant looks innocuous at the beginning of his reign, he grows to create enormous disadvantages for his people later (5.92). These three pictures of tyranny taken together form a pattern, a tyrannical template, so to speak. In other shorter passages too, Herodotus makes

T.3a   For more on the Philaid and Alkmeonid fami-
        lies in Herodotus, see Appendix L, Aristocratic
        Families in Herodotus, §2–4, 8, 11, 15.

clear the Greek preference for freedom over autocracy. He comments that the Athenians who were weak under their tyrants grew strong when they became a democracy and could work for themselves (5.66, 5.78, 5.91). Comments of the same sort made either by Herodotus or people within the narrative are scattered elsewhere throughout the *Histories*.[a]

§5. However, other passages in the *Histories* complicate this picture of tyranny as clearly bad for a city and its citizens. Some rulers, both Greek and non-Greek, refer to their own reigns as tyrannies and themselves as tyrants, or Herodotus refers to them in passing as tyrants without any great disapproval.[a] This suggests that the semantic field of the word (perhaps originally a Lydian word) originally implied little more than "reigning monarch." In the highly competitive aristocratic world of Archaic Greek lyric poetry, one can see that an Archilochus, Simonides, or Alkaios might indeed use the word "tyrant" against a fellow aristocrat who looked too ambitious or behaved in a high-handed fashion. Moreover, Herodotus also praises the deeds of some Greek tyrants: Periandros is depicted defending Miletus, distributing justice, and acting as an interstate arbitrator (1.20, 1.24, 5.95); the rulers of Miletus are chosen by the Parians because their farms have been well run (5.29), Peisistratos is praised for the beautification of Athens and the fact that he followed its customary laws (1.59), Miltiades the Athenian tyrant from the Chersonese becomes the architect of Athenian success at Marathon (6.109–111). As Herodotus depicts it, Greek tyrants in the sixth century are dangerous primarily because they often bring Persian overlordship with them (most notoriously after the collapse of the Ionian cause at Lade, 6.9, 6.25, 6.32).

§6. So the tyrant in Herodotus is an ambiguous figure. On the one hand, tyrants are often dangerously oppressive figures mistreating their citizens, and implicated in the even greater perils posed by large-scale Eastern autocracy as it attempts in the later books of the *Histories* to extend its control into Greece. On the other hand, the individual Greek tyrants as Herodotus portrays them also exhibit that self-motivated initiative that Herodotus believes is allied to the distinctively Greek love of individual liberty and that lies at the heart of the Greek ability to resist Persian imperial domination at the beginning of the fifth century.[a]

Carolyn Dewald
Professor of Classical and Historical Studies
Bard College
Annandale-on-Hudson, NY

T.4a Comments on Greek preference for freedom as against autocracy can be found at 4.137, 6.5.5, 7.101–105, 7.135, 7.234–235, and 8.142.

T.5a References to tyrants without disapproval are: 1.86, 3.53, 5.98, 5.113, 7.52, 7.99, 8.137.

T.6a I have written more fully on this subject in the article from which the above is largely drawn: C. Dewald, "Form and Content: The Question of Tyranny in Herodotus," in *Popular Tyranny: Sovereignty and Its Discontents in Ancient Greece*, ed. K. Morgan (Austin: University of Texas, 2003), 25–58.

APPENDIX U

On Women and Marriage in Herodotus

§1. Apart from Sappho, we possess almost no female voices from the ancient Greek world. Nonetheless, thanks to a generation and more of cultural studies, many of them undertaken from a feminist orientation, we now understand a fair amount about ancient women's lives—certainly more than we did when the field of ancient history was defined in Thucydidean terms as the political and military adventures of important citizen males. Unless they were members of royal dynasties or great aristocratic families, individual women in ancient Greece rarely exercised powerful public roles. As Thucydides' Pericles famously puts it in the funeral oration at the end of the first year of the Peloponnesian War, briefly addressing Athenian women who have been left war widows: "Great will be your glory in not falling short of your natural character; and greatest will be hers who is least talked of among the men whether for good or for bad" (*Thucydides* 2.45). We now understand that in the context of the family, and the broader societal structures represented by religion, medicine, or the economy of the *oikos* (household), women played a variety of vital and active roles in the poleis (cities) of the classical world, even if they were rarely explicitly discussed.[a]

§2. Herodotus' frequent comments about women preserve for us one well-traveled Hellenic man's observations and assumptions about women's multiple and complex roles not just in Greece but throughout the fifth-century eastern Mediterranean world. There are polished and expansive narratives about powerful queens like Artemisia, Tomyris, Pheretime, Amestris, or the unnamed wife of Kandaules, but also brief and tantalizing passing mentions of people like Croesus' baker, the beard-growing priestess of Pedasa (twice!), or the Mendean woman who was said to have had sex with a goat in public.[a] A substantial number of women mentioned in the *Histories* are anonymously described in ethnographic contexts, when a whole culture is being sketched out, so to speak, in the context of an impending Persian invasion.[b]

U.1a Women tended to be described in overtly ideological contexts, for instance in ancient oratory, where they were depicted as innocent or corrupt depending on whether they were in the speaker's or the opponent's family.

U.2a Artemisia (7.99, 8.87–93, 8.101–103), Tomyris (1.205–206, 1.211–214), Pheretime (4.162.5, 4.165, 4.167, 4.201, 4.205), Amestris (7.114.2,

9.109, 9.110, 9.112), the wife of Kandaules (1.8–12), Croesus' baker (1.51.5), the priestess of Pedasa (1.175, 8.104), and the Mendean woman (2.46.3).

U.2b See R. Munson, *Telling Wonders. Ethnographic and Political Discourse in the Work of Herodotus* (Ann Arbor: University of Michigan Press, 2001).

§3. A couple of decades ago I counted every mention of a woman or groups of women in Herodotus and came up with 375 instances in all: 128 passages where they are presented as passive figures, either in a family context (97) or in civic groups (31); 212 passages depicting active women, either in the context of a polis (12), as part of the family (40), in the public sphere (22), in an ethnographic description (76), or in a religious context (62); and, finally, 35 mentions of the feminine depicted as an abstraction.[a] These last occur in discussions of geography (see especially 4.45), generalizations about male and female behavior (for example, 2.102, where Herodotus comments that Sesostris is supposed to have left pillars with female genitalia engraved on them at sites where he thought his enemies proved weak or cowardly), or in connection with dreams or visions in which females occur (6.61.4, 6.107, 8.84). As these categories show, Herodotus' women are quite variegated; this is the product of the breadth and variety of his sources, but also the catholicity of his own interests.

§4. When women are mentioned not as actors but merely in passing, as parts of a family or civic structure, they often appear in the context of a threat posed to the safety of the family or city. When the Ionians lose the battle of Lade in 494 (6.14ff.), the Persians kill their men and enslave and scatter their women and children; Babylonian men wishing to revolt from Persia decide to kill off their own women to save resources for their revolt (3.50, 3.159); when Polykrates of Samos wants to coerce his enemies, he shuts up their women and children in a warehouse and threatens to burn them alive (3.45). Within the family, and in the context of the family's ability to reproduce itself over time, they are mentioned when they cannot bear children, are crippled themselves, or bear children who will be problems (1.59, 1.107–108, 5.39–40, 5.92.γ–δ, 6.61). Families and communities are built through marriage connections, and Herodotus also pays particular attention to the stresses posed by exogamy itself. Women sometimes bear children who remain loyal to their mother's family and turn against their father (3.50). Several stories testify to the anxieties that powerful marriage connections could cause a man. Croesus is obliged, he feels, to avenge his brother-in-law Astyages' defeat (1.73–75); according to Herodotus, Alexander of Macedon is forced to marry his sister to a powerful Persian, and to become part of a Persian political alliance, because he has killed noble Persians intent on violating his female relatives (5.20–21).

§5. In Attic tragedy, women who are active agents in their city or family sphere are often portrayed as plotting against relatives or otherwise causing trouble, but Herodotus rarely depicts them in this way. Cyno the cowherd's wife saves baby Cyrus and is the only individual in the whole story of his grandfather's attempt to kill him who articulates a thoughtful and human rationale for her actions and takes responsibility for them; Intaphrenes' wife saves more of her family than Darius ini-

---

U.3a   C. Dewald, "Women and Culture in Herodotus' *Histories*," in *Reflections of Women in Antiquity*, ed. H. Foley (New York: Gordon and Breach, 1981), 120–125.

tially intended, through her clever retort to Darius that her first choice would be to save a brother (a retort that Sophocles adopts for his *Antigone*). Strong queens—Kandaules' wife, Tomyris, Artemisia, Amestris—do act ruthlessly, but they also give reasons for their actions. Except for Artemisia, they present themselves as following the *nomoi*, or customs, of their cultures, and all of them are more successful than most male actors in the *Histories* at defending themselves against threats to their person and/or position. Less prominent women too, like Labda mother of Kypselos, the Lacedaemonian women married to Theran husbands, or the Egyptian Nitokris, act in unexpected ways, but they do so in order to preserve family members from disaster or to avenge their deaths. Even Pheretime of Cyrene, famous (and punished by the gods) because she takes vengeance to an inhuman extreme, does so to avenge the violent death of her son. And there is also the example of the Egyptian thief who is forced by his mother to rescue the body of his decapitated brother even at great risk to himself (2.121). Women in Herodotus tend to be more successful than their powerful masters, husbands, fathers, and brothers in getting their way, often through unconventionally clever means. Herodotus enjoys reporting on the ease with which people of inferior status of either sex succeed in manipulating men in power, often by exploiting their blindness to their own vulnerabilities; such stories also connect to Herodotus' desire to report *erga megala te kai thomasta* (1.1), strange and remarkable deeds of all kinds.

§6. Women play essential roles in Herodotus' ethnographic descriptions. He says the war chariots of the Zauekes of Libya are driven by their women (4.193). He delights in telling us that the Egyptians do everything backward from the rest of the world; that their men work indoors while their women sell things in the market; that Egyptian men urinate sitting down, the women standing up, etc. (2.35.2–3). He gives a long and fascinating account of Sauromatian origins (the Scythians want the Amazons as wives for their sons, and send the young men to woo them), which serves almost as a sophistic teaching parable about the necessity for complementarity and mutual adjustments between the sexes (4.110–117). And it is interesting that Herodotus does not disapprove of sexual mores that are quite different from the rigidly controlled female sexuality of the Greek model; in cultures where near promiscuity is practiced, he emphasizes that there are rules governing privacy and the assignment of paternity to the group's offspring.[a] He is quick to point out parallel behavior in a culture's men and women; for example, when the Athenians stone one of their council members to death because he proposed that they accept a Persian alliance, their wives in Salamis rush to stone the man's wife and children (9.5). And a "Lemnian deed," Herodotus says, refers not just to the famous mythic slaying of men by Lemnian women, but also to an act committed by Lemnian men, who kill their Attic concubines because of the threat that their half-Attic children pose to the children of their Lemnian wives (6.138). This story also testifies to the power

U.6a   For examples of these rules, see 1.216, 4.104,
       4.172, 4.180.

women have to transmit cultural values not only to their children but to other family members as well.

§7. Women figure frequently in Herodotus in a religious context. In four passages women are founders of cults;[a] others are priestesses or instruments of the divine to particular men or cities, or are depicted celebrating religious festivals like the all-female Thesmophoria. If one counts the role rather than the individual human actor, the priestess at Delphi appears more frequently than any other woman in the *Histories*. Forty-five times she advises cities or individuals; the advice she gives, however, is not her own but the god's, and Herodotus comments twice on the corrupt actions of a particular Delphic priestess (5.63, 6.66). His views on religion are currently subject to considerable controversy, and here especially his sources' opinions and religious beliefs may color his account, as well as his own desire to report anything remarkable, even if he does not believe it. A snake goddess in Scythia in one story holds Herakles to a hard bargain (4.9), the daughter of Polykrates has a portentous dream about her father's death (3.124), and Labda the Bacchiad in Corinth is an agent of a divine plan (5.92.δ). Herodotus generally reports such stories at face value, but it is difficult not to see a sly, skeptical humor in his account of Demaratos' mother's description of a divine impregnation, particularly since Demaratos himself flees to Persia instead of trying to convince his fellow Spartans of the improbable tale (6.67–70).

§8. This brings up a final necessary observation, germane to almost all Herodotean narrative but perhaps particularly striking in his treatment of women. Herodotus seems to find sexual roles and conventions interesting and entertaining. It is difficult not to read the long, rationalizing series of mutual abductions of women at the beginning of the *Histories* as a humorous one, although it also has the serious historiographical purpose of showing that all *logoi* from long ago are partisan. The story of Gyges, Croesus' ancestor and the founder of his dynasty, contains at least a strong element of sexually based irony. He is ordered by his royal master to hide behind the bedroom door and view the queen's nakedness, and then "chooses to live" when the queen legalistically faces him with the fact that only one man gets to see her naked, and it's up to him to decide whether he or the king will die (1.11.2–4). Herodotus enjoys telling us about Pheretime, nagging a Cypriot prince for an army and given a golden spindle instead (4.162.3–4); he enjoys even more reporting Artemisia's unconventional and even bizarre (but effective!) military behavior. Her decision to sink an allied ship, to persuade the pursuing Athenians that they have mistakenly identified her own ship (8.87–88), is clearly a shocking story that Herodotus ironically appreciates.

§9. In sum, it is difficult to account for the full range of Herodotus' treatment of women without returning to some of his most basic historiographic convictions: to report the remarkable, to "seek out side issues" (4.30), to grid an enormous road

U.7a See 2.54–55, 2.171, 2.182, 4.33–35.

map of *ta anthropeia*, human matters, in all their fascinating particulars. More than any other ancient author, Herodotus resists easy categorization in his omnivorous curiosity.

Carolyn Dewald
Professor of Classical and Historical Studies
Bard College
Annandale-on-Hudson, NY

Bibliography

Blok, J. "Women in Herodotus' *Histories*." In E. Bakker, I. de Jong, H. van Wees, eds., *Brill's Companion to Herodotus* (Leiden: Brill, 2002), 225–242.

Fantham, E., H. Foley, N. Kampen, S. Pomeroy, H. A. Shapiro, eds. *Women in the Classical World* (Oxford: Oxford University Press, 1994).

GLOSSARY

Achaimenids: royal family of Persian empire. Founded by Cyrus in 550.

acropolis: the citadel or high point of a Greek city; often the site of the original settlement, and in historic times well stocked with temples and sacred sites, enclosed by its own set of defensive walls.

Aeolians: an ethnic group of Greeks, inhabiting Aegean islands and the west coast of Asia Minor north of Smyrna.

aegis: Athena's shield or short cloak, with a fringe of snakes and device of Medusa's head.

Agiads and Eurypontids: Spartan royal hereditary families, each one supplying one of the two reigning kings of Sparta.

agora: the agora was the civic center of a Greek polis where all political, commercial, and much social activity took place. A fundamental feature of every Greek city, it was a marketplace where citizens could buy and sell goods, gossip, and discuss politics or other topics.

akinakes: a type of Persian and Scythian sword. An *akinakes* was short and straight.

Amphiktyonic League/Amphiktyones: a league made up of representatives from mostly neighboring states who were selected to maintain, protect, and defend the sanctuary of Delphi. They had responsibility for administering the sanctuary, and could impose fines, declare sacred wars, and award contracts for building projects.

angareion: a system organized by the Persians of mounted couriers riding in relays to swiftly carry royal messages.

archon: a magistrate at Athens, chosen by lot in the later fifth century. The nine archons were concerned with administering justice, overseeing foreign residents of Athens, adjudicating family property disputes, and carrying out a variety of other tasks. The eponymous archon gave his name to the civil year.

Argonauts/*Argo*: the subject of an ancient Greek epic legend with common themes. To rid himself of Jason, a dangerous pretender to the throne, King Pelias of Iolkoss in Thessaly, sends him far away on a journey to bring back the Golden Fleece. Jason gathers a group of noble Minyans, together with other heroes such as Herakles and Orpheus, and sails off in a ship built by the hero Argos, and called the *Argo*, to Colchis on the Black Sea, where the fleece is located. After many harrowing adventures they arrive at Colchis, where King Aeetes gives them further dangerous tasks to accomplish. With the help of Medea, the king's daughter, they successfully complete the tasks and obtain the Golden Fleece. Then, taking Medea with them, Jason and the Argonauts return to Greece.

battos: a North African word for king.

Bosporus: a narrow strait separating two lands—Thracian Bosporus separates Europe from Asia, the Cimmerian Bosporus separates the Crimea from Eastern Scythia.

Council of Elders/the Gerousia: the senate and highest council of Sparta. The Council was made up of thirty members over the age of sixty, although it included the two reigning kings of Sparta at any age. Members, who were limited to certain aristocratic families, were elected and served for life.

chthonian deities: the nether or earth gods, regarded as dwelling in or under the earth.

demos: "common people" and "people" are translations the Greek word *demos*. The basic sense of the word is "district," which extends then to people of a district, especially the common people of the country districts surrounding the urban center; and then, in a political context, the sovereign people. When Kleisthenes reformed the Athenian government in 508/07, he set up a system of demes in both rural and urban areas, which became formal political units of the Athenian state.

dithyramb: a choral hymn sung at festivals in honor of Dionysus.

Dorians: an ethnic group or Greeks speaking and writing a distinctive dialect of Greek and sharing certain customs and rituals.

Eleusinian mysteries: an initiatory cult in honor of Demeter and Persephone at Eleusis in Attica.

ephor: one of five annually elected powerful magistrates at Sparta. An individual could only be elected to it once in his lifetime.

Eurypontids and Agiads: Spartan royal hereditary families, each supplying one of the two reigning kings of Sparta and both tracing their lineage back to Herakles.

guest-friendship (*xenia*): a hallowed institution of ancient Hellas (and Herodotus would have us believe of Persia also). It was a formal relationship, usually formed between eminent citizens of different states, but sometimes between an individual and a whole state. The parties committed themselves to profound mutual obligations, including hospitality, advice, and support, which were not taken lightly; these commitments could pass to succeeding generations.

hecatomb: originally, as the name implies, a sacrifice of one hundred oxen (hekaton, bous); then any particularly large number of victims destined for public sacrifice.

hegemony/hegemon: leader, preponderant authority of a state over other states.

Hellenes: the name by which the Greeks called themselves.

Hellespont: the modern Dardanelles, the southern section of the straits between the Propontis and the Black Sea.

helots: the original Greek inhabitants of Laconia and Messenia, now held in serfdom by their Spartiate masters, whom they greatly outnumbered.

hoplite: a heavily armed Greek citizen foot-soldier, who fought in a phalanx formation.

The Iakhos cry: it was made by the initiates into the mysteries celebrated at Eleusis, the site of the famous shrine to Demeter.

Immortals: an elite Persian infantry force of 10,000 serving both as a bodyguard to the King and as a crack unit for special missions.

Ionians: an ethnic group of Greeks, inhabiting Attica and an important segment of the Aegean coast of Asia Minor called Ionia.

Isthmus of Corinth: the narrow strip of land that connects the northern Greek mainland to the Peloponnese.

klerouchs: a type of colony used by the Athenians in ruling their empire. *Klerouchs* were Athenian citizens allotted plots of land appropriated from allies, who retained their Athenian citizenship and thus did not establish a typical Greek colony.

Lacedaemon: territory of the polis of Sparta, including Messenia and Laconia. The inhabitants of Lacedaemon were called Lacedaemonians.

Magi: the Magi were Median priests and seers.

Medes: a north-Iranian people often confused by Greeks with Persians. The Medes once ruled Persia but at the time of Herodotus they were ruled by the Persians.

medizing/medism: describes those Greek states or individuals who sided with the Persians. This is an example of the Greek practice of using the names "Persian" and "Mede" interchangeably.

Ocean: the great river surrounding the known land mentioned by the poets, whose existence was doubted by Herodotus.

oligarch/oligarchy: rule by the few, the rich, the well born, but not necessarily the best, as in aristocracy.

Olympia: major shrine to Zeus in northwest Peloponnese. Quadrennial athletic games and contests here were part of the rites and were the most celebrated contests in Greece.

ostracism: a political procedure by which an Athenian citizen could be honorably banished from Athens and her empire for ten years without loss of property or citizenship. He was ostracized if, after the Athenians had chosen to hold such a vote, he received the most votes out of a total of at least 6,000 votes cast. Votes were noted on shards of pottery called *ostraka*.

paean: a hymn or cry of praise, originally to Apollo, but later with wider application. Often sung by warriors marching into battle or after a military success.

penteconter: a warship propelled by fifty oars.

perioikoi: literally the "dwellers around Sparta;" inhabitants of neighboring towns, who were Spartan citizens, though of lesser status and with fewer rights than full Spartiates.

Persians: inhabitants of central and southern Iran who created a great empire under talented kings like Cyrus and Darius. They were often confused by the Greeks with the Medes, a nearby group who once ruled over the Persians.

Plataea: a small Boeotian town on the border between Attica and Thebes who allied with the Athenians and fought with them against the Persians. It is not to be confused with a small island off the coast of Africa named Plateia.

polemarch: originally a "war leader" but later just the title of one of the archons in Athens. In Sparta the polemarch commanded a mora, the largest unit in the Spartan army.

polis: the most important ancient Greek political unit; an independent city with its surrounding territory. At one time there were almost 1,000 of them.

proskynesis: Persian practice of lowering oneself to the ground before the King or other superior. Greeks considered such abasement unseemly to do before men, and just barely appropriate to do before gods.

proxenos: a citizen and resident of one state who served as a friend or representative of a foreign state (much like a modern honorary consul). He provided assistance and attempted to protect the interests of the citizens of his designated city. The office was often hereditary.

Pythia: the priestess of Apollo at Delphi who pronounced oracles.

Pythioi: special sacred delegates who were sent to Delphi to consult on behalf of Sparta with the Pythia for oracular advice and predictions. They dined with the king at public expense and shared knowledge of the oracles that pertained to the state with the king.

satrap: Persian viceroy or governor of a large province or territory called a satrapy.

Spartiate: a full citizen of Sparta; numbers were limited by strict regulations as regards qualifications, which included lineage and submission to the famous Spartan Agōgē, or "upbringing." There were other citizens of Sparta, like *perioikoi*, who did not have full political rights.

Thebes: hegemonic city of Boeotia, medized in the Persian Wars.

tithe: the practice of reserving one tenth of received revenue, confiscated property, or spoils of war, for the service of the god or gods.

triaconter: a thirty-oared ship. They were used as messenger ships in Xerxes' fleet.

trireme: the standard warship of Herodotus' time, powered by 170 rowers arrayed in three tiers, and armed with marines, archers, and a ram.

twelve gods: the most important gods of the Greek pantheon—Zeus, Hera, Poseidon, Demeter, Apollo, Artemis, Hephaistos, Athena, Ares, Aphrodite, Hermes, and Histia. They shared a central altar in the agora, from which distances to other sites were reckoned.

tyrant: one who ruled a state as an absolute monarch without traditional or other constraints or sanctions.

ANCIENT SOURCES

Aelian (c. 170–235 C.E.): Roman author and teacher of rhetoric, author of *Historical Miscellany*.

Aeschylos (525/24–426): Athens' most successful early tragic playwright. He fought the Persians at Marathon and probably at Salamis. The titles of 82 plays that he wrote are known to us, but only seven have survived in their entirety. One of those plays *The Persians*, is the only eyewitness account we have of the battle of Salamis.

Aesop: supposed sixth-century author of instructive fables, but there is doubt that he ever existed as one person.

Alkaios: an aristocrat from Mytilene on Lesbos who wrote lyric poetry c. 620–580. Only fragments of his work survive. They include drinking songs, love songs, hymns and political songs. The work mentioned by Herodotus in 5.95.2 has survived.

Alkman (fl. 654– 611): lyric poet who lived in Sparta.

Anaximander (610–547): Greek philosopher and mathematician. A friend and pupil of Thales.

Archilochus: Greek lyric poet who flourished c. 650.

Ctesias: a late-fifth-/early-fourth-century doctor at the Persian court, author of a history of Persia, a geographical treatise, and the first separate work on India, now all lost except for a few fragments.

Diodorus Siculus (fl. 60–30): wrote a world history in 40 books, which reproduces elements of many historians, such as Hekataios, Ctesias, and others.

Hekataios: author of geographical and historical accounts of Asia Minor and the East, late sixth century, and a source both used and criticized by Herodotus. He also plays a role in Herodotus' account of Ionian history. See 5.36, 5.125–126, and 6.137.

Hesiod: flourished c. 700. Poet and author of two works which have come down to us: *Works and Days* and *Theogony*.

Homer: the poet who the Greeks believed to be the author of the epic poems Iliad and Odyssey, which are thought to have been composed and compiled in the late eighth or early seventh century.

Isocrates: Athenian speechwriter and pamphleteer of the fourth century; he encouraged Greeks to unite and attack Persia, even under Macedonian leadership.

Pausanias: a travel writer of the second century A.D. who wrote *Description of Greece* (*Periegesis Hellados*).

Pindar (518–438): a lyric poet active in the first half of the fifth century until c. 446. He was especially known for the victory odes he composed for victorious athletes throughout the Greek world.

Pliny the Elder (c. 23–79 C.E.): Roman encyclopaedic writer; author of both a history (lost) and a *Natural History* which has come down to us.

Plutarch (46–120 C.E.): author of a series of biographies known as *Plutarch's Lives*, and a large number of essays (*Moralia*) which have survived.

Sappho (c. 612–550): the most famous Ancient Greek poetess. She appears to have lived in Mytilene in Lesbos.

Semonides: seventh-century verse author of local and Samian history.

Simonides of Ceos (c. 556–468): poet most famous for epigrams.

Strabo (63 B.C.E.–24 C.E.): Greek historian and geographer. His historical work has not survived, but his *Geographica*, a vital work for our knowledge of his world, has come down to us almost intact.

Thucydides (c. 460–401): Athenian historian, successor to Herodotus, author of *The Peloponnesian War*, focused on analytic military and political history.

Xenophon (c. 430–356): Greek soldier, historian, essayist; born at Athens, he fought with Cyrus the Younger's expedition to Mesopotamia, and later enlisted in the Spartan mercenary force formed by Agesilaus, with whom he served for many years. He wrote several books and a number of essays which have come down to us.

Thales (c. 640–546): born at Miletus, he was a natural philosopher who made contributions to many fields. He is said to have invented geometry, but he was also active in politics, engineering, geography, astronomy, and mathematics.

BIBLIOGRAPHY FOR
THE GENERAL READER

Bakker, Egbert J., Irene. J. F. de Jong, and Hans van Wees, eds. *Brill's Companion to Herodotus* (Leiden and Boston: Brill Publishers, 2002).

The Cambridge Ancient History, 2nd ed. (New York: Cambridge University Press):
    Vol. 3, *The Expansion of the Greek World, Eighth to Sixth Centuries* B.C. (1982).
    Vol. 4, *Persia, Greece, and the Western Mediterranean c. 525–479* B.C. (1998).
    Vol. 5, *The Fifth Century* B.C. (1992).

Cartledge, Paul. *Thermopylae, The Battle that Changed the World* (Woodstock and New York: Overlook Press, 2006).

Cawkwell, George L. *The Greek Wars* (New York: Oxford University Press, 2005).

Dewald, Carolyn, and John Marincola, eds. *The Cambridge Companion to Herodotus* (Cambridge: Cambridge University Press, 2006).

Evans, J. A. S. *Herodotus: Explorer of the Past: Three Essays*. Princeton: Princeton University Press, 1991.

Gould, John. *Herodotus.* (New York: St. Martin's Press, 1989).

Green, Peter. *The Greco-Persian Wars* (Berkeley and Los Angeles: University of California Press, 1996).

Holland, Tom. *Persian Fire: The First World Empire and the Battle for the West* (London: Little, Brown, 2005, and Abacus, 2006).

Hornblower, Simon, and Anthony Spawforth, eds. *The Oxford Classical Dictionary*, 3rd ed. (New York: Oxford University Press, 1996).

Lateiner, Donald. *The Historical Method of Herodotus* (Toronto: University of Toronto Press, 1989).

Munson, Rosaria Vignolo. *Telling Wonders: Ethnographic and Political Discourse in the Work of Herodotus* (Ann Arbor, MI: University of Michigan Press, 2001).

Myers, John. *Herodotus: Father of History* (Oxford: Oxford University Press, 1958).

Redfield, James. "Herodotus the Tourist," *Classical Philology* 80 (1985): 97–118.

Romm, James. *Herodotus* (New Haven: Yale University Press, 1998).

Strauss, Barry. *The Battle of Salamis: The Naval Encounter that Saved Greece and Western Civilization* (New York: Simon & Schuster; Reprint, 2005).

Talbert, Richard J., ed. *Barrington Atlas of the Greek and Roman World* (Princeton, NJ: Princeton University Press, 2000).

Thomas, Rosalind. *Herodotus in Context* (Cambridge: Cambridge University Press, New ed., 2002).

Waters, K. H. *Herodotos* [sic] *the Historian. His Problems, Methods and Originality* (London: Croom Helm, 1984).

West, Martin L. *Greek Epic Fragments from the Seventh to Fifth Centuries B.C.* (Cambridge, MA: Harvard University Press, 2003).

EDITIONS AND COMMENTARIES

Asheri, David, et al. *Le storie: Erodoto.* 9 vols. (Milan: Fondazione Lorenzo Valla: A. Mondadori, 1988–1998).

Blakesley, J. W. *Herodotus, Vol. I* (London: Whittaker and Co., 1854).

Godley, A. D., ed. *Herodotus, with an English Translation by A. D. Godley.* (Cambridge: Harvard University Press, 1920–1925). Perseus Digital Library Project. Gregory R. Crane, ed., October, 2008. Tufts University. December, 1999. http://www.perseus.tufts.edu.

How, W. W., and J. Wells, *A Commentary on Herodotus, With Introduction and Appendixes,* 2 vols. (Oxford: Clarendon Press, 1928.)

Hude, Carolus. *Herodoti Historiae.* 3rd ed. (Oxford: Clarendon Press, 1927).

Larcher, P. H. *Historical and Critical Comments on the History of Herodotus.* New ed., with corrections and additions by William Desborough Cooley (London: Whittaker and Co., 1844).

Lloyd, Alan B. *Herodotus, Book II. 3 vols. Etudes préliminaires aux religions orientales dans l'Empire romain* (Leiden: E. J. Brill, 1975–1988).

Macan, R. W. *Herodotus, the fourth, fifth, and sixth books* (London: Macmillan, 1895).

_____. *Herodotus, the seventh, eighth, and ninth books* (London: Macmillan, 1908).

McNeal, R. A., ed. *Herodotus Book I.* (Lanham, Md.: University Press of America, 1986).

Powell, J. Enoch, *A Lexicon to Herodotus,* 2nd ed. (Hildesheim: Georg Olms, 1960).

Rosen, H. B. *Herodotus Historiae,* Vol. 1 (Leipzig: Teubner, 1987).

Sayce, A. H. *The Ancient Empires of the East: Herodotus I–III* (New York: C. Scribner's Sons, 1896).

Waddell, W. G. *Herodotus Book II* (London: Methuen and Co., 1939).

Woods, Henry George. *Herodotus Book I* (London: Rivingtons, 1871).

_____. *Herodotus Book II* (London: Rivingtons, 1873).

UNPUBLISHED WORKS

Wheeler, Everett L. Unpublished essay on Greeks in the Black Sea region (August, 2006).

Figure Credits

Frontispiece	Musée de l'Agora Antique d'Athènes, no. S270, GNU Free Documentation License
1.1	Johannes Laurentius, Bildarchiv Preussischer Kulturbesitz/Art Resource, NY
1.14, 6.117b, 9.39, 9.81b, 9.82	© The Trustees of the British Museum
1.31, 1.52, 2.55, 2.124a–b, 4.15, 7.129, 7.139, 8.53	Robert B. Strassler
1.47, 7.211 (right)	Bildarchiv Preussischer Kulturbesitz/Art Resource, NY
1.51	Musée Châtillon-sur-Seine
1.91, 1.92	A. Furtwängler and K. Reichhold, *Griechische Vasenmalerei: Auswahl hervorragender*
1.93	Shane Solow, Lost Trails
1.106	Tehran Museum, Iran, as reproduced in *Forgotten Empire, The World of Ancient Persia*, ed. John Curtis and Nigel Tallis, The British Museum, 2005
1.161	Ersin Alok, *Architecture in Asia Minor*, James Steele, Academy Editions, London, 1992
1.162a–b	Avraham Hay, *The Conquest of Lachish by Sennacherib*, David Ussishkin, Institute of Archaeology, Tel Aviv University, 1982
1.193 (left)	Hajor, GNU Free Documentation License; (right) David White, www.socialstudiesforkids.com
2.67	© Museum of Fine Arts, Boston, Hay Collection
2.97, 2.124c	Courtesy of the Fine Arts Library, Harvard College Library
2.129	© Museum of Fine Arts, Boston, Harvard University-Museum of Fine Arts Expedition
2.138	Rita Freed
3.8a–b	Gösta Hellner/Eleutherios, German Archaeological Institute, Athens
3.8c	After Kienast, German Archaeological Institute, Athens
3.57, 4.169 (right), N.1–3	Photo Hirmer, München
3.88	E. Böhm, Mainz, *Hellas, The Civilization of Ancient Greece*, K. Branigan, M. Vickers, McGraw-Hill, New York, 1980
3.91	Archibald Cary Coolidge Fund, The Museum of Fine Arts, Boston
4.9, 4.46, 4.74, 4.78 (right), 4.174	Renate Rolle, *The World of the Scythians*, C. J. Bucher Verlag, München, 1980
4.78 (left)	Vinogradov-Krujiski, *Eine altgriechische Stadt im nordwestlichen Schwarzmeer*, Brill, 1995
4.152a (left)	Alan Kaiser
4.152a (right)	By permission of Oxford University Press
4.152b (left), 5.92, 4.169 (left)	© Museum of Fine Arts, Boston, Theodora Wilbour Fund
4.152b (right)	© MSM, France, Musée du Châtillonnais
5.101	© Ernst Wasmuth Verlag, Tübingen
6.102, 7.22	Elsevier, *Atlas of the Greek World*, Peter Levi, Phaidon Press Ltd., Oxford, 1980
6.117a (left)	Eva-Maria Czakó, German Archaeological Institute, Athens
6.117a (right)	Gösta Hellner, German Archaeological Institute, Athens
6.117c	Archaeological Society of Athens
6.132, J.1	The Ashmolean Museum, Oxford
6.137a	American School of Classical Studies at Athens, Alison Frantz collection
6.137b	Martin von Wagner-Museum, Würzburg
7.5, S.2	*Warfare in the Classical World*, John Warry, St. Martins Press, New York, 1998
7.36 (left)	Ekdotike, Athens, *The Greco-Persian Wars*, Peter Green, University of California Press, Berkeley, 1996
7.36 (right)	Victor A. Lazzaro
7.143	Werner Forman/Art Resource, NY
7.193	Green Hill Books
7.211a	The Wadsworth Atheneum Museum of Art, Hartford
8.10, S.1, S.3	The Trireme Trust: (S.1) Paul Lipke, (S.3) John F. Coates
8.79	American School of Classical Studies at Athens: Agora Excavations
8.84	John Bradford Collection, *Atlas of the Greek World*, Peter Levi, Phaidon Press Ltd., Oxford, 1980
9.62a	The Royal Scottish Museum
9.62b	Bibliothèque Nationale, Paris, Seyrig Collection, *Persia and the West*, John Boardman, Thames and Hudson, London, 2000
9.81a	German Archaeological Institute, Istanbul
E.1	Vittorio Merico, as reproduced in *Erodoto, Le Storie*, Libro IV, ed. Aldo Corcella, Fondazione Lorenzo Valla, Arnoldo Mondadori Editore, 1993
N.4	Martin von Wagner Museum, Würzburg
S.4	German Archaeological Institute, Athens

INDEX

battos, a North African word for king, 4.155; *see also* individual kings named Battos

Battos (I) of Thera, is instructed by Pythia to found a city in Libya, 4.150; he founds Cyrene, 4.155–157

Battos (II) the Blessed, king of Cyrene, **4.**159.2

Battos (III) the Lame, king of Cyrene, 4.161–163

bay trees, Apollo's statue in Metapontum surrounded by, 4.15.3

beacons
fire beacons used to inform Greek fleet at Artemision of fate of ships fleeing Persians, 7.183.1
Mardonios hopes to notify Xerxes in Sardis by signal beacons that Athens has been taken, 9.3.1
Persians will not attack Greeks until they receive signal from ships sent round Euboea, 8.7.2

beans, Egyptians do not eat, 2.37.5

bears, as rare in Egypt, 2.67

beaver, Boudini cloaks trimmed with heads of, 4.109.2

beef, Egyptian priests eat every day, 2.37.4

bees
nest in severed head of Onesilos, leading to his being venerated by Amathousians, 5.114
as unlikely beyond the Ister due to cold, 5.10

betrayal, *see* treachery

Bias of Priene, dissuades Croesus from attacking Aegean islands, 1.27.1–4; advises Ionians to settle in Sardinia, 1.170.2

birds, migration of, 2.22.4

birth, *see* childbirth

births, monstrous, in Sardis, concubine of King Meles gives birth to a lion cub, 1.84.3; in Babylon, mules gives birth before city falls to Darius, 3.151.2, 3.153.1; occur as Xerxes crosses the Hellespont, 7.57

Bithynians, name for Asiatic Thracians, 7.75

Biton and Cleobis of Argos, regarded by Solon as happiest and most prosperous of men next to Tellos, 1.31

bitumen
Babylon, hot bitumen used as mortar in building walls of, 1.179.2; bitumen obtained from River Is, 1.179.4
Carthaginians describe how on Cyrauis gold is gathered with tarred feathers, 4.195.2
Eretrian captives settled near well producing, 6.119.2–4

Black Cloaks, 4.20.2, 4.102.2, 4.107; refuse to join Scythians against Persians; the Persians and Scythians invade their territory and wreak havoc, 4.119.1, 4.125.2–5

blasphemy, *see* sacrilege

blindness
the blind king of Egypt hides in the marshlands, 2.140
Epizelos is struck blind after Marathon, 6.117
Pheros king of Egypt cured of through washing his eyes with urine of a faithful woman, 2.111

blood guilt, Croesus admits Adrastos to his household to purge, 1.35, 1.41, 1.44

blood oaths
Arabians, 3.8
Greek and Carian mercenaries drink blood of Phanes' slaughtered sons, 3.11.2
Medes and Persians, 1.74.4
Scythians, 4.70

blood sports, Cambyses pits a lion cub against a puppy, 3.32.1

boars, Lydian fields ravaged by, 1.36.1; Atys killed in hunt for, 1.43; Samian ships' prows decorated with boar heads, 3.59.3

boat bridges, Cyrus begins building over Araxes River, 1.205.2; Darius builds over the Ister River, 4.97, 4.118.1; Ionians to guard it, 4.98; deceive Scythians by partially dismantling it, 4.139–141; *see also* Hellespont, boat bridge

boats
Amazons know nothing about sailing, 4.110.2
Assyria, reed boats and river commerce, 1.194
Bosporus, Mandrokles constructs bridge of boats for Darius, 4.87.1, 4.88; Darius crosses into Thrace, 4.89.3
Egypt, Nile craft, 2.96

Boeotia/Boeotians, expel Kadmeians (Phoenicians) and Gephyraians, 5.57.2; Kadmeian remains include inscriptions in sanctuary of Ismenian Apollo in Thebes, 5.58–61; join Spartan attack on Athenians, 5.74.2; assist Chalcidians against Athenians but are overwhelmed; 700 prisoners are ransomed, 5.77; when Persians advance, all except Thespians and Plataeans submit to Xerxes, 7.132; Xerxes invades on march to Athens, 8.34, 8.50.1; Macedonians protect the city from Persians by showing it has medized, 8.34; Athenians had expected to find Peloponnesians waiting in, 8.40.2; Boeotians join Persian army, 8.66.2; Xerxes returns to after Salamis, 8.113.1; Athenians urge Spartans to do battle against Mardonios, 8.144.5, 9.7.β; Mardonios marches to since Attica is unsuited for cavalry and fortifies his base along Asopos River, 9.14.3, 9.15, 9.17, 9.19.3; lament death of Masistios at Erythrai, 9.24; at Plataea, oppose Athenians, 9.31.5, 9.46.2, 9.47; fight bravely against Athenians and their cavalry protect Persian army's flight, 9.67–68; at Mycale, rumors spread of Greek victory in Boeotia, 9.100.1

Boges governor of Eion, praised by Xerxes for taking his own life rather than surrendering to Greeks, 7.107

Boreas, Athenian sacrifices to are credited with bringing wind that destroys Persian navy, 7.189

Borysthenes River, course and fertility of plain of, 4.52–54; Greek trading posts, 4.24; peoples living to the north of, 4.17–18; Zeus' union with daughter of produces first Scythian, 4.5.1

Borysthenites (Scythian farmers), 4.17.1, 4.18; Skyles adopts Greek customs in town of, 4.78.4, 4.79.1

Bosporus (Cimmerian), 4.12.1; freezes over, 4.28.1

Bosporus (Thracian), geography and dimensions of, 4.85–86; Darius orders construction of a bridge, which is built by Mandrokles of Samos, 4.83, 4.87.1, 4.88; *see also* Hellespont

Bottiaia/Bottiaians, provide troops to Xerxes' army, 7.185

Boubares son of Megabazos, supervises building of Mount Athos Canal, 7.22.2

Boubastis, festival of Artemis, 2.59.1, 2.60; elevation of, 2.137.5; sanctuary of, 2.127.5

Boudinoi, 4.21, 4.108–109; support Scythians in resisting Persians, 4.119.1; Persians destroy their city's wooden ramparts, 4.123

Boulis son of Nikolaus, volunteers to be executed by Persians to atone for Spartans' murder of heralds, 7.134–137

Bousiris, festival of Isis, 2.40, 2.59.1–2, 2.61

Bouto, temple of, 2.156

Branchidai, *see* Didyma

accounts of priests of Hephaistos in Memphis, 2.3.1; Eridanus is a Greek word so that proves the city was not called that by barbarians but was invented by some poet, 3.115.1–2; if one can judge from this evidence, Pelasgians spoke a barbarian language, 1.57.2; Greeks produce no evidence to support belief that the Ocean flows round the entire earth, 4.8.2; cannot provide proof of judgment as to who was most courageous, 9.71.2; uses the visible as basis for judgements about the unknown, inferring course of Nile from that of Danube, 2.33.2–34.2

sources:
Archias of Sparta, has met grandson of, 3.55; Arion, corroboration of story of, 1.23.8; Aristaios the poet, things Herodotus heard in Proconnesus and Cyzicus, 4.14.1; Chaldaians describe statue of Zeus in Babylon, 1.183.3; Cretans' view of origins of Carians, 1.171.5; Cyrenians report what the Ammonian king Etearchos told them, 2.32.1, 2.33.1; Dodona, priestess of, 2.52.1, 2.53.3, 2.55.1; Egypt, own observation, judgment and research, together with words of Egyptians, 2.99.1; that Gephyraians were originally Phoenician is known from Herodotus' own investigations, 5.57.1; Heliopolis, priests of, 2.3.1; Hephaistos, priests of, 2.2.5; Isagoras, unable to find details on origins of, 5.66.1; Issedones are the only source of information about what lies beyond them, 4.27; oracle of Ammon confirms Herodotus' account of Egypt as all the land watered by the Nile, 2.18; Persian authorities of the past, 1.1.1, 1.2.1; Persian information, up to this point, was based on certain knowledge, 1.140.1; Pontine Greeks tell story of Herakles and the snakewoman, 4.8–10; Sais, scribe in sacred treasury of Athena was knowledgeable about source of the Nile, 2.28.1; Scythia, no eyewitness accounts exist for lands north of, 4.16; Thebes, priests of, 2.3.1, 2.54; Thesander of Orchomenos recounts Persian prediction of defeat, 9.16.5; Tymnes, chief official of Ariapeithes, 4.76.6; the Zopyros who deserted Persia for Athens may have been, 3.160.2

view of history: prosperity of cities waxes and wanes, 1.5.3–4

Hesiod, as contemporary with Homer and defining theogony, 2.53.2; Hyperboreans mentioned by, 4.33.2

Himera (Sicily), battle of between Greeks and Carthaginians, 7.165–167

Hipparchos son of Peisistratos, had once driven Onomakritos out of Athens for inserting a prediction into the oracles of Mousaios, 7.6.4; dreams he will be killed and is murdered by Gephyraians, 5.55, 5.56, 5.62.1; his murder drives surviving Peisistratids to savagery, 6.123.2

Hippias son of Peisistratos, advises Peisistratos to try to regain tyranny of Athens after his expulsion, 1.61; rules harshly as tyrant of Athens after murder of his brother Hipparchos, 5.62.2; Spartans send for to persuade their allies to restore tyranny in Athens, 5.91, 5.93; had thorough and unrivalled knowledge of oracles, 5.93.2; returns to Sigeion and appoints his son Hegistratos as tyrant, 5.94; slanders Athenians to the Persians, who attempt to secure his return to Athens, 5.96.1; leads Persians to Marathon as region of Attica most suited to cavalry, 6.102, 6.107; dreams of his mother and interprets loss of his tooth to

mean barbarian invasion will fail, 6.107; Miltiades threatens that Athenians will be handed over to Hippias if Persians are not defeated, 6.109.3

Hippocrates father of Peisistratos, receives portent at Olympic games that he should disown his son, 1.59.1–3

Hippocrates tyrant of Gela, sons of are defeated by Gelon, 7.155

Hippocrates tyrant of Rhegion, captures Zancle in Sicily, 6.23

Hippokleides son of Teisandros, disgusts Kleisthenes with his shameless dancing, so loses contest for his daughter, 6.129.3–4

hippopotamus, description of, 2.71

Histiaia, Persians seize and overrun after Greeks leave Artemision, 8.23.2

Histiaios son of Lysagoras, tyrant of Miletus, persuades Ionians to hold the bridge over the Ister; deceives Scythians by pretending to destroy it and allows Darius to escape, 4.137–142; Darius rewards for his help by giving him Myrkinos in Edonia to found a city, 5.11, 5.23.1; warned of his increasing power in Thrace, Darius summons him back to Sardis, 5.23–25.1; encourages Aristagoras to revolt, sending a secret message tattooed on a slave's head, 5.35.2–4; Darius sends to quell Ionian Revolt, believing his promises that he will do so, 5.106–107; attempts to convince Artaphrenes that he was ignorant of reason for Ionian Revolt; flees to Chios since he is known to have been complicit, 6.1–2; Milesians refuse to allow him to return as they have tasted liberty, 6.5.1; Lesbians supply with eight triremes; he sails to Byzantium, 6.6; overcomes Chians at the Hollows but is defeated by the Persians at Atarneus, 6.26–28; Artaphrenes orders his execution, 6.30; Darius buries his head and remembers him as a benefactor, 6.30; as capable of destroying Persian power when he had joined other tyrants instead of opposing them, 7.10.γ

Histiaos son of Tymnes, tyrant of Termera, arrested by Iatragoras, 5.37.1

Homer
Cypria are not the work of, 2.117
Epigonoi, Homer may not be their author, 4.33.2
gods' characteristics defined by, 2.53.2
Helen, rejects story of her detention in Egypt though he knew of Alexandros' wanderings in Egypt, 2.116
Hesiod as contemporary with, 2.53.2
Iliad and *Odyssey* describe wanderings of Alexandros, 2.116.2–6
Ocean river, idea probably invented by, 2.23
Odyssey, lambs in Libya said to grow horns from birth, 4.29
Sicyonian bards celebrate Argives in Homeric verses, 5.67.1

honey
Babylonians use to preserve bodies, 1.198
in Egyptian sacrificial rites, 2.40.3
Gyzantes produce in quantity, 4.194
Samians sustain rescued Corcyraean boys with, 3.48.3

honey cake, offering to snake said to guard Acropolis at Athens, 8.41.2–3

hoplites
Aristeides brings Athenians stationed near Salamis to Psyttaleia, where they annihilate Persian occupiers, 8.95

Zopyros' self-mutilation deceives the Babylonians, 3.156–158

fortification, *see* walls

morale: Athenian prowess greatly increased after the fall of their tyrannical government, 5.78; when told the Persian arrows darkened the sun, Spartan Dienekes replied "all the better, we shall fight in the shade," 7.226.2; Greeks much heartened by having repulsed the Persian cavalry, 9.25; Greeks at Mycale encouraged by rumor of victory at Plataea, 9.101

scorched earth:

Alyattes attacks Miletus by burning crops and siezing livestock, 1.18–19, 1.25

in Phocis, Persians plunder and burn everything in their path, 8.33

Scythians destroy wells and crops before Persian advance, 4.120

sieges, *see under* sieges

milk, as only drink of Ethiopians, 3.23.1; Scythians compel blinded slaves to stir mares' milk, 4.2

millet

cultivated in Persia, 3.117.4

Herodotus knows but will not mention Assyrian and Babylonian returns from cultivation of, 1.193.4

raised and eaten by Kallipidai, Greek Scythians, 4.17.1

Miltiades son of Kimon, seizes control of Chersonese, marries daughter of Oloros, king of the Thracians, but flees Scythian invasion, 6.39–40; evades Phoenicians, taking refuge in Imbros, and returns to Athens, 6.41; in Athens, he is tried for tyranny in the Chersonese; he is acquitted and elected to be one of the ten generals commanding Athenian forces, 6.103, 6.104; wins debate to attack at Marathon, 6.109–110; after Marathon, he attacks Paros with fleet of 70 ships, 6.132–134; is tried for deception but because of his popularity the death penalty is commuted to a fine of 50 talents, 6.136; conquers Lemnos, sailing from Chersonese on the Etesian winds, and drives out Pelasgians, 6.137–140; injures his leg in violating sanctuary of Demeter on Paros and contracts gangrene, from which he dies, 6.134.2, 6.136.2–3

Miltiades son of Kypselos, descent and wealth of, 6.35.1; leads expedition to Chersonese to escape rule of Peisistratos, 6.35.3; becomes tyrant of Chersonese at request of the Dolonci, 6.34–36; walls off Chersonese isthmus, 6.36.2; Croesus secures release of when captured by Lampsacenes, 6.37; Ister bridge, proposes Ionians allow Scythians to capture Darius and thereby free Ionia, 4.137.1; dies childless and his wealth passes to his half brother Stesagoras son of Kimon; the Chersonese honor his memory with commemorative games, 6.38–39

Milyas/Milyans, in Darius' first provincial district, 3.90.1; in Persian army of invasion, 7.77

Min, first king of Egypt, 2.4.2–3, 2.99

mina (sum equal to 100 drachmas)

Boeotians pay Athenians ransom of two minas for each of 700 captives, 5.77.3;

Greeks living in Egypt donate 20 minas to rebuilding temple of Delphi, 2.180.2

among Peloponnesians, two minas is customary ransom for a prisoner of war, 6.79.1

mining, *see also* gold mines; siege mining

Alexandros of Macedon's mine produces a talent of silver per day, 5.17.2

Laureion silver mines produce new revenues, Themistokles persuades Athens to use the funds to build a fleet of 200 triremes, 7.144

Libya, salt mines along Atlas ridge, 4.185.2–3

Mount Pangaion, gold and silver mines, 7.112

Siphnos very wealthy from productive gold and silver mines, 3.57.2

Thasos obtains great wealth from mines on island and mainland, 6.46.2–3

Minos, first Greek to attempt to control the sea, 3.122.2; Greeks failed to help Cretans avenge his death, 7.169.2

Minyans, imprisoned in Sparta after seeking excessive influence; they escape to Calliste (renamed Thera), 4.145–150

Mitradates (Median slave), with his wife Kyno, shelters the infant Cyrus, 1.110–113; confesses to Astyages under torture, 1.116

Mitrobates governor of Dascyleium, reproaches Oroites for murder of Polykrates and is killed by him, 3.120, 3.126.2

Moeris king of Egypt, memorials built by, 2.101

money, *see also* drachma; mina; stater; talent

Aryandes, Persian governor of Egypt, strikes silver coins of highest purity and is executed by Darius, 4.166

Babylonian, Darius uses for payment in silver, 3.89.2

Cheops prostitutes his daughter when he runs short of money, 2.126.1

Darius, tribute to, 3.89.2, 3.90–97; converts tribute of satrapies to fixed sum, 3.89.2–3; strikes coins from stores of molten gold, 3.96.2; strikes gold coins of highest purity but executes Aryantes for producing purest silver coins, 4.166; Daric stater, Pythios son of Atys gives Xerxes nearly four million for the war against Greece, 7.28–29

Democedes the physician is hired by Aeginetans, Athenians and Polykrates, 3.131.2

Gelon of Syracuse sends money to Delphi since he is unable to help Greeks directly, 7.165

Lydians as first people to use gold and silver coins, 1.94.1

Oroites seeks to lure Polykrates with, 3.122.3–123.2

Plataea, Greeks divide Persian spoils, 9.81.2

Polykrates, passion for, 3.123.1; said to have bribed Spartans with gilded lead coins, 3.56.2

pyramids, cost of, 2.125.6, 2.134

monkeys, Gyzantes said to eat, 4.194

monogamy, Egyptians and Greeks practice, 2.92.1

monuments, *see* memorials; statues

morale, *see* military morale

morality, Darius proves Pindar's statement that custom is king of all, 3.38

mortality, Xerxes weeps at the brevity of human life, 7.46.2; as a mere mortal, Xerxes is doomed to experience a mixture of adversity in his life, 7.203.2

Moschians, in Darius' nineteenth provincial district, 3.94.2; in Xerxes' army of invasion, 7.78

mosquito nets, used in Egypt, 2.95

Mossynoikians, in Darius' nineteenth provincial district, 3.94.2; in Persian army of invasion, 7.78

mounds (Persian siege tactic), *see* earthworks

sanctuaries, violation of
Aeginetans sever hands of rebel at shrine of Demeter and are cursed, 6.91.2
Alkmeonids persuade Kylon and fellow suppliants to move from statues of the gods before killing them, 5.71.2
Apollo paradoxically tells Cymaeans to give up suppliant Paktyes and be destroyed, 1.159.3
Argos, Kleomenes drives suppliants from sacred grove by fire, 6.75.3, 6.79–80
Artayktes brings women into sanctuary of Protesilaos at Elaious, 7.33; had intercourse with women in the inner shrine, 9.116.3
Athens, Persians murder those who had taken refuge in megaron, 8.53.2
Dorieus and Euryleon of Sparta are killed despite taking refuge at altar of Zeus, 5.46.2
Kleomenes ravages shrine of Eleusis, 5.74–76; burns sacred grove of Argos, 6.75.3, 6.79–80
Miltiades leaps over the wall into sanctuary of Demeter at Paros, 6.134.2
Mykerinos is condemned to an early death because he refused to follow his people's fate and make them suffer 150 years, 2.133.2–3
Paktyes is torn from temple of Athena and handed over to Persians, 1.160.3–5
Persians destroy: Abai, 8.33, Athens, murdering those who had taken refuge in megaron, 8.53.2, 8.54; Didyma (Branchidai), 6.19.3; Eleusis, 9.65; Eretria, 6.101.3; Naxos, 6.96
Samos, Otanes' troops kill citizens regardless of sanctuary, 3.147.2
Selinuntines kill Euryleon at shrine of Zeus of the Agora, where he had taken refuge, 5.46.2
Sandanis the Lydian, warns Croesus that Persians are poor and rough, 1.71
Sandokes of Cyme, punished by Darius for delivering an unjust verdict but released in light of his good service to the crown, 7.194
Sane, Greek city becomes starting point of Persian canal across Mount Athos peninsula, 7.22.3, 7.23.1
Sappho, denounces her brother Charaxos for freeing the courtesan Rhodopis, 2.135.5
Sarangians, in Darius' fourteenth provincial district, 3.93.2
Sardanapolos, underground treasury at, 2.150.3
Sardinia (also known as Sardo), Histiaios deceives Darius over attempt to conquer, 6.2; Ionians reject Bias of Priene's advice to migrate there, 1.170.1–2; Sardinians among Hamilcar's forces in Sicily, 7.165
Sardis/Sardians
Alyattes reigns in, 1.19, 1.22.2
Ardys reigns in, 1.7
Aristagoras organizes expedition against, 5.99.2; Ionians capture and burn, 5.100–101
Artaphrenes appointed governor of, 5.25.1, 5.106.1, 5.123; is not deceived by Histiaios when he returns there, 6.2; executes Histiaios, 6.30.1; compels Ionians to accept peaceful arbitration of disputes, 6.42
Asias tribe in, 4.45.3
Athenians send embassy to seek alliance with Persians against Spartans, 5.73; their messengers fail to persuade Artaphrenes to reject Hippias, 5.96.2
Cimmerians capture except for acropolis, 1.15

REFERENCE MAPS
Directory

This directory lists all the sites known, or possibly known (?) that appear in Herodotus' text. Places mentioned only in the Introduction or appendices have not been included. Places mentioned in the text, but whose locations are not known are not listed. Names given are the ancient ones used in the text. The numbers that follow each name indicate the reference map (Ref.1–5) or the map within the text (identified by book and chapter) on which the location can be found. Letters, if any, indicate map coordinates.

Abai, Ref.5, BX
Abdera, Ref.2, AX
Abydos, Ref.2, AY
Acarnania, 1.59, BX
Achaea, Ref.2, CW
Achaea Phthiotis, Ref.5, AX
Achelous River, Ref.2, BW
Acheron River, 8.47, AX
Achilleion, 5.97, AY
Achilles, Racecourse of, 4.53, inset
Acropolis, 6.105, inset
Adramyttium, 7.42
Adramyttium, Gulf of, 7.42
Adriatic Sea, Ref.1, AX
Adyrmachidians, 4.175, BY
Aegae, 1.149, AY
Aegean Sea, Ref.1, BX
Aegina, Ref.5, CY
Aeolis, Ref.2, BY
Aetolia, Ref.2, CW
Agathyrsoi, Ref.1, AX
Aglauros Cave, 8.47, inset
Agora, 8.47, inset
Agrianes River, Ref.2, AY
Agrianians, 5.14
Agylla (Caere), 1.166
Aigai, 1.146, AY
Aigaleos, Mount, 8.86, inset
Aige, 7.123, BY
Aigeira, 1.146, BX
Aigilia?, 6.105, AY
Aigion, 1.146, AX
Aigospotamos, 9.107, inset
Aineia, 7.123, BX
Ainos, Ref.2, AY
Aiolidai?, 8.32, BY
Aisa, 7.123, BX
Akanthos, Ref.2, AX
Akragas, Ref.3, BX
Akraiphiai, 8.134, inset
Akrothooi, Ref.2, BX
Alabanda, Ref.2, CY
Alalie, Ref.1, AW
Alarodians, Ref.1, BY
Alazones, 4.53

Aleion Plain, 7.75
Alopeke (deme), 5.63
Alpenos, Ref.5, AX
Amathous, 5.108, inset
Ambracia, Ref.2, BW
Ammonion, Ref.1, CX
Ampelos Promontory, 7.123, BY
Amphiareion, Ref.5, BZ
Amphikleia, 8.32, AX
Amphipolis, Ref.2, AX
Amphissa, 8.32, BX
Anactorium, Ref.2, BW
Anagyrous (deme), 8.86, inset
Anaphlystos (deme), 4.93, inset
Anaua, 7.34
Andros, Ref.2, CX
Angites River, 7.111, AX
Angrus River?, 4.53, AX
Anopaia Path, 7.213, inset
Anopaia, Mount, 7.213, inset
Antandros, 5.31, AY
Anthela, 7.213, inset
Anthemous, 5.97, AX
Anthylla, 2.97, inset
Antikyra?, Ref.5, AX
Anysis?, 2.165, inset, AY
Aparytai, 3.94, AY
Aphetai?, Ref.5, AY
Aphidna (deme), Ref.5, BZ
Aphrodisias Island, 4.165
Aphytis, 7.123, BX
Apidanos River, Ref.2, BW
Apis, 2.19
Apollonia (Hellas), Ref.2, AW
Apollonia (Thrace), Ref.1, AX
Apsinthis, Ref.2, AY
Arabia, Ref.1, CY
Arabian Gulf, 2.155
Arados, 7.98, locator
Aral Sea, Ref.1, AY
Araxes River, Ref.1, BY
Arcadia, Ref.2, CW

Archandropolis, Ref.4, AX
Areia, Ref.1, BZ
Areiopagos, 8.47, inset
Argilos, 7.111, AX
Argos, Ref.5, DX
Argos, Gulf of, Ref.5, DX
Arisba, 1.149, AX
Armenia, Ref.1, BY
Artace, Ref.2, AY
Artemision, Ref.5, AY
Asbystaians, 4.175, BY
Ascalon, 1.103, BX
Asia, Ref.1, BY
Asian Thrace, 3.90
Asine, 8.72, BX
Assa?, 7.123, BY
Assyria, Ref.1, BY
Atarbechis, Ref.4, BY
Atarneus, Ref.2, BY
Athena Skiras, 8.86, inset
Athens, Ref.5, CZ
Athos (peninsula), 7.123, BY
Athos Canal, Ref.2, AX
Athos, Mount, Ref.2, BX
Athribites, Nome, 2.165, BY
Athrys River, 4.53, AX
Atlantic Ocean, Ref.1, AW
Attica, Ref.5, CZ
Augila, 4.175, BY
Auschisians?, 4.175, BY
Auseans, Ref.1, BW
Axios River, Ref.2, AX
Axos, 4.150, BY
Azania, 6.125, BX
Aziris, 4.165
Azotos, 2.155

Babylon, Ref.1, BY
Babylonia, 3.94, BX
Bakalians?, 4.175, BY
Baktria, Ref.1, AZ
Baktrians, 3.94, AY
Barke, Ref.1, BX
Belbina, Ref.5, DZ

Bermion, Mount, 8.134, AX
Bisaltia, Ref.2, AX
Bisanthe, 7.98, AY
Bistones, 7.111, AY
Bistonis, Lake, 7.111, AY
Bithynia, Ref.2, AZ
Black Cloaks?, Ref.1, AY
Black Gulf, 7.58
Black River, 7.58
Boebeis, Lake, 7.128, BY
Boeotia, Ref.5, BY
Bolbitinic Mouth, Ref.4, AX
Borysthenes (Olbia), Ref.1, AX
Borysthenes River, Ref.1, AX
Bosporus (Cimmerian), Ref.1, AY
Bosporus (Thracian), Ref.2, AZ
Bottiaia, Ref.2, AX
Boubastis, Ref.4, BY
Boubastites, Nome, 2.165, BY
Boudinoi?, Ref.1, AY
Boura, 1.146, AX
Bousiris, Ref.4, AY
Bousirites, Nome, 2.165, AY
Bouto, Ref.4, AY
Brauron, 6.136
Brindisi, Ref.3, AY
Brongus River?, 4.53, AX
Brygoi?, 7.186, AX
Bucolic Mouth, Ref.4, AY
Bybassian Peninsula, 1.173, inset
Byzantium, Ref.2, AZ

Caere/Agylla, 1.166
Caicus River, Ref.2, BY
Camarina, Ref.3, BX
Canal (Egypt), Ref.4, BZ
Canobic Mouth, Ref.4, AX
Canopus, Ref.4, AX
Cappadocia, Ref.1, BY
Caria, Ref.2, DZ

Carthage, Ref.1, BW
Casius, Mount, Ref.4, AZ
Caspian Sea, Ref.1, AY
Caucasus Mountains, Ref.1, AY
Caunus, Ref.2, DZ
Cayster River, Ref.2, CY
Cephallania, Ref.2, CW
Cephisus River, 8.32, AX
Chaeronea, 6.34
Chalastra, 7.123, AX
Chalcedon, Ref.2, AZ
Chalcidice, Ref.2, AX
Chalcis, Ref.5, BZ
Chalybes, 7.75
Charadra, 8.32, AX
Chemmis, Ref.4, AY
Chemmites?, Nome, 2.165, AX
Chersonese (Thracian), Ref.2, AY
Chios, Ref.2, CY
Choaspes River?, 1.183
Chorasmia, 3.110
Chorasmians, Ref.1, AZ
Cilicia, Ref.1, BY
Cimmerian Bosporus, Ref.1, AY
Cimmerians?, Ref.1, AY
Cithaeron, Mount, Ref.5, CY
Cnidus, Ref.2, DY
Colchis, Ref.1, AY
Colophon, Ref.2, CY
Colossae, 7.34
Copais, Lake, 8.134, inset
Corcyra, Ref.2, BW
Corinth, Ref.5, CX
Corinth, Isthmus of, Ref.5, CY
Coronea, 6.34
Corsica/Kyrnos, Ref.1, AW
Cos (island), Ref.2, DY
Crathis River, Ref.3, AY
Crete, Ref.1, BX
Crimea, 4.18, BX
Croton, Ref.3, AY

W X

Atlantic Ocean

Borysthenes R.

Ister R.

Hypanis R.

Tyras R.

Gherla

Agathyrsoi

SCYTHIA

Olbia

EUROPE

Tyras

Karkine?

Rhone R.

Kerkinitis

A

PYRENEES MTNS.

VENETIA

Histria

Massalia

Getai

Ligurians

Corsica/Kyrnos

ITALY

Euxine (Black) Sea

IBERIA

ETRURIA

Alalie

Mesembria

Adriatic Sea

Apollonia

PAPHLAGONIA

TARTESSOS

3

2

HELLESPONT

Cape
Soloeis

Sardinia

Croton

Aegean Sea

5

*Pillars of
Herakles*

Sicily

Athens

B

Carthage

Syracuse

Mediterranean Sea

*Lake
Tritonis?*

Auseans

Kydonia

Crete

Machlyes?
Lotus-eaters?
Gindanes?

Kinyps R.

Makai

Barke

Cyrene

Euesperides

4

NILE
DELTA

*Gulf of
Syrtis*

Plynos

Nasamones

*Lake
Moeris*

LIBYA

Ammonion

EGYPT

Nile R.

C

Chemmis

D

0   800 km   800 mi

Ref. 1

Y   Z

Boudinoi?

Black Cloaks?   *Aral*
Kremnoi *Tanais R.*   *Sea*   *Jaxartes R.*
immerians?   •Sauromatai
Lake   Chorasmians   Sacae   A
Maeotis
•SINDIKE   Sogdians
Cimmerian   CAUCASUS MTNS.   *Oxus R.*   BAKTRIA   Dadikai
Bosporus   COLCHIS   *Caspian*   Massagetai   Gandarians
Euxine (Black) Sea   —Phasis R.   *Sea*   Paktyike?
•Sinope   Moschians   *PARTHIA*
                     Makrones   *Indus R.*—
CAPPADOCIA   Saspeires? *Araxes R.*   HYRCANIA   *AREIA*
Halys R.   ARMENIA   Alarodians   INDIA   B
ASIA   Matienians
CILICIA   •Nineveh   •Ecbatana
Cyprus   SYRIA   ASSYRIA   MEDIA   •Sakai
HOENICIA   *Tigris R.*   Parikanians?
 •Sidon   *Euphrates R.* •Babylon •Susa
 •Tyre   KISSIA?   *PERSIA*
PALESTINE   •Persepolis•
 •Gaza

ARABIA   Mykians?

                                                                                                              C
Thebes

Elephantine

ETHIOPIA

Nile R.
                                                      Erythraean
 •Meroe   *Sea*
                                                                                                              D

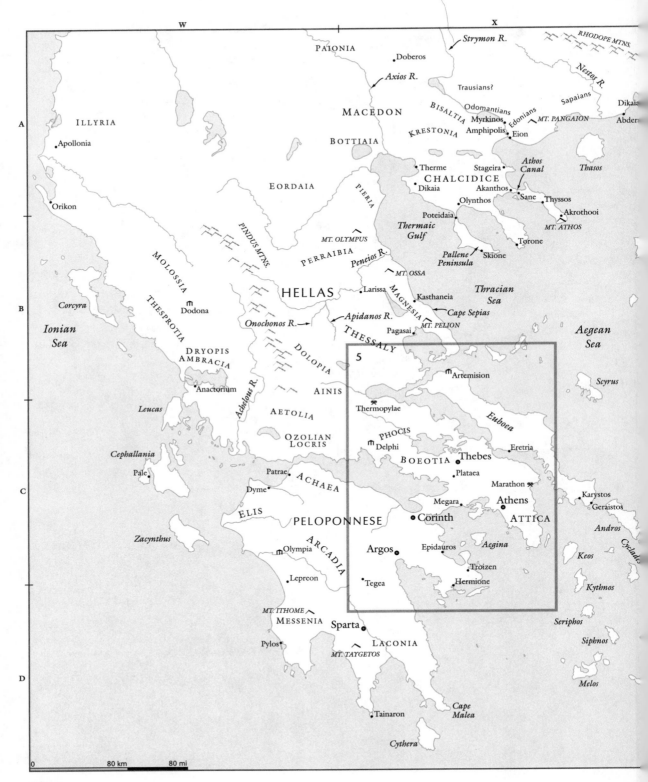

W   X

RHODOPE MTNS.

PAIONIA

• Doberos

Strymon R.

Axios R.

Trausians?

Nestos R.

BISALTIA

Odomantians

Sapaians

• Dikaia

MACEDON

KRESTONIA

Myrkinos

Edonians

MT. PANGAION

• Abdera

A

ILLYRIA

BOTTIAIA

Amphipolis

Eion

• Apollonia

• Therme

• Stageira

Athos Canal

Thasos

EORDAIA

CHALCIDICE

• Dikaia

Akanthos

• Orikon

Olynthos

Sane

Thyssos

Poteidaia

Akrothooi

PINDUS MTNS.

PIERIA

Thermaic Gulf

MT. ATHOS

MT. OLYMPUS

Pallene Peninsula

• Skione

• Torone

MOLOSSIA

PERRAIBIA

Peneios R.

B

Corcyra

THESPROTIA

Dodona

MT. OSSA

• Larissa

MAGNESIA

Thracian Sea

Kasthaneia

Aegean Sea

Ionian Sea

DRYOPIS

Apidanos R.

• Pagasai

Cape Sepias

AMBRACIA

Onochonos R.

THESSALY

MT. PELION

DOLOPIA

• Anactorium

Leucas

AINIS

5

Cephallania

AETOLIA

Achelous R.

Artemision

Scyrus

OZOLIAN LOCRIS

Thermopylae

Euboea

• Pale

PHOCIS

Eretria

• Delphi

• Patrae

BOEOTIA

Thebes

ACHAEA

• Plataea

C

• Dyme

Marathon

Karystos

ELIS

PELOPONNESE

Megara

Athens

Geraistos

Corinth

ATTICA

Zacynthus

ARCADIA

Andros

Olympia

Argos

• Epidauros

Aegina

Keos

Cyclades

• Lepreon

• Troizen

Kythnos

• Tegea

Hermione

MT. ITHOME

Seriphos

MESSENIA

Sparta

Siphnos

• Pylos

LACONIA

MT. TAYGETOS

D

Melos

• Tainaron

Cape Malea

Cythera

0   80 km   80 mi

REF.2

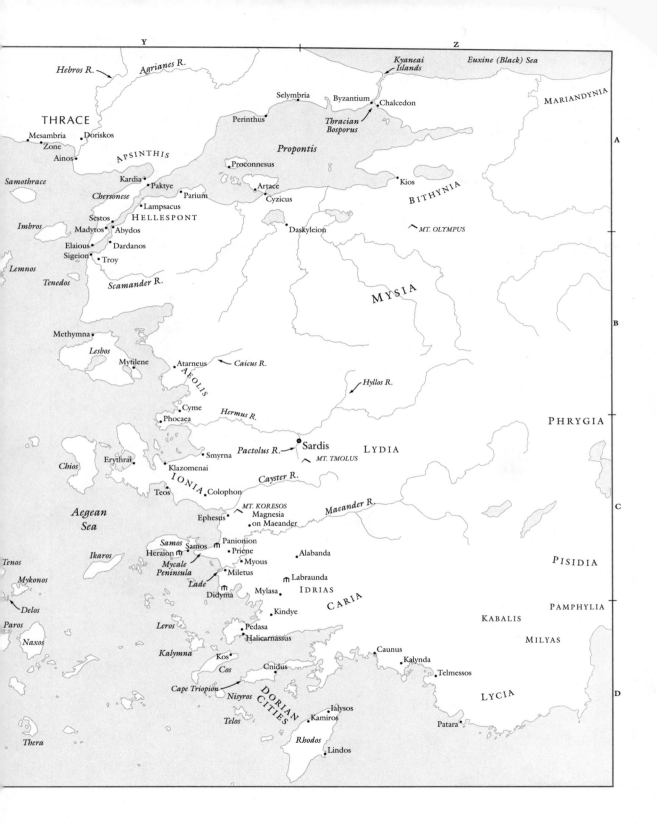

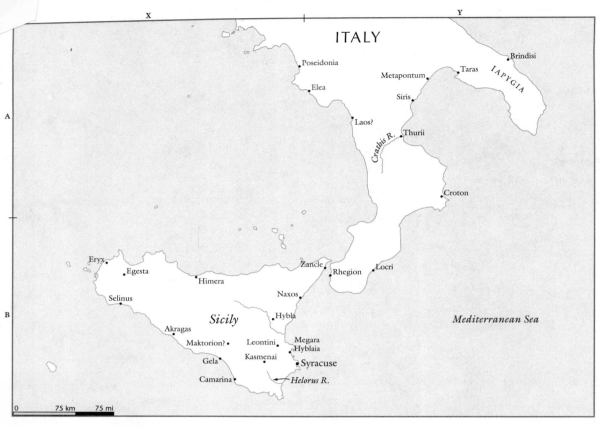

X   Y

ITALY

•Poseidonia

Metapontum•   Taras•

•Elea   Siris•

•Brindisi

IAPYGIA

A

Laos?•   *Crathis R.*

•Thurii

•Croton

Eryx•   •Zancle

•Egesta   Rhegion•   •Locri

•Himera

Selinus•   •Naxos

Sicily   •Hybla

Mediterranean Sea

B

Akragas•

Maktorion?•   Leontini•   Megara
Hyblaia•

Gela•   Kasmenai•   •Syracuse

Camarina•   *Helorus R.*

0   75 km   75 mi

REF.3

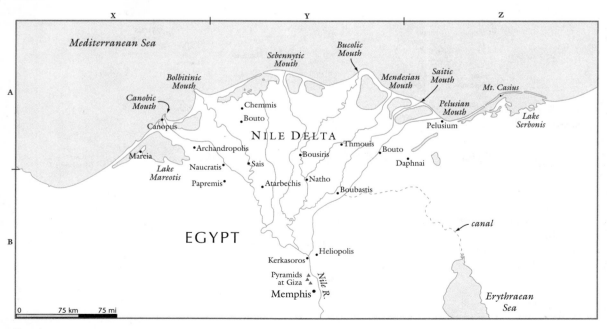

X   Y   Z

Mediterranean Sea

*Sebennytic
Mouth*   *Bucolic
Mouth*

*Bolbitinic
Mouth*   *Mendesian
Mouth*   *Saitic
Mouth*

Mt. Casius

A

*Canobic
Mouth*   •Chemmis   *Pelusian
Mouth*

Canopus•   •Bouto   Pelusium•

*Lake
Serbonis*

NILE DELTA

•Archandropolis   •Thmouis

Mareia•   •Bousiris   •Bouto

*Lake
Mareotis*   Naucratis•   Sais•   •Daphnai

Papremis•   Atarbechis•   •Natho

•Boubastis

canal

B

EGYPT

Heliopolis•

Kerkasoros•

Pyramids
at Giza▲▲   *Nile R.*

Memphis •

*Erythraean
Sea*

0   75 km   75 mi

REF.4

X   Y   Z

Halos ⋔

Aphetai?

Sciathus

ACHAEA
PHTHIOTIS

Artemision ⋔

Histiaia

Aegean Sea

A

MALIS

Malian Gulf

Antikyra?
Trachis
TRACHIS Alpenos
Thermopylae

DORIS Drymaia OPUNTIAN
LOCRIS

Euboea

MT. PARNASSUS

Abai ⋔

PHOCIS

Tamynai

Daulis Panopeos Orchomenus
Ptoios ⋔

Euripos
Chalcis

B

Delphi ⋔

Lebadeia

Eretria

BOEOTIA

Thebes ⊙

Tanagra Oropos
Amphiareion ⋔

Thespiai *Asopos* R.

Plataea Erythrai

Hysiai *MT. CITHAERON*

Aphidna

Dekeleia

Marathon

Styra

Pellene

Eleusis

Pallene

Sicyon *Isthmus of
Corinth*

Megara

Athens

MT. KYLLENE

Salamis

Peiraieus

Paiania

C

Corinth ⊙

Phaleron

ATTICA

Phleious

Aegina

*Cape
Zoster*

Orchomenos Mycenae

Argos ⊙

Epidauros

*Cape
Sounion*

Mantineia Tiryns

MT. PARTHENION

Troizen

Belbina

D

Tegea

THYREA *Gulf of
Argos*

Hermione

Halieis

REF.5